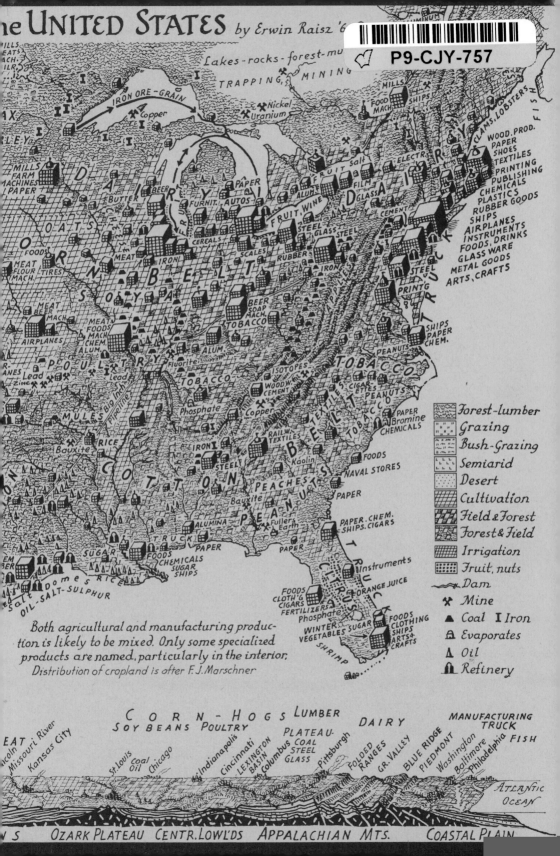

he UNITED STATES by Erwin Raisz '6

Both agricultural and manufacturing production is likely to be mixed. Only some specialized
products are named, particularly in the interior.
Distribution of cropland is after F. J. Marschner

Legend:
- Forest-lumber
- Grazing
- Bush-Grazing
- Semiarid
- Desert
- Cultivation
- Field & Forest
- Forest & Field
- Irrigation
- Fruit, nuts
- Dam
- Mine
- Coal I Iron
- Evaporates
- Oil
- Refinery

THE GROWTH OF THE AMERICAN REPUBLIC

FRANKLIN DELANO ROOSEVELT *by Douglas Chandor*

THE GROWTH OF THE

AMERICAN REPUBLIC

VOLUME TWO

SAMUEL ELIOT MORISON

AND

HENRY STEELE COMMAGER

NEW YORK · OXFORD UNIVERSITY PRESS

1962

PRINTED IN THE UNITED STATES OF AMERICA

PREFACE

The Growth of the American Republic appeared in 1930 as a single volume, beginning the story in 1763 and terminating it in 1917. In 1936–37 we carried the story down to the second inauguration of President Franklin D. Roosevelt. In the third edition of 1942, we extended the story backward to the origin of man in America and forward to cover America's entry into World War II. The fourth edition of 1950 covered that conflict as well, and ended with the presidential election of 1948. For the fifth edition we have rewritten the entire book, and carried the narrative through the presidential election of 1960. By eliminating some of the data on earlier periods that no longer seem significant, this fifth edition is not substantially longer. Throughout, the text has been revised to correct errors and the bibliographies have been reduced in length, owing to the appearance of *The Harvard Guide to American History* in 1954. A select General Bibliography will be found at the end of this volume.

In this edition, Morison is responsible for Vol. I, excepting the chapters on the Civil War, and for the chapters on World War II in Vol. II. Commager is responsible for the rest of Vol. II and for the chapters on the Civil War in Vol. I.

Our sincere thanks are extended to the many readers who have notified us of mistakes in earlier editions; to our colleagues who have read parts of the copy; to authors and publishers severally mentioned in the footnotes, who have allowed us to quote passages from prose and poetry.

We write for young men and women of all ages, for whom economy in truth-telling is neither necessary nor appropriate. We believe that history embraces the whole of a people's activity: economic and social, literary and spiritual, as well as political and military. We have endeavored therefore to give such stress to these different aspects that our story will be that of a growing and changing civilization in an expanding United States of America.

This new edition is dedicated to the rising generation. May they continue to further the Growth of the American Republic!

SAMUEL ELIOT MORISON
HENRY STEELE COMMAGER

June 1961

CONTENTS

LIST OF MAPS

ALL MAPS HAVE BEEN PREPARED AND DRAWN
FOR THIS EDITION BY ERWIN R. RAISZ.

ILLUSTRATIONS

THE GROWTH OF THE AMERICAN REPUBLIC

The Aftermath of the War

1. THE HERITAGE OF WAR

Bow down, dear land, for thou hast found release!
  Thy God, in these distempered days,
  Hath taught thee the sure wisdom of His ways
And through thine enemies hath wrought thy peace!
  Bow down in prayer and praise!
No poorest in thy borders but may now
Lift to the juster skies a man's enfranchised brow;
O Beautiful! My Country! Ours once more!

THUS James Russell Lowell, at the Harvard commemoration service of 1865, saluted, as he believed, a reunited nation purged by
war of all grossness that had accompanied its rise to power. But the
fierce passions of warfare had burned good with evil; and in the
scorched soil the new growth showed more tares than wheat. Lowell
was, in fact, delivering the swan song of the New England intellectuals and reformers. In the generation to come that region would no
longer furnish the nation with reformers and men of letters, but
with a mongrel breed of politicians, sired by abolition out of profiteering. Industry and commerce had the Middle States firmly in their
grasp and were extending tentacles throughout the Middle West.
The old simplicity and idealism retreated beyond the Mississippi,
and materialism soon overtook them there.

The war had been fought for the preservation of the Union, yet
this was not the sole object of the war. The nation whose endurance
was to be tested was, as Lincoln said in his Gettysburg Address, 'a
nation conceived in liberty and dedicated to the proposition that all
men are created equal.' After 1862 the abolition of slavery came to
be a second acknowledged objective of the war. And to many people,
in Europe as in America, the maintenance of a 'government of the
people, by the people, for the people' came to be a third. Union, freedom, and democracy, these things were legitimate objectives of the

war, and it is proper to inquire to what extent they were achieved, and at what cost.

Union had been preserved, but it could not be said that the old Union had been restored. The long dispute over the nature of the Union had been settled, at last, in favor of the nationalist contention, but the settlement had been brought about by force; soon it was to be sanctioned by constitutional guarantees and accepted by common consent. Nor had sectionalism disappeared. The natural influences of geography and climate which had gone to create Northern and Southern sectionalism remained, and in the generation after the war a third powerful section came into existence — the trans-Mississippi West, whose regional consciousness, like that of the South, was accentuated by its politico-economic exploitation by the Northeast. Until the turn of the century, American life was conditioned by this tripartite sectional division of North, South, and West.

Slavery, to be sure, was gone and no more would politicians proclaim the sophistry that black servitude was necessary for white freedom. But emancipation, too, had been brought about by violence rather than by reason or by natural law. Perhaps this was the only way it could have been brought about, but even the most ardent champions of freedom were forced to admit that the method was painful for white and black alike. Emancipation ended slavery, and that was a momentous thing, but it did not solve the Negro problem. For slavery it substituted not freedom but a kind of peonage, and though in the weird metamorphosis of race relations that followed Appomattox, the Negroes did have some voice in their own destiny, for the most part they merely obeyed new masters. Not for another hundred years were Negroes to enjoy even in part those rights which the war and the new constitutional amendments had attempted to assure them.

And what shall we say of the third objective — government of, by, and for the people? Democracy, indeed, had not 'perished from the earth,' yet for a decade to come the essentials of self-government were denied to the South, and Americans witnessed what they had never known before: military government in time of peace. The Civil War had destroyed slavery and the slaveholding class; but within a few years it strengthened corporate industry and sharpened class dissensions in the victorious North. Twenty years after the attack on Fort Sumter the railroads alone represented a greater investment and con-

centration of power than had ever the slave interest, and their influence in politics and in the economic activities of free men were
scarcely less far-reaching. The Civil War may have advanced democracy in the South because there slavery was destroyed and almost
everyone reduced to a uniform poverty; but in the North and the
West it furnished an opportunity for the development of powerful
industrial and financial interests with which democracy had to grapple, as it had with slavery. As early as 1873 Walt Whitman, apostle of
democracy, looked out upon *Democratic Vistas* and was moved to
solemn warning:

> Shift and turn the combinations of the statement as we may, the prob-
> lem of the future of America is in certain respects as dark as it is vast.
> Pride, competition, segregation, vicious wilfulness, and license beyond
> example brood already upon us. Unwieldy and immense, who shall hold
> in behemoth? who bridle leviathan? Flaunt it as we choose, athwart and
> over the roads of our progress loom huge uncertainty, and dreadful threat-
> ening gloom. It is useless to deny it: Democracy grows rankly up the
> thickest, noxious, deadliest plants and fruits of all — brings worse and
> worse invaders — needs newer, larger, stronger, keener compensations
> and compellers.

There was poetic exaggeration here, and a failure to realize that the
evils complained of were common to mankind, not unique to America. Yet years later Justice Harlan of the Supreme Court, looking
back upon this period, remembered that ' there was everywhere
among the people generally a deep feeling of unrest. The nation had
been rid of human slavery . . . but the conviction was universal that
the country was in real danger from another kind of slavery, namely
the slavery that would result from aggregations of capital in the
hands of a few.'

The major objectives of the war, then, had been achieved, but only
in a partial and inconclusive manner, and the post-Civil War generation was to learn what our own generation has learned, that war always creates as many problems as it solves. The cost, too, had been
colossal, though Lincoln alone of the statesmen of that day seems to
have realized how great it was and how hard its payment. ' Fondly
do we hope,' he had said, ' fervently do we pray, that this mighty
scourge of war may speedily pass away. Yet if God wills that it continue until all the wealth piled by the bondsman's two hundred and
fifty years of unrequited toil shall be sunk, and until every drop of

blood drawn with the lash shall be paid by another drawn by the sword, as was said three thousand years ago, so still it must be said, " The judgments of the Lord are true and righteous altogether." '

It is impossible, now, to compute with exactness the cost of the Civil War, but Lincoln's tragic fears were fulfilled. Deaths from all causes in the Union army totaled some 360,000, and in the Confederate army some 260,000. The number of wounded who recovered was far larger: but no reliable figures have ever been compiled. How many lives were lost because of malnutrition, disease, and the chaotic conditions of 1865 and 1866, it is impossible to say, nor can we count the cost in lives shattered by destruction and demoralized by defeat.

The money cost of the war was staggering; proportionally higher, indeed, than the money cost of World War I. Loans and taxes raised by the Federal Government came to a little less than $3 billion, and the interest on the Civil War debt came to an additional $2.8 billion. The Confederacy floated loans of over $2 billion, but the total financial loss of the South, in property confiscated, depreciated, and destroyed, in the losses of banks and insurance companies and businesses, and in the expense of reconstruction, was incalculable. Many states, North and South, went heavily into debt for the prosecution of the war. And although these debts have long been extinguished, the country continued to pay for the war well into the twentieth century: pensions paid by the United States government came to a little less than $8 billion, and additional sums were paid to Confederate veterans by Southern states. The total money cost of the war to North and South may be estimated at well over $20 billion.

This does not mean the total cost. The war left a heritage not only of death, desolation, and debt, but of practical problems of far-reaching importance and enormous complexity. The Union and Confederate armies had to be demobilized and upwards of 1.5 million men returned to the pursuits of peace. The administrative activities of the War Department and the Provost General's office had to be curbed and the supremacy of civil government restored. Currency and industry needed deflation to a peace basis and re-inflation to provide for the needs of an expanding nation. There were staggering financial burdens of the war to be liquidated. Four million former slaves had to be adjusted to their new condition. Equally serious were the problems presented by the new industrial revolution in the North and the agricultural revolution in the South and the West. And foreign affairs of a most urgent nature, both in Europe and in the Americas, called for immediate action.

The material problems of the war could be solved and the material devastation repaired; the moral devastation was never wholly repaired. The North was emboldened by victory, the South demoralized by defeat. During the war violence and destruction and hatred had been called virtues; it was a long time before they were again recognized as vices. The war had been brutalizing in its effects on combatants and non-combatants alike. Ruthlessness and wastefulness, extravagance and corruption, speculation and exploitation, had accompanied the conflict, and they lingered on to trouble the postwar years. Above all, the war left a heritage of misunderstanding and even of bitterness that colored the thinking and conditioned the actions of men, Northern and Southern, for over a generation.

Modern America emerged from the period usually called ' Reconstruction.' In the fiery cauldron of the Civil War not only the Old South was melted down but the old America — the federal republic of Thomas Jefferson and Andrew Jackson — was volatilized. The Civil War, itself a political revolution, speeded up an inevitable revolution in material economy, society, and civilization.

2. THE REVOLUTION

The fall of the Confederacy dealt an extremely heavy blow to the planter and political aristocracy that had guided the destinies of the South since the days of Thomas Jefferson. A large part of this class was excluded, for some years, from participation in the government, and for some of the abler leaders such as Davis and Lee the disability was never removed. Slave property valued in 1860 at over $2 billion evaporated, and the savings and sacrifices represented by Confederate securities were lost. A labor system which was the very basis of Southern economy was overthrown, the agricultural regime which it served was disarranged, and a new system, no less wasteful and scarcely less oppressive, was established in its stead.

The old planter aristocracy had suffered in the war more severely than any other group; for if the war had been ' a poor man's fight,' the poor white had nothing to lose, and his condition was no worse in 1870 than it had been in 1850. But the planters lost not only their youth but often their means of recuperation. The blows of reconstruction, as staggering as those of defeat, wasted those impalpable moral values which had been accumulated during a century or more of stewardship. Well they learned what the Knights of Aristophanes declared twenty-four centuries ago:

There are things, then, hotter than fire, there are speeches more shameless still
Than the shameless speeches of those who rule the City at will.

Many gave up the struggle to maintain themselves on the land. A few fled to England, Mexico, or Brazil, others migrated to the Northern cities or started life anew in the West; many moved to the towns and adapted themselves to business or professional life. At the same time the small farmers and poor whites took advantage of the prevailing disorder to enlarge their farms, better their conditions, and elect men of their own kind, who shared instead of scorning their prejudices, to high office. A little while and the Tillmans, Watsons, and Rankins would sit in the seats of the Calhouns, the Cobbs, and the Clays.

The most clean-cut stroke of the revolution in the South was the emancipation of 4 million Negro slaves. This process of emancipation had begun during the war; it was consummated by three amendments to the Constitution. The Thirteenth, ratified in 1865, abolished slavery in places not reached by the Emancipation Proclamation. The Fourteenth Amendment extended federal protection to the freedmen for their personal and property rights, and the Fifteenth Amendment attempted to assure them the franchise. ' The bottom rail was on top,' in the salty phrase of the time, but the whites did not let it stay there long.

While the old pattern of Southern society and economy was being rearranged into a new one, a corresponding revolution was effected in the North. With the representatives of the planter class out of Congress, the spokesmen of industry, finance, and of free Western lands were unopposed, unless by one another. During the war they pushed through legislation to fulfill the arrested hopes of the 'fifties, and after victory they garnered the fruits thereof.

The moderate tariff of 1857 gave way to the Morrill tariff of 1861, and that to a series of war tariffs with duties scaling rapidly upward, and carefully adapted to meet the need and greed of Northern business. By the National Banking Acts of 1863 and 1864 the Independent Treasury system of 1846 was swept away in favor of one more attractive to private finance; and an act of 1865 imposed a tax of 10 per cent on all state bank notes, a fatal blow which none would regret. The money question which long agitated American politics was settled as the financial interests of the East wished, by the rejection of greenback inflation, the resumption of specie payments, and eventually by the establishment of the gold standard. That there might be no shortage of labor, Congress in 1864 permitted the importation of contract labor from abroad, and though this act was repealed within a few years, the practice itself was not discontinued until the decade of the 'eighties. At the same time the policy of internal improvements at national expense found expression in subsidies to telegraph and cable lines and in generous grants of millions of acres out of the public domain to railroad promoters and financiers.

While Northern industry and finance were reaping the fruits of loyalty and victory, the century-old ambition of Western farmers was ostensibly satisfied by the passage of the Homestead Law in 1862. This act, limited temporarily in its application to those who ' have never borne arms against the United States Government,' granted a quarter-section (160 acres) of public domain to anyone who would undertake to cultivate it. The Morrill Act, passed the same year, subsidized agricultural education through public lands. At the same time easier access to the West was assured through the government-subsidized railroads. This legislation carried out the promise of the Republican party platform and helped bring to that party support from the agricultural West.

In order to secure this body of legislation and the support of those who benefited from it, the Republican party managed to throw about it constitutional guarantees. The Fourteenth Amendment, originally designed to protect the freedmen, with its provision that no state could deprive any person of life, liberty, or property without due process of law, was used to protect business interests from state regulation, and taught those interests to look to the Federal Government and the Republican party for protection. The Fifteenth Amendment, granting the franchise to the freedmen, was designed to secure the Negro vote to the Republican party.

Partly as a result of this legislation the Republican party, a sectional and, in all probability, a minority party,[1] was for two decades entrenched in power. But the support which came from industry, finance, agriculture, pensioned veterans, and the Negro does not wholly explain the long tenure of power by that party. Perhaps equally important was the fact that the Republicans could claim to be the party that had saved the Union, and that they could brand the Democrats with the odium of secession. With a single exception, every candidate whom the Republican party named for the presidency between 1868 and 1900 had been an officer in the Union army. For a generation Republican orators rang the changes on Fort Sumter and Andersonville prison, and ' waved the bloody shirt of the rebellion,' and no appeal was more effective than that voiced by Colonel Robert Ingersoll in the campaign of 1876:

Every State that seceded from the United States was a Democratic State. Every ordinance of secession that was drawn was drawn by a Democrat. Every man that endeavored to tear the old flag from the heaven that it enriches was a Democrat. Every man that tried to destroy this nation was a Democrat. Every enemy this great Republic had for twenty years has been a Democrat. Every man that shot Union soldiers was a Democrat. . . . Every man that loved slavery better than liberty was a Democrat. The man that assassinated Abraham Lincoln was a Democrat. . . . Every man that wanted the privilege of whipping another man to make him work for him for nothing, was a Democrat. . . . Every man that impaired the credit of the United States, every man that swore we would never pay the bonds, every man that swore we would never redeem the greenbacks, every maligner of his country's credit, or his country's honor, was a Democrat.[2]

The war, then, developed the revolution in industry, transportation, and finance that was already under way, and strengthened the political party which came to be committed to these interests. Most of this development might have come about eventually by peaceful means, but the war accelerated the process and gave to it a drastic character. Industrial America, Alexander Hamilton's embodied vi-

[1] It is interesting to note that in four out of the five presidential elections between the end of reconstruction in 1876 and 1892, the Democratic candidate polled a larger popular vote than did the Republican. In the fifth election, that of 1880, the Republican candidate polled some 7000 more votes than the Democratic. Or, to use another method of calculation, the total Democratic vote, from 1872 when for the first time all the Southern states voted, to 1892, was larger by some 4000 than the total Republican vote.

[2] *Works,* IX, p. 156.

sion, swaggered in under the cloak of patriotism, with the bayonet as a substitute for the slow process of education and economic revolution.

3. The Prostrate South

Physical devastation without parallel until 1914–18 preceded the social and economic revolution in the South. Over large sections of the country, Union and Confederate armies had tramped and fought, and parts of Virginia, Tennessee, South Carolina, Georgia, Alabama, and Arkansas had the appearance of enormous battlefields. Sherman had left a broad belt of blackened ruin from Atlanta to Savannah and from Savannah to Raleigh: ' where our footsteps pass,' wrote one of his aides, ' fire, ashes, and desolation follow in the path.' From Fairfax Courthouse to Petersburg the region was such a wilderness that nature came back and deer ran wild in the forests. Sheridan had swept down the fertile Shenandoah valley like an avenging fury, leaving a trail of wreckage and ruin. ' We had no cattle, hogs, sheep, or horses or anything else,' wrote a native of Virginia. ' The fences were all gone . . . the barns were all burned; chimneys standing without houses and houses standing without roofs, or doors, or windows . . . bridges all destroyed, roads badly cut up.' In the West, conditions were just as bad. ' The Tennessee Valley,' wrote Robert Somers, an English observer, ' consists for the most part of plantations in a state of semi-decay and plantations of which the ruin is total and complete.' The Governor of Arkansas wrote of his state: ' The desolations of war are beyond description. . . . Besides the utter desolation that marked the tracks of war and battle, guerilla bands and scouting parties have pillaged almost every neighbourhood. . . . It would be safe to say that two thirds of the counties in the State are in destitute circumstances.'

Some of the cities presented a picture as appalling as the rural regions. Charleston, once the proudest city of the South, had been bombarded and partially burned; a Northern visitor painted it as a city of ' vacant houses, of widowed women, of rotting wharves, of deserted warehouses, of weed-wild gardens, of miles of grass-grown streets, of acres of pitiful and voiceless barrenness.' Of Richmond, the capital of the Confederacy, we read ' all up and down, as far as the eye could reach, the business portion of the city lay in ruins. Beds of cinders, cellars half filled with bricks and rubbish, broken and blackened walls, impassable streets deluged with *débris.*' In Atlanta, Sidney Andrews found masses of brick and mortar, charred timber, scraps of tin roofing, engine bolts and bars, cannonballs, and long shot filling the ruined streets. Mobile, Galveston, Vicksburg, and numerous other cities of the South were in a similar plight.

With the collapse of the Confederacy, civil government and administration all but disappeared throughout the South. There was no money for the support of government and no authority which could assess or collect taxes. The postal service was paralyzed and it was fully two years before normal service was restored. There were no courts, no judges, no sheriffs, no police officers with any authority, and vandalism went unrestrained except by public opinion or by lynch law. ' Our principal danger,' observed George Cary Eggleston, ' was from lawless bands of marauders who infested the country, and our greatest difficulty in dealing with them lay in the utter absence of constituted authority of any sort.' Fraud and peculation added to the universal distress. United States Treasury agents seized hundreds of thousands of bales of cotton, and other property as well. ' Agents frequently received or collected property which the law did not authorize them to take,' admitted Secretary McCulloch. ' Lawless men, singly and in organized bands, engaged in general plunder; every species of intrigue and peculation and theft was resorted to.' No less than 40,000 claimants were subsequently reimbursed by the Federal Government because of illegal confiscation of their property.

The economic life of the South was shattered and even agriculture was slow to revive. Alabama produced 989,955 bales of cotton in 1860 and only 429,472 in 1870; Mississippi produced 1,202,507 bales in 1860 and 564,938 in 1870. Not until 1879 did the seceding states produce a cotton crop as large as that of 1860. The rice industry of South Carolina and Georgia all but disappeared, and so too the sugar cane industry of Louisiana. In 1870 the tobacco crop of Virginia was one-third that of 1860 and the corn and wheat crop one-half. Between 1860 and 1870 the total value of farm property in the seceding states declined 48 per cent.

What manufacturing there was had been all but destroyed. Few Southern banks were solvent, and it was years before the banking system was even partially restored. Confederate securities into which the people had sunk their savings were now as worthless as Continental currency. Shops were depleted of goods, and almost everything had to be imported from the North on credit. Labor was demoralized and property depreciated in value. Farm land that had once sold for $100 an acre went begging at $5, and in Mississippi alone almost 6 million acres of land were sold for non-payment of taxes. In the decade between 1860 and 1870 the estimated real value of all property in the eleven Confederate states decreased from $5,202,055,000 to $2,929,350,000: during the same period the estimated value of all property in the rest of the country more than doubled.[3]

The transportation system of the region was in a state of collapse. Roads were all but impassable, bridges destroyed or washed away, ditches filled in, river levees broken. What steamboats had not been captured or destroyed were in a state of disrepair. Railroad transportation was paralyzed, and most of the railroad companies bankrupt. Over a stretch of 114 miles of railroad in Alabama ' every bridge and trestle was destroyed, cross-ties rotten, buildings burned, water-tanks gone, ditches filled up, and tracks grown up in weeds and bushes.' A similar story could be told for the railroads of Virginia, the Carolinas, and Georgia. Except in Texas, public lands were not made available for Southern railway construction, and the railroad system of the South was not properly restored for almost a generation.

Starvation was imminent in certain sections. In Richmond half the population was dependent upon government rations, doled out by federal relief; in Columbia 10,000 people were fed by the army and at Atlanta the army commissary distributed food to 50,000 needy whites and blacks of the surrounding territory. The Negroes suffered most, being less able to adjust themselves to the new situation. The Freedmen's Bureau and other Northern relief agencies did what they could to alleviate the suffering, but as late as December 1865 it was estimated that in Alabama, Mississippi, and Georgia there were over half a million people without the necessities of life.

Social disorganization was scarcely less complete. Much of the educational system of the South had been deranged. Schools were closed, pupils and teachers scattered; school funds had been used up in the war, endowments for colleges and universities squandered or confis-

---

[3] Few things are more confusing or more unreliable than estimates of property values. It must be recalled that slaves were counted as property in the census of 1860. It is probable, too, that the values of 1860 were somewhat inflated, those of 1870 somewhat deflated. These estimates are not the same as the figures for assessed property value: the assessed values in the South reveal a more drastic depreciation.

cated. Churches had been destroyed and church money dissipated. Young men of family who had interrupted their education to fight for Southern independence had to labor in the fields to keep their families from starving; and a planter's family which still had young men was deemed fortunate. Seventy-year-old Thomas Dabney, once a proud Mississippi planter, did the family wash for years after the war. General Pendleton plowed his few acres and General Anderson worked as a day laborer in the yards of the South Carolina Railroad. George Fitzhugh, the philosopher of slavery who had lectured at Harvard and Yale, lived in a poor shanty among his former slaves. William Gilmore Simms, the South's leading man of letters, lost not only his ' house, stables, barns, gin house, machine and threshing houses, mules, horses, cattle, wagons, ploughs, implements, all destroyed ' but what was probably the finest private library in the South. ' Pretty much the whole of life has been merely not dying,' wrote the Southern poet, Sidney Lanier.

4. The Triumphant North

To the North the war brought not only victory, but unprecedented prosperity, a sense of power, a spirit of buoyant confidence, and exuberance of energy that found expression in a thousand outlets. Never before had the American people exhibited greater vitality, rarely since has their vitality been accompanied by more reckless irresponsibility. To the generation that had saved the Union everything seemed possible: there were no worlds, except the worlds of the spirit, that could not be conquered. Men hurled themselves upon the continent with ruthless abandon as if to ravish it of its wealth. Railroads were flung across mountain barriers, and settlers crowded into half a continent, while cattle swarmed over the grasslands of the High Plains. Forests were felled, the earth gutted of coal, copper, iron ore, and precious metals; petroleum spouted from untended wells. Telegraph wires were strung across the country and cables stretched from continent to continent; factories sprang up overnight; new industries were established and old industries took on new form; speculators thronged the floors of stock and produce exchanges, inventors flooded the patent office with applications for new devices with which to conquer nature and create wealth. Cities grew so fast

HAMILTON FISH *by Thomas Hicks*

that no one could keep track of them, and the mansions of the rich were as vulgar as the tenements of the poor were squalid. Year after year, from every hamlet and farm, countrymen hurried into the cities, and immigrants poured into the mines and the mills, all anxious to participate in what Vernon Parrington called the great barbecue. Well might Walt Whitman ask, ' Who shall hold in behemoth? who bridle leviathan? '

Despite four years of war the resources of the North seemed little impaired. Population and wealth had increased; the output of factory and farm had not declined despite the drain on manpower. The national debt was close to $3 billion, but no one doubted the solvency of the government, and the debt was in fact paid off in record time. More money was in circulation than at any time in our history, and the census of 1870 revealed that the per capita wealth of the North had doubled in ten years. Sectional antipathies were for the time moderated, and East and West joined in the common enterprise of exploitation. There was a universal feeling that the resources of the continent were as yet untapped. ' The truth is,' wrote Senator Sherman to his brother, the General, ' the close of the war with our resources unimpaired gives an elevation, a scope to the ideas of leading capitalists far higher than anything ever undertaken in this country before. They talk of millions as confidently as formerly of thousands.'

The war, like all wars, made special demands on some industries and depressed others, and created new opportunities for the amassing of private wealth. The business of supplying the armies with food and clothing and munitions was immensely profitable. More profitable still was the business of financing the war. Government bonds bore from 5 to 7 per cent interest in gold. During the war they had sold at a discount; after the war they brought a premium, and many a fortune was founded upon speculation in these bonds. The National Banking Act, too, afforded a legitimate means to wealth, and in 1870 some 1600 banks reported earnings of $60 million on a capitalization of $425 million, while President Johnson estimated that banks which held government bonds received an aggregate of 17 per cent interest annually upon their investment. The rewards of railroad organization, financing, and construction were even greater. At the end of the war there had been some 35,000 miles of railroad in the country; ten years later the figure was 74,000, and the profits of con-

struction and operation had gone, often by devious means, to establish the fortunes of Vanderbilt and Gould, Huntington and Stanford,
and other multimillionaires.[4]

No less spectacular was the exploitation of natural resources. Oil
was struck in western Pennsylvania in 1859, and soon thousands of
fortune-hunters stampeded into the oil-soaked triangle between the
Allegheny river and Oil Creek, and the stock of hundreds of new oil
companies was hawked from town to town. During the war years the
production of oil increased from 21 million to 104 million gallons,
and the capitalization of new oil companies was not far from half a
billion dollars. Equally stirring was the story of silver. In the year
of Lincoln's election the production of silver was a paltry $150,000;
by the end of Reconstruction the annual production had reached
$38 million, and the silver barons of the West had come to exercise
an influence in politics comparable to that of the bankers and industrialists in the East. Though the production of basic minerals
barely held its own during the war, the postwar years saw a great
upswing: coal production trebled, and iron ore production in the
Lake Superior region alone increased more than tenfold.

Business, which had been slowed down by the war, responded to
new and cheaper markets with renewed vigor. Old factories expanded, and new factories were built, and in the decade of the 'sixties
the number of manufacturing establishments in the entire country
increased by 80 per cent. Wherever we dip into the economic statistics of the postwar years we emerge with the same result. During
the 1860's the value of manufactured products in Maine more than
doubled, in Illinois it trebled, and in Michigan it increased fourfold.
Four times as much timber was cut in Michigan, four times as much
pig iron was smelted in Ohio, four times as much freight was handled
by the Pennsylvania Railroad, four times as many miles of railroad
track were laid, in 1870 as in 1860. Once the war was over, the
woolens, the cotton, the iron, the lumber, the meat, and the milling
industries all showed a steady and even a spectacular development.
Three times as many patents were granted in 1870 as in 1860, and
the transactions in the New York clearing house multiplied fivefold.
And while property values in the South were suffering a cataclysmic
decline, the census reported an increase in the total property value of

---

[4] Each of these fortunes was eventually returned to the public in the form of philanthropy.

the North and West from $10 billion in 1860 to over $25 billion a decade later.

Accompanying this extraordinary development of business enterprise was a steady growth in the population of cities and in immigration. Older cities such as New York and Philadelphia, Boston and Baltimore, continued the growth which had begun back in the 'forties, and newer cities such as Chicago and St. Louis, Cleveland and Pittsburgh, St. Paul and San Francisco, more than doubled their population in ten years. Immigration, too, responded to the new opportunities. Even during the war years some 800,000 immigrants had found their way to the United States, and in the ten years after Appomattox no less than 3.25 million immigrants flooded into the cities and the farms of the North and the West.

Industry, transportation, banking, speculation, the exploitation of natural resources and of labor, all contributed to the wealth of the country and to the wealth of individuals. Already observers began to remark upon that concentration of wealth in certain fortunate areas and certain favored groups. In 1870, for example, the wealth of New York State alone was more than twice as great as the combined wealth of all the ex-Confederate states; in that same year only 276,000 persons paid a tax on incomes of $1000 or over. Every business grew its own crop of millionaires, and soon the names of Morgan and Jay Cooke, Vanderbilt and Jay Gould, Armour and Swift, McCormick and Pillsbury, came to be as familiar to the average American as the names of his statesmen. A new plutocracy emerged from the War and Reconstruction, masters of money who were no less self-conscious and no less powerful than the planter aristocracy of the Old South. The war, which had gone far to flatten out class distinctions in the South, tended to accentuate class differences in the North.

BIBLIOGRAPHY

1. GENERAL. William A. Dunning, *Reconstruction, Political and Economic;* John Hope Franklin, *Reconstruction;* Allan Nevins, *The Emergence of Modern America;* Ellis P. Oberholtzer, *History of the United States since the Civil War,* vol. 1; James G. Randall & David Donald, *The Civil War and Reconstruction;* James F. Rhodes, *History of the United States,* vol. 5.

2. THE PROSTRATE SOUTH. Sidney Andrews, *The South since the War;* Myrta L. Avary, *Dixie After the War;* E. M. Coulter, *The South During Reconstruction;* John W. DeForest, *A Union Officer in the Reconstruction;* Francis B.

Leigh, *Ten Years on a Georgia Plantation;* Elizabeth W. Pringle, *Chronicles of Chicora Wood;* Whitelaw Reid, *The Southern States since the War;* Robert Somers, *The Southern States since the War;* Albion Tourgee, *A Fool's Errand, by One of the Fools;* J. T. Trowbridge, *The South.*

3. THE TRIUMPHANT NORTH. Victor S. Clark, *History of Manufactures in the United States 1860–1914;* Charlotte Erikson, *American Industry and the European Immigrant 1860–1885;* E. D. Fite, *Social and Cultural Conditions in the North During the Civil War;* Allan Nevins, *The Emergence of Modern America.*

4. DOCUMENTS. H. S. Commager (ed.), *Documents of American History,* nos. 241, 250; H. S. Commager, *The Blue and the Gray,* chaps. 21, 26, 29, 31; Walter L. Fleming, *Documentary History of Reconstruction* (2 vols.).

For further references, *Harvard Guide,* ¶ 195.

Reconstruction, Political and Constitutional

1. RECONSTRUCTION DURING THE CIVIL WAR

RECONSTRUCTION had been a subject of discussion in the North ever since the beginning of the war. As usual with American political issues involving sectional balance, the discussion took place on the plane of constitutional theory. It turned largely on two questions: whether the seceded states were in or out of the Union when their rebellion was crushed and whether the process of restoration was presidential or congressional. From the Northern premise that secession was illegal, strict logic reached the conclusion that former states of the Confederacy had always been and were now states of the Union, with all the rights and privileges pertaining thereto. If, on the contrary, secession was valid, the South might consistently be treated as conquered territory, without any legal rights that the Union was required to respect. Both sides adopted the proper deductions from the other's premise. Radical Republicans, the most uncompromising nationalists, managed to prove to their satisfaction that the Southern states had lost or forfeited their rights, while former secessionists insisted that their rights in the Union from which they had seceded were unimpaired!

But the question of the status of the Southern states was to be decided not in accordance with theory but in accordance with political and economic necessities. Lincoln, with his customary clarity, saw this, and saw, too, how dangerous was any theoretical approach to the problem. In his last speech, on 11 April 1865, he insisted that this question whether the Southern states were in or out of the Union was ' bad as the basis of a controversy, and good for nothing at all — a merely pernicious abstraction . . . Finding themselves safely at home, it would be utterly immaterial whether they had ever been abroad.' Obviously, these states were 'out of their proper practical relation with the Union'; the object of all should be to 'get them into their proper practical relation' again.

Lincoln had been pursuing this eminently sensible policy since the beginning of the war. As early as 1862 he had appointed provisional military governors in Tennessee, Louisiana, and North Carolina whose duty it was to re-establish loyal governments in those states. The North Carolina experiment came to naught, but in Tennessee Governor Andrew Johnson and in Louisiana General Banks made impressive progress toward the restoration of federal authority, and after the fall of Vicksburg, Arkansas was similarly restored. Encouraged by this success, Lincoln, in a proclamation of 8 December 1863, formulated what was to be the presidential plan of reconstruction.

The object of this plan was to get the seceded states back into their normal relations with the Federal Government as quickly and as painlessly as possible; the means was the presidential power to pardon. The plan itself provided for a general amnesty and restoration of property to all who would take a prescribed oath of loyalty to the Union. Furthermore whenever 10 per cent of the electorate of 1860 should take this oath they might set up a state government which Lincoln promised to recognize as the true government of the state. Whether Congress would recognize any such state government, or not, was of course a matter over which the Executive had no control.

This magnanimous plan, known as the 10 per cent plan, was promptly adopted in Louisiana and Arkansas. Thousands of voters, many of them cheerfully perjuring themselves, swore that they had not willingly borne arms against the United States; they were then duly registered. They held constitutional conventions, drew up and ratified new constitutions abolishing slavery, and their states then prepared to reassume their place in the Federal Union. But all was not to be such easy sailing. Congress, which was the judge of its own membership, refused to admit the representatives of these reconstructed states, and in the presidential election of 1864 their electoral votes were not counted.

The congressional leaders had a plan of their own for reconstructing the seceded states; it carefully retained control of the entire process in congressional hands. This plan was embodied in the Wade-Davis Bill of 8 July 1864, which provided that Congress, not the President, was to have jurisdiction over the processes of reconstruction, and that a majority of the electorate, instead of merely 10 per cent, was required for the reconstitution of legal state governments. When Lincoln averted this scheme by a pocket veto, he brought down upon himself the bitter excoriation of the Wade-Davis Manifesto. ' The President . . . must understand,' said the two Congressmen, ' that the authority of Congress is paramount and must be respected . . . and if he wishes our support he must confine himself to his executive duties — to obey and execute, not make the laws — to suppress by arms armed rebellion, and leave political reorganization to Congress.' Here was the real beginning of that rift between the President and the extremists of his own party who came to be called Radicals. The term has no connotations of liberalism, but refers to those who were determined to punish the South for secession and war, give civil and political rights to the freedmen, and establish the supremacy of the Republican party in national politics and of the Congress in the federal administration. Though at first small, the Radical faction included such formidable leaders as Thaddeus Stevens of Pennsylvania, Ben Wade of Ohio, Zachary Chandler of Michigan, and Charles Sumner of Massachusetts, and during the Johnson administration it managed to dominate the Republican party.

With the publication of the Wade-Davis Manifesto, then, the issue between the President and the congressional Radicals was fairly joined, and it was not to be settled until a President had been impeached, a Supreme Court intimidated, and the Constitution altered. Congressional opposition to Lincoln's plan was due in part to legislative *esprit de corps,* in part to the hatreds engendered by the war, and in part — it must be admitted — to persuasive constitutional considerations, for it seemed only logical that Congress, which had the power to admit new states and was the judge of its own membership, should control reconstruction. Nor should we ignore the emotional factor: to the Radicals it seemed monstrous that traitors and rebels should be readmitted to full fellowship in the Union they had repudiated and tried to destroy. But the strongest motives behind Radical intransigence were probably political and economic. If the Southern states returned a solid Democratic contingent to Congress, as appeared inevitable, the reunited Democratic party would have a majority in both Houses and would be strong enough to repeal a good part of the tariff, railroad, banking, and money legislation which the Republicans had placed upon the statute books. It would be the Union as in Buchanan's time, administered by ' rebels ' and ' Copperheads ' for the benefit of the agrarian South and West. Even Northerners who were quite willing to admit that Davis and Stephens were honorable men did not care to see them at their old desks in the Senate, shouting for state rights. As Thaddeus Stevens put it, the Southern states ' ought never to be recognized as capable of acting in the Union, or of being counted as valid states, until the Constitution shall have been so amended . . . as to secure perpetual ascendancy to the party of the Union.' The amendment which Stevens had in mind was that providing for Negro suffrage, which would fulfill the moral obligation to the freedmen, satisfy the humanitarian and liberal wing of the Republican party, and create a flourishing Republican party in the South.

If all this seems narrow and ungenerous, we should ask ourselves what other nation in history has ever turned over control of the government and of the spoils of victory to the leaders of a defeated rebellion?

If Lincoln had lived, there is some likelihood that his policy of wisdom, justice, and magnanimity would have prevailed; for even after his death the Radicals had great difficulty in imposing their policy upon the country, and in the end had to make many compromises and concessions. For about six weeks after the assassination there was a petty reign of terror, directed by Secretary Stanton and supported by President Johnson, who had always been in favor of hanging ' traitors ' when apprehended. Only the stern intervention of Grant prevented the seizure of Lee and other Confederate generals. Large rewards for the apprehension of Davis and his cabinet, as alleged promoters of the murder of Lincoln, resulted in their capture and temporary imprisonment. But the charge of complicity in the murder was quickly seen to be preposterous, and since it was obviously impossible to get a Virginia jury to convict Davis of treason, that charge was quietly directed to the circumlocution office. Thirst for vengeance appeared to be slaked by the shooting or suicide of the assassin Booth, by hanging his three accomplices and the unfortunate woman who had harbored them, after an extra-legal trial by a military tribunal, and by hanging the miserable Henry Wirz, commander of the infamous Andersonville prison, for the ' murder ' of Union prisoners.

All this was cause for shame, but again it is proper to observe that no other great rebellion of modern times has been suppressed with so little loss of life or formal punishment of the vanquished. For generations Southerners have rung the changes on the theme of Northern ruthlessness and Southern wretchedness during the Reconstruction years, and many historians, looking at this chapter of our history entirely through American eyes, have concluded that the North imposed upon the South a ' Carthaginian peace.' Yet we have only to recall the suppression of the Peasants' Revolt in Germany in the sixteenth century, the ravages of Alva in the rebelling Low Countries, the punishments inflicted on the Irish by Cromwell and on the Scots after Culloden, the vengeance exacted by victors over vanquished in the French Revolution, the Napoleonic Restoration, the great Chinese Rebellion of the mid-nineteenth century, or the Russian, Nazi, and Spanish revolutions of our own time, to appreciate how moderate was the conduct of the triumphant North after 1865.

2. ANDREW JOHNSON TAKES CHARGE

The results of the election of 1864 indicated that the country was still willing to follow ' Father Abraham,' and up to the eve of his death Lincoln persisted in applying his own policy of reconstruction. Lincoln's political astuteness might have defeated the sharp-witted leaders of the Radicals, but the situation was drastically altered by his assassination and the accession to the presidency of Andrew Johnson.[1]

Like Tyler in 1841, Johnson was the nominal head of a party of which he was not really a member. A War Democrat from a seceded state, he had been placed on the same ticket with Lincoln to emphasize the Unionism of the Republican party in 1864. Of origin as humble as Lincoln's, in early life a tailor in a Tennessee mountain village and unable to write until taught by his wife, he possessed many of Lincoln's virtues but lacked his ability to handle men. Self-

---

[1] Some of the Radicals rejoiced in the removal of Lincoln and the accession of Johnson. ' I spent most of the afternoon in a political caucus,' wrote Representative Julian of Indiana, ' and while everybody was shocked at his murder, the feeling was nearly universal that the accession of Johnson to the Presidency would prove a godsend to the country. Aside from Mr. Lincoln's known policy of tenderness to the Rebels . . . his . . . views of the subject of Reconstruction were as distasteful as possible to radical Republicans.'

educated and self-trained, he possessed a powerful though not well-disciplined mind, fine oratorical abilities, and a trenchant pen that was time and again to cast consternation into the ranks of his opponents. United with these intellectual qualities were the virtues of personal integrity, devotion to duty, and courage. Johnson had been the ablest spokesman of Southern democracy, and no truer democrat ever occupied the presidential chair. Yet he is perhaps the most maligned of all our Presidents. In the historical literature of the half-century after the war he is represented at the best as a pugnacious ignoramus, at the worst as a drunken ruffian. Actually he had most of the civil and moral virtues, and caution rather than pugnacity was his failing. No President was ever in a more difficult situation. He had no personal following either in the South or in the North, none of the prestige that came to Lincoln from the successful conduct of the war, and no party organization behind him, for he had broken with the Democratic party and he had not been accepted by the Republican. The Radicals, including most of the professional Republican politicians, controlled the party machinery; and the civil service looked to them for leadership. Seward and Welles were loyal to Johnson, but Stanton, with his customary duplicity, used the machinery of the War Department against him, and kept the Radicals posted on cabinet secrets. And Johnson's personality and policies soon antagonized not only the professional politicians but the financial and business interests, the press, and the pulpit as well.

Immediately upon his accession to the presidency, Johnson appeared to be willing to co-operate with the Radicals. ' Treason is a crime and must be punished,' he said; ' treason must be made infamous, and traitors must be impoverished,' and bluff Ben Wade exclaimed exultantly, ' Johnson, we have faith in you. By the gods, there will be no trouble now in running this government.' But soon there was trouble enough, and Wade was one of those who made it. After a brief interval of vindictiveness, Johnson, influenced no doubt by Secretary Seward and sobered by responsibility, swung around and made Lincoln's policy of reconciliation his own.[2] While Congress was out of session he proceeded to carry on Lincoln's reconstruction program. The theory underlying his policy was the indestructibility of the states. Johnson, like Lincoln, held that the

---

[2] When this happened Representative Julian of Indiana called him a ' genius in depravity.'

Southern states never had been out of the Union, and that their constitutional relations to the Federal Government were unaffected; but that until loyal governments were re-established their vitality was suspended.

Beginning with North Carolina, therefore, Johnson proceeded to appoint provisional civil governors in all the Confederate states where Lincoln had not already done so. These governors were enjoined to summon state constitutional conventions, which were to be elected by the ' whitewashed rebels ' — former citizens of the Confederacy who took the oath of allegiance required by the presidential proclamation. Fourteen specified classes, assumed to be inveterate rebels, were excluded from this general amnesty and required to make personal application for pardon.[3] Although many of those thus proscribed did receive special pardons from President Johnson, the general effect was to exclude natural leaders and experienced statesmen from participation in the task of establishing the new state governments. Broadly speaking, these were middle-class and poor-white governments.

The constitutional conventions declared invalid the ordinances of secession, repudiated the state war debts — which they could not in any event have paid — declared slavery abolished, and wrote new state constitutions. Not a single one of these granted the vote to even the most enlightened Negroes. Elections were promptly held under these new or amended constitutions, and by the autumn of 1865 regular civil administrations were functioning in all the former Confederate states except Texas.

Almost inevitably the ease and the speed with which reconstruction was being consummated excited distrust in the North. That distrust was exacerbated by the enactment of the Black Codes, and by the understandable but impolitic alacrity with which Southern voters elected their former Confederate leaders to high offices. As

[3] Including all civil and diplomatic officers of the Confederacy, and state governors, general officers of the Confederate Army, former U.S. Army officers and naval officers who had resigned their commissions, Congressmen and judges who had resigned their seats, and other Confederates worth over $20,000. To these classes were eventually added all who had held federal office before 1861 — coroners, constables, notaries public, and sextons of cemeteries — and who had afterwards entered the Confederate service or given aid and comfort to the rebellion. Confederate common soldiers were not disfranchised under this or any subsequent plan of reconstruction although they were ineligible for office under the congressional plan.

James G. Blaine later wrote, ' If the Southern men had intended, as their one special and desirable aim, to inflame public opinion of the North against them, they would have proceeded precisely as they did.' Certainly many Northerners came to believe that political reconstruction had been accomplished before any genuine reconciliation had been achieved, and that the South was neither repentant for her sins nor reconciled to defeat. There were many in the North who professed to fear that the rebellious spirit of the South had been scotched, not crushed, and the rewards of victory were being wasted. It was to meet this criticism that Johnson, in the fall of 1865, sent a number of observers to report on conditions in the South and to advise him on policies. These reports, as well as other information made public at this time, went far to prove that Southerners had fairly ' accepted defeat ' and its logical consequences.

' I am satisfied that the mass of thinking people in the South accept the situation of affairs in good faith,' wrote General Grant to the President. ' Slavery and State rights they regard as having been settled forever by the highest tribunal — arms — that man can resort to. . . .' Other observers, such as Harvey Watterson and Benjamin Truman concurred in this opinion; at the same time General Sherman was writing to his brother, the Senator, ' No matter what change we may desire in the feelings and thoughts of the people South, we cannot accomplish it by force. . . . You hardly yet realize how completely this country has been devastated, and how completely humbled every man of the South is.' In one sense, it is clear that Grant and Sherman were right. Without in the least confessing that her cause had been wrong the South acknowledged her defeat as final and irrevocable, and definitely put aside all thought of reopening the issue of slavery or secession. The South accepted the advice of Lee, that her allegiance was now due to the United States, and that her duty was to create a new and better South within the Union. Lee himself set a noble example to his countrymen by his serene acquiescence in trial by battle, and by devoting the rest of his life to service as president of Washington College in Lexington, Virginia.

Yet this did not mean, as many Northerners somewhat credulously supposed, that the South accepted the logical consequences of freedom for the Negro. ' Refusing to see that a mighty cataclysm had shaken the profoundest depths of national life,' says Professor Coulter, ' they did not expect that many things would be made anew but rather looked for them to be mended as of old, — that Humpty Dumpty might after all be put back on the wall.' [4] This misunderstanding about the implications of the phrase ' accepting defeat' was fraught with danger for the future.

This was the situation then, when Congress prepared to meet in December 1865. The South had ' accepted ' the verdict of Appomattox; the North was not inclined to take advantage of its victory. Slavery was irrevocably gone, and the wounds of war were healing. The presidential policy had apparently triumphed over Radical congressional policy, and the process of political reconstruction seemed all but complete. In his first annual message President Johnson announced with pride the restoration of an indissoluble Union of indestructible states. Such was the fact; yet within a few months all Lincoln's and Johnson's work of reconstruction was undone, and the Southern states once more were cast into the political crucible.

3. CONGRESS INTERVENES

The Congress which met for the first time on 4 December 1865 showed its temper by forbidding the clerk of the House even to read the names of the members-elect from the reconstructed states at the first roll call. The Radicals shrewdly postponed any definite decision on the status of these states on the ground that Congress was not yet properly informed. A joint committee of both Houses was appointed with authority to investigate and report on the title of Southern members-elect to be received. This Joint Committee of Fifteen, a resurrection of the old Committee on the Conduct of the War, was controlled by a Radical majority who soon proved themselves the most astute and skillful group of parliamentarians in our history. It was this committee which formulated the theory and set the pace of congressional reconstruction, dictated the tactics of the struggle against the President, and elaborated the Fourteenth Amendment to the Constitution. The chairman of the committee was the mild-mannered Fessenden of Maine, but the man who dominated its actions was Thaddeus Stevens of Pennsylvania, leader of the Republicans in the House, and for two years the virtual ruler of the United States.

A sincere democrat, lifelong spokesman for the poor and the oppressed, and tireless champion of public education, Stevens was now

---

[4] E. M. Coulter, *The South During Reconstruction*, p. 46.

a harsh embittered old man of seventy-four nursing an implacable enmity toward the Southern slaveocracy and President Johnson, who, he thought, stood between them and their just deserts. ' The punishment of traitors,' he said, in a speech in Congress in the spring of 1867, ' has been wholly ignored by a treacherous Executive and a sluggish Congress. To this issue I desire to devote the small remnant of my life.' And he did. ' Strip a proud nobility of their bloated estates,' he demanded; ' reduce them to a level with plain republicans; send them forth to labor and teach their children to enter the workshops or handle a plow, and you will thus humble the proud traitors.' Partly out of sincere devotion to the Negro,[5] partly out of a passionate conviction that the welfare of the Union was identical with the triumph of the Republican party, Stevens was determined to impose Negro suffrage on the states of the South. ' I am for Negro suffrage in every rebel State,' he said. ' If it be just it should not be denied; if it be necessary it should be adopted; if it be punishment to traitors, they deserve it.' The argument that Congress lacked the constitutional authority to impose its will on Southern states that were now back in the Union Stevens brushed aside as irrelevant, for he regarded the Southern states as nothing more than conquered provinces and insisted that Congress should treat them as such. Upon the basis of this theory Congress could do just about as it pleased with the former Confederate states, and this theory underlay much of the reconstruction of the next two years.

Charles Sumner of Massachusetts, Republican leader in the Senate, was not on the Joint Committee, but next to Stevens he was the most powerful figure in congressional reconstruction. An idealist by conviction, and a reformer by training, he was a pedant and a doctrinaire, but in his way quite as sincere as Stevens. Against the ex-Confederates he held no vindictive feelings, but without personal knowledge of the Negroes he believed them no exception to the dogma of equality, and that they wanted only the vote to prove it.

[5] In his devotion to the Negro, Stevens was consistent to the last. He arranged to be buried in a Negro cemetery, and wrote his own epitaph:

> I repose in this quiet and secluded spot,
> Not from any natural preference for solitude
> But, finding other Cemeteries limited as to Race by Charter Rules,
> I have chosen this that I might illustrate in my death
> The Principles which I advocated through a long life:
> EQUALITY OF MAN BEFORE HIS CREATOR.

Sumner advanced the theory that the Southern states had committed political suicide, had extinguished their standing as states, and were in the position of territories subject to the exclusive jurisdiction of Congress. Vain, humorless, and irritable, Sumner nevertheless had a distinguished record as a champion of good causes: the New England intellectuals looked to him for leadership, his polished orations impressed the commonalty, he was widely admired in England and on the Continent, and he gave to the Radical movement a tinge of idealism and altruism which it badly needed.

The theory of reconstruction upon which Congress ultimately acted was not precisely that formulated either by Stevens or Sumner, but a hybrid of the two. As drafted by the joint committee it announced that ' the States lately in rebellion were . . . disorganized communities, without civil government and without constitutions or other forms by virtue of which political relation could legally exist between them and the federal government,' that they had ' forfeited all civil and political rights and privileges under the federal Constitution,' and that they could be restored to their political rights only by Congress. In other words, the states were intact, but the state governments were, for most but not for all purposes, in a condition of suspended animation. Under this interpretation it was possible for Congress at once to deny representation to the Southern states and to accept the ratification of the Thirteenth Amendment by the legislatures of these same states!

The policy of Congress, then, was unequivocally opposed to that of the President. Johnson threw down the gauntlet to Congress in February 1866 by his veto of the Freedmen's Bureau Bill, and the war was on. Having accepted the issue Johnson should at once have remodeled his cabinet, and removed federal officials who were working against him. But he did not have the courage to split his adopted party. Consequently the Radicals were able to unfold their program with no opposition save the President's vetoes.

What was the Radical program? It can be summarized briefly. 1. To keep the ex-Confederate states out of the Union until they had set up governments that could be regarded as ' republican ' in nature. 2. To require them, as a prerequisite for readmission to the Union, to repeal their Black Codes, disqualify those who had been active in rebellion from holding state office, guarantee the Negro his civil rights and give him the right to vote and to hold office. What this meant was ratification of the Fourteenth and Fifteenth Amendments. 3. By these means to assure permanence to that body of tariff, railroad, agricultural, and money legislation which had been written into the statute books during the war years. To achieve these ends the Radicals were prepared to frustrate and, if necessary, paralyze opposition from the President or the Supreme Court.

The Radicals were unable to command enough votes to override the presidential veto of the first Freedmen's Bureau Bill,[6] but this initial victory of the President was almost his last. Within a month Stevens and Sumner pushed through a Civil Rights Bill which forbade the states to discriminate between citizens on the ground of race or color, and when Johnson rejected this bill as both inexpedient and unconstitutional, it was passed over his veto.

Yet even the Radicals were dubious of the constitutionality of this measure, and it was in part to allay these doubts that the Committee of Fifteen drafted the Fourteenth Amendment and presented it to the Southern states as a *sine qua non* of readmission to Congress. This amendment, the most important that was ever added to the Constitution, was designed to guarantee the civil rights of the Negro against unfavorable legislation by the states, reduce congressional representation in proportion to the denial of suffrage to Negroes, disqualify ex-Confederates who had formerly held state or federal office, invalidate the Confederate debt, and validate the federal debt. It was the first article of the amendment, that was particularly significant. This article first defined citizenship, and then provided that ' No State shall make or enforce any law which shall abridge the privileges or immunities of citizens of the United States; nor shall any State deprive any person of life, liberty, or property, without due process of law; nor deny to any person within its jurisdiction the equal protection of the laws.' It thus for the first time clearly threw the protection of the Federal Government around the rights of life, liberty, and property which might be invaded by the states, reversing the traditional relationships between these governments which had from the beginning distinguished our federal system. Ostensibly designed to protect the Negro, this provision came increasingly to be interpreted as extending the protection of the Federal Government to corporations whose property rights were threatened by state legisla-

---

[6] A second Freedmen's Bureau Bill was subsequently passed over the presidential veto, 16 July 1866.

tion. There is no evidence that the framers of the amendment anticipated any such interpretation of this article.

The issue was now joined between the President and the majority
in Congress. Everything turned on the election of a new Congress in
the autumn of 1866, one of the most important congressional elections in our history. A National Union Convention of moderate men
from both sections pledged support of the President but it did not
form a new party or create party machinery. Hence in most congressional districts in the North voters had to choose between a Radical
Republican and a Copperhead Democrat. Faced with this prospect
most of the moderate Republicans like Lyman Trumbull and John
Sherman went over to the Radical camp. The business interests, concerned with the maintenance of tariff, railroad, and banking legislation, followed suit, and almost all the powerful papers in the country
swung into line.

Johnson did not manage his campaign well. He failed to capitalize
the underlying economic issues and permitted the Radicals to make
the campaign one of personalities and of passions. He seemed incapable of advocating a policy of tolerance in a tolerant manner, and
his ' swing around the circle,' a stumping tour of the Middle West,
became in many instances an undignified exercise in vituperation. He
was, said Seward, the best stump speaker in the country, but as Secretary Welles shrewdly remarked, the President should not be a stump
speaker. Instead of appealing to the memory of Lincoln, and to the
finer popular instinct, he called names and rattled the dry bones of
state rights. Probably no orator, the New York *Nation* caustically
observed, ever accomplished so much by a fortnight's speaking. The
Radicals, on the other hand, proved themselves remarkable political
generals. Soft-pedaling the economic issues and concealing their intention to force Negro suffrage on the South, they made ' patriotism '
the single issue. Reiterated tales of Southern defiance and atrocity,
lurid reports of race riots at Memphis and New Orleans for which
Southern leaders were held responsible, bewildered Northern opinion.

In such circumstances it is not surprising that the Northern voters
returned a majority sufficient to override the presidential vetoes.[7]

Johnson has been criticized for not bowing to the ' will of the peo-

[7] The Congress that met in March 1867 contained 143 Republicans and 49 Democrats
in the House; 42 Republicans and 11 Democrats in the Senate.

ple ' and advising the Southern state governments to ratify the Fourteenth Amendment in order to mollify Northern sentiment and get
their representatives admitted. But Johnson was a stubborn man. He
knew perfectly well that Congress had no intention of receiving
Southern representatives until Negro suffrage had been established
and Northern supremacy written into the Constitution; he thought
the first of these objectives unconstitutional and the second undesir-
able. So Johnson nailed his colors to the mast, and defied Congress
to do its worst.

4. Congressional Reconstruction

While the campaign was still under way, in August 1866, President
Johnson formally declared the ' insurrection ' at an end, and that
' peace, order, tranquillity, and civil authority now exist in and
throughout the whole of the United States.' But the Radicals took
the results of the fall elections as a vindication of their ' thorough '
policy, and under the implacable leadership of Thaddeus Stevens a
series of measures of far-reaching importance were whipped through
a complaisant Congress. These measures undid the whole of presidential reconstruction, placed the Southern states back where they
were in April 1865, and temporarily revolutionized our political
system by substituting a quasi-parliamentary for a presidential system
of government.

The most important of these measures, indeed the most important
piece of legislation of the entire period, was the First Reconstruction
Act of 2 March 1867. This act declared that ' no legal government '
existed in any Southern state except Tennessee, and divided the territory of the South into five military districts subject to military commanders who were charged with the responsibility of protecting life
and property throughout their districts. For this purpose they might
use, at their discretion, the ordinary civil tribunals or military tribunals. Escape from this military regime and restitution of state rights
were promised on condition that a constitutional convention, chosen
by universal male suffrage, set up governments based on black and
white suffrage; and that the new state legislatures ratify the Fourteenth Amendment.

Johnson returned the bill with a scorching message arguing the
unconstitutionality of the whole thing, and the most impartial students have agreed with his reasoning. Yet the President thought that

he had no choice but to enforce this and subsequent Reconstruction Acts. In March 1867 military rule replaced in the South the civil governments that had been operating for over a year. The military governors ruled with a firm hand, sometimes with a flagrant disregard for the civil rights of the inhabitants. Confederate veteran organizations, parades, and even historical societies, were suppressed. Thousands of local officials were removed to make way for carpetbaggers or Negroes; the governors of six states were displaced and others appointed in their place; civil courts were superseded by military tribunals; the legislatures of Georgia, Alabama, and Louisiana were purged of conservatives; state legislation was set aside or modified; and an army of occupation, some 20,000 strong and aided by a force of Negro militia, kept the South safe for democracy but highly unsafe for the Democracy.

The rule of the major generals was harsh but had the merits of honesty and a certain rude efficiency. Particularly important were the efforts made by the military to cope with economic disorganization and to regulate the social life of their satrapies. Thus in South Carolina General Sickles abolished imprisonment for debt, stayed foreclosures on property, made the wages of farm laborers a first lien on crops, prohibited the manufacture of whiskey, and ended discrimination against the Negroes. Similar regulations were enforced in other military districts.

The principal task incumbent upon the military commanders was the creation of new electorates and the establishment of new governments. In each of the ten states over which they had jurisdiction — Tennessee, it will be remembered, was ' reconstructed ' in 1866 — the commanders enrolled a new electorate; in South Carolina, Alabama, Florida, Mississippi, and Louisiana the black voters outnumbered the white. This electorate chose in every state a constitutional convention which, under the guidance of Northern carpetbaggers, drafted new state constitutions enfranchising the blacks and disfranchising ex-Confederate leaders,[8] and guaranteeing civil and political equality to the freedmen.

---

[8] Because this provision for the disfranchisement of ex-Confederates led to the defeat of the constitutions in some states, Congress permitted Southerners to vote on — and defeat — them separately. In any event the Amnesty Act of 1872 re-enfranchised all except some 500 Southerners who had held high office in the Confederate government. Not until 1898 were all disabilities finally repealed.

These new state constitutions represented, in almost every instance, a definite advance upon the older constitutions. The Constitution of South Carolina, for example, set up a far more democratic, humane, and efficient system of government than that which had obtained during the ante-bellum regime. In addition to providing for universal manhood suffrage it abolished property qualifications for office-holding, reapportioned representation in the legislature, drew up a new and more elaborate Bill of Rights, abolished all ' distinctions on account of color,' reformed local government and judicial administration, outlawed dueling and imprisonment for debt, protected homesteads from foreclosure, enlarged the rights of women, and provided — on paper at least — a system of universal public education.

By the summer of 1868 reconstructed governments had been set up in eight of the Southern states: the other three — Mississippi, Texas, and Virginia — were reconstructed in 1870.[9]

After the legislatures of the reconstructed states had duly ratified the Fourteenth and Fifteenth Amendments, Congress formally readmitted them to the Union, seated their elected Representatives and Senators, and, as soon as the supremacy of the new governments appeared reasonably secure, withdrew the army. Yet congressional reconstruction was by no means complete, and Congress reserved to itself, and occasionally exercised, the right of interfering in the domestic affairs of the reconstructed states.

Congressional reconstruction was by no means confined to the South, nor were the Radicals content with securing the temporary ascendancy of their party in the South through Negro suffrage. They aimed ultimately at establishing congressional supremacy in the American governmental system. The majority of Congress, not the Supreme Court, was to be the final judge of the powers of Congress; the President a servant of Congress. This new dispensation was implicit in the Reconstruction Act of 2 March 1867 and in two other pieces of legislation pushed through Congress the same day. The first of these, the Command of the Army Act, virtually deprived the Executive of control of the army by requiring that he issue all military orders through the General of the Army, who was protected against

---

[9] Georgia, readmitted in 1868, was once again cast into the limbo of suspended animation when her legislature unseated some duly elected Negro members; she was not finally readmitted in good standing until 1870.

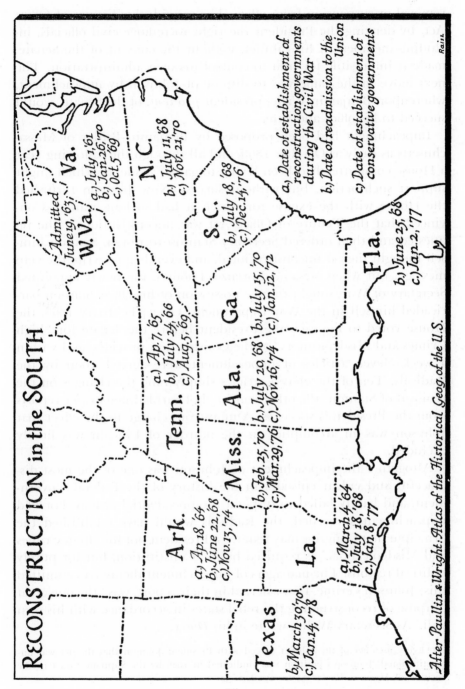

RECONSTRUCTION in the SOUTH

Va.
a.) July 1, '61
b.) Jan. 26, '70
c.) Oct. 5, '69

Admitted June 19, '63 j. W.Va.

N. C.
b.) July 11, '68
c.) Nov. 21, '70

S. C.
b.) July 18, '68
c.) Dec. 14, '76

Tenn.
a.) Ap. 7, '65
b.) July 24, '66
c.) Aug. 5, '69

Miss.   Ala.   Ga.
b.) Feb. 25, '70 b.) July 20, '68 b.) July 15, '70
c.) Mar. 29, '76 c.) Nov. 16, '74 c.) Jan. 12, '72

Fla.
b.) June 25, 68
c.) Jan. 2, '77

Ark.
a.) Ap. 18, '64
b.) June 22, 68
c.) Nov. 13, '74

La.
a.) March 4, '64
b.) July 18, '68
c.) Jan. 8, '77

Texas
b.) March 30, '70
c.) Jan. 14, '78

a.) Date of establishment of reconstruction governments during the Civil War

b.) Date of readmission to the Union

c.) Date of establishment of conservative governments

Raisz.

After Paullin & Wright: Atlas of the Historical Geog. of the U.S.

35

removal or suspension from office. The second, the Tenure of Office Act, by denying the President the right to remove civil officials, including members of his cabinet, without the consent of the Senate, made it impossible for him to control his own administration. The next move in the game was to dispose of Johnson by impeachment, whereupon Benjamin Wade, president *pro tem.* of the Senate, would succeed to his office and title.

Impeachment had been proposed by Benjamin Butler of Massachusetts as early as October 1866, and all through the following year a House committee had been trying to gather evidence which might support such action, but without success. Now Johnson furnished the House with the excuse for which it had so long waited. Convinced that the Tenure of Office Act was unconstitutional [10] he requested and then ordered Secretary Stanton to resign. Stanton himself thought the act unconstitutional, and even helped write the veto message, but when General Lorenzo Thomas, the newly appointed Secretary of War, sought to take possession of his office, Stanton barricaded himself in the War Department. On 24 February 1868, the House voted to impeach the President before the Senate for ' high Crimes and Misdemeanors ' as the Constitution provides, and within a week eleven articles of impeachment were agreed upon by the Radicals. Ten of the eleven articles simply rang the changes on the removal of Stanton; the other consisted of garbled newspaper reports from the President's speeches. A monstrous charge to the effect that Johnson was an accomplice in the murder of Lincoln was finally excluded.

Altogether the impeachment of Johnson was one of the most disgraceful and vulgar episodes in the history of the Federal Government, and barely failed to suspend the presidential system. For had impeachment succeeded, the Radicals would have established the principle that Congress may remove a President not for ' high Crimes and Misdemeanors,' as required by the Constitution, but for purely political reasons. The managers of impeachment themselves admitted this; Johnson's crime, they asserted in their report, was ' the one great purpose of reconstructing the rebel states in accordance with his own will.' As Secretary Welles wrote in his *Diary,*

[10] Every member of the cabinet agreed with President Johnson that the act was unconstitutional. Johnson's position was vindicated in 1926 by the Supreme Court in the decision of *Myers v. United States* 272 U.S. 52.

The Radical leaders are revolutionary, and many of their associates of better mind and temper have become tainted, corrupted, and distempered. They have called the President so many vile names, applied to him such vile epithets, that they persuade themselves he must be in fault, yet they designate nothing except that he does not lend himself and the Government to their party schemes and usurpations. They denounce him as a traitor because he adheres to the Constitution, holds firmly to his own belief, and refuses to surrender his own judgment to their dictation.[11]

The President was defended by able counsel including William M. Evarts, leader of the American bar, and Benjamin R. Curtis, formerly a justice of the Supreme Court. These tore the case of the prosecution to shreds and it was soon apparent to all but the most prejudiced that there were no valid grounds, legal or otherwise, for impeachment. Yet the Radicals would have succeeded in their object but for Chief Justice Chase who insisted upon legal procedure, and for seven Republican Senators who sacrificed their political future by voting for acquittal.[12] One more affirmative vote and Ben Wade — who himself voted for conviction — would have been installed in the White House. Then, in all probability, the Court would have been battered into submission, and the Radicals would have triumphed over the Constitution as completely as over the South.

When the trial took place, Johnson had less than one year to serve; and the Republican nominating convention met shortly after his acquittal. There was no longer any effective opposition to the Radicals within the party ranks, and the reconstructed states gave them faithful delegates. In the ensuing election General Grant was victorious over his Democratic rival, but his popular majority was dangerously narrow. Indeed, the election revealed unmistakably that the people were growing tired of Radical reconstruction and wanted a return to the traditions and practices of representative government. To the Radicals it indicated likewise that if the Republican party was to hold its gains it was necessary to ensure Negro suffrage by Constitutional amendment. Within four months the Fifteenth Amendment to the Constitution, that ' the right of citizens of the United States to vote shall not be denied or abridged by the United States or by any State on account of race, color, or previous condition of servitude,'

[11] Entry of 15 May 1868, III *Diary*, 355.

[12] Fessenden, Grimes, Trumbull, Ross, Van Winkle, Fowler, and Henderson. Fessenden died in 1869; none of the others was re-elected to the Senate!

was passed by both Houses of Congress and sent to the states for ratification.

5. RECONSTRUCTION AND THE CONSTITUTION

At no time in American history has the Constitution been subjected to so severe or prolonged a strain as during the era of reconstruction. The theory *intra arma silent leges* had been tacitly accepted during the actual conflict without serious impairment of the laws; it remained to be seen whether reconstruction would be carried through on the same legal theory. There arose at once a number of knotty problems concerning the legal character of the war, the legal status of the seceded states after Appomattox, and the status of persons who had participated in the rebellion. There arose, too, with equal urgency, the problem of the division of powers in the Federal Government — whether Congress or the President was the proper authority to direct reconstruction, and how far the courts could go in moderating or arresting programs primarily political. Finally — and in the long run most important — there came the question of the meaning of the three constitutional amendments that were pushed through during reconstruction, particularly the Fourteenth. Some of these legal questions were settled by the courts at the time, others, especially those affecting the freedmen, lingered on into our own day, and still others remained unsettled except by rude extra-legal forces.

Throughout the war President Lincoln maintained the legal principle that the states were indestructible; that they were never out of the Union for the simple reason that they could not be. This theory, though vigorously controverted by the Radical leaders, received judicial support in the leading case of *Texas v. White,* in 1869, in which Chief Justice Chase, speaking for the majority, said:

The Constitution, in all of its provisions, looks to an indestructible Union composed of indestructible States. . . . Considered, therefore, as transactions under the Constitution, the ordinance of secession . . . and all the acts of her legislature intended to give effect to that ordinance, were absolutely null. They were utterly without operation in law. The obligations of the State, as a member of the Union, remained perfect and unimpaired. It certainly follows that the State did not cease to be a State, nor her citizens to be citizens of the Union. If this were otherwise, the State must have become foreign, and her citizens foreigners. The war must have ceased to be a war for the suppression of rebellion, and must have become a war for conquest and subjugation. . . . Our conclusion therefore is, that Texas continued to be a State, and a State of the Union.[13]

Upon what theory, then, could reconstruction proceed? If the states were still in the Union, it was only the citizens who were out of their normal relations with the Federal Government, and these could be restored through the pardoning power of the President. This at least was Lincoln's theory, and Johnson took it over from him; when, in a series of proclamations, Johnson declared the insurrection at an end, the Supreme Court accepted his proclamations as legally binding.

But if the insurrection was at an end, by virtue of what authority did Congress proceed to impose military government upon Southern states, and set up military courts? The Supreme Court had already passed upon this question of military courts in *ex parte Milligan*. In this famous case involving the validity of military courts in Indiana, the Court laid down the doctrine that ' martial rule can never exist where the courts are open, and in the proper and unobstructed exercise of their jurisdiction '; and to the argument of military necessity the Court said, ' No doctrine involving more pernicious consequences was ever invented by the wit of man than that any of the [Constitution's] provisions can be suspended during any of the great exigencies of government. Such a doctrine leads directly to anarchy or despotism.' [14] Yet within a year, in clear violation of this decision, Congress established military tribunals throughout the South; and when the validity of this legislation was challenged, in the McCardle case, Congress rushed through a law depriving the Court of jurisdiction over the case, while the Supreme Court sat idly by.

While brushing aside embarrassing legal obstacles, Radical leaders nevertheless sought refuge in constitutional dialectics. The maintenance of military rule in the South and the insistence upon ratification of the Fourteenth Amendment, and later the Fifteenth Amendment, before re-admission, were based theoretically upon the clause in the Constitution that ' the United States shall guarantee to every State a Republican Form of Government.' For three-quarters of a century this clause had been interpreted to mean that Congress would sustain the pre-existing governments, but now the Radicals wrenched it away from this traditional meaning and insisted that

[13] 7 Wallace 700 (1869) .   [14] 4 Wallace 2 (1866) .

— for the Southern states at least — a ' republican ' form of government included Negro suffrage; and the Court supported them to the extent of declaring that ' the power to carry into effect the clause of guarantee is primarily a legislative power, and resides in Congress.' Yet at this very time only six Northern states permitted the Negro to vote, and two new states — Nebraska and Colorado — tried to come into the Union with suffrage limited to whites!

Some of the acts which Congress passed in order to carry into effect its reconstruction policy were palpably unconstitutional, but the attitude of the Radicals was well expressed by General Grant when he said of this legislation that ' much of it, no doubt, was unconstitutional; but it was hoped that the laws enacted would serve their purpose before the question of constitutionality could be submitted to the judiciary and a decision obtained.' This hope was indeed well founded, for the validity of some of the reconstruction measures never came before the courts, and others were not passed upon until long after they had ' served their purpose.' In his messages vetoing the Freedmen's Bureau Bill, the Civil Rights Act, and the Reconstruction Acts of 2 March, 23 March, and 19 July 1867, President Johnson argued their unconstitutionality with monotonous insistence. Nevertheless, once they were passed over his veto, he believed that he was required to carry out their provisions. It remained then for the aggrieved victims of these and other acts to test their validity in the courts. This object was sought in a number of cases, but in every instance the federal courts succeeded in escaping responsibility for a decision. Mississippi asked for an injunction restraining President Johnson from carrying out the Reconstruction Acts, but the Supreme Court refused to accept jurisdiction. Georgia then brought suit against Secretary of War Stanton and General Grant, but once again the Court refused to intervene in what it termed a political controversy.

Individuals fared somewhat better. Though some of the Radicals wanted to prosecute the leaders of the Confederacy for treason it was soon apparent that no jury would convict them, and the terms of military surrender guaranteed that there would be no military trials. Efforts to punish participants in the rebellion by discriminatory legislation were equally unsuccessful. Thus in *ex parte Garland* the operation of the federal test oath to exclude lawyers who had participated in the rebellion from practicing in federal courts was declared invalid because *ex post facto;* and in *Cummings v. Missouri* similar state legislation was held invalid on the same grounds.[15] For practical reasons it proved almost impossible to challenge the constitutionality of the confiscation of cotton or other property seized from those who were assumed to be rebels, but one notable case vindicated the right of the individual against lawless action even when committed in the name of the United States government. During the war Robert E. Lee's splendid estate at Arlington, Virginia, had been seized for non-payment of taxes and bid in by the Federal Government, which then used it as a national cemetery. Long after the war the heirs of Lee succeeded in testing this seizure and sale in the federal courts. By a five to four vote the Supreme Court held that it would hear a suit against a sovereign — or its agents — and that the original seizure was illegal. Constitutionally, the significance of the decision lies in the assertion that no official of the government can cloak himself in the immunity of sovereignty for his illegal acts.[16]

More important was the judicial emasculation of the various acts to enforce the Fourteenth and Fifteenth Amendments which made clear that the courts could not be relied upon to secure for the Negroes the rights presumably guaranteed to them.[17]

The delicate question to which department of the government, executive or legislative, appertained the task of reconstruction, has never been legally settled, though at the time the legislative branch was victorious. The truth is that the separation of powers played havoc with the realities of the situation. In the conflict between these two departments of the government President Johnson was scrupulous in his concern for the observance of the limitations on congressional power, while Congress rode roughshod over such limitations, and the courts played a negative and ineffectual role.

6. Radical Reconstruction in the South

The period from 1868 to 1877 was one in which the Radicals were in control, for varying periods, of most of the reconstructed states of

[15] 4 Wallace 333 (1867); and 4 Wallace 277 (1867).

[16] *United States v. Lee* 106 U.S. 196 (1882). When one of the judges asked Lee's counsel, Judge Shipman, if a claimant might eject the Government from a lighthouse, Shipman replied, ' Far better extinguish all the lighthouses in the land than put out the light of the Law.'

[17] See below, Chapter IV.

the South. This period is sometimes called ' Black Reconstruction,' but the term is misleading, for it implies that the reconstruction process was directed by Negroes. But in no state were the Negroes ever in control of the government, and only in South Carolina — where Negroes outnumbered whites four to three — did they have even a temporary majority in the legislature. There were no Negro governors, and very few Negroes in high position in the executive branch or in administration. It is a simple statistical fact that at no time and in no state did the Negro have a representation proportional to his numbers in any branch of any government.

Radical control of Southern states was exercised by an uneasy coalition of three groups — Negroes, ' carpetbaggers,' and ' scalawags.' Both of the latter words are, of course, heavily loaded. The one conjures up the image of an impecunious Yankee adventurer descending on a prostrate South with a carpetbag to be stuffed full of loot; the other was a word commonly applied to runty cattle and, by implication, to the lowest breed of men. There were disreputable adventurers among the carpetbaggers, but most of them were Union veterans who had returned to the South to farm, businessmen looking for good investments, government agents who for one reason or another decided to stay on in the South, schoolteachers who thought of themselves as a kind of ' peace corps ' to the freedmen. As for the ' scalawags ' — the largest single element in the Radical coalition — these were the men who had opposed secession in the first place and were now ready to return to the old Union and to take in the Negroes as junior partners in the enterprise of restoration.

It was the participation of the Negroes in the politics of the Southern states that arrested the attention of contemporaries, and has commanded the interest of students ever since. What Charles Sumner and Wendell Phillips had elaborated in their studies, and what Thaddeus Stevens and Ben Wade had contrived for political purposes, was put briefly into effect. Yet the experiment was never given a fair trial, nor were the auspices under which it was conducted even remotely favorable. The great majority of the freedmen were wholly unprepared for the exercise of political responsibility; they were catapulted into politics without preparation, and this at a time which would have tried the statesmanship of the wisest political leaders; they were abandoned by the best men of the South and deceived by the worst; and their innocence and inexperience betrayed them into the hands of mischievous spoilsmen who exploited them for selfish ends.

The Radical governments that flourished briefly in the Southern states in these years were, in many cases, incompetent, extravagant, and corrupt. The corruption was pervasive and ostentatious. In Florida, for example, the cost of public printing in 1869 exceeded the total cost for all of the state government in 1860; in South Carolina the state maintained a restaurant and bar-room for the legislators at a cost of $125,000 for a single session, and under the head of ' legislative supplies ' provided Westphalia hams, Brussels carpets, and ornamental cuspidors to the fortunate legislators; in Arkansas clerical costs of the auditor's office alone increased from $4000 to $92,000 in a single year; and in Louisiana the youthful Governor Warmouth managed to garner a fortune of half a million dollars during four years of office, while bartering away state property and dissipating school funds. But corruption did not begin with the advent of the Radicals, nor did it cease when they were forced from office. The Louisiana state convention of 1864, for example, spent $9400 on liquor and cigars for its members, and $156,000 for printing the journal of the convention; in 1873 the state treasurer of Virginia was indicted for looting the treasury, and as late as 1883 the treasurer of Tennessee absconded with $400,000 of state monies; while the land and railroad legislation of some of the ' Redeemer ' governments was no less corrupt and considerably more expensive than anything that the Radical governments indulged in. Corruption was confined to no class, no party, and no section: the corruption and extravagance of the Tweed Ring in New York City and the Gas Ring in Philadelphia made the Southern Radicals look like the feckless amateurs that most of them were.

Radical reconstruction was expensive, and taxes and indebtedness mounted throughout the South. In Alabama taxes increased fourfold, in Louisiana eightfold, and in Mississippi fourteenfold. Here, too, however, it is essential to keep a sense of perspective. Thus, in Mississippi where the new taxes were described as ' awful, monstrous, and ruinous,' the fourteenfold increase meant that taxes went up from 1 mill — or one-tenth of a cent — on the dollar, to 14 mills, or 1.4 cents on the dollar. We should keep in mind, too, a number of mitigating circumstances. With emancipation the population requiring public services had almost doubled; the task of repairing the damages of the war was a herculean one and made unprecedented demands on government; the Radical governments for the first time tried to set up public schools for all children; much of the property that had customarily borne the burden of taxation — banks, railroads, and industries — had been destroyed by the war, leaving almost the whole burden of taxation to fall on real estate. And while it may be true that the Radicals added some $131 million to the indebtedness of the eleven ex-Confederate states, it must be remembered that money was depreciated and prices inflated; that most of the states were forced to float their bonds in the North at ruinous discounts; and that some two-thirds of the total new indebtedness was in the form of guarantees to railroads and other industries. In this extravagant and often corrupt policy of underwriting railroads, there was no perceptible difference between Radicals and Redeemers. Actually the conservative governments which succeeded the Radicals spent, or pledged, more money on railway subsidies than had the Radicals. In Texas, for example, a grant of $6 million in public lands to the Texas and Pacific Railroad was carried by Democratic votes over the veto of the Radical governor. Of the situation in Alabama, John Hope Franklin says, ' there was no marked difference when the Republicans came to power in 1868 or when a Democratic governor was elected in 1870, or when the Republicans were finally driven from power in 1874. Corruption was bisectional, bipartisan and biracial.'

More important than all this was the constructive side of Radical reconstruction. Much of this was directed to sheer physical rehabilitation required by the ravages of the war, but in almost every one of the Southern states a good deal of progressive legislation was written onto the statute books by the Radicals. In South Carolina, for example, the Radical legislature reformed the system of taxation, provided relief for the poor, distributed homesteads to Negroes, established numerous charitable and humane institutions, encouraged immigration, and, for the first time in the history of the state, provided free public schools and compelled attendance of all children from six to sixteen. It was in the realm of public education that the Radical governments made their most significant contribution, and it was here, too, that the Redeemer governments — in part out of impatience with Negro education and in part for reasons of economy — reversed their predecessors most dramatically. In general the Radical legislatures advanced political democracy and inaugurated social reforms, and these contributions go far to justify a favorable judgment upon them. So, too, does the consideration that the Radical legislatures enacted no vindictive or punitive legislation against the former slave-owners.

Notwithstanding these real accomplishments, the Negro was unable to make any serious dent on Southern white hostility or prejudice. Convinced that the Negro was incompetent politically, Southern whites blamed on him all the ills and burdens and humiliations of reconstruction. And because the experiment of Negro participation in politics had been associated with the Republican party, Southerners concluded that the Democratic party was the party of white supremacy and fastened upon the South a one-party system. Because some progressive legislation was identified with carpetbag and Negro rule, they came to distrust such legislation and found reassurance in the return to office of an ultra-conservative Democracy. Because extravagance and high taxes had accompanied Radical rule, they came to believe that economy and good government were synonymous, and renewed their ante-bellum suspicion of governmental expenditure, even for schools. And, finally, the readiness with which the colored people had lent themselves to exploitation by unprincipled white men cost them the support of many of their quondam Northern champions, and helped foster the notion that Negro participation in politics had been premature.

7. The Undoing of Reconstruction

Inevitably Radical reconstruction aroused vigorous and determined opposition throughout the South. This opposition took both legal and illegal form. In some states where whites greatly outnumbered blacks, the Democrats recaptured control of the state governments by regular political methods almost at once. Thus Virginia and North Carolina were ' redeemed ' in 1870 and Georgia in 1871. Elsewhere it was thought necessary to resort to intimidation and terror to destroy the combination that made possible Radical success. Carpetbaggers and scalawags soon felt the heavy weight of economic pressure or the sharp sting of social ostracism. Negroes were dealt with more ruthlessly, by playing on their timidity and superstition or by methods that were frankly terroristic.

Much of this violence was perpetrated by secret societies, of which the most famous, though not the largest, was the Ku Klux Klan. ' The origin of the Klan,' wrote a Southern editor, ' is in the galling despotism that broods like a nightmare over these Southern States.' Actually its origin was more prosaic. When a social *kuklos* (circle) of young men in Pulaski, Tennessee, discovered that their initiation garb of sheets and pillow-cases made them appear to the Negroes as authentic spirits from another world, they spread the word, and the *kukloi* multiplied. In 1867 they organized as the ' Invisible Empire of the South,' with elaborate ritual and ceremonial. The KKK described itself as an institution of ' chivalry, humanity, mercy and patriotism,' but it was in fact quite simply an institution for the maintenance of white supremacy. Military reconstruction gave a sharp impetus to its growth, and during the next three or four years the KKK and other secret societies — notably the Knights of the White Camellia and the White Leagues of Louisiana and Mississippi — policed ' unruly ' Negroes in the country districts, discouraged them from serving in the militia, delivered spectral warnings against using the ballot, and punished those who disregarded the warnings. There can be no doubt that the Klan and other secret societies were guilty of innumerable crimes, and that their secrecy was often a cloak for lawlessness and outrages directed against the blacks and even against recalcitrant whites. Thus the Ku Klux Klan investigation of 1871 reported 153 Negroes murdered in a single Florida county that year; over 300 murdered in parishes outside New Orleans; bloody race riots in Mississippi and Louisiana; a reign of terror in parts of Arkansas; and in Texas, ' murders, robberies and outrages of all kinds.' It was, says the historian of reconstruction, Ellis P. Oberholtzer, ' a reign of outrage and crime which, all taken together, forms a record of wrong among the most hideous in the history of any modern state.' Not all of this could be laid at the doors of the Klan or the White Leaguers, or even of the whites, but the evidence is conclusive that they were responsible for most of the violence that afflicted the South during these turbulent years.

Under the impact of all this, Negro participation in politics declined sharply, and even whites began to desert the Radical cause. But the Radicals had no intention of acquiescing tamely in the undoing of reconstruction. Their answer was first a series of state laws which sought to break up the secret societies and, when these proved

THE VERDICT OF THE PEOPLE *by George Caleb Bingham*

unavailing, an appeal to Washington for help. The Grant administration responded with renewed military occupation of evacuated
districts, the unseating of Democratic administrations on the ground
of fraud, and a new crop of supervisory laws of which the most important were the Force Acts of 1870 and 1871 and the drastic Ku
Klux Klan Act of 1871 authorizing the President to suspend the writ
of habeas corpus and suppress violence by military force. Altogether
some 7000 indictments were found under these acts, and over 1000
convictions, but it would be an exaggeration to say that they fulfilled
their purpose. In large areas of the South — notably in South Carolina, Louisiana, and Mississippi — violence flourished throughout
the entire reconstruction period.

The fact is that public opinion in the North was no longer willing to sustain federal intervention in the affairs of the South. Much
of the idealism that had gone into the anti-slavery movement had
petered out, or been deflected into new channels, and the North was
increasingly willing to leave the Negroes to their fate. The country
was tired of the ' Southern question '; even the *Nation,* long a spokesman for ardent Radicalism, confessed that ' every Republican has
become disgusted with military control of the States, and thoroughly
convinced that a State government which cannot support itself
should not be propped up by national soldiers.' A substantial segment of the Republican party opposed the continuance of the Radical policy in the South, and in the election of 1872 this group threw
its support to Horace Greeley, who was pledged to put an end to the
Southern problem. In his day an implacable foe of the slaveocracy,
Greeley now called for a cessation of ' talk about rebels and traitors.'
Grant was elected, but two years later the Democrats captured the
lower House, and the repudiation of Radicalism was all but complete. Meantime all the Southern states had been readmitted to Congress, and by the Amnesty Act of 1872 almost all Southern whites
who were still disfranchised were restored to full political privileges.

In the South, too, the Radicals were in full retreat. Frightened by
the violence they inspired, and weary of being pawns in the party
struggle, Negroes were deserting their Republican allies. The merchants and businessmen who had taken over from the planters wanted
peace, too — peace within the Republican party if that were necessary, but better yet peace at the expense of that party. Meantime,

factional struggles between carpetbaggers and scalawags split the Republican party in almost every Southern state. As the power of the Radicals waned, demands for military intervention by Washington became more insistent, but Grant himself revolted against these demands. ' The whole public,' he protested, ' are tired out with the annual autumnal outbreaks in the South, and the great majority are ready now to condemn any interference on the part of the government.'

So in state after state the conservative whites recaptured control of the political machinery, until by the end of 1875 only South Carolina, Louisiana, and Mississippi were still under Radical control, and even in these states that control was precarious. The process of ' redemption ' was by no means a simple matter of keeping the Negro and the carpetbagger away from the polls and restoring ' white supremacy.' Almost everywhere the struggle was also between rival economic groups, and the prizes were railroad and corporate franchises. Thus in Virginia much of the politics of reconstruction polarized about two rival groups of railroad promoters led by John W. Garrett, president of the Baltimore and Ohio Railroad, and General William Mahone, hero of ' the Crater ' and president of the Southside line — later the Norfolk and Western Railroad. The prize was control of the Virginia and Tennessee Railroad which gave a connection across the mountains to the West. The victory for Mahone was at once a victory for the Southside Railroad and for the ' Redeemers,' though Mahone himself found no difficulty in going over to the Republicans a few years later! So too in Alabama the political struggle was for control of the railroad that tapped the rich Birmingham coal and iron fields, rather than between ' Radicals ' and ' Redeemers ' — between a group of Democratic businessmen backed by the powerful Louisville and Nashville Railroad and the Belmont interests in New York, and a rival group connected with the Alabama and Chattanooga Railroad and supported by the Jay Cooke interests in Philadelphia. The collapse of the House of Cooke meant the triumph of the Louisville and Nashville group, and of the Democratic Redeemers.

Thus by one means or another conservatives triumphed. Negroes were eliminated from politics, carpetbaggers scared out, scalawags won over — and ' home rule ' was restored. The Redeemer governments then proceeded to reduce expenditures and taxes — often at the expense of school children — and to wipe a good deal of progressive legislation off the statute books; it is suggestive that they did not find it necessary to draft new constitutions but mostly continued with those written by the Radicals. But acting on the assumption that the Radicals had saddled their states with fraudulent debts, and on the fact that in some instances the railroads, for whose benefit the debts had been contracted, had not carried out their part of the bargains, the Redeemers proceeded to repudiate a good part of the state obligations. By this convenient method Southern states rid themselves of perhaps $100 million of debts; efforts to collect these debts in the federal courts ran into the stone wall of the Eleventh Amendment.

When Rutherford B. Hayes was inaugurated President, 4 March 1877, the carpetbag regime had been overthrown in all the Southern states save South Carolina and Louisiana, where it was still upheld by federal bayonets. In South Carolina an army of Confederate veterans known as Red Shirts organized white voters, kept Negroes away from the polls, and elected the beloved Confederate General Wade Hampton governor and a Democratic legislature. A Republican returning board, however, sustained by federal soldiers, threw out the ballots of two counties, canceled thousands of others, and declared the carpetbag Governor D. H. Chamberlain duly re-elected to the governorship. The Democratic members then organized their own House, and with Speaker, clerks, and sergeant-at-arms forced their way into the representatives' chamber where the Radicals were sitting. During three days and nights the rival Houses sat side by side, every man armed to the teeth and ready to shoot if the rival sergeant-at-arms laid hands on one of his colleagues. At the end of that time the Democrats withdrew, leaving Governor Chamberlain in possession of the state house. For four months the two legislatures glared at each other, but the people of the state paid their taxes to Hampton's government. Chamberlain hastened to Washington to appeal for aid, but in vain. Faithful to the compromise by which he had been elected, President Hayes broke the deadlock by withdrawing the troops from Columbia, and the Democrats took possession. Two weeks later, when federal troops evacuated New Orleans, white rule was completely restored throughout the South. That restoration represented a victory of order over disorder, of the South over the Federal Government, of conservative business interests over elements of reform, and of the principle of white supremacy over the interests of the Negro.

Reconstruction left deep physical and moral scars upon the South — the white South and the black alike. Politics were forced into an unnatural radical groove, allegiance to the Democratic party became synonymous with white supremacy, and from 1876 to 1916 the South presented a united front politically. Race relations were poisoned, as the annual crop of outrages and lynchings attested. The colored people were retarded at least a generation in their progress toward responsible citizenship, and toward economic self-sufficiency, and even longer in their progress toward social equality. Southern society remained relatively static, immune to modern movements in education and social regeneration, and in the twentieth century the South was hardly more prepared to meet the industrial invasion than New England had been a century before.

BIBLIOGRAPHY

1. PRESIDENTIAL RECONSTRUCTION. Howard Beale, *The Critical Year;* Howard Beale (ed.), *The Diary of Gideon Welles* (3 vols.); Jonathan Dorris, *Pardon and Amnesty under Lincoln and Johnson;* W. A. Dunning, *Reconstruction, Political and Economic* and *Essays on the Civil War and Reconstruction;* John Hope Franklin, *Reconstruction;* William B. Hesseltine, *Lincoln and the War Governors;* Charles McCarthy, *Lincoln's Plan of Reconstruction;* Eric McKitrick, *Andrew Johnson and Reconstruction;* George Fort Milton, *The Age of Hate;* James G. Randall, *Constitutional Problems under Lincoln.*

2. CONGRESSIONAL RECONSTRUCTION. Thomas B. Alexander, *Political Reconstruction in Tennessee;* George Bentley, *A History of the Freedmen's Bureau;* Willie M. Caskey, *Secession and Restoration in Louisiana;* Walter L. Fleming, *Civil War and Reconstruction in Alabama;* J. W. Garner, *Reconstruction in Mississippi;* Matthew Josephson, *The Politicos, 1865–1896;* Roger Shugg, *Origins of the Class Struggle in Louisiana;* F. B. Simkins & R. H. Woody, *South Carolina during Reconstruction;* David Y. Thomas, *Arkansas in War and Reconstruction;* C. M. Thompson, *Reconstruction in Georgia.*

3. RECONSTRUCTION AND THE CONSTITUTION. W. A. Dunning, *Essays on the Civil War and Reconstruction,* chaps. 1–3; Harold Hyman, *The Year of the Oath;* Joseph B. James, *The Framing of the Fourteenth Amendment;* John M. Mathews, *Legislative and Judicial History of the Fifteenth Amendment;* Jacobus ten Broek, *Antislavery Origins of the Fourteenth Amendment;* Charles Warren, *The Supreme Court of the United States,* vol. 2.

4. RADICAL RECONSTRUCTION. Fawn Brodie, *Thaddeus Stevens;* Richard N. Current, *Old Thad Stevens;* Jonathan Daniels, *Prince of Carpetbaggers:*

Life of M. S. Littlefield; Mary Dearing, *Veterans in Politics: the G.A.R.;* D. M. De Witt, *Impeachment and Trial of Andrew Johnson;* David Donald, *Charles Sumner* (2 vols.) ; W. E. B. DuBois, *Black Reconstruction;* Harold Hyman, *Edwin M. Stanton;* Ralph Korngold, *Thaddeus Stevens;* George F. Milton, *The Age of Hate;* Henry White, *Life of Lyman Trumbull.*

5. UNDOING OF RECONSTRUCTION. W. G. Brown, *The Lower South in American History;* H. J. Eckenrode, *Rutherford B. Hayes, Statesman of Reunion;* Stanley Horn, *The Invisible Empire, the Story of the Ku Klux Klan;* Henry T. Thompson, *Ousting the Carpetbagger;* C. G. Welles, *Hampton and His Red Shirts;* C. Vann Woodward, *Reunion and Reaction* and *Origins of the New South.*

6. DOCUMENTS. H. S. Commager, *Documents,* nos. 245–67, 269–73, 278, 284; W. L. Fleming, *Documentary History of Reconstruction* (2 vols.) ; Benjamin Kendrick (ed.) , *Journal of the Joint Committee of Fifteen on Reconstruction;* Samuel Klaus (ed.) , *The Milligan Case.*

For further references, *Harvard Guide,* ¶¶ 189–90.

Politics of the Grant Administration

1. THE ELECTION OF 1868

EVEN as the Senate sat in solemn judgment on President Johnson, the triumphant Republicans met in party convention to nominate his successor, and to promise a continuation of Radicalism in politics and conservatism in economic policy. Any number of favorite sons were willing to accept the crown which sat so uneasily upon Johnson's head, but only one was considered worthy of that honor: General Grant. Before the Civil War he had seldom taken the trouble to vote, and the army was not a good school of politics. Such political principles as he professed had inclined him toward the Democratic party, but after McClellan's candidature it was inconceivable that he should have tied up with the Democrats. He had been to Lincoln a faithful subordinate, but to Johnson less than faithful, and after his break with Johnson he had been captured by the shrewd Radical politicians who saw in him an unbeatable candidate.[1] On the first ballot Grant received a unanimous nomination; the selection of ' Smiling ' Schuyler Colfax of Indiana as his running mate did nothing to strengthen the ticket.

The Republican platform pledged the party to continue Radical reconstruction in the South, repudiated the ' Ohio idea ' of payment of the government debt in greenbacks, committed the party to hard money, and preserved an eloquent silence on the tariff issue. The adoption of this platform indicated that the Republican party of Frémont and Lincoln was now controlled by a coalition of political Radicals (in the then special sense of that word) and economic conservatives.

[1] As Gideon Welles observed, ' A feeling of gratitude for military services, without one thought of his capacity, intelligence, or experience in civil affairs, has enlisted popular favor for him, and the conspirators have availed themselves of it, though the knowing ones are aware of his unfitness for administrative duties. They expect to use him; he intends to use them.' Entry 21 May 1868, III *Diary*, 363.

No such unanimity characterized the Democratic convention which met in New York City some weeks later, for the deep gash cut in that party in 1860 had not yet fully healed. The Democrats still labored under the odium of secession, and were embarrassed by the leadership of the discredited President Johnson. Harassed by conflicting counsels and confused by rival claims for leadership, they adopted a platform that emphasized equally the reconstruction and the money issues. That platform arraigned the Radical Republican party ' for its disregard of right, and the unparalleled oppression and tyranny which have marked its career,' charged it with ' corruption and extravagance ' exceeding anything known to history, and declared its Reconstruction Acts ' unconstitutional, revolutionary, and void.' In addition the platform committed the Democratic party to the so-called ' Ohio idea ' — that, wherever possible, the public debt of the United States should be paid in greenbacks rather than in gold. If the campaign was to be fought on the reconstruction issue, Andrew Johnson was the obvious candidate; if on the money issue, the logical candidate was ' Gentleman George ' Pendleton, sponsor of the ' Ohio idea '; if on the issue of loyalty, General Hancock of Pennsylvania. With an evasiveness that was coming to appear characteristic, the party chose instead a man who could not dramatize the reconstruction issue, who was committed to a hard money policy, and whose wartime record had associated him with the Copperheads — the weak and the ineffectual Horatio Seymour, former Governor of New York.

The campaign that followed was one of the most bitterly fought in our history. The stakes of victory were large. To Republicans success promised an indefinite tenure of power, during which the party might be given a national basis through the extension of Negro suffrage to the South, and an untrammeled continuation of the economic program through tariff, banking, and railroad policies already begun. To the Democrats victory promised the relegation of the Negro problem to local politics, the restoration of Southern states to the Union, and the modification of some of the economic legislation which had been written into the statute books during the Civil War years. Republican strategy made reconstruction the major issue and the efforts of the Democrats to distract attention to economic issues proved unavailing. Again the Republicans waved the ' bloody shirt of the rebellion,' even more effectively than in 1866. When the electoral vote was counted, it was found that Grant had carried all the states but eight, but that his popular majority was only 300,000. It was the Negro vote of some 450,000 that gave Grant his popular majority, and it was the exclusion of three Southern states [2] and the control of six others through reconstruction laws that assured him his large electoral college majority. Only by a willful misreading could the election be interpreted as a vote of confidence for the Radicals or even an endorsement of Grant. The statistics of the election strengthened the Radicals in their determination to assure the vote of the Negro and nourish a Republican party in the South, and excited Southerners to believe that restoration of home rule would mean the triumph of the Democratic party not only in the liberated states of the South but nationally as well.

2. President Grant

The problems which Grant faced were varied and complex, but he brought to their solution neither understanding nor competence. Of the new economic forces that were shaping the United States, he was completely unaware. With less equipment for the presidency than any predecessor except Harrison, his temperament unfitted him for high political office, and he was unable or unwilling to overcome his temperamental deficiencies. Although a leader of men, he was not a good judge of men, and the very simplicity which had carried him safely through the intrigues of the Civil War exposed him to the wiles of politicians whose loyalty to himself he mistook for devotion to the public weal.

Brilliance, subtlety, urbanity — these qualities were not expected of Grant, but it came as a shock that he seemed to have lost the qualities he had shown in the war — a sense of order and of command, directness, resoluteness, consistency, and intellectual honesty. He was vacillating and undignified; his judgment was incalculable, his prejudices implacable. The magnanimous victor of Appomattox revealed himself in office petty, vindictive, and shifty. He was naïve rather than innocent, simple rather than unsophisticated, and his simplicity, as Henry Adams remarked, ' was more disconcerting than the complexity of a Talleyrand.'

[2] Mississippi, Texas, Virginia.

Untutored in politics, his political sense was as primitive as that of a Sioux Indian. He was ignorant of the law and even of the Constitution, and he never came to understand properly the relations of the executive to his cabinet or to the other departments of the government. Nor did he ever come to understand the character of the presidential office. To the end he regarded the presidency as a personal prerogative, a reward for services rendered rather than a responsibility, and he failed entirely to grasp the real character of the pressure groups who lobbied so successfully for favorable legislation on tariffs, finance, public lands, and even foreign affairs. He had, apparently, but one political principle — faith in his friends. It was a faith often mistaken and often betrayed.

Without qualifications for his office, Grant's only hope lay in the wisdom and integrity of his advisers. These were chosen with bizarre irresponsibility. Grant's cabinet contained some men of ability and two or three of real talent, but these were accidents, and in time Grant came to regard them as errors. Altogether, during his eight years of office, Grant appointed no less than twenty-six men to his cabinet.[3] Six — Hoar, Cox, Creswell, Jewell, Bristow, and Fish — proved to be men of intelligence and integrity, and of these Grant managed to dismiss all but one, Secretary of State Fish.

It was fortunate, indeed, that Grant was able to command, throughout the eight years of his administration, the talents of Hamilton Fish. A New York aristocrat, Grant's third choice for the State Department, and relatively unknown when he took office, Fish proved himself one of the shrewdest men who have ever directed the foreign affairs of the nation. He had what most of his colleagues in Grant's cabinet lacked, integrity of character, disciplined intelligence, learning, experience, urbanity, and a tact and patience sufficient to win and retain the confidence of his chief. To Fish must be ascribed responsibility not only for the achievements of the admin-

[3] ' He picked his cabinet officers to suit himself, and so clumsily that the group had to be reorganized before it could function. The state department he gave to a personal friend, Elihu B. Washburne, to gratify his pride; he allowed a military aide, John A. Rawlins, to appropriate the War Department to reward himself; he picked a great merchant with whom he had dined well, Alexander T. Stewart, to fill the treasury post, only to discover that his appointee was legally incompetent. The other places he passed around with no reference to the existence of a party that fancied it had a right to rule, or to popular sense of fitness in appointment; and he could not understand or forgive criticism of himself because of this.' F. L. Paxson in *Dictionary of American Biography* (article on Grant).

istration in the field of foreign affairs but also for preventing many egregious mistakes in domestic policies.

Yet for all his obvious defects of character and of mind, Grant wielded an immense power. The devotion which he commanded from millions of men was devotion to something stronger than integrity or political wisdom or character or intellectual pre-eminence. It was devotion to an ideal. 'The plain man,' as Allan Nevins observes, 'had not elected Grant; he had elected an indestructible legend, a folk-hero. . . . Mention that monosyllabic name, and the prosaic laborer, farmer, clerk, or business man for once in his life saw a vision. It was a vision of four years of terror and glory. Painted on the clouds above his farm or shop, he saw the torrent of muddied blue uniforms rallying on the bluffs of Shiloh . . . he saw the night ripped by shells and rockets as gunboats spouting fire raced past Vicksburg; he saw the lines at Lookout Mountain waver, reform and go on up; he saw two armies wait as Lee walked into the parlor at Appomattox.' It was well for Grant that he brought to the presidency this imperishable glamor, for he brought little else.

3. FOREIGN AFFAIRS

Thanks to Seward the Johnson administration was at its best in the realm of foreign affairs. Thanks to Hamilton Fish the Grant administration likewise won its most notable successes in this area. During almost the whole of Grant's two terms of office, American foreign relations were in a delicate and critical state. The outbreak of revolution in Cuba threatened to involve the United States in war with Spain; the activities of the Fenians along the Canadian border embarrassed our relations with Canada; and the unwillingness of Lord Russell to arbitrate American claims against Great Britain for alleged failure to observe neutrality during the Civil War strained Anglo-American friendship to the breaking-point.

Many vexatious foreign questions had grown out of the Civil War. Some had been liquidated; others remained to plague the Grant administration. Seward, by his firm attitude toward the French in Mexico and the Spaniards in Santo Domingo, had vindicated the Monroe Doctrine, and by his able strokes of diplomacy had advanced his policy of imperialism in the Pacific. Spain's attempted conquest of Santo Domingo broke down of its own accord, but the Spanish withdrawal from the ill-fated island in 1865 appeared to be a diplomatic victory for Seward. It was not until two years later that Seward persuaded Napoleon III of the necessity of abandoning the Mexican venture: in June 1867 the puppet-Emperor Maximilian slumped before a firing squad and the cardboard empire collapsed. Russia had long been eager to get rid of Alaska, and in 1867 Sumner in the Senate and a well-oiled lobby in the House permitted Seward to buy that rich domain, known at the time as ' Seward's Folly,' for $7,200,-000. To round out his expansionist policy Seward annexed the Midway Islands west of Hawaii, and, with a view to the construction of an isthmian canal at some future date, acquired the right of transit across Nicaragua. When he surrendered his office, a treaty for the purchase of the Danish West India islands (the present Virgin Islands) was pending in the Senate — which promptly rejected it.

President Grant, although indifferent to the Danish West Indies, was enormously interested in another of Seward's Caribbean projects — the annexation of Santo Domingo. This hare-brained proposal had originated with two Yankee fortune-hunters who planned to secure for themselves half the wealth of the island. They managed to draw into their conspiracy powerful financial and commercial interests and bought the support of such men as Ben Butler, John A. Rawlins, and Grant's personal secretary, Orville Babcock; these in turn persuaded the President to commit himself to the project. Grant sent Babcock on a tour of inspection to Santo Domingo, and Babcock returned with a treaty of annexation in his pocket. The treaty was eventually formalized and submitted to the Senate only to encounter the implacable hostility of Charles Sumner and Carl Schurz and fail of ratification. It was the most severe defeat that the administration was to suffer.

The Santo Domingo episode was not in itself of importance, but its consequences were. It revealed how easily Grant could be won over to projects of a dubious character and how naïve his understanding of foreign affairs. It led to the deposition of Charles Sumner from his position as chairman of the Senate Committee on Foreign Affairs and caused a rift in the Republican party that widened, by 1872, into a complete breach. It distracted the attention of Grant and the Radicals from the Cuban situation and enabled Secretary Fish to sidetrack the demand for a recognition of Cuban belligerency and preserve peace with Spain.

A Cuban rebellion had broken out in 1868 and dragged on for ten dreadful years before it was finally suppressed. From the beginning the sympathy of most Americans was with the rebels, and when the Cuban junta in New York spread stories of Spanish barbarism — stories for the most part true — sympathy flamed into indignation. Early in 1869 the House passed a resolution of sympathy for the Cubans, but the movement for recognition of Cuban belligerency encountered the firm opposition of Fish. Recognition would have been a serious mistake, for it would have gravely compromised pending American claims against Great Britain for premature recognition of the belligerency of the Confederate states. As it was, the two nations came to the very brink of war in 1873 over the unhappy *Virginius* affair. The *Virginius,* a ship flying the American flag and carrying arms for the Cuban insurgents, was captured on the high seas by a Spanish gunboat; fifty-three of her seamen, including eight Americans, were summarily executed for ' piracy.' When Spain disowned the barbarous deed and paid an indemnity, and when it was discovered that the ship had no right to her American papers or to fly the American flag, the crisis was averted and the danger of war evaporated.

To the northward as well as to the southward relations were strained. During the war Canada had furnished an asylum for Confederate plotters and a base for Confederate raids on Vermont and New York. In time of peace the Fenians, or Irish Revolutionary Brother-Republics, took similar liberties in the United States. Two rival Irish republics were organized in New York City, each with its president, cabinet, and general staff in glittering uniforms of green and gold. Each planned to seize Canada with Irish veterans of the Union army, and hold it as hostage for Irish freedom. From 1866 to 1870 the Fenians harassed the Canadian border. The first invasion, in April 1866, was promptly nipped by federal authorities at Eastport, Maine, but the ensuing howl from the Irish vote frightened President Johnson and his cabinet. Before the Attorney-General and the Secretaries of War and of the Navy could decide who should take on the onus of stopping him, ' General ' John O'Neil led 1500 armed Irishmen across the Niagara river. The next day, 2 June 1866, the Canadian militia gave battle, and fled; but the Fenians fled farther — to New York State, where they were promptly arrested and as promptly released. During the following three years the Fenians collected arms and money and girded themselves for a new attack, and in the spring of 1870 tatterdemalion armies moved on Canada from St. Albans, Vermont, and Malone, New York. This time both governments were ready for them. United States marshals arrested the Fenian leaders, and the armies disintegrated. Ridiculous as they were, the Fenian forays caused Canada much trouble and expense for which she was never reimbursed by the United States.

The greatest achievement of the Grant administration was the liquidation of all outstanding diplomatic controversies with Great Britain. The sympathy of the English governing classes for the Confederacy and the lax enforcement of neutrality by the British government had aroused deep resentment in the United States. For some years after the war the psychological atmosphere was such that no calm adjudication of American claims was possible. The most important of these claims had to do with the alleged negligence of the British government in permitting the Confederate cruisers *Alabama, Shenandoah,* and *Florida* to be armed in, and escape from, British ports. Seward's persistent advocacy of these claims was finally rewarded in the last months of Johnson's administration by the socalled Clarendon Convention for their adjudication. But nothing that President Johnson did could then find favor with the Republican party. In April 1869 the Senate rejected this convention as insufficient, after Sumner had charged Great Britain with responsibility for half the total cost of the war: a mere $2,125 million. Sumner's speech shocked his English friends who so faithfully had sustained the Union cause; nor were they much comforted by his explanation that the cession of Canada would be an acceptable form of payment.

After Sumner was eliminated as a result of the Caribbean question, negotiations went forward more successfully. By this time England was ready to make amends for her wartime support to the Confederacy. For, whatever her legal position (which was weak), she realized that her conduct had created a precedent for fitting out warships in American or other neutral waters that might be used to destroy British commerce in any future war. So the Canadian Sir John Rose staged with Hamilton Fish a diplomatic play of wooing and yielding that threw dust in the eyes of extremists on both sides. The covenant thus secretly arrived at was the famous Treaty of Washington (8 May 1871). It provided for submission to arbitration of boundary disputes, the fisheries question, and the *Alabama* claims; determined rules of neutrality that should govern the arbitral tribunal; and contained an expression of regret for the escape of the *Alabama* from British waters — a friendly gesture for which Americans had long been waiting.

In presenting its case to the arbitral tribunal at Geneva the United States claimed compensation not only for actual damage inflicted by the Confederate cruisers, but for the numerous transfers of registry occasioned by fear of capture. Hamilton Fish had no intention of pressing these ' indirect claims,' which he was anxious only to be rid of; but English opinion was deeply stirred by their presentation. Prime Minister Gladstone would have withdrawn from the arbitration on that issue had not Charles Francis Adams, the American member, proposed that the Geneva tribunal should rule out the indirect claims in advance. This was done, and the arbitration proceeded smoothly to its conclusion: an award of $15 million for depredations committed by the *Alabama, Florida,* and *Shenandoah.* Even this sum was in excess of the actual direct damage, and part of it was never handed out to claimants.

Although the United States was thereby vindicated, the greater victory was for arbitration and peace. No threat of force affected the issue, for American ironclads had lost their primacy by 1871. Never before had questions involving such touchy matters of national honor been submitted to a mere majority vote of an international tribunal; and the good grace with which England as a whole accepted the verdict smoothed out the ill-tempered dissenting opinion of Sir Alexander Cockburn. Of other persons involved, Charles Francis Adams never forgot that he was judge not advocate. President Grant by his unwavering support of peaceful methods showed a quality not unusual in statesmen who know war at first hand; and in a later message to the Arbitration Union of Birmingham he confessed his guiding principle: ' Nothing would afford me greater happiness than to know that, as I believe will be the case, at some future day, the nations of the earth will agree upon some sort of congress which will take cognizance of international questions of difficulty, and whose decisions will be as binding as the decisions of our Supreme Court are upon us. It is a dream of mine that some such solution may be.'

4. Domestic Politics

No such idealism animated Grant in his handling of the more pressing problems of domestic politics. Three of these problems, reconstruction, the money question, and the tariff, were of urgent national importance; a fourth, civil service reform, was taken seriously only by a small group, but that group included many of the ablest men in American political life.

' Let us have peace,' the concluding phrase of Grant's letter accepting the presidential nomination, had encouraged the country to believe that Grant would abandon Radical reconstruction and adopt toward the South a more conciliatory policy. In the beginning this hope seemed justified. The President suggested to his cabinet a sweeping amnesty proclamation and urged Congress to complete the reconstruction process in Virginia, Mississippi, and Texas. By 1870 representatives from these three laggard states again took their places in Congress. But despite this good beginning it was soon clear that Grant, who had ardently supported the impeachment of Johnson, was still in the Radical camp. In his first annual message he recommended to Congress a drastic reconstitution of the legislature of Georgia, and Congress responded with appropriate legislation. He gave his approval to the Force Acts and the Ku Klux Act and applied them with uncompromising rigor. Faced with a revolt throughout the South against the carpetbag regime he fell back upon his military idea of restoring order, which he identified with Radical government. In South Carolina, Alabama, Mississippi, Louisiana, and Arkansas, Grant supported the worst of the carpetbaggers and authorized the use of federal troops to overthrow duly elected Democratic governments and keep these states in the Radical Republican ranks. None of this — it should be added — was inspired by concern for the Negro.

The money question, like the Southern question, had been inherited from previous administrations. During the war the government had issued $450 million of legal tender notes, and at the close of the war some $400 million of these so-called greenbacks were still in circulation. The presence of greenbacks in the currency gave rise to two issues that divided public opinion along class and sectional rather than party lines. The first involved the medium of payment of the interest and principal of government bonds. These bonds had been purchased with depreciated greenbacks, and it was urged that they should be redeemable in greenbacks unless otherwise specified. Farmers and workingmen who would ultimately pay most of the taxes for the redemption of these bonds supported this proposal as just. Bondholders and the business interests which they represented opposed it as a betrayal of national honor.

The Democratic party, as we have seen, endorsed this idea of the payment of government securities in greenbacks. President Johnson, in his last annual message went even farther and proposed that future interest payments be applied to the liquidation of the principal of the debt. Pointing out that bondholders received 6 per cent in gold which was 9 per cent in currency, that government bonds were exempt from state and federal taxes, and that they could be converted into national bank capital bearing another 6 per cent interest, Johnson argued that bondholders were in fact receiving 17 per cent return on their investment. ' It may be assumed,' he said, ' that the holders of our securities have already received upon their bonds a larger amount than their original investment, measured by the gold standard.' He proposed that the 6 per cent interest paid by the government be applied to the reduction of the principal which in sixteen years and eight months would liquidate the entire national debt. ' The lessons of the past,' he added, ' admonish the lender that it is not well to be overanxious in exacting from the borrower rigid compliance with the letter of the bond.' But Democratic defeat meant that this plan was discredited. In his first inaugural address Grant committed himself to payment of all government obligations in gold, and the first measure passed by the new Congress (18 March 1869) pledged the faith of the United States to such payment.

The second question raised by the presence of greenbacks concerned the policy of the government toward the contraction of the greenback currency and the resumption of specie payments. The inflation of the currency through greenbacks had tended to raise commodity prices, make credit easier and money cheaper. The farmer and the debtor therefore favored inflation and regarded with dismay any proposal for the contraction of the currency by calling in these greenbacks. Business interests, on the contrary, looked upon contraction as financially sound and economically advantageous. Representatives of the farmer interest urged, correctly enough, that more rather than less money was needed to serve the needs of a rapidly growing nation. Representatives of business interests insisted, with equal correctness, that inflation, if it got out of hand, might prostrate the business of the nation and destroy the credit of the government. They demanded that, in any event, the government should stabilize the currency by pledging itself to redeem greenbacks with gold and thus bring greenbacks to par.

A powerful argument for stabilization of the currency was that constant fluctuation in the value of greenbacks opened a wide door to speculation. Because greenbacks were not legal tender for all purposes and because it was uncertain whether the government would ever redeem them in gold, they circulated at a discount which varied from month to month. In 1862 the gold value of a greenback dollar had been 90 cents; in 1865 it fell to 50 cents; by the time Grant assumed office it had risen to 73 cents. In September 1869 two notorious stock gamblers, Jay Gould and Jim Fisk, took advantage of this fluctuation in the value of money to organize a ' corner ' in gold. With the passive connivance of persons high in the confidence of the President and the Secretary of the Treasury, the nefarious scheme was almost successful. On ' Black Friday,' 24 September 1869, the premium on gold rose to 162, and scores of Wall Street brokers faced ruin. Then the government dumped $4 million in gold on the market, and the ' corner ' collapsed. The whole country was aroused, and men everywhere blamed Grant for criminal incompetence in permitting himself to be enmeshed in the sordid affair. ' The worst scandals of the 18th century,' wrote Henry Adams, ' were relatively harmless by the side of this which smirched executive, judiciary, banks, corporate systems, professions, and people, all the great active forces of society.'

Yet the episode reflected not so much upon Grant's character as upon his judgment. The fact is that Grant knew little about finance and understood less, and the policy of the administration was from the beginning vacillating. Grant favored a resumption of specie payments but he was opposed to contraction of the currency and disposed to accept greenbacks as a permanent part of the currency. Chief Justice Chase — who as Secretary of the Treasury had originally issued them — announced that greenbacks were not legal tender for obligations entered into prior to the emission of the notes, and even made the alarming suggestion that they were completely invalid; [4] the government promptly moved for a rehearing of the case. Two vacancies on the Supreme Court afforded Grant a propitious opportunity to strengthen the government's position. In Joseph P. Bradley and William Strong, Grant found jurists upon whose faith in the constitutionality of the greenbacks he could with confidence rely.[5] He was not disappointed. In the second Legal Tender decision, *Knox v. Lee*,[6] the Court reversed itself and sustained the constitutionality of the Civil War greenbacks. Thirteen years later, in an even more sweeping decision, *Julliard v. Greenman*,[7] it proclaimed the right of the government to issue legal tender even in time of peace.

The Court having sustained the constitutionality of legal tenders, Secretaries Boutwell and Richardson found it proper to increase their number. When Grant assumed office there were in circulation $356 million in greenbacks; by 1874 the total had been raised to $382 million. Congress, frightened by the deflationary effect of the panic of 1873, voted to increase the total to $400 million. The sum was not in itself too large, but the gesture toward inflation alarmed the business community. Grant vetoed the bill, and the threat passed. Encouraged by the firm stand of the President and dismayed by the prospect of Democratic control of the lower House, Congress in 1875 finally provided for the resumption of specie payments on 1 January 1879. This act settled, for the time being, the legal tender question, but it did not settle the money question. That remained to plague the next generation.

The tariff question was also settled to the satisfaction of the business interests, though it must be remembered that those interests were by no means uniform or monolithic, but diverse and often conflicting. The Civil War tariffs, raising duties to unprecedented heights, were originally regarded as emergency revenue measures; protected industries soon came to regard them as permanent. After Appomattox, Western farmers and Eastern progressives joined hands

---

[4] *Hepburn v. Griswold* 8 Wallace 603 (1870).

[5] It was charged at the time, and later, that Grant had 'packed' the Court. Like all Presidents he appointed to the Court men who were broadly sympathetic to his point of view; aside from this there is no evidence of any impropriety in the two appointments.

[6] 12 Wallace 457 (1871).

[7] 110 U.S. 421 (1884).

in demanding tariff reduction, but the protected interests had no intention of yielding to a demand which they regarded as sentimental folly. In 1867 duties had actually been raised on a number of items, and throughout the following years Congress passed a series of ' pop ' tariff bills which continued the upward course of protective duties. The administration was definitely hostile to tariff reform. Secretary Cox was forced out of the cabinet in part because of his sympathy for it, and David A. Wells, the able economist who was a special commissioner of revenue, had to resign for the same reason. The approach of a presidential election, however, scared the administration into temporary virtue on this issue, and in 1872 Grant signed a bill providing for a horizontal slash of 10 per cent on many protected articles. At the same time, the last of the Civil War income taxes were repealed. In 1875 tariff duties were restored to their earlier status, but no effort was made to restore the income tax.

Nor did civil service reform fare better. In no department was the record of Grant's administration more discreditable. Dissatisfaction with the spoils system was widespread, and when voiced by such leaders as Carl Schurz, Lyman Trumbull, and Charles Sumner it could not be disregarded. In the beginning it appeared that the reformers had Grant's support. The appointment of Jacob Cox to the Interior Department was a gesture toward reform, and when in 1871 a Civil Service Commission, headed by George William Curtis, submitted a list of desirable reforms, Grant promised that ' at all events the experiment shall have a fair trial.' But Cox was forced out of the cabinet, and Grant soon scuttled the commission and jettisoned the reform. The recommendations of the commission were ignored, the civil service packed with party henchmen, and the system of assessments on officeholders brought to a high state of efficiency. ' There is an utter surrender of the Civil Service to the coarsest use by the coarsest men,' observed Whitelaw Reid, and reformers everywhere echoed the sentiment. Curtis, wearied of shadow-boxing with the spoilsmen, resigned in disgust, and in 1875 the commission itself was discontinued. With the appointment of the Republican boss, Zachary Chandler, to the Department of the Interior the administration abandoned even the pretense of interest in civil service reform and surrendered itself to the spoilsmen.

5. THE LIBERAL REPUBLICAN MOVEMENT

The Civil War had obscured the deep differences within the Republican party, and Reconstruction served as a smoke-screen behind which Radicals captured control of the party organization. Grant had commanded the support of Eastern and Western business and farming interests alike, but his record soon forfeited the favor of those who looked to him to reform and to nationalize the party. Within less than a year after his assumption of office, revolt was in full swing.

Causes for dissatisfaction were numerous. The full measure of administrative corruption was as yet unknown, but enough was suspected to outrage men who cherished standards of political decency. Grant's Southern policy was a failure, his Caribbean policy an affront, while his repudiation of civil service and tariff reform alienated even some of his own followers. Above all there was a growing distrust of Grant himself, a distrust which found dramatic expression in Sumner's famous speech of May 1872 wherein the President was scored for taking and giving bribes, nepotism, neglect of duty, lawless interference with the business of the other departments of the government, and for half a dozen other misdemeanors. Sumner's disapproval was something which all Presidents had had to face, and was not taken too seriously; but soon many of the most distinguished of the elder statesmen were following his lead. Grant's abuse of the civil service alienated Cox and Schurz, his Southern policy antagonized Lyman Trumbull and Gideon Welles, his tariff policy cost him the support of David A. Wells, while outside the ranks of the politicians such men as Chief Justice Chase, Horace Greeley, Charles Francis Adams, and E. L. Godkin came to regard the President as unfit for high office.

This revolt against Grant was started by liberals and reformers, but old-line politicians and disappointed factional leaders soon flocked to it in embarrassing numbers. In the end it consisted of as heterogeneous a group as was ever gathered together in one political party. Free-traders like David A. Wells and high protectionists like Horace Greeley, Eastern conservatives like Charles Francis Adams and Western radicals like Ignatius Donnelly, civil service reformers like Carl Schurz and practical politicians like Reuben Fenton of New York, were all in the same boat. The one idea that animated them all

was distrust or dislike of President Grant. It was a movement of opposition rather than of positive reform; and therein lay its chief
weakness.

When the Liberal Republican convention met at Cincinnati
1 May 1872, this weakness became apparent. It was impossible for
the discordant elements to agree upon a satisfactory platform or a
logical candidate; 'coherence,' as one of its ardent supporters,
'Marse' Henry Watterson observed, 'was a missing ingredient.'
The platform as finally adopted called for the withdrawal of troops
from the South, civil service reform, and a resumption of specie payments; as for the tariff, the convention 'recognizing that there are
in our midst honest but irreconcilable differences of opinion' re-
manded 'the discussion of the subject to the people in their congressional Districts.'

The task of choosing a candidate proved even more difficult. There
were available half a dozen able men, any one of whom might have
carried the new party to victory. The most obvious choice was
Charles Francis Adams, son and grandson of Presidents, Minister to
England during the critical days of the Civil War, and a man of distinguished intellect and irreproachable character. An equally satisfactory nominee would have been Lyman Trumbull, whom Lincoln
had helped elect to the Senate back in 1855 and who had been for
almost twenty years one of the ornaments of the Republican party.
Two Supreme Court Justices, S. P. Chase and David Davis, were
eager for the nomination, and Jacob Cox of Ohio and B. Gratz
Brown of Missouri had their champions. Intrigues and jealousies
defeated all of these, however, and in the end the convention was
stampeded to Horace Greeley of New York.

No man in the country was better known than Horace Greeley,
for over thirty years editor of the powerful New York *Tribune,* but
he was known as an editor not as a statesman. A Vermont Yankee
who had kept his homespun democracy and youthful idealism in the
atmosphere of New York, Greeley persistently championed the cause
of the underprivileged, the worker, and the farmer. He had long
been a power in the councils of the Whig and Republican parties,
and his advocacy of high tariff, liberal land laws, and abolition had
helped to shape the course of American history. Yet for all his intellectual abilities and idealism, Greeley lacked the first qualifications for responsible political position. He was impulsive and un-

predictable, ambitious and intriguing, vain and vindictive. Worst of all, his eager promotion of every reform, his crotchets and caprices and carefully cultivated idiosyncrasies, laid him open to ridicule and caricature. He had championed Fourierism and vegetarianism, spiritualism and temperance, and a dozen other fads, and the average man saw in these things not the expression of consistent social philosophy but rather the vagaries of a visionary and impractical nature.

The nomination of Greeley, engineered by a coalition of journalists and ' practical ' politicians, came as a shock to the reformers who had organized the Liberal Republican movement, and many of them hastened to retreat from a position which they thought untenable. But the dismay of the reformers was as nothing to the dismay of Southern Democrats. For thirty years Greeley had castigated the South and the Democratic party, and much of the responsibility for anti-slavery and, later, for Radical reconstruction could justly be laid at his door. Democrats might well feel that an endorsement of Greeley would be more stultifying than an endorsement of Grant. Yet they had no alternative, and bitterly they swallowed the strange pill presented to them by the Liberal Republicans and made Greeley their nominee.

Greeley proved himself, surprisingly enough, an excellent campaigner, but the odds against him were insuperable. Grant could command the support not only of the rank and file of the Republican party, veterans of the Union armies, the colored vote North and South, and most of the German vote, but, above all, of the business and banking interests. These came to his aid in handsome fashion. Banking houses such as Jay Cooke and Company, and Henry Clews and Company, the iron interests of Pennsylvania, and the ' Whiskey Ring ' in St. Louis, all contributed generously to the Republican campaign funds. Yet it is probable that Grant would have been re-elected even without these contributions. When the votes were counted it was found that Grant had carried all the states but six and that he had a popular majority of over 700,000. Three weeks later Horace Greeley died, broken-hearted, and the promising experiment in political liberalism which had excited such high hopes collapsed.

6. Scandal and Stagnation

' It looks at this distance,' wrote Senator Grimes to Lyman Trumbull, ' as though the Republican party were going to the dogs. . . . Like all parties that have an undisturbed power for a long time, it has become corrupt, and I believe that it is to-day the [most] corrupt and debauched political party that has ever existed.' When this was written, in July 1870, it was an exaggeration, but within a few years a series of sensational exposures went far to prove its accuracy. While the campaign of 1872 was still under way the country was startled by charges of wholesale corruption in connection with the construction of the Union Pacific Railroad, charges which reflected upon men high in the councils of the Republican party. The promoters of the Union Pacific, in order corruptly to divert the profits of construction to themselves, had organized a construction company, the Credit Mobilier of America. To this company the directors of the Union Pacific awarded contracts of a fantastically profitable nature. As a result of this neat arrangement the Union Pacific was forced to the verge of bankruptcy while the Credit Mobilier paid in a single year dividends of 348 per cent. Fearing lest Congress might interpose, the directors placed large blocks of Credit Mobilier stock ' where they would do most good.' Exposure of the scheme brought disgrace to a number of representatives, and to Vice-President Schuyler Colfax, while others such as Wilson of Massachusetts and Garfield of Ohio were never able to explain away their connection with the unsavory affair.

Scarcely less excusable was the so-called Salary Grab. In the closing days of Congress, February–March 1873, Ben Butler pushed through a bill doubling the salary of the President and increasing by 50 per cent the salary of Congressmen. This could be justified; what particularly affronted public opinion was that the increases granted to Congressmen were made retroactive for two years: thus each Congressman voted to himself $5000 of back salary out of public funds. The bill was an evasion if not an outright violation of the Constitution, but Grant signed it without demur. A storm of indignation against this ' steal ' swept the country, and in the following session Congress hastened to restore the old salary scale.

The Credit Mobilier and the Salary Grab were merely the most sensational of the exposures which indicated the demoralization of the administration. It soon appeared that the executive department as well as the legislative was honeycombed with corruption.

The Navy Department sold business to contractors, and Secretary Robeson managed to accumulate a fortune of several hundred thousand dollars during his tenure of office. The Department of the Interior was working hand in glove with land speculators. The Treasury Department farmed out uncollected taxes to one J. D. Sanborn who promptly proceeded to highjack some $425,000 out of railroad companies and other corporations, one-half of which he took for himself. The American Minister to England, Robert Schenck, lent his name and position to the Emma Mine swindle, and the Minister to Brazil, J. W. Webb, defrauded the Brazilian government of $50,000 and fled to Europe, leaving the United States Government to refund the money, with apologies. The Custom House in New York was a sink of political corruption, and when Collector Thomas Murphy was finally forced out Grant accepted his resignation ' with regret,' while at the same time the skulduggery of Collector Casey of the Port of New Orleans was rewarded by Casey's reappointment to the office which he had disgraced. In the national capital ' Boss ' Shepherd, head of the local ring, ran up a debt of $17 million, a large part of which was graft, and found himself appointed by a grateful President to be chairman of the Board of Public Works! It was Shepherd, too, who was largely responsible for the failure of the Freedmen's Bank, a failure which worked cruel hardship upon thousands of trusting Negroes who had deposited their savings in an institution supposedly philanthropic.

All of this was bad enough, but worse was still to come. The Democrats carried the congressional elections of 1874, and the following year a Democratic House, the first since the Civil War, set afoot a series of investigations designed to cleanse the government and to furnish campaign material for the impending presidential contest. In the Treasury Department and the War Department investigators uncovered sensational frauds. For years a ' Whiskey Ring ' in St. Louis had systematically defrauded the government of millions of dollars in taxes on distilled whiskey. It was inescapably clear that the Ring had operated with the collusion of Treasury officials and of the President's private secretary, Babcock. When Grant was appraised of the situation he said, ' Let no guilty man escape. Be especially vigilant against all who insinuate that they have high influence to protect or to protect them.' But most of them did escape — Babcock with the President's connivance. No sooner had the 'Whiskey Ring' been exposed than the country was confronted with a new scandal. Exploitation of the Indians for political and financial graft had long been notorious. In the spring of 1876 Secretary Bristow found irrefutable proof that Secretary of War Belknap had sold Indian post-traderships. Faced with impeachment, Belknap hurried to resign, and his resignation was accepted 'with great regret' by the President whom he had betrayed. Impeachment proceedings were instituted, but the Secretary was finally acquitted on the technical ground that the Senate no longer had jurisdiction over his case.

Corruption was by no means confined to the national government. It could be found in state and municipal governments, in business and finance and transportation, and even in the professions. There was almost everywhere a breakdown of old moral standards, and to many it seemed that integrity had departed from public life. Much of the idealism of the prewar years had been burnt out in the flames of the war and reconstruction. The industrial revolution, the building of transcontinental railroads, and the exploitation of new natural resources had called into existence a class of new rich untrained to the responsibilities of their position. Never before and only once since — after World War I — have public morals fallen so low.

State legislatures, too, were guilty of gross corruption. The systematic looting in which the Southern governments indulged was matched in the Northern and Western states. In the fierce struggle between Daniel Drew and Cornelius Vanderbilt for control of the Erie Railroad the legislature of New York State was auctioned off to the highest bidder, and both the bar and the bench proved that they too were for sale. In Pennsylvania the powerful Cameron machine bought and sold legislation with bare-faced effrontery. In Illinois a corrupt legislature jammed through, in disregard of the Constitution, over 700 acts of incorporation. In Wisconsin, Minnesota, and California it was charged that the legislatures were controlled by railroads, and the charges were not hard to substantiate; in Iowa the money for the Agricultural College realized from land-grant sales was stolen. The cities, too, presented a sorry spectacle. The brigandage of the Tweed Ring cost New York City not less than $100 million, and the ravages of the Gas Ring in Philadelphia and of Boss Shepherd in Washington were scarcely less thorough.

This political corruption was symptomatic of corruption in the business world. The rise of the corporation as the chief instrument of business brought a diffusion and weakening of responsibility. Defalcations, bankruptcies, stock watering, wildcat investment schemes, railway wrecking, were accepted parts of commercial life. Oil wells, gold and silver mines, and, above all, railroad construction offered rich fields for speculation, and the absence of statutory regulation of business practices made speculation and trickery fairly safe.

The panic of 1873 was partly a consequence of these malpractices. The causes of business depressions are always obscure, but it is safe to say that reckless speculation in railroads and wholesale stock watering in many industries played an important part in precipitating this panic. Other causes were perhaps equally important. The depression was world-wide: Germany, France, and England all felt the hard times, and European investors proceeded to call in their American loans. The unfavorable balance of trade, which had persisted all through the war and the postwar years, mounted during the early 'seventies: the total deficit for the years 1870 to 1876 was $789 million. Too rapid expansion of the agricultural West produced surplus crops which, after the Franco-Prussian War, could not be marketed abroad at satisfactory prices. The war and expansion had led to a shift of capital from productive to more speculative enterprises. Credit was overextended, currency inflated, and public finances deranged by the conflicting claims of greenbacks and of gold. With an immense self-confidence the country had mortgaged itself to the future; now it found itself unable to pay either interest or principal.

The crash came 17 September 1873 with the failure of the great banking house of Jay Cooke and Company — the house that had helped finance the war and the Northern Pacific Railroad. Soon one substantial business firm after another toppled, and the New York Stock Exchange took the unprecedented step of closing its doors for ten days. Soon the panic lengthened into a depression. Industrial plants shut down, railway construction declined sharply, and over half the railroads defaulted on their bonds. Long bread lines began to appear in the larger cities — there was no notion of public relief — and tramps swarmed the countryside. Commercial failures increased to almost 6000 in 1874, almost 8000 in 1875, and over 9000 in 1876.

As always, the workers and the farmers were the worst sufferers. As unemployment mounted the promising labor organizations of the Civil War years disintegrated and union membership declined from about 300,000 to one-fourth that figure. With the guerrilla warfare waged by the Molly Maguires in the coal fields of Pennsylvania, and the open violence in the great railroad strikes of 1878, class warfare came to the United States. Farmers, who had greatly overextended themselves during the war and postwar years, were hard hit by the familiar combination of falling prices and fixed charges; the result was the first organized farmers' crusade in American history — the Granger crusade.[8]

7. The Disputed Election of 1876

Republican defeat seemed certain in 1876 as the bankruptcy of the Grant administration became increasingly apparent. James G. Blaine of Maine, in a speech deliberately calculated to arouse sectional animosities, tried to deflect public attention from corruption to the reconstruction issue. The attempt might have succeeded better had not the well-timed exposure of Blaine's corrupt connection with the Little Rock and Fort Smith Railroad hopelessly damaged his claim to leadership. In the Cincinnati Convention the Republicans passed up the magnetic Blaine and chose instead the respectable but uninspiring Rutherford B. Hayes. Hayes had been thrice Governor of Ohio, and his record was good enough to command the support of the Liberal Republicans; the Old Guard had no alternative but to support the one man who might save the party from disaster. The Democrats, determined to make reform the issue of the campaign, nominated Samuel J. Tilden of New York, who had exposed and broken the notorious Tweed Ring and then, as Governor of New York, smashed the ' Canal Ring.' [9]

When the first reports came in Tilden appeared to have won a sweeping victory. He carried New York, New Jersey, Connecticut, Indiana, and, apparently, the Solid South, and piled up a popular plurality of over 250,000. But, scanning the returns, the Republican campaign managers became convinced that the election might yet be

8 See below Chapter XI.

9 The newly organized Greenback party nominated the venerable philanthropist, Peter Cooper of New York; he received 81,740 votes.

swung to their candidate. The votes of four states — South Carolina, Florida, Louisiana, and Oregon — were apparently in doubt. Without the vote of these states Tilden had only 184 electoral votes; 185 were necessary for election. On the morning after election the Republican stalwart, Secretary Zachary Chandler, dispatched telegrams to each of the doubtful states, ' Can you hold your state? ' — and that afternoon he announced, ' Hayes has 185 electoral votes and is elected.'

The situation was highly involved, and highly precarious. In all three of the Southern states there had been intimidation and fraud on both sides. Hayes appeared to have carried South Carolina, but, in Florida and Louisiana, Tilden seemed to have a safe majority. Republican returning boards threw out about 1000 Democratic votes in Florida and over 13,000 in Louisiana, and gave certificates to the Hayes electors. In Oregon a Democratic governor had displaced a Republican elector on a technicality and appointed a Democrat to his position. From all four states came two sets of returns.

The Constitution provides that ' The President of the Senate shall, in the presence of the Senate and the House of Representatives, open all certificates and the votes shall then be counted.' But counted by whom? If the President of the Senate did the counting, the election would go to Hayes; if the House counted the votes, Tilden would be President. And if the two houses could not agree on the procedure, there would be no President. Was the nation then to drift, distraught and confused, without a chief executive? Was the long agony of war and reconstruction to reach a new climacteric in the frustration of those constitutional mechanisms provided by the Fathers and in a new wave of violence and war?

Conservatives, North and South, hastened to head off such a crisis. By this time both sections were thoroughly tired of the bickering and quarreling, disorder and violence that interfered with the re-creation of traditional political alignments, the resumption of economic progress, and the restoration of social harmony. The solution of the immediate crisis was hinted at by Representative Garfield in a letter to Hayes. Some of the extremists on both sides, he wrote, were prepared to make trouble, but ' in the meantime two forces are at work. The Democratic businessmen of the country are more anxious for quiet than for Tilden; and the old Whigs are saying that they have seen war enough, and don't care to follow the lead of their northern

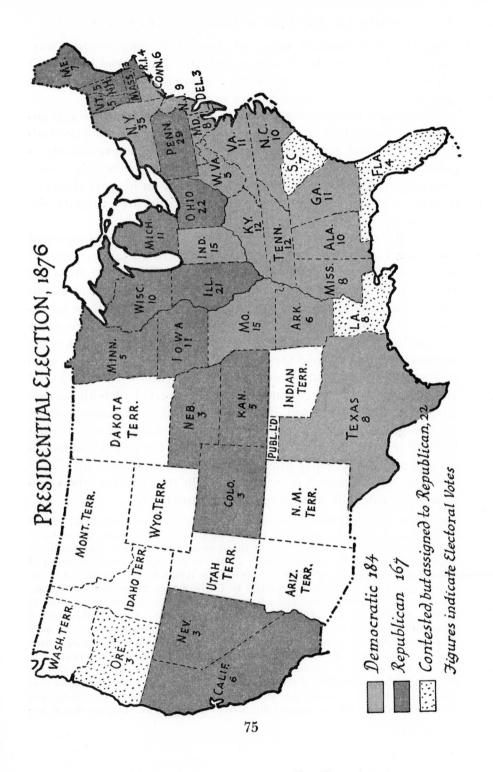

PRESIDENTIAL ELECTION, 1876

ME. 7
VT. 5
N.H. 5
MASS. 13
R.I. 4
CONN. 6
N.Y. 35
PENN. 29
N.J. 9
DEL. 3
MD. 8
VA. 11
W.VA. 5
N.C. 10
S.C. 7
FLA. 4
OHIO 22
MICH. 11
IND. 15
KY. 12
TENN. 12
GA. 11
ALA. 10
WISC. 10
ILL. 21
MO. 15
ARK. 6
MISS. 8
LA. 8
MINN. 5
IOWA 11
KAN. 5
INDIAN TERR.
TEXAS 8
DAKOTA TERR.
NEB. 3
PUBL. LD.
COLO. 3
N.M. TERR.
MONT. TERR.
WYO. TERR.
UTAH TERR.
ARIZ. TERR.
WASH. TERR.
IDAHO TERR.
NEV. 3
ORE. 3
CALIF. 6

Democratic 184
Republican 167
Contested, but assigned to Republican, 22
Figures indicate Electoral Votes

75

associates.' And Garfield suggested that 'if in some discreet way, these southern men who are dissatisfied with Tilden and his violent followers, could know that the South is going to be treated with kind consideration,' they might acquiesce in Hayes's election.

What Southern conservatives wanted was an end to military reconstruction, the restoration of ' home rule,' some voice in the Hayes administration, and generous subsidies for internal improvements — particularly railroads. If these concessions were forthcoming, they were prepared to concede the presidency. And on his part Hayes — or those who spoke for him — were equally prepared to make the concessions.

Under these uncertain auspices, and with the reluctant support of Governor Tilden, Congress was able to act. On 29 January 1877 it set up an Electoral Commission of fifteen members — five from the House, five from the Senate, and five from the Supreme Court — to pass on the credentials from the four states whose votes were in dispute. It was originally planned to appoint to this committee seven Democrats and seven Republicans and, as the fifteenth member, the non-partisan Judge David Davis of Illinois. At the last moment, however — and not by inadvertence — the legislature of Illinois elected Judge Davis to the Senate and, with the approval of both parties, Judge Bradley was named in his place. And as it turned out it was Judge Bradley who named the next President of the United States. For on all questions submitted to it the Electoral Commission divided along strict party lines, and Judge Bradley voted invariably with the Republicans.[10] By a straight eight to seven vote the Commission awarded all four contested states to Hayes.

[10] There is reason to believe that Judge Bradley's vote represented neither his original opinion nor his conviction. Abram S. Hewitt, Democratic leader of the House, wrote of Judge Bradley's vote: ' The history of this opinion forms an important feature in the final outcome of the electoral count. . . . Mr. Stevens was the intimate friend of Judge Bradley. He passed the night previous to the rendition of the judgment in the Florida case at my house. About midnight he returned from a visit to Judge Bradley and reported . . . that he had just left Judge Bradley after reading his opinion in favor of counting the vote of the Democratic electors of the state of Florida. Such a judgment insured the election of Tilden to the Presidency with three votes to spare above the necessary majority. We parted, therefore, with the assurance that all further doubt as to the Presidency was at rest. I attended the delivery of the judgment the next day without the slightest intimation from any quarter that Judge Bradley had changed his mind. In fact, the reading of the opinion, until the few concluding paragraphs were reached, was strictly in accordance with the report of Mr. Stevens. The change was made between midnight and sunrise. Mr. Stevens afterwards informed me that it was

Would the Democrats accept a solution which seemed so partisan and so unfair? For a time it was touch and go. Public indignation was intense, for Tilden had a clear majority over his rival, and the vote had constituted a sharp rebuke to the Republican administration. The Northern wing of the party was prepared to filibuster long enough to prevent Congress from opening and counting the votes. Such a filibuster actually flourished in the closing weeks of the Grant administration, and with a little encouragement from Tilden and Hewitt it might have continued to the close of Congress. But in the end wiser counsels prevailed. With renewed assurances from Hayes that he would abide by the understanding reached by his intermediaries, enough Southern Democrats deserted the Northern intransigents to permit the Congress to count the ballots, and on 2 March 1877 Hayes was declared formally elected by a majority of one vote.

On the whole this famous compromise worked well, and reflected credit on the good sense of those who contrived it. There was no inclination to challenge Hayes's title to his office, or to punish him or his party for what many Democrats regarded as a travesty of constitutional processes. In the perspective of history, it can be seen that none of those directly involved suffered as a consequence of their moderation. The real victim of the compromise was the Southern Negro, for it had been made at his expense, and delayed for three generations the enforcement of those guarantees written into the Fourteenth and Fifteenth Amendments. What the Negro thought of the results of the compromise is not on record, but it is not too difficult to imagine.

BIBLIOGRAPHY

1. GRANT AND DOMESTIC POLITICS. Henry Adams, *The Education of Henry Adams;* Herbert Agar, *The Price of Union;* D. C. Barrett, *Greenbacks and the Resumption of Specie Payments;* James G. Blaine, *Twenty Years of Congress;* Louis Boudin, *Government by Judiciary,* vol. 2, chap. 25; W. A. Cate,

due to a visit to Judge Bradley by Senator Frelinghuysen and Secretary Robeson, made after his departure. Their appeals to Judge Bradley were said to have been reinforced by the persuasion of Mrs. Bradley. Whatever the fact may have been, Judge Bradley himself in a subsequent letter addressed to the Newark *Daily Advertiser* admitted that he had written a favorable opinion which on subsequent reflection he saw fit to modify.' ' Secret History of the Election, 1876–77,' *Selected Writings of Abram S. Hewitt,* edited by Allan Nevins, pp. 172–3.

L. Q. C. Lamar; C. H. Coleman, *The Election of 1868;* D. R. Dewey, *Financial History of the United States;* Martin Duberman, *Charles Francis Adams;* C. R. Fish, *The Civil Service and the Patronage;* W. B. Hesseltine, *U. S. Grant, Politician;* Matthew Josephson, *The Politicos, 1865–1896* and *The Robber Barons;* Henrietta Larsen, *Jay Cooke, Private Banker;* Hugh McCulloch, *Men and Measures of Half a Century;* Stewart Mitchell, *Horatio Seymour;* Wesley C. Mitchell, *A History of Greenbacks;* Allan Nevins, *Hamilton Fish: Inner History of the Grant Administration;* A. B. Paine, *Thomas Nast and His Pictures;* E. D. Ross, *The Liberal Republican Movement;* Joseph Schafer, *Carl Schurz, Militant Liberal;* Charles Warren, *History of the Supreme Court,* vol. 2, chap. 31.

2. FOREIGN AFFAIRS. Frederic Bancroft, *William H. Seward;* S. F. Bemis (ed.), *Secretaries of State and Their Diplomacy,* vol. 7; J. M. Callahan, *The Alaska Purchase;* F. E. Chadwick, *Relations of the United States and Spain: Diplomacy;* C. L. Jones, *Caribbean Interests of the United States;* J. B. Moore, *History and Digest of International Arbitrations,* vol. 1, chap. 14 and *Cambridge History of British Foreign Policy,* vol. 3; Allan Nevins, *Hamilton Fish: Inner History of the Grant Administration;* L. S. Shippee, *Canadian-American Relations 1849–1874;* Goldwin Smith, *The Treaty of Washington, 1871;* C. C. Tansill, *The United States and Santo Domingo 1789–1873;* Sumner Welles, *Naboth's Vineyard* (2 vols.) , (Santo Domingo) .

3. THE ELECTION OF 1876. H. J. Eckenrode, *Rutherford B. Hayes, Statesman of Reunion;* A. C. Flick, *Samuel Jones Tilden;* Paul L. Haworth, *The Hayes-Tilden Election;* Allan Nevins, *Abram S. Hewitt with Some Account of Peter Cooper;* James Ford Rhodes, *History of the United States,* vol. 7; L. B. Richardson, *William E. Chandler, Republican;* C. R. Williams, *Life of Rutherford B. Hayes* (2 vols.) ; C. Vann Woodward, *Reunion and Reaction.*

4. DOCUMENTS. Ruhl J. Bartlett, *Record of American Diplomacy,* chaps. 19–20; H. S. Commager, *Documents,* nos. 276–97; W. L. Fleming, *Documentary History of Reconstruction,* vol. 2.

For further references, *Harvard Guide,* ¶¶ 192–194.

The Negro and the New South

1. THE FREEDMEN

IN Reconstruction the Negro was the central figure and the most difficult problem. Upwards of a million colored people had in one way or another become free before the end of the war; victory and the Thirteenth Amendment liberated about 3 million more. Never before in the history of the world had civil and political rights been conferred at one stroke on so large a body of men, nor had any people ever been less prepared to assume a new status. Many Negroes thought that freedom meant no more work and proceeded to celebrate an endless ' day ob jubilo '; others were led to believe that every Negro would be given ' forty acres and a mule ' by the government, or that the property of their former masters would be divided among them. ' Emancipation having been announced one day,' wrote Tom Watson about his Georgia home, ' not a Negro remained on the place the next. The fine old homestead was deserted. Every house in " the quarter " was empty. The first impulse of freedom had carried the last of the blacks to town.' Thousands took to the woods or to the road, or clustered around the United States army posts, living on doles or dying of camp diseases. As the most famous of colored leaders, Frederick Douglass, said, the Negro ' was free from the individual master but a slave of society. He had neither money, property, nor friends. He was free from the old plantation, but he had nothing but the dusty road under his feet. He was free from the old quarter that once gave him shelter, but a slave to the rains of summer and the frosts of winter. He was turned lose, naked, hungry, and destitute to the open sky.' Deaths among the black men from starvation, disease, and violence in the first two years of freedom ran into the tens of thousands.[1] Those who continued to work on the old plantation were

[1] The Negro and white populations of Charleston, S.C., were substantially the same, but in the years from 1866 to 1871 Negro mortality was twice that of white, and infant mortality among the Negroes of the city was three times that of the whites.

more fortunate than those who took to the road or followed the Union armies.

To the average Southerner emancipation changed the position of the Negro legally rather than socially or economically. Few whites of the South were able to realize the implications of freedom or willing to acquiesce in anything approaching race equality. The Negro was still thought of as an inferior being, incapable of real independence, impossible to teach. Some of the former slaveholders tried sincerely and with some success to assist the Negro in adjusting himself to his new status, and observers agreed that the planter was the Negro's best friend. But the small farmers and the poor whites were determined to ' keep the Negro in his place,' by laws if possible, by force if necessary. J. T. Trowbridge, for example, writing shortly after the war, remarked that ' there is at this day more prejudice against color among the middle and poorer classes . . . who owned few or no slaves, than among the planters, who owned them by the hundred,' and it was the universal opinion that emancipation sharply accentuated racial antipathies in the South.

Most planters sought to keep their former slaves as hired help or as tenant farmers, or on the sharecrop system, and the Southern states attempted to assure this by a series of laws collectively known as the ' black codes,' which embodied the Southern solution to the Negro problem. Tennessee had none; the codes of the other states varied widely in scope and in character. The codes of Virginia and North Carolina, where the whites were in secure control of the situation, were mild; those of South Carolina, Mississippi, and Louisiana, where the Negroes outnumbered the whites, were severe.

These black codes conferred upon the freedmen fairly extensive privileges, gave them the essential rights of citizens to contract, sue and be sued, own and inherit property, and testify in court, and made some provision for education. In no instance, however, were the freedmen accorded the vote or made eligible for juries, and for the most part they were not permitted to testify against white men. Because of their alleged aversion to work they were required to have some steady occupation, and subjected to special penalties for violation of labor contracts. Vagrancy and apprenticeship laws were especially harsh, and lent themselves readily to the establishment of a system of peonage. The penal codes provided harsher and more arbitrary punishments for blacks than for whites, and some states permitted individual masters to administer corporal punishment to ' refractory servants.' Negroes were not allowed to bear arms, or to appear in certain public places, and there were special laws governing the domestic relations of the Negroes. In some states laws that closed to the freedmen every occupation save domestic and agricultural betrayed a poor-white jealousy of the Negro artisan, and this practice of excluding the Negro from some industries and professions grew as the South became increasingly industrialized and the Negroes more competitive.

Southern whites, who had never dreamed it possible to live side by side with free Negroes, professed to believe that these laws were liberal and generous. But the philosophy which animated them was the philosophy of the Old South, and every one of the codes confessed a determination to keep the freedmen in a permanent position of tutelage, and of social and political inferiority. The Southern point of view was succinctly expressed by a writer in the most influential of Southern journals, *De Bow's Review:*

We of the South would not find much difficulty in managing the Negroes, if left to ourselves, for we would be guided by the lights of experience and the teachings of history. . . . We should be satisfied to compel them to engage in coarse common manual labor, and to punish them for dereliction of duty or nonfulfillment of their contracts with sufficient severity to make the great majority of them productive laborers. . . . We should treat them as mere grown-up children, entitled like children, or apprentices, to the protection of guardians and masters, and bound to obey those put above them in place of parents, just as children are so bound.[2]

It was scarcely surprising that Northerners regarded the black codes as palpable evasions of the Thirteenth Amendment, and conclusive evidence that the South was not prepared to accept the ' verdict of Appomattox.' So the chief significance of the black codes was the demand from the North that the Federal Government step in to protect the former slaves. This object, eventually embalmed in the Fourteenth and Fifteenth Amendments and the various civil rights bills, was first pursued through the agencies of the Freedmen's Bureau and the military governments.

The Freedmen's Bureau of the War Department was created by Congress 3 March 1865, for a period of one year after the close of the

[2] June 1866, Vol. 1 (n.s.) , 578.

war — later extended to 1869 — and was given general powers of relief and guardianship over Negroes and refugees, and the administration of abandoned lands. General O. O. Howard, the ' Christian soldier,' was in charge of its activities, and hundreds of its agents were distributed throughout the South charged with responsibility for aiding the Negro to adjust himself to freedom. The chief activities of the bureau were relief work for both races, administration of justice in cases involving freedmen, and the establishment of schools for colored people. During its brief existence the Freedmen's Bureau set up over a hundred hospitals, gave medical aid to half a million patients, distributed over 20 million rations to the destitute of both races, and maintained over 4000 schools for Negro children.

Opinion on the character and achievements of the bureau differed sharply. Northern observers were lyrical in its praise, Southerners vituperative in criticism. In the opinion of Carl Schurz, ' no other agency . . . could have wielded that moral power . . . so necessary to prevent southern society from falling at once into the chaos of a general collision between its different elements,' while Governor Humphreys of Mississippi thought that ' four years of cruel war were scarcely more blighting and destructive . . . than has resulted from the administration of this black incubus.' However, the bureau soon ceased to fulfill its original purposes and became increasingly a political machine of the Republican party, or, as the failure of the Freedman's Bureau Bank, wiping out the savings of thousands of freedmen, revealed, an opportunity for men of low character to enrich themselves at the expense of both races.

The most important work of the bureau was educational. As rapidly as schools were provided the freedmen took advantage of them. ' It was a whole race trying to go to school,' wrote Booker T. Washington, the greatest of Negro educational leaders. ' Few were too young and none too old to make the attempt to learn. As fast as any kind of teachers could be secured, not only were day schools filled, but night schools as well. The great ambition of the older people was to try to learn to read the Bible before they died.' Most of these freedmen's schools were taught by Northern women who volunteered for what W.E.B. DuBois has called the Ninth Crusade:

Behind the mists of ruin and rapine waved the calico dresses of women who dared, and after the hoarse mouthings of the field guns rang the rhythm of the alphabet. Rich and poor they were, serious and curious,

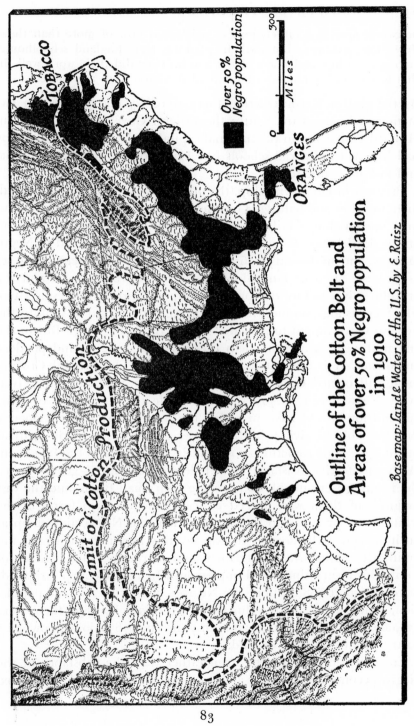

Outline of the Cotton Belt and
Areas of over 50% Negro population
in 1910

Basemap: Land & Water of the U.S. by E. Raisz

TOBACCO

ORANGES

Limit of Cotton Production

Over 50%
Negro population

0   300
Miles

bereaved, now of a father, now of a brother, now of more than these, they came seeking a life work in planting New England schoolhouses among the white and black of the South. They did their work well. In that first year they taught one hundred thousand souls and more.[3]

By the end of Reconstruction there were 600,000 Negroes in elementary schools in the South; the Federal Government had set up Howard University in the national capital, and private philanthropy had founded industrial schools like Hampton Institute in Virginia, and Fisk in Tennessee.

Progress in land-ownership, the other great ambition of the freedmen, was slow and halting. This was one of the most egregious — and most inexcusable — failures of reconstruction. During the war, land on the Sea Islands off the Carolina coast had been assigned to Negro farmers, and in January 1865 General Sherman had tentatively set aside large areas of land along the South Carolina coast and the St. John's river in Florida, for the freedmen. Northern statesmen, too, like Stevens and Sumner, had encouraged the Negro to look to the Federal Government to provide ' forty acres and a mule.' But in the end nothing was done to help the Negro become an independent landowner. It is difficult to understand this. The Federal Government still owned enough public land in the South to have given every Negro family a 40-acre farm, while the cotton tax of some $68 million would have provided the mule! Certainly a Congress that was able to give 40 million acres of land to a single railroad might have done something to fulfill its obligation to the freedmen. Without effective assistance from federal — or state — governments, the Negroes were unable to purchase even small farms, and the vast majority of them were forced to lease land on such terms as the whites were prepared to grant. And when the Negro did set up as an independent landowner he was severely handicapped by his unfamiliarity with farm management and marketing, and his lack of capital for farm animals and implements. In 1888 Georgia farmlands were valued at $88 million; the Negroes, who were half the population, owned land to the value of $1.8 million. By 1890 there were 121,000 Negro landowners, and ten years later 187,000 who owned a paltry 13 million acres of land.

Emancipation altered the form rather than the substance of the Negro's economic status for at least a generation after Appomattox.

[3] *The Souls of Black Folk* (1961 ed.), p. 38.

The transition from slave to independent farmer was a long and painful one, made usually through the medium of tenancy, and for many it was never completely made. Without the requisite capital, without credit except such as was cautiously extended by white bankers or storekeepers on usurious terms, and without agricultural skills the vast majority of freedmen were unable to rise above the sharecropper or tenant class. They continued to work in the cotton or tobacco fields, to live in the shacks provided for them by the former master or by his children, and on credit provided by the same hands. Some of the more ambitious drifted westward to the fertile lands of Texas or joined that curious exodus to Kansas in the late 'seventies that proved so futile. A very few achieved something more — a business or a profession which brought them social standing as well as livelihood. After 1890 some Negroes became laborers in the coal mines or the steel mills or tobacco factories that began to spring up in parts of the South; others drifted northward to work in industrial centers while their wives and daughters found work as ' domestics.' But the majority remained on land that belonged to others, plodding behind the plow in spring and picking cotton in the fall, reasonably sure of food and shelter and clothing, a Saturday afternoon in town, a Sunday at revival meetings, continuing in the ways of their fathers.

2. The Undoing of Reconstruction

When, in 1873, the Supreme Court was called upon for the first time to interpret the esoteric phrases of the Fourteenth Amendment, Justice Miller, speaking for the Court, reviewed the history of the three Civil War Amendments and observed of them that

No one can fail to be impressed with the one pervading purpose found in them all, lying at the foundation of each, and without which none of them would have been even suggested; we mean the freedom of the slave race, the security and firm establishment of that freedom, and the protection of the newly made freedman and citizen from the oppressions of those who had formerly exercised unlimited dominion over him.[4]

At the time this seemed the common sense of the matter, and even the judges who dissented from the decision of the Court did not chal-

----

[4] 16 Wallace 36.

lenge this general interpretation of the Amendments; indeed they enlarged upon it. The Fourteenth Amendment, said Justice Bradley,

was an attempt to give voice to the strong national yearning for that time and that condition of things, in which American citizenship should be a sure guaranty of safety, and in which every citizen of the United States might stand erect in every portion of its soil, in the full enjoyment of every right and privilege belonging to a freeman, without fear of violence or molestation.

The war had been fought, in part, to free the slave; the Thirteenth Amendment had been added to the Constitution to guarantee his freedom; the Fourteenth Amendment to protect him in his civil rights; the Fifteenth Amendment to assure him the vote. Each of these Amendments contained the unusual provision that ' Congress shall have power to enforce this article by appropriate legislation.' And, beginning with the ill-fated Civil Rights Act of 1866, Congress enacted a series of laws designed to do just that. The most important of these were the Enforcement Acts of 31 May 1870 and 28 February 1871 which threw the protection of the Federal Government over the Negro's right to vote; the Ku Klux Klan Act of 20 April 1871 which made it a federal offense to conspire to deprive Negroes of the equal protection of the laws; and the Civil Rights Act of 1 March 1875 which undertook to wipe out social as well as political discrimination and to secure the Negro ' full and equal enjoyment of the accommodations, advantages, facilities, and privileges of inns, public conveyances on land or water, theatres, and other places of public amusement,' as well as the right to serve on juries.

During the brief period of Radical Reconstruction the Negro did enjoy both civil and political rights. He was freed from the restrictions of the black codes; he exercised the vote; he held office. Nor did he suffer severe economic or social discrimination. Most of the jobs that he could do were freely open to him, and that large apparatus of social indignities that came later to be called ' Jim Crow ' had not yet been applied, or invented.

The withdrawal of troops by President Hayes in 1877 marked not only the abandonment of formal reconstruction, but the abandonment of the Negro as well. Congress, which had enacted three constitutional amendments and half a dozen Enforcement Acts all designed to protect the freedman, now threw in the sponge, and turned the ' Negro problem ' over to the South. That was what the South demanded as the price of reunion, and as the price would be paid by the Negro, the North did not find it exorbitant. There were three generally recognized parts to the unwritten agreement: that the North would hereafter keep hands off the ' Negro problem '; that the rules governing race relations in the South would be written by the whites; and that these rules would concede the Negro limited civil rights, but neither political nor social equality. The principle underlying this relationship was set forth succinctly by Henry Grady of the Atlanta *Constitution:* ' The supremacy of the white race of the South must be maintained forever, and the domination of the Negro race resisted at all points and at all hazards, because the white race is superior.' It was as simple as that.

Abandoned by the Congress and the President, the Negro was now repudiated by the courts. If the ' one pervading purpose ' of the Civil War Amendments was, indeed, the protection of the freedman from oppression, then it failed. Beginning with the Slaughterhouse case of 1873 the Supreme Court proceeded systematically to riddle the structure of Negro rights until in the end it was — in the words of John Marshall — ' a magnificent structure to look at, but totally unfit for use.' In the Slaughterhouse case the Court, distinguishing between the privileges and immunities derived from national and from state citizenship, asserted that all the important ones came from state citizenship and that it was not the purpose of the Fourteenth Amendment to try to extend federal protection over these.[5] The Cruikshank case of 1875, which involved a mob attack on Negroes who were trying to vote, carefully restricted the reach of the Fourteenth Amendment to state — not private — interference with Negro rights, and to such interference as was clearly directed against Negroes on account of their race or color. ' Inasmuch,' said Chief Justice Waite with nice irony, ' as it does not appear . . . that the intent of the defendants was to prevent these parties from exercising their right to vote on account of their race, it does not appear that it was their intent to interfere with any right granted or secured by the Constitution or laws of the United States. We may suppose that " race " was the cause of the hostility, but this is not so averred.' [6] When an election official in Kentucky — one Reese — refused to receive a Negro vote, the Court held that Congress did not have au-

[5] 16 Wallace 36 (1873).   [6] 92 U.S. 542 (1875).

thority to protect the right to vote generally, but only where that right was denied by the *state,* and on grounds of *race* or *color.*[7] In 1878 the Court provided the legal foundation for segregation by striking down a Louisiana statute forbidding discrimination in transportation, as an unlawful interference with congressional authority over interstate commerce! [8] In the *United States v. Harris,* a case in which a Tennessee mob had lynched four Negro prisoners, the Court returned to the well-worn theme that the national government could protect the Negro only against acts by the *state,* and that for protection against violence by individuals or by mobs the Negro must look to the state authorities.[9] The crucial test came with the Civil Rights Cases of 1883, where the Court, in effect, wiped off the statute book the Civil Rights Act of 1875 forbidding discrimination against Negroes in public facilities.

It would be running the slavery argument into the ground [said Justice Bradley] to make it apply to every act of discrimination which a person may see fit to make as to the guests he will entertain, or as to the people he will take into his coach or cab or car, or admit to his concert or theatre, or deal with in other matters of intercourse or business.

And the Court added, somewhat gratuitously, that

When a man has emerged from slavery and by the aid of beneficent legislation has shaken off the inseparable concomitants of that state, there must be some stage in the progress of his elevation when he takes the rank of a mere citizen, and ceases to be the special favorite of the laws, and when his rights as a citizen, or a man, are to be protected in the ordinary modes by which other men's rights are protected.[10]

This was the thesis, too, of the famous *Plessy v. Ferguson* decision of 1896 which, by accepting — or inventing — the doctrine of ' separate but equal accommodations,' threw the mantle of judicial approval over segregation.

The object of the 14th Amendment [said the Court] was undoubtedly to enforce the absolute equality of the two races before the law, but in the nature of things, it could not have been intended to abolish distinctions based upon color, or to enforce social as distinguished from political equality, or a commingling of the two races upon terms unsatisfactory to either.[11]

[7] 92 U.S. 214 (1876).
[8] *Hall v. De Cuir* 95 U.S. 485 (1878).
[9] 106 U.S. 629 (1883).
[10] 103 U.S. 3 (1883).
[11] 136 U.S. 537 (1896).

This jettisoning of the civil rights program did not go without protest from within the Court itself. It was Justice Harlan of Kentucky who was the spokesman of a construction of the Constitution broad enough to embrace the rights of all citizens, Negro and white alike. His classic dissent in the Civil Rights Cases applied to the whole body of judicial construction which had by now paralyzed the effectiveness of the wartime Amendments:

The opinion in these cases proceeds . . . upon grounds entirely too narrow and artificial. I cannot resist the conclusion that the substance and spirit of the recent amendments of the Constitution have been sacrificed by a subtle and ingenious verbal criticism. . . . Constitutional provisions, adopted in the interest of liberty, and for the purpose of securing, through national legislation, if need be, rights inhering in a state of freedom, and belonging to American citizenship, have been so construed as to defeat the ends the people desired to accomplish, which they attempted to accomplish, and which they supposed they had accomplished by changes in their fundamental law.[12]

And, observing that the ' separate but equal ' doctrine of the Plessy case would, in time ' be quite as pernicious as the decision in the Dred Scott case,' Harlan wrote prophetically that

The destinies of the two races in this country are indissolubly linked together, and the interests of both require that the common government of all shall not permit the seeds of race hate to be planted under the sanction of law. What can more certainly arouse race hate, what more certainly create and perpetuate a feeling of distrust between these races, than state enactments which in fact proceed on the ground that colored citizens are so inferior and degraded that they cannot be allowed to sit in public coaches occupied by white citizens.

What all this meant — the end of Reconstruction, the restoration of white rule, the watering down of the Enforcement Acts and their judicial nullification — was that the Southern Negro was exiled to a kind of no-man's land halfway between slavery and freedom. He was no longer a slave; he was not yet free. He was tied to the soil by the sharecrop and crop-lien systems. He was excluded from most professions and from many jobs. He was fobbed off not only with segregated schools, but with schools that were palpably inferior, and with ' separate ' accommodations that were rarely ' equal.' Socially he was relegated to a position of clear inferiority, and expected not only to

[12] Civil rights cases, above.

accept that position without protest, but to rejoice in it by playing the role of ' Uncle Tom.' At first gradually, then with dramatic speed, he was rendered politically impotent: ' grandfather ' clauses, literacy tests, poll taxes, and — where these failed — naked intimidation, deprived him of the vote. In 1885 the Louisiana novelist, George Washington Cable, was able to write that

There is scarcely one public relation of life in the South where the Negro is not arbitrarily and unlawfully compelled to hold toward the white man the attitude of an alien, a menial, and a probable reprobate, by reason of his race and color. One of the marvels of future history will be that it was counted a small matter, by a majority of our nation, for six millions of people within it, made by its own decree a component part of it, to be subjected to a system of oppression so rank that nothing could make it seem small except the fact that they had already been ground under it for a century and a half. . . . It heaps upon him in every public place the most odious distinctions, without giving ear to the humblest plea concerning mental or moral character. It spurns his ambition, tramples upon his languishing self-respect, and indignantly refuses to let him either buy with money or earn by any excellence of inner life or outward behavior, the most momentary immunity from these public indignities.[13]

Thus stripped of power, of rights, and of dignity, the Negro was exposed, naked and helpless, to the mounting aversion of the white tenant farmers and mill-villagers, who regarded him as a potential rival, and to the merciless enmity of popular leaders like James Vardaman, Cole Blease, and Tom Watson, who exploited racial fears and hatreds for political purposes. And to add to all these injuries the Negro was abandoned by his quondam friends in the North. ' The fact is,' wrote the editor of *The Century Magazine,* ' that the Negroes constitute a peasantry wholly untrained in, and ignorant of, those ideas of constitutional liberty and progress which are the birthright of every white voter; that they are gregarious and emotional, and are easily led in any direction by white men of energy and determination.'

Southerners generally congratulated themselves that they had persuaded the North to concede them almost complete control of their domestic institutions, and that they were now permitted to settle the race question in accordance with the principles they thought right. Yet the cost of the restoration of white rule on these terms was

[13] G. W. Cable, ' The Freedman's Case in Equity,' *The Century Magazine,* January 1885.

high, for white as well as for black, and for North as well as for South. By denying basic rights to the Negro, Southerners did Negroes an irreparable injury, weakened their own sense of justice, and exposed themselves and their nation to the charge of hypocrisy. By sanctioning the use of fraud and evasion to deny the Negro his legal rights, they sanctioned fraud in politics, and weakened the moral standards of public life and the moral fiber of their people. By limiting Negro voting they discouraged and limited white voting, and thus struck a heavy blow at democracy in their section of the country. By identifying white supremacy with the Democratic party they saddled a one-party system upon the South, and threw that party into the hands of the least enlightened elements of their society.

3. THE NEW SOUTH: AGRICULTURE

It is easier for an agricultural than for an industrial society to recover from the devastation of war, for though factories may be destroyed and capital dissipated, the land remains. All through the spring of 1865 veterans of the armies of Lee and Johnston beat their way back to their farms and plantations and, with courage and hope, took up the task of knitting together the shattered economy of their section. 'The soldier stepped from the trenches into the furrow,' said Henry Grady, ' horses that had charged Federal guns marched before the plow, and fields that ran red with human blood in April were green with the harvest in June.' The old plantation regime, based as it was on slavery, was gone, but gradually the Southern landscape took on its familiar appearance. Fields bloomed white with cotton bolls; houses, roads and fences were repaired; the wandering Negro returned to his farm, as a sharecropper, now, or tenant. Farmers managed to raise more than 2 million bales of cotton for market in 1865, yet not until 1875 did the cotton crop surpass that of 1859. By the end of the century it was more than doubled.

The most striking feature of postwar agriculture was the widespread redistribution of the land and the emergence of revolutionary new patterns of land-tenure. The planter class had been badly crippled by war and emancipation, and during Reconstruction thousands of planters were forced to the wall. Out of this came the most far-reaching transfer of land-ownership since the Revolution, as yeoman farmers, small merchants and businessmen, Northern soldiers and carpetbaggers, and investors, snapped up what looked like bargains in land. On the surface this meant not only a redistribution of land-ownership but the breakup of plantations into small farms and a striking increase in land-ownership. Thus in 1860 there were 33,171 farms in South Carolina, 55,128 in Alabama, and 17,328 in Louisiana; twenty years later the figures were 93,328 for South Carolina, 135,864 for Alabama, and 48,292 for Louisiana. Altogether the census reported that between 1860 and 1880 the number of farms in nine cotton states increased from approximately 450,000 to approximately 1,110,000, while the average size of farms declined from 347 to 156 acres, and the number of farms under ten acres jumped almost twentyfold.

But these figures are misleading. What happened in the years after the war was not a revolution in land-ownership but in farm labor. The number of large farms (or plantations) remained about the same, but now they were divided up into small ' holdings '; and farmed not by slaves but by sharecroppers and tenants. Thus in Louisiana — where we have pretty full statistics — the percentage of farms over 100 acres actually went up in the two decades after secession from 34 to 70 and a census of Louisiana parishes of 1910 which took account of *ownership* rather than of *tenancy* reported the average farm to be 904 acres. In short, if we look to ownership rather than to cultivation the agricultural revolution — like the famous Cheshire cat — fades away, all but the grin. As Vann Woodward concludes, the agricultural revolution was in fact

the plantation minus such scant efficiency, planning, responsible supervision, and soil conservation as the old system provided . . . minus the ordinary minimum of economic virtues associated with proprietorship . . . minus even an owner who lived on its soil, and spent the profits of another's labor on his own family. The evils of land monopoly, absentee ownership, soil mining, and the one-crop system, once associated with and blamed upon slavery, did not disappear, but were instead, aggravated, intensified, and multiplied.[14]

The explanation was to be found in the operation of the sharecrop and the crop-lien systems.

These twin evils emerged as a response to the breakdown of the old labor system, and the collapse of credit after the war. The sharecrop system was an arrangement whereby planters could obtain la-

[14] *Origins of the New South*, pp. 179–80.

bor without paying wages and landless farmers could get land without paying rent. Instead of an interchange of money for labor and rent, there was a sharing of crops. The planter furnished his tenant with land and frame cabin, and, generally, with seed, fertilizer, a mule, a plow, and other farm implements; in return he received at the end of the year one-half of the crop which the tenant raised. The tenant furnished his labor, and received, in return, the rest of the crop as well as whatever he could raise for himself in his vegetable garden. At the close of the war most of the freedmen and many of the poorer white [15] farmers entered into just such an arrangement with the landowners. This system, which appeared at first to be mutually advantageous, was really injurious to all. The sharecropper was rarely able to escape from the tenant class into the farm-owning class; the planter was seldom able to farm profitably or scientifically with sharecrop labor. The method was, said the U.S. Commissioner of Agriculture, ' the best possible plan to destroy fertility and profit and demoralize labor.' With every year the number of tenant farmers increased, the profits from farming and the fertility of the soil decreased. In 1880, when the first records were made, one-third of the farmers of the cotton belt were tenants; forty years later the proportion had increased to two-thirds.

The crop-lien system was perhaps even more disastrous in its economic and social consequences. Under this system the farmer mortgaged his ungrown crop in order to obtain supplies for the year. Rates of interest were usuriously high, and the merchant who supplied food, clothing, seed, and other necessities customarily charged from 20 to 50 per cent above the normal price. Because cotton and tobacco were sure money crops, creditors generally insisted that most of the land be planted to one of these, thus discouraging diversification of crops and bringing about exhaustion of the soil. As early as 1880 two-thirds of the farmers of South Carolina had mortgaged their ungrown crops, and by 1900 this proportion was applicable to the entire cotton belt. Sharecrop and crop-lien systems served to keep the poorer farmers of the South in a state of perpetual bondage to the large planters, country storekeepers and bankers — a state from which few were ever able to extricate themselves. For when the cropper's share failed to meet the inflated charges against

[15] Four-fifths of the Negro farmers were tenants or sharecroppers, but probably less than one-half the white farmers.

him at the country store, he was forced to renew the lien on his next crop to the same merchant — and often on more onerous conditions. When this happened, wrote Matthew Hammond, the sharecropper

passed into a state of helpless peonage. . . . With the surrender of this evidence of indebtedness he has also surrendered his freedom of action and his industrial autonomy. From this time until he has paid the last dollar of his indebtedness, he is subject to the constant oversight and direction of the merchant. Every mouthful of food he purchases, every implement that he requires on the farm, his mules, cattle, the clothing for himself and family, the fertilizers for his land, must all be bought of the merchant who holds the crop-lien, and in such amounts as the latter is willing to allow.[16]

The result of all this was an increasing impoverishment of the farm population, a growing stratification of class lines, and a relative decline in the agricultural prosperity of the entire section. By the turn of the century ' Tobacco Road ' was spreading throughout the entire South.

Despite the reorganization of the large plantation and the emancipation of the Negro, the Cotton Kingdom of 1900 was in many essential respects much what it had been before the Civil War. The old-fashioned planter was gone — except from the pages of romantic fiction — but in his place was the merchant, banker, or loan-agent, controlling large aggregations of tenant farms. The farm-labor force showed fewer changes than in other parts of the country: the Negro slave was no more, but in his place was the sharecropper. The South was still a stable-crop section, less self-sufficient agriculturally in 1900 than in 1860, and what Rupert Vance has called the ' cotton culture complex ' still dominated the psychology of that section. The application of science and invention to farming had wrought fewer changes in the Cotton Kingdom than elsewhere, for cotton was the one important crop that refused to yield to machinery; the boll weevil proved invincible; and proportionately less money was invested in machinery here than in any other section of the country.

4. THE NEW SOUTH: INDUSTRY

Urban recovery was slower than agricultural, but once under way went faster and farther. Not until the mid-seventies did many of the

[16] Matthew B. Hammond, *The Cotton Industry*, p. 149.

ruined cities of the South make a real comeback. Norfolk was long stagnant; Galveston lost population; Columbia and Charleston were too shattered to rebuild properly for years, and Charleston exported less in 1880 than she had in 1860. New Orleans took a generation to recover from the combined impact of the decline of Mississippi steamboating, Union occupation, the mismanagement of the Reconstruction governments, and yellow fever; and the stricken city of Memphis suffered so severely from the war and the ravages of yellow-jack that she temporarily disappeared as a city. But new cities like Birmingham and Chattanooga and Durham sprang into existence, and Atlanta rose from her ashes to a more vigorous life and by 1880 boasted a population four times as large as at the outbreak of the war. ' Chicago in her busiest days,' wrote a visitor, ' could scarcely show such a sight as clamors for observation here.'

Here was the ' New South ' — the South of cities, factories, and blast furnaces. When, all through the 1880's, Henry Grady proclaimed the New South, what inspired enthusiasm was not so much his celebration of the Union, or his tribute to Lincoln, or even his insistence that the South would take care of the Negro, but his glorification of the new industrial order — cities, factories, immigrants, tariffs, and all. ' Think of it,' he said in a rapturous outburst —

In cotton a monopoly. In iron and coal establishing swift mastery. In granite and marble developing equal advantages and resources. In yellow pine and hard woods the world's treasury. Surely the basis of the South's wealth and power is laid by the hand of Almighty God!

But two things were necessary before the South could achieve wealth and power: capital and transportation. Capital presented the most difficult problem. The South itself had no surplus, and the fiscal policies of the Reconstruction governments, Radical and Redeemer alike, were not calculated to inspire confidence in Northern or foreign investors. But gradually the South attracted, or accumulated, money. The Freedmen's Bureau and the army spent large sums of money; the government appropriated millions for internal improvements; Northerners bought up farms and plantations, and Northern capital went into railroads, timberlands, coal and iron industries. Gradually, too, the South re-entered the world market with her exports, and lifted herself by her financial bootstraps. By the 'eighties money was pouring into the South from the North and from abroad.

Much of this went to rebuilding, modernizing, and expanding the railroads. Some of these roads — notably the Louisville and Nashville — had weathered the war in good shape, and others were speedily repaired. During the 'seventies the South added 5000 miles to her railroad network, and in the 'eighties no less than 23,000 miles, much of it in Texas, but over 14,000 miles east of the Mississippi. It is suggestive that the Louisville and Nashville was controlled by Northern capital, and that of the twenty directors of the South's largest railroad system, the Terminal, seventeen were New Yorkers.

For two generations Southerners had sent their cotton to the mills of Old and New England where the manufacturing establishments, labor, capital, and facilities for world marketing were well organized. The 'fifties saw the beginnings of a textile industry in Georgia and South Carolina, and some of the new mills — those of William Gregg at Graniteville, South Carolina, for example — flourished all through the war. Not until the 'seventies, however, did the South seriously challenge the monopoly of New England mills. Proximity to raw materials and to water power, cheap labor, freedom from legal restraints, low taxes, and eager community support all gave Southern mills an initial advantage. By the end of Reconstruction over 100 Southern mills had almost half a million spindles; twenty years later some 400 mills boasted over 4 million spindles. Yet this was only a beginning. By 1920 the textile industry had moved south, and North Carolina, South Carolina, and Georgia ranked second, third, and fourth among the textile states of the nation.[17]

The rapid growth of the textile industry in the South necessitated grave social and economic readjustments. It introduced to Southern economy a labor problem of an explosive nature; to Southern society a social problem that long defied solution; to Southern politics new pressures that acted as a solvent on the old political solidarity. Because Southerners had no experience with the industrial revolution, or with the regulation of industry and of free labor, they blundered as badly as had the English at the beginning of the nineteenth century, and took even longer to recover from their blunders.

The pattern of the Southern textile industry differed in important ways from that of New England. Small mills were on the outskirts of scores of little Carolina and Georgia towns, financed by lo-

[17] In 1957 each of these states had more spindles than all the New England states combined.

cal capital, managed by local enterprise, supported by local pride, and worked by white labor recruited from the neighborhood. The mill-workers, mostly from the poor-white class, welcomed the opportunity to exchange their drab and impoverished existence for the dubious attractions of the mill village.

To such people [wrote Holland Thompson] the cotton-mill offered a means of escape from bitter poverty. . . . The whole family had worked on the farm, as families have done since farming began, and for the family to work in the mill seemed a natural procedure. The usual result was that the children worked, though the father often failed to find employment and became a hypochondriac or a loafer.[18]

The great majority of mill-workers were women, and children between the ages of ten and fifteen; these worked an average of seventy hours a week, for a weekly wage of about three dollars. No laws limited the hours of labor of women, and such child labor laws as were enacted were universally unenforced.

Though such cities as Gastonia and Winston-Salem in North Carolina, Columbia and Greenville in South Carolina, West Point, Georgia, and Elizabethtown, Tennessee, became major textile centers, the industry was less concentrated and much less specialized in the South than in New England. The establishment of local mills introduced a new element into many an old Southern town — the ' mill village,' inhabited by laborers recruited from nearby farms, its very existence often ignored by respectable people. A Northern visitor has described the appearance of a typical Georgia mill village in the 'eighties:

Flung as if by chance beside a red clay road that winds between snake fences, a settlement appears. Rows of loosely built, weather-stained frame houses, all of the same ugly pattern and buttressed by clumsy chimneys are set close to the highway. No porch, no doorstep even, admits to these barrack-like quarters; only an unhewn log or a convenient stone. To the occupants suspicion, fear, and robbery are unknown, for board shutters stretched swagging back leave the paneless windows great gaping squares. A shackling bed, tricked out in a gaudy patchwork, a few defunct ' split-bottom ' chairs, a rickety table, and a jumble of battered crockery keep company with the collapsed bellows and fat pine knots by the hearth. The bare floors are begrimed with the tread of animals, and the muddy

[18] ' The Southern Textile Situation,' *South Atlantic Quarterly*, April 1930.

outline of splayed toes of all shapes and sizes betoken inmates unused to shoes and stockings. Yard there is none, nor plant, nor paling, nor out-house, in the whole community . . .[19]

The mill village gathered around the factory as a medieval village clustered about a feudal castle, and the mill manager ruled his community as a feudal lord ruled his manor. The company ordinarily owned the entire village — houses, stores, streets, the school, the church; needless to add, it effectively owned the workers, the shop-keepers, the teachers, and the preacher as well. Labor organizers could be denied access to the village, trouble-makers could be evicted, and teachers or preachers who indulged in criticism of the system could be sent packing. By the opening of the twentieth century the New South had gone a long way toward substituting industrial autocracy for the old agrarian feudalism.

It was not until the late 'seventies and 'eighties that the pattern of Southern economy took on a more varied appearance. The South had manufactured most of the nation's tobacco even before the war, and after Appomattox the tobacco industry made a swift comeback. As with the textile industry, it enjoyed the advantages of the proximity of raw material, low transportation costs, and cheap labor; unlike the textile industry, it was concentrated in large cities such as Richmond and Louisville, and used Negro labor. Two circumstances account in large part for the great prosperity it enjoyed: the invention, in 1880, of a cigarette-making machine by James Bonsack of Virginia, and the organizing genius of James Buchanan Duke. Starting as a boy peddling his father's tobacco to North Carolina farmers, young Duke rose to be the Rockefeller of the tobacco industry, made his native town of Durham, North Carolina, the tobacco capital of the world, and in 1890 welded together the gigantic American Tobacco Company, whose operations — conducted in New York City — stretched from the tobacco fields of the American South to Europe, Egypt, India, and China. The 'eighties saw, too, the beginnings of a flourishing coal and iron industry centered on Birmingham, Alabama, which quickly became the Pittsburgh of the South, and a lumber industry which moved south from the timber stands of New York and Michigan to exploit and devastate the pine forests of Louisiana and Mississippi. And after the opening of the new century

[19] Clare de Graffenried, in *The Century Magazine*, February 1891.

the plains of Texas and Oklahoma, once the domain of the Indians and the cattlemen, became part of the domain of oil.

The industrialization of the South carried with it changes in the political outlook of that section. The leaders of the New South were no less sensitive to the demands of industry than the leaders of the Old South had been to the demands of slavery. The 'Bourbons' who ruled the South from Reconstruction to the turn of the century were, for the most part, wholeheartedly committed to a program of industrialization, and it was not long before the South, as well as the North, could boast its 'railroad Senators' and its 'coal and iron Senators.' William Mahone, for example, who was active in Virginia politics for almost twenty years after the war, was a railroad builder and industrialist who used parties and politics for his business purposes. The three men who controlled Georgia politics in the postwar years, General Colquitt, General John Gordon, and Governor Joseph E. Brown, were all deeply involved in railroad promotion, manufacturing, real estate, and other forms of speculation. Louisiana politics were dominated by the Lottery Ring, which hired distinguished Confederate veterans like General Beauregard and General Jubal Early as fronts, while it debauched legislatures and corrupted the press to make fabulous profits. Through Milton Smith and General Basil Duke the Louisville and Nashville Railroad controlled Kentucky politics for over twenty years; when in 1900 a reformer, Governor William Goebel, threatened that control, he was assassinated.

It was this combination of developments — the emergence of the small farmer and of the free Negro, the rise of industry, and the growth of cities — that persuaded contemporaries that there was indeed a 'New South.' Thus in 1881 Bishop Atticus Haygood asked, rhetorically,

Does History record an example in any race or age where a people of strong character went so far in fifteen years as the Southern people have gone since 1865 in the modification of opinions, in the change of sentiments that had been, through generations, firmly fixed in all their thinking and feeling? The change of opinions and sentiments of the Southern people since 1865 is one of the most wonderful facts of history.

Yet we must not be deceived by the glib phrase, as so many Southerners were. Industrialization is common to the entire post-Civil War United States, and there was no more a 'New' South than there was

a ' New ' North or a ' New ' West. Indeed the Middle West and the
Pacific coast both advanced more rapidly along the path of industry
than did the seaboard South, and the South of 1900 accounted for a
smaller proportion of the total manufacturing product of the country than did the South of 1860. Far more than other sections, the
South escaped those two concomitants of industry — urbanization
and immigration. The South was still, in 1900 as in 1860, predominantly rural, and the population of the Southern states remained
almost entirely native-born. Notwithstanding the experience of the
Civil War, the South was still almost wholly a staple-crop — and
even a one-crop — section; if King Cotton had been deposed he was
still a lively pretender, and the South of 1900 still imported meat,
butter, milk, and other farm products from the North. The problem
of black and white still hung like a dark cloud on the Southern horizon, and the necessity of keeping his a ' white man's country ' still
dominated the Southerner's psychology, and his politics as well.
South of the Mason-Dixon Line was still the ' Bible belt ' — the
home of orthodoxy and revivalism. And notwithstanding the bargain
of '77 and the policy of *rapprochement* pursued by the Republican
party, from 1880 to the new century the Republicans failed to carry
a single Southern state.

Actually the ' New ' South was not to come for another half century, and then it was a world war, and the Negro, that ushered it in,
with a substantial part of the South still fighting it.

Nor was the ' New ' South the only preoccupation of Southerners
of this generation. Along with ever-mounting enthusiasm for the
New South went ever-deepening nostalgia for the Old, and the more
ardently Southerners committed themselves to the real world of
railroads and business and machinery, the more passionately they wal-
lowed in nostalgia for the dream world of the Old South of plantations and romance. The dream of the Old South was a phantasma-
goria of the wide-spreading plantation and the white-pillared manor
house, of families always old and distinguished, of aristocratic colo-
nels and great ladies and girls who were lovelier and purer than girls
elsewhere, of happy slaves singing in the cotton fields or dancing in
the quarters on Saturday nights, of an independent yeomanry and
picturesque mountaineers given to Elizabethan speech, of a special
hospitality, a special grace, a special sense of chivalry and code of
honor, a Cause forever right and forever Lost. The Old South was,

in short, mankind before the Fall, but it was Southern mankind, not Yankee — a special moral and historical experience which Providence had vouchsafed to Southerners and which set them apart. As, with the passing years, the contrast between the dream of the Old South and the reality of the New — between the myth of plantation and slavery and the reality of tenant-farming and the mill villages — grew ever more ostensible, Southerners grew more defiant about it and more insistent upon it, for it was not only a myth but an emotional outlet and a moral salve. What is perhaps most remarkable is that in the end the South imposed this myth not only on itself, but on the North as well; even now, repudiated by Southern scholars and novelists, it still flourishes in Hollywood and along Madison Avenue, testimony to the pervasive romanticism of the American people.

BIBLIOGRAPHY

1. THE NEGRO AS FREEDMAN. P. A. Bruce, *The Plantation Negro as Freedman;* George W. Cable, *The Negro Question,* ed. by Arlin Turner; Wilbur J. Cash, *The Mind of the South;* Henderson H. Donald, *The Negro Freedman;* W. E. B. DuBois, *Black Reconstruction* and *The Souls of Black Folk;* John Hope Franklin, *Reconstruction;* Rayford W. Logan, *The Negro in American Life and Thought, 1877–1901;* Basil Mathews, *Booker T. Washington;* Gunnar Myrdal, *An American Dilemma* (2 vols.) ; William Peters, *The Southern Temper;* Arthur Raper, *Preface to Peasantry;* Otis Singletary, *Negro Militia and Reconstruction;* S. R. Spencer, Jr., *Booker T. Washington and the Negro's Place in American Life;* Booker T. Washington, *Up from Slavery;* Charles H. Wesley, *Negro Labor in the United States, 1850–1925;* Vernon Wharton, *The Negro in Mississippi;* Carter G. Woodson, *A Century of Negro Migration.*

2. THE NADIR OF NEGRO RIGHTS. Robert J. Harris, *The Quest for Equality;* Joseph B. James, *Framing of the Fourteenth Amendment;* Milton Konvitz, *The Constitution and Civil Rights* and *A Century of Civil Rights;* Paul Lewinson, *Race, Class, and Party;* Samuel D. Smith, *The Negro in Congress, 1870–1901;* Gilbert T. Stephenson, *Race Distinctions in American Law;* Jacobus Ten Broek, *Antislavery Origins of the Fourteenth Amendment;* C. Vann Woodward, *The Strange Career of Jim Crow.*

3. THE EMERGENCE OF THE NEW SOUTH. W. K. Boyd, *The Story of Durham, City of the New South;* R. P. Brooks, *The Agrarian Revolution in Georgia, 1865–1912;* P. A. Bruce, *The Rise of the New South;* Paul Buck, *The Road to Reunion;* Wilbur Cash, *The Mind of the South;* Virginius Dabney, *Liberalism in the South;* John Dollard, *Caste and Class in a Southern Town;* W. B. Hesseltine, *Confederate Leaders in the New South;* John W. Jenkins, *James B. Duke: Master Builder;* V. O. Key, *Southern Politics in State and Nation;* Broadus Mitchell, *Rise of Cotton Mills in the South;* Herman C. Nixon, *Forty*

Acres and Steel Mules; R. B. Nixon, *Henry W. Grady;* Benjamin Ratchford, *American State Debts;* Fred Shannon, *The Farmer's Last Frontier;* Roger W. Shugg, *Origins of the Class Struggle in Louisiana;* Holland Thompson, *From Cotton Field to Cotton Mill;* Rupert Vance, *Human Factors in Cotton Culture* and *Human Geography of the South;* C. Vann Woodward, *The Origins of the New South.*

4. DOCUMENTS. Herbert Aptheker (ed.), *A Documentary History of the Negro in the United States;* H. S. Commager, *Documents,* nos. 245–247, 251–253, 271–273, 291–293, 297; Rayford Logan, *The Negro in the United States.*

For further references, *Harvard Guide,* ¶¶ 195, 212.

The American Mind During the Reconstruction Years

1. THE IMPACT OF WAR

THOSE who fight wars customarily console themselves with the expectation, or the hope, that war is not wholly destructive, that it is in some way creative. War, they urge, quickens the scientific spirit, inspires intellectual activity, calls forth new moral energies. This expectation was not wholly without foundation in American experience: the American Revolution, after all, loosened the floodgates of political talent, and the war of 1812 was followed by ferment in the intellectual world and by a new birth of nationalism. Would the Civil War leave the American people exhausted and embittered or would it discover new ideas and excite new energies? Would defeat produce an intellectual revival in the South or destroy initiative and hope? Would the immense organization of power and the heady sense of victory exalt the mind of the North or would habits of materialism and ruthlessness born of the war persist into the postwar era?

Emerson saw the Civil War as a ' frosty October which shall restore intellectual and moral power to these languid and dissipated populations,' and James Russell Lowell

> looked to see an ampler atmosphere
> By that electric passion-gust blown clear . . .

Both lived to confess themselves disillusioned. Walt Whitman welcomed the war more realistically:

> Beat! Beat! Drums! — blow! bugles! blow!
> Through the windows — through doors — burst like a ruthless force
> Into the solemn church, and scatter the congregation,
> Into the school where the scholar is studying;

Leave not the bridegroom quiet — no happiness must he have now with
   his bride,
Nor the peaceful farmer any peace, ploughing his field or gathering his
   grain,
So fierce you whirr and pound you drums — so shrill you bugles blow.

   Defeat at the hands of Napoleon had inspired an intellectual renaissance in Prussia in the first years of the century; Denmark had
emerged from the catastrophe of 1815 into a golden age of literature
and philosophy; defeated France flourished far more vigorously after
1871 than did victorious Germany. But the defeated South experienced no such renaissance of spirit or of culture. Everywhere the
war had ' burst like a ruthless force,' but it was in the South that it
scattered the congregations and put an end to happiness and peace.
The cultural life of the South was irretrievably damaged by the war
and by reconstruction, and did not recover for over a generation.
Schools, colleges, libraries, and churches were destroyed or impoverished, and the intellectual life was paralyzed by poverty, by the preoccupation with sheer survival, and by obsession with the past and with
defeat. ' You ask me to tell you the story of my last year,' wrote the
poet Henry Timrod. ' I can embody it all in a few words: beggary,
starvation, death, bitter grief, utter want of hope.' And the Kentucky-
born scientist, Nathaniel Shaler, wrote that

Not only did the Civil War maim the generation of Kentuckians to which
I belonged, it also broke up the developing motives of intellectual culture of the commonwealth. Just before it I can see that while the ideals
of culture were in a way still low and rather carnal, there was an eager
reaching-out for better things; men and women were seeking, through history, literature, the fine arts, and in some measure through science, for a
share in the higher life. Four years of civil war, which turned the minds
of all towards what is at once the most absorbing and debasing interest of
man, made an end of all this. . . .[1]

Many of the intellectual leaders of the South — like the novelist
Simms and the poet Paul Hamilton Hayne and the sociologist George
Fitzhugh — retired to live with poverty and bitterness for the rest
of their lives. Others fled the South for the more prosperous or hos-
pitable North and West: thus Frederick Barnard left the University
of Mississippi to become president of Columbia University; the
LeConte brothers gave up their scientific work in South Carolina and

---

[1] Shaler, *Autobiography*, pp. 76-7.

moved to the new University of California; the novelist George W. Cable of Louisiana took refuge in Massachusetts; the brilliant young architect Henry Hobson Richardson moved from New Orleans — via Paris — to Boston and New York; the Greek scholar Basil Gildersleeve and the poet-musician Sidney Lanier, both veterans of the Confederate army, found careers in the Johns Hopkins University in Baltimore. Such physical energies as the South was able to summon up went into material reconstruction and the building of the New South; such intellectual energies as it discovered were devoted chiefly to the elegiac celebration of the Lost Cause, or the defense of a Southern way of life.

Meantime the North, lusty and arrogant, its power undiminished and its wealth enhanced by the war, was pushing forward to ever greater power and wealth. The decade after Appomattox was a period of relentless materialism and almost limitless expansion, when, blindly but unashamed, men were getting and spending and laying waste their powers, creating a new America of giant industry and finance capitalism, and sprawling, unlovely cities. The war had strengthened the materialistic forces of American life, while it coarsened and, in some respects, corrupted the American character.

Certainly these were years of tawdriness and vulgarity. It was the era of the Tweed Ring and Black Friday and the Molly Maguires in the coal fields of Pennsylvania; of Anthony Comstock ' the Roundsman of the Lord,' and the flamboyant Roscoe Conkling, and the railroad-wrecking Daniel Drew; of lachrymose novels like Augusta Evans's *St. Elmo* and Elizabeth Phelps's *Gates Ajar,* and the pious tales of Horatio Alger; of Rogers's plaster-cast statues and Currier and Ives lithographs and massive choruses of 10,000 voices shouting the Anvil Chorus to the accompaniment of cannon fired by electricity. It was the period of the brownstone front, the mansard roof, the stained-glass window, and the ' House Beautiful ' described by Mark Twain in one of the happiest chapters of *Life on the Mississippi.*

The editor of *The Nation,* E. L. Godkin, called this a ' chromo civilization,' and Walt Whitman pronounced it:

Cankered, crude, superstitious, and rotten. . . . Never was there, perhaps, more hollowness of heart than at present, and here in the United States. Genuine belief seems to have left us . . . I say that our New World democracy, however great a success in uplifting the masses out of their sloughs, in materialistic development, products, in a certain highly deceptive superficial popular intellectuality, is so far an almost complete failure in its social aspects, and in really grand religious, moral, literary and esthetic results.[2]

All true enough, yet we must not accept these verdicts too quickly or uncritically. In his ' Song of the Exposition,' written the same year as *Democratic Vistas,* Whitman celebrated the ' great cathedral sacred industry ' as ' mightier than Egypt's tombs, Fairer than Grecia's, Roma's temples, Prouder than Milan's statued, spired cathedral.' And the very next year came ' Thou Mother with Thy Equal Brood ' — the most exultant tribute to America that any poet has ever penned:

Beautiful world of new superber birth that rises to my eyes,
Like a limitless golden cloud filling the western sky,
Emblem of general maternity lifted above all,
Sacred shape of the bearer of daughters and sons, . . .
Thou wonder world yet undefined, unform'd, neither do I define thee, . . .
Land tolerating all, accepting all, not for the good alone, all good for thee,
Land in the realms of God, to be a realm unto thyself,
Under the rule of God to be a rule unto thyself.

For Whitman recognized what we are only now coming to appreciate, as we uncover the artifacts of culture beneath the debris of reconstruction, that along with so much that was tawdry and vulgar there was, in these years, an immense vitality, resourcefulness, enterprise, and imagination. For if the war had coarsened the characters of some, it had refined the spirits of others, and there was truth in the noble words of Justice Oliver Wendell Holmes, who bore the wounds of three battles:

The generation that carried on the war has been set aside by its experience. Through our great good fortune, in our youth our hearts were touched with fire. It was given to us to learn at the outset that life is a profound and passionate thing. . . . We have seen with our own eyes, beyond and above the gold fields, the snowy heights of honor, and it is for us to bear the report to those who come after us.

2. LITERARY CURRENTS

And bear the report they did. The literary record of the war, North and South, was varied and rich. No public man of the nine-

---

[2] *Democratic Vistas,* 1871.

teenth century wrote more eloquently than Lincoln, and a handful of his public papers can be ranked as world literature. The memoirs of the great captains like Grant and Sherman, Longstreet and Gordon, are unfailingly interesting but rarely possess the literary qualities that we find in the recollections of some of the lesser figures: Joshua Chamberlain's *The Passing of the Armies,* for example, or Thomas W. Higginson's *Army Life in a Black Regiment,* or General Taylor's brilliant *Destruction and Reconstruction.* Nor has any American war produced more memorable poetry. Henry Timrod and Paul Hayne sang the cause of the South — Lanier did not turn to poetry until after the war — and Walt Whitman was the laureate of the Union. In his poems we can read much of the history, and the meaning, of the war, from ' Eighteen Sixty-one ':

> Arm'd year — year of the struggle,
> No dainty rhymes of sentimental love verses for you terrible year, . . .

to the lovely elegy for President Lincoln: ' When Lilacs Last in the Dooryard Bloom'd.'

Whitman spanned the whole period from the 'fifties to the 'eighties, linking together in his own philosophy and his poetic experiments the romanticism of the Golden Day and the naturalism of the Gilded. It was in the years after the war that he wrote many of his greatest and most enduring poems — the ' Memories of President Lincoln,' ' Whispers of Heavenly Death,' ' Thou Mother with Thy Equal Brood,' and ' Passage to India.' These years, too, saw the emergence of the three great writers who were to dominate the American literary scene for almost half a century — Mark Twain, William Dean Howells, and Henry James — as well as minor writers like Bret Harte, whose sentimental stories of life in the mining camps appealed vastly to his generation, Sidney Lanier, and Emily Dickinson, whose exquisite genius awaited later recognition.

All three of the major literary figures who made their debuts during these years reached maturity only after the end of reconstruction; of the three Mark Twain alone belongs indubitably to the era which he named. Born in frontier Missouri where North meets South and East meets West, Sam Clemens spent his boyhood on the banks of the river whose epic he was to write, absorbing the rich human drama that passed before him. Before he was twenty-five he had worked as a journeyman printer and a newspaperman, and served an apprenticeship as a Mississippi pilot, learning the great river and the varied country that it traversed and the society that floated on its muddy waters. When the war came he enlisted, briefly, in a volunteer Confederate company, then — like his own Huck Finn — lit out for the Territory. It was there, in Nevada and California, that he found the material for his early stories, like ' The Celebrated Jumping Frog of Calaveras County,' and for *Roughing It,* the first full-length novel about the Far West. In 1867 he sailed on the *Quaker City* to the Mediterranean and the Holy Land: *Innocents Abroad* (1869) gave him a reputation as a ' humorist ' which he never quite lived down, and struck a note familiar in American literature and thought — the theme of American innocence and Old World corruption. *The Gilded Age* (1874), like *Roughing It,* drew on his acquaintance with the frontier, and with the Washington of Grant's administration. Thereafter it was the Mississippi river that provided inspiration for his greatest books. From the steamboat leadsmen's cry at two fathoms, ' by the mark, twain! ' he took his literary name, and on the river were born his three immortal characters, Tom Sawyer, Huck Finn, and the Negro Jim. These early books — *Roughing It, Innocents Abroad, Old Times on the Mississippi* (later *Life on the Mississippi*), and *Tom Sawyer,* all written before 1877 — were, as Van Wyck Brooks observes, ' germs of a new American literature with a broader base in the national mind than the writers of New England had possessed. By his re-creation of the frontier life in the great central valley, by his skill in recapturing its speech and its turns of mind, Mark Twain pre-empted for later writers a realm that was theirs by right of birth but might never have been theirs for literature if he had not cleared the way.' [3]

The second figure of the triumvirate, William Dean Howells, was, like Mark Twain, a son of the Middle Border and, like Mark Twain too, came out of a background of printing and journalism into literature. In 1860, at the age of 23, Howells wrote an undistinguished campaign biography of Lincoln and was rewarded with the consulship at Venice. There he had time to immerse himself in European letters, and to study America from the vantage point of the Old World. Returning home at the close of the war he wrote critical essays for *The Nation* and travel sketches, stories, and theatricals for a wider public; in 1871 the Ohio printer's devil became editor-in-

[3] *The Times of Melville and Whitman,* p. 297.

chief of the *Atlantic,* and made that house-organ of the Brahmins
into a national periodical. Somehow he found time to carry on his
editorial and critical work, while a steady stream of novels and stories
flowed from his pen. As with Mark Twain, Howells's early books anticipate his later themes: the conflict in manners, and in standards,
of Boston and the hinterland (*A Chance Acquaintance,* 1873), the
impact of the Old World on unsophisticated Americans (*A Foregone
Conclusion,* 1875 and *The Lady of the Aroostook,* 1879), and the
morality of the commonplace and the immorality of what passed
for 'romance.' As Henry James wrote of him:

He thinks scarcely anything too paltry to be interesting, that the small
and vulgar have been terribly neglected, and would rather see an exact
account of a sentiment or a character he stumbles against every day than
a brilliant evocation of a passion or a type he has never seen. He adores
the real, the natural, the colloquial, the optimistic, and the democratic.

Henry James, born eight years after Mark Twain and six after
Howells, was the last of the three to make his literary bow, but he,
too, published his first important work during these reconstruction
years. Like Howells — with whom he maintained an abiding friendship — he cut his teeth on *The Nation* and the *Atlantic Monthly,*
and, like Howells too, he indulged in travel sketches to which he
added a new dimension of insight. Educated mostly abroad, James
was never thereafter at home in America. 'It is a wretched business,' he wrote, 'this virtual quarrel of ours with our own society,' and he spoke for a whole generation of American writers and
artists. 'Quarrel' was too strong a word in his case, for though James
could not come to terms with America, all his life he remained loyal
to its virtues. What fascinated him was the contrast between the simplicity and innocence of America and the rich, dense, complex, and
often evil pattern of Europe. 'It is a complex fate being an American,' he said, 'and one of the responsibilities it entails is fighting
against a superstitious veneration of Europe.' James's first story, 'A
Passionate Pilgrim' (1871), was a variation on a theme exploited
by his master, Hawthorne — the theme of the American pilgrim
seeking his Old Home and suffering cruel repudiation. The theme
of his first major novel, *Roderick Hudson* (1876), was a similar one:
the demoralizing effect of the Old World — in this case the 'golden
haze' of Italy — on the artistic integrity of a young American sculp-

tor. Here were already two of the great moral themes with which
James was to be preoccupied for the remainder of his long and distinguished career — the theme of New World innocence and Old
World corruption, and of the preservation of the integrity of the
artist.

3. JOURNALISM

In the 'sixties and 'seventies New York City was the newspaper
center of the nation. Though such local papers as the *Springfield Republican,* the *Boston Transcript,* the *Toledo Blade,* and the *Cincinnati Commercial* were comparatively more influential than provincial
papers of the present time, it was the great New York dailies — the
Tribune, Sun, Evening Post, and *Times* — that held a commanding
position.

The dean of American newspapermen was the venerable William
Cullen Bryant, for half a century editor of the *Evening Post.* The
just fame of Bryant had been obscured by emphasizing his poetry at
the expense of his journalistic talents. Few more vigorous, discriminating and far-sighted critics have dealt with the American scene than
this poet-editor who combined respectability with a zeal for righteousness. He lifted American journalism to a higher literary and ethical plane than it had heretofore occupied, and gave not only his editorial column but his entire paper a dignity that assured it the
leading place in American journalism. But he lacked the talent to
appeal to a broad popular audience, and his influence was limited
almost entirely to the intellectual elite.[4]

At the farthest remove from Bryant in ability to gauge and to influence popular opinion and to create a broad national paper, was
Horace Greeley of the *Tribune,* by common consent the greatest of
American editors. Greeley was the spokesman of the plain people,
not of New York alone but of the entire North. Practical, liberal,
open-minded, fearless, and with boundless faith in democracy, he
was a social reformer who fashioned a great paper as an instrument
for social purposes. He founded the *Tribune* in 1841, drove its circulation up over the hundred thousand mark, and until the close of

[4] Says Allan Nevins, historian of the *Evening Post,* ' his journalistic vein had something of the narrowness which marked his poetic genius, and though the Post's editorials, political news, literary articles, and foreign correspondence were of the highest
merit, they were for the few and not for the many.'

WALT WHITMAN *by Thomas Eakins*

the Civil War exerted a greater influence over public opinion north of the Mason-Dixon Line than any other editor — and possibly than any other private citizen in the country. The weekly edition of his paper was read all the way from Maine to Minnesota, and its fierce denunciations of the slave power did as much to inflame Northern opinion against that institution as all the agitation of the professional abolitionists. Greeley's erratic course during the war cost him some popularity, and his vindictive attacks upon President Johnson contrasted unpleasantly with the more tolerant attitude of Bryant and of Raymond of the *Times*. Yet throughout the whole of his long career Greeley found room in his paper for the liveliest literary intelligence, the most varied points of view, and the most extreme reforms. His thirty years of editorial leadership of the *Tribune* still constitutes the greatest achievement of personal journalism in our history. In 1872 Greeley abandoned his newspaper for politics, with disastrous results. Within a few weeks of the election he was dead; his successor, Whitelaw Reid, reversed his liberal and crusading policies and fashioned the *Tribune* into a voice for conservatism.

A very different paper was *The Sun*, after 1868 under the control of Charles A. Dana, graduate of Harvard College and of Brook Farm. Dana had been trained to journalism under Greeley; he had seen service in the war under Grant, and was close to the center of power. When he took over *The Sun* he announced that it would ' study condensation, clearness, point, and will endeavor to present its daily photograph of the whole world's doings in the most luminous and lively manner.' By emphasizing news and feature articles, and by attracting to his staff some of the most skillful journalists of the day, Dana soon made *The Sun* the most popular paper in the country. With the passing of years, however, Dana grew increasingly cynical and even capricious, equally hostile to political corruption and to civil service reform, to organized capital and to organized labor; in the end he frittered away his influence and condemned his paper to sterility.

Less sensational than either Greeley or Dana was Henry J. Raymond of the New York *Times*. When he took over the paper he announced that he meant to ' navigate it into a position of independent thought and speech,' and that is what he did. The *Times*, under Raymond, was to its generation pretty much what the *Times* of today is to ours: intelligent, accurate, impartial, liberal, and judicious — and well-edited. In politics the *Times* tried to play a moderate and a moderating role. Raymond had been one of the earliest of Lincoln's supporters, and during the war he exercised considerable influence in the councils of the Republican party, writing much of the Republican platform of 1864 and helping arrange the candidacy of Johnson. After the war Raymond, like Greeley, nursed political ambitions, and like Greeley, he was a failure. But through all the buffetings of politics, he kept his ideal of a newspaper that was honest and impartial. ' It probably came nearer the newspaper of the good time coming than any other paper in existence,' wrote Godkin of *The Nation*.

The most powerful newspaper in the country outside New York City was probably the *Springfield Republican,* edited from 1844 to 1915 by three generations of Samuel Bowleses. Like the *Tribune,* the *Republican* was issued in a weekly as well as a daily edition, and the weekly had a much wider circulation, spreading the liberal principles of its editors throughout New England and even west into the Ohio and Mississippi valleys. The second Samuel Bowles had charge of the paper during the critical years of the war and reconstruction; he supported Lincoln, advocated a magnanimous policy toward the defeated South; fought corruption under Grant, and held fast to principles of independence and honesty. One signal service of the *Republican* was to demonstrate the nation-wide influence that a provincial journal might wield, and set an example that was later to be followed by such editors as William Allen White with the Emporia (Kansas) *Gazette,* and Evan P. Howell with the Atlanta *Constitution*.

More influential than many of the great daily papers, were the weekly journals of opinion such as *The Nation, The Independent,* and *Harper's Weekly*. Of these three *The Nation,* under the Irish-born E. L. Godkin, was for the thirty years after 1865 easily the most influential journal. A great editor, fearless, incisive, and vigorous, with high literary and intellectual standards, Godkin made his weekly the organ for enlightened liberalism, and for the discussion of new ideas in every field of politics, literature, and science. What made *The Nation* the liveliest and most effective journal of its day was, above all, Godkin's matchless talent for enlisting the support of the best minds in the country: Henry James and William James, Henry Adams, James Russell Lowell, William Dean Howells,

C. W. Eliot and Daniel C. Gilman, Asa Gray and John Fiske — the list reads like an intellectual Who's Who of America. It was Lowell's considered opinion that ' the *Nation*'s discussion of politics had done more good and influenced public opinion more than any agency, or all others combined, in the country.' Yet for all his high-mindedness, his unremitting hostility to corruption and low standards, Godkin found himself increasingly out of touch with the political and economic realities of his adopted country. His liberalism was doctrinaire; he had no understanding either of the farmer or the workingman, and was as bitter in his criticism of the Granger movement or organized labor as in his attacks on political or business corruption. ' He couldn't imagine a different kind of creature from himself in politics,' wrote William James shrewdly, and it is significant that the most fervent appreciation of Godkin came from his New England and English friends who, like him, often mistook good taste for good morals.

More securely in the American tradition was *Harper's Weekly,* long edited by the versatile and scholarly civil service reformer, George William Curtis. A family magazine, designed for entertainment rather than agitation, it was nevertheless a force for political decency, and Curtis came in time to occupy the position formerly held by Bryant. *Harper's Weekly* is chiefly remembered today for its lively coverage of the Civil War and for Winslow Homer's early drawings, as well as for being a vehicle of Thomas Nast's incomparable political cartoons. Less important than *Harper's Weekly* was *The Independent,* the leading religious paper of the postwar years, ably edited by Theodore Tilton and the famous Brooklyn preacher, Henry Ward Beecher.

The *Atlantic* and *Harper's Monthly,* high-minded but somewhat parochial, had for some time almost pre-empted the field of the monthly magazine. After the war they were joined by a number of newcomers which quickly made a place for themselves in the public affections. First in the field was *The Galaxy,* deliberately designed to compete with the *Atlantic.* Mark Twain wrote for it, and Henry James, and many of the most popular English authors of the day, and it gave extensive space to new developments in science. In 1878 *The Galaxy* was absorbed by the *Atlantic.* More interesting was California's bid for literary attention, the *Overland Monthly,* edited briefly by the brilliant Bret Harte whose ' Luck of Roaring Camp ' and ' Outcasts of Poker Flat ' first appeared in its fascinated pages. Harte abandoned the magazine at the end of a year, and though it lingered on for a long time it never lived up to its initial promise. A happier fate was reserved for that best of all children's magazines, the beloved *St. Nicholas*. Founded in 1873 by Mary Mapes Dodge — she had already written *Hans Brinker and the Silver Skates* — *St. Nicholas* managed to attract to its pages almost every distinguished author on both sides of the Atlantic, and many of the most talented artists and engravers as well. No magazine — not even *The Nation* — was better edited, and none ever gave more pleasure.

A decade that saw the launching of *The Nation*, the *Overland Monthly*, and *St. Nicholas* compares not unfavorably with any subsequent decade in the history of American journalism.

4. EDUCATION

The effect of the war on education in the South was little less than disastrous. Schoolhouses had fallen into ruin; teachers were killed or scattered; the impoverished South, less able to bear heavy taxes than at any time, now faced the additional burden of providing a public education for white and Negro alike. Higher education was all but paralyzed; many private institutions had lost part or the whole of their endowment; the very buildings of others had been destroyed; and few states were able to support their state universities. The University of North Carolina closed its doors for some years during reconstruction; the University of Louisiana was kept alive only by the heroic self-denial of a few professors who refused to abandon the stricken institution. Southern education did not fully recover from the effects of the war and reconstruction until the twentieth century.

In the North, by contrast, the temper and energy of the war and the postwar years stimulated education at almost every level. By the middle of the century the responsibility of the community to provide schooling for all its children was generally acknowledged, but that responsibility was faithfully discharged only in the realm of elementary education. In 1870, for example, there were only 200 public high schools in the entire country; a decade later the number had increased to some 800. As late as the 1870's it was still possible to challenge the propriety and even the legality of public support to high

schools, and not until 1874 was this question forever laid to rest by
the decision of Justice Cooley of the Michigan Supreme Court in
the Kalamazoo case.[5]

The student body of today, accustomed to a wide variety of courses,
lavish equipment, well-trained teachers, and elaborate extracurricular activities, would find the schools of this postwar era shockingly
primitive in almost every respect. Most children went to a ' little red
schoolhouse ' — more picturesque than efficient — where some student working his way through a nearby college, or a girl too young
to marry, taught all subjects and all grades. Teaching was largely by
rote, discipline was capricious but severe, corporal punishment taken
for granted, and extracurricular activities limited to games of marbles or of crack-the-whip on a muddy school ground. The backbone
of the curriculum, a term which few of the teachers would have
recognized, was the ' three R's ' — reading, writing, and arithmetic. Children learned spelling, and many other things, out of Noah
Webster's Blue Backed Spellers, which had already done service for
three generations of American boys and girls, and ' spelling-bees '
were as exciting a part of school life as basketball games today.
More important even than Webster's Spellers were the McGuffey
Readers, of which over 100 million were sold in the years between
1836 and the end of the century. In an age when schools did not
have libraries, and few children had any books at home, McGuffey's
Readers, by introducing children to ' selections ' from the best of
English and American literature, set the popular literary standard
for two or three generations. The novelist Hamlin Garland, who
went to country schools in Iowa during these years, remembered
that ' from the pages of McGuffey's Readers I learned to know and
love the poems of Scott, Byron, Southey, Wordsworth, and a long
line of English masters, and got my first taste of Shakespeare.' The
average schoolteacher of that day was no less concerned with molding
character than with molding mind, and to this purpose the McGuffey
Readers, with their pious axioms of conduct and their moral tales,
made their contribution.

The average teacher was a schoolma'am. The war had drawn men
from teaching into the ranks of the army, or to industry and business,
and the feminization of teaching was in full swing. By 1870 almost
two-thirds of the public schoolteachers were women — a number

[5] 30 Michigan Reports 69 (1874).

which increased through the rest of the century. Though Horace Mann had established the first ' normal ' school for teachers at Lexington, Massachusetts, as early as 1839, there were only twelve in the entire country at the outbreak of the Civil War. The great majority of teachers were untrained, and it was generally supposed that any girl not otherwise occupied was competent to teach school. In due course states created boards of education designed to establish minimum requirements for teaching and to maintain standards of a sort, and gradually teaching took on some of the characteristics of a profession. During the reconstruction years nine states provided for compulsory school attendance for at least part of the year, and some even enforced these laws.

In 1867 Congress created the office of United States Commissioner of Education to ' collect statistics and facts concerning the conditions and progress of education ' and ' to diffuse information regarding the organization and management of schools and methods of teaching.' Though the office was reduced to the status of a bureau, and systematically starved by a niggardly Congress, it managed nevertheless to attract to its service a number of distinguished educators: first Henry Barnard, founder and editor of the famous *American Journal of Education* and dean of educational statesmen; then the learned philosopher, William T. Harris, long-time superintendent of schools of St. Louis. It was under Harris's auspices that the first public kindergarten in the country was opened, in 1873, and it was Harris, too, whose long series of annual reports on public schools did for his generation what Horace Mann's Reports had done for an earlier generation, providing a rationalization of public education in an industrial age.

What was later known as ' progressive ' education received its formulation and earliest application during these years. The doctrines of the Swiss Johann Pestalozzi, and of the German Friedrich Froebel, had been introduced to America in the years just before the war; now they triumphed in the work of Edward A. Sheldon of the famous Oswego State Normal School, whose graduates carried the new gospel from that upstate New York Zion throughout the East and the Middle West. Almost equally important was the work of Colonel Francis Parker who had studied pedagogy in Germany, returned to be superintendent of schools in Quincy, Massachusetts, and, with the support of Charles Francis Adams, quietly carried through a revolution in education whose philosophy and techniques anticipated, and deeply influenced, John Dewey two decades later.

Higher education in the North, meantime, experienced something of a renaissance. This renaissance can be traced to a number of factors: the enactment of the Morrill Land Grant Act of 1862; the demand of business and the professions for specialized knowledge and skills; the new pressures for educational facilities for those heretofore neglected; and the emergence of a remarkable group of educational statesmen, most of them deeply influenced by German educational ideas and practices.

As early as 1850 the legislature of Michigan had petitioned Congress for help in founding a college of agriculture; three years later Jonathan Turner, tireless champion of agricultural education, persuaded the legislature of his state of Illinois to second the appeal. Thereafter the idea gathered force, and in 1859 a bill looking to federal support to agricultural education passed both houses of Congress only to be vetoed by President Buchanan. Three years later President Lincoln gladly signed a similar but more generous bill sponsored by Justin Morrill of Vermont. The Morrill Land Grant Act of 1862 gave to each state 30,000 acres of public land for each Congressman, to be used as endowment or support of a college of agricultural and mechanical arts. Under the terms of the act some 13 million acres of public domain were given to the states; because the original grant favored populous Eastern states like New York and Pennsylvania, new Western states were later recompensed with additional land grants and compensation. The Morrill Act was undoubtedly the most important piece of educational legislation passed in this country in the nineteenth century, and was to serve as a precedent for far-reaching programs of federal aid to education in the twentieth century. Under its generous provisions land grant colleges were founded in every state of the Union. Some states gave their lands to existing institutions; others to private universities; most established new agricultural and mechanical schools. Such varied universities as the University of Illinois, Purdue University, the Massachusetts Institute of Technology, and Cornell University — all founded during the reconstruction years — profited from the far-sighted wisdom of Jonathan Turner and Justin Morrill.

The scientific revolution and the growing complexity of American economic life gave rise to a demand for education more closely related to the needs of the day. One result of this was that the natural sciences were encouraged at the expense of classical and humanistic studies. Another was the establishment of numerous professional and vocational schools, and soon schools of law, medicine, architecture, and engineering began to turn out graduates fitted by special training to the demands of the new economy. Some of the older states assigned their Morrill Land Grant money to schools of science or engineering at existing institutions: thus Sheffield got Connecticut's share; Massachusetts turned her money over to the new Institute of Technology; and New York's princely grant of 1 million acres provided a large part of the endowment of the new Cornell University. Meantime private philanthropy created a series of new engineering schools: Columbia's School of Mines in 1864, Lehigh University in 1865, Stevens Institute in 1870, and even a School of Mines in Colorado as early as 1874 — two years before that Territory was admitted as a state!

Once the old universities had gone outside the bounds of the four traditional faculties, into such things as engineering and architecture, the establishment of new professional schools of education, journalism, and business was probably inevitable. The earliest and most interesting development along these lines was the attempt to provide in America the kind of facilities for graduate study that had long flourished abroad. Ever since George Ticknor and George Bancroft had led the way to Göttingen University back in the second decade of the century, eager graduates of American colleges had poured over to Berlin, Jena, Halle, Leipzig, and Munich in ever-growing numbers, bringing back with them admiration for German scholarship, the seminar, and the Ph.D. degree. Yale awarded the first Ph.D. granted in America in 1861, and ten years later organized a graduate school, and Harvard followed in 1872, while President Andrew D. White, who had studied at Berlin, made provision for graduate studies on the German model at the newly founded Cornell. With the opening of the Johns Hopkins University in 1876 the German model was firmly transplanted in the New World.

The third influence — a quickened sense of equalitarianism — required provision for higher education for women and for Negroes. Wesleyan Academy for girls had opened at Macon, Georgia, as early as 1836, and the gallant Mary Lyon had persevered against heavy odds to found Mount Holyoke College at South Hadley, Massachusetts, in

1837, while Oberlin — pioneer in this as in so many things — adopted coeducation in the late 1830's. The war and postwar years saw the founding of a number of new colleges for women: Vassar, the gift of a rich brewer of Poughkeepsie, New York, opened its doors in 1867; Wellesley College dates from 1870 and Smith College from 1871, while Hunter College in New York City, destined to be one of the largest women's colleges in the world, was likewise chartered in 1870. Meantime Iowa led the way among the state universities in adopting coeducation, and most of the state and municipal universities in the North followed her example. At a time when Englishmen were anxiously debating the propriety of establishing their first college for women — Girton, in Cambridge — the United States could boast a dozen flourishing women's colleges, and a growing acceptance of coeducation as the common sense of the matter.

Oberlin College had admitted Negroes almost from its foundation, and before the Civil War the Negroes had founded a university of their own at Wilberforce, Ohio. Few Negroes in the South were prepared to take advantage of higher education in the decade after emancipation, and the institutions that were established for them were largely industrial training colleges. Thus General Clinton Fisk, who had been a colonel of a colored regiment during the war, opened a training school for Negroes in Nashville, Tennessee, in 1866 which eventually evolved into Fisk University. In 1868 General Samuel Armstrong — he too had led a Negro regiment and had worked with the Freedmen's Bureau — established Hampton Institute in Virginia; a few years later its most distinguished graduate, Booker T. Washington, was to found his famous school at Tuskegee, Alabama.

A fourth contribution to the educational renaissance was the emergence, during these postwar years, of the most remarkable group of statesmen in the history of higher education in America. In 1869 Harvard departed from her long tradition of clerical presidents and elected a 35-year-old chemist, Charles W. Eliot, to the presidency. Eliot summed up in himself many of the new forces that were quickening educational thought in America: he had spent some time observing universities in Germany, he was a scientist rather than a theologian, and a scientist prepared to accept the teachings of Darwinian evolution, he was peculiarly sensitive to the changes brought about by the Civil War and the industrial revolution and determined to bring Harvard abreast of those changes. He signalized his advent to the presidency by a revolution in the organization, curriculum, and academic policies of the university. Though he was not the first to advocate the elective system, his tireless championship of freedom of choice, and donations that made it possible to add new subjects to the curriculum, established the system in public favor. Of greater ultimate significance was Eliot's rehabilitation of the schools of law and medicine, which he placed upon a sound professional basis. So significant was his achievement, and so widespread his influence — through his public statements, his famous ' five-foot shelf ' of books, his service on national committees — that he came to be regarded as the first citizen of his country.

While Eliot was transforming Harvard, two other remarkable educational statesmen were making new universities. Even as Grant was hammering at the lines around Richmond, the industrialist-philanthropist, Ezra Cornell, joined hands with the statesman-scholar Andrew Dickson White, to create a university far above Cayuga's waters, at Ithaca, New York. The new Cornell University, based on income from the Morrill Land Grant and on gifts from Ezra Cornell, was to be both public and private and thus to pioneer in a new pattern of higher education. Cornell induced White to accept the presidency of the new institution. Graduate of Yale College, student at Paris and Berlin, professor at the University of Michigan, chairman of the New York State committee on education, White had long dreamed of a university that should be the equal of those of Germany and France, and now he was given a free hand to create one. He decided that Cornell would have no barriers of color, sex, or faith; it would treat students like adults, encourage mature scholarship, maintain professional standards for the study of engineering and agriculture, and be a stronghold of academic freedom. Opened in 1868, Cornell set a pattern, later followed by Hopkins and Chicago, of springing to life full-panoplied in academic armor.

The third major educational statesman was Daniel Coit Gilman, who created the new Johns Hopkins University. A classmate of White's at Yale, Gilman had studied abroad and then returned to Yale to help found the Sheffield Scientific School, and to dream of doing for Yale what Eliot was doing for Harvard. When in 1871 the Yale Corporation elected a staunch champion of academic conservatism, Noah Porter, to the presidency, Gilman went west to take the presidency of the new University of California. In 1874 a Baltimore

philanthropist, Johns Hopkins, left $7 million to found a university
and a hospital; when the trustees of the university turned to President Eliot of Harvard, White of Cornell, and Angell of Michigan
for advice, each one recommended that they make Gilman president
and give him a free hand. They did. Gilman created a university
largely on a German model, with emphasis on graduate study and
scholarship. He put his money in men, not buildings, and collected
not only a distinguished faculty but a distinguished group of younger
' Fellows ' — among them the future President Woodrow Wilson,
Josiah Royce and John Dewey, leaders of two schools of philosophy,
J. Franklin Jameson and Frederick Jackson Turner, historians, Walter Hines Page and Newton D. Baker, to be prominent in the public
life of the next generation. Woodrow Wilson said, later, of Gilman
that he was ' the first to create and organize in America a university
in which the discovery and dissemination of new truth were conceded a rank superior to mere instruction.' In all this Gilman set a
standard which most great universities were to follow in the next
century.

5. SCIENTIFIC INTERESTS

' Amid the din of war, the heat of party, the deviltries of politics,
and the poison of hypocrisy,' wrote the Harvard mathematician,
Benjamin Peirce, ' science will be inaudible, incapable, incoherent
and inanimate.' The war greatly speeded up the application of science to practical problems, but retarded science itself. Out of the
war came marked improvements in rifles, artillery, naval ordnance,
torpedoes, and bridge building; and distinguished engineers like
Washington Roebling of Brooklyn Bridge fame and James B. Eads,
who spanned the Mississippi at St. Louis, learned much from their
Civil War experiences. The war provided, too, a mass of experience,
and of statistical data useful later for the study of medicine and especially of surgery. But, inevitably, the war drew scientists from their
laboratories, interrupted the work of universities and of government
bureaus and expeditions, and tended to put a premium on what was
destructive in science. Yet — as with education — forces released by
the war, as well as new ideas from abroad, stimulated scientific
thought and achievement during the reconstruction years.

Tocqueville had observed that a democracy almost inevitably addressed itself to what was practical and immediate in science; that

generalization was, for the most part, valid for this period. These years witnessed a series of large-scale geological and topographical explorations of the Far West; the organization of research at the Lawrence and Sheffield scientific schools and at government bureaus in Washington; far-reaching developments in geology, paleontology, botany, and ethnology; and the popularization of science by men like John Fiske and Edward Youmans.

The Far West had been acquired only in the 1840's, and much of it was still unexplored and unmapped; indeed the myth of the 'Great American Desert' still persisted for much of the Far West. With settlement ready to penetrate the Last West, the need for exploring its geology and geography, its flora and fauna, was urgent, and in the decade after the war the Federal Government undertook to fill the need. The Wilkes Exploring Expedition of the 'forties, the Railroad Surveys and Boundary Surveys and Coastal Surveys of the 'fifties, provided the pattern. First in the field was the army-sponsored Geological Survey of the Fortieth Parallel under the leadership of the gifted Clarence King of the Sheffield Scientific School, whom John Hay called 'the best and brightest man of his generation.' Meanwhile the Corps of Engineers launched a large-scale expedition to explore the territory west of the 100th meridian; this was entrusted to an army engineer, George M. Wheeler, who took with him a staff of geologists, ethnologists, and zoologists and whose 40-odd volumes of reports were of immense value to American science. The Hayden Geological Survey of the Territories, sponsored by the General Land Office and directed by a distinguished professor from the University of Pennsylvania, mapped much of the *terra incognita* of the Far West and uncovered much of its mineral and botanical resources. Easily the most dramatic of the Western expeditions was that headed by the remarkable John Wesley Powell, a one-armed veteran of the Civil War who had already piloted four boats down the 900 miles of the Green and Colorado rivers of the West. In 1870 the Department of the Interior launched him upon a series of expeditions into the West, and in 1875 he directed the Survey of the Rocky Mountain Regions. Out of all this came not only a new discovery of the American West, but, in 1879, the creation of the United States Geological Survey headed first by Clarence King and then by Powell.

An important part of the discovery of America was the emergence of a new and more scientific interest in its native races. As Major Powell wrote, in 1878, ' The field of research is speedily narrowing because of the rapid change in the Indian population now in progress; all habits, customs, and opinions are fading away; even languages are disappearing; and in a very few years it will be impossible to study our North American Indians in their primitive condition, except from recorded history.' Lewis Morgan had led the way with his study of the Iroquois; in the 'seventies he turned his attention to the Indians of the West and the Southwest, and in 1877 published *Ancient Society,* an argument for the common origin and evolution of all races which owed a great deal to Darwin. During these same years the historian Hubert Howe Bancroft published his five-volume *History of the Native Races of the Pacific Coast,* and the Swiss-born Adolphe Bandelier launched his pioneering studies of the archaeology of ancient Mexico and the pueblo Indians of the Southwest which led — among other things — to his fascinating novel, *The Delight Makers.* The year 1879 saw, too, the establishment of the United States Bureau of Ethnology and the founding of the Archaeological Institute of America.

Meantime these same productive years witnessed notable contributions from the universities — particularly from Yale, Harvard, and Pennsylvania. At Harvard Asa Gray, stout champion of the Darwinian theory, brought to completion his *Flora of North America.* In the midst of the war James Dwight Dana, dean of academic geologists, published his famous *Manual of Geology,* which reflected the evolutionary findings of the great Charles Lyell in England. Dana's colleague at Yale, the paleontologist Othneil Marsh, organized a series of scientific expeditions into the West, and published his famous study *Vertebrate Life in America,* which placed the study of fossils on a scientific basis. At the Smithsonian Institution the veteran zoologist Spencer Baird brought to completion his *History of North American Birds.*

All of this was part not only of the discovery of America, but of a growing awareness of the urgent necessity of conserving its resources. Everyone could see that the native races were being wiped out, or losing their identity, nor did it take much perspicacity to appreciate the disappearance of the buffalo and the wild pigeon and the beaver. More serious was the threat to soil, forest, and water, and other natural resources. Pioneer in alerting the American people to this threat was the versatile George Perkins Marsh, diplomat, historian, philologist, and scientist. From observing the waste of soil and forest in his native Vermont, and from experience in Turkey and Asia Minor, he came to appreciate the consequences of the violation of nature's laws by the misuse of her resources. In 1864 he published his masterpiece, *Man and Nature* (later published as *The Earth as Modified by Human Action*), which has justly been called the most influential American geographical work of the nineteenth century. It dealt, in a broad way, with ' man as a disturbing agent,' described the destruction of animal and vegetable life by men, and argued with special emphasis the importance of conservation of forests. Once the forest is removed, he pointed out, ' the face of the earth is no longer a sponge, but a dust heap. Stripped of its vegetable glebe, the soil grows less and less productive, and less able to protect itself by weaving a new network of roots to bind its particles together, a new carpeting of turf to shield it from wind and sun and scouring rain.' Marsh's book exerted a powerful influence on contemporaries in America and Europe, and contributed largely to the crystallization of conservation sentiment. Ferdinand Hayden carried it with him on his exploratory expedition, and John Wesley Powell applied its central thesis to his study of the problem of land and water on the High Plains. As early as 1874 he had warned Congress that much of the territory west of the 100th meridian, comprising some two-fifths of the entire nation ' has a climate so arid that agriculture cannot be pursued without irrigation.' Four years later he brought out his memorable *Report on the Arid Regions of the West* which warned against the application of Eastern techniques of farming to the High Plains, argued the necessity of farm units of not less than 2500 acres, emphasized the paramount importance of water and access to water supplies, and insisted that the right to water should inhere in the land.

These fermenting years were distinguished, too, by contributions to both pure science and popular science. In 1876 Edward Pickering became director of the astronomical observatory at Harvard, and began that remarkable photographic record of the stellar universe which was to command world-wide interest. At Yale Willard Gibbs, the most gifted mathematician of his generation, made fundamental contributions to mathematical physics with his papers on the equilibrium of heterogeneous substances. William James opened the first psychological laboratory in America in the early 'seventies, and there began those studies that were to culminate in the publication of his epoch-making *Principles of Psychology.* Meantime at the other end of the scientific spectrum, John Fiske was engaged in reconciling Darwinian evolution, Spencerian sociology and liberal religion in the *Outlines of Cosmic Philosophy* that sprawled through four volumes, and his friend Edward Youmans was popularizing the findings of the new science through the *Popular Science Monthly* and — more substantially — the many volumes of his International Scientific Series.

6. THE FINE ARTS

Even before the Civil War the architectural renaissance sponsored by Thomas Jefferson and Benjamin Latrobe, and its offspring the Greek Revival, had petered out, and the most promising of American architects, James Renwick and Richard Upjohn, had turned to Gothic. Renwick's Grace Church and St. Patrick's Cathedral, and Upjohn's Trinity Church and Church of the Ascension, all in New York City, gave promise of a Gothic revival like that which flourished in the England of Ruskin and Gilbert Scott. What came instead was a kind of pseudo-Gothic that takes its name from Queen Victoria or, at a more popular level, from Charles Eastlake, whose *Hints on Household Taste* enjoyed an astonishing vogue in America. Victorian Gothic was used in many large public buildings, such as the Smithsonian Institution in Washington, and had a peculiar fascination for college trustees, who littered the academic landscape from Maine to California with pseudo-Gothic structures such as Harvard's Memorial Hall or Walker Hall at Amherst College. The enraptured John Fiske of Harvard urged that ' we honestly confess our stupidity and show some grain of sense by copying the Oxford and Cambridge buildings literally.' Harvard did not accept this advice but Trinity College in Hartford, Connecticut, did, and Knox College out on the Illinois prairies, and a few years later the new University of Chicago reproduced Oxford, ' battlemented towers ' and all.

By the 'sixties, says Lewis Mumford, ' architectural anarchy had reached a point at which disorder had resulted almost in physical brutality, and ugliness conducted a constant assault and battery wherever one turned one's eye. When one beholds some of the famous buildings of the period, one must charitably assume that they were built by the blind for a generation that dwelt in darkness.' Like much of the oratory of the period, this American Gothic was florid, vain, and empty. Just as the oratory substituted rhetoric for ideas, so the architecture substituted ostentatious ornamentation for function and sincerity. Spires and battlements, gables and buttresses, stained glass windows and gargoyles, jig-saw scroll work, ornate fireplaces and mantels, elaborate hangings, endless bric-a-brac — all this proclaimed the emptiness and insincerity of the architects of that generation and confessed the decline in American taste since the simplicity and dignity of Jefferson and Bulfinch.

Along with a yearning for the medieval went a yen for the exotic. It was a day when the *Rubáiyát* of Omar Khayyám represented the highest reaches of philosophy to many a village Socrates; when romantic ladies swooned over Bayard Taylor's *Poems of the Orient;* when P. T. Barnum erected his fantastic *Iranistan* outside Bridgeport in Indo-Persian style, and the painter Frederick Church built the dazzling *Olana* on the banks of the Hudson in Persian style, complete wtih minarets and domes and spires and a roof of green, red, and black; when Peter Wight created the National Academy of Design in New York to display a multitude of styles, and the eccentric Erastus Salisbury projected a ten-story ' Historic Monument of the American Republic ' with each story in a different architectural style; and when James McNeill Whistler and Mary Cassatt were revealing the beauties of Japanese art and Henry Adams and John La Farge discovering the South Seas.

Out of all this welter of the archaeological and the exotic two distinguished architects emerged: Henry Hobson Richardson and Richard Morris Hunt. It was Richardson who ushered in the new day of American architecture. Born in New Orleans he had gone to Paris for his training, and brought back not the renaissance style then so popular in France, but the influence of the great medievalist Viollet-le-Duc. Richardson's fame is associated with the attempt to transplant Romanesque architecture to the United States — an attempt, it would seem, foredoomed to failure. Yet by contrast with the jerry-built structures of so many of his contemporaries, Richardson's buildings have an integrity that goes far to explain their popularity. Such was Richardson's power that he enjoyed a personal success greater than any other figure in American architecture before Frank Lloyd

Wright. ' To live in a house built by Richardson,' wrote one art historian, ' was a cachet of wealth and taste; to have your nest-egg in one
of his banks gave you a feeling of perfect security; to worship in one
of his churches made one think one had a pass key to the Golden
Gates.' John Hay and Henry Adams employed Richardson to build
their joint house on Lafayette Square, Washington, D.C., and while
Adams took for granted that anywhere an Adams lived was better
than the White House, he was happy to know that his house really
was better! Richardson's greatest monuments were Trinity Church,
Boston, for which John La Farge did the stained-glass windows, Austin Hall of Harvard University, and the fortresslike Marshall Field
warehouse in Chicago. Although it was these public buildings that
contemporaries most prized, later critics have been more impressed
by Richardson's influence on domestic architecture, particularly in
his use of shingles to create low, rambling houses which adapted
themselves to the landscape of the New England seacoast, and which
anticipated some of the innovations of Frank Lloyd Wright.

Contemporary with Richardson and, like him, trained in the École
des Beaux Arts, was Richard Morris Hunt, brother of the eminent
painter. Hunt was the favored architect of the new American plutocracy. He introduced to America the beauty and lavishness of the
French Renaissance, and built for American millionaires magnificent
country houses patterned after French châteaux, or palatial town
houses that resembled French hôtels-de-ville. Yet French châteaux
were no more suited to the genius of America than Romanesque for-
tresses, and Hunt's influence remained limited.

Viollet-le-Duc had prophesied an architecture of metal and glass,
and even as Richardson and Hunt wrought in their derivative styles,
these materials were working a revolution in architecture. There had
been anticipations abroad — London's great Crystal Palace of 1851,
for example — but the first American building boldly to employ
these new materials was the old Grand Central railroad station in
New York, whose train-shed was modeled on those of London and
Paris stations. More important architecturally was the work of the
bridge-builders, notably John Roebling and his son Washington, who
all through the 'sixties and 'seventies supervised the construction of
that *stupor mundi*, the Brooklyn Bridge.

These years saw, too, the beginning of the organization and pro-
fessionalization of art and architecture in the United States. The

American Institute of Architects had been founded in the late 'fifties, and the National Academy of Design in the early 'sixties. In that decade, too, the Massachusetts Institute of Technology, and then Cornell University, offered the first formal training for architects, and before long Pennsylvania and Columbia followed their example. In 1874 Harvard appointed the gifted but reactionary Charles Eliot Norton to the first chair of fine arts at any American university. The early 'seventies saw the beginnings of three of the greatest of American museums. Boston opened her Museum of Fine Arts; a group of New York philanthropists chartered the Metropolitan Museum of Art; and in the national capital William Corcoran — son of an Irish immigrant — built and endowed the gallery that bears his name.

Important, too, in the artistic history of the postwar generation was the development of landscape architecture and of city planning associated so largely with the work of Frederick Law Olmsted. Before the war Olmsted had won a reputation as a sociological interpreter of the South, and of England. In 1858 he was appointed chief architect of the proposed Central Park in New York City, and quickly became absorbed in the three closely related problems that were to command his attention for the rest of his life: city planning, landscape architecture, and the preservation of the natural beauties of the nation. He laid out Central Park, Prospect Park in Brooklyn, the Capitol grounds in Washington, the park system of Boston and, eventually, the Chicago World's Fair of 1893. He was chiefly instrumental in preserving Yosemite valley as a national park and in protecting Niagara Falls from the worst ravages of commercialization. Through his books, editorials, and lectures he dramatized to his generation the consequences of heedless urban growth and of the reckless expropriation of the natural resources of the nation.

The most distinguished of the American landscape painters of the prewar years, George Inness, revisited Italy in the years after the war and found not only new subjects for his gifted brush, but new techniques as well. Inness's last years were in many respects like those of Whitman: the spreading canvas of ' Peace and Plenty,' painted in 1865, was the counterpart in paint of Whitman's ' Thou Mother with Thy Equal Brood.' In the next decade Inness painted a whole series of panoramic landscapes that rank among the best of their kind in American art: ' Harvest Scene in the Delaware Valley,' for example, and ' The Approaching Storm,' and Italian scenes such as ' Tivoli,' and ' Lake Albano.'

The war itself produced one of the major American artists. Trained as a lithographer, Winslow Homer had been sent to the front to do sketches for *Harper's Weekly;* his wartime drawings were the best to come out of the war — 'Prisoners at the Front' and 'The Sharpshooter,' for example, or some of his Negro sketches. In the postwar years — his middle period — Homer turned to genre painting and lifted that difficult art to the highest level it had attained in America: 'Morning Bell' (1866), and 'High Tide at Long Branch' (1869), and the beloved 'Snap-the-Whip' (1872), and the colorful 'The Carnival' (1875). Homer's greatest period, however, was still ahead.

Meantime the most original genius among American painters was experimenting with new techniques and new subjects. Thomas Eakins had studied at the École des Beaux Arts, but that artistic finishing school left little impression on him. Back in Philadelphia in 1870 he began to turn out pictures whose unashamed realism forfeited for him the popularity that his talent merited: paintings of swimmers, fishermen, oarsmen, and professional men and women busy with their work. 'Respectability in art,' said Eakins, 'is appalling' and his own art was marked by a homespun realism, and a lack of respectability reminiscent of the best of Dutch painting of the seventeenth century. A professor of anatomy at the University of Pennsylvania, Eakins brought to his art a scientific knowledge of the human body, and portrayed it with an intimacy that shocked many of his contemporaries. His great achievement during these early years was 'The Gross Clinic' (1875); it was hung in the Centennial Exposition, not in the art collection — it was thought to be too unpleasant for that — but in the medical building! In the 'seventies Eakins turned from teaching anatomy to teaching art, and though ignored by the fashionable collectors of his own day deeply influenced the whole next generation of American painters: Sloane, Henri, Pennell, Glackens, and many others acknowledged him their master.

In art, as in literature and education, this was an era of popularization. John Adams had written, in 1780, that he must study politics so that his grandchildren might study painting, music, and architecture; and now the grandchildren were hungry for just these things, and if their taste was still untutored that was just what Tocqueville had predicted for a democratic people! When in the 1860's the Beecher sisters advised American women on the decoration of their homes, they recommended an expenditure of no less than $30 on chromos to be hung in the parlor: ' Miss Oakley's charming cabinet picture of The Little Scrap-book Maker; Eastman Johnson's Barefoot Boy, Newman's Blue Gentian, and Albert Bierstadt's Sunset in the Yosemite Valley.' If the frames were too expensive, the Beecher sisters added, the decorators ' could make rustic frames of twigs with the bark still on them, and glue on these a cluster of acorns or pine cones at the corners.' No wonder Godkin called this a ' chromo civilization '; certainly Currier and Ives seemed to dominate the artistic scene. Equally characteristic were the famous Rogers groups — plaster casts, fashioned by the talented John Rogers, to illustrate some familiar event in history or some homely story: ' The Emancipation Proclamation,' or ' The Slave Auction,' or ' The Checker Game,' or ' Fetching the Doctor.' Rogers himself deprecated his ' art,' but a writer in one of the popular magazines asserted confidently that ' what Hogarth is in the pencil, Canova and Michelangelo in marble, Reynolds and Landseer on canvas — all the excellences of these masters in art have their illustration in the plaster of John Rogers.' Altogether Rogers sold over 100,000 of his plaster figures in the generation after the war.

Popular art reached its climax — or its nadir — at the Centennial Exposition which opened in Fairmont Park, Philadelphia, in May 1876. It was America's first world exposition, and designed to dramatize cultural independence as much as to celebrate political: Bayard Taylor wrote an ode for the occasion, the venerable Whittier composed a Hymn, Sidney Lanier provided a cantata, and Richard Wagner composed a special march. The 10 million visitors who swarmed through the fair grounds that summer could feast their eyes on a rich display of architecture: Memorial Hall — ' a noble edifice of Renaissance design ' — a Turkish building ' of true Oriental type,' a Moorish Pavilion, a Tunisian Bazaar, and a Japanese pagoda. The American state buildings, most of them in Victorian Gothic, were almost as bizarre as the Oriental. Most Old World nations sent over examples of their art, and a large exhibit of American paintings included not only old masters like Stuart and Copley but younger painters like Winslow Homer and John La Farge and Alden Weir. What made the deepest impression on the visitors, however, was the exhibit of industrial art and of machinery. As William Dean Howells wrote, ' it is still in these things of iron and steel that the national

genius most freely speaks; by and by the inspired marbles, the
breathing canvases, the great literature; for the present America is
voluble in the strong metals and their infinite uses.' And an English
reporter, contemplating the many inventions and machines on display, wrote that ' the American mechanizes as the old Greeks sculp-
tured and as the Venetians painted.'

Two of America's major poets used the Centennial to reflect on
the significance of America in history. James Russell Lowell was
satirical and bitter: Columbia

> puzzled what she should display
> Of true home-make on her Centennial Day

asked Brother Jonathan, who advised her:

> Show 'em your Civil Service, and explain
> How all men's loss is ever'body's gain. . . .
> Show your State Legislatures; show your Rings;
> And challenge Europe to produce such things
> As high officials sitting half in sight
> To share the plunder and to fix things right. . . .

Sidney Lanier's Cantata was more philosophical. When Columbia
asked how long she would survive, her ' Good Angel ' answered:

> Long as thine Art shall love true love,
> Long as thy Science truth shall know,
> Long as thine Eagle harms no Dove,
> Long as thy Law by law shall grow,
> Long as thy God is God above,
> Thy brother every man below,
> So long dear Land of all my love,
> Thy name shall shine, thy fame shall glow.[6]

---

[6] Lowell's poem can be found in *The Nation,* 5 August, 1875; it is not reprinted in
his *Collected Works.* Lanier's Cantata is in the appendix to the *Poems of Sidney Lanier,*
edited by his wife.

BIBLIOGRAPHY

1. LITERATURE. Henry Adams, *The Education of Henry Adams;* Van Wyck
Brooks, *New England: Indian Summer* and *The Times of Melville and Whitman;*
John B. Clark, *Life and Letters of John Fiske* (2 vols.) ; Joseph Dorfman, *Eco-
nomic Mind in American Civilization,* vol. 3; Leon Edel, *Henry James: The
Untried Years;* Ralph Gabriel, *Course of American Democratic Thought;* James
Hart, *The Popular Book in America;* William Dean Howells, *Literary Friends
and Acquaintances, My Mark Twain,* and *Years of My Youth;* F. O. Matthiessen,
American Renaissance; Lewis Mumford, *The Brown Decades;* Vernon L. Par-

rington, *Main Currents of American Thought,* vol. 3; Stowe Persons, *American Minds;* Aubrey H. Starke, *Sidney Lanier;* Dixon Wecter, *Sam Clemens of Hannibal.*

2. JOURNALISM. Harry Baehr, *The New York Tribune since the War;* H. S. Commager (ed.), *The St. Nicholas Anthology;* Elmer Davis, *A History of the New York Times;* Frank L. Mott, *A History of American Magazines, 1865–1885* and *American Journalism;* Allan Nevins, *The Evening Post: A Century of Idealism* and *American Press Opinion;* F. M. O'Brien, *The Story of the Sun;* Rollo Ogden, *E. L. Godkin* (2 vols.) ; James Parton, *Life of Horace Greeley;* Gustav Pollak, *Fifty Years of American Idealism* (*The Nation*) ; Candace Stone, *Dana and the Sun;* Glyndon Van Deusen, *Horace Greeley: Nineteenth Century Crusader.*

3. EDUCATION. Lawrence A. Cremin, *The Transformation of the School, 1876–1957;* Ellwood P. Cubberley, *Public Education in the United States;* Merle Curti, *Social Ideas of American Educators;* Charles W. Eliot, *Educational Reform;* Daniel C. Gilman, *University Problems;* Hugh Hawkins, *Pioneer: A History of the Johns Hopkins University, 1874–1889;* Paul Monroe (ed.), *Cyclopaedia of Education* (5 vols.) ; S. E. Morison, *The Development of Harvard University, 1869–1929;* Allan Nevins, *Illinois* and *The Land-Grant Colleges;* George Pierson, *Yale College: An Educational History, 1871–1921;* Henry Pochmann, *German Culture in America;* Andrew D. White, *Autobiography,* vol. 1.

4. SCIENCE. Edward S. Dana, *et al., A Century of Science in America;* W. C. Darrah, *Powell of the Colorado;* A. Hunter Dupree, *Science in the Federal Government* and *Asa Gray;* C. L. & M. A. Fenton, *Giants of Geology;* John Fiske, *Excursions of an Evolutionist* and *Edward Livingston Youmans;* Donald Fleming, *John W. Draper and the Religion of Science;* Daniel C. Gilman, *Life of James Dwight Dana;* Asa Gray, *Darwiniana: Essays and Reviews;* David Lowenthal, *George Perkins Marsh;* Muriel Rukeyser, *Willard Gibbs;* Wallace Stegner, *West of the 100th Meridian;* Benjamin J. Stern, *Lewis Henry Morgan, Social Evolutionist.*

5. THE FINE ARTS. Lloyd Goodrich, *Winslow Homer* and *Albert P. Ryder;* Henry R. Hitchcock, *The Architecture of H. H. Richardson;* James Jackson Jarves, *Art Thoughts;* John Kouwenhoven, *Made in America;* Oliver Larkin, *Art and Life in America;* Russell Lynes, *The Tastemakers;* James D. McCabe, *History of the Centennial Exposition;* Elizabeth McCausland, *George Inness;* Roland McKinney, *Thomas Eakins;* Harriet Monroe, *John Wellborn Root;* Lewis Mumford, *The Roots of Contemporary Architecture, The Brown Decades,* and *Sticks and Stones;* Fairfield Porter, *Thomas Eakins;* E. P. Richardson, *Painting in America;* Montgomery Schuyler, *Architectural Writings* (2 vols.) ; Francis Steegmuller, *The Two Lives of James Jackson Jarves;* M. G. Van Rensselaer, *Henry Hobson Richardson.*

6. DOCUMENTS. Richard Hofstadter & Wilson Smith, *American Higher Education,* vol. 2, parts 7–10; Lewis Mumford (ed.), *Roots of Contemporary American Architecture;* Allan Nevins, *American Press Opinion.*

For further references, *Harvard Guide,* ¶¶ 217–18.

The Passing of the Frontier

1. THE LAST WEST

THE roaring vitality, the cascading energy of the American people
in the postwar years, is nowhere better illustrated than in the
history of the West. The generation after the Civil War witnessed the
most extensive movement of population in our history; a doubling
of the settled area; the rapid development of this population from
primitive social and economic conditions to contemporary standards
of civilization; the final disappearance of the wild Indian; the rise and
fall of the mineral empire and of the cattle kingdom; the emergence
of new types of agriculture and of economic life articulated to the
geography and climate of the High Plains and the Rocky Mountains;
and the organization of a dozen new states with a taste for social and
political experiment.

The most notable of these achievements was the conquest of the
Great Plains — that region extending roughly from longitude 98 to
the Rocky Mountains, and from Texas to the Canadian border. This
vast area, comprising roughly one-fifth of the United States, had long
interposed a formidable barrier to settlement. In the decade of the
'forties the westward moving frontier had reached the edge of the
Plains. Then, instead of moving progressively westward as it had
always heretofore done, the frontier leaped 1500 miles to the Pacific
coast. For 30 years the intervening territory was practically unin-
habited except by Indians and Mormons; not until the decade of the
'seventies did permanent settlers begin to close in on the Plains and
Mountain regions; then the process went on with unprecedented
rapidity until by 1890 it was almost complete and the frontier had
disappeared.

The Plains region had long been known as ' the Great American
Desert '; it was not, of course, a desert, but the designation was not
without justification. For over 200 years the American pioneer had

moved westward from one woodland frontier to another, and in all that time it had never been necessary for him to make any radical readjustment to forest and prairie and stream. But when the pioneer came to the edge of the Great Plains he found an environment fundamentally different from that to which he was accustomed. Here was an immense grassland, sparsely wooded, with few navigable streams, and with a rainfall seldom sufficient for farming as practiced in the East. When the pioneer farmer tried to apply here the experience he had gained and the tools he had developed in the wooded East, he failed. ' The attempt,' as Walter P. Webb has said, ' of a migrating people to cross this line of the 96th or 98th meridian resulted in social chaos and economic ruin which continued until, through invention and much experiment, new weapons were adopted, new implements invented, new methods devised for getting water, making fences, and farming, until new institutions were evolved or old ones modified to meet the needs of a country that was level, devoid of timber, and deficient in rainfall; until a plainscraft took the place of woodcraft.'

Not until the 1870's did the industrial revolution, science, and invention come to the aid of the farmer and enable him successfully to invade the High Plains. Before the farmer could establish himself permanently on the Plains four things were necessary: the elimination of the Indian; new methods of farming to cope with inadequate rainfall; a substitute for traditional wooden fencing; and transportation to take the crops to market. The army and the destruction of the buffalo took care of the Indian; barbed wire solved the fencing problem; the windmill, dry farming, and irrigation went far to overcome the effect of insufficient rainfall and intermittent droughts; and the railroad furnished transportation.

In the course of this long and arduous struggle with the Plains environment, the miner, the cattleman, and the farmer evolved social and economic institutions that differed markedly from those which had obtained in the woodlands of the East. The Plains environment necessitated a modification not only of the tools and methods of farming, but of social attitudes, economic concepts, political and legal institutions as well. ' The physical conditions which exist in that land,' as Major John Wesley Powell of the U.S. Geological Survey said, ' and which inexorably control the operations of men, are such that the industries of the West are necessarily unlike those of the East and their institutions must be adapted to their industrial wants. It is thus that a new phase of Aryan civilization is being developed in the western half of America.'

Thus there emerged in this last American West a regional consciousness as distinct and characteristic as that of the Old South: a common feeling that expressed itself not only in politics and economics but in social attitudes, legal institutions, art and literature. This sectionalism of the last West, rooted in geography, was cultivated by the impact of the industrial revolution on the process of settlement, and was exacerbated by the manner in which the various stages of economic development — mining, cattle raising, and farming — all came to be controlled by outside interests. This interplay of basic local forces with absentee political and economic interests in the creation of this last West makes a fascinating study in the history of sectionalism.

2. THE INDIAN PROBLEM

The first step in the conquest of the last West was the solution of the Indian problem. The Indians of the Great Plains and the Rocky Mountain regions, perhaps 225,000 in number, presented a formidable obstacle to white settlement. The strongest and most warlike of the tribes that the whites encountered were the Sioux, Blackfeet, Crow, Cheyenne, and Arapahoe in the north; the Comanche, Kiowa, Ute, Southern Cheyenne, Apache, and Southern Arapahoe in the south. Mounted on swift horses, admirably armed for Plains warfare, and living on the millions of buffalo that roamed the open range, these tribes for generations had maintained a stubborn and successful resistance to white penetration of their hunting grounds.

The first serious invasion of these hunting grounds came with the great migrations of the 1840's. The fate of the California Indians after the gold rush was prophetic of what was to happen elsewhere in the West. There were approximately 100,000 Indians in California in 1850; ten years later the number had been reduced to 35,000, and the Commissioner of Indian Affairs could write that ' despoiled by irresistible forces of the land of their fathers; with no country on earth to which they can migrate; in the midst of a people with whom they cannot assimilate; they have no recognized claims upon the government and are compelled to become vagabonds — to steal or to starve.' The advance of the miners into the mountains, the building of the transcontinental railroads, and the invasion of the grasslands by cattlemen, threatened the other Indian tribes of the West with the same fate. Most serious was the wanton destruction of the buffalo, indispensable not only for food but for hides, bowstrings, lariats, fuel, and a score of other purposes. Scarcely less ruinous were two other developments: the perfection of the Colt repeating revolver, fearfully efficient in Plains warfare, and the spread of smallpox and venereal diseases among the Indians.

It would be useless to trace in any detail the melancholy story of Indian relations in the period from 1860 to 1887, the year of the passage of the Dawes Act. It is a tale of intermittent and barbarous warfare, broken pacts and broken promises, greed and selfishness, corruption and maladministration, of alternating aggression and vacillation on the part of the whites, of courageous defense, despair, blind savagery, and inevitable defeat for the Indians. The sober historian, accepting neither the myths and legends that have clustered around the ' noble redman ' nor the bitterly prejudiced interpretation of Indian character by frontiersmen, must subscribe to President Hayes's indictment of our Indian relations in his annual message of 1877:

The Indians were the original occupants of the land we now possess. They have been driven from place to place. The purchase money paid to them in some cases for what they called their own has still left them poor. In many instances, when they had settled down upon lands assigned to them by compact and begun to support themselves by their own labor, they were rudely jostled off and thrust into the wilderness again. Many, if not most, of our Indian wars have had their origin in broken promises and acts of injustice on our part.

Until 1861 the Indians of the Plains had been relatively peaceful, but in that year the invasion of their hunting grounds by thousands of frantic and ruthless miners, and the advance of white settlers along the upper Mississippi and Missouri frontier, together with dissatisfaction at their treatment by the government and the breakdown of the reservation system, resulted in numerous minor conflicts. In 1862 the Sioux of the Dakota region went on the warpath, devastated the Minnesota frontier, and massacred and imprisoned almost a thousand white men, women, and children. Retribution was swift and terrible and fell indiscriminately upon the innocent and the guilty. For the next 25 years Indian warfare was a constant of Western history, each new influx of settlers driving the redskins to acts of desperation which brought on renewed outrage and punishment. In 1864 the Cheyenne, banished from their hunting grounds to the wastes of southeastern Colorado, attacked Ben Halliday's stage and harried the mining settlements to the north; they were persuaded to abandon their depredations and concentrate at Indian posts, and at one of these posts Colonel Chivington ordered a savage slaughter of the Indian men, women, and children which sent a thrill of horror through the nation. Two years later a small force under Colonel Fetterman was in turn massacred by the embittered Sioux. All through the following decade the Sioux fought desperately for their hunting grounds. The climax came in 1875 when prospectors discovered gold in the Sioux reservation in the Black Hills. That summer General Sheridan was able to hold back the importunate gold-seekers, but the next spring they broke through and flooded over the area. Under Sitting Bull and Crazy Horse the Sioux struck back. In June 1876 they ambushed the impetuous 'glory-hunter,' General George Custer on the Little Big Horn, and annihilated his whole command of 264 men; for two generations, millions of children got their notions of the Indians from the Currier and Ives lithograph of the gory massacre. Punishment was swift; the Sioux were scattered and Crazy Horse captured and murdered by his guard.

In the mountains, as on the plains, the Indians were driven from their ancient homes. In Montana the Crow and the Blackfeet were ejected from their reservations; in Colorado the vast holdings of the Utes were confiscated and opened to settlement; in the Southwest ten years of warfare ended in the capture of the intractable Apache chief, Geronimo, and the practical destruction of the Apache tribe. The discovery of gold on the Salmon river in western Idaho precipitated an invasion of the lands of the peaceful Nez Percés. The Indians refused to surrender the lands once guaranteed to them, and fifteen years of intermittent warfare culminated in the decision to drive the recalcitrant tribe entirely out of their hunting grounds. Chief Joseph struck back, but in vain, and in 1877 there began a retreat eastward over 1500 miles of mountain and plain that remains the most memorable feat in the annals of Indian warfare. In the end the feeble remnant of the Nez Percés tribe was captured and exiled to Oklahoma, and Chief Joseph spoke for all his race:

I am tired of fighting. Our chiefs are killed. Looking-Glass is dead. Too-hul-hut-sote is dead. The old men are all dead. It is the young men now who say ' yes ' or ' no.' He who lead the young men is dead. It is cold and we have no blankets. The little children are freezing to death. My people, some of them, have run away to the hills and have no blankets, no food. No one knows where they are, perhaps freezing to death. I want to have time to look for my children and see how many of them I can find. Maybe I can find them among the dead. Hear me, my chiefs. My heart is sick and sad. I am tired.

Altogether the Indian wars between 1865 and 1880 cost the government millions of dollars and the lives of hundreds of men. Yet, in 1881, President Arthur could affirm:

We have to deal with the appalling fact that though thousands of lives have been sacrificed and hundreds of millions of dollars expended in the attempt to solve the Indian problem, it has until within the past few years seemed scarcely nearer a solution than it was half a century ago.

A large part of this failure was no doubt inherent in the problem, but part of it rests squarely upon the Federal Government. The theory that each Indian tribe constituted a sovereign though dependent nation, to be dealt with as such through treaties, was completely divorced from reality. The Indians frequently failed to understand the terms of the treaties, nor did individual Indians consider themselves bound by tribal treaties. A further and fruitful source of difficulty was the fact that authority over Indian affairs was divided between the Departments of War and of the Interior, and that both departments pursued a vacillating and uncertain policy, the one failing to live up to treaty obligations, the other failing to protect the Indians on their reservations from the aggressions of white settlers.

That aggression often took the form of fraud and chicanery as large areas of Indian lands were alienated by ' treaty ' or by ' sale ' to railroads and other speculators. One railroad acquired 800,000 acres of Cherokee lands in southern Kansas by methods that the governor of the state denounced as ' a cheat and a fraud in every particular,' but nothing was done to cancel the arrangement, and the railroad resold the lands to settlers at 100 per cent profit. The Pottawatomie Indians sold 340,000 acres of land to the Santa Fe Railroad at one dollar an acre; within a few years the railroad had doubled its investment and managed to retain a good part of the land for future rise in value. Only the intervention of the Secretary of the Interior prevented a particularly crass deal whereby the Osage Indians were to sell 8 million acres of land to a railroad for 20 cents an acre.

These conflicting policies pursued by different departments of the government were expressive of the conflicting policies embraced by the American people as a whole. Frontiersmen, in general, still subscribed to the traditional idea that the only good Indian was a dead Indian, and most soldiers were inclined to agree with them. But Easterners, removed by a century from the Indian menace, had developed a different attitude. Here churchmen and reformers united to urge a policy of humanitarianism toward Indian wards. Statesmen like Carl Schurz, religious leaders like Bishop Whipple, literary figures like Helen Hunt Jackson, whose *A Century of Dishonor* stirred the nation's conscience, were loud in their criticism of the government's treatment of the Indian, and their attitude was effective in bringing about important changes in Indian policy.

In 1865, in the breathing space permitted by the conclusion of the Civil War, Congress had created a Committee on the Condition of the Indian Tribes which recommended, among other things, the practice of dealing with the Indians as individuals and concentrating them in reservations. This substitution of a ' peace ' policy for the more belligerent one of the 1860's was dictated partly by humanitarian considerations, and partly by the more cogent argument of economy — for it was obviously cheaper to herd the Indians into government reservations and feed them than it was to fight them. The new plan was carried forward under the administrations of Hayes, Arthur, and Cleveland, and culminated, in 1887, in the passage of the Dawes Act which established the Indian policy for a half-century.

The Dawes Act was the first serious attempt to civilize the Indian, teach him the practices of agriculture and social life, and merge him in the body politic of the nation. It provided for the dissolution of the tribes as legal entities and the division of the tribal lands among the individual members. To protect the Indian in his property the right of disposal was withheld for a period of 25 years; upon the expiration of this probationary period, the Indian was to become the unrestricted owner and to be admitted to full citizenship in the United States. In October 1901 the Five Civilized Nations of Oklahoma, already assimilated to American social and political institutions, were admitted to citizenship and in 1924 Congress granted full citizenship to all Indians.

The Dawes Act was hailed at the time as an Indian Emancipation

Act; it might better have been compared to Appomattox. Under the operation of this misguided act, Indian holdings decreased in the next half-century from 138 to 48 million acres, half of these arid or semi-arid, with no compensating advantages. Indian timber land was seized by speculators, and in 1917 the Indian commissioner explained blandly that ' as the Indian tribes were being liquidated anyway it was only sensible to liquidate their forest holdings as well.' Tribal funds amounting to more than $100 million were diverted from their proper use to meet the costs of the Indian Bureau — including the costs of despoiling the Indians of their lands. And during the Harding administration, which marked the nadir of Indian welfare, the egregious Secretary Fall tried to take their oil lands away from the Navajo Indians as well.

Thus the proud savages who once undisputed ruled the American continent were settled on some 200 government reservations, eking out an existence on government doles, cut off from the free life of an earlier day, losing the power to fend for themselves, disintegrating economically and physically, tragic remainders of the race which had helped the white man to adjust himself to the American scene, descendants of the Hiawathas and Pocahontases who for so long fired the imagination of the American people.

3. The Mining Frontier

The vast territory between the Missouri and the Pacific had first been explored by the fur traders of the American and the Rocky Mountain fur companies, and it had been crossed and recrossed by emigrants along the great trails, but it was the miners who first revealed to the nation the resources and possibilities of this country. The first frontier of the last West was the miners' frontier. In 1849 the lure of gold had drawn to California a turbulent, heterogeneous throng of miners who later formed the nucleus of a large permanent population and who developed the varied agricultural resources of the state. This process was to be repeated time and again in the decade of the 'sixties: in Colorado, Nevada, Arizona, Idaho, Montana, and Wyoming. In each case precious metals were the magnet that attracted the first settlers and advertised the resources of the territory; then, as the big pay dirt was exhausted, the mining population receded, and its place was taken by ranchers and farmers who established, with the aid of the railroads and the government, the permanent foundation of the territory.

In 1859 the discovery of gold in the foothills of the Rockies, near Pike's Peak, drew thousands of eager prospectors from the border settlements and from California, bent on repeating here the fabulous story of California gold. Within a few months the roads from Council Bluffs and Independence to western Kansas were crowded with wagons bearing the slogan ' Pike's Peak or Bust ' scrawled on their canvas. Soon brash little mining camps dotted the hills all along Cherry Creek, a branch of the South Fork of the Platte. Denver City, Golden, Boulder, and Colorado City arose almost overnight, the Territory of Jefferson — changed later to Colorado — was organized, and the census of 1860 recorded a population of some 35,000. The mining boom soon spent itself, and the development of Colorado was somewhat retarded by the Civil War and Indian uprisings as well as by inadequate transportation and a failure to appreciate the agricultural and grazing resources of the country. During the ensuing decade population barely held its own, and it was not until the advent of the railroads in the 1870's, the influx of farmers, and the readjustment of the region to a new economic basis, that the foundations for a sounder development were laid.

In the same year that gold was discovered in Colorado, came the announcement of a rich strike of silver on the eastern slopes of the Sierra Nevada, near Lake Tahoe. Here was located the Comstock Lode, one of the richest veins in the world. Within a year the roaring towns of Virginia City, Aurora, and Gold Hill sprang up in the desert waste, the Territory of Nevada was carved out of Utah, and 10,000 men were digging frantically in the bowels of the earth for the precious silver stuff.

Nevada furnishes the most extreme example of a mining community; nowhere else in history do we find a society so completely and continuously dependent upon mineral wealth. And the history of this mining commonwealth for the first decade of its existence is largely that of the Comstock Lode. Within 20 years the lode yielded no less than $306 million. Very little of this enormous wealth, however, remained in Nevada, most of it going to California mining companies or to speculators in the East. The Comstock Lode is notable not only as the foundation of the mineral wealth of Nevada, but as the location of one of the greatest engineering enterprises of the nineteenth century — the Sutro Tunnel. It was this tunnel, built by Adolph Sutro over a period of eight years and penetrating into the heart of the mountain to the depth of three miles, that made possible the continuous and profitable mining of the fabulous lode.

The application of engineering skill, machinery, and capital to mining the Comstock illustrates a process that was universal in the history of the mining kingdom. Panning and placer mining as practiced in the diggings of early California and Colorado was not only wasteful, but entirely unsuitable for getting the silver out of the quartz veins of such a mine as the Comstock. It was necessary to change from placer mining to quartz mining, and this change required the purchase of expensive machinery, the hiring of engineering skill, and the organization of mining as a big business. So outside capital came in and took over the mining industry; the miners became day laborers working for wages, and the profits went to stockholders scattered throughout the United States and Europe. Mining actually added nothing to the wealth of the state. It did not create permanent industries or cities, nor provide foundations for healthy growth. This was the history of Comstock, and it was to a greater or less extent the history of most of the mines of the West in the following decade.

The story of Idaho and Montana runs parallel to that of Colorado and Nevada. Gold was discovered in 1860 on the Nez Percés reservation in the extreme eastern part of Washington Territory. Within a year a wave of prospectors from Washington and Nevada was rolling into the region. Lewiston and, farther to the south, Boise City, sprang into existence; and in 1865 the Territory of Idaho was carved out of Washington and Montana. ' The Idaho miners,' wrote the historian of the West, H. H. Bancroft, ' were like quicksilver, a mass of them dropped off in any locality, broke up into individual globules, and ran off after any atom of gold in the vicinity. They stayed nowhere longer than the gold attracted them.' But mining furnished a most insubstantial foundation for the development of Idaho, and the census of 1870 showed a population of only 15,000 for the Territory.

Gold was discovered east of the Continental Divide along the headwaters of the Missouri, and in the Bitter Root valley in the eastern part of Washington Territory, and soon Alder Gulch (later Virginia City), Last Chance Gulch (Helena), and Bannack City enjoyed a flush rivaling that of the Colorado and Nevada camps. Al-

The Last of the Buffalo by *Albert Bierstadt*

though Montana produced over $100 million in precious metals in the first decade, the mining kingdom was short-lived, and the census of 1870 recorded a population of only slightly over 20,000. Like other mining camps, those of Montana soon died out or were transformed into respectable towns, with schools, churches, and other institutions of civilization. For a brief time the activities of the notorious Henry Plummer and his gang of highway robbers and cutthroats threatened the prosperity of the Montana camps, and it required a vigilante organization such as that which had arisen in California fifteen years earlier to restore law and order. Virginia City, which may well serve as typical of the mining towns of the West, was thus described by N. P. Langford in his *Vigilante Days and Ways:*

This human hive, numbering at least ten thousand people, was the product of ninety days. Into it were crowded all the elements of a rough and active civilization. . . . Gold was abundant, and every possible device was employed by the gamblers, the traders, the vile men and women that had come in with the miners to the locality, to obtain it. Nearly every third cabin in the town was a saloon where vile whiskey was peddled out for fifty cents a drink in gold dust. Many of these places were filled with gambling tables and gamblers, and the miner who was bold enough to enter one of them with his day's earnings in his pocket, seldom left until thoroughly fleeced. Hurdy-gurdy dance-houses were numerous, and there were plenty of camp beauties to patronize them. . . . Not a day or night passed which did not yield its full fruition of fights, quarrels, wounds, or murders. The crack of the revolver was often heard above the merry notes of the violin. Street fights were frequent, and as no one knew when or where they would occur, everyone was on his guard against a random shot.

Sunday was always a gala day. . . .Thousands of people crowded the thoroughfares, ready to rush in any direction of promised excitement. Horse-racing was among the most favored amusements. Prize rings were formed, and brawny men engaged at fisticuffs until their sight was lost, and their bodies pummelled to a jelly, while hundreds of onlookers cheered the victor. . . . Pistols flashed, bowie-knives flourished, and braggart oaths filled the air, as often as men's passions triumphed over their reason. This was indeed the reign of unbridled license, and men who at first regarded it with disgust and terror, by constant exposure soon learned to become part of it, and forgot that they had ever been aught else. All classes of society were represented at this general exhibition. Judges, lawyers, doctors, even clergymen, could not claim exemption. Culture and religion afforded feeble protection, where allurement and indulgence ruled the hour.[1]

[1] N. P. Langford, *Vigilante Days and Ways* (1912 ed.) , pp. 222-4.

' But,' Langford adds, ' underneath this exterior of recklessness, there was in the minds and hearts of the miners and business men of this society a strong and abiding sense of justice — and that saved the Territory.' It would indeed be a mistake to picture the mining camps as mere nests of lawlessness or to argue from the accounts of Easterners an abandonment of the institutions of civilized society. They had, to be sure, few of the institutions taken for granted in the East — churches, schools, newspapers, theaters, and so forth — but they hastened to establish these institutions as quickly as they could. Nor did the ' Argonauts ' — as the first miners were known — conform to the standards of society or of law which obtained elsewhere; instead they very sensibly formulated their own social standards and developed their own laws. The evolution of common law institutions in the miners' camps is one of the most illuminating chapters in the history of American law. Each miners' camp was an administrative and a judicial district. It had its own executive officers, judges, recorders, it voted laws and regulations suited to its own peculiar needs, and it enforced these laws through public opinion and police officers.

The Argonauts [said Senator Stewart, himself once a miner] found no laws governing the possession and occupation of mines but the common laws of right. . . . They were forced to make laws for themselves. The reason and justice of the laws they formed challenge the admiration of all who investigate them. Each mining district . . . formed its own rules and adopted its own customs. The similarity of these rules and customs throughout the entire mining-region was so great as to attain the beneficial results of well-digested general laws. These regulations were thoroughly democratic in character. . . .

The legal codes and practices of these mining communities were eventually recognized in the American courts and many of them were incorporated into the constitutions and laws of the Western states.

The early development of Wyoming and Arizona followed the same general lines of the other mining communities. The mines along the Sweetwater river at South Pass City, Pacific City, and Miners' Delight were soon played out, and after 1865 the future of Wyoming Territory was almost wholly dependent upon cattle and sheep. In the Southwest, silver had been mined by the Spaniards in the Santa Cruz valley of the New Mexican Territory and by Americans in the Gadsden Purchase for many years, but the brisk development of mining which began along the Bill Williams fork of the Colorado river was a by-product of the Civil War. Though a few mushroom mining towns sprang up in the Arizona and New Mexico deserts, the majority of the prospectors had poor luck and soon limped back to more promising territory to the north.

Not gold and silver but copper proved the chief resource of Montana, and of Arizona, too. In the 1870's William Clark, a speculator who had turned storekeeper and banker, bought up property around Butte that proved fabulously rich in copper. In 1881 he opened the Anaconda mine, and in the next half-century he and his associates took over two billion dollars' worth of copper out of this ' richest hill in the world.' To control this and other copper mines, Clark, Marcus Daly, and other ' copper kings ' bought legislatures and senatorships, corrupted the public life of the state for a generation, and engaged in open warfare with each other. In the end Clark got a senatorship, $100 million, and a mansion on New York's Fifth Avenue with 121 rooms and 31 baths. After the turn of the century, copper mining shifted to Arizona where the Phelps-Dodge interests dominated the economy of the state, and where the single Copper Queen mine at Bisbee yielded more money than all the gold and silver mines of the Territory.

The last domestic gold rush came in the Black Hills region of western Dakota Territory, on the reservations of the Sioux. In 1874 the news of the discovery of gold here rioted along the frontier and through the mining kingdom, and precipitated a frantic and lawless invasion. The railroad to Bismarck and the stagecoach from Cheyenne gave access to this region, and 4000 feverish prospectors rushed into the desolate hills between the forks of the Cheyenne. Deadwood had its brief day of glory; here ' Calamity Jane ' enjoyed her merited notoriety; here ' Wild Bill ' Hickok handed in his checks; here a stock company played Gilbert and Sullivan's *Mikado* for a record run of 130 nights. Within a short time heavily capitalized companies, like the Homestead, took over the mining, and the days of glamor were gone.

The history of the last gold rush is as gaudy as that of California or Colorado, but belongs as much to Canadian as to American history. The discovery of gold along the waters of the Klondike, which flows from Yukon into Alaska, came in 1896; the next year ships from San Francisco were unloading avid fortune-hunters all along the frozen coast. By 1898 there were 30,000 fortune-hunters in the Yukon, washing the icy waters of the Klondike and tributary streams. The gold strike in the Klondike had interesting repercussions. By depressing the price of gold and raising that of silver, it took Bryan's issue away from him for the campaign of 1900. It gave rise to a boundary controversy between Canada and the United States, which President Roosevelt agreed to arbitrate only on condition that all the issues were settled his way. It furnished material for a dozen red-blooded novels which gave Jack London an international reputation; inspired Robert Service to write and a million hams to recite ' The Shooting of Dan McGrew '; and provided the background for Charlie Chaplin's wonderful movie *The Gold Rush*. More important, it brought in a wave of population that left some deposits even after it had receded, and thus marked the beginnings of modern Alaska.

Ephemeral as it was, the mining frontier played an important part in the development of the West, and of the nation. The miners familiarized the American people with the country between the Missouri and the Pacific, and advertised its magnificent resources. They forced a solution of the Indian problem, dramatized the need for railroads, and laid the foundations for the later permanent farming population. Out of the necessities of their situation they developed codes of law admirably suited to their needs, and contributed much of value to the legal and political institutions of the West. They produced, in the 30 years from 1860 to 1890, a total of $1,241,827,032 of gold and $901,160,660 of silver, enabled the government to resume specie payments, precipitated ' the money question ' which was for well-nigh twenty years the major political issue before the American people, and then solved it. They added immeasurably to American folklore, enriched the American idiom, and in the stories of Bret Harte and Mark Twain inspired lasting contributions to American literature.

4. THE CATTLE KINGDOM

One of the most dramatic shifts in the screen-picture of the West was the replacement of millions of buffalo that had roamed the Great Plains by cattle, and of the Indian by the cowboy and the cattle king. The territory between the Missouri and the Rockies, from the Red river of the South to Saskatchewan — an area comprising approximately one-fourth of the United States — was the cattle kingdom, the last and most picturesque American frontier. Here millions of cattle — Texas longhorns, full-blooded Herefords, Wyoming and Montana steers — fatted on the long luscious grasses of the public lands. The cowboys and their liege lords, the cattle barons who ruled this vast domain, developed therein a unique culture, folklore, and society, and then passed away forever.

The development of the cattle industry on a large scale was due to a peculiar combination of factors: the opening up of the public domain after the Civil War, the elimination of the Indian danger and the annihilation of the buffalo, the extension of the railroads into the High Plains, the decline in the number of cattle raised in the Middle West and the East, the increased consumption of meat here and abroad, the invention of the refrigerator car, and the growth of great packing centers and of world markets.

Since the days when the American Southwest belonged to Spain, the sturdy Texas longhorn, descendant of Spanish *toros* from the plains of Andalusia, had grazed on the limitless prairie grasses north of the Rio Grande. Wild as the buffalo they supplanted, and valued only for their hides, it was not until 1846 that the first herd was driven northward to Ohio, though long before that many had found their way to California. In 1856 a drove of Texas cattle reached Chicago, but not until the middle 'sixties did the ' long drive ' to the region of rich grasses and good prices cease to be an experiment. In 1867 the Kansas Pacific began to reach out in the Plains, and in the same year J. G. McCoy established the first of the cow towns, Abilene, Kansas, from which live cattle were shipped to slaughter houses in Chicago. The refrigerator car, in common use by 1875, delivered the western dressed beef to the great eastern centers of population.

On the first of the organized long drives, 35,000 longhorns pounded up clouds of dust all along the famous Chisholm Trail, across the Red and Arkansas rivers and into the land of the Five Nations, to Abilene, Kansas. Two years later no less than 350,000 longhorned kine made their way along the Chisholm and Goodnight trails to fatten on the long northern grasses and find a market at one of the several roaring cattle towns on the Kansas and Pacific Railroad: Abilene, Dodge City, or Newton. Later the ' long drive ' extended north to the Union Pacific and even to the Northern Pacific.

In after years [writes the historian of the cattle kingdom] the drive of the Texas men became little short of an American saga. To all who saw that long line of Texas cattle come up over a rise in the prairie, nostrils wide for the smell of water, dust-caked and gaunt, so ready to break from the nervous control of the riders strung out along the flanks of the herd, there came a feeling that in this spectacle there was something elemental, something resistless, something perfectly in keeping with the unconquerable land about them.[2]

Altogether some 6 million cattle were driven up from Texas to winter on the High Plains of Colorado, Wyoming, and even Montana, between 1866 and 1888. It was this new industry of fattening cattle on the Great Plains that produced the last phase of the Wild West, and the highest and most picturesque development of the ancient art of cattle droving. The experience of cattlemen along the Oregon and California trails in the decade of the 'forties had long proved the practicability of wintering cattle in the northern ranges. Now Easterners and Englishmen of a sporting or speculating turn put their money into cattle, establishing their headquarters anywhere from the Rio Grande to the Canadian border, and in the absence of law managed their affairs through some *de facto* commonwealth such as the Wyoming Stock Growers' Association. Texas borderers who learned their horsemanship and ' cowpunching' from the Mexican *vaqueros* were the first and the best *bucaroos* or cowboys. Every spring they rounded up the herds in designated areas, all the way from Texas to Wyoming and the Dakotas, identified their owners' cattle by the brands, and branded the calves, dividing up pro rata the strays or ' mavericks.' The breeding cattle were then set free for another year while the likely three- and four-year-olds were conducted on the ' long drive ' to the nearest cow town on a railway. Each ' outfit ' of cowboys attended its owner's herd on the drive, protecting it from wolves and cattle rustlers, sending scouts ahead to locate water and the best grazing. The long drive seems romantic in retrospect, but to the cowboys it was hard and often hazardous work. Andy Adams, later one of the cattle barons of Texas, describes a dry drive along the Old Western Trail:

Good cloudy weather would have saved us, but in its stead was a sultry morning without a breath of air, which bespoke another day of sizzling heat. We had not been on the trail over two hours before the heat became almost unbearable to man and beast. Had it not been for the condition of the herd, all might yet have gone well; but over three days had elapsed without water for the cattle, and they became feverish and ungovernable.

[2] E. S. Osgood, *The Day of the Cattleman*, p. 26.

The lead cattle turned back several times, wandering aimlessly in any direction, and it was with considerable difficulty that the herd could be held on the trail. Our horses were fresh, however, and after about two hours' work, we once more got the herd strung out in trailing fashion; but before a mile had been covered, the leaders again turned, and the cattle congregated into a mass of unmanageable animals, milling and lowing in their fever and thirst. . . . No sooner was the milling stopped than they would surge hither and yon, sometimes half a mile, as ungovernable as the waves of an ocean. After wasting several hours in this manner, they finally turned back over the trail, and the utmost efforts of every man in the outfit failed to check them. We threw our ropes in their faces, and when this failed, we resorted to shooting; but in defiance of the fusillade and the smoke they walked sullenly through the line of horsemen across their front. Six-shooters were discharged so close to the leaders' faces as to singe their hair, yet, under a noonday sun, they disregarded this and every other device to turn them, and passed wholly out of our control. In a number of instances wild steers deliberately walked against our horses, and then for the first time a fact dawned upon us that chilled the marrow in our bones — *the herd was going blind.*

The bones of men and animals that lie bleaching along the trails abundantly testify that this was not the first instance in which the plain had baffled the determination of man.[3]

The cowboy developed his own lingo, folklore, and customs. His high-horned Mexican saddle, lariat, broad-rimmed sombrero, high-heeled boots, and shaggy chaparajos were perfectly adapted to his work. His jangling spurs with their enormous rowels were not too severe for his bronco — vicious little mustang of Spanish origin, hardy as a donkey and fleet as an Arab. The clownish posturing of film heroes has obscured the authentic cowboy: spare of frame and pithy of speech, reserved and courteous as the true gentleman that he was, yet with the cavalier's eternal swagger; alert with the sort of courage needed to fight Indians and bad men, to break broncos and rope steers, or to deal with stampedes and prairie fires; enduring and uncomplaining, asking no better end than to die with his boots on. Finest of our frontier types, he flourished for a brief score of years, and faded into legend with the passing of the open range.

Wyoming was the most typical of the cattle states as Nevada was the most typical of the mining states. Here was a country admirably suited by nature for large-scale ranching, but almost entirely unsuited for farming, and here the great cattle companies ruled supreme. The cattlemen seized most of the public and much of the Indian lands,

---

[3] Andy Adams, *The Log of a Cowboy*, Houghton Mifflin Co., pp. 63–4.

controlled the politics and wrote the laws of the Territory. For almost 20 years the powerful Wyoming Stock Growers' Association was the *de facto* government of the Territory; it formulated laws and regulations governing land and water rights, the round-up, the disposition of estrays, breeding, and similar matters, and enforced them on members and non-members alike; it agitated ceaselessly for the revision of the land laws of the West, and for the recognition of the prior rights of cattlemen; it attempted, by fraud, intimidation, and violence, to keep Wyoming the exclusive preserve of the ranchers.

This proved impossible. The most dangerous threat to the cattle kingdom, in Wyoming as elsewhere through the West, was not, at first, the farmer but the lowly sheepherder. Before the Civil War, Vermont had been the leading sheep-raising state of the Union; during the war sheep moved west to Ohio. Then came competition from Australia and the Argentine, which Ohio farmers, who had to pay $50 an acre for their lands and had to buy winter forage, could not meet; and the sheep kingdom shifted to the Far West and Southwest. The Spaniards had raised sheep on the limitless lands of the Southwest and of Alta California. After the Civil War the sheep moved in from these grazing grounds, and from Oregon and the East as well, onto the rich grasses of Colorado, Wyoming, and Montana. Sheep, like cattle, could graze free on Uncle Sam's inexhaustible lands; labor costs were negligible; and the wool clip, protected by high tariffs, was increasingly valuable. The cattlemen, who resented the invasion of their lands by the sheepherders and were convinced that sheep ruined the grass by close cropping, waged open war on their rivals. The Tonto Basin War in northern Arizona, like Kentucky feuds, dragged on for years and ended only when ranchers and sheepherders had wiped each other out; the so-called Johnson County War in Wyoming was halted only by the timely arrival of federal troops; and in the Horn Basin War of Montana, cattlemen wiped out 5000 sheep and killed several sheepherders before the authorities moved in and made peace. But in the end the sheepmen triumphed over the cattlemen, even in Wyoming. In the decade after the great blizzard the number of cattle in that state declined from 900,000 to about 300,000, while the number of sheep increased to some 3 million. Montana, too, counted 675,000 cattle but over 3 million sheep. By that time sheep could safely graze. Oddly enough, though the sheepherder is an older and more beloved figure than the rancher, and one with many Biblical associations, sheep raising never caught the American imagination, or acquired a folklore or a literature.

It is clear that a system of laws based upon conditions in the well-watered and well-wooded East, and designed to encourage family farming, was not suitable for the needs of the semi-arid West, nor for the purposes of ranching or sheep raising. As early as 1879 Major Powell of the U. S. Geological Survey had recommended to Congress a thorough revision of the laws governing Western lands, based on realities — on a recognition of the paramount importance of water rather than mere acreage and on the abandonment of the rectangular survey. These recommendations were ignored, and the land-office continued its misguided effort to confine the cattle industry as well as farming within the framework of sections and quarter-sections. It was perhaps inevitable that cattlemen and sheepmen should flout these laws, and make their own. By hook or by crook the cattle companies seized control of the grasslands. They leased millions of acres from Indians, strung barbed wire fences around other millions of acres — or across roads and around the approaches to streams and water holes, denying water to farmers who were entitled to it. In 1886 Secretary Lamar reported that ' substantially the entire grazing country west of the 100th meridian ' was fenced in by cattlemen. Cleveland moved with characteristic energy to destroy these illegal enclosures, and in the end the forces of the law and the inexorable advance of the farmer forced the cattlemen to accommodate themselves to the law.

The cattle boom reached its height about 1885. By that time the range had become too heavily pastured to support the long drive, and was beginning to be crisscrossed by railroads and the barbed wire fences of homesteads. By that time, too, the range had ceased to be a frontier industry and had become a corporate enterprise, organized, capitalized, and directed in the East or in Britain. New factors had begun to increase enormously the hazards of ranching. The rapid fencing-in of the open range, the appearance of cattle diseases and the passage of state quarantine laws, the conflict between the cattlemen and sheepherders, between northern and southern cattlemen, and between cattlemen and settlers, and the determination of the Federal Government to enforce its land laws in the West — all these factors presaged the decline of the cow kingdom. Then came the two terrible winters of 1885–86 and 1886–87 which almost annihilated the herds on the open ranges. Cattle owners began to stake out homestead claims in the names of their ' outfit ' and to fence off their lands. Almost in a moment the cattle range replaced the open ranges. Cowboy custom and tradition died hard; in ' dude ranches ' they still flourish; but the cowboy turned cattleman or ranch employee, penned in behind wire and knowing not the joys and dangers of the long drive, was a clipped eagle.

5. The Disappearance of the Frontier

What marked the end of the picturesque mining and cattle kingdoms, and of the old, romantic ' Wild West,' was the pressure of farmers, swarming by the hundreds of thousands out onto the High Plains and into the mountain valleys, subduing this wilderness of prairie and mountain land to cultivation and civilization. During the Civil War the discoveries of precious ores, the necessity of maintaining communication with the Pacific coast, and the insatiable demand for wheat, all served to advertise the West. War dangers and uncertainties, especially in the border states, induced many to try their luck in the new regions, while the liberal provisions of the Homestead and later land acts, the low cost of railroad lands, and the high rewards of farming proved an irresistible magnet for thousands of others. During the war years the population of nine Western states and Territories increased by over 300,000, while the agricultural states of Illinois, Wisconsin, Minnesota, Iowa, Kansas, and Nebraska received 843,000 immigrants from Europe and the East. It is recorded that in the year 1864 no less than 75,000 persons passed westward bound through Omaha alone. From Council Bluffs, Iowa, eastern terminus of the Union Pacific, the Reverend Jonathan Blanchard wrote in 1864:

When you approach this town, the ravines and gorges are white with covered wagons at rest. Below the town, toward the river side, long wings of white canvas stretch away on either side, into the soft green willows; at the ferry from a quarter to a half mile of teams all the time await their turn to cross. Myriads of horses and mules drag on the moving mass of humanity toward the setting sun; while the oxen and cows equal them in number.

All this seems incredibly remote from the Wilderness and marching through Georgia. It was one of the great pulses of American life that went on beating amid the din of arms.

The close of the war brought a sharp acceleration of this movement. It was in part the absorbing power of the West which enabled a million soldiers to resume civilian life without serious economic derangements. Southerners by the tens of thousands, despairing of recouping their fortunes in the war-stricken South, migrated westward although excluded temporarily from the privileges of the Homestead Act. Immigrants, mostly from northern Europe, found their way to the prairies of Iowa and Minnesota and eastern Dakota by the hundreds of thousands.

It was the twenty years following 1870 that witnessed the greatest expansion of the West, the overwhelming of the mining and cattle kingdoms, the taking up of most of the good public and railroad lands, and the disappearance of the frontier. The railroads, crossing the continent along half a dozen lines, and immigration, which reached a total of 8 million in these 20 years, were the most influential factors in the process. Not only did the railroads provide transportation and ensure markets, but they were the active colonizing agents of the time. Whole Territories, such as the Dakotas, came into existence largely by virtue of the railways, while scores of towns and cities, such as Cheyenne, Council Bluffs, Kansas City, Spokane, Portland, and Seattle, were created by and completely dependent upon them.

But it was not enough to provide land and transportation for eager immigrants to the West. Some method had to be found for overcoming the natural handicaps to agriculture in the semi-arid Plains region. The first and most urgent problem was to provide fencing. Even in the East, where timber was available, the cost of fencing was an important item: in 1870 the Department of Agriculture estimated that the total cost of fencing in the entire country was not far from $2 billion and that the annual upkeep consumed almost $200 million. In the Plains, where lumber had to be imported, the cost of timber-fencing a quarter-section of land was prohibitive. Yet if cattle were to be controlled, manure saved, crops protected from the ravages of cattle, and water holes preserved, fencing was absolutely necessary. Plains farmers experimented for years with various substitutes such as earth embankments and almost impenetrable osage orange hedges. In 1874 J. F. Glidden of DeKalb, Illinois, put barbed wire on the market and the fencing problem was solved! By 1883 Glidden's company was turning out 600 miles of barbed wire daily, and the expense of fencing had been reduced to a mere fraction of its former cost. The importance of barbed wire to the development of the Great Plains was comparable to that of the cotton gin in the development of the South.

Fencing made farming on the High Plains possible, but not necessarily profitable. There was still the question of water. ' The Great Plains,' wrote an observer from the Department of Agriculture, ' can be characterized as a region of periodical famine. . . . Year after year the water supply may be ample, the forage plants cover the ground with rank growth, the herds multiply, the settlers extend their fields, when, almost imperceptibly, the climate becomes less humid, the rain clouds forming day after day disappear upon the horizon, and weeks lengthen into months without a drop of moisture. The grasses wither, the herds wander wearily over the plains in search of water holes, the crops wilt and languish, yielding not even the seed for another year.' The great droughts and dust storms of 1934–37 brought home to our generation in dramatic fashion the dangers that have always threatened farmers in the Plains.

Scientific farming and invention modified, though they did not overcome, the menace of drought. For a time irrigation promised to solve the farming problem of the West. The Pueblo Indians were familiar with irrigation, and the Mormons had reclaimed millions of acres of arid land by this ancient method. In 1894 Congress passed the Carey Act, turning over to the western states millions of acres of public lands to be reclaimed through irrigation. The act was ineffective, and by the Reclamation Act of 1902 the Federal Government took charge of irrigation. By the turn of the century some 5 million acres had been reclaimed: 20 years later this acreage under irrigation had been multiplied fourfold. Yet irrigation was not an unqualified success, and its effects were limited to a comparatively small area of the mountainous West and to California.

Far more effective than irrigation was the use of deep-drilled wells and of the windmill, and the practice of dry farming. By drilling from 100 to 500 feet below the surface it was possible to tap ground water. Such water was brought to the surface not in the romantic

' old oaken bucket ' lowered and raised by hand, but in slender metal cylinders lowered and raised by never failing windmills. Windmills were introduced to the Plains in the middle 'seventies; within a short time they became a familiar feature on the Plains landscape, and assured the Plains farmer a steady though sometimes meager supply of water. Dry farming — the scientific conservation of moisture in the soil through the creation of a dust blanket to prevent evaporation — made it possible to grow cereal crops successfully over large parts of the Plains area, though in the more arid sections it failed to bring satisfactory results.

As a result of all these factors: transportation, immigration, the growth of domestic and foreign markets, new methods of fencing and of soil cultivation, the settlement of the last West went on with unprecedented rapidity. In the 20-year period from 1870 to 1890 the population of California doubled, that of Texas trebled, that of Kansas increased fourfold, of Nebraska eightfold, of Washington fourteenfold, and of Dakota Territory fortyfold. Altogether, the population of the trans-Mississippi West rose from 6,877,000 in 1870 to 16,775,000 in 1890. General Phil Sheridan described the process with prophetic pen:

As the railroads overtook the successive lines of frontier posts, and settlements spread out over the country no longer requiring military protection, the army vacated its temporary shelters and marched into remote regions beyond, there to repeat and continue its pioneer work. In the rear of the advancing line of troops the primitive ' dug-outs ' and cabins of the frontiersmen were steadily replaced by the tasteful houses, thrifty farms, neat villages and busy towns of a people who knew how best to employ the vast resources of the great West. The civilization from the Atlantic is now reaching out toward that rapidly approaching it from the direction of the Pacific, the long intervening strip of territory, extending from the British possessions to Old Mexico, yearly growing narrower; finally the dividing lines will entirely disappear and the mingling settlements absorb the remnants of the once powerful Indian nations, who fifteen years ago, vainly attempted to forbid the destined progress of the age.

These ' dividing lines ' which were 1000 miles apart when Sheridan wrote, had, by 1880, become so irregular as to be well-nigh untraceable, and ten years later, in his annual report for 1890, the Superintendent of the Census announced that

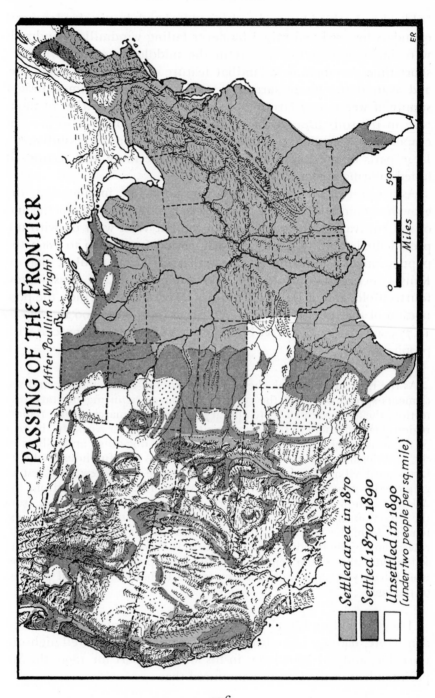

PASSING OF THE FRONTIER
(After Paullin & Wright)

Settled area in 1870

Settled 1870 · 1890

Unsettled in 1890
(under two people per sq. mile)

0   500
Miles

ER

Up to and including 1880 the country had a frontier of settlement, but at present the unsettled area has been so broken into by isolated bodies of settlement that there can be hardly said to be a frontier line.

The ' disappearance of the frontier ' was shortly hailed by a great American historian, Frederick Jackson Turner, as the close of a movement that began in 1607, and the beginning of a new era in American history.

The decade of the 'nineties did constitute a watershed in American history, but the ' passing of the frontier ' was not a distinctive or significant feature of that watershed. If the frontier represented an opportunity to stake out a farm in the West, that opportunity did not disappear in the 1890's. Over a million new farms were settled in the last decade of the century, and more land was patented for homestead and grazing purposes in the generation after 1890 than in the previous generation. The great wheat fields of western Canada continued to offer opportunities to American farmers. The westward movement of population, too, continued unabated. Thus, while in the years 1890 to 1930 population increased in the flourishing Middle Atlantic and North Central States by about 90 per cent, in the Mountain and Pacific States it increased threefold, and the greatest era in the history of the westward movement of population was still to come.[4] And if the frontier represented, as one distinguished historian has said, ' not merely a staked claim to a farm, but a state of mind, and a golden opportunity,' then it is clear that the ' golden opportunity ' — if it ever really existed — went glimmering when the overhead of farming in the West came to equal or to exceed that in the East, and that the psychological change was not an effect of the passing of the frontier but a cause.

The driving force which swept the pioneer westward from the Alleghenies to the Pacific, the dynamic energy which for two generations concentrated on the taking up of land, has changed direction. The frontier as a possible safety valve for economic discontent, a social laboratory, a democratizing process, a spur at once to individual initiative and to collective social action, and a psychological attitude, has disappeared; but its disappearance is more the result of complex economic and psychological forces than a cause of great changes. The relatively lower returns from agriculture than from other forms of

[4] In the years from 1940 to 1960 the Mountain and Pacific coast states increased their population by not far from 14 million.

industry, the heavier cost of labor and the higher risks of farming, the greater social and cultural attractiveness of urban than of rural life, the transformed values and standards of living in the last forty or fifty years, have made Americans shun rather than seek the great open spaces, except for purposes of play. The ideal of the sturdy, self-sufficient, independent farmer, so seldom realized in fact, was by the 1920's supplanted by the ideal of the middle-class city-dweller, enjoying the security of a permanent job, drawing a good salary, and making money on the stock market.

This change in ideals is associated with a sense of frustration and of dissatisfaction that was part of the westward movement and of pioneer life. Both have been the subject of so much romantic sentimentality that we are apt to overlook some of the more realistic aspects. The continuous exodus of a large part of the population meant the unsettling, in a social sense, of the more settled regions of the East and South. Western colonization went on at the expense of older communities and contributed to that process of social and cultural disintegration which has long been one of the characteristics of American life. What it meant for the men and women who participated in it is more difficult to determine, but glimpses of it can be caught from the moving pages of Garland's *Main-Travelled Roads,* Rölvaag's *Giants in the Earth,* the brutal pages of Sandoz's *Old Jules,* or the nostalgic *Grandmother Brown's Hundred Years.* Often it meant release from hardship, a chance to be a man among men, and grow up with a new country. Often, too, it meant the exchange of an ordered, civilized, neighborly community with hard-won standards of propriety, for primitive conditions, an unequal contest with the wilderness, with loneliness and fear and disease. To break new pathways into the West and to wrest a living from the soil was not easy; and the process laid a heavy hand upon those who were not rough-hewn for pioneering. The pioneer women, laboring under intolerable burdens, denied the homely pleasures of social intercourse, cut off from aid in time of need, suffered the most, as the stories of Hamlin Garland and of Rölvaag have revealed. The terrible toll that pioneering exacted from the men and women who engaged in it can be neither discounted nor overlooked in any evaluation of the westward movement and the significance of the frontier.

6. POLITICAL ORGANIZATION

In 1860 something over one-third of the area of the United States was divided into Territories and under the control of the Federal Government. From Minnesota to Oregon, from Texas to the Canadian border, there were no states. Within 30 years all this territory, comprising something over a million square miles, was organized politically, and the major part of it included in states. Statehood was an important step in the assimilation of the West. Federal political control and the frontier disappeared simultaneously.

The admission of Nevada in 1864 had been dictated by the desire to obtain its three electoral votes for Lincoln. The inhabitants of Colorado had rejected the proffer of statehood in the same year, but in 1876 Colorado was admitted as the Centennial State. Nebraska was brought into the Union in 1867 over President Johnson's veto, in time to cast her vote for the impeachment of that unfortunate chief magistrate. With the creation of Wyoming Territory in 1868 the territorial subdivisions of the West had been rounded out, but few of these Territories, most of them based upon mineral wealth, showed any prospects of being prepared for statehood in the immediate future.

The building of the transcontinental railroads, however, put an entirely different face upon the situation, for they brought to the Western Territories a permanent farmer population and a solid economic foundation for statehood. This became apparent first in the northernmost tier of Territories. In 1870 the population of the Dakota, Idaho, and Washington Territories was only 75,000; by 1890, after the Northern Pacific had been completed and the Great Northern almost completed, their population had increased to 1 million. The influence of the railroads, both in bringing a permanent population and in providing markets, was a controlling factor in the creation of most of the other Western states.

Agitation for statehood, especially in the Dakotas and Washington Territory, was continuous. It is somewhat difficult, however, to distinguish between popular enthusiasm and that of professional politicians, eager to become congressmen and state officials. The situation in both Washington and Dakota was complicated: the inhabitants of Washington sought to incorporate the Idaho panhandle in their state, and in Dakota Territory there was a strong popular demand for a separation into two states. Though these and other Territories were amply entitled to statehood, on the score of population, action was held up for a full decade by political differences in Congress. The decisive influence of Colorado's vote in the disputed presidential election of 1876 brought the statehood question into party politics. Except for the two years of the Forty-seventh Congress, 1881–83, control of the government was divided between the two parties during the entire period from Hayes to Harrison. Favorable action upon the demand of the Dakotas for admission in 1881 was held up by Eastern fear of Western radicalism, and Eastern resentment over the repudiation of certain railway bonds by Yankton county. Senator Ingalls of Kansas was led to exclaim, ' I believe that all the objections which have been hitherto urged against the passage of that bill are purely partisan, and malignant.' But by playing politics with the fortunes and the futures of the Western Territories, both parties forfeited the confidence of these embryo states and made them the more willing to follow the banner of Populism in the early 1890's.

The so-called blockade, however, came to an end abruptly in 1888, with the election of Harrison and the prospect of complete Republican control of the government. Both parties and both Houses then made frenzied efforts to get the credit for the admission of the Western states. The result of this eager rivalry was the Omnibus Bill of 1889 which, in its final form, provided for the admission of North and South Dakota, Montana, and Washington. No provision had been made in the Omnibus Bill for Wyoming and Idaho, but in both of these Territories constitutional conventions met without specific authority, and a few months later both were admitted by a debate-weary and vote-hungry Republican Congress.

With the admission of these six states there existed for the first time a solid band of states from the Atlantic to the Pacific. The same year that the Omnibus Bill was passed, the government purchased a large part of the lands of the Five Civilized Tribes and threw Oklahoma open to settlement under the provisions of the homestead laws. The fertility and accessibility of its soil attracted thousands of prospective settlers and speculators, and when the gun was fired on 22 April 1889 there ensued a scene without parallel in the history of the West. Let Edna Ferber's Yancey Cravat describe it:

Well, eleven o'clock and they were crowding and cursing and fighting for places near the line. They shouted and sang and yelled and argued, and the sound they made wasn't human at all, but like thousands of wild animals penned up. The sun blazed down. It was cruel. The dust hung over everything in a thick cloud, blinding you and choking you. The black dust of the prairie was over everything. We were a horde of fiends with our red eyes and our cracked lips and our blackened faces. Eleven-thirty. It was a picture straight out of hell. The roar grew louder. People fought for an inch of gain on the Border. . . . Eleven-forty-five. Along the Border were the soldiers, their guns in one hand, their watches in the other. Those last five minutes seemed years long; and funny, they'd quieted till there wasn't a sound. Listening. The last minute was an eternity. Twelve o'clock. There went up a roar that drowned the crack of the soldiers' musketry as they fired in the air as the signal of noon and the start of the Run. You could see the puffs of smoke from their guns, but you couldn't hear a sound. The thousands surged over the Line. It was like water going over a broken dam. The rush had started and it was devil take the hindmost. We swept across the prairie in a cloud of black and red dust that covered our faces and hands in a minute, so that we looked like black demons from hell.[5]

The towns of Guthrie and Oklahoma City sprang up overnight. By November, Oklahoma had 60,000 settlers and the following year it was organized into a Territory. Within a decade the population had reached almost 800,000 and the question of statehood became urgent. The problem of the disposition of the Indians of Indian Territory complicated matters considerably, and it was not until 1907, when the population was larger than that of any other Territory on admission, that Oklahoma and Indian Territory were admitted as one state.

It was in 1890 that the Mormon government in Utah accepted the inevitable and promised to abandon polygamy, thus removing the last objection to its admission to statehood. Under the able administration of the Mormon Church the Latter-day Saints had prospered amazingly, and when Utah was finally admitted to statehood, in 1896, it was with a flourishing population of some 250,000. The Territories of Arizona and New Mexico, both containing a large admixture of Mexicans and Indians, had rejected joint admission as a single state in 1907, and it was five years before they were admitted individually.

Thus was completed a process inaugurated by the Northwest Ordinance of 1787. Since that time the United States had grown from 13 to 48 states, embracing the whole continental domain; Alaska and Hawaii were admitted just half a century later. Texas came in as an

---

[5] Edna Ferber, *Cimarron*, Doubleday, Doran, pp. 23–5.

independent Republic, Maine and West Virginia were separated from other states, Vermont and Kentucky were admitted without previous Territorial organization; but all the others, after passing through the Territorial stage, were admitted as states in a Union of equals, in accordance with the policies laid down by the enlightened ordinance. The greatest experiment in colonial policy and administration of modern times had been brought to a conclusion successful beyond the wildest dreams of those who inaugurated it.

The constitutions of the new states differed little from those of the older states; for Americans, on the whole, have hesitated to exploit the opportunity for political experiment and differentiation offered by the federal system. What differences there were took a democratic form. The constitutions of Wyoming [6] and Utah provided for woman suffrage from the beginning, and Colorado and other Western states incorporated this provision in their constitutions shortly after. Some of the states provided for the initiative, the referendum, and the Australian ballot, and Arizona went so far as to legalize the recall of judges — a provision which persuaded President Taft to veto her admission to the Union on the ground that it was ' destructive of free government.' All of the new constitutions contained lengthy provisions for the regulation of railroads and other corporations, and most of them reflected the more liberal attitude of the 'nineties toward labor and social reform. There were provisions for the eight-hour day, the limitation of the hours of labor for women and children, arbitration of labor disputes, and employer liability, and prohibitions against the use of the blacklist. In form, too, these new constitutions differed from those of the Eastern states; they were remarkably long and detailed; they strengthened the executive at the expense of the legislative power; and they encouraged the growth of the ' fourth branch ' of the government by providing for numerous boards and commissions to supervise new governmental functions. On the whole they resembled codes of law rather than statements of basic principles of government, and constituted documents in ' the case of the American People *versus* Themselves.'

Yet it would be an error to suppose that the governments of the

---

[6] The Wyoming proviso was attacked on the floor of the House as a violation of the guaranty clause of the Constitution, for, as one Congressman from Georgia observed, ' female suffrage and the right of females to hold office are antagonistic to republican institutions.'

new states were more liberal, during these years, than those of the old. The contrary was more commonly true: after all it was easier for vested interests to capture control of thinly populated and politically immature Western states than of the great states of the East. For years the Southern Pacific dominated the politics of California — it was ' The Octopus ' of Frank Norris's famous novel; the Anaconda Copper Company ruled Montana as a feudal fief; the Wyoming Stock Growers' Association gave the law to that territory; and the copper companies and land speculators controlled by the ' Anglos ' imposed their rule on the Native Peoples of New Mexico. Railroads bought and sold state legislatures; mining companies kept labor in its place; timber and cattle overlords despoiled the public domain; and later on oil companies were strong enough to control not only the states but Congress when their own interests were at stake. And once the Populist impulse had spent itself, nowhere were the authorities more ready to put down radicalism, nowhere was religious fundamentalism more ardent, nowhere was there less interest in racial equality, than in the Far West. If it is not quite true that the Western farmer held no grievances that dollar wheat wouldn't cure, it is true of the West in general that it was far more interested in economic panaceas than in political freedom, and that it was scarcely interested in intellectual freedom at all.

BIBLIOGRAPHY

1. GENERAL. Ray Billington, *Westward Expansion;* Harold E. Briggs, *Frontiers of the Northwest;* John C. Caughey, *History of the Pacific Coast;* Dan E. Clark, *The West in American History;* Everett Dick, *The Sod House Frontier, 1854–1890;* Emerson Hough, *The Passing of the Frontier;* James G. Malin, *The Grassland of North America;* Allan Nevins, *The Emergence of Modern America;* Glenn C. Quiett, *They Built the West;* A. M. Sakolski, *The Great American Land Bubble;* Fred A. Shannon, *The Farmer's Last Frontier;* Walter P. Webb, *The Great Plains.*

2. THE INDIAN PROBLEM. E. D. Branch, *The Hunting of the Buffalo;* John Collier, *Indians of the Americas;* James H. Cook, *Fifty Years on the Old Frontier;* George Crook, *General George Crook: His Autobiography;* Chester A. Fee, *Chief Joseph;* Grant Foreman, *The Five Civilized Tribes;* G. B. Grinnell, *The Story of the Indian* and *The Cheyenne Indians* (2 vols.) ; Helen Hunt Jackson, *A Century of Dishonor;* J. P. Kinney, *A Continent Lost, a Civilization Won;* F. E. Leupp, *The Indian and His Problem;* E. P. Priest, *Uncle Sam's Stepchildren 1865–1887;* B. N. Richardson, *The Comanche Barrier to the South Plains Settlement;* Flora W. Seymour, *Indian Agents of the Old Frontier;* Philip Sheridan,

Personal Memoirs (2 vols.) ; Walter P. Webb, *The Texas Rangers;* Paul Wellman, *Death on the Prairie, Death in the Desert,* and *The Trampling Herd.*

3. THE MINING FRONTIER. Hubert H. Bancroft, *Popular Tribunals* (2 vols.) ; Dan De Quille, *The Big Bonanza;* C. B. Glassock, *Gold in Them Hills, The War of the Copper Kings,* and *The Big Bonanza;* Nathaniel P. Langford, *Vigilante Days and Ways;* George D. Lyman, *Saga of the Comstock Lode;* Effie M. Mack, *Nevada, a History of the State;* W. P. Morrell, *The Gold Rushes;* Paul C. Phillips (ed.), *Forty Years on the Frontier: Journals and Reminiscences of Granville Stuart* (2 vols.) ; Glenn C. Quiett, *Pay Dirt, a Panorama of American Gold Rushes;* T. A. Rickard, *The History of American Mining;* W. J. Trimble, *The Mining Advance into the Inland Empire;* Mark Twain, *Roughing It;* G. F. Willison, *Here They Dug the Dirt.*

4. CATTLE KINGDOM. Andy Adams, *The Log of a Cowboy;* Leonard J. Arrington, *Great Basin Kingdom;* E. D. Branch, *The Cowboy and His Interpreters;* Merrill Burlingame, *The Montana Frontier;* Robert Cleland, *Cattle on a Thousand Hills;* Edward E. Dale, *The Cattle Range Industry;* J. Frank Dobie, *A Vaquero of the Brush Country;* Joe B. Frantz & Julian Choate, *The American Cowboy: the Myth and the Reality;* G. R. Hebard & E. A. Brininstool, *The Bozeman Trail* (2 vols.) ; Stuart Henry, *Conquering Our Great American Plains;* Emerson Hough, *The Story of the Cowboy;* Winifred Kupper, *The Golden Hoof: the Story of the Sheep of the Southwest;* John Lomax, *Cowboy Songs* and *Songs of the Cattle Trail and Cow Camp;* Ernest S. Osgood, *The Day of the Cattlemen;* O. B. Peake, *The Colorado Cattle Range Industry;* Louis Pelzer, *The Cattleman's Frontier, 1850–1890;* Samuel P. Ridings, *The Chisholm Trail;* P. A. Rollins, *The Cowboy;* Fred Shannon, *The Farmer's Last Frontier;* Walter Webb, *The Great Plains;* Paul I. Wellman, *The Trampling Herd;* Edward Wentworth, *America's Sheep Trails* and *Shepherd's Empire.*

5. PASSING OF THE FRONTIER AND THE ORGANIZATION OF THE WEST. Mary Austin, *The Land of Little Rain;* Harold E. Briggs, *Frontiers of the Northwest;* Willa Cather, *O Pioneers, My Ántonia,* and *A Lost Lady;* Robert Cleland, *California* (2 vols.) ; Everett Dick, *Vanguards of the Frontier;* Edna Ferber, *Cimarron;* Dixon Ryan Fox (ed.), *Sources of Culture in the Middle West: Backgrounds versus Frontier;* Hamlin Garland, *A Son of the Middle Border* and *Boy Life on the Prairie;* Paul W. Gates, *Frontier Landlords and Pioneer Tenants;* Roy Gigginter, *Oklahoma;* Alfred B. Guthrie, *The Big Sky* and *The Way West;* John D. Hicks, *The Constitutions of the Northwest States;* John Ise, *Sod and Stubble; the Story of a Kansas Homestead;* Marquis James, *Cherokee Strip;* Richard Lillard, *Desert Challenge: An Interpretation of Nevada;* James C. Malin, *Winter Wheat in the Golden Belt of Kansas;* J. C. Parish, *The Persistence of the Westward Movement;* R. N. Richardson, *Texas, The Lone Star State;* Roy Robbins, *Our Landed Heritage;* Ole Rölvaag, *Giants in the Earth;* Robert Taft, *Artists and Illustrators of the Old West, 1850–1900;* Frederick J. Turner, *Significance of the Frontier in American History.*

6. DOCUMENTS. H. S. Commager, *Documents,* nos. 302, 304, 315; Stanley Vestal, *New Sources of Indian History.*

For further references, *Harvard Guide,* ¶¶ 196, 198, 199, 208.

Transportation and Its Control

1. THE RAILWAY KEY

ECONOMICALLY the era after the Civil War was marked by the application of machine power, in constantly increasing units and over a widely expanded area, to the processes of industry and of agriculture. Transportation was the key; mass production the result. We have already seen how railroads developed from the local feeders into the Eastern trunk lines, which connected the Mississippi valley with the northern Atlantic coast and helped the North to win the war. Immediately after the war came mechanical improvements such as the gradual replacement of the old type of engine (which looked like a wash boiler hitched to a big funnel and a cow-catcher) by coal-burning expansion-cylinder locomotives, the Pullman sleeping car (1864), the safety coupler, and the Westinghouse air brake. This last, invented in 1869, did more than any other invention to transform the original string of boxes on tracks to the modern train, and to make possible safe operation at high speeds. But it was the old wood-burning, spark-belching ' bullgine,' gay with paint and sporting a name instead of a number, tugging unvestibuled coaches with swaying kerosene lamps and quid-bespattered wood stoves, which first wheezed across the Great Divide and linked the Atlantic to the Pacific.

There were 35,000 miles of steam railway in the United States in 1865, practically all east of the Mississippi. During the next eight years as many more were constructed. In the years 1874–87 some 87,000 additional miles of track were laid, and in 1900, with just under 200,000 miles in operation, the United States had a greater railway mileage than all Europe.

A transportation system such as this required state and federal legislation, colossal sums of money, and a sure supply of cheap labor. It affected the fortunes of almost everyone in the country, and of millions abroad as well. It gave a new wrench to the body politic, already distorted by the war. Railway expansion touched American life at countless points. It closely interacted with western migration and settlement, with the iron and steel industry, and with agriculture; it greased the way for big business and high finance, helped to pollute politics, and gave birth to new problems of constitutional law and of government policy and governmental mechanisms. A later revolution in transportation, wrought by the internal combustion engine, the motor car, and the airplane, so overshadowed the railroads that it is difficult now to realize how completely they dominated the industrial and political world for almost fifty years after the Civil War.

We have seen how the agitation for transcontinental railroads affected the fortunes of Stephen A. Douglas, and helped the Republican party to ride into power on a wholly different series of issues; how competing routes were advocated and surveyed, but deadlocked by sectional jealousy and politics. While the Civil War was wrecking the railway system of the South, it accelerated railway development in the North and across the continent. As a connection between the Mississippi valley and the Far West, Halliday's Overland Stage was more picturesque than efficient; but military necessity brought the dream of Asa Whitney to fulfillment. With the active co-operation of the War Department, and under the supervision of Generals Dodge and Sherman, the first transcontinental line was projected and constructed.

On 1 July 1862 President Lincoln signed the first Pacific Railway Act. This bill provided for the construction of a transcontinental railroad by two corporations — the Union Pacific which would build westward from Council Bluffs, Iowa, and the Central Pacific, which was to build eastward from Sacramento, California. It pledged liberal aid in the form of alternate sections of public lands to the depth of ten miles (and later twenty) on either side of the road, and of loans ranging from $16,000 to $48,000 for every mile of track completed. Active construction of the Union Pacific, financed by the notorious Credit Mobilier,[1] and directed by General Grenville Dodge as chief engineer, began in 1865, and the road was pushed rapidly westward from Omaha through Nebraska and Wyoming Territories, near the line of the old Oregon and Mormon Trails, and

1 See Chap. III.

across the Wasatch range of the Rockies into the Great Salt Basin. In the meantime the Central Pacific, chartered in 1858, and directed by Collis P. Huntington and Leland Stanford, built eastward over the difficult grades of the Sierras and across the arid valleys of Nevada to meet the Union Pacific. The lurid details of their race have lost nothing in their telling by Zane Grey, but there is no need to exaggerate or to idealize this spectacular achievement. The obstacles to be overcome seemed almost insuperable: engineering problems, labor and financial difficulties, the constant struggle with mountain blizzard and desert heat, and — in the mountains — with the Indians as well. As General Dodge recalled:

All the supplies for this work had to be hauled from the end of the track, and the wagon transportation was enormous. At one time we were using at least ten thousand animals, and most of the time from eight to ten thousand laborers. The bridge gangs always worked from five to twenty miles ahead of the track, and it was seldom that the track waited for a bridge. To supply one mile of track with material and supplies required about forty cars, as on the plains everything — rails, ties, bridging, fastenings, all railway supplies, fuel for locomotives and trains, and supplies for men and animals on the entire work — had to be transported from the Missouri River. Therefore as we moved westward, every hundred miles added vastly to our transportation. Yet the work was so systematically planned and executed that I do not remember an instance in all the construction of the line of the work being delayed a single week for want of material.[2]

That the obstacles were overcome must be attributed not only to the indomitable energy and perseverance of men like Dodge and Huntington, but also to the courage and devotion of the thousands of laborers — the ex-soldiers, Irish immigrants, and Chinese coolies — upon whose brawny shoulders the heaviest part of the task rested.

When I think [wrote Robert Louis Stevenson] of how the railroad has been pushed through this unwatered wilderness and haunt of savage tribes . . . ; how at each stage of construction, roaring, impromptu cities full of gold and lust and death sprang up and then died away again, and are now but wayside stations in the desert; how in these uncouth places pigtailed Chinese pirates worked side by side with border ruffians and broken men from Europe, talking together in a mixed dialect mostly oaths, . . . how the plumed hereditary lord of all America heard in this last fastness the scream of the " bad medicine wagon " charioting his foes; and then when I go on to remember that all this epical turmoil was con-

[2] Grenville Dodge, *How We Built the Union Pacific*.

ducted by gentlemen in frocked coats, and to nothing more extraordinary than a fortune and a subsequent visit to Paris, it seems to me . . . as if this railway were the one typical achievement of the age in which we live. . . . If it be romance, if it be contrast, if it be heroism that we require, what was Troy town to this.[3]

Both the Union and the Central Pacific roads were pushed forward in record time, 20,000 laborers laying as much as eight miles of track in a day in the last stages of the race. The prime motive for this feverish haste was the greed of each group of promoters to obtain the lion's share of federal bounties and land grants. When, amidst universal rejoicing, the two sets of rails were joined with a golden spike at Promontory Point, Utah, 10 May 1869, the Union Pacific was regarded as the winner, but the Central Pacific promoters had made enough to enable them to buy the state government of California.

Meantime there was a wild scramble among other groups of promoters for charters and favors, and within a few years Congress chartered and endowed with enormous land grants three other lines: (1) the Northern Pacific — from Lake Superior across Minnesota, through the Bad Lands of Dakota up the valley of the Yellowstone, across the Continental Divide at Bozeman, to the headwaters of the Missouri, and by an intricate route through the Rockies to the Columbia river and Portland; (2) the Southern Pacific — an outgrowth and development of the Central Pacific and the short-lived Atlantic and Pacific — from New Orleans across Texas to the Rio Grande, across the Llanos Estacado to El Paso, and through the territory of the Gadsden Purchase to Los Angeles, up the San Joaquin valley to San Francisco; (3) the Santa Fe — following closely the old Santa Fe Trail, from Atchison, Kan., up the Arkansas river to Trinidad, Colo., across the Raton spur of the Rockies to Santa Fe and Albuquerque, through the country of the Apache and the Navajo, parallel to the Grand Canyon of the Colorado — which thrusts its impassable barrier for 300 miles athwart the southern railway routes — and across the Mojave desert to San Bernardino and San Diego. The Southern Pacific link was completed in 1881; the Northern Pacific and Santa Fe both reached the Pacific in 1883. Thus within twenty years of the Pacific railway legislation there were four transcontinentals; a fifth, the Great Northern, was completed in the next decade.

3 *Across the Plains*, pp. 50–52.

2. THE RAILROADS AND THE WEST

These transcontinental lines were promoted largely with a view to profit from construction and from manipulation of securities, but the peopling of the vast region between the Missouri and the Pacific proved to be their most valuable function. In this respect they performed a work comparable with that of the Virginia Company of 1606 and the Ohio Company of 1786.

At the end of the Civil War the Plains west of eastern Kansas and Nebraska, the High Plains, and the Rocky Mountain regions were practically unpeopled, save for mining towns in Colorado and Nevada and the Mormon settlements in Utah. Mail coaches of the Overland Stage Line required at least five days to transport passengers and mails from the Missouri river to Denver, where flour was sold for 20 cents a pound and potatoes for $15 a bushel. Prewar pioneers had been confined to subsistence farming until the railway connected them with markets; but the transcontinental railways pushed out into the Plains far in advance of settlers, advertised for immigrants in the Eastern states and Europe, transported them at wholesale rates to the prairie railhead, and sold them land at from $1 to $10 an acre. Thus James J. Hill settled his great domain in the Far Northwest, his agents scouring Europe for settlers and meeting new arrivals at the piers in New York City; Henry Villard of the Northern Pacific employed almost a thousand agents in England and continental Europe, and their advertising literature painted the climate and the soil of the Northwest in such roseate colors that the Union Pacific lands were popularly known as Jay Cooke's banana belt. The immigration department of the Santa Fe Railroad brought to Kansas, in 1874, 10,000 German Mennonites whose ancestors had colonized the Ukraine, and these in turn brought with them not only piety and industry but the Red Turkey wheat which made Kansas prairies bloom like a garden. Thousands of section-hands entered a free homestead right, saved their wages to buy farm equipment and a team of horses, built a sodhouse or cabin, and became permanent settlers as soon as the steel road was built. The termini and eastern junction points of these lines — like Omaha, opposite the old Council Bluffs of the Indians; Kansas City, hard by the old jumping-off place for the Oregon Trail; Duluth, the 'Zenith City of the Unsalted Seas'; Oakland on San Francisco bay; Portland, Oregon; Seattle and Tacoma, Washington — places non-existent or mere villages before the Civil War — became in thirty years metropolitan cities.

Railroading was the biggest business of a big era, and the railway builders were of the mettle that makes leaders and conquerors. The new Northwest was the domain of James J. Hill, the 'Empire Builder,' and the Great Northern Railway his individual path of empire. St. Paul was a small town on the edge of the frontier when he migrated thither from eastern Canada just before the Civil War, and Minneapolis a mere village at the St. Anthony falls of the Mississippi. Such importance as they had was due to their position at the end of a trail from the Red river of the North, which connected Winnipeg with the outside world. Long trains of two-wheeled ox-carts transported the peltry and supplies in 40 or 50 days' time. In the winter of 1870 Donald Smith, resident governor of the Hudson's Bay Company, started south from Winnipeg, and James J. Hill north from St. Paul, both in dog-sleds. They met on the prairie and made camp in a snowstorm; and from that meeting sprang the Canadian Pacific and the Great Northern railways.

In the panic of 1873 a little Minnesota railway with an ambitious name, the St. Paul and Pacific, went bankrupt. Hill watched it as a prairie wolf watches a weakening buffalo, and in 1878, in association with two Canadian railway men, wrested it from the Dutch bondholders by a mere flotation of new securities.

The day of land grants and federal subsidies was past, and Hill saw that the Great Northern Railway, as he renamed his purchase, could reach the Pacific only by developing the country as it progressed. ' We consider ourselves and the people along our lines as co-partners in the prosperity of the country we both occupy,' said Hill, ' and the prosperity of the one should mean the prosperity of both, and their adversity will be quickly followed by ours.' So this empire builder undertook to enhance the prosperity of what came to be known as the ' Hill country '; he introduced scientific farming, distributed blooded bulls free to farmers, supported churches and schools, and assisted in countless ways the development of the communities of the Northwest. ' It was,' observes one commentator, ' largely due to his unceasing interest in all that pertained to getting the most out of the soil that the " Hill country " developed more evenly and with fewer tragedies than any other large-scale land enterprise of these years.'

In the construction of his railroad Hill showed equal forethought and shrewdness. Construction costs were low, the financial management was skillful and conservative, and the Great Northern was the one transcontinental line that managed to weather every financial crisis. Hill first made connection with Winnipeg by the Red river valley; then, anticipating a diversion of Winnipeg traffic by the Canadian Pacific, he struck almost due west across the Dakota plains, sending out branches in order to people the region and carry its wheat to market. In the summer of 1887 he made a record stride, 643 miles of grading, bridging, and plate-laying from Minot, North Dakota, to the Great Falls of the Missouri, at the rate of over three miles per working day. Two years later, the Rockies yielded their last secret, the Marias pass, to a young engineer named John F. Stevens. In 1893 the trains of the Great Northern reached tidewater at Tacoma, Washington. Ten years more, and Hill had acquired partial control of the Northern Pacific Railroad, had purchased joint control of a railway connecting its eastern termini with Chicago, and was running his own fleets of steamships from Duluth to Buffalo, and from Seattle to Japan and China.

The Great Northern, the Northern Pacific, and the Union Pacific (which sent a taproot northwesterly) were responsible for the opening of the great ' Inland Empire ' between the Cascades and the Rockies, and for an astounding development of the entire Northwest. This once isolated Oregon country, with its rich and varied natural resources, magnificent scenery, and thriving seaports, became as distinct and self-conscious a section of the Union as New England. The three states of this region — Washington, Oregon, and Idaho — increased their population from 282,000 in 1880 to 763,000 in 1890, and 2,140,000 in 1910. California, which contained only half a million people when the golden spike was driven in 1869, kept pace with them: it stood twenty-fourth in population in 1870, and twelfth in 1910; fifty years later it was crowding New York for first place. The population of Kansas, Nebraska, and the Dakotas, starting at the same level in 1870, increased sixfold in two decades; Utah and Colorado, where there was a great mining boom in the 1870's, rose from 125,000 to 624,000 in the same period; Oklahoma and the Indian Territory, where not a white man was enrolled in 1880, had over a million and a half palefaces in 1910; and Texas, with the aid of a network of railways and the discovery of oil wells that were seemingly inexhaustible, foreshadowed its future growth by doubling its population between 1880 and 1910.

King Cotton's crown passed to King Wheat, whose dominions increased. Railway penetration of the Far Northwest, improved farm machinery, new strains of rust-resistant wheat, techniques of dry farming, the trans-shipment to lake or ocean steamers by grain elevator companies, and a new milling process which ground Northern spring wheat into superfine flour — all these factors combined to move the center of wheat production north and west from Illinois and Iowa into Minnesota, the Dakotas, Montana, Oregon, and the prairie provinces of Canada.

Villard and Dodge, Huntington and Hill, connected the Atlantic and the Pacific. Meantime another enterprise, no less heroic, was connecting the two shores of the Atlantic. As early as the 1840's Samuel F. B. Morse, inventor of the telegraph, and the famous oceanographer Matthew Maury, had proposed laying a telegraphic cable under the Atlantic Ocean. But it was Cyrus Field of New York, member of one of America's most distinguished families, who took up the notion and carried it through. In 1856 he enlisted the financier Peter Cooper, British scientists and investors, and the British and American governments in a bold plan to string a giant cable from westernmost Ireland to Trinity Bay, Newfoundland. He quickly connected Trinity Bay with New York, and by summer 1857 two men-of-war were playing out a giant cable off the Irish coast. It broke in midocean — the first of a long series of cruel disappointments. In 1858 a cable was finally laid over 2000 miles of ocean bed, but even as two continents indulged in an orgy of rhetoric and rejoicing, the cable ceased to transmit messages. The Civil War put a stop to further experiments, but after the war the indomitable Field once more took up the project, enlisting this time the scientific genius of Lord Kelvin and the engineering talent of the railroad builder Isambard Brunel. With the fabulous *Great Eastern* — the world's largest ship — playing out a vastly improved cable, a firm connection between the continents was finally established in 1866. It cost $5 a word to send a message across the ocean, and the public was duly impressed when the Emperor Maximilian of Mexico cabled a message to the Empress

Carlotta at a cost of $4780, but soon the price was reduced and the messages improved.

3. FEDERAL AND LOCAL AID

When railroads began to supplant rivers and canals as highways of commerce, connect isolated rural regions with markets, and open up new land to settlement, they were looked upon as an unmixed blessing, and their promoters were regarded as public benefactors. Since every route decided upon by surveyors and railway promoters brought prosperity to some communities and threatened ruin to others, towns, counties, and states outdid one another in bidding for the iron tracks. The Federal Government, too, having definitely abandoned strict construction theories that had embarrassed an earlier generation, regarded the roads as military and postal necessities and aided them with a liberality which at the time seemed commendable but which a later generation came to regard as excessive.

This policy of government aid to internal improvements had its beginnings in grants of land to canal, turnpike, and railroad companies in the decades before the Civil War. In the 1850's no less than 28 million acres of public lands were granted to states for the purpose of subsidizing railroad construction; the Illinois Central alone got some 2.6 million acres in the states through which it passed. With the enactment of the Pacific Railway Acts of 1862 and 1864 the Federal Government inaugurated the practice of making land grants directly to railway corporations. Certainly few of the Western railroads could have been built by private capital alone without generous aid from federal, state, and local governments.

Besides charters and rights of way across the territories, federal aid was extended to the roads in a number of ways, the most important of which were land grants, loans, subsidies, and tariff remission on rails. The land grants were the most lavish and the most valuable. The Union Pacific was given some 20 million acres of public lands, in alternate sections along its track; the Santa Fe got 17 million acres from the Federal Government and additional millions from the state of Texas; the Central Pacific and the Southern Pacific each got 24 million acres; while the Northern Pacific obtained the enormous total of 44 million acres, an area equal to the entire state of Missouri. Altogether the Federal Government gave the railroads 155,504,994 acres, of which over 40 million were forfeited because the roads failed to fulfill the conditions of the grants, leaving a net total of 131,350,534 acres from this source.

But this was by no means the whole of the land subsidy to the Western roads. The states — notably Texas and Minnesota — gave the railroads an additional 48,883,372 acres. Other millions of acres were obtained by purchase or chicanery under the easy terms of the Desert Land Act of 1877 and the Timber and Stone Act of 1878, and the Forest Lieu Act of 1897, which enabled the railroads to exchange barren land for well-timbered land elsewhere on the public domain. Vast acreages were acquired at absurdly low prices from Indian tribes, or from states disposing of their swamp lands or their land-grant college scrip.

As most of this land was worth nothing to the roads until it produced crops to be hauled to market, and because they were in urgent need of money, the railway companies generally disposed of it as rapidly as possible, and at a price of between $4 and $5 an acre. Some of the land, however, covered extensive deposits of coal or oil, or other minerals, and much of it was heavily timbered. So while disposing rapidly of their agricultural and grazing lands, the roads consistently followed the policy of reserving mineral lands, timber lands, and potential town sites for speculative purposes, and in this policy they were encouraged by amiable interpretations of the law by successive land commissioners. Some of these holdings — the Williston Oil Basin, for example, still controlled by the Northern Pacific — proved fabulously rich. All in all, these land grants, designed to assist railroads in financing construction where as yet there was no basis for revenue, paid a considerable part of the total construction costs. The lands granted the Illinois Central, for example, brought in a sum equal to the entire construction cost of that railroad. It cost some $70 million to build the Northern Pacific, but in 1917 that road reported gross receipts from land sales of over $136 million, with a substantial part of its most valuable lands still unsold. The lands granted to both the Union Pacific and the Central Pacific brought in enough money to have covered all legitimate costs of building these roads.

Direct financial aid was given by the Federal Government only to the Union Pacific and the Central Pacific railways and their subsidiaries in the form of a loan for every mile of track. These loans, aggregating $64 million, were repaid in 1899 with interest of about $100 million, but the controversy involving their repayment troubled American politics for a decade.

The Federal Government received substantial benefits in return for its largess. Land-grant railroads were required to carry government mail at a reduced price, and also to transport military personnel and supplies at less than normal charges: an arrangement of considerable importance during the First World War. Spokesmen for the railroads estimated the accumulated value of these benefits at more than the total value of the land grants, but those who have ventured into the labyrinths of this accounting have never been known to emerge.

Aid from states, counties, and municipalities, often competing with one another, was equally lavish and more reckless. The states often granted tax exemption, protection from competition, and liberal charters; some lent the roads their credit, others subscribed outright to the stock of railway companies. Many states made extensive land grants, sometimes under pressure: thus the La Crosse Railroad managed to get a grant of one million acres from the state government by a judicious distribution of $900,000 in railroad stock to the governor, the legislature, and state judges. Counties and municipalities subscribed liberally to railroad stock, and often donated money outright. Counties and towns in Kentucky incurred a debt of over $13 million for railroad construction; 86 counties in Illinois subsidized railroads to the extent of over $16 million; the municipalities of Kansas contributed well over $12 million to the railroads of that state. Many railroads ' reorganized ' or went bankrupt before they could build the promised roads, but cities and counties were held to their commitments. Careful estimates of total subsidies to railroads by various governmental agencies of Western states indicate that Kansas contributed about $75 million, Nebraska and Iowa each about $60 million, and Wisconsin over $30 million. It is impossible to avoid the conclusion that the aggregate subsidies received by the Western railroads from federal, state, and local governments amply covered the legitimate cost of construction.

Yet it would be unfair to conclude on a note that echoes the tale of exploitation and chicanery. Two other observations are called for. First, short of government construction and operation — something unimaginable to Americans of that generation — this was probably the only way to get the Western railroads built at all. The roads were built; they linked together the sections; they hastened the settlement of the High Plains and the Rockies, and vastly increased the wealth of those sections. Second, the policy of governmental subsidy to transportation is as old as the Republic and as recent as the last session of Congress. The Populists and Progressives were shocked at the spectacle of private profit from government subsidies, but a generation that has seen Congress vote hundreds of millions to subsidize the merchant marine, spend billions on highways used by trucks, and vote additional billions to build airports and subsidize airlines, does not find it so difficult to understand the methods — however incompetent and corrupt — whereby our forebears built the transcontinentals.

4. ABUSES AND STATE REGULATION

This rapid extension of the railroads was not followed by the expected wave of prosperity — except for the insiders who built the roads. On the contrary, within a few years the farmers of the West began to feel the effects of the postwar deflation, followed by the panic of 1873, and many laid the blame on the railroads. The advantages for which Westerners had paid so handsomely seemed to bring only hard times. How far the railroads were responsible for the hard times of the early 1870's through stimulating production ahead of market needs, is a matter of dispute; but there is no question of the reality of grave abuses connected with railway expansion in the generation after the Civil War.

To the farmer the most grievous of the abuses were the high freight rates charged by the Western roads — rates so exorbitant that the farmers at times burned their corn for fuel rather than ship it to market. The whole question of rates is, of course, inextricably connected with the question of the capitalization upon which the roads undertook to earn dividends. The railway masters argued that they were barely able to maintain dividend payments, and it is true that in periods of depression, such as those following upon the panics of 1873 and 1893, a good many roads were in receivership. Yet it is equally true that profits, either in the form of dividends, stock splits, or other devices, were often exorbitant, and that both the extortionate freight rates and the financial troubles of the roads were traceable to such things as over-high construction costs, fraudulent purchase of other properties at inflated prices, fraudulent manipulation of stock, and incompetent management.

Thus the total construction cost of the Central Pacific, for example, from Sacramento to Ogden, Utah, was something over $90 million, and upon this investment the directors of the road expected to pay dividends; but a congressional committee estimated that ' a road similar to that of the Central Pacific could probably be built for $22,000,000.' The same committee estimated the cost of the five transcontinental lines at $634 million, and that these same roads could be duplicated for $228 million. The reason construction costs were so high was partly the pressure under which many of the roads were built in order to get land grants, but chiefly because costs were artificially increased by dummy construction companies in order to provide profits for the directors. The evil of illegally padded costs and of overcapitalization was by no means confined to the West; the chicanery of the Credit Mobilier [4] could be matched by the even more flagrant chicanery of Jay Gould and Jim Fisk in systematically milking the Erie Railroad, which did not finally recover until the 1940's. This technique of using dummy construction corporations is illustrated by the career of the short-lived Southern Pennsylvania Railroad. This little road was started by Vanderbilt in order to force the Pennsylvania Railroad to buy it. A contractor offered to build it for $6.5 million, but instead Vanderbilt organized a corporation consisting of his clerks, who received $15 million to build the road; the syndicate who furnished them with this money were paid with $40 million in railroad shares. The Pennsylvania, which eventually had to buy this property, not unnaturally expected to earn dividends on the cost of acquiring all this! No wonder Poor's Railroad Manual for 1885 estimated that approximately one-third of all railroad capitalization in the country that year represented water.

Other abuses against which complaint was loud and persistent were: the creation of railroad ' pools ' which did away with competition in large areas by fixing prices and dividing up profits in accordance with agreed-on schedules; discrimination in rates and in services with secret rebates to powerful shippers which put the small shippers at a hopeless disadvantage; the long-and-short-haul evil, which consisted in slashing freight rates at competitive points and making up the losses at non-competitive points; railroad control of

4 See Chap. III.

warehouses and other facilities, which enabled the railroads to
'grade' the grain and to fix prices on beef; retention of railroad
lands for speculative purposes; and corrupt activities of railroads in
politics.

A single illustration must suffice for each of these. (1) The most
famous 'pool' was that organized by Albert Fink of the Louisville
and Nashville Railroad which divided up the business of the entire
South, eliminated competition, and increased rates. (2) Discrimination in favor of powerful shippers was well-nigh universal: the most
notorious example was the rebate granted the Standard Oil Company of 40 cents on each barrel of oil shipped to Cleveland, and an
additional drawback on each barrel shipped by any competitor.
(3) The practice of charging more for short hauls than for long hauls
was designed to make up at non-competitive points losses incurred in
competition; thus goods traveling from Boston to Denver direct paid
$1.70 a hundredweight, but if they traveled from Boston to San Fran-
cisco and then back to Denver, they went for $1.50. (4) The rail-
roads controlled all the great grain elevators in Chicago and through
them fixed the price they would pay for wheat from the hinterland;
they owned, too, the Union stockyards which enabled them pretty
well to control the price of beef in the Mid-West. (5) As we have
seen, the Northern Pacific kept valuable oil and timber lands for future rise in value; the Southern Pacific retained valuable lands in
cities like Los Angeles. (6) As for political corruption it is sufficient
to note that the Union Pacific agent in Nebraska's state capital admitted that he ordinarily gave out over 400 passes a year to those who
might influence legislation.

The fact is that the power of the Western railways over their exclusive territory was nearly absolute, for until the age of the automobile the West had no alternate means of transportation. Railways
could make an industry or ruin a community by a few cents more or
less in a rate on wheat or cattle or oil. The money at their disposal,
often created by financial manipulation, enabled them to influence
both public opinion and legislatures. Railway builders and promoters had the point of view of feudal overlords. Railroading, in
their opinion, was a business wholly private in its nature, no more a
fit subject for government regulation than a retail store. 'There is
no foundation in good reason,' said Leland Stanford to his stockholders in 1878, 'for the attempts made by the General Government

and by the States to especially control your affairs. It is a question of might, and it is to your interest to have it determined where the power resides.'

The determination of this question was not difficult. Leland Stanford, Collis P. Huntington, and their associates who built the Central Pacific and controlled the Southern Pacific, had the might, and in the exercise of that might they were indifferent to all save considerations of gain for themselves and their roads. By distributing free passes to state representatives, by paying campaign expenses, and by downright bribery, they prevented just taxation of their railroad properties and evaded most regulation. By discriminating in freight charges between localities, articles, and individuals, they terrorized merchants, farmers, and communities ' until matters reached such a pass, that no man dared engage in any business in which transportation largely entered without first . . . obtaining the permission of a railroad manager.' [5] Through the press, the professions, and even the pulpit they wielded a power over public opinion comparable to that of the slave-owners over the old South. The same methods were imitated by the railroad magnates in the rest of the country. Thus President Milton Smith of the Louisville and Nashville Railway regarded all regulation as a form of demagoguery, and for years openly defied legislatures and court orders in four states. The New York Central and the Erie Railroads corrupted not only the Albany legislature but the state courts as well.[6] In New Hampshire, as in California, a ' railroad lobby,' ensconced in an office near the state capitol, acted as a chamber of initiative and revision; and, as the novelist Winston Churchill tells us in his *Coniston* and *Mr. Crewe's Career*, few could succeed in politics unless by grace of the Boston and Maine. ' The railroad corporations,' asserted Governor Larrabee of Iowa, ' were in fact rapidly assuming a position which could not be tolerated. Shel-

[5] Report of the U.S. Pacific Railway Commission (1887), Vol. I, p. 141.

[6] ' War is the natural state of an American railway towards all other authorities and its own fellows, just as war was the natural state of cities towards one another in the ancient world. And as an army in the field must be commanded by one general, so must this latest militant product of an eminently peaceful civilization. The president of a great railroad needs gifts for strategical combinations scarcely inferior to those, if not of a great general, yet of a great war minister — a Chatham or a Carnot. If his line extends into a new country he must be quick to seize the best routes. . . . He must know the Governors and watch the legislatures of the States or Territories through which his line runs; and must have adroit agents at the State capitals well supplied with the sinews of war. . . .' James Bryce, *The American Commonwealth*, Vol. II, pp. 651–2.

tering themselves behind the Dartmouth College decision, they practically undertook to set even public opinion at defiance. . . . They
thoroughly got it into their heads that they, as common carriers, were
in no way bound to afford equal facilities to all, and indeed, that it
was in the last degree absurd and unreasonable to expect them to
do so.'

These exactions and abuses of power were tolerated by the American people with what Europeans deemed a remarkable patience, so
imbued were they with laissez-faire doctrine, so proud of progress,
improvement, and development, and so averse to increasing the
power of government. But the deflation of the postwar years and the
panic of 1873 brought an inevitable reaction against the roads. This
reaction centered in the Mid-Western states of Illinois, Iowa, Wisconsin, Minnesota, Missouri, and Nebraska, but it also found expression in Eastern states such as Massachusetts and in Western states
such as California. It took several forms: prohibition of further state
aid, as in the constitutions of California, Kansas, and Missouri; recovery of land grants; prohibition of specific abuses such as rebates
and passes; and positive regulation of rates and services. The Eastern
state governments inclined to supervision by special railway commissions, and that of Massachusetts, under the leadership of the
gifted Charles Francis Adams, Jr., attracted widespread attention and
became the conservative model for numerous states.

The Mid-Western states were more direct in their methods. The
Illinois Constitution of 1870 contained a clause directing the legislature to ' pass laws to correct abuses and to prevent unjust discrimination and extortion in the rates of freight and passenger tariffs on
the different railroads of the state.' Pursuant to this clause the legislature of Illinois prohibited discrimination, established a maximum
rate, and created a Railway and Warehouse Commission to regulate
roads, grain elevators, and warehouses. These laws, though bitterly
denounced as socialism throughout the East, served as models for
similar legislation in other states. At the demand of the farmers, the
example of Illinois was followed in 1874 by Iowa and Minnesota, and
by Wisconsin with its drastic Potter law.

Thus within a few years the railroads of the Middle West found
their independence severely circumscribed by a mass of highly restrictive regulatory legislation. The day of individualism and laissez-
faire theories was passing away.

The validity of this legislation, shortly contested in the courts, was upheld in the ' Granger ' cases. The first and most important of these was *Munn v. Illinois* (1876) involving the constitutionality of a statute regulating the charges of grain elevators. The warehouse owners contended that the act was a deprivation of property without due process of law and thus constituted a violation of the Fourteenth Amendment. In one of the most far-reaching decisions in American law, Chief Justice Waite upheld the validity of the Illinois statute. Basing his opinion upon the historical right of the state, in the exercise of its police power to regulate ferries, common carriers, inns, etc., he announced that

When private property is affected with a public interest it ceases to be *juris privati* only. . . . Property does become clothed with a public interest when used in a manner to make it of public consequence, and affect the community at large. When, therefore, one devotes his property to a use in which the public has an interest, he, in effect, grants to the public an interest in that use, and must submit to be controlled by the public for the common good, to the extent of the interest he has created.[7]

The warehouse owners not only challenged the right of the state to regulate their business but contended further that rate-fixing by a legislative committee did not constitute ' due process of law.' This contention the Court disposed of in cavalier fashion:

It is insisted, however, that the owner of property is entitled to a reasonable compensation for its use . . . and that what is reasonable is a judicial and not a legislative question. . . . The controlling fact [however] is the power to regulate at all. If that exists, the right to establish the maximum charge, as one of the means of regulation, is implied. . . . We know that this is a power which may be abused; but that is no argument against its existence. For protection against abuses by legislatures, the people must resort to the polls, not to the courts.

On the same day that the Court sustained the validity of the Illinois statute, it handed down decisions in the important cases of *Peik v. Chicago & Northwestern R.R., Chicago, Burlington & Quincy R.R. v. Iowa,* and *Winona & St. Peter R.R. v. Blake.* These cases involved the validity of Granger laws establishing maximum freight and passenger rates. The laws had been attacked not only on the ground that they violated the Fourteenth Amendment, but also on the ground that they invaded the exclusive control over interstate

[7] *Munn v. Illinois* 94 U.S. 113 (1876).

commerce by the Congress. The Court, however, sustained the validity of these laws against both charges. The railroad, said the Court,

is employed in state as well as interstate commerce, and until Congress
acts, the State must be permitted to adopt such rules and regulations as
may be necessary for the promotion of the general welfare of the people
within its own jurisdiction, even though in so doing those without may
be indirectly affected.

Thus the Court announced three major principles of constitutional law: first, the right of government to regulate all business affected with a public interest; second, the right of the legislature to
determine what is fair and reasonable; third, the right of the state, in
areas of concurrent authority, to act where Congress has failed to act.
These decisions gave laissez faire the air, and inaugurated the modern era of public regulation of public utilities. They aroused, however, a storm of protest from conservative and financial circles in the
East. They were branded as socialistic and revolutionary, and as irreparable blows to private enterprise. Within a decade the composition of the Supreme Court became more conservative, and two of the
three Granger principles were duly modified. Thus, in 1886, in the
Wabash case, the Court retreated from the third principle by holding
invalid an Illinois statute prohibiting the ' long-and-short-haul ' evil,
on the ground that it infringed upon the exclusive power of Congress over interstate commerce. In the same year, in the case of *Stone
v. Farmers' Loan Co.*, the Court intimated that the reasonableness
of the rate established by a commission might be a matter for judicial rather than legislative determination. Three years later this
obiter dictum became the basis for a decision declaring rate regulation by a legislative commission invalid.[8] These decisions dealt a
heavy blow to state regulation of roads and rates, and placed the burden squarely upon the Federal Government. Congress responded
with the Interstate Commerce Act of 1887.

5. The Advent of Federal Regulation

Agitation for federal rather than state regulation of railroads began with the Senate report of the Windom Committee in 1874,
which advocated federal construction and operation of railways to

[8] *Chicago, Milwaukee and St. Paul Railroad Co. v. Minnesota* 134 U.S. 418 (1889) .

compete with the private roads. In the same year the House passed and the Senate rejected the McCrary Bill providing for federal regulation of rates charged by interstate carriers. Three years later Congressman Reagan of Texas introduced a bill looking to the elimination of railway abuses, and got it through the House in 1878, but again the Senate, influenced by a powerful railroad lobby, failed to take action.

In the meantime interest had shifted somewhat from the problem of rates to that of pools and discrimination. The report of the Cullom Committee of 1886 made clear the need for immediate reform in these matters. ' The paramount evil chargeable against transportation systems,' observed the committee, ' is unjust discrimination between persons, places, commodities, on particular descriptions of traffic.' Almost equally dangerous, in the view of the committee, was the effect of pooling agreements in creating regional monopolies and sustaining high charges.

The Wabash decision of 1886 made congressional action imperative. The Interstate Commerce Act of 4 February 1887 represented in its substance a compromise between the Massachusetts or supervisory type of regulation and the Granger or coercive type of regulation. It specifically prohibited pooling, rebates, discrimination of any character, and higher charges for a short haul than for a long haul. It provided that all charges should be ' reasonable and just ' but failed to define either of these ambiguous terms. Perhaps most important of all, it established the first permanent administrative board [9] of the Federal Government, the Interstate Commerce Commission, to supervise the administration of the law. Enforcement was left to the courts, but a large part of the burden of proof and prosecution was placed upon the commission. Although the bill was popularly regarded as a victory for the public, it had the support of the railroads, and railway stocks rose in the market upon its passage.

Administrative regulations, however, were still so foreign to the American conception of government that the federal courts insisted upon their right to review orders of the Interstate Commerce Commission, and took the teeth out of the act by a series of decisions. In

[9] Unless the Civil Service Commission, established in 1883, but spectacularly ineffective, should be regarded as the first. Since 1887 the commissions have become so numerous as to constitute a ' fourth department ' of the government.

the Maximum Freight Rate case (1897), the Supreme Court held that the commission did not have the power to fix rates, and in the Alabama Midlands case of the same year it practically nullified the long-and-short-haul prohibition. It was found almost impossible to require agents of the railroads to testify about railroad malpractices, and it was customary for witnesses to introduce into the court new testimony which had been withheld from the commission, thus requiring an entirely new adjudication of the case. Reversals of the commission's rulings were frequent; in the entire period from 1887 to 1905 fifteen of the sixteen cases appealed to the Supreme Court were decided adversely to the commission. Even where the rulings of the commission were sustained it was found almost impossible for shippers to collect refunds from recalcitrant roads: down to 1897 shippers had succeeded in getting refunds in only five out of 225 cases. Indeed, the roads evaded the provisions of the act so successfully that Justice Harlan declared the commission to be a ' useless body for all practical purposes,' and the commission itself, in its annual report for 1898, confessed its failure. Nevertheless the principle of federal regulation of railroads was established, and the machinery for such regulation created. It remained for a later administration to apply the principle and make the machinery effective.

6. THE DECLINE OF STEAMBOATING

I saw the boat go round the bend,
Good-by, my lover, good-by!
All loaded down with gentlemen,
Good-by, my lover, good-by!

The generation that flung the iron tracks across the prairies and mountains of Western America witnessed the passing of one of the most characteristic and colorful phases of American life — steamboating. From the eventful day that Henry Shreve launched the *George Washington* on the Ohio (1817) until the Civil War, steamboats were the major means of inland transportation. For fifty years the waters of the Mississippi and her tributaries floated hundreds of steamboats great and small, their main decks laden with cotton and cattle, grain and furs, and ' fellows who have seen alligators and neither fear whiskey nor gunpowder '; their upper decks, which to the simple dwellers of the valley, appeared ' fairy structures of Oriental gorgeousness and splendor,' bearing planters, merchants, dandies, and fine ladies. Swift passenger steamers raced each other recklessly on the lazy Father of Waters or the riotous Missouri, lashing the waters into foam with their churning paddles. While the North and East followed the fortunes and compared the records of the Yankee clippers, the people of the interior bet their shirts on the *Robert E. Lee* and the *Natchez* in their historic race from New Orleans to St. Louis, won by the *Lee* in the record time of three days, eighteen hours, and fourteen minutes. Mark Twain has preserved for us the talk in the pilot-house, the jabber of the Negro roustabouts, the glamor of gilded cabins and the tense excitement of steamboat racing, in his immortal *Life on the Mississippi*.

It was in the decade of the 'fifties that river traffic reached its zenith. The value of the river trade at New Orleans was over $289 million in 1860. In those piping times before the war hundreds of new steamboats were launched on the inland waters, and on the outbreak of the conflict there were over 2000 of them on the Ohio-Mississippi system alone. Before the coming of the railroads the steamboat almost succeeded in tying the upper part of the great valley to the Cotton Kingdom. At one time 80 per cent of the pork and grain from Cincinnati was floated down the Ohio, and Southern Congressmen so far waived their strict-construction principles as to vote over $3 million for river improvements.

The greater part of the produce that came down-river was re-shipped by sea to Atlantic ports and to Europe. In the 1850's the Eastern trunk lines provided a short cut, right across this roundabout route, and struck at the fancy profits of river steamboating just as on the high seas the steamships got the cream from the clipper ships. As in that rivalry, so in this, the Civil War accelerated the movement tremendously. Southern shipping was destroyed, and some of the Southern ports as well, and control of the cotton trade passed to the North. The steamboat fought gallantly for life, readjusting itself to new circumstances, compromising with new conditions. As Mark Twain tells it:

Boat used to land — captain on hurricane roof — mighty stiff and straight — iron ramrod for a spine — kid gloves, plug hat, hair parted behind — man on shore takes off hat and says:
' Got twenty-eight tons of wheat, Cap'n — be great favor if you can take them.'
Captain says:
' I'll take two of them ' — and don't even condescend to look at him.

But nowadays the captain takes off his old slouch and smiles all the way around to the back of his ears, and gets off a bow which he hasn't got any ramrod to interfere with, and says:

' Glad to see you, Smith, glad to see you — you're looking well — haven't seen you looking so well for years — what you got for us.'

' Nuthin,' says Smith; and keeps his hat on, and just turns his back and goes on talking with somebody else.

But the river captains were not always as unsuccessful as this. Although passenger traffic almost disappeared from the inland waters, the opening up of the wheat, timber, and iron-ore regions of the Northwest brought an absolute, though not a relative, gain in freight traffic. In 1879 no fewer than 3372 boats and 1320 barges passed Winona, Minnesota, loaded down with lumber and grain, and 1880 witnessed the high-water mark of freight transportation for the lower Mississippi, with over a million bales of cotton unloaded at the levee at New Orleans. After that the decline of river shipping was precipitous. In 1880 two-thirds of the cotton at New Orleans came by river; by 1910 only one-tenth.

Shipping on the Great Lakes was a different story. The enormous iron-ore deposits of the Lake Superior region, the products of the forests, and the wonderfully productive soil of the Northwest now brought under cultivation, increased Great Lakes tonnage from 500,000 in 1869 to 2.6 million in 1920. In 1885 traffic through the newly built Sault Ste. Marie canals amounted to 3,256,628 tons; by 1920 it had increased to almost 80 million tons, surpassing the tonnage of both the Suez and the Panama Canals. Both river and Great Lakes transportation exhibited the same tendencies we have observed in the railroads: combination, absorption of the weaker by the stronger lines, and pressure for local and federal aid. Thus, for example, after the railroads had effectually destroyed traffic on the historic Erie Canal, New York State tried to rehabilitate it by the construction of a parallel Barge Canal, at a cost of $230 million.

With the decline of the steamboat passed another phase of American frontier life as unique and as rich as the cattle kingdom. Only a few rusty, battered stern-wheelers survive to bring down cotton, hops, and pipestaves from the tributaries and remoter reaches of the Black, the Arkansas, and the Ouachita rivers. There, as Roark Bradford's stories remind us, we may still see the Negro roustabouts toting heavy burdens with their peculiar shuffling gait, the ' coonjine,' and hear them sing:

De Coonjine, jine de Coonjine!
De Coonjine, jine de Coonjine!
Roll dat cotton bale down de hill,
De Coonjine, jine de Coonjine.

BIBLIOGRAPHY

1. GENERAL. G. D. Bradley, *Story of the Santa Fe;* Stuart Daggett, *Chapters on the History of the Southern Pacific;* J. P. Davis, *The Union Pacific Railroad;* Carl Russell Fish, *Restoration of the Southern Railroads;* Paul Gates, *The Illinois Central Railroad and Its Colonization Work;* Edward Hungerford, *The Story of the Baltimore and Ohio Railroad* (2 vols.); George Kennan, *Life of E. H. Harrison* (2 vols.) ; Edward C. Kirkland, *Men, Cities and Transportation, 1820–1900* (2 vols.); Wheaton Lane, *Commodore Vanderbilt;* Oscar Lewis, *The Big Four;* John Moody, *The Railroad Builders;* E. H. Mott, *Between the Ocean and the Lakes: the Story of Erie;* J. G. Pyle, *James J. Hill* (2 vols.) ; William Z. Ripley, *Railroads: Rates and Regulations* (2 vols.) and *Railroads, Finance and Organization;* E. L. Sabin, *Building the Pacific Railway;* Eugene Smalley, *History of the Northern Pacific Railroad;* Nelson Trottman, *History of the Union Pacific.*

2. RAILROADS AND THE WEST. Thomas Cochran, *Railroad Leaders, 1845– 1890;* Thomas Donaldson, *The Public Domain;* L. H. Haney, *Congressional History of Railways, 1850–1887;* J. B. Hedges, *Henry Villard and the Railways of the Northwest;* R. C. Overton, *Burlington West: A Colonization History of the Burlington Railroad;* J. R. Perkins, *Trails, Rails and War: The Life of Grenville Dodge;* Glenn C. Quiett, *They Built the West;* Robert E. Riegel, *The Story of the Western Railroads;* Robert L. Thompson, *Wiring a Continent.*

3. RAILROAD ABUSES AND REGULATION. Charles F. Adams, *Railroads;* Solon J. Buck, *The Granger Movement;* E. G. Campbell, *The Reorganization of the American Railroad System 1893–1900;* F. A. Cleveland & F. W. Powell, *Railway Promotion and Capitalization;* E. S. Corwin, *The Commerce Power Versus States Rights;* J. B. Crawford, *The Credit Mobilier of America;* Felix Frankfurter, *The Commerce Clause under Marshall, Taney and Waite;* Matthew Josephson, *The Robber Barons* and *The Politicos;* William Larrabee, *The Railroad Question;* Frederick Merk, *Economic History of Wisconsin;* Allan Nevins, *Emergence of Modern America;* W. Z. Ripley, *Railroads: Rates and Regulations;* Fred Shannon, *The Farmer's Last Frontier;* I. L. Sharfman, *The Interstate Commerce Commission* (5 vols.) ; Charles Warren, *History of the Supreme Court,* vol. 2.

4. THE DECLINE OF STEAMBOATING. Norman Beasley, *Freighters of Fortune;* G. A. Cuthbertson, *Freshwater: A Narrative of the Great Lakes;* G. E. Eskew, *Pageant of the Packets;* Walter Havighurst, *The Long Ships Passing;* W. J. Petersen, *Steamboating on the Upper Mississippi;* Herbert Quick, *Mississippi Steamboating;* Mark Twain, *Life on the Mississippi.*

5. DOCUMENTS. H. S. Commager, *Documents,* nos. 215, 294, 314, 318, 319; A. R. Ellingwood & W. Coombs (eds.) , *The Government and Railroad Transportation;* W. Z. Ripley, *Railway Problems.*

For further references, *Harvard Guide,* ¶¶ 197, 200.

The Economic Revolution

1. HAMILTON WINS

IT was the dream of Jefferson that his country — 'with room enough for our descendants to the hundredth and thousandth generation' — was to be a great agrarian democracy. 'While we have land to labor,' he wrote, ' let us never wish to see our citizens occupied at a work bench, or twirling a distaff,' for ' those who labor in the earth are the chosen people of God.' It is one of the ironies of our history that the Sage of Monticello himself, through his pet embargo, should have given the first impetus to factory development in America, and that his own party should have passed the first protective tariff. Within two generations of Jefferson's death the value of American manufactured products was almost treble that of the agricultural, and the spokesmen of big business were appealing to his laissez-faire principles against the regulatory ideals of his rival Hamilton. For a hundred years America progressed economically in the direction that Alexander Hamilton wished: that of a diversified, self-sufficing nation, ruled by the people who controlled the nation's prosperity. When the census of 1920 recorded over 9 million industrial wage-earners producing commodities to the value of some $62 billion, and over 50 per cent of the population crowded into towns and cities, surely Hamilton was able to collect some bets from Jefferson in the Elysian Fields!

By 1910 the United States, hitherto a debtor nation of extractive and predominantly agricultural industry, had become the leading industrial and manufacturing power in the world. The First World War made it the leading financial power as well. But the responsibilities which this achievement thrust upon the United States were but imperfectly apprehended by her people.

What were the bases of this economic revolution? It rested on seven or eight obvious factors: the discovery and large-scale exploitation of natural resources such as iron ore, coal, natural gas, copper, gold and silver, and oil; the application of science, invention, and machine power to the processes of extraction and manufacture; the recruitment of a labor supply sufficiently large, steady, and cheap for the purposes of industry; the construction of a transportation system adequate to the needs of an industrialized nation of continental dimensions; the growth of the domestic market and the immense expansion of foreign markets; the creation of capital at home and the ability to borrow abroad; and the perfection of new techniques of corporate organization such as trusts, pools, and holding companies. In addition, the economic revolution was fostered and aided by the Federal Government, positively through protective tariffs and other indirect subsidies, and negatively through a policy of laissez faire.

The consequences of this revolution are not so easy to summarize, but some of them are by now sufficiently clear. It enhanced national wealth, raised standards of living, produced cycles of prosperity and depression with attendant periodical unemployment, and eventually called in the government to redress the economic balance. It depressed agriculture and speeded up urbanization, encouraged immigration, and stimulated the more rapid growth of population. It led to mechanization and standardization of social life, modified social institutions such as that of the family and the church, and changed the intellectual outlook of the people. It plunged the United States into world affairs, economically and politically, shifted the balance of international payments, helped make the United States a creditor nation, and emphasized American nationalism. It led to a concentration of wealth and placed the control of the natural resources and the machinery of production and distribution in the hands of a small group of men, so creating, in a nation brought up on Jeffersonian principles, a whole series of antagonisms and difficulties which the teachings of the Fathers did little to illuminate.

It is one of the ironies of our history that the South, which cherished the agrarian tradition, and which had most to fear from the industrialization of America, should have greatly accelerated its coming by her secession and the consequent Civil War, and that after the war she should have embraced industrialism with a fervor equal to that of the North. It is now so evident what the Civil War accomplished in the long run that one school of historians, under the leadership of Charles Beard, has asserted that industrialization was the

conscious purpose of the Republican party or at least of those who
supplied the brains and the funds of the party during the era of
the war and the reconstruction. There is no persuasive evidence
either of purpose or of conspiracy. It was simply another case of what
Euripides said, through the chorus in the *Medea,* twenty-four centuries ago:

> And the end men looked for cometh not,
> And a path is there where no man thought;
> So hath it fallen here.

America, where society was fluid, and neither established Church
nor feudal aristocracy stood up for the ancient ways, and where success had always been its own justification, was the land first destined
for conquest by the industrial Moloch. Yet England, Germany, and
France, where all the forces of resistance were entrenched in government and society, all fell; Jefferson's America must fall sooner or
later. But the Civil War, like every great war, depressed the forces
which were declining in the nation's life, and gave tenfold vigor to
those which were active, flourishing, and positive.

The issue of the war, while not absolutely unfavorable to farming
and the farmer class, was so highly profitable to manufacturing and
finance that small-scale subsistence farming was doomed. War needs
enormously stimulated manufacturing and banking in the North,
and a complaisant government prolonged the high profits of the war
period with tariff and banking legislation largely dictated by the interests which were benefited. The hard-money policy of Congress
played into the hands of bankers and speculators, and the income
tax — never very burdensome — was shortly abandoned altogether.
At the same time the immigration policy of the government enabled
industry to import cheap labor and thus keep wages down. The construction of the great transcontinental railroads opened up new
markets for exploitation and furnished employment for additional
capital. Within thirty years the ultimate control of a large part of the
transportation system of the country was in the hands of a few banks
and corporations in the East.

Yet after all, the Civil War was a mere speeding-up process which
eliminated the weak and strengthened the strong. The fundamental
factors were the march of science and invention, the exploitation of
new resources of iron and power, and the availability of a labor force
both industrious and intelligent.

2. The Age of Invention

The United States Patent Office was created in 1790 largely through the efforts of one of the greatest American inventors, John Stevens of Hoboken, New Jersey. So numerous were the patents granted to ingenious Americans in the following years that in 1833, it was said, the head of the Patent Bureau decided to resign because he felt that everything of importance had been invented! Yet the 36,000 patents granted before 1860 were but a feeble indication of the flood of inventions that was to inundate the Patent Office in the years following the Civil War. In the period from 1860 to 1890 no less than 440,000 patents were issued, and in the first quarter of the twentieth century the number reached the staggering total of 969,428. The average number of inventions patented in any one year since 1900 equals or exceeds the total number patented in the entire history of the country before 1860.

While the beginnings of many important inventions can be traced to the late eighteenth and early nineteenth centuries, their application on a large scale to the processes of industry and agriculture came after the Civil War. Thus James Watt in Glasgow and Oliver Evans in Philadelphia developed the steam engine before the close of the eighteenth century, but it was not until the construction of the railroad system and the introduction of the De Laval steam turbine in 1882 that steam reached its peak in American development. And even at this time, the age of electricity was portended. A hundred years earlier Franklin, Galvani, and Oersted had experimented with electricity; Michael Faraday of England and Joseph Henry of the Smithsonian Institution had developed the principle of the dynamo as early as 1831, but it was not until after 1880 that the genius of Thomas A. Edison, William Stanley, Charles Brush, and a host of others revolutionized American life with the dynamo. Thus Charles Goodyear discovered the secret of the vulcanization of rubber in 1839, but it was not until the coming of the automobile that it assumed an important place in the economic order. Elias Howe invented the sewing machine in 1846, but it did not come into general use until popularized by Isaac Singer after 1860, and was first applied to the making of shoes by Gordon McKay in 1862. Eli Whitney of cotton-gin fame adapted for firearms the revolutionary principles of standardization and interchangeability of parts as early as 1798, but the general application of this principle to manufacturing, which has given precedence to American mass production, did not come until after the achievements of Kelly, Holley, and Bessemer ushered in the age of steel. Dr. N. A. Otto of Germany invented the internal combustion engine in 1876, but it did not mean much to the average American until Henry Ford in 1908 placed a motorcar on the market that was not a rich man's toy but a poor man's instrument.

A reference to some of the more important inventions developed since the Civil War will indicate something of their dominant place in modern American life. In the field of railway transportation the Westinghouse air brake of 1869, the Janney automatic coupler of 1871, the interlocking block signals introduced on American railroads in 1874, and the wide use of all-steel trains after 1900 ensured a higher degree of safety to passengers, while the introduction of the Pullman car, in 1864, changed traveling from an ordeal to a pleasure. The use of refrigerator cars after 1875 revolutionized the slaughtering and meat-packing industry of the country.

At the same time other forms of transportation — the electric railway, the automobile, and the airplane — were being developed. Between 1870 and 1880 Stephen Field and Thomas A. Edison in America and the Siemens firm in Berlin were perfecting the first electric railway, and inside of ten years there were 769 miles in operation in the United States. Then within a short time the streetcar, the elevated and subway train, all based upon the dynamo, accelerated that concentration of population in cities which is one of the characteristics of modern America. It is one of the dramatic things in our history that the steam railway dispersed population all over the land, and the electric railway and motorcar then pulled it, for working-day purposes at least, into a few hundred civic centers, and concentrated one-twelfth of the population of the country in a single metropolitan conglomeration, New York.

George Selden of Rochester, New York, had experimented with gasoline cars as early as 1879, but it was not until the turn of the century that the industry of Henry Ford and the genius of Charles Duryea bore fruit in the modern automobile. By 1920 Ford was making more than 6000 cars a day in his Detroit factories, and the automobile industry ranked first in the country in the value of its finished products. ' Darius Green and his flyin' machine ' was a favorite comic recitation in the gay 'nineties; ' God never intended man to fly ' was a serious conviction in 1900. Yet the vision of Samuel P. Langley and the perseverance of the Wright brothers and Glenn Curtiss lifted the airplane out of the experimental stage into the practical, around 1908. Langley died broken-hearted in 1906 at the failure of his flying machine; in 1919 two Englishmen, John Alcock and Arthur Brown, made the first non-stop trans-Atlantic flight from St. Johns, Newfoundland, to Clifden, Ireland; and in 1927 Charles Lindbergh made his non-stop flight from New York to Paris.

Other forms of communication, the telegraph, the cable, the telephone, and wireless telegraphy, helped to revolutionize modern life. It was in 1844 that Samuel Morse, a Yankee painter with a talent for mechanics, flashed over the wires from Washington to Baltimore the first telegraphic message: ' What hath God wrought! ' In 1856 the Western Union Company was organized and soon the whole country was crisscrossed with a network of wires. In 1858 the duplex telegraph was invented, and on the modern multiplex telegraph over 100,000 words can be transmitted within an hour. In 1866, the courage of Cyrus Field and the faith of Peter Cooper were rewarded, and communication between Europe and America became a matter of seconds; and in 1896 an Italian, Marconi, discovered the secret of wireless telegraphy.

In the centennial year of 1876 Emperor Dom Pedro of Brazil, attending the Philadelphia Exposition, sauntered up to the booth of young Alexander Graham Bell; he picked up the cone-shaped instrument on display there, and as he placed it to his ear Bell spoke through the transmitter. ' My God, it talks! ' exclaimed His Majesty; and from that moment the telephone became the central feature of the Exposition. Within half a century 16 million telephones had profoundly affected the economic and social life of the nation. The tempo of business life was enormously quickened, too, by the invention in 1867 of the typewriter by an erratic printer, Christopher Sholes of Milwaukee; of the cash register in 1897 by James Ritty; of the adding machine by Burroughs in 1888; of the dictaphone — an outgrowth of the phonograph — by Edison; and hundreds of other office and business accessories. The linotype composing machine invented by Ottmar Mergenthaler and first used by Whitelaw Reid in 1886 in printing the New York *Tribune,* Hoe's rotary press, the web press, and folding machinery, have made it possible to print as many as 240,000 eight-page newspapers in an hour; and the electrotype has worked a comparable change in the printing of magazines and books. This revolution — plus the benevolent policy of the postal authorities in allowing cheap postal rates — shortly made it possible for new magazines like the *Reader's Digest* and *Time* to reach a mass market heretofore unsuspected.

Just as science and invention revolutionized transportation, communication, business, and the conditions of urban living, so they wrought profound changes in agriculture and in the daily life of the American people. Postponing to another chapter the influence of the new machinery on the development of American agriculture, we merely note here a few of the inventions that carried the industrial revolution to the farm and the countryside. In 1868 a Scotch immigrant, James Oliver, perfected the chilled plow; in the 1870's John Appleby took out a series of patents for a twine binder; in 1881 Benjamin Holt turned out the first combined harvester and thresher, designed for the bonanza farms of the Far West; in 1888 A. N. Hadley invented a combined corn cutter and shocker; and after the opening of the twentieth century, gasoline power was widely applied to farm machinery. Thus the industrial revolution went beyond the walls of the factory and the streets of the city, transforming the basic processes of farming.

Meantime a host of inventions affected the daily life of the American people, especially those who flocked to the towns. The ' Wizard of Menlo,' Thomas Edison, gave the world the incandescent lamp in 1880, and within a few years millions of homes were supplied with better, safer, and cheaper light than had ever been known before. It was Edison, too, who perfected the talking machine — which was in time to become a music-playing machine — and in conjunction with George Eastman developed the motion picture. And D. W. Davis's invention of the refrigerator car in the late 1860's changed the diet of the American people, as did the deep-freeze of almost a century later.

The immediate material consequences of the application of machinery and of the inventive genius to the processes of extraction and manufacture are not difficult to ascertain. Machinery, science, and invention have enabled man to increase his productivity a hundredfold and — it may be added — to exploit with hundredfold efficiency the natural resources of the continent. Thus in 1830 it was estimated that the production of a bushel of wheat required something over three hours of human labor; by the turn of the century the application of machine labor — machine seeders and harrows, steam reapers and threshers — had reduced the time to less than ten minutes. Thus under primitive conditions of weaving it required 5605 hours of labor to produce 500 yards of cotton sheeting; by 1900 cotton manufacturers were able to produce the same amount with only 52 hours of human labor, and in the last 30 years machinery has materially reduced even this time requirement. One hundred and fifty years ago Adam Smith celebrated the efficiency of machine production with his famous illustration of the pin. Without machinery, he observed, a workingman would need a full day to make a single pin, but machinery then enabled a workingman to manufacture 5000 pins in a single day. A century later the great economist might have pointed his moral even more effectively, for then a single workingman could supervise the manufacture on automatic machines of 15 million pins each day.

Such illustrations could be multiplied indefinitely, but it is unnecessary to belabor a point so obvious. The economic and cultural consequences of machinery and invention, however, are less easy to determine. That improvements in the processes of manufacture produce technological unemployment cannot be denied; it is equally true that until our own generation, at least, invention and machinery created more jobs than they destroyed. It is asserted, too, that recognition of the importance of machinery has tended to subordinate men to machines and to dehumanize industry. It is not certain whether industry today is less humane than it was in the eighteenth or early nineteenth century or that other values have not compensated workingmen for the alleged blunting of the creative instinct. But if we look away from the question of cultural values to that of social consequences, it is clear that invention and scientific discoveries have presented to us a series of complex social problems and have required, inescapably, a series of readjustments.

Social institutions [a group of distinguished sociologists observed in the 1920's] are not easily adjusted to inventions. The family has not yet adapted itself to the factory; the church is slow in adjusting itself to the city; the law was slow in adjusting to dangerous machinery; local governments are slow in adjusting to the transportation inventions; international relations are slow in adjusting to the communication inventions; school curricula are slow in adjusting to the new occupations which machines create. There is in our social organizations an institutional inertia and in our social philosophies a tradition of rigidity. Unless there is a speeding up of social invention or a slowing down of mechanical invention, grave maladjustments are certain to result.[1]

Actually these years had witnessed a series of ' social inventions ' more important than 999 out of every 1000 mechanical inventions that managed to get a patent out of the Patent Office. Perhaps these should not be called ' inventions ' at all, but rather ideas about the nature and organization and administration of the economy, or about the relations of society and government to the economy. A dozen of these invite our consideration. Two of them can be ascribed to Henry Ford: the use of the ' assembly line ' technique that cut the time required to assemble a Ford car from 11.5 to 1.5 hours; and the idea that the way to make money was to reduce prices and reach out to mass markets. Closely allied to these was a third invention — that of modern advertising, which discovered that business was not limited to supplying familiar wants, but could itself create new wants which it then undertook to fill. This, in turn, led to, or required, a fourth concept, that of planned obsolescence: the recognition that if industry made things to last it would collapse, and that prosperity depended, therefore, on making houses, automobiles, and clothing that would rapidly deteriorate or become out-of-date. Associated with this was a new attitude toward money — an attitude which, to be sure, did not achieve fashionableness until the 1920's. Thrift, which had been both an economic necessity and a moral virtue, became increasingly unfashionable, and business undertook to persuade the American people that they had a moral duty to spend what they had and to anticipate future earnings by installment buying. A sixth invention was designed to make spending easier and more attractive: the chain store and the supermarket, both of them products of the twentieth century and both of them destined to have far-reaching social as well as economic implications. In this same category of ideas contributing directly to the felt needs of business was Frederick W. Taylor's elaborate formula for ' scientific management ' — a formula which brought more happiness to the hearts of industrialists and factory managers than to the workers.

Other inventions, or concepts, less clearly in the service or the interests of business, nevertheless served it well. There was, for ex-

[1] *Findings of the President's Research Committee on Social Trends,* Vol. I, p. xxvii.

ample, the legal fiction of 'liberty of contract' which gave a kind of sanctity to the wages and hours and conditions of work which industry could force workingmen to accept. There were the two far-reaching legal devices for the elimination of embarrassing competition: the trust, invented by Samuel Dodd of the Standard Oil Company; and the holding company, invented by James B. Dill and sanctioned by New Jersey law in 1888.

Finally there were three great ideas that lent themselves readily to institutionalization. First was the idea that it was possible to solve problems and to discover new ideas by co-operative research, which could be institutionalized not only in the laboratories of universities but also in the industrial research carried on by such corporations as Bell Telephone, General Electric, and Eastman Kodak. Second was the idea, imperishably associated with the names of the two greatest industrial leaders of the day, of organized philanthropy that should look not only to the alleviation of present suffering but to the solution of the basic problems of society and government. This idea was institutionalized in the Carnegie Endowment of 1911 and the Rockefeller Foundation of 1913, prototypes of scores of similar foundations today. And third there was the idea — or the policy — that government could use the instrument of taxation quite deliberately to encourage or discourage economic and social practices, to redistribute wealth, encourage a particular kind of investment, stimulate education or research or whatever seemed socially desirable. These ideas did not have full play until well into the twentieth century, but their origins can be found in the nineteenth.

3. IRON AND STEEL

'The consumption of iron,' wrote the great ironmaster, Abram S. Hewitt, 'is the social barometer by which to estimate the relative height of civilization among nations.' If this is true, the progress of civilization in the United States from the Civil War to World War I was indeed remarkable. The works of man in the United States of 1860 were constructed of wood and stone, with a little brick and iron; by 1920 this had become a nation of iron, steel, and concrete. The United States of 1860 produced less than one million tons of pig iron; 60 years later production had mounted to almost 36 million tons and the United States was easily foremost in the manufacture of

iron and steel products among the nations of the world. This transformation resulted from the exploitation of new resources of iron,
the discovery of new processes for converting it into steel, the contribution by the government of indirect subsidies in the form of a prohibitive tariff, and the rise of a group of ironmasters with a genius
for organization and production.

Iron ore had been mined in the Appalachians from early colonial
days; in the early nineteenth century the industry was concentrated
in eastern Pennsylvania and northern New Jersey. By the middle of
the century the Trenton Iron Works, controlled by the philanthropist Peter Cooper, was producing 35,000 tons of iron annually, but
even then the industry was moving westward to the Pittsburgh region
and geologists were hunting eagerly for new iron-ore deposits. In the
late 1840's enormous iron-ore deposits were discovered in the northern Michigan peninsula, and the year of the rush to the California
gold diggings witnessed a rush to the iron-ore fields around Mar-
quette scarcely less spectacular and no less significant for the American economy. Transporting the ore by rail was expensive; a water
route was essential. Far-sighted empire-builders had already proposed
a canal connecting Lakes Huron and Superior, but Henry Clay,
father of the ' American system,' pronounced the idea preposterous.
The driving energy of young Charles Harvey, however, built the
canal, and it was open to Great Lakes shipping in 1855. Soon a series
of new iron-ore discoveries more than justified the enterprise. In the
1870's the Menominee range in the upper Michigan peninsula was
opened, and then ten years later the vast Gogebic range lying just
below the western end of Superior. That greatest of lakes proved to
be rimmed by iron. In the mid-1880's Charlemagne Tower of Philadelphia opened up the rich Vermilion iron range on the north side
of the lake, pushed a railroad through from Duluth, and within a
few years was shipping one million tons annually through the Soo
Canal. To the west and north lay even richer iron-ore fields. As early
as 1844 lumbermen had stumbled on the Missabe (or Mesabi) iron
range west of the lake, but it was not until almost fifty years later
that the fortitude and faith of the seven Merritt brothers, and the or-
ganizational genius of Rockefeller, made the ore commercially available and guaranteed the supremacy of the American steel industry
for another half-century. For within a short time this region proved
to be the greatest ore producer in the world. The ore of the Mesabi

region had, in addition, two inestimable advantages: it lay on the surface of the ground and was therefore easy and cheap to mine, and it was remarkably free of those chemical impurities that made conversion into steel difficult. In 1860 the tonnage of vessels passing through the Soo Canal between Lakes Superior and Huron was 403,000, and in 1870 only 691,000, but in 1901 it was almost 25 million and in 1920, 58 million, and ore furnished the bulk of these increasing burdens.

The ore fields of the Lake Superior region are hundreds of miles distant from coal deposits, but cheap lake and railway transportation brought the two together. Ore and coal met in smelters of Chicago where the first American steel rails were rolled in 1865, and in Cleveland, Toledo, Ashtabula, and Milwaukee. Much of the ore was carried to Pittsburgh, center of the great Appalachian coal fields and strategically located with reference to water and rail transportation. In the 'eighties the iron and coal beds of the southern Appalachians were first exploited, and soon Birmingham, Ala., became a southern rival to Pittsburgh and Chicago, and in the twentieth century Colorado with apparently inexhaustible resources of minerals came to be the Western center of the steel industry.

The Bessemer and open-hearth processes and the application of chemistry and electricity to the making of steel were as fundamental as the new ore beds. The Bessemer process, which consists in blowing air through the molten iron to drive out the impurities, was anticipated in America by William Kelly of Kentucky, a prophet without honor in his own country; but it was not until Henry Bessemer had demonstrated the utility of his process in England that American iron manufacturers adopted it. The Bessemer process gave to American steel manufacturers one incalculable advantage: it was effective only where the phosphorus content of the iron ore was less than one-half of 1 per cent; comparatively little of the English iron ore was thus free from phosphorus, but practically all the ore of the Lake Superior region was. By 1875 Carnegie had recognized the advantages of the Bessemer process and adopted it in his great J. Edgar Thomson steel works. Shortly after the Civil War, Abram Hewitt had introduced to this country the Siemens-Martin open-hearth method of smelting, and despite the increased time and expense it involved, the superiority of the steel it produced was soon apparent. In 1880 ten times as much steel was manufactured by the Bessemer as by the open-hearth process, but by 1910 the latter method accounted for 20,780,000 tons of steel and the Bessemer for only 10,328,000 tons. The Bessemer and open-hearth processes not only made steel of superior quality and in enormous quantities but reduced the price from $300 to $35 a ton.

The application of chemistry to steel making introduced further economies and solved many technical problems. ' Nine-tenths of all the uncertainties were dispelled under the burning sun of chemical knowledge,' affirmed Andrew Carnegie. The introduction of electric furnaces has made it possible to produce hard manganese steel for automobiles and machines and ' high-speed ' steel for tools. Carnegie could boast with truth:

Two pounds of iron stone mined upon Lake Superior and transported nine hundred miles to Pittsburgh; one pound and one-half of coal mined and manufactured into coke, and transported to Pittsburgh; one-half pound of lime, mined and transported to Pittsburgh; a small amount of manganese ore mined in Virginia and brought to Pittsburgh — and these four pounds of materials manufactured into one pound of steel, for which the consumer pays one cent.

Well might the great ironmaster congratulate himself on this combination of engineering and technical skill, science and business enterprise. By 1890 the United States had passed Great Britain in the production of pig iron; by 1900 American furnaces produced as much steel as those of Great Britain and Germany combined; and this supremacy in iron and steel manufacture, once attained, was never surrendered. Yet it would be naïve to suppose that this supremacy was due entirely to the combination of raw materials, science, and business enterprise. An important element in the growth of the iron and steel industry was the protective tariff. From the beginning the ironmasters of Pennsylvania had insisted upon protection for their infant industry, and long after that industry had outgrown its swaddling clothes it continued to enjoy the blessings of government paternalism. It was this tariff which enabled American manufacturers to compete successfully with their English and German competitors and to pile up fabulous profits. Abram Hewitt, himself one of the greatest of the ironmasters, put the matter succinctly: ' Steel rails . . . were subject to a duty of $28 a ton. The price of foreign rails had advanced to a point where it would have paid (the manufacturer) to make rails without any duty, but of the duty of $28 a ton he added $27 to his price and transferred from the great mass of the people $50 million in a few years to the pockets of a few owners who thus indemnified themselves in a very short time, nearly twice over, for the total outlay which they had made in the establishment of their business.' Even Carnegie himself, when his company showed a profit of $40 million in a single year, felt that the time had come to abandon protection.

The story of the steel industry cannot be told without reference to those titans of industry who presided at its birth and nurtured its giant growth. Alexander Holley of Troy, N.Y., was the first to apply the processes of Kelly and Bessemer in America, and for a decade after the Civil War he was active in introducing these processes to steel manufacture throughout the country. Equally active in laying the foundations of the industry, and a pioneer in the use of the open-hearth process, was Abram S. Hewitt of New York, whose distinguished career in industry was matched by a career no less distinguished in politics. But the greatest leader in the American iron and steel industry and the archetype of the industrial age was undoubtedly Andrew Carnegie. A poor immigrant boy from Scotland, he followed and helped to perpetuate the American tradition of rising from poverty to riches, and his success he ascribed entirely to the political and economic democracy which obtained in this country. By dint of unflagging industry and unrivaled business acumen and resourcefulness, and especially through his extraordinary ability to choose as his associates such men as Charles Schwab, Henry Frick, and Henry Phipps and to command the devotion of his workmen, Carnegie built up the greatest steel business in the world, and retired in 1901 to chant the glories of ' Triumphant Democracy ' and to give away his enormous fortune of $450 million. This was made possible by the sale of his holdings to a rival organization, directed by the Chicago lawyer Elbert Gary and the New York banker J. Pierpont Morgan. The result was the United States Steel Corporation, a combination of most of the important steel manufacturers in the country, capitalized at the colossal sum of $1400 million — a sum greater than the total estimated national wealth of the United States in 1800. Seven hundred million of this capitalization was ' water,' but by 1924 the company had earned aggregate net profits of $2,108,-848,640 and no one could deny that its sponsors were vindicated in their business acumen.

4. TRUSTS AND MONOPOLIES

The organization of the United States Steel Corporation in 1901 came as the climax to an economic movement which had been under way for a generation. This was the concentration of industry and transportation in large units — a concentration taking various forms such as pools, trusts, corporations, and holding companies.

The advantages of combination were numerous. It tended to eliminate competition, removing many of the hazards of unregulated competitive production and facilitating great economies in manufacture, transportation, marketing, administration, and finance. Through combination, capital reserves could be built up as a means to stabilize or expand industry. Where combination was along horizontal lines — the combination, for example, of all manufacturers of rubber or of typewriters — it was easy to control production and price. Where combination was along vertical lines — the control, by one corporation, of all the elements of raw materials, transportation, manufacture, marketing, and finance of a single product, like the Ford car — it gave a degree of independence and of power that no isolated industry could expect to enjoy. In the steel and the oil industries, combination was both horizontal and vertical, and created industrial sovereignties as powerful as states.

The creation of an industrial monopoly did not require that all the plants under one control be concentrated at a particular place, but only that legal control be concentrated in the hands of a particular group. The primary legal instrument of this process was incorporation. Business corporations were not new in our history, but the widespread use of the corporate device came in the years after the Civil War. Incorporation gives permanence of life and continuity of control, elasticity and easy expansion of capital, limited liability for losses in case of disaster, the concentration of administrative authority and the diffusion of responsibility, and the ' privileges and immunities ' of a ' person ' in law and in interstate activities. With these immense privileges went responsibilities, but corporations often chose to recollect their privileges and ignore their responsibilities until these were called to their attention by legislative or judicial bodies.[2]

[2] See below, p. 218 ff.

Already as early as 1873 a Congressional Investigating Committee had announced that

The country is fast becoming filled with gigantic corporations wielding and controlling immense aggregations of money and thereby commanding great influence and power.

Yet at this time the trust movement was only in its infancy. In 1860, 140,433 manufacturing establishments turned out products to the value of $1,895,861,000. In 1900 the number of establishments had increased slightly to 207,514,[3] while the value of their products had increased eightfold to $11,406,977,000. Even more illuminating are the statistics of concentration of manufacturing in particular industries. In 1860, 2116 manufacturers of agricultural machinery turned out products which averaged $9845 in value; 40 years later the number of companies had been reduced by two-thirds to 715 but the average product had increased fifteenfold. In 1860, 542 iron and steel companies produced goods with an average value of a little less than $100,000; by 1900 the number of companies had increased very slightly but the average product had increased more than twelvefold. The number of establishments engaged in tanning and curing leather in 1880 was 5425; 20 years later this number had declined to 1306, but the value of the product had been multiplied five times.

If we direct our attention to the growth of large establishments at the expense of smaller ones, the statistics are equally significant. In 1904, 98 per cent of all the manufacturing establishments in the country had an annual output of less than $1 million, while but 1 per cent of the establishments boasted an annual output of over that sum. The former, however, turned out 62 per cent of the manufactured products of the country, while the latter turned out no less than 38 per cent, and of these no less than 33 manufactured products to the value of over $100 million each. Yet even this concentration was but a faint indication of the concentration that was to come in the first quarter of the twentieth century.[4]

The trust movement grew out of the period of fierce competition following hard upon the Civil War. Competing railways cut freight rates between important points, in the hope of obtaining the lion's

[3] The comparison here is only relatively accurate because the method of ascertaining what constituted a ' manufacturing establishment ' was changed.

[4] See below, Chap. XVII.

share of business, until dividends ceased and railway securities became a drug on the market. The downward trend of prices from 1865 to 1895, specially marked after 1873, put a premium on labor-saving machinery, on new processes of manufacture, and on greater units of mass production, just as did the downward trend of 1929–35. Pooling — 'gentlemen's agreements' between rival producers or railroad directors to maintain prices and divide business, or even to pro-rate profits — was characteristic of the period after 1872. But on the whole it was found so difficult to maintain these rudimentary monopolies that a 'gentlemen's agreement' came to be defined as one that was certain to be violated. Pools were forbidden in the Interstate Commerce Act of 1887, and the prohibitions of the Sherman law were extended to them in the Trans-Missouri Freight Association case of 1897. By that time they were no longer necessary.

In the 1880's pools were superseded by trusts — a form of combination in which affiliated companies handed over their securities to be administered by a board of trustees. The trust device was 'invented' by a Standard Oil lawyer, Samuel Dodd, in 1882; first adopted by the great oil combination it quickly became the pattern followed by combinations of every kind in the business world. The term itself shortly outgrew its purely technical meaning, and came to be used as a description of all large-scale combinations. According to the economist Eliot Jones, 'a trust may be said to exist when a person, corporation, or combination owns or controls enough of the plants producing a certain article to be able for all practical purposes to fix its price.' How much is 'enough' is something that not even the courts have been able to determine, and in some ways Mr. Dooley's definition of a trust is more accurate: 'A trust,' he said, 'is somethin' for an honest, ploddin', uncombined manufacturer to sell out to.'

The Standard Oil Company was not only the first trust and — as Allan Nevins observes — 'the largest and richest industrial organization in the world'; it was also in its relations to the industry it dominated, to its rivals, and to the public, the most characteristic, and it provides us with the classic example of the advantages and dangers, the costs and rewards of this form of organization. It was built on the exploitation of a great natural resource; it prospered by the astute application of technology and of scientific management; it combined control of almost every economic activity that affected its welfare — raw material, transportation, wholesale and retail trade, and finances; it was deeply involved in overseas operations; it influenced, perhaps corrupted, the political processes; it inspired, and frustrated, anti-trust legislation and litigation; it piled up unparalleled fortunes for its astute founders and beneficiaries, most of which were poured back into the channels of philanthropy.

Oil had provided light from almost the beginning of history; the America of the 1850's was lighted by candles, and by lamps that used whale oil, coal oil, and the petroleum that was just coming onto the market in small quantities: all of these were expensive. The Seneca Indians of northwestern Pennsylvania had long been familiar with the green viscous fluid that shimmered on the surface of the streams and pools of the Allegheny valley, and as ' Seneca oil ' it was sold by traveling medicine men to gullible purchasers at a dollar a bottle as a cure-all for most of the ailments to which the flesh is heir. In 1854 a group of New Yorkers and New Englanders who had organized the Pennsylvania Rock and Coal Company to exploit this surface oil sent a sample of it to Professor Benjamin Silliman of Yale College; his *Report on the Rock Oil or Petroleum from Venango County, Pennsylvania* which predicted the industrial possibilities of the petroleum was a kind of scientific charter for the oil industry. Four years later Edwin Drake, prospecting along Oil Creek, near Titusville, Pennsylvania, sunk a shaft some 70 feet into the ground and struck oil. The word echoed through the east like the cry of ' Gold ' in 'forty-eight. Within two years tens of thousands of frantic prospectors were sinking wells along the hillsides and in the gullies of the forsaken countryside that now came to be known as the ' Regions.' The life of the ' Regions ' was like that of a mining camp in Nevada or Montana. When a prospector struck oil at Pithole Creek, a town of almost 15,000 grew up overnight, with 50 hotels, theaters, and concert halls, dance halls and brothels, newspapers and churches; five years more and the place was deserted. As prospectors denuded the hills of trees they erected a forest of derricks; the open wells sometimes caught fire, and a pall of smoke hung over the valley at most times; railroads pushed their way into what had been an unprofitable wilderness, and enterprising oil men ran miniature pipelines to the swollen Allegheny, where the barrels were filled and floated down to Pittsburgh.

In nearby Cleveland a young commission-merchant, John D. Rockefeller — he was not yet twenty-five — watched the birth of the oil industry with shrewd understanding, and in 1863 sold out his commission business and acquired an oil refinery. Two years later his was the largest refinery in Cleveland, and in 1870 he and his partners incorporated as the Standard Oil Company of Ohio. Two years later he organized the South Improvement Company to do battle with, or absorb, his competitors in Pittsburgh and Philadelphia. With ample financial backing he weathered the panic of 1873; he bought up weaker competitors or forced them to their knees; he entered into arrangements with shippers that put him in an invulnerable position; he went into the pipeline business and soon had a virtual monopoly on the pipelines of the East. Within a decade he was master of the oil business of the nation.

What accounts for this spectacular achievement? Rockefeller's own explanation of it might apply to almost any one of the major industrial monopolies of the day:

I ascribe the success of the Standard to its consistent policy to make the volume of its business large through the merits and cheapness of its products. It has spared no expense in finding, securing, and utilizing the best and cheapest methods of manufacture. It has sought for the best superintendents and workmen and paid the best wages. It has not hesitated to sacrifice old machinery and old plants for new and better ones. It has placed its manufactories at the points where they could supply markets at the least expense. It has not only sought markets for its principal products, but for all possible by-products. . . . It has not hesitated to invest millions of dollars in methods of cheapening the gathering and distribution of oil by pipe lines, special cars, tank steamers and tank wagons. It has erected tank stations at every important railroad station to cheapen the storage and delivery of its products. It has spared no expense in forcing its products into the markets of the world among people civilized and uncivilized. It has had faith in American oil, and has brought together millions of money for the purpose of making it what it is, and holding its markets against the competition of Russia and all the many countries which are . . . competitors against American oil.[5]

What Rockefeller failed to mention in this testimony was what made Standard Oil feared and hated by his contemporaries. By playing competing railways one against another, he obtained rebates from their published freight rates, and even forced them to pay to

[5] Report of the U. S. Industrial Commission, I, 796–7 (1899).

the Standard rebates from competitors' freight payments. If competing oil companies managed to stagger along under such handicaps, they were ' frozen out ' by cutting prices in their selling territory until the Standard had all the business. The situation was so notorious that the Hepburn Committee of New York reported in 1880 that the Standard Oil

owns and controls the pipe lines of the producing regions that connect with the railroads. It controls both ends of these roads. It ships 95 per cent of all the oil. . . . It dictates terms and rebates to the railroads. It has bought out and frozen out refiners all over the country. By means of the superior facilities for transportation which it thus possessed, it could overbid in the producing regions and undersell in the markets of the world. Thus it has . . . absorbed and monopolized this great traffic.

The Pennsylvania legislature annulled the charter of the South Improvement Company almost as soon as it had been granted; and in 1892 the Supreme Court of Ohio dissolved the trust on the ground that it had violated its charter, only to have it reorganize under the more lenient laws of New Jersey a few years later.

Rockefeller himself sincerely believed that his work was beneficial not only to the oil industry but to society as a whole. He had in effect created a new industry; he had brought order out of chaos; he had immensely enhanced the wealth of the country; he had worked in harmony with Natural Law:

This movement [he said] was the origin of the whole system of modern economic administration. It has revolutionized the way of doing business all over the world. The time was ripe for it. It had to come. . . . The day of combination is here to stay. Individualism has gone, never to return.

And Samuel Dodd, who had invented the trust, was even more dithyrambic:

You might as well endeavor to stay the formation of the clouds, the falling of the rains, or the flowing of the streams, as to attempt by any means or in any manner to prevent organization of industry, association of persons, and the aggregation of capital to any extent that the ever-growing trade of the world may demand.[6]

The Standard Oil trust was soon followed by a number of similar business combinations. The movement for consolidation gathered

[6] Both quotations can be found in Allan Nevins, *John D. Rockefeller*, Vol. I, p. 622, and Vol. II, p. 358.

momentum in the 1880's and early 1890's, receded during the depression, and reached its climax in the years of prosperity around the Spanish War. Altogether in this period something over 5000 industrial establishments were consolidated into about 300 trusts or corporations, and of these no less than 198 were formed in the period from 1898 to 1902. The combined capitalization of the consolidations formed in the single year of 1899 was no less than $2,243,-995,000 — a sum greater than the total national debt at the time. The most important of the industrial combinations, besides the Standard Oil Company and the United States Steel Corporation, were the Amalgamated Copper Co., the American Sugar Refining Co., the American Tobacco Co., the United States Rubber Co., the United States Leather Co., the International Harvester Co., and the Pullman Palace Car Co., no one of which had a capitalization under $50 million.

Nor was the process of combination confined to the field of industrial manufacturing. In the exploitation of natural resources of coal, iron, oil, gas, copper, and timber, in transportation by land and by sea, in communication by telegraph and by telephone, in banking and finance, the same tendency toward combination and concentration was discernible. In no field was it more impressive, nor were its consequences more serious, than in transportation. By the turn of the century the major part of the railroad mileage and the railroad business of the country was in the hands of six groups: the Morgan and the Morgan-Belmont group controlling 24,035 miles, the Harriman group with 20,245 miles, the Vanderbilt group with 19,517 miles, the Pennsylvania group with 18,220 miles, the Gould group with 16,074 widely scattered miles, and the Hill group with 10,373 miles of track flung across the Northwest. Of the total railway mileage in the country only some 40,000 was still in the hands of independents. So, too, with other forms of transportation and communication: the expressing business of the country was apportioned out between three companies which by their united influence prevented the United States mails from taking parcels until 1912; the Western Union, until the rise of the Postal Telegraph, had a virtual monopoly on the telegraph business; and the American Telephone and Telegraph Company, capitalized in 1900 at one-quarter of a billion dollars, was already on its way to becoming the greatest of modern combinations.

   The role of New York City bankers in putting together many of
these great railroad and industrial combinations led many Americans
to fear that the greatest and most elusive of all trusts was in the making — the 'money trust.' The House of Morgan, which played a
leading role in substituting combination for competition, was exhibit A in this argument. In 1864 Junius Spencer Morgan, long a
leader in marketing American securities in England, placed his son
John Pierpont in charge of the American branch of the firm. Within
a few years young Morgan had tied up with the old banking house of
Drexel in Philadelphia, and soon was challenging the supremacy of
Jay Cooke and Company. The failure of Cooke in the panic of 1873
put the House of Morgan in a position of immense power. In the
1880's Morgan formed a close association with the New York Central
Railroad, and all through that decade and the next the House of
Morgan organized and reorganized railroads, extending its influence
through the South and even into the Far West where, after the turn
of the century, it formed an alliance with the Hill group. Meantime
Morgan interests had spread into many other fields, until in the new
century there was scarcely a major business which it did not touch
except those controlled or influenced by the rival Rockefeller interests. The House of Morgan had financed the Federal Steel Company, and in 1901 put through the gigantic deal that created the
United States Steel Corporation. Morgan had brought together the
warring manufacturers of agricultural instruments, and emerged
with the International Harvester Company. He organized American
shipping in the ill-fated Mercantile Merchant Marine combine, and
helped finance the American Telephone and Telegraph, the General
Electric, the New York Rapid Transit Company, and a dozen other
giants. He had spent — wasted, his critics said — millions on the attempt to consolidate the whole of New England transportation into a
single system. He and his associates controlled a dozen major banks in
New York and other leading cities — the Hanover, the Chase, the
First National, the Bankers' Trust, and others; more important, from
the fiscal point of view, they had tied up with three of the greatest
insurance companies — the New York Life, the Mutual Life, and the
Equitable. In 1912 the Pujo Committee reported that the House of
Morgan held 341 directorships in railroads, shipping, utilities, in-
surance, steel, copper, and iron, with resources of some $22 billion.
Was this a money trust?

COMMUNITY OF INTEREST AMONG RAILROADS IN THE UNITED STATES

Lines	Miles	Lines	Miles
I.—Vanderbilt Group		**V.—Gould Group**	
New York Central lines............	10,016	Missouri Pacific.................	5,326
Delaware, Lackawanna and Western..	951	Texas and Pacific................	1,599
Chicago and Northwestern..........	8,550	St. Louis and Southwestern........	1,265
	19,517	International and Great Northern...	825
		Denver and Rio Grande...........	1,675
II.—Morgan Group		Missouri, Kansas and Texas........	2,423
Southern Railway.................	6,807	Rio Grande Western..............	603
Mobile and Ohio..................	879	Wabash	2,358
Queen and Crescent...............	1,115		16,074
Central of Georgia................	1,835		
Georgia Southern and Florida.......	285	**VI.—Hill Group**	
Macon and Birmingham...........	97	Great Northern..................	5,185
Philadelphia and Reading...........	1,891	Northern Pacific.................	5,188
Lehigh Valley....................	1,404		10,373
Erie............................	2,271		
Central of New Jersey..............	677	**VII.—Belmont Group**	
Atlantic Coast Line................	1,812	Louisville and Nashville...........	3,235
	19,073	Nashville, Chattanooga and St. Louis	1,195
			4,430
III.—Harriman Group			
Illinois Central...................	5,000	**VIII.—Belmont-Morgan**	
Union Pacific.....................	3,029	Georgia Railroad.................	307
Oregon Railroad and Navigation Co...	1,137	Atlanta and West Point...........	87
Oregon Short Line.................	1,498	Western of Alabama..............	128
Chicago and Alton................	918		532
Southern Pacific..................	7,723		
Kansas City Southern..............	833	**IX.—Independent Systems**	
Chicago Terminal Transfer..........	107	Seaboard Air Line................	2,591
	20,245	Plant System....................	2,170
		Chicago, Milwaukee and St. Paul....	6,592
IV.—Pennsylvania Group		Rock Island.....................	3,819
Pennsylvania system...............	10,031	Chicago, Burlington and Quincy....	8,070
Buffalo, Rochester and Pittsburgh....	650	Atchison, Topeka and Santa Fe.....	7,808
Western New York and Pennsylvania..	633	St. Louis and San Francisco (K. C. M.	
Chesapeake and Ohio..............	1,476	& B.).......................	3,000
Norfolk and Western...............	1,671	Chicago & Great Western..........	1,023
Baltimore and Ohio system..........	3,156	Colorado Southern...............	1,142
Long Island......................	603	Pere Marquette..................	1,762
	18,220		37,977

SUMMARY

Groups	Mileage	Groups	Mileage
Vanderbilt.......................	19,517	Belmont........................	4,430
Morgan..........................	19,073	Belmont-Morgan.................	532
Harriman........................	20,245		
Pennsylvania.....................	18,220		108,464
Gould...........................	16,074	Independent.....................	37,977
Hill	10,373		

From the *Final Report* of Industrial Commission of 1900, p. 308.

If by a 'money trust' [reported the committee] is meant an established
and well defined identity and community of interest between a few
leaders of finance which has been created and is held together through
stock holdings, interlocking directorates, and other forms of domination
over banks, trust companies, railroad, public service and industrial corporations, and which has resulted in a vast and growing concentration of
control of money and credit in the hands of a comparatively few men —
your committee has no hesitation in asserting as a result of its investigation that this condition . . . exists in this country today.

These facts and figures spelled the doom of local industry, of the
local self-sufficient community. They bespoke the concentration of
manufacturing in large corporation-owned factories where economies
could be attained through the elimination of unnecessary duplication and through centralized control. They reveal an ever-increasing
specialization in industry, both of the community and of the individual laborer, and indicated an ever-increasing burden upon the transportation system of the country and greatly increased costs of distribution. The economic implications of these developments are writ large
in the census reports; the social implications can best be read in such
novels as Louis Bromfield's *Green Bay Tree,* or in Sherwood Anderson's *Poor White:*

In the days before the coming of industry, before the time of the mad
awakening, the towns of the Middle West were sleepy places devoted to
the practice of the old trades, to agriculture and merchandising. In the
morning the men of the towns went forth to work in the fields or to the
practice of the trade of carpentry, horse-shoeing, wagon-making, harness
repairing, and the making of shoes and clothing. They read books and
believed in a God born in the brains of men who came out of a civilization much like their own. On the farms and in the houses in the towns
the men and women worked together toward the same ends in life. They
lived in small frame houses set on the plains like boxes, but very substantially built. The carpenter who built a farmer's house differentiated it
from the barn by putting what he called scroll work up under the eaves
and by building at the front a porch with carved posts. After one of the
poor little houses had been lived in for a long time, after the children had
been born and men had died, after men and women had suffered and had
moments of joy together in the tiny rooms under the low roofs, a subtle
change took place. The houses became almost beautiful in their old
humanness. Each of the houses began vaguely to shadow forth the personality of the people who lived within its walls. . . . A sense of quiet
growth awoke in sleeping minds. It was the time for art and beauty to
awake in the land.

Instead the giant, Industry, awoke. Boys, who in the schools had read of Lincoln, walking for miles through the forest to borrow his first book . . . began to read in the newspapers and magazines of men who by developing their faculty for getting and keeping money had become suddenly and overwhelmingly rich. Hired writers called these men great, and there was no maturity of mind in the people with which to combat the force of the statement, often repeated. . . .

Out through the coal and iron regions of Pennsylvania into Ohio and Indiana, and on westward into the States bordering on the Mississippi River, industry crept. . . .

A vast energy seemed to come out of the breast of the earth and infect the people. Thousands of the most energetic men of the Middle States wore themselves out in forming companies, and when the companies failed, immediately formed others. In the fast-growing towns, men who were engaged in organizing companies representing a capital of millions lived in houses thrown hurriedly together by carpenters who, before the time of the great awakening, were engaged in building barns. It was a time of hideous architecture, a time when thought and learning paused. Without music, without poetry, without beauty in their lives or impulses, a whole people, full of the native energy and strength of lives lived in a new land, rushed pell-mell into a new age.[7]

5. TRUST REGULATION

It was not until the 1880's that the American public began to demand effective regulation of the trusts; and the problem of regulation was seriously complicated by the federal form of government. Corporations are chartered by the states, not the nation. The constitutions of many states contained general prohibitions of monopolies or conspiracies in restraint of trade — and it was Ohio that broke up the first great trust — but most state prohibitions were singularly ineffective, especially after the federal courts began to interpret broadly the congressional authority over interstate commerce and to limit severely the kind of regulation permitted the states under the first article of the Fourteenth Amendment.[8]

A corporation chartered by one state has the right to do business in every other state. Hence it was easy for corporations to escape the restrictions or limitations of strict state laws by incorporating in states such as New Jersey, West Virginia, or Delaware where the laws as to issuing stock, accountability of directors, and the right to hold

[7] *Poor White*, p. 131 ff. Reprinted by permission of the author and Viking Press.

[8] '. . . nor shall any State deprive any person of life, liberty, or property, without due process of law. . . .'

stock in other corporations were very lax. Furthermore a corporation is a ' person ' before the law, and enjoys the inestimable privilege of protection by the Federal Government from state legislation which might be thought to deprive it of property ' without due process of law.' And in its ordinary operations the average corporation came into contact only with state and municipal governments. Railway companies, except certain transcontinental lines, obtained all their privileges from the states, and were taxed only by them, but where they engaged in interstate commerce they could not be regulated by the states nor, after the Fourteenth Amendment, could they be assessed a confiscatory or even a punitive tax. Lighting and water companies and street railways, on the other hand, depended for their very existence on municipalities. Hence the corrupt alliance that was cemented after the Civil War between politics and business. Plain bribery was often practiced with municipal councils, which gave away for nothing franchises worth millions, while their cities remained unpaved, ill-lit, and inadequately policed. As Brand Whitlock, reform mayor of Toledo, Ohio, observed:

Out of these privileges to conduct public utilities, e.g., privileges to absorb social values, enormous fortunes were made, with all the evils that come with a vulgar newly rich plutocracy. To keep, extend, and renew these privileges, they must have their lawyers, and their newspapers to mislead and debauch the public mind; they must go into politics, organize and control the machines of both parties, bribe councilmen and legislators and jurors; and even have judges on the bench subservient to their will, so that the laws of the state and the grants of the municipality might be construed in their favor.

Opposition to trusts and monopolies, however, was not aroused so much by corruption and dishonest practices, which were looked upon with a leniency characteristic of the American people, as by the fear that the natural resources of the country were being ruthlessly exploited and rapidly exhausted by a group of men who used them for the aggrandizement of their own fortunes. Equally effective was the hostility of labor to powerful corporations, the opposition of the small businessman who in many instances was faced with the choice of surrender or ruin, and the widespread disapproval of the growth of great fortunes and the concentration of wealth.

All who recall the conditions of the country in 1890 [said Mr. Justice Harlan in the Standard Oil case] will remember that there was everywhere among the people generally a deep feeling of unrest. The nation had been rid of human slavery . . . but the conviction was universal that the country was in real danger from another kind of slavery, namely the slavery that would result from the aggregation of capital in the hands of a few . . . controlling, for their own advantage exclusively, the entire business of the country, including the production and sale of the necessities of life.

In the 'eighties began the first concerted attack upon monopolies and upon the theory and practice of laissez faire behind which monopolies flourished. This attack had been anticipated by such radicals as Wendell Phillips and Peter Cooper, but the animadversions of Henry George, Edward Bellamy, and Henry Demarest Lloyd reached a wider audience and inspired a more effective protest.[9] Soon the spokesmen of labor, which found itself at an enormous disadvantage in bargaining with gigantic corporations, took up the cry and, supported by small businessmen and by many plain people, forced the issue into politics. The Populist party was the first instrument of control, and Populist sentiment forced a dozen Southern and Western state legislatures to enact anti-trust laws. President Cleveland raised the issue in his tariff message of 1887 and the next year stressed it with even greater urgency.

As we view the achievements of aggregated capital [he wrote] we discover the existence of trusts, combinations and monopolies, while the citizen is struggling far in the rear or is trampled to death beneath an iron heel. Corporations which should be carefully restrained creatures of the law and servants of the people, are fast becoming the people's masters.

And that same year the platforms of both the major parties pledged them to oppose trusts and monopolies.

The result of this widespread agitation was the Sherman Anti-Trust Act of 1890. This famous law, the joint product of Senators Sherman of Ohio, Edmunds of Vermont, Hoar of Massachusetts, and George of Mississippi, passed Congress by an almost unanimous vote and received the signature of President Harrison 2 July 1890. Its central provisions are to be found in the first two articles:

1. Every contract, combination in the form of trust or otherwise, or conspiracy, in restraint of trade or commerce among the several States, or with foreign nations is hereby declared to be illegal. . . .

[9] See Chap. XVI, The Progressive Movement.

2. Every person who shall monopolize, or attempt to monopolize . . . any part of the trade or commerce among the several States, or with foreign nations, shall be deemed guilty of a misdemeanor. . . .

It is difficult to determine what was the precise purpose of this bill. At the time it was alleged that the purpose was to give to the federal courts common law jurisdiction over the crime of monopoly and conspiracy in restraint of trade; if so the law should have been interpreted in accordance with common law precedents to the effect that only *unreasonable* restraints of trade, or monopolies contrary to public interest, were illegal. But there were no such qualifications in the provisions of the act itself. Nor were there any definitions of the terms ' trust,' ' conspiracy,' and ' monopoly,' while the phrase ' in the form of trust or otherwise ' left much to the imagination. In all probability the provisions of the act were purposely couched in general and indefinite terms, leaving to the courts the task of interpreting and applying them. In thus placing responsibility upon the courts the legislators evaded the problem, and put off its solution indefinitely, for judicial regulation proved singularly ineffective. Indeed as a weapon against trusts, the Sherman law was a broken reed.

The first important case involving the interpretation and application of the anti-trust law was that instituted by the government against the whiskey trust. This suit, *United States v. Greenhut,* was summarily dismissed by the Court on the ground that no restraint in trade had been proven. Discouraged by this rebuff, the Federal Government abandoned the prosecution of the whiskey trust and allowed an indictment against the cash register trust to lapse. The attempt to dissolve the powerful sugar trust met with an even more serious reverse. In this case, *United States v. E. C. Knight and Company,*[10] the Court held that the mere control of 98 per cent of the sugar refining of the country did not in itself constitute an act in restraint of trade:

Doubtless [said Chief Justice Fuller] the power to control the manufacture of a given thing involves in a certain sense the control of its disposition, but this is a secondary and not a primary sense; and although the exercise of that power may result in bringing the operation of commerce into play, it does not control it, and affects it only incidentally and indirectly. Commerce succeeds to manufacture, and is not a part of it.

[10] 156 U.S. 1 (1895).

The vigorous dissenting opinion of Justice Harlan was fraught with significance, for he warned that

Interstate traffic . . . may pass under the absolute control of overshadowing combinations having financial resources without limit and audacity in the accomplishment of their objects that recognize none of the restraints of moral obligations controlling the action of individuals; combinations governed entirely by the law of greed and selfishness — so powerful that no single State is able to overthrow them and give the required protection to the whole country, and so all-pervading that they threaten the integrity of our institutions.

But the government was not similarly concerned, and Attorney-General Olney wrote complacently, ' You will observe that the government has been defeated in the Supreme Court on the trust question. I always supposed it would be, and have taken the responsibility of not prosecuting under a law I believed to be no good.'

Obviously, when the Attorney-General came so near as this to sabotaging the Sherman law, it could not be effective. In case after case the courts emasculated or nullified the act, leading Theodore Roosevelt to declare, later, that the ' courts . . . had for a quarter of a century been . . . the agents of reaction and by conflicting decisions which, however, in their sum total were hostile to the interests of the people, had left both the Nation and the States well-nigh impotent to deal with the great business combinations.' Yet responsibility for the failure of the anti-trust law should not be charged exclusively to the judiciary. The legislature failed to amend the act; the executive failed to enforce it. Altogether only seven suits under the Sherman Act were instituted by Harrison, eight by Cleveland, and three by McKinley; these suits were equally ineffective in reversing or even slowing down the movement toward consolidation. Only when the law was applied to labor unions — happily embraced in the ambiguous term ' or otherwise ' — was it somewhat effective; here the government won a series of victories. But more business combinations were formed during the McKinley administration than in any years of our history until the 1920's.

The persistent and uniform failure of the anti-trust laws and of the machinery of enforcement — failures which persisted into the Roosevelt and Taft administrations — inevitably gave rise to the suspicion that the whole trust-busting movement was something of a sham. Americans were, in fact, caught on the horns of a dilemma.

On the one hand their traditions and habits, drawn from a rural background, exalted individualism and idealized the independent yeoman, the self-reliant artisan and shopkeeper; they were firmly convinced that if you made a better mousetrap the world would really beat a path to your door! On the other hand all those forces of technology and science, which Americans so deeply admired, advertised the incomparable advantages of large-scale organization and the elimination of wasteful competition. Had the American people really wished to strike down trusts and liquidate monopolies, they could have done so easily enough by taxing them out of existence. Had they believed wholeheartedly in bigness and efficiency, they could have stimulated these by permitting consolidation to proceed without legal interference. But wanting the best of both worlds — the pastoral world of the eighteenth century and the technological world of the twentieth, they contented themselves with ceremonial gestures. They satisfied their moral scruples by donning the armor of anti-trust legislation and undertaking, from time to time, ritualistic skirmishes against the trusts; they satisfied their passion for efficiency and profits by permitting and even encouraging whatever combinations could be regarded as ' reasonable,' and by supporting them with lavish land-grants, protective tariffs, friendly incorporation laws, and easygoing tax policies. As Thurman Arnold observes:

In order to reconcile the ideal with the practical necessity, it became necessary to develop a procedure which constantly attacked bigness on rational, legal and economic grounds, and at the same time never really interfered with combinations. Such pressures gave rise to the anti-trust laws which appeared to be a complete prohibition of large combinations. The same pressures made the enforcement of the anti-trust laws a pure ritual. The effect of this statement of the ideal and its lack of actual enforcement, was to convince reformers either that large combinations did not actually exist, or else that if they did exist, they were about to be done away with just as soon as right-thinking men were elected to office. Trust busting therefore became one of the great moral issues of the day, while at the same time great combinations thrived and escaped regulation.[11]

It is perhaps the crowning irony of this situation that when Mr. Arnold himself was put in charge of the anti-trust division of the Department of Justice, he displayed quite exceptional zeal in the ritualistic enforcement of the Sherman Act!

[11] Thurman Arnold, *Folklore of Capitalism*, p. 208.

6. Big Business and Its Philosophy

The age was memorable not for statesmen, as in the early years of the Republic, or for reformers and men of letters, as in the middle years, or for soldiers as during the Civil War, but for titans of industry and masters of capital. Schoolboys today who have difficulty in remembering the names of any Presidents between Grant and Theodore Roosevelt identify readily enough the names of John D. Rockefeller, Andrew Carnegie, or John Pierpont Morgan. Few novelists of these years blunted their pens on the portrayal of the political scene, but the most distinguished novels of the age portray the world of business and industry, from Mark Twain's *The Gilded Age* and William Dean Howells's *The Rise of Silas Lapham* to Theodore Dreiser's *The Titan* and Henry James's *The Ivory Tower*. At no other period of our history has the businessman exercised a comparable power. Earlier generations had not offered sufficient scope to his talents; the twentieth century learned how to harness those talents to social usefulness. But during this half-century the great captains of industry and finance could say, with Frederick Townsend Martin, ' We are rich. We own America. We got it, God knows how, but we intend to keep it.'

Everything seemed arranged to enhance their sense of power and gratify their sense of magnificence. Nature and man conspired to prosper and to exalt them. A boundless continent lay open and ready for their exploitation; willing legislators gave them first chance, and amiable judges confirmed them in what they had won or seized. Gold and silver, copper and oil, forest and stream, all the bounties of nature which in the Old World had belonged, as a matter of course, to the crown — that is, to the commonwealth — were allowed to fall into the hands of strong men and powerful corporations. Clever lawyers worked out new devices for legal aggrandizement of wealth — pools, trusts, holding companies, and similar mechanisms; legislators made these devices available in their states, and co-operative courts held that the principle of interstate comity applied to corporations as to individuals. No income tax impeded the swift accumulation of private fortunes or deprived the rich of what they had earned by the sweat of their brows or the cunning of their brains; no labor laws or workmen's compensation laws interfered with their profits; no government officials told them how to run their business;

no public opinion penetrated the walls of their conceit. When they chose to extend their empires abroad — to Mexico, Cuba, or the Near East — a willing government gave their activities the protection of the American flag, and fought their battles for them. They had their own political system, their own culture, their own society, and even their own morality.

Political power and social prestige naturally gravitated to the rich. As a matter of course they exerted a decisive influence on politics and parties. They controlled newspapers and magazines; wrote party platforms; subsidized candidates; bought legislation and even judicial decisions. The greatest of them, such as John D. Rockefeller or J. P. Morgan, treated state governors as servants, and Presidents as equals, in the exercise of power. And as wealth came to dominate the political scene, so it came in time to dominate the social scene. The new rich moved into the great cities, hired architects to build French châteaux or English country houses on New York's Fifth Avenue or Cleveland's Euclid Avenue or San Francisco's Nob Hill, and undertook to indulge themselves in luxuries which Benjamin Franklin had called ' more curious than useful ' and which Thorstein Veblen was to designate as ' conspicuous waste.' They filled their houses with paintings and tapestries from the Old World to delight the eye and gratify their pride; they staffed their palaces with innumerable servants and gave parties which they thought were like those of Versailles; they patronized museums and the opera. They built Gothic churches, and listened gladly to the gospel as expounded by a Bishop Lawrence who assured them that ' godliness is in league with riches '; they built schools like Groton to train up an elite that should govern America as Eton and Winchester governed England. Thus strengthened they crashed the gates of society. ' I remember very well,' wrote Frederick Martin, ' the first great march of the suddenly rich upon the capitals of the nation. Very distinctly it comes back to me with what a shock the fact came home to the sons and daughters of what was pleased to call itself the aristocracy of America, that here marched an army better provisioned, better armed with wealth, than any other army that had ever assaulted the citadels of Society.'

Business even formulated a philosophy which drew impartially on history, law, economics, religion, and biology in order to justify its acquisitiveness and its power: we give this philosophical potpourri the name Social Darwinism. At its most full blown it was made up of five not wholly harmonious ingredients. First, the principle drawn from Jeffersonian agrarianism and Manchester liberalism, that that government was best which governed least, and that government should keep its hands off business. ' All experience,' wrote the most vigorous of the Social Darwinists, Professor William Graham Sumner of Yale, ' is against state regulation and in favor of liberty. The freer the civil institutions are, the more weak and mischievous state regulation is.' Second, the principle of the peculiar sanctity of property — including, of course, corporate charters and franchises — in our constitutional and economic system. This principle was, presumably, written into the Fourteenth Amendment's prohibition of the deprivation of life, liberty, and property without due process of law, and was applied with uncompromising rigor by jurists like Justice Field, and lawyers like Joseph Choate, long leader of the American bar. Third, the quasi-religious principle that the acquisition of wealth was a mark of divine favor, and that the rich therefore had a moral responsibility both to get richer and to direct the affairs of society. At its most grotesque, this appeared in the notorious observation by President George Baer of the Reading Railroad that the rights of labor could safely be trusted to those whom God in His infinite wisdom had given control of the property of the country. Judge Elbert Gary, who had refused to talk to representatives of steel workers who worked twelve hours a day seven days a week in his mills, put it more simply: ' Moral principles,' he said, ' are the base of all business success.' Distinguished churchmen, too, endorsed this view; Bishop Lawrence, for example, assured his parishioners that ' in the long run it is only to the man of morality that wealth comes.'

Fourth was the principle of white, and Nordic, supremacy which seemed to justify the exploitation of the Negro by Southern whites, and of newly arrived immigrants from Italy, Poland, Rumania and other non-Nordic countries by industry, and which, on a larger scale, was invoked to throw a halo around imperialism and the White Man's Burden. The findings of social workers and the teaching of sociologists commonly supported this principle of Nordic supremacy, for somehow all of these findings went to show that ' new ' immigrants and Negroes contributed far more than their share to crime and vice and poverty and disease. That such findings indicated more a measure of opportunity than of character would not occur to a Carnegie or a Rockefeller who had made their own opportunities.

Fifth, and perhaps most persuasive of all, was the pseudo-scientific principle of 'the survival of the fittest,' derived from Darwinian biology and applied to the affairs of mankind by the great English philosopher Herbert Spencer and by his many American disciples. ' If we do not like the survival of the fittest,' wrote Professor Sumner, ' we have only one possible alternative, and that is the survival of the unfittest. The former is the law of civilization; the latter is the law of anti-civilization.' When Henry Demarest Lloyd launched his first attack on the Standard Oil Company, the president of one of the great railroads wrote to a distinguished journalist, Charles Atkinson, ' The donkeys who can't see the operation of natural laws in fixing the rates of transportation now, rely mainly on the Standard Oil Company as an example. It would answer an extremely useful purpose if as able a pen as yours would show what I suppose to be the fact, that the Standard Oil Company is simply a product of natural laws which it is not safe to touch.' John D. Rockefeller stated his own case even more simply. ' The American beauty rose,' he said, ' can be produced in the splendor and fragrance which bring cheer to its beholder only by sacrificing the early buds which grow up about it. This is not an evil tendency in business. It is merely the working out of a law of Nature and of God.' Neither Rockefeller nor the American public seemed to realize that what the social reformers wanted was precisely the kind of intervention that produced the American beauty rose; after all it was not nature but man who sacrificed the buds in order to get the perfect flowers!

These doctrines of Social Darwinism were popularized from the pulpit, the press, and in popular literature. No one was more influential here than Edward Youmans, founder and editor of the immensely influential *Popular Science Monthly* which skillfully submitted the scientific basis and social implications of Spencer's doctrines. And to generations of American boys, Horatio Alger supplied an endless series of stories of poor boys who made good by hard work and honesty and marrying the boss's daughter. In the end all this added up not so much to an apology for business as to the inescapable conclusion that America itself was a business civilization — and should be kept that way.

BIBLIOGRAPHY

1. GENERAL HISTORIES. Victor S. Clark, *History of Manufactures in the United States 1860–1914;* Thomas Cochran & William Miller, *The Age of Enterprise;* Harold U. Faulkner, *The Quest for Social Justice;* Louis M. Hacker, *Triumph of American Capitalism;* Samuel P. Hays, *The Response to Industrialism;* Edward C. Kirkland, *A History of American Economic Life* and *Industry Comes of Age: Business, Labor and Public Policy, 1860–1897;* Lewis Mumford, *Technics and Civilization;* Sidney Ratner, *American Taxation as a Social Force;* Fred A. Shannon, *America's Economic Growth;* Ida Tarbell, *The Nationalization of Business;* Chester Wright, *Economic History of the United States.*

2. SPECIAL INDUSTRIES AND INDUSTRIAL LEADERS. Frederick L. Allen, *The Great Pierpont Morgan;* R. A. Clemen, *American Live Stock and Meat Industry;* A. H. Cole, *The American Wool Manufacture* (2 vols.) ; Lewis Corey, *The House of Morgan;* Richard Current, *The Typewriter and the Men Who Made It;* Paul de Kruif, *Seven Iron Men;* Paul Giddens, *The Birth of the Oil Industry* and *The Standard Oil Company of Indiana;* Burton J. Hendrick, *Andrew Carnegie* (2 vols.) ; Ralph and Muriel Hidy, *Pioneering in Big Business: The Standard Oil Company of New Jersey;* William T. Hutchinson, *Cyrus McCormick* (2 vols.) ; Meyer Jacobstein, *The Tobacco Industry;* Marquis James, *Alfred I. DuPont;* Henrietta Larson, *Jay Cooke: Private Banker;* John Moody, *Masters of Capital;* S. E. Morison, *The Ropemakers of Plymouth;* Allan Nevins, *John D. Rockefeller: The Heroic Age of American Enterprise* (2 vols.) and *Abram Hewitt: With Some Account of Peter Cooper;* Allan Nevins & F. E. Hill, *Henry Ford* (3 vols.) ; C. C. Rister, *Oil: Titan of the Southwest;* F. P. Wirth, *Discovery and Exploitation of the Minnesota Iron Lands.*

3. TRUSTS AND TRUST REGULATION. A. A. Berle & G. S. Means, *Modern Corporation and Private Property;* J. D. Clark, *Federal Trust Policy;* John R. Commons, *Legal Foundations of Capitalism;* Eliot Jones, *The Trust Problem in the United States;* Dexter Keezer & Stacy May, *Public Control of Business;* O. W. Knauth, *The Policy of the United States towards Industrial Monopoly;* Harry W. Laidler, *Concentration of Control in American Industry;* Henry D. Lloyd, *Wealth Against Commonwealth;* John Moody, *The Truth About the Trusts;* G. W. Nutter, *Extent of Enterprise Monopoly;* W. Z. Ripley, *Trusts, Pools, and Corporations;* H. R. Seager & G. A. Gulick, *Trust and Corporation Problems;* Hans B. Thorelli, *Federal Anti-Trust Policy: Origin of an American Tradition;* Albert Walker, *History of the Sherman Law.*

4. INVENTIONS. Roger Burlingame, *Engines of Democracy;* T. K. Derry & Trevor Williams, *A Short History of Technology to* A.D. *1900;* Siegfried Giedion, *Mechanization Takes Command;* Harry Jerome, *Mechanization in Industry;* Matthew Josephson, *Edison;* Waldemar Kaempffert, *Popular History of American Inventions* (2 vols.) ; J. W. Oliver, *History of American Technology;* Michael Pupin, *From Immigrant to Inventor;* Holland Thompson, *The Age of Invention.*

5. BIG BUSINESS AND ITS PHILOSOPHY. Charles Barker, *Henry George;* F. B. Copley, *Frederick Taylor: Father of Scientific Management;* Jerome Davis, *Capitalism and Its Culture;* Sigmund Diamond, *The Reputation of the American*

Businessman; Joseph Dorfman, *Economic Thought in American Civilization,* vol. 3; Sidney Fine, *Laissez Faire and the General Welfare State;* E. L. Herrmance, *The Ethics of Business;* Richard Hofstadter, *Social Darwinism in the United States;* Edward C. Kirkland, *Business in the Gilded Age: The Conservative's Balance Sheet* and *Dream and Thought in the Business Community 1860–1900;* Robert G. McCloskey, *American Conservatism in the Age of Enterprise;* William G. Sumner, *The Forgotten Man and Other Essays;* Thorstein Veblen, *Theory of Business Enterprise;* Lester Ward, *Psychic Factors in Civilization;* Irvin Wyllie, *The Self-Made Man in America.*

6. DOCUMENTS. H. S. Commager, *Documents,* nos. 215, 231, 320, 339; H. U. Faulkner & F. Flügel, *Readings in the Economic History of the United States.*

For further references, *Harvard Guide,* ¶¶ 202, 206, 210.

Labor

1. GENERAL CONSIDERATIONS

THE efforts of society and government to adjust themselves to the rise of big business and the nationalization of industry were energetic and fairly successful; the efforts of labor to effect a similar adjustment were convulsive and on the whole unsuccessful. American labor was unable to achieve a satisfactory adjustment to industrial capitalism during the years following the Civil War largely because it was unable to act as a unit, or to agree upon the nature of the problem, the instruments of action, or the proper objectives. Throughout the nineteenth century and well into the twentieth, labor debated whether to accept or reject capitalism, whether to welcome or sabotage inventions, whether to trust laissez faire or seek government patronage, whether to organize on a broadly industrial or on a narrow craft basis, whether to embrace unskilled as well as skilled, Negro as well as white workers, within its organizations.

Although labor is fundamental to industry, the labor problem has been set by industry rather than the other way around. From the beginning of the industrial revolution in America, labor has been exposed to a series of influences which if they did not fix its course of development may nevertheless be said to have conditioned it. Some of these influences date back to the beginnings of the factory system in the early years of the Republic; others appeared after the Civil War; all made themselves felt with augmented force in the years after 1890. Among these influences the most important were the increased mechanization of industry, the evolution of the giant corporation as employer, the nationalization of much of industry and of the transportation system, the decline of agriculture as a potential safety valve, the change in the character of internal migration and of immigration, and a popular psychology which regarded unsympathetically the efforts of labor to achieve its objectives and which persistently refused to regard the labor problem realistically or to admit the existence of class divisions.

During most of the nineteenth century the benefits of the application of science and invention to industry redounded to the advantage of society as a whole, but more especially to capital rather than to labor. Machinery made enormous savings in manufacturing and a vast increase in productivity, but only a small proportion of these savings was passed on to labor in the form of wages, and the decrease in the hours of labor did not keep pace with the increase in productivity. Such decreases as were wrested from employers were in part nullified by the increasing fatigue and nervous strain of modern machine labor. As early as 1886 the United States Commissioner of Labor, Carroll Wright, observed that ' If the question should be asked, has the wage-earner received his equitable share of the benefits derived from the introduction of machinery, the answer must be, no,' and not until a generation later was there any justification for an answer to the contrary.

That the increasing mechanization of industry had in general the effect of lowering the standards of skilled labor, there seems to be no reason to doubt. The skill and experience of the craftsman no longer had their old-time value or gave the skilled worker any considerable advantage over the unskilled. It takes little training to tend machines. In 1922 Henry Ford estimated that 43 per cent of the jobs in his automobile factories required only one day of training, and only 15 per cent of the jobs required as much as one month of training.

The creative instinct of craftsmanship was eroded, and working-men were more and more reduced to a mere part of a mechanical process, automata performing a hundred times a day some monotonous operation. Upton Sinclair described it:

Each one of the hundreds of parts of a mowing machine was made separately, and sometimes handled by hundreds of men. Where Jurgis worked there was a machine which cut and stamped a certain piece of steel about two square inches in size; the pieces came tumbling out upon a tray, and all that human hands had to do was to pile them in regular rows, and change the trays at intervals. This was done by a single boy, who stood with eyes and thoughts centered upon it, and fingers flying so fast that the sounds of the bits of steel striking upon each other was like the music of an express train as one hears it in a sleeping car at night. . . . Thirty thousand of these pieces he handled every day, nine or ten millions every year — how many in a lifetime it rested with the gods to say. Near by him sat men bending over whirling grind-stones, putting the finishing touches to the steel knives of the reaper; picking them out of a basket with the right hand, pressing first one side and then the other against the stone, and finally dropping them with the left hand into another basket. One of these men told Jurgis that he had sharpened three thousand pieces of steel a day for thirteen years.[1]

It was because artisans recognized that machinery threatened their only asset — skill — that they turned, in self-protection, to organization along craft lines, and it was from the ranks of such groups as the shoemakers, tailors, iron-molders, typesetters, stonecutters, cigar-makers, and machinists, that the impetus for organization first came. The Knights of St. Crispin, for example, was composed of shoe-makers, the National Labor Union was organized by iron-molders, and the Knights of Labor by garment-cutters, while the American Federation of Labor had its genesis among cigar-makers.

As machinery came to represent a large part of capital investment, it was thought necessary to accommodate the worker to machinery rather than machinery to the worker. Thus if economy required that machines be run twenty-four hours a day and seven days a week, workers were expected to adjust themselves to that requirement regardless of the social desirability of such a schedule. Furthermore machinery constituted a fixed capital charge which could not well be reduced; when economies were necessary there was a temptation to effect them at the expense of labor. Finally the introduction of increasingly efficient machinery resulted in throwing large groups of laborers out of work. While most of these were eventually absorbed in other industries, and while in the long run mechanization more than balanced losses in factory jobs by increases in clerical and service jobs, the process worked severe hardship on the individual workingman and was accompanied by a staggering social waste. At the same time the increasing efficiency of machinery sometimes resulted in the production of more commodities than the public could or cared to buy, thus creating unemployment and lowering of wages and standards of labor. Industrial unemployment was, of course, a product of the machine age, and grew proportionately with the development of the machine economy until governments intervened to control it.

[1] Upton Sinclair, *The Jungle.*

The rise of the giant corporation as employer had consequences for labor almost as serious as those which flowed from the mechanization of industry. Such corporations subjected the laborer to a new set of circumstances, impersonal and complex as those introduced by the machine. The fiction that a corporation was a person had a certain legal usefulness, but every laborer knew that the distinguishing characteristic of a corporation was precisely its impersonality. A person was responsible for his acts to his own conscience; a corporation was responsible to its stockholders. As individuals, the directors of a corporation might be willing to make concessions to labor, even at personal sacrifice; but as directors they could not indulge themselves in this pleasure, for their first duty was to maintain the solvency of their business and dividend payments. Stockholders, too, might be willing to make concessions, but the gap between ownership and management was so great, and the machinery for bridging that gap so cumbersome, that it was almost impossible for stockholder opinion to become articulate or effective.

It was in relation to the bargaining power of labor that the change from individual employer to impersonal corporation was most keenly felt. It was one thing for an iron-puddler in the mid-nineteenth century to strike a bargain about wages and hours with the owner of a small ironworks; it was a very different thing for a ' roller ' in the twentieth century to strike a bargain with the United States Steel Corporation. Theodore Roosevelt put the matter with characteristic clarity:

The old familiar relations between employer and employee were passing. A few generations before, the boss had known every man in his shop; he called his men Bill, Tom, Dick, John; he inquired after their wives and babies; he swapped jokes and stories and perhaps a bit of tobacco with them. In the small establishment there had been a friendly human relationship between employer and employee.

There was no such relation between the great railway magnates, who controlled the anthracite industry, and the one hundred and fifty thousand men who worked in their mines, or the half million women and children who were dependent upon these miners for their daily bread. Very few of these mine workers had ever seen, for instance, the president of the Reading Railroad. . . . Another change . . . was a crass inequality in bargaining relation between the employer and the individual employee standing alone. The great coal-mining and coal-carrying companies, which employed their tens of thousands, could easily dispense with the services of any particular miner. The miner, on the other hand, could not dispense with the companies. He needed a job; his wife and children would starve if he did not get one. What the miner had to sell — his labor — was a perishable commodity; the labor of today — if not sold — was lost forever. Moreover, his labor was not like most commodities — a mere thing; it was part of a living, breathing human being. The workman saw that the labor problem was not only an economic but also a moral, a human problem.[2]

It was in response to this situation that laborers organized ' to secure,' as Roosevelt says, ' not only their economic but their simple human rights.' Here, too, the giant corporations possessed immense advantages not vouchsafed to the small employers. Great corporations representing the combined wealth and strength of scores of companies and thousands of stockholders could afford to fight a strike for months, import strike-breakers, hire Pinkerton detectives, carry their battle through the courts with highly paid lawyers, buy the press and influence politicians, and, if necessary, close down their plants and starve the workers into submission. Until the rise of the C.I.O., labor was least successful in building up and maintaining unions in those industries dominated by great corporations — the coal, the iron and steel, the oil, and the automobile industries.

At the same time the giant corporation sometimes exercised an industrial dominion menacing not only to labor but to American society. Corporations were able to acquire mining or manufacturing properties and, not infrequently, whole towns and counties; they became, to all intents and purposes, sovereignties within states. Many textile companies in the South came to own the villages in which mills are located — the streets, houses, stores, schools, churches, and utilities — and to control, inevitably, the local administration and police; the inhabitants of such mill villages, most of them operatives in the mills, could remain and work only on sufferance of the mill owners. Similar conditions, in even more aggravated form, were to be found in Colorado, Kentucky, and Pennsylvania mining communities and in many of the lumber camps of the South and the West. In 1914 a United States congressman testified that he had to have a pass to enter one of the towns of Colorado situated on the property of the Colorado Fuel and Iron Company; in the 1920's the Constitution was suspended in Harlan County, Kentucky, and as late as 1933 the Secretary of Labor, Frances Perkins, was forcibly prevented from

2 *Theodore Roosevelt: An Autobiography*, Scribners, pp. 470–71.

speaking in the streets of a Pennsylvania coal town. Thus there developed in certain major industries a species of industrial feudalism in which the laborer occupied a position in many respects less secure than that of the medieval serf.

In two ways the nationalization of industry and transportation operated to the disadvantage of labor. It made labor competition nation-wide, and tended to establish labor standards at the lowest common denominator. With flexibility of capital and an efficient transportation system, it became possible for some industries to take advantage of cheap labor wherever it was available and thus largely to eliminate the influence of local conditions and to nullify the gains which labor might make under such conditions. The shift of the textile industry from New England to the South is a case in point, but such shifts were not generally necessary. Labor was as mobile as capital, and the importations of cheap labor from southern Europe to the industrial East, and of cheap Negro labor from the South to the North, were continuous and effective. In the second place the nationalization of industry and transportation, and the growing interdependence of industries, tended to make labor disturbances national rather than local in character, thus bringing into play forces of public opinion and of government which were, before the New Deal, more likely to be hostile to labor than to capital. A reduction of wages in a single corporation might affect tens of thousands of workers in widely separated parts of the country and a strike against a corporation, such as the Pullman strike of 1894 or the coal strike of 1902 or the steel strike of 1919, affected not only the workers and stockholders in that industry but the workers and stockholders in scores of related industries, and became, inevitably, a matter of grave national concern. Thus the three great railroad strikes of 1877, 1894, and 1922 were all national in character and in effect, and on each occasion the Federal Government intervened in a manner harmful to the interests of the strikers.

The extent to which agriculture and the frontier functioned as safety valves for labor discontent is difficult to determine because we have no statistics on motivation. Probably only a small percentage of discontented laborers actually threw up their jobs and trekked to the open lands of the West. There is little evidence that the existence of cheap farm land operated in any effective fashion to raise wages or standards of labor. For the workingman, indeed, the alternative between industrial labor and farming was rarely a real one; after 1865 it became almost wholly unreal. Throughout the period of industrialism the movement of population — including, of course, European immigrants — from the country to the city has been greater than the movement from the city to the country, and the movement from agriculture to industry greater than that from industry to farming.

Despite these essential qualification of the safety-valve theory, the significance of open land to labor cannot be wholly ignored. The real significance of the frontier to labor is that it attracted to agriculture substantial numbers of immigrants and discontented or adventurous farm boys from the East and the South who might otherwise have been forced into the ranks of industrial labor. The passing of good cheap farm land in the 1890's, the increasing specialization and mechanization of agriculture, the rising investment and overhead costs and the declining economic and social returns, all combined to eliminate agriculture as an effective alternative to industrial labor for the immigrant and the farmers and villagers of the East in the twentieth century. The 'new' immigrants from Italy, Russia, and Poland settled down in the mining and industrial regions of the East; the sons and daughters of Eastern and Southern farmers moved to the city instead of going West; and when in the second decade of the new century Negroes began to stream to the North in large numbers, it was invariably to the great cities and industrial regions. All of these groups swelled the ranks of industrial labor, and made the labor problem increasingly acute.

Immigration presented the most urgent problem with which labor had to contend, and the most conspicuous. In the single generation from 1880 to 1910 almost 18 million persons entered the United States; most of the men were farmers or unskilled workers from the countries of southern and eastern Europe. Unable or unwilling to undertake farming, these 'new' immigrants took what work they could find in the factories and sweatshops of Northern cities, or in the mines of Pennsylvania or Illinois or Michigan. Even subtracting the large number of immigrants who returned to their Old World homes, and the women and children who did not enter industry (and many of them did) there remained several hundred thousand industrial workers who annually had to be absorbed into the body of American labor. Since the great majority of these new recruits to American labor were unskilled, they formed a body of cheap laborers whose presence tended to depress labor standards generally. This

danger might have been mitigated if labor had been as quick to organize them as were political parties, but in part because of the racial
and religious antagonisms that embittered relations between native-
and foreign-born workers and between various immigrant groups,
partly because organized labor was by this time committed to the
principle of craft unions, the labor unions made no serious effort to
enlist the immigrants. Almost inevitably labor experienced its most
serious difficulties in those industries where the proportion of foreign-
born workers was highest — the meat-packing, iron and steel, and
mining industries. In the circumstances it is not surprising that organized labor campaigned continuously for immigration restriction.

Finally, the development of labor and the solution of the labor
problem were conditioned by nineteenth-century attitudes that persisted well into the twentieth. The tradition that America was a land
of equal opportunity for all, that in America there were not and
never would be any classes, and that here any laboring man could
rise by his own efforts — the tradition, in short, of rugged individualism — was a tenacious one. The average American, and not the
native-born alone, looked with suspicion upon any tendency to consider the problems of labor as distinct from those of capital or to develop class consciousness among workingmen, and regarded with
deep distrust the entry of labor into politics. Most labor organizations shared these views.

These attitudes were not unreasonable, but from them flowed certain corollaries distinctly injurious to the interests of labor. Throughout the nineteenth century there was a widespread hostility toward
labor unions and the closed shop, and even so open-minded a man as
President Eliot of Harvard could assert that the closed shop was un-
American. The strike, which as late as the 1840's was regarded as a
conspiracy against the public interest, continued to be in bad repute,
and in 1886 the New York banker, Henry Clews, identified the strike
with treason. ' Strikes may have been justifiable in other nations,' he
said, ' but they are not justifiable in our country. The Almighty has
made this country for the oppressed of other nations, and therefore
this is the land of refuge . . . and the hand of the laboring man
should not be raised against it.' If the strike was looked upon as un-
patriotic, picketing and the boycott were regarded as downright illegal, and not really until the 1930's did labor win immunity from
judicial interference with the use of these weapons.

The climate of opinion in which these ideas flourished was hostile to organized labor, and not until comparatively recent years was that climate moderated by new intellectual currents. Meantime there developed in the late nineteenth century a double standard of social morality for labor and capital. Combination of capital was regarded as in accordance with natural laws; combination of labor as a conspiracy. Monopoly was good business, and businessmen denounced or evaded the Sherman Act, but the closed shop was un-American. It was the duty of government to aid business and to protect business interests, but government aid to labor was socialism. That business should go into politics was common sense, but that labor should go into politics was contrary to the American tradition. Property had a natural right to a fair return on its value, but the return which labor might enjoy was to be regulated strictly by the law of supply and demand. Appeals to protect or enhance property interests were reasonable, but appeals to protect or enhance labor interests were demagogic. Brokers who organized business combines were respectable public servants, but labor organizers were agitators. The use of Pinkerton detectives to protect business property was preserving law and order, but the use of force to protect the job was violence, and for labor to call in the militia or federal troops to protect its property in jobs was quite unthinkable. To curtail production in the face of an oversupply of consumers' goods was sound business practice, but to strike for shorter hours in the face of an oversupply of labor was unsound. The list might be extended, but the principle is more interesting than the practice. The double standard was illogical, but it was real, and labor had the choice of conforming to it, defying it, or changing it. Conformity was not to be expected, and defiance was generally suicidal, so labor naturally directed its efforts toward changing it. The story of the gradual modification of this double standard can be read in the history of labor organization and in the record of social legislation of state and federal governments over the past fifty years.

2. The Rise of Organized Labor

Organized labor passed through phases of bewildering complexity before it won the power to meet organized capital on nearly equal terms. There was little continuity of leadership from the ante-bellum period: wage-earners of the 1840's had largely become farmers, shopkeepers, and small capitalists by the 'seventies. Their places were taken by farmers' sons, discharged soldiers lured by the attractions of urban life, and a new wave of immigrants, continental rather than British. Ignorant of what had been tried before, the American labor leaders passed through the same cycle of experiment as in the 1830's and 1840's. There were national trade unions and local trade unions; efforts to escape from the established order through co-operation, to ameliorate it by devices like the single tax, to break it down with socialism; political activities; and attempts to form one big union. Yet, the ideas of Marx, Lassalle, and Bakunin exerted less influence than did those of Owen, Cabet, and Fourier in the 'forties.

Labor began to turn away from Utopian escapes and humanitarian panaceas to the more practical agencies of trade unionism and collective bargaining as early as 1850 when the National Typographical Union was founded. Within a few years the hat-finishers, stone-cutters, iron-puddlers, and machinists had formed national organizations. These and other national unions were in a flourishing condition in the early 'fifties, but the panic of 1857 devitalized the entire labor movement, and by 1861 only a few struggling unions maintained a precarious existence.

The Civil War speed-up to industrial development created new opportunities for labor organization, while the sky-rocketing cost of living and currency inflation made organization imperative, if labor wished to protect the gains which war demands made possible. A score of new craft unions were established and workingmen experimented with local trade assemblies representing different crafts. By 1863 these mixed assemblies of trades' councils had been established in all the larger cities of the East and the next year witnessed the brief appearance of an International (Canadian and United States) Industrial Assembly. More important were the new labor organizations that appeared during the period of brief prosperity after the war: the National Labor Union, founded at Baltimore in 1866, the Knights of St. Crispin, established in Milwaukee the following year, and the Knights of Labor, founded in 1869, and many others. By 1873 there were 25 national unions in the field with an uncertain membership of a little less than 200,000.

The National Labor Union was a curious conglomeration of trades' assemblies, national and local unions, farmers' societies, women's suffrage leagues, and various other reform groups, with a program as miscellaneous as its membership. It lasted only six years, but attained a maximum membership of over 600,000 and helped to push through two laudable pieces of federal legislation: the eight-hour law for employees on government works, and the repeal of the Contract Labor law of 1864. The Knights of St. Crispin, a shoe-makers' union, had some 50,000 members, scattered from Massachusetts to Wisconsin. Its policy was reactionary, for it tried to maintain the old apprenticeship system under guild control, and it opposed the introduction of shoe machinery; both efforts were unsuccessful.

By far the most important of the early labor organizations was the Noble Order of the Knights of Labor, founded in 1869 by a Philadelphia tailor, Uriah S. Stephens. Native American in leadership and largely in personnel, it was an attempt to unite the workers of America into one big union, under centralized control. Membership was open to all workers — men and women, white and black, skilled and unskilled, laborers and capitalists, merchants and farmers. Only liquor dealers, professional gamblers, lawyers, and bankers were excluded! The professed object of the order was ' To secure to the toilers a proper share of the wealth that they create; more of the leisure that rightfully belongs to them; more societary advantages; more of the benefits, privileges, and emoluments of the world; in a word, all those rights and privileges necessary to make them capable of enjoying, appreciating, defending, and perpetuating the blessings of good government.' The Order hoped to secure these laudable but somewhat vague ends by co-operation, arbitration of industrial disputes, an eight-hour day, the abolition of child labor, and many other social and economic reforms that were eventually incorporated into state and federal laws and accepted by even the most conservative.

The growth of the Knights of Labor was nothing short of phenomenal. When a Pennsylvania machinist named Terence V. Powderly became Grand Master in 1878, the membership was under 50,000. Powderly was an idealist who disliked the tactics of combative unionism and believed in producers' co-operation; but it was the fate of the Order to become powerful not through co-operation, but by winning a great railroad strike in the Southwest in 1885. Capital then, for the first time, met labor on equal terms, when the New York financier, Jay Gould, conferred with the Knights' executive board and conceded their demands. The prestige of this victory was so great that the Order reached a membership of over 700,000 the following year. The Knights helped to push the Chinese Exclusion Act through Congress in 1882, and were largely responsible for the law of 1885 forbidding the importation of contract labor.

Parallel with the rise of the Knights of Labor, non-political trade unions of skilled workers grew and multiplied, as did a few unions affiliated with the ' Black ' International, an anarchistic organization introduced into the United States in the early 'eighties by the German Johann Most. Local units of the Knights of Labor, trade unions, and socialist unions struck for the eight-hour day in 1886, in an era of comparative prosperity. A general strike called for 1 May 1886 was climaxed by a tragedy only indirectly connected in origin with the eight-hour movement, the Haymarket bomb explosion in Chicago. A long drawn-out lockout and strike in the McCormick Harvester Company culminated, on 3 May, in a riot in which the police killed and wounded half a dozen labor demonstrators. On the following day when the police broke up a mass meeting held to protest this massacre, someone threw a bomb into their midst; seven persons were killed and over sixty injured. Though the actual perpetrator of the outrage could not be found, Judge Joseph E. Gray of the Cook County Criminal Court held that those who incited the deed by word or action were equally guilty with those who committed the actual murder. Under this ruling the jury found eight anarchists guilty of murder, and sentenced one to imprisonment and seven to death. Of these seven one committed suicide, four were executed, and the other two had their sentences commuted to life imprisonment. Six years later Governor Altgeld came to office. Alleging that ' the record of this case shows that the judge conducted the trial with malicious ferocity,' he pardoned the three anarchists who were still serving prison sentences. Although there was, and is, no possible doubt of the innocence of these men, Altgeld was denounced from coast to coast as an aider and abetter of anarchy. The Knights of Labor was in no way responsible for the Haymarket affair and Powderly had even attempted to disassociate the Order from the eight-hour movement, but the popular revulsion against radical organization of any kind embraced them uncritically, and their influence began to wane. Indiscriminate strikes, all failures, the mismanagement of Powderly, and the difficulty of holding skilled and unskilled labor in the same union made serious inroads in their ranks. By the end of the decade membership in the Order had dwindled to about 100,000 and, after a brief and half-hearted flirtation with the Populists, the Knights practically disappeared.

Thus the first experiment of one big union ended disastrously, yet the Knights contributed much of lasting value to the American labor movement. It contributed the democratic idea of the solidarity and unity of all labor, in contrast to the more exclusive principle of trade unionism. Through emphasis on education and social democracy it advanced the status and dignity of labor and prepared the public mind for the K. of L. reforms which were achieved after its demise.

As the Knights of Labor declined in membership and prestige, its place in the van of the labor movement was usurped by a new and more vigorous organization, the American Federation of Labor. This body, which was to dominate the American labor scene for the next half-century, definitely rejected the idea of one big union and returned to the principle of unions of skilled workers on craft lines. The two organizations differed in other respects as well: the A. F. of L. was opportunistic and practical where the K. of L. had been idealistic and vague in its aims; the new organization abjured politics and relied on the traditional weapons of the strike and the boycott, whilst the old Order had, on occasion, embraced politics and theoretically discouraged strikes. The Federation from the beginning accepted capitalism and chose to work within the framework of the established economic order, whilst the Knights was tinged with revolutionary radicalism and looked forward to a co-operative republic of workers.

The A. F. of L., distinctively American as it is, issued from the brain of a foreign-born worker in the polyglot section of New York. In the late 'sixties a bullet-headed young man named Samuel Gompers, a British subject of mixed Hebrew and Flemish ancestry, was working in a highly unsanitary cigar-making shop in the lower East Side, and speaking at the meetings of a cigar-makers' union — the famous Local No. 144. Cigar making was then a sociable handicraft. The men talked or read aloud while they worked, and both shop and union included German and Hungarian immigrants who could discuss socialism or Darwinism with equal facility. Gompers, as he rose in the councils of his fellow workers, learned to concentrate on the economic struggle and to fight shy of intellectuals who would ride union labor to some private Utopia. He determined to divorce unionism from politics, which dissipated its energy, and from radicalism, which served only to arouse the fear of the public and the fury of the police. In the hard times of the 'seventies he experienced cold and hunger, the futility of charity, and the cowardice of politicians. At all times he had reason to bewail the lack of discipline in the labor movement. By 1881 he and other local labor leaders had thought their way through to a national federation of craft unions, economic in purpose, evolutionary in method, and contending for the immediate objects of shorter hours and better wages. Five years later the A. F. of L. was born, and as the Knights of Labor declined the Federation became the fighting spearhead of the American labor movement.

There is a rough analogy between the A. F. of L. and the Federal Government. Each national union in the Federation has complete power to contract with or strike against employers within its own jurisdiction. The Federation decides matters of jurisdiction, prevents — or tries to prevent — the establishment of rival unions in the same trade, and relies on salaried organizers and a labor press to keep the ranks of the workers solid. Opportunistic rather than idealistic, animated by the philosophy of the job, the Federation is a purely economic organization of wage-earners for the business of collective bargaining. 'At no time in my life,' said Gompers, 'have I worked out definitely articulated economic theory,' and Gompers's co-worker, Adolph Strasser, was even more emphatic. 'We have no ultimate ends,' he testified. 'We are going on from day to day. We are fighting only for immediate objects — objects that can be realized in a few years.' In 1918 the economic platform of the Federation included opposition to the injunction in labor disputes; an eight-hour day and a six-day week; municipal ownership of public utilities; factory inspection; workmen's compensation laws; abolition of child labor; the initiative, referendum, and recall; free schools, free textbooks, and compulsory education — objectives that had already been realized in many states. State federations, cutting across the national unions, were created within the A. F. of L. in order to obtain legislation of this nature by bargaining with local political leaders.

Despite the loss of the great Homestead strike against the Carnegie Steel Company in 1892 and failure to co-operate in the Pullman strike, the A. F. of L. weathered the hard times of 1893–97 and turned the century with a membership of over half a million. The piping years of the T. R. Roosevelt administration brought prosperity to labor as well as to industry, and by 1904 this membership was trebled and ten years later it reached 2 million. The World War stimulated American industry just as had the Civil War, and the stimulus was promptly reflected in the growth of the Federation. When in 1917 the United States entered World War I, the membership was almost 2.5 million, and the Federation embraced 111 national unions, 762 city central bodies, and 26,761 local unions.

This rapid growth of the Federation was in great part due to the leadership of Gompers who for 40 years guided its destiny, impressed it with his personality, permeated it with his ideas, inspired it with his stubborn courage, held it steadily to the course of aggressive self-interest, and steered it clear of the shoals of politics upon which so many earlier labor movements had grounded. ' We must be partisan for a principle,' said Gompers, ' and not for a party.' From time to time the A. F. of L. threw its influence to some candidate who was favorable to the labor program or supported a party which adopted a good labor platform. Thus in 1908 Gompers supported Bryan and in 1912 Wilson; and the Federation frequently made its power felt in local or state contests. But it never listened to radical counsels or yielded to radical leadership, never formally tied up with the Socialist or the Socialist Labor parties, never, except in 1924, entered politics in any organized fashion.

Although the American Federation of Labor was for 40 years the acknowledged spokesman of American labor, at no time did its membership embrace a majority of the working class. It was not merely that some of the more powerful craft unions such as the aristocratic Four Brotherhoods, or the Amalgamated Garment Workers, kept their independence; more to the point, the A. F. of L. itself never made any effort to organize the great mass of unskilled workers. As late as 1920, for example, when the Federation was strongest, only 23 per cent of the workers in manufacturing plants, 25 per cent in the building trades, and 37 per cent in transportation were organized, and nothing at all had been done for miners and smelters, lumberjacks and migratory farm workers, women in domestic service or in textile mills or tobacco factories, immigrants and Negroes in packing houses, the flotsam and jetsam of American labor.

The Knights, with their philosophy of industrial unionism, had made uncertain gestures toward these people, but with the decline of

STEELWORKERS' NOONTIME by *Thomas Anschutz*

the Knights there was no one to champion them. The void was only partially filled by ragged unions that sprang up spontaneously in the mining camps of the West and eventually coalesced into the Industrial Workers of the World. The origin of this militant organization, which acted as a catalytic agent in American labor, was the labor warfare in the Coeur d'Alene mines of Idaho in the early 'nineties. To meet assaults upon them, the miners organized the Western Federation of Miners, which in turn conducted a long series of strikes through the West. Theirs was from the beginning a fighting existence. Themselves prone to violence, they were met by violence from mine operators, vigilante committees, and government officials. Thus when the Federation went out on strike at the Cripple Creek mines in Colorado in 1903 and 1904, the governor declared martial law and rushed in state troops without even pausing to investigate; the military commander arrested workers without preferring charges against them, destroyed miners' camps, cooped the miners up in bull pens, deported several hundred of them from the state, seized supplies of food sent in for their relief, shut down offending newspapers, and forced operators who had managed to keep their mines open to discharge union workers.

Out of all this, in 1905, came the Industrial Workers of the World (the I.W.W., or ' Wobblies,' as they came to be known). It was the first labor organization formally committed to the principle of class warfare. This principle was set forth in the preamble of its constitution:

The working class and the employing class have nothing in common. There can be no peace so long as hunger and want are found among millions .of working people, and the few, who make up the employing class have all the good things of life.

Between these two classes a struggle must go on until all the toilers come together on the political as well as on the industrial field, and take and hold that which they produce by their labor, through an economic organization of the working class, without affiliation with any political party.

In its fifteen years of existence the I.W.W. tried to organize the migratory farm workers of the Great Plains, lumbermen of the Far Northwest, copper miners in Arizona, and dock hands along the Pacific waterfront. In 1912 it ventured east to take charge of the textile strike in Lawrence, Massachusetts, where the mill-owners had countered a new state law reducing hours to 54 hours a week by slashing wages, which then stood at $8.56 a week. The I.W.W. won this strike, but lost a parallel strike in the textile town of Paterson, New Jersey. Before its demise in 1918 it had conducted almost 150 strikes, winning an astonishingly large number of them. When its activities threatened to interfere with the war in 1917 and 1918, it was destroyed. For a long time no other organization tried to do what it had done with such explosive violence. Not until 1936, when John L. Lewis of the United Mine Workers founded the Committee for Industrial Organizations, was there any serious effort to organize the great mass of unskilled and semi-skilled workers.

3. INDUSTRIAL CONFLICT

As, after the Civil War, labor shifted its objectives from social reform to wages and the job, it resorted with increasing frequency to the weapons of industrial warfare — the strike and the boycott — and business retaliated with the lockout, the blacklist, the injunction, and the employment of company police or the National Guard. The result was an uninterrupted industrial conflict that frequently broke out into violence and assumed the ominous character of warfare. In 1900 the Industrial Commission concluded that strikes and lockouts were far more prevalent in the United States than in other industrial countries — possibly a tribute to the independent spirit of the American workingman as well as to the growing pains of big business and big labor; the experience of the next 30 years furnished no ground for modifying the sobering estimate.

The basic causes of the American industrial conflict are not hard to ascertain. There was everywhere among the workers a persistent feeling that labor was being denied its proper share of the benefits that accrued from the exploitation of natural resources and of the savings made possible by machinery. The great majority of strikes that occurred after the 1870's involved either hours or wages or both. Given the conditions which confronted the average workingman, this is easy to understand.

Agitation for the eight-hour day began in the 1860's, but as late as 1900, 70 per cent of the industrial workers in the country worked ten hours or more each day, and ten years later only 8 per cent were on an eight-hour day. In many industries the hours were shockingly long: the steel industry had a twelve-hour day and a seven-day week, and this schedule was maintained for many steel workers until 1923. Hours in the textile industry ranged from 60 to 84 a week, even for the women and little children who constituted a large part of the working force. In New York City bakers were expected to put in 84 hours or more each week; when the state finally got around to limiting the hours to 60 a week the Supreme Court threw the law out with the disdainful comment, ' There is no reasonable ground for interfering with the liberty of persons or the right of free contract by determining the hours of labor in the occupation of a baker.'

The wage situation was not much better. Investigation after investigation disclosed that in the decades from 1880 to 1910 the unskilled laborer commonly earned less than $10 a week and the skilled worker rarely more than $20, while the earnings of women ranged from a low of $3.93 a week in Richmond to a high of $6.91 in San Francisco. During the whole of this 30-year period the average annual family income of industrial workers was never more than $650, or of farm laborers more than $400, figures considerably below that fixed as necessary for a decent standard of living. When we recall that unemployment averaged 10 per cent during the entire period and was often higher,[3] that even those employed rarely enjoyed continuous work through the year, and that with the growth of cities the vegetable garden, fruit trees, chicken-coop, and family cow that had supplemented earlier family incomes disappeared, we can understand better the deep discontent of labor and the resort to conflict and even to violence.

The strike had been a recurrent phenomenon in our history ever since the 1790's but before the Civil War strikes had been localized and, on the whole, peaceful, partly because they were long regarded as ' conspiracies ' at common law, and strikes subject to jail sentences. The first great industrial conflict in our history came in 1877 when the four Eastern trunk railroads jauntily announced a wage-cut of 10 per cent, the second since the panic of 1873. Without adequate organization the railway employees struck, and with the support of a huge army of hungry and desperate unemployed, the strike flared up into something that seemed to respectable folk like rebellion.

[3] In 1898, for example, 14 per cent of the workers in manufacturing and transportation were unemployed. In the same year the average miner in the bituminous coal mines worked 211 days a year, and in the anthracite mines 152 days a year. In 1908 and 1914 average unemployment in manufacturing was 16 per cent. These were not depression years.

During one week in July traffic was entirely suspended on the trunk lines and demoralized elsewhere in the country, and every large industrial center from the Atlantic to the Pacific was in turmoil. In Baltimore, Pittsburgh, Martinsburg, Chicago, Buffalo, San Francisco, and elsewhere, there were pitched battles between militia and the mob, and order was restored only by federal troops. Pittsburgh was terrorized for three days; fatalities ran into the scores, and property damage was estimated at $10 million. American complacency received a shock which was only partially alleviated by the notion, so precious to Americans then and since, that foreign agitators alone were responsible for the disorder. Only the most far-sighted realized that the country had reached a stage of industrial evolution which created a labor problem, and that the ' Great Strike ' of 1877 would be only the first of a long series of battles between labor and capital.

The decade of the 'eighties was a turbulent one, and almost 400,000 workers participated in the eight-hour movement of 1886 that ended so disastrously in the Haymarket riot. Not until 1892 was the nation again to witness so menacing an outbreak in the labor field. In that year occurred the terrible strike in the Homestead works of the Carnegie Steel Company which culminated in a pitched battle between infuriated strikers and an army of Pinkerton detectives hired by the president of the Carnegie Company, Henry C. Frick. The strikers won the sanguinary battle, but the attempted assassination of Frick alienated public opinion and state militia broke the backbone of the strike.

Two years later the country was distracted by a strike against the Pullman Palace Car Company in the model town of Pullman, Illinois. The strike resulted originally from the arbitrary refusal of Mr. Pullman to discuss grievances with representatives of his employees, but it came eventually to involve far larger issues. The cause of the Pullman workers was taken up by the American Railway Union, a powerful body of railway workers under the leadership of the magnetic Eugene V. Debs. When this union voted a boycott against all Pullman cars, the cause of the Pullman Company was as promptly championed by the newly organized General Managers' Association of Railroads. The result was a paralysis of transportation throughout the North. Disorder was widespread and the situation was explosive. The railroads succeeded in enlisting the sympathies of President Cleveland and the aid of Attorney-General Olney, a former railroad attorney who had not forgotten his earlier obligations to the railroads nor failed to consider the railroad's future obligations to him. On 1 July Olney appointed as special counsel for the United States a prominent railway attorney named Edwin Walker, at whose suggestion the federal circuit court at Chicago served on the officers of the American Railway Union a ' blanket injunction ' against obstructing the railways and holding up the mails. Hooligans promptly ditched a mail train, and took possession of strategic points in the switching yards. Walker as promptly called for federal troops. Cleveland declared that he would use every dollar in the Treasury and every soldier in the army if necessary to deliver a single postcard in Chicago. On 4 July he ordered a regiment of regulars to the city. The effect was like that of sending British regulars to Boston in 1768.

Cleveland's antagonist in this conflict was not so much Debs and the Railway Union as Governor John P. Altgeld. This honest and fearless statesman had already been marked for destruction by big business because he had helped Jane Addams to obtain factory regulations in Illinois and because he had pardoned the men imprisoned for presumed responsibility in the Haymarket bomb outrage of 1886. During the Pullman strike Altgeld was ready and able to protect law and order with state militia. He sent troops to every point in the state where the authorities called for them, and had an ample force ready to use in Chicago, where, as yet, there was no disorder with which police and militia were unable to cope. The real reason Walker called for a federal injunction and federal troops was to break the strike, not to preserve order; and the most serious disorder came after the federal injunction had been issued. Altgeld's eloquent protest against this gratuitous interference by the Federal Government and his demand for the withdrawal of federal troops was cavalierly disregarded. Debs defied the injunction, a prosecution for conspiracy failed, but he was given six months' imprisonment for contempt of court. By early August the strike was smashed.

The dramatic events of this Pullman strike raised weighty questions of law, and placed the Federal Government in direct opposition to union labor. The President simply saw the issue of law and order, but through permitting Olney to appoint a railroad attorney special counsel of the government, he played into the hands of those who wanted federal troops to break a strike, and not state militia to preserve order. Governor Altgeld had no desire to foment disorder; but his stout protest against a dubious assumption of federal authority placed him in the position of a rebel. Debs was merely trying to help the Pullman employees by boycotting the company; but the movement got out of his hands and became something like a labor insurrection. The Supreme Court of the United States, to which Debs appealed his sentence, upheld the government, declaring that even in the absence of statutory law it had a dormant power to brush away obstacles to interstate commerce — an implied power that would have made Hamilton and Marshall gasp.[4] Yet the whole affair was not without a certain educational value to all concerned. Debs, in his prison cell, studied socialism and in time became the organizer and leader of the Socialist party in America; the workers learned the real meaning of the Sherman Anti-Trust Act; business awoke to the potentialities of the injunction in labor disputes; and the country at large was taught a new interpretation of the sovereign powers of the Federal Government. Only George Pullman emerged innocent of new ideas.

Scarcely less spectacular than the Pullman strike was the outbreak in the anthracite coal fields of Pennsylvania in 1902. Then, as later, the coal industry was in a chaotic condition, and the position of the miners was depressed and insecure. In the 'nineties organization had made some progress in the bituminous fields, but the racial antipathies among the miners and the bitter hostility of the railway-controlled operators delayed unionization among the anthracite miners. In 1898, however, the youthful John Mitchell became president of the United Mine Workers union which then numbered some 40,000 members. Within two years he whipped it into shape, extended its membership to the anthracite fields, and wrested favorable terms from the powerful coal companies of eastern Pennsylvania. Two years later the operators abrogated this agreement, and the miners struck for recognition of their union, a nine-hour day, and an increase in wages. The operators were obdurate, and for four tense months the strike dragged on while the strikers maintained an unbroken front and won the support of public opinion. It was in the course of this struggle that President George F. Baer of the Philadelphia and Reading Railroad announced that 'the rights and interests of the laboring man will be protected and cared for, not by the labor

[4] *In re Debs* 158 U.S. 564 (1895).

agitators, but by the Christian men to whom God in His infinite wisdom, has given control of the property interests of the country.' In October, with both a congressional election and a coal-less winter looming up, Roosevelt brought pressure on miners and operators to arbitrate. The miners were willing, but not Mr. Baer, who rebuked the President for ' negotiating with the fomenters of anarchy.' Outraged by this attitude Roosevelt then threatened to take over the mines and run them with militia unless the stubborn operators came to terms with the miners. This threat, and the force of public opinion, persuaded the mine-owners to arbitrate, and the strike ended in a signal victory for the miners, enhancement of the prestige of John Mitchell and of President Roosevelt, and a triumph for the cause of arbitration.

Labor unrest in the coal fields was chronic. The murderous activities of the Molly Maguires in the eastern Pennsylvania coal fields in the early 'seventies had given the American people their first premonition of class warfare and had helped create a stereotype of the ' alien agitator ' that did service for half a century or more. In 1903–04 came a terrible outbreak in the Rockefeller-owned coal fields of Colorado which was crushed by the military. Ten years later the United Mine Workers union tried to unionize the Colorado Fuel and Iron Company; the company resisted, armed guards were called in and broke up the miners' camps, and the conflict ended in the ' Ludlow massacre ' — a pitched battle between miners and soldiers that plunged Colorado into something like civil war, aroused nation-wide sympathy for the striking miners, and led, eventually, to far-reaching reforms. West Virginia, too, experienced prolonged struggles in the coal fields which burst out into something like civil war in 1919 and 1920, while the struggle in the coal mines of southern Illinois came to an awful climax in the ' Herrin massacre ' of 1922. In the twenty years from 1910 to 1929 no less than 4 million coal miners were out on strike at one time or another. In the 1920's came a concerted effort on the part of the mine operators to destroy the United Mine Workers and put mines on an open-shop basis, and this program met with considerable success; by the end of the decade the U.M.W. was fighting for its life. Tempered in the flames of these conflicts, leaders like John L. Lewis came out hard as steel.

The statistics of strikes and lockouts during these years go far to justify the conclusion of a recent student of our economy that

'American labor history has been principally a fighting history.' Statistics are not available for every year, but in the 25 years from 1881 to 1906 there occurred some 38,000 strikes and lockouts, involving almost 200,000 establishments and over 9.5 million workers. World War I and the postwar years saw some abatement of the industrial conflict, but the 26,000 strikes that broke out between 1916 and 1935 indicated that the struggle was a continuous one. And during almost the whole of this period the forces of law and of government, and usually of public opinion as well, were thrown to the support of business and against labor.

4. LABOR LEGISLATION AND THE COURTS

It is a truism that until the 1930's American social legislation lagged almost a generation behind that of the more progressive European states like Denmark and Germany and behind such Commonwealth nations as Australia and New Zealand. It should be remembered that the difficulties of dealing with the various social and economic and constitutional aspects of the problem are greater in the United States than in England or continental Europe. This is due largely to four factors. First is the tradition of rugged individualism which made businessmen reluctant to acquiesce in legislative regulations and disposed the public to associate welfare legislation with socialism. Second is the tradition of the classless society, where every man and every economic group were supposed to fend for themselves: Gompers himself subscribed to this principle. 'I tell the politicians,' he said, 'to keep their hands off and thus to preserve voluntary institutions and opportunity for individual and group initiative and leave the way open to deal with problems as the experience and facts of industry shall indicate.' Third was a written constitution whose limitations and restrictions were interpreted strictly by a conservative Court; and fourth the existence of a federal rather than a centralized state where it was possible for corporations to take advantage of states with easy-going corporation and labor laws.

The very existence of organized labor has often been threatened; its chief weapons, the strike and the boycott, have frequently been paralyzed by injunction or judicial decision. Early in the nineteenth century labor unions were held to be illegal in themselves, but by the time of the Civil War the right of workingmen to organize was everywhere accepted.[5] Yet the strike remained at best an uncertain weapon. Business and government invoked the injunction against it time and again — in the great railroad strike of 1877, in the Pullman strike of 1894, and on scores of other occasions. The Clayton Anti-Trust Act of 1914 contained a special article forbidding the use of the injunction in labor disputes, except ' to prevent irreparable injury '; but the intent of this article was defeated by a series of Court decisions,[6] and eight years after its enactment the United States Attorney-General broke the railway trainmen's strike with the most sweeping injunction in American history — not until 1932 did the Norris-LaGuardia anti-injunction bill erect apparently invulnerable safeguards against the issue of the injunction in labor disputes. The boycott of employers who would not accept union terms was adjudged an unlawful conspiracy in restraint of trade, and thus a violation of the Sherman Act, in two leading cases,[7] and the secondary boycott, too, came under the judicial ban.[8] The Supreme Court even held that unincorporated labor organizations might be prosecuted for violations of the Anti-Trust act.[9] So, too, the practice of picketing was so hedged about with judicial restrictions as to be until recently practically impotent.[10]

Probably more has been accomplished by labor through legislation than through strikes or other violent methods. Before the 1930's this included the establishment of an eight-hour day in most industries, limitation of the hours and regulation of the conditions of women's labor, abolition of child labor, factory inspection, safety and sanitation regulation, arbitration of industrial disputes, workmen's compensation, and restriction of immigration and protection of native labor against foreign competition. Thereafter came a flood of labor and welfare legislation whose character and impact we will analyze later.

Outside the field of interstate commerce — a term which the Court was inclined to interpret narrowly during these years — and except

[5] *Commonwealth v. Hunt* (Mass. Reports, 4 Metcalf, 45, 1842) is the leading case.

[6] Especially *Duplex Printing Press Co. v. Deering* 254 U.S. 443 (1921).

[7] *Gompers v. Bucks Stove and Range Co.* 221 U.S. 418 (1907) and the famous *Danbury Hatters'* case, 208 U.S. 274 (1908), where the court assessed triple damages against individual members of the union.

[8] *Bedford Cut Stone Co. v. Journeymen Cutters Association* 274 U.S. 37 (1927).

[9] *United Mine Workers v. Coronado Coal Co.* 259 U.S. 344 (1922).

[10] *Truax v. Corrigan* 257 U.S. 312 (1921) in which the Supreme Court held unconstitutional a law of Arizona forbidding the use of the injunction in labor disputes.

for federal employees, the Federal Government was thought to have no jurisdiction over many of these matters, and it was not until the New Deal that ways were found to achieve indirectly what could not be achieved directly. As early as 1868 Congress established an eight-hour day on public works, and in 1892 enacted an eight-hour day for all government employees. The Adamson Law of 1916 extended this boon to all railway employees. In many other ways, too, the Federal Government responded to the demands of organized labor or of reformers. In 1884 a Bureau of Labor was created, and this was elevated to cabinet rank in 1913 and assigned to a stalwart of the labor movement, William B. Wilson. An act of 1885 prohibited the importation of contract labor, and thereafter a whole series of laws regulated, restricted, or excluded immigration. In 1898 Congress passed the Erdman Act providing for the arbitration of labor disputes on interstate carriers, and in 1908 an Employers' Liability Act whose provisions were likewise confined to railway employees. The LaFollette Seaman's Act of 1915 elevated seamen for the first time to the full status of free men. Twice Congress attempted to prohibit child labor through statutory enactment — in 1916 under the guise of a regulation of commerce, and again in 1919 through the medium of taxation, but both laws were nullified by the Court.[11] Within two years of the failure of the second attempt, opponents of child labor succeeded in pushing through a Constitutional amendment; then a Supreme Court reversal of the first child-labor decision validated federal legislation and made ratification of the amendment less urgent.

Before the 1930's, however, labor and social legislation lay for the most part in the domain of the individual states, and here there was progress in certain lines, particularly in more progressive states such as Massachusetts, New York, Oregon, and Washington. The first labor law to be adequately enforced was the Massachusetts Ten-Hour Act of 1874 for women and children in factories. It was not so hard to get such laws passed as it was to provide proper administrative machinery for their enforcement; and until judges began to lose their laissez-faire prepossessions, there was constant danger of judicial nullification. The Massachusetts law was sustained, but similar laws in Illinois and New York were voided by the courts. An historic ex-

[11] *Hammer v. Dagenhart* 247 U.S. 251 (1918) and *Bailey v. Drexel Furniture Co.* 259 U.S. 20 (1922).

ample of judicial intervention in social legislation was the nullification of the New York Act of 1882 prohibiting the manufacture of
cigars in tenement houses which Gompers persuaded young Theodore Roosevelt to sponsor and Grover Cleveland to sign. It was intended as an entering wedge to break up the ' sweating ' system, a
rapidly growing menace. The highest state court in New York, however, threw it out on the ground that it interfered with the profitable
use of real estate without any compensating public advantage. ' It
cannot be perceived how the cigarmaker is to be improved in his
health or his morals by forcing him from his home and its hallowed
associations and beneficent influences to ply his trade elsewhere,' declared the court.[12] Roosevelt, who had personally inspected these one-
room ' homes ' where whole families and their lodgers ate, slept, and
rolled cigars, then began to revise his conception of justice and of the
role of the courts in American economy.

It was this case [he recorded in his autobiography] which first waked me
to a dim and partial understanding of the fact that the courts were not
necessarily the best judges of what should be done to better social industrial conditions. The judges who rendered this decision were well-meaning men. They knew nothing whatever of tenement-house conditions;
they knew nothing whatever of the needs, or of the life and labor, of
three-fourths of their fellow-citizens in great cities. They knew legalism,
but not life . . . This decision completely blocked tenement-house reform
legislation in New York for a score of years, and hampers it to this day. It
was one of the most serious setbacks which the cause of industrial and
social progress and reform ever received.[13]

By what theory did the courts declare such labor and welfare laws
unconstitutional? It is forbidden in most state constitutions and in
the Fourteenth Amendment to the federal Constitution to deprive
persons of liberty or property without due process of law. As no reform can be effected without depriving someone of something that
he may deem to be a liberty or a property right, American courts
(following English precedents) early elaborated the doctrine of a
superior ' police power ' — the reserved right of the state to protect
the people's health, safety, morals, and welfare. The police power
was held to justify even confiscatory legislation such as the prohibition of lotteries or of the sale of alcoholic liquors. But when labor

12 *In re Jacobs* 98 N.Y. 98 (1885).
13 *Theodore Roosevelt: An Autobiography*, Scribners, p. 81.

and factory laws began to appear on the statute books, judges began to have second thoughts about the scope of this police power. Corporations engaging the best lawyers found it easy to convince courts that such laws were not a proper exercise of the police power but rather a violation of the 'due process' clause of the Fourteenth Amendment.

For half a century after Reconstruction such judges as Field and Brewer, Peckham and Sutherland, and their disciples in the state courts, turned the judicial bench into a dike against which the surging tides of welfare legislation beat in vain. They interpreted the Constitution as a prohibition rather than an instrument, and read into it limitations on the scope of governmental authority which were in fact merely the conclusions of natural law syllogisms. Insisting that they were without discretion, and that their functions were purely mechanical, they struck down hundreds of state police laws on the theory that they deprived somebody of property or of liberty of contract without due process of law, and when outraged legislators pointed to the laws themselves, judges answered that laws that deprived corporations of a fair return or workers of the right to work when and where they pleased were arbitrary and therefore without 'due process.' Two assumptions pervaded these decisions. First, they assumed that the provisions of the Constitution were axiomatic, inflexible, and indisputable, and that the judges were the only persons competent to apply them to particular cases. Second, they held that whenever social or economic facts conflicted with the theoretical assumptions of natural law, the facts must give way to the assumptions.

Behind all this was the judicial fear that labor and welfare laws constituted 'an assault upon capitalism' or 'the first step towards socialism,' and they wrote their fears into legal doctrine. In 1913 Justice Holmes could observe that 'When twenty years ago a vague terror went over the earth and the word socialism began to be heard, I thought and still think that fear was translated into doctrines that had no proper place in the Constitution or the common law.'

The record bore this out. A Pennsylvania act forbidding payment of workers by orders on company stores was voided as an 'infringement on natural inherent rights and an insulting attempt to put the laborer under a legislative tutelage,' and a West Virginia court, confronted by a similar act, held that 'the evil was in the hands of the employee since he is not compelled to buy from the employer' —

this in the face of the fact that the company owned the town, the houses, and the stores. A New York act fixing the hours of labor for municipal contracts was struck down because it ' created a class of statutory laborers ' and a Colorado act regulating hours in the smelting industry was voided as an interference with liberty of contract. The New York Court of Appeals voided a workmen's compensation law because ' it did nothing to conserve the health, safety or morals of employees,' and an amendment was required to enable the legislature to deal with this urgent problem. An Illinois court declared unconstitutional a statute limiting the hours of labor for women in sweatshops on the ground that women had the same liberty of contract as men, a decision which inspired the Chicago *Evening Post* to protest that ' when Dora Windeguth, her employer at her elbow, says that she cannot earn enough in ten hours to live, our whole chivalry rises to her defense; let her work twelve hours then. We have always contended that nobody need starve in America! ' [14] And a few years later the New York Court of Appeals declared void a law prohibiting night work for women. ' When it is sought,' said Judge Gray on behalf of the court, ' under the guise of a labor law, arbitrarily, as here, to prevent an adult female citizen from working any time of day that suits her, I think it is time to call a halt.' In 1905 the Supreme Court of the United States in the case of *Lochner v. New York* took a similar view of a New York statute prescribing the hours of labor in bakeries.[15] If, said the Court in effect, long hours of bakers could be shown to affect the quality of bread, something might be said for the regulation under the police power; but bakers were sufficiently intelligent to make their own labor contracts in their own interest, and ' we think the limit of the police power has been reached and passed in this case.' Justice Holmes, however, entered a vigorous dissenting opinion in which he observed that ' This case is decided upon an economic theory which a large part of the country does not entertain. . . . The Fourteenth Amendment does not enact Mr. Herbert Spencer's *Social Statics.*'

14 The *Post* continued: ' It is interesting to reflect that while Dora's feudal forebears fought for the right to work, it has been left for Dora's generation to fight for the right to work overtime. But there is still a chance — if we all stick together — to save this state from the fate of Massachusetts . . . and other commonwealths, which, given the choice between healthy womanhood and cheap paper boxes, are now going without paper boxes.'

15 198 U.S. 45 (1905).

Many of these illiberal decisions have since been reversed, and all of the states today have laws carefully regulating conditions and hours of labor for women and children, and in all dangerous occupations. As early as 1898 the Supreme Court, in the case of *Holden v. Hardy* [16] accepted a Utah law limiting to eight the hours of labor in mines, and this precedent has been commonly followed, though judges have differed on the question of what constituted a hazardous or fatiguing occupation. An Oregon law of 1903 limiting to ten the hours of employment for women was upheld in the Supreme Court in the notable case of *Muller v. Oregon* [17] — notable not alone for the apparent change of attitude on the part of the Court, but because the mass of scientific, sociological, economic, and physiological data introduced by the counsel for Oregon, Louis D. Brandeis, was admitted as evidence. Thus the principle was established that the courts could take cognizance of the special circumstances that justified the exercise of the police power. This did not necessarily mean that the courts would accept expediency as a legal argument, but rather that they would acquiesce in legislative findings of reasonableness. By 1930 almost every state in the Union had limited the hours of labor for women, and most states either strictly regulated or wholly prohibited the labor of children under fourteen years of age. Under the impact of such legislation child labor declined from almost 2 million in 1910 to less than three-quarters of a million in 1930.

Legislative enactments of minimum wages were for a long time less successful. Organized labor itself long opposed such legislation as tending to level the general wage scale down rather than up, but in time labor withdrew its opposition to minimum wages for women and children. Following Australian and British precedents, Massachusetts in 1912 enacted the first minimum wage law for women and children, and within a few years fourteen states had followed suit. In 1916 the learning and logic with which Louis Brandeis and Felix Frankfurter had argued in the state court persuaded the Supreme Court to accept the Oregon minimum wage act,[18] and thereafter all seemed clear sailing. Seven years later, however, in one of the most remarkable reversals in our judicial history, the Court found a Dis-

[16] 169 U.S. 366 (1898).

[17] 208 U.S. 412 (1908).

[18] *Stettler v. O'Hara* 243 U.S. 629 (1916). On this case the Court divided four to four, thus sustaining the act.

trict of Columbia minimum wage law unconstitutional,[19] and on this rock of judicial intransigence the program of minimum wage legislation was temporarily wrecked. When in 1933 the legislature of New York attempted to fix minimum wages for women in laundries, the Court, by a five to four decision, invalidated the law, stating that legislatures are 'without power by any form of legislation to prohibit, change or nullify contracts between employers and adult women workers as to the amount of wages to be paid.'[20]

Another series of laws was designed to safeguard the health and lives of workers. In no other industrial nation were the hazards of industry so great or the accident and death rate so high as in the United States. In 1907, for example, there were 4534 fatal accidents and 87,644 non-fatal injuries among railroad workers alone, and in 1917 fatal accidents in manufacturing establishments amounted to 11,338 and non-fatal to the astonishing total of 1,363,080. The most elementary task here was to require the installation of safety devices and to provide for sanitary and fire inspection. It proved easier to pass laws and draw up regulations than to enforce them. Not until inspection was taken out of the hands of spoilsmen and entrusted to civil servants was there any perceptible improvement in the safety situation. The next task was to secure compensation for the injured or incapacitated victims of industry. Before this could be done it was necessary to get rid of the monstrous common law doctrines which made it almost impossible for the injured workingman or his family to collect compensation for injuries or death: if the worker had willingly assumed the risks of his job, if his accident resulted from his own negligence or that of a fellow worker, the company was not responsible! Most European and Commonwealth nations had workmen's compensation legislation by the turn of the century; alone of major industrial nations the United States lagged behind. Congress provided workmen's compensation for interstate railroad workers but when the states — Maryland leading the way — enacted similar laws the courts declared them void. Not until 1917 when the Supreme Court sustained New York's new compensation act[21] were the states able to go ahead with full-dress programs. Within a few years

[19] *Adkins v. Children's Hospital* 261 U.S. 525 (1923).
[20] This decision was in turn reversed and state minimum wage laws held valid. *West Coast Hotel Co. v. Parrish* 300 U.S. 379 (1937).
[21] *New York Central R.R. v. White* 243 U.S. 188 (1917).

most states outside the South had legislated workmen's compensation.

Veterans of industry were as much the responsibility of society as casualties, but few industries or businesses made the least provision for workers who had outlived their usefulness: they were supposed to fend for themselves, or to live on the charity of their children. The palpable injustice and inefficiency of this had led Britain and all the advanced European countries to provide unemployment and old-age pension programs even before the turn of the century. Here, too, the United States lagged behind. A few railroads experimented with contributory old-age pension plans in the late nineteenth century, and some years later the Carnegie Steel Company and the Standard Oil Company set up pension schemes. During the First World War, Congress provided retirement pensions for federal employees, and in the 'twenties a number of states experimented with ineffective pension schemes, but nothing was really done until after the inauguration of the second Roosevelt. So, too, with unemployment insurance. Ohio had set up employment offices early in the century, and other states had followed, but this did little to alleviate the problem for the unemployable. Here, too, Wisconsin, so often in the forefront of progressivism, led the way with a plan drafted by the distinguished economist, John R. Commons, and during the depression other states followed suit. But unemployment was by its very nature a national problem, and did not yield to state palliatives. Not until 1935 was this grievous problem finally put on the road to solution.

BIBLIOGRAPHY

1. GENERAL. F. T. Carlton, *History and Problem of Organized Labor;* John R. Commons, *et al., History of Labor in the United States,* vols. 3 and 4; C. R. Daugherty, *Labor Problems in American Industry;* Joseph Dorfman, *Economic Mind in American Civilization,* vol. 3; Foster R. Dulles, *Labor in America;* Harold U. Faulkner, *The Decline of Laissez Faire;* A. L. Harris, *The Black Worker;* Herbert Harris, *American Labor;* Edward C. Kirkland, *Industry Comes of Age: Business, Labor and Public Policy, 1860–1897;* L. L. Lorwin, *The American Federation of Labor;* Selig Perlman, *History of Trade Unionism in the United States* and *A Theory of the Labor Movement;* Philip Taft, *The A. F. of L. in the Time of Gompers;* Frank Tannenbaum, *A Philosophy of Labor;* Norman J. Ware, *Labor Movement in the United States 1860–1895;* Charles H. Wesley, *Negro Labor in the United States 1850–1925;* Leo Wolman, *Growth of American Trade Unions 1880–1923.*

2. LABOR LEADERS AND LEADERSHIP. Jane Addams, *Twenty Years at Hull House;* Charles Barker, *Henry George;* Harry Barnard, *Eagle Forgotten* (John P. Altgeld); C. R. Geiger, *The Philosophy of Henry George;* Ray Ginger, *The Bending Cross* (Eugene V. Debs); Elsie Glück, *John Mitchell;* Samuel Gompers, *Seventy Years of Life and Labor* (2 vols.); Jonathan Grossman, *William E. Sylvis;* R. E. Harvey, *Samuel Gompers;* Tom Johnson, *My Story;* Caro Lloyd, *Henry Demarest Lloyd* (2 vols.); A. E. Morgan, *The Philosophy of Edward Bellamy;* Terence Powderly, *The Path I Trod;* Lincoln Steffens, *Autobiography* (2 vols.); Graham Taylor, *Pioneering on Social Frontiers.*

3. LABOR CONFLICTS AND INDUSTRIAL VIOLENCE. Louis Adamic, *Dynamite;* Paul W. Brissenden, *The I. W. W.;* J. R. Brooks, *American Syndicalism;* J. W. Coleman, *The Molly Maguire Riots;* J. R. Commons, *et al., History of Labor in the United States,* vol. 4; Henry David, *History of the Haymarket Affair;* Carter Goodrich, *The Miner's Freedom;* Harry W. Laidler, *Boycott and Labor Struggles;* Almont Lindsey, *The Pullman Strike;* G. S. Mitchell, *Textile Unionism in the South;* C. H. Parker, *The Casual Laborer and Other Essays;* Benjamin Rastall, *Labor History of the Cripple Creek District;* Tom Tippett, *When Southern Labor Stirs;* Samuel Yellen, *American Labor Struggles.*

4. NOVELS PORTRAYING LABOR. Sherwood Anderson, *Marching Men;* Frank Harris, *The Bomb;* John Hay, *The Breadwinners;* Robert Herrick, *Memoirs of an American Citizen;* William D. Howells, *A Hazard of New Fortunes;* Jack London, *The Iron Heel;* Ernest Poole, *The Harbour;* Upton Sinclair, *The Jungle.*

5. LABOR LEGISLATION AND THE COURTS. Edith Abbott, *Women in Industry;* Edward Berman, *Labor and the Sherman Act;* M. C. Cahill, *Shorter Hours: A Study of the Movement since the Civil War;* M. R. Carroll, *Labor and Politics;* John R. Commons & J. B. Andrews, *Principles of Labor Legislation;* John R. Commons (ed.), *History of Labor in the United States,* vol. 3; Paul Douglas, *Social Security in the United States;* E. H. Downey, *Workmen's Compensation;* Merle Fainsod & Lincoln Gordon, *The Government and the American Economy;* Felix Frankfurter & N. V. Greene, *The Labor Injunction;* Ernst Freund, *The Police Power;* R. Fuller, *Child Labor and the Constitution;* G. G. Groat, *Attitude of American Courts on Labor Cases;* Clyde E. Jacobs, *Law Writers and the Courts;* John Lombardi, *Labor's Voice in the Cabinet;* A. T. Mason, *Organized Labor and the Law;* I. M. Rubinow, *Social Insurance;* John Spargo, *Bitter Cry of the Children;* H. L. Sumner & E. A. Merritt, *Child Labor Legislation in the United States;* Edward E. Witte, *The Government in Labor Disputes.*

6. DOCUMENTS. Edith Abbott (ed.), *Immigration: Select Documents and Case Records;* H. S. Commager, *Documents,* nos. 233, 295, 301, 326, 334–6, 364–6, 368; John R. Commons (ed.), *Documentary History of American Industrial Society,* vols. 4–6; A. R. Ellingswood & W. Coombs, *The Government and Labor;* James M. Landis, *Cases on Labor Law;* Carl Rauschenbush & Emmanuel Stein, *Labor Cases and Materials.*

For further references, *Harvard Guide,* ¶¶ 205, 210.

Immigration

1. A NATION OF NATIONS

IMMIGRATION is the oldest and most persistent theme in American history, and though the character of American immigration changed in the twentieth century, the process has remained essentially the same throughout our history. For 300 years immigrants to America shared common experiences: the English, Dutch, and French of the seventeenth century, the German, Scotch, Irish, and Scandinavian of the eighteenth and nineteenth, the Italian, Slav, Hungarian, and Greek of the twentieth, all had to uproot themselves from Old World homes, break away from familiar folkways, and adjust themselves to a new environment and new institutions in a New World. With the early settlers the process of adjustment was largely physical. Of their experience we can say with Robert Frost

> The land was ours before we were the land's.
> She was our land more than a hundred years
> Before we were her people. . . .

For those who came after the pattern of American life had been in some measure fixed, the adjustment was more largely social and economic; but the cultural and psychological implications of the process of uprooting and transplanting were substantially the same for all. And all through these years, from the founding of the Republic to 1917, the United States welcomed all comers, and invited all of them to membership in its political and social community. If the United States was not precisely a melting pot, as the earlier metaphor asserted, it was a loom on which the domestic warp and the imported weft were woven into a pattern in which all the threads, except perhaps the black, blended harmoniously into each other.

The transfer of peoples from the Old World to the New was the most extensive and successful experiment of its kind in modern history, carried out on a larger stage and over a longer period and with fewer convulsive reactions than any comparable enterprise. Yet it would be a mistake to think it unique. The emigration of 40 million Europeans to the United States was part of a much larger emigration from the Old World to Canada, Australia, South Africa, the Argentine, Brazil, and many others parts of the globe. And while it is true that in the past century and a half more emigrants went to the United States than to any other country, it is worth noting that Argentina and, for long periods, Canada actually received larger numbers of immigrants in proportion to their population, and that since the mid-'twenties it is France that has been the chief magnet for emigrants from other European countries.[1]

What explains the readiness of tens of millions of Europeans to embark upon the arduous adventure of emigration? Persistent poverty for the peasants, recurrent hard times for workers, war and the constant threat of military service for young men, political oppression, religious persecution, a class system which closed the door of opportunity to the vast mass of the poor and denied education to their children — these were, for 200 years, the major motivations. As for the magnetic attraction of America, that is even more easily explained: open land, work for all who were willing to work, a higher standard of living for ordinary folk than was known in Europe, religious freedom, political democracy, social equality, a second chance for the young — these were the lodestars that drew millions from the Old World to the New. Ballads and songs, the accounts of travelers printed in the local newspapers, the tales of those who revisited their old homes and boasted of their new-found wealth, a million ' America-letters ' — all told the same story:

> They give you land for nothing in jolly Oleana,
> And grain comes leaping from the ground in floods of golden manna,
> And ale as strong and sweet as the best you've ever tasted,
> It's running in the foamy creek, where most of it is wasted . . .[2]

Men and women foregathered in the mill towns of Scotland or the fishing villages of Norway, or along the sanguinary banks of the Danube, to sing some new ballad about America, or listen to the latest

[1] See Frank Thistlethwaite, ' Migration from Europe Overseas in 19th and 20th Centuries,' Reports of the 11th International Conference of Historical Sciences, Vol. V, for a fascinating analysis.

[2] ' Oleana,' translated by Theodore Blegen, *Norwegian Emigrant Songs and Ballads*, U. of Minnesota Press.

America-letter: in America you eat meat every day; in America everybody is equal; in America you do not pull your forelock to the priest
or take your hat off to the mayor — he takes his hat off to you; in
America women do not work in the fields; in America all the children go to school; in America no one makes you serve in the army.
When Andrew Carnegie was a little boy in Dumfermline, Scotland,
he used to hear his father and mother sing

> To the West, to the West, to the land of the free,
> Where the mighty Missouri rolls down to the sea;
> Where a man is a man if he's willing to toil,
> And the humblest may gather the fruits of the soil;
> Where children are blessings, and he who hath most
> Has aid for his fortune and riches to boast.
> Where the young may exult and the aged may rest,
> Away, far away, to the land of the West.

It was this song that induced the elder Carnegie to migrate to Amer-
ica, where all of his dreams came true. The Swedish immigrant,
Hans Mattson — who eventually became Secretary of the State of
Minnesota — put the matter simply:

Much has been said of the causes of immigration. These are numerous
but the chief cause I have found to be that the people of the Old World
are now being aroused to the fact that the social conditions of Europe
with its aristocracy and other inherited privileges, are not founded on
just principles, but that the way to success ought to be equally open for
all, and determined, not by privileges of birth, but by the inherent worth
of man. And here in America is found a civilization which is, to a large
extent, built on equality and the recognition of personal merit. This, and
the great natural resources of the country, the prospects for good wages,
which a new continent affords, and in many cases greater religious liberty,
draws the people of Europe to this country.[3]

Other countries, to be sure, were potentially as attractive — Canada, Australia, the Argentine — but of them all it was the United
States alone that — until the end of the nineteenth century — combined a liberal land policy, abundant opportunities for work, complete religious freedom, and cheap access across the Atlantic by
sailing ship and steamer and into the interior by railroad.

The decades of the 'forties and 'fifties had seen the influx of immense numbers of immigrants from Ireland, Germany, and Scandinavia. The Civil War deflected the stream of immigration, but after

[3] Hans Mattson, *Reminiscences, the Story of an Emigrant*, p. 296.

Appomattox the waters flowed once again into familiar channels. In the next three-quarters of a century some 33 million emigrants sought American shores,[4] swarming out onto the rich prairie lands of the West, transforming the cities into enormous cosmopolitan bee-hives, performing the back-breaking labor that made possible the economic expansion of the nation, creating new problems of social assimilation and adaptation, and bringing to the United States the richest and most varied cultural heritage vouchsafed any modern na-tion — though one all too often dissipated. This immigration from the Old World to the New represents the greatest folk movement in history, ancient or modern. After a century and a half of colonization and unprecedented natural increase the population of the English colonies in America was but slightly over 2 millions; every decade from 1850 to 1930 witnessed an immigration large enough to replace this entire population.

In attempting to analyze and interpret the significance of this immigration it may be well to dispose of some misconceptions at the outset. Neither immigration nor racial heterogeneity is a recent de-velopment; immigration was as large, proportionately, in the later colonial period as in the latter part of the nineteenth century, and the population of the colonies on the eve of the Revolution, though predominantly English and African, represented six or seven nation-alities and three or four languages. Nor was there ever any ground for fearing that the ' native stock ' would succumb to the alien inva-sion, or that the foreign infiltration would upset the equilibrium of the American population. Despite the fecundity of many of the im-migrant groups, and the very general intermarriage of native- and foreign-born, the number of Americans of foreign or mixed parent-age constituted only one-fifth of the population in 1920, and de-clined steadily thereafter. And though the number of foreign-born in the country more than doubled in the 50 years after 1880, so, too, did the population, and the foreign-born made up a smaller per-centage of the population in 1930 than in 1880, while by 1960 the number had fallen to about 5 per cent. Less unreasonable was the fear that the changing sources of immigration after 1880 would im-

---

[4] Total immigration from 1820 to 1930 was 37,762,102. There has been, however, a continuous return emigration to the Old World, and in the decade 1930–40 this more than equaled immigration. One authority has estimated that the total net increase from immigration from 1820 to 1930 may be placed at 26,180,000.

pede the processes of assimilation and Americanization; yet the experience of World War II did not justify these fears. Certainly there is no evidence that recent immigrant stock has shown itself less intelligent politically than the earlier stock, or less faithful to democracy. At one time the notion that the foreign-born element in the population was largely responsible for crime and disease, and the perpetual object of charity, was widely prevalent, but a more careful examination of this question has not substantiated this belief. That the foreign-born figures more largely than the native-born in the statistics of crime and charity was clearly an index of opportunity rather than of character. Nor is there any scientific ground for holding that those of Northern European stock are in any important respects different from those of the South, and by now the theory of Nordic supremacy is interesting only as an historical curiosity. Cheap immigrant labor unquestionably threatened the gains of organized labor, and tended to depress money wages, and this accounts for the persistent agitation by labor for some kind of restriction on immigration. Yet the material standard of living in America generally kept ahead of that in Europe, and after half a century of large-scale immigration remained higher than in all but a very few countries, such as Denmark and Sweden. The infiltration of new blood into a given industry generally makes the people already there ambitious to move on and up; yesterday's pick-hand becomes today's riveter and tomorrow's construction boss or company vice-president. Standards of living for a long time remained lower among the Anglo-Saxon mill hands in the South, where there was no push from below, than among the Finnish and Polish and Lithuanian textile workers in New England; and Polish tobacco farmers in the Connecticut valley boasted cars, radios, and modern plumbing at a time when ' Nordic ' farmers in Georgia could not afford electric light. And as for the immigrant ' taking advantage ' of his adopted country, official and unofficial estimates of the simple monetary value of each immigrant to the American economy ranged from $1000 to $10,000.

2. The ' Old ' Immigration and the ' New '

The facts and figures of immigration can be told briefly; their implications are not so easy to evaluate. In the decade from 1850 to 1860 about 2.5 million immigrants came to this country; in the 40

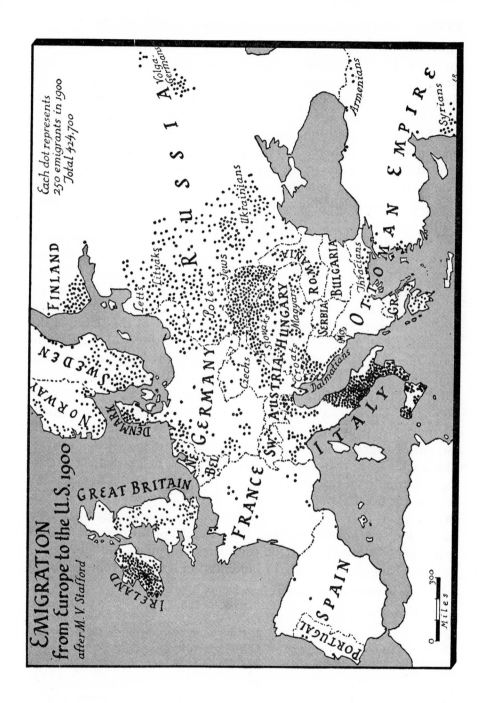

EMIGRATION
from Europe to the U.S. 1900
after M.V. Stafford

Each dot represents
250 emigrants in 1900
Total 424,700

GREAT BRITAIN

IRELAND

NORWAY
SWEDEN
DENMARK
FINLAND

NETH.
BEL.
GERMANY
FRANCE
SW.
AUSTRIA-HUNGARY
Czechs
Slovaks
Croats
Maygars
Dalmatians
SERBIA
MON.
BULGARIA
ROMANIA
GREECE
Thracians

ITALY
SPAIN
PORTUGAL

R U S S I A
Finland
Letts
Littvaks
Poles
Jews
Ukrainians
Volga-Germans

Armenians
OTTOMAN EMPIRE
Syrians

0 300
Miles

261

years from 1860 to 1900 about another 14 million; in the first
30 years of the twentieth century over 18 million. Of these 35 million immigrants the largest number were from the United Kingdom — some 8.5 million in all — of which over 4.5 million came
from Ireland. Germany accounted for approximately 6 million, Canada for almost 3 million, and the three Scandinavian countries for
2.25 million. The largest number of immigrants from northern and
western Europe came in the generation immediately after the Civil
War — there was a notable decline in immigration from Germany
and the United Kingdom after 1890 and from Scandinavia after
1910.

The racial ingredients that made up the American population in
1870 were not markedly different either in character or in relative
strength from those which had made up the population a hundred
years earlier. But already in the 1870's there began to appear new
types among the thousands who swarmed in at Castle Garden, New
York. Austrians and Hungarians from the valley of the Danube, Bo-
hemians from the river Moldau, Poles from the Vistula, and Serbs
from the river Save, blue-eyed Italians from the banks of the Arno
and olive-skinned Italians from the plains of Campania or the mountains of Sicily, Russians from the Volga and the Dnieper and the
steppes of Ukraine, all poured to the promised land. Almost 75,000
of the many peoples of the old Dual Monarchy came over in the
'seventies, over 50,000 Italians and as many Russians. By the 'eighties
this trickle from southern and eastern Europe had become a stream,
by the 'nineties a torrent, and in the early years of the new century
a veritable flood. Altogether, in the 50 years between 1880 and 1930,
Italy sent us over 4.5 million emigrants, Austria, Hungary, and the
succession states over 4 million, Russia and Poland perhaps another
4 million — a total from these countries alone of 13 million.[5]

This change in the source of immigration is to be accounted for by

[5] Change in source of immigration from Europe, 1860–1930.

Period	Total Admitted	Northern and Western Europe		Southern and Eastern Europe	
1861–70	2,314,824	2,031,624	87.8%	33,628	1.4%
1871–80	2,812,191	2,070,373	73.6	201,889	7.2
1881–90	5,246,613	3,778,633	72.0	958,413	18.3
1891–1900	3,687,564	1,643,492	44.6	1,915,486	51.9
1901–10	8,795,386	1,910,035	21.7	6,225,981	70.8
1911–20	5,735,811	997,438	17.4	3,379,126	58.9
1921–30	4,107,209	1,284,023	31.3	1,193,830	29.0

overpopulation in southern and eastern Europe, the desire to escape military service, and the persecution of Jews, Poles, Czechs, and other minority groups, and also by the insatiable demand of American industry for cheap labor and by the importunate advertising of railroads and steamship companies. . . .[6] It is the conclusion of John R. Commons that the demand for cheap labor, the competition for steerage passengers, and the need of the transcontinental railroads to unload their large landholdings, brought more immigrants here than were sent by the hard conditions in the Old World; in fact these causes were largely complementary.

The distribution of these elements in the American population is important. Immigrants from northern Europe tended to go West and take land. Large numbers of Germans, it is true, congregated in the cities of the Middle West, giving a distinctive flavor to such places as Cincinnati, St. Louis, and Milwaukee which lingers on into the twentieth century. Among the Norwegians and Swedes the tendency to go out to the land was marked; the great agricultural states of Minnesota, Illinois, North and South Dakota, Nebraska, and Iowa still have a substantial Scandinavian population, and the single state of Minnesota displays no less than 400 Swedish place names, while the influence of these industrious and intelligent farmers was felt south to Texas and west to California. Some of the Irish went west — in 1860 there were 50,000 of them in Wisconsin, and large numbers in Iowa. Although most of the Irish who came here were farmers, the technique of American agriculture was strange to men who for generations raised only potatoes and cattle; there was a demand for their labor in the cities and on the railroads, and many of their religious leaders, like Bishop Hughes, feared that dispersion would destroy the faith and impair the moral standards of Catholics. As a consequence, most of them remained in the cities of the Eastern seaboard, where their group loyalty and talent for politics in a democratic medium made them the first and most enduring of racial blocs in American politics. Their control of the local government of New York was long proverbial, and their conquest of New England was so complete that in 1915 the Irish mayor of Boston could boast that his people had first ' made Massachusetts a fit place to live in,' and get away with it.

[6] Two leading steamship lines had 5000 to 6000 ticket agents in Galicia alone in the early years of the century.

The later immigrants — Italians, Russians, Austrians, Poles, Jews, and others from southern and eastern Europe — likewise chose, or got stuck in, the cities. Most of them were far too poor to buy a farm or invest in the machinery and stock necessary for modern agriculture, and peoples whose language, customs, and religion were very different from those of the older stock naturally tended to live together in colonies rather than isolate themselves on farms or in small towns. For many of them, too, as for many Irish and Danes and Norwegians, migration to America was their urban movement — inspired by the same notions that took native Americans from the farms to the cities. In 1900 two-thirds and in 1930 three-fourths of the foreign-born were living in towns and cities. The proportion of foreign-born in such large cities as New York, Chicago, Cleveland, and Detroit was impressive, but the concentration in the smaller industrial cities, such as Passaic and Paterson, New Jersey, or Lawrence and Fall River, Massachusetts, was even more extraordinary. In 1930 it was not New York City but the industrial town of Hamtramck, Michigan, that had the largest percentage of foreign-born in its population. But New York City, with the largest Jewish population of any city in the world, with almost 500,000 Italians and Russians, 250,000 Poles and Germans, and large numbers of every European and some Asiatic nationalities, presented the most varied racial picture. The Danish-born journalist Jacob Riis thus describes the city in 1890 when the new immigration was just beginning on a large scale:

A map of the city, colored to designate nationalities, would show more stripes than on the skin of a zebra, and more colors than any rainbow. The city on such a map would fall into two great halves, green for the Irish prevailing in the West Side tenement districts, and blue for the Germans on the East Side. But intermingled with these ground colors would be an odd variety of tints that would give the whole the appearance of an extraordinary crazy-quilt. From down in the Sixth Ward . . . the red of the Italian would be seen forcing its way northward along the line of Mulberry Street to the quarter of the French purple on Bleeker Street and South Fifth Avenue, to lose itself, after a lapse of miles in the ' Little Italy ' of Harlem. . . . Dashes of red would be seen strung through the District, northward to the city line. On the West Side the red would be seen overrunning the Old Africa of Thompson Street, pushing the black of the Negro rapidly uptown. . . . Hardly less aggressive than the Italian, the Russian and the Polish Jew . . . is filling the tenements of the old Seventh Ward to the river front, and disputing with the Italian every foot of available space in the back alleys of Mulberry Street. . . . Between the dull gray of the Jew, and the Italian red, would be seen squeezed in on the map a sharp streak of yellow marking the narrow boundaries of Chinatown. Dovetailed in with the German population the poor but thrifty Bohemian might be picked out by the sombre hue of his life as of his philosophy. . . . Down near the Battery the West Side emerald would be soiled by a dirty stain, spreading rapidly; like a splash of ink on a sheet of blotting paper, headquarters of the Arab tribe. Dots and dashes of color here and there would show where the Finnish sailors worship their God, the Greek pedlars the ancient name of their race, and the Swiss the goddess of thrift. . . .[7]

The same character could be observed in Boston, Chicago, San Francisco, and the other big cities of the country. Problems of housing, sanitation and health, and education inevitably arose. American cities came to have their 'ghettos,' their 'little Italy' or their 'Chinatown,' and 'slum' became a familiar word in the American vocabulary. By the decade of the 'eighties tenement conditions in American cities were as sordid as in the industrial centers of the Old World: breeding places for vice, crime, and epidemics. In 1890 two-thirds of the population of New York City was crowded into tenements. The situation was so serious that civic authorities, churches, and private philanthropies were aroused to remedy or eradicate the problem. Jacob Riis, who had gained the confidence of Police Commissioner Theodore Roosevelt, told the story of *How the Other Half Lives,* and led a crusade that wiped out the worst of the tenements; and the Henry Street Settlement was established under the energetic leadership of Lillian D. Wald. In Chicago, Jane Addams founded the famous Hull House, a social settlement which served as a clearing house for social reform throughout the Middle West. Miss Addams, at one point, even took on the job of garbage collector in order to show what could be done to rescue the slums from filth and disease by honest civic services. The tenement problem, however, touched important property interests, and while hundreds of the worst tenements were condemned, housing conditions among the foreign-born, and later among the Negroes who drifted up from the South, remained disgraceful.

Desperately poor, illiterate, without industrial or mechanical skills, and unable to strike out for themselves in a new country, the immigrants from southern and eastern Europe became, for the most part, unskilled laborers in mine, in factory, or on the railroad.

[7] Jacob Riis, *How the Other Half Lives,* pp. 25–7.

Historically, [according to a government report] the American origin of the more recent immigration . . . seems to have been the desire of certain Pennsylvania anthracite mine owners to replace the employees that they had found hard to deal with, and especially the Irish, with cheaper and more docile material. Strikes were a frequent cause of friction . . . and it was natural that employers should be on the lookout for new sources of labor supply. In a number of places these raw recruits of industry seem to have been called in as the result of a strike, and there probably were plenty of instances of sending agents abroad to hire men or of otherwise inducing labor to immigrate either under contract or with an equivalent understanding.

The Italians, Magyars, Slovaks, Hebrews, Czechs, Croats, Poles, and others who came over in the 'nineties, took what work was available, in the steel mills of Pennsylvania or the mines of West Virginia, in the lumber camps or the iron mines of Michigan, in the stockyards of Chicago or the sweatshops of New York. In 1907 a study of the Carnegie steel works revealed that of 23,337 laborers, 15,858 were foreign-born; two years later a survey of the workers in the bituminous mines of Pennsylvania discovered 76 per cent to be of foreign birth, and of these 92 per cent from southern and eastern Europe. The ' new ' immigration was crowding out the native and Irish laborers in the field of unskilled labor, but though this worked hardship in individual cases, it was in general advantageous; until the great depression of the 'thirties, there was work enough for all in American industry. The ever-ready supply of unskilled and unorganized foreign labor at the beck and call of industry was a serious obstacle to American labor organizations, and it is not a coincidence that the corporation that only in the 'thirties abandoned the open shop system — the United States Steel Corporation — recruited its labor force largely from immigrants of southern and eastern European extraction. The presence of large numbers of unskilled workers in manufacturing states such as Pennsylvania, Illinois, and Michigan and mining states such as West Virgina and Colorado tended to accentuate the grave industrial problems already pressing for solution, and these states achieved a distressing notoriety in the frequency and seriousness of their industrial disturbances. Yet the tendency to ascribe social unrest to the ' foreign agitator ' or the unassimilated laborer is for the most part sophistry.

Two other groups of immigrants came into the United States in increasing numbers after the turn of the century: Canadians and

Mexicans. It was easy for Canadians to drift into the United States, and after the Civil War many of them, attracted by the opportunities for work in the textile or lumber mills, or in the woods, found their way to northern New England, the Great Lakes states, and the Far Northwest. Canadian immigration first took on major proportions after 1910; in the next 20 years 1.5 million Canadians, one-third of them French and about two-thirds of them English-speaking, crossed over the border, cementing the strong ties already binding the two neighboring democracies. It should be added that especially in the prairie lands of the West there was a good deal of movement the other way as well, that between 1890 and the coming of the War perhaps a million American farmers moved into Canada, and that the tier of states on either side of the border from Minnesota to Montana and from Manitoba to Alberta came to constitute something of a social as well as an economic unit.

Immigration from Canada did not raise any problems of assimilation or Americanization, except among some of the French, but immigration from Mexico was a more serious matter. The census of 1930 revealed that not far from 750,000 Mexicans were domiciled in the United States, the majority of them in the border states of Texas, New Mexico, Arizona, and California. For the most part poor and illiterate, casual laborers who worked under shocking conditions in the cotton, rice, and beet-sugar fields of Colorado and the Southwest, they presented an urgent problem of labor and race relations. Immigration exclusion laws did not apply to the countries of the Western Hemisphere, and in so far as Mexican immigration was regulated at all, it was under the general provisions giving immigration officials the power to exclude those who ' might become public charges.' A strict application of this provision cut the Mexican-born population to a mere 372,000 by 1940.

On the surface the differences between the ' old ' and the ' new ' immigration were striking, and sometimes below the surface as well. Immigrants from northern and western Europe were usually literate, and often well-educated; they were predominantly Protestant; many of them were skilled workers or farmers, and a substantial number of them were from the professional classes. The vast majority of them came to stay, learned the language of their adopted country, took out their citizenship papers, and were soon indistinguishable from their American neighbors. Immigrants from southern and eastern Europe were often illiterate and unskilled; they were for the most part Catholic, Greek Orthodox, or Jewish in religious faith; they congregated in the slums of large cities where they retained their native language and customs; many of them were birds of passage rather than permanent settlers.[8] Yet these differences, obvious as they were, were the products of history and economy rather than manifestations of character. Almost all of them disappeared with the second generation.

All through our history there have been zealots who persuaded themselves that love of country comes only from birth not from adoption, and who were agitated about the ability of American society to absorb these newcomers, and about their loyalty to America. These sponsored the alien laws of 1798, joined the Know-Nothing party in the 1850's, rallied to the American Protective Association in the 1890's, signed up with the Ku Klux Klan of the 1920's, and gave aid and comfort to McCarthyism in the 1950's and to the John Birch Society a few years later. Yet the process of assimilation was not difficult, not even for Orientals and Mexicans who long seemed to present a special problem — after all it was not the Japanese-Americans who caused trouble during the Second World War but the super-patriots whose misguided zeal was responsible for putting them in concentration camps; nor was it the ' native peoples ' of New Mexico who looted the national domain, but the ' Anglos.' Assimilation did not necessarily mean the supplanting of native culture with an artificial American one, but the acceptance of American social and political institutions and practices. The opposition of certain patriotic groups to what Theodore Roosevelt called ' hyphenated Americanism ' led frequently to efforts to crush those heritages of foreign cultures that would give variety and richness to American life.

Actually what is impressive is not the resistance of immigrants to Americanization, but the extreme eagerness of most newcomers to abandon their Old World loyalties and profess those of the New. Americanization has not been the achievement of filio-pietistic groups winning over reluctant aliens — if anything these groups slowed the processes of Americanization — but the product of hu-

---

[8] Thus in the years 1908–10, of every 100 immigrants, ten of the ' old ' stock returned to their native country and 38 of the ' new.' In the decade 1900–1910, 45 out of every 100 ' old ' immigrants were women, but only 27 of the ' new,' which suggests that many of the immigrants did not come to stay.

man nature and of history. In other countries — Brazil, Chile, India, South Africa, Poland, Tunisia, for example — European aliens have been able to preserve their languages and their customs, but not in America. Here everything conspired to root out old attachments and supplant them with new: the vastness of the country which broke up compact settlements; the economy which rewarded speedy acquisition of the American language; the political system which encouraged naturalization and voting; the habit of voluntary association which welcomed most newcomers into political parties, labor unions, granges, and a hundred other organizations; and perhaps most effective of all, the public schools. What the public school meant is movingly recalled by the Russian Jewess, Mary Antin:

> Education was free. That subject my father had written about repeatedly, as comprising his chief hope for us children, the essence of American opportunity, the treasure that no thief could touch, nor even misfortune or poverty. It was the one thing that he was able to promise us when he sent for us; surer, safer than bread or shelter. On our second day I was thrilled with the realization of what this freedom of education meant. A little girl from across the alley came and offered to conduct us to school. My father was out, but we five between us had a few words of English by this time. We knew the word school. We understood. This child, who had never seen us till yesterday, who could not pronounce our names, who was not much better dressed than we were; was able to offer us the freedom of the schools of Boston! No application made, no questions asked, no examinations, rulings, exclusions; no machinations, no fees. The doors stood open for every one of us. The smallest child could show us the way.[9]

It is customary to interpret immigration from the point of view of the native American, but the persons chiefly affected by it were of course the immigrants themselves. The story of immigration cannot be read in the cold statistics of the Census Bureau, in the reports of labor surveys, of charity organizations, or of educational institutions. To the American already here, immigration has been merely one of a number of challenges to his social and political institutions. But for the immigrant who has torn up his roots from the Old World and transplanted them to new soil, who has abandoned the familiar ways and fields of his forefathers and is attempting to adapt himself to new and strange conditions, this is the great adventure of his life. Few historians have yet cut through the statistics of immigration to the psy-

[9] Mary Antin, *The Promised Land,* Houghton Mifflin Co.

chological realities that underlie them and give them meaning, but
the stirring and often splendid story can be read in the pages of
Rölvaag's *Giants in the Earth,* of Jacob Riis's *Making of an American,* of Mary Antin's *The Promised Land,* of Michael Pupin's *From
Immigrant to Inventor,* and many other novels and autobiographies.

These books, all by immigrants, emphasize the immigrant contribution to American society.

> We came not empty-handed here
> But brought a rich inheritance [10]

wrote one of the immigrant poets, and no student of American culture can fail to appreciate the validity of the boast. The immigrant
contribution of muscle and brawn is obvious; the contribution to
politics and public affairs, industry and labor, science and education,
arts and letters, is scarcely less apparent, though to be sure, in these
fields it has been an individual rather than a group contribution. To
remember the achievements of Carl Schurz and John Peter Altgeld
in politics, Jacob Riis and Nathan Straus in social reform, Joseph
Pulitzer, James Gordon Bennett, and E. L. Godkin in journalism,
Andrew Carnegie, James J. Hill, and Henry Villard in business,
Samuel Gompers and William B. Wilson in labor, Alexander Graham Bell, John Ericson, and Nikola Tesla in the field of invention,
Louis Agassiz, Albert Michelson, and Michael Pupin in science, Francis Lieber and Herman Von Holst in scholarship, Karl Bitter and
Augustus St. Gaudens in sculpture, and Theodore Thomas and Wal-
ter Damrosch in music,[11] is to realize the extent to which the foreign-
born have enriched American life.

[10] The Danish poet, Adam Dan.

[11] The foreign-born have, from the beginning, exercised almost a monopoly over
musical activities in the United States; only in the last generation is this changing. A
partial list of conductors of the leading symphony orchestras in the country illustrates
the situation in the 1930's:

Boston	Serge Koussevitsky
Buffalo	Lajos Shuk
Chicago	Frederick Stock
Cincinnati	Eugene Goossens
Cleveland	Artur Rodzinski
Detroit	Ossip Gabrilowitch
Kansas City	Karl Kreuger
Los Angeles	Arnold Schonberg
Minneapolis	Eugene Ormandy
New York	Arturo Toscanini
	John Barbirolli

THE LAST OF ENGLAND *by Ford Madox Brown*

3. PUTTING UP THE BARS

The story of governmental regulation of immigration, important as it is, can be told briefly. It is a suggestive fact that though, in our constitutional system, the regulation of immigration is a function of the Federal Government, it was not effectively exercised for well-nigh a hundred years. From the first, regulation of immigration was left largely to the states, and shortly after independence the states undertook to exclude ' undesirables.' South Carolina, for example, passed an Act for Preventing the Transportation of Malefactors in 1788, and Pennsylvania a simlar law in the following year. For the next half-century the states of New York, Massachusetts, and Pennsylvania, to whose ports most of the arrivals came, attempted, through the exercise of the police power, to exclude criminals, paupers, and diseased immigrants. The constitutionality of such legislation was sustained, but when New York State, faced with the heavy burden of receiving and protecting the throngs of immigrants who poured in during the 'thirties and 'forties, assessed a small head tax on each immigrant, the Supreme Court declared the tax unconstitutional as an interference with the congressional control of commerce.[12] It was obviously unjust for one or two states to carry the entire burden of welfare work which unrestricted immigration entailed, but the Federal Government steadfastly refused to assume any part of that burden.

It was not until 1882 that Congress finally undertook to regulate immigration, and then it acted only because its hand was forced by a situation which was rapidly getting beyond control. This was the threat of an inundation of the Pacific coast by Chinese coolies. It was the discovery of gold in 1849 and the consequent demand for cheap labor that first brought the Chinese to California, and the great Taiping rebellion of 1850 accelerated the movement. By 1852 there were about 25,000 Orientals on the Pacific coast, and thereafter they

Omaha	Rudolph Ganz
Philadelphia	Leopold Stokowski
Portland	William van Hoogstraten
Rochester	José Iturbi
St. Louis	Vladimir Golschmann
San Francisco	Pierre Monteux
Syracuse	André Polah
Washington	Hans Kindler

[12] *The Passenger cases,* 7 Howard 283 (1849) .

came at the rate of 4000 a year, their numbers augmented in the 'sixties by the demand for laborers on the Central Pacific Railroad. By the end of the 'seventies there were almost 150,000 Chinese in California alone, and their low standards of living, long hours of labor, and tractability were said to constitute a serious menace to native labor. At the same time they aroused racial prejudice by their obstinate adherence to the Chinese ways of life and religion, their exotic appearance, customs, and language, and their obvious intention to return to China with their savings.[13] As a result of these factors an anti-Chinese movement developed in the 'seventies under the leadership of an Irish agitator, Dennis Kearney. Taken up by the California Workingmen's party, it culminated in discriminatory legislation and a demand for the prohibition of further Oriental immigration.

It was in response to this demand that Congress, in 1882, passed an act excluding Chinese laborers for a period of ten years — a prohibition that was extended in 1890 and again in 1902 until it became permanent. As a result of this policy of exclusion the Chinese population of the country declined from 107,000 to 75,000 in 1930, and with that decline came a virtual disappearance of the anti-Chinese agitation that had for some time disturbed the relations of the United States and China.

Japanese immigration did not become a serious problem until some years later. There were less than 25,000 Japanese in the country at the beginning of the twentieth century, but when the following decade witnessed an extraordinary upturn in immigration from the Nipponese Empire, the Pacific coast became alarmed and demanded that the policy of exclusion be extended to embrace the Japanese as well as the Chinese. Anti-Japanese agitation crystallized into discriminatory legislation, and in order to avoid an international crisis, President Roosevelt, in 1907, reached a 'gentlemen's agreement' with the Japanese government whereby it pledged itself to continue

[13] Wrote Robert Louis Stevenson: ' Of all stupid ill-feelings, the sentiment of my fellow-Caucasians towards our companions in the Chinese car was the most stupid and the worst. They seemed never to have looked at them, listened to them, or thought of them, but hated them *a priori*. The Mongols were their enemies in that cruel and treacherous battlefield of money. They could work better and cheaper in half a hundred industries, and hence there was no calumny too idle for the Caucasians to repeat, and even to believe. They declared them hideous vermin and affected a kind of choking in the throat when they beheld them.' *Across the Plains,* 1879.

' the existing policy of discouraging emigration of its subjects of the laboring classes to continental United States.' Despite this agreement a small stream of Japanese continued to trickle into the Pacific coast, and between 1911 and 1913 California and other Western states enacted a series of laws designed to prevent Japanese from owning or even leasing real estate. Once again a diplomatic rupture was threatened. The personal intervention of Secretary of State Bryan was effective in softening the language though not in modifying the meaning of the California laws, and the crisis was temporarily averted. Ten years later when Congress was assigning mathematical quotas for immigration — an arrangement which would have admitted 246 Japanese a year — it went out of its way specifically to exclude Japan from the operation of the system and to ban Japanese immigration completely. The State Department expostulated in vain against this deliberate affront to a wartime ally. ' Our friends in the Senate have in a few minutes spoiled the work of years,' said Secretary Hughes, ' and done lasting injury to our common country.' All in all, by its long record of racial prejudice, segregation in schools, prohibition of land-holding, and discrimination in immigration, the United States managed to stockpile for itself a formidable arsenal of ill-will and bitterness among the Japanese people.

Once embarked upon a policy of regulation, Congress was faced with a number of alternatives among which to choose. Should it adopt a policy of selection, of regulation, or of exclusion? If selection, upon what basis should it be made? If restriction, how far should the government go in denying entry to prospective immigrants? The first general immigration law, that of 1882, was based upon the theory of selection; it imposed a head tax of 50 cents on each immigrant admitted, and excluded convicts, idiots, and persons likely to become public charges. From this time on a long series of federal acts elaborated the policy of selection, increased the head tax, and prohibited contract labor, considerably extended the classes excluded, and provided for more efficient enforcement of the laws. In a general way the new laws excluded the sick and diseased, paupers, polygamists, prostitutes, anarchists, alcoholics, and — by the Act of 1917 — persons with constitutional inferiority complexes!

While this policy of selection afforded protection against some unwelcome additions to the population, it made no dent on the total number who clamored to come in. Beginning early in the century there arose an insistent demand for some plan designed to reduce the total number who would be admitted and to select those thought to be best. Agitation for exclusion came from three disparate groups. First, and most powerful, was organized labor which had long looked upon unrestricted immigration — especially the immigration of unskilled workers — as a major threat. Second were social reformers like E. A. Ross of Wisconsin who had come to the conclusion that there could be no solution of the problems of slums, public health, and the exploitation of the poor as long as illiterate immigrants poured into the great cities. Third were the traditionalists who had been taken in by the doctrines of Nordic supremacy and who deplored the

> Accents of menace alien to our air,
> Voices that once the Tower of Babel knew.[14]

The fallacy of Nordic supremacy had already been used to justify Jim Crow laws in the South, and ' manifest destiny ' in the Philippines; now it was called on to rationalize the exclusion of the peoples from southern and eastern Europe.

The criterion of selection was to be literacy, and an historic battle was waged over this issue. A bill incorporating a literacy test passed one of the two Houses of Congress no less than 32 times, and on four occasions it was passed by both Houses and went to the President, only to be vetoed each time. Cleveland, in 1897, characterized the measure as ' a radical departure from our national policy.' Taft, in 1913, declared that a literacy test violated a principle which he believed should be maintained. Wilson in 1915 and again in 1917 denounced it as a test of opportunity rather than of character or fitness. On this last occasion, however, the bill was passed over the presidential veto and became a law. By its term no alien over 16 years of age who could not read English or some other language was to be admitted to the United States. When we note that in the first decade of the century less than 3 per cent of the ' old ' immigrants were illiterate, but over half of those from Sicily and southern Italy, we can see that the literacy test provided an easy and certain method of discrimination on racial and national lines.

The Immigration Act of 1917, in method selective, in purpose restrictive, marks the transition from the earlier to the modern policy

[14] Thomas Bailey Aldrich, ' Unguarded Gates.' ' A Poem,' wrote Aldrich, ' in which I mildly protest against America becoming the cesspool of Europe.'

of immigration regulation — regulation which became increasingly restrictive until it finally reached the point of exclusion. During the First World War immigration from Europe fell off sharply, but the fear of a renewal of the influx on an unprecedented scale after the cessation of arms led Congress to abandon the policy of selection for one of absolute restriction. By the Immigration Act of 1921, the number of aliens admitted from any European, Australasian, Near Eastern, or African country [15] was to be limited to 3 per cent of the total number of persons of that nationality residing in the United States in 1910. This so-called quota system, specifically designed to reduce the number of immigrants from southern and eastern Europe, drastically restricted the total number that could be admitted in any one year to 357,802. Even this act was criticized because it admitted too many immigrants and it failed to discriminate sufficiently in favor of northern and western Europeans. Consequently a new and more drastic law was passed in 1924 which reduced the annual quota from 3 to 2 per cent, and which, by taking the census of 1890 as a basis, more effectively favored English, Irish, German, and Scandinavian, and discriminated against Italian, Austrian, Russian, and other southern and eastern European immigration. Finally by the National Origins Act of 1929 the total number of immigrants who might be admitted in one year was reduced to 150,000 to be apportioned among the various European countries in proportion to the ' national origins ' of the American people in 1920.[16] Immigration from other American countries was left undisturbed, except by a Department of Labor ruling that no immigrants should be admitted who might become public charges.

The enactment of the first quota law of 1921 ended an era. In a hundred years the tide of immigration had risen to a flood, engulfing the whole country and depositing millions of people from every land and the cultural accretions of centuries. Then suddenly it ebbed. The Statue of Liberty still stood guard over New York harbor, its beacon light held proudly aloft, the inscription on its base not yet erased:

> Give me your tired, your poor,
> Your huddled masses yearning to breathe free,

[15] The Act of 1917 created a Barred Zone, including India, Siam, Indo-China, and other parts of Asia, from which no immigrants were to be admitted.
[16] See Table in Appendix.

The wretched refuse of your teeming shore,
Send these, the homeless, tempest-tost to me:
I lift my lamp beside the golden door.

But it was a symbol of things strange, and but faintly remembered.

BIBLIOGRAPHY

1. GENERAL. H. S. Commager (ed.), *Immigration and American History;* John R. Commons, *Races and Immigrants in America;* Maurice Davie, *World Immigration;* Oscar Handlin, *The Uprooted* and *Immigration as a Factor in American History;* Marcus Hansen, *The Atlantic Migration* and *The Immigrant in American History;* J. W. Jenks & W. J. Lauck, *The Immigration Problem;* Mary R. Keely (ed.), *Selected Articles on Immigration;* Carl Wittke, *We Who Built America.*

2. SPECIAL GROUPS. K. C. Babcock, *Scandinavian Element in the United States;* Rowland Berhoff, *British Immigration to Industrial America 1790–1850;* Kenneth O. Bjork, *West of the Great Divide: Norwegian Migration to the Pacific Coast;* Theodore C. Blegen, *Norwegian Migration to America* (2 vols.) ; Thomas Capek, *The Czechs in America;* Mary Coolidge, *Chinese Immigration;* Jerome Davis, *The Russian Immigrant;* A. B. Faust, *German Element in the United States* (2 vols.); Robert Foerster, *The Italian Emigration of Our Times;* Manuel Gamio, *Mexican Immigration to the United States;* Oscar Handlin, *Adventure in Freedom: Three Hundred Years of Jewish Life in America;* Florence E. Janson, *The Background of Swedish Immigration 1846–1930;* Bruno Lasker, *Filipino Immigration;* Henry S. Lucas, *Netherlanders in America 1789–1950;* William Mulder, *Homeward to Zion: Mormon Migration from Scandinavia;* Henry Pochmann, *German Culture in America;* George Potter, *To the Golden Door: the Story of the Irish in Ireland and America;* C. C. Qualey, *Norwegian Settlement in the United States;* Arnold Schrier, *Ireland and the American Emigration 1850–1900;* Wilbur S. Shepperson, *British Emigration to North America;* Carl Wittke, *The Irish in America.*

3. IMMIGRATION RESTRICTION. William Bernard (ed.), *American Immigration Policy — A Reappraisal;* Jane P. Clark, *Deportation of Aliens from the United States to Europe;* Edward Corsi, *The Shadow of Liberty;* Robert A. Divine, *American Immigration Policy 1924–1952;* R. L. Garis, *Immigration Restriction;* S. L. Gulick, *The American Japanese Problem;* John Higham, *Strangers in the Land: Patterns of American Nativism;* E. G. Mearns, *Resident Orientals on the Pacific Coast;* Rodman Paul, *The Abrogation of the Gentlemen's Agreement;* Barbara Solomon, *Ancestors and Immigrants.*

4. IMMIGRANT AUTOBIOGRAPHIES, LETTERS, AND NOVELS. Louis Adamic, *Native's Return;* Mary Antin, *The Promised Land;* Theodore C. Blegen, *Land of Their Choice: The Immigrants Write Home;* Abraham Cahan, *The Rise of David Levinsky;* Willa Cather, *My Ántonia;* Alan Conway, *The Welsh in America: Letters from Immigrants;* Henry S. Lucas, *Dutch Immigrant Memoirs and Related Writings* (2 vols.) ; Michael Pupin, *From Immigrant to Inventor;* Jacob Riis, *How the Other Half Lives* and *The Making of an American;* Ole

Rölvaag, *Giants in the Earth* and *Peder Victorious;* Theodore Saloutos, *They Remember America;* Gustaf Unionius, *A Pioneer in Northwest America 1841–1858: Memoirs* (2 vols.) .

5. DOCUMENTS. Edith Abbott (ed.) , *Historical Aspects of Immigration Problems* and *Immigration: Select Documents and Case Records;* H. S. Commager, *Documents,* nos. 233, 257, 306–7, 387, 404, 422, 453.

For further references, *Harvard Guide,* ¶¶ 211, 226.

Agriculture and the Farm Problem

1. THE AGRICULTURAL REVOLUTION

WHILE manufacturing, transportation, and business were advancing with giant strides in the half-century following the Civil War, agriculture still remained the basic industry, and the one which engaged the labor of the largest number of people and upon which industrial development largely rested. But agriculture itself was undergoing a revolution brought about through the operation of four basic factors: the expansion of the agricultural domain; the application of machinery and science to the processes of farming; the use of modern transportation to convey the products to world-wide markets; and the assumption by the Federal Government of major responsibility for the welfare of the farmers. This revolution meant a shift from husbandry to machine-farming, and from subsistence to commercial farming; made agricultural an intimate though subordinate part of the industrial system; exposed the farmer to the vicissitudes of the industrial economy and the world market; and brought a vast increase in productiveness and efficiency which did not always bring comparable returns.

In the years from 1860 to 1910 the number of farms in the United States trebled, increasing from 2,033,000 to 6,361,000; the acreage more than doubled, from 407,212,000 to 878,798,000, and the acreage of improved farm land trebled. The production of wheat rose from 173 to 635 million bushels, of corn from 838 to 2886 million bushels, and of cotton from 3,841,000 to 11,609,000 bales. More land was brought under cultivation in the 30 years after 1860 than in all the previous history of the nation. While the value of farms and farm products increased, they did not keep pace with returns from manufacturing and business, and there were serious decreases in parts of New England and the South. In 1900 the farmers' share in the national wealth was less than half that of 1860. Farm population increased absolutely, but the proportion of people living on farms declined; while the agricultural domain expanded, the relative political and social position of the farmer contracted.

In the half-century after the Civil War farming had been subjected to a series of shocks. The first, which we have already studied, was the impact of the war and reconstruction on the South, involving the partial destruction of the plantation system, the redistribution of land, and the rise of the crop-lien and the sharecrop systems. The second came from opening up the High Plains and the West, and the over-rapid extension of farming westward, with a consequent depression of farming in the Middle West and the East. American crops moved westward with the American people. In 1860 Illinois, Indiana, and Wisconsin were the leading wheat-producing states; 50 years later the cereal empire had passed to North Dakota, Kansas, and Minnesota. In 1860 the heart of the corn belt was the Ohio valley; in 1910 it was the Mississippi valley from the Wabash to the Platte. In 1860 Ohio led the nation in the production of wool; by 1900 Wyoming and New Mexico were the leading woolen states. In 1860 Mississippi was the leading cotton state of the South; by the turn of the century the Cotton Kingdom's capital was somewhere on the plains of Texas. All this meant drastic readjustment in the older states and the transition to truck or dairy farming or — as in much of New England — to mere subsistence farming.

A third shock was the rapid growth of world markets, and of world competition, as the productivity of the American farm outstripped America's capacity to consume. Wheat then competed with the wheat of the Argentine, Australia, and Russia; beef and wool with the products of Australia, New Zealand, and the Argentinian pampas; cotton with Egypt and India. Fourth, and scarcely less disturbing to the agricultural equilibrium was the impact of new machinery and of new crops, and new techniques of farming.

Except in isolated regions like the Southern highlands or the rich Pennsylvania and Maryland country, the average farm ceased to be a self-sufficient unit, where a man and his family raised most of what they ate, wore, and used, and provided their own amusement in neighborhood groups. It became, like the West Indian sugar plantations, a cog in an industrial system, devoted to the raising of a staple crop, mechanized, and tied up with banking, railroading, and manufacturing.

One thing, however, did not greatly change until after the First World War. American agriculture continued to be, as it had always been, extensive rather than intensive, robbing the land of its fertility and leaving desolation behind. Because land was abundant, fertile, and cheap, the American farmer of the early Republic had found it easier and more profitable to take up new land than to conserve the resources of the old. Just as speculators recklessly exploited mineral resources, so the farmer used up the soil, and the lumberman cut down the forest, leaving nature to do the replacing unaided. Almost everything conspired to encourage the farmer in his gutting of the soil: not only machinery and world markets, but constant change in farm ownership, unskilled Negro labor in the South, an increase in absentee ownership and in tenancy which destroyed the sense of responsibility toward the land, and a laissez-faire policy of government, both state and federal, toward the land and its resources. Not until the sharp rise in farm land values in the early years of the new century dramatized the passing of cheap good land did the government realize the necessity for conservation, or the farmer the necessity for scientific farming. Then it was almost too late. When economists came to count the cost of our exploitative agriculture they found that 100 million acres of land — an area equal to Illinois, Ohio, North Carolina, and Maryland — had been irreparably destroyed by erosion; that another 200 million acres were badly eroded; that over large areas the grass lands of the Great Plains had been turned into dust, and that the forest resources of the Eastern half of the country were rapidly disappearing. It remained to be seen whether science and technology could repair the material devastation, whether the drastic remedies of the economists could heal the economic malaise, and whether the expedient of government support could rehabilitate the farmer class.

The first and most important gesture was the Homestead Act.

2. THE USE AND ABUSE OF THE HOMESTEAD ACT

During the entire period from 1862 to the Theodore Roosevelt administration the Federal Government went through the motions of giving the public lands of the West — and of the South — to the people. The Homestead Act of 1862 was the triumphant climax of a struggle that had been going on ever since the 1780's. Over the years the forces of liberalism had gradually brought about a more demo-cratic land policy, forcing reluctant governments to sell public lands in smaller lots, and at lower prices, and to recognize the claims of pre-emption. Now the long struggle was at an end, and the public domain belonged to the people! Under the terms of the Homestead Act any citizen, except one who had served in the Confederate army, could obtain 160 acres on the public domain by living on it or culti-vating it for five years. Not content with this, and recognizing, some-what grudgingly, that the neat little rectangular farm of the East was not really suitable to the West, Congress had passed a complex series of land laws enlarging the areas that could be patented, facilitating entry and final acquisition, providing government aid to reclama-tion, and so forth. Thus the Timber Culture Act of 1873, the Desert Land Act of 1877, the Timber and Stone Act of 1878, the Carey Irrigation Act of 1894, the Enlarged Homestead Act of 1909, and so forth.

All of this should have meant that the immense public domain — perhaps 1 billion acres in 1860 — should have gone into the hands of the independent yeoman who, ever since Jefferson's day, had been the ideal American figure. Nothing of the kind happened. When the smoke of battle and the dust of the great plains blew away and statis-ticians came to account for the operation of the land system, it was clear that something between one-sixth and one-tenth of the public domain had gone to Homesteaders, and that all the rest had not been given away but sold — or held off the market by speculators, or by the government itself. Thus by the end of the century Home-steaders had patented about 80 million acres, but the railroads had received — from federal and state governments — 180 million acres, the states had been given 140 million acres, and another 200 million acres — much of it Indian lands — had been put up for sale to the highest bidders.

What accounted for the frustration of the Homestead policy? What accounted for it was a combination of confusion, incompetence, chi-canery, and fraud. Actually the Homestead policy was never suited to the needs of the landless workingman or immigrant; after all, how was he to move himself and his family to the West, build a house and barn, buy farm equipment and cattle, and keep going for a year until the money for his crops came in? Nor was the 160-acre farm suitable for the kind of farming profitable on the plains of the West, or in the mountains. Perhaps more important than either of these considerations was the fact that government policy was never really consistent; that for all their professed interest in the independent yeoman, Congress and the states showed themselves a good deal more interested in satisfying the demands of business and speculator groups. In land policy as in trust policy, the Federal Government contented itself with ceremonial gestures. Just as Congress could have broken up trusts at any time by the simple device of taxation, so Congress could have made sure that the public domain went to genuine farmers, either by refraining from lavish land grants to corporations or by the calculated use of taxation.

Instead, as the Commissioner of Lands stated in 1901, 'immense tracts of the most valuable lands, which every consideration of public interest demanded should be preserved for public use, have become the property of a few individuals and corporations.' The railroads were the most favored beneficiaries, but they were by no means the only ones who enjoyed privileged treatment. Lumber companies, ranchers' associations, emigration and colonization companies, individual speculators like Ezra Cornell of New York or Amos Lawrence of Boston got princely domains. Over 40 per cent of public lands in Kansas, for example, were withdrawn from the operation of the Homestead law and sold to railroads or speculators.

Most of these sales were legal, but many of them were accompanied by fraud. When Cleveland's reform land commissioner, William J. Sparks, came to examine the operation of the land system in 1885, he reported that

I found the magnificent estate of the nation in its public lands had been to a wide extent wasted under defective and improvident laws, and through a laxity of public administration astonishing in a business sense if not culpable in recklessness of official responsibility. The widespread belief of the people of this country that the land department has been very largely conducted to the advantage of speculation and monopoly, private and corporate, I have found supported by developments in every branch of the service. It seems that the prevailing idea running through this office and those subordinate to it was that the government had no distinctive rights to be considered and no special interests to protect. . . . I am satisfied that thousands of claims without foundation in law or equity, involving millions of acres of public land, have been annually passed to patent upon the single proposition that nobody but the government had any *adverse* interest. . . . The vast machinery of the land department appears to have been devoted to the chief result of conveying the title of the United States to public lands upon fraudulent entries, under strained constructions of imperfect public land laws, and upon illegal claims under public and private grants.[1]

An illuminating example of what happened when enthusiasm for Homesteaders gave way to concern for business is afforded by the history of the disposition of public lands in the South after the War. In 1866 Congress had set aside some 47 million acres of public lands in five Southern states for 80-acre homesteads. Ten years later the pressure of Northern lumber interests forced a repeal of these arrangements, and the land was thrown open to purchase by speculators. One Congressman hastened to acquire 111,000 acres in Louisiana; a Michigan firm got 700,000 acres of pine lands. In Louisiana alone Northern businessmen picked up over a million acres, and in Mississippi another 900,000 acres of timber. English firms, too, hurried to be in on the kill. One English company bought 2 million acres of timbered land in Florida, another bought 1.3 million acres in the Yazoo Delta country, and a London firm called the North American Land and Timber Company got 1.5 million acres in Louisiana for 45 cents an acre. In 1906 a government expert could conclude that the exploitation of the South by these and other companies was 'probably the most rapid and reckless destruction of forests known to history.'

Cleveland instituted some far-reaching reforms in the disposal of public lands, and these were carried further under Harrison. An act of 1889 put an end to all cash sale of public lands, and the next year the government limited land acquisitions to 320 acres; in 1891 came the first act setting aside forest reservations on public lands. But these modifications of the land system were both too little and too late.

3. MACHINERY

It is a curious and suggestive fact that the application of machinery to agriculture lagged fully a century behind the application of machinery to industry. The eighteenth century witnessed a thoroughgoing mechanization of many mining and manufacturing operations, but Henry Adams could truthfully observe of the America of 1800 that

---

[1] Quoted in Paul Gates, 'Homestead Law in an Incongruous Land System,' 41 *Am. Hist. Rev.* 655.

The Saxon farmer of the eighth century enjoyed most of the comforts known to Saxon farmers of the eighteenth. . . . The plough was rude and clumsy; the sickle as old as Tubal Cain, and even the cradle not in general use; the flax was unchanged since the Aryan exodus; in Virginia, grain was still commonly trodden out by horses.[2]

Mechanization of agriculture did not really begin until the 'thirties and 'forties, when Obed Hussey and Cyrus McCormick were experimenting with a reaper, A. D. Church and George Westinghouse with a thresher, and John Lane and John Deere with a chilled plow. Agricultural machinery, moreover, remained relatively unimportant, except in parts of the upper Middle West, before 1860. The Civil War, robbing the farms of their laborers and increasing the price of grain, induced farmers generally to adopt machines such as the reaper, which enabled a woman or even a boy to perform the work of several men. Over 100,000 reapers were in use by 1861 and during the four years of the war the number increased by a quarter of a million. After the war came countless new inventions — there were over 12,000 patents on plows alone before 1900 [3] — and the pressure of competition eventually made the use of agricultural machinery almost universal in the North. Soon almost every operation from preparing the ground to harvesting the product was transformed by machinery. The Oliver chilled plow, finally perfected in 1877, meant an enormous saving in time and money; within a few years the simple plow had been developed into the wonderfully efficient rotary plow which plowed and harrowed the soil and drilled the grain in a single operation. In 1878 the Deering Company marketed George Appleby's twine binder which greatly increased the amount of grain a farmer could harvest, and at the same time the steam threshing machine was perfected to a point where it was both efficient and safe. Within twenty years the bonanza farms of California were using 'combines' which reaped, threshed, cleaned, and bagged the grain in a single operation. During these same years the mowing machine, the corn planter, corn binder, husker and sheller, the manure spreader, the four-plow cultivator, the potato planter, the mechanical hay drier, the poultry incubator, the cream separator, and innumerable other machines entirely transformed the ancient practices of agriculture, lightened the drudgery, decreased the amount of

[2] Henry Adams, *History of the United States*, Vol. I, p. 16.

[3] Also 5319 on thrashers, 5801 on harrows and diggers, 9156 on seeders and planters, 12,519 on harvesters — and 1038 on instruments of bee culture!

labor, and increased efficiency. At the same time the steady reduction in the price of windmills, the invention of a vane that turned the wheel to the wind, and the mass production of barbed wire, speeded up the conquest of the Plains.

How great a saving in labor was made possible by the use of farm machinery can best be discovered from a few specific examples. In 1830 it required something over half an hour to prepare the ground and sow one bushel of wheat; in 1900 two minutes sufficed for this operation. With the hand cradle of 1830 a man could harvest 20 bushels of grain in 61 hours; by 1900 he could perform the same work in less than three hours. It took 21 hours to harvest a ton of timothy hay in 1850; half a century later, four hours. It was this vast saving in labor which made it possible for a proportionately smaller number of farmers to feed an ever-increasing number of city-dwellers and have a surplus left over for export.

In the twentieth century came a further development of industrialization with the application of steam, gasoline, and electricity to the farm. The huge ' combines,' formerly drawn by 20 or 30 horses, were propelled by gasoline tractors, and in 1930 almost 1 million tractors were in use on the farms of the United States: the kindly beasts which have accompanied mankind from the dawn of civilization, and whose care, training, and breeding have entered into human discipline, and culture, have been forsaken in favor of impersonal machinery. This substitution of power for horses has released not less than 30 million acres formerly devoted to pasture and forage. Electric power came to be used in all up-to-date dairies. The motor truck altered marketing conditions, and the motor car — especially after Henry Ford reduced its price to below $400 — the telephone, and the radio enlarged the social radius of the farm and led farmers to forget their rich heritage of folklore and song in favor of canned entertainment.

Varied farming persisted in many parts of the country, for mechanization was not profitable in much of New England, with its rolling topography and little specialties, or in the South where cotton and tobacco farming did not take readily to the use of machinery. The value of farm implements and machines in the whole country increased from about $246 million in 1860 to $750 million in 1900, and then, swiftly, to $3595 million in 1920. This increase was distinctly sectional in character. It was the Middle West and the Far

West that absorbed the reapers, mowers, tractors, harvesters, and threshers as fast as they could be turned out of the factories. In 1910 the value of machinery on Northern farms was $800 million, and by 1920 this had increased to over $2300 million, while the corresponding figures for the South were $293 million and $771 million. In 1920 the average value of farm implements and machinery on each South Dakota farm was $1500; on each farm in the cotton belt it was $215.

Farming as a way of life gave way to farming as a business. The farmer became increasingly an industrial worker, as much bound up in the complex industrial and fiscal system of the country as if he had a boss over him. A stout heart and willing hands were no longer the essential equipment of farming, or a cabin roof and the sky the only ' overhead.' Increase in land values, heavy costs of machinery, and the substitution of chemical fertilizer for manure required capital, and commonly involved the farmer in heavy indebtedness. The small diversified farm of the 1860's, with fields of wheat, corn, oats, and barley, orchard and vegetable garden, pasture mowing and woodlot, gave way to the large farm specializing in staple crops which could be produced with one kind of machinery, and sold for cash. Another result was the ominous increase in farm mortgages and in tenancy: by 1930 almost every second farmer was a tenant, and one-fifth of the total value of American farms was mortgaged.

4. Scientific Agriculture

There had been considerable interest in scientific agriculture in the second half of the eighteenth century, both in Europe and in America. Progressive Virginia planters like Washington and Jefferson adopted the new methods and implements which had been proved in England, and added some of their own; agricultural societies had been formed in all the thirteen original states by 1800. The rise of the Cotton Kingdom after the invention of the cotton gin in 1793, however, made it more profitable to take up virgin land in the newer South than to reclaim farms in Virginia and the Carolinas. Interest in scientific agriculture waned, except in New England where agricultural societies founded in the eighteenth century are still flourishing, where Elkanah Watson inaugurated the agricultural fair, where the first agricultural school in the United States opened in 1822, and where Benjamin Bussey's will anticipated the Morrill

Act by twenty-five years. The *American Farmer*, the first agricultural journal in the United States, was established in Baltimore in 1819. By 1840, when the prevalence of ' old-field ' land worn out by successive cropping with tobacco had become an eye-sore in tidewater Virginia and Maryland, Edmund Ruffin of Virginia began to devote himself to disseminating knowledge of scientific agriculture; and much of the abandoned land was regenerated by the use of marl. Lord Playfair's translation of Baron von Liebig's great treatise, *Chemistry in Its Application to Agriculture and Physiology* (1840), was read with avidity by the more progressive farmers. By 1860 there were 50 farm papers in the country, many of them in the South; and if the Civil War had not broken out, the teachings of Ruffin and De Bow would undoubtedly have borne fruit in a more diversified and economical agriculture in the South. For Southern energies were diverted away from specialization, just as in the last generation they have been directed toward it.

Yet the average farmer had little patience with scientific agriculture, and some of them doubtless read with approval the dictum of one book on farming that was published in 1860: ' Scientific agriculture stands today with phrenology and biology and magnetism. No farmer ever yet received any benefit from any analysis of the soil and it is doubtful if any one ever will.' As long as there was an abundance of cheap land and a shortage of labor — a condition which obtained until some time after the Civil War — it was more economical for farmers to abandon worn-out soil and move on to virgin land than to cultivate intensively and invest in expensive fertilizers. The passing of these conditions led inevitably to scientific agriculture, conservation, and reclamation.

Scientific agriculture in the United States has depended largely upon government aid. A number of states subsidized agriculture in one way or another even before the Civil War. The Constitution gives Congress no explicit jurisdiction over agriculture but as early as 1839 Congress made its first appropriation, $1000, for agricultural research. One of the most useful results of the loose-constructionist thinking in the Republican party was the creation by Congress in 1862 of a Department of Agriculture, under the direction of a commissioner with the happy name of Isaac Newton. In 1889 this department was raised to executive grade with a secretary of cabinet rank.

The activities and influence of the Department of Agriculture grew steadily until by 1930 it included some 40 subdivisions and bureaus, and operated with an appropriation of almost $100 million.[4] Its Bureau of Plant Industry introduced over 30,000 foreign plants including alfalfa from Liberia, short-kernel rice from Japan, seedless grapes from Italy, and grass from the Sudan to cover the High Plains; its Bureau of Entomology had field laboratories in every state to fight plant diseases; its Bureau of Animal Husbandry fought and conquered hog cholera, sheep scab, and Texas fever in cattle. It was the first government department to undertake extensive research and was, for a time, the leading research institution in the country. Nor was all of its research confined to the laboratory. In 1903 the department employed perhaps the most distinguished of agricultural scientists, Seaman Knapp of Iowa, to set up 'demonstration' farms throughout the South, and to fight the boll-weevil plague with techniques that every farmer could understand and use.

In the year 1862, which saw the passage of the Homestead Act and Pacific Railway Act, Congress passed the most important piece of agricultural legislation in American history, and perhaps the most important educational as well — the Morrill Land-Grant College Act. This far-sighted law, the joint product of Justin Morrill of Vermont and Jonathan B. Turner of Illinois, provided for the appropriation of public land to each state for the establishment of agricultural and industrial colleges. The act discriminated heavily in favor of the more populous states of the East — where farming was of less importance — and against the agricultural states of the West: thus New York State got almost a million acres of Western lands, while Kansas, which depended entirely on agriculture, got 90,000 acres. Seventeen of the states, including Illinois, Wisconsin, and Minnesota, turned the Morrill land-grant money over to the existing state universities; others, like Iowa, Indiana, and Oregon, chose to set up independent agricultural and mechanical colleges. This made for expensive duplication of facilities, but assured educational experiments and paid dividends when the rush of college students got to be more than any one state institution could handle. At first agricultural colleges were looked upon by the practical farmer with suspicion, but in time farmers learned their value and came to take pride in them. Milburn Wilson, an Iowa farm boy later active in the Department of Agriculture, recalled that

4 The 1961–62 budget was $82.1 billion!

When I went to Ames (Iowa) to study agriculture in 1902 I was not the first boy in my Iowa neighborhood to go to college, but I was the first boy from that neighborhood to go on to an agricultural college. Ten or fifteen years later it was becoming an accepted thing for all who could afford it. A few farmers began to keep books, count costs, and calculate where profit came and loss occurred. Still more farmers began to feed their stock scientifically, following the advice from Feeders' Hints columns in the farm journals. Alfalfa came in, and farmers became aware of nitrogen needs of the soil. Dairymen began building up new herds of high-producing Holsteins. Hardy and rust-resistant strains of wheat were accepted eagerly by more farmers. Hog men improved their stock, and inoculated against cholera. Finally came the popular demand for county agents — for thoroughly trained men to bring to farmers the advantages of scientific training.[5]

Scarcely second to the Morrill Act in importance is the Hatch Act of 1887. Influenced by the valuable work performed by the experimental station of Wesleyan University in Middletown, Connecticut, Congress provided in this act for the creation of agricultural experiment stations in every state in the Union; since that time Congress has steadily supported and expanded the work of education and experimentation in the field of agriculture. In 1930 sixty experiment stations were carrying on scientific research of incalculable benefit to the nation. For the most part the experiment stations concentrate their efforts on local problems: the boll weevil in Alabama, red rust in Minnesota, dry farming in the West.

Scientific farming, the conquest of plant and animal diseases, the surmounting of natural obstacles, and the adaptation of plants to American conditions — each has its roll of pioneers and heroes. Mark Alfred Carleton who experienced on the Kansas plains the devastations of wheat rust and rot and the vagaries of Kansas weather, scoured the wilds of Asia for a wheat strong enough to withstand the rust, the droughts, and the frosts of the Middle West. He returned with the famous Kubanka wheat and later introduced the Kharkov wheat to the American farmer. Within a few years these plants demonstrated their superiority to the domestic variety, and by 1919 over one-third of the American wheat acreage was of the varieties introduced by Carleton. William Saunders and Angus Mackay of Canada succeeded in crossing Red Fife with Calcutta wheat, and produced the hardy Marquis, thus opening up millions of acres of land in the

[5] *Agriculture in Modern Life,* Harper Bros., pp. 223-4.

Canadian Northwest to winter wheat. Niels Ebbesen Hansen of the South Dakota Agricultural College explored the steppes of Turkestan and the plateaus of inner Mongolia and brought back a yellow-flowered alfalfa that would flourish in the American Northwest. From Algeria and Tunis and the oases of the Sahara came the famous white Kaffir corn, introduced by Dr. J. H. Watkins, and admirably adapted to the hot dry climate of the great Southwest. George Hoffer conquered the insidious rot that destroyed the corn of the Middle West; Marion Dorset found the remedy for hog cholera; and George Mohler helped to stamp out the dread hoof and mouth disease that threatened to wipe out a large part of American livestock. Dr. Stephen M. Babcock saved the dairy farmers of the nation millions of dollars through the use of the Babcock milk test which determined the amount of butter fat contained in milk; he gave the patent to the University of Wisconsin. Seaman Knapp found in the Orient varieties of rice wonderfully adapted to the Gulf region, and today Louisiana exports rice to China and Japan. Luther Burbank, working in his experimental garden at Santa Rosa, California, succeeded in creating a host of new plants by skillful crossing. David A. Coker, on his South Carolina experimental farm, improved upland cotton and added immeasurably to the wealth of his section, and George Washington Carver of the Tuskegee Institute developed hundreds of new uses for the peanut, the sweet potato, and the soy bean. To be sure, the cinch bug, the boll weevil and his cousin the alfalfa weevil, and many other insect pests and plant blights have so far refused to yield to science, but the triumphs of science over plant and animal diseases have been as notable as the triumphs of medicine over the diseases which afflict mankind.

Scientific agriculture, whose benefits were world-wide, made it possible to raise more and better crops on less land, and even before the turn of the century the American farmer was plagued by over-production. But the impulse that had for generations sent American pioneers out looking for virgin soil persisted. Tantalized by the vision of millions of acres of land in the West that needed only a little damp to blossom like a garden, the farmers undertook, or persuaded the government to sponsor, ambitious projects of irrigation and reclamation. Artificial irrigation had been practiced by the Pueblo Indians even before the coming of the white man, and later by the Spanish missions of the Southwest, but it first came into general use with the Mormon settlements in Utah. Major Powell had suggested, in his famous Report of 1878, that much of the arid land of the West could be reclaimed by irrigation and had proposed that the Federal Government establish irrigation colonies comparable to those that already flourished in Utah and Colorado. Out of all this came the Carey Act of 1894 and the Newlands Reclamation Act of 1902. Together these opened up some millions of acres of Western land through state-federal co-operation. By 1910 some 14 million acres of land were under irrigation — a figure which increased by only 5 million in the next twenty years.

5. THE FARM PROBLEM

> When we've wood and prairie land,
> Won by our toil,
> We'll reign like kings in fairy land,
> Lords of the soil.

So sang Richard Garland and the ' trail-makers of the Middle Border ' as they pushed hopefully westward from the forests of Maine to the coulees of Wisconsin, the prairies of Iowa, and the sun-baked plains of Kansas, Nebraska, and the Dakotas. They won their wood and prairie land, but often won it for others — for absentee landlords, railroads, banks, and mortgage companies — and they lingered on as slaves, not lords, of the soil. Within a generation the ' marching song of the Garlands ' gave way to a different tune:

> There's a dear old homestead on Nebraska's fertile plain,
> There I toiled my manhood's strength away:
> All that labor now is lost to me, but it is Shylock's gain,
> For that dear old home he claims today.

And when young Hamlin Garland wrote his *Main Travelled Roads* he dedicated it to ' my father and mother, whose half-century of pilgrimage on the main travelled road of life has brought them only pain and weariness.' [6]

The history of a half-century of American agriculture is implicit in the story of the Garlands, and well might the student ask why the pilgrimage of the farmer toward the sunset regions should have ended in weariness and pain, why the conquest of a continent and the cre-

[6] Garland completes the story in *Trailmakers of the Middle Border* and *A Son of the Middle Border*.

ation of a great agricultural domain should have resulted not in the realization of Jefferson's dream of a great agrarian democracy, but in a ' farm problem.' For sixty years after 1870, the farm problem was a constant in American history, and during the whole of that time it not only ruffled the surface of American politics but churned up the vasty depths.

We can distinguish, for purposes of convenience, four aspects of the farm problem. There was the physical problem of soil exhaustion and erosion, drought and frost and flood, plant and animal diseases; the economic problem of over-expansion and over-production, rising costs and declining returns, exploitation in the domestic market and competition in the world market, mortgages and tenancy; the social problem of isolation and drabness, inadequate educational, religious, medical, and recreational facilities, narrowing opportunity and declining prestige. Finally there was the political problem of wresting remedial legislation from intransigent state and federal governments, which were much more responsive to the demands of industry, transportation, and finance than to the appeals of the farmer.

Of all these problems, the physical problem was the most intractable. The reckless mining of the soil, the cultivation of staple crops, the destruction of the forests, resulted in soil erosion and flood. The use of unskilled Negro labor, the concentration upon cotton and tobacco which exhaust the soil more rapidly than other crops, and heavy rainfall, made the problem of soil erosion peculiarly grave in the South. Almost 100 million acres of that section — approximately one-sixth of the total — had been hopelessly lost or seriously impaired through erosion, and in some sections of the Piedmont as much as half of the arable land had been swept of its topsoil by 1930. Early travelers in the South recorded that the streams were as clear as those of New England, but by the twentieth century the rivers of the South, which every year carried out to the ocean over 50 million tons of soil, were mud-black or clay-red. The abuse of the Southern uplands, says one distinguished geographer, ' is well nigh incredible under the cotton economy, and the necessary breaking of that socio-economic pattern if the country is not ultimately to be left to the foxes and the briars is about as tough a task of regeneration as one can imagine.' Southern farmers have tried to replenish their worn-out soil with fertilizer, but that means an intolerable financial burden on the agricultural overhead. South Carolina, for example, long spent 15 per cent of its total farm income on fertilizer, and the proportion was almost as great in the other seaboard states. Not until the TVA began to produce cheap fertilizer and the New Deal to provide low-cost farm loans, was the South able to inaugurate a program of reclamation and restoration.

In the grasslands of the West, too, erosion reached staggering proportions, necessitating irrigation and dry farming, and making the farmer helpless before dust storms and droughts.

> The primeval sod [writes Stuart Chase] has been burned, over-grazed, plowed up and destroyed. Where dry farming for wheat lands has been practised on the Great Plains, the Dust Bowl spreads. Where corn has been planted on the slopes of the tall grass regions, water erosion spreads. The sharp hooves of too many cattle and the close cropping of the grass by too many sheep have torn the cover from the open grazing lands, loosened the ancient sod, and started gullies and dunes of both water and wind erosion. One hundred and sixty-five million acres of grazing lands has been serious depleted.[7]

Closely connected with erosion, and more serious to the individual farmer, were the recurrent droughts which brought crop failures, bankruptcy, and ruin to the farmers of the High Plains ever since they first ventured out on that forbidding land. Mari Sandoz has graphically described for us the effect of drought in western Nebraska in the early 'nineties:

> The drought exceeded all probability. Corn did not sprout. On the hardland fringe the buffalo grass was started and browned before the first of May. Even lighter soil south of the river produced nothing. The sandhills greened only in stripes where the water-logged sand cropped out. The lake beds whitened and cracked in rhythmical patterns. Grouse were scarce and dark-fleshed. Rabbits grew thin and wild and coyotes emboldened. Covered wagons like gaunt-ribbed, gray animals moved eastward, the occupants often becoming public charges along the way.[8]

Since that time the drought has been an ever-present menace. So hazardous, indeed, was farming in parts of the High Plains that in the 1930's officials of the Department of Agriculture concluded that nature did not design this section for intensive agriculture, and seriously proposed the abandonment of farming over large areas.

---

[7] *Rich Land, Poor Land*, McGraw-Hill, p. 41.
[8] *Old Jules*, Little, Brown & Co., p. 179.

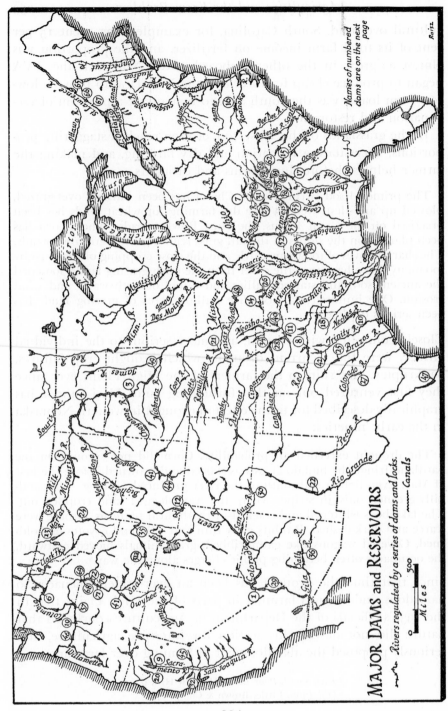

MAJOR DAMS and RESERVOIRS

⌇ Rivers regulated by a series of dams and locks. ═══ Canals

Names of numbered
dams are on the next
page

Reisz

MAJOR DAMS AND RESERVOIRS IN THE U.S.

Purpose

F—Flood control I—Irrigation N—Navigation *Capacity in*
P—Power WS—Water supply *1000 acre-feet*

A. BUREAU OF RECLAMATION AND CORPS OF ENGINEERS PROJECTS

1.	Hoover, Ariz.–Nev.	F, I, N, P	29830
2.	Glen Canyon, Ariz.	F, I, N, P	28040
3.	Oahe, S.D.	F, N, P	23600
4.	Garrison, N.D.	F, I, N, P	23000
5.	Ft. Peck, Mont.	F, I, N, P	19400
6.	Grand Coulee, Wash.	F, I, N, P	9402
7.	Wolf Creek, Ky.	F, P	6089
8.	Denison, Tex.–Okla.	F, N, P, WS	5530
9.	Shasta, Calif.	F, I, P, WS	4500
10.	McGee Bend, Tex.	F, P, WS	4480
11.	Eufaula, Okla.	F, N, P	3850
12.	Flaming Gorge, Utah (in constr.)	F, I, P	3789
13.	Hungry Horse, Mont.	F, I, P	3468
14.	Table Rock, Mo.	F	3462
15.	Hartwell, Ga.	F, N, P, WS	2858
16.	John H. Kerr, Va.	F, P, WS	2808
17.	Buford Dam, Ga.	F, N, P, WS	2554
18.	Texarkana, Tex.	F, P, WS	2509
19.	John Day, Ore.–Wash.	F, I, N, P	2500
20.	Trinity, Calif.	F, I, P	2500
21.	Tuttle Creek, Kansas	F	2280
22.	Elephant Butte, N.M.	F, I, P	2206
23.	Center Hill, Tenn.	F, P	2092
24.	Canyon Ferry, Mont.	F, I, P	2051
25.	Whitney, Tex.	F, P, WS	2017
26.	Norfolk, Ark.	F, P	1983
27.	Marshall Ford, Tex.	F, I, P	1951
28.	Keystone, Okla.	F, N, P, WS	1879
29.	Parker-Davis, Ariz.–Nev.	I, P, WS	1818
30.	Navajo, N.M.	I, P	1709
31.	Dale Hollow, Tenn.	F, P	1706
31a.	Minidoka, Idaho	I, P	1700
32.	Solano, Calif.	I, P, WS	1602
33.	Sardis, Miss.	F	1569
34.	Oologah, Okla.	F, N, P, WS	1519
35.	Palisades, Idaho	I, P	1402
36.	Theo. Roosevelt, Ariz.	F, I, P	1382
37.	McNary, Ore.–Wash.	F, I	1345
38.	Grenada, Miss.	F	1337
39.	Tiber, Mont.	F, I, P	1337
40.	Tenkiller Ferry, Okla.	F, P, WS	1230
41.	Owyhee, Ore.	F, I, P	1120
42.	Lewisville, Tex.	F, I, P, WS	1016
43.	Pathfinder, Wyo.	F, I, P	1016
44.	Seminoe, Wyo.	F, I, P	1012
45.	Folsom, Calif.	F, I, P, WS	1010

B. OTHER NOTABLE DAMS

46. Bonneville, Wash.–Ore.
47. Falcon, Tex.–Mexico
48. Bagnell, Mo.
49. Fort Randall, S.D.–Neb.
50. Jim Woodruff, Fla.

C. TENNESSEE VALLEY AUTHORITY DAMS

51. Kentucky
52. Pickwick
53. Wilson
54. Wheeler
55. Guntersville
56. Hales Bar
57. Chickamauga
58. Watts Bar
59. Fort Laudon
60. Norris
61. Cherokee
62. Douglas
63. Fontana
64. Hiwassee, etc.

D. ST. LAWRENCE RIVER LOCKS AND DAMS

65. Beauharnois, Que.
66. Long Sault, Ont.–N.Y.
67. Iroquois, N.Y.–Ont.

E. SNAKE RIVER DAM

68. Mountain Sheep
69. Nez Perce
70. Brownlee
71. Oxbow
72. Hells Canyon

Outraged nature took her revenge on the farmer not only in erosion, dust storms, and droughts, but in floods. The long-continued practice of denuding the land of topsoil and trees exposed the land to a series of calamitous floods, such as those which inundated the Middle States in the spring of 1936 and the great flood on the Ohio river which inflicted incalculable damage throughout its entire valley in the winter of the following year.

The ravages of insect pests have been scarcely less serious than erosion, drought, and flood. ' Every year,' writes Dr. L. O. Howard of the Bureau of Entomology, ' the damage wrought by insects nullifies the labor of a million men.' Before the attack of the cinch bug and the corn borer, the boll weevil and the alfalfa weevil, the average farmer was all but helpless, and the plagues of grasshoppers have been like the locust plagues of ancient Egypt. Who that has read Rölvaag's *Giants in the Earth* can forget how the grasshoppers destroyed not only the wheat but the morale of the farmers of the West:

And now from out the sky gushed down with cruel force a living, pulsating stream, striking the backs of the helpless folk like pebbles thrown by an unseen hand. . . . This substance had no sooner fallen than it popped up again, crackling and snapping — rose up and disappeared in the twinkling of an eye; it flared and flittered around them like light gone mad; it chirped and buzzed through the air; it snapped and hopped along the ground; the whole place was a weltering turmoil of raging little demons; if one looked for a moment into the wind, one saw nothing but glittering, lightning-like flashes — flashes that came and went, in the heart of a cloud made up of innumerable dark-brown clicking bodies. All the while the roaring sound continued. . . . They whizzed by in the air; they literally covered the ground; they lit on the heads of grain, on the stubble, on everything in sight — pepping and glittering, millions on millions of them. The people watched it stricken with fear and awe.[9]

More complex, but more readily susceptible to remedial action, was the economic problem of the farmer. Put in its simplest terms, this was the problem of rising costs and falling prices. So long as farm land increased in value it was possible for individual farmers to sell out at a profit and thus have something to show for a lifetime of toil. But except for this increase in land values — an increase closely related to the general increase in the cost of living — American farming, for most of this period, operated at a loss.

The factors that account for this economic malaise were numerous,

[9] *Giants in the Earth,* Harper & Bros., pp. 342–3.

and we can do no more than list them in some logical sequence. In the generation after the Civil War the agricultural domain expanded too rapidly. This expansion into the West and Southwest brought ruin to the farmers of New England and the seaboard South, but it did not bring prosperity to the farmers of the West, for it was paralleled by a no less remarkable expansion of the agricultural domain of Canada, the Argentine, Australia, Russia, and Brazil. So long as farming was primarily for subsistence and while the market was largely domestic, this situation was not serious. But when the American farmer grew more than the American market could absorb — a condition with which the cotton planter was long familiar — he had to sell his product in the world market, and the price which he received, at home as abroad, was determined by the world market. Industry, which could regulate its production and which operated behind tariff walls, bought in a world market and sold in a protected market; agriculture, which could not effectively regulate its production and very little of which could benefit from tariffs, bought in a protected market and sold in a world market.

There were two possible means by which the farmers might have overcome these disadvantages. The first was organization, looking to a limitation upon production. Transportation, finance, manufacturing, power, even labor, organized for self-protection, but the farmers were never able to organize successfully or to work out any voluntary limitation upon crops which would be at once effective and profitable. The second alternative was governmental action which would afford the farmers the same kind of protection and subsidy as that which the tariff gave to industry. Such action was proposed in the 1920's, only to encounter insuperable political opposition. Not until the administration of Franklin D. Roosevelt did the government undertake to aid agriculture as it had long aided industry, through loans, subsidies, and price guarantees.

Furthermore, as agricultural technology expanded, the farmer found himself more and more the victim rather than the beneficiary of the industrial revolution. The expansion of agriculture into the West meant an absolute dependence upon railroads, and freight charges came to consume an increasingly large share of the farmer's income. The *Prairie Farmer* asserted in 1867 that Iowa corn cost eight or ten times as much at Liverpool as the farmer received for it at the local grain elevator; thus corn that sold for 70 cents a bushel in the East might bring the farmer only ten or fifteen cents at the local exchange, and it was sometimes cheaper for him to burn his corn as fuel than to ship it to market. In 1880 wheat fetched almost a dollar in the Chicago pit, but it cost 45 cents to ship a bushel of wheat from central Nebraska to Chicago. Almost equally burdensome were certain railroad practices against which the farmer protested in vain. The railroads came to control the warehouse facilities of the West, fixed the price for storage, and controlled grading. In the late 1890's Governor Thayer of Nebraska asserted that 'There is no question in my mind but that the farmers of Nebraska have been defrauded of hundreds of thousands of dollars within the last few years by the wrongful classification of corn at Chicago and other great corn centers.'

The farmer sold his product in a competitive market, but purchased supplies, equipment, and household goods in a market which was protected against competition. The cost of his transportation was fixed by the railroads, of his fertilizer by a fertilizer trust, of his farm implements by the McCormick Harvester Company, of his fencing by a barbed wire trust. The prices which he paid for daily necessities — for furniture and clothing, for lumber and leather goods — were artificially raised by the operation of protective tariffs. Above all, the price which he paid for money was prohibitively high. Some states attempted, through usury laws, to fix low interest rates, but such laws were flouted or evaded, and interest rates in the farm belts of the South and the West were seldom below 10 per cent and in the 'nineties much higher. Inadequate banking facilities were in part responsible for this situation. In 1880, for example, the per capita banking power of the Eastern states was $176, of the Central states $27, and of the Southern states $10. Furthermore, with the rise in the value of money after the Civil War, the farmers' debt appreciated steadily. It took approximately 1200 bushels of wheat, corn, oats, barley, and rye to buy a $1000 mortgage in the years 1867 to 1869; between 1886 and 1888 it took approximately 2300 bushels of the same crops to repay that mortgage.

This was the heart of the matter. During most of the thirty years after the Civil War the farmer of the South and West was the victim not only of rising costs but of falling prices. Wheat which netted the farmer $1.45 a bushel in 1866 brought only 76 cents in 1869, 69 cents in 1889 and 49 cents in 1894, so that while the wheat crop in 1878 and again in 1889 was double what it had been in 1867 the farmers received approximately the same amount on the three crops. Corn which brought 75 cents at Chicago in 1869 fell to 38 cents in 1879 and to 28 cents in 1889. Twenty-three million bushels of rye brought $23 million in 1867 and 28 million bushels brought only $12 million in 1889. Cotton sold at 31 cents a pound in 1866, 9 cents in 1886 and 6 cents in 1893; less than 6 million bales of cotton sold, in 1884, for some $241 million; and approximately 10 million bales sold, in 1894, for $220 million.

The result was to be read in the figures of farm values, farm income, mortgages, and tenancy. Agriculture, which represented not quite half of the national wealth in 1860, accounted for but one-fifth of the national wealth half a century later. The value of manufactured products was 50 per cent higher in 1870 than the value of all farm products; by 1910 it was over twice as large. The farmer received 30 per cent of the national income in 1860, 19 per cent in 1890, 18 per cent in 1910, 13 per cent in 1920 and after the collapse of the early 'thirties, 7 per cent in 1933. Farm mortgages and tenancy increased correspondingly: 27 per cent of the farms operated by their owners were mortgaged in 1890; by 1910 the number had increased to 33 per cent; and by 1930 to 42 per cent. The total mortgage indebtedness on these owner-operated farms increased from $1726 million in 1910 to $4080 million in 1930, while the mortgage indebtedness for all farms operated increased during the same period from $3.5 billion to $9.5 billion. As a large part of these farm mortgages were held by mortgage companies, banks, and insurance companies in the East, the interest payment drained the rural sections for the benefit of the urban sections of the country; to many farmers this annual interest charge came to seem more like a tribute than a just payment for services rendered. Even more alarming were the mounting figures of farm tenancy. In 1880 one-fourth of all American farmers were tenants; by the turn of the century one-third of all farmers were tenants; thirty years later almost half the farmers of the nation were cultivating land which they did not own. In the beginning tenancy was largely confined to the Negroes of the South, but in the early years of the twentieth century it spread rapidly throughout the Middle West, and in the census of 1930 five of the leading Mid-Western farming states — Illinois, Iowa, Kansas, Nebraska, and South Dakota — showed over 40 per cent tenant farmers.

The social problem of the American farmer lends itself less readily to statistical analysis, but its significance can be read in the pages of such stories as Garland's *Main Travelled Roads*, Rölvaag's *Giants in the Earth*, Willa Cather's *My Ántonia*, Ruth Suckow's *Folks*, and Ellen Glasgow's *Barren Ground*. It is abundantly clear that in the years before the First World War, farming yielded not only decreasing economic returns but also decreasing social returns. Before the coming of the automobile, the telephone, and the radio, the isolation of the farm was a real and a fearful thing. Thousands of families were cut off from companionship and conviviality, church and school. Thousands of mothers died in childbirth, thousands of children died through lack of simple medical care. Hamlin Garland tells us that when he wrote *Main Travelled Roads*, he determined ' to tell the truth.'

> But I didn't. Even my youthful zeal faltered in the midst of a revelation of the lives led by the women on the farms of the middle border. Before the tragic futility of their suffering, my pen refused to shed its ink. Over the hidden chamber of their maternal agonies I drew the veil.

And when he revisited the Dakota country, he

> revolted from the gracelessness of its human habitations. The lonely box-like farm-houses on the ridges suddenly appeared to me like the dens of wild animals. The lack of color, of charm in the lives of the people anguished me. . . . All the gilding of farm life melted away. The hard and bitter realities came back upon me in a flood. Nature was as beautiful as ever . . . but no splendor of cloud, no grace of sunset could conceal the poverty of these people, on the contrary they brought out, with a more intolerable poignancy, the gracelessness of these homes, and the sordid quality of the mechanical daily routine of these lives.[10]

It was the women who suffered most from the niggardliness and narrowness of farm life. The confession of Benét's John Vilas might have been that of a whole generation of pioneers:

> I took my wife out of a pretty house,
> I took my wife out of a pleasant place,
> I stripped my wife of comfortable things,
> I drove my wife to wander with the wind.[11]

---

[10] The quotations are from *A Son of the Middle Border*, Macmillan, pp. 356–65, 416.
[11] *John Brown's Body*, p. 143.

No wonder it was so often the wives and the mothers who inspired the revolt against the farm, who encouraged their sons and daughters to try their fortunes in the cities.

It was inevitable that with the rise of the city, the social and cultural attractions of rural life should have been contrasted unfavorably with those of urban life. The cities offered not only business and professional opportunities, but facilities for education and recreation that were not to be found in the average rural community. City life conferred, too, a certain social prestige that no longer attached to farm life. The farmers, who had once been regarded as ' the chosen people of God,' came to be looked upon as ' hayseeds ' and 'hicks,' fit subjects for the comic strip or the vaudeville joke. An ever increasing number of young people, unwilling to accept the drudgery and frustration that their parents had suffered, left the farms for the cities. The same thing was happening in the Old World, and this movement from the farm to the city was a significant part of that immense ferment that brought millions of European peasants to American cities during these years. Between 1870 and 1930 the rural population declined from over 80 to less than 40 per cent of the total, and the decline in the actual farm population was even more precipitous.

It must not be supposed that the farmer made no effort to save himself from the social and economic difficulties that were rapidly crowding him to the wall. For almost every problem he had a solution, one that was usually reasonable and intelligent. But those solutions generally required legislative action from state or federal government, and in the generation after the Civil War the farmer was seldom in a position to obtain legislative action. From Jefferson to Jefferson Davis the politics of the nation had been guided chiefly by those who were responsible to the farmers, and where agrarian legislation had failed, such failure was to be charged rather to sectional conflict than to class conflict. But with the shift in population from the farm to the city, the rise of giant railroad and industrial corporations, and the concentration of financial power in the East, this situation changed. The farmers still constituted the largest single economic group in 1870, but they could not bridge the sectional barrier. Although the problems of the Southern planter and the Middle Western farmer were in many essentials the same, for a generation the Southerner insisted on voting Democratic, and the Western farmer just as stubbornly voted Republican. Railroad, banking, and industrial interests, however, were perturbed by no such sectional cleavage, but presented a united front to matters that concerned them; and political parties, always sensitive to economic forces, became increasingly subservient to these interests. Farmers everywhere wanted railroad regulation, but the railroad was the most powerful single interest in New Hampshire as in California, in Nebraska as in Georgia, and except for the brief Granger interlude the efforts of farmers to enact railroad rate bills met with stubborn political and legal obstacles. The vast majority of farmers wanted cheap money and a more flexible banking system, but even Bryan was unable to overcome the well-financed propaganda of the banking interests of the East or to make any serious impression upon the tradition of loyalty to the Republican party which flourished among the farmers of the North. Nor were the farmers more successful in placing their representatives in state legislatures or in Congress. Lawyers and businessmen constituted the majority of the legislatures even in such states as Georgia and Nebraska, while in the halls of Congress a 'dirt' farmer was something of a curiosity. It is suggestive that in the whole period from 1860 to 1928 no candidate of a major party was a genuine farmer and that only one candidate nominated to the presidency by either major party came from west of the Mississippi, and he was not elected.

Failing to make any dent upon either major political party, the farmers inevitably turned to organizations of their own. These organizations were not always political in character, but they sought to do by common action what the government failed to undertake. From the Granger movement of the late 'sixties to the farm bloc of the Hoover administration, the story of the farmers' revolt can be told largely in terms of these organizations.

6. AGRARIAN REVOLT

The bubble of Civil War prosperity burst in 1868 as did that of World War I in 1920, and the collapse of farm prices resulted in the first agrarian revolt. This revolt took various forms: the election of legislatures, governors, and often congressmen sympathetic to the farmers' demands; the passage of laws regulating freight and elevator charges; the organization of co-operative societies and eventually of local and even national political parties.

The first and most important of the societies that grew out of agrarian distress was the Patrons of Husbandry, commonly known as the Grange. It was in 1866 that President Johnson sent Oliver H. Kelley, a clerk in the Bureau of Agriculture, on a tour of investigation through the South. Kelley returned deeply impressed with the poverty, isolation, and backwardness of the farmers of that section of the country, and determined to organize a farmers' society which might in part ameliorate these evils. In 1867 he and a group of government clerks in Washington, D.C., founded the Patrons of Husbandry, and in the following year the first permanent Grange of this society was established in Fredonia, New York. By the end of 1870 there were Granges in nine states of the Union and when the panic of 1873 burst, the Grange had penetrated every state but four. Two years later it boasted a membership of over 800,000, organized in some 20,000 local Granges, most of them in the Middle West and the South.

The purpose of the Grange, as set forth in its 1874 declaration, was ' to develop a better and higher manhood and womanhood among ourselves. To enhance the comforts and attractions of our homes, and strengthen our attachments to our pursuits. To foster mutual understanding and co-operation. . . . To buy less and produce more, in order to make our farms self-sustaining. To diversify our crops, and crop no more than we can cultivate. . . . To discountenance the credit system, the mortgage system, the fashion system, and every other system tending to prodigality and bankruptcy.' The major function of the Grange, as conceived by its founders and announced in its declarations, was social, and it was as a social institution that it made its most useful contribution. One secret of the success of the order was the policy of admitting women to membership, and for farmers' wives the Grange, with its monthly meetings and picnics, lectures and entertainments, offered an escape from the loneliness and drudgery of the farm. To the women of the Middle Border the Grange, and later the Alliance, suggested a more abundant, a more generous life, and when the heroine of Garland's *A Spoil of Office* spoke at the farmers' picnic, it was the cultural aspects of the movement that she stressed:

I see a time [said Ida Wilbur] when the farmer will not need to live in a cabin on a lonely farm. I see the farmers coming together in groups. I see them with time to read, and time to visit with their fellows. I see them enjoying lectures in beautiful halls, erected in every village. I see them gather like the Saxons of old upon the green at evening to sing and dance. I see cities rising near them with schools, and churches, and concert halls and theatres. I see a day when the farmer will no longer be a drudge and his wife a bond slave, but happy men and women who will go singing to their pleasant tasks upon their fruitful farms. When the boys and girls will not go west nor to the city; when life will be worth living. In that day the moon will be brighter and the stars more glad and pleasure and poetry and love of life come back to the man who tills the soil.[12]

This social program was remote — and innocuous. Not so with the political and economic program of the Grange. The Grange was formally non-political in character, but it was inevitable that the Grangers should use their influence on politics, and almost from the beginning the movement took on a distinctly political character. In Illinois, Iowa, Wisconsin, Minnesota, Kansas, California, and elsewhere the farmers entered politics, elected their candidates to legislatures and judgeships, and agitated for farm relief through railway and warehouse regulation. The result was the so-called Granger laws limiting railroad and warehouse charges and outlawing some of the grosser railway abuses.[13] Though these laws proved in the long run ineffective, they did teach the farmers the value of co-operation in politics and dramatize for the nation the necessity of political curbs on business and transportation.

Not only did the Grangers venture into politics; they embarked upon business enterprises as well. In an attempt to eliminate the middleman, they established hundreds of co-operative stores on the Rochdale plan — a plan whereby profits were divided among the shareholders, in proportion to their purchases. They set up co-operative creameries, elevators, and warehouses, organized farmers' insurance companies, and entered the manufacturing field, buying up patents and constructing their own factories which turned out excellent reapers, sewing machines, wagons, and similar things for half the price charged by private concerns. Kelley from the first opposed such business activities. ' This purchasing business,' he said, ' commenced with buying jackasses; the prospects are that many will be *sold*.' In the end his sour prophecy was justified. Owing to the relentless opposition by business and banking interests, the individual-

---

12 *A Spoil of Office*, p. 14.
13 See Chap. VII for the legislative and judicial history of the Granger laws.

ism of the farmers, over-expansion and mismanagement, most of the co-operative enterprises failed. Yet some good resulted from the foray of the Grangers into business. Prices were reduced, thousands of farmers saved money, and with the establishment of Montgomery Ward and Company in 1872 specifically ' to meet the wants of the Patrons of Husbandry ' the mail-order business came into existence.

Prosperity returned to the farm in the late 'seventies, and membership in the Grange dwindled rapidly, until by 1880 it had fallen to 100,000. A revival began in that year but, chastened by experience, the Grange confined itself thereafter largely to social activities. Its place was taken by the more aggressive Farmers' Alliances, and the history of agrarian revolt during the 'eighties and early 'nineties is largely the history of the Alliance movement.

There were, from the beginning, a number of Alliances, but by the late 'eighties the process of consolidation and amalgamation had resulted in the creation of two powerful groups, the Northwestern Alliance, and the Farmers' Alliance and Industrial Union, commonly known as the Southern Alliance. The first effective organization of the Northwestern Alliance was undertaken by Milton George, editor of the *Western Rural Magazine,* and the platform which he drew up in 1880 proposed to ' unite the farmers of America for their protection against class legislation, and the encroachments of concentrated capital and the tyranny of monopoly.' The Northwestern Alliance was particularly strong in Kansas, Nebraska, Iowa, Minnesota, and the Dakotas, and during the hard times of the late 'eighties it increased its membership by leaps and bounds and became a major power in the politics of the Middle Border. The origin of the Southern Alliance dates back to a cattlemen's association in Lampasas County, Texas, in the middle 'seventies. Within a decade this Texas Alliance had spread throughout the state and in the late 'eighties, under the guidance of the astute C. W. Macune, it began to absorb farmers' organizations in other Southern states such as the Arkansas Wheel and the Louisiana Farmers' Union, and affiliated with the powerful Colored Farmers' National Alliance. By the early 'nineties the Southern Alliance boasted a membership of over a million and was the most powerful farmers' organization in the country. Despite an obvious community of interest between the Northern and the Southern Alliances, all efforts to achieve an amalgamation of the two organizations foundered on the rocks of sectionalism.

The activities of the Alliances were as diverse as those of the Grange. Social activities embraced not only the customary meetings and picnics, but farmers' institutes, circulating libraries, and the publication of hundreds of farm newspapers and dozens of magazines, so that the Alliance became, in the words of one observer, a farmers' national university. The economic enterprises of the Alliance were more substantial and ambitious than those of the Grange. The Texas Alliance undertook co-operative buying and selling, the North Dakota Alliance underwrote co-operative insurance, the Illinois Alliance organized co-operative marketing. Thousands of farmer's ' exchanges ' were established, and it was estimated that in 1890 the various Alliances did a business of over $10 million.

But historically the significance of the Alliance is to be found in its political rather than its social and economic activities. From the first the Alliances entered more vigorously into politics than had the Grange, for the Alliance programs required political action. Those programs varied from year to year and from state to state, but in general they embraced demands for strict regulation or even government ownership of railroads and other means of communication, currency inflation, the abolition of national banks, the prohibition of alien land ownership and of trading in futures on the Exchange, a more equitable taxation, and various progressive political reforms. An original contribution of the Alliance was the so-called Sub-Treasury scheme, which provided that the government should establish warehouses where the farmers might deposit non-perishable farm produce, receiving in exchange a loan of legal tender money up to 80 per cent of the market value of the produce, which might be redeemed when the farmer had sold his produce. This scheme had the triple advantage of enabling the farmer to borrow at a low rate of interest on his farm produce, sell his produce at the most favorable market price, and profit by an expanded and flexible currency. At the time when it was first advanced, it was regarded as merely a socialistic aberration; the Warehouse Act of 1916 adopted a similar proposal as a national policy.

Between 1890 and 1892, the Alliance became absorbed into the Populist party.[14] The failure of the Populists to perfect and maintain a party organization brought about the disintegration not only of that party but of the Alliance, and induced an abiding distrust of

14 For the political history of the Populist movement, see Chap. XIII.

direct political action on the part of the farmer. He snapped back into voting Republican if of the North or West, and Democratic if of the South or Southwest. The first two decades of the twentieth century brought prosperity to the farmer, and though the value of agricultural products continued to be disproportionately low, a four-fold increase in the value of much of the farm land largely compensated him for his relatively low income.

After the debacle of the Alliance and the Populist movements, farmers turned once more from political to social and economic objectives. The Grange increased rapidly in membership, but confined itself largely to educational and social activities. The conservative American Farm Bureau Federation, with a membership of not far from a million, concerned itself principally with problems of marketing and distribution, and sponsored co-operative organizations of grain and cotton growers. In the 1920's farmers' co-operatives flourished among the fruit growers of California, the wheat farmers of the Northwest, and the cotton planters of the South, and by 1929 almost 700,000 farms reported co-operative sales.

During the Wilson administration the Farmers' Non-Partisan League, organized in North Dakota, spread into fifteen states of the West. In 1916 the League captured control of the government of North Dakota and in the ensuing years enacted a farm relief program of a far-reaching nature. This legislation provided for state-owned warehouses and elevators, a state bank, exemption of farm improvements from taxation, creation of a hail-insurance fund and a Home Building Association to encourage home ownership, and the establishment of an industrial commission to organize state-owned and state-financed industries. These laws, like the Granger and Populist laws of an earlier generation, were loudly denounced as class legislation throughout the East, for no axiom of politics was more deeply cherished in that section than the one axiom that legislation for farmer or labor interests was ' class ' legislation, while legislation for manufacturing, banking, railroad, and shipping interests was national.

BIBLIOGRAPHY

1. GENERAL. L. H. Bailey, *Cyclopedia of American Agriculture* (4 vols.) ; O. E. Baker (ed.) , *Atlas of American Agriculture;* Ernest L. Bogart, *Economic History of American Agriculture;* David Cohn, *Life and Times of King Cotton;* Benjamin H. Hibbard, *A History of Public Land Policies;* Merrill Jarchow, *The*

Earth Brought Forth: Minnesota Agriculture to 1885; Howard Odum, *Southern Regions of the United States;* E. L. Peffer, *The Closing of the Public Domain;* Willard Range, *A Century of Georgia Agriculture;* Roy Robbins, *Our Landed Heritage: the Public Domain;* Aaron Sakolski, *The Great American Land Bubble;* Joseph Schafer, *Social History of American Agriculture* and *History of Agriculture in Wisconsin;* Fred A. Shannon, *The Farmer's Last Frontier;* U. S. Dept. of Agriculture, *Yearbook, 1889: Progress of Agriculture in the United States* and *Yearbook, 1940: American Agriculture, the First Three Hundred Years;* Rupert Vance, *Human Geography of the South;* Walter Webb, *The Great Plains;* Harold Wilson, *The Hill Country of Northern New England;* C. Vann Woodward, *Origins of the New South.*

2. FARM PROBLEM AND AGRARIAN REVOLT. A. M. Arnett, *Populist Movement in Georgia;* R. P. Brooks, *The Agrarian Revolution in Georgia;* Solon J. Buck, *The Granger Movement* and *The Agrarian Crusade;* J. B. Clark, *Populism in Alabama;* Everett Dick, *The Sod House Frontier;* Elmer Ellis, *Henry Moore Teller: Defender of the West;* Nathan Fine, *Labor and Farmer Parties in the U. S.;* P. R. Fossum, *The Agrarian Movement in North Dakota;* Paul Gates, *Fifty Million Acres: Conflicts over Kansas Land Policy;* Marion Harrington, *Populist Movement in Georgia;* John D. Hicks, *The Populist Revolt;* O. M. Kile, *Farm Bureau Movement;* Charles Otken, *The Ills of the South;* D. M. Robinson, *Bob Taylor and the Agrarian Revolt in Tennessee;* Theodore Saloutos & J. D. Hicks, *Agrarian Discontent in the Middle West;* Fred Shannon, *Farmer's Last Frontier;* Roger Shugg, *Origins of the Class Struggle in Louisiana;* F. P. Simkins, *The Tillman Movement in South Carolina;* F. E. Weaver, *James Baird Weaver;* William Allen White, *Autobiography;* C. Vann Woodward, *Tom Watson: Agrarian Rebel.*

3. MACHINERY, SCIENCE, AND THE GOVERNMENT. R. L. Ardrey, *American Agricultural Implements;* Joseph Bailey, *Seaman A. Knapp;* H. N. Casson, *The Romance of the Reaper;* Paul de Kruif, *Hunger Fighters;* Philip Dorf, *Liberty H. Bailey;* L. W. Ellis & E. A. Rumeley, *Power and the Plow;* Rackham Holt, *George Washington Carver;* L. O. Howard, *Fighting the Insects;* William T. Hutchinson, *Cyrus Hall McCormick* (2 vols.) ; D. S. Jordan & V. Kellog, *The Scientific Aspects of Luther Burbank's Work;* Waldemar Kaempffert, *Popular History of American Inventions,* vol. 2; Louise Peffer, *Closing of the Public Domain;* Leo Rogin, *Introduction of Farm Machinery in Its Relations . . . to Labor;* E. D. Ross, *Democracy's College: The Land Grant Movement in the Formative Stage;* W. H. Shepardson, *Agricultural Education in the United States;* William E. Smythe, *Conquest of Arid America;* Ray P. Teile, *Economics of Land Reclamation in the United States;* George Thomas, *Development of Institutions under Irrigation;* A. C. True & V. A. Clark, *Agricultural Experiment Stations in the United States;* W. L. Wanlass, *The United States Department of Agriculture.*

4. NOVELS. Louis Bromfield, *The Farm;* Gladys Hasty Carroll, *As the Earth Turns;* Willa Cather, *My Ántonia, O Pioneers!* and *A Lost Lady;* Dorothy Dondore, *The Prairie and the Making of Middle America;* Edna Ferber, *American Beauty;* Hamlin Garland, *Boy Life on the Prairie, Son of the Middle Border,* and *A Spoil of Office;* Ellen Glasgow, *Barren Ground;* Lucy Hazard, *The Frontier in American Literature;* Ed Howe, *The Story of a Country Town;* Frank

Norris, *The Octopus;* Herbert Quick, *Vandemark's Folly* and *The Hawkeye;* Ole Rölvaag, *Giants in the Earth;* Thomas Stribling, *The Forge* and *The Store;* Ruth Suckow, *Folks* and *Iowa Interiors;* William Allen White, *The Heart of a Fool;* Margaret Wilson, *The Able McLaughlins.*

5. DOCUMENTS. H. S. Commager, *Documents,* nos. 214, 216, 316, 323–5; L. B. Schmidt & E. E. Ross, *Readings in the Economic History of American Agriculture.*

For further references, see *Harvard Guide,* ¶¶ 199, 209.

Politics

1. MASKS IN A PAGEANT

THERE is no drearier chapter in American political history than
that which records the period from the end of Reconstruction
to the Populist revolt of the early 1890's. The high political passions
of the 'fifties throw a fitful gleam upon the administrations of that
triumvirate of nonentities, Fillmore, Pierce, and Buchanan, while
the rascality and ineptitude of the 1920's give a morbid interest to
the administrations of Harding, Coolidge, and Hoover. But the monotonous administrations of Hayes, Arthur, Cleveland, and Harrison are relieved neither by grand political passions nor by excess of
virtue or of vice, but merely by labor troubles and a depression. Civil
War issues were dead, though politicians continued to flay the
corpses. National politics became little more than a contest for power
between rival parties waged on no higher plane than a struggle
for traffic between rival railroads. The vital interests of the era lay
mostly outside politics, and for that reason must be studied separately.

During the whole of this period the electorate played a game of
blind man's buff. There were no clearly defined issues between the
major parties, and the political leaders preferred to raise fake ones
and attempt to be all things to all men, rather than tie up parties to
the real forces that were transforming the country, which in any
case they did not understand. Perhaps they were right, for the last
time that a major party had adopted a vital issue, the country had
been torn apart, and nobody wanted another Civil War. But the result was to make national politics unreal, and, except for electoral
clowning and congressional buncombe, very dull.

America was emerging from her isolation and becoming a part
of the community of nations, but there was no intelligent appreciation of the responsibilities which this new position involved, and

Blaine's gestures toward Pan-Americanism were all but futile. The country had recovered from the Civil War, but instead of encouraging sectional friendliness, politicians on both sides exploited patriotic and sectional animosities for the grossest purposes. The industrial revolution, as it unfolded, made traditional ideas of laissez faire less and less valid; but politics and law were still conducted on this outmoded principle and politicians still prated of individualism as if it were a reality in the economic and social spheres as in biology. Big business was growing bigger, trusts were becoming super-trusts, railroad monopolies placed unparalleled power in the hands of a few men, and the conflict of 'wealth against commonwealth' which Henry D. Lloyd was soon to dramatize, was recognized by thoughtful men; but political leaders showed no appreciation of the implications of these developments, and laws such as the Interstate Commerce Act or the Anti-Trust Act raised only the flimsiest of barriers against the onward march of privilege. Agriculture was facing a series of grave crises and the independent American farmer was threatened on all sides by forces over which he could exercise no effective control; but politicians in Washington lacked the imagination to understand even the existence of a farm problem until it was called to their attention by political revolt. The money question, with its far-reaching consequences to the fortunes of that generation, demanded the most careful and impartial study; but it was either ignored or, when that was no longer possible, dealt with as a moral rather than economic problem. There were issues enough before the American people, issues involving in the most vital way the fortunes of the Republic and presenting valid alternatives, but candidates commonly evaded them and fought political campaigns on the basis of personality, party or inherited prejudice. Few fundamental political issues were agitated, few new policies were inaugurated, no problems were solved, except by being left behind.

And what of the lawmakers and political leaders, whose tattered banners Americans followed with such uncritical enthusiasm? It is a drab procession that passes before the historian, inspiring wonder and weariness, for the politicians of this era were mostly sad, solemn fellows. Clowns went out of fashion with Benjamin Butler and Parson Brownlow, and did not return until the swashbuckling imperialists of 1898 introduced a new note of humor into American politics. The titular leaders — Hayes, Garfield, Arthur, Cleveland, Harrison — were estimable men, who contributed nothing of lasting importance to American politics or American life. Orators extolled their virtues in oceans of words and biographers have embalmed their reputations in scores of books, but with the exception of Grover Cleveland it is not apparent that American history would have been in any essential different had none of them ever lived.

Behind these titular leaders were the real rulers — men who sat in committee rooms listening to the demands of lobbyists, bosses who sat in caucus selecting candidates, ' boys ' who ' fried the fat ' out of reluctant corporations, hucksters who flooded the country with ' educational ' literature or with the poison of sectional hatred or with the stench of scandal — all so that their candidates might gain office. At the head of the ranks of those who really ran the country were great bosses like Conkling and Hill of New York, Cameron and Quay of Pennsylvania, Hanna and Brice of Ohio. Then there were the representatives of special interests — Standard Oil senators, sugar trust senators, iron and steel senators, and railroad senators, men known by their business rather than their political affiliations, like Aldrich of Rhode Island, Depew of New York, Elkins of West Virginia, Sawyer of Wisconsin, Mahone of Virginia, and Clark of Montana. Running through all ranks were the spoilsmen, interested only in office and patronage, like Platt and Fenton of New York, Alger of Michigan, Foraker of Ohio, Logan of Illinois, Ingalls of Kansas, and Allison of Iowa. Yet there was always a small group of men in politics who preserved an old-fashioned integrity, patriotism, sense of duty, and responsibility which transcended personal interest and occasionally even party interest — men like George F. Hoar of Massachusetts, John G. Carlisle of Kentucky, Lucius Q. C. Lamar of Mississippi, Abram Hewitt of New York, Lyman Trumbull of Illinois, and Carl Schurz of Missouri.

James G. Blaine of Maine, Congressman, Senator, twice Secretary of State, and perpetual aspirant to the presidency, was typical of this era, as Clay and Webster were of an earlier one. A man of indubitable intellectual power and of immense personal magnetism, Blaine was possibly the most popular figure in American politics between Clay and Bryan. Year after year thousands of men marched, shouted, and sang for ' Blaine of Maine ' whom devoted followers pictured as the ' Plumed Knight,' paladin of all virtues and defender of the true Republican faith. For thirty years he exercised a controlling power in the councils of his party, in legislation, foreign and domestic policies, party platforms and candidates. The perfect politician, he never forgot a name or a friend and always knew how to influence votes and manipulate committees. He was a magnificent orator and could inspire a frenzy of enthusiasm by twisting the British lion's tail or solemnly intoning the platitudes of party loyalty. Yet aside from his personality he made no impression upon American politics except to lower its moral tone. He was assiduous in cementing a corrupt alliance between politics and business. Deliberately and violently he fanned the flames of sectional animosity, waving the ' bloody shirt of the rebellion ' for partisan and personal purposes. His name is connected with no important legislation; his sympathies were enlisted in no forward-looking causes. He was as innocent of economic as of political ideas and ignored the interests of the laboring and the farming classes when he did not oppose them. His vision was narrow and selfish, his methods the methods of the spoilsman, his ambitions personal and partisan. Nevertheless, for his little faith in democracy and his power to stimulate emotions and hatreds that a statesman would have laid at rest, he was rewarded with votes, office, power, and almost with the presidency.

Politics was largely a Punch and Judy show, but though the puppets and even the voices changed, the hands that held the strings were the same. Business ran politics, and politics was a branch of business. The country, said John Sherman after the election of 1888, had ' reached the last stages in the history of the Roman Empire when offices were sold at public auction to the highest bidder,' and when some years later David Graham Phillips wrote *The Treason of the Senate* he merely recorded what was common knowledge as to the intimate relations of business and politics. The story can be read in the biographies of captains of industry like Carnegie and Rockefeller, of masters of capital like Morgan and Gould, of politicians like Blaine and Aldrich, and, told with more imagination but essential accuracy, in such novels as Henry Adams's *Democracy,* Winston Churchill's *Coniston,* William Allen White's *A Certain Rich Man,* and Theodore Dreiser's *The Financier.* The system was set forth most nakedly, perhaps, by Frederick T. Martin:

It matters not one iota what political party is in power or what President holds the reins of office. We are not politicians, or public thinkers; we are the rich; we own America; we got it, God knows how, but we intend to keep it if we can by throwing all the tremendous weight of our support, our influence, our money, our political connections, our purchased Senators, our hungry Congressmen, and our public-speaking demagogues, into the scale against any legislation, any political platform, any Presidential campaign, that threatens the integrity of our estate.[1]

Since politics was a branch of business, the ethics of business became the ethics of politics. It was illogical of reformers to be shocked at corrupt practices in the one and not in the other. It is for this reason that much of the civil service reform movement, which looms so large in the history of these years, appears today unreal. Business had no party preferences except insofar as it preferred to invest in successful rather than unsuccessful candidates; it contributed more generously to the Republican than to the Democratic coffers because the Republicans were more often victorious, but Democratic senators like Hill of New York, Gorman of Maryland, and Brice of Ohio could command the support of business quite as effectively as Morton of New York, Cameron of Pennsylvania, or Foraker of Ohio. Only rarely did parties divide along economic lines; for the most part both major parties straddled every important issue. Railroad and trust legislation were not party questions; both parties ostensibly favored regulation, neither gave such regulation sincere or intelligent support. Labor was not a political issue: Hayes in the ' Great Strike ' of 1877 and Cleveland in the Pullman strike of 1894 permitted the use of the injunction and sent federal troops to protect business interests. Both parties were committed to a liberal and democratic land policy, but when it came to enforcing the provisions of the land laws and to stopping the frauds that made a mockery of those laws, Cleveland encountered bitter opposition from his own party and so did Theodore Roosevelt. The Republicans espoused protection and the Democrats low tariff, but once in office the Democrats were unwilling to make any significant concessions to tariff reform. Both parties avoided the money question as long as they could; when evasion was no longer possible, they split along geographical lines.

Yet if the surface of the political waters was placid, underneath the currents flowed swift and treacherous, and when the ship of state, manned by an incompetent crew, drifted out of the quiet stretch of the 'eighties into the dangerous 'nineties, it was buffeted and battered and all but capsized.

[1] *Passing of the Idle Rich,* Doubleday, Page & Co., p. 149.

2. GLIMMERINGS OF REFORM

The administrations of Hayes and Arthur illustrate and emphasize some of these generalizations. A well-educated lawyer, officer in the Union army, elected twice to Congress and for three terms governor of Ohio, Rutherford B. Hayes was honest and able, but he was from the beginning seriously handicapped in his efforts to effect constructive measures or to inaugurate necessary reforms. Not only the Democrats but even many of his own party followers believed that he had achieved office through fraud, and he was never able to count on the moral support of the nation or to anticipate a second term in which he might consolidate his position. The factional disputes which had wrecked the harmony of the second Grant administration and of the Convention of 1876 were not allayed, and from the beginning Hayes incurred the animosity of Blaine and the implacable hostility of Conkling and his followers. The elections of 1876 had preserved Democratic control of the lower House, and two years later this opposition party captured control of the upper House as well. In the circumstances it is a tribute to Hayes that his administration was not a total failure.

That it was not a complete failure can be credited to the courage with which Hayes tackled the two immediate problems of reconstruction and civil service reform. The first and most important act of his administration was the recall of the federal troops from the South, an act which marked the technical end of political and military reconstruction. In order to dramatize the reconciliation of the sections, the President appointed an ex-Confederate, David M. Key, to his cabinet. Yet, with an inconsistency that was almost obtuse, Hayes refused to countenance the repeal of the hated Force Acts either directly or through ' riders ' on appropriation bills, and the acts remained on the statute books to trouble future relations between the North and the South.

Hayes's second task was to cleanse his party of the corruption which had so seriously damaged it during the Grant administrations and to fulfill his pledges of civil service reform. The appointments of the civil service reformer, Carl Schurz, to the Interior Department and of William M. Evarts, one of President Johnson's counsellors, to the State Department, were evidence of Hayes's sincerity. Yet excellent as his intentions were, he seriously compromised himself from the beginning by the scandalous manner in which he rewarded every member of the notorious Louisiana returning board as well as others who had been instrumental in awarding him the presidency. Although he thereafter made genuine efforts toward reform, removing some of Grant's most offensive appointees and cleaning up the New York custom house, he was never able to win the complete confidence of the civil service reformers.

Indecisive as it was, Hayes's struggle with the spoilsmen had considerable effect on American political history. That struggle was precipitated by Hayes's attempt to oust Chester A. Arthur and Alonzo B. Cornell from the New York custom house which they had turned into a political machine of the most corrupt and disreputable character. Senator Conkling, already outraged by Hayes's Southern policy and embittered because he had not received the recognition which he thought was his due, took the removals as a personal affront and persuaded the Senate to reject the nominations of those whom the President appointed to succeed Arthur and Cornell. What was involved in this unseemly squabble was not merely a falling-out between two factions in the Republican party, or ' Senatorial courtesy,' but a larger issue of the American form of government. During the Johnson administration Congress had inaugurated a quasi-parliamentary form of government, and Grant had offered no effective resistance to the continuation of this parliamentary system. Congress, since the Civil War, had so largely eaten into the presidential prerogative that the chief executive was by way of becoming a mere figurehead, like the President of the French Republic.[2] Under Hayes a senatorial cabal, led by Conkling, Platt, Cameron, Ferry, Chandler, Boutwell, and Edmunds, proposed to continue their domination of the government. Against this plan the President set himself with adamantine stubbornness, and in the end, with the support of the Democrats, he was successful. His appointees were renominated and confirmed and Conkling retired from the struggle, only to renew it in the next administration, without success. The normal and constitutional relationship between President and Congress was thereby restored.

For the larger task of articulating the government to the new eco-

[2] This tendency was exposed in a book entitled *Congressional Government*, published in 1885 by young Dr. Woodrow Wilson who later did much to correct the evil.

nomic forces, Hayes was not prepared. His only solution of the labor problem presented by the ' Great Strike ' of 1877 was to send federal troops to put down the strikers. The resumption of specie payments, voted in 1875, caused an appreciation in the value of greenbacks that was hard on debtors, and when Congress tried a different solution of the money problem — the Bland-Allison Silver Act of 1878 — Hayes interposed his veto, an interposition which was quite unsuccessful. To the problems of railroad malpractices, trusts, and land frauds he gave no attention. He later confessed that ' the money-piling tendency of our country . . . is changing laws, government and morals, and giving all power to the rich, and bringing in pauperism and its attendant crimes and wickedness like a flood,' but when President he did not even hang out danger signals. His administration, for all its political drama, was largely a negative one.

As the election of 1880 approached, the ' stalwart ' Republicans who had been supporters of Grant's throne proposed the General for a third term. He was willing, but the Republican nominating convention was not; and a ' dark horse ' from Ohio, General James A. Garfield, obtained the nomination. Garfield was an educated gentleman with a good military record and long experience in Congress; but his party made a greater virtue of his log-cabin birth and early exploits as a canal bargee. The nomination was a blow to Conkling, who had supported Grant; and in order to placate the New York Senator the convention named his henchman, Chester A. Arthur, to the vice-presidency. The Democrats, to confirm their loyalty, nominated General Winfield Scott Hancock of Pennsylvania, and the Greenback party, which had polled over a million votes in 1878, put up a third Civil War veteran, General James B. Weaver of Iowa. The campaign was fought largely on personalities and trumped-up issues. Although General Hancock, who had helped save the day at Gettysburg, had a far more distinguished Civil War record than Garfield, the Republicans once more waved ' the bloody flag of the Rebellion ' to discredit the rival party. Thus one of the Republican campaign songs:

> Treason may make its boast, my boys,
> And seek to rule again;
> Our Jim shall meet its host, my boys,
> And strike with might and main!

> Once more he'll crush the foe, my boys,
> With arm and bosom bare!
> And this shall be his field, my boys,
> The Presidential Chair.

With these auspices presiding, Garfield won a thumping victory in the electoral college but his popular plurality was less than 10,000 in a total of over 9 million votes, and Weaver polled the largest vote of any third-party candidate until the twentieth century.

Four months after his inauguration, while still struggling with questions of patronage, Garfield was shot by a disappointed office-seeker who boasted, ' I am a Stalwart; Arthur is now President of the United States.' After a gallant struggle for life, Garfield died on 19 September 1881. The new President, Chester A. Arthur, was a prominent lawyer and machine politician of New York, long a satellite of the lordly Conkling, and with nothing in his record to justify the hope that he would make more than a mediocre executive and much to arouse fear that he would make a very bad one. Handsome and affable, liked by businessmen and women of the world, he gave Washington its only ' society ' administration between those of Buchanan and Theodore Roosevelt. Unexpectedly he developed a genuine independence and became something of a reformer. He severed his connections with the worst of the spoilsmen, vetoed an eighteen million dollar river and harbor bill, and prosecuted, with some vigor, the so-called Star Route frauds in the Post Office Department which had cost the government millions of dollars. Above all, his administration is memorable for the enactment of the Pendleton Civil Service Reform Bill.

Every President since Polk had complained of the demands that patronage made on his time, energy, and judgment, and Lincoln had expressed fears that the spoils system was ' going to ruin republican government.' Scandal had followed scandal in the civil service; yet the spoils system had been extended even to scrubwomen in the public offices. Rotation in office was never complete, and a large residuum of trained servants was left undisturbed; but in general the federal service had become permeated with a class of men who were strongly tempted to anticipate future removal by present corruption. Federal officeholders were regularly assessed for campaign contributions and were expected to spend a good part of their time and energy in party activity.

The spoils system had been subjected to heavy criticism for two decades before Arthur's accession to office. As early as 1864 Sumner had introduced a bill looking to civil service reform, and three years later Representative Jenckes of Rhode Island, long the spokesman of the reform group, attempted to secure congressional endorsement for a classified civil service modeled along English lines. Jenckes had the support of a number of Eastern intellectuals — men of the type of E. L. Godkin of *The Nation*, G. W. Curtis of *Harper's Weekly*, and Thomas Wentworth Higginson, as well as active politicians like Carl Schurz, Senator Hoar, and Lyman Trumbull. In 1871 Grant came unexpectedly to the assistance of the reformers with a recommendation for a law governing ' the manner of making all appointments,' and in that same year a Civil Service Commission was established which was empowered to prescribe rules and regulations for admission into the civil service. Grant's enthusiasm was short-lived, and so was the commission.

Hayes, as we have seen, had grievously disappointed party regulars by his friendliness toward the movement. He announced in his acceptance speech his determination to institute reforms, and shortly after becoming President he informed Secretary of the Treasury John Sherman that

party leaders should have no more influence in appointments than other equally respectable citizens. No assessment for political purposes on officers or subordinates should be allowed. No useless officer or employee should be retained. No officer should be required or permitted to take part in the management of political organizations, caucuses, conventions, or election campaigns.

This sounds like the Hatch Act of 1939, but it was only an expression of opinion; yet Sherman supported Hayes's efforts at reform, and Secretary Schurz introduced new standards of honesty and efficiency into the Department of the Interior and cleaned up the nauseating corruption which disgraced the administration of the Indian Bureau.

All this aroused the bitter hostility of politicians like Conkling, whose attitude toward civil service is indicated by his classic observation: ' When Dr. Johnson defined patriotism as the last refuge of a scoundrel, he ignored the enormous possibilities of the word *reform*.' The Stalwarts now looked to Arthur to undo the progress which his predecessors had made, but to their chagrin Arthur allied himself with the reform element, and in his first annual message to Congress came out squarely for the merit system.

It was the manner of Garfield's death that made possible the achievement that reformers and Civil Service Leagues had been advocating for years. Public opinion was finally aroused to the real dangers of the spoils system, and politicians were galvanized into action. Late in December 1882 the Senate passed, by a vote 38 to 5, a Civil Service Bill drafted by Dorman Eaton, life-long champion of reform, and sponsored by ' Gentleman ' George Pendleton of Ohio, who gave it his name. The House majority was equally decisive, and on 16 January 1883, the bill became law. The Pendleton Act created a Civil Service Commission to administer a new set of rules which required appointments to be made as a result of open competitive examinations, and prohibited assessments on officeholders for political purposes. By law these new rules were applied only to some 14,000 positions, about 12 per cent of the total, but the President was empowered to extend them to other parts of the service at his discretion. At the turn of the century there were not far from 100,000 in the classified civil service; at the end of Theodore Roosevelt's administration the number had more than doubled, and at the end of Wilson's administration it had increased to almost half a million.[3] At the same time most states were passing civil service laws of their own. The emoluments were not sufficiently high to attract university graduates and other able men from business and the professions, but there was a great improvement in morale and efficiency. It was fortunate that the merit principle was adopted before the twentieth century when administrative expansion greatly increased the need of honest men and expert service.

In only one other field did the Arthur administration make any contribution to the development of the nation. The War of the Pacific between Peru, Bolivia, and Chile, and the rising interest in an isthmian canal, awakened the American people to a realization of the decrepitude of their navy.[4] Twenty years after the building of

3 In 1940, 726,827 out of a total of 1,014,117 federal employees were in the classified civil service.

4 ' " I don't think I should like America." — " I suppose because we have no ruins and no curiosities," said Virginia, satirically. — " No ruins! no curiosities! " answered the Ghost; " You have your navy and your manners." ' — Oscar Wilde, *The Canterville Ghost.*

the *Monitor* it was inferior to the navy of every principal European country, and to that of Chile. After long discussion Congress authorized on 5 August 1882 ' two steam cruising vessels of war . . . to be constructed of steel of domestic manufacture.' These were the *Chicago* and the *Boston,* which entered active service in 1887, and a new era in American naval history was begun.

3. THE ADMINISTRATION OF GROVER CLEVELAND

Arthur's placid administration ended in the most exciting presidential campaign since the Civil War, although the only real issue between the parties was possession of the government. The Greenback party was first in the ring, nothing daunted by the steady decline in its strength since the high point of the 1878 congressional elections. Unable to find a candidate identified with their program, they accepted the ever-willing Benjamin Butler of Massachusetts, familiarly known throughout the South as ' beast Butler ' for his conduct as captor of New Orleans. Butler had been a Democratic governor and a Republican congressman and it was only natural that he should now try a third party. The Republicans, disappointed in Arthur, turned to the magnetic Blaine who had so narrowly missed the nomination in 1880. He had served for a few months as Secretary of State under Garfield and Arthur, and had retired to write *Twenty Years of Congress,* a thousand-page celebration of the virtues and triumphs of the Republican party. Now it was his turn, and he was not to be denied; four ballots sufficed to give him the nomination. But Blaine was more than conscientious Republicans could swallow. To the rank and file of the party he may have been a ' Plumed Knight,' but to upright and intelligent Republicans, who were sick of the prevailing corruption, he was a simple grafter. The principal charge against him was the prostitution of the speakership to personal gain; in that connection he had never been able to explain the missive to a certain Fisher with the damning postscript, ' Burn this letter.' Even Conkling, when asked to campaign for Blaine, had replied, ' I don't engage in criminal practice.' Under the leadership of Carl Schurz and George William Curtis the reform wing of the party bolted from the convention, promised to support any decent nomination the Democrats might make, and proudly

accepted the name ' Mugwump ' which was given them in derision.[5]
As bolting was the great offense in American political ethics, few of
the Mugwumps managed to resume a political career; younger and
shrewder politicians like Henry Cabot Lodge and Theodore Roosevelt, who supported Blaine while admitting the worst about him, had
their reward.

With the Promised Land at last in sight, the Democrats made an
admirable nomination. Grover Cleveland was a self-made man who
as reform mayor of Buffalo and governor of New York had distinguished himself for firmness and integrity, to the disgust of Tammany Hall. ' We love him for the enemies he has made,' said General
E. S. Bragg of Wisconsin in the nominating speech, and it required
only two ballots for the convention to endorse this tribute. Powerful
journals such as the New York *Times,* the *Springfield Republican,*
The Nation, and *Harper's Weekly,* with Nast's telling cartoons,
shifted over to Cleveland, as did scores of independents and liberal
Republicans of the stripe of Charles Francis Adams, James Russell
Lowell, and Carl Schurz. No campaign since the Civil War had
played such havoc with party regularity.

As the campaign proceeded it became noisy and nasty. Cleveland
was charged, among other things, with having an illegitimate child,
which he admitted, to the consternation of his supporters. But, as one
of them concluded philosophically, ' We should elect Mr. Cleveland
to the public office which he is so admirably qualified to fill, and
remand Mr. Blaine to the private life which he is so eminently fitted
to adorn.' Democratic torchlight processions paraded the streets,
shouting,

> Blaine, Blaine, James G. Blaine,
> The continental liar from the State of Maine
> *Burn this letter!*

To which Republican processions retorted:

> Ma! Ma! Where's my pa?
> Gone to the White House,
> *Ha! Ha! Ha!*

The contest was bitterly fought throughout the North; Hendricks,
the Democratic vice-presidential nominee, added to the strength of
the ticket in the critical state of Indiana, and the Mugwumps played

---

[5] ' Mugwump ' is the word for ' great captain ' in Eliot's Indian Bible, applied on this
occasion by the New York *Sun.*

an important role in New Jersey and Connecticut. But New York was the decisive state. Here Blaine had a strong following among the Irish-Americans, which he lost at the eleventh hour through the tactless remark of a clerical supporter. As spokesman for a visiting delegation, a hapless parson named Burchard described the Democracy as the party of ' Rum, Romanism, and Rebellion.' Blaine neglected to rebuke this insult to the faith of his Celtic friends; Cleveland carried New York by a plurality of 1149 in a vote of over a million; and New York's electoral votes gave him the presidency.

For a person of such generous bulk, Grover Cleveland was remarkably austere, unbending, and ungenial. He was a man of integrity, courage, and steadfast devotion to duty; but singularly lacking in imagination and never quite at home in the rough and tumble of party politics. Though brought up in rural communities he never understood the problems of the farmers of the South and the West or the reasons for their discontent, but at least he made the effort. Conservative but not reactionary, he did not conceive of the government as an instrument for social reform but rather as a mediator between conflicting interests. Elected at a period when subservience to the popular will was supposed to be the first political virtue, he remained inflexible in the right as he saw it, and made few departures from his preconceived notions on any subject.

It was character that made Cleveland's administration the most respectable between Lincoln's and Theodore Roosevelt's. He alone of the presidents of this generation had some suspicion of the significance and direction of the economic changes that were transforming the country and made some effort to grapple with the problems created by changes. He alone of the titular leaders of either party had sufficient courage to defy the privilege groups and the pressure groups that were using the government for selfish purposes and to risk his political career in defense of what he thought was honest and right. He supported and advanced civil service reform; challenged the predatory interests that were engrossing the public lands of the nation; denounced the evils of protection and dramatized the tariff issue so effectively that it could not be evaded; and called a halt to the raids on the Treasury by war veterans and their lobbyists. If the total achievements of his administration were negative rather than positive, that was something of a virtue at a time when most politicians were saying ' yes ' to the wrong things.

Shortly after Cleveland's inauguration the question of patronage arose. Deserving Democrats, deprived of the sweets of office for twenty-five years, demanded as clean a sweep as the law would allow — 88 per cent clean; virtuous Mugwumps insisted on no sweep at all. ' I have a hungry party behind me,' the President remarked sadly, and on another occasion he broke out, more expressively, ' the d — d everlasting clatter for office continues to some extent, and makes me feel like resigning, and Hell is to pay generally.' Congress repealed the Tenure of Office Act, which left the President free again to remove incumbents without permission of the Senate; and by the end of his term, Cleveland, despite his intense dislike for the spoils system, had replaced nearly all the postmasters, and about half the other officials. Yet Cleveland did more for civil service reform than any President before Theodore Roosevelt. When he entered office some 43,000 places were filled by the merit system; when he left, in 1897, this was the case for 86,932 out of a total of about 200,000. And in the end the Democrats were not satisfied, and the Mugwumps were not pleased.

Cleveland stirred up the old soldiers by appointing General Lucius Quintus Cincinnatus Lamar, C.S.A., Secretary of the Interior; by proposing to return to their states the captured Confederate battle flags; and above all by his attitude toward private pension claims and pension legislation in general. The pension situation already was scandalous; it was shortly to become preposterous. The first general Civil War pension bill had been passed in 1862 and was based upon the sound theory that it was the duty of the government to pension veterans who suffered from disabilities contracted while in military service, and to assist the widows and children of these veterans. Under this law not far from 900,000 claims had been filed by veterans or their dependents prior to the accession of Cleveland to the presidency. Of these some 520,000 had been allowed; the rest had been rejected as invalid. Many of those whose claims were thus rejected had recourse to private pension bills which were presented by greedy pension attorneys and pushed through by Congressmen anxious to make political capital. This particular form of raid on the public treasury disgusted right-thinking men everywhere. Charles Francis Adams wrote scathingly, ' We had seen every dead-beat, and malingerer, every bummer, bounty-jumper, and suspected deserter . . . rush to the front as the greedy claimant of public bounty. If there was any man whose army record had been otherwise than creditable . . . we soon heard of him as the claimant of a back pension . . . or as being in the regular receipt of his monthly stipend.' Cleveland actually signed no less than 1453 of these private pension bills — a larger number than any of his predecessors — but it was his vetoes that were remembered.

Soon a second pension theory emerged — a theory which insisted that all veterans who suffered from any physical disability, regardless of its origin or its cause, were entitled to pensions. This theory had the solid support of the Grand Army of the Republic, of thousands of pension agents, and of business interests anxious to dispose of surplus revenue in order that there might be no downward revision of the tariff. The G.A.R. which by the middle 'eighties boasted a membership of almost half a million, was one of the most powerful pressure groups in the country and had long maintained an intimate alliance with the Republican party. It flooded the country with propaganda, bullied Congressmen, threatened presidents, and intimidated political parties.

We flatter ourselves [said Senator Saulsbury in 1884] that we are great men. We are the Senators of the United States who make laws for the people; but behind us there is another power greater than ourselves, controlling our action if not our judgment. The pension agents who sit around this Capitol issue their circulars and decrees, and petitions come up for pensions, and the Senators of the United States, great and mighty as they may be, bow to the behests of the pension agents and vote the money that they require, and they are afraid not to do it for fear that they would lose political status at home. We all know it, and the country knows it.

In 1887 Congress, at the dictation of the G.A.R. and the pension agents, passed the Dependent Pension Bill granting pensions to all veterans suffering from any disabilities, regardless of how contracted. Cleveland vetoed the bill, and his veto was an important factor in defeating him for re-election the following year.

There was a roar of protest, too, from the predatory interests that were despoiling the lands and forests of the West when the President ordered an investigation into the fraudulent practices of cattle ranchers, railroads, timber companies, and squatters on Indian reservations. Lamar and his Land Office Commissioner, William A. Sparks, uncovered frauds that staggered the imagination. Most railroad lands had been granted on terms calling for forfeiture in the event of the non-fulfillment of the contract within a stated time, but during preceding administrations these forfeiture clauses had been blandly ignored. More serious, where railroad grants happened to embrace lands already settled, the railroads had been permitted either to take over the homesteader's land, with all improvements, or to indemnify themselves from valuable forest or mineral lands elsewhere. Lamar put an end to these practices and instituted suits to recover millions of acres of land from the railroads. He proceeded with equal energy against powerful lumber companies like the Sierra Lumber Company and the Montana Improvement Company, subsidiary of the Northern Pacific Railroad, who were ruthlessly despoiling the national forests. He nullified fraudulent leases of Indian lands like that whereby one cattle company leased from the Cherokees 6 million acres for which it paid an annual rental of only $100,000 and which it then subleased for five times that amount. He ordered cattle barons to take down their barbed wire fences enclosing millions of acres of public lands, and instituted reforms long overdue in the administration of the Land Office. Altogether, during his first administration, Cleveland forced the restoration of some 81 million acres of public lands. At the same time the Interstate Commerce Act of 1887 and the Dawes Act of 1887 furnished useful points of departure for the more effective regulation of the railroads and of Indian affairs.

More dramatic was Cleveland's effort to force action on the tariff problem. In this effort he was moved by two considerations. The high tariff, adopted originally as an emergency Civil War measure, had come to be accepted as a permanent part of national policy. As such it had contributed, in Cleveland's opinion, not only to a general increase in the price level of protected goods, but to the encouragement and development of trusts. Government revenues had shown a consistent surplus over ordinary expenses of almost $100 million annually all through the decade of the 'eighties, and this surplus was a standing temptation to extravagance of the pork barrel and pension grab variety. Yet the tariff, which had divided parties so sharply before the Civil War, had almost ceased to be a party issue, or even a political issue. The Civil War tariffs had raised the average duties from 18 to 40 per cent, and successive tinkerings in 1867, 1870, 1872, and 1875 had not changed levels in any substantial way, though there had been a gradual upward trend on iron ore and woolens. Yet aside from the protests of the Liberal Republicans in 1872 there had been singularly little agitation on the subject. In 1880, however, the Democrats had demanded a ' tariff for revenue only ' and soon the clamor for reform became so insistent that the Tariff Commission of 1882, composed though it was of protectionists, recommended a downward revision of not less than 20 per cent.[6] Congress responded the following year with a ' mongrel tariff ' that lowered some duties and raised others — a tariff which had the support not only of Republican protectionists like ' Pig Iron ' Kelley of Pennsylvania but also of conservative Democrats like Randall of Pennsylvania and Mahone of Virginia.

This was the situation when Cleveland came to office. During the first two years of his administration the Democrats made no sincere effort to redeem their platform pledges of a downward revision of the tariff. In 1887, Cleveland, despite warnings to avoid the explosive subject, startled the nation by devoting his annual message exclusively to the tariff. He denounced the fantastic extremes to which the principle of protection had been pushed, derided the ' infant industry ' theory of high tariffs, emphasized the intimate relation of the tariff to trusts, and demanded a reduction which would be in harmony with the interests of society as a whole. ' Our progress toward a wise conclusion,' he wrote, ' will not be improved by dwelling upon theories of protection and free trade. It is a condition which confronts us, not a theory.' Reformers everywhere took heart. The New York *Nation* characterized the message ' the most courageous document that has been sent from the White House since the Civil War.' But Blaine denounced it as pure ' free trade,' and the Republicans prepared joyously to make this the issue of the forthcoming campaign. A House bill looking to a downward revision of the tariff bill was duly deadlocked by Senate Republicans. Yet Cleveland had accomplished his purpose. He had brought the tariff issue sharply to the attention of the country and he had forced his own party to espouse tariff reform as the paramount issue.

[6] ' The Commission,' so read the report, ' became convinced that a substantial reduction of tariff duties is demanded, not by a mere indiscriminate popular clamor, but by the best conservative opinion of the country. . . . Such a reduction of the existing tariff the Commission regards not only as a due recognition of public sentiment and a measure of justice to consumers, but one conducive to the general industrial prosperity, and which . . . will be ultimately beneficial to the special interests affected by such reduction.'

4. THE CLIMAX OF REACTION

Cleveland was renominated by the Democrats in 1888 without great enthusiasm, but with little opposition except from some of the disgruntled politicians, and the platform pledged the party to ' the views expressed by the President in his last message to Congress.' The Republicans pitched on the innocuous Benjamin Harrison of Indiana as the most available and least offensive candidate, since he came from a critical state and had distinguished ancestry and a war record. The tariff was the issue of the campaign, but it did not decide the event. More important were such factors as Tammany's betrayal of Cleveland in the critical state of New York, the Republican campaign fund of over $4 million, and the conversion of the G.A.R. to an instrument of the Republican party. The Democrats tried to round up the California vote by a bill which in effect denied treaty rights to Chinese immigrants; the Republicans, now that the issue of sexual immorality, so useful in the last campaign, was played out, resorted to the charge that the President beat his wife! Neither of these expedients had any effect, but another trick was more successful. The Irish vote had helped defeat Blaine in 1884; now it was turned against Cleveland. A naturalized Anglo-American was inspired to inquire of the British Minister, Sir Lionel Sackville-West, how he should vote in order to serve the mother country. Sir Lionel, with incredible stupidity, advised him by letter to vote for the Democrats. Two weeks before the election, his letter was published, and the mischief was done. Though Cleveland's popular vote exceeded Harrison's by 100,000 the Republicans carried New York State by a few thousand votes, and again New York was decisive.

Benjamin Harrison, grandson of the hero of Tippecanoe, was an Indiana lawyer who made a dignified figurehead in the presidency from 1889 to 1893. Aloof and aristocratic, honest and conscientious, he lacked the insight to comprehend the economic and imperialistic problems of a new day and the ability to control the spoilsmen of his party. Despite his character and attainments he made singularly little impression upon his own or later generations. James G. Blaine, who still considered himself the leader of the party, became his Secretary of State; the rest of the cabinet were nonentities. With the autocratic ' Czar ' Thomas B. Reed as Speaker of the House, and with a majority in both Houses, the way was clear for constructive legisla-

tion. But the Republican party wanted little legislation that was not
a raid on the treasury or a hold-up on the consumer, and in this administration statesmanship reached a new low-water mark.

The Republicans returned to office with heavy political debts to
pay. The machine politicians had performed yeoman service in
rounding up votes, and they expected to be rewarded with the spoils
of office. The old soldier vote had proved decisive in critical states,
and the soldiers counted on more generous pensions. Business and
manufacturing interests had contributed liberally to the campaign
fund, and they expected to be rewarded with an upward revision of
the tariff. To all these demands the administration showed itself remarkably complaisant. Rarely before in our history had an administration been more responsive to pressure groups; never since, unless
in the 1920's, has the connection between government and business
been more openly avowed and frankly accepted.

Harrison had said, in his acceptance speech, that ' only the interest
of the public service should suggest removals from office,' but it was
quickly apparent that such interest required a clean sweep of Democratic officeholders. Within a year Postmaster-General Wanamaker
had removed over 30,000 postmasters, more than double the number
that Cleveland had dismissed in the same period. Cleveland had
placed the railroad mail service under civil service rules, but Harrison suspended the operation of the rules until the service could be
filled with Republicans, and at the same time refused to extend the
rules to the new Census Bureau. Theodore Roosevelt was appointed,
as window-dressing, to the Civil Service Commission, but the Civil
Service Reform League denounced the President for violation of his
campaign pledges and the New York *Nation* characterized him as a
' subservient disciple of the spoils doctrine.'

Harrison, during his campaign, had announced that ' it was no
time to be weighing the claims of old soldiers with apothecary's
scales,' and he lived up to the implications of that statement. ' God
help the Surplus,' said Corporal Tanner who was appointed to the
office of Pension Commissioner, and whose liberal interpretations of
the existing pension legislation cost the Treasury millions of dollars.
In 1890 Congress passed and the President signed a Disability Pension Act which provided pensions to all veterans who had served 90
days and who were unable to perform *manual* labor, or suffered from
any disability ' not the result of their own vicious habits.' Even the

G.A.R. was satisfied for a time. 'While not just what we asked,' the pension committee of that organization reported, 'it is the most liberal pension measure ever passed by any legislative body in the world, and will place upon the rolls all of the survivors of the war whose conditions of health are not practically perfect.' Yet in course of time the veterans came to demand, and politicians found it expedient to grant, still more. After the turn of the century came a system of Universal Service Pensions, and by a presidential ruling, in 1904, all veterans were granted pensions on the basis of service alone. By 1936 the Civil War pension bill had come to a little less than $8 billion.

The year 1890 is memorable, politically, for the passage of the Disability Pension Act, the Sherman Anti-Trust Act, the Sherman Silver Purchase bill, the McKinley tariff, and for the admission of the last of the 'omnibus' states. Of these we have already discussed the Anti-Trust Act and the omnibus states, and will reserve for later consideration the Silver Purchase bill. That the Harrison administration should fulfill its campaign promises by new tariff legislation was inevitable. Yet it was by no means clear, in the light of Cleveland's popular plurality, that the country wanted a higher tariff, nor was it certain that the administration could muster a majority on this issue. The McKinley tariff bill of October 1890 was pushed through as the result of a bargain between Western Republicans who wanted silver legislation and Eastern Republicans who wanted tariff legislation. Its provisions were formulated chiefly by William McKinley of Ohio and Nelson W. Aldrich of Rhode Island, but the important schedules were dictated by such interested groups as the National Association of Wool Manufacturers, the Tin Plate and Iron and Steel Associations, and the Louisiana sugar growers. The bill was a frank recognition of the protective principle: it sought not only to protect established industries, but to foster 'infant industries' and, by prohibitory duties, to create new industries. It embodied three new and interesting provisions: it reached out for the farmers' vote with protective rates upon products of agriculture, duties which proved completely ineffective in the forthcoming agricultural depression; it put raw sugar on the free list and compensated the Louisiana and Kansas beet sugar growers with a bounty of two cents a pound — a provision which all but wrecked the Hawaiian sugar industry and brought on a revolution in that island kingdom; it included a reciprocity section which gave the President authority to place duties on sugar, molasses, tea, coffee, and hides if he thought that nations exporting those articles to the United States were imposing unequal and unreasonable duties on American goods.

Pension legislation and tariff legislation helped to liquidate the troublesome surplus, and further support to this happy policy was found in additional legislation of a less important character. Postal subsidies to steamship lines were increased; the direct taxes collected during the Civil War were generously returned to the states where they had been paid; outbreaks among the Sioux, culminating in the massacre of Indians at Wounded Knee Creek and the murder of Sitting Bull, required enlarged expenditures for the army and the Indian Bureau; and finally Secretary Windom's policy of using surplus treasury funds to buy up and cancel government bonds took some $275 million before the policy was reversed by Windom's successor. The total expenditures of the Fifty-first Congress, 2 December 1889 to 3 March 1891, reached the unprecedented sum of almost a billion dollars. ' This is a Billion Dollar country,' was the retort attributed to ' Czar ' Reed.

The unpopularity of the McKinley tariff was largely responsible for the political revolution in the congressional elections of 1890. Only 88 Republicans were returned to the new House, as against 235 Democrats and nine Populists; and the Republican majority in the Senate was reduced to eight unstable votes from the Far West. Even rock-ribbed Republican states like Michigan and Massachusetts went Democratic, and McKinley himself failed of re-election. There was more to this verdict, however, than revulsion from the tariff and disgust at Republican chicanery and corruption. It registered a deep-lying unrest that was presently to break forth into a movement that carried Bryan to prominence, Roosevelt to achievement, and Wilson to apotheosis.

BIBLIOGRAPHY

1. GENERAL. Herbert Agar, *The Price of Union;* Charles A. and Mary R. Beard, *Rise of American Civilization,* vol. 2; James Bryce, *The American Commonwealth* (2 vols.) ; Harold U. Faulkner, *Politics, Reform and Expansion 1890–1900;* Sidney Fine, *Laissez Faire and the General Welfare State;* Eric Goldman, *Rendezvous with Destiny;* Richard Hofstadter, *American Political Tradition;* Matthew Josephson, *The Politicos;* Charles E. Merriam, *American Political Ideas;* Horace Merrill, *Bourbon Democracy in the Middle West 1865–1896;* Russel B.

Nye, *Midwestern Progressive Politics 1870–1950;* Ellis P. Overholtzer, *History of the United States since the Civil War,* vol. 4; Harry Thurston Peck, *Twenty Years of the Republic;* James Ford Rhodes, *History of the United States from Hayes to McKinley;* Edward Stanwood, *American Tariff Controversies;* H. C. Thomas, *Return of the Democratic Party to Power;* Charles Warren, *History of the Supreme Court,* vol. 2; Leonard D. White, *The Republican Era 1865–1900;* William A. White, *Masks in a Pageant* and *Autobiography.*

2. REFORM. Edward Cary, *George William Curtis;* Carl Russell Fish, *The Civil Service and the Patronage;* Claude Fuess, *Carl Schurz;* W. H. Glasson, *Federal Military Pensions in the United States;* E. L. Godkin, *Problems of Modern Democracy;* H. F. Gosnell, *Boss Platt and the New York Machine;* Allan Nevins, *Grover Cleveland: A Study in Courage;* A. B. Sageser, *Two Decades of the Pendleton Act;* Carl Schurz, *Reminiscences* (one-vol. ed. by Wayne Andrews) ; F. M. Stewart, *National Civil Service Reform League.*

3. BIOGRAPHIES. Harry Barnard, *Eagle Forgotten: Life of John P. Altgeld;* James J. Barnes, *John G. Carlisle;* Herbert Croly, *Mark Hanna;* Claude Fuess, *Carl Schurz;* Mark A. Hirsch, *William C. Whitney;* George Hoar, *Autobiography of Seventy Years;* Walter Johnson, *William Allen White's America;* Margaret Leech, *In the Days of McKinley;* David S. Muzzey, *James G. Blaine;* Allan Nevins, *Grover Cleveland;* William A. Robinson, *Thomas B. Reed;* T. C. Smith, *Life and Letters of James A. Garfield* (2 vols.) ; Nathaniel W. Stephenson, *Nelson Aldrich;* Charles R. Williams, *Life of Rutherford B. Hayes* (2 vols.) .

4. DOCUMENTS. H. S. Commager, *Documents,* nos. 297, 299, 300, 303, 308, 312, 317.

For further references, see *Harvard Guide,* ¶¶ 193, 203, 204.

The Battle of the Standards

1. THE POPULIST REVOLT

IN 1890 American politics lost their steady beat, and began to dip and flutter in an effort to maintain equilibrium among strange currents of thought that issued from the caverns of discontent.

Almost a generation had passed since the Civil War. The older Republicans had come to revere their 'Grand Old Party' only less than the Union and the flag, and indeed they often identified party loyalty with patriotism. They had come to regard their leaders as the beloved generals of a victorious army. It was difficult for the politicians to believe that anything was amiss. The Ohio and Middle Western men, average and representative of the party, had grown up with the country. Their experience of life had been utterly different from that of any European statesman. They had seen the frontier of log-cabins, stumpy clearings, and razor-back hogs replaced by frame houses and great barns, well-tilled farms, and sleek cattle. Towns with banks, libraries, high schools, mansions, and 'opera houses' had sprung up where once as barefooted boys they had hunted squirrel and wild cat; and the market towns of their youth had grown into great manufacturing cities. As young men they had enlisted in the crusade for the Union, and returned to take their part in progress, development, and expansion. The railroad, the telegraph, the sewing machine, oil and gas lighting, and a hundred new comforts and conveniences had come within reach of all but the poorest and remotest during their lifetime. If discontented workmen and poverty-stricken farmers sometimes intruded into the picture, it must be foreign agitators or the law of supply and demand that were to blame. How could there be anything wrong with a government which had wrought such miraculous changes for the better, or with a Grand Old Party which had saved the nation from disunion?

The Democratic party, too, was in danger of becoming conservative and content. The oldest, and during most of this period the largest, political party,[1] it embraced the most diverse elements and was compelled to reconcile those elements by avoiding controversial issues. Its stronghold was in the most conservative sections of the country — the South and the industrial centers; and its strength in these sections rested not on any policies it might embrace but upon race, tradition, and the loyalty of local organizations. There was little reason to believe that the Bourbon Democrats of the South would be friendly to new ideas of a liberal or radical character; there was no reason to suppose that Tammany Hall and kindred organizations in the North would be open to any ideas. The Solid South, irrevocably committed to the one principle of maintaining white supremacy, hung like a dead weight on party leadership; the local machines in the North, no less irrevocably committed to the single principle of getting and keeping office, were willing to sell out on any other issue to the highest bidder. There were independents, of course, in the Democratic as in the Republican party, men like Cleveland in New York, Thurman in Ohio, John Carlisle in Kentucky, and Lamar in Mississippi, but only rarely could they carry their party with them on any controversial issue.

Yet the quarter-century of exploitation had its suffering victims, who felt that something was radically wrong and were groping for a remedy. Industrial unrest was acute; 1890 witnessed the largest number of strikes recorded in any one year of the nineteenth century, and the Homestead strike of 1892 recalled the scenes of violence and terrorism of the ' Great Strike ' of 1877. Immigrants from southern and eastern Europe were pouring into the country in unprecedented numbers, threatening the wages and the standards of American workingmen. Railroad regulation had proved all but futile, and the anti-trust law was to prove effective only against labor organizations. Discontent with the McKinley tariff was widespread, and the prospect of any effective tariff reduction was dim. Money was tight, credit inflexible, banking facilities inadequate, and the Sherman Silver Purchase Act did little to satisfy the advocates of free and unlimited coinage of silver and less to settle the money question. The political machinery was not geared to democracy: the Senate, chosen not by popu-

[1] Note that the Democratic party polled a plurality of the popular vote in the presidential elections of 1876, 1884, 1888, and 1892.

BAPTISM IN KANSAS *by John Steuart Curry*

lar vote but by state legislatures, was the stronghold of special interests; the Supreme Court reflected the ideas of the privileged.

Dissatisfaction was most acute on the farms of the South and the
West. The Middle Border began, in 1887, to suffer the devastating
effects of deflation after a great land boom. Virgin prairie land, and
peak prices of wheat and corn in 1881, had induced an excessive construction of railroads, largely financed locally, and an oversettlement
of the comparatively arid western part of Kansas, Nebraska, and the
Dakotas. Small towns and counties indulged in lavish expenditure,
and their citizens speculated wildly in building lots. These new farms
were created largely on credit granted by mortgage companies in the
East; in Kansas there was one mortgage, on the average, to every
other adult in the state, and the situation in Nebraska and Iowa was
almost as bad. After several years of excessive rainfall there came in
1887 a summer so dry that the crops withered all along the border
of the Plains. In the four years from 1889 to 1893 over 11,000 farm
mortgages were foreclosed in Kansas alone and in fifteen counties of
that state over three-quarters of the land was owned by mortgage
companies. During these years the people who had entered that new
El Dorado trekked eastward again; on their wagons one could read
the scrawl, ' In God we trusted, in Kansas we busted.' William Allen
White described some of these picturesquely.

There came through Emporia yesterday two old-fashioned mover
wagons, headed east. . . . These movers were from western Kansas. . . .
They had come from that wilderness only after a ten years' hard vicious
fight, a fight which had left its scars on their faces, had beat their bodies,
had taken the elasticity from their steps and left them crippled to enter
the battle anew. For ten years they had been fighting the elements. They
had seen it stop raining for months at a time. They had heard the fury of
the winter wind as it came whining across the short burned grass and cut
the flesh from their children huddling in the corner. These movers have
strained their eyes watching through long summer days for the rain that
never came. . . . They have tossed through hot nights wild with worry,
and have arisen only to find their worst nightmares grazing in reality on
the brown stubble in front of their sun-warped doors. They had such high
hopes when they went out there; they are so desolate now — no, not now,
for now they are in the land of corn and honey. They have come out of
the wilderness, back to the land of promise.

Others, made of sterner stuff, struggled on through the 'eighties and
the 'nineties to better times. What was true along the Middle Border

was almost equally true of other agricultural regions. In an Eastern state a survey of 700 representative farms discovered an average annual yield of $167. In the older Middle West farmers were glad to exchange places with immigrant factory hands who had at least a dollar a day. And in the South cotton growers struggled on from year to year against a falling market, overproduction, and the improvidence of Negro tenants, while mortgage indebtedness and tenancy grew at an ominous rate.

The stage was set for the entrance of a party of revolt, and with gratifying promptness the Populist party made its appearance. The rank and file of the new party was recruited from the Farmers' Alliances, Greenbackers, Knights of Labor, free-silverites, disciples of Edward Bellamy, and followers of Henry George; the leadership, drawn almost exclusively from the Alliances, furnished a refreshing contrast to the dismal leadership of the major parties during the 'eighties and 'nineties. There was ' Pitchfork Ben ' Tillman of South Carolina, who placed himself at the head of the underprivileged farmers of the Palmetto state, won the governorship from the ' Bourbon ' Wade Hampton, pushed a series of reforms through the state legislature, and created a political machine to do his bidding. There was the demagogic Tom Watson of Georgia, apostle of the new Jeffersonianism, who championed the cause of the tenant farmers and the mill hands — but not the Negroes — ran for the presidency on the Populist ticket, wrote biographies of Jefferson and Napoleon, and earned the dubious title of the ' Sage of Hickory Hill.' There was David H. Waite, Governor of Colorado, friend of the farmers and the miners and of all the underprivileged of the earth, known by his admirers as the ' Abraham Lincoln of the Rockies ' and by his critics as ' Bloody Bridles Waite ' because he had said that it was better ' that blood should flow to the horses' bridles rather than our national liberties should be destroyed.' Minnesota boasted the Sage of Nininger, the inimitable Ignatius Donnelly, discoverer of the lost Atlantis, advocate of the Baconian theory, author of the prophetic *Caesar's Column,* undismayed champion of lost causes and desperate remedies. From Iowa came the upright and dignified James Baird Weaver who gave respectability to heterodoxy and who undertook the thankless job of representing the Greenbackers in the canvass of 1880 and the Populists in 1892, and who had every quality but magnetism. Abolitionist Kansas, where, as William Allen White remembered, the farm revolt became ' a religious revival, a crusade, a pentecost of politics in which the tongue of flame sat upon every man and each spake as the spirit gave him utterance ' was most prolific of leadership. Here the sad-faced Mary Lease went about advising farmers to ' raise less corn and more Hell.' Here Jerry Simpson, the sockless Socrates of the prairie, espoused the doctrines of Henry George and exposed the iniquities of the railroads. Here Senator William A. Peffer of the hickory-nut head and long flowing beard, whom Roosevelt, with his usual impetuosity denounced as ' a well-meaning, pin-headed, anarchistic crank,' presented with logic and learning *The Farmer's Side, His Troubles and Their Remedy*. And from Nebraska came the greatest of all the farmers' leaders, the Jefferson of the new dispensation, William Jennings Bryan.

Although the new party was not formally organized until 1891, it got under way in 1890, and that year succeeded in capturing control of the Democratic party in a number of Southern states and in effecting a working alliance with the Democrats in the West. As a result of this strategy it emerged from the fall elections of 1890 with four Senators and over fifty Congressmen and with partial or complete control of the legislatures of a dozen states. Flushed with this initial success the triumphant leaders prepared, through a series of conferences and conventions, to organize the new party in a formal fashion and to present a full ticket in the elections of 1892.

The Populist convention that met in Omaha on Independence Day of 1892 presented a sharp contrast to the conventions of the two major parties. Decorum and apathy had marked these conventions, and the nominations of Cleveland and Harrison had excited neither surprise nor enthusiasm. But a camp-meeting atmosphere characterized the convention of the People's party, and the speeches which the oddly assorted delegates greeted with such ' tumultuous applause ' were old-fashioned camp-meeting harangues. The platform, drawn up by the eloquent Ignatius Donnelly, raked both the major parties and painted a melancholy picture of the American scene:

We meet in the midst of a nation brought to the verge of moral, political, and material ruin. Corruption dominates the ballot-box, the legislatures, the Congress, and touches even the ermine of the bench. The people are demoralized; . . . The newspapers are largely subsidized or muzzled; public opinion silenced; business prostrated; our homes covered with mortgages; labor impoverished; and the land concentrating in the

hands of the capitalists. The urban workmen are denied the right of
organization for self-protection; imported pauperized labor beats down
their wages; a hireling standing army, unrecognized by our laws, is
established to shoot them down, and they are rapidly degenerating into
European conditions. The fruits of the toil of millions are boldly stolen
to build up colossal fortunes for a few, unprecedented in the history of
mankind; and the possessors of these in turn, despise the republic and
endanger liberty. From the same prolific womb of governmental injustice
we breed the two great classes — tramps and millionaires.

Specifically, the platform demanded the free and unlimited coinage
of silver; a flexible currency system, controlled by the government
and not by the banks, with an increase in the circulating medium to
$50 per capita; a graduated income tax; the sub-treasury scheme;
postal savings banks; public ownership and operation of railroads,
telegraph, and telephones; prohibition of alien land ownership and
reclamation of railroad lands illegally held; immigration restriction;
the eight-hour day for labor; prohibition of the use of labor spies;
the direct election of Senators, the Australian ballot, the initiative
and referendum. The platform was regarded throughout the East as
little short of communism, yet within a generation almost every one
of the planks was incorporated into law in whole or in part. The
Populist party was the seed-bed of American politics for the next
half-century.

For their standard-bearer the Populists chose James B. Weaver of
Iowa, a veteran of the reform movement too well known to excite
curiosity and too respectable to justify abuse. The ensuing three-
cornered campaign was less exciting than might have been expected,
but the election offered some suggestive comments on American politics. Cleveland swept the Solid South and seven Northern states, including New York, and for the third successive time received a popular plurality. Harrison polled a smaller vote than he had in his first
campaign, and the labor and tariff policies for which his party was
held responsible forfeited the support of the industrial states of the
East. Weaver received over a million popular votes and 22 electoral
votes, but his efforts to rally the farmers of the nation to his standard
had been successful only in the region of the High Plains. Southern
farmers, regardless of grievances, preferred to vote for the party
which to them represented white supremacy. It remained to be seen
whether a Democrat could perform in 'ninety-six what a Populist had
failed to achieve in 'ninety-two — the renewal of the traditional alli-

ance of South and West which had been shattered by the Civil War, and the creation of an agrarian party which could command the support of labor.

2. THE MONEY QUESTION

American society appeared to be dissolving, but the same old Grover Cleveland, a little stouter and more set in his ideas, was inaugurated President on 4 March 1893. A large proportion of his vote had come from suffering farmers who looked for relief to the Democracy rather than to the Populists. Cold comfort they got from the inaugural address! The situation, as the President saw it, demanded ' prompt and conservative precaution ' to protect a ' sound and stable currency.'

The trouble was, of course, that men disagreed violently as to the nature of ' a sound and stable currency,' and from that time to the present neither historians nor economists have been able to reach any agreement. No problem is of a more controversial character, and no controversy was ever more interpenetrated with emotion or more confused by the application of moral attitudes. But the money question, for all its complexity, had the merit of cutting athwart party lines and reflecting sectional and class alignments as did no other political issue of that time — not even the tariff. Yet it would be an error to suppose that party loyalties were completely shattered by the realignment over this question. Even at the height of the controversy, traditional party loyalties continued to animate millions of voters; and that such predominately agricultural states as Iowa, Minnesota, and North Dakota cast their electoral votes for McKinley rather than for Bryan in 1896 must be credited, in the last analysis, not to economic determinism but to political habit and inheritance.

Put in its simplest terms — and nothing is more difficult to put in simple terms — the money question involved the relation of money to commodity prices, wages, and investments, and the function of the government in regulating that relation. The orthodox or classical theory of money, entertained by the business and investor classes generally, was the bullion theory. This theory held that money was actually only a token of coin, that its value was determined by the bullion which was held as security for its redemption, and that any interference by government with this value was economically unsound. It required therefore that all money in circulation have behind it some substantial metallic value, and that government confine itself to issuing money on security of bullion actually in the treasury vaults, either directly or indirectly through banks. As long as the ratio between gold and silver remained relatively stable, the bullion theory of money accepted a bimetallic standard; when the decline in the value of silver disrupted that long-established ratio, orthodox economists turned to the single gold standard. This classical theory of money was part of the philosophy of laissez faire which was so widely accepted in the whole field of economy and politics in the first half of the nineteenth century.

In the second half of the century, and especially after the Civil War, a new theory of money gained many adherents, a theory which regarded money as a token of credit rather than of bullion, and which maintained that it was the proper business of the government to regulate money in the interests of society at large. Advocates of this theory pointed out that bullion, and especially gold, did not provide a sufficiently large or flexible basis for the money needs of an expanding nation, and that any financial policy which tied money to gold placed the whole monetary system of the nation at the mercy of a fortuitous gold production. They insisted that bullion security for money was unnecessary or necessary only in part; that the vital consideration was the credit of the government, and that ' the promise to pay ' of the United States was sufficient to sustain the value of any money issued by that government. These proponents of credit money demanded that currency be expanded whenever essential to provide for the business needs of the country and to hold commodity prices stable. Enthusiastic support for this school of economic thought was found among the farmers of the South and the West, and among the debtor groups everywhere — groups who had favored easy money since the days of the Massachusetts land bank scheme and Shays's Rebellion of the eighteenth century.

The roots of the money question are to be found in the financing of the Civil War. At that time, it will be remembered, the Federal Government issued $450 million in greenbacks — money with no security but the promise of the government to pay. These greenbacks were legal tender for all purposes except customs duties and interest on certain government bonds. In part because of this discrimination against them, in part because of lack of confidence in the ability or the willingness of the government to redeem them in coin, they promptly depreciated in value. Yet though the fluctuation in the value of greenbacks was a constant temptation to speculation, they served nevertheless a useful purpose and came in time to command the confidence of a large part of the people. They not only helped to finance the war, but by expanding the currency they served to lower interest rates and to raise commodity prices.

On the conclusion of the war conservative business interests presented three demands: the resumption of specie payments on all government obligations; the retirement from the currency of all legal tender notes; and the refunding of the national debt on a gold basis. These demands aroused the bitter opposition of such men as Thaddeus Stevens and Wendell Phillips, but they were in large part complied with. Congress, in 1869, pledged the faith and credit of the United States to the payment of the principal and interest of government bonds in gold; the amount of legal tender notes was contracted to $346,681,000; and on 1 January 1879, the government resumed specie payments.

As a result of these policies, so their critics averred, commodity prices fell sharply and the public debt burden was vastly increased. The arguments which the greenbackers advanced to support this charge are not hard to follow. As per capita circulation of money declined from $31 in 1865 to $19 in 1875, money became tight and therefore dear. Since there were fewer dollars to go around in 1875 than there had been a decade earlier, it took more corn, wheat, and cotton to buy a dollar, than it had formerly taken. And as for the public debt, it was argued that as the government had borrowed greenback dollars worth anywhere from 50 to 80 cents in gold, it was not morally obliged to pay back dollars worth a dollar in gold.

The Specie Resumption Act of 1875, however, ended the greenback question as a practical political issue. A Greenback party, to be sure, entered the field; in 1878 it polled a million votes, and in 1880 and 1884 it offered presidential candidates to an indifferent electorate. But after the middle 'seventies the zeal of the inflationists was transferred from greenbacks to silver, and for the next twenty years ' free silver ' was the most exciting and significant political issue before the American people. This shift from greenbacks to silver was brought about by three considerations. In the first place silver satisfied the requirement that there should be some substantial security behind money, for to the conservative economists silver bullion seemed a sounder security than the mere promise of the government to pay. In the second place, dependence upon gold and silver would ensure a reasonable expansion of the currency but guard against any such reckless inflation as might result from the use of mere legal tender notes. In the third place, silver had behind it the silver-mine owners and investors, a powerful group, vitally interested in silver legislation and prepared to finance ' educational ' and political campaigns looking to such legislation.

In 1861 the mines of the country had produced approximately $43 million worth of gold but only $2 million worth of silver. The coinage ratio between silver and gold of 15.988 to 1 actually undervalued silver, and in consequence silver was sold for commercial purposes and only gold was carried to the mints for purposes of coinage. During the 'sixties and early 'seventies, however, came the discoveries of immense deposits of silver in the mountains of the West; by 1873 the value of silver mined in the United States had increased to $36 million while the value of gold had declined to the same figure. As a result of this relative and absolute increase in silver production, the price of silver gradually slumped until by 1873 it reached approximately the legal ratio. The next year, for the first time since 1837, it fell below the legal ratio, and it became profitable to sell silver to governments for coinage purposes instead of selling it for commercial purposes.

But when the silver-mine owners turned to governments, they found their market gone. Germany in 1871 adopted a gold standard; the Latin Union consisting of France, Italy, Switzerland, Belgium, and Greece hastened to suspend the free coinage of silver; and all the other European states came tumbling after. Worst of all, from the point of view of the silver interests, the United States had, by the coinage act of 1873, demonetized silver. This demonetization had been effected by the simple device of omitting from the act any specific provision for the coinage of silver dollars. Silverites hotly charged a trick, and the act became known as ' the Crime of '73.' It is immaterial now to determine whether the demonetization of silver was without malice or guile; the significant fact is that for a quarter-century a large part of the population sincerely and passionately believed that demonetization was part of a ' gold conspiracy ' and that it constituted the ' greatest crime in history.'

According to my views of the subject [said John G. Carlisle, who later became Cleveland's Secretary of the Treasury] the conspiracy which seems to have been formed here and in Europe to destroy by legislation and otherwise from three-sevenths to one-half of the metallic money of the world, is the most gigantic crime of this or any other age. The consummation of such a scheme would ultimately entail more misery upon the human race than all the wars, pestilences, and famines that ever occurred in the history of the world.

And the schoolmaster in *Coin's Financial School* — a book which was to the free silver crusade what *Uncle Tom's Cabin* was to the anti-slavery crusade — described the act in even more hysterical terms:

It is known as the crime of 1873. A crime, because it has confiscated millions of dollars worth of property. A crime, because it has made tens of thousands of tramps. A crime, because it has made thousands of suicides. A crime, because it has brought tears to strong men's eyes and hunger and pinching want to widows and orphans. A crime because it is destroying the honest yeomanry of the land, the bulwark of the nation. A crime because it has brought this once great republic to the verge of ruin, where it is now in imminent danger of tottering to its fall.

From the middle 'seventies to the middle 'nineties, then, the money question took the form of a demand for the free and unlimited coinage of silver. In 1878 the silverites pushed through, over a presidential veto, the Bland-Allison Act which provided that the government must purchase each month not less than $2 million nor more than $4 million worth of silver, to be coined into silver dollars at the existing legal ratio with gold. Successive secretaries of the treasury followed the minimum amount, and the addition to the currency was not sufficient to increase in any appreciable way the per capita circulation of money or to halt the steady decline in the price of silver in the world market.

The hard times of the late 'eighties brought a renewal of the silver agitation, a demand from the farmers and the silver interests that the government abandon the faint-hearted gesture of the Bland-Allison Act and commit itself irrevocably to the policy of unlimited coinage of silver. Domestic production of the white metal increased from $36 million in 1873 to $57 million by 1890, and the increase in world production was proportionately great. This increase, of course, depressed the price of silver and raised the price of gold. At the same time per capita circulation of money in the United States barely held its own, and in some sections of the country declined sharply. The relation between the limited coinage of silver and the low price of silver was not lost upon silver-mine interests. The connection between low commodity prices and high gold prices, between low per capita circulation of money and high interest rates, was not lost upon the farmers.

Yet silver agitation might have come to nought had it not been for the admission of the ' Omnibus ' states. The enabling acts of 1889 and 1890 brought into Congress representatives from six new Western states, and the Senate at once became the stronghold of silver sentiment. The result was the enactment of a new and more generous silver bill — the Sherman Silver Purchase Act of 1890. This curious measure, the product of a bargain whereby Western Republicans voted for a tariff bill which they disliked and Eastern Republicans voted for a silver bill which they feared, satisfied no one. It provided that the Treasury Department purchase each month 4.5 million ounces of silver, at the market price, paying for such silver with Treasury notes of the United States. It contained further the fateful provision that ' upon demand of the holder of any of the Treasury notes . . . the Secretary of the Treasury shall, under such regulations as he may prescribe, redeem such notes in gold or silver coin, at his discretion, it being the established policy of the United States to maintain the two metals on a parity with each other upon the present ratio.'

The Democrats opposed this measure not only on party grounds but because they regarded it as a futile and dangerous compromise. In this they were correct. The Sherman Act failed not only to increase the price of silver; it failed equally to increase the amount of money in circulation or to affect the steady decline in the prices of farm commodities. The failure of the Sherman Act to effect these ends was variously explained by two opposing schools of thought. Gold monometallists insisted that the act revealed the hopelessness of the effort to do anything for silver, and that it proved that the price of silver could not be raised artificially by government action. Silverites argued that the act proved the futility of compromise and the necessity for free and unlimited coinage. The act provided, to be sure, for the purchase of practically the entire domestic production of silver. But the world production was almost three times the domestic production, and as long as there were huge quantities of silver seeking a market, the price would be sure to slump. The solution, said conservatives, was to abandon silver to its fate and return to the gold standard. The solution, said the silverites, was to open our mints to unlimited coinage of silver, and peg the price at the traditional ratio of 16 to 1.

It is impossible now to determine which alternative was the better. In the end the gold standard was victorious, and before the 1930's historians were inclined to regard that victory as providential. Yet logic, at least, would seem to be with the bimetallists. Certainly if the United States stood ready to exchange, with all comers, one ounce of gold for sixteen ounces of silver, no one would sell silver for less than that sum. That is, if the United States could absorb all the silver that would be brought to her mints, she could peg the price, and bimetallism would be an established fact. But that *if* was crucial. The success of the operation depended upon the ability of the United States to pay out gold for silver until speculators were convinced of the futility of trying to break the price, or until the increased demand for silver raised its commercial value.

There was a third solution, one upon the desirability of which both monometallists and bimetallists were agreed. That was international bimetallism. If the United States could persuade the other great powers of the world to co-operate with it in re-establishing bimetallism, the normal market for silver would be restored, silver would rebound to its traditional price, and the money question would be solved. Hopefully, year after year, delegates journeyed to International Monetary Conferences. Practically every conference concluded that international bimetallism was economically expedient and financially sound. But on the political expediency of bimetallism there was no agreement. Each nation distrusted the sincerity of its neighbors, and no nation was ready to take the plunge. International bimetallism therefore served only the dubious purpose of furnishing bimetallists with arguments and permitting monometallists to hedge on the money question.

If bimetallism were to be tried, then, it would have to be tried as a national policy. The mere statement of this fact created an emotional tension unfavorable to the intelligent consideration of the question. On the one hand conservatives insisted that national finance and trade were so intimately connected with world finance and trade that it would be ruinous for the United States to embark upon a policy which might lead to economic isolation, and they painted in lurid colors the fearful consequences of such a development. On the other hand the silverites made the issue one of nationalism and patriotism, and the battle-cries of the Revolution echoed curiously across the plains of Nebraska and Texas. ' It is the issue of 1776 over again,' said Bryan. ' Our ancestors when but three million in number, had the courage to declare their political independence of every other nation; shall we, their descendants, when we have grown to 70 millions, declare that we are less independent than our forefathers? '

Consideration of the money question was confused not only by irrelevant issues of patriotism and nationalism, but of morals and ethics. ' Gold-bugs ' talked of an ' honest dollar,' and, smugly appropriating all honesty to themselves, denounced their opponents as wicked and immoral men. ' The eagerness of the advocates of free silver,' wrote the conservative economist, J. Laurence Laughlin, ' is founded on an appeal to dishonesty and cheating on the part of those who would like to repudiate and scale one-half of their obligations.' Silverites retorted by branding the monometallists as ' Shylocks ' and ' vampires,' and hurled back at them the charge of dishonesty. ' A dollar approaches honesty,' argued Mr. Bryan, ' as its purchasing power approaches stability. . . . Society has become accustomed to some very nice distinctions. . . . The poor man who takes property by force is called a thief, but the creditor who can by legislation make a debtor pay a dollar twice as large as he borrowed is lauded as the friend of sound currency. The man who wants the people to destroy the Government is an anarchist, but the man who wants the Government to destroy the people is a patriot.'

We can see now that the issue was both deeper and less dangerous than contemporaries realized. It was deeper because it involved a struggle for the ultimate control of government and of economy between the business interests of the East and the agrarian interests of the South and the West — a struggle in which gold and silver were mere symbols. It was less dangerous because, in all probability, none of the calamities so freely prophesied would have followed the adoption of either the gold or the silver standard at any time during these years. When the gold standard was finally adopted in 1900, the event made not a ripple on the placid seas of our economic life. When the gold standard was abandoned by Great Britain and by the United States, a full generation later, the event led to no untoward results. Historical parallels and analogies are always dangerous, but we are safe in saying that in the light of the experience of the 1930's much of the high-flown discussion of the 1890's was fantasy.

3. THE PRESIDENT AND THE PANIC

The Cleveland administration was just two months old when the failure of the National Cordage Company inaugurated the panic of 1893. The fundamental causes of this panic, as of all panics, are obscure, and the explanation that it was an inevitable curve of the business cycle merely begs the question. Yet it is possible to suggest some of the factors which contributed to the collapse of 1893. The long drawn-out agricultural depression which began in 1887 had seriously curtailed the purchasing power of one large group of consumers, and had similarly affected railway income. The collapse of our markets abroad, owing to business distress in Europe and Australia, had serious repercussions on American trade and manufacturing. Overspeculation attendant upon the organization of trusts and combines endangered the stability of the business world, while industrial disorders like the Homestead strike and the Coeur d'Alene strike reduced profits and cut down purchasing power. Finally the silver policy of the government impaired confidence in the business world at home and abroad, and persuaded many European creditors to dump their American securities on the market and drain the nation of its gold.

By midsummer of 1893 the panic was in full swing. The Reading Railroad failed early in the spring. In July came the failure of the Erie, and shortly thereafter the Northern Pacific, the Union Pacific, and the Santa Fe all went into the hands of receivers. Within two years one-fourth of the railroad capitalization of the country was under control of bankruptcy courts, and 60 per cent of railroad stocks had suspended dividend payments. Banks everywhere felt the strain and called in their loans, often with consequences fatal to business firms and individuals unable to meet their obligations; over 15,000 failures were recorded for the year 1893. In the rural sections banks toppled like card-houses; of the 158 national bank failures in 1893, 153 were in the South and the West. ' Men died like flies under the strain,' wrote Henry Adams, ' and Boston grew suddenly old, haggard, and thin.' Adams was thinking of the Boston financiers; the characterization was equally applicable to the 4 million jobless who, by the summer of 1894, walked the streets of factory towns in a vain search for work.

Convinced that monetary uncertainty was the chief cause of the panic, President Cleveland summoned a special session of Congress to repeal the Sherman law, and to enact legislation which should ' put beyond all doubt or mistake the intention and the ability of the Government to fulfill its pecuniary obligations in money universally recognized by all civilized countries.' The result was the liveliest session of Congress in a generation. The administration forces were led by William L. Wilson of West Virginia and the eloquent Bourke Cockran of New York; silver was championed by the veteran ' Silver Dick ' Bland and by young William Jennings Bryan of Nebraska.

On the one hand [said Bryan] stand the corporate interests of the United States, the moneyed interests, aggregated wealth and capital, imperious, arrogant, compassionless. . . . On the other side stand an unnumbered throng, those who gave to the Democratic party a name and for whom it has assumed to speak. Work-worn and dust-begrimed, they make their mute appeal, and too often find their cry for help beat in vain against the outer walls, while others, less deserving, gain ready access to legislative halls.

Bryan's conclusion was right, however dubious the logic. Cleveland's discreet manipulation of the patronage provided enough Democratic votes to help the Republicans repeal their own silver-purchase act at the request of a Democratic President and a bimetallist Secretary of the Treasury! Business and finance breathed more freely, but the farmers cried out betrayal, and Bland warned the President that Eastern and Western Democrats had finally come to ' a parting of the ways.'

Nor did the repeal of the Sherman Act bring about that restoration of prosperity so hopefully anticipated and so confidently predicted. The Treasury Department was freed of its obligations to purchase silver but Secretary Carlisle's troubles had just begun. Distrust of the monetary policy of the government was by no means allayed, and there began a steady raid on the gold reserves of the Treasury. The Sherman Act had provided that silver certificates might be redeemed in gold or silver coin and had announced the ' established policy of the United States to maintain the two metals at a parity with each other. Holders of silver certificates, fearful for the future, began to bring their certificates to the Treasury and ask for gold.

Cleveland and Carlisle agreed that the government had no legal right to refuse their request. The resultant drain on the gold reserve not only carried that reserve below the established mark of $100 million, but threatened to wipe it out altogether. To the frightened President it seemed that the hour was fast approaching when the government would be unable to meet its legal obligations in gold and would therefore be pushed onto the silver standard. There was, so he thought, but one recourse: to sell government bonds for gold. When the public market for $50 million worth of government bonds proved unresponsive, Carlisle turned in desperation to the New York bankers. A banking syndicate, headed by the House of Morgan, took the issue, and a howl went up that the administration had sold out to Wall Street. Worst of all, this bond sale did not permanently help the Treasury. Purchasers of the bonds simply drew from it the gold with which to pay for their bonds. An 'endless chain' was thus set in operation, and the gold supply of the Treasury was depleted at one end as fast as it was replenished at the other. More bond sales thus became inevitable, and twice again, in November 1894 and February 1895, the same thing happened. Cleveland thought that he was doing the right thing; Morgan and his fellow bankers thought that they were doing the patriotic thing; but the farmers of the country were convinced that a traitor was in the White House and a Judas in the Treasury Department. Finally in 1896, the Treasury floated a $100 million bond issue through popular subscription. With the success of this fourth and last bond issue, the crisis was passed.

The financial difficulties of the government were ascribable not only to the gold drain, but to a sharp decline in government revenues. The McKinley tariff had actually reduced income from customs duties, and the depression cut into internal revenues, while the 'billion dollar Congress' had committed the government to a number of new and heavy expenditures. As a result the surplus of 1890 became a deficit of $70 million by 1894. In the face of this situation Cleveland tried to force the Democratic party to redeem its pledge of tariff reduction. But vested interests had been built up under Republican protection, and Democratic Senators from the East were no less averse to tariff reduction than their Republican colleagues. The Wilson tariff as prepared by the House represented an honest effort to reduce duties, but when it emerged from the joint committee of the House and the Senate it was no longer recognizable. Protectionist Democrats like Gorman of Maryland and Brice of Ohio had introduced no less than 634 changes, most of them upward. The new tariff abolished the sugar bounty, but restored the tariff on raw sugar, and fixed rates on refined sugar that were entirely satisfactory to the Sugar Trust — but ruinous to Cuban sugar planters. Cleveland, who had insisted that ' a tariff for any other purpose than public revenue is public robbery,' denounced the bill as smacking of ' party perfidy and party dishonor.' Believing, however, that the Wilson-Gorman tariff was some improvement on the McKinley bill, he allowed it to become a law without his signature.

The sponsors of the Wilson bill had anticipated a reduction in customs duties, and they had wisely added a provision for a tax of 2 per cent on incomes above $4000. This income tax upon which the administration had confidently relied for necessary revenue was, however, declared unconstitutional by a five to four decision of the Supreme Court which fifteen years earlier had passed favorably and unanimously upon the war income tax. As some of the opinions, notably that of Mr. Justice Field,[2] were characterized by gross prejudice and as it happened to be known that one judge had changed his mind at the eleventh hour, this decision seemed a further proof to the farmers and workingmen that they had no voice in their government.

Even while the Senate was debating the Wilson bill and the House was making futile gestures toward free silver, one proposal was advanced which pointed the way to a statesmanlike solution of some of the most pressing problems created by the money stringency and the depression. This proposal came from ' General ' Jacob Coxey, a wealthy quarry owner of Massillon, Ohio, who with his wife and his infant son, Legal Tender Coxey, was shortly to lead an army of unemployed on a march to Washington. Coxey's attack on the depression and the money question was a double-barreled one: non-interest-bearing bonds for public works and appropriations for good roads. One bill provided that any county or town desiring to undertake public improvements might issue non-interest-bearing bonds which should be deposited with Secretary of the Treasury in exchange for

2 *Pollock v. Farmers' Loan and Trust Co.* 158 U.S. 601 (1895) . ' The present assault upon capital,' said Mr. Justice Field, ' is but the beginning. It will be but the stepping-stone to others, larger and more sweeping, till our political contests will become a war of the poor against the rich. . . .'

legal tender notes, and which must be retired by taxation within twenty-five years. Public improvements thus financed were to be a form of work relief, employment being guaranteed to any jobless man at not less than $1.50 for an eight-hour day. The Good Roads Bill called for an issue of $500 million of legal tender notes to be used for the construction of a county road system throughout the country at the same rate of pay. These measures were designed to inflate the currency, bring down interest rates, inaugurate much-needed public improvements especially in the rural regions, and provide work for the unemployed. The program was not unlike that later inaugurated by Franklin D. Roosevelt, but at the time it excited only contempt or amusement. Governor Greenhalge of Massachusetts, for instance, declared that it was immoral to tax people for public works that were not imperatively needed. Unemployment was an act of God!

This year, 1894, year of the Wilson tariff and the income tax decision, was the darkest that Americans had known for thirty years. Everything seemed to conspire to convince the people that democracy was a failure. Prices and wages hit rock-bottom and there seemed to be no market for anything. Half a million laborers struck against conditions which they thought intolerable, and most of the strikes were dismal failures. Ragged and hungry bands of unemployed swarmed over the countryside, the fires from their hobo camps flickering a message of warning and despair to affrighted townsfolk. Coxey's army, consisting of broken veterans of the armies of industry, inspired by the pathetic delusion that a ' petition on boots ' might bring relief, marched on Washington where they were arrested for trespassing on the Capitol grounds — a charge which somehow was never preferred against silk-hatted lobbyists who there presented their petitions for higher tariffs. The corn crop was a failure; wheat fell below 50 cents a bushel, cotton to 6 cents a pound, and bitterness swept over the West like a prairie fire. Never did the government seem more unfriendly, or democratic processes more futile. The Pullman workers struck for a living wage, and every agency of the government was enlisted to smash the strike. Representatives of the people in the lower House tried to reduce tariff duties, and representatives of privilege in the Senate made a farce of the effort. Congress passed an anti-trust law and it was enforced not against the trusts but against labor unions; when the great Sugar Trust was finally called into court, the Attorney-General of the United States sabotaged the prosecution. Congress enacted an income tax and it was voided in the highest court. And the President sold bonds to Wall Street, while silver, the poor man's friend, was disinherited and disgraced!

No wonder the Populists rolled up a vote of almost a million and a half in the congressional elections of 1894. In countless country schoolhouses and Grange halls toil-worn men and women read from the graphic pages of *Coin's Financial School* the story of the Crime of '73, and auditors applauded with delight when the author refuted all the arguments of the ' gold-bugs.' Tenant farmers cheered lustily as ' Pitchfork Ben ' Tillman demonstrated how he would stick his fork into the ribs of Grover Cleveland, and the rebel yell resounded again in the red hills of Georgia as flaming Tom Watson denounced the vampires of Wall Street. On the plains the ' Kansas Pythoness ' Mary Lease warned the East that ' the people are at bay, let the bloodhounds of money beware,' and in Nebraska young William Jennings Bryan the ' Boy Orator of the Platte ' rallied the farmers to a new crusade. There was ferment, too, in the intellectual world. Everywhere men were discussing the revelations of Lloyd's *Wealth against Commonwealth,* the first great broadside against the trusts. Edward Bellamy's Utopian novel, *Looking Backward,* sold by the hundred thousand, and a chain of Nationalist Clubs, inspired by that book, planned hopefully for a new and saner world. Jacob Riis told the sordid story of *How the Other Half Lives* and respectable people, who had scarcely known the meaning of the word slum, were shocked into a realization of conditions in their own backyards. And William Dean Howells, who had described American society in so many placid novels, wrote a poem called ' Society ' which was published in the sedate pages of *Harper's Magazine.*

> I looked and saw a splendid pageantry
> Of beautiful women and of lordly men,
> Taking their pleasure in a flowery plain,
> Where poppies and the red anemone,
> And many another leaf of cramoisy,
> Flickered about their feet. . . .
> I looked again, and saw that flowery space
> Stirring, as if alive, beneath the tread
> That rested now upon an old man's head,
> And now upon a baby's gasping face,
> Or mother's bosom, or the rounded grace

Of a girl's throat; and what had seemed the red
Of flowers was blood, in gouts and gushes shed
From hearts that broke under that frolic pace,
And now and then from out the dreadful floor
An arm or brow was lifted from the rest,
As if to strike in madness, or implore
For mercy. . . .

4. BRYAN, BRYAN, BRYAN, BRYAN

The party in power is always blamed for hard times. The congressional elections of 1894 resulted in a complete reversal of the political scene. Not only did the Republicans win an overwhelming majority in the House and a plurality in the Senate, but the Populists made heavy inroads upon the Democratic vote in the South and the West. The Democratic party seemed on the verge of disintegration, and it was apparent that one of two courses was open to it. Either the silver wing of the party would capture control of the organization and unite all silver forces under the Democratic banner, or the silverites would secede to the lusty young Populist party and make that one of the great major parties. An analogous situation in the 1850's had resulted in the demise of the Whigs and the creation of the Republican party; in the 1890's, fate and Bryan decreed a different solution.

It was Cleveland's insistence upon the repeal of the Sherman Act that drove the first wedge into the Democratic party. ' Silver Dick ' Bland then warned the President that ' We have come to the parting of the ways. . . . I believe I speak for the great masses of the great Mississippi Valley when I say that we will not submit to the domination of any political party, however much we may love it, that lays the sacrificing hand upon silver.' In 1893–94 silver Democrats everywhere effected a fusion with the Populists, and in many Western states it was difficult to distinguish between the two parties. But the silver leaders were unwilling to abandon the party without a final effort to mold it to their way of thinking. In the closing days of the Fifty-third Congress, March 1895, Bryan and Bland drew up an eloquent ' Appeal of the Silver Democrats ' calling upon the ' rank and file ' of the Democratic party to seize control of the party organization. The tactics thus suggested were promptly put into effect, with results described by Bryan in his ' Cross of Gold ' speech a year later:

Then began the struggle. With a zeal approaching the zeal which inspired the Crusaders . . . our silver Democrats went forth from victory unto victory. . . . In this contest brother has been arrayed against brother, father against son. . . . Old leaders have been cast aside when they have refused to give expression to the sentiments of those whom they would lead, and new leaders have sprung up to give direction to this cause of truth.

Cleveland, of course, fought back, but his attempts to stay the tide of silver sentiment within his party were as futile as the efforts of King Canute to stay the tides of the ocean.

While the Democratic party was being torn apart, the Republicans looked on with complacency. Never were Republican prospects brighter. The three years of Democratic administration had been depression years, and the Republicans did not fail to point the moral of that coincidence. The Democratic party had failed to solve the money question, or to reform the tariff; it had antagonized labor and the farmers without conciliating big business. So certain were the Republicans of victory in 1896 as to boast that any Republican could be elected — a boast that Mark Hanna made a prophecy.

Marcus Alonzo Hanna was the last great representative figure of the Ohio dynasty. A big business man satiated with wealth but avid for power, naturally intelligent though contemptuous of learning, personally upright but tolerant of corruption, shrewd and cynical in his management of men, but capable of deep loyalties and abiding friendships, Mark Hanna was the nearest thing to a national ' boss ' that ever emerged in this country. Hanna was genuinely convinced that the business interests should govern the country, and he believed ardently in the mission of the Republican party to promote business activity, whence prosperity would percolate to the farmers and wage-earners below. Since 1890 he had been grooming for the presidency his friend William McKinley, whom he rescued from bankruptcy in the hard times of 1893. Other Republicans like ' Czar ' Reed of Maine and Shelby Cullom of Illinois were abler and more experienced, but the Ohio tradition and Ohio management prevailed. One by one McKinley's competitors were eliminated, as ' Uncle Mark ' won over the delegations from the Southern and Mid-Western states. When the convention met, ' Bill McKinley, author of the McKinley Bill, advance agent of prosperity,' was nominated on the first ballot, 18 June 1896. Only one untoward event marred the unanimity and jollity of the occasion: as the convention committed itself to the gold standard, the venerable Senator Teller of Colorado bade farewell to the party which forty years earlier he had helped to found. And up in the press gallery William Jennings Bryan looked on with palpitating interest as Teller led a grim band of twenty-two silver delegates from the convention hall.

Three weeks later, when the Democratic convention met at Chicago it became apparent that the tactics of Bryan and Bland had been successful. Instead of going over to the Populists, the silver Democrats had captured control of the party organization and were prepared to write a silver platform and name a silver candidate. Trainload after trainload of enthusiastic delegates swarmed into the streets of the Windy City, silver badges gleaming from their lapels, silver banners fluttering in the breeze. ' For the first time,' wrote one Eastern delegate, ' I can understand the scenes of the French Revolution! ' It was indeed a revolution; the Democratic party had been taken over by the farmers of the South and the West. On the opening day of the convention the Eastern wing was snubbed by the election of Senator Daniel of Virginia as temporary chairman. The credentials committee was controlled by the silverites; the resolutions committee was controlled by the silverites. What of the candidate?

' All the silverites need,' said the New York *World* on the eve of the Convention, ' is a Moses. They have the principle, they have the grit, they have the brass bands and the buttons and the flags, they have the howl and the hustle, they have the votes, and they have the leaders, so-called. But they are wandering in the wilderness like a lot of lost sheep, because no one with the courage, the audacity, the magnetism and the wisdom to be a real leader has yet appeared among them.' The lament was premature. In the person of William Jennings Bryan of Nebraska, the silver forces found a leader with courage, audacity, magnetism, and wisdom.

Only 36 years of age, Bryan had already distinguished himself as the most aggressive and eloquent spokesman of silver in the country. Elected to Congress in 1890 he had received the extraordinary tribute of appointment to the powerful Ways and Means Committee on his first appearance in that body; his speeches on the tariff, the income tax, and silver had attracted national attention and made him one of the leaders of his party. Defeated for election to the Senate in

the landslide of 1894, he had turned his cascading energies and oratorical talents to the task of whipping up silver sentiment, organizing
the silver forces within the party, and clearing the way for his own
nomination. His preconvention campaign was thorough and shrewd;
his convention strategy astute; his nomination came as a surprise to
the East only because the East did not know what was going on elsewhere in the country.

Bryan's opportunity came in the debate on the platform. Hill of
New York and William E. Russell of Massachusetts had spoken eloquently for the gold plank; ' Pitchfork Ben ' Tillman had failed to
do justice to silver, and the great throng of 20,000 sweltering men
and women were anxious and impatient. Bryan's was the closing
speech, and as he made his way nervously down the aisle, a great
shout went up, and Bryan banners appeared miraculously in every
part of the great hall. His opening words, clear and mellifluous,
stilled the vast throng and set the tone of his speech — dignified but
impassioned:

> It would be presumptuous, indeed, to present myself against the dis-
> tinguished gentlemen to whom you have listened if this were a mere meas-
> uring of abilities; but this is not a contest between persons. The humblest
> citizen in all the land, when clad in the armor of a righteous cause, is
> stronger than all the hosts of error. I come to speak to you in defense of
> a cause as holy as the cause of liberty — the cause of humanity.

Bryan reviewed the contest between the silver and the gold forces
within the party, and reminded the delegates that they were ' now assembled, not to discuss, not to debate, but to enter up the judgment
already rendered by the plain people of this country.' That judgment
might run counter to the interests of Big Business, but,

> when you come before us and tell us that we are about to disturb your
> business interests, we reply that you have disturbed our business interests
> by your course. We say to you that you have made the definition of a busi-
> ness man too limited in its application. The man who is employed for
> wages is as much a business man as his employer; the attorney in a coun-
> try town is as much a business man as the corporation counsel in a great
> metropolis; the merchant at the crossroads store is as much a business
> man as the merchant of New York; the farmer who goes forth in the
> morning and toils all day, who begins in the spring and toils all summer,
> and who by the application of brain and muscle to the natural resources
> of the country creates wealth, is as much a business man as the man who
> goes upon the Board of Trade and bets on the price of grain; the miners

who go down a thousand feet into the earth, or climb two thousand feet upon the cliffs, and bring forth from their hiding places the precious metals to be poured into the channels of trade, are as much business men as the few financial magnates who in a back room, corner the money of the world. We come to speak for this broader class of business men.

And they came, said Bryan, not as petitioners, but as a victorious army.

We have petitioned, and our petitions have been scorned; we have entreated and our entreaties have been disregarded; we have begged, and they have mocked when our calamity came. We beg no longer; we entreat no more; we petition no more. We defy them.

The convention had found its spokesman at last, and every sentence was punctuated by a frenzied roar of applause. Like a skillful fencer Bryan found the weakness in the gold armor and drove home every thrust. Swiftly he reviewed the minor planks in the platform — the income tax which was ' not unconstitutional until one of the judges changed his mind, and we cannot be expected to know when a judge will change his mind '; the bank-note plank — ' the issue of money is a function of government, and banks ought to go out of the governing business '; the tariff, which was less important than the money question, for while ' protection has slain its thousands, the gold standard has slain its tens of thousands.' For the paramount issue was the gold standard. Then followed the peroration which drew the class and sectional lines:

You come to us and tell us that the great cities are in favor of the gold standard; we reply that the great cities rest upon our broad and fertile prairies. Burn down your cities and leave our farms, and your cities will spring up again as if by magic; but destroy our farms and the grass will grow in the streets of every city in the country. . . . Having behind us the producing masses of the nation and the world, supported by the commercial interests, the laboring interests and the toilers everywhere, we will answer their demand for a gold standard by saying to them: You shall not press down upon the brow of labor this crown of thorns, you shall not crucify mankind upon a cross of gold.

Bryan might have been nominated even without the ' Cross of Gold ' speech, but that speech made his nomination a practical certainty. Yet five ballots were necessary before Bland's support disintegrated and the ' Boy Orator of the Platte ' was selected as the Democratic standard-bearer in the Battle of the Standards.

Not only on the silver issue, but on banks, trusts, the injunction, and other issues, the Democrats had stolen the Populist thunder. When the People's party met in St. Louis the fusionists were in complete control. Under the skillful leadership of men like Weaver and Senator Allen of Nebraska, the Populists chose Bryan as their candidate, and then confused the situation by naming Tom Watson of Georgia for the vice-presidency. Within a short time silver Republicans bolted to Bryan; gold Democrats named a separate ticket but actually threw their support to McKinley. For the first time in thirty years the country divided roughly along class and sectional lines, and the electorate was confronted with a clean-cut issue. And that was not merely the money issue, but the more fundamental one of the control of the government by the business interests of the East or the agrarian interests of the South and the West.

In Bryan the agrarians had an ideal leader:

> Prairie avenger, mountain lion,
> Bryan, Bryan, Bryan, Bryan,
> Gigantic troubadour, speaking like a siege gun,
> Smashing Plymouth Rock with his boulders from the West.[3]

Radical only on economic questions of money, banks, and trusts, strictly orthodox in matters of morality and religion, Bryan was an honest, emotional crusader for humanity, with the forensic fervor and the political shrewdness that would have carried him to the presidency in the age of Clay and Jackson. More fully than any other candidate since the Civil War he represented the average middle class American, and it was because he was the common denominator of the American people of his generation that he was able to retain his extraordinary hold upon their affections for so many years. Everything about him illustrated that quality which justified his title, ' the Great Commoner.' Born in a small farming town in southern Illinois, he came from mixed Scotch, Irish, and English stock, from both North and South. One of his parents was Baptist, one Methodist; he himself joined the Presbyterian church. For generations his family had participated in the westward movement — from the Virginia tidewater to the Valley, from the Valley to the banks of the Ohio, from the Ohio to the Mississippi valley; he himself continued the process by moving out to the last frontier in Nebraska. He attended

[3] Vachel Lindsay, ' Bryan, Bryan, Bryan, Bryan,' *Collected Poems*, Macmillan.

a small denominational college, studied law, dabbled in politics, and finally found himself in the championship of a great popular cause. A man of no mean intellectual abilities, at least as well read as the average politician, enjoying a tremendous physical vitality, realist enough to appreciate the significance of the economic revolution, and astute enough to appeal to man's emotions as well as interests, he was thoroughly equipped for politics. But it was his qualities of character rather than of mind that won for him such emotional loyalty as no other leader of his generation could command. Irreproachable in private and in professional life, his career was characterized by sincerity, courage, audacity, faith in the wisdom of the plain people and the processes of democracy, religious belief in the identity of morals and politics, and an undismayed conviction that the right must eventually triumph over the wrong.

The campaign was such a one as the country had not witnessed since Jackson and would not see again until 1928. For the farmers, wrote William Allen White,

It was a fanaticism like the Crusades. Indeed the delusion that was working on the people took the form of religious frenzy. Sacred hymns were torn from their pious tunes to give place to words which deified the cause and made gold — and all its symbols, capital, wealth, plutocracy — diabolical. At night, from ten thousand little white schoolhouse windows, lights twinkled back vain hope to the stars. . . . They sang their barbaric songs in unrhythmic jargon, with something of the same mad faith that inspired the martyr going to the stake. Far into the night the voices rose — women's voices, children's voices, the voices of old men, of youths and of maidens, rose on the ebbing prairie breezes, as the crusaders of the revolution rode home, praising the people's will as though it were God's will and cursing wealth for its iniquity.

Big business, fearing for its privileges, acted as if the Hun were thundering at the gates. Bryan's object was to reform government and curb privilege, not to reconstruct society; but the Republicans stressed the ' danger to our institutions,' and charged that the Democratic platform was animated by a spirit that would ' organize sedition, destroy the peace and security of the country.' Others were not so mild in their remarks. The New York *Tribune* denounced ' the wretched rattle-pated boy, posing in vapid vanity and mouthing resounding rottenness,' and ' Marse ' Watterson of Kentucky described Bryan as ' a dishonest dodger . . . a daring adventurer . . . a political fakir.' The churches were enlisted in the campaign of abuse;

one clergyman announced, 'The Chicago platform was made in Hell.' 'Good and high-minded men,' observed Theodore Roosevelt justly, ' in their panic played into the hands of the ultra-reactionaries of business and politics.'

Mark Hanna, who was managing the Republican campaign, shook down metropolitan banks, insurance companies, and railroad corporations for colossal campaign contributions. His committee reported campaign expenditures of 3.5 million, but estimates of the amount

PRESIDENTIAL ELECTION, 1896

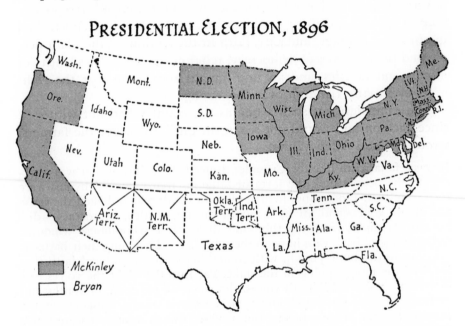

McKinley

Bryan

actually spent by local and national organizations ran as high as $16 million. Employees were ordered to vote for McKinley on pain of dismissal, and their fears were aroused by the prospect of receiving wages in depreciated dollars or by the even more serious danger of wage-slashes and unemployment. On Wall Street there was even talk of an Eastern secession if Bryan should win. The silver-mining interests contributed to the Democratic funds, but their contributions were niggardly and the Democrats had not one-tenth of the ' sinews of war ' that their opponents commandeered. Bryan alone bore the brunt of the battle; traveling day and night, speaking ten, twenty times a day to vast throngs, he inaugurated a new kind of campaign and struck terror into the hearts of his opponents. Had the election been held in August he might have carried the country. But there were bumper crops that year throughout the West, and a crop failure in India, and farm prices bounded upward. The results of the election proved that the fears of conservatives had been somewhat exaggerated. Bryan carried the late Confederacy and most of the Far West; but the electoral votes of the populous East and the Middle West together with the trans-Mississippi states of Iowa, Minnesota, North Dakota, Oregon, and California gave McKinley an emphatic victory.[4]

The great fight is won [wrote Mrs. Henry Cabot Lodge] a fight conducted by trained and experienced and organized forces, with both hands full of money, with the full power of the press — and of prestige — on one side; on the other, a disorganized mob, at first, out of which burst into sight, hearing, and force — one man, but such a man! Alone, penniless, without backing, without money, with scarce a paper, without speakers, that man fought such a fight that even those in the East can call him a Crusader, an inspired fanatic — a prophet! It has been marvellous. Hampered by such a following, such a platform . . . he almost won. We acknowledge to 7 millions campaign fund, against his 300,000. We had during the last week of the campaign 18,000 speakers on the stump. He alone spoke for his party, but speeches which spoke to the intelligence and hearts of the people, and with a capital P. It is over now, but the vote is 7 millions to 6 millions and a half.[5]

The significance of the campaign, indeed, was not lost upon contemporaries. The election of McKinley constituted a triumph for big business, for a manufacturing and industrial rather than an agrarian order, for the Hamiltonian rather than the Jeffersonian state. ' For a hundred years,' Henry Adams observed, ' the American people had hesitated, vacillated, swayed forward and back, between two forces, one simply industrial, the other capitalistic, centralizing, and mechanical. . . . The issue came on the single gold standard, and the majority at last declared itself, once and for all, in favor of a capitalistic system with all its necessary machinery. All one's friends, all one's best citizens, reformers, churches, colleges, educated classes, had joined the banks to force submission to capitalism; a submission long foreseen by the mere law of mass.'

Equilibrium was restored. Nothing had ever been the matter with the Grand Old Party. Now for high protection, plenty and prosper-

---

[4] The electoral vote was McKinley 271; Bryan 176.

[5] Quoted in Stephen Gwynn, *Letters and Friendships of Sir Cecil Spring Rice*, Vol. 1.

ity. Actually the election of a Democratic administration could have served no useful purpose. The Democrats were not prepared, nor was the country ripe, for measures to bring financial giants under control, and the enormously increased production of gold in Australia and the Klondike soon made the money question, in its traditional form, one of mere historical interest. Yet Bryan's campaign had a significance quite independent of any question as to the soundness of its first principles. It was not only the last protest of the old agrarian order against industrialism, it was also the first attempt of the new order to clean house. Bryan was the bridge between Andrew Jackson and Franklin D. Roosevelt.

BIBLIOGRAPHY

1. GENERAL. Joseph Dorfman, *Economic Mind in American Civilization*, vol. 3; Harold U. Faulkner, *Politics, Reform and Expansion, 1890–1900* and *The Decline of Laissez Faire*; Sidney Fine, *Laissez Faire and the General Welfare State*; Eric Goldman, *Rendezvous with Destiny*; Richard Hofstadter, *The Age of Reform*; Matthew Josephson, *The Politicos* and *The President Makers*; Edward C. Kirkland, *Industry Comes of Age*; H. S. Merrill, *Bourbon Democracy in the Middle West*; Allan Nevins, *Grover Cleveland*; Arthur Schlesinger, *The Rise of the City*; William Allen White, *Masks in a Pageant*.

2. THE MONEY QUESTION AND THE PANIC OF 1893. James A. Barnes, *John C. Carlisle, Financial Statesman*; A. S. Bolles, *Financial History of the United States*, vol. 3; Louis Boudin, *Government by Judiciary*, vol. 2; William J. Bryan, *The First Battle*; David R. Dewey, *Financial History of the United States*; Matilda Gresham, *Life of Walter Q. Gresham* (2 vols.) ; Mark D. Hirsch, *William C. Whitney, Modern Warwick*; W. J. Lauck, *Causes of the Panic of 1893*; J. Lawrence Laughlin, *History of Bimetallism in the United States*; D. L. McMurray, *Coxey's Army*; Wesley C. Mitchell, *A History of Greenbacks*; Alexander D. Noyes, *Forty Years of American Finance, 1865–1907*; Sidney Ratner, *American Taxation*; Charles Warren, *The Supreme Court*, vol. 2; F. B. Weberg, *Background of the Panic of 1893*; M. S. Wildman, *Money Inflation in the United States*.

3. THE POPULIST REVOLT. Alex M. Arnett, *The Populist Movement in Georgia*; Harry Barnard, *Eagle Forgotten: John Peter Altgeld*; John B. Clark, *Populism in Alabama*; John D. Hicks, *The Populist Revolt*; Russel B. Nye, *Midwestern Progressive Politics*; Fred A. Shannon, *The Farmer's Last Frontier*; William D. Sheldon, *Populism in the Old Dominion*; Francis Simkins, *The Tillman Movement in South Carolina*; C. Vann Woodward, *Tom Watson: Agrarian Rebel*.

4. BRYAN AND THE ELECTION OF 1896. William J. Bryan, *Memoirs* and *The First Battle*; Herbert Croly, *Marcus Alonzo Hanna*; Elmer Ellis, *Henry*

Teller; Paul W. Glad, *The Trumpet Soundeth: William Jennings Bryan 1896–1912;* Paxton Hibben, *W. J. Bryan: The Peerless Leader;* Allan Nevins, *Grover Cleveland;* Mark Sullivan, *Our Times: The Turn of the Century;* Wayne Williams, *William Jennings Bryan.*

5. DOCUMENTS. W. J. Bryan, *The First Battle;* H. S. Commager, *Documents,* nos. 280, 289, 299, 300, 311, 321–5, 327, 328, 332, 333, 337, 338, 341–3, 353.

For further references, *Harvard Guide,* ¶¶ 201, 209, 210.

Philosophy, Arts, and Letters

1. PHILOSOPHY AND RELIGION

FROM the year 1859, when Darwin published his *Origin of Species*, we can date a revolution in thought as in science. The leaders of practically every Christian sect except the Unitarian fought hard for the book of Genesis and special creation, and Louis Agassiz of Harvard University attacked evolution of species on scientific grounds. But with the support of scientists like Asa Gray and of popularizers like Edward Youmans and John Fiske, the doctrine of evolution spread rapidly, and by the 'eighties had triumphed in most scientific and intellectual circles, and was making heavy inroads on the popular consciousness.

This doctrine of evolution was chiefly responsible for the abandonment of transcendentalism, and the formulation of a new philosophy known as instrumentalism or pragmatism. Rooted in the eighteenth century, transcendentalism was a kind of philosophical romanticism, and celebrated many of the things dear to the romanticists: Nature, the divinity of Man, individualism, intuition, spontaneity, the imagination. Transcendentalist philosophy rested upon primal intuitions not susceptible to proof, such as the benevolence of God and of Nature, and the divinity of Man, and preferred the assurances of *a priori* principles to the findings of the laboratory.

Such a philosophy, unscientific and basically anti-intellectual, was clearly irrelevant to the kind of universe unveiled by Charles Darwin and described by the sociologist Herbert Spencer. Truth could no longer be something plucked from the inner consciousness of man, nor yet what God revealed to man; it must be a hypothesis that would stand laboratory tests. Moral standards, when discovered to be the product of social evolution and environment, could no longer be absolute, and must change. Laws, by the same test, were neither eternal nor cosmic; they were the expression of a social conscience derived from the social needs of the day. Fixed ideas were out of place in politics and economics as in science and religion.

Between transcendentalism as expounded by Kant and Coleridge and Emerson, and the new doctrine of organic evolution as expounded by Darwin and Huxley and John Fiske, there could be no logical compromise. The St. Louis school of philosophy, founded in the 1860's by the German immigrant Henry Brockmeyer and the educator William T. Harris, simply ignored the new science and devoted itself to the futile task of sowing the seeds of Hegelian idealism in the unfertile soil of the Middle West. The Scottish, or ' common sense,' school of philosophy, represented in the United States by President McCosh of Princeton, attempted to effect a compromise between science and theology by arguing that ' evolution proceeded from a universal causation — namely God '; this did not prove very helpful. It was clearly necessary to formulate a new philosophy which would harmonize with science and yet avoid the pitfalls of materialism, explain an organic world and a dynamic society. This task was undertaken by a remarkable group of philosophers who came to maturity in the last third of the nineteenth century: Chauncey Wright, Charles Peirce, William James, and John Dewey—all from New England. Pragmatism is the name of the philosophy that they formulated; and although European philosophers cried out with one voice that its concern with consequences was just a piece of American sordidness, it may yet be admitted that pragmatism was one of the really important novelties in the history of thought through the ages.[1]

It is not easy to define pragmatism; the Italian Papini observed that pragmatism was less a philosophy than a method of doing without one. James certainly, and Dewey probably, would have admitted the validity of this criticism, for they insisted that pragmatism was less an independent system of thought than a method of thinking about philosophical questions. The philosophy which they elaborated was meant not for the schoolroom but for the world of affairs. ' Better it is,' wrote Dewey, ' for philosophy to err in active participation in the living struggles and issues of its own age and times than to maintain an immune monastic impeccability.' The pragmatists regarded truth not as an absolute, but as a social achievement, and James sometimes summed up his point of view in the phrase ' Damn

---

[1] Parts of it were as old as the fifth century B.C., when Protagoras was exiled from Athens for proclaiming the universal right of every man to find his own truth.

the absolute!' Truth was not fixed, but rather something that each society and each thinking individual had to make for himself. 'The truth of an idea,' wrote James, ' is not a stagnant property inherent in it. Truth *happens* to an idea. It becomes true, it is *made* true by events. Its verity is in fact an event, a process; the process, namely, of its verifying itself, its *verification.*' The test of truth then was to be found in its consequences; the business of the philosopher was to find out what worked to the best possible purposes. 'The ultimate test of what a truth means,' wrote James, ' is the conduct it dictates or inspires.'

The pragmatists conceived of our world as still in the making. They accepted the fullest implications of organic evolution, and applied them to the field of morals and thought, as to social and political institutions; here again their test was the test of consequences. The effect of such an attitude on politics, law, economics, social institutions, education, art, and morals was little less than revolutionary, and the revolution, inaugurated in the 'eighties, is still going on. Its influence was not limited to America, but it was far greater in America than in other parts of the world, for it accommodated itself readily to the American environment and admirably expressed the American style. ' It is beyond doubt,' wrote John Dewey, ' that the progressive and unstable character of American life and civilization has facilitated the birth of a philosophy which regards the world as being in a constant formation, where there is still place for indeterminism, for the new, for a real future.'

What all this meant was a shift from the deductive to the inductive, from the intuitive to the experimental, from form to function, from pattern to process, from the static to the dynamic, from principle to practice.

Progressive teachers abandoned the idea that education was the mere acquiring of a body of information, and tried to make it a function of society. Political scientists talked less about abstractions such as ' sovereignty ' and the ' state ' and more about institutions like the ' political party ' and the ' spoils system.' Jurisprudents ceased to regard the law as a body of changeless truth and sacred precedent, and accepted the doctrine that law was a creation of society and that every generation must make its own precedents. Economists reluctantly surrendered axioms which they had long regarded as inviolable, and ' economic laws ' like supply and demand went down the

WILLIAM JAMES *by Ellen Emmet* (Rand)

drain. Sociologists came to reject the dour doctrine that man is the creature of his environment, and taught instead that man could transform and master his environment. Moralists ceased to speak so pontifically of ' self-evident ' truths; liberal clergymen cited the Old Testament less frequently than the New; even historians admitted that historical truth was relative to each generation. That is one reason why textbooks so quickly become out-of-date!

It was the Protestant churches whose doctrines were based exclusively on the Bible that suffered most from the new philosophy. Beginning with the Tübingen school in Germany in the 1830's, theological scholars had applied to the Bible critical standards long accepted in other fields of scholarship, testing the Scriptures by the facts of history, philology, geology, archaeology, and other sciences. In the hands of such devout ministers as Theodore Parker this ' higher criticism ' was employed to justify an allegorical rather than a literal interpretation of sacred Scriptures. This application of the scientific method to religion paved the way for the rejection of much that seemed incongruous to modern life, and for a liberal religion based upon ethics rather than upon revelation. In the course of time the ' higher criticism ' came to be accepted by many Protestant churches, and for them the Bible lost its Divine authority. Much was lost in this process, for when the Bible ceased to be regarded as God's word, it was no longer assiduously read, and one of the priceless heritages of English literature which had imparted beauty, wisdom, and imagination for three centuries was neglected.

The Protestant churches were more afraid of Darwinism than of the ' higher criticism,' and several Southern states actually passed laws forbidding the teaching of evolution in the public schools. For a time leaders of almost all denominations joined in the hue and cry against evolution, and a famous battle raged along the whole intellectual front. Orthodox defenders of the faith quoted with approval Disraeli's famous declaration, ' Is man an ape or an angel? I, my Lords, am on the side of the angels.' Stout champions of science countered with vigorous attacks upon what they denominated religious bigotry: John William Draper's *History of the Conflict Between Religion and Science* (1874) and Andrew D. White's ' Warfare of Science ' [2] (1876) ran through innumerable editions, while the professional agnostic,

[2] Elaborated later (1896) into the two-volume *History of the Warfare Between Science and Theology.*

Colonel Robert Ingersoll, lectured on 'Some Mistakes of Moses' to rapt audiences in all parts of the country. Moderates on both sides, meantime, attempted to effect a reconciliation between religion and evolution. The task was undertaken first by the English scientists, Huxley and Tyndall, who lectured widely in the United States. It was shortly taken up by a group of American scholars of whom the most successful was the philosopher John Fiske. Fiske, a very behemoth of a scholar, who wrote on history, ethnology, and sociology, expounded a reconciliation of science and religion to the students of Harvard College as early as the 'sixties, published his elaborate *Outlines of Cosmic Philosophy* in 1874, and thereafter, by books and lectures throughout the North, spread his message that evolution was simply God's way of doing things. Soon the most popular of American preachers, Henry Ward Beecher, announced his conversion, and shortly thereafter such distinguished clergymen as President James McCosh of Princeton, James Freeman Clarke of Boston, and William Tucker of the Andover Seminary came over to the side of the evolutionists.

While 'higher criticism' and Darwinism caused some churchmen to gird on armor and do battle for their faith, others chose to meet a third challenge of the times, that of the industrial revolution which was making it increasingly difficult for people to lead the life that Christ commanded. And those who chose to meet this challenge simply discarded all but the essentials of the gospel and concentrated on making the Church an instrument of social reform. As early as the 'forties William Ellery Channing and Theodore Parker had prepared the way for the 'social gospel' by their emphasis on the duty of the Church to the 'perishing' and the 'dangerous' classes of society. Now in the postwar years a host of their disciples made the churches effective instruments for wide-ranging social reforms. From his parsonage in Columbus, Ohio, Washington Gladden championed the cause of industrial peace and succeeded in persuading labor and capital to arbitrate their differences. The venerable Edward Everett Hale of Boston — he had written 'The Man Without a Country' — was Parker's successor in rescuing the dangerous and perishing classes of Boston. The presses teemed with such volumes as George Herron's *The Christian Society*, Shaler Matthews's *Social Teachings of Jesus*, and Washington Gladden's *Applied Christianity;* and millions of copies were sold of Charles Sheldon's *In His Steps*, describing a congregation which followed consistently the teachings of Jesus. Probably the most influential books were those from the pen of the gifted Walter Rauschenbusch, who came out of the same theological background that later produced Reinhold Niebuhr. As a young man Rauschenbusch had done social work in New York's 'Hell's Kitchen'; he supported the single-taxer Henry George and the socialist Eugene Debs, and worked with Jacob Riis to humanize life for the 'other half'; when he went as professor to the Rochester Theological Seminary it was to train up a generation of preachers imbued with his social gospel, and to produce a series of books, the most notable of which was *Christianity and the Social Crisis* (1907).

Competitive commerce [he wrote] exalts selfishness to the dignity of a moral principle. It pits men against one another in a gladiatorial game in which there is no mercy, and in which ninety per cent of the combatants finally strew the arena. It makes Ishmaels of our best men and teaches them that their hand must be against every man, since every man's hand is against them. It makes men who are the gentlest and kindliest friends and neighbors relentless taskmasters in their shops and stores who will drain the strength of their men and pay their female employees wages on which no girl can live without supplementing them in some way.

Meantime, of course, the fundamentalist churches closed their doors — and their minds — to the new currents of thought that were sweeping across the country. In a world that trembled and reeled beneath them they clung with passionate faith to the simple orthodoxies of the past, content with Henry Lyte's great prayer

> Swift to its close ebbs out life's little day;
> Earth's joys grow dim, its glories pass away;
> Change and decay in all around I see;
> O Thou who changest not, abide with me.

The intellectual history of the Protestant churches in the second half of the nineteenth century is the story of an almost convulsive effort to harmonize dogma and revealed religion with the new forces of science and society. The Roman Catholic Church was under no pressure to conform to the new science, and specifically repudiated 'modernism' in the papal encyclical *Pascendi Dominici Gregis* of 1907, although in the encyclical *Rerum Novarum* of 1891 the Church had sharply attacked the evils of unregulated capitalism and encouraged far-ranging social and economic reforms.

Perhaps in the long run the most important development of these years was neither the reconciliation of science and religion, which was never complete or harmonious, nor the formulation of the Social Gospel, but the growth of American Catholicism. In 1890 the Roman Catholic Church counted some 9 million communicants in the United States; thirty years later the number had doubled, and every sixth person and every third church member was Catholic. This growth coincided with and was in large part the product of the flood of immigration which brought 16 million people from the Old World to the New during these years; well over half of these came from the Catholic countries of central and southern Europe. No church that had been in the Americas a century before the Jamestown plantation could be called an immigrant church, but probably the majority of Catholic communicants were first- or second-generation Americans, while the Church hierarchy was long dominated by those who were Irish in background or in origin; thus Cardinal Gibbons of Baltimore and Archbishop Ireland of St. Paul. The unassailable unity of the Catholic Church, its centralized control and discipline, its elaborate organization, its refusal to compromise with modernism or nationalism, its rejection of ecclesiastical co-operation with non-Catholic bodies, its comprehensive control of education from the parochial school through the seminary and the university, all contrasted sharply with the secularism, liberalism, decentralization, and fragmentation of Protestantism. Finally the geographical concentration of Catholicism in the North and East, and in the larger cities, gave it a potential power — political, cultural, and economic — enjoyed by no other denomination except the Church of the Latter-day Saints in Utah.

As in the past the growth of Catholicism gave rise to anti-Catholic movements that were inspired in part by religious considerations, in part by racial and economic. Most prominent of these was the American Protective Association which flourished, chiefly in the Middle West, during the 'nineties. Like the Know-Nothing Movement of the 'fifties and the later Ku Klux Klan of the 1920's, the A.P.A. was wholly lacking in intellectual content and wholly negative in character; unlike them it did comparatively little damage.

2. Social and Legal Thought

The eighteenth century — the Age of Reason — had believed that government, society, and economy were subject to the same great laws of Nature that governed the physical universe, and those monarchs who aimed to be ' enlightened ' brought in philosophers to conduct the affairs of state in accordance with these laws. Romanticism, with its exaltation of the imaginative, the subjective, and the irrational, dealt a heavy blow to this philosophy. The doctrine of evolution, however, appeared to restore to it something of its former lustre, for it argued progress not as conformity to great natural laws, but as part of the long process of evolution itself — an inevitable consequence of the survival of the ' fittest ' in the long struggle for existence. This, as we have seen, was the teaching of Herbert Spencer, and of his American disciples, William Graham Sumner, Edward Youmans, and John Fiske.

The trouble with this doctrine was that while it guaranteed ' progress,' it did so only as a reward for acquiescence in a process that required several thousand years to work itself out.[3] Meantime Frank Lester Ward, the father of American sociology, formulated a philosophy which, while fully accepting Darwinian evolution in the realm of Nature resolutely rejected its authority in the realm of human nature. Man, he argued — and he was a distinguished zoologist and paleontologist — is not subject to the same iron laws that govern the animal world, for while environment, or Nature, masters and transforms the animal world, man masters and transforms Nature. What is more, he does this not by a blind struggle for existence, but by cooperation and applied intelligence.

We are told [wrote Ward] to let things alone, and allow nature to take its course. But is not civilization itself, with all it has accomplished, the result of man's *not* letting things alone, and of his *not* letting nature take its course. . . . Every implement or utensil, every mechanical device . . . is a triumph of mind over the physical forces of nature in ceaseless and aimless competition. All human institutions — religion, government, law, marriage, custom — together with innumerable other modes of regulating

[3] Discussing corruption in New York City politics, Henry George said to Youmans, ' What do you propose to do about it? ' ' Nothing,' replied Youmans, ' You and I can do nothing at all. It's all a matter of evolution. Perhaps in four or five thousand years evolution may have carried men beyond this stage of things.'

industrial and commercial life are only so many ways of meeting and checkmating the principle of competition as it manifests itself in society.[4]

Ward called, therefore, for a sociology that would recognize that progress was something to be achieved, and that would rely confidently on education and on government as the means whereby it was to be achieved. Though neglected in his own lifetime, he raised up a school of disciples, and his arguments came in time to be accepted as the common sense of the matter.

It was one of the original leaders of philosophical pragmatism, Charles Peirce, who in 1893 observed that ' soon a flash and a quick peal will shake economists out of their complacency.' What afflicted the economists of that day was not only complacency but the same feeling that prevailed among the sociologists: passive acquiescence in a series of iron laws that controlled the whole of the economy. The full-throated attack upon this notion came from a new generation of academic economists — most of them followers of Lester Ward — who repudiated the teachings of ' classical ' economics and turned to the study of the economy as it actually functioned — men like Richard Ely and John R. Commons of the University of Wisconsin, Simon Patten of the University of Pennsylvania, and above all, Thorstein Veblen, a rugged individualist who was too independent to stay long with any institution. These taught that the laws of economics could be amended or rewritten by government, and the economy bidden to do service for man and society.

A Norwegian farm-boy who had grown up in the Middle West, Veblen was all his life something of an outsider, and able therefore to look at institutions and practices of the American economy without emotional or intellectual commitments. This he did in *The Theory of the Leisure Class* (1899) and *The Theory of Business Enterprise* (1904) and in a long series of volumes dealing with the more ostentatious manifestations of the economy and the social system. Veblen's books constituted an uncompromising attack on orthodox laws of economics — indeed on the notion that there are any such laws — and on the stereotypes and clichés with which the privileged groups described and adorned their economic and social practices. Veblen himself emphasized the irrational element in the economy; the role of conspicuous leisure, conspicuous consumption, and conspicuous

[4] *Psychic Factors of Civilization*, p. 262.

waste; the conflict between the instinct for craftsmanship and the instinct for pecuniary gain, the engineer and the price system. Those engaged in industry, he argued, were subject to the discipline of tools and of the machine, dealt with facts, were impatient of mere doctrines and conventions; those who engaged in business were given to ' de jure rather than de facto arguments,' exalted precedent and convention, and were interested not in production but in mere pecuniary gain. Veblen called for an economy which would serve what he held to be the real interests and desires of men, and which would be controlled by the engineers and technicians rather than by businessmen or financiers.

Evolution and pragmatism profoundly affected the interpretation of politics and history as well. There was a widespread revolt against Newtonian concepts of government — against the tyranny of abstract concepts like sovereignty, the state, the separation of powers, and the illusion that there could be such a thing as ' a government of laws and not of men.' Instead scholars and statesmen turned to the analysis of constitutions and governments as they actually functioned: to the Constitution as a mechanism that often broke down and had to be tinkered with rather than as a sacred Covenant which (as one judge put it) meant precisely the same in his day as it had meant in 1787! They studied actual administration rather than impersonal government; analyzed what presidents and judges did rather than abstractions called The Executive Power or The Judiciary; explored the battlefields of party politics or the misty fogs of public opinion rather than the formal documentary record. Woodrow Wilson, who was a professor of politics at the time, explained the revolution with characteristic clarity:

Government is not a machine but a living thing. It falls not under the theory of the universe, but under the theory of organic life. It is accountable to Darwin, not to Newton. It is modified by its environment, necessitated by its tasks, shaped to its functions by the sheer pressure of life. . . . Government is not a body of blind forces; it is a body of men. Living political constitutions must be Darwinian in structure and in practice.[5]

History, in many ways closer to literature than to the social sciences, responded somewhat more sedately to the new teachings. In the 'nineties the elder statesmen who had dominated the historical

[5] *Constitutional Government in the United States*, pp. 56–7.

stage for two generations were passing from the scene. The venerable George Bancroft completed the Author's Last Revision of his great history just in time to have it go out of date on publication. Nicolay and Hay brought out their pious ten-volume monument to Lincoln in 1890. In 1892 the indomitable Francis Parkman published the last panel of his great historical series on the struggle between the French and English peoples for the control of North America — the most impressive achievement of the age of historical romanticism. With the death of Bancroft in 1891 and of Parkman in 1893 the golden age of American history came to an end and the iron age set in. Three names dominate the new generation. In 1890 Captain Alfred Mahan published the remarkable *Influence of Sea Power upon History;* the next year Henry Adams completed his brilliant nine-volume study of the administrations of Jefferson and Madison and turned from the writing of history to the study of historical forces; in 1893 young Frederick Jackson Turner announced a frontier interpretation of American history that was to bemuse the imagination of American historians for another half-century. These historians — and others of their generation — shared a rejection of romanticism, of all special laws and dispensations, and of moral considerations in history, to-gether with a primary interest in history as a science, in the role of environment, and in the potentialities of evolution.

Of all the social sciences it was law that responded most decisively to evolution and pragmatism. Under the compelling pressures of the new exegesis Natural Law gave way to historical jurisprudence, and this in turn to sociological jurisprudence. It was a development which Dean Roscoe Pound of the Harvard Law School characterized as 'a movement for pragmatism as a philosophy of law; for the adjustment of principles and doctrines to the human conditions they are to gov-ern rather than to assumed first principles; for putting the human fac-tor in the central place and relegating logic to its true position as an instrument.'

This concept of the law as a living, growing organism owes much to the learning and genius of the most distinguished American jurist of his generation, Oliver Wendell Holmes, who sat on the Supreme Court of Massachusetts and that of the United States for half a cen-tury, from 1882 to 1932. A product of Harvard, and of the Union Army, Holmes had early associated with Charles Peirce, William James, John Fiske, and other members of the Metaphysical Club of

Cambridge, and he took in pragmatism as naturally as his father, the famous Dr. Holmes of the Harvard Medical School, took in the new teachings about antisepsis. From the beginning he confessed the pragmatist's distrust of systems and absolutes. ' The life of the law has not been logic,' he wrote in that famous treatise *The Common Law,* which he published in 1881, ' it has been experience. The felt necessities of the time, the prevalent moral and political theories, intuitions of public policy, avowed or unconscious, even the prejudices which judges share with their fellow men, have had a good deal more to do than the syllogism in determining the rules by which men should be governed. The law embodies the story of a nation's development through many centuries and cannot be dealt with as if it contained only the axioms and corollaries of a book of mathematics.'

In the hands of jurists like Justices Holmes and Brandeis and Cardozo and of scholars like Professors Pound, Ernst Freund, and Felix Frankfurter, sociological jurisprudence was a program as well as a method. It held that the truth of law, like truth in general, was something to be found by experience; that good law was what worked best for society; and that the actual day-by-day workings of the law were more important than its abstract theoretical content. It brought law squarely into the social sciences and required that it conform to social ends; it emphasized administration and enforcement — the cop on the beat as well as the judge on the bench; it affirmed that the past had exhausted neither the inventive nor the creative capacities of jurists and lawmakers; it insisted that law was concerned with the collective good of society and embraced in its scope the whole range of social interests and needs.

If law was an organic growth rather than a body of fixed principles, it could be studied as a science rather than as a ' brooding omniscience in the sky ' — the phrase is Holmes's. The creating of a science of law was the special function of the law schools, the most notable of which were the Harvard Law School, revitalized by the appointment of C. C. Langdell as Dean in 1870, and the new University of Chicago Law School which called Ernst Freund to its faculty in 1894. Langdell introduced the case method of the study of law — a method which speedily supplanted the older lecture and textbook method throughout the United States, though it has not yet been accepted in Europe — while Freund established administrative law as a major di-

vision of jurisprudence and, by his studies of the police power, paved
the way for the ' legal realism ' of our own day.

3. LITERATURE

The three writers who had emerged during the Civil War and Reconstruction years continued to dominate the literary scene: Mark
Twain, William Dean Howells, and Henry James. In background,
character, temperament, literary interests, and style they seemed to
have little in common: Mark Twain, a child of the frontier, product
of the rough and tumble mining camps and of life on the Mississippi;
Howells, so proper and respectable, editor of the dignified *Atlantic*
and the no less dignified *Harper's Monthly;* Henry James, fastidious
and elegant, an exile from his own country spiritually as well as
physically, preoccupied with problems of social and moral relationships too subtle for Mark Twain and too eccentric for Howells. Yet
these three in fact had much in common: a revolt against the pervasive romanticism which plagued so much of the speech and the style
of the time; a concern with the relations between the New World
and the Old — all three of them were obsessed by this subject and
all three lived much of their lives abroad; disillusionment with many
aspects of American society; and a common concern for moral issues
and values.

Mark Twain had published *Tom Sawyer* in 1876; now he entered
into the era of his greatest productivity and his highest achievement.
In the course of the following twenty years he wrote *The Prince and
the Pauper,* an enlarged version of *Life on the Mississippi, A Connecticut Yankee at the Court of King Arthur, Pudd'nhead Wilson,
Joan of Arc,* and, of course, the immortal *Adventures of Huckleberry
Finn.*

Huckleberry Finn (1884) is, by common consent, the greatest of
Mark Twain's books and one of the two or three greatest of American
novels. The wonderful device of the raft floating down the Mississippi through the heartland of America enabled Mark Twain to pass
in review the whole of American society at mid-century, or, if not
the whole of it, the most characteristic segments of it. Huck's voyage
is the Odyssey of American literature; not even the voyage of Melville's *Pequod* can compare with it. It is not a pleasant society that we
see through the eyes of the two innocents, Huck Finn and his friend

Jim, escaping, as they think, from slavery; it is a society ravaged by cruelty, violence and greed, pretentiousness, hypocrisy, and superstition, with only occasional glimmerings of decency and kindness. Mark Twain's disillusionment with ' the damn'd human race' was implicit in *Huckleberry Finn*.

All modern American literature comes from *Huckleberry Finn*, said Ernest Hemingway, and if we emphasize the word *American* there is a good deal of truth in the aphorism. For *Huckleberry Finn* is the first American novel so unmistakably American in subject matter, setting, characters, idiom, and style, that it could not have been written elsewhere. Though Mark Twain himself was the product of the frontier he was, in a deeper sense, the product of the whole of America of the Gilded Age — the America of business and speculation and politics as well as of mining and river-boating. In his fresh and idiomatic speech, his exuberant style, his wild imagination, his extravagant humor, he was indubitably American, and so too in his philosophy. ' Emerson, Longfellow, Lowell, Holmes, I knew them all, and all the rest of the sages, poets, seers, critics, humorists,' wrote Howells. ' They were like one another and like other literary men. But Mark Twain was sole, incomparable, the Lincoln of our literature.'

For the generation that came after his own *Gilded Age,* Mark Twain was a symbol not only for what he was but for what he failed to be and to do. Though he made his countrymen rock with laughter at the conventions and follies of the Old World, he accepted most of the conventions and follies of American materialism without protest. Magnificently ' natural ' and, to the end of his life, irrepressibly boyish, he settled down to respectable society in Hartford, Connecticut, devoted himself to business and money-making, curbed his Rabelaisian humor, and aspired to be accepted by the ' genteel ' literary figures of New England. Yet he was never really content with any of his roles — humorist, novelist, lecturer, businessman — or, for that matter, with life itself. Increasingly he was embittered not so much by particular follies and immoralities as by human nature itself. ' I have been reading the morning paper,' he wrote to Howells. ' I do it every morning, well knowing that I shall find in it the usual depravities and basenesses and hypocrisies and cruelties that make up civilization and cause me to put in the rest of my day pleading for the damnation of the human race.' This note recurred increasingly as the

years took their toll of him in failures and betrayals, in public dis-
illusionments and private tragedies. As Henry Adams found some
consolation for his misery in contemplating the cathedrals of Mont
St. Michel and Chartres, so Mark Twain took refuge in adoration of
the Maid of Orleans or in flight to Italy and Switzerland. To these
last years belong his sentimental *Personal Recollections of Joan of
Arc,* the savage *Man that Corrupted Hadleyburg,* and the allegorical
Mysterious Stranger with its comforting conclusion that, after all,
nothing was real.

Strange, indeed, that you should not have suspected that your universe
and its contents were only dreams, visions, fiction! [says Satan to the boy
Theodor] Strange because they are so frankly and hysterically insane. . . .
It is all a dream — a grotesque and foolish dream. Nothing exists but you.
And you are but a thought — a vagrant thought, a useless thought, a
homeless thought, wandering forlorn among the empty eternities.

For forty years Mark Twain carried on a literary love affair with
William Dean Howells. ' You are really my only author,' he wrote
to his Boston friend and mentor, ' I am restricted to you. I wouldn't
give a damn for the rest.' Howells responded with affection and understanding. He was the first major critic to recognize that Mark
Twain was not just a humorist but an authentic genius, just as he
was the first to recognize talent in his young friend Henry James.

Howells's relationships with Mark Twain and with James illustrates something of the position he held in American intellectual society. Not the greatest novelist of his generation, nor the most profound critic, nor the most talented editor, nor the most perspicacious
biographer, he combined these roles more successfully than any
other individual, and for almost half a century functioned as Dean
— or Pope — of American letters. He had begun, pleasantly enough,
with essays and travel sketches — *Venetian Life,* for example —
then had turned to recording ' the more smiling aspects of American life,' and then gone on to describe and interpret that life in almost every aspect. In some forty novels, thirty plays, a dozen books
of criticism, and a score of biography and travel, Howells provided
the most comprehensive description of middle-class Victorian America to be found in our literature, and his Mr. Homos from Altruria
could readily have reconstructed from the writings of his creator
a large part of the American scene about which he was so curious. In these volumes Howells drew genre pictures of New Eng-

land villages and Ohio towns, of the frontier and of the summer resort, of autumnal Boston and vigorous New York, of suburbia and
Bohemia, and of the trans-Atlantic ship and European watering
places; he crowded his literary canvas with farmers and workingmen,
journalists and clergymen, timorous maidens and elderly spinsters,
criminals and reformers, the new poor and the new rich — representative samples of American society north of the Potomac and east
of the Mississippi. ' Stroke by stroke,' wrote Henry James, ' and book
by book, your work was to become for this exquisite notation of our
whole democratic light and shade and give and take, in the highest
degree documentary.' Howells was the American Balzac, fascinated
by the homely details of social and class relationships. *A Foregone
Conclusion* and *The Kentons* were concerned with the contrast between American and European manners; *The Rise of Silas Lapham*
drew a classic portrait of the self-made man; *A Modern Instance* interpreted a Victorian marriage and its breakdown; *A Hazard of New
Fortunes* dramatized industrial conflict in New York City, and *Annie
Kilburn* work in the New England mill towns; *Dr. Breen's Practice*
dealt with the new woman; *The Leatherwood God* returned to
the Ohio frontier of the past, and *Through the Eye of a Needle*
looked to a utopian future. In all of this, as James wrote, ' he adores
the real, the natural, the colloquial, the moderate, the optimistic, the
domestic, and the democratic.'

The ' optimistic ' note was there, but gradually it died out as Howells came up against ' the riddle of the painful earth.' More and more
he was caught up in the economic conflicts of the day — the Haymarket riot, the Populist revolt, the rights of labor, socialism. In the
late 'eighties he moved to New York, and thereafter devoted himself
increasingly to commentary on the economic order. ' After fifty years
of optimistic content with civilization and its ability to come out all
right in the end,' he wrote, ' I now abhor it, and feel that it is coming
out all wrong in the end, unless it bases itself anew on a real equality.' Yet while Howells criticized the America of his day more sharply
than did Mark Twain, he never suffered the desperate bitterness that
ravaged the author of *The Man that Corrupted Hadleyburg*. Thus,
Howells wrote *A Traveler from Altruria* to show what men could do
to save themselves, while Mark Twain wrote *The Mysterious Stranger* to show that man wasn't worth saving.

Howells was not only an American Balzac, he was an American

Sainte-Beuve as well. 'Yours is the recognized critical Court of Last Resort in the country,' Mark Twain wrote him, and few would have challenged the statement. If realism triumphed over romanticism, much of the credit goes to Howells. He did more than any one else to obtain a hearing for the rebellious younger novelists who were coming to the fore: he found a publisher for Stephen Crane's *Maggie, a Girl of the Streets,* wrote an introduction to Hamlin Garland's *Main Travelled Roads,* championed Thorstein Veblen and Edward Bellamy, and welcomed a host of European naturalists like Henrik Ibsen, Bjornsen, Turgenev, Thomas Hardy, and Émile Zola.[6]

Where Mark Twain wrote of rivermen and miners and small-town boys and slaves, and Howells of the proper middle classes, Henry James took for his theme the sophisticated relationships of an aristocratic — or sometimes merely a very rich — international society. Life in America, he felt, was thin and arid, lacking color and drama and intensity and the marrow of literature; life in the Old World, he thought, was rich and dense and intricately patterned. After 1875 James lived mostly abroad, and though a few of his novels — *The Bostonians, Washington Square,* and *The Ivory Tower,* for example — have an American setting, generally he set his stories in the great houses, the hotels, or the boulevards of London, Paris, and Rome. He was fascinated by the trappings and machinery of society — houses, gardens, dinners, teas, travel, manners, and ceremonies — but only because these reflected, or concealed, traditions and values with a deeper moral significance. A long shelf of novels and stories — and James wrote almost as voluminously as Howells — elaborates on two basic themes: the interaction of New World innocence and Old World sophistication, and the interaction of the values of the artist and of fashionable society. The first of these is the theme of the greatest of his books — *The American* (1877), *The Portrait of a Lady* (1881), *The Ambassadors* (1903), *The Wings of the Dove* (1903), *The Golden Bowl* (1904) — all exploring with subtlety and compassion the complex moral relationships of the American and the European, innocence and corruption, renunciation and moral tri-

[6] One disgruntled romanticist, Thomas Bailey Aldrich, wrote:

> The mighty Zolaistic Movement now
> Engrosses us — a miasmatic breath
> Blown from the slums. We paint life as it is,
> The hideous side of it, with careful pains,
> Making a god of the dull Commonplace . . .

umph. The second — the theme of the artist and society — permeates much of these books as well as *Roderick Hudson* (1876), *The Aspern Papers* (1888), *The Lesson of the Master* (1892), *The Ivory Tower* (1917), and others. Because James wrote of subjects and characters far removed from the interest of the average American, and in a style intricate and contrived, he had few readers in his own lifetime and but little honor in his own country. Like Melville, he has been rediscovered in our time, and is now generally acknowledged to be one of the great masters of the modern novel and one of the glories of American letters.

These three novelists grew to literary maturity during the period of the Darwinian controversy, but their writings do not reflect the new evolutionary philosophy. Few of the younger men of letters, born after the Civil War, enjoyed a comparable immunity. Almost all of these were deeply influenced by Darwin's teachings, some bemused by the notion of evolutionary progress, others fascinated by the principle of the struggle for existence and the survival of the fittest. Thus, among the first, the poet William Vaughn Moody (b. 1869) in the sardonic ' The Menagerie ':

> Survival of the fittest, adaptation,
> And all their other evolution terms,
> Seem to omit one small consideration,
> To wit, that tumblebugs and angleworms
> Have souls; there's soul in everything that squirms . . .

So, too, the philosopher-poet George Santayana held that Nature

> hath not made us, like her other children,
> Merely for peopling of her spacious kingdoms,
> Beasts of the wild, or insects of the summer,
> Breeding and dying
> But also that we might, half knowing, worship
> The deathless beauty of her guiding vision . . .

The most philosophical poet of his generation, Edwin Arlington Robinson (b. 1869), accepted evolution and scientific determinism but, like his contemporaries in Victorian England, refused to acquiesce in mere negation or despair. Fascinated by failure and renunciation, he peopled his Tilbury Town (really his own town of Gardiner, Maine) with a wonderful gallery of misfits and derelicts — Luke Havergal and Richard Cory and the famous Miniver Cheevy and others — who were unable to cope with life but often triumphed over misfortune and tragedy. Himself a confirmed bachelor, Robinson gave us, in his Arthurian trilogy — *Merlin, Lancelot,* and *Tristram* — the greatest love poetry in our literature, poetry which celebrates not so much the high noon but the twilight of passion, not the failure of men to live up to their own expectations but the enduring of the expectations. Robinson agreed with Mark Twain that man's fate was tragic, but he admonished man to meet the fate with fortitude and wrest from material defeat some spiritual victory. As he wrote in the autobiographical ' Captain Craig ':

> It is the flesh
> That ails us, for the spirit knows no qualm,
> No failure, no down-falling; so climb high
> And having set your steps regard not much
> The downward laughter clinging at your feet . . .
> only know
> As well as you know dawn from lantern light
> That far above you, for you, and within you
> There burns and shines and lives, unwavering
> And always yours, the truth. Take on yourself
> But your sincerity, and you take on
> Good promise for all climbing; fly for the truth
> And hell shall have no storm to crush your flight.

Meantime a host of less philosophical writers were carried away by the literary possibilities of the doctrine of the survival of the fittest. Not a subtle idea, it made few demands upon the mind or the imagination; mostly it took the literary form of celebrating passion, self-indulgence, violence, or malign fate. It can be found in such varied works as Stephen Crane's *Maggie,* which shocked readers in 1893, and Frank Norris's *McTeague* and *Vandover and the Brute,* where the central character reverts to a kind of animal brutality. It riots unrestrained through twenty volumes of Jack London's tales of the Arctic North and the Wild West. It infects alike the mordant poems that make up Edgar Lee Masters's *Spoon River Anthology* and those stories in which Sherwood Anderson presented *Winesburg, Ohio,* as a kind of charnel house. The argument was put crudely by Jack London's Wolf Larsen:

I believe that life is a mess. It is like a yeast, a ferment, a thing that moves or may move for a minute, an hour, a year, or a hundred years, but that in the end it will cease to move. The big eat the little that they may continue to move, the strong eat the weak that they may retain their strength. The lucky eat the most and move the longest, that's all.

So too Frank Norris in the best of his books, *The Octopus,* the story of the struggle of the sheep-ranchers against the Southern Pacific:

Force only existed — Force that brought men into the world — Force that crowded them out of it to make way for the succeeding generation — Force that made the wheat grow — Force that garnered it from the soil to give way to the succeeding crops.

With Theodore Dreiser, however, determinism is more sophisticated than with London or Norris, and survival is not so much an elementary physical achievement as a matter of wits. To Dreiser, man was not so much a mere animal as a poor fool, victim of his own vagrant impulses, pitiful vanities, insatiable lusts and greeds. Like London, Dreiser was obsessed with power, but it was the complicated power of control over social and economic machinery: the city provided his background, and his characters pitted their cunning and ruthlessness against their fellow men in the desperate battlefields of business or of love. Frank Cowperwood, the hero — if we can use that word — of *The Titan* and *The Financier* is a far more sophisticated creature than Wolf Larsen, or McTeague, but not therefore more admirable. Through a quarter-century of writing, from *Sister Carrie* (1900) to *An American Tragedy* (1925), Dreiser played variations on this theme of determinism.

Determinism was by its very nature amoral, but few of the writers who subscribed to it could regard the contemporary scene with scientific detachment; not only London and Norris and Dreiser but most of the other poets and novelists of their day found themselves protesting against just those malpractices of business and politics which they had explained away as inevitable. The note of protest was struck by representatives of the old order, in a vocabulary which accorded ill with the modern temper. Thus as early as 1875 the romantic Lanier had asked:

> Yea, what avail the endless tale
> Of gain by cunning and plus by sale?
> Look up the land, look down the land,
> The poor, the poor, the poor, they stand
> Wedged by the pressing of Trade's hand . . .
> Does business mean, Die you — live I?
> Then ' trade is trade ' but sings a lie:
> 'Tis only war grown miserly.

And so too William Vaughn Moody in his ' Gloucester Moors ' (1900):

> But thou, vast outbound ship of souls,
> What harbour town for thee?
> What shapes, when thy arriving tolls
> Shall crowd the banks to see?
> Shall all the happy shipmates then
> Stand singing brotherly?
> Or shall a haggard ruthless few
> Warp her over and bring her to,
> While the many broken souls of men
> Fester down in the slavers' pen
> And nothing to say or do?

Lanier and Moody spoke to limited audiences. A lesser poet, Edwin Markham, caught the popular fancy with his moving protest against the exploitation of man in ' The Man with the Hoe ':

> Through this dread shape humanity betrayed,
> Plundered, profaned and disinherited
> Cries protest to the Judges of the World,
> A protest that is also prophecy.

There was a many-sided revolt against the city, the iniquities of capitalism, the mistreatment of workingmen, political spoilsmen. Mark Twain had led the way with *The Gilded Age,* a picture of chicanery in Washington and in the West too. Henry Adams had grown up in a world far removed from Hannibal, Missouri, but his portrait of Washington politics, ironically called *Democracy*, did not differ in substance from Mark Twain's. John Hay, who moved in the best circles — including the White House — described labor troubles in the pages of *The Breadwinners,* as his friend Howells did in *A Hazard of New Fortunes.* Robert Herrick, professor at the new University of Chicago, drew a somber picture of Chicago life against the background of the Haymarket riot in the *Memoirs of an American Citizen,* and a savage indictment of the delinquencies of business in *The Common Lot.* Brand Whitlock, soon to be mayor of Toledo, Ohio, portrayed municipal corruption in *The Thirteenth District,* and William Allen White of the *Emporia Gazette* dramatized national corruption in ' The Mercy of Death.' Even the incurably romantic Booth Tarkington, in the best of his novels — *The Magnificent Ambersons* and *Alice Adams* — drew a picture of what happened to a gracious small town, his own Indianapolis, when it grew into an unlovely big city.

Long years of agrarian distress, the cruel contrast between the high ideal of the independent, self-sufficient farmer and the tragic reality of farm life on the middle border, brought a literary revolt similar to that against the industrial order. Something of this realistic attitude had already been expressed in the stories of Joseph Kirkland and Edward Eggleston; but Edward Howe's grim *Story of a Country Town* (1884) fixed the type in our literature. It was Hamlin Garland who was destined to be the literary spokesman of the middle border. In his first and best book of short stories, *Main Travelled Roads,* he presented farm life in Wisconsin and Iowa in all its unprepossessing actuality, ' with a proper proportion of the sweat, flies, heat, dust and drudgery of it all.' *Prairie Folks* and *Rose of Dutcher's Coolly* followed. Eventually Garland achieved eminence and prosperity, settled in the East, and in his old age waved the magic wand of romance over the scenes of his boyhood and enveloped them in a nimbus of romance and of beauty. The result was *A Son of the Middle Border,* a classic narrative of life in the West, recounting the heroic saga of the pioneer. But if Garland himself had abandoned the hot realism of his youth, others had taken it up. Willa Cather in novels which lifted her to a high position in American literature — *My Ántonia* and *O Pioneers!* — painted the Nebraska prairie-land in somber hues, ' its fierce strength, its peculiar savage kind of beauty, its uninterrupted mournfulness '; and in that exquisite and moving portrayal of *A Lost Lady* she presented a memorable example of the spiritual disintegration that was a part of the pioneering process. And the Norwegian-American, O. E. Rölvaag, in *Giants in the Earth* (1927) wrote the epic story of the immigrant farmer in the Dakota country. *Giants in the Earth* chronicled, as no other volume has, that combination of physical and spiritual experiences which are the warp and the woof of the westward movement; but instead of being the proud story of man's conquest of the earth, it is the record of earth's humbling of man.

4. JOURNALISM

In the evolution of the newspaper of Greeley's and Bennett's day into the New York *Times* or the Chicago *Tribune* of the twentieth century, we can see not only the material growth of the nation and the expansion of its interests, cultural as well as political, but many other characteristically American factors. First there was the subordination of politics to ' news,' with a consequent development of the highly efficient machinery of reporting and news-gathering, made possible largely by improvements in the telephone, telegraph, cable, and printing machinery. Second we note the passing of the personal element in journalism and the growth of editorial anonymity. With few exceptions newspapers ceased to be vehicles of opinion and became great impersonal business enterprises, and the center of gravity shifted from the editorial to the news pages. Third there was centralization and standardization through the creation of chains, the elimination of competition, and the use of syndicated editorials and features. This was, in effect, the horizontal trust extended to the area of journalism, through such agencies as the Hearst and the Scripps-Howard chains; a bit later came the beginnings of the vertical trust in journalism through the centralized control of all processes of newspaper-making from wood-pulp to distribution. Further factors were the enlargement and improvement in the appearance of the newspapers, and in features, services, and techniques of news-gathering, accomplished in large part through improved machinery such as the Hoe rotary press, the Mergenthaler linotype and rotogravure processes, the organization of news-gathering agencies such as the United Press and the Associated Press, and the immense growth of advertising which gave newspaper-owners the money to install expensive machinery and maintain elaborate services. And last, the co-operation of the Federal Government in the form of low postal rates for newspapers and magazines, and rural free delivery. Thus those processes of consolidation, standardization, the scientific revolution, and governmental co-operation which characterized American life as a whole were rapidly changing the nature of American journalism.

The late 'seventies and 'eighties marked a dividing line in American journalism. Adolph Ochs bought the Chattanooga *Times* in 1878, and used it as a kind of trial run for the New York *Times*, which he acquired in the mid-'nineties. Joseph Pulitzer took over the moribund St. Louis *Post-Dispatch* that same year, and the New York *World* in 1883; Frank Munsey descended on New York in 1882; William Randolph Hearst acquired the San Francisco *Call* in 1887 and was already launched on a gaudy career in journalism and politics when he entered the New York newspaper arena a few years later.

No one better represented the methods and objectives of the new journalism than Joseph Pulitzer. A Hungarian-German-Jew, trained under Carl Schurz, he first made the St. Louis *Post-Dispatch* a respectable newspaper, then moved on to New York where he acquired the almost defunct *World* from the speculator Jay Gould. By elaborating on the sensationalism of James Gordon Bennett, Pulitzer pushed the circulation of the *World* up to unprecedented figures, passing the million mark during the hectic days of the Spanish-American War. His paper, popular in appeal, played up crime, scandal, and sensational news in screaming headlines and illustrations, while its bold political program recommended it to the poor. Yet the *World* under Pulitzer was never merely a ' yellow ' journal. There was a wide gap between the news stories and the editorial page, which was conducted on a high intellectual and moral plane. Pulitzer's ambition was to reach the masses through sensationalism, and then indoctrinate them with his liberalism — an ideal which did not work out very well. In the course of time the *World*, like the *Herald* and the *Sun*, became entirely respectable; after the retirement of Pulitzer and the accession of Frank I. Cobb to the editorship it became the leading Democratic organ in the country, a position which it maintained under the able direction of Walter Lippmann until its lamented demise in 1931.

The success of Pulitzer in tapping substrata of newspaper readers was contagious. Hearst, who had inherited a vast mining fortune, bought the New York *Journal* in 1896 — the same year in which Adolph Ochs acquired the New York *Times*. Soon Hearst was out-sensationalizing Pulitzer himself, and there ensued one of the fiercest and most dramatic struggles in the history of American journalism — a struggle which sent the circulation of both papers soaring, but degraded the press. Hearst, in the *Journal*, and in the nation-wide chain of papers he subsequently acquired, brought ' yellow ' journalism to its most extreme development, but without the editorial compensations offered by the *World*. Lavish use of enormous black leaders, colored paper, blaring full-page editorials, and colored cartoon strips assured the Hearst papers an extraordinary popularity, but sensationalism became a national menace when, in order to boost the circulation of his papers, Hearst exploited the Cuban revolution to whip up popular demand for war with Spain. E. L. Godkin, in one of his last editorials, hotly denounced ' a regime in which a blackguard boy with several millions of dollars at his disposal, has more influence on the use a great nation may make of its credit, of its army and navy, of its name and traditions, than all the statesmen and philosophers and professors in the country.'

Pulitzer and Hearst, for all their faults, were real journalists, and Pulitzer at least contributed greatly to making journalism a respected profession. Not so the third powerful figure on the national journalistic scene, Frank A. Munsey. It was in 1882 that Munsey came down to New York City from Portland, Maine, and began to deal in magazines and newspapers the way Daniel Drew had dealt in stocks. An entrepreneur, who at one time owned more valuable newspaper properties than anyone else in the country, Munsey had no interests outside business, subscribed to no ascertainable policies beyond an uncritical attachment to the status quo, and recognized no responsibility to the public. Shrewd, single-minded, and possessed by a driving ambition to make money, Munsey was not a builder but a speculator who bought and sold newspapers and magazines as he bought and sold real estate. Those he did not sell he frequently killed off, for he thought that American journalism was over-competitive, and believed in the survival of the fittest, by which he meant, of course, the most profitable. At one time or another Munsey owned the New York *Press, Sun, Mail, Globe, Herald,* and *Telegram,* the Baltimore *American* and *News,* the Philadelphia *Times,* the Washington *Times,* and the Boston *Journal;* most of these he merged or killed. 'Frank Munsey,' wrote William Allen White in one of the bitterest of obituaries, 'contributed to the journalism of his day the talent of a meat packer, the morals of a money changer, and the manners of an undertaker. He and his kind have about succeeded in transforming a once-noble profession into an eight per-cent security.' It should be added that although during his lifetime Munsey showed not the faintest interest in art, he left a fortune of $20 million to the Metropolitan Museum of Art, so that the rubble of a score of newspapers and magazines went to build the foundations for new art collections.

Despite this vulgarization of the press, the professional standards and ethics of journalism were on the whole improving during these transition decades. This was brought about in part through voluntary agreements, in part through the establishment of schools of journalism — of which those at Columbia and Missouri Universities were the most influential — and in part through the example of such papers as the New York *Times.* When Ochs bought the *Times* in

1896, it was bankrupt and on the verge of collapse; by printing only the news 'that's fit to print,' eschewing sensationalism, insisting on standards of integrity in reporting as high as those for the editorial page, and building up a staff of skillful correspondents around the world, Ochs made the *Times* at once the American counterpart of *The Times* of London and the Manchester *Guardian,* and an immensely profitable enterprise. The vigorous growth of other papers such as the St. Louis *Post-Dispatch,* the Baltimore *Sun,* and the Chicago *Daily News,* went far to offset the strident inroads of cheap journalism and the low standards of the mass circulation press, and to make journalism respectable and useful.

The 'eighties saw something of a revolution in magazines as well. The magazine field had long been dominated by respectable family journals like *Harper's, Scribner's,* the *Atlantic Monthly* and the *Century,* content with a modest circulation and catering to middle-class readers whose tastes and interests were primarily literary. In 1886 came the *Forum,* designed — as its title announced — for the discussion of controversial issues. Three years later Benjamin Flower launched the lively *Arena,* which opened its pages to radicals, socialists, reformers, and heretics of all stamps. Then came a flood of weekly and monthly magazines devoted to agitation rather than to entertainment — Bryan's *Commoner,* for example, and *LaFollette's Weekly,* and a revived and revised *Independent.* In 1912 Oswald Garrison Villard obtained control of the *Nation,* and transformed it into a radical weekly of opinion. The *New Republic,* launched two years later under the auspices of Herbert Croly, and with an editorial staff that included Walter Lippmann and Randolph Bourne, was designed ' to start little insurrections,' and assumed at once a commanding position among the magazines of the country.

5. EDUCATION

No nation was ever more fully committed to the ideal of education, free, universal, and comprehensive, than the United States, and the statistics of school enrollment and expenditures are eloquent of a continuous striving toward that ideal. As early as the 1840's Horace Mann, Henry Barnard, and others had laid the foundations for public educational systems in most of the states of the North, but progress was slow. In 1870 only 6,871,000 pupils were enrolled in the public

schools of the country, and of these only 80,000 were in the high
schools.[7] Even these figures were misleading, for the average daily attendance was barely four million, while the average number of days
of schooling for each pupil was seventy-eight. By 1900, however, enrollment had increased to 15,503,000 and by 1920 to 21,578,000,[8] of
whom over two million were in the high schools. In the same half-
century the percentage of children between five and seventeen who
were in school increased from 57 to 78, while the average daily attendance increased fivefold. Equally impressive was the upswing in
expenditures for public education. In 1870 Americans spent some
$63 million on their public schools; by 1920 expenditures had passed
the billion mark. In the half-century from 1870 to 1920 the per capita
expenditure for public education rose from $1.64 to $9.80; and the
sum spent on each pupil rose from $9 to $48.

The qualitative changes were more important than the quantitative: education responded to the same currents of science and philosophy that affected most other social and cultural institutions and
with results as startling. Progressive education, anticipated in the
'seventies in the experiments of Elizabeth Peabody and Colonel
Francis Parker, now came into its own. It owed much to the teachings
of German educational philosophers from Pestallozi to Froebel,
and something to Herbert Spencer, but it was fundamentally indigenous, and Froebel himself was to say that only in America did
his *Kindergarten* reach its ideal condition. The leaders in the transformation of the school were the sociologist Lester Ward, who
thought education 'the great panacea' for all social ills and the
mainspring of progress; William James, whose *Principles of Psychology,* published in 1890, provided inspiration for the new dispensation; G. Stanley Hall, first professional psychologist in America
and president of Clark University, who wrote a pioneer work on
Adolescence; Edward Thorndike of Columbia University's new
Teachers' College, who carried out psychological and educational experiments which went far to transform the whole learning process;
and above all John Dewey, who was in time to be not only the philosopher but the symbol of the whole progressive education move-

---

[7] Compare, however, Great Britain, which had a population roughly two-thirds that
of the United States, only 1,450,000 children were enrolled in schools, and the number
who attended was much smaller.

[8] Non-public school enrollment for 1900 was 1,334,000 and for 1920 was 1,700,000.

ment, and on whose benign head has been heaped praise for all the achievements and blame for all the shortcomings of progressive education.

The revolution that these men and their disciples carried through was really no ' revolution ' at all but an application of common sense to education. It involved a shift from emphasis on instruction to emphasis on the processes of learning, from subject matter to the training of the pupil, from teaching by rote to teaching by experience, from education as a preparation for life to education as life itself. It called for actual participation in the learning process by the children themselves — the original principle of the *Kindergarten* — through such activities as woodwork, cooking, printing, map-making, and so forth; did away with much of the formality of the classroom and in the relationship between teacher and child; greatly broadened the curriculum, often at the expense of thoroughness and discipline; encouraged children to play an active role in such things as music, games, and student government; and attempted to make each school, in the words of Dewey, ' an embryonic community life, active with types of occupations that reflect the life of the larger society.' Within a short time Dewey and his associates at Columbia's Teachers' College succeeded in imposing their educational philosophy on a large part of the country, and ' progressive education ' came to be accepted as normal. In the second quarter of the twentieth century, and noticeably after the death of Dewey in 1952, it fell into some disrepute, but we can safely say that if it is indeed buried, it is buried beneath the ruins of its own triumph.

Developments in higher education were scarcely less important than those in elementary and secondary. Here too, there was an immense quantitative expansion: the 52,000 students who attended some five hundred colleges in 1870 — all of them financially and most of them intellectually impoverished — increased to 157,000 by 1890; when the census of 1920 showed no less than 600,000 students in institutions of ' higher learning ' (more than in all the universities of the Old World), it was impossible for Americans to contain their gratification. The terms ' college ' and ' university ' still had the most varied meaning: in no other country, we may be sure, did education run quite so broad a gamut from the ridiculous to the sublime as in the United States. Yet in 1888 Bryce was able to find ten or twelve institutions in the New World that he thought worthy to be ranked with the older universities of Britain and the European continent.

Soon this number increased, for the habit of building new universities overnight, from the ground up, was contagious. In 1889 John D. Rockefeller made the first of his munificent gifts to create the new University of Chicago, which promptly took its place at once among the leading institutions of learning of the New World. In the 1880's, too, the railroad magnate, Leland Stanford, endowed a university at Palo Alto, California, in memory of his son; supported by an initial gift of some $20 million the Leland Stanford, Jr., University became at once the leading private institution of learning west of the Mississippi — an area heretofore committed almost entirely to public education. A third major creation of private benevolence was Clark University in Worcester, Massachusetts, which, under the guidance of the eminent psychologist G. Stanley Hall, undertook to be a New England version of the Johns Hopkins University. From these new universities came many educational innovations: the quarter system, for example, the summer session, extension divisions, the university press and the creation of new graduate and professional schools.

Perhaps more important, in the long run, and certainly prophetic of future educational developments, was the rapid growth of state universities which, after the turn of the century, began to attract students in ever increasing numbers. California, which attracted only 197 students in 1885, enrolled over six thousand in 1915; during the same period student enrollment at the University of Illinois increased from 247 to 5500, at Minnesota from 54 to 4500, and at Ohio State from 64 to 4600. Pressures from state legislatures often required these institutions to be general service stations, and pressures from public opinion tended to lower academic standards and encourage an unwholesome emphasis upon competitive athletics. But many of the best state institutions, such as Michigan, Wisconsin, Illinois, and California, were able to hold their own academically with the older private universities.

Some of the educational pioneers of the earlier generation lived on into the new — President Eliot of Harvard, for example, and Andrew Dickson White of Cornell; and new educational statesmen came to the fore. William Rainey Harper, a Hebrew scholar from Yale, new-made the University of Chicago, gathering about him on Chicago's

Midway perhaps the most remarkable group of scholars to be found in America in the 1890's and inaugurating far-reaching educational experiments that contrasted sharply with the traditional Gothic architecture of the institution. Nicholas Murray Butler, founder and first director of Teachers' College, was elected President of Columbia University in 1901, and for over forty years directed the destinies of that institution, changing it from a small residential college to one of the largest of the world's universities and the leading center for graduate research in the country. These men — like Gilman and Eliot — were influenced, directly or indirectly, by the example of German universities; they were interested primarily in graduate and professional training and in the university as a center for research. Woodrow Wilson who came to the presidency of Princeton just as Butler took over the helm at Columbia, favored the English rather than the German model for his university. He raised standards, toughened the intellectual fiber of the college, and introduced something like the Oxford tutorial system, all with marked success; when he was defeated in his attempt to add on top of this a great graduate school, he resigned to become Governor of New Jersey.

One important feature of the educational upsurge of these years was the interest in adult education and in the organized popularization of culture. Bishop John Vincent founded Chautauqua in 1874, on the principle that 'mental development is only begun in school and college, and should be continued through all of life.' Though the emphasis of Chautauqua was originally on religion, the institution became increasingly secular, and devoted more and more of its energies to the popularization of literature, the arts, music, and drama. With permanent headquarters on the shores of Chautauqua Lake in western New York, Chautauqua was peripatetic, carrying its message of cultural good cheer to every small town in the country. With the coming of the movies and the radio, and with a growing sophistication in the rural and small town population of the country, the influence of Chautauqua declined, and it withdrew to its lakeside refuge.

An essential instrument of education, and of popular culture, was the library — public, school, and university. Libraries were not uncommon even in the Colonial period, and several subscription libraries, such as the New York Society Library and the Library Company of Philadelphia, were flourishing even before the Revolution, while the Boston Athenaeum, founded in 1807, was long the most famous of New England libraries. But the free public library, supported by taxation and open to all comers on equal terms, is a more recent development. The first of the great modern public libraries was founded in Boston in the 'fifties, and soon attracted not only public support but generous private bequests. The Chicago Public Library was developed around the gift of 7000 volumes presented after the great fire of 1871 by Thomas Hughes of England, author of *Tom Brown at Rugby*. The New York Public Library, which quickly became the largest of its kind in the Western world, was formed by the merger of three privately endowed libraries — the Astor, the Lenox, and the Tilden — with the library resources of the city. The Library of Congress was built around the nucleus of Thomas Jefferson's private library; it is not only the largest and the most effective library in the world, but through its famous Library of Congress classification system simplifies the tasks of scholars everywhere.

The major impulse to the public library movement came not from official sources or from public demand, but from the generosity of Andrew Carnegie. Inspired by a genuine passion for education, persuaded that the public library was the most democratic of all highways to learning, and mindful of his own debt to books and his love of them, the Pittsburgh iron-master devoted some $45 million of his vast fortune to the construction of library buildings throughout the country. His philanthropies were not only munificent but far-sighted, for by requiring a guarantee of adequate support to the libraries he built he laid the foundation for healthy growth of library facilities after his own gifts had served their initial purpose.

If the United States did not ' invent ' the public library, it did, in a very real sense, invent library science. Three things were essential here: trained librarians and the development of librarianship as a profession; adequate systems of cataloguing and classification to make the vast and disparate literary records available to students; and a new philosophy that invited the public into the library, put books in circulation, and generally dedicated the library to public service. By 1900 these objectives were achieved, thanks in large part to three remarkable men who dominated the library scene from the 'seventies to the turn of the century. Charles Cutter, long librarian of the Boston Athenaeum, devised a *Dictionary Catalogue* which was largely responsible for systemizing and giving uniformity to library cataloguing. Melvil Dewey, librarian at Amherst College and at Columbia University, not only invented the famous Dewey Decimal system of book classification — a system still used in almost every public library in the country — but launched the American Library Association and the first professional library journal, and set up the first school of library science. And at Newark, New Jersey, John Cotton Dana showed how a public library could be made an effective instrument of the cultural life of the whole community.

If, as most Americans from Jefferson to John Dewey confidently believed, education could be counted on to provide a sound basis for ' a happy and a prosperous people,' Americans at the turn of the century had reason to be cautiously optimistic. The principle of universal free public education from kindergarten through the university had been established; it only remained for the practice to catch up with the principle. That would take another half century or so.

6. Art and Architecture

The advance in American architecture might be measured by comparing the buildings of the Centennial Exposition of 1876 with those of the Columbian Exposition at Chicago in 1893. The first had been a helter-skelter of frame and iron buildings without either design or harmony — doubtless the ugliest collection of buildings ever deliberately brought together at one place in the United States. The Chicago Exposition, by contrast, was carefully planned and elaborately designed. Neither Richardson nor Hunt had been involved in the Centennial Exposition; by the time arrangements were made for the Columbian Exposition Richardson had passed from the scene, but the planning was assigned to the gifted Hunt. Hunt promptly enlisted the aid of the most distinguished artists and architects in the country: Daniel Burnham of Chicago, Stanford White of the ubiquitous firm of McKim, Mead, and White, and the brilliant young Louis Sullivan among the architects; Augustus Saint-Gaudens, Daniel Chester French, and Frederick MacMonnies among the sculptors; Gari Melchers, Edwin Blashfield, and Mary Cassatt as painters; while the famous Frederick Law Olmsted was put in charge of the landscaping of the exhibition — a task which he carried out with dazzling success. Saint-Gaudens's outburst at one of the planning sessions, ' Look here, old fellow, do you realize that this is the greatest meeting of artists since the fifteenth century? ' was not wholly rhetorical.

Together these artists created along the shores of Lake Michigan the best designed and most beautiful exposition of modern times. Yet the design was conventional and the beauty mostly derivative. The over-all plan was classical, for the Fair was to represent the beauty of Greece and the grandeur of Rome. As Richard Watson Gilder exclaimed:

> Say not, ' Greece is no more,'
> Through the clear morn
> On light wings borne
> Her white-winged soul sinks on the New
>   World's breast
> Ah, happy West —
> Greece flowers anew, and all her temples soar!

The individual buildings were almost uniformly good, but they were good archaeologically rather than functionally. Hunt's Administration Building was a brilliant copy of St. Paul's Cathedral in London; Charles Atwood's Art Building had been unequalled — so Burnham said — since the Parthenon. Almost everything reminded the visitor of something he had read about or heard about, and most of the buildings had all the virtues of the originals except originality. The whole exposition proclaimed that there had been little advance in architecture since Rome. The most promising artist of the Fair, Louis Sullivan, whose exquisitely decorated Transportation Building did reveal originality, said of the Exposition that it was a ' fraudulent and surreptitious use of historical documents.' That was a palpable exaggeration. There was nothing surreptitious about the adoption of Roman classicism and little that was fraudulent. The fact is that Americans had not yet developed an indigenous architectural style, and if classicism was less appropriate to the New World than the Georgian of the late eighteenth century or the Palladian and Italianate of the early nineteenth, it was probably an improvement on both the Gothic and the Romanesque. In any event, under the influence of the World's Fair, and under pressure from the now dominant firm of McKim, Mead, and White, the classical style spread over the whole United States. As Burnham said to the young Frank Lloyd Wright: ' The American people have seen the Classics on a grand scale for the first time. I can see all America constructed along the lines of the Fair, in noble, dignified classic style.' He was a good prophet. Washington adopted the classical as the official style; soon most public buildings, railroad stations, libraries, banks, and college dormitories were being constructed in this style. In 1894 McKim and Burnham established the American Academy at Rome where architects and artists could learn at the source; in 1897 the citizens of Nashville voted to build a replica of the Parthenon in their city; within a few years state legislatures were crowning their capitols with domes; and in time even the homespun Lincoln was to find himself in a memorial more fitting for a Caesar than for a rail-splitter from Illinois.

It was Louis Sullivan who, more clearly than any other architect of his time, saw the connection between architecture and society, and tried to articulate the one to the other. ' What people are within,' he wrote, ' the buildings express without; and inversely what the buildings are objectively is a sure index to what the people are subjectively.' This interpretation of the functional character of architecture was not meant to flatter Americans of the 'nineties; Sullivan added that ' the unhappy, irrational, heedless, pessimistic, unlovely, distracted and decadent structures which make up the bulk of our contemporaneous architecture point with infallible accuracy to qualities in the heart and soul of the American people.' The most gifted architect of his generation — he built the great Auditorium Building in Chicago, and the Carson, Pirie, and Scott store with its daring use of glass and metal and its rich ornamentation — Sullivan failed in the end to sustain this early promise. It remained for his student and disciple, Frank Lloyd Wright, to vindicate his philosophy and realize his vision.

Born in 1869 and trained in the architectural office of Adler and Sullivan, Wright had helped Sullivan on the famous Transportation Building of the World's Fair, and taken to heart Sullivan's guiding principle that function determines form and form follows function. He conceived a building not as something superimposed upon the landscape, but as part of an organic whole embracing the structure and its furnishings, the grounds and gardens about it, the people who use it or live in it, and even the community of which it is a part. He began to apply these ideas in the 'nineties as soon as he set up on his own, in such early prairie-style buildings as the Isabel Roberts House at River Forest, Illinois, the Coonley House at Riverdale, and the famous Robie House on Chicago's Woodland Avenue, as well as in the first Taliesin House at Spring Green, Wisconsin, where he worked and taught. In 1906 he built the Unity Temple in Oak Park, Illinois, the first of those remarkable churches which did so much to revolutionize ecclesiastical architecture in the United States. At the same time he was putting up office buildings and factories, among them the dazzling Larkin Building in Buffalo. All this was but preparation for those masterpieces of the later years — houses like Falling Waters near Pittsburgh where the rocks and waterfalls were incorporated into the house itself; the Imperial Hotel in Tokyo built to withstand earthquakes — but not bombing; office buildings like the futuristic Johnson wax works in Racine, Wisconsin; desert residences like his own Taliesin West in Arizona. Not only as a master architect — indubitably the greatest produced in the New World — but as a highly articulate social philosopher, Wright waged a lifelong war against all that was meretricious, derivative, and imitative, against exploitation of the land for profit, and the megalomania of the skyscraper. His artistic life spanned two generations; he tied together the world of Louis Sullivan and the world of Mies van der Rohe; he did more than any other single person to change the character of American architecture.

Three major figures dominated American painting during the transition years: Winslow Homer, Albert Ryder, and Thomas Eakins. Fed up with his genre paintings, Homer went abroad in the early 'eighties, and returned to take up a solitary residence on the Maine coast and devote himself to painting the sea and the wilderness. In one great canvas after another — ' The Life Line,' ' Fog Warning,' ' Lost on the Banks,' ' The Undertow,' ' Eight Bells,' and ' Gulf Stream ' — he portrayed the struggle of man against the elements with a vigor and a craftsmanship without equal in American painting. By the 'nineties Homer was the acknowledged dean of American painting, but without a school or disciples.

Albert Ryder, like Herman Melville, lived obscurely in New York, and came into his own only after his death. Like Melville, too, he lived in ' a dark, moon-ridden world, stirring with strange beauty that indicated unexplored realities, deeper than the superficial levels of being.' [9] His imagination was lyrical and mystical, and he trans-

---

[9] The phrase is from Mumford's The Brown Decades; it is suggestive that Mumford is also the biographer of Melville.

THE COUNTRY SCHOOL *by Winslow Homer*

ferred to his varnish-covered canvases the mysterious world of his imagination — clouds flitting across the moon, ships forever lost scudding before the wind, dim figures out of the mythological past — thus his ' Death on a Pale Horse,' ' The Flying Dutchman,' ' Jonah,' ' Siegfried and the Rhine Maidens,' which make us fancy for a moment, in Justice Holmes's phrase, ' that we heard a clang from behind phenomena.'

It was in these years, too, that the Philadelphia artist Thomas Eakins reached maturity, providing for the future historian of the American character the most comprehensive and faithful pictorial record, since Copley, of American men going about their daily affairs. A kind of Thorstein Veblen among artists, Eakins had no use for the salon or the academy; he was fascinated by the spectacle of men and women at their normal activities; by the body, not as an aesthetic object, but at work and at play. (As Mumford says, ' He made art face the rough and brutal and ugly facts of our civilization, determined that its values should grow out of these things, and should not look for its themes to the historic symbols of Europe.') He thought no subject without interest or dignity. Thus he gave us young men swimming, oarsmen rowing, professors lecturing, surgeons operating, singers on the concert stage, scientists in their laboratories. When he painted President Hayes it was at his desk, working, and in his shirt sleeves; as presidents were not supposed to have shirt sleeves, the painting was rejected! ' I never knew but one artist, and that's Tom Eakins, who could resist the temptation to see what they think ought to be rather than what is,' said Walt Whitman, whose portrait is one of Eakins's masterpieces.

It was a group of Eakins's disciples who, in the first decade of the new century, launched the ' Realistic ' movement in American painting. Robert Henri, George Luks, Everett Shinn, William Glackens, and John Sloane had all studied at the Philadelphia Academy under Eakins's disciple, Thomas Anschutz, and had absorbed Eakins's philosophy and something of his technique as well. Most of them had worked as pictorial reporters on the old Philadelphia *Press,* where they had come to know the seamy side of life in the great cities; most of them had studied in Paris where they had come under the influence not of the Impressionists but of Daumier and Toulouse Lautrec. During the 'nineties they drifted to New York where they formed a loose-knit brotherhood of independents, and were joined by other young rebels and independents like George Bellows and Maurice Prendergast. The leader of the group was the gifted Robert Henri, who conducted a famous school that was as much philosophical as artistic.

When we packed our paint boxes and journeyed to the new Henri School [wrote one of his pupils] it was equivalent to throwing our gauntlets in the face of the old order. Life seemed somehow to flow richer and freer in Bowery bars and flop houses than at Sherry's or the Waldorf, and the mother who wrapped her baby in a tattered shawl seemed a more poignant embodiment of maternity than her more fortunate sisters. . . . In the Henri School we learned that art was only another medium for interpreting life, and we were taught that all the arts are kindred and relevant to painting.

The philosophy of the group was that of Walt Whitman — unpretentious, robust, and equalitarian:

See in my poems immigrants continually coming and landing . . .
See in my poems cities, solid, vast, inflamed, with
     paved streets, with iron and stone edifices,
     ceaseless vehicles, and commerce . . .
Hear the loud echoes of my songs, there, read the
     hints come at last.

Affectionately and sensitively they painted the color of the great city — McSorley's Bar, boys swimming off East River piers, children dancing in the teeming streets of the Five Corners; Bowery bums lounging under the ' El '; Yeats dining at Petipas; girls drying their hair on the roofs of tawdry tenements; a prize-fight at Sharkey's; the Staten Island ferry. With Jacob Riis they showed *How the Other Half Lives;* with Jane Addams they celebrated *The Spirit of Youth in the City Streets;* with O. Henry they chronicled the simple annals of the *Four Million.*

It was in 1908 that these Manhattan realists gave their first exhibition at the Macbeth Galleries in New York, and were promptly dubbed the ' Ash-Can School.' When two years later they gave an Exhibition of Independent Artists, two thousand visitors tried to crash the gates on opening day. These exhibits mark the beginnings of modern art in America as truly as the much-touted Armory Show of 1913.

Meantime another group of painters — they cannot be denominated a school — took up impressionism, that new technique, vision, and philosophy of painting which artists like Monet, Manet, Degas, and Renoir were revealing to an enraptured world. Inness had anticipated something of impressionism in his later years, and so, too, the remarkable John La Farge, who was equally talented in oils, water colors, murals, and stained glass and who had returned from Paris in the 'sixties determined that his paintings ' indicate very carefully in every part the exact time of day and circumstance of light.' In 1874 Mary Cassatt — whose brother was President of the Pennsylvania Railroad — settled permanently in Paris, where she studied with Degas, exhibited with the Impressionists, bought their paintings, and saw to it that they were to be found in American collections; and herself experimented both with impressionism and with techniques of Japanese art. Others who revealed the influence of the Impressionists were the enormously successful Childe Hassam, who painted the New England countryside in shimmering light and New York City in its gayer and more colorful moods; the frail Theodore Robinson, who had studied at Giverney with Monet and whose early death deprived his country of its most promising Impressionist; and John Twachtman, who preferred the melting snows, the frozen waterfall, the purple light on snow to the warmer landscapes that attracted his fellow Impressionists.

The most successful of all American painters belonged to no school — unless it was the school of Velasquez — and to no country. John Singer Sargent was born in Florence, Italy; studied in Dresden, Venice, and Paris; kept studios in London and Boston; traveled incessantly in the Old World and the New; painted hundreds of portraits, acres of murals, and preferred to do water-colors. The most dazzling technician of his generation, he became society's idol — and victim. The rich and the great flocked to his studios: the President, millionaires, and the leaders of society; and to be painted by Sargent became as essential to social success as to be presented at Court. A Bostonian by adoption, Sargent provided Boston with a pictorial record rarely equaled in the history of any city.

In sculpture as in architecture American artists had first struck roots in the classical soil of Greece or Italy, and then moved to modern France. Heretofore sculpture, like architecture, had been mostly derivative. The statues and decorations of Hiram Powers, Thomas Crawford, and Horatio Greenough had been faithful copies of Canova or Thorwaldsen, and so, for the most part, had the designs of that odd combination of lawyer, poet, dramatist, and sculptor, William Wetmore Story. The first American sculptor to give evidence of originality was John Quincy Adams Ward, whose statues of Henry Ward Beecher and President Garfield were completely divorced from neo-classical insipidity. But modern American sculpture begins with the work of Augustus Saint-Gaudens, who for a generation towered over all of his artistic contemporaries. Born in Ireland of Irish and French parentage, he nevertheless recorded the American genius with rare sympathy and understanding. His Lincoln, in Lincoln Park, Chicago, with its intuitive comprehension of the combination of rugged shrewdness and spirituality, is so convincing that ' no one, having seen it, will conceive him otherwise thereafter.' The Farragut Monument (1881), its base executed by Stanford White, and the Shaw Memorial (1897) in Boston established him as indubitably the foremost monumental sculptor of his day. The loveliest of Saint-Gaudens's statues is the figure he made for the tomb of Mrs. Henry Adams. ' From Prometheus to Christ, from Michael Angelo to Shelley,' wrote Henry Adams, ' art had wrought on this eternal figure almost as though it had nothing else to say.'

Less powerful and less original than Saint-Gaudens, American trained and in the American grain, was Daniel Chester French who made his reputation with the colossal figure of The Republic at the Columbian Exposition and brought it to a climax with the enormous bronze Lincoln for the Lincoln Monument in Washington. Frederick MacMonnies, a student of Saint-Gaudens and of Falguière in Paris, did the great foundation The Ship of State for the World's Fair, and soared at once to spectacular popularity; his playful but unmistakably shameless Bacchante which was considered too improper for the Boston Public Library found more appropriate refuge in the court of the New York Public Library. Equally impressive were contributions from George Gray Barnard, a disciple of Rodin who is best known for his collection of medieval art appropriately housed in The Cloisters overlooking the Hudson River; Karl Bitter, director of sculpture of three major Expositions; and Lorado Taft, whose towering statue of Blackhawk overlooking the Rock River in Illinois is one of our most impressive historical monuments and whose large and intricate memorial foundations are to be found in many American cities. And already younger and more original sculptors such as Paul Manship and Jo Davidson were on the way.

BIBLIOGRAPHY

1. PHILOSOPHY AND RELIGION. James Bryce, *The American Common-wealth*, part. VI; Mary Ellen Chase, *A Goodly Heritage;* Stewart Cole, *A History of Fundamentalism;* H. S. Commager, *The American Mind;* Merle Curti, *The Growth of American Thought;* John Dewey, *Influence of Darwin on Philosophy;* Washington Gladden, *Recollections;* C. H. Hopkins, *The Rise of the Social Gospel, 1865–1915;* William James, *Pragmatism, A Pluralistic Universe,* and *The Will to Believe;* Henry F. May, *The End of Innocence* and *The Protestant Churches and Industrial America;* Theodore Maynard, *The Story of American Catholicism;* Ralph Barton Perry, *The Thought and Character of William James* (2 vols.) ; Stow Persons (ed.), *Evolutionary Thought in America* and *American Minds;* George Santayana, *Character and Opinion in the United States* and *Winds of Doctrine;* Herbert Schneider, *A History of American Philosophy* and *Religion in Twentieth Century America;* Anson P. Stokes, *Church and State in the United States* (3 vols.) ; Harvey Townsend, *Philosophical Ideas in the United States;* William J. Tucker, *My Generation;* Morton G. White, *Social Thought in America;* Philip Wiener, *Evolution and the Founding of Pragmatism.*

2. SOCIAL AND LEGAL THOUGHT. Herbert Agar, *The Price of Union;* Charles and Mary Beard, *The American Spirit;* Samuel Chuggerman, *Lester Ward: The American Aristotle;* John R. Commons, *Legal Foundations of Capitalism;* Bernard Crick, *The American Science of Politics;* Merle Curti, *Growth of American Thought;* Chester M. Destler, *American Radicalism 1865–1901;* Joseph Dorfman, *Thorstein Veblen and His America;* Felix Frankfurter, *Mr. Justice Holmes and the Supreme Court;* Edward C. Hayes (ed.), *Recent Developments in the Social Sciences:* Richard Hofstadter, *Social Darwinism in America;* Oliver W. Holmes, *Collected Legal Papers;* William Jordy, *Henry Adams: Scientific Historian;* Max Lerner (ed.), *The Mind and Faith of Justice Holmes;* Walter Lippmann, *The Good Society;* Howard Odum (ed.), *American Masters of Social Science;* Ernest Samuels, *Henry Adams: The Middle Years;* Harris E. Starr, *William Graham Sumner;* William G. Sumner, *The Forgotten Man and Other Essays;* Benjamin Twiss, *Lawyers and the Constitution;* Thorstein Veblen, *The Theory of the Leisure Class;* Lester Ward, *Psychic Factors in Civilization;* Charles Warren, *History of the American Bar.*

3. LITERATURE. Henry Adams, *The Education of Henry Adams;* Van Wyck Brooks, *New England: Indian Summer, Howells: His Life and World,* and *The Ordeal of Mark Twain;* Edwin H. Cady, *William Dean Howells: The Road to Realism;* Oscar Cargill, *Intellectual America* and *The Novels of Henry James;* Everett Carter, *Howells and the Age of Realism;* Harry H. Clark (ed.), *Transitions in American Literary History;* Malcolm Cowley, *After the Genteel Tradition;* Dorothy Dudley, *Forgotten Frontiers: Theodore Dreiser and the Land of the Free;* Maxwell Geismar, *Ancestors and Rebels;* William Dean Howells, *My Mark Twain;* Alfred Kazin, *On Native Grounds;* Francis O. Matthiessen, *The James Family* and *Henry James: The Major Phase;* Emery Neff, *Edwin A. Robinson;* Vernon L. Parrington, *Beginnings of Critical Realism in America;* Henry Nash Smith & William Gibson (eds.), *Mark Twain-Howells Letters* (2 vols.) ; Robert E. Spiller, *et al., Literary History of the United States,* vol. 2; Walter

Taylor, *The Economic Novel in America;* Edmund Wilson, *Axel's Castle;* Yvor Winters, *E. A. Robinson.*

4. JOURNALISM. Thomas Beer, *The Mauve Decade;* George Britt, *Forty Years, Forty Millions: A Biography of Frank Munsey;* Oliver Carlson, *Hearst: Lord of San Simeon;* Elmer Davis, *The New York Times;* Gerald Johnson, *An Honorable Titan: Adolph Ochs;* Frank Luther Mott, *American Journalism* and *History of American Magazines,* vol. 3; Don Seitz, *Joseph Pulitzer: His Life and Letters;* W. A. Swanberg, *Citizen Hearst;* John Tebbel, *George Horace Lorimer and the Saturday Evening Post;* Oswald G. Villard, *Some Newspapers and Newspapermen;* William Allen White, *Autobiography.*

5. EDUCATION. Howard Beale, *Are American Teachers Free?;* John L. Childs, *American Pragmatism and Education;* Lawrence Cremin, *The Transformation of the School;* Merle Curti, *Social Ideas of American Educators;* Charles W. Dabney, *Universal Education in the South* (2 vols.) ; John Dewey, *The School and Society* and *Democracy and Education;* Richard Hofstadter & Walter Metzger, *Academic Freedom in the United States;* Henry James, *Charles W. Eliot* (2 vols.) ; Edward Krug, *Charles W. Eliot and Popular Education;* Thomas LeDuc, *Piety and Intellect at Amherst College;* Robert D. Leigh, *The Public Library in the United States;* Paul Monroe (ed.) , *Cyclopedia of Education* (5 vols.) ; S. E. Morison, *Development of Harvard University 1869–1929;* Allan Nevins, *The Land Grant Colleges;* George Pierson, *Yale College, 1871–1921;* E. D. Ross, *Democracy's College.*

6. ART AND ARCHITECTURE. Wayne Andrews, *Architecture in America* and *Architecture, Ambition, and Americans;* Virgil Barker, *American Painting;* Cecilia Beaux, *Background with Figures;* John Burchard & Albert Bush-Brown, *The Architecture of America;* Alan Burroughs, *Limners and Likenesses;* H. S. Commager, *The American Mind;* Royal Cortissoz, *Augustus St. Gaudens* and *John La Farge;* W. H. Downes, *John Singer Sargent;* James Marston Fitch, *American Building: The Forces that Shape It;* Siegfried Giedion, *Space, Time and Architecture;* Ira Glackens, *William Glackens and the Ash-Can Group;* Lloyd Goodrich, *Albert Ryder* and *Winslow Homer;* Talbot Hamlin, *The American Spirit in Architecture;* John Kouwenhoven, *Made in America;* Oliver Larkin, *Art and Life in America;* Russell Lynes, *The Tastemakers;* Roland McKinney, *Thomas Eakins;* C. H. Moore, *Daniel H. Burnham, Architect and Planner of Cities;* Lewis Mumford, *Roots of Contemporary Architecture, The Brown Decades, Sticks and Stones,* and *The South in Architecture;* Jerome Myers, *Artist in New York;* E. P. Richardson, *Painting in America;* Marjorie Ryerson (ed.) , *The Art Spirit: Robert Henri;* Augustus St. Gaudens, *Reminiscences;* Homer St. Gaudens, *The American Artist and His Times;* Montgomery Schuyler, *American Architecture* (2 vols.) ; Frederic Sherman, *Albert Pinkham Ryder;* Lorado Taft, *History of American Sculpture;* William Walton, *Art and Architecture at the World's Columbian Exposition* (2 vols.) ; Frank Lloyd Wright, *Autobiography, Modern Architecture,* and *Writings and Buildings.*

Imperialism and World Power

1. The United States in World Affairs

WRITING in 1889 Henry Cabot Lodge, later to win distinction as one of the most chauvinistic of American politicians, observed that ' our relations with foreign nations today fill but a slight place in American politics, and excite generally only a languid interest.' This generalization applied with equal force to the whole generation which had come to maturity since Reconstruction. From the settlement of the Alabama Claims and the successful weathering of the *Virginius* crisis to the eruption of Hawaii and Venezuela into American politics in the 1890's, the relations of the United States with the outside world were singularly placid. The American people, proverbially parochial in their outlook, were busy with their internal affairs — repairing the devastations of the war, settling the continent, constructing their transportation and industrial system, absorbing new racial groups, and enjoying the game of politics.

The change came in the 'nineties, and it was more than mere coincidence that it synchronized with the passing of the frontier, the shift from the ' old ' to the ' new ' immigration, the rise of the city, and the coming of age of our industrial system. As fast as the population of the United States grew, the productivity of its agricultural and industrial organization grew still more rapidly. Almost every year before 1876 the United States suffered an unfavorable balance of trade; almost every year thereafter the balance was decidedly in its favor. In 1865 the foreign trade of the United States had been $404 million; by 1890 it had reached $1635 million. More important than this quantitative increase was the fact that the increase in the export of manufactured goods was proportionately far greater than the increase in the export of agricultural products. The significance of this was obvious, and every President, from Grant to McKinley, was concerned with the expansion of our foreign markets.

Nor was the emergence of the United States as a world power an isolated phenomenon. The closing years of the nineteenth century witnessed everywhere the rise of a new imperialism that was part of an international struggle for new markets and sources of supply, such as had led to the colonization of America. Great Britain, after a long and sated indifference, was fired once more with enthusiasm for expansion and power; France found compensation for defeat by Germany in consolidating her African empire; Germany, having proved herself the strongest Continental power, demanded her share of colonial pickings; Japan startled the world with her smashing victory over China in 1895 and won recognition as a great power by her spectacular defeat of Russia in 1905. Europe, having almost completed the partitioning of Africa, began, in rivalry with Japan, to break pieces from the weak Chinese Empire. But in the Western Hemisphere the Monroe Doctrine stood as an insuperable barrier against fresh acquisition of American territory by European powers, although it did not prevent the exploitation of Latin America by European or North American capital. To European and African affairs the American people were completely indifferent; into the maelstrom of Far Eastern affairs they were drawn almost in spite of themselves. But the United States regarded affairs of this hemisphere as her particular concern; in time, as her exclusive province.

After the Civil War the two traditional policies in American foreign relations — the Monroe Doctrine and expansion in the Pacific area — persisted. American interest in the Pacific and the Far East dated back to the old China trade and became vital with the acquisition of Oregon and California. As early as 1844 Caleb Cushing negotiated a treaty with China granting trade and tariff concessions similar to those enjoyed by Great Britain. Nine years later Commodore Perry steamed past the forts at Yedo Bay and opened Japan to the commerce of the Western world. ' It is self-evident,' wrote Perry, who anticipated much of our subsequent Pacific policy, ' that the course of coming events will ere long make it necessary for the United States to extend its jurisdiction beyond the limits of the western continent,' and he recommended a naval base in the Far East.

But the United States was not yet ready to go this far. Secretary Seward first inaugurated a clean-cut Pacific policy in the late 'sixties. Declaring that our commerce in the East had ' already brought the ancient continents near to us and created necessities for new positions — perhaps connections or colonies there,' Seward embarked upon a design grandiose in conception. The purchase of Alaska was one element in this design; other parts of it called for the cementing of friendly relations with China, an isthmian canal, and the annexation of Hawaii and other coaling stations available in the Pacific such as the Midway Islands.

Hawaii, or the Sandwich Islands, had been discovered by Captain Cook in 1778, and early served as a convenient port of call in the China trade and recruiting station for Yankee whalers. By 1840 Honolulu, with whalemen and merchant sailors rolling through its streets, shops filled with Lowell shirtings, New England rum, and Yankee notions, orthodox missionaries living in frame houses brought around the Horn, and a neo-classic meeting house built of coral blocks, was a Yankee outpost. As early as 1842 Webster assured the islanders that the United States could not permit Hawaii to become the possession of any other foreign power; but it just missed becoming a British protectorate in 1843. A few years later, Secretary Marcy negotiated with King Kamehameha III a treaty of annexation which failed of ratification because by its terms Hawaii was to be made a state of the Union. Seward, too, moved toward annexation, but despite the approval of President Johnson and later of Grant, nothing was done. In 1875, however, the United States concluded with the Hawaiian monarch a reciprocity treaty which granted exclusive trading privileges to both nations and guaranteed the independence of the islands against any third party; nine years later a new treaty renewed these privileges and ceded Pearl Harbor on the island of Oahu to the United States.

These treaties greatly stimulated the sugar industry, which the sons of thrifty missionaries had established in Hawaii, on lands donated by the native princes for religious objects. American capital poured in, sugar production increased fivefold within a decade, and by 1890, 99 per cent of the Hawaiian exports, then valued at $20 million, went to the United States. The islands had, in fact, become an American commercial appendage. In 1881 Secretary Blaine declared Hawaii to be part of the ' American system ' and announced somewhat cryptically that if Hawaiian independence were endangered, the United States ' would then unhesitatingly meet the altered situation by seeking an avowedly American solution for the grave issues presented.' Even Cleveland, anti-imperialistic as he was, declared his 'unhesitating conviction that the intimacy of our relations with Hawaii should be emphasized.'

Then came the McKinley tariff which by providing a bounty of 2 cents a pound to domestic sugar dealt a catastrophic blow to the Hawaiian economy. Sugar fell overnight from $100 to $60 a ton, and property values collapsed. Only annexation could restore to Hawaiian sugar interests their American market on equal terms.

This was the situation when, in 1891, Queen Liliuokalani came to the throne, and inaugurated a policy looking to the elimination of American influence, and the restoration of autocracy. This policy, which threatened the position of the powerful American element, excited a prompt counteroffensive. After marines had been landed from the U.S.S. *Boston,* with the connivance of the American minister John L. Stevens, a Committee of Safety consisting largely of missionaries' sons deposed the hapless Queen on 17 January 1893. A provisional government under Chief Justice Sanford B. Dole was set up, which promptly opened negotiations for annexation to the United States. 'I think we should accept the issue like a great Nation,' wrote Minister Stevens, 'and not act the part of pigmies nor cowards'; [1] he did his part by hoisting the American flag over the government house at Honolulu. President Harrison, in full sympathy with this attitude, accepted a treaty of annexation on 14 February; but before the Senate got around to it, Grover Cleveland became President, and hearkened to the appeal of 'Queen Lil.' 'I mistake the Americans,' he said, 'if they favor the odious doctrine that there is no such thing as international morality; that there is one law for a strong nation and another for a weak one.' He withdrew the treaty from the Senate, sent out a special commissioner to investigate the situation, and, when the commissioner reported that the Hawaiian revolution was the work of American interests, aided by Minister Stevens, denounced the affair, and endeavored to persuade the provisional government to step down. The gesture was ineffective and, under the presidency of an American, the provisional government

---

[1] Compare Tennyson's birthday tribute to Queen Victoria:

> We sailed wherever ship could sail;
> We founded many a mighty state;
> Pray God our greatness may not fail
> Through craven fear of being great.

became a permanent one, and Cleveland was forced to recognize the Republic of Hawaii.

Between 1893 and 1898 two developments in the Far East sharpened the demand for the annexation of the Hawaiian islands. The first was the rise of Japan to world power, and the fear of a Japanese inundation of the islands. The second was the prospective annexation of the Philippines, which gave Hawaii a new significance as a naval base. Toward annexation McKinley had no such scruples as had animated his predecessor, but there was still sufficient opposition in the Senate to necessitate action through a Joint Resolution instead of through the normal method of a treaty — as in the case of Texas half a century earlier. Annexation was finally consummated by the Joint Resolution of 7 July 1898. An organic act of 1900 conferred American citizenship on all subjects of the short-lived republic, and the full status of a Territory of the United States, eligible for statehood, on the islands. The government was of the usual territorial form, except that, as in the case of Puerto Rico, the governor could make appropriations by his own authority for current expenses of government in case the territorial legislature refused to do so. A similar provision in the charters of the Thirteen Colonies might have changed the course of history.

Our official relations with Samoa were equally confused. The Samoan, or Navigators, Islands were to the South Pacific what the Hawaiian were to the North Pacific, and from the 1830's on they had offered refuge to whalers and a virgin field for missionary activities. Not until the late 'sixties did American commercial interests with the islands become sufficiently important to attract official attention; and in 1872 an American naval officer negotiated a treaty with some native chieftains granting to the United States exclusive control of the harbor of Pago Pago in the island of Tutuila. The treaty failed of confirmation, but the policy which it embraced was nevertheless adopted, and within six years a similar treaty was duly ratified. Shortly thereafter Great Britain and Germany secured comparable concessions in the islands, and there followed ten years of ridiculous rivalry for supremacy among the three powers, each supporting a rival claimant to the native kingship. The danger of involving the United States in serious international complications was averted by the establishment of a tripartite protectorate guaranteeing the independence and neutrality of the islands and confirming American rights to Pago Pago. Unimportant as this episode was, it constituted nevertheless, in the words of Secretary of State Gresham, ' the first departure from our traditional and well established policy of avoiding entangling alliances with foreign powers in relation to objects remote from this hemisphere.' President Cleveland asked Congress to withdraw from the agreement, but his request was ignored. After another embarrassing native civil war, the tripartite agreement was abrogated in 1900, and the islands divided between Germany and the United States, Great Britain obtaining compensation elsewhere.

Thus, President Cleveland turned his back on the ' manifest destiny ' to which his party had once summoned the United States, and the Republicans, reflecting the expansive forces of American life, somewhat timidly began to play the imperialist game. Before long there was to be another turn of the wheel, and the positions of the parties were once again reversed.

In the years between Polk and Lincoln, the Monroe Doctrine had lapsed into something approaching desuetude; Seward's vigorous action against the French in Mexico proved that it was still a basic factor in American foreign policy. Other objectives of our foreign policy were to maintain the leadership of the United States in all American questions, promote the commercial interests of the country, and keep peace, all of which involved diplomatic controversies with powers who still had colonies and capital in America.

A new contribution to our policy was Pan-Americanism; as formulated by James G. Blaine, it was primarily economic in character. Although the high priest of protection, Blaine realized that protective tariffs injured commercial relations between the United States and Latin America, because those countries, still regions of extractive industries, sold to us an excess of raw materials such as coffee, sugar, and cocoa, but purchased their manufactured articles in the cheaper markets of Europe. Since 87 per cent of Latin American exports to the United States entered duty free, Blaine threatened to clamp a tariff on them unless the Latin American countries lowered their duties on United States products. What he had in mind was a Pan-American customs union, a series of uniform tariffs which would give reciprocal preference to American products or goods in all American countries; and it was with this in view that he called a Pan-American Conference in 1881. President Garfield's death was followed by a change in the State Department, and Blaine's successor revoked the invitations. Eight years later President Harrison placed Blaine once more in a position to advance his cherished project. In October 1889 the first International American Conference, representing eighteen countries, convened at Washington to consider Blaine's proposals for a Pan-American customs union and the arbitration of international disputes. To the Latin Americans both seemed like the invitation of the spider to the fly, and were politely rejected. His ardor for Pan-Americanism somewhat dampened, Blaine endeavored to secure the same thing through reciprocity provisions in the McKinley tariff of 1890. Under the terms of this law reciprocity agreements were secured with ten nations. These agreements were abrogated by the Wilson tariff of 1894, but under the Dingley tariff of 1897 provision was made for a new series of reciprocity arrangements which were effected not only with the Latin American states but with European countries. On the eve of his assassination President McKinley announced his conversion to reciprocity as a universal policy:

The period of exclusiveness is past. The expansion of our trade and commerce is the pressing problem. Commercial wars are unprofitable. A policy of good will and trade relations will prevent reprisals. Reciprocity treaties are in harmony with the spirit of the times; measures of retaliation are not. If perchance some of our tariffs are no longer needed for revenue or to encourage and protect our industries at home, why should they not be employed to extend and promote our markets abroad?

In spite of this persuasive argument from a high source, the Republican Senate, sensitive to the interests of American manufacturers, stubbornly refused to ratify any of the reciprocity treaties that were negotiated.

Although the Pan-American Conference did not accept arbitration as a formal policy, the principle itself was often invoked. President Hayes had arbitrated the Argentine-Paraguay boundary dispute; Cleveland arbitrated a similar dispute between the Argentine and Brazil; and Secretary Blaine intervened in no less than four boundary disputes. In another quarter, too, there was a victory for the principle of arbitration. This was in connection with the fur-sealing controversy in the Bering Sea. Anxious to prevent the ruthless extermination of the seal in Alaskan waters, and convinced that Canadian practices violated both property rights and morals, Blaine sought to extend American jurisdiction over the whole of the Bering Sea, and ordered the seizure of Canadian fishing vessels operating in these waters. He was right in principle but wrong in law, and the controversy took an ugly turn. But at this juncture (1891) the United States and Great Britain had the good sense to resort to arbitration. The tribunal decided all points of law adversely to the United States, but implicitly admitted the wisdom of Blaine's efforts to save the seal by drawing up regulations looking to that end.

Far more important than this sealing controversy was the dispute over the Venezuela boundary which afforded an opportunity both for an emphatic reaffirmation of the Monroe Doctrine and for an application of the principle of arbitration. The dispute over the boundary line between British Guiana and Venezuela was one of long standing, but the whole question was suddenly given new importance by the discovery of gold in the hinterlands of both countries. Overnight Great Britain extended her claims deep into the heart of Venezuela; Lord Salisbury refused to submit the question to arbitration because of Venezuela's counterclaim to more than half the British colony, and sent troops to the disputed area. Secretary of State Olney promptly dispatched a note which gave a definition of the Monroe Doctrine that alarmed Latin America, insulted Canada, and challenged England:

Today the United States is practically sovereign on this continent, and its fiat is law upon the subjects to which it confines its interposition. . . . Distance and three thousand miles of intervening ocean make any permanent political union between a European and an American state unnatural and inexpedient.

Lord Salisbury allowed four months to go by before acknowledging this astonishing note — and rejecting it. On 17 December 1895 President Cleveland informed Congress of Salisbury's refusal, asked Congress to set up a commission to determine the proper boundary line, and added that in his opinion any attempt by Britain to assert jurisdiction beyond that line should be resisted by every means in the nation's power. Panic ensued in Wall Street, dismay in England, and an outburst of jingoism in the United States.

No facts of the controversy could justify these extreme claims and provocative language. Why did Olney and Cleveland use it? Some have said that it was to win the Irish-American vote, or to create a new issue for the approaching presidential campaign. Cleveland's character was such as to stifle any suspicion of his playing to the gallery. Probably Palmerston's seizure of Belize (British Honduras) was at the back of their minds, as the British seizure of the Nicaraguan customs in April 1895 was certainly in the fore. They feared that England was procrastinating, and that Venezuela, if abandoned to her own expedients, would declare a war in which the United States would be forced to participate. Seventeen years later Olney explained his language on the ground that ' in English eyes the United States was then so completely a negligible quantity that it was believed only words the equivalent of blows would be really effective.'

Actually it was only the felt necessity for friendship with the United States that induced the Salisbury government to let this challenge lie. Of the British navy's numerical strength over the American — at least five to one — there was no doubt. But ' Great Britain,' as Bayard wrote, ' has just now her hands very full in other quarters of the globe. The United States is the last nation on earth with whom the British people or their rulers desire to quarrel. . . . The other European nations are watching each other like pugilists in the ring.' And so they were. The first Boer War was already in the making, and England was beginning to find ' splendid isolation ' a bit precarious. On 2 January 1896 came Jameson's raid in the Transvaal, and the next day the whole world was reading that masterpiece of diplomatic blundering, Kaiser Wilhelm's congratulatory telegram to the Boer leader Kruger.

There was now a dramatic shift in English public opinion that the government shortly reflected. On 25 January, Joseph Chamberlain declared that war between the two English-speaking nations would be an absurdity as well as a crime, and two weeks later Salisbury made a conciliatory statement in the House of Lords. After some secret diplomacy at London and Washington, a treaty was concluded between Great Britain and Venezuela submitting the boundary question to an arbitral tribunal, to be governed by the rule that ' adverse holding or prescription during a period of fifty years shall make a good title.' Thus Cleveland and Olney secured their principle that the whole territory in dispute should be subject to arbitration, and Salisbury his, that the British title to *de facto* possessions should not be questioned.

The tribunal, which included the Chief Justices of Great Britain and the United States, gave a unanimous decision in 1890, substantially along the line of the original British claim. So the Monroe Doctrine was vindicated, arbitration triumphed, and Anglo-American friendship was restored. But outbursts of bad feeling like this always leave their mark; and the abusive language in the American press so affected Rudyard Kipling, then living in Vermont, that for the rest of his life references to the United States were sarcastic and bitter.

2. Manifest Destiny in the 'Nineties

It is clear that in the 'nineties, the spirit of ' manifest destiny,' long dormant, was once more abroad in the land. The precise manifestations of that destiny differed, but the ideology was fundamentally the same as that which had animated an earlier generation. The phrase had once served as a rationalization for the conquest of Texas and California; it was now to serve as a rationalization for a ' large policy ' in the Caribbean, the Pacific, and the Far East. Now that the continent was conquered, it was the ineluctable destiny of the United States to become a world power. ' Whether they will or no,' wrote Captain A. T. Mahan, the naval philosopher of the new imperialism, ' Americans must now begin to look outward.' The idea was echoed, in a great variety of forms, by a large number of politicians, businessmen, and scholars. The combination was irresistible. The scholars furnished the scientific and historical argument; the businessmen pointed to the potential profits; the politicians rang the changes on national honor and glory and party advantage. The Republican platform of 1892 called for ' the achievement of the manifest destiny of the Republic in its broadest sense.' When, after a decade of tumult and shouting, the noise died down, the United States found herself in fact a world power, owning the extraterritorial lands of Puerto Rico, Hawaii, Wake, Guam, Tutuila, and the Philippines, exercising protectorates over Cuba, Panama, and Nicaragua, and asserting interest and influence in the Far East.

This policy, which within half a century carried the United States to world responsibility and world leadership, was merely one manifestation of a world-wide trend toward imperialism. Britain, France, and Germany were busy carving up Africa, and Russia and Japan joined them in scrambling for special concessions in China. Everywhere, too, historians, journalists, poets, novelists, and clergymen provided a convenient rationalization of what came to be called, quite simply, the ' white man's burden.' Nowhere was such rationalization more full-blown than in the United States. Captain A. T. Mahan, whose influence was world-wide, demonstrated in his brilliant series on the history of seapower that not the meek, but those who possessed big navies, inherited the earth. Professor John W. Burgess of Columbia University popularized the German philosophy of nationalism and discovered that Teutonic nations were ' peculiarly endowed with the capacity for establishing national states, and are especially called to that work; and therefore that they are entrusted, in the general economy of history, with the mission of conducting the political civilization of the modern world.' Even the clergy joined in the argument, and the Reverend Josiah Strong, author of the enormously popular tract, *Our Country,* asked rhetorically, ' Does it not look as if God were not only preparing in our Anglo-Saxon civilization the die with which to stamp the peoples of the earth, but as if he were massing behind that die the mighty power with which to press it? '

The politicians and the journalists found all this a gospel of good tidings. Political imperialism was not confined to any one party: Republicans, Democrats, and even Populists joined in the hue and cry for more land, more trade, and more power. Henry Cabot Lodge analyzed ' Our Blundering Foreign Policy ' for one of the popular magazines, and concluded that

From the Rio Grande to the Arctic Ocean there should be but one flag and one country. . . . In the interests of our commerce . . . we should build the Nicaragua canal, and for the protection of that canal and for the sake of our commercial supremacy in the Pacific, we should control the Hawaiian islands, and maintain our influence in Samoa. England has studded the West Indies with strong places which are a standing menace to our Atlantic seaboard. We should have among those islands at least one strong naval station, and when the Nicaragua canal is built, the island of Cuba . . . will become a necessity.

And Senator Cullom of Illinois put it more simply:

It is time that some one woke up and realized the necessity of annexing some property. We want all this northern hemisphere, and when we begin to reach out to secure these advantages we will begin to have a nation, and our lawmakers will rise above the grade of politicians and become true statesmen.

Other young Republicans like Theodore Roosevelt and Albert J. Beveridge were equally emphatic, but neither Democrats nor Populists were inclined to permit the Republicans to make political capital out of so popular an issue. Although Cleveland set his face sternly against imperialism, Democrats like Morgan of Alabama and even Bryan supported an expansionist policy which was bound to eventuate in imperialism; Populists like Allen of Nebraska and Teller of Colorado were no less enthusiastic.

From the newspapers came the frankest expressions of imperialism and the most candid defense of a ' large policy.' It was not only the New York *Journal* and the New York *World* which fed the flames of chauvinism; throughout the country, editors called upon Americans to take up new responsibilities. Some editors, like Pulitzer and Hearst, had circulation in mind, but most of those who clamored so loudly for expansion sincerely reflected what they thought to be the temper of the American people. No better commentary on that temper was furnished than an editorial in the Washington *Post* published on the eve of the Spanish War:

A new consciousness seems to have come upon us — the consciousness of strength — and with it a new appetite, the yearning to show our strength . . . ambition, interest, land hunger, pride, the mere joy of fighting, whatever it may be, we are animated by a new sensation. We are face to face with a strange destiny. The taste of Empire is in the mouth of the people even as the taste of blood in the jungle. It means an Imperial policy, the Republic, renascent, taking her place with the armed nations.

Of course if the United States was to be a world power, she would have to be able to act like one in a crisis. In the 'eighties, as we have seen, Americans awoke with something of a shock to the discovery that their navy was, in the words of the *Army and Navy Journal*, ' a heterogeneous collection of naval trash.' Cleveland's energetic Secretary of the Navy, William C. Whitney, pushed through an ambitious program reorganizing the Navy Department, and starting construction on some thirty armored ships — a program which was sweetened for the American businessman by his very sensible requirement that the armor be of American manufacture. And all through the 'nineties Captain Mahan made clear, in a flood of books and articles, that historically the command of the seas was the price of survival, and his friends, Theodore Roosevelt and Henry Cabot Lodge, spread his gospel where it would do most good — in legislative chambers and executive departments. In 1880 the U.S. Navy had ranked twelfth among the navies of the world; by 1900, with 17 battleships and 6 armored cruisers, it was third.

3. Cuba Libre

It was the Cuban revolution of 1895 that brought all of this chauvinism to a head, and furnished a focus for the imperialistic ambitions of the American people. From the days of Jefferson, Cuba had been an object of peculiar interest to the United States, and regarded as properly within the American sphere of influence. As long as Spain owned the island, most Americans were inclined to let matters rest, but the possibility of ultimate acquisition was never out of the minds of American statesmen. ' In looking forward to the probable course of events,' wrote John Quincy Adams, ' it is scarcely possible to resist the conviction that the annexation of Cuba to our Federal Republic will be indispensable to the continuance and integrity of the Union itself.' Polk had tried to purchase the island, and the effort was renewed under the Pierce administration, but without results other than the aggravation of sectional hostilities in the United States. On the very eve of the Civil War a Senate Committee announced that ' the ultimate acquisition of Cuba may be considered a fixed purpose of the United States.' Yet curiously enough, when the opportunity came, during the Ten Years' War of 1868–78, the United States was coy.

That Ten Years' War was characterized by all the disorder, cruelty, and affronts to American interests and honor that later marked the course of the revolution of 1895. Yet in the first instance the United States carefully avoided any commitment to the cause of the rebels, and in the second it entered the war on their side. How did it happen that the inhumanities of the 'sixties did not shock American sensibilities as did those of the 'nineties, that the spectacle of Spanish tyranny did not affront the spirit of American democracy in the 'sixties as in the 'nineties, and that the necessity for order and stability appeared so much less urgent in the earlier than in the later period? How did it happen that the murder of the crew of the *Virginius* in 1873 did not create a demand for war while the explosion of the *Maine* in 1898 was followed by a wave of war hysteria? How did it happen, finally, that the destiny which necessitated American control of the Caribbean in the 'nineties, was not manifest in the 'sixties? The explanation of this change in the temper of the people and in the policy of the government is fourfold.

In the first place — as we have seen — Americans of the 'nineties came to share with the British, Germans, and French a willingness to take up ' the white man's burden,' and to this added their own special sense of ' manifest destiny.'

In the second place, the technique of journalism had become enormously elaborated and the methods of journalism increasingly sensational. Newspaper editors found that circulation responded to atrocity stories, and it became immensely profitable to exploit them. The New York *World* and the New York *Journal*, then engaged in a titanic struggle for circulation, were the worst offenders in the business of pandering to the popular taste for sensation, but they were by no means alone. Most of the metropolitan papers throughout the country bought news service from the New York papers, and most of them subscribed to the Associated Press, which served up daily concoctions of atrocities for the delectation of the public. For three years, from 1895 to 1898, this campaign of propaganda went on until at last the American people were brought to the point where they demanded intervention on behalf of ' humanity.'

In the third place, the economic stake of the United States in Cuba had increased enormously during these thirty years. That economic stake did not consist merely of the $50 million invested in Cuban sugar and mining industries, though these investments were important. More important was our trade with Cuba, which by 1893 had passed the $100 million mark, and all the varied business and shipping interests dependent upon that trade. Finally the American people and American business had adjusted themselves to the Cuban sugar economy; the destruction of the Cuban sugar industry which resulted from the insurrection seriously affected that adjustment. As the American Minister to Spain told one of his diplomatic colleagues: ' the sugar industry of Cuba is as vital to our people as are the wheat and cotton of India and Egypt to Great Britain.'

In the fourth place, the United States had developed a new set of world interests which made it seem necessary that the entire Caribbean area be under American control. American interests in the Pacific and the Far East enhanced the importance of an isthmian canal, and the prospect of having to defend an isthmian canal made the islands that guarded the route strategically important. A big navy was necessary to protect our far-flung island possessions; new island possessions were necessary in order to provide harbors and coaling stations for our navy. Cuba was not the only object of American concern in the Caribbean area. During this same decade President Cleveland asserted the Monroe Doctrine on behalf of Venezuela; Senator Morgan championed a Nicaraguan canal; Senator Lodge agitated for the purchase of the Danish West Indies; and the State Department considered a revival of the proposal to lease Samana Bay in Santo Domingo.

It is in the light of these changing attitudes and interests and philosophies that we must interpret the events leading up to the War of 1898. That war was fought for the liberation of Cuba, but it did not begin until the Cubans had already fought three years for their own liberation. The fundamental cause of the Cuban revolution which broke out in 1895 was Spanish political oppression and economic exploitation; the immediate cause was the prostration of the sugar and tobacco industries which resulted from the operation of tariffs, both in the United States and in Spain. The Wilson-Gorman tariff, by raising duties on tobacco and abolishing the duty on raw sugar, dealt a heavy blow to the Cuban tobacco planters and encouraged the extension of sugar plantations. Between 1889 and 1894 the production of sugar increased from 630,000 tons to 1,054,000 tons. The following year the Wilson tariff which taxed sugar up to 40 per cent went into operation, and the bottom fell out of the sugar market. The price of sugar which had been 8 cents per pound in 1884 fell to 2 cents in 1895. The consequent poverty and misery in Cuba furnished the impetus for the revolution.

From the beginning the United States was inextricably involved in the Cuban revolution. The United States made little effort to enforce neutrality: a Cuban ' junta ' in New York, spread propaganda and sold bonds, and scores of filibustering expeditions sailed out from American ports. Americans with property interests in Cuba clamored for intervention to protect those interests; Cubans with suspiciously fresh citizenship papers, claimed the protection of the United States government. When, within a fortnight of the outbreak of war, a Spanish gunboat fired upon an American vessel, the *Alliance,* an outburst of jingoism revealed the temper of the country. ' It is time,' said Senator Cullom of Illinois, ' that some one woke up and realized the necessity of annexing some property,' a point of view echoed by others prominent in public life. Thereafter one incident after another aggravated the already tense relations between the United States and Spain and excited American sympathies for the insurrectionists, and if there happened to be a dearth of such incidents, they were brazenly fabricated by the yellow press.

In the face of a mounting demand for intervention, President Cleveland remained imperturbable and unmoved. He issued a proclamation of neutrality, recognizing the existence of a state of rebellion but not the belligerency of the rebels, and he did his best to enforce neutrality laws and protect American interests. Beyond that he would not go, and when Congress, in April 1896, passed a concurrent resolution recognizing the belligerency of the Cubans, Cleveland ignored it, and in the summer of 1896 he confessed that ' there seemed to be an epidemic of insanity in the country just at this time.' Yet by the end of that year even Cleveland's patience had been strained well-nigh to the breaking point, and in his annual message to Congress he warned Spain that if the war went on and degenerated into a hopeless struggle the United States would have to intervene.

McKinley had been elected on a platform calling for Cuban independence, yet at first he too moved with circumspection. ' You may be sure,' he confided to Carl Schurz, ' that there will be no jingo nonsense under my administration,' and shortly after his inauguration he pledged his opposition ' to all acquisitions of territory not on the mainland — Cuba, Hawaii, San Domingo, or any other.' In September 1897 McKinley tendered the good offices of the United States to restore peace to Cuba, but even though a new and more liberal government had come to power in Spain the American overture was rejected. Nevertheless the Spanish government did inaugurate some long overdue reforms. General Weyler, who had earned the unenviable title of ' Butcher Weyler ' was recalled; the policy of herding Cubans into concentration camps, where many of them died of disease and mistreatment, was disavowed; all political rights enjoyed by peninsular Spaniards were extended to the Cubans, and a program looking to eventual home rule for Cuba was inaugurated.

Home rule no longer satisfied the Cubans. Reforms which might have headed off the revolution had they been offered in 1895 were now unacceptable, and the war of extermination continued. Yet the sincere desire of the Spanish government for peace did much to moderate the attitude of the American government if not of the American people. In his annual message of December 1897 McKinley repudiated the idea of intervention and urged that Spain ' be given a reasonable chance to realize her expectations and to prove the asserted efficacy of the new order of things to which she stands irrevocably committed.' It was not to the interest, however, of the Cuban junta to permit a policy of neutrality, and on 9 February 1898 the New York *Journal* printed a private letter to Washington from the Spanish Minister, Enrique de Lôme, which had been stolen from the Havana post office. ' McKinley's message,' wrote the tactless Minister, ' I regard as bad. . . . It once more shows what McKinley is, weak and a bidder for the admiration of the crowd, besides being a would-be-politician who tries to leave a door open behind himself while keeping on good terms with the jingoes of his party.' De Lôme resigned at once, but the relations of the United States and Spain were exacerbated.

At this juncture the nation was horrified by the news that in the night of 15 February 1898 the battleship *Maine* was blown up in Havana harbor with the loss of 260 lives. ' Public opinion,' Captain Sigsbee wired, ' should be suspended until further report,' but when a naval court of inquiry reported that the cause of the disaster was an external explosion by a submarine mine, ' Remember the Maine! ' went from lip to lip. Without a dissenting vote Congress rushed through a bill appropriating $50 million for national defense, and McKinley sent to Madrid what turned out to be his ultimatum, suggesting an immediate armistice, the final revocation of the concentration policy, and American mediation between Spain and Cuba. Spain's formal reply was unsatisfactory, but the Sagasta government, anxious to avoid war, moved toward peace with a celerity unusual at Madrid. Orders were given revoking the concentration policy and a desperate effort was made to persuade the Pope to request a suspension of hostilities — a request to which the Spanish government could agree without loss of face. The American Minister at Madrid cabled to know whether such a solution would be satisfactory to McKinley. ' I believe,' he said, ' that this means peace, which the sober judgment of our people will approve long before next November and which must be approved at the bar of final history. I believe that you will approve this last conscientious effort for peace.' But McKinley's reply was non-committal. On 9 April the Spanish government caved in completely; hostilities were suspended, and the American Minister cabled from Madrid that if nothing were done to humiliate Spain further the Cuban question could be settled in accordance with American demands.

Any President with a backbone would have seized this opportunity for an honorable solution. McKinley, a veteran of 1861, was averse to war. Mark Hanna, Wall Street, big business, and the leaders of the Republican Old Guard backed him up. With such support McKinley needed less firmness than John Adams had shown in the XYZ affair or Grant in the *Alabama* case to preserve peace. But Congress, the press, and the country were clamoring for war. Theodore Roosevelt wrote in a private letter, ' the blood of the murdered men of the *Maine* calls not for indemnity but for the full measure of atonement, which can only come by driving the Spaniard from the New World.' McKinley became obsessed with the notion that if he did not give way, he would forfeit his leadership in the party. After long prayer and hesitation, he decided to yield to popular demand. One year later he recorded his conviction that ' if he had been left alone, he could have concluded an arrangement with the Spanish government under which the Spanish troops would have withdrawn from Cuba without a war.'

On 11 April the President sent Congress the war message which he had already prepared. At the very conclusion of that message he added a casual reference to the fact that Madrid had capitulated on every point at issue.

This fact, with every other pertinent consideration, will, I am sure, have your just and careful attention in the solemn deliberations upon which you are about to enter. If this measure attains a successful result, then our aspirations as a Christian, peace-loving people will be realized. If it fails, it will be only another justification for our contemplated action.

That action, of course, was war.

4. Exit Spain

Lightheartedly the United States entered upon a war that brought quick returns in glory, but new and heavy responsibilities. It was emphatically a popular war. Although imperialistic in result, it was not so in motive, as far as the vast majority of its supporters were concerned. To the Joint Resolution of 20 April 1898, authorizing the use of the armed forces of the nation to liberate Cuba, had been added the self-denying Teller Amendment, declaring that 'The United States hereby dis-claims any disposition or intention to exercise sovereignty, jurisdiction or control over the said Island, except for the pacification thereof, and asserts its determination, when that is accomplished, to leave the government and control of the Island to its people.'

With what generous ardor the young men rushed to the colors to free Cuba, while the bands crashed out the chords of Sousa's ' Stars and Stripes Forever! ' And what a comfortable feeling of unity the country obtained at last, when Democrats vied in patriotism with Republicans, when William J. Bryan had himself appointed Colonel and donned a uniform alongside the irrepressible T. R.; when the South proved as ardent as the North for the fight, and Joe Wheeler, the gallant cavalry leader of the Confederacy, became a high commander of the United States Army in Cuba! It was more close and personal to Americans than World War I; it was their own little show for independence, fair play, and hip-hip-hurrah democracy, against all that was tyrannical, treacherous, and fetid in the Old World. How they enjoyed the discomfiture of the Continental powers, and how they appreciated the hearty good will of England! Every ship of the smart little navy, from the powerful *Oregon,* steaming at full speed round the Horn to be in time for the big fight, to the absurd ' dynamite cruiser ' *Vesuvius,* was known by picture and reputation to every American boy. And what heroes the war correspondents created — Hobson who sank the *Merrimack,* Lieutenant Rowan who delivered the ' message to Garcia,' Commodore Dewey (' You may fire when ready, Gridley '), Captain Philip of the *Texas* (' Don't cheer, boys, the poor fellows are dying ') , and Teddy Roosevelt with his horseless Rough Riders! [2]

This was no war of waiting and endurance, of fruitless loss and hope deferred, of long casualty lists and ' vacant chairs.' On the first

[2] Roosevelt's volume celebrating the deeds of the Rough Riders was the inspiration for one of Mr. Dooley's choice comments:

' I haven't time f'r to tell ye the wurruk Tiddy did in ar-hmin' an' equippin' himself, how he fed himself, how he steadied himself in battles an' encouraged himself with a few well-chosen worruds whin th' sky was darkest. Ye'll have to take a squint into the book ye'erself to l'arn thim things.'

' I won't do it,' said Mr. Hennessy. ' I think Tiddy Rosenfelt is all r-right an' if he wants to blow his horn lave him do it.'

' True f'r ye,' said Mr. Dooley . . . ' But if I was him I'd call th' book " Alone in Cubia." '

day of May, one week after the declaration, Dewey steams into
Manila Bay with the Pacific squadron and without losing a man reduces the Spanish fleet to old junk. The Fifth Army Corps safely
lands in Cuba, and wins three battles in quick succession. Admiral
Cervera's fleet issues from Santiago Bay and in a few hours' running
fight is completely smashed, with the loss of a single American sailor.
Ten weeks' fighting, and the United States had wrested an empire
from Spain.

Prince Bismarck is said to have remarked, just before his death,
that there was a special providence for drunkards, fools, and the
United States of America. On paper Spain was a formidable power.
If the United States had more battleships, Spain had more armored
cruisers and torpedo craft. Spain had almost 200,000 troops in Cuba
before the war. The American regular army was as good as any in
the world, but included less than 28,000 officers and men, scattered
in small detachments from the Yukon to Key West. So weak were
the harbor defenses of the Atlantic coast, and so apprehensive were
the people of bombardment, that the North Atlantic fleet was divided: the one-half blockading Havana and the other, reassuringly
called ' the Flying Squadron,' stationed at Hampton Roads. Against
any other nation such strategy might have been disastrous. But the
Spanish navy was inconceivably neglected, ill-armed, and untrained;
while the United States Navy — a new creation of the last fifteen
years — was smart, disciplined, and efficient. John D. Long, Secretary
of the Navy, was honest and intelligent; and when the energetic
assistant secretary, Roosevelt, left to lead the Rough Riders, his place
on the board of naval strategy was taken by Captain Mahan.

In a military sense the United States was entirely unprepared. An
elderly jobbing politician was at the head of the War Department.
There were enough Krag rifles for the Regulars, but the 200,000 volunteers, whom the President insisted on calling to the colors, received Springfields and black powder. There was no khaki cloth in
the country, and thousands of troops fought a summer campaign in
Cuba clothed in the heavy blue uniform of winter garrison duty.
The Commissary Department was disorganized, and soldiers complained that they were fed on ' embalmed beef.' Volunteers neglected
even such principles of camp sanitation as were laid down in Deu-
teronomy, and for every one of the 386 men killed or mortally
wounded in battle, 14 died of disease. Transporting 18,000 men to

Cuba caused more confusion than conveying 2 million men to France twenty years later. The Regulars were encamped at Tampa, Florida, but there was no adequate railroad connection between Tampa and Port Tampa, nine miles distant, and no adequate pier or transport facilities at the latter place. General Miles recorded his impression of conditions at Tampa:

Several of the volunteer regiments came here without arms, and some without blankets, tents, or camp equipage. The 32nd Michigan, which is among the best, came without arms. General Guy V. Henry reports that five regiments under his command are not fit to go into the field. There are over 300 cars loaded with war material along the roads about Tampa. . . . To illustrate the confusion, fifteen cars loaded with uniforms were side-tracked twenty-five miles away from Tampa, and remained there for weeks while the troops were suffering for clothing. Five thousand rifles, which were discovered yesterday, were needed by several regiments. Also, the different parts of the siege train and ammunition for the same, which will be required immediately on landing, are scattered through hundreds of cars on the side-tracks of the railroads.

Yet the little expeditionary force which finally got under way was allowed to land on the beach at Daiquiri without opposition (20–25 June), and the Captain-General of Cuba, with six weeks' warning, and with almost 200,000 men on the island and 13,000 in the city of Santiago, was able to concentrate only 1700 on the battlefields of Las Guasimas, El Caney, and San Juan, against 15,000 Americans. These 1700 Spaniards, well armed and entrenched, gave an excellent account of themselves, and helped to promote Theodore Roosevelt from a colonelcy to the presidency.

It was the navy, however, that clinched the conquest of Cuba. Late in April the Spanish Admiral, Cervera, with four armored cruisers and three destroyers, had steamed out of the Cape Verde Islands to destinations unknown. There was panic all along the Atlantic coast, and timid people hurried their valuables to points of safety well in the interior. But Cervera was not bound on offensive operations. On 19 May he sneaked into the narrow land-locked harbor of Santiago Bay, and was promptly bottled up by the American navy under Admiral Sampson and Commodore Schley. With the army closing in on Santiago, Cervera had no alternatives but surrender or escape, and he chose the latter. On 3 July the Spanish battle-fleet sailed forth from Santiago Bay to death and destruction:

> Haste to do now what must be done anon
> Or some mad hope of selling triumph dear
> Drove the ships forth: soon was *Teresa* gone
> *Furór, Plutón, Vizcaya, Oquendo,* and *Colón.*[3]

Not since 1863 had there been such a Fourth of July in America as that Monday in 1898 when the news came through. Santiago surrendered on the 16th and except for a military promenade in Puerto Rico, which Mr. Dooley described as ' Gin'ral Miles' Gran' Picnic and Moonlight Excursion,' the war was over.

The most important event of the war had occurred not in the Caribbean but in the Far East. Two months before the actual declaration of war Theodore Roosevelt, then Assistant Secretary of the Navy, had taken it upon himself to outline naval strategy and direct national policy. On 25 February he had cabled to Commodore Dewey in command of the Asiatic Squadron: ' Secret and confidential. Order squadron to Hong Kong. Keep full of coal. In the event of declaration of war Spain, your duty will be to see that the Spanish squadron does not leave the Asiatic coast, and then offensive operations in Philippine Islands.' As soon as war was declared, Dewey set out under full steam for the Philippines, and on the night of 30 April he slipped through the narrow channel of Boca Grande and into the spacious waters of Manila Bay, where a Spanish fleet was anchored. Gridley fired when ready; they all fired; and when the smoke and mist cleared away it was apparent that the Spanish fleet had been utterly destroyed. Dewey moved on the shore batteries, which promptly displayed a white flag, and the battle of Manila Bay was over. Not until 13 August — one day after the signing of the peace protocol — did an American expeditionary force, with the support of Aguinaldo's Filipino army, take the city of Manila.

The collapse of her military and naval power everywhere forced Spain to sue for terms of peace. McKinley dictated them on 30 July — immediate evacuation and definite relinquishment of Cuba, cession of Puerto Rico and an island in the Ladrones, and American occupation of the city, harbor, and bay of Manila pending the final disposition of the Philippine Islands. Spain signed a preliminary peace to that effect on 12 August, sadly protesting, ' This demand strips us of the very last memory of a glorious past and expels us . . . from the Western Hemisphere, which became peopled and civilized through

[3] ' Spain in America ' in *Poems* by George Santayana, Scribner, p. 118.

the proud deeds of our ancestors.' But John Hay wrote to his friend Theodore Roosevelt in a very different vein: ' It has been a splendid little war; begun with the highest motives, carried on with magnificent intelligence and spirit, favored by that fortune which loves the brave.'

5. THE FRUITS OF VICTORY

In the formal peace negotiations which began at Paris on 1 October 1898, the United States was represented by a commission consisting of Whitelaw Reid, editor of the powerful New York *Tribune,* Secretary of State Day, and three Senators. Four of these commissioners had already committed themselves to a ' large policy ' of imperialism and expansion; the fifth, Senator Gray, came around eventually to the majority point of view. To the American demand for the independence of Cuba and the cession of Puerto Rico and Guam, the Spanish representatives interposed no objections, and they even agreed to assume the Cuban debt of some $400 million. The question of the disposition of the Philippines, however, offered serious difficulties. If they had been contented under Spanish rule, there would have been no question of annexing them. An insurrection had just been partially suppressed when the Spanish War broke out, but Dewey had encouraged Emilio Aguinaldo, leader of the *insurrectos,* to return from exile after the battle of Manila Bay; and upon the fall of the city of Manila the Filipino leader had organized the ' Visayan Republic ' in the province of Luzon and made a bid for foreign recognition. The obvious thing to do was to turn the Philippines over to the Filipinos, as Cuba to the Cubans. But Dewey cabled that the ' republic ' represented only a faction, and was unable to keep order within its nominal sphere. Yet the fact remained that Aguinaldo represented government in the islands, and that if the United States expected to retain the Philippines it would first have to conquer them.

McKinley was in a quandary. In his message of December 1897 he had laid down with respect to Cuba the rule that ' forcible annexation . . . can not be thought of. That, by our code of morality, would be criminal aggression.' Did the same rule hold good for the Philippines? The question was to be answered not by logic, but by a combination of interest and emotion. Already the newspapers were clamoring ' Keep the Philippines.' Already navalists were emphasizing the military importance of the islands and suggesting the danger to American interests should Germany or Japan annex them. Senator Beveridge was speaking hopefully of ' China's illimitable markets ' and Whitelaw Reid of the New York *Tribune* wrote that the Philippines would ' convert the Pacific ocean into an American lake.' Popular feeling was being aroused by the cry, ' Don't haul down the flag,' and when McKinley returned from a trip through the Middle West he found ' a very general feeling that the United States is in a situation where it cannot let go.' The President's instructions to the Peace Commission presented all of these considerations:

The Philippines stand upon a different basis. The presence and success of our arms at Manila imposes upon us obligations which we cannot disregard. The march of events rules and overrules human action . . . We cannot be unmindful that, without any desire or design on our part, the war has brought us new duties and responsibilities which we must meet and discharge as becomes a great nation . . . Incidental to our tenure in the Philippines is the commercial opportunity to which American statesmanship cannot be indifferent.

Yet there were still several alternatives. The United States might simply guarantee and protect the independence of the Philippines as it was to guarantee and protect the independence of Cuba. It might take only the island of Luzon, leaving the rest of the archipelago to the Filipinos. It might take the Philippines in trust, as it were, with a promise of independence — the principle of the Bacon bill that was defeated only by the casting vote of the Vice-President in the Senate. Or it might annex all the Philippines.

McKinley hesitated long and prayerfully, but finally concluded to fulfill manifest destiny by taking them all. ' One night it came to me this way,' he told his Methodist brethren, ' (1) that we could not turn them over to France or Germany, our commercial rivals in the Orient — that would be bad business and discreditable; (2) that we could not give them back to Spain — that would be cowardly and dishonorable; (3) that we could not leave them to themselves — they were unfit for self-government, and they would soon have anarchy and misrule over there worse than Spain's was; and (4) that there was nothing left for us to do but take them all, and to educate the Filipinos and uplift and Christianize them.' So Spain was required to part with the islands for $20 million, and on 10 December 1898 the Treaty of Paris was signed and the United States became, officially, a world power.

But the prospect of the annexation of an alien people without their consent aroused the fierce indignation of many Americans who thought it a monstrous perversion of the ideals which had inspired our crusade for Cuba. Old-fashioned Senators like Hoar of Massachusetts girded on their armor to fight for the principles of the Declaration of Independence, and for two months the fate of the treaty hung in suspense. Lodge led the fight for ratification, and he was particularly concerned with the disgrace involved in repudiating what the President, through his envoys, had concluded in Paris. ' I confess,' he wrote, ' I cannot think calmly of the rejection of that Treaty by a little more than one-third of the Senate. It would be a repudiation of the President and humiliation of the whole country in the eyes of the world, and would show we are unfit as a nation to enter into great questions of foreign policy.' The administration invoked patronage and party regularity to save the treaty, and in its efforts, it received unexpected aid from William Jennings Bryan. Bryan was unalterably opposed to imperialism, but he thought that a question of such magnitude as this should be decided on its own merits, and not as part of the general question of peace, and that it should be submitted to the verdict of the people at large.[4] On 6 February 1899 the necessary two-thirds majority for ratification was obtained, but Lodge called it ' the hardest fight I have ever known.'

McKinley, in 1897, had rejected a proposal to buy Cuba because he did not care to buy an insurrection; the United States now found that it had purchased, for $20 million, a first-class Filipino insurrection. For the Filipinos, who had been good Catholics for over three centuries, did not wish to be ' uplifted and Christianized' by the Americans; but when, on 4 February 1899, Aguinaldo's troops disregarded the command of an American sentry to halt, the United States army undertook to ' civilize them with a Krag.' Before the Philippine insurrection was stamped out it had cost the United States almost as many lives as the Spanish War, and more scandals; for a war between white soldiers and semi-civilized men of color is something worse than what Sherman said it was. Within a short time

[4] The charge that Bryan was primarily interested in creating a campaign issue for 1900 is unfounded.

the United States found itself doing in the Philippines precisely what it had condemned Spain for doing in Cuba. Soon stories of concentration camps and ' water-cures ' began to trickle back to the United States, and public opinion, already highly skeptical of a venture dubious alike in origin, method, and purpose, became inflamed. The result was a vigorous anti-imperialism crusade which commanded the support of men from all parties and all walks of life. It was not inappropriate that the nineteenth century should be ushered out with a passionate appeal to the Declaration of Independence, and the twentieth century ushered in with a victory for the forces of imperialism.

Rarely in our history has any reform movement attracted a more distinguished group of supporters than that which rallied to the banner of anti-imperialism. Party lines were disregarded: Republicans like Senators Hoar and Edmunds, Secretary Sherman, and Speaker Reed joined hands with Democrats like Cleveland and Bryan, Ben Tillman and John G. Carlisle. Samuel Gompers spoke for labor, and Andrew Carnegie paid the bills. The press was represented by E. L. Godkin of *The Nation* and Bowles of the *Springfield Republican*. President Eliot of Harvard spoke for the intellectuals of New England and President David Starr Jordan of Leland Stanford combatted jingoism on the Pacific coast. Philosophers like William James, clergymen like Henry Van Dyke, social workers like Jane Addams, all worked together for a common cause. Effective aid came from the men of letters. Mark Twain was deeply embittered by our conquest of the Philippines, and in his letter ' To the Person Sitting in Darkness ' he charged McKinley with ' playing the European game ' of imperialism, and suggested that Old Glory should now have ' the white stripes painted black and the stars replaced by the skull and cross bones.' Through the inimitable Mr. Dooley, Finley P. Dunne passed in scathing review the whole imperialistic venture, and soon the whole country was laughing at his observation that ' 'tis not more thin two months since ye larned whether they were islands or canned goods,' and pondering his conclusion that ' they'se wan consolation; an' that is, if th' American people can govern thimsilves, they can govern anything that walks.' The most powerful indictment of imperialism came from the young poet, William Vaughn Moody. In ' An Ode in Time of Hesitation,' he appealed from the chauvinistic spirit of the 'nineties to the idealism of the 'sixties:

JUST BEFORE THE ENGAGEMENT *by William Glackens*

Lies! lies! It cannot be! The wars we wage
Are noble, and our battles still are won
By justice for us, ere we lift the gage.
We have not sold our loftiest heritage.
The proud republic hath not stooped to cheat
And scramble in the market-place of war . . .
Ah no!
We have not fallen so.

We are our fathers' sons: let those who lead us know! . . .
Tempt not our weakness, our cupidity!
For save we let the island men go free,
Those baffled and dislaureled ghosts
Will curse us from the lamentable coasts
Where walk the frustrate dead . . .
O ye who lead,
Take heed!
Blindness we may forgive, but baseness we will smite.[5]

The argument against the annexation of the Philippines rested
not only on an old-fashioned repugnance to government without the
consent of the governed and a humanitarian revulsion against the
manner in which the war of conquest was conducted, but on political,
constitutional, and economic grounds as well. It was asserted that the
possession of colonies in the Pacific would require for their protection a larger military and naval establishment and would involve us
in the whole complex of Far Eastern politics; and the assertion was
sound. It was pointed out that the conquest, defense, and administration of the Philippines would cost us far more than the islands
would ever bring in return; and the prediction proved to be correct.
It was alleged that the flouting of the principles of democracy in the
Philippines would impair the vitality and integrity of democracy at
home; and the prophecy was justified. Finally it was argued that the
Constitution did not permit the acquisition of extraterritorial possessions and the government of alien peoples without their consent.
This last argument was eventually rejected by the Supreme Court,
but in a series of decisions so contradictory that no one has ever been
able to unravel their logic.

Bryan's leadership of the Democratic party was unchallenged and
he determined to make imperialism the paramount issue of the campaign of 1900. The Democratic platform announced that

[5] William Vaughn Moody, *Selected Poems,* Houghton Mifflin, 1931.

all governments instituted among men derive their just powers from the consent of the governed; that any government not based upon the consent of the governed is a tyranny; to impose upon any people a government of force is to substitute the methods of imperialism for those of a republic.

The Republicans were glad to accept this issue, and they went before the electorate with the rallying cry, ' Don't haul down the flag.' ' Who,' asked Bryan, in vain, ' will haul down the President? ' But the real issue of the election was not imperialism, but prosperity. The Republicans held all the trump cards, and played them well. An upswing in foreign trade and the discovery of extensive new gold deposits in the Klondike had enabled them to settle the money question. Under the protection of the Dingley tariff of 1897, industry was flourishing and wages were up. Higher prices for wheat, corn, and cotton allayed agricultural discontent, and McKinley's claim to be the ' advance agent of prosperity' appeared to be justified. The Republican party had carried the nation through a victorious war and raised its prestige in the eyes of the world. There was no inclination to repudiate the results of that war or the party that capitalized those results. The country was prosperous, contented, and weary of idealism. The election proved that Bryan had misjudged the temper of the American people just as Wilson misjudged the popular temper in 1920. McKinley's victory was far more impressive in 1900 than it had been in 1896; in the electoral college he received 292 votes to 155 for Bryan, and his popular plurality was almost 900,000.

6. The Open Door

It was feared by many Americans and assumed by most Europeans that the annexations of the year 1898 were only a beginning; that the United States was destined to become a great colonial power. Imperialism in the Roman sense did not, however, make any permanent appeal to the American people; even the word signified a reproach. The political control of islands densely populated with inhabitants of foreign tongue and alien race was a very different matter from the traditional expansion into sparsely inhabited regions capable of full fellowship in the Union; the ready evacuation of Cuba, the Jones Act of 1916, and the 1934 decision to give up the Philippines indicate how superficial was the imperialism of 1898.

The Japanese victory over China in the War of 1894–95 had revealed to the world the weakness of China: to forestall the danger of Japan's securing political and economic ascendancy in that empire, the European powers hurried to obtain for themselves special concessions and spheres of influence. ' The various powers,' said the Dowager Empress of China, ' cast upon us looks of tiger-like voracity, hustling each other in their endeavors to be the first to seize upon our inner-most territories.' Japan had already taken Formosa and established her ascendancy in the ' Hermit Kingdom ' of Korea; in 1897 and 1898 Russia took Port Arthur and the Liaotung Peninsula, which gave her access to the interior of Manchuria; Germany seized Kiaochow in Shantung, France consoled herself with a lease to Kwangchow bay, adjoining Indo-China; Italy got Sanmun bay, south of the Yangtze river; and England added to her holdings the port of Wei-hai-wei. Along with these leases went valuable railway concessions, which promised to give to the European powers all but complete control over the internal trade of China.

Since the Cushing mission of 1844 the United States had demanded for itself the same commercial and extraterritorial privileges that were granted to other powers, and in this policy it had been entirely successful. Now with the acquisition of the Philippines, American interest in the Chinese trade was vastly increased, and so, too, American strategic interest in the command of the western Pacific. The carving up of China into foreign concessions, protectorates, and spheres of influence appeared to threaten American trade, especially in Manchuria, and to nullify part of the value of the Philippines. The United States was not alone in its concern over the consequences of the partition of China. Great Britain, who had long enjoyed a privileged position in the Far East, saw her markets threatened and her prestige damaged by the entry of the other powers into the game. Like the United States, she wanted an ' open door ' in China and, as in 1823, she made overtures to the American government for a joint declaration of policy. These formal overtures were rejected. Meantime, however, an ' old China hand,' the Englishman Alfred E. Hippisley, had enlisted his friend W. W. Rockhill, State Department adviser on Chinese affairs, in a similar project. Together they drafted a proposal urging all the major powers to accept the principle of trade equality in China, and to refrain from violations of Chinese territorial integrity. Almost casually, Secretary John Hay accepted these proposals and incorporated some of them into his own ' open door ' policy for China. In a circular note of 6 September 1899 addressed to the major European powers, Hay recognized the existence of the ' spheres of influence,' and requested from each power a declaration that each, in its respective sphere, would maintain the Chinese customs tariff, and levy equal harbor dues and railway rates on the ships and merchandise of all nations. All the powers but Russia expressed approval, but only Great Britain formally agreed; Hay, however, promptly announced the agreement of all the powers as ' final and definitive.'

The ' open door ' policy, as originally announced, was concerned solely with safeguarding American commercial interests in China. Within less than a year, however, it was given a new and far-reaching interpretation. The brazen exploitation of China by the great powers had created a deep antipathy to foreigners, and in June 1900 a secret organization called the Boxers tried to drive the ' foreign devils ' out of China. Within a short time the Boxers had massacred some 300 foreigners, mostly missionaries and their families; others were driven into Peking, where they took refuge in the British legation. An expeditionary force to rescue the beleaguered Europeans was hurriedly organized, and the United States co-operated with some 5000 soldiers. There was grave danger that the relief expedition might deteriorate into a general war, and Hay bent all his energies to localizing the conflict. On 3 July, in a circular note to all the powers, he tried to limit the objectives of the joint intervention:

The policy of the government of the United States is to seek a solution which may bring about permanent safety and peace to China, preserve Chinese territorial and administrative entity, protect all rights guaranteed to friendly powers by treaty and international law, and safeguard for the world the principle of equal and impartial trade with all parts of the Chinese Empire.

These were not the objectives that were entertained in the chancelleries of Berlin, St. Petersburg, and Tokyo, but these powers, fearful of each other and of war, found it easy to concur. The danger of war was averted, and the Chinese government permitted the joint expedition to save the legations. Punishment, however, was exacted from the guilty Boxers, and China saddled with an outrageous indemnity of $333 million. Of this some $24 million went to the United States; half of it was eventually returned to the Chinese government which established therewith a fund for sending Chinese students to American colleges.

Now the United States was committed not only to an ' open door ' to China, but to the maintenance of the political integrity of that decrepit empire. Yet what did the commitment mean? Only by alliance with some European power like England could the United States have enforced this policy, and at no time did the exigencies of American politics permit an open alliance. American public opinion rejoiced in the spectacle of the United States teaching a moral lesson to the wicked imperialists of the Old World, but as Secretary Hay himself said, ' the talk of the papers about our pre-eminent moral position giving us the authority to dictate to the world, is mere flapdoodle.' And when, in 1901, Japan made cautious inquiries about the American reaction to Russian encroachments in Manchuria, Hay assured them that the United States was not prepared ' to attempt singly, or in concert with other Powers, to enforce these views in the east by any demonstration which could present a character of hostility to any other Power.' In short the United States wanted an ' open door ' but would not fight for it.

Yet we cannot dismiss the ' open door ' policy quite this easily. It faithfully expressed American sentimental interest in China — an interest represented by long-standing religious, medical, and cultural missions. It may have delayed for a time the attack on China from Japan. It probably enhanced American prestige in China and other parts of the globe. It was part of that unwritten agreement whereby American support to England's Far Eastern policy bought English support to the American Caribbean policy. And it came, in time, to take on a symbolical character — just as did the Monroe Doctrine — a phrase which meant that America would not have any part in imperialistic designs on China and would discourage such designs in others. It helped build up popular support for President Wilson's China policy, and for resistance against Japanese aggression in China, and this in turn exacerbated Japanese attitudes toward the United States.

7. THE SUPREME COURT AND THE INSULAR CASES

The annexation of extra-continental territory, already thickly populated by alien peoples, created new problems in American politics and government. The petty islands and guano rocks that had already been annexed had never raised, as Puerto Rico and the Philippines did, the embarrassing question of whether the Constitution followed the flag, or the difficult question of the nature and extent of congressional control. The Treaty of Paris had provided that ' The civil rights and political status of the native inhabitants hereby ceded to the United States shall be determined by Congress ' but this provision threw little light on the subject. Opinions of the Supreme Court in the ' Insular Cases ' left the status of the new possessions very unclear, but eventually, as in the British Empire, a theory was evolved from practice. Insular possessions are of two categories: incorporated and unincorporated; and the question of what constitutes incorporation is one to be determined on the basis of fact and intention as revealed in congressional legislation. Thus at the turn of the century Alaska was held to be incorporated,[6] but Puerto Rico was unincorporated, and this despite the fact that after 1917 its inhabitants became citizens of the United States.[7] Unincorporated territories are not foreign, however, and their exports are not controlled by American customs duties unless by special act of Congress.[8] But Congress may, nevertheless, impose such duties as it sees fit.[9] This meant, according to a dissenting opinion by Chief Justice Fuller, that

if an organized and settled province of another sovereignty is acquired by the United States, Congress has the power to keep it like a disembodied shade, in an intermediate state of ambiguous existence for an indefinite period: and more than that, after it has been called from that limbo, commerce with it is absolutely subject to the will of Congress, irrespective of constitutional provisions.[10]

Thus the Republican party was able to eat its cake and have it; to indulge in territorial expansion and yet maintain the tariff wall against such insular products as sugar and tobacco which might compete with the home-grown products.

The question of the civil and political rights of the inhabitants of these new territorial possessions was even more perplexing. Organic acts of Congress are the constitutions of the Philippines, Hawaii, and

[6] *Rasmussen v. United States* 197 U.S. 516 (1905).

[7] *Balzac v. Porto Rico* 258 U.S. 298 (1924). In 1952 Puerto Rico became a Commonwealth associated with the United States.

[8] *De Lima v. Bidwell* 182 U.S. 1 (1901).

[9] *Hawaii v. Mankichi* 190 U.S. 197 (1903); *Dorr v. U.S.* 195 U.S. 138 (1904); *Balzac v. Porto Rico* 258 U.S. 298 (1924).

[10] *Downes v. Bidwell* 182 U.S. 224 (1901).

Puerto Rico, but to what extent was Congress bound, in passing these acts, and the courts, in interpreting them, by the provisions of the Constitution and the Bill of Rights? How far, in short, did the Constitution follow the flag? To this question the Court returned an ingenious answer. It distinguished between ' fundamental ' rights and ' formal ' or ' procedural ' rights. Fundamental rights are extended to all who come under the sovereignty of the United States, but mere procedural rights, such as trial by jury or indictment by grand jury, are not extended to the inhabitants of unincorporated territories unless Congress chooses so to extend them. Thus, in fact, the President and Congress, though limited in power within the United States, possess powers that are practically absolute over American dependencies — powers limited only by the moral sanction of principles of natural justice. The parallel with the old British Empire is suggestive; and the government at Washington, like that of eighteenth-century England, was reluctant to admit the existence of an empire. No colonial office was established or colonial secretary appointed, and the administration of what we must call our ' non-colonies ' was characterized by diversity and opportunism.

BIBLIOGRAPHY

1. GENERAL. S. F. Bemis, *A Diplomatic History of the United States;* S. F. Bemis & G. G. Griffin, *Guide to the Diplomatic History of the United States,* contains elaborate bibliographies; J. Bartlett Brebner, *The North Atlantic Triangle: The Interplay of Canada, the United States and Great Britain;* Foster R. Dulles, *America's Rise to World Power 1898–1954, The Imperial Years,* and *America in the Pacific;* John W. Foster, *American Diplomacy in the Orient;* Lionel Gelber, *The Rise of Anglo-American Friendship 1898–1906;* Robert E. Osgood, *Ideals and Self-Interest in America's Foreign Policy;* Dexter Perkins, *Hands Off! A History of the Monroe Doctrine;* A. K. Weinberg, *Manifest Destiny: A Study in Nationalist Expansionism;* Arthur Whitaker, *The Western Hemisphere Idea: Its Rise and Decline;* B. M. Williams, *Economic Foreign Policy of the United States;* William A. Williams, *The Tragedy of American Diplomacy.*

2. RISE OF IMPERIALISM AND MANIFEST DESTINY IN THE 'NINETIES. Harry C. Allen, *Great Britain and the United States;* Howard K. Beale, *Theodore Roosevelt and the Rise of America to World Power;* E. J. Carpenter, *America in Hawaii;* R. E. Chadwick, *The Relations of the United States with Spain: Diplomacy;* P. E. Corbett, *The Settlement of Canadian-American Disputes;* Tyler Dennett, *Americans in Eastern Asia;* William Livezey, *Mahan on Sea Power;* A. T. Mahan, *From Sail to Steam;* Ernest May, *Imperial Democracy;* Elting E. Morison & John Blum (eds.) , *The Letters of Theodore Roosevelt* (8 vols.) ; Allan Nevins, *Henry White: Thirty Years of American Diplomacy;*

Gordon O'Gara, *Theodore Roosevelt and the Rise of the Modern Navy;* Earl S. Pomeroy, *Pacific Outpost: American Strategy in Guam;* Julius Pratt, *Expansionists of 1898;* Henry Pringle, *Theodore Roosevelt;* W. D. Puleston, *Admiral Mahan;* G. H. Ryden, *The Foreign Policy of the United States in Relation to Samoa;* Harold and Margaret Sprout, *The Rise of American Naval Power;* S. K. Stevens, *American Expansion in Hawaii 1842–1898;* Richard West, *Admirals of American Empire.*

3. THE SPANISH WAR. E. J. Benton, *International Law and Diplomacy of the Spanish-American War;* Stephen Bonsal, *The Fight for Santiago;* F. E. Chadwick, *Relations of the United States and Spain: The War* (2 vols.) ; George Dewey, *Autobiography;* Orestes Ferrara, *The Last Spanish War;* H. E. Flack, *Spanish-American Diplomatic Relations Preceding the War of 1898;* Frederick Funston, *Memories of Two Wars;* Jennette Keim, *German-American Political Relations;* A. T. Mahan, *Lessons of the War with Spain;* Walter Millis, *The Martial Spirit;* J. W. Pratt, *Expansionists of 1898;* B. A. Reuter, *Anglo-American Relations During the Spanish American War;* Theodore Roosevelt, *The Rough Riders;* H. S. Sargent, *The Campaign of Santiago de Cuba* (3 vols.) ; W. S. Schley, *Forty-five Years under the Flag;* J. R. Spears, *Our Navy in the War with Spain;* R. S. West, *Admirals of American Empire;* Joseph Wheeler, *The Santiago Campaign;* Joseph Wisan, *The Cuban Crisis as Reflected in the New York Press.*

4. IMPERIALISM AND ANTI–IMPERIALISM. William J. Bryan, *The Second Battle;* Andrew Carnegie, *Autobiography;* Royal Cortissoz, *Life of Whitelaw Reid* (2 vols.) ; Merle Curti, *Bryan and World Peace;* Tyler Dennett, *John Hay;* Elmer Ellis, *Henry Teller;* Margaret Leech, *In the Days of McKinley;* Ernest R. May, *Imperial Democracy;* William V. Moody, *Poems,* ed. by Robert M. Lovett; Richard F. Pettigrew, *The Course of Empire;* Arthur S. Pier, *American Apostles to the Philippines;* Julius Pratt, *Expansionists of 1898;* Moorfield Storey & M. P. Lichanco, *The Conquest of the Philippines by the United States;* A. K. Weinberg, *Manifest Destiny.*

5. THE OPEN DOOR. Joseph Barnes (ed.) , *Empire in the East;* M. J. Bau, *Open Door Doctrine in Relation to China;* J. M. Callahan, *American Relations in the Pacific and in the Far East;* Charles Campbell, Jr., *Special Business Interests and the Open Door Policy;* H. Chung, *The Oriental Policy of the United States;* P. H. Clemens, *The Boxer Rebellion;* Tyler Dennett, *Americans in Eastern Asia;* Tyler Dennett, *John Hay;* Alfred L. P. Dennis, *Adventures in American Diplomacy;* Foster R. Dulles, *China and America since 1784* and *America in the Pacific;* John W. Foster, *American Diplomacy in the Orient;* A. W. Griswold, *The Far Eastern Policy of the United States;* William L. Langer, *The Diplomacy of Imperialism,* vol. 2; C. O. Paullin, *Diplomatic Negotiations by American Naval Officers;* Paul S. Reinsch, *An American Diplomat in China;* Alfred Vagts, *Deutschland und die Vereinigten Staaten in der Weltpolitik* (2 vols.) ; Paul A. Varg, *Open Door Diplomat — The Life of William W. Rockhill;* W. W. Willoughby, *Foreign Rights and Interests in China.*

6. IMPERIALISM AND THE CONSTITUTION. Charles B. Elliott, *The Philippines, to the End of the Military Regime;* C. E. Magoon, *Legal Status of the Territory Acquired by the U.S. during the War with Spain;* C. F. Randolph,

Law and Policy of Annexation; Charles Warren, *The Supreme Court in U.S. History,* vol. 2; W. F. Willoughby, *Territories and Dependencies of the U.S.*

7. DOCUMENTS. R. J. Bartlett (ed.), *The Record of American Diplomacy;* H. S. Commager, *Documents,* nos. 268, 281, 305, 329–31, 340, 345–52; Insular Cases, House Documents, 56 Cong. 2nd Sess. no. 509.

For further references, *Harvard Guide,* ¶¶ 220–25.

The Progressive Movement

1. The Promise of American Life

A T THE TURN of the century, Americans could look back over three generations of progress unparalleled in history. The nation had advanced, in Jefferson's prophetic words, to ' destinies beyond the reach of mortal eye.' The continent was subdued, the frontier was gone, and already Americans were reaching out for new worlds to conquer. From a small struggling republic, menaced on all sides, the nation had advanced to the rank of a world power, its hegemony in the Western Hemisphere undisputed, its influence in the Eastern everywhere acknowledged. The political foundations upon which the nation had been established had endured the vicissitudes of foreign and civil war, of prosperity and depression. No standing army menaced personal liberty; no permanent bureaucracy endangered political liberty; and the institution of slavery, which had threatened to destroy not only the Union but democracy, had been itself destroyed. Population had increased from 5 to 76 million, and 28 million Europeans of all races had been absorbed without impairing racial integrity or warping social institutions. In the half-century from 1850 to 1900 national wealth had increased from $7 to $88 billion, and the standard of living for the common man compared favorably with that to be found anywhere else on the globe. In agriculture and in industry the American people had advanced with giant strides, and progress in science and invention had been equally spectacular. Nor were the achievements of Americans merely material. The ideal of free public education had been realized; the ideal of a free press had been maintained; the ideal of religious freedom had been cherished. In literature, art, and science, Americans had made contributions of enduring value, and by almost every test of character or of achievement, America had proved herself worthy of her opportunities. When, in 1888, James Bryce finished his magisterial survey of

The American Commonwealth, he concluded that life was better for the common man in America than elsewhere on the globe.

Yet thoughtful Americans did not look with complacency upon their social, economic, and political institutions. For, as Woodrow Wilson said in that inaugural address which ushered in the ' New Freedom ':

> The evil has come with the good, and much fine gold has been corroded. With riches has come inexcusable waste. . . . We have been proud of our industrial achievements, but we have not hitherto stopped thoughtfully enough to count the cost, the cost of lives snuffed out, of energies overtaxed and broken, the fearful physical and spiritual cost to the men and women and children upon whom the dead weight and burden of it all has fallen pitilessly the years through. . . . With the great Government went many deep secret things which we too long delayed to look into and scrutinize with candid, fearless eyes. The great Government we loved has too often been made use of for private and selfish purposes, and those who used it had forgotten the people.

The indictment was a general one, but it was all too easy to substantiate it with a bill of particulars. The continent had been conquered, but the conquest had been attended by reckless exploitation of soil, forest, and water. The agricultural domain had grown beyond the dreams of even a Jefferson, but the farmer was on the verge of ruin. The industrial revolution had made the United States the greatest of manufacturing nations, but the process had been accompanied by iniquitous practices in the employment of women and children and in the treatment of the aged, the incompetent, and the infirm. Unemployment and child labor went hand in hand; machinery was marvelously efficient, but no other industrial nation confessed to so many industrial accidents. The nation was fabulously rich, but its wealth was gravitating rapidly into the hands of a small portion of the population, and the power of wealth threatened to undermine the political integrity of the Republic. In a land of plenty there was never enough of food, clothing, and shelter for the underprivileged; and cyclical depressions, apparently unavoidable, plunged millions into actual want. In the great cities the slums grew apace, and from the slums spread dirt and disease, crime and vice. Science taught how to control many of the diseases that plagued mankind, but poverty interposed between science and health, and tuberculosis, hookworm, malaria, and other diseases of want and ignorance took an annual toll that ran into the millions. The churches taught the Ten Commandments and philosophers the Golden Rule, but man's inhumanity to man was still illustrated in the penal code, in prison conditions, in the treatment of the aged, the poor, the incapacitated, the defective, and the insane, and in the attitude toward the criminal and the prostitute. The Civil War had ended slavery but ' white superiority ' still flourished throughout the South, and the degradation and exploitation of the Negro was a blot on American civilization. The educational system was an object of pride, but its benefits were unevenly distributed, and the census of 1900 discovered over 6 million illiterates. Everyone gave lip service to the principles of democracy, but political corruption poisoned the body politic from head to foot. On all sides thoughtful men feared that the nation which Lincoln had called ' the last best hope of earth ' would prove instead the world's illusion.

Against the crowding evils of the time there arose a full-throated protest that was neither unrealistic nor ineffective. It is this protest which gives a peculiar character to American politics and thought from approximately 1890 to World War I. Its manifestations were as varied as the evils toward which it was directed. It took the form of an agrarian revolt, and in that form attempted to adapt the principles of Jeffersonian agrarianism to the facts of a modern industrial economy. It demanded the centralization of power in the hands of a strong government and the extension of regulation or control over industry, finance, transportation, agriculture, labor, and even morals. It found expression in a new concern for the poor and the underprivileged, for women and children, for the immigrant, the Indian, and the Negro. It called for new standards of honesty in politics and in business, the reform of political machinery, and the restoration of business ethics. It formulated a new social and political philosophy, which rejected political laissez faire and justified public control of social and economic institutions on the principles of liberal democracy. This protest can be studied in political debates and campaign speeches; laws and constitutions; sermons and editorials; the treatises of sociologists, historians, economists, and philosophers; fiction, drama, and poetry; and in the voluminous writings of the journalists who came to be known as ' muckrakers.'

This progressive revolt of the 'nineties and the early years of the new century was clearly in the American tradition. It did not essentially differ either in its motivations or in its manifestations from the reform movement of the 'forties and 'fifties, and if it was on the whole more superficial than this earlier movement, the explanation can be found in the greater complexity of the problems which it attacked and the greater urgency of the reforms which it agitated. The new progressivism, like the old, had a distinctly moral flavor, and its leaders — Bryan, LaFollette, Roosevelt, Wilson — were moral crusaders. It was, for all its nationalism, Jeffersonian rather than Hamiltonian in character; it was liberal rather than radical; it was optimistic rather than desperate. Its roots went deep into American experience, but it profited from the teachings and the practices of the more enlightened European nations. It was romantic in its philosophical implications, but realistic in the sense that it recognized the economic bases of politics. It was basic in its criticism, but opportunistic in its program, accepting in practice Justice Holmes's dictum that ' legislation may begin where an evil begins.' Its accomplishments, both social and legislative, were impressive, and though many of those accomplishments were forfeited in the war and the postwar years, it may be said to have laid both the philosophic and the legislative foundations for the New Deal of the 1930's.

2. CHALLENGES TO AMERICAN DEMOCRACY

The problems which faced reformers on the threshold of the new century were many and complex. For the sake of convenience we may note six major problems which embraced, in one form or another, practically all of the particular evils which the progressives hoped to improve. The first of these was the confusion of ethics which resulted from an attempt to apply the moral code of an individualistic, agrarian society to the practices of a highly industrialized and integrated social order. The second was the rise of big business and the control of the natural resources and the labor of the country by trusts and monopolies with the consequent exploitation of social wealth for private aggrandizement. The third was the grossly unequal distribution of wealth and the creation of social and class divisions along economic lines. The fourth was the rise of the city with its demand for a new type of social engineering. The fifth was the breakdown of political honesty and administrative system and the application of antiquated administrative institutions to the new problems of government. And sixth was the denial to the Negro of his elementary constitutional and political rights, and the persistence of gross social and economic discriminations against him and against other minority groups.

The chief factors in the ethical confusion which overtook American society in the industrial age were the growing complexity and interdependence of the social organism and the diffusion of personal responsibility through the use of the corporate device. In a simple agrarian society, personal and social morals were much the same thing, and the harm that a bad man could do was pretty well limited to crimes against individuals. Such crimes — mainly violations of the Ten Commandments — were easy to recognize and comparatively easy to control. But in a highly complex industrial society personal crimes and social sins were very different things, and the old moral standards were no longer applicable. As society grew more interdependent, it grew more vulnerable. Society could be hurt in a thousand new ways, and many of them not recognized in the old moral codes, or in the law codes. ' The growth of credit institutions,' wrote the sociologist E. A. Ross, whose *Sin and Society* attracted the attention of such men as Theodore Roosevelt and Justice Holmes, ' the spread of fiduciary relations, the enmeshing of industry in law, the interlacing of government and business, the multiplication of boards and inspectors — all invited to sin. What gateways they open to greed! What fresh parasites they let in on us! How idle in our new situation to intone the old litanies! '

The men who were guilty of the new sins against society were for the most part upright and well-intentioned gentlemen, often quite unaware of the consequences of their actions. ' Unlike the old-time villain,' Ross observed, ' the latter-day malefactor does not wear a slouch hat and a comforter, breathe forth curses and an odor of gin, go about his nefarious work with clenched teeth and an evil scowl. . . . The modern high-powered dealer of woe wears immaculate linen, carries a silk hat and a lighted cigar, sins with calm countenance and a serene soul, leagues or months from the evil he causes. Upon his gentlemanly presence the eventual blood and tears do not obtrude themselves.' These men were caught in the meshes of a business system which had not yet developed a moral code of its own and to which the old codes were irrelevant. The manufacture and sale of impure foods, dangerous drugs, infected milk, poisonous toys, might produce disease or death, but none of those involved in the process —

retailers, wholesalers, manufacturers, advertisers, corporation directors, or stockholders — realized that they were guilty of murder. Misleading advertisements, the use of the shoddy in manufacture, improper inspection, and short-weight packages, all might cheat purchasers, but none of those involved in the process realized that they were guilty of theft. Failure to observe fire regulations, to install safety appliances in factories and in mines and on railroads, to inspect unseaworthy boats, might take a fearful toll in lives, but none of those involved in the process realized that they were guilty of manslaughter. Improper inspection of banks, insurance companies, and trust companies, false statements in a company prospectus, speculation in stocks, in gold, or in grain, might bring poverty and misery to thousands, but none of those involved in the process realized that they were guilty of larceny. Business competition might force the employment of children of eight or nine years of age in mines and in mills or dictate the use of woman labor in sweatshops, but none of those involved in the process realized that they were guilty of maintaining slavery. The purchase of votes, the corruption of election officials, the bribing of legislators, the lobbying of special bills, the flagrant disregard of laws, might threaten the very foundations of democracy, but none of those involved in the process realized that they were guilty of treason to representative government.

For the new social sins were impersonal and without evil intent, and consequently produced no sense of guilt. The explanation of this may be found largely in the operation of the corporate device. It is the essence of the corporation that it is a person for legal purposes but not for moral purposes. ' The corporation,' said Ross, ' is an entity that transmits the greed of investors, but not their conscience, that returns them profit, but not unpopularity.' Corporation employers were responsible to the management, the management was responsible to the directors, the directors were responsible to the stockholders, and the stockholders were too far removed from the business to exercise any effective control over its ethics even had they been inclined to do so. Occasionally there was a mild protest against ' tainted money ' or against corporation malpractices, but for the most part it remained true that ' there is nothing like distance to disinfect dividends.'

The impersonality of ' social sin,' the diffusion of responsibility, presented perhaps the gravest problem which the reformers had to face. It was necessary for them to formulate a new social ethics and to educate the people to that new ethical code, and much of the work of the 'muckrakers' was directed toward this end. It was necessary to devise new administrative machinery for discovering the consequences of industrial malpractices and new legal machinery for fixing responsibility, and the effort to do this can be read in the struggle over trust, labor, factory, pure food, housing, and similar legislation. In the end many of the progressive reformers, persuaded that even 'good' men would not acquiesce in reforms that cut into their profits, despaired of any effective improvement within the framework of the capitalistic system. But that despair was premature.

We have already traced the second problem — the rise of big business, the growth of trusts and monopolies, and the efforts to bring combinations of capital and industry under the control of the government. A large part of the reform movement was concerned with the problems that flowed from the new industrial order — problems of child labor, factory inspection, unemployment, the exploitation of immigrant workers, the use of natural resources for private or corporate aggrandizement. Roosevelt's reputation as a progressive rests upon his gestures toward 'trust-busting,' railroad regulation, conservation, the 'square deal' for labor, and similar efforts to grapple with the industrial revolution. Wilson's 'New Freedom' was largely directed toward these same ends: freedom of competition for the small businessman, freedom from monopolistic control of prices for the public, freedom from industrial feudalism for the laborer. LaFollette inaugurated his reform career by attacking the railroads and the lumber interests that controlled Wisconsin, and throughout his long career labored for social democracy through the regulation of industrial and financial monopolies. Bryan, after abandoning the money issue and imperialism, concentrated his energies upon the task of regulating business, industry, and finance. A host of lesser leaders in the progressive movement — Hughes of New York, Pingree of Michigan, Tom Johnson of Ohio, Altgeld of Illinois, Johnson of California, to name only a few — comprehended with equal realism the economic basis of the reform movement and fought the campaign for democracy by a series of flank attacks on the citadels of industrial and financial privilege. Political reformers learned that to cleanse politics it was necessary to regulate the business interests that controlled politics; social reformers learned that to eliminate child labor or the sweatshop or the slums it was essential to control the industrial and corporate interests that profited by these evils; humanitarian reformers discovered that the improvement of race relations, of penal conditions, and even of morals depended in the last analysis upon the improvement of general economic circumstances. The 'Promise of American Life,' as interpreted by Herbert Croly, editor of *The New Republic,* was not so much the promise of political democracy as of economic independence for the common man. And Henry Demarest Lloyd concluded his analysis of *Wealth Against Commonwealth* with the prophetic observation: ' The word of the day is that we are about to civilize industry.'

No less serious than the problems created by the industrial revolution, and intimately connected with them, was the third problem — that of the distribution of wealth. Benjamin Franklin had found in the American economic order ' a general happy mediocrity.'

There are few great proprietors of the soil [he wrote] and few tenants; most people cultivate their own lands, or follow some handicraft or merchandise; very few are rich enough to live idly upon their rents or incomes or to pay the high prices given in Europe for Paintings, Statues, Architecture, and other works of Art, that are more curious than useful.

In the early years of the Republic there was little wealth and little poverty. Wealth was chiefly in land, and many of the greatest landowners, like Washington and Jefferson, were actually ' land poor.' The first half of the nineteenth century saw the rise of a few large fortunes, most of them either in land or in shipping, and the wealthy men of the time, like John Jacob Astor or James Lenox, were designated ' landlords ' or ' merchant princes ' rather than ' captains of industry ' or ' titans of finance.' Moses Yale Beach of the New York *Sun* who published in the 1850's a pamphlet on ' Wealthy Men of New York ' discovered only nineteen who could be called millionaires, and the richest, John Jacob Astor, boasted a fortune of only $6 million.

The Civil War, the industrial revolution, and the railway expansion into the West changed all this. Men discovered a hundred new ways of making money, and many of the new fortunes were gained through speculation, and carried with them no sense of responsibility, only a sense of power. In 1888 Bryce warned Americans that they were developing greater extremes of wealth and poverty than were to be found even in England. The statisticians confirmed the fears of the critics. An estimate made in 1890 indicated that one-eighth of the people of the country owned seven-eighths of the property. Subsequent surveys revealed that this estimate was perhaps too moderate. Writing in 1896, Charles B. Spahr concluded that 1 per cent of the population owned over half the total national wealth, and that 12 per cent owned almost nine-tenths. This disparity between the rich and the poor did not decrease during the next twenty years, and when O. Henry contrasted New York's Four Million with her 'Four Hundred' the proportions were felt to be too embarrassingly close to the truth for the purposes of humor.

The great fortunes of the day were obtained not from land but from the exploitation of natural resources, manufacturing, banking, and speculation. When in 1892 the New York *Tribune* compiled figures on the millionaires of the country, it discovered that almost 1000 had earned their fortunes in 'merchandising and investment,' over 600 in manufactures, over 300 in banking and brokerage, over 200 in transportation. Some hint of the concentration of natural resources in the hands of the few could be found in the fact that the *Tribune* counted 178 millionaires in the lumber industry, 113 in coal and lead mining, 73 in gold and silver mining, and 72 in oil. Sixty-five lawyers had become millionaires, but only 26 farmers had made the grade, and most of them were absentee landlords. It was clear that a handful of men had jockeyed themselves into a position where they could control most of the natural resources and almost all of the processes of extraction, manufacture, transportation, and finance whereby those resources were converted into the finished product. As the Chief Justice of Wisconsin had pointed out as early as 1873, 'the accumulation of individual wealth seems to be greater than it ever has been since the downfall of the Roman Empire. . . . For the first time in our politics, money is taking the field as an organized power.'

Actually this third problem — the unequal distribution of wealth — though it seemed formidable, proved in the end the easiest to solve. The solution was twofold. First was the income tax — permitted by the Sixteenth Amendment and enacted in 1913 — which made possible the orderly control of great fortunes. The second was a development unplanned and unforeseen which came only after the Second World War — the general leveling up of incomes so that the great majority of Americans could enjoy the benefits of an affluent society.

The fourth problem which challenged the ingenuity of the progressives was the rise of the city. In the generation from 1860 to 1900 the urban population had increased from 16 to 33 per cent, but it was not so much the general increase in urban population as the increase in the size of the largest cities that created difficulties. Cities were growing far more rapidly than small towns and villages. In the twenty years from 1880 to 1900 the population of New York City increased from a little less than two to almost three and a half millions; Chicago grew from half a million to a million and a half, and became the second city in the nation; such cities as Detroit, Cleveland, Buffalo, Milwaukee, Indianapolis, Columbus, Toledo, Omaha, and Atlanta more than doubled in size. In 1880 there were 19 cities with a population of 100,000 or more; by 1900 the number had increased to 36, and by 1910 to 50.

This rapid urbanization resulted from two streams of immigration, one from the country, one from abroad. Those who came to the great cities, either from the farms or from foreign lands, had torn up their roots, and the process of transplantation was often a painful one. The movement to the cities, like the movement to the West, created new and healthy communities, but both reflected a social disintegration of older and more stable communities, and both suffered from the consequences of that disintegration.

The rapid and unregulated growth of cities created problems of a new and complex character. How should the teeming thousands who thronged into the towns be housed? What provision could be made to guard against the diseases and epidemics that resulted from impure water, inadequate sewage disposal, filth, congestion, and poverty? What measures should be adopted to control crime and vice; what measures to prevent the recurrence of fires such as that which devastated Chicago in 1871 and Boston in 1872? Could the cities build enough schools for their children, and find room between the crowded streets for playgrounds? All of these tasks of housing, sanitation, fire protection, policing, traffic regulation, education, devolved upon the city governments. Under their impact the administrative machinery of many cities broke down completely, and many governmental functions had to be assumed by purely private agencies. Yet private agencies, no matter how well intentioned or well financed, could not permanently carry on the administrative work of the great cities. What was needed was a new science of municipal government, a new philosophy of social engineering. In no department was the progressive movement more vigorous than in the realm of municipal reform, and cities like New York, Cleveland, Toledo, and Detroit were the training grounds for many reformers who later achieved national importance. In no other department did the progressive movement borrow more liberally from European and especially English experience, and the cities were the experimental laboratories in which many of the new progressive ideas were tested.

But whether working within the framework of municipal, state, or federal government, the reformers were always under the necessity of operating through the established political channels, and allying with the major parties. This was the fifth major problem — the struggle against political corruption.

Observers like James Bryce, critics like E. L. Godkin, feared that inertia and corruption would, in the long run, destroy democracy, and the exposures of the ' muckrakers ' proved that their fears were not wholly unfounded. What was the explanation of the phenomena of corruption in American politics? Corruption was not, of course, unique to the United States, but that it flourished more shamelessly in the United States than in other democratic nations, none could doubt. Its prevalence was to be explained in part by the American tradition of lawlessness, inherited from the revolutionary era and from successive frontiers; in part by the unstable character of American social life which resulted from continuous social disintegrations involved in the westward movements, the movement from the country to the city, and the immigration from the Old World to the New World; in part by the absence in America of a ' patriciate ' — a class with the habits, the leisure, and the skill for public service. It was associated with a pragmatic philosophy which emphasized results rather than methods, and which made success the criterion of measurement.

There were, too, more practical explanations. First, the administrative organization, inherited from an older and simpler day, broke down from sheer weight of the new and complex duties placed upon it. It took a long time for the science of government to catch up with the problems of government. Second, the deep-rooted belief, inherited from the Jacksonian period, that any honest man could fill any office, and the fear of a permanent bureaucracy, kept the expert out of politics and made municipal and state administration a paradise for the incompetent and a happy hunting ground for privilege. Third, the legitimate financial rewards of politics were so meager that able men preferred business or the professions, and incompetents brought the prestige of office so low that 'gentlemen' did not go into politics.

A considerable part of the energy of the reform movement was dissipated in fighting corruption, and so spectacular did this struggle become that it seemed at times to be an end in itself. The result was that after the reformers had won a victory over the local 'ring' or the state 'boss,' the public often lost interest in the house-cleaning that followed, and permitted corrupt groups to regain lost ground. The exposure of the 'Shame of the Cities' or of dishonesty in state politics loomed large in the newspapers and magazines of the time, but was actually of little importance. Far more important was the effort of progressives to devise new political techniques and administrative agencies to ensure a more effective operation of democracy.

Sixth was the Negro problem. In the generation after the restoration of self-government to the white South, the position of the freed man had steadily worsened. The vast majority of Southern Negroes were every year more deeply sunk in the tenancy-mortgage morass. The flickering promise of better educational facilities that Reconstruction had held out was not fulfilled; as late as 1900 only some 8000 Negro boys and girls were in the high schools of the entire South. Political and civil rights presumably guaranteed by the Fourteenth and Fifteenth Amendments were eroded by judicial interpretation or flouted by public opinion, and in 1896 *Plessy v. Ferguson*[1] stamped judicial approval on the 'separate but equal' theory which gave segregation a spurious respectability. Thereafter 'Jim Crow' became almost universal, and segregation took on the character of a cosmic law. With the decline of the old planter class and the rise to power of the classes represented by Ben Tillman and Hoke Smith, and the ineffable Vardaman of Mississippi, racial prejudice and violence became the order of the day: in the fifteen years after 1885 almost 2500 Negroes were lynched. Nor were conditions much better in the North. Negroes who found their way to Northern cities were herded into ghettos, segregated in most public places, fobbed off

[1] 163 U.S. 537 (1896).

with inferior schooling, cold-shouldered by labor unions, and consigned to the most menial and ill-paid jobs.

3. The Era of the Muckrakers

It was in 1906 that President Roosevelt applied to those engaged in uncovering corruption in American society the epithet ' muckrakers ':

In Bunyan's *Pilgrim's Progress,* you may recall the description of the Man with the Muck-rake, the man who could look no way but downward with the muck-rake in his hands; who was offered the celestial crown for his muck-rake, but would neither look up nor regard the crown he was offered, but continued to rake the filth of the floor.

Like many other epithets — Puritan, Quaker, Democrat — the term became in time almost a title of nobility. For the muckrakers did the work that no one else was prepared to do. They exposed the particular iniquities that afflicted American life, stirred public opinion to the point where it was willing to support men like Roosevelt and Wilson in their reform programs, and planted the seeds of progressivism which the politicians were to harvest. These muckrakers at whom Roosevelt hurled his anathema included journalists, novelists, historians, economists, sociologists, and philosophers. The task which they set themselves, consciously or unconsciously, was that of saving political and economic democracy and realizing what Herbert Croly called the ' Promise of American Life.' Insofar as the progressive movement achieved this end, the credit belongs in part to the muckrakers.

The literature of exposure and protest did not begin in the Roosevelt administration. Its beginnings can be traced back to the 'eighties and the 'nineties, to the period of the agrarian revolt and the radical labor movement and the protest against the trusts. But not until after the turn of the century, when widely read magazines like *McClure's, Everybody's, Cosmopolitan, Collier's,* and the *American Magazine* opened their pages to the literature of exposure, did the muckrakers really achieve popularity and influence. In its early phrases muckraking was more philosophical and less spectacular, more concerned with fundamental economic and social problems and less with specific grievances; and the difference may be explained in part by the fact that the later muckraking was to some extent a journalistic stunt.

Most of the literature of protest was ephemeral, but some of it was permanent and most of it of considerable significance. Philosophically the most important were contributions from three of the seminal minds of that generation: Henry George, Lester Ward, and Thorstein Veblen.

Henry George's *Progress and Poverty,* published in 1879, is one of the great books of the nineteenth century, but like most great books its influence was provocative rather than didactic. George, who was one of the few original economic thinkers that this country had produced, set himself to resolve the paradox of progress and poverty through a 'formula so broad as to admit of no exceptions.' The formula which he found was the Single Tax — a tax which would wipe out unearned increment on land, ensure equal access to the land and its resources, and thus destroy monopoly, eliminate speculation, and restore economic equality in all classes of society. George's diagnosis of the causes of poverty and inequality was more profound than his single-tax cure, and a whole generation of progressives confessed their indebtedness to this 'Bayard of the Poor' — men like Hamlin Garland, Tom Johnson, Clarence Darrow, and Brand Whitlock in the United States, Sidney Webb and Bernard Shaw in England, Tolstoy in Russia, and Sun Yat-sen in China. Nor was George's influence confined to the intellectuals. Over 2 million copies of his book were sold, and on the dusty plains of Kansas, in the slums of Liverpool and of Moscow, on the banks of the Ganges and of the Yangtze, poor men painfully spelled out the message of *Progress and Poverty* to grasp a new vision of human society.

Lester Ward, too, exercised a far-reaching influence on his generation, at home and abroad. A distinguished scientist who worked most of his life for the U.S. Geological Survey and made capital contributions to geology, zoology, and paleontology, Ward turned in his middle age to the study of society, and became the 'father' of American sociology. He was the first truly revolutionary sociologist, the first to apply the teachings of Darwin with scientific rigor to the study of human affairs. Where amateurs like Herbert Spencer and William Graham Sumner translated Darwinian evolution into political and economic laissez faire, Ward's more rigorous reading led him to precisely the opposite interpretation. He saw that all civilization was a product of the triumph of man over the forces of nature, and that only by organizing the human faculties could man hope to achieve progress. ' We are told to let things alone,' he wrote,

and allow nature to take its course. But has intelligent man ever done this? Is not civilization the result of man's not letting things alone, and of his not letting nature take its course? . . . Every implement or utensil, every mechanical device, is a triumph of man over the physical forces of nature in ceaseless and aimless competition. All human institutions — religion, government, law, marriage, custom . . . are broadly viewed only so many ways of meeting and checkmating the principle of competition as it manifests itself in society.

In book after book — *Dynamic Sociology, Applied Sociology, Psychic Factors in Civilization* — Ward hammered home this scientific moral: that although for all other creatures environment controlled life, man alone was able to control his environment. It was the fittest who survived, to be sure, but fitness meant the application of organized intelligence, and the institution best qualified to organize man's intelligence was government.

Thorstein Veblen enjoyed neither the popularity of Henry George nor the acclaim and honor that came to Ward, but his long-range influence may have been greater than that of either of these contemporaries. Those able to fight their way through his intricate style could discover in the *Theory of the Leisure Class* (1899) and the *Theory of Business Enterprise* (1904) the most severe indictment of modern business that had yet been fashioned with the tools of scholarship. Veblen distinguished sharply between ' business ' and ' industry '; the first, he contended, was concerned merely with profits and was therefore antisocial; the second was concerned with organizing the technological processes of production, and was therefore socially beneficial. It is impossible to follow here the ramifications of Veblen's thesis, but it is pertinent to point out that his books furnished many of the reformers with their most telling arguments against ' predatory wealth,' absentee ownership, and the profit system.

Discontent took a different form of literary expression in utopianism. The 'nineties saw the publication of almost 50 utopian romances, but it is suggestive that the utopianism of the 'nineties, unlike that of the 'thirties and 'forties, spent itself in literary exercises. The most famous of the utopian romances was Edward Bellamy's *Looking Backward, 2000–1887.* Bellamy's utopia was a co-operative industrial society, where not only profit but even money was eliminated: in some respects it resembled the industrial order set up in Soviet Russia in the 1920's. The book enjoyed an enormous popularity, and hundreds of Nationalist Clubs, dedicated to the nationalization of industries and natural resources, were established throughout the country. ' In those days,' wrote William Dean Howells, ' the solution of the riddle of the painful earth through the dreams of Edward Bellamy, through the dreams of all the generous visionaries of the past, seemed not impossibly far off.' Howells added his own fantasy to the dream, *A Traveler from Altruria*, a novel in which Mr. Homos contrasted the inequities of American life with the ideal society of Altruria.

Exposure of corporate malpractices and political corruption — and of the connection between the two — was the most characteristic form of muckraking. This literature of exposure was voluminous, but we must content ourselves with a few representative samples. As early as 1894 Henry Demarest Lloyd of Chicago fixed the type and the method of the later muckraking literature with his *Wealth Against Commonwealth,* a vigorous assault on the malpractices of the Standard Oil Company. Ten years later Ida Tarbell stumbled on the same theme when she was free-lancing for *McClure's Magazine:* the result was the classic *History of the Standard Oil Company,* which analyzed with a wealth of statistical data the methods whereby Standard Oil had crushed competitors, seized natural resources, and purchased legislative favors. Within a few years appeared a whole cluster of books of this type: Charles Edward Russell's *Greatest Trust in the World,* an attack on the beef trust; Thomas Lawson's *Frenzied Finance,* the story of the Amalgamated Copper by a Wall Street insider; Burton J. Hendrick's *Story of Life Insurance,* which did much to create public demand for regulation of that business; and Gustavus Myer's *History of the Great American Fortunes,* which surveyed American fortunes from the colonial era to the twentieth century and concluded that many of them were based on fraud or favor. Soon came protests from more respectable sources. Andrew Carnegie announced that it was a disgrace to die rich; the conservative Senator Beveridge demanded an income tax to curb ' unhealthy fortunes '; and President Roosevelt denounced ' malefactors of great wealth ' and confided to Jacob Riis his determination ' to favor the diffusion of wealth in such a manner as will measurably avoid the extreme of swollen fortunes and grinding poverty.'

Equally virulent were the exposures of political corruption, and of the alliance between business and politics. The most notable of all these was doubtless the series of articles on municipal misrule which Lincoln Steffens, greatest of the muckrakers, wrote for *McClure's Magazine* and gathered into the classic *Shame of the Cities*. Studying one city after another — ' Philadelphia: Corrupt and Contented '; ' Pittsburgh, a City Ashamed '; ' The Shame of Minneapolis '; ' The Shamelessness of St. Louis ' — Steffens found everywhere conditions remarkably similar, and he worked out something like a law of municipal politics. Privilege, Steffens concluded, controlled politics and neither morals nor laws had anything to do with the matter. Analyzing conditions in Colorado, Judge Ben Lindsey found the same rule applicable to state politics, and in *The Beast* told with compelling fervor the story of corporation control of the Centennial State. Nor were national politics immune from the muckraker's rake; in *The Treason of the Senate* written for the *Cosmopolitan* the novelist David Graham Phillips called the roll of Senators he found loyal to their business masters but traitors to their constituents: Depew of New York, Aldrich of Rhode Island, Gorman of Maryland, Lodge of Massachusetts, Elkins of Virginia, and others of the same stamp.

At no other time in our history has literature been more vitally concerned with social problems, or contributed more to the popular understanding of those problems. Book for book the novelists matched the journalists, and for every volume of sociological analysis there was a companion volume of fiction reaching a wider audience and often making a more lasting impression. Stephen Crane's *Maggie: A Girl of the Streets* supplemented Riis's *How the Other Half Lives;* Jack London's *The Road* was a fictional version of Coxey's ' Petition on Boots.' Theodore Dreiser's *The Financier* and *The Titan* made it easier to understand *Frenzied Finance,* as his leading character, Frank Cowperwood, was a fictional portrait of the Chicago speculator Charles Yerks. Frank Norris's *The Octopus* was a companion to Bryan's attacks on the railroad monopolies, and Norris's picture of wheat speculation in *The Pit* explained much of the agrarian protest. Brand Whitlock's picture of municipal corruption in Toledo, *The Thirteenth District,* anticipated Lincoln Steffens's *Shame of the Cities,* and his *Turn of the Balance* was the most effective plea of that decade for penal reform. Russell's exposure of the meat trust was not nearly as effective as Upton Sinclair's famous picture of life in the stockyards, *The Jungle* — a book which contributed directly to the enactment of the Pure Meat Act. David Graham Phillip's best novel, *Susan Lenox: Her Fall and Rise,* came a good many years after George Kibbe Turner's exposure of the white slave traffic, *Daughters of the Poor,* and was more widely read. And the story of corruption in politics was never better told than in Winston Churchill's *Coniston* and *Mr. Crewe's Career.* One critic has characterized this literature of protest as the ' minority report of the novelists.' As we note its sweep and depth and trace its influence, we must conclude that it represented rather a majority report.

4. Humanitarian Reform

' The world is too full of amateurs who can play the golden rule as an aria with variations,' wrote H. D. Lloyd in 1894. ' The only field for new effects is in epigrams of practice.' Into this field the reformers entered with buoyant enthusiasm. For every evil there was to be a remedy, and men and women banded together in innumerable charitable and rescue and humane societies to ameliorate social injustice. The methods of big business were introduced into the organization of philanthropy, and the study of social pathology became a science, with its own professional standards, technique, and vocabulary. Private philanthropy poured millions of dollars into the channels of reform; the churches adjusted themselves to the demands of ' socialized Christianity ' and the state supplemented the work of private agencies through legislative regulations and appropriations. Inspired by the example of Toynbee Hall in London, social workers established settlement houses in the slums of the great cities. The most famous of these special oases were Hull House in Chicago, Henry Street Settlement in New York, and South End House in Boston, but altogether almost a hundred such settlement houses had been founded by the turn of the century. Designed originally to familiarize social workers at first-hand with the lives of the poor, they became in time elaborate social service agencies and foci for social reforms. The experience of Hull House is typical:

We early found ourselves [wrote Jane Addams] spending many hours in efforts to secure support for deserted women, insurance for bewildered widows, damages for injured operators, furniture from the clutches of the installment store. The Settlement is valuable as an information and interpretation bureau. It constantly acts between the various institutions of the city and the people for whose benefit these were erected. The hospitals, county agencies, and State asylums are often but vague rumors to the people who need them most. Another function of the Settlement to its neighborhood resembles that of the big brother whose mere presence on the playground protects the little one from bullies.

The influence of the social settlements was felt in time not only in the slums but in the legislative chambers, in labor reforms, in health and sanitation, in arts and handicrafts. Social workers, regarded by politicians and businessmen as misguided zealots, came to be recognized as the most effective reformers of their generation. Certainly that was true of Jane Addams, who founded Hull House in 1887. With its day nursery, boys' club, gymnasium, music and drama and art schools, handicrafts shop, and many other activities, that wonderful institution quickly became a laboratory for social work. Not content with charity or rescue work, Miss Addams — and her associates like Julia Lathrop and Dr. Alice Hamilton — spearheaded drives for effective regulation of the labor of women and children, the establishment of the first Juvenile Court, protection for immigrant girls, improved sanitary inspection, and improved schools. Hull House attracted the attention of university sociologists and economists, of jurists interested in the reform of the law, of professional students of education, and even of politicians. Presidents listened to what Miss Addams had to say, and legislatures did her bidding. Hull House became in time a world institution, and Jane Addams more nearly a world figure than any other woman of her day.

The settlement houses were generally located in the most congested and the poorest parts of the great cities, and settlement workers early engaged in a ' battle with the slums.' Probably the most difficult of all the problems that had attended the growth of the city was that of housing. It was impossible to build dwellings fast enough to house the teeming thousands who poured in from the Old World and from the countryside to such cities as New York, Boston, and Chicago. Furthermore, land values and construction costs were so high that poor immigrants could not afford individual houses, even had they been available. Out of this situation came the tenement house of malodorous fame — a huge, compact structure of five or six stories, with scores and often hundreds of rooms and apartments. The rooms were small, dingy, airless, and sunless; the halls long and dark;

the sanitation shockingly primitive; and many of the tenements were fire traps. As early as 1866 a report of the New York City Council described the ' filth, overcrowding, lack of privacy and domesticity, lack of ventilation and lighting, absence of supervision, and sanitary regulation ' prevalent in the tenements, and in the following decades conditions became worse. By 1890 over a million New Yorkers were packed into 32,000 tenements; some of these were decent apartment houses, but many were ' crazy old buildings, rear yards, dark, damp basements, leaking garrets, shops, outhouses, and stables converted into dwellings though scarcely fit to shelter brutes.'

Doctors had long warned that these tenements were breeding places of disease and vice, and statistics revealed a death rate in New York and Boston 50 per cent higher than that of London. But it was not until 1890, when a Danish immigrant, Jacob Riis, published *How the Other Half Lives,* that public opinion was thoroughly aroused to the menace of the slums. Riis told of one of these tenements which housed over 700 and confessed a death rate of 75 per 1000. One typical block in New York's Lower East Side contained ' 2,781 persons on two acres of land, nearly every bit of which was covered with buildings. There were 466 babies in the block, but not a bathtub, except one that hung in an air-shaft. Of the 1588 rooms, 441 were dark, with no ventilation to the outer air; 635 rooms gave upon " twilight air-shafts." In five years 32 cases of tuberculosis had been reported from that block, and in that time 660 different families in the block had applied for charity.' The names of some of these tenement blocks — Blind Man's Alley, Murderers' Alley, Poverty Gap, Misery Row, and Penitentiary Row — were as eloquent of their character as pages of description.

The public response to these revelations led to ' a battle with the slums ' and with the anti-social property owners who profited from the rents derived from tenements. For as financial investments, tenements stood high. Of the tenement described above, for example, Riis remarked ' the rent-roll was all right. It amounted to $113,964 a year.' Despite opposition from vested interests, public opinion rallied to the reformers. A tenement house commission, appointed by Governor Theodore Roosevelt, made a series of recommendations for reform, and most of these were incorporated in the model tenement house law of 1901 which did away with the old lightless and airless ' dumbbell ' tenements and ensured more decent housing for the poor. State after state followed the example of New York, and by 1910 most of the great cities had inaugurated housing reform. Yet though the worst conditions were eliminated, the slums remained, and it was not until the 1930's that Americans were willing — though apparently not able — to tackle the problem of slum clearance in any realistic fashion.

This same period witnessed the climax of the movement for the organization of charity. The unemployment and misery which accompanied the panic of 1873 had led to the establishment of a National Conference of Charities and Correction in the following year. Soon almost every large city in the country had a Charity Organization Society similar to that founded in New York in 1882 and designed to introduce science and efficiency into the haphazard administration of charity by scores of private agencies. These charity societies maintained shelters for homeless men, undertook the care of dependent children, engaged in rescue work among delinquent girls, provided legal aid to the poor, fought loan sharks, and attempted in scores of ways to alleviate the burden of poverty. Boards of Charity were created in almost every state, and cities made generous appropriations to supplement the contributions of private philanthropy. Professional social work started with Mary Richmond of Baltimore, who gave training to young women prepared to make social service a career. In 1909 the Russell Sage Foundation established a Charity Organization Department to serve as a clearing house for this work and inaugurated a series of far-reaching investigations into the causes of poverty, crime, and disease.

Particularly notable was the solicitude for women and children. The latter, especially, were the innocent victims of urban growth and industrialism. High ground rents forced children out into the streets or into littered alleyways to play, tenements deprived them of air and light, and industry exploited them as a cheap source of labor. Two of Jacob Riis's most effective tracts were *Children of the Poor* and *Children of the Tenements,* while John Spargo, echoing *The Bitter Cry of the Children,* told of little girls working 16 hours a day in factories and nine-year-old ' breaker boys ' working ten hours a day picking slate out of moving coal. And Jane Addams's *The Spirit of Youth and the City Streets* was the best argument yet made for playgrounds and parks. Society was aroused and there was a concerted effort to eliminate the grosser abuses of child labor, to protect the health and morals of children. About the turn of the century the movement for community playgrounds gained headway, and soon most of the large cities provided parks and playgrounds to take the children off the streets; by 1915 over 400 cities had opened such playgrounds. Baby clinics and day nurseries were established for the benefit of mothers who had to work; free milk was distributed at milk depots; settlement houses and Visiting Nurses' Associations gave medical care to children; and eventually medical and dental examination became a part of most public school routine.

The problem of juvenile delinquency was an especially vexatious one. At common law, children above seven were held capable of crime, and those above fourteen had the same responsibility as an adult; as late as 1894 these common law principles were incorporated into the penal code of New York. Children were tried by the same laws as were applied to adults and, when convicted, were jailed with adult offenders, and thus schooled in a career of crime. In 1899 Miss Addams persuaded Illinois to establish special courts for children, and soon the institution spread throughout the country. Most notable of those who labored for a more humane attitude toward the juvenile delinquent was Judge Ben Lindsey of the Denver Juvenile Court, whose judicial practices and writings eventually commanded international attention.

The ' emancipation ' of women had proved a mixed blessing; for many, emancipation from the drudgery of the home merely meant a change to the worse drudgery of the sweatshop. The shift from the country home to the city apartment and the declining size of the family circumscribed the domestic activities of women, but when they turned their energies and talents into industry or business or the professions, they found discrimination everywhere. The principle of equal pay for equal work of the two sexes did not yet obtain in business or industry, and women who wished to enter the legal, medical, or clerical professions found themselves at a heavy disadvantage. Scarcely less serious were the legal and political discriminations against women. In few states did married women enjoy the same property rights as men; marriage and divorce laws worked to their economic and social disadvantage; and they were denied that participation in politics whereby they might improve their status. Socially, too, women suffered from discrimination. The strict social and moral codes of the time meant that a double standard of morality was almost everywhere accepted. Even in the field of education women by no means enjoyed the opportunities open as a matter of course to men.

The most spectacular aspect of the struggle for women's rights is that which led to the Nineteenth Amendment (1920) granting woman suffrage. Equally important, however, was the achievement of equality in the schools and in some of the professions, the improvement in the legal status of married women, the reform of marriage and divorce laws, the enactment of legislation regulating the hours and conditions of woman labor, the development of prenatal care and maternity aid, and the growth of the woman's club movement, which not only provided new outlets for the energies and talents of women but created an instrument for bringing their influence to bear on public affairs.

Society's misfits as well as society's wards excited the concern of humanitarians, and particular attention was given to prison and penal reform. Everywhere efforts were made to improve prison conditions, mitigate the penalties of the law, and humanize the administration of justice. Since the 1840's the United States had been peculiarly ' the home of penitentiary science.' Under the leadership of Frederick Wines, the Cincinnati Prison Conference of 1870 inaugurated a new era in penal and prison reform, and within a generation many of the recommendations of that conference had been incorporated into law. Altgeld had written a slashing attack on *Our Penal Machinery and Its Victims* as early as 1884; as Governor of Illinois he did much to reform that machinery and rescue its victims. It was a reading of Altgeld's book that started Clarence Darrow on his life-long career as champion of the underdogs and the misfits of society. The fundamental idea that ' the supreme aim of prison discipline is the reformation of criminals,' was everywhere acknowledged in principle, though rarely in practice. Reformatories were established for juvenile delinquents; first offenders were separated from hardened criminals; the indeterminate sentence and the parole system were widely adopted; state prison farms were established; convict labor and the lease system were outlawed in some states at least; some of the most barbarous features of the penal codes were repealed, and a campaign against capital punishment led to its abolition in several states. The relation of feeble-mindedness to vice and crime was argued by studies such as Dugdale's *The Jukes* and McCulloch's *The Tribe of Ishmael,*

SIXTH AVENUE ELEVATED AT THIRD STREET *by John Sloan*

and eugenicists began to urge the sterilization of the feeble-minded as a policy fundamental to the protection of society.

Most importunate of all the crusades of this generation was that against the Demon Rum. The origins of the temperance movement in the United States date back to the early days of the Republic. Before the Civil War the fight against liquor was carried on through personal appeals for total abstinence. Temperance orators like Neal Dow and John Gough persuaded hundreds of thousands of men and children to 'sign the pledge,' and the Washingtonian Society for reformed drunkards had lodges throughout the country. As early as 1851 the temperance forces had established prohibition in Maine and had won minor victories in other states.

The traffic in liquor was growing by leaps and bounds, investment in the liquor business increased almost sevenfold between 1860 and 1880, and by the end of the century New York, Chicago, St. Louis, and other large cities with heavy Irish and German populations contained one saloon for every 200 inhabitants. Not only was intemperance on the increase, but the liquor business entered everywhere into an alliance with vice and, through the National Protective Association, with politics. It was this development which aroused the temperance workers to renewed efforts. The churches denounced drinking as a sin; women attacked the saloon as a menace to the American home and the welfare of the women and children of the nation; reformers exposed the unholy alliance of the liquor business with crime and the connection between intemperance and poverty; businessmen discovered that drinking affected the efficiency of the workingman and increased the dangers of industrial accidents; while in the South it was urged that Negro sobriety was necessary for the protection of the whites. These various elements represented a public opinion so powerful that it could not long be denied.

The progress of prohibition, as distinct from temperance, was furthered by three well-organized agencies: the Woman's Christian Temperance Union, founded in 1874 and long dominated by Frances Willard; the Anti-Saloon League, founded in Oberlin, Ohio, in 1895 and financed by churches and businessmen; and the Methodist Church, most active of all religious denominations. By the turn of the century these organizations, working through the schools, the press, the church, and politics, had succeeded in drying up five states, all of them predominantly rural. A sixth state, South Carolina, had embarked upon the experiment of a state dispensary system not dissimilar from that subsequently adopted in Sweden, but the experiment did not prove a success. In the first fifteen years of the new century the cause of prohibition advanced with rapid strides, and by the time the United States entered World War I over two-thirds of the states were dry, and almost three-fourths of the population lived under ' local option ' dry laws. The large cities, however, continued to be wet and from them supplies of liquor flowed unimpeded into thirsty dry areas.

The demand for national prohibition arose out of the ease with which liquor could be imported from wet into dry territory and the inadequacy of local enforcement machinery. State legislation restricting the importation of liquor had been held unconstitutional as early as 1888,[2] and subsequent efforts by Congress to delegate to the states control over the interstate liquor traffic proved ineffective. ' The Interstate Commerce Clause,' said the U.S. Attorney-General, ' has been made a weapon of offense by which the liquor producing States have compelled prohibition States to receive intoxicating liquors willy-nilly, and thus have made the endorsement of local prohibition substantially impossible.' To remedy this intolerable situation Congress passed, in 1913, the Webb-Kenyon Act penalizing the shipment of liquor into any state where the sale of such liquor was illegal. During World War I, Congress, allegedly for reasons of national economy and efficiency, prohibited the wartime manufacture or sale of all intoxicants. While this law was still in force Congress wrote prohibition into the Constitution in the form of the Eighteenth Amendment. With a unanimity and promptness unique in our constitutional history up to that time, forty-six of the states ratified the amendment.[3]

The achievements of the humanitarians were impressive, yet much that they did was palliative rather than curative. Increasingly, as one of the reformers confessed, the conviction was becoming more widespread

that poverty would take care of itself if external conditions were made fairly tolerable, if children were not put at work prematurely, if exploitation of employees and purchasers were impossible, if sanitary homes were insured, if congestion . . . were controlled, if preventable diseases and

---

[2] *Bowman v. Chicago & Northwestern R.R.* 125 U.S. 465; and *Leisy v. Hardin* 135 U.S. 100.

[3] For the subsequent history of prohibition, see Chap. XXIII.

accidents were prevented . . . if savings were safe, and schools provided an education, the police gave protection, the courts administered justice and charities relief.[4]

There was a growing impatience among the reformers themselves and they concentrated upon consequences rather than upon the causes of the social and economic malaise. The changing attitude is illustrated in the career of one of the most distinguished of the social workers, Josephine Shaw Lowell. Founder of the New York Charity Organization Society, active in work for dependent children, for delinquent girls, and for the insane, she decided finally to withdraw from much of this work. Explaining her decision to resign from the State Board of Charities, she wrote:

If the working people had all they ought to have, we should not have the paupers and the criminals. It is better to save them before they go under than to spend your life fishing them out when they're half drowned and taking care of them afterwards.

It was as a result of this more realistic attitude toward the problem of social reform that progressives turned from organized charity and humanitarianism to political and legislative action. The progressive movement in municipal, state, and national politics was associated at every point with the program of the social reformers.

5. PROGRESSIVISM IN POLITICS

In its political manifestations the progressive movement was directed toward a broader democracy and a greater efficiency in administration. It is clear that the reformers, however acute their disappointment in the actual functioning of political and economic institutions, were not inclined to despair of democracy. There was none of that tendency, so marked in European nations, to achieve order at the cost of liberty, to substitute efficient dictatorship for inefficient popular government. On the contrary most of the progressives had a boundless faith in the efficacy of democracy, and for all the ailments that assailed American institutions their panacea was more democracy. The abandonment of traditional doctrines of laissez faire in favor of the principle of governmental regulation revealed

---

[4] Edward T. Devine, quoted in F. D. Watson, *Charity Organization Movement in the United States*, p. 331.

not so much a disillusionment with liberty as a new confidence in government, and the growth of federal centralization pointed in the same direction. Yet the progressives were acutely aware that the administrative machinery inherited from a simpler age had broken down under the weight of new burdens, and they directed their energies toward the creation of more adequate administrative machinery and the formulation of a science of government. The effort to achieve democracy took the form of agitation for woman suffrage, the Australian ballot, direct primaries, direct election of Senators, the initiative, referendum and recall, municipal home rule, and governmental regulation of railroads, utilities, labor, banking, and finance. The attempt to improve administrative efficiency took the form of agitation for civil service reform, the short ballot, regulation of campaign expenditures, executive leadership, tax reform, and the commission and city manager plan for municipal government.

In the arena of national politics, the progressive movement was organized by Bryan and LaFollette, Roosevelt and Wilson. Bryan inherited much of his progressivism from the Populists, with whom he was early affiliated, and throughout his long political career he ceaselessly advocated the extension of governmental regulation over business, and the adoption of ' anything that makes the government more democratic, more popular in form, anything that gives the people more control over the government.' LaFollette, working through the state university, made Wisconsin an experimental laboratory for progressive ideas and, in the Senate, applied those ideas to the problems of national politics. Roosevelt made a reputation as a reformer by his support of trust and railway regulation, civil service reform, the ' square deal ' for labor, and the conservation of natural resources, and in 1912 he named his new organization the ' Progressive Party ' and adopted the whole of the reform program indicated above. Wilson announced that society stood ready to attempt a ' radical reconstruction ' and that ' political society may itself undergo a radical modification in the process.' Originally a Manchester liberal, and sharing Louis Brandeis's distrust of ' big government,' he came to adopt a good part of the program of nationalism, and, as President, wrote much of it into the federal statute books.

It was in state and municipal politics that the progressives achieved some of their most notable results. The constitutions of the Omnibus States had incorporated many of the items of the reform program, and the constitutions of Oklahoma, New Mexico, and Arizona went even further in this direction. Some of the older state constitutions were thoroughly revised; others were liberalized by amendments, over 900 of which were adopted in the first two decades of the new century. South Dakota in 1898, Utah in 1900, and Oregon in 1902 adopted the initiative and referendum, and by the time of the First World War over 20 states had provided in some form or other for the use of these devices. In 1908 Oregon committed itself to the re-call, and within six years its example was followed by ten states, all west of the Mississippi but one. At first confined to executive officers, the recall was extended by Arizona to judges, and by Colorado to judicial decisions, and this latter application of the recall received the approval of Roosevelt in his presidential campaign of 1912. The campaign for direct primaries was even more successful. Governor LaFollette, who had been twice defeated for the governorship by a boss-ridden convention, persuaded Wisconsin to adopt this reform in 1903; Oregon followed in 1905, and within a decade two-thirds of the states had enacted direct primary and presidential preference laws. Yet the direct primary, which had aroused the enthusiasm of LaFollette and Roosevelt and Wilson, proved a distinct disappointment, for professional politicians quickly found ways to control the primaries, and by 1912 one advocate of the plan confessed that 'some bosses are wondering why they feared the law, and some reformers why they favored it.' No such dissatisfaction followed the adoption of the Australian or secret ballot which soon became universal. More popular than any of these was the demand for the direct election of Senators. Like so many of the progressive reforms, this one had its origins in the Populist movement of the 'nineties. As early as 1899 Nevada formulated a method for circumventing the constitutional requirement of election by state legislatures, and by 1912 some thirty states had provided for the expression of popular opinion in the choice of Senators. The Seventeenth Amendment, ratified in 1913, was therefore rather a recognition of an accomplished fact than an innovation.

From New York to California reform governors gave their support not only to these measures but to enlarging the scope of governmental control over business. Charles Evans Hughes, elected Governor of New York after exposing spectacular corruption in the great insurance companies, obtained the establishment of a public utilities commission; Woodrow Wilson in New Jersey pushed through almost the whole progressive program and made that state, temporarily, a model of administrative efficiency and democracy. In Illinois John Peter Altgeld reformed the penal code, the prisons, and the eleemosynary institutions and fought the Yerkes interests that were trying to secure a perpetual franchise for the street railways in Chicago. In Wisconsin Robert LaFollette broke the power of the bosses, regulated railroads and public utilities, reorganized the system of taxation, established an industrial commission, made the state university an effective instrument of the social and economic regeneration of the state, and reconstructed the administration along more democratic lines. Hazen Pingree in Michigan, Albert Cummins in Iowa, and Hiram Johnson in California shattered the domination of the railways over state politics and brought the roads under strict governmental supervision. Even the South was not immune from the contagion of reform. Charles B. Aycock made North Carolina into the most progressive of Southern commonwealths, Charles A. Culberson brought Texas into the main current of the reform movement, and ' Alfalfa Bill ' Murray, who had played a leading role in the Constitutional Convention of 1907, made Oklahoma for a brief time an experimental laboratory of Bryan democracy.

The same story can be repeated for municipal as for state politics. From Boston to San Francisco party bosses had captured control of city governments and used them for purposes of party advantage and personal gain. Venality, maladministration, and extravagance were the order of the day. Vice and crime were protected, public utility franchises sold for a song, and government was handed over to groups of cutthroats who had no interest but to serve themselves and their henchmen. Lord Bryce, in his *American Commonwealth,* observed that municipal government was the one conspicuous failure of American democracy, and the revelations of Lincoln Steffens and his fellow muckrakers abundantly substantiated this generalization. Corruption played a large part in the breakdown of municipal government, but it was not the whole of the story. The framework of American municipal governments had been designed for smaller and simpler communities and few cities were prepared to undertake the new tasks of traffic, lighting, sanitation, fire prevention, policing, education, and other costly and complex functions which the great cities demanded. Nor were the cities always able to adapt their administrations to these new duties.

The ills from which our cities suffer [wrote Brand Whitlock, reform mayor of Toledo] are not the ills incident to democracy; they are ills incident to a lack of democracy. The American city is not fundamentally democratic, because it is governed from without. . . . Cities are ruled by legislatures from the State capital; they are governed, that is, by men from the country who know nothing of city problems or city life, and have indeed no real conception of just what cities need. In league with them . . . are the public utility corporations and political machines. The first requisite, therefore, for municipal reform, is home rule.[5]

It was for municipal home rule that men like Brand Whitlock of Toledo and Tom Johnson of Cleveland fought, but their efforts were only partially successful, and most large American cities today suffer from absentee government and from gross under-representation in state legislatures.

Far more spectacular was the revolt against the boss rule and corruption which Steffens had described. Tom Johnson, a wealthy manufacturer who had come under the influence of Henry George, rescued Cleveland from the grip of the utilities and the domination of Mark Hanna and made it, for a time, the best governed city in the country. He left as his disciples two young men who later figured prominently in national politics: Frederic Howe and Newton D. Baker. In Toledo, Ohio, ' Golden Rule ' Jones administered the city in accordance with his interpretation of the Golden Rule, and after his death Brand Whitlock carried on the work of reform — including municipal ownership of public utilities — in the same spirit and with even more acute understanding of the nature of the problem of municipal government. Emil Seidel, Socialist mayor of Milwaukee, gave that city a government as efficient and honest as was the government of the state. In Jersey City Mark Fagan fought the corrupt alliance of bosses and utility interests, and in San Francisco Fremont Older exposed the skulduggery of a political ring controlled by the president of the Union Pacific. Even New York, under mayors like Seth Low and John Purroy Mitchell, lapsed into respectability, only to repent and reinstate the Tammany Tiger.

More fundamental than these crusades against corruption were the

[5] *The Letters of Brand Whitlock,* edited by Allan Nevins, p. 114.

efforts to find a permanent solution to the vexatious problems of city government. The merit system was extended into municipal administration, and bureaus of municipal research inaugurated the study of the science of municipal government. Various schemes to divorce city government from politics were proposed, and two eventually found wide favor: the city manager and the city commission plans. Both plans were first adopted as a result of emergencies that necessitated honest and efficient administration. The commission plan grew out of the Galveston flood of 1900; adopted with modifications by Houston, Texas, and Des Moines, Iowa, it was soon widely copied throughout the country. The council-manager plan was Dayton's solution for a similar crisis — the Dayton flood of 1913. Both forms made rapid progress in the early years of the century, especially in cities of medium size. By 1940, some 332 cities had adopted the commission form of government, and 315 cities the council-manager.

Much of this progressive zeal was naïve, some of it was misguided. The reformers were fundamentally moralists, and progressivism adopted a moral approach to politics. It assumed that most of the failings of government could be ascribed to Bad Men — bosses, spoilsmen, vested interests, malefactors of great wealth — and it assumed, too, that if only Men of Good Will would devote themselves to public service, all would be well. There were no evils in politics that would not yield to intelligence and morality — to throwing the Rascals out and putting the Honest Men in. Progressivism had a touching faith, too, in mechanical contrivances like the initiative and referendum, or the direct primary, or the short ballot — even Wilson, who was more realistic than many of his followers, once said that the ' short ballot was the key to the whole problem of the restoration of popular government in this country.' The progressive ideal was really that which Bryan never ceased to expound — the independent yeoman, the honest shopkeeper, the sturdy workingman, law-abiding and God-fearing, who did his duty and did not exploit his fellow man. The reformers put their faith, too, in moral gestures and clichés, even in the international arena: thus the New Nationalism, or the New Freedom, or the Open Door, or Making the World Safe for Democracy.

It is a mistake, of course, to exaggerate their naïveté: much of what seems naïve to us was merely a matter of vocabulary. Reformers like Jane Addams, Lincoln Steffens, Louis Brandeis, and Robert La-

Follette were certainly as hard-headed as any of their successors. If their faith failed to move mountains, it did remove many of the obstacles in the way of effective popular government; if their achievements never quite came up to expectations, they were far from negligible. Insofar as politics was more honest, the economy more just, society more enlightened, in 1914 than in 1890, much of the credit goes to the embattled and indefatigable progressives.

6. The Struggle for Negro Rights: Washington and DuBois

The most conspicuous failure of the progressive movement was in the area of race relations. After the arduous struggle for abolition, the convulsions of war, and the confusions of Reconstruction — which somehow associated the cause of the freed man with Radicalism and Grantism — Northern liberals wearied of the Negro problem and turned to more manageable issues. Southerners who were ' liberal ' on the race question — like the novelist George Washington Cable — found it healthier to go North. Worse yet, in the decade of the 'nineties and the early years of the new century, Southern progressives themselves often exploited the race issue in their appeal to tenant farmers and mill workers; men like Tom Watson of Georgia, Ben Tillman of South Carolina, and Josephus Daniels of North Carolina, who on most matters went along with Bryan and LaFollette, readily sacrificed the Negro to their political ambitions.

Clearly then it was up to the Negro to fend for himself. Two schools of thought emerged, one represented by Booker T. Washington of Tuskeegee Institute in Alabama, the other by the Massachusetts-born W. E. B. DuBois of Atlanta University. The issues these two towering figures raised, the controversies they agitated, the programs they sponsored, have dominated Negro thought and thought about the Negro to this day.

Born in slavery, raised in abject poverty, catching an education as best he could at the new Hampton Institute in Virginia, Booker T. Washington came to be in truth the Washington of his people, the most distinguished leader of his race since Frederick Douglass, and one of the most influential men in the country between Reconstruction and the First World War. Persuaded that the Negro must win economic independence before he could expect to command social or political equality, Washington opened the Tuskeegee Normal and Industrial School for Negroes in 1881, with the object of teaching the Negroes habits of work and of thrift and of good citizenship.

About eighty-five per cent of the colored people in the Gulf States [he wrote] depended upon agriculture for their living. Since this was true we wanted to be careful not to educate our students out of sympathy with agricultural life, so that they would be attracted from the country to the cities and yield to the temptation of trying to live by their wits. We wanted to give them such an education as would fit a large proportion of them to return to the plantation districts and show the people there how to put new energy and new ideas into farming as well as into the intellectual and moral and religious life of the people.

Over a period of almost forty years Washington counseled progress by evolution rather than by agitation or violence, temporary acquiescence in policies of segregation, and co-operation with the ruling white class. ' In all things that are purely social,' he said, in a notable speech at the Atlanta Cotton Exposition of 1895, ' we can be as separate as the fingers, yet one as the hand in all things essential to mutual progress.' The rapt whites who applauded the new dispensation failed to note the qualification: ' purely ' social. To win his immediate objectives of economic progress Washington was prepared to forego not only agitation for the vote, but for social equality as well. ' The wisest among my race,' he said, ' understand that the agitation of questions of social equality is the extremest folly and that progress in the enjoyment of all privileges that will come must be the result of severe and constant struggle rather than artificial feeding.' This philosophy won the enthusiastic support of the white community, and with that support Washington was able to fix the pattern of race relations for most of his lifetime. In time he came to command the confidence of Presidents, who consulted him about patronage; he influenced newspaper editors throughout the country; and he interested Northern philanthropy in the betterment of the Negro.

At the beginning of the century the young W. E. B. DuBois, trained at Harvard and Berlin, challenged this Washingtonian program of compromise and concession.

So far as Mr. Washington apologizes for injustice, North or South, does not rightly value the privilege and duty of voting, belittles the emasculating effects of caste distinctions, and opposes the higher training and ambition of our brighter minds — so far as he, the South, or the Nation does this — we must unceasingly and firmly oppose him. By every civilized and peaceful method we must strive for the rights which the world accords to men.

It was folly, said DuBois, to suppose that Negroes could ever win economic security without the vote, or achieve self-respect as long as they acquiesced in a position of inferiority, or attain true equality as long as they preferred vocational to intellectual training. In 1905 DuBois and his followers met at Niagara Falls to inaugurate what came to be called the Niagara Movement, designed to impose a very different solution for the Negro problem. The Niagara platform, as elaborated at subsequent meetings, asserted that

We want the laws enforced against rich as well as poor; against Capitalist as well as Laborer; against white as well as black. We are not more lawless than the white race, we are more often arrested, convicted, and mobbed. . . . We want the Constitution of the country enforced. We want Congress to take charge of Congressional elections . . . We want the Fourteenth Amendment carried out to the letter. . . .

Three years later, in 1909, with the aid of distinguished reformers like John Dewey, Jane Addams, Joel Spingarn, and Moorfield Storey of Boston, the Niagara group founded the National Association for the Advancement of Colored People which for the next half-century was the spearhead of the struggle for Negro rights.

The creation of the NAACP in a sense marked the victory of the DuBois over the Washington philosophy. Yet the passing years showed how deeply indebted the Negro was to both of these great leaders. The struggle of the 1950's vindicated DuBois's argument that the vote was essential to economic progress, but also Washington's contention that economic pressure could be the most persuasive of arguments.

BIBLIOGRAPHY

1. GENERAL. Thomas N. Carver, *Essays in Social Justice;* Herbert Croly, *Progressive Democracy* and *The Promise of American Life;* Chester M. Destler, *American Radicalism 1865–1901;* B. P. De Witt, *The Progressive Movement;* Joseph Dorfman, *Economic Mind in American Civilization,* vol. 3, and *Thorstein Veblen and His America;* Louis Filler, *Crusaders for American Liberalism;* Thomas H. Greer, *American Reform Movements since 1865;* Richard Hofstadter, *The Age of Reform: From Bryan to F.D.R.;* Matthew Josephson, *The President Makers;* Edward C. Kirkland, *Industry Comes of Age: Business, Labor and Pub-*

lic Policy; Arthur Mann, *Yankee Reformers in the Urban Age;* Charles E. Merriam, *American Political Ideas 1865–1917;* V. L. Parrington, *The Beginnings of Critical Realism in America;* C. C. Regier, *The Era of the Muckrakers;* Arthur M. Schlesinger, *The Rise of the City* and *The American Reformer.*

2. POLITICAL REFORM AND ERA OF THE MUCKRAKERS. Claude Bowers, *Beveridge and the Progressive Era;* R. C. Brooks, *Corruption in American Politics and Life;* James Bryce, *The American Commonwealth,* part V; Edward N. Doan, *The LaFollettes and the Wisconsin Idea;* A. H. Eaton, *The Oregon System;* D. D. Egbert & Stow Persons (eds.), *Socialism and American Life* (2 vols.); Elmer Ellis, *Mr. Dooley's America: Life of Finley Peter Dunne;* Louis Filler, *Crusaders for American Liberalism;* Edward A. Fitzpatrick, *McCarthy of Wisconsin;* W. A. Flint, *The Progressive Movement in Vermont;* W. D. Foulke, *Fighting the Spoilsmen;* Carter Harrison, *Stormy Years;* Fred E. Haynes, *Third Party Movements in the United States;* Fred Howe, *Wisconsin: An Experiment in Democracy* and *The City, the Hope of Democracy;* Ira Kipnis, *The American Socialist Movement 1897–1912;* A. D. Kirwan, *The Revolt of the Rednecks: Mississippi Politics 1876–1925;* B. C. and L. LaFollette, *Robert M. LaFollette* (2 vols.); C. C. McCarthy, *The Wisconsin Idea;* G. E. Mowry, *The Era of Theodore Roosevelt;* R. E. Noble, *New Jersey Progressivism before Wilson;* C. W. Patton, *The Fight for Municipal Reform;* Henry F. Pringle, *Theodore Roosevelt;* Howard Quint, *The Forging of American Socialism;* C. C. Regier, *The Era of the Muckrakers;* D. A. Shannon, *The Socialist Party of America;* Lincoln Steffens, *The Shame of the Cities* and *Autobiography;* Arthur and Lila Weinberg (eds.), *The Muckrakers: An Anthology;* Brand Whitlock, *Forty Years of It;* Harold Zink, *City Bosses.*

3. HUMANITARIAN REFORM. Edith Abbott, *The Tenements of Chicago 1908–1935;* Jane Addams, *Forty Years at Hull House;* W. D. P. Bliss (ed.), *New Encyclopedia of Social Reform;* Robert H. Bremner, *From the Depths: The Discovery of Poverty in the United States;* Merle Curti, *The Peace Crusade;* R. D. DeForest & L. Veiller, *The Tenement House Problem;* Paul Kellogg, *The Pittsburgh Survey;* Josephine Shaw Lowell, *Public Relief and Private Charity;* Jacob Riis, *The Battle with the Slum* and *Out of Mulberry Street;* Arthur M. Schlesinger, *The Rise of the City;* Lillian Wald, *The House on Henry Street* and *Windows on Henry Street;* F. D. Watson, *The Charity Organization Movement in the U.S.;* Robert A. Woods, *The City Wilderness: A Settlement Study;* Robert A. Woods & A. J. Kennedy, *The Settlement Horizon;* Winifred E. Wose, *Jane Addams of Hull House.*

4. THE STRUGGLE FOR NEGRO RIGHTS. B. G. Brawley, *Social History of the Negro;* George W. Cable, *The Silent South* and *The Negro Question;* W. J. Cash, *The Mind of the South;* W. E. B. DuBois, *Dusk of Dawn, The Philadelphia Negro, Color and Democracy,* and *The Souls of Black Folk;* Eli Ginzberg (ed.), *The Negro Potential;* Alain Locke, *The New Negro: An Interpretation;* Rayford W. Logan (ed.), *What the Negro Wants;* Basil Matthews, *Booker T. Washington;* Gunnar Myrdal, *An American Dilemma* (2 vols.); Saunders Redding, *The Lonesome Road;* Booker T. Washington, *Up From Slavery* and *The Story of the Negro;* Walter White, *How Far the Promised Land?;* Vann Woodward, *Strange Career of Jim Crow.*

5. BIOGRAPHIES AND PERSONAL LITERATURE. Daniel Aaron, *Men of Good Hope: A Story of American Progressives;* Jane Addams, *My Friend Julia Lathrop;* Oscar Ameringer, *If You Don't Weaken;* Ray Stannard Baker, *An American Chronicle;* Charles Barker, *Henry George;* Claude Bowers, *Beveridge and the Progressive Era;* John R. Commons, *Myself;* Joseph Dorfman, *Thorstein Veblen and his America;* George P. Geiger, *Philosophy of Henry George;* Josephine Goldman, *Impatient Crusader: Florence Kelley;* Frederic Howe, *Confessions of a Reformer;* Tom Johnson, *My Story;* Ben Lindsey, *The Beast;* Arthur E. Morgan, *Philosophy of Edward Bellamy;* Fremont Older, *My Story;* Theodore Roosevelt, *Autobiography;* Lincoln Steffens, *Autobiography* (2 vols.) ; Mary Heaton Vorse, *A Footnote to Folly;* William Allen White, *Autobiography;* Brand Whitlock, *Forty Years of It.*

6. IMAGINATIVE LITERATURE. Henry Adams, *Democracy;* Winston Churchill, *Coniston* and *Mr. Crewe's Career;* Jon W. DeForest, *Honest John Vane;* Theodore Dreiser, *The Titan* and *The Financier;* Paul L. Ford, *The Honorable Peter Stirling;* Edgar Lee Masters, *A Spoon River Anthology;* David G. Phillips, *The Plum Tree;* Booth Tarkington, *In the Arena;* Mark Twain, *The Gilded Age;* W. A. White, *A Certain Rich Man* and *The Quality of Mercy;* Brand Whitlock, *The Thirteenth District* and *The Turn of the Balance;* Richard Wright, *Native Son.*

7. SOURCES AND DOCUMENTS. C. A. Beard & B. E. Shultz, *Documents on Initiative, Referendum and Recall;* H. S. Commager, *Documents,* nos. 301, 313, 371, 376, 384, 406, 407, 432, 433; R. W. Logan (ed.), *The Negro in the United States;* Arthur and Lila Weinberg, *The Muckrakers: An Anthology.*

For further references, *Harvard Guide,* ¶¶ 212–15.

The Reign of Roosevelt

1. THEODORE ROOSEVELT

WHEN McKinley had been renominated to the presidency in 1900, the Republican Old Guard had named as his running mate the brilliant and bellicose young Governor of New York, Theodore Roosevelt. This action was dictated by three considerations: the desire to strengthen the ticket, the desire to head off Roosevelt's ambitions in national politics, and the desire to fill the New York governorship with a pliable figurehead. With a show of reluctance which was probably sincere, Roosevelt accepted the nomination to this high but inconspicuous office and the political oblivion that it usually meant, and prepared to study law for a professional career. But President McKinley was shot by an anarchist on 6 September 1901, six months after his second inauguration. Eight days later he died, and Theodore Roosevelt became President of the United States.

Roosevelt at forty-three was the youngest by several years in the line of Presidents; yet few have been better equipped to administer the office. Building on a broad paternal inheritance of wealth, culture, and public service, he had already achieved prominence as a naturalist, a man of letters, a soldier, and a statesman. He had served his political apprenticeship as a member of the New York State Assembly and, later, as Civil Service Commissioner under Harrison and Cleveland, and in both capacities, he had identified himself with the reform element of his party. In between he had found time to write the four-volume *Winning of the West,* and to win a bit of it himself as a Dakota ranchman. In 1895 he had returned to New York City and accepted the thankless post of Police Commissioner. His achievements up to this point were more sensational than permanent, but this work served to throw him into intimate contact with the social reformers and to give him a lasting sympathy with the underprivileged. Two years later McKinley was persuaded to offer him the position of Assistant Secretary of the Navy, but this office proved too confining for his ebullient energies and with the outbreak of the Spanish War he organized the famous Rough Riders and fought his way to fame and glory at San Juan Hill. Elected Governor of New York in 1898 on his return from war, he had struck at corruption in that state with such vigor that in self-defense Boss Platt and the machine politicians had boomed him for the vice-presidency. His accession to the presidency, regarded with dismay by the conservatives of his party,[1] inaugurated a new era in American politics in which his personality was a decisive factor.

No American of his time was more national in his interests or universal in his friendships than was Roosevelt. University men and the well-to-do in the Eastern states regarded him as one of themselves. He had identified himself with the West by ranching in the Bad Lands of Dakota, leading the Rough Riders, and writing Western history. The South remembered that his Bulloch uncles had been warriors in the Lost Cause. People everywhere knew him as a red-blooded, democratic American whose every action showed good sportsmanship and dynamic vitality. Impetuous, temperamental, pugnacious, brilliant, Roosevelt promised to be the most colorful personality in American politics, and within a short time he had amply fulfilled that promise.

Like Bryan and Wilson, Roosevelt was a moralist in politics, a crusader for righteousness. Elihu Root accused him of imagining that he had discovered the Ten Commandments, and others remarked his tendency to see all questions as moral issues. His morality was positive, but not subtle; he was never in doubt as to the right or wrong of any question, and he regarded those who differed with him as either scoundrels or fools. His habit of injecting moral considerations into political and economic questions served to dramatize the need for reform, but tended to confuse rather than to clarify the problems with which he coped. He was a man of fixed convictions and implacable prejudices, but political realism and a positive talent for opportunism saved him from becoming doctrinaire. He was an

[1] H. H. Kohlsaat tells of riding in the McKinley funeral train with Mark Hanna. ' He was in an intensely bitter state of mind. He damned Roosevelt and said, " I told William McKinley it was a mistake to nominate that wild man at Philadelphia. I asked him if he realized what would happen if he should die. Now look, that damned cowboy is President of the United States." ' *McKinley to Harding*, p. 101.

ardent nationalist, but his idea of nationalism was to some extent a matter of flags and martial airs. He was a faithful Republican, looked upon Democrats with deep suspicion and, until he himself bolted his party in 1912, upon bolters with positive loathing. He was a sincere progressive, but his progressivism was circumscribed by a limited understanding of economics. He was a thorough democrat, but his democracy was a matter of intellectual conviction rather than of instinct, and he was always faintly embarrassed by his patrician background. He took a just pride in his versatility and in the catholicity of his taste: he could lasso a bucking steer, turn out an historical essay, hunt lions, run a political convention, play tennis, lead a regiment, and hypnotize an audience with equal facility; he could hold his own in the company of cowboys, ward politicians, Methodist clergymen, newspaper reporters, foreign diplomats, and Henry Adams. He read widely, and his judgments on questions of literature and science were as dogmatic as his judgments on questions of politics and morals. He had a talent for friendship, and commanded a loyalty as near to hero-worship as that which was given to Bryan, and more personal. Wonderfully energetic, bubbling over with good spirits, fascinating in private intercourse, and magnetic in public, he communicated to the American people something of his own wholesome enthusiasm for morality, his own zest for ' the strenuous life.' In time the legend grew that Roosevelt was the ' typical American.' Actually he was less typical, in background, in character, in mind, than Bryan or LaFollette or Wilson, but he was more exciting than any of them.

Roosevelt's genuine progressivism was always qualified by his distaste for most progressives. His own program was general rather than specific, moral rather than realistic. He advocated ' trust-busting,' but his moral sense led him to distinguish between ' good ' trusts and ' bad ' trusts, and actually the trusts were more powerfully entrenched when he left than when he entered office. He espoused more effective railway regulation, but was unwilling to support measures which might have made such regulation possible. He denounced ' malefactors of great wealth ' but was critical of the ' muckrakers ' who exposed their malefactions, and took no positive steps to curb individual fortunes or to secure a more equitable distribution of wealth through taxation. He demanded a ' square deal ' for labor, but no one in the country was more vitriolic in his denunciation of men like Altgeld, Debs, and Bryan, who tried to inaugurate the ' square deal.' He dramatized popular issues and avoided dangerous ones such as tariff and banking reform; and even on those issues to which he had committed himself, like trust and railway regulation, pure food, and labor reform, he was usually ready to compromise on ' half a loaf ' rather than risk a break with the Old Guard of his party. His chief service to the progressive cause was to dramatize the movement and make it respectable. Yet Roosevelt's dramatics often distracted attention from the big tent to the side shows, and his respectability required a conformity that seriously impaired the integrity of a reform movement. After the seven years of tumult and shouting had passed, many reformers came to feel that they had been fighting a sham battle and that the citadels of privilege were yet to be invested.

2. THE TRUSTS

' It shall be my aim,' said the new President immediately upon his accession to office, ' to continue absolutely unbroken the policy of President McKinley for the peace, prosperity and honor of our beloved country.' But aside from reciprocity, in which Roosevelt had no interest, McKinley had formulated no policy except that of standing pat, and it was inconceivable that Roosevelt should emulate him in this. Indeed, despite this gesture of respect, it was clear that Roosevelt's conception of the presidency was utterly different from McKinley's. McKinley had been willing to follow the leadership of Congress, but Roosevelt believed in executive leadership and gave an exhibition of it that recalled Andrew Jackson and anticipated his own cousin Franklin. According to his conception of the presidency, ' it was not only his right but his duty to do anything that the needs of the Nation demanded, unless such action was forbidden by the Constitution or by the laws,' and he soon indicated his conviction that the needs of the nation were multifarious. McKinley had been content to let well enough alone in business and politics, but Roosevelt was acutely discontented with existing practices in both, and demanded reform all along the line. In his first message to Congress he gave the country a sample of his political program: the regulation of trusts, railroads, and banks, the creation of a Department of Commerce, new immigration legislation, more conservation, irrigation and reclamation, improvement of the merchant marine, a larger army and navy, construction of an isthmian canal, civil service reform, more generous support to the Smithsonian Institution and the Library of Congress, reform in the consular service and the Indian service, and fifteen or twenty additional items.

What particularly arrested the attention of the country was the demand for a more effective enforcement of the anti-trust laws and for additional legislation empowering the Federal Government to regulate all corporations engaged in interstate business. It was clear that the Sherman law had neither retarded the growth of trusts and monopolies nor stamped out the abuses which accompanied such growth. The revival of prosperity after the Spanish War, indeed, had been the occasion of a frenzy of consolidation that threatened to give control of business development to a few powerful interests. A governmental investigation of 1900 revealed the existence of 185 manufacturing combinations, with a total capitalization of over $3 billion. Seventy-three of these trusts had a capitalization in excess of $10 million. Four years later John Moody surveying the scene discovered a total of 318 manufacturing combinations with a total capitalization of over $7 billion — altogether some two-fifths of the manufacturing capital in the country. As 184 of these trusts had been organized since 1898, it was clear that anti-trust laws were not taken seriously. This process of consolidation was even more marked in the realm of transportation, the control and exploitation of natural resources, and especially of finance. Gradually in the course of the first decade of the century, horizontal consolidations and vertical combinations came under the control of great banking houses located for the most part in New York City. The Houses of Morgan, Rockefeller, Vanderbilt, and Baker came to exercise an influence over the economic life of the nation comparable to that of the Houses of Bardi and of Fugger in the age of the Renaissance. Moody struck a popular note when he concluded that ' viewed as a whole, we find the dominating influences in the trusts to be made up of an intricate network of large and small capitalists, many allied to one another by ties of more or less importance but all being appendaged to or parts of the greater groups which are themselves dependent on and allied with the two mammoth, or Rockefeller and Morgan groups. These two mammoth groups jointly . . . constitute the heart of the business and commercial life of the nation.' [2]

2 John Moody, *The Truth about the Trusts*, p. 493.

In many cases the merger of competing or complementary industries marked a technical advance. But trust methods, however suitable for industries such as meat packing and oil refining, were also extended to others where they were less suitable; and the economies of mass production were not often shared with laborer or consumer. The United States Steel Corporation combined the already swollen corporations of Gates, Rockefeller, Carnegie, and others in a trust capitalized at $1400 million, of which nearly one-half was water, and nearly one-tenth was issued to promoters for their services. Prices were maintained, although 10 to 12 per cent was being earned on the real capitalization, and the wages of steel workers were kept down by importing cheap labor from southern Europe. The great insurance companies of New York, instead of reducing premiums for their policyholders, paid salaries of $100,000 or more to executives who were often mere figureheads, used their profits recklessly to form industrial consolidations, and corruptly to influence legislation. E. H. Harriman purchased the bankrupt Union Pacific Railway in 1893 with reserve funds of the Illinois Central system that he controlled, and made it one of the best railways in the country; but other lines which he absorbed were sucked dry and cast aside after the stockholders had been ruined. J. Pierpont Morgan, successful in reorganizing railroads and savings banks, came a cropper when at the end of his career he tried to unite all the transportation lines of New England under one management; his effort to consolidate the major transatlantic steamship companies into the International Mercantile Marine was equally disastrous to the stockholders.

As the Sherman law had not been effectively invoked against these practices either by the Cleveland or the McKinley administrations, the public suspected corrupt collusion, and labor threatened to leave the guidance of Gompers for some more revolutionary dispensation, such as that offered by the Socialist leader 'Gene Debs. Roosevelt himself pointed out that ' the power of the mighty industrial overlords of the country had increased with giant strides, while the methods of controlling them . . . through the government, remained archaic.' Much the same thing, to be sure, was going on in England and in Europe, but not to such an extent. The American theater was so vast, and American resources so boundless, that financial or industrial consolidations found richer materials to work with. American financiers and industrialists were more sanguine and audacious than their transatlantic contemporaries; and the American government was decentralized, constantly changing in personnel, lacking organic strength and administrative traditions.

Roosevelt proceeded with caution and circumspection. He had not come into power as an opposition leader, but was President ' by act of God,' and titular head of the party of big business. To most Republican leaders the election of 1900 appeared a mandate to let business alone, and Roosevelt knew that no one of the four Vice-Presidents who had previously succeeded to the presidency had obtained the party nomination at the next election. He knew too, however, that the conscience of the people was aroused and their temper ripe for action. He tried to steer his way cautiously between laissez faire and socialism, to differentiate between trusts and monopolies, and to distinguish between the use and the abuse of corporations, and he had the common sense to see that the problem was complicated. ' In dealing with the big corporations we call trusts,' he said in 1902, ' we must resolutely purpose to proceed by evolution and not by revolution. . . . Our aim is not to do away with corporations; on the contrary these big aggregations are an inevitable development of modern industrialism. . . . We can do nothing of good in the way of regulating and supervising these corporations until we fix clearly in our minds that we are not attacking the corporations, but endeavoring to do away with any evil in them. We are not hostile to them; we are merely determined that they shall be so handled as to subserve the public good.' [3] To this end the President recommended the creation of a Department of Commerce, and a thorough investigation of the business of corporations. Both recommendations were accepted by Congress. In 1903 a Department of Commerce and Labor was established with cabinet rank, and a Bureau of Corporations was authorized to investigate the operations and conduct of interstate corporations. At first the new bureau was innocuous, but even-

---

[3] Roosevelt's practice of arguing both sides of this question inspired one of Mr. Dooley's happiest comments: ' " Th' thrusts " says he [Roosevelt], " are heejous monsthers built up by th' inlightened intherprise ov th' men that have done so much to advance progress in our beloved counthry," he says. " On wan hand I wud stamp them undher fut; on th' other hand, not so fast. What I want more thin th' bustin' iv th' thrusts is to see me fellow counthrymen happy an' continted. I wudden't have thim hate th' thrusts. Th' haggard face, th' droopin' eye, th' pallid complexion that marks th' inimy iv thrusts is not to me taste. Lave us be merry about it an' jovial an' affectionate. Lave us laugh an' sing th' octopus out iv ixistence." '

tually it investigated the oil, packing, tobacco, steel, and other industries and furnished material for prosecution under the anti-trust laws.

More dramatic was Roosevelt's decision to re-invigorate the Sherman law. ' As far as the Anti-Trust Laws go,' he announced, ' they will be enforced . . . and when suit is undertaken it will not be compromised except upon the basis that the Government wins.' In 1902 he shocked Wall Street by instructing Attorney-General Philander C. Knox to enter suit against the Northern Securities Company, a consolidation of the Hill-Morgan and the Harriman railways which embraced the Northern Pacific, the Great Northern, and the Chicago, Burlington and Quincy systems. Morgan and Hanna hurried to Washington to dissuade the President, but their intervention was futile.[4] Nor was their distinguished counsel more successful in the Supreme Court. By a five to four vote the Court sustained the government and overruled its previous decision in the E. C. Knight case,[5] thereby stopping a process of consolidation that Harriman proposed to continue until every important railway in the country came under his control. To Chief Justice White's lament that the parallel between the Knight and the Northern Securities cases was complete, Roosevelt replied that Mr. Justice White ' was entirely correct. . . . It was necessary to reverse the Knight case in the interests of the people against monopoly and privilege just as it had been necessary to reverse the Dred Scott case in the interest of the people against slavery.' This decision gave a serious setback to the use of the holding company device for the consolidation of businesses, aroused consternation in financial circles,[6] proved to the nation that industrial magnates were not immune from the law, and enormously enhanced the popularity of the President.

The trusts needed regulation more than dissolution, but Roosevelt was unable to get any legislation from Congress in the right direction. Bills initiated by his supporters in the House died in the

---

[4] On the conclusion of this interview, according to Roosevelt's biographer, J. B. Bishop, the President said to Mr. Knox, ' That is a most illuminating illustration of the Wall Street point of view. Mr. Morgan could not help regarding me as a big rival operator, who either intended to ruin all his interests, or else could be induced to come to an agreement to ruin none.' *Theodore Roosevelt and His Time*, Vol. I, p. 184.

[5] *Northern Securities Co. v. U.S.* 193 U.S. 197 (1904).

[6] ' It seems hard,' wrote J. J. Hill, ' that we should be compelled to fight for our lives against the political adventurers who have never done anything but pose and draw a salary. . . .'

Senate. A large part of the metropolitan press attacked his very moderate program as socialistic and subversive of the common weal, and himself as a reckless demagogue. The President, however, was steadily growing in popularity. Merely by being himself — greeting professors and pugilists with equal warmth, teaching his boys to ride and shoot, leading major-generals on a point-to-point ride, exercising with his ' tennis cabinet,' praising the good, the true, and the beautiful and denouncing the base, the false, and the ugly, preaching in scores of short addresses all over the country, with vigorous gesture and incisive utterance, the gospel of civic virtue and intelligent democracy — Roosevelt became an institution. Even the journals most opposed to his policies were forced to advertise him in their columns. When the election of 1904 came around, the Old Guard would have preferred to nominate Mark Hanna; but ' Uncle Mark ' died, and Roosevelt was nominated for the presidency by acclamation. The Democrats, hoping to attract the disgruntled reactionaries, discarded Bryan and put up a conservative New York judge, Alton B. Parker. Roosevelt swept the country by a majority of over 2.5 million votes, and on 4 March 1905 became ' President in his own right.'

Encouraged by this mandate, Roosevelt turned with new enthusiasm to the enforcement of his trust policies. In the first two years of his second term, big business was further discredited by the muckrakers' attacks on Standard Oil, the beef trust, and the railroads, by the shocking disclosures of the New York insurance investigations of 1905, by the discovery that the sugar trust had swindled the government out of $4 million in customs duties and false weights, and by the panic of 1907. In that year Roosevelt sent Congress a pungent message in which he attributed the panic to ' the speculative folly and flagrant dishonesty of a few men of great wealth,' described the current malpractices of business and industry, and concluded that ' our laws have failed in enforcing the performance of duty by the man of property toward the man who works for him, by the corporation toward the investor, the wage-earner, and the general public.' Yet legislation giving the Federal Government plenary power to regulate all corporations engaged in interstate business was not forthcoming. Consequently Roosevelt could do little else than demand continued prosecutions under the Sherman law. Altogether there were forty-five such prosecutions, and in notable instances they were successful, but they simply punished the grosser mischief after it had been committed and did not always do that. The beef trust was dissolved, but managed somehow to reintegrate; the fertilizer trust was dissolved but miraculously reappeared some years later in different form; the American Tobacco Company was dissolved, but the constituent parts continued to maintain a community of interest.

Unscrambling the eggs, indeed, proved to be a delicate and often impossible operation. Roosevelt was forced to conclude that the mere size and power of a combination did not necessarily render it illegal; there were ' good trusts ' such as the International Harvester Company, which traded fairly and passed on their economies to consumers; and there were ' bad trusts ' controlled by ' malefactors of great wealth.' This moral distinction was soon raised to the dignity of a legal one when the Supreme Court, in the Standard Oil case of 1911, accepted the common-law doctrine that only those acts or agreements of a monopolistic nature ' unreasonably ' affecting interstate commerce were to be construed as in restraint of trade under the anti-trust law. Justice Harlan, in a vigorous dissenting opinion, denounced this ' rule of reason ' as ' judicial legislation ' and a ' perversion of the plain words of an Act in order to defeat the will of Congress.' But the ' rule of reason ' became the guiding rule of decision, notably in the case against the United States Steel Corporation in 1920. Subsequent prosecutions have been based not on size or power, or community of interest — which came in time to be encouraged rather than discouraged — but on unfair, dangerous, or illegal use of power.

3. THE EXTENSION OF GOVERNMENT REGULATION

' The great development of industrialism,' said Roosevelt early in 1905, ' means that there must be an increase in the supervision exercised by the Government over business enterprise.' In his efforts to regulate the trusts the President had already given a foretaste of this ' increase in supervision,' but the application of the new philosophy of government was not confined to this matter. Early in his first administration Roosevelt had extended the scope of supervision into the realm of labor relations. ' I found the eight hour law a mere farce,' he wrote. ' This I remedied by executive action.' Other aspects of the labor problem likewise felt the impact of ' executive action.'

On demand of the President, Congress enacted a workmen's compensation law for all government employees, factory inspection and child labor laws for the District of Columbia, and safety appliance legislation for interstate carriers. But the most notable example of 'executive action' was Roosevelt's high-handed settlement of the anthracite coal strike of 1902, a settlement which revealed a resourcefulness that no former executive had possessed.[7] Yet despite his enthusiasm for the 'square deal' in labor, and for 'social and industrial justice,' Roosevelt failed to support Senator Beveridge in his struggle for national legislation against child labor.

The railways provided the clearest example of the extension of government supervision; indeed they furnished the fireworks for the second Roosevelt administration as the trusts had for the first. Abandoned by Congress, ignored by Presidents Harrison, Cleveland, and McKinley, and emasculated by court decisions, the Interstate Commerce Act of 1887 had proved all but useless. Yet the necessity for regulation was as urgent in the first decade of the new century as it had been in the 1880's. Concentration of control was growing: by 1904 six major railway systems, representing a combination of almost 800 independent roads and a capitalization of over $9 billion, controlled approximately three-fourths of the mileage in the country.[8] After the Spanish War, freight charges had increased sharply without any corresponding increase in wages or improvement in service, while rebates, discrimination, and favoritism, forbidden by the Act of 1887, continued unabated and the activities of railroad lobbies in politics were notorious. And the railroads still enjoyed a practical monopoly on transportation. Only river and lake steamboats furnished any competition; the day of motor and air competition was still far ahead.

The railroads themselves were anxious to make the prohibition of rebates effective, and in 1903 they supported the Elkins Act, described as 'a truce of the principals to abolish piracy.' This act made the published freight rates the lawful standard, substituted civil for criminal penalties, and provided that shippers were equally liable with the railroads for obtaining rebates. Under the provisions of this act Attorney-General Moody instituted prosecutions against

---

7 See above, Chap. IX.
8 The Vanderbilt, Morgan-Belmont, Harriman, Pennsylvania, Gould, and Hill systems. See p. 210.

the Chicago & Alton and the Burlington for granting rebates and against a group of Chicago packing houses for accepting them. Soon the government went after bigger game. In 1907 Judge Kenesaw Mountain Landis assessed a fine of $29,240,000 against the Standard Oil Company for accepting rebates, but the sentence was set aside by a higher court.

In 1904 Roosevelt announced that railway regulation was the ' paramount issue.' The House promptly passed an act authorizing the Interstate Commerce Commission to fix railway rates, but the Senate refused to concur and substituted instead a bill providing for an investigation of the entire subject. Testimony before the investigating committee revealed the continuation of malpractices and rallied the country behind the President. Roosevelt charged Congress that ' the most important legislative act now needed . . . is this act to confer on the Interstate Commerce Commission the power to revise rates and regulations, the revised rate to at once go into effect, and stay in effect unless and until the court of review reverses it.'

Congress responded with the Hepburn Act of 1906, a compromise between the House demand for radical reform and the Senate desire for innocuous regulation. This act made rate regulation for the first time possible and extended it to include storage, refrigeration, and terminal facilities, sleeping car, express, and pipeline companies; regulation was further extended in 1910 to include telephone and telegraph companies. It authorized the Interstate Commerce Commission to determine and prescribe maximum rates and order conformity therewith after thirty days. The railroads could appeal, but the burden of proof was now on the carrier, not the commission. Free passes were prohibited for other than railroad employees, and by the ' commodity ' clause the railways were required to disgorge most of the steamship lines and coal mines which they had bought up to stifle competition — a requirement which they managed to evade. The Hepburn Act represented a substantial advance in railway regulation; within two years the commission heard almost twice as many complaints as in the previous nineteen years, and by 1911 it had reduced almost 200,000 rates by as much as 50 per cent. Yet as Senator LaFollette contended, it did not get to the heart of the matter, for it failed to give the commission power to evaluate railroad properties and the cost of service by which alone it could determine rates that were reasonable *per se*. Not until 1913 was provision made for any valuation of the railroads, and another decade was to elapse before that valuation came to be used for purposes of rate-making. By that time the problem had taken on an entirely new character.

Another gesture toward federal centralization was the extension of governmental supervision over foods and drugs. Since 1890 there had been federal inspection of meat designed for export, but there was no inspection of meat or food consumed in the United States. Yet investigations of Dr. Harvey Wiley, chief chemist of the Department of Agriculture, and others revealed an almost universal use of adulterants and preservatives in canned and prepared foods. One chemist, analyzing the adulterants used in common foods, found that an average menu for breakfast, dinner, and supper might contain forty different doses of chemicals and dyes! As early as 1905 Dr. Wiley had persuaded Roosevelt of the necessity of pure food legislation, and in his annual message for that year the President specifically recommended congressional action. The packing interests fought tooth and nail against ' socialistic ' interference with the sacred maxim of *caveat emptor,* but in March 1906 Upton Sinclair published *The Jungle* with its descriptions of loathsome conditions in the Chicago stockyards, and a shocked public demanded action. Representatives of the packing interests were forced to toe the mark, and in June 1906 a federal meat inspection law was placed on the statute books.

Of the same nature was legislation designed to protect the American public against dangerous drugs and patent medicines. In 1904 the *Ladies' Home Journal* inaugurated a campaign against poisonous patent medicines and misleading advertising, and in the same year Samuel Hopkins Adams contributed to *Collier's Weekly* a series of articles on ' The Great American Fraud.' The American Medical Association placed itself squarely behind the campaign and despite the frantic efforts of the Liquor Dealers' Association and the patent-medicine interests, Congress enacted in 1906 a Pure Food and Drugs Act which was strengthened in 1911 by an amendment forbidding misleading labeling of medicines. Though this legislation still left much to be desired, it did give American consumers better protection than the laws of any other country then afforded.

4. CONSERVATION

Unquestionably the most important achievement of the Roosevelt administrations was in the conservation of the natural resources of the nation. Roosevelt's love of nature and knowledge of the West gave him a sentimental yet highly intelligent interest in the preservation of soil, water, and forest; and from the beginning ' conservation ' became one of his leading policies. In his first message to Congress he announced that ' the forest and water problems are perhaps the most vital internal problems of the United States ' and called for a far-reaching and integrated program of conservation, reclamation, and irrigation. It was high time to put some brake on the greedy and wasteful destruction of natural resources that was encouraged by existing laws. Of the original 800 million acres of virgin forest, less than 200 million remained when Roosevelt came to the presidency; four-fifths of the timber in this country was in private hands, and 10 per cent of this was owned by the Southern Pacific, the Northern Pacific, and the Weyerhaeuser Timber Company. The mineral resources of the country, too, had long been exploited as if inexhaustible.

As early as 1873 the American Association for the Advancement of Science had called attention to the reckless exhaustion of our forest resources, but public opinion remained apathetic, and the majority of Americans continued to hug the comfortable delusion that our resources were infinite. It was not until 1891 that Congress was induced to pass a Forest Reserve Act authorizing the President to set aside timber lands. Under this authority Harrison withdrew some 13 million, Cleveland 25 million, and McKinley 7 million acres of forest from public entry. Despite this promising beginning, and the work of faithful public servants like Gifford Pinchot, Chief Forester of the United States, and R. H. Newell, the process of exploitation was going on more rapidly than that of conservation when Roosevelt assumed office. The official attitude, too, was distinctly hostile to conservation.

A narrowly legalistic point of view toward the natural resources obtained in the Departments [Roosevelt later wrote] and controlled the Governmental administrative machinery. Through the General Land Office and other Governmental bureaus the public resources were being handled and disposed of in accordance with the small considerations of petty legal formalities instead of for the large purposes of constructive development, and the habit of deciding, whenever possible, in favor of private interests against the public welfare was firmly fixed.

Taking advantage of the law of 1891 Roosevelt set aside almost 150 million acres of unsold government timber land as national forest reserve, and on the suggestion of Senator LaFollette withdrew from public entry some 85 millions more in Alaska and the Northwest, pending a study of their mineral and water power resources by the United States geological survey. The discovery of a gigantic system of fraud by which railroads, lumber companies, and ranchers were looting and devastating the public reserve enabled the President to obtain authority for transferring the national forests to the Department of Agriculture, whose forest bureau, under the far-sighted Gifford Pinchot, administered them on scientific principles.

Realizing the necessity for arousing public opinion to the imperative need for conservation, Roosevelt secured wide publicity for the work of the Forest Service, and enlisted the co-operation of local and state groups throughout the country. In 1907 he appointed an Inland Waterways Commission to canvass the whole question of the relation of rivers and soil and forest, of water power development, and of water transportation. Out of the recommendations of this Commission grew the plan for a national conservation conference; in 1907 Roosevelt invited all the state governors, cabinet members, justices of the Supreme Court, and notables from the fields of politics, science, and education to such a conference at the White House. This conference, one of the most distinguished gatherings in American history, focused the attention of the nation upon the problem of conservation, and gave to the movement an impetus and a prestige that enabled it to survive later setbacks. The conference issued a declaration of principles stressing not only the conservation of forests but of waters and minerals, and the problems of soil erosion and irrigation as well. It recommended the retention by the government of all lands containing coal, oil, phosphate, natural gas, and power sites, the separation of title to surface and sub-surface, the regulation of timber-cutting on private lands, the improvement of navigable streams and the conservation of watersheds. As a result of its recommendations a number of states established conservation commissions, and in 1909 a National Conservation Association, with President Eliot of Harvard as chairman, was organized as a center for propaganda and education. Another outgrowth of the conference was a National Commission, headed by the indefatigable Gifford Pinchot, which undertook an inventory of the natural resources of the nation. Roosevelt realized that the problems of conservation were international in character, and through a North American Conservation Commission he succeeded in securing the co-operation of the other American states in the great work which he had at heart.

The hostility of the West to the program of conservation, aroused by the war on land-frauds and by the requirement that cattlemen take down their illegal fences on the public domain and pay for grazing on public lands, was allayed by a series of irrigation projects. The Carey Act of 1894, giving the states the right to appropriate public lands for irrigation, had proved inadequate, and in 1902 Roosevelt secured the enactment of the Newlands Reclamation Act which provided that irrigation should be financed out of the proceeds of public land sales under the supervision of the Federal Government. A new Reclamation Service, of which Frederick Newell was the guiding spirit, was established. Under the terms of this act the government undertook the construction of the great Roosevelt dam in Arizona, the Arrowrock dam in Idaho, the Hoover dam on the Colorado river, the Grand Coulee on the Columbia river, and a dozen other dams. At the same time Roosevelt put an end to the acquisition of water-power sites by private utility interests, withdrew over 2000 such sites from entry, and granted others only on fifty-year leases. In addition Roosevelt created five new national parks together with four game preserves and over fifty wild bird refuges.

Much had been accomplished, but much remained to be done. The American people were still prodigal with their magnificent resources. Hundreds of millions of tons of coal were wasted yearly by inefficient methods of mining; hundreds of millions of barrels of oil wasted by unscientific and criminally reckless drilling and piping; billions of cubic feet of natural gas permitted to escape annually through improvidence and inefficiency. Forest fires continued to lay waste millions of acres yearly, and soil erosion destroyed additional millions. Lumber companies devastated the timber areas of the East and the South, and over 50 per cent of the annual cut was wasted by inefficient methods; while both lumber and coal companies soon resumed, under more friendly auspices, their depredations on the public domain. Alone of our Presidents up to this time, Theodore Roosevelt had grasped the problem of conservation as a whole and comprehended its basic relationship to national welfare, and until the accession of Franklin D. Roosevelt to the presidency, none of his successors had the boldness or the breadth of vision to carry on the work he so hopefully inaugurated.

5. THE BIG STICK

' There is an old adage that says, " speak softly, and carry a big stick, and you· will go far." ' This quotation from one of the President's earlier speeches provided cartoonists with another Rooseveltian attribute that proved most appropriate for his foreign policy. Not that the ' big stick ' was used to incite war. It was Roosevelt who gave the Hague Tribunal its first case — the Pious Fund dispute with Mexico — who instructed his delegation at the second Hague Conference to work for the restriction of naval armaments, who was responsible for the return of the Boxer indemnity, who smoothed over a dangerous controversy with Japan, participated in the Algeciras Conference, and won the Nobel peace prize for successful mediation between Russia and Japan.

Roosevelt inherited from McKinley a Secretary of State, John Hay, whose experience as ambassador in London made him eager to meet halfway the new British policy of friendship. And that friendship persisted, despite English alarm over the invasion of their country by American boots and shoes, steel rails and cottons, and despite some dissatisfaction with Roosevelt's belligerent attitude in the Alaskan boundary and the Venezuela controversies. There is no truth in the oft-repeated rumor of a secret Anglo-American alliance, but there was in effect, during the entire progressive era, an Anglo-American understanding. Downing Street readily conceded to Washington a free hand in the New World; and in return the State Department under Hay, Root, and Knox, refrained from any act or expression that would unfavorably affect British interests, and supported British diplomacy in the Far East. The entente, if we may so call it, was consummated by the appointment of the author of *The American Commonwealth*, James Bryce, to the Washington embassy in 1907.

A first fruit of this understanding was the Panama Canal. The voyage of the U.S.S. *Oregon* round the Horn in 1898 touched the popular imagination; and new island possessions in the Caribbean and the Pacific made the construction and operation of an interoceanic canal appear vital to American interests. The Clayton-Bulwer Treaty of 1850 stood in the way of its realization, but not the government of Lord Salisbury. John Hay negotiated with Sir Julian Pauncefote in 1899 a treaty which the Senate, much to his chagrin, rejected because it prohibited fortifying the canal and suggested instead an international guarantee. With the informal aid of Senator Lodge, chairman of the Committee on Foreign Relations, a new Hay-Pauncefote Treaty was signed on 18 November 1901, and promptly ratified. This abrogated the earlier agreement, permitted the United States to construct a canal and control it, and provided that the canal would be open to all nations on equal terms.

The project for an isthmian canal was no new thing; it had been talked of since the sixteenth century, and had entered into United States foreign policy since Polk's administration. In 1876 French interests purchased from Colombia the right to build a canal across Panama, and by 1889 DeLesseps, engineer of the Suez canal, had spent over $260 million in a vain effort to cut a canal through the mountains and jungles of Panama. DeLesseps's company was forced into bankruptcy, but a new organization, the Panama Canal Company, was formed for the sole purpose of selling the dubious assets of the old to the United States.

With the quickening of interest in the canal project Congress became a battleground of rival groups: the new Panama Company, which wished to sell its concession on the Isthmus, and an American syndicate which had purchased a concession from the Republic of Nicaragua. McKinley appointed a commission to investigate the merits of the rival routes and that commission, finding that the Panama Company wanted $109 million for its concession, reported in favor of the Nicaragua canal route which had the added advantage of sea-level rather than lock construction. The Panama Company countered by reducing its price to a mere $40 million and by engaging the services of a prominent New York lobbyist, William Nelson Cromwell, who tactfully contributed $60,000 to the Republican campaign fund and enlisted the powerful support of Senator Hanna. Heaven itself came to the aid of the Panama Company; in May 1902, while Congress was considering the rival routes, Mont Pelé in Martinique erupted with a loss of 30,000 lives. Mont Monotombo in Nicaragua followed suit, and when the Nicaraguan government denied that an active volcano existed in that republic, the Panama lobbyists triumphantly presented each Senator with a Nicaraguan postage stamp featuring a volcano in full action. Under these genial auspices Congress on 28 June 1902 passed the Spooner Act. This act authorized the President to acquire the French concession for $40 million if the Colombian Republic would cede a strip of land across the Isthmus of Panama, ' within a reasonable time ' and upon reasonable terms; if not, the President was to open negotiations with Nicaragua. On 22 January 1903 Secretary Hay induced the Colombian chargé at Washington to sign a treaty granting the United States a hundred-year lease of a ten-mile-wide canal zone, for the lump sum of $10 million and an annual rental of $250,000.

The Colombian government procrastinated about ratifying the treaty — as other governments have been known to do — in spite of a truculent warning from Hay that something dreadful would happen in case of amendment or rejection. We need not take too seriously the constitutional scruples of the Colombian government, since after the dreadful thing did happen the President of the Republic offered to summon a congress with ' new and friendly members,' and rush the treaty through. Nor need we give much weight to Roosevelt's argument that ' foolish and homicidal corruptionists' placed him in a dilemma, the other horn of which was the inferior Nicaragua route. The real obstacle to ratification was the $40 million coming to the Panama Canal Company, whose financial affairs were now in the expert hands of the banking house of J. P. Morgan. That company had no right to sell its concession without the permission of Colombia, and there is some ground to believe that the charter of the company would have expired within a year, leaving it without anything to sell! There is no good evidence that Colombia attempted to ' hold up ' the United States for a higher price than the treaty provided, although its chargé at Washington had not obtained the conditions required by his instructions.

Colombia's recalcitrance outraged Roosevelt. ' I do not think the Bogotá lot of obstructionists should be allowed permanently to bar one of the future highways of civilization,' he exclaimed to Hay. Neither did Mr. Cromwell nor the Panama junta, dominated by the colorful Philippe Bunau-Varilla, a former agent for the French canal company; and in July 1903 there was held at New York an informal meeting of Panama businessmen, agents of the Panama Company, and United States army officers, to plan a way out. That was, of

THEODORE ROOSEVELT *by Joseph R. De Camp*

course, the secession of Panama from the Republic of Colombia. Without making any promise or receiving any of the plotters, Roosevelt and Hay let their intentions become so notorious that Bunau-Varilla advised the revolutionary junta at Panama to proceed in perfect assurance of American assistance.[9] On 19 October three United States war vessels were ordered to the probable scene of hostilities, and on 2 November their commanders were instructed to occupy the Panama railway if a revolution broke out, and to prevent Colombia from landing troops within fifty miles of the Isthmus. The acting Secretary of State cabled the United States consul at Panama, 3 November 1903, ' Uprising on Isthmus reported. Keep Department promptly and fully informed.' The consul replied that afternoon, ' No uprising yet. Reported will be in the night '; and a few hours later, ' Uprising occurred tonight 6; no bloodshed. Government will be organized tonight.'

The description was brief but accurate. The revolution had come off according to schedule. The Governor of Panama consented to being arrested, the Colombian Admiral on station was bribed to steam away, and United States warships prevented troops from being landed by the Colombia government to restore authority. Three hundred section hands from the Panama Railroad and the fire brigade of the city of Panama formed the nucleus of a revolutionary army commanded by General Huertas, former commander-in-chief of Colombian troops. On 4 November a Declaration of Independence was read in the Plaza, and General Huertas addressed his soldiers. ' The world,' he said, ' is astounded at our heroism. President Roosevelt has made good.' Two days later Secretary Hay recognized the Republic of Panama, which by cable appointed Mr. Bunau-Varilla its plenipotentiary at Washington. With him, twelve days later, Hay concluded a treaty by which the Canal Zone was leased in perpetuity to the United States. And while these negotiations were under way, Roosevelt wrote to his son: ' I have had a most interesting time about Panama and Colombia. My experiences in these matters

[9] ' Of course,' Roosevelt wrote some months later, ' I have no idea what Bunau-Varilla advised the revolutionists, or what was said in any telegrams to them as to Hay or myself; but . . . he is a very able fellow, and it was his business to find out what he thought our Government would do. I have no doubt that he was able to make a very accurate guess and to advise his people accordingly. In fact he would have been a very dull man had he not been able to make such a guess.' J. B. Bishop, *Theodore Roosevelt and His Time*, Vol. I, p. 295.

give me an idea of the fearful times Lincoln must have had in dealing with the great crisis he had to face.'

As Roosevelt afterwards declared in a speech, ' I took Panama.' Considering the circumstances, one would wish that he had not defended himself by citing a treaty of 1846 with Colombia in which she guaranteed to the United States the right of transit and in return was guaranteed her ' right of sovereignty and property over the said territory.' It would also have been better taste on Mr. Roosevelt's part to have refrained from hurling opprobrious epithets at fellow citizens who questioned the righteousness of his action. After all, the only issue at stake was the money to be paid to the speculators who controlled the Panama Canal Company and the construction of the canal might well have waited six months or a year. Colombia was hit by the big stick, but all Latin America trembled. Subsequently, in 1921, the United States paid $25 million to quiet Colombia; it would have been better to have paid this sum eighteen years earlier.

Roosevelt was most anxious to secure the Panama Canal as a permanent monument to his administration. ' The people of the United States,' he said, ' and the people of the Isthmus and the rest of mankind will all be better because we dig the Panama Canal and keep order in the neighbourhood. And the politicians and revolutionists at Bogotá are entitled to precisely the amount of sympathy we extend to other inefficient bandits.' Roosevelt certainly was not ' inefficient,' but, overeager to ' make the dirt fly,' he made some ill-considered appointments to the first Canal Zone Commission. The dirt would have flown to little purpose if he had not appointed Colonel George Goethals chief engineer and autocrat of the Canal Zone in 1907. Open to commercial traffic in August 1914, and formally completed six years later, the Panama Canal was a triumph of American engineering and organization. No less remarkable was the sanitary work of Colonel Gorgas, which gave one of the world's greatest pestholes a lower death rate than any American city, while Colonel George Goethals converted the spot described by Froude as ' a hideous dung-heap of moral and physical abomination ' into a community of healthy workers.

Elsewhere in the Caribbean area Roosevelt wielded the big stick with redoubtable energy. In 1902 a crisis arose over the question of international intervention for the collection of the Venezuelan debt. Great Britain, Germany, and Italy established a blockade to force the recalcitrant dictator, General Castro, to come to terms. Castro appealed to Roosevelt to arbitrate the claims, but inasmuch as American rights were involved, Roosevelt very properly refused. Yet he deprecated the use of force for the collection of debts, and looked askance at the potential threat to the Monroe Doctrine. A crisis was avoided, however, when Germany, breaking away from the lead of Great Britain, agreed to submit her claims to arbitration. The Hague Tribunal settled the dispute satisfactorily, scaling down the demands from some $40 million to $8 million,[10] and accepting the doctrine of the Argentinian jurist Luis Drago which denied the propriety of coercion for the collection of claims. Roosevelt expressed the general satisfaction with this solution in a speech in which he said ' Both powers (England and Germany) assured us in explicit terms that there was not the slightest intention on their part to violate the Monroe Doctrine, and this assurance was kept with an honorable good faith which merits full acknowledgement on our part.' [11]

6. THE AMERICAN COLONIAL SYSTEM

Cuba was not a colony, but until 1902 the island was ruled by the United States Army, with General Leonard Wood as military governor. The outstanding feature of this military regime was the remarkable clean-up of Havana under the direction of Major William C. Gorgas which cut the average annual death rate in half. In 1900 came one of the worst yellow-fever epidemics in years. A commission of four army surgeons under Dr. Walter Reed was appointed to investigate the cause. Working on the theory advanced by a Cuban physician, Dr. Carlos Finlay, they proved that the pest was transmitted by the stegomyia mosquito; and two of them, Dr. James Caroll and Dr. Jesse W. Lazear, proved it with their lives. Major Gorgas then declared war on the mosquito; and in 1901 there was not a single case of yellow fever in Havana. One of the greatest scourges of the tropics was at last under control.

[10] The United States claims were reduced from some $4 million to $81,000.

[11] Many years later Roosevelt gave an entirely different version of this incident. According to the story in his autobiography, Germany was the ringleader in the intervention, and Roosevelt forced her to submit to arbitration only by threatening to send Dewey's fleet to Venezuela waters inside of twenty-four hours if the Kaiser did not back down. The evidence to support this version of the story is conflicting and unconvincing.

By the Teller Amendment the United States had disclaimed any intention of exercising sovereignty over Cuba, and had promised to leave the government in the hands of the Cuban people. Few persons in Europe expected the United States to live up to this altruistic promise, and many Americans regarded it with skepticism. But on the conclusion of the war General Wood provided for the meeting of a constitutional convention to draw up a form of government. The convention met in November 1900 and drafted a constitution modeled upon that of the United States, but without any provision for future relations with that country. The American government was unwilling to acquiesce in this situation, and discreet pressure was applied to induce the Cubans to add a series of provisions known collectively as the Platt Amendment, and formulated by Roosevelt's Secretary of War, Elihu Root. The chief provisions of the Platt Amendment were those giving to the United States an ultimate veto over the diplomatic and fiscal relations of Cuba with foreign powers, recognizing the right of the United States to intervene to preserve Cuban independence and to protect life and property, and committing Cuba to sell or lease a naval base on the island.

Under terms of the Platt Amendment the United States leased and built the naval base at Guantanamo, which she retained even after the Amendment itself was abrogated. The right of intervention was first exercised in 1906, upon the request of the President of Cuba, Estrada Palma. Roosevelt sent his Secretary of War, William Howard Taft, to take charge of the island. When peace and stability were restored, the United States withdrew, leaving the affairs of Cuba in sound condition. At the same time Roosevelt somewhat gratuitously warned the islanders that ' if elections become a farce and if the insurrectionary habit becomes confirmed . . . it is absolutely out of the question that the Island remain independent; and the United States, which has assumed the sponsorship before the civilized world for Cuba's career as a nation, would again have to intervene, and see that the government was managed in such an orderly fashion as to secure the safety of life and property.'

Even more important as a precedent was Roosevelt's intervention in Santo Domingo, and the enunciation of what came to be called the ' Roosevelt corollary ' to the Monroe Doctrine. The financial affairs of the Dominican Republic were in a desperate state, and in 1904 the Dominican Minister appealed to Roosevelt ' to establish some kind of protectorate' over the island and save it from its European creditors. Roosevelt had no desire to get involved in the affairs of the Republic — 'about the same desire,' he said, 'as a gorged boa constrictor might have to swallow a porcupine wrong-end-to' — but he agreed that something had to be done to avoid anarchy and European intervention. He set forth his solution in an open letter to Elihu Root: 'If a nation shows that it knows how to act with decency in industrial and political matters, if it keeps order and pays its obligations, then it need fear no interference from the United States. Brutal wrongdoing, or an impotence which results in a general loosening of the ties of civilizing society may finally require intervention by some civilized nation; and in the Western Hemisphere the United States cannot ignore this duty.' [12] In February 1905 he signed a protocol with the Dominican Republic placing an American receiver in charge of Dominican customs, and arranging that 55 per cent of the customs receipts should be applied to the discharge of debts, and 45 per cent to current expenses. The Senate refused to ratify the protocol, but Roosevelt went ahead anyway, and in 1907 the Senate came around. In a little more than two years Santo Domingo was transformed from a bankrupt island to a prosperous and peaceful country, with revenues more than sufficient to discharge its debts and pay its expenses, and Roosevelt congratulated himself that he had 'put the affairs of the island on a better basis than they had been for a century.' But a dangerous precedent had been established, and within a decade the United States found herself deeply involved in the domestic as well as the foreign affairs of other Caribbean and Central American nations. So burdensome did this responsibility become, that a quarter-century later the 'Roosevelt corollary' to the Monroe Doctrine was officially repudiated by the Department of State.

The problem of the Philippine Islands presented peculiar difficulties, especially since from the beginning it was felt that our tenure of these islands was temporary. The Bacon Resolution, promising immediate independence upon the establishment of a stable government, had been defeated by the casting vote of Vice-President Hobart, but the McEnery Resolution had been adopted in its stead. This Resolution announced that 'it is not intended . . . permanently to annex said islands as an integral part of the territory of the United

[12] See, too, his annual message of 1904 for an expression of the same policy. See H. S. Commager (ed.), *Documents*, No. 462.

States; but it is the intention of the United States to establish on said islands a government suitable to the wants and conditions of the inhabitants . . . to prepare them for local self-government. . . . ' There was, to be sure, a certain ambiguity about this declaration of intention, but the Filipinos were early given to understand that their aspirations for independence would have the sympathy and support of the United States. The first Philippine Commission, for example, was instructed to emphasize ' upon all occasions the just and beneficent intentions of the United States ' and to represent ' the good-will, the protection, and the richest blessings of a liberating rather than a conquering nation.'

The Filipino Insurrection dragged on until 1902, but as early as 1900 military government was succeeded by a civil Philippine Commission. William Howard Taft was chairman of the Commission and first Governor-General of the islands. The Commission was entrusted with executive, legislative, and judicial powers, and authorized to reconstruct the government of the islands from the bottom up; that the interests of the natives might be represented in this work, the Commission was shortly enlarged by the addition of three Filipinos, and the Commission was instructed to ' bear in mind that the government which they are establishing is designed . . . for the happiness, peace and prosperity of the people of the Philippine Islands, and the measures adopted should be made to conform to their customs, their habits, and even their prejudices ' so far as was consistent with the principles of good government. This executive arrangement was soon regularized by the passage of the Organic Act of 1 July 1902. This act recognized the islands as unincorporated territory of the United States, and the inhabitants as ' citizens of the Philippine Islands ' and thus entitled to the protection of the United States; and provided for the ultimate creation of a bicameral legislature the lower house of which should be popularly elected.

American rule in the Philippines has been compared with that of Great Britain in India, with disparagement to the latter which is unfair; for America had simpler problems. The insular population in 1900 was about seven million, of whom only 4 per cent were Mohammedans and 5 per cent wild pagan tribes. Christian Filipinos, the ' little brown brothers ' who comprised 85 per cent of the total, were a fairly homogeneous group, law-abiding and intelligent. Their ideas of justice and administration were Oriental, but caste distinctions were lacking; their thirst for education was keen, and Tammany Hall could teach them little in the way of politics. Under American rule they made a remarkable advance in education, well-being, and self-government. Through Taft's diplomacy at Rome, the United States acquired title to vast areas of agricultural land from the religious orders, and sold them on easy terms in small holdings to the peasants. ' Uncle Sam ' provided the islands with honest, intelligent, and sympathetic, if somewhat expensive, administrators such as Taft and W. Cameron Forbes; with schools, sanitation, good roads, a well-trained native constabulary, a representative assembly, and baseball. The number of pupils attending school rose from 5000 in 1898 to over a million in 1920, and all but three hundred of the teachers at that date were native. The infant death rate in Manila declined from 80 to 20 per thousand between 1904 and 1920; and smallpox and cholera were practically stamped out. Although the entire cost of civil administration was defrayed by the islanders, their per capita taxation in 1920 was only \$2.50, and their per capita debt, \$1.81. Civilization penetrated to parts of the interior where the Spaniards had never ventured. Remote forest glades where savage tribes once met in deadly combat were transformed into baseball diamonds and the jungle resounded to cries of ' Strike him out! '

7. WORLD POLITICS

For the first time the United States had a President the rulers of Europe looked upon as one of themselves, and who could play their game with their weapons. Roosevelt, like Edward VII, loved to inject his personality into world politics. The most conspicuous instance of this was his mediation in the Russo-Japanese War, undertaken at the suggestion of the Japanese and the German Emperors. Secretary Hay was then in his last illness, and the President negotiated directly with premiers and crowned heads. He brought the two belligerents together and broke the deadlock, from which the Treaty of Portsmouth emerged; but not every one will admit the wisdom of that treaty. Roosevelt preserved for the time being the integrity of China, but the Treaty of Portsmouth merely substituted Japan for Russia in Manchuria and embittered the Japanese people toward the United States. Yet Roosevelt's action had been dictated by friendship for Japan, and he himself later declared that he had served notice on France and Germany that the United States would support Japan if either power went to the aid of Russia.[13] It is difficult to find any difference between this sort of thing and the system of secret treaties and balance-of-power diplomacy that Roosevelt, like other Americans, professed to abhor. He played the game of world politics with native audacity and amateur skill, sounding out every step in advance; but if something had gone wrong the American people would have found themselves morally committed by their President to a fighting membership in the Anglo-Japanese alliance. Yet it is inconceivable that the American people would have accepted any such commitments, and if the door held open by John Hay swung to shortly after his death it was, according to Tyler Dennett, because Roosevelt's policy ' could not be continued except at the expense of the Constitution of the United States.'

By the conclusion of the Treaty of Portsmouth, Roosevelt established for his country a right that she did not at that time want — to be consulted in world politics. Again, in the Moroccan crisis of 1905–06, he quietly intervened to preserve peace with justice. French policy of hegemony in Morocco threatened a war with Germany that might easily have become a world conflagration. At the suggestion of the German Emperor Roosevelt urged France to consent to a conference on the North African question, and the American representative, Henry White, was in large part responsible for the Algeciras Convention which, whatever its inadequacies, did keep peace for some years. The Senate ratified the Convention, but with the qualifying amendment that ratification did not involve any departure ' from the traditional American foreign policy which forbids participation by the United States in the settlement of political questions which are entirely European in their scope.' It is interesting to note, by contrast, that President Taft carefully refrained from any participation in the second Moroccan crisis of 1911.

Roosevelt's growing radicalism had alienated conservatives and moderates even of his own party, and his willingness to compromise had forfeited the confidence of doctrinaire liberals and professional reformers, whom he denounced as ' muckrakers.' His vigorous assertion of executive leadership had antagonized Congress and powerful party leaders; and his sense of what constituted fair

---

[13] It is difficult to know whether Roosevelt really made such a threat, or whether his memory played tricks on him, as with the Venezuela episode.

play brought down upon him at one time or another the wrath of labor and of capital, of Negroes and of the Southern whites. Yet no President since Jackson was so popular with the ' plain people.' Only fifty years old in 1908, and at the height of his power and popularity, Roosevelt could have been renominated if he had only said the word. But he had declared in 1904 that ' under no circumstances ' would he be a candidate to succeed himself; and in deference to the third-term tradition he contented himself with nominating his successor. Secretary of State Elihu Root, Charles E. Hughes of New York, and William Howard Taft were the most available candidates, but Taft was closer to the President than any other man in high public office. Roosevelt held the Republican convention in the hollow of his hand, and Taft was duly nominated. After Parker's calamitous defeat in 1904 Bryan's control over the Democratic party was no less complete, and he was nominated by a convention subservient to his every wish. The differences between the two parties were insignificant, and except for charges and counter-charges of financial irregularities, the campaign was apathetic. Bryan carried only the Solid South, Kansas, Nebraska, Colorado, and Nevada, but his popular vote was a million more than that of Parker in 1904, and 43 per cent of the total. The Republicans captured not only the presidency but both houses of Congress.

To Taft, then, on 4 March 1909, Roosevelt handed over a government that had grown rapidly in prestige and power during the last seven years, and a government that was by way of becoming once more a servant of the people. The entire civil service had been stimulated by Roosevelt's vitality no less than by the knowledge that efficiency and intelligence would be recognized and rewarded. The whole tone and temper of public life had changed for the better, and popular interest in public affairs had never been more keen or intelligent. Yet in one respect Roosevelt had failed as a leader. He inspired loyalty to himself, rather than to his ideals and policies. With the conceit of a strong man he had forced and fascinated men of other beliefs to his and the public's service, while neglecting to build up a progressive staff within the Republican party. It would never be quite the same old party again; but the Old Guard drew a sigh of relief when Roosevelt took ship to Africa.

For Bibliography for this Chapter see Bibliography at end of Chapter XVIII, page 519.

The Taft Administration

1. INEPTITUDE AND INSURGENCY

STRONG-WILLED Presidents of the United States have generally managed to nominate their successors; and if Roosevelt, unlike Jefferson and Jackson, did not bequeath the office to his Secretary of State, it was because his Secretary of War was more ' available.' William Howard Taft, fifty-one years old when he became President, had no less experience in public affairs than Elihu Root. He had been an admirable circuit court judge, Governor of the Philippines, Canal-Zone administrator, and Secretary of War. The President loved him as a brother, and believed him the ideal person to carry out his policies. Many progressives welcomed the change; for except in the realm of conservation the last year of Roosevelt's administration was without achievement; as soon as the Republican leaders in Congress had learned that Roosevelt would retire in 1909, they ignored alike his recommendations and his threats. ' Big Bill ' Taft, it was hoped, would apply the emollient of his humor and good nature to the wheels of legislation.

If Roosevelt appeared to be less conservative than he really was, Taft appeared more so. He genuinely wished to clinch the Roosevelt policies, but in his own fashion; and he was unprepared to go forward with a program of his own. Roosevelt was primarily a man of action, Taft essentially a man of deliberation. As a constitutional lawyer he could not share Roosevelt's view that the President could do anything not forbidden by law; rather, the executive could do only those things for which he had specific authority under the Constitution. This difference in attitude between the two was much like the difference between Jackson and Buchanan, or, in our own time, Truman and Eisenhower. Roosevelt had given the presidency an organic connection with Congress; under Taft the relationship became formal, almost diplomatic, and the initiative passed to House and Senate leaders who thought reform had gone far enough, if not too far. In this they were wrong, but Taft was not prepared to disabuse them of their error.

Cautious and vacillating, Taft was by instinct conservative, by training 'regular.' In theory he agreed with much of the insurgent program; actually he was unwilling to antagonize the Old Guard upon whom he relied increasingly for counsel and support. And it was during the first two years of the Taft administration that the Old Guard reached the zenith of its power. 'Uncle Joe' Cannon of Illinois was its representative in the House, Nelson W. Aldrich of Rhode Island in the Senate, and so certain were these men of their power that they openly professed a contempt for democracy.

Roosevelt went to Africa in March 1909, as much to avoid embarrassing the new President by his presence as for the pleasure of big game hunting. The new President and the old parted with warm expressions of trust and affection. But Roosevelt returned fifteen months later to find the Republican party divided, the progressive program halted, and liberals alienated; and in fifteen months more the two old friends were exchanging bitter reproaches before the public. That this happened was in large part President Taft's fault; the manner in which it happened was Roosevelt's.

The Republican platform of 1908 contained a pledge to revise the tariff: an issue that Roosevelt had gingerly avoided, fearing lest it should disrupt his party. Revision was popularly understood as reduction, and Taft had specifically committed himself to this interpretation. For a downward revision there was, by 1909, pressing need. The cost of living was rising, and the average worker was no better off than he had been a decade earlier. Trusts, which many thought were spawned by high tariffs, were growing stronger every year, and the investigations of the Pujo Committee were soon to reveal the existence of a 'money trust' unsuspected by most Americans. President Taft proposed in his inaugural address that 'a tariff bill be drawn in good faith in accordance with the promises made before the election,' and he suggested that the new tariff should afford merely a protection equal to the difference between the cost of production at home and abroad. Any consequent deficiency in the revenue, he added, might be made up by a graduated inheritance tax. In order to shorten the uncertainty of businessmen, he summoned a special session of Congress for immediate legislation along these lines.

When Congress assembled, Sereno Payne of New York was ready with a tariff bill which placed iron ore, flax, and hides on the free list and reduced duties on steel, lumber, and numerous other items. The bill promptly passed the House and went to the Senate, where representatives of interested industries fell upon it. When it emerged from the Senate as the Payne-Aldrich tariff it was seen that of the 847 changes, some 600 were upward and that the free list was a joke.[1] 'I have never come so close to tariff making before,' wrote Senator Lodge, 'and the amount of ruthless selfishness that is exhibited on both sides surpasses anything I have ever seen.' The progressive Republicans were outraged, and LaFollette, rapidly emerging as the leader of American progressivism, organized his fellow liberals in the Senate to fight the proposed measure item by item. There followed one of the most stirring debates in American political history. LaFollette attacked the woolens schedule, Beveridge the tobacco, Cummins the steel, Bristow the sugar, Dolliver the cotton, and if in the end their efforts failed to change the tariff, they did at least furnish the country with an enlightening analysis of the connection between tariffs and trusts, and laid the dynamite for the political explosion of 1910. The President was perturbed. The insurgents urged him to veto the bill as a violation of party pledges, but after painful vacillation he decided to sign it. And shortly after, in a most unfortunate speech at Winona, Minnesota, he aggravated his offense by pronouncing the Payne-Aldrich bill ' the best tariff bill that the Republican party ever passed.'

The progressive Republicans, led by LaFollette, Beveridge, and Norris of Nebraska, who would be heard from later, began to suspect Taft of playing traitor to the Roosevelt policies, and their suspicions were confirmed by Taft's conservation policy. James R. Garfield, Roosevelt's lieutenant in conservation, had been supplanted in the Interior Department by R. A. Ballinger, who was presently charged by chief forester Gifford Pinchot with letting the Guggenheim interests obtain reserved coal lands in Alaska. The President referred this quarrel in his official family to the House of Representatives, which

[1] ' Th ' Republican party,' explained Mr. Dooley to Mr. Hennessy, ' has been thrue to its promises. Look at th' free list if ye don't believe it. Practically ivrything necessary to existence comes in free. Here it is. Curling stones, teeth, sea moss, newspapers, nux vomica, Pulu, canary bird seed, divvy-divvy, spunk, hog bristles, marshmallows, silk worm eggs, stilts, skeletons, an' leeches. Th' new tariff bill puts these familyar commodyties within th' reach iv all.' Mr. Dooley on The Tariff in *Mr. Dooley Says*, p. 148.

white-washed Ballinger, upon which Pinchot was dismissed. This action was naturally mistakenly interpreted as a dramatic reversal of Roosevelt's conservation program. Actually Taft was not unfriendly to conservation. He was the first President to withdraw oil lands from public sale. He asked for and obtained from Congress the authority to reserve the coal lands which Roosevelt had reserved without specific authority, and set up the Bureau of Mines as guardian of the nation's mineral resources. Pinchot was replaced by the head of the Yale School of Forestry, and his policy was continued by the purchase, in 1911, of great timbered tracts in the Appalachians.

The indignation of the progressives was directed not only against the President but against the Old Guard upon whom he depended. In the Senate, LaFollette, Beveridge, and Dolliver excoriated Aldrich to such effect that he decided not to stand for re-election. In the House, insurgency took the form of a revolt against Speaker Cannon, ' a hard, narrow old Boeotian,' who controlled a well-oiled legislation mill which rejected progressive grist. On 18 March 1910 George Norris offered a resolution depriving the Speaker of membership on the powerful Committee on Rules, and making that committee elective. Democrats joined with progressive Republicans to pass the resolution, and Taft's prestige fell. The progressive cause gained, but legislative efficiency lost. Authority was needed to enforce party discipline in a body so unwieldy and fluctuating as the House of Representatives, and the Speaker's whip in due course was transferred to the floor leader.

The ineptitude of Taft's administration and the growing revolt against him must not blind us to his achievements. During his term much valuable legislation was enacted. The Mann-Elkins Act of 1910 strengthened the Interstate Commerce Commission by empowering it to suspend any rate increases until and unless the reasonableness thereof was ascertained, and created a new Commerce Court to hear appeals from the commission. The Department of Commerce and Labor, established at Roosevelt's instance in 1903, was wisely divided. A postal savings bank and a parcel post — conveniences long overdue, much wanted by the people, but opposed by selfish interests — were provided. A Commission of Economy and Efficiency to examine into the national administration was created, and an act requiring publicity for campaign expenditures passed. The merit system was expanded by the addition of second- and third-class postmasters to the civil service list. A Federal Children's Bureau was established, and its activities entrusted to Julia Lathrop of Hull House. Alaska, peevish and discontented since the collapse of the Klondike gold bubble, at last obtained full territorial government in 1912. New Mexico and Arizona, last of the continental Territories except Alaska, became the forty-seventh and forty-eighth states of the Union. Here again Taft unnecessarily antagonized the progressives by refusing to certify the admission of Arizona until it expunged from its constitution a provision for the popular recall of judges; once admitted as a state, Arizona promptly restored the device. Approximately twice as many prosecutions for violation of the Sherman Act were instituted during Taft's four years in office as during Roosevelt's seven.

Significant of the rapidly expanding envelope of law were two amendments to the Constitution. As James Bryce pointed out, the difficulties of this process were such that the Constitution had not been amended since 1802, excepting ' in the course of a revolutionary movement which had dislocated the Union itself.' The Sixteenth, or income-tax, Amendment and the Seventeenth Amendment, which transferred the election of United States Senators from state legislatures to the people, were adopted by Congress in 1909 and 1912 respectively and ratified by the requisite number of states in 1913.

It is difficult to believe that Taft, and the Republicans who supported the first of these amendments, appreciated its revolutionary potentialities, yet the Sixteenth Amendment has some claim to being considered the most radical of all amendments to the Constitution. For the income tax provided a peaceful and legal method of putting an end to great fortunes, and redistributing the wealth of the people. One indication of the fundamental conservatism of the American people is that it has not been deliberately used for these purposes. Though tax rates rose consistently they never became confiscatory, nor did great fortunes disappear. It was fortunate that the amendment was passed and ratified when it was, for it is difficult to see how the country could have financed the First World War — to say nothing of the Second — without it.

From direct election of Senators much had been expected. It would make that body more democratic; it would put an end to indirect corruption; it would open more widely the door to talent, even to impoverished talent. Few of these expectations were realized. The Senate may have become more representative, but the cost of elections has gone up, and it is not certain that the general level of ability has.

Little of all this legislation could be credited directly to the Taft administration. The public was more concerned with mid-term elections of 1910. Democrats and progressive Republicans won a smashing victory. The Democrats gained an impressive majority in the House and very much narrowed the Republican majority in the Senate. Democratic governors were elected in several Eastern states such as Maine, Massachusetts, Connecticut, and New York; and in New Jersey Dr. Woodrow Wilson, late president of Princeton University, made his first step toward a larger presidency.

2. CANADIAN RECIPROCITY AND DOLLAR DIPLOMACY

With a lawyer in the White House and in the Department of State, American diplomacy returned to its traditional channels. By an exchange of notes in 1908, Japan and the United States had agreed to support the independence and integrity of China, and the ' open door.' Japan, nevertheless, with the full approval of the Triple Entente, began to consolidate her position in Manchuria. Secretary Knox attempted to meet this situation by proposing, in 1909, that the United States and European powers lend China sufficient money to buy back all the railroads controlled by foreign interests. This, said Knox, ' was perhaps the most effective way to preserve the undisturbed enjoyment by China of all political rights in Manchuria and to promote the development of those Provinces under a practical application of the policy of the open door.' But he had not felt out the Powers, as Roosevelt would have done, and his plan was rejected somewhat contemptuously by Russia and Japan. Failing in this effort to assist China out of her difficulties, Taft insisted that American bankers be allowed to participate in a four-power consortium to finance railway construction in the Yangtze valley, ' in order that the United States might have equal rights and an equal voice in all questions pertaining to the disposition of the public revenues concerned.' But this plan, innocent enough in purpose, was repudiated by Wilson within two weeks of his accession to office.

It was fear of Japan, too, which provoked the so-called Lodge corollary to the Monroe Doctrine. In 1911 an American company proposed to sell Magdalena Bay in Lower California to a Japanese fishing syndicate. On hearing of the proposal, Senator Lodge, suspicious that the syndicate might be a cover for the government itself, introduced and the Senate passed a resolution announcing that the purchase or control by any non-American government of any part of the American continents which had a potential naval or military value would constitute an unfriendly act. Though Taft declared that he was not bound by the resolution it further aggravated Latin American public opinion, already exasperated by Roosevelt's Panama and Caribbean policy.

A comparison of the Roosevelt and Taft policies in Central America recalls the old adage that some persons can make off with a horse, while others cannot look over the stable wall. Secretary Knox signed treaties with Nicaragua and Honduras similar to Roosevelt's treaty with Santo Domingo, underwriting American loans by guaranteeing the bankers against revolution and defalcation. But the Knox treaties were rejected by the Senate, and Taft's policy both in Central America and the Far East was denounced as ' dollar diplomacy.' In 1911 Taft, a warm friend to international peace, concluded treaties with both England and France for the arbitration of all disputes, including those involving ' national honor.' The German-American press and the professional Irish-Americans broke out into shrieks of dissent. A presidential election was approaching, and the Senate rejected the treaties.

Again it was Taft's misfortune, not his fault, that tariff reciprocity with Canada failed. In November 1910 three United States commissioners concluded with two members of the Dominion Parliament a reciprocity agreement to be adopted by identical legislative acts. The agreement provided free trade in primary food products, which would naturally flow from Canada southward, and a large reduction on manufactures, which would obviously go the other way. It was a sincere and statesmanlike effort by President Taft to cement friendly relations: but bad politics. The insurgent Republicans, representing for the most part Western agrarian states, were able to argue that reciprocity was a good bargain only for the trusts, which would gain a new market and free raw materials at the farmer's expense; oddly enough Eastern industrialists and manufacturers opposed it too. Democratic votes pushed the bill through Congress. In the debate,

Champ Clark, the new Democratic Speaker, said, 'I am for it because I hope to see the day when the American flag will float over every square foot of the British North American possessions clear to the North Pole.' Mr. Clark awoke the next day to find himself notorious. His words may have been a joke, as he feebly explained; more likely they were spoken for effect, and certainly they expressed no current American sentiment. But they aroused the fighting spirit of Canadian loyalty, were repeated in Parliament, and awoke to loud entreaty Rudyard Kipling's lyre. Sir Wilfrid Laurier, the Canadian Premier, was forced to appeal to his country. Canadian manufacturers, who feared to lose the protected home market they had so carefully built up, financed the conservative opposition, and in September 1911 the treaty and Sir Wilfrid went down to defeat.

3. ROOSEVELT AND THE PROGRESSIVE PARTY

Theodore Roosevelt, after enjoying good hunting in Africa and a triumphal progress through Europe, returned to New York in June 1910. Greeted with an hysterical enthusiasm that somewhat dismayed him, he insisted on settling down at Sagamore Hill to pursue his many non-political interests. The *Outlook* made him associate editor, and afforded him an organ. But the role of sage was not congenial to 'Teddy,' and the public would not be denied the delight of seeing and hearing their hero. Before the summer was over, he was making public addresses in the West which showed unmistakably that shooting lions and dining with crowned heads had not dulled his fighting edge for reform. His ideas, clarified and systematized as the 'New Nationalism,' included not only the old Roosevelt policies of honesty in government, regulation of big business, and conservation of natural resources, but the relatively new conception of social justice — the reconstruction of society by political action. This principle involved some vigorous and wholly justified criticism of recent Supreme Court decisions, which had nullified social legislation in the states. In his Osawatomie speech of 31 August 1910, T. R. announced, 'I stand for the square deal . . . I mean not merely that I stand for fair play under the present rules of the game, but that I stand for having those rules changed so as to work for a more substantial equality of opportunity and of reward for equally good service.' 'We must drive special interests out of politics,' he said, and hinted that unless the railroads behaved themselves the government might eventually be forced into a policy of public ownership. That autumn, at the request of Governor Hughes of New York, Roosevelt actively promoted the adoption of the direct primary, and soon found himself in the thick of the state gubernatorial campaign.

Conservative Republicans shuddered at the ' New Nationalism ' and feared a split in the party. President Taft was worried. ' I have had a hard time,' he confessed to his old friend. ' I have been conscientiously trying to carry out your policies, but my method of doing so has not worked smoothly.' Roosevelt visited the President at the temporary summer capital, continued a friendly correspondence for several months, and refrained from public criticism of his administration. Yet the two men were being pulled apart. Insurgents and displaced progressives like Pinchot were continually telling Roosevelt that the President had surrendered to the Old Guard, and entreating him to be a candidate in 1912. Taft, on the other hand, was surrounded by friends and relatives whose advice resembled that of George III's mother: ' George, be a King! '

After the Democratic victories of 1910 and the Republicans' loss of the House and the Old Guard revolt on the reciprocity issue, it was clear that Taft could not succeed himself. In December 1910 Senator LaFollette, spokesman for the insurgents, drafted a declaration of principles for a Progressive Republican League, and the next month the league was formally organized for the purpose of liberalizing the Republican party. On obtaining what he thought was Roosevelt's assurance that he would not enter the contest, LaFollette became a candidate for the Republican nomination, and his prospects improved as the schism in the party deepened. His strength, however, was confined largely to the Mississippi valley, and his radicalism frightened many who agreed in theory with the principles that he advocated. In the midst of a speech on the ' money trust,' on 2 February 1912, LaFollette collapsed. He recovered by the following day, but insurgents who had used him as a stalking horse for Roosevelt promptly deserted and went over to the old leader.

Roosevelt had declared in 1904 that ' under no circumstances ' would he again be a candidate for the presidency. Taft was his friend and his own choice; to oppose Taft would be to impeach his own judgment. But if he must confess that his judgment had been wrong, LaFollette was the obvious alternative. As late as 20 December 1911 Roosevelt wrote, ' I do not want to be President again, I am not a candidate, I have not the slightest idea of becoming a candidate.' This was true only in a purely technical sense, for Roosevelt had already assured his friend Lodge that if the nomination should be presented in the form of a patriotic duty, he would not decline. Even before LaFollette's candidacy fell flat, Roosevelt was planning how best to get into the race. At his own suggestion the Republican governors of seven states addressed to him, on 10 February 1912, an open letter urging that he announce his candidacy. A few days later President Taft publicly denounced persons who had supported the ' New Nationalism ' as destructive radicals, ' political emotionalists,' and ' neurotics.' These words touched Roosevelt on the raw, since a rumor that he was losing his reason was being circulated. They were exactly the sort of challenge to dissolve his lingering doubts, and arouse a violent spirit of combat. ' My hat is in the ring,' he announced on 21 February.

That same day he delivered an address before the Ohio Constitutional Convention which was the opening speech of his campaign. He urged that democracy be given economic as well as political connotations, that the rich man ' holds his wealth subject to the general right of the community to regulate its business use as the public welfare requires,' and that the police power of the state be broadened to embrace all necessary forms of regulation. Further, he advocated not only the initiative and the referendum, but the recall of judicial decisions. ' It is both absurd and degrading,' he said, ' to make a fetish of a judge or of any one else.' His radicalism alienated thousands of Republican voters, cost him the support of friends like Lodge, Knox, Root, and Stimson, and made his nomination by the Republicans extremely improbable.

LaFollette stayed in the fight, and the three-cornered contest for the Republican nomination became unseemly and bitter. Taft accused Roosevelt of appealing to class hatred, Roosevelt accused Taft of biting the hand that fed him, and many other things were said that would better have been left unsaid. Roosevelt knew that he could not win over the regular party organization, but wherever the law permitted he entered the presidential preference primaries in the hope that a display of popularity among the rank and file of the party might frighten the Old Guard. Thirteen states chose their delegates to party conventions through popular primaries, and in these states Roosevelt obtained 278, Taft 46, and LaFollette 36 delegates. There was no doubt that Roosevelt had the overwhelming support of the rank and file of the Republican party, but the bosses were with Taft. Where delegates were chosen by conventions, the President was almost uniformly successful, and the Southern districts, the Republican rotten boroughs, returned a solid block of Taft delegates who represented little more than the federal officeholders in that region. The credentials of some 200 delegates were in dispute. By electing Elihu Root temporary chairman, the conservatives retained control of the convention machinery, and awarded practically all the contested seats to Taft men. On the ground that his legitimate majority had been stolen, Roosevelt instructed his delegates to take no further part in the proceedings; and Taft was renominated by a strong majority.[2]

Roosevelt and his followers at once took steps to found a new party. Local organizations were rapidly formed, and on 5 August 1912 the first Progressive party convention met at Chicago amid scenes of febrile enthusiasm that recalled Populism and the early days of the Republican party. ' We stand at Armageddon, and we battle for the Lord,' announced Roosevelt to his enraptured followers, who paraded around the convention hall singing ' Onward Christian Soldiers ' and

> Follow! Follow!
> We will follow Roosevelt,
> Anywhere! Everywhere,
> We will follow on.

The convention adopted a platform embracing almost the whole of the progressive program and nominated Roosevelt by acclamation. A phrase of the beloved leader, ' I am feeling like a bull moose,' gave the new party an appropriate symbol, beside the Republican elephant and the Democratic donkey.

[2] This question of the contested delegates is so enmeshed in precedent and party technique as to be almost insoluble for the layman. It is asserted on the one hand that the same ' steam roller ' methods were used by Roosevelt in 1904 and 1908; on the other that there was no precedent for the action taken by Root. It seems on the whole probable that even if all the contests had been fairly decided, Roosevelt would not have had a majority. Yet if Roosevelt had allowed his avowed delegates to vote, it is possible though not probable that they might have won enough Taft votes to obtain the nomination. As one member said, the Negro delegates were ' straining on the leash ' to vote for Roosevelt.

In the perspective of history the formation of the Progressive party appears to have been a mistake from every point of view save that of the Democrats. Roosevelt's secession with his following lost many good men their political careers, and ended all chance of liberalizing the Republican party in that generation; for although the Progressives eventually returned to the fold, it was with their tails between their legs. The true progressive strategy of the moment was that of LaFollette — to remain within the party, let the Old Guard lead it to defeat, and wait for 1916. Roosevelt's mistake was so colossal and irreparable, and so contrary to his long-settled principles of party regularity, that one naturally asks whether an appetite for power was not his moving force. Like the elder Pitt, Roosevelt believed that he, and he alone, could save the country; unlike Pitt, he did not win the opportunity to justify his faith.

The Progressives hoped that they would break into the Solid South. But Roosevelt had antagonized Southern whites by inviting the Negro leader, Booker T. Washington, to lunch at the White House, and appointing a Negro collector of the port at Charleston. And the South had a candidate of her own.

4. WOODROW WILSON AND THE ELECTION OF 1912

The young men of the South who lived through the dark days of Reconstruction without allowing the bitterness of it to enter their souls came out clean as tempered steel. Such men were Chief Justice Edward D. White, Walter Hines Page, and Thomas Woodrow Wilson. The year after Taft entered Yale, and the year before Roosevelt entered Harvard, Woodrow Wilson, son and grandson of Scots Presbyterian ministers, came up to Princeton. At the Hasty Pudding Club of Harvard, ' Teddy ' would become so excited in debate as to lose the power of articulation. ' Tommy ' was remembered at Whig Hall, Princeton, for having lost an interclub debating contest rather than defend protection against free trade. Before graduating from Harvard, Roosevelt wrote his first book, *The Naval History of the War of 1812,* which sounded the note of preparedness for war upon which his life closed. In his last year at Princeton, Wilson published an article exposing the irresponsibility of congressional government, which he later did so much to remedy. Roosevelt entered public life in 1881; Wilson, after a brief and unprofitable practice of law, took his doctorate at Johns Hopkins, and began a quiet career of teaching and scholarship. In 1890, the year after Roosevelt was appointed to the Civil Service Commission, Wilson became a professor of political science at Princeton; and in 1902, the year after Roosevelt became President of the United States, Wilson was chosen president of Princeton University.

While Roosevelt fought political privilege in the nation, Wilson contended with social privilege at Princeton. Originally an austere Presbyterian college, Princeton had become a haven of the well-to-do, where young bloods monopolized the amenities of university life. Wilson attempted somewhat arbitrarily to transform the aristocratic undergraduate clubs into more democratic dormitory groups. Dean Andrew F. West, a classical scholar, spoiled the symmetry of the scheme, and Wilson met his first defeat. Soon arose an even more important dispute over the organization and control of the graduate school which Wilson insisted must be integrated with the college. The whole country was interested when Wilson refused a bequest of half a million dollars which carried qualifying provisions that he deemed fatal to the proper functioning of the graduate school. The issue, to Wilson, was more than academic; it went to the very heart of the problem of democracy. ' The American college,' he said, ' must become saturated in the same sympathies as the common people. The colleges of this country must be reconstructed from the top to the bottom. The American people will tolerate nothing that savours of exclusiveness. . . . The people are tired of pretense, and I ask you . . . to heed what is going on.' But Princeton refused to heed what was going on; and when a new bequest of several million dollars was placed at the disposal of Wilson's enemies, he stepped out of the academic picture.

As a scholar, publicist, and leader in education Wilson enjoyed a national reputation; but active politics was considered a closed sphere to professors. George Harvey, editor of *Harper's Weekly,* in search of a Democratic candidate for the presidency, mentioned Woodrow Wilson in 1906. The suggestion was greeted with jeers, but the professor took it to heart. In 1910 the Democrats of New Jersey — an amorphous state, half bedroom to New York and half to Philadelphia, controlled by corporations attracted by the laxity of its laws — wished to achieve respectability with a new sort of candidate. They had long been out of power and their none too savory reputation might be sweetened by a scholar. At George Harvey's suggestion the bosses nominated Wilson, and the people elected him governor. Chosen for the job of window-dressing, Wilson proceeded to clean up the shop. Within a year he had repudiated the bosses, broken the power of the sinister ' Jim ' Smith, won the enthusiastic allegiance of reformers like George Record and Joseph Tumulty, and written more progressive legislation into the statute books than had been enacted in the previous half-century. He broke away from Harvey, but a silent politician from Texas, Colonel Edward M. House, took him up; and Wilson became a leading candidate for the presidential nomination of 1912.

When the Democratic convention met in Baltimore, June 1912, the promised land was at last in sight. The split in the Republican party ensured a Democratic victory on the single condition that the Democrats nominate a Progressive candidate on a Progressive platform. Bryan, thrice defeated, but still the most powerful figure in the party, made it his business to see that this condition was fulfilled. When the convention organized he dramatized his purpose by opposing his old rival Alton B. Parker for the temporary chairmanship. By a narrow margin Parker won, but the reaction from the country was critical, and Bryan emerged from this preliminary skirmish stronger than ever. The real battle came on the nomination. The largest number of delegates were pledged to Champ Clark of Missouri, the candidate of the party regulars and of William Randolph Hearst. Judge Harmon of Ohio had the support of Tammany Hall, Underwood of Alabama represented the Bourbon Democracy of the South, Governor Wilson commanded the progressive wing of the party. Before the balloting got under way Bryan forced the convention to adopt a resolution renouncing ' any candidate who is the representative of or under obligation to J. Pierpont Morgan, Thomas F. Ryan, August Belmont, or any other member of the privilege-hunting and favor-seeking class.' From the beginning Clark led the field, but when on the tenth ballot Tammany Hall threw its vote to the Missourian, Bryan in a dramatic repudiation of any candidate who had the support of the New York bosses, transferred his vote from Clark to Wilson. Once again the ' folks back home ' were heard from, and as the balloting dragged on one delegate after another followed Bryan's lead. On the forty-sixth ballot Woodrow Wilson was nominated.

The presidential election, then, became a three-cornered contest between Taft, Roosevelt, and Wilson; but really between the two last, as rival bidders for the popular support against privilege. It was a year of social unrest. The I.W.W. took charge of a great strike in the polyglot textile city of Lawrence, Massachusetts, and displayed to the shocked middle class red banners with lawless mottoes. The Socialist nominee Eugene Debs was attracting more support than ever before in the history of the party. Samuel Gompers, analyzing the Progressive platform as mere eye-wash for Caesarism, advised labor to vote for Wilson, but reformers generally were divided. Taft and the Republicans clearly represented the ultra-conservatives, but there was little to choose between in the Democratic and the Progressive platforms. Both denounced the Payne-Aldrich tariff, but the Democratic platform had the more clean-cut tariff plank. The Progressive platform was more explicit on social and industrial reforms, but the influence of Roosevelt's financial backers, Frank Munsey and George W. Perkins, could be detected in the prudent avoidance of the trust issue, which the Democrats emphasized. It was on the regulation of business that Roosevelt and Wilson differed most sharply. Roosevelt believed that big business was here to stay, and that concentration was inevitable; his solution of the problem was effective regulation. Wilson subscribed rather to the doctrine of Louis Brandeis, that bigness was a curse, and that the responsibility of government was to break it down and to restore genuine competition. The solution, as Brandeis saw it, was regulated competition instead of regulated monopoly — this was the heart of Wilson's New Freedom. However similar their platforms, their methods of campaigning had no more in common than had their personalities. Roosevelt's tone was that of a fighting parson; Wilson already showed some glint of the spiritual quality of Lincoln. Roosevelt, with biblical imagery and voice like a shrilling fife, stirred men to wrath, to combat, and to antique virtue; Wilson, serene and confident, lifted men out of themselves by phrases that sang in their hearts, to a vision of a better world. It was the Old Testament against the New, and the New won.

Wilson polled only 42 per cent of the vote, but won an overwhelming victory in the electoral college. Roosevelt, with 27 per cent, carried six states. Taft, with 23 per cent, carried only Utah and Vermont. Nine hundred thousand voted for Debs! Technically, Wilson was a minority President, as Lincoln had been; actually the progressive principles which he, Roosevelt, and Debs alike espoused, commanded the support of over three-fourths of the voters.[3] The Democrats swept Congress, carrying the House by 290 to 145 and the Senate by 51 to 45, and they were victorious in twenty-one of the state gubernatorial contests. It was a complete repudiation of the old order.

Progressives thought of 1856 and were confident of triumph in 1916. The Grand Old Party, as they saw it, had gone the way of the Whig party — killed by a great moral issue that it would not face. Another bland Buchanan was in the White House. But the Old Guard neither died nor surrendered. The Progressives were little more than a candidate and his following, certainly not an organic party. And Woodrow Wilson, instead of playing the part of Buchanan, welded his party into a fit instrument of his great purpose ' to square every process of our national life again with the standards we so proudly set up at the beginning and have always carried at our hearts.'

BIBLIOGRAPHY

1. GENERAL: ROOSEVELT AND TAFT. Henry Adams, *The Education of Henry Adams;* John Blum, *The Republican Roosevelt;* Claude Bowers, *Beveridge and the Progressive Movement;* Nicholas Murray Butler, *Across the Busy Years* (2 vols.) ; Archie Butt, *Taft and Roosevelt Intimate Letters;* Herbert Croly, *The Promise of American Life;* Lewis Einstein, *Roosevelt: His Mind in Action;* Harold U. Faulkner, *The Decline of Laissez Faire;* Eric Goldman, *Rendezvous with Destiny;* Stephen Gwynn (ed.) , *Letters and Friendships of Sir Cecil Spring-Rice* (2 vols.) ; Philip Jessup, *Elihu Root* (2 vols.) ; Walter Johnson, *William Allen White's America;* Matthew Josephson, *The President Makers;* Henry Cabot Lodge (ed.) , *Selections from the Correspondence of Theodore Roosevelt and Henry Cabot Lodge* (2 vols.) ; A. T. Mason, *Bureaucracy Convicts Itself: The Ballinger-Pinchot Controversy;* E. E. Morison & J. M. Blum (eds.) , *The Letters of Theodore Roosevelt* (8 vols.) ; George E. Mowry, *The Era of Theodore Roosevelt;* Allan Nevins, *Henry White;* Gifford Pinchot, *Breaking New Ground;* Henry F. Pringle, *Theodore Roosevelt* and *Life and Times of William Howard Taft* (2 vols.) ; James Ford Rhodes, *The McKinley and Roosevelt Administrations;* R. M. Stahl, *The Ballinger-Pinchot Controversy;* Nathaniel W. Stephenson, *Nelson W. Aldrich;* Henry Stimson, *On Active Service in Peace and War;* O. S. Straus, *Under Four Administrations: From Cleveland to Taft.*

2. THE EXTENSIONS OF GOVERNMENT REGULATION. Frederick L. Allen, *The Great Pierpont Morgan;* F. B. Clark, *Constitutional Doctrines of Justice Harlan;* James D. Clark, *The Federal Trust Policy;* Sidney Fine, *Laissez Faire and the General Welfare State;* Samuel P. Hays, *Conservation and the Gospel of Efficiency 1890–1920;* B. H. Hibbard, *History of Public Land Policies;*

---

[3] 11,334,324 voted for the Progressive candidate, 3,483,922 for Taft.

H. L. Hurwitz, *Theodore Roosevelt and Labor in New York State;* Eliot Jones, *The Trust Problem in the United States;* D. M. Keezer & Stacy May, *The Public Control of Business;* B. H. Meyer, *A History of the Northern Securities Case;* Gifford Pinchot, *The Fight for Conservation;* Philip Taft, *The A.F. of L. in the Time of Gompers;* W. H. Taft, *The Anti-Trust Act and the Supreme Court;* Hans B. Thorelli, *The Federal Anti-Trust Policy;* C. R. Van Hise, *Conservation of Natural Resources;* A. H. Walker, *History of the Sherman Act;* H. W. Wiley, *An Autobiography.*

3. FOREIGN AFFAIRS: GENERAL. Eugene N. Anderson, *The First Moroccan Crisis;* Howard K. Beale, *Theodore Roosevelt and the Rise of America to World Power;* Samuel F. Bemis, *The United States as a World Power, 1900–1950;* Joseph B. Bishop, *Theodore Roosevelt and His Times* (2 vols.) ; Charles S. Campbell, *Anglo-American Understanding 1898–1903;* Herbert Croly, *Willard Straight;* Tyler Dennett, *John Hay: From Poetry to Politics;* L. E. Ellis, *Reciprocity, 1911;* Lionel M. Gelber, *The Rise of Anglo-American Friendship;* W. H. Haas, *The American Empire;* Philip Jessup, *Elihu Root* (2 vols.) ; J. L. Keenleyside & G. S. Brown, *Canada and the United States;* Allan Nevins, *Henry White;* G. C. O'Gara, *Theodore Roosevelt and the Rise of the Modern Navy;* Alfred Vagts, *Deutschland und die Vereinigten Staaten in der Weltpolitik* (2 vols.) .

4. FOREIGN AFFAIRS: PANAMA DIPLOMACY. K. W. Abbott, *Panama and the Canal;* J. B. Bishop, *The Panama Gateway;* J. B. and F. Bishop, *Goethals, Genius of the Panama Canal;* Miles Du Val, *Cadiz to Cathay* and *And the Mountains Will Move;* M. C. Gorgas & B. J. Hendrick, *W. C. Gorgas: His Life and Work;* W. D. McCain, *The United States and the Republic of Panama;* H. G. Miller, *The Isthmian Highway;* Dwight Miner, *The Fight for the Panama Route.*

5. FOREIGN AFFAIRS: MEXICO AND THE CARIBBEAN. W. H. Callott, *The Caribbean Policy of the United States;* V. S. Clark, *et al., Porto Rico and Its Problems;* H. P. Davis, *Black Democracy;* Russell J. Fitzgibbon, *Cuba and the United States 1900–1935;* Henry C. Hill, *Roosevelt and the Caribbean;* C. M. Knight, *Americans in Santo Domingo;* David Lockmiller, *Magoon in Cuba: History of the Second Intervention;* Knowlton Mixer, *Porto Rico;* Dana G. Monroe, *The United States and the Caribbean;* J. Fred Rippy, *The United States and Mexico* and *The Capitalists and Colombia;* G. H. Stuart, *Cuba and Its International Relations;* Frank Tannenbaum, *The Mexican Agrarian Revolution;* Sumner Welles, *Naboth's Vineyard* (2 vols.) ; Arthur P. Whitaker, *The United States and South America: The Northern Republics.*

6. FOREIGN AFFAIRS: THE PACIFIC AND THE FAR EAST. Thomas A. Bailey, *Theodore Roosevelt and the Japanese-American Crisis;* George H. Blakeslee, *Conflicts of Policy in the Far East;* J. H. Blount, *American Occupation of the Philippines 1898–1912;* P. H. Clemens, *The Boxer Rebellion;* Tyler Dennett, *Roosevelt and the Russo-Japanese War* and *Americans in Eastern Asia;* C. B. Elliott, *The Philippines to the End of Commission Government* (2 vols.) ; Alfred W. Griswold, *The Far Eastern Policy of the United States;* S. L. Gulick, *The American Japanese Problem;* Hermann Hagedorn, *Leonard Wood* (2 vols.) ; F. B. Harrison, *The Cornerstone of Philippine Independence;* Grayson Kirk,

Philippine Independence; R. D. McKenzie, *Oriental Exclusion;* H. K. Norton, *China and the Powers;* J. G. Reid, *The Manchu Abdication and the Powers 1908–1912;* C. F. Remer, *Foreign Investments in China;* J. S. Reyes, *Legislative History of America's Economic Policy Towards the Philippines;* Nicholas Roosevelt, *The Philippines;* S. K. Stevens, *American Expansion in Hawaii;* Dean C. Worcester, *The Philippines, Past and Present.*

7. THE ELECTION OF 1912. Ray S. Baker, *Woodrow Wilson, Life and Letters,* vol. 3; William J. Bryan, *A Tale of Two Conventions;* Champ Clark, *My Quarter Century of American Politics* (2 vols.) ; Josephus Daniels, *The Wilson Era: Years of Peace, 1910–1917;* Kenneth W. Hechler, *Insurgency: Personalities and Politics of the Taft Era;* Arthur Link, *Woodrow Wilson and the Progressive Era* and *Woodrow Wilson: The Road to the White House;* George Mowry, *Theodore Roosevelt and the Progressive Movement;* Victor Rosewater, *Backstage in 1912;* Mark Sullivan, *Our Times,* vol. 3.

8. DOCUMENTS. R. J. Bartlett (ed.), *The Record of American Diplomacy;* P. H. Clyde (ed.), *United States Policy Towards China;* H. S. Commager, *Documents,* nos. 345–52, 355, 356, 360–63, 367, 369–87, 412, 446; J. W. Gantenbein, *Evolution of Latin American Policy,* passim.

For further references, *Harvard Guide,* ¶¶ 220–25, 236–39.

The New Freedom

1. The Inaugural

FEW men have ever come to high office in the United States so un-prepared politically as was Woodrow Wilson, but no man ever showed a firmer grasp of the problems of statemanship with which he had to cope, or a shrewder understanding of the game of politics which he was to play. Before he became President he had held only one elective office. Possibly his most remarkable characteristic was his capacity for growth, his ability to immerse himself in new prob-lems, to master them and to re-interpret them in the light of the past and of his own convictions. By birth and training a conservative and a Hamiltonian, he became the greatest leader of the plain people since Lincoln, and a democrat who accommodated the ideals of Jef-fersonian democracy to the conditions of a new day.

Few even of the new President's friends expected more than a re-spectable presidency. Wilson lacked the common touch, and loved humanity in the abstract rather than people in particular. Unlike T.R., he could not descend into the market-place or emulate the prize-ring; throughout his eight years of office he was always aloof and often alone; no one ever called him W.W. or Tommy! His hu-mor and warm affections appeared only to a few intimate friends. The obstinacy that had been his undoing in the academic world was not likely to be a useful virtue in the presidency, if Cleveland's career was a fair test; and it was clear that Wilson would not sacrifice a principle either for friendship or for political expediency. ' Wilson is clean, strong, high-minded and cold-blooded,' wrote F. K. Lane, the warm-hearted man who became his Secretary of the Interior; but he was also the kind of person to take refuge from facts in generali-ties. In an era of fierce contention, and without Lincoln's ability to express himself in simple, homely language, he was certain to be misunderstood.

The Democratic party for which he was now the spokesman had undergone little change since Andrew Jackson's time. The elements in it that counted were the emotional and somewhat radical Western wing represented by Bryan; Irish-Americans of the industrial states, who wanted the power and office denied them during the Republican dynasties; a large segment of labor and the Solid South, including almost every white man in the late Confederacy, and many in the new Southwest — Oklahoma, New Mexico, and Arizona. Tradition, habit, and common suspicion of Big Business and Wall Street held these sections together, and the issues of liquor and religion that almost split the party in 1924 and again in 1928 had not yet arisen; the small farmers of the South and West had much in common while the rural tories of the South could sympathize with rebels against the Northern industrial bosses.

In only one election since Reconstruction had the Democratic party polled less than 42 per cent of the popular vote cast for a President, and in five of the ten presidential elections it received a plurality. But the party wanted leadership. Cleveland's victories had proved barren, Bryan had thrice failed, and the majority leaders in Congress were elderly and timid. For the task of leadership Wilson proved himself peculiarly equipped. He had inherited a Calvinistic philosophy which placed the halo of moral necessity on expediency, and he had developed an intellectual arrogance which inclined him to rely largely upon his own judgment, while from a prolonged professional study of the science of government he had learned the necessity of executive leadership in the modern state. This conclusion emerged from all three of his earlier scholarly works, *Congressional Government,* *The State,* and *Constitutional Government in the United States,* and it was basic to his political thinking and practice. ' We have grown more and more inclined,' he said in 1908, ' to look to the President as the unifying force of our complex system, the leader both of his party and of the nation.' He had tested his theory of executive leadership in New Jersey and found it good; he was now prepared to justify it in a larger sphere.

Wilson's inaugural address, striking a note of high idealism and couched in words reminiscent of Jefferson's first inaugural, aroused the hopes and enthusiasm of liberals everywhere.

No one can mistake the purpose for which the Nation now seeks to use the Democratic Party. It seeks to use it to interpret a change in its plans and point of view. Some old things with which we had grown familiar, and which had begun to creep into the very habit of our thought and of our lives, have altered their aspect as we have latterly looked critically upon them, with fresh, awakened eyes. . . . Some new things . . . have come to assume the aspect of things long believed in and familiar, stuff of our own convictions. We have been refreshed by a new insight into our own life.

It was by the light of this new vision that Wilson examined the processes by which America had achieved her greatness and revealed the ruthlessness, waste, and corruption, and reckoned anew the cost, not by the balance sheet of business but in the ledger of social well-being.

We have been proud of our industrial achievements, but we have not hitherto stopped thoughtfully enough to count the human cost of lives snuffed out, of energies over-taxed and broken, the fearful physical and spiritual cost to the men and women and children upon whom the dead weight and burden of it all has fallen pitilessly the years through. The groans and agony of it all had not yet reached our ears, the solemn, moving undertone of our life, coming up out of the mines and factories and out of every home where the struggle had its intimate and familiar seat. . . . The great Government we loved has too often been made use of for private and selfish purposes, and those who used it had forgotten the people.

The inaugural, however, was not just a jeremiad, but a program of constructive reform. ' Our duty,' said Wilson, ' is to cleanse, to reconsider, to restore, to correct the evil without impairing the good, to purify and humanize every process of our common life.' And he itemized with some degree of particularity the things that ought to be altered. These included the tariff, ' which makes the Government a facile instrument in the hands of private interests '; an antiquated and inadequate banking and currency system; a burdensome and wasteful industrial system, which ' exploits without renewing or conserving the natural resources of the country '; an inefficient and neglected agricultural system; ' water-courses undeveloped, waste places unreclaimed, forests untended, unregarded waste heaps at every mine.' Government was not negative —

it must be put at the service of humanity, in safeguarding the health of the Nation, the health of its men and its women and its children, as well as their rights in the struggle for existence. . . . There can be no equality of opportunity . . . if men and women and children be not shielded in their lives, their very vitality, from the consequences of great industrial and social processes, which they can not alter, control, or singly cope with. . . . Sanitary laws, pure food laws and laws determining conditions of labor which individuals are powerless to determine for themselves are intimate parts of the very business of justice and legal efficiency. The Nation has been deeply stirred by a solemn passion, stirred by the knowledge of wrong, of ideals lost, of government too often debauched and made an instrument of evil. The feelings with which we face this new age of right and opportunity sweep across our heartstrings like some air out of God's own presence, where justice and mercy are reconciled and the judge and the brother are one.

And the Calvinist in Wilson visualized the contest as one between the forces of good and of evil.

No administration of modern times has been inaugurated with a greater passion for righteousness and justice. Yet it was not in the nature of American politics to move on a high level of idealism, nor to surrender without a struggle the stakes of battle. Nor was Wilson himself either a fighting progressive like LaFollette, a spokesman for agrarian and labor discontent like Bryan, or a doctrinaire liberal like the editors of the *New Republic* and the *Nation*. He was rather an old-fashioned liberal, suspicious of bigness, suspicious of special interests whether they were of Wall Street or of the Grange or the labor union. And he was by no means prepared to forego the advantages of partisanship; he considered himself not only the head of the nation, but the head of his party as well, and no more consummate political strategist ever cracked the whip of party regularity. It was Wilson's fortune during his first administration to have behind him a reasonably united party, eager to follow his leadership. It was his misfortune during his second administration to conjure up the most bitter political and personal antagonisms in recent American history, and to have a large part of his reform program imperiled by the intervention of war.

2. THE UNDERWOOD TARIFF

Colonel E. M. House elected himself the political liaison officer of the Wilson administration. The cabinet was selected with his advice, though not by his dictation, in order to reunite a party considerably torn by the contest for the presidential nomination. It was an able if not a brilliant cabinet, as good as any since the Hayes administration. Bryan was the inevitable choice for the State Department, not only by reason of his contribution to Wilson's nomination but because he would ensure the support of his immense following. William G. McAdoo, Wilson's campaign manager and future son-in-law, became Secretary of the Treasury. L. M. Garrison as Secretary of War proved too warlike for his chief, and was dropped after three years for the more pacific Newton D. Baker, reform mayor of Cleveland. Franklin K. Lane, Canadian by birth and Californian by residence, became the ideal Secretary of the Interior to reconcile the Far West to conservation. The appointment of Josephus Daniels, a North Carolina editor, to the Navy Department caused criticism, but he proved himself a satisfactory administrator and a faithful ally in the fight for progressive legislation, and allowed his young assistant-secretary, Franklin D. Roosevelt, to take care of routine naval matters. David F. Houston, like Wilson a scholar and a university president, was the choice for the Department of Agriculture and William B. Wilson, who had begun life as a miner and was most acceptable to labor, was appointed to the newly created Labor Department. For the important post of Attorney-General, Wilson wanted Louis Brandeis, but was dissuaded; the substitution of J. C. McReynolds, a Tennessee lawyer, was a mistake which Wilson compounded by promoting him to the Supreme Court. Finally Wilson wanted ' one thorough-going politician ' in his cabinet, and in A. S. Burleson of Texas, as Postmaster-General, he found a man who had no other qualifications. Four members of the cabinet were from the South, and two from the West; New England was not represented although Massachusetts, for the first time since 1820, had voted with Virginia.

When Congress met on 7 April 1913 President Wilson revived a practice abandoned by Jefferson, of addressing both Houses in person. A slight thing in itself, this act caught the popular imagination. It restored the President's initiative in lawmaking and established a relation between the ' two ends of Pennsylvania Avenue ' in the best sort of way. For Wilson's power over men left him when he stepped off the rostrum; unlike Roosevelt, he could not persuade or browbeat Congressmen in private conversation.

On the very day he took office, Wilson had summoned Congress to special session, as in 1909, to revise the tariff. It was a dangerous issue; in the preceding twenty years only one tariff revision had not resulted in defeat at the polls, and the fate of the Wilson-Gorman tariff was as familiar to Democrats as the fate of the Payne-Aldrich to Republicans. But there was no hesitation, no compromise, in Wilson's position. ' The tariff duties must be altered,' he said. ' We must abolish everything that bears even the semblance of privilege, or of any kind of artificial advantage, and put our business men and producers under the stimulation of a constant necessity to be efficient, economical and enterprising.' Hearings on the new tariff bill had begun as early as January 1913, and House leaders such as Underwood of Alabama, Kitchin of North Carolina, and Hull of Tennessee were ready with a bill. After a brief debate, the Underwood tariff, as it came to be known, passed the House by a strict party vote, 281 to 139. The real struggle, as everyone anticipated, came in the Senate.

On 8 May the Underwood tariff went to the Senate, which prepared to exercise its ancient prerogative of rewriting the House measure. To assist in this task, representatives of vested interests descended upon Washington. Senator Thomas of Colorado described the scene:

By telegram, by letter, by resolutions of commercial and industrial associations and unions, by interviews, by threat, by entreaty, by the importunities of men and the clamor of creditors, by newspaper criticism and contention, by pamphlet and circular, by the sinister pressure of a lobby of limitless resources, by all the arts and power of wealth and organization, the Senate has been and will be besieged, until it capitulates or the Underwood bill shall have been enacted.

Wilson did not intend that the circumstances of the Wilson-Gorman and the Payne-Aldrich tariffs should be duplicated. In a public statement of 26 May he lashed out at the sinister activities of the lobbyists. ' It is of serious interest to the country,' he said, ' that the people at large should have no lobby, and be voiceless in these matters, while great bodies of astute men seek to create an artificial opinion and to overcome the interests of the public for their private profit.' His appeal was effective, and consideration of the tariff bill went forward in a more wholesome atmosphere. Through the hot months of a Washington summer the President held Congress to its appointed task. He himself set an example of ceaseless vigilance, scrutinizing every section of the measure with meticulous care and appearing with embarrassing frequency at the Senate committee rooms to participate in conferences. In September the bill passed the Senate, and

on 3 October 1913 it received the signature of the President, who announced that ' we have set the business of this country free from those
conditions which have made monopoly not only possible, but in a
sense easy and natural.'

The Underwood tariff was far from a free-trade measure, but it
did reverse a tariff policy which had been almost unchallenged for
fifty years. The average duties were reduced from some 37 per cent
to some 27 per cent, but more important than this were reductions
in specific schedules and additions to the free list. Duties were reduced on 958 articles, raised on 86, and maintained on 307. Reductions embraced important raw materials such as cotton and woolen
goods, iron and steel, while wool, sugar, iron ore, steel rails, agricultural implements, hides, boots, cement, coal, wood and wood pulp, as
well as many agricultural products were to enter duty free. To meet
the anticipated reduction in revenues, the bill provided for a graduated tax on incomes of $4000 and over, ranging from 1 to 6 per cent.
For all the jeremiads of the business interests, the new tariff worked
admirably during the brief period of peace in which it could be
tested, and the income tax brought sufficient revenue to balance the
budget.

3. BANKING AND CURRENCY REFORM

As an administrative measure, reform of the banking and currency
system was second only in a strictly chronological sense, for Wilson
had from the first envisioned such legislation as an integral part of
the reform program. In his inaugural address he had called attention
to ' a banking and currency system based upon the necessity of the
Government to sell its bonds fifty years ago and perfectly adapted to
concentrating cash and restricting credits,' and in his tariff message
of 8 April he had promised to call to the attention of Congress ' reforms which should press close upon the heels of the tariff changes
. . . of which the chief is the reform of our banking and currency
laws.' Actually the President presented his proposal for a reorganization of the banking system while Congress was still wrestling with
the Underwood tariff.

The need for a thorough overhauling of our banking and currency
system was almost universally recognized. The election of 1896 and
the Gold Act of 1900 had settled only one aspect of the ' money
question '; credit and banker control over money and credit re-

mained to vex businessmen as well as farmers. The ' bankers' panic ' of 1907 reflected no basic unsoundness in the economic system, but a ruinous shortage of currency and inelasticity of credit; only by hasty importations of gold from abroad and by resort to extra-legal forms of currency was business able to weather the crisis. Out of this panic emerged the Aldrich-Vreeland bill which provided for a somewhat more flexible asset currency, based upon state and municipal securities and commercial paper. Recognizing that the whole question of banking and currency required further study, Congress created a National Monetary Commission, whose final report listed no less than seventeen serious defects in the American banking system, among them a ' concentration of surplus money and available funds in New York ' which ' imposes upon the banks of that city the vast responsibilities which are inherent in the control of a large proportion of the banking resources of the country.'

The extent of that concentration of money and credit was not fully realized until the investigations of the Pujo Committee of 1912 were made public. Those investigations revealed that the firm members or directors of two sets of New York banks, controlled by the Morgan and Rockefeller interests, held:

One hundred and eighteen directorships in 34 banks and trust companies having total resources of $2,679,000,000 and total deposits of $1,983,000,-000.

Thirty directorships in ten insurance companies having total assets of $2,293,000,000.

One hundred and five directorships in 32 transportation systems having a total capitalization of $11,784,000,000 and a total mileage (excluding express companies and steamship lines) of 150,000.

Sixty-three directorships in 24 producing and trading corporations having a total capitalization of $3,339,000,000.

Twenty-five directorships in 12 public utility corporations having a total capitalization of $2,150,000,000.

In all, 341 directorships of 112 corporations having aggregate resources of capitalization of $22,245,000,000.

Wilson himself was acutely aware of this condition, and of its significance to the agriculture and industry of the nation. ' The great monopoly in this country,' he had said in 1911, ' is the money monopoly. . . . The growth of the nation, and all our activities, are in the hands of a few men who . . . are necessarily concentrated upon the great undertakings in which their own money is involved, and who necessarily . . . chill and check and destroy genius and economic freedom.'

To this question, then, the new administration promptly addressed itself. Upon the necessity of reform all were agreed, but upon the precise nature of that reform there was widespread disagreement. Conservatives, even within the President's own party, wanted legislation along the lines of the Aldrich Act which would establish a central bank such as the old Bank of the United States without its branches, and place control of credit in the hands of the bankers. Bryan's followers, on the other hand, were determined that the power to issue notes should be a government not a private function, and that control of the new banking system should be exclusively governmental. Wilson was unfamiliar with the technical aspects of banking but, as Carter Glass later wrote, ' there was never a moment when he did not know what he wanted done or know what he would not permit to be done in this currency proceeding.' On 23 June he appeared before Congress to outline his own program for banking and currency reform.

We must have a currency, not rigid as now, but readily, elastically responsive to sound credit. . . . And the control of this system of banking and of issue which our new laws are to set up must be public, not private, must be vested in the Government itself, so that the banks may be the instruments, not the masters of business and of individual enterprise and initiative.

Carter Glass was ready with a bill which carried out these general principles, and for six months Congress wrangled over this administration measure while metropolitan bankers and Western farmers criticized it with equal severity. Wilson had little to fear from the opposition of the bankers, but he could not afford to forfeit the support of Bryan and his followers, and in the end the provisions of the new law recognized both of Bryan's demands: that there should be no banker representation on the banking board, and that all Federal Reserve currency should be governmental obligations.

The Federal Reserve Act of 23 December 1913 provided for the creation of a new national banking system upon regional lines. The country was divided into twelve districts,[1] each with a Federal Reserve Bank owned by the member banks, which were required to sub-

[1] District banks were established at Boston, New York, Philadelphia, Cleveland, Richmond, Atlanta, Chicago, St. Louis, Minneapolis, Kansas City, Dallas, and San Francisco.

scribe 6 per cent of their capital. These regional banks acted as agents for their members. All national banks were required and state banks permitted to join; within a decade one-third of the banks, representing 70 per cent of the banking resources of the country, were members of the Federal Reserve system. A Federal Reserve Board, consisting of the Secretary and the Comptroller of the Treasury and six others appointed by the President, was to supervise the business of the regional banks. A new type of currency was authorized: Federal Reserve notes secured by short-term commercial paper and backed by a 40 per cent gold reserve. The new system was designed to introduce greater elasticity into the credit of the country, a sounder distribution of banking facilities, and more effective safeguards against speculation. All of these ends were realized, and in time the bankers themselves admitted that the Federal Reserve system had added immeasurably to the financial stability of the country.

One of the purposes of the Federal Reserve Act was to provide easier credit for farmers, but the act did little to bring down farm interest rates or ease farm credit. These objects were partially achieved however, by the Federal Farm Loan Act of May 1916 which purposed to ' reduce the cost of handling farm loans, place upon the market mortgages which would be a safe investment for private funds, attract into agricultural operations a fair share of the capital of the nation, and lead to a reduction of interest.' Specifically the act created a Federal Farm Loan Board and 12 regional Farm Loan banks similar in general character to the Federal Reserve banks. These Farm Loan banks were authorized to extend loans on farm lands, buildings, and improvements up to 70 per cent of their value to co-operative farm loan associations. Loans were to run from 5 to 40 years, interest rates not to exceed 6 per cent, and profits were to be distributed to the members of the subscribing farm loan associations. By 1930 over 4000 such farm loan associations had been established and over a billion dollars of farm mortgages were held by the Farm Loan banks. A further step toward the creation of better credit facilities for farmers was taken in the enactment of the Warehouse Act of 1916 authorizing licensed warehouses to issue against farm products warehouse receipts which might be used as negotiable paper. Thus were the Populists vindicated a quarter-century after their subtreasury scheme had been rejected with contempt.

4. THE REGULATION OF BUSINESS

With the enactment of the Underwood tariff and the Federal Reserve Act the Democrats had gone far toward translating their platform promises into law, but the most emphatic of the party pledges was as yet unfulfilled. 'A private monopoly,' said the platform, 'is indefensible and intolerable. We therefore . . . demand the enactment of such additional legislation as may be necessary to make it impossible for a private monopoly to exist in the United States.' In the campaign, too, Wilson had stressed the trust problem as the paramount issue; and the heart of the 'New Freedom,' as he had elaborated it in his speeches, was the freedom of the consumer from monopolies and the restoration of competition.

Additional anti-trust legislation was long overdue. Roosevelt had recognized the need, but had failed to obtain such legislation from a recalcitrant Congress; Taft had not even tried. Yet the findings of the Pujo Committee of 1913 and of the Commission on Industrial Relations of 1915 revealed that trusts were more numerous and monopolies more powerful in 1913 than at the beginning of the century. Reliance upon the Sherman law was clearly futile, and Wilson, in his acceptance speech, had called for 'new laws' to meet 'conditions that menace our civilization.'

As soon as the tariff and banking reform bills were disposed of, Wilson appeared before Congress to ask for legislation on trusts and monopolies. His address of 20 January 1914 included five specific legislative recommendations: the prohibition of interlocking directorates of corporations, banks, railroads, and public utilities; the grant of authority to the Interstate Commerce Commission to regulate the financial operations of railways; the explicit definition of the meaning of the anti-trust laws; the creation of a federal interstate trade commission to supervise and guide business; and the penalization of individuals, not business, for violations of the anti-trust laws. Congress responded with three bills designed to meet executive specifications: the Federal Trade Commission Act, the Clayton Anti-Trust Act, and the Rayburn Securities Act. The first two became law in September and October 1914; the third was defeated in the Senate and was not successfully revived until 1933.

The Federal Trade Commission Act was preventive rather than punitive in character. It replaced Roosevelt's Bureau of Corporations with a new non-partisan commission of five, appointed by the President for seven-year terms. Unfair methods of competition were declared unlawful, and the commission was authorized to investigate alleged violations of the anti-trust laws and to issue ' cease and desist ' orders against any corporation found guilty of unfair methods of competition. During Wilson's administration the commission heard some 2000 complaints and issued 379 ' cease and desist ' orders against such malpractices as misleading advertising, bribery, adulteration, and unfair competition. In co-operation with the Department of Justice it brought about the dissolution of the International Harvester Company and the Corn Products Refining Company, and its subsequent investigations of electric light and power companies materially aided President Franklin D. Roosevelt in obtaining more adequate regulation of public utilities.

The Clayton Act, though far from radical in character, encountered bitter opposition. It prohibited discriminations in price which might tend to lessen competition or create monopoly and ' tying ' agreements limiting the right of purchasers to deal in the products of competing manufacturers. It forbade corporations to acquire stock in competing concerns, and outlawed interlocking directorates in corporations with a capital of more than $1 million and banks with a capital of more than $5 million. In accordance with the President's recommendation, officers of corporations were made personally responsible for violations of the act. Labor unions were exempted from the terms of the act as long as they sought legitimate objectives, and the use of the injunction in labor disputes ' unless necessary to prevent irreparable injury to property . . . for which there is no adequate remedy at law ' was explicitly forbidden. Gompers hailed these provisions as ' labor's charter of freedom,' yet the act did not outlaw the notorious ' yellow-dog ' contracts or, unlike the British Act of 1906, relieve unions from corporate responsibility for damage caused by their members; and subsequent developments were to reveal its inadequacy.

' With this legislation,' said Wilson optimistically, ' there is clear and sufficient law to check and destroy the noxious growth [of monopoly] in its infancy.' But the courts reserved to themselves the right to determine what constituted ' unfair methods of competition ' just as they reserved the right to interpret the phrase 'irreparable injury to property,' and in the war and postwar years judicial rulings became increasingly conservative. The effort to enforce the provision making directors responsible for corporation malpractices broke down when the government failed to prove its case against the directors of the New Haven Railroad. During the war the Clayton Act was tacitly suspended, and in the postwar period of Republican ascendancy it was seldom invoked, while the Federal Trade Commission, by encouraging the formulation of codes of trade practices, entered into something suspiciously like an alliance with the trusts. When, twenty years after the enactment of the Wilsonian anti-trust legislation, Franklin D. Roosevelt came into office, the trusts were as numerous and monopolies as powerful as ever, and the whole problem had to be studied afresh. Perhaps all this merely demonstrates the validity of Thurman Arnold's theory that the function of anti-trust agitation and legislation is purely ceremonial — that it provides us the satisfaction of declaiming against the ' evil ' part of a ' necessary evil ' while retaining what is necessary about it. Yet if the legislation did not break up trusts or curb monopolies, it may well have imposed on them a pattern of good behavior.

By 1914 the major part of Wilson's program had been achieved, and Wilson, who was not at all a social reformer of the LaFollette type, was content to rest on his oars. He had used his influence to moderate the terms of the Clayton Act, appointed notorious conservatives to the Federal Reserve Board and the Federal Trade Commission, and displayed indifference toward the child labor bill and the LaFollette Seamen's bill, both of which hung fire in Congress. And until alarmed by the storm of liberal disapproval, he had permitted members of his cabinet to practice racial discrimination in several government departments — including the Post Office — and acquiesced in racial policies dictated by the reactionary wing of the Democratic party in the South. His instinct for moderation was strengthened by the congressional elections of 1914 which reduced the Democratic majority in the House from 73 to 25, and gave several of the industrial states of the East to the Republicans.

Wilson would doubtless have continued his cautious drift to the right had it not been for the collapse of the Progressive party in 1916, and the threat that Roosevelt's ardent following might follow him back into the Republican fold. If the election of 1912 had meant anything, it meant the endorsement of progressivism by the great majority of American voters. And if one thing was clear, in 1916, it was that Wilson could not hope to outbid the Republican party in conservatism. Confronted by this situation, Wilson once more turned to the left. In rapid succession came the appointment of the distinguished labor-lawyer, Louis D. Brandeis, to the Supreme Court, the enactment of a Workmen's Compensation Law for the federal civil service, of a law excluding the products of child labor from interstate commerce, of the Federal Farm Loan Bill, and of the Adamson Act establishing an eight-hour day on all interstate railways. That fall the Democratic party was able to go to the country with a record of constructive legislation which compared favorably with that of any previous administration in history. If it all looked more like T.R.'s New Nationalism than like Wilson's New Freedom, it could be noted that T.R. himself had abandoned the New Nationalism so that it was a fair case of ' finders keepers.'

In four years Wilson had reasserted presidential leadership, converted a state-rights party to enlightened nationalism, convinced the average citizen that the government was at last his servant, and made clear that progressivism transcended party lines.

5. Neighbors and Dependencies

Wilson had not mentioned foreign affairs in his inaugural address nor had he discussed them in his campaign; yet his first administration was concerned largely, his second almost exclusively, with problems of international relations. When he assumed office the United States was at peace with the world, but faced with many vexatious controversies which demanded early attention. Japanese aggressions in Manchuria threatened the open door policy, and Japan was assuming a menacing attitude toward the anti-alien land laws of the Pacific coast states; Colombia was still sore over the Panama episode, and England was aggrieved at our discrimination in favor of American coastwise shipping through the Panama Canal; American marines controlled Nicaragua, and conditions elsewhere in the Caribbean were unsettled, while Mexico was in the throes of a revolution which vitally affected American interests. To the solution of these difficulties the new President brought neither experience nor detailed information, but a body of broad principles which not only required the maintenance of peace but American leadership in that effort. And to those principles, most of which he might justly claim to be his own, Secretary Bryan subscribed with enthusiasm. For while Wilson was for the most part his own Secretary of State, Bryan's contribution to Latin-American policy was not negligible; his interpretation of the problem of neutrality, when that arose, was, however, less realistic than that of his chief.

In principle and to a lesser extent in practice, Wilson reversed much of the foreign policy of his predecessors. The first hint of that reversal was the statement of 19 March 1913 withdrawing support from the proposed bankers' loan to China as incompatible with Chinese sovereignty. This was widely interpreted as a formal repudiation of 'dollar diplomacy.' Shortly thereafter came recognition of the new Chinese Republic. At the same time Secretary Bryan launched that program of conciliation treaties which he had been advocating ever since 1905 and in whose success he had a touching faith. Altogether Bryan concluded thirty agreements submitting all disputes — including those involving questions of ' national honor ' — to arbitration, and providing a ' cooling-off ' period of one year before resort to arms; of the major powers only Germany refused to sign such an agreement.

Bryan had campaigned in 1900 on a platform promising independence to the Philippines, and in 1912 the party had once again pledged itself to that policy. In 1914 a Bryan follower, Representative Jones of Virginia, introduced an act largely drafted by young Felix Frankfurter granting immediate self-government to the Filipinos and promising complete independence in the near future. Under pressure from the War Department, which was alive to the strategic importance of the Philippines, and from Catholics who feared confiscation of church property in the islands, Wilson maneuvered for a less drastic bill. There was a brief tug-of-war between the Bryan followers who wanted to write into the bill a specific time-limit on American control, and the conservatives of both parties who were reluctant to commit themselves — or the Philippines — so definitely. In the end the conservatives won. The Jones Act, passed in 1916, formally pledged the United States to withdraw from the Philippines ' as soon as a stable government can be established therein,' and inaugurated far-reaching political and administrative reforms. It abolished the Philippine Commission, provided for a legislature of two houses, both elected by popular vote, and gave the legislature authority to reorganize the government. At the same time Governor-General Harrison filled the civil service with native Filipinos and encouraged the Philippine government to establish state-controlled railroads, banks, mines, and manufacturing industries. Under these auspices the Filipinos made such progress that President Wilson, in his last annual message, reminded Congress that the time had now come to fulfill the promise of the Jones Act. But the incoming Republican administration had no sympathy with such a program. A new commission, dominated by General Leonard Wood, reported that the islands were not ready for independence, and Wood, who stayed on as Governor-General, reversed practically all of Harrison's enlightened policies. In 1927 Wood died, but not before he had destroyed in large part the reputation he had made in Cuba; his successor, Henry L. Stimson, returned to the policy of conciliation which had been so successful. Not until 1934 did Congress finally pass a bill providing for Philippine independence; not until 1946 did the bill take effect.

It was Latin America, however, that provided the crucial test of the new policy, and that furnished the arena for its triumph and its defeat. Nothing better illustrates the high-mindedness of the new administration than Wilson's reaction to two Panama Canal problems that he had inherited from his predecessors. The first was the long-standing dispute with Colombia, which still bitterly resented the part that President Roosevelt had played in detaching Panama and setting her up as an independent state in 1903. In 1914 Bryan negotiated a treaty with Colombia which expressed ' sincere regret ' for whatever injury the United States might have inflicted, paid an indemnity of $25 million, and granted Colombia free use of the Panama Canal. That a powerful nation should apologize to a weak one was something new in international relations. To Roosevelt it was nothing less than an outrage, and his friend Senator Henry Cabot Lodge led a successful fight against ratification of the obnoxious treaty, thus delaying for seven years the restoration of good relations with Colombia and getting in some good practice for his more ambitious battle against the Versailles treaty a few years later.

The second dispute grew out of the special exemption which Congress had granted American coastwise shipping from paying tolls on the canal. The British protested this as a violation of earlier treaty agreements. Convinced that the British were right, Wilson persuaded Congress to repeal the exemption. There were practical considerations here,[2] but the moral aspects were not lost to observers.

Within two weeks of his inauguration Wilson announced that ' one of the chief objects of my administration will be to cultivate the friendship and deserve the confidence of our sister Republics of Central and South America.' A few months later, in a speech at Mobile, Alabama, he announced that the foreign policy of his administration would be concerned more with ' human rights, national integrity and opportunity ' than with ' material interests,' and promised that ' the United States will never again seek one additional foot of territory by conquest.' Yet despite these entirely sincere protestations of altruism, Wilson and Bryan continued without modification the Caribbean policies of Roosevelt and Taft. The marines remained in Nicaragua, a new and exacting bankers' loan received the approval of the State Department, and in 1914 Bryan negotiated a treaty leasing the Gulf of Fonseca, the Great Corn and Little Corn Islands, and granting the United States the right to intervene to maintain orderly government and protect property, which so seriously infringed on Nicaraguan sovereignty that it was denounced by the Central American Court of Justice. In Santo Domingo Bryan authorized ' an enlargement of the sphere of American influence beyond what we have before exercised '; and as minister to that hapless Republic he sent an ex-pugilist named James Sullivan who introduced the worst Tammany methods into Dominican politics, exploited his office for personal profit, deliberately misled the State Department about the true condition of affairs, and in the end helped precipitate a revolution. In 1916 Wilson ordered a military occupation of the Dominican Republic, which lasted for eight years. Anarchy in Haiti, too, led to American intervention. In 1915 the United States Marine Corps occupied the island after fighting which cost the lives of over 2000 Haitians. Under the terms of the treaty which the Wilson administration dictated to the helpless Haitians, American control was continued until 1930 when public opinion in the United States forced its discontinuance.

Elsewhere in the Caribbean, relations were less troubled. During the First World War Cuba experienced an unprecedented prosperity, but that prosperity was accompanied by extravagance and corrup-

2 See below, p. 541.

tion. At the close of the war the Cuban sugar market collapsed, and Cuban politics reflected the economic and financial disorder. President Wilson sent a personal representative, General Enoch Crowder, to help the Cubans out of their troubles. Crowder, for all his abilities, was only partially successful, and when prosperity returned he was discredited by the Cuban nationalists who resented his extralegal status and feared the economic implications of his advisory activities — fears not unjustified by the rapid growth of American investments and banking influence in the island. Crowder's anomalous position was soon regularized by his appointment as ambassador to Cuba, and thereafter Cuban-American relations returned, for a time, to a less troubled basis. Under the long regime of the tyrant, Gerardo Machado (1925–33), unrest was chronic, but even when that unrest broke out into revolution, the United States avoided any official intervention. The fact is that by the 1920's the rising tide of Cuban nationalism made intervention in Cuban affairs a highly dangerous business. There was a growing feeling under Coolidge and Hoover that the Platt Amendment had outlived its usefulness, but not until 1934 was President Roosevelt able to negotiate a treaty with the liberal Mendieta regime abrogating the amendment — except for the provision permitting the maintenance of a naval base.

Puerto Rico, like Cuba, was governed for a time by the United States military, but in 1900 the Foraker Act had established civil government of the old crown colony type: an elective assembly, with an executive council appointed by the President acting as an upper house. This, too, was contrary to the Wilsonian philosophy, and in 1917 Congress passed an act granting American citizenship to the inhabitants of the island, and a semi-responsible government. Not until 1947 were the islanders permitted to elect their own Governor, but in 1952 the island achieved Commonwealth status, whatever that term might mean in American constitutional law.

Intervention in Nicaragua, Santo Domingo, and Haiti, then, were balanced, in a sense, by a more enlightened policy toward Cuba and Puerto Rico. The real test of Wilson's Latin American policy was presented by Mexico, and one of the achievements of the Wilson administration was the maintenance of peace with that distraught Republic. In 1911 Porforio Diaz, dictator of Mexico for thirty-five years, resigned as a result of a revolutionary movement that he could no longer suppress. Diaz had given his country order at the expense of every sort of liberty. The national domain of 135 million acres was cut up into latifundia, or used to augment the already swollen estates of less than a thousand great landowners. At the same time Diaz pursued a policy resembling the enclosures of eighteenth-century England, expropriating and allotting in severalty the communal lands of the Indian villages. The new owners were able to exact forced labor from the landless peons by keeping them in perpetual debt for food and supplies. Education remained in the hands of the Catholic Church. The government was autocratic, the ruling class concentrated and powerful, the condition of the common people desperate. Foreign, especially English and American, mining and business interests, to which Diaz gave generous concessions and protection, enthusiastically supported his rule.

The revolution of 1910–11 was conducted by a small doctrinaire middle class under Francisco I. Madero, but supported by the peons in the hope of recovering their communal lands. Madero was installed as constitutional President in 1911, but neither kept order nor satisfied the aspirations of the landless. A counter-revolution of the landowners, supported by foreign investors, displaced him by assassination in February 1913, and installed Victoriana Huerta as President. Although unable to exert his authority over the greater part of the country, which was fast falling into anarchy, Huerta was promptly recognized by Great Britain and most of the Powers. Strong pressure was exerted on President Wilson by the American ambassador and by American business interests to do the same. How powerful those business interests were is indicated by reports of a congressional committee which calculated American investments in Mexico at $1.5 billion and estimated that Americans owned 78 per cent of the mines, 72 per cent of the smelters, 58 per cent of the oil, 68 per cent of the rubber plantations, and some two-thirds of the railroads of Mexico.

But President Wilson refused to be moved by the importunities of business. In his statement of 11 March he anticipated his refusal to recognize Huerta:

We hold that just government rests always upon the consent of the governed, and that there can be no freedom without order based upon law and upon public conscience and approval. . . . We can have no sympathy with those who seek to seize the power of government to advance their own personal interests or ambition.

Such a policy, importing moral considerations into the realm of international law, was a departure from the traditional practices of the United States as well as of other nations. The easier course would have been to accord the Huerta government *de facto* recognition, and leave to the Mexicans the solution of their problems of constitutional law and democracy. The other policy was fraught with peril, for it placed upon the United States the responsibility of deciding which government was a moral one, and of supporting that government. Furthermore in the event that Huerta failed to back down, Wilson was faced with the awkward alternatives of some kind of intervention, which would be an invitation to imperialism, or of a serious loss of prestige.

The situation also threatened to becloud Anglo-American relations, for the United States government had reason to believe that the British support for Huerta was dictated by considerations of oil, vital to the Royal Navy. As we have seen, relations between the United States and Britain were momentarily strained by the exemption of American coastal shipping from Panama Canal tolls. Colonel House met Sir Edward Grey in July 1913 in order to talk these matters over. At a series of private and informal conferences in Washington the President agreed to press Congress to repeal the obnoxious legislation in return for the British Foreign Office's withdrawing support from Huerta. The agreement, quietly conducted over the heads of the State Department and the British embassy, was carried out. Congressional leaders fumed, but acquiesced. Equality of tolls was restored by an Act of 15 June 1914, and from that date the British followed the American lead in Mexican affairs. It was well that this misunderstanding was cleared up, for within two months Europe was swept by war, and Britain needed American friendship and understanding.

Wilson was now ready for a showdown with Huerta. On 3 February 1914 he revoked the arms embargo and permitted American arms to go to the leader of the Constitutional forces, Venustiano Carranza. The landed aristocracy and the Catholic Church rallied to Huerta, and the situation seemed as insoluble as ever. What could Wilson do short of outright intervention — an intervention that would have rallied both the Huerta and the Carranza forces against the invader? At this juncture the zeal of a Mexican colonel made history. When the paymaster and crew of an American warship landed, without permission, at Tampico they were arrested. The Mexican commander instantly apologized and returned the men, but Admiral Mayo demanded not only an apology but a salute to the American flag, and President Wilson, eagerly looking for an excuse to intervene, backed him up. Inasmuch as the United States refused to recognize the Huerta government, the situation presented obvious and embarrassing legal difficulties. Huerta, hoping that American aggression might consolidate Mexican sentiment behind him, refused to budge further — though he did sardonically promise to exchange salute for salute! On 21 April a force of American marines landed at Vera Cruz which they took with slight loss to themselves but at the cost of several hundred Mexican casualties. Almost everybody expected that a second war with Mexico was about to begin. It did not begin, partly because Wilson realized that his legal case was ridiculous and his moral case far from strong, but chiefly because he wished above all to help the Mexican people find themselves. He tried to distinguish between the Mexican people and the Mexican government — just as he later distinguished between the German people and the German government — and insisted that ' if armed conflict should unhappily come . . . we should be fighting only General Huerta and those who adhere to him.'

The situation was growing acute when the President was rescued by a proposal from Argentina, Brazil, and Chile for a joint mediation. The President gladly took this way out of the impasse, especially as he was confident that he could control the proceedings, and a conference with these 'A.B.C.' powers met at Niagara Falls in May 1914 to compose the differences between the warring Mexican factions. The conference — the first of its kind in the history of the Americas — averted war and proposed a new constitutional government for Mexico. Huerta stood out stiffly against the terms of the mediation; unable, however, to obtain arms or credit from the United States or from an otherwise-occupied Europe, he was forced out of office. Late in July he fled the country, and on 20 August Venustiano Carranza, leader of the Constitutional party, entered Mexico City and took over the presidency.

But there was to be no peace for stricken Mexico. No sooner had Carranza won Mexico City than his ablest lieutenant, Francisco Villa, raised the standard of revolt. With incomparable ineptitude the Wilson administration now decided to back Villa, mistakenly supposing him more tractable than the stubborn and independent Carranza. Carranza, however, took the field, and shattered the Villa forces, and the United States had no alternative but to accord him recognition.

During the five years that followed there were occasional outbreaks of peace in Mexico. Fundamentally the trouble was that the underlying force of the revolution — the land hunger of the peasants — was unable to find a leader with the honesty to adopt fundamental reforms and the ability to carry them through. All other policies having failed, President Wilson adopted a policy of ' watchful waiting,' while endeavoring, without much success, to create a Pan-American machinery for dealing with the situation. The State Department advised all Americans to withdraw from the country, and some 40,000 did so. Many who remained to protect their property suffered at the hands of the revolutionists and bandits. Estimates of American losses vary, but it is probable that between 1910 and 1922 over 400 American civilians lost their lives in Mexico or along the Mexican border, and that property losses totaled not far from $200 million. It is relevant to note that not all the losses were on one side: the Mexicans, too, suffered loss of life and property from American intervention.

Defeated by Carranza and abandoned by the United States, Villa took to banditry. In 1916 he launched repeated raids across the border on American towns. Wilson mobilized the regular army along the Rio Grande border and in March sent an expeditionary force under General John Pershing to capture Villa. Pershing's force, 6000 strong, pursued Villa deep into the interior but failed to capture him. The practice it afforded the army was hardly worth the cost, for this violation of Mexican soil outraged Carranza and aroused the suspicion of most of the peoples of South America.

When American troops and Mexican regulars clashed at Carrizal, war seemed unavoidable. War, and even annexation, would have been popular with vociferous groups in the United States, but once again Wilson refused to take advantage of Mexican weakness. Instead he sent a commission to Mexico to try to patch things up. The commission was not very successful, but it gained time, and time was decisive. By 1917 the United States was drifting into a major war on her southern border; there was nothing she wanted less. In March 1917, Wilson formally recognized the Carranza government.

Carranza had proved himself more determined even than Wilson.

As for Wilson, despite the vagaries and blunders of his Mexican policy, what his biographer Arthur Link says is true, that

he, almost alone, stood off Europe during the days of the Huerista tyranny, withstood the powerful forces in the United States that sought the undoing of the Revolution, and refused to go to war at a time when it might have insured his re-election.

BIBLIOGRAPHY

1. WOODROW WILSON. Ray S. Baker, *Woodrow Wilson: Life and Letters* (8 vols.), vols. 1–4; Herbert C. Bell, *Woodrow Wilson and the People;* John M. Blum, *Joe Tumulty and the Wilson Era;* Josephus Daniels, *The Wilson Era: Years of Peace, 1910–1917;* William E. Dodd, *Woodrow Wilson;* Charles Forcey, *The Crossroads of Liberalism: Weyl, Croly and Lippmann and the Progressive Era;* John L. Heaton, *Cobb of the World;* Burton J. Hendrick, *Life and Letters of Walter Hines Page* (3 vols.) ; David F. Houston, *Eight Years with Wilson's Cabinet;* Harold L. Ickes, *The Autobiography of a Curmudgeon;* James Kerney, *The Political Education of Woodrow Wilson;* Robert LaFollette, *Autobiography;* Arthur Link, *Woodrow Wilson* (3 vols.) ; Henry May, *The End of American Innocence;* William G. McAdoo, *Crowded Years;* Frederick Palmer, *Newton D. Baker* (2 vols.) ; Frederick L. Paxson, *The Pre-War Years;* Charles Seymour (ed.) , *The Intimate Papers of Colonel House* (4 vols.) ; Oswald G. Villard, *Fighting Years;* Arthur Walworth, *Woodrow Wilson* (2 vols.) .

2. DOMESTIC POLICIES. Cyrus Adler, *Jacob H. Schiff: His Life and Letters* (2 vols.) ; Thomas C. Blaisdell, *The Federal Trade Commission;* Louis D. Brandeis, *Other People's Money and How the Bankers Use It;* John D. Clark, *The Federal Trust Policy;* William Diamond, *Economic Thought of Woodrow Wilson;* Carter Glass, *An Adventure in Constructive Finance;* W. P. G. Harding, *Formative Period of the Federal Reserve System;* Seymour E. Harris, *Twenty Years of Federal Reserve Policy* (2 vols.) ; W. S. Holt, *The Federal Farm Loan Bureau;* E. W. Kemmerer, *The A.B.C. of the Federal Reserve System;* Thomas Lamont, *Henry P. Davison;* J. Laurence Laughlin, *The Federal Reserve Act;* Miriam E. Loughran, *Historical Development of Child-Labor Legislation in the United States;* Frederick L. Paxson, *The Pre-War Years;* Frank W. Taussig, *The Tariff History of the United States* and *Some Aspects of the Tariff Question;* Charles Van Hise, *Concentration and Control: A Solution of the Trust Problem;* Paul M. Warburg, *The Federal Reserve System* (2 vols.) and *Essays on Banking Reform in the United States.*

3. FOREIGN AFFAIRS. Edward Buehrig, *Woodrow Wilson and the Balance of Power;* Howard F. Cline, *The United States and Mexico;* R. W. Curry, *Woodrow Wilson's Far Eastern Policy;* Merle Curti, *Bryan and World Peace;* Sidney Gulick, *The American Japanese Problem;* C. W. Hackett, *The Mexican Revolution and the United States;* Stanley Hornbeck, *Contemporary Politics in the Far East;* T. Iyenage & K. Sato, *Japan and the California Problem;* E. G. Mears, *Resident Orientals on the Pacific Coast;* Harley Notter, *Origins of the Foreign Policy of Woodrow Wilson;* Paul S. Reinsch, *An American Diplomat in China;*

J. Fred Rippy, *The United States and Mexico;* George Stephenson, *John Lind of Minnesota;* Frank Tannenbaum, *The Mexican Agrarian Revolution;* Charles C. Tansill, *The Purchase of the Danish West Indies.*

4. DOCUMENTS. H. S. Commager, *Documents,* nos. 389–98, 402, 404, 410–12; *Report of the Industrial Commission of 1915,* 64 Cong. 1st Sess. Sen. Doc. no. 415; *Report of the Pujo Committee,* 62 Cong. 3d Sess. House Rep. no. 1593.

For further references, *Harvard Guide,* ¶¶ 235, 237, 238.

The Road to War

1. THE UNITED STATES AND THE WORLD WAR:
FACTORS AND CONDITIONS

SINCE the early years of the twentieth century Europe had been preparing for war, and hoping to avoid it. Peace was maintained only by a precarious balance between two sets of alliances: the Triple Alliance or Central Powers (Germany, Austria-Hungary, Italy) and the Triple Entente (France, Russia, and Great Britain). A general war had been threatened on several occasions: by the Moroccan question in 1905, when Germany backed down; by the Agadir crisis of 1911; and two or three times during the Balkan War of 1912–13. The result of that local war was to lessen the prestige of the Central Powers which backed the wrong horse, and to increase both the power and the bumptiousness of Serbia and Rumania, the Balkan kingdoms that obtained the lion's share of the loot. And as soon as the war was over, Serbia went fishing in the troubled waters of the Dual Monarchy.

On 28 June 1914 the shot was fired that closed an era of progress, liberalism, and democracy and inaugurated the age of warfare, destruction, revolutionary upheavals, and dictatorships, which is not yet ended. Archduke Franz Ferdinand, heir to the throne of Austria-Hungary, was assassinated at Sarajevo in the province of Bosnia. The murderer belonged to a Serbian revolutionary group active in breaking up the Dual Monarchy, but that was not generally known until after the war. Austria determined once and for all to put an end to the Slavic threat and, supported by Germany, presented stringent demands with which Serbia could not comply save at the cost of losing her independence. She made several concessions which Austria deemed insufficient, and on 28 July Austria declared war on her. Russia, as the leader of the Slavic world, could not stand by while Serbia, whom she had secretly encouraged, was crushed; she mobilized her army. Germany, fearing to be caught between two enemies, declared war first (1 August) on Russia and then (3 August) on France, which was bound to come to Russia's aid in any case. In order to crush France before unwieldy Russia fairly got going, Germany struck at her through Belgium, whose neutrality she and the other powers were bound by treaty to respect. Great Britain then (4 August) declared war on Germany. The First World War was on.[1]

President Wilson at once tendered American good offices, which were politely but firmly rejected, and proclaimed the neutrality of the United States. 'The occasion is not of our making,' he said in his message to Congress of 4 September 1914. 'But it is here. It affects us directly and palpably almost as if we were participants in the circumstances which gave rise to it. . . . We shall pay the bill, though we did not deliberately incur it.' The statement was exact and the warning prophetic. From the very beginning the United States was vitally affected by the war. The most powerful of nations that remained neutral, we were likewise the most vulnerable. Our population included representatives of every racial group whose homelands were involved in the war, and their emotions were naturally aroused. Our commercial and financial relations extended to every European nation, and were particularly bound up with England and Germany. Our cultural relations were very close with England and France. And no European war in which England was involved could fail to raise problems of neutral rights, which, as the experience of Jefferson's time recalled, might easily become points of national honor.

Yet in 1914 the suspicion hardly dawned on the average American that his country might be drawn into the war, and there was an almost universal determination to stay out. A century had passed since the Treaty of Ghent and the fall of Napoleon; a hundred years for the sentiment of isolation from the ' broils of Europe ' to deepen; a century of unparalleled growth in the power to maintain isolation. And although the United States, in view of her wars with the Indians and with Mexico and Spain, could hardly be called a pacific nation,

[1] Turkey joined the Central Powers about a month later. Italy disregarded her alliance with the Central Powers, and after a highly profitable neutrality and much astute bargaining, threw in her lot with the Entente Allies in 1915. Japan also joined the Allies before the United States came in, but confined her efforts to the Far East. Rumania and Portugal joined the Allies; Bulgaria, the Central Powers. Greece tried to remain neutral, but the Allies occupied Salonica as a base, and finally she joined their side.

she had early taken the lead in the peace movement and from the beginning of her history had subscribed to the principle of the arbitration of international controversies. The Jay Treaty, the Rush-Bagot agreement, the Treaty of Guadalupe-Hidalgo, the Geneva arbitration, the arbitration of the fur-sealing, the Canadian and the Venezuela boundary controversies, the provisions of various Pan-American conferences declaring arbitration to be a principle of ' American international law,' the Root and Bryan treaties, all testified to the persistence and the sincerity of American faith in this method of settling disputes.

There was a long American tradition of neutrality and neutral rights, and one of the most important of these rights was freedom of the seas. From the Franco-American treaty of 1778, the United States made it a consistent policy to enlarge the right of neutrals and decrease the power of belligerents to disturb the peaceful part of the world. She went to war with England in 1812 to protect her rights as a neutral. She adhered to the Declaration of Paris of 1856, which adopted the principle that free (neutral) ships make free goods; took part in the Hague Conventions of 1899 and 1907, and helped draft the Declaration of London of 1909, which drew up a code of naval warfare based on the Declaration of Paris. American determination to preserve and enforce neutrality traversed class, sectional, and party lines, and found eloquent expression from the President, who pleaded with the country to ' be neutral in fact as well as in name . . . impartial in thought as well as in action.'

There is no easy answer to the question of why we fought, and those who look for simple explanations will be disappointed or misled. It is possible to discover the causes of wars such as that of 1812 or the one with Mexico, but after a century and a half, no two scholars are agreed upon the precise causes of the American Revolution; and the schoolboys of North Dakota and South Carolina grow up with very different notions of responsibility for the Civil War. The immediate provocations of these wars, to be sure, can be fixed; the underlying causes are still in dispute. So, too, with our entry into the First World War: the provocation is easy to discover, but the fundamental causes are lost in a maze of controversy, and most of the available literature on the subject is tinged by emotion. We must guard against reading back into the period 1914–17 our present-day judgments and preconceptions. And if our generation is disillusioned about ' making the world safe for democracy ' we must not assume that the phrase was insincere or the ideal naïve.

Let us then retrace the path to war. It is necessary that we keep in mind several considerations of a general character as well as a particular train of facts and circumstances. For while it is true that American entry into the war was precipitated by the German submarine warfare, and that without this we probably should not have fought, it is important to know why Germany resorted to submarine warfare, and why the United States reacted to it as she did.

From the outbreak of World War I American public opinion was predominantly favorable to the Allies. This is a fact of primary importance. It matters little how much of this opinion was due to Allied propaganda, since propaganda can be really effective only on friendly hearts and receptive minds. American friendship with England and France, and suspicion of Germany, was no sudden and artificial growth. It went deeper than that. The majority of Americans were English-speaking, and regarded some part of the British Empire as their mother country, with whom war would have seemed immoral. For one thing, it would have involved us in war with our sister democracy, the Dominion of Canada. Ties of language and literature, law and custom, as well as those of a more personal character, bound America to the British Empire in a hundred ways. With France our relations were more sentimental than intimate, but the tradition of Franco-American friendship went back to the Revolution: Lafayette's gallantry was one thing that schoolchildren did not forget when they grew up, and Colonel Stanton's ' Lafayette, we are here ' was something more than dramatics. With Germany and her allies, on the other hand, American relations were amicable but not cordial. To be sure, the presence of millions of Germans in America made for understanding and even sympathy with the German people; but many even of these were critical of their fatherland's policies, and few, as Ambassador von Bernstorff lamented, were inclined to place the interest of Germany before that of the United States. And since the Spanish War, there had grown up in America a feeling that the German government was militaristic, hostile to democracy, and unfriendly to the United States. To many Americans there was something ridiculous in the posturings and saber-rattlings of William II, when they were not even odious.

This basic friendliness for the Allies and suspicion of Germany made our entry into the war on the side of Germany unthinkable, our entry on the side of the Allies not inconceivable. Wilson himself furnished an illustration of this attitude. Of mixed Scots and English ancestry, steeped in English literature and history, and an admirer of British political institutions, he found it easier to grasp the British than the German point of view, and his emotional and intellectual sympathies were from the first enlisted on the side of the Allies. He tried to be neutral, but he was willing to endure almost any provocation rather than risk a war with England; and Bryan was right in protesting that the President was quicker to hold Germany than England to ' strict accountability ' for violations of neutral rights. And when Russia — temporarily — went republican, just as we were about to enter the war, Wilson found it easy to identify the cause of the Allies with that of democracy and of civilization itself.

American suspicion of Germany was intensified by her cynical violation of Belgian neutrality, and by the widespread conviction, supported by seemingly irrefutable documentary evidence, that she alone was responsible for the war. American opinion was further alienated by the sinking of the *Lusitania* and exacerbated by Germany's persistence in her U-boat policy, which most Americans regarded as a flagrant violation of international law and of morality. With Belgium and the *Lusitania* in mind, it was easy for Americans to believe the anti-German propaganda which the Allies sponsored. Yet we must not exaggerate the importance of Allied propaganda: that propaganda probably did not hasten by a day the decision to fight. It did break down resistance in some quarters and silence it in others, and encourage Americans to rationalize their war on broad humanitarian grounds. No one now believes the more preposterous atrocity stories, to the authenticity of which even Lord Bryce lent his name; but the hatred that they engendered served to give the war the moral character of a wolf hunt.

France was the most popular of the countries at war. Germany had declared war upon her, apparently without the slightest provocation, caught her unprepared, and taken an unfair advantage by striking through Belgium; and the French armies aroused admiration by their desperate stand along the Marne. American novelists such as Edith Wharton and correspondents such as Frank Simonds glorified France. A group of wealthy young Americans formed the *Lafayette Escadrille* in the French flying corps; thousands of other youngsters enlisted in the British and Canadian armies and air forces — among them William Faulkner — and their letters and articles all stimulated the feeling that the least America could do was not to let our historic ally be crushed by insisting on too strict a neutrality. While the American friends of France worked for her, the British issued first-class propaganda for themselves. They had an initial advantage in speaking the same language as the Americans and having much the same modes of thought. The Allies, moreover, controlled the most important avenues of communication, had ready access to American newspapers and journals, and could command the services of many intellectuals and leaders of American society. German propaganda, designed largely for groups that were favorable anyway, such as German-Americans and the anti-British Irish-Americans, was by contrast inept and ineffective. Its arguments were legal and technical, rather than emotional. And whenever the German propaganda began to get going nicely, something happened — the sinking of the *Lusitania* or the deportation of Belgian civilians in 1916 — that undid everything. After the *Lusitania* the German ambassador confessed ' our best plan is frankly to acknowledge that our propaganda in this country . . . has completely collapsed.' Subsequent resort to sabotage in munitions works and to acts of violence merely emphasized the growing German desperation.

Next in importance to the emotional was the economic factor. Even before the war a large part of American trade was with the Allied nations. On the outbreak of the war the Allies began to apply trade-restriction measures — commonly called the blockade — to the Central Powers; and they were very shrewd in developing these restrictions progressively. Cotton, for instance, was added to the list of contraband only after the *Lusitania* was sunk; and when a Southern Senator complained, Senator Lodge remarked that he was more moved by the spectacle of American women and children drowning in the ocean than by that of American cotton sitting on a wharf. Trade with Germany became negligible; trade with Great Britain and France mounted impressively. This increase in our foreign trade, in full swing by the middle of 1915, rescued the United States from a commercial depression that had lasted a year. Cotton, wheat, and beef, as well as manufactures, found a ready and highly profitable market; and when the Allies seized American cargoes destined directly or indirectly for Germany, it was possible to claim and eventually to collect damages. Within a year after the outbreak of the war the whole fabric of our economic life was so closely interwoven with the economy of the Allies that any rupture would have been ruinous. It was the realization of this, in addition to sympathy for the Allies, that persuaded Wilson and his cabinet to reject an embargo on munitions of war.

This trade in munitions was particularly important. Countenanced by international law it was open alike to all belligerents. But this impartiality was theoretical rather than real. Allied sea power prevented the Central Powers from procuring American munitions; the Allies got all they wanted; and our munitions exports increased in value from some $40 million in 1914 to $1290 million in 1916, and our total trade to the Allied countries from $825 million to $3214 million. Germany never officially denied the legality of this trade, but she protested that it did violate the spirit of neutrality. To the suggestion that the United States place an embargo upon munitions exports, the American government replied that it could not change the rules of neutrality to the advantage of one belligerent while the war was in progress. As a technical defense this was sound; but both belligerents were changing the rules of war, and it was within the rights of Congress to stiffen our neutrality requirements as, for instance, the Dutch did, by treating armed merchantmen as warships and interning them. The point is, neither Congress nor public opinion wished to do so.

Credit was essential for trade; without credit the belligerents could not buy American goods. At the beginning of the war the United States was a debtor nation; this situation was promptly reversed as foreign investors dumped their securities on the American market. Soon the Allies found it advisable to finance their purchases in the United States through loans floated in Wall Street. This scheme Bryan opposed. 'Money,' he said, 'is the worst of all contrabands because it commands everything else.' For this and other reasons the State Department on 15 August 1914, informed American bankers that 'in the judgment of this Government, loans by American bankers to any foreign nation which is at war are inconsistent with the true spirit of neutrality.' Yet within a month this position was modified to authorize 'credit loans,' and bank credits were promptly extended to belligerent governments. By the late summer of 1915 Bryan was out of the cabinet, and his successor Secretary Lansing, as

well as Secretary McAdoo, warned the President that the country was
'face to face with what appears to be a critical economic situation.'
'Popular sympathy,' wrote Lansing, 'has become crystallized in
favor of one or another of the belligerents to such an extent that the
purchase of bonds would in no way increase the bitterness of partisanship or cause a possibly serious situation.' Before this united pressure, Wilson gave way, and on 14 September 1915 the State Department withdrew altogether its opposition to loans. By the time the
United States entered the war, over $2 billion had been lent by the
American public to the Allied governments, as opposed to only
$27 million to the Central Powers.

In 1934–35 the Nye Committee of the Senate made public a vast
body of data bearing on the relations between American bankers and
munitions manufacturers and the Allies. These data were more sensational than significant. That the American financial stake in an
Allied victory may have influenced some people is possible. But the
financial community as a whole, it was well known at the time, favored American neutrality rather than American participation, for
neutrality afforded Wall Street all the profits of war without the
corresponding sacrifices and taxation. And there is not a shred of evidence to support the allegations that Wilson himself was at any time
influenced by the financial stake in his relations with Germany, or
that the decision to fight in April 1917 would have been retarded or
reversed had financial relations been otherwise. It was neither trade,
nor munitions, nor loans, nor propaganda that persuaded the administration of the necessity of war; it was the German submarine
policy.

2. The Struggle for Neutral Rights

From the beginning the United States was engaged in a losing
struggle for the preservation of her rights as a neutral. There were
two fundamental difficulties: lack of international law to deal with
unforeseen conditions and circumstances; and the immensity of the
stakes and the savagery of the fighting which made the belligerents
ready to flout law or morality if that was necessary for their survival.
Laws purporting to protect the rights of neutrals had been formulated with reference to the last naval war, the Russo-Japanese conflict of 1905; but at that time the big naval powers were neutral, and
the technique of offense developed so fast in World War I that there

was no generally recognized law to deal with it. The Declaration of London of 1909 represented a hopeful effort to codify and modernize the laws of neutrality, but that declaration had been rejected by Great Britain as too favorable to neutral rights, and had no legal standing. With reference, therefore, to many controversial matters international law was vague; with reference to new problems presented by the submarine, it was silent. And as Lloyd George subsequently remarked: ' Nations fighting for their lives cannot always pause to observe punctilios. Their every action is an act of war, and their attitude to neutrals is governed, not by the conventions of peace, but by the exigencies of a deadly strife.'

America's first and most prolonged dispute was with Great Britain. Promptly upon the outbreak of the war, Britain blockaded Germany. This was no mere policing of German ports, but a new type of blockade which involved a considerable extension both of the contraband list and of the ' continuous voyage ' doctrine which justified confiscating cargoes of enemy destination in neutral ships, even when billed for neutral ports; and a declaration that the North Sea and the English Channel were ' military areas.' The Allies' command of the sea enabled them to enforce these Orders in Council, even when their diplomacy was hard put to justify them on legal grounds. American direct trade with the Central Powers was entirely, and her indirect trade largely, cut off. In addition the Allies employed such devices as the rationing of trade to neutrals and the blacklisting of firms suspected of trading with the Central Powers.

Against these palpable violations of American neutral rights, the United States protested in vain. England's determination to enforce her own interpretation of neutral rights was inflexible. Three possible courses of action were open to the United States: war, an embargo partial or complete, or temporary acquiescence accompanied by formal protest. But from the start our means of defense and retaliation were circumscribed by pro-Allies sentiment; and by 1916 they were still further restrained by the economic tie-up with the Allied cause which affected farmers and businessmen alike. And it was inconceivable that the United States should have gone to war over questions affecting property rights alone.

Wilson and the State Department certainly had no intention of taking a stand for neutral rights which, if persisted in, might land us in war on the side of autocracy, as had happened in 1812. They remembered that Jefferson's embargo had hurt us more than it had the belligerents in 1808. So they chose the course of protest and persuasion, a course designed to keep the record clear while avoiding the catastrophe of war.

The British and French continued to violate neutral rights, and the State Department to protest, until the beginning of 1917. At any time after the middle of 1915 a real threat of an embargo on munitions of war would probably have brought the Allies to heel. Their own factories were unable to supply the enormous demand of their armies for high explosives; the cutting off of supplies from America would have lost them the war. Jefferson's embargo had not accomplished anything, but Madison's non-intercourse, it will be remembered, forced the repeal of the Orders in Council; and the situation of 1915–17 was analogous to that of 1811–12, not to that of 1807–9.

Faced with economic strangulation, Germany struck back with the only weapons at her disposal: mines and submarines. As early as August 1914 she began to plant mines in the North Sea and the Irish Sea, and on 4 February 1915 she announced that all the waters around the British Isles constituted a war zone in which all commerce with the Allies would be destroyed. Thus was inaugurated the submarine warfare which eventually forced the United States into war. That the sinking of unarmed neutral ships was a clear violation of existing international law, Germany did not deny; but she justified her policy on the ground that it was necessitated by the equally lawless British blockade.

To Wilson, and to most Americans, the distinction between British and German violations of neutral rights was clear. As Mr. Asquith said, ' Let the neutrals complain about our blockade and other measures taken as much as they may, the fact remains that no neutral national has ever lost his life as the result of it.' But the U-boat warfare took a toll of 209 American lives on the high seas — twenty-eight of them on American ships.[2] Damages for property losses entailed by Allied violations of American rights could be settled after the war; damages for American lives that had been lost in the U-boat campaign could never be adequately paid.

Alarmed at the threat of submarine warfare, Wilson informed the

[2] Borchard and Lage give the number as 195. Other neutrals suffered far more. During the war over 3000 Norwegian sailors lost their lives through submarine and mine, and over 50 per cent of the Norwegian merchant marine was destroyed.

German government on 10 February 1915 that 'the United States would be constrained to hold the Imperial German Government to a strict accountability' for 'property endangered or lives lost.' Thereby the Wilson administration took the stand that must inevitably lead to war, unless either the United States or Germany backed down.

The trouble with requiring submarines to follow the time-honored procedure of visit and search was that U-boats were extremely vulnerable; and a merchantman armed with a single 6-inch rifle could sink any that appeared above the surface. The Dutch government early in the war adopted the principle for which there was ample precedent in earlier naval wars, that armed merchantmen were warships, and refused to allow them to trade with the Netherlands. If the United States had adopted and enforced a similar law, the Allies would have had to stop arming their merchantmen, and the German submarines in that event could have afforded to observe the proprieties and humanities when making captures at sea. Our government might also have warned American citizens against traveling on belligerent merchant ships. But we must remember that they had the right, as neutrals, to do that, and to expect that if the ship they traveled in was sunk they would first be placed in safety. And the American public, with its strong tradition of defending neutral rights, would have treated any failure to hold the U-boats to 'strict accountability' as pusillanimous and the Democratic party would have lost the election of 1916. As it was, Wilson was accused of insincerity, cowardice, and pro-Germanism by the Republican press and also by the growing proportion of the American people who sincerely believed that the Allies must win, or the Prussian heel would be upon our necks.

Soon came a test of the meaning of 'strict accountability.' On 28 March 1915 an American citizen went down with the British ship *Falaba;* on 29 April an American merchant vessel, the *Cushing,* was attacked by a German airplane; and on 1 May the American tanker *Gullflight* was torpedoed. Germany offered to make reparations for an 'unfortunate accident' but refused to abandon submarine warfare.

Matters were brought to a head when on 7 May the crack Cunard liner *Lusitania* was torpedoed off the coast of Ireland with a loss of over 1100 lives, including 128 American citizens. Germany justified the sinking as one of the hazards of war: the *Lusitania* was a 'semi-warship' carrying munitions and troops, passengers had been duly warned, and if Americans were unprepared to take the risks of war they could have sailed on American vessels instead. Yet the sinking was a violation of international law as it then stood, and it was a piece of criminal folly as well. Nothing except the invasion of Belgium did so much to inflame American sentiment against Germany. Public leaders like Theodore Roosevelt clamored for war, and the press took up the cry. That, as it turned out, might have been the best moment for the United States to have entered the war. Had we been able to bring our strength to bear in 1916, the war would probably have been over within a year, and the disastrous loss of life, the destruction of spiritual values, and the breakdown of civilized standards would have ceased two years earlier than it did. But the country was not yet mentally prepared for war, and Wilson in 1915, like Jefferson in 1807, refused to be stampeded into any irrevocable act. On 13 May he demanded that the German government disavow the sinking of the *Lusitania,* 'make reparation so far as reparation is possible for injuries that are without measure, and take immediate steps to prevent the recurrence of anything so obviously subversive of the principles of warfare.' But Germany, persuaded that Wilson was playing to the gallery, tried to drag out the issue by a series of technical objections. Impatient of procrastination, Wilson sent, on 9 June, a second peremptory note; this brushed aside German extenuations and technicalities and insisted upon a formal disavowal of the outrage. Bryan, who felt that this protest was dangerously close to an ultimatum, resigned from the cabinet rather than sign the note. His own solution for the difficulty was to renounce responsibility for the lives of Americans who chose passage on belligerent ships. 'Germany,' he said, 'has a right to prevent contraband from going to the Allies, and a ship carrying contraband should not rely upon passengers to protect her from attack — it would be like putting women and children in front of an army.' This plausible argument, not without precedent in our own history, commanded the support of many of the most influential congressional leaders — Senators Stone and Gore, Congressmen Clark, Lindbergh, Kitchin, and McLemore, among them. It was embodied, early in 1916, in the Gore-McLemore Resolutions refusing passports to American citizens who purposed to travel on the armed ships of belligerents. Wilson moved promptly to defeat the resolutions. 'Once accept a single abatement of right,' he wrote to Senator Stone, 'and many other humiliations would certainly follow, and the whole fine fabric of international law might crumble under our hands piece by piece.' As a result of executive pressure, the resolutions were defeated, and the ' whole fine fabric of international law ' was saved — for the moment.

On 19 August 1915, before the *Lusitania* controversy had been settled, the English liner *Arabic* was torpedoed with the loss of two American lives. A diplomatic rupture seemed inescapable, but Bernstorff, fully alive to the seriousness of the situation, hastened to disavow the action, and to promise that in the future ' liners will not be sunk by our submarines without warning and without safety of the lives of non-combatants.' A month later his disavowal was confirmed by the German government, and the crisis passed. For six months American relations with Germany were undisturbed by any new U-boat sinkings, but this peaceful interlude was rudely shattered when in February 1916 the German government announced a renewal of submarine warfare on armed merchant vessels. On 24 March the unarmed channel steamer *Sussex* was torpedoed without warning. Outraged at this violation of the pledge which had been given after the *Arabic* affair, Wilson warned Germany that unless she immediately abandoned her submarine warfare against freight and passenger vessels the United States would be forced to break off diplomatic relations. Faced with this threat, the German government capitulated, promising, on 4 May, that henceforth no more merchant vessels would be sunk without warning, provided the United States held England also to ' strict accountability.' The State Department continued to protest England's violations, and German submarines spared merchant vessels until February 1917; during the intervening nine months American relations with Germany were less disturbed than at any time since the *Lusitania* tragedy.

3. PREPAREDNESS AND THE ELECTION OF 1916

Despite this apparent settlement of the U-boat controversy, President Wilson became more and more persuaded that the only way in which the United States could avoid war was to end the war. Proffers of good offices and of mediation had been repeatedly rejected, but all through 1916 Wilson labored to bring about a peace on the basis of mutual compromises and concessions. The task was hopeless from the first, for none of the belligerents wanted such a peace; none of

WOODROW WILSON *by F. Graham Cootes*

the politicians dared face their peoples without some compensation for their terrible sacrifices. In all Europe there was no statesman with vision to foresee and courage to proclaim the disastrous consequences of a Pyrrhic victory.[3] Wilson alone appreciated the ultimate cost of a dictated peace to victors and vanquished alike; he alone had the courage to call for a ' peace without victory.'

So eager was Wilson to achieve peace that he went to the somewhat inconsistent extreme of offering to fight for it. In February 1916 Lord Grey, after a series of conferences with the ubiquitous Colonel House, was able to assure his government that ' President Wilson was ready . . . to propose that a Conference should be summoned to put an end to the war. Should the Allies accept this proposal, and should Germany refuse it, the United States would probably enter the war against Germany. . . . If such a Conference met, it would secure peace on terms not unfavorable to the Allies; and if it failed to secure peace, the United States, would probably leave the Conference as a belligerent on the side of the Allies, if Germany was unreasonable.' For reasons that were not entirely clear, the British cabinet rejected this overture, and it was never renewed. Efforts to enlist the interest both of France and of Germany were equally fruitless.

Profoundly discouraged, Wilson turned early in 1916 toward a program of military preparedness. This policy was the result in part of conviction, in part of political expediency. A presidential campaign was in the offing, and the Democrats could not afford to permit their Republican opponents to capitalize on the popular issue of national defense. As early as November 1915 Wilson had set forth a program of preparedness, justifying his conversion by a reference to Ezekiel xxxiii: ' But if the watchman see the sword come, and blow not the trumpet, and the people be not warned; if the sword come, and take any person from among them, he is taken away in his iniquity; but his blood will I require at the watchman's hand.' And in the following months Wilson blew the trumpet, and the people were

---

[3] 3 January 1917. ' The Allies' reply to the peace overture of Germany is published today; about as weak a document as could be imagined. Neither the German proposal nor the Allies' response rises to any level of statesmanship. The chancelleries of Europe, so far as character is concerned are bankrupt, and the conceptions of the men in them are no higher than those of the fish-wives down at the Fish Market; they plot and wrangle all the time.' Allan Nevins, ed., *The Letters and Journal of Brand Whitlock*, ii, 341. Cf. the situation in our own Civil War, Vol. I.

warned. A series of monster preparedness parades in Eastern cities indicated support from the business and industrial sections of the country, but the South and the Middle West were lukewarm. Nevertheless, during the summer of 1916, the administration urged through Congress a series of acts strengthening the military and naval forces of the nation. The National Defense Act of 3 June enlarged the regular army to some 220,000, integrated the national guard into the National Defense system, and provided for an officers' reserve corps; the Naval Appropriation Bill of 29 August authorized the construction of a large number of new battleships and cruisers. The handicap American trade was under, from having to depend on belligerent or Scandinavian merchantmen to carry its exports, persuaded the Democratic party of the need to build up an expensive merchant marine, and the United States Shipping Board Act of 7 September 1916 appropriated $50 million for the purchase or construction of merchant ships. To co-ordinate industries and resources, Congress created a Council for National Defense, and an advisory board drawn from the ranks of industry and labor.

Having thus made appropriate gestures toward the more militant elements, the President embarked upon a campaign for re-election under the slogan, ' He kept us out of war.' As a statement of fact it was accurate; those Americans who read into it a promise of future policy failed to consider the possibility of a change in the circumstances on which the promise was conditioned.

The Republican party was pro-Allies in leadership, but dared not avow it for fear of losing the German-American vote; the Progressive party was moribund. Progressives hoped that the Republican convention would nominate Roosevelt, but the Republicans wished to punish him for his secession and feared the effect on German-American voters of his vigorous support of the Allies and of preparedness. Instead, Charles Evans Hughes, Justice of the Supreme Court, was placed in nomination; and Roosevelt dismissed the last Progressive convention with the advice that they follow him back to the Grand Old Party. Some did; others, more concerned than he with the problems of domestic reform, went over to the Democrats.

By adding together the Republican and Progressive votes of 1912 Justice Hughes appeared certain of victory. All the well-known portents — the September election in Maine, the trend in New York, the betting odds of ten to seven — indicated a Republican victory.

But Hughes proved a disappointing candidate; Wilson's progressive reforms were not forgotten; and hundreds of thousands of Socialists, more loyal to peace than to party, gave their votes to the candidate who had kept us out of war. When the early returns showed that Mr. Hughes had carried New York, New Jersey, and Indiana, his election was taken for granted. But the Far West was not yet heard from; and the electoral vote of the Far West had grown with its population. Mr. Hughes had made several errors during an electioneering tour of California. He lost that state by less than 4000 votes, and its electoral vote was just sufficient to give a majority in the electoral college to Wilson. The margin was uncomfortably narrow, but Wilson's popular plurality of 600,000 was a better indication of the relative strength of the two candidates, and the increase of almost 3 million in his popular vote since 1912 was a measure of the extent to which he had won the confidence of the American people.

4. WAR

As soon as his re-election was assured, Wilson determined to renew his appeal to the belligerents for a negotiated peace. Such an appeal seemed well-timed. The Battle of the Somme cost a million casualties; the Russian offensive in Galicia a million and a half more. Unfortunately, Wilson postponed his overture a week too long. Germany, having beaten Rumania to her knees in a quick summer campaign, issued an invitation to the Allies to open direct negotiations (12 December 1916). Six days later President Wilson addressed to every belligerent government a note asking for a statement of ' the precise objects which would, if attained, satisfy them and their people that the war had been fought out.' Coming at that time, this seemed an echo of the German invitation, which queered the Wilson overture in the sight of the Allies. Lloyd George announced that Britain's terms would be ' complete restitution, full reparation, and effectual guarantees ' for the future; Germany's terms, announced confidentially to Washington, included a slice of France, economic control of Belgium, parts of Russian Poland, and plenty of indemnities. Clearly there could be no getting together on either basis; and although Wilson had at his hand one weapon — embargo — that could have forced the Allies to a conference, he had as yet no means to compel Germany.

Faced with this intransigence on the part of the belligerents, and convinced that the time had come when the United States must co-operate in securing and maintaining world peace, Wilson, in a memorable speech on 22 January 1917, formulated the conditions upon which such co-operation might be extended. Those conditions, anticipating in a general way the subsequent ' Fourteen Points,' included government by the consent of the governed, freedom of the seas, limitation of military and naval armaments, and a League to enforce peace. Fundamental to all of these principles was the requirement that the peace must be a ' peace without victory.' Victory, said the President prophetically,

would mean peace forced upon the loser, a victor's terms imposed upon the vanquished. It would be accepted in humiliation, under duress, at an intolerable sacrifice, and would leave a sting, a resentment, a bitter memory upon which terms of peace would rest, not permanently, but only as upon quicksand. Only a peace between equals can last.

This appeal fell upon deaf ears, and even in the United States the phrase ' peace without victory ' was criticized as pusillanimous. There was no hope that the Allies, bound hand and foot by secret treaties, or that Germany, now that Rumania was crushed and Russia reeling, would agree to a reasonable settlement; and though Wilson proposed, the Allies disposed. Yet it was not pressure from the Allies, or even from American interests favorable to the Allies, which within two months swept the United States into war. Actually the die was cast, even before Wilson made his ' peace without victory ' speech. Late in August 1916 the war-lords Hindenburg and Ludendorff had been elevated to the supreme military command in Germany. Determined to break the blockade and to destroy British morale, they insisted upon the reopening of unrestricted U-boat warfare, and on 7 October the German Reichstag approved their demand, though an announcement of this change of policy was delayed until Wilson had exhausted the possibilities of mediation.

The decision to embark upon unrestricted submarine warfare was made with a full comprehension of its effect upon relations with the United States. ' I know full well,' wrote Chancellor Bethmann-Hollweg to Bernstorff, ' that by taking this step we run the danger of bringing about a break and possible war with the United States. We have determined to take this risk.' And on an official Admiralty memorandum suggesting that war with the United States might be avoided if submarines ' overlooked ' American boats, the Kaiser penciled, ' Now, once and for all, an *end* to negotiations with America. If Wilson wants war, let him make it, and let him then have it.' The German high command believed that American participation in the war would not materially increase their contributions of money, munitions, and supplies, and like their Nazi successors 25 years later they discounted American naval and military assistance. With over 120 submarines ready for service they calculated to a nicety the destruction of British and neutral merchant tonnage and promised a victory in six months. In that time, the United States, it was thought, could do nothing important.

On 31 January 1917 Bernstorff informed the American government that beginning the next day German submarines would sink on sight all merchant vessels, armed or unarmed, within a military zone around the British Isles and in the Mediterranean. Diplomatic relations between the two nations were promptly severed, and though Wilson still shrank from war, and hoped that Germany would not commit the supreme folly of aggressive acts against the United States, the nation prepared for war. Wilson himself took the first step in this direction by calling upon Congress for authority to arm American merchant vessels; he was apparently thinking in terms of the armed neutrality of 1798 that fell just short of war. A Senate filibuster, led by LaFollette and what Wilson described as ' a little group of willful men,' prevented congressional action until the adjournment of 4 March, when the President discovered a piracy statute of 1819 that authorized him to act. But events moved so rapidly that armed neutrality was soon forgotten. Late in February the British secret service handed over to the United States State Department a copy of the incredibly stupid ' Zimmermann note ' in which the German government proposed that, if the United States declared war, Mexico conclude an offensive alliance with Germany and Japan; Mexico to have Texas, New Mexico, and Arizona for her share of the loot. This note was released to the newspapers on 1 March and immensely strengthened the popular demand for war. On 17 March came the news that a revolution in Russia had overthrown the Tsar and established a provisional republican government; the last taint of autocracy in the Allied cause disappeared. When, also during March, German submarines torpedoed five American merchant vessels, Wilson decided that Germany was warring upon the United

States and that the time had come to proclaim the existence of this war.

In the 'twenties and 'thirties that decision was denounced as a mistake. American participation, it was argued, made Allied victory possible, but that victory was not sealed by a just peace and in the end the war brought the United States nothing but debts and disappointments. Yet what was the alternative? We must not let ourselves be deceived by wishful thinking into the theory that a fair and lasting peace would have been negotiated in 1917 if the United States had stayed neutral. Those who indulge in that hypothesis are invited to examine the terms of the Treaty of Brest-Litovsk that Germany imposed upon Russia early in 1918. The Russian revolution took that great country out of the war. The submarine campaign would shortly have starved England. France, unable to budge the German armies from the Hindenburg line, had shot her bolt; there were mutinies on the Western front even after the United States entered. Germany would have won the war had the United States not come in; and the resulting peace settlement would have left Imperial Germany — which was essentially the Germany of Hitler, with slightly better manners and without the venomous anti-Semitism — bestride the narrow world like a colossus. Men at some times are masters of their fates; but April of 1917 was not one of those times. The hour for negotiated peace had passed. Mankind was destined to a year and a half more of warfare that did more to destroy the accumulated values of civilization than what had already occurred. President Wilson, looking ahead, and faced by the most terrible alternative that any statesman since Lincoln had faced, doubtless felt that the lesser evil was for America to join the conflict and try to direct the peace that must eventually come into channels that would justify the sacrifice. Few doubt now that he was right.

Turning to the United States alone, and assuming that we could afford to be indifferent to a German victory, it is true that Wilson could have kept the United States out of the war had he been determined to preserve peace at the going price and had the American people been willing to pay the price. It was a price that not very many Americans were willing to pay, since it involved not only an embargo upon American shipping with disastrous consequences to American economy, but a complete submission to German demands and a consequent surrender of national honor. In January 1916 Wilson had warned his countrymen that considerations of national honor might require participation in the war:

> I know that you are depending upon me to keep this Nation out of the war. So far I have done so and I pledge you my word that, God helping me, I will — if it is possible. But you have laid another duty upon me. You have bidden me see to it that nothing stains or impairs the honor of the United States, and that is a matter not within my control; that depends upon what others do, not upon what the Government of the United States does. Therefore there may at any moment come a time when I cannot preserve both the honor and the peace of the United States. Do not exact of me an impossible and contradictory thing.

The preservation of both honor and peace, in March 1917, seemed to Wilson an ' impossible and contradictory thing.' Whatever others might think of the desirability of war in order to protect investments, enhance munitions profits, or preserve gains in trade, Wilson himself did not respond to these considerations, and it was Wilson who made the decision to fight. To him the logic of that decision was crystal clear. ' The United States entered the war,' he said,

> not because our national interests were directly threatened or because any special treaty obligations to which we were parties had been violated, but only because we saw the supremacy, and even the validity, of right everywhere put in jeopardy and free government likely to be everywhere imperilled by the intolerable aggression of a power which respected neither right nor obligation. . . . We entered the war as the disinterested champions of right.

That Wilson's faith in a peace without victory was betrayed, that his vision of a new and better world order was dissipated, was not his fault, but the fault of the European and American peoples who proved themselves incapable of living up to his ideal. Wilson's error was in failing to take a sufficiently realistic view of human nature, and it was an error that a later generation found difficult to condone.

And yet, even here, the evidence is conflicting. It is folly to suppose that Wilson, a student of history and a practical politician, was unfamiliar with the character of war or with its consequences. On the night before he delivered his war message to Congress he summoned Frank Cobb of the New York *World* to the White House. Cobb's recollection of that visit, as reported by Maxwell Anderson, is worth quoting:

He said war would overturn the world we had known; that so long as we remained out, there was a preponderance of neutrality, but that if we joined with the Allies the world would be off the peace basis and onto a war basis.

It would mean that we should lose our heads along with the rest and stop weighing right and wrong. It would mean that a majority of the people in this hemisphere would go war-mad, and quit thinking and devote their energies to destruction. The President said a declaration of war would mean that Germany would be beaten, and so badly beaten that there would be a dictated peace, a victorious peace.

'It means,' he said, 'an attempt to reconstruct a peacetime civilization with war standards, and at the end of the war there will be no bystanders with sufficient peace standards left to work with. There will be only war standards.' . . .

'Once lead this people into war,' he said, 'and they'll forget there ever was such a thing as tolerance. To fight you must be brutal and ruthless, and the spirit of ruthless brutality will enter into every fibre of our national life, infecting Congress, the courts, the policeman on the beat, the man in the street.' Conformity would be the only virtue, said the President, and every man who refused to conform would have to pay the penalty.

He thought the Constitution would not survive it; that free speech and the right of assembly would go. He said a nation couldn't put its strength into a war and keep its head level; it had never been done.[4]

Despite his keen intelligence and sensitiveness, Wilson did not sufficiently appreciate the strength of Old World diplomatic traditions or of New World traditions of isolation. He did not contemplate the betrayal of his peace program by the Allies or realize that his own power and influence would be drained from him by repudiation at home, nor, needless to say, was he aware of those qualities in his own character that would contribute so much to that repudiation.

So on 2 April 1917, President Wilson appeared before Congress and read his message asking for a declaration of war:

It is a fearful thing to lead this great peaceful people into war, into the most terrible and disastrous of all wars, civilization itself seeming to be in the balance. But the right is more precious than peace, and we shall fight for the things which we have always carried nearest our hearts, — for democracy, for the right of those who submit to authority to have a voice in their own Government, for the rights and liberties of small nations, for a universal dominion of right by such a concert of free peoples as shall bring peace and safety to all nations and make the world itself at last free. To such a task we can dedicate our lives and our fortunes, every-

4 John L. Heaton, *Cobb of ' The World,'* pp. 268–70.

thing that we are and everything that we have, with the pride of those who know that the day has come when America is privileged to spend her blood and her might for the principles that gave her birth and happiness and the peace which she has treasured. God helping her, she can do no other.

In the small hours of Good Friday morning, 6 April 1917, Congress passed a joint resolution declaring war on the German Empire.

BIBLIOGRAPHY

1. GENERAL. Alex Arnett, *Claude Kitchin and the Wilson War Policies;* Ray Stannard Baker, *Woodrow Wilson: Life and Letters,* vols. 5 and 6; R. S. Baker & W. E. Dodd (eds.), *The Public Papers of Woodrow Wilson* (6 vols.); Charles A. Beard, *The Idea of National Interest;* C. H. Cramer, *Newton D. Baker;* Stephen Gwynn (ed.), *Letters and Friendships of Sir Cecil Spring-Rice* (2 vols.); Burton J. Hendrick, *Life and Letters of Walter Hines Page* (3 vols.); Allan Nevins (ed.), *The Letters and Journals of Brand Whitlock* (2 vols.); Harley Notter, *Origins of the Foreign Policy of Woodrow Wilson;* R. E. Osgood, *Ideals and Self-Interest in America's Foreign Relations;* Frederick L. Paxson, *American Democracy and the World War,* vol. 1; Charles Seymour, *American Neutrality, 1914–1917* and *American Diplomacy During the World War;* Charles Seymour (ed.), *The Intimate Papers of Colonel House* (4 vols.).

2. STRUGGLE FOR NEUTRAL RIGHTS. Thomas A. Bailey, *The Policy of the United States Towards Neutrals;* Newton D. Baker, *Why We Went to War;* Edwin M. Borchard & W. P. Lage, *Neutrality for the United States;* Merle Curti, *Bryan and World Peace;* Sidney B. Fay, *Origins of the World War* (2 vols.); James W. Gerard, *My Four Years in Germany;* Hugh Gibson, *Journal from Our Legation in Belgium;* Malbone Graham, *Controversy Between the United States and the Allied Governments Respecting Neutral Rights;* C. Hartley Grattan, *Why We Fought;* Joseph Grew, *Turbulent Era: A Diplomatic Record of Forty Years;* Walter Millis, *The Road to War;* Alice Morrisey, *American Defense of Neutral Rights 1914–1917;* Maurice Prendergast & R. H. Gibson, *The German Submarine War;* Bernadotte E. Schmidt, *The Coming of the War* (2 vols.); Charles Seymour, *American Neutrality 1914–1917;* Arno Spindler, *La Guerre Sous-Marine* (3 vols.); Charles Tansill, *America Goes to War;* Edgar Turlington, *Neutrality: The World War Period.*

3. PROPAGANDA. Thomas A. Bailey, *The Man in the Street: Impact of American Public Opinion on American Foreign Policy;* C. J. Child, *The German-American in Politics 1914–1917;* L. Gelber, *Rise of Anglo-American Friendship;* Harold D. Lasswell, *Propaganda Technique in the World War;* H. C. Peterson, *Propaganda for War;* Arthur Ponsonby, *Falsehood in War Time;* Armin Rappaport, *British Press and Wilsonian Neutrality;* James M. Read, *Atrocity Propaganda 1914–1917;* C. E. Schieber, *Transformation of American Sentiment Toward Germany 1898–1914;* J. D. Squires, *British Propaganda at Home and in the United States 1914–1917;* George Sylvester Viereck, *Spreading Germs of Hate;*

Johann von Bernstorff, *My Three Years in America;* Franz Rintelen von Kleist, *The Dark Invader.*

4. DOCUMENTS. H. S. Commager, *Documents,* nos. 400, 405, 408, 409, 416–18; *Official German Documents Relating to the War* (2 vols.) ; *Papers Relating to the Foreign Relations of the United States, 1914–1917* (6 vols.) ; *The Lansing Papers* (2 vols.) ; Carleton Savage (ed.), *Policy of the United States Toward Maritime Commerce in War* (2 vols.) .

For further references, *Harvard Guide,* ¶¶ 240, 241.

War and Peace

1. INDUSTRIAL AND FINANCIAL MOBILIZATION

'IT is not an army that we must shape and train for war,' said President Wilson, ' it is a nation.' The real history of American participation in the First World War is not so much the story of Belleau Wood and St. Mihiel and Château-Thierry as of mobilizing industrial resources at home. The task was not only gigantic, but urgent. In April 1917 German submarine warfare was succeeding beyond the expectations of the Germans themselves, and the Allies were almost at the end of their tether. Few Americans realized at the time the gravity of the situation, and Admiral Sims, who had been dispatched to consult with the British Admiralty, recorded his own consternation when Admiral Jellicoe assured him that the Germans would win unless the U-boat losses were stopped. Shortly, Allied commissions came to the United States with the same story of desperate need for ships, food, munitions, and credit.

It was not easy to transform the individualistic American economic system into a well-integrated military machine, but the task was performed with surprising speed and efficiency. Spurred by necessity Congress conferred upon the President extensive powers to commandeer essential industries and mines, requisition supplies, control distribution, fix prices, and take over and operate the entire system of transportation and communication. The President in turn delegated these powers to a series of boards, organized under the general supervision of the Council for National Defense. These boards mobilized America's industrial, agricultural, and even intellectual resources for war purposes.

The first task was to provide ships to replace the tonnage which the submarines were destroying at the rate of over half a million tons monthly. Fortunately, the United States Shipping Board Act of 1916 had already called into existence an organization prepared to deal with the problems of a government-owned and government-operated merchant marine. On 16 April 1917 Congress authorized the creation of an Emergency Fleet Corporation with broad powers to acquire and operate ships without limitation. By seizing interned German ships, commandeering or buying neutral ships, taking over all private shipping, constructing enormous new shipyards at Hog Island in the Delaware river and elsewhere, building steel ships, wooden ships, fabricated ships, even concrete ships, the Emergency Fleet Corporation succeeded in increasing the available tonnage from 1 million to 10 million tons.[1] By thus laying down two ships for every one sunk by the U-boats, the submarine danger was circumvented and even overcome.

Scarcely less important was the reorganization of transport within the United States. Under the impact of war orders and troop movements the American railroad system broke down. On 26 December 1917 the government took it over, and proceeded to operate the railroads as a unified system, guaranteeing adequate compensation to the owners. William G. McAdoo, undismayed by his duties as Secretary of the Treasury, took over administration of the railroads as well. By consolidating terminal facilities, standardizing equipment, shutting down little-used lines, discouraging passenger traffic, and co-ordinating freight traffic, he succeeded in bringing the railroads to a peak of effectiveness heretofore unknown. Because the rental paid was too high, and the freight rates too low, this experiment in federal ownership and operation of the railroads cost the government $714 million. During the war the government also took over other agencies of transportation and communication — terminals, express companies, sleeping-car companies, elevators, warehouses, and telephone, telegraph, and cable lines.

Mobilization of the nation's industrial resources was carried through by the War Industries Board under the direction of Bernard Baruch, for two years almost economic dictator of the country. The task of this board was to regulate all existing industries that produced war materials, develop new industries, facilities, and sources of supply, enforce efficiency and eliminate waste, fix prices, determine priorities of production and delivery, and manage all war pur-

---

[1] 'Appalling prices,' wrote Secretary McAdoo, 'were paid for everything that had to do with a ship. Engines and other equipment were purchased at such a staggering cost that I fancied more than once that the machinery we were buying must be made of silver instead of iron and steel.' *Crowded Years.*

chases for the United States and the Allies. The production of some 30,000 articles came under the supervision of the War Industries Board, and that supervision was almost incredibly minute. In order to save coal, the service of elevators was regulated even to the number of stops and the number of passengers they must carry. Baby carriages were standardized; traveling salesmen limited to two trunks; and the length of uppers on shoes was cut down. New regulations for the manufacture of corsets released 8000 tons of steel annually; the elimination of tin from children's toy carts saved 75,000 tons of this metal. Ordinary peacetime production all but ceased, the government forbidding any work which might interfere with war manufacturing and conscripting labor to war purposes. It was such a regimentation of national economy as had never before been known; yet it was carried through with little friction and accepted in good spirit.[2]

The Food Administration more than any other government agency brought the war home to the American people. Herbert Hoover, who had carried through Belgian relief and whose prestige was second only to the President's, was put in charge of the work. Mr. Hoover's task was to increase production and decrease the consumption of food in America so that the Allies might have enough. In accomplishing this task he displayed extraordinary ingenuity. By law he was empowered to fix prices of staples, license food distributors, co-ordinate purchases, supervise exports, prohibit hoarding or profiteering, and stimulate production. His administration fixed the price of wheat at $2.20 a bushel, established a grain corporation to buy and sell it, organized the supply and purchase of meat, and corralled the supply of sugar. Meantime a systematic campaign persuaded the American people to cut down food consumption. ' Wheatless Mondays,' ' Meatless Tuesdays,' and ' Porkless Thursdays ' became an accepted part of the national regimen, and Americans experimented with such unattractive comestibles as sugarless candy, vegetable lamb chops, and shark steak. As a result of ' Hooverizing ' the United States was able to export in 1918 approximately three times her normal amounts of breadstuffs, meats, and sugar.

These were the most important of the new war agencies, but they by no means exhaust the list. A fuel administration, under the direction of Harry A. Garfield, introduced daylight saving and ' Fuelless

---

[2] The two men chiefly instrumental in working out the details of this mobilization of industrial and agricultural resources were Hugh S. Johnson and George Peek, who later applied to the NRA and AAA the technique they learned under Baruch.

Mondays,' banned electric displays and closed down non-essential manufacturing plants in an effort to conserve coal. A war trade board licensed exports and imports and black-listed firms suspected of trading with the enemy. A labor administration regulated relations between capital and labor, fixed hours and wages in certain industries, and banned strikes contrary to public interest. A war finance corporation supervised the flotation of all security issues of $100,000 or over and in addition was empowered to underwrite loans to industries engaged in the production of war materials.

The financial problem was crucial too. It was necessary to find money not only for our own but for Allied expenses. As early as July 1917 the British Chancellor of the Exchequer, Lord Northcliffe, informed Colonel House that ' our resources available for payments in America are exhausted. Unless the United States government can meet in full our expenses in America . . . the whole financial fabric of the alliance will collapse.' During and immediately after the war the United States Government lent some $10 billion to the Allies and associated governments, practically all of which was spent in this country. American expenditures to October 1919 came to $26 billion. The total direct cost of the war was therefore about $36 billion; indirect costs in the form of interest on the national debt, pensions, soldiers' bonuses, and so forth brought the total to well over $42 billion by 1936.

Approximately one-third of the war cost was financed by taxation, two-thirds by loans. Income, inheritance, corporation, and excess profits taxes were stepped up, and new taxes laid on transportation, spirits, gasoline, amusements and entertainments of all kinds, and almost every other source which the ingenuity of Treasury Department officials could discover. Wartime prosperity had made so many new millionaires and prosperous workingmen that these taxes were borne without protest. That the nation was enjoying unprecedented prosperity was evident from the success of the five war loans which were floated between May 1917 and May 1919: four Liberty loans and one Victory loan: all were handsomely oversubscribed.

2. Mobilizing Public Opinion

Yet when war was declared, a very large part of the public was indifferent to the issues, and an important minority disaffected. The leaders of opinion, to be sure, were more than ready for the fray; but the boy on the farm and the man in the street who were to do the fighting, the girl in the factory who was to make supplies, and the woman in the kitchen who was to do the saving, had very little idea what the war was about, and needed to be told. By an act of 14 April 1917 Congress established the Committee on Public Information. Its chairman, George Creel, combined, as Mark Sullivan observed, ' incredibly efflorescent imagination, fertile ingenuity, and prodigious energy.' He undertook to mobilize the mind of America as Baruch was mobilizing industry and Baker the man power. Artists, advertisers, poets, historians, photographers, educators, actors were enlisted in the campaign and the country was inundated with a flood of propaganda pamphlets, posters, magazines, and newspapers. Altogether over 100 million pieces of ' literature ' were distributed by the indefatigable Creel, while 75,000 ' four-minute men ' let loose a barrage of oratory at movie houses and public gatherings which all but paralyzed the intelligence of the country. Motion pictures displayed to horrified audiences the barbarities of the ' Hun '; pamphlets written by learned professors proved to the more skeptical that the Germans had always been a depraved people; and thousands of canned editorials taught the average man what to think about the war. In this campaign none was neglected: school children learned to lisp the vocabulary of hatred; women's clubs were titillated by atrocity stories; and foreigners were taught to be ashamed that they had not been born in America. Nor were the delights of education confined to the United States; no people was safe from Creel's zeal, no country too remote for his concern. Three hundred Chinese newspapers supplied the palpitating Celestials with ' the truth about the war '; pictures of the American President and the American flag hung on walls of cottages of Russian peasants and Peruvian *mestizos*.

Equally important was propaganda directed toward breaking down the will to fight in the Central Powers. From the first Wilson had tried to distinguish between the German people and their government, and had held out to minority races of the Dual Monarchy the hope of independence from the Hapsburgs. In his war message of 2 April he had announced that ' we have no quarrel with the German people. We have no feeling toward them but one of sympathy and friendship,' and throughout the war he reiterated his policy of ' war on the German government, peace with the German people.' The war was, he said, ' a war for freedom and justice and self-government amongst all the nations of the world, a war to make the world safe for the peoples who live upon it and have made it their own, the German people themselves included.' In all this Wilson was entirely sincere, and his policy was designed to achieve two ends: to establish a moral basis for peace upon which all belligerents — including the Allies — must agree, and to sow dissatisfaction among the peoples of Germany and Austria-Hungary.

These purposes were in Wilson's mind when he announced, on 8 January 1918, the Fourteen Points upon which it would be possible to formulate terms of peace. Since the Fourteen Points subsequently served as the basis for the peace negotiations and the Versailles Treaty, they are worth noting in detail:

1. Open covenants openly arrived at.
2. Freedom of the seas alike in peace and in war.
3. The removal of all economic barriers and the establishment of an equality of trade conditions among all nations.
4. Reduction of national armaments.
5. A readjustment of all colonial claims in which the interests of the population concerned must have equal weight with the claims of the government whose title is to be determined.
6. The evacuation of Russian territory and the independent determination by Russia of her own political development and national policy.
7. The evacuation and restoration of Belgium.
8. The evacuation and restoration of France and the return of Alsace-Lorraine.
9. A readjustment of the frontiers of Italy along national lines.
10. Self-determination for the peoples of Austria-Hungary.
11. A redrawing of the boundaries of the Balkan states along historically established lines of nationality.
12. Self-determination for the peoples under Turkish rule and freedom of the Dardanelles under international guarantees.
13. The independence of Poland with free access to the sea guaranteed by international covenant.
14. The formation of a general association of nations under specific covenants for the purpose of affording mutual guarantees of political independence and territorial integrity to great and small states alike.

Wilson's appeal to the German people, assiduously circulated throughout Germany, helped to drive a wedge between the people and the government, and when Ludendorff's army met defeat on the Western front, Germany hastened to comply with Wilson's insistence upon a popular government, and opened negotiations for an armistice upon the basis of the Fourteen Points.

3. CIVIL LIBERTIES IN WARTIME

Propaganda justifying the war at home and abroad was not enough. It was thought necessary to search out disloyalty and punish it. Despite large and active disloyal groups, North and South, both Confederate and federal governments had managed to get through the Civil War without enacting sedition laws, but in 1917–19 the people of the United States abandoned themselves to a hysteria of fear of German conspiracies and of Communist subversion, and the government indulged in greater excesses than at any previous crisis of our history. The Espionage Act of 15 June 1917 fixed a maximum fine of $10,000 and 20 years' imprisonment for anyone who interfered with the draft or encouraged disloyalty. The Espionage Act of May 1918 extended these penalties to anyone who should obstruct the sale of United States bonds, incite insubordination, discourage recruiting, ' wilfully utter, print, write or publish any disloyal, profane, scurrilous or abusive language about the form of government of the United States, or the Constitution, or the flag, or the uniform of the Army or Navy, or bring the form of government . . . or the constitution . . . into contempt . . . or advocate any curtailment of production of anything necessary to the prosecution of the war.' In addition a Trading with the Enemy Act of October 1917 gave the President authority to censor all international communications, and the Postmaster-General power over the foreign-language press in the United States.

Under these harsh laws the government instituted widespread censorship of the press; banned two Socialist newspapers from the mails; held up circulation of a tax-journal, *The Public,* because it advised that more of the costs of the war should be borne by taxation; and banned Thorstein Veblen's *Imperial Germany and the Industrial Revolution* — while Creel's committee was using it for propaganda purposes! A hapless film-producer was sentenced to ten years in jail for producing a film on the American Revolution called *The Spirit of Seventy-six,* because it was thought that it might excite anti-British sentiments; a Vermont minister was sentenced to fifteen years' imprisonment for citing Jesus as an authority on pacifism; South

Dakota farmers went to jail for petitioning for a referendum on the war and on the payment of war costs through taxation; the son of a Chief Justice of New Hampshire was convicted for sending out private letters upholding the German interpretation of U-boat warfare; and a New Hampshire judge, trying a radical who said that ' this was a Morgan war and not a war of the people,' observed that ' out West they are hanging people for saying such things,' and vindicated New Hampshire justice by jailing the man for only three years. A drive against conscientious objectors, who were theoretically excluded from the draft, netted 4000 men, of whom more than 400 were hurried to military prisons.

Altogether, under the Espionage and Sedition laws there were over 1500 prosecutions. Among those convicted, the two most distinguished were Eugene V. Debs and Victor Berger. Debs had been four times a candidate for the presidency of the United States; in 1912 he had polled almost 900,000 votes and in 1920 he was to poll almost a million. He was sentenced to 20 years in jail for a speech which was held to have a tendency to bring about resistance to the draft, though there was no evidence to prove that it did. Berger, editor of the Milwaukee *Leader* and Congressman from Milwaukee, was also given a 20-year sentence for editorials in his newspaper branding the war as a capitalist conspiracy. Twice re-elected by his constituents he was twice refused his seat by Congressmen who had forgotten, if they ever knew, the case of John Wilkes in the days of George III. C. T. Schenck, General Secretary of the Socialist party, was convicted on the same charge; Justice Holmes's opinion sustaining the conviction is memorable because it announced for the first time the ' clear and present danger ' test which was to stand as a safeguard for freedom of speech until whittled away in the 'fifties by the counter-doctrine of the ' balance of interests.' ' The question in every case,' wrote Holmes,

is whether the words are used in such circumstances and are of such a nature as to create a clear and present danger that they will bring about the substantive evils that Congress has a right to prevent. It is a question of proximity and degree.[3]

No less disturbing than this official crusade against sedition was the unofficial witch-hunting that engaged the energy of sundry old ladies

[3] *Schenck v. United States* 249 U.S. 47.

of both sexes and of members of filiopietistic organizations. It was a great opportunity to bring patriotism to the aid of personal grudges and neighborhood feuds; the independent-minded sort of citizen who was known to his conforming neighbors as a ' Tory ' in the Revolution, a ' Jacobin ' in 1798, a ' Copperhead ' in the Civil War, became a ' pro-German traitor ' in 1917 and a ' Bolshevik ' in 1918, and was lucky if he did not have garbled scraps of his conversation sent in to the Department of Justice, or flashes from his shaving mirror reported as signals to German submarines. German-Americans, the vast majority of them loyal to the United States, were subjected to all sorts of indignities. Schools dropped German from their curricula, and even some universities abolished their German departments; German books were withdrawn from public library circulation and German publications driven under cover. The Governor of Iowa decreed that ' conversation in public places, on trains, or over the telephone ' should be in the English language. Frederick Stock, distinguished conductor of the Chicago Symphony Orchestra, was deprived of his baton; the patriotic mayor of Jersey City refused to allow Fritz Kreisler to appear on the concert stage; and some universities revoked degrees they had conferred on distinguished Germans, thus giving academic sanction to the doctrine of retroactive guilt.

' The only way to keep men from agitating against grievances,' said President Wilson in 1919, ' is to remove the grievances. An unwillingness even to discuss these matters produces only dissatisfaction and gives comfort to the extreme elements in our country which endeavor to stir up disturbances in order to provoke Governments to embark upon a course of retaliation and repression. The seed of revolution is repression.' It would be difficult to improve on this as a short description of what actually happened. Yet it was Wilson who signed the Espionage and Sedition Acts and supported A. Mitchell Palmer's request for an even more extreme Sedition Act in 1919; who refused to release men like Eugene Debs or Victor Berger from the savage sentences pronounced on them in wartime; and who sat by while Palmer carried through his high-handed raids and deportations in 1919 and 1920.[4] Wilson's melancholy prophecy that ' to fight you must be brutal and ruthless, and the spirit of ruthless brutality will enter into the very fibre of our national life, infecting Congress, the courts, the policeman on the beat, the man in the street ' was fulfilled

4 See below, Chap. XXIII.

to the letter, and this high-minded scholar who read and admired those great libertarians, John Stuart Mill and Walter Bagehot, was an instrument in its fulfillment.

4. Naval and Military Operations

' Force to the utmost, force without stint or limit ' had been Wilson's promise, yet the Germans had deliberately discounted America's military and naval contribution and the Allied powers clearly expected little aid from the United States. In one sense the German estimate was correct; it was fully a year after the declaration of war before American soldiers were available in sufficient numbers to affect the military situation on the Western front, and the Germans confidently expected to win the war in less than a year. When American military aid did come, it was decisive. But even before American soldiers turned the tide at Château-Thierry, the navy had co-operated to destroy the effectiveness of German submarine warfare, and thus prevented U-boats from winning a decision.

General Joffre early assured American officials that half a million soldiers was the largest number the Allies expected the United States to send to France, but the government organized its military machine upon a far more ambitious basis. Within eighteen months the United States created an effective army of 4 million men, transported over 2 million to France, and placed 1.3 million on the firing line. This was a tribute to the organizing genius of Newton D. Baker, who, despite pacifist inclinations, proved himself one of the ablest of all secretaries of war.

Even before the actual declaration of war, General Hugh L. Scott, Chief of Staff, had convinced Mr. Baker of the necessity of raising an army by conscription rather than by the volunteer system, and in turn won over Wilson. Although our experience with the Civil War draft had not been happy, European experience in the First World War proved conscription to be a necessity. The Selective Service Act of 18 May 1917 provided that all men between the ages of twenty-one and thirty must register for service. Some Congressmen, recalling the New York draft riots of 1863, prophesied that conscription would be attended by ' rioting all over the United States,' and that ' we will never get a conscript on the firing line in France,' but these predictions proved erroneous. When the registration offices closed at sundown on 5 June, 9,586,508 men had registered and there had not been the slightest disorder or opposition. Subsequent registrations of all men between the ages of eighteen and forty-five brought the total registration up to 24,234,021. Of these, 2,180,296 were inducted into the army. The regular army, national guard, navy, and marine corps continued to be recruited by voluntary enlistment. Including these and 'minor branches of service,' the total number of men in the armed forces of the United States at the end of the First World War was about 4 million.

Raising an army was only a part of the military task which the United States was called upon to perform. It was necessary to provide clothing, arms, ammunition and explosives, light and heavy artillery, gas and gas masks, airplanes and balloons, and a hundred other things equally essential. It was necessary to build a ' bridge ' across the Atlantic, build dockage facilities and provide railroad, motor, and horse transportation in France, string thousands of miles of telephone wires, create a vast medical and nursing corps, and construct hundreds of hospitals in the United States and overseas. No task of similar magnitude had ever been attempted before by this nation.

When the war broke out the United States had actual military equipment for an army of approximately half a million men. Notwithstanding an enormous upsurge of industrial production the American army depended heavily on English and French arms and supplies. Before the end of the war American factories had produced only 64 tanks, the Liberty aviation engine was just getting into production, field artillery was almost exclusively supplied with French 75 mm. field guns, and more American troops went to Europe in British than American transports.

The first American contingent, the 1st Infantry Division, arrived in France in June 1917, and on Independence Day paraded through the streets of Paris. The purpose of this and subsequent contingents in 1917 was chiefly to bolster up Allied morale, and for this purpose the Americans were distributed among French and English troops along the quieter sectors of the front. By the end of 1917 some 200,000 American soldiers were in France, but only a few Engineer Regiments of the 1st Division had seen active service at the front, in the Cambrai offensive.

The U.S. Navy had been, somewhat unwillingly, in the war from mid-April 1917. Although Secretary Daniels and his Assistant-Secretary, Franklin D. Roosevelt, had done a great deal to build up the morale and efficiency of the fleet, the new construction provided for in the summer of 1916 was still mostly in the blueprint stage and the ' bridge ' of merchant ships to France was as yet largely a bridgehead, at Hog Island on the Delaware. Admiral William S. Benson, the Chief of Naval Operations, had no war plan ready when war was declared, and the one he promulgated on 11 April looked to little more than a defensive patrol by battleships and cruisers on the American side of the Atlantic, and a considerable Pacific Fleet to watch Japan — which was an ally! Fortunately, the President had been prevailed upon by Ambassador Page to send the gifted and energetic Rear Admiral William S. Sims to London a few days ahead of the declaration of war; and the situation, as Sims pungently described it in his despatches, was so appalling that the navy almost completely altered its plans.

Admiral Jellicoe, First Lord of the Admiralty, told Sims that sinkings of Allied merchant vessels averaged almost 570,000 tons per month in February and March, and bade fair to reach 900,000 tons in April 1917.[5] There was only a three weeks' supply of grain on hand in England, the German U-boats were increasing in numbers and efficiency, and if something was not done promptly to stop these losses and repair the life line, the Allies would have to throw in the sponge before the end of the year. Sims found, to his surprise, that the Allies had not yet adopted the convoy system of operating merchant ships in groups so that they could be protected from submarine attack by an escort of cruisers and destroyers. Sims threw his influence on the side of convoys, they were promptly adopted, the predicted frictions and collisions proved to be few and unimportant, and the convoy system, more than any single factor (and this was as true of World War II as of World War I), enabled American troops and supplies to cross the Atlantic safely.[6]

[5] Compare figures for World War II: only in six months of 1942 and in March 1943, did sinkings by submarines in the Atlantic and Arctic pass 500,000 tons, the highest being 637,000 tons in November 1942. Morison, *Battle of the Atlantic*, p. 412.

[6] The comparatively small U-boats of 1917–18 had so short a cruising range that it was necessary to convoy vessels for only a few hundred miles west of Europe. It is true that the German navy, as a stunt, sent six submarines into U.S. coastal waters in 1918, but they sank only 24 ships of 2000 tons and over and their operations were little more than a nuisance raid which failed even to disrupt coastal shipping.

Sims also persuaded the navy to send as many destroyers as it could spare to Queenstown, Ireland, to be operated for escort-of-convoy and anti-submarine patrol under the British. The first six of them arrived on 4 May and went right to work; by 5 July there were 34 American destroyers at Queenstown together with several ancient 400-ton torpedo boats of the Asiatic Fleet, which Lieutenant Commander Harold R. Stark had brought halfway around the world.

This was the first time in history that American warships had operated under British, or indeed any foreign command. The British commander, Vice Admiral Sir Lewis Bayly, was an austere, crusty old sea-dog, but the experiment was a success. The American destroyer officers (including in their junior ranks such men as Nimitz, Halsey, Carpenter, Hewitt, and Lee, who emerged as distinguished admirals in World War II) came to have a feeling amounting almost to veneration for ' Uncle Lewis.'

These destroyers experimented successfully with listening gear that detected submarines' propellers, and with depth charges (' ashcans ') which could destroy a submerged U-boat if properly placed; both were primitive in comparison with the sonar and depth weapons of World War II, but effective against the small submarines of World War I. It was not until 17 November that American destroyers made their first kill of a U-boat, but in the meantime the new convoy tactics and aggressive patroling had reduced Allied monthly shipping losses from 881,000 tons (April) to 289,000 tons (November) ; the losses were more than replaced by new construction; submarine operations now became very hazardous and the United States could send troops and supplies abroad with confidence that they would arrive. Not one loaded transport was lost. In several other ways, too, the U.S. Navy contributed to put the squeeze on Admiral Tirpitz's underwater fleet. A fleet of 120 SC's (subchasers) was sent to European waters, commanded entirely by naval reservists fresh out of college; these boats proved their value against the Austrian navy in the Adriatic. Naval aviators, flying the old Curtiss float planes that few would dare to fly now, began operating in Europe, and by the end of the war the United States had some 500 planes and three ' blimps ' on 27 different European bases, reporting U-boats, and before the end of the war they joined the army air force in bombing raids on Germany. Finally, it was the U.S. Navy that initiated, planned, and executed the colossal mine barrage across the North

Sea which, beginning in June 1918, practically closed that exit to enemy submarines.

Previous to the laying of this barrage, an American battle fleet under Rear Admiral Hugh L. Rodman, with a complement of destroyers, was sent to augment the British Grand Fleet at Scapa Flow in the Orkney Islands. These combined fleets were more than sufficient to contain the German high-seas navy in port and to reduce its efficiency and morale to a point that contributed strongly to the German surrender in November 1918.

Without the work by the U.S. Navy, the Allies might have been defeated before American ground forces could have arrived. Nevertheless, it was the American Expeditionary Force which, in conjunction with the British, French, and (to a limited extent) Italian armies, secured Allied victory.

Late in 1917 the military situation turned radically against the Allies. In October the Italian army cracked at Caporetto and the Austrians poured onto the plains of Friuli; the Italians dug in along the Piave, but it was necessary for the Allies to hurry troops from the Western front to stem the Austrian tide. A month later came the Bolshevik revolution in Russia; the new Soviet government sued for peace, and the inauguration of negotiations at Brest-Litovsk, 22 December 1917, released hundreds of thousands of German soldiers for the Western front. By the spring of 1918 the Germans had a clear numerical superiority in the West, and the German high command prepared with confidence for a drive on Paris that would end the war.

A Macedonian cry went up for American troops, and there began a ' race for France.' Could the United States speed up her troop shipments sufficiently to restore the numerical balance between the Allies and the Central Powers? ' Would she appear in time to snatch the victor's laurels from our brows? ' asked Hindenburg. ' That, and that only was the decisive question! I believed I could answer it in the negative.' Troop shipments were given right of way over supplies, new transports were pressed into service, and soldiers were rushed from American training camps to France. In March 80,000 troops were shipped abroad, in April 118,000, in May 245,000. Altogether, during the critical months from March to October 1918, 1,750,000 American soldiers landed in France. ' America,' wrote the German

Commander-in-Chief von Ludendorff, 'thus became the decisive power in the war.'

The great German offensive began on 21 March 1918 with a terrific assault on the British line from Arras to La Fère. Within a week the Germans had severely crippled the British Fifth Army, captured 90,000 prisoners, and rolled the British line back 25 miles. On 9 April came the second offensive; once again the British were hurled back on a broad front from Ypres to Armentières, and General Haig issued his famous appeal, 'Every position must be held to the last man: there must be no retirement. With our backs to the wall and believing in the justice of our cause, each one of us must fight on to the end.' In late May and early June the Germans launched their third offensive, this time against the French armies along the sector between Noyon and Rheims. Within a week the Germans smashed supposedly impregnable defenses, captured 40,000 prisoners and 650 guns and, standing on the right bank of the Marne, threatened Paris. At this crisis of the war the Allies placed General Foch in supreme command of all their forces, and the premiers of Great Britain, France, and Italy warned the United States that 'as there is no possibility of the British and French increasing the numbers of their divisions . . . there is great danger of the war being lost unless the numerical inferiority of the Allies can be remedied as rapidly as possible by the advent of American troops.'

American troops were already supporting the English and French at the front lines. Pershing, Baker, and Wilson were all determined that the American army in France should eventually form a separate and independent unit, but temporarily Pershing waived this claim and placed all his forces at the disposal of Foch, who dispersed them among the Allied armies where they were most needed. On 28 May the famous 1st Division helped to repulse the German drive on Montdidier and in a counter-attack captured the heights of Cantigny. A few days later a marine brigade of the 2nd Division was rushed to the front to stop the German onslaught at Château-Thierry; for 96 hours the marines, assisted by the French colonials, fought off the Germans, hurling them back to the right bank of the Marne. On 5 June the 2nd Division took the offensive at Belleau Wood, and after three weeks of fighting succeeded in clearing the woods of Germans and penetrating their lines to a depth of over three miles. The

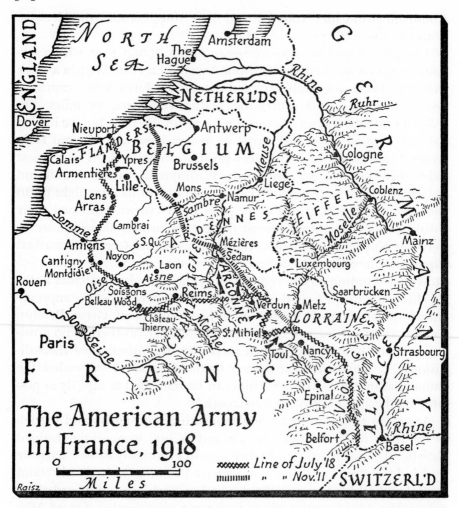

The American Army in France, 1918

xxxxxxx Line of July '18
ıııııııı   "   " Nov. 11

Raisz

actual military importance of these engagements was not great, but their morale importance was incalculable.

On 15 July came the fourth and last phase of the great German offensive, known as the Second Battle of the Marne. The Germans launched their heaviest attack at the Château-Thierry salient; had they broken through, Paris could not have been saved. American troops, 275,000 strong, supported the French in stemming a tide which at first seemed irresistible. In three days the German attack was played out, and on 18 July, without giving the enemy an opportunity to consolidate his position, Foch called upon the 1st and 2nd

American and the First French Morocco Divisions to form the spearhead of a counter-attack. It was brilliantly executed and completely successful and, said General Pershing, ' the tide of war was definitely turned in favor of the Allies.' The German Chancellor Hertling later confessed that ' at the beginning of July 1918, I was convinced . . . that before the first of September our adversaries would send us peace proposals . . . That was on the 15th. On the 18th even the most optimistic among us knew that all was lost. The history of the world was played out in three days.'

With the passing of the crisis on the Marne, Pershing revived his cherished plan for an independent American army. The Allied command of necessity acquiesced and on 10 August the American army began its official existence. It was assigned the task of straightening out the St. Mihiel salient, south of Verdun. St. Mihiel, which had been in the possession of the Germans since September 1914, was strategically important because it commanded the Mézières-Sedan-Metz railway and the great Briey iron basin. The Germans were preparing to withdraw when, early in the morning of 12 September, blanketed by a heavy fog, the American army of over half a million men went into battle. ' The rapidity with which our divisions advanced overwhelmed the enemy,' wrote Pershing, ' and all objectives were reached by the afternoon of September 13.' In two days the American army wiped out the St. Mihiel salient, captured 16,000 prisoners and over 400 guns and established their line in a position to threaten Metz, all with only 7000 casualties.

General Foch was unwilling to authorize a continuation of the St. Mihiel offensive because he had other plans for the American army. These involved American co-operation in a gigantic Allied offensive all along the line from Ypres to Verdun. The time was propitious for such a drive. The last Austrian offensive against Italy had ended in failure and the revived Italian army was prepared to take the offensive; Bulgaria had cracked up in September, and Turkey was about to follow; while the uninterrupted Allied success all along the Western front since July proved the disintegration of German morale. American contingents were fighting alongside the Belgians in the north and played an important part in the British offensive on the Somme, but for the main attack the American First Army was assigned the sector between the Meuse and the Argonne Woods, with Sedan and the Sedan-Metz railway as the ultimate objective.

The Meuse-Argonne battle, launched on 26 September, was the greatest in which American troops had been engaged so far. It was stretched out over a period of 40 days, engaged 1,200,000 soldiers, 840 airplanes, and 324 tanks, and cost 117,000 American casualties.

Despite stout resistance from the badly depleted German troops, the entire movement was a complete success. The famous Hindenburg line was broken, and day by day the American troops pushed toward their objective. In the course of the battle American forces and their French allies captured over 25,000 prisoners, 874 cannon, and 3000 machine guns, and inflicted over 100,000 casualties on the enemy. Similar success attended the Allied offensive along the whole front from Flanders to Rheims.

As early as August it was apparent to Ludendorff, if not to the Allied high command, that the end was near. The Allies had now regained numerical superiority. Foch was planning for a new offensive in the spring of 1919, and Pershing was asking for an army twice the size of that already under his command. On 2 October Ludendorff informed the German government that the army could not hold out 48 hours. In this he was, as events proved, mistaken, but the German government was panic-stricken. In the hope of conciliating Wilson [7] a parliamentary system was hastily established and Prince Max of Baden was called upon to form a liberal government. On 3 October Prince Max addressed to President Wilson the first overture for peace — on the basis of the Fourteen Points. After a month of diplomatic fencing, in which the Germans were necessarily worsted, Foch was instructed by the Allied governments to negotiate for an armistice. Mutiny in the German navy and revolution in Munich, the Rhine cities, and Berlin, rendered the Germans impotent to offer further resistance; but in the vain hope that a complete change in the form of government might win milder terms of peace, the Kaiser was forced to abdicate, and on 9 November he fled across the border to Holland. Two days later an armistice was officially proclaimed, and the greatest and most costly war that the world had yet known came to an end.[8]

---

[7] Austria-Hungary had inaugurated peace overtures as early as 14 September, but without success.

[8] For casualties, see Statistical Table in the Appendix.

5. The Russian Revolution and the Siberian Misadventure

It is difficult now to unravel the tangled skein of American politics, diplomacy, and military enterprise in the fateful years 1918–20 that enmeshed American relations with Russia for decades to come. Of all our political decisions of that era intervention in Russia was the most ill-considered, of all diplomatic adventures the most maladroit, of all military escapades the most misguided.

The collapse of Russia in November 1917 and the separate treaty of Brest-Litovsk the following March administered a double shock to American, and Allied, opinion. First, not only was Russia out as a military ally, but her defeat released scores of veteran German divisions for service in the spring offensives on the Western front. Second — and in the long run this seemed even more alarming to many of the Allied statesmen — the Bolshevik revolution was by its very nature world-wide in scope and in thrust, and threatened the very bases of Western political and economic institutions.

What, then, should be the American policy toward the Bolsheviks, fighting to stay afloat in the turbulent seas of war, revolution, invasion, famine, and civil strife? There were two alternatives. The policy of bolstering up the moderate Alexander Kerensky had failed, but it might still be possible to bolster up the Bolsheviks themselves, so they could continue to fight the Germans. This, of course, meant recognition of Bolshevism and taking the chance that it might spread throughout Europe, and beyond. The other policy was to support the White Russians, or any other forces hostile to the Bolsheviks, including the Japanese, who promised to continue the war against Germany.

From the beginning the French and British, speaking through the Supreme Allied Command, favored the second course. Alone of major statesmen, President Wilson counseled patience with the Russian people and set himself against intervention in any form. There was a brief interlude in the early months of 1918 when some of the American representatives in Russia — notably the old-time Progressive, Raymond Robins — tried to work out some arrangement with Lenin and Trotsky whereby the Russians would keep on fighting in return for American military and economic aid. But it was pretty clear that by this time neither side could deliver: the United States could not get aid through to Russia, and if the Bolsheviks took up arms again, the Germans would sweep into Moscow and Petrograd. In any event Robins was recalled, and Ambassador David Francis and the influential Edgar Sisson, who held a somewhat ambiguous position as director of American propaganda, won the ear of the President. Sisson's contribution was to ' prove ' with documents palpably forged, that Lenin and Trotsky were ' German agents.' [9]

Wilson himself was torn by indecision. ' I have been sweating blood over the question of what is right and feasible to do in Russia,' he wrote. ' It goes to pieces like quicksilver under my touch.' All of his instincts counseled him to sympathize with the Russian masses in their hour of agony, and his training taught him to mistrust anything that smacked of imperialistic ventures in Europe or Asia. On the other hand he was unalterably hostile to Bolshevism, and he found the pressure from the British and French for intervention almost impossible to resist. As he explained to his Secretary of War, he felt obliged to do it, because the British and French were pressing it on his attention so hard, and he had refused so many of their requests that they were beginning to feel that he was not a good associate, much less a good ally.

Out of all this came a series of compromises and improvisations by which the United States managed to get the maximum of trials and tribulations with the minimum of advantages. In July Wilson agreed to send a token force to the Arctic front which the British were trying to establish at Murmansk and Archangel, on condition that they were to be used only ' to guard military stores and make it safe for Russian forces to come together in organized bodies in the north,' and not for offensive operations. As there were no military stores, and no Russian forces to come together, it was not surprising that the British naval commander ignored these reservations. So that in September some 5000 bewildered American infantrymen from Michigan and Wisconsin, who had been headed for France, found themselves fighting in the frozen forests of Arctic Russia, for purposes

---

[9] These documents played a decisive role in the conviction of Jacob Abrams and his associates for printing leaflets calling on American workers to refuse to have any part in the invasion of Russia — conduct which earned them 20-year sentences. If we were not technically at war with Russia such advice could not be a violation of the Espionage Act, which penalized conduct designed to hinder the conduct of the war. The Court got around this by assuming, on the basis of the Sisson documents, that the Russian Revolution was all a German plot! See Zechariah Chafee, *Free Speech in the United States,* chap. III.

never clear, and against an enemy who had never officially been recognized as such.

There was a similar situation with the more important venture in far-eastern Siberia. Here a special situation of unusual complexity had developed. Fifteen thousand Czech prisoners, who had been released after the collapse of Russia, had seized the Trans-Siberian railroad and were fighting their way across thousands of miles of Russia and Siberia to Vladivostok, where they expected to embark for the Western front, in France. When this plan proved impracticable, they 'captured' Vladivostok — with the aid of the Japanese who had moved in to keep an eye on things generally — and then prepared to take the offensive against alleged armies of German and Austrian prisoners in eastern Siberia.

Here, quite fortuitously, was a justification for Allied intervention: they could come to the aid of the heroic Czechs and enable them to return to the Western front! Besides, it was a good idea to be on hand and see to it that the Japanese did not dig in too deeply in Russian Siberia or in Manchuria. Once again France and Britain brought pressure on Wilson; once again he yielded to pressure — but in his own way. There was to be no 'intervention' in Russia, and no fighting the Bolsheviks; the American expeditionary force was to be limited to helping the Czechs, and to this laudable purpose the United States and Japan would each contribute not more than 7000 troops. It was riding the tiger, and we ended up inside.

The situation speedily got out of hand; as George Kennan says, 'the American forces had scarcely arrived in Russia when history invalidated at a single stroke almost every reason Washington had conceived for their being there.' The Czechs had won their freedom and were no longer in need of help; as there were no Germans or Austrians to fight, they were fighting the Bolsheviks instead. The Japanese sent in not 7000 men, as agreed, but 72,000. The American General Graves found himself, in 1919, fighting the wrong war, at the wrong time, in the wrong place, and against the wrong enemy.

The Archangel and Siberian adventures attracted very little attention at a time when the war had entered its final stages. But its long-term consequences were formidable. Americans forgot the intervention, but the Bolsheviks did not. What it meant to them was that the United States had joined the capitalist countries of the Old World in an attempt to destroy them at a time when they were struggling for their life. 'The Siberian situation,' wrote Secretary Baker, 'will always illustrate the eccentricities of a remote and irrational emanation from the central madness of a warring world.'

6. THE PEACE CONFERENCE, THE TREATY, AND THE LEAGUE

Wilson had been successful in carrying the war to a victorious conclusion; he was to discover that it was easier to win a war than to make a peace. Like Lincoln, he failed to guard against the forces of vindictiveness, hatred, and greed that are inevitably loosed by war. Yet the problems which faced Wilson were infinitely more complex than those which faced Lincoln and Johnson at the close of the Civil War, and the opposition which he encountered at home and abroad more powerful and more firmly entrenched, and more brazen. Nor was Wilson well equipped for the task of overcoming or outwitting this opposition. The only statesman representing a major power who combined intelligence, magnanimity, and vision, he was nevertheless constitutionally unable or unwilling to play the game of politics and of diplomacy as it was being played in the United States and in Europe. His only weapons were intellectual conviction and moral inspiration; he was 'too proud to fight' with the piratical weapons used by his opponents.

Yet though Wilson himself was guiltless of vindictiveness or greed, he was not without responsibility for inspiring these emotions in others or for creating a situation in which they would have free play. He had acquiesced in the suppression of liberalism, of freedom of speech and of the press in the United States; he had supported George Creel's campaign to inoculate Americans with the germs of hatred for the Central Powers; and against his better judgment had acquiesced in the Russian ventures.

Even before the armistice Wilson determined to shatter precedent by taking personal charge of the peace negotiations. On 24 October 1918 he had appealed to the American electorate for a vote of confidence: 'If you have approved of my leadership and wish me to continue to be your unembarrassed spokesman in affairs at home and abroad, I earnestly beg that you will express yourselves unmistakably to that effect by returning a Democratic majority to both the Senate and House of Representatives.' Two weeks later Americans went to

SIGNING THE TREATY OF VERSAILLES *by John Johanssen*
(STANDING, L-R: ORLANDO, KLOTZ; EMIR FEISUL, TSENG T. LOU, PADEREWSKI;
VENIZELOS, PERSHING. SEATED, L-R: TARDIEU, PICHON, FOCH, BLISS, HOUSE, WHITE,
LANSING, WILSON, CLEMENCEAU, LLOYD GEORGE, BRATIANO, BALFOUR, BOTHA,
HUGHES. FRONT, L-R: SMUTS; MULLER, BELL.)

the polls and chose a majority of Republicans for both houses of Congress. The damage to Wilson's prestige was irreparable, and when on 13 December he sailed for France, ex-President Roosevelt warned ' our allies, our enemies and Mr. Wilson himself ' that ' Mr. Wilson has no authority whatever to speak for the American people at this time. His leadership has just been emphatically repudiated by them.'

As members of the American peace delegation Wilson took with him Secretary of State Lansing, General Tasker H. Bliss, Colonel House, and Mr. Henry White, a career man in the diplomatic service. It was not a strong delegation. Prudence would have counseled the appointment of representatives of the Senate and of the Republican party; common sense would have dictated the appointment of men of international repute and experience such as William H. Taft, Elihu Root, or A. Lawrence Lowell. Along with the American delegation went hundreds of experts to assist in the historical, ethnographical, and economic work of the peace commission. The Paris Conference, whatever its defects, had the benefit of more expert advice than any political arrangement ever concluded.

In the preliminary armistice negotiations with the Allies, Wilson had been made painfully aware of the conflict in war aims between the United States and the Allied powers. While he had clung tenaciously to his Fourteen Points, he had been forced to admit qualifications with respect to the important items of ' freedom of the seas ' and reparations. Clearly, he knew of the existence of the secret treaties which in part nullified the Fourteen Points, but he persuaded himself to ignore their significance. These secret treaties, which had been revealed by the Soviet government in Russia to discredit imperialist diplomacy, had been concluded between the major Allies and powers like Japan, Italy, and Rumania, in order to induce them to join the Allied side. This did not indicate any peculiar obliquity on the part of the Allies — for Italy and Rumania would certainly have joined the Central Powers otherwise — but the treaties were contrary in spirit and letter to the principle of self-determination, and Wilson should have tried to obtain formal abrogation or modification of them before sending American troops to Europe. Why he did not attempt to do so, why the Department of State remained indifferent to them, is still a mystery.

In the Peace Conference which held its first formal session 18 January 1919, all the Allied and associated powers were represented, but

the ' Big Four ' — England, France, Italy, and the United States —
made the important decisions. Like the conference at Brest-Litovsk,
this one gave the defeated powers no part in the negotiations; they
were merely called in when the treaty was ready and ordered to sign
on the dotted line. Nor was Russia officially represented, since the Allies hoped that the Soviet government would shortly collapse. Moreover, the jingo atmosphere of Paris and the personalities of the leaders made a just peace exceedingly difficult to attain. David Lloyd
George, the British prime minister who represented his country was
an able leader, but a self-seeker and demagogue. He had won a general election since the armistice on the slogans ' Hang the Kaiser ' and
' Make Germany Pay '; he was to learn before the conference was over
that you could not do either. Georges Clemenceau, the ' tiger ' of
French politics, was an able and disillusioned old man who regarded
Wilson liberalism with complete skepticism and assailed it with mordant wit: ' Mr. Wilson bores me with his Fourteen Points; why, God
Almighty has only ten! ' Clemenceau cared only for France, and France
wanted but one thing, security; the English and Americans were never
able to convince the ' logical ' French that the worst way to security
was the way that had always made for insecurity in the past — a
humiliating peace that placed intolerable burdens on the vanquished. Orlando, the prime minister who represented Italy, was the
exponent of *sacro egoismo,* the prisoner of his own propaganda; he
must bring home the Austrian bacon to Rome. All four leaders were
responsible to the public opinion of democratic states, and had to
work in a democratic medium; this meant that the most enlightened and generous statesmen had to reduce the standards of their
own thoughts to the level of popular feeling. People everywhere had
been outraged, impoverished, and wounded by a war which they
regarded as entirely Germany's fault; they were in no mood to support the sort of peace that Wilson wanted and that would have saved
us from most of the postwar agony.

Wilson, who had insisted that ' punitive damages, the dismember-
ment of empires, the establishment of exclusive economic leagues, we
deem . . . no proper basis for a peace of any kind,' stood out as best
he could for his Fourteen Points. Once, exasperated by the intransigence of his three associates, he was on the point of giving up and
going home. But it is easy to see why he stayed. His departure would
have been a confession of failure, and would have laid him open to

the charge of caring more for Germany than for the Allies — a charge that leading Republicans were already making. And, above all, there was the menace of Bolshevism that hung over Paris like a dark cloud. Everyone was thinking of it; many were talking of it. At one point Hungary went Bolshevik, rumors that Germany and Italy were slipping kept coming in, the entire bourgeois-capitalist world was terrified! Any peace was better than prolonging the uncertainty, and if America deserted the Allies would not Bolshevism reap the profit? So Wilson stayed. In the end he was forced to acquiesce in many compromises, but he imposed upon his colleagues something of his own ideas of a ' just ' peace, and wrung from them some concessions. Perhaps no one could have done more.

The Treaty of Versailles to which the Germans affixed their signature on 28 June, after a peace conference of over six months' duration, was not as drastic as France wanted, nor harsh enough to keep Germany down. It required Germany to admit her war guilt, stripped her of all colonies and commercial rights in Africa and the Far East, of Alsace-Lorraine, Posen, and parts of Schleswig and Silesia, rectified the Belgian boundary line, confiscated the coal mines of the Saar basin, imposed military and naval disarmament upon her, saddled her with an immediate indemnity of $5 billion and a future reparation bill of indeterminate amount, and placed practically the whole of her economic system under temporary Allied control. Other treaties drawn up simultaneously or shortly after recognized Czechoslovakia, greatly enlarged the territories of Italy, Rumania, and Serbia at the expense of the old Dual Monarchy, and from the historic Polish territories that had been parts of three empires, created a new Poland with a corridor to the sea.

Wilson successfully resisted some of the more extreme demands of the Allies. He prevented France from annexing the Saar basin, substituting instead a temporary control under League mandate — eventually the Saar went back to Germany. He denied Fiume to Italy — an action which caused Orlando to withdraw from the conference in a huff. He protested against the cession of Shantung to Japan, and finally wrung from her the promise of an early evacuation of that province — a promise which was fulfilled. He refused to permit the Allies to charge Germany with the whole cost of the war — a sum which Lloyd George estimated at approximately $120 billion — pointing out that this was ' clearly inconsistent with what we deliberately led the enemy to expect.' He resisted Clemenceau's desire to detach the entire Rhineland from Germany, the Polish demand for East Prussia, and the desire of many to intervene actively in Russia. And finally he wrote into the treaty the covenant of the League of Nations. This, he felt, was the heart of the treaty, the part that justified the whole. ' The settlements,' he said, ' may be temporary, but the processes must be permanent.'

It was Wilson who insisted that the League should be an integral part of the treaty, and on 25 January the Peace Conference sustained him and assigned to a special committee, of which he was chairman, the task of drawing up the league covenant. For this task he and his advisers were abundantly prepared. Since 1915 the idea of a League to Enforce Peace had been agitated in the United States and in Great Britain. The American society of that name, a British committee, and various individuals like Colonel House had plans, and all these contributed something to the final draft of the league covenant, drawn up by Sir Cecil Hurst and David Hunter Miller. This Hurst-Miller draft was adopted by the Peace Conference on 14 February 1919.

The function of the League of Nations, as set forth in its preamble, was ' to promote international co-operation and to achieve international peace and security.' Membership was open to all nations and self-governing dominions; every member nation should be represented and have an equal vote in the Assembly, which was a deliberative body, while the United States, Great Britain, France, Italy, and Japan should be permanent and four other nations temporary members of the Council, which was more largely an executive body. A secretariat, attached to the League at Geneva, and an independent Permanent Court of International Justice, established at the Hague, completed the machinery for world organization. The members of the League pledged themselves to ' respect and preserve as against external aggression the territorial integrity and existing political independence of all Members of the League ' (Art. X) ; to bring to the attention of the League any circumstance threatening international peace; to give publicity to treaties and to armaments; to submit to inquiry and arbitration all disputes threatening international peace, breaches of treaties, and questions of international law, and refrain from war until three months after the award by the arbiters; to refrain from war with the nations complying with the award of the League; and to employ on the recommendation of the League Coun-

cil, military, naval, financial, and economic sanctions against nations resorting to war in disregard of their covenants under the
League. The Council was further authorized to make plans for the
reduction of armaments; give publicity to treaties; exercise mandates
over the former colonies of Germany and Turkey; and set up an International Labor Bureau which should have jurisdiction over conditions of labor, traffic in women and children, drugs, arms, and
munitions, and the control of health. The covenant specifically recognized ' the validity of . . . regional understandings like the Monroe
Doctrine.'

The President called Congress into special session to consider the
treaty and the League of Nations, but when he returned to the
United States, early in June, he found debate already under way and
the Senate in an ugly mood. Opposition to the League had been
growing from the time of the armistice, and prospects for ratification
seemed unfavorable. The opposition was compounded of diverse
elements: personal hostility to Wilson, partisanship, and senatorial
pique; indignation of German-Americans who felt that their country
had been betrayed, Italian-Americans angry over Fiume, Irish-
Americans stirred up against England, then engaged in trying to suppress the Sinn Fein revolution; conservative disapproval of what was
alleged to be leniency toward Germany, liberal disapproval of severity toward Germany; and a general feeling that Wilson and America
had been tricked, and that he should avoid future European entanglements. In the Senate three groups could be discerned. At one
extreme were the ' irreconcilables ' — Lodge, Borah, Johnson, Knox,
Moses, McCormick, LaFollette, and others who were adamant against
any departure from the traditional policy of isolation and determined to undo the whole of Wilson's handiwork; at the other extreme were the faithful followers of the President who were ready
to ratify the treaty as it stood. In between was a large number of
moderates, made up of members of both parties, who believed in the
wisdom of a few reservations to protect American interests. At all
times, during the prolonged debate over the treaty, more than three-
fourths of the members of the Senate were ready to accept membership in the League in some form or other.[10]

But Wilson, unwilling to accept any but the mildest ' interpreta-

[10] See the careful analysis of the votes in W. S. Holt, *Treaties Defeated by the Senate*,
pp. 294–301.

tions,' showed himself almost as stubborn as the irreconcilables. Failing to make headway against the senatorial clique, he resorted to a policy which he had often before employed with spectacular success — a direct appeal to the people. On 4 September he set out on a speaking tour which carried him through the Middle West and Far West. He spoke with superb eloquence and passionate conviction, but against the rising tide of isolationism and illiberalism he made little headway, and much of the effect of his speeches was spoiled by the counter-arguments of the irreconcilables who stalked him relentlessly from city to city. On 25 September he spoke at Pueblo, Colorado; that night as his train sped eastward to Wichita he suffered a physical collapse. And with his collapse went all the hopes of ratification.

On 19 November 1919, the Treaty of Versailles was defeated in the Senate, both with and without reservations. Yet it was clear that a large majority of Senators favored ratification with some kind of reservations, as did a large majority of the American people. Senator Lodge would not budge; would Wilson? Colonel House urged him to accept reservations in order to save the treaty, but his letters went unread; Bryan pleaded with him, and so did the Democratic leader, Senator Hitchcock, but in vain; the British sent over Sir Edward Grey to urge compromise, but the President would not see him. The treaty was brought up for reconsideration again in February 1920, but another full-dress debate did nothing but exacerbate tempers. The final vote came on 19 March. Twenty-three Democrats joined the twelve Republican irreconcilables to defeat ratification with reservations by a vote of 49 to 35; a change of seven Democratic votes would have approved the treaty and put the United States in the League of Nations.

' If the President desires to make a campaign issue on the treaty,' said Senator Lodge, ' the Republicans are willing to meet that issue.' The President did so desire. Calling for a ' solemn referendum ' on the League of Nations, Wilson and his followers made that the issue of the presidential campaign of 1920, and went down to defeat. On 25 August 1921, almost three years after the armistice, Congress by joint resolution officially declared the war with Germany at an end.

Thus were the hopes for a new world order condemned to frustration and defeat. It is not the business of the historian to pronounce moral judgment on the past, but it is proper to attempt to fix responsibility for those fateful decisions that seem to affect the destinies of man. Responsibility for the defeat of the League lies first on the Republican irreconcilables who were animated by blind partisanship, personal vindictiveness, or misguided parochialism; next on President Wilson, shattered in body but not in will, uncompromising and implacable, insulated in his own sense of virtue, and prepared to sacrifice the present for vindication by History; third on the handful of Democrats also lacking in courage to break with their chief and vote their convictions. Thus was sacrificed to short-sightedness, stubbornness, and vindictiveness, the fairest prospect for world order which had yet been opened to mankind. Thus was the world condemned to seek solutions once more along those dire paths which had always, in the past, led to slaughter and ruin.

BIBLIOGRAPHY

1. MOBILIZATION. Arthur Bullard, *Mobilizing America;* J. M. Clark, *Costs of the World War to the American People;* G. B. Clarkson, *Industrial America at War;* John R. Commons, *et al., History of Labor,* vol. 4; Benedict Crowell & Robert F. Wilson, *How America Went to War* (6 vols.) ; Samuel Gompers, *American Labor and the War;* William G. McAdoo, *Crowded Years;* A. D. Noyes, *The War Period of American Finance;* Frederick Palmer, *Newton D. Baker: America at War* (2 vols.) ; F. L. Paxson, *American Democracy and the World War,* vols. 1 and 2; P. W. Slosson, *The Great Crusade and After;* Mark Sullivan, *Our Times,* vol. 5; G. S. Watkins, *Labor Problems and Labor Administration During World War* (2 vols.) ; W. F. Willoughby, *Government Organization in War Times and After.*

2. PUBLIC OPINION AND CIVIL LIBERTIES. G. G. Bruntz, *Allied Propaganda and the Collapse of the German Empire;* Zechariah Chafee, *Free Speech in the United States;* George Creel, *How We Advertised America;* Max Lerner (ed.), *The Mind and Faith of Justice Holmes;* J. R. Mock & Cedric Larson, *Words that Won the War;* James M. Read, *Atrocity Propaganda 1914–1917;* Harry Scheiber, *The Wilson Administration and Civil Liberties;* Norman Thomas, *Conscientious Objectors in America;* Nathaniel Weyl, *Treason.*

3. MILITARY AND NAVAL HISTORY. Leonard Ayres, *The War with Germany: A Statistical Summary;* John S. Bassett, *Our War with Germany;* R. L. Bullard, *Personalities and Reminiscences of the War;* Josephus Daniels, *Our Navy at War;* Thomas G. Frothingham, *Naval History of the World War* (3 vols.) and *American Re-enforcement in the World War;* R. H. Gibson & M. Prendergast, *German Submarine War 1914–1918;* Louis Guichard, *The Naval Blockade 1914–1918;* J. G. Harbord, *The American Army in France;* Liddell Hart, *A History of the World War;* Edward Hurley, *The Bridge to France;* John Bach McMaster, *The United States in the World War* (2 vols.) ; Elting Morison, *Admiral Sims and the Modern American Navy;* Allan Nevins (ed.) , *The Letters*

and Journals of Brand Whitlock (2 vols.) ; Frederick Palmer, *America in France: Our Greatest Battle* (the Meuse-Argonne) and *Bliss: Peacemaker;* John J. Pershing, *My Experiences in the World War* (2 vols.) ; Edouard Requin, *America's Race to Victory;* W. S. Sims & B. J. Hendrick, *The Victory at Sea;* George S. Viereck (ed.), *As They Saw Us.*

4. INTERVENTION IN RUSSIA. Thomas A. Bailey, *America Faces Russia;* William S. Graves, *America's Siberian Adventure 1918–1920;* George Kennan, *Russia Leaves the War: Soviet-American Relations 1917–1920* and *Russia and the West under Lenin and Stalin;* Arthur S. Link, *Wilson the Diplomatist;* Betty M. Unterberger, *America's Siberian Expedition 1918–1920;* Robert D. Warth, *The Allies and the Russian Revolution;* W. A. Williams, *American-Russian Relations 1781–1947.*

5. THE TREATY, THE LEAGUE, AND THE PEACE. Selig Adler, *The Isolationist Impulse;* Thomas Bailey, *Woodrow Wilson and the Lost Peace* and *Woodrow Wilson and the Great Betrayal;* R. S. Baker, *Woodrow Wilson and World Settlement* (3 vols.) and *What Wilson Did at Paris;* Bernard M. Baruch, *The Making of the Reparations and Economic Sections of the Treaty;* John S. Bassett, *The League of Nations;* Robert C. Binkley, " Ten Years of Peace Conference History," *Journal of Modern History,* I, 607; Paul Birdsall, *Versailles Twenty Years After;* Allan Cranston, *The Killing of the Peace;* Donald F. Fleming, *The United States and the League of Nations* and *The United States and the World Court;* John Garraty, *Henry Cabot Lodge: A Biography;* W. S. Holt, *Treaties Defeated by the Senate;* E. M. House and Charles Seymour (eds.) , *What Really Happened at Paris;* Robert Lansing, *The Peace Negotiations: a Personal Narrative;* Henry Cabot Lodge, *The Senate and the League of Nations;* David Hunter Miller, *The Drafting of the Covenant* (2 vols.) ; Harold Nicholson, *Peace Making, 1919;* K. F. Nowak, *Versailles;* Frederick Palmer, *Bliss: Peacemaker;* H. R. Rudin, *Armistice, 1918;* James T. Shotwell, *At the Paris Peace Conference;* Frank Simonds, *How Europe Made Peace without America;* A. Tardieu, *The Truth about the Treaty;* Harold W. V. Temperley, *et al., History of the Peace Conference* (6 vols.) .

6. DOCUMENTS. Ray S. Baker, *Woodrow Wilson and World Settlement* (3 vols.) ; R. J. Bartlett, *Record of American Diplomacy;* H. S. Commager, *Documents,* nos. 418, 423–9, 435, 436, 442; John H. Latané, *Development of the League of Nations Idea: Documents and Correspondence of Theodore Marburg* (2 vols.) ; James B. Scott, *Official Statements of War Aims and Peace Proposals;* James T. Shotwell (ed.), *Origins of the International Labor Organization* (2 vols.) .

For further references, *Harvard Guide,* ¶¶ 242–3.

World Politics

1. The League, the World Court, and Peace

THE foreign policy of the Republicans, who guided the affairs of the nation from 1921 to 1933, was largely dictated by facts rather than theories. Committed in theory to isolation, they were in fact forced to participate in the liquidation of old problems and the solution of new ones that vitally affected American interests: war debts and reparations, armaments, Japanese aggression in the Far East, and the peace movement. Subscribing to the policy of economic nationalism and the erection of trade barriers, they were forced in the interests of their supporters to fight for raw material and markets with the weapons of reciprocal bargains and trade agreements. Actually, therefore, despite professions to the contrary, we can discern considerable continuity in American foreign policy throughout the whole period from Wilson to the first administration of Franklin D. Roosevelt.

In their relations with the Old World the Republicans repudiated the spirit of Wilson, yet in time accepted the substance; in their relations with Latin America they repudiated the substance, but acknowledged the spirit. The same basic interests that shattered American isolation after 1914 continued to operate after 1920; the same considerations that seemed to justify Wilson's retreat from the Far East in 1917 dictated the diplomatic retreat of the Washington Conference in 1922; the same factors that inspired Wilson's Mobile address and 'watchful waiting' toward Mexico in the end brought about the retreat from 'dollar diplomacy' and the 'Roosevelt corollary' that marked the administrations of Coolidge, Hoover, and F. D. Roosevelt. For, as Secretary of State Hughes pointed out:

Foreign policies are not built upon abstractions. They are the result of practical conceptions of national interest arising from some immediate exigency or standing out vividly in historical perspective. . . . They express the hopes and fears, the aims of security or aggrandizement, which have become dominant in the national consciousness and thus transcend party divisions and make negligible such opposition as may come from particular groups.

And 'practical conceptions of national interest' indicated the espousal of policies not dreamed of in the Republican philosophy of 1920.

Upon one thing, the Republicans were agreed: that Wilson's League was 'intolerable.' Aside from that, however, the Republican policy was shrouded in an impenetrable obscurity unclarified by the floundering explanations of candidate Harding. The Republican platform committed the party to 'an international association' to 'secure instant and general conference whenever peace shall be threatened by political action,' and promised to bring about 'such agreement with the other nations of the world as shall meet fully the duty of America to civilization and humanity in accordance with American ideals.' Harding, in the course of his campaigning, approved of the League with reservations, suggested the substitution of a new organization for the existing League, and denounced any League. His masterly obfuscation of the issue was his supreme intellectual achievement.[1] To add to the general confusion, 'irreconcilables' assured the electorate that the election of Harding would mean the end of the League of Nations while 32 distinguished Republicans, including Hughes, Taft, Root, Hoover, President Butler of Columbia, and President Lowell of Harvard, announced that the election of Harding was the surest way to 'bring America into an effective league to preserve peace.'

Although the new Vice-President, Calvin Coolidge, expressed doubt whether 'any particular mandate was given in the last election on the question of the League of Nations,' Harding entertained no such doubts. The issue, he said, was a closed one; the League — then composed of 48 nations — was 'deceased.' Secretary Hughes adopted a policy of calculated disparagement toward the League; for

[1] One Republican commentator observed with pardonable pride that: 'One half of the speeches were for the League of Nations if you read them hastily, but if you read them with care every word of them could have been read critically against the League of Nations. The other half were violent speeches against the League of Nations if you read them carelessly, but if you read them critically every one of them could be interpreted as in favor of the League of Nations.'

months communications from that body were ignored until at last the situation became both embarrassing and ridiculous. Then, pushed by circumstances into the bold policy of recognizing the existence of the League, the Harding administration found it convenient to co-operate with it. In 1922 the United States began to send ' unofficial observers' to League conferences on the white slave and opium traffic, and by 1925 this policy had been extended to the point where the United States was officially represented at the League conference on traffic in arms and munitions.

From that time to 1939 co-operation with the League was continuous. The United States was represented at numerous League conferences, participated in many of its social and cultural activities, contributed, publicly and privately, to its work, and established a permanent secretariat at Geneva to co-ordinate American and League activities. In 1934 the United States officially joined the International Labor Organization. On several occasions it supported the efforts of the League to enforce peace. In 1932 an American representative sat on the commission which investigated Japan's invasion of Manchuria, and the next year Norman Davis, speaking for President Franklin D. Roosevelt, announced that if the United States concurred in the wisdom and justice of sanctions against an offending nation, ' we will refrain from any action tending to defeat such collective effort which these states may make to restore peace.' This promise of support was shortly implemented by congressional legislation looking to the imposition of an embargo against Italy during the Ethiopian crisis of 1935. Since 1920 no party had dared advocate membership in the League of Nations, but the United States had gone far toward active co-operation with that organization.

American traditions dictated effective co-operation for disarmament and the outlawry of war. In the first year of office President Harding, pursuant to a senate resolution sponsored by Senator Borah, called a conference of the nine powers with interests in the Pacific area to consider a limitation on armaments. On 12 November 1921 delegates from the United States, Great Britain, France, Italy, Belgium, Holland, Portugal, China, and Japan heard Secretary Hughes propose an itemized plan for scrapping warships and limiting naval armaments to prevent a naval ' race.' The United States, Great Britain, Japan, France, and Italy finally agreed upon a program calling for the maintenance of a naval ratio of 5–5–3 for the first three countries and 1.7 for the others, the scrapping of designated ships, and a ten-year naval holiday in the construction of capital ships.[2]

At the time, this Washington Treaty of 1922 and the London Naval Treaty of 1930, which extended its provisions to some non-capital classes of ships, were regarded as outstanding victories for peace. Yet no well-meaning reform of the twentieth century, except prohibition, was so disappointing as naval limitation. The United States sacrificed an opportunity to become the world's greatest naval power, which in the troublous years ahead could have made her an effective keeper of the world's peace. The U.S. Navy scrapped 15 new capital ships on which over $300 million had already been spent, and no other nation had a comparable building program with which to match this sacrifice. Britain retained the prestige of parity at the expense of weakening the naval power that in a few years' time would be essential to her existence. And, in order to induce Japan to consent to the 5–5–3 ratio, the United States and Great Britain had to agree not to strengthen any of their fortifications and naval bases in the Pacific between Singapore and Hawaii. This action virtually doubled the value of Japanese tonnage quotas for naval operations in the Orient and rendered the defense of Guam, Singapore, and the Philippines virtually impossible. Moreover, in spite of these concessions, Japan was insulted rather than appeased; their militarists used the slogan ' 5–5–3 ' much as in other days we had used ' 54–40 or fight,' to discredit the liberal government which had accepted limitation, and to get into power. When that had been accomplished, at the end of 1934 Japan denounced the naval-limitation treaties and started a frenzied building program which, by the time war broke out in the Pacific, rendered the Japanese navy more powerful in every type of ship than the United States and British Pacific and Asiatic fleets combined. And American and British budgets, now geared to meager naval appropriation, followed suit slowly and reluctantly.

Naval limitation saved the American taxpayer of 1922–37 millions of dollars, but the taxpayer after 1941 paid a hundredfold for this

---

[2] The agreement proposed to scrap 1,878,000 tons of capital ships, built, building, or planned, and permitted the following tonnage to be built over the next ten years: Britain, 558,950 tons; United States 525,850 tons; Japan 301,320 tons; France 221,170 tons; Italy 182,800 tons.

futile gesture. If the United States had gone ahead resolutely with the Daniels building program of 1916, the Japanese militarists might have been kept within bounds; Anglo-American naval power was the only force they feared.[3]

Equally soothing at the time, but of no practical effect in preventing World War II, were the various treaties for the arbitration of international disputes and the outlawing of war that the United States sponsored in the 1920's and 1930's. Arbitration, as we have seen, was in the American tradition.

The United States submitted to the Hague Tribunal its first case — the Pious Fund case from the Philippines. Both Taft and Wilson had attempted to extend the scope of arbitration to embrace disputes of all kinds, even those involving ' national honor.' The Taft treaties had been amended beyond recognition, but those which Secretary Bryan proposed had successfully hurdled all Senate opposition. By the time of the First World War Bryan had negotiated with thirty nations treaties providing for a commission to investigate all disputes not otherwise arbitrable and for a ' cooling-off ' period of one year pending the settlement during which neither party to the dispute should resort to any act of force.

It was in part disillusionment with the futility of these treaties, and in part the general isolationist mood, that prevented the United States from adhering even to the Permanent Court of International Justice — commonly called the World Court — throughout this period, although repeatedly urged to do so by Presidents Harding, Coolidge, Hoover, and Roosevelt. The Senate was prepared to ratify, but only on condition that the Court would not give any advisory opinion affecting the interests of the United States without American consent. Yet notwithstanding our failure to join the Court, an American has been one of the judges on the Court from its beginning.

When in 1927 the French Premier, Aristide Briand, offered a bilateral treaty to the United States for the outlawry of war, Secretary of State Frank B. Kellogg countered with the suggestion of a multilateral treaty of the same character. The result of these negotiations was the Pact of Paris, sometimes known as the Kellogg Peace Pact, of 27 August 1928. It provided that the contracting powers ' condemn

[3] For other treaties that emerged from the Washington Conference, see below, section 3.

recourse to war for the solution of international controversies, and renounce it as an instrument of national policy,' and that ' the settlement or solution of all disputes or conflicts of whatever nature or of whatever origin they may be . . . shall never be sought except by pacific means.' Adhered to eventually by 62 nations, it was ratified by the United States on 15 January 1929 by a vote of 81 to 1. The most thoroughgoing commitment to peace that great powers had ever made, the Pact of Paris may fairly be called an attempt to keep peace by incantation.

All these methods of preserving the peace — by limitation, by incantation, and (in the next administration) by negation (the Neutrality Acts) — would have been effective among nations that wanted peace. They were worse than useless in a world in which three nations — Germany, Italy, and Japan — wanted war; for they merely served to lull the democracies into a false feeling of security, while giving the militarists elsewhere a chance to plot, plan, and prepare for a war that would enable them to divide up the world.

2. WAR DEBTS AND REPARATIONS

However aloof America professed to be from European politics, it was of necessity deeply interested in European economy. During the First World War the United States Government had lent to the Allies something over $7 billion, practically all of which was spent in the United States. These were the original ' war debts,' but after the armistice loans and credits to the sum of $3.25 billion more were extended to our late associates and to some of the succession states. These were used for purposes of reconstruction, and were ' peace ' rather than ' war ' debts. The original terms of these loans provided for payment of 5 per cent interest; in 1922 Congress provided that the loans should not run longer than to 1947 and fixed the rate of interest at 4.25 per cent.

The payment of war debts was complicated by two other factors. The first, of minor importance, was the existence of a system of interallied debts. Thus Great Britain, who owed the United States over $4 billion, had extended loans to her allies to the sum of $10.5 billion; France had borrowed some $7 billion and loaned some $3.5 billion; Italy had borrowed almost $5 billion and loaned a little less than $400 million. Italy and France would clearly profit from an all-round cancellation of war debts; Great Britain, though her credits were $6 billion more than her debts, would profit, directly because she had little prospect of collecting debts owing to her and indirectly because speedy restoration of purchasing power and world trade would bring her prosperity. As early as August 1922 Balfour approached the United States with a proposal for a general cancellation of war debts and at the same time announced that Great Britain would not attempt to collect from her debtors more than enough to cover her own debts to the United States. The United States, refusing to be embarrassed by this attempt to shift responsibility, ignored the proposal.

The second factor affecting the war-debt situation was reparations. From the beginning it was the avowed intention of the debtor nations to pay all their debts out of German reparations. Precisely how large those reparations were to be was not settled until 1921 when a Reparations Commission fixed the total at $33 billion, a sum more than sufficient to cover all debts to the United States. It was one thing, however, to exact reparations; another to collect them. The burden was probably not too heavy for Germany to carry, but within a year payments were in default. So too, since the Allies insisted upon coupling reparations with war debts, were payments to the United States.

The United States showed itself willing to refund the war debts at a more reasonable rate of interest and to co-operate in attempts to solve the reparations problem. In June 1923 a settlement was negotiated with Great Britain and thereafter with other debtors, markedly easing the terms of payment. Based upon the original 5 per cent interest rate, these funding arrangements represented a total cancellation of approximately 50 per cent, ranging from 30 per cent for Great Britain to 80 per cent for Italy. Americans considered these arrangements generous; most Europeans regarded them as proof that ' Uncle Shylock ' was grasping and mercenary.

The necessity of getting money from Germany with which to pay these newly funded debts led to a reconsideration of the whole problem of reparations. France, less patient with German failure to meet her obligations than was the United States with her debtors, attempted to compensate herself by occupation of the Ruhr, but this coercion was a dismal failure. At the suggestion of American Secretary of State Hughes a committee of experts under the chairmanship of Charles G. Dawes worked out a new and less onerous scale of reparations payments, arranged for a loan to stabilize German currency, and recommended the evacuation of the Ruhr. Under this so-called Dawes Plan Germany faithfully met her reparations payments until 1928, but only by extensive borrowing in the United States. When in 1929 the rival attraction of stock-market speculation dried up American loans, Germany once again faced default. To avert this disaster a new reparations committee, headed by the American financier Owen D. Young, came up with a new plan under which the total reparations bill was reduced to approximately $27 billion with payment spread over fifty-nine years. The Young plan specifically recognized the connection between reparations and the Allied war debts by providing that reparations payments might be scaled down in the same proportion that the United States permitted the scaling down of the war debts.

Additional borrowings in the United States financed reparations until 1931, when the depression put an end to this simple method, and Germany once more defaulted, never to resume payments. Altogether Germany had paid in reparations, $4,470,300,000, and had borrowed in the United States, $2,475,000,000. During this same period the Allies had paid to the United States only $2,606,340,000. The United States therefore had paid over half the reparations bill and almost the whole war-debt bill.

The year 1931 brought a major banking crisis in Austria which spread throughout Europe, forcing Germany to abandon further reparations payments and Great Britain to abandon the gold standard. Faced with a collapse of the world financial structure, President Hoover advised, and Congress ratified, a one-year moratorium on all intergovernmental payments. A conference at Lausanne then drastically reduced reparations payments to a mere $750 million. Great Britain and France at once made overtures to the United States for a revision of the war debts. Hoover replied that ' reparations are a solely European question in which the United States is not concerned.' But when war-debt payments fell due in June 1933 there was a general default. Some states paid nothing, some made ' token ' payments, Finland alone met her obligations in full. Faced with this effective if one-sided cancellation of the war debts, Congress in April 1934 passed the Johnson Act forbidding Americans to make loans to any foreign government which was in default on its debts to the United States, the first of a series of fateful neutrality acts.

The question of voluntary cancellation of the war debts was intricate and controversial. On the one hand it was alleged that most of the money advanced to the Allied and associated powers was spent in the United States, that a good part of it might reasonably be regarded as America's financial contribution to winning the war, that wartime prosperity brought to the United States more money than was loaned, that the American tariff policy was responsible for the inability of European nations to meet their obligations, that payment would prolong the world depression and adversely affect the United States, and that in any event the debtor nations were quite unable to make payments. On the other hand it was asserted that the American financial contribution to the war was proportionately greater than that of any of the Allies, that at least one-third of the debt was extended after the armistice for constructive purposes and a good part of it to nations with which we were not associated in the war, that while the Allies were pleading poverty they were spending huge sums on armaments and themselves lending large sums to satellite states, that they did not even turn over to the United States what they obtained from Germany in reparations, and that if the European nations failed to pay their debts, the burden would be transferred to the American taxpayer. Into this maze of conflicting assertions it is difficult for the historian to enter. One thing, however, is clear: the average American took the attitude expressed in President Coolidge's classic remark, ' They hired the money, didn't they? ' and no American political party dared come out openly in favor of cancellation.

3. FAR EASTERN AFFAIRS

Acquisition of the Philippines and the ' open door ' policy in China had excited the liveliest expectations of an upswing in trade and investments in the Far East. These were disappointed. The Siberian misadventure, almost ceaseless civil war in China, the growing power and aggressiveness of Japan, all these contributed to persuading most Americans that Far Eastern power-politics were dangerous and that Far Eastern diplomacy was as distasteful as European, and even more mysterious.

Certainly Far Eastern politics were loaded with dynamite, but there was nothing very mysterious about them. There were three major elements to deal with. First there was the great and ancient empire of China, nominally a republic on the Western model since 1912 but actually, since 1920, torn by civil wars between generals that left little power to the national government. Second there was the ancient but streamlined empire of Japan, nominally a constitutional monarchy but actually at the mercy of the Emperor's army leaders whenever they chose to assert their authority. Japan by 1920 had acquired an economic position in the Orient similar to that of Britain in the Occident a century earlier; by technique learned in the West, combined with native energy, the so-called Mitsu-bishi group of interests had built up an industrial empire in textiles, steel, and consumer goods that was capturing the former European-dominated markets all around the Pacific. Underneath all this modern industrial skill, however, Japan was a country of primitive ideas, where the military were venerated, *Bushido* (the code of the warrior) was the highest morality, and *Hakko Ichiu* — ' bringing the eight corners of the world under one roof,' the probably mythical slogan of a possibly mythical Emperor in 600 B.C. — was in the back of the popular mind. This meant that, unless Westernized liberal elements kept control of the Japanese government, Japan, like Germany in 1914, would not be content with industrial expansion but would go in for foreign conquest. And third, there was the colossus of Russia, shattered by war and torn by revolution, on whose Siberian steppes ' ignorant armies clashed by night.' Her new leaders had not forgotten the humiliating defeat that Japan had inflicted upon their nation in 1905; they burned with resentment against all the Allied powers who had invaded her territories in her hour of mortal peril; they were conscious of a great historical past and determined to have a greater future.

American policy toward the Orient remained substantially the same after World War I as before it: to keep the peace, maintain the ' open door ' policy both for business and missionary effort, and by diplomacy to check the ambitions of Japan, Russia, or any other power that tried to take advantage of Chinese weakness. There was no ' retreat ' from our earlier policy, but there was less vigor in maintaining it, little understanding of what it might involve, and no disposition whatever to enlarge our own sphere of influence. The Tydings-McDuffie Act of 1934, promising independence to the Philippines in 1946, looked like a retreat, but in reality it was a wise advance step toward the withdrawal of Western control from the Orient, one that all Western nations were forced to take after World War II.

The Anglo-Japanese alliance gave Japan a welcome excuse to participate in World War I, from which she profited greatly. First she seized the islands in the North Pacific and the German concessions in Shantung. Then she took advantage of the involvement of the European powers and the isolation of the United States to consolidate her position in Manchuria and to browbeat China into submission to her will.

Early in 1915 the Japanese government presented to China, in the form of an ultimatum, Twenty-one Demands, that would give her a practical protectorate over China more complete than any the United States had ever exercised over Cuba. They were a clear violation of the Root-Takahira agreement of 1908 to maintain the independence and territorial integrity of China, and the 'open door' for commerce. Bryan protested, but he protested from a position of weakness rather than of strength. For it was just at this time that California, contemptuously rejecting President Wilson's plea for moderation, went ahead with its program of forbidding Japanese to own land in the state. Such discriminatory legislation clearly violated the most-favored nation agreement with Japan, and inevitably outraged Japanese public opinion, which found it difficult to distinguish between an affront from the United States and one from one of its sovereign states. Therefore, when Bryan informed the Japanese government that the United States would not recognize any impairment of American rights, or of the territorial integrity or political sovereignty of China, the Japanese abandoned a few of their extreme demands, forced China to accept the others, and continued a stealthy but sure advance toward domination of the Far East. Secret agreements with the European powers secured support for the Japanese claim to Shantung, the German islands in the Pacific, and special concessions in China. In 1917 Viscount Ishii came to the United States on a special mission to quiet American apprehension of Japanese policies and obtain definite recognition of Japan's 'paramount' interest in China. From the point of view of the Japanese, the Lansing-Ishii Agreement of 2 November 1917 accomplished just that, but the American

interpretation of the agreement was very different. It reaffirmed the
' open door,' pledged both nations to respect the independence and
territorial integrity of China, and disclaimed any desire for ' special
rights or privileges.' At the same time, however, it specifically recognized that ' territorial propinquity creates special relations, and that
Japan has special interests in China, particularly in that part to which
her possessions are contiguous.'

In 1918 Japan took advantage of the collapse of Russia to intervene
in eastern Siberia. The United States, as we have seen, joined this
intervention. But by 1920 the United States and other Allied powers
had withdrawn their forces from Siberia; Japan alone stayed on. And
at the Versailles Conference Japan succeeded in legalizing her claims
to Shantung and the former German islands in the Pacific.

This, then, was the situation which confronted President Harding
in 1921. The ' open ' door had been partly shut, the territorial integrity and political sovereignty of China had been impaired, and
Japan had entrenched herself firmly in Shantung, Manchuria, Mongolia, and eastern Siberia. Most of the agreements, declarations, and
understandings by which the United States had sought to impose her
own policy upon Japan had proved to be scraps of paper, and short
of war — which nobody wanted — there was no way by which she
could enforce them. From this embarrassing situation the United
States tried to extricate herself by the Washington Conference.

The Washington Conference was designed to achieve two major
objectives: disarmament and an avoidance of conflict in the Far East.
The first we have already discussed; the second was attempted by converting bilateral into multilateral understandings, thus freeing the
United States from sole responsibility for a policy which she could
not in any event enforce and making that responsibility a common
one. By the Four Power Treaty (13 December 1921) the United
States, Great Britain, France, and Japan engaged mutually to ' respect their rights in relation to their insular possessions in the region
of the Pacific Ocean ' and pledged themselves to settle any controversy that might arise over these rights by a joint conference. By the
Nine Power Treaty (6 February 1922) the same powers plus Italy,
Belgium, the Netherlands, Portugal, and China, in order to ' stabilize
conditions in the Far East ' and ' to safeguard the rights and interests
of China,' agreed to respect China's sovereignty, independence, and
territorial and administrative integrity, maintain the principle of

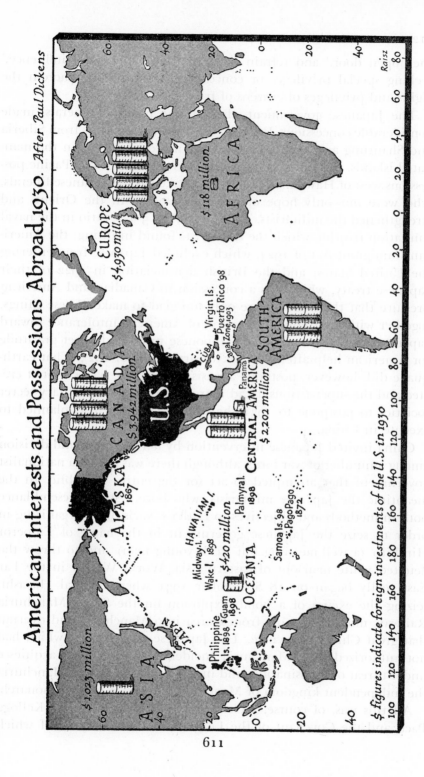

American Interests and Possessions Abroad, 1930. *After Paul Dickens*

Raisz

EUROPE
$4,930 mill.

AFRICA
$118 million.

ASIA
$1,023 million

CANADA
$3,942 million

ALASKA
1867

U.S.

SOUTH
AMERICA

CENTRAL AMERICA
$2,202 million

JAPAN

HAWAIIAN I.
Midway I.
Wake I. 1898
$420 million
Palmyra I.
1898
Philippine
Is. 1898 Guam
1898
OCEANIA

Samoa Is. 98
PagoPago.
1872

Cuba
Virgin Is.
Puerto Rico 98
Canal Zone, 1903
Panama

$ figures indicate foreign investment of the U.S. in 1930

the ' open door,' and refrain from creating ' spheres of influence,' seeking special privileges or concessions, or abridging therein the rights and privileges of citizens of friendly states.

The Japanese government, then in the hands of liberals, made considerable concessions. It forced the army to withdraw from Siberia and Shantung and agreed to construct no fortifications in the mandated islands, in return for our not fortifying any of our Pacific possessions west of Hawaii. Three things weakened the Japanese liberals, who were our only hope of preserving peace in the Orient, and strengthened the militarists. These were, the 5–5–3 ratio in the naval limitation treaties, which the militarists found insulting; the American Immigrant Act of 1924, which excluded Japanese from entering the United States; and the British denunciation in 1922 of their Japanese treaty, which was a concession to Canadian and American pressure that the British were only too glad to make. These things, together with too frequent instances of American intolerance toward Japanese-Americans, offended Nipponese pride and offset gratitude for American help after the Tokyo earthquake of 1923. That earthquake did, however, postpone a crisis because the havoc that it created and the superstitious dread it aroused caused the military secret societies to postpone to 1931 the *coup d'état* they had planned to execute in China.

China invited Japanese intervention by her weakness and division among a number of war lords, although there was always a nationalist government that attempted to act for the entire Republic. In the meantime the Japanese militarists, who bore a strong resemblance both in methods and objectives to Hitler's Nazis, were organizing in order to seize the Japanese government in the name of Emperor Hirohito (a well-meaning but weak young man) and to throw the detested white man out of eastern Asia. World War II in the Far East really began on 18 September 1931 when General Hayashi, seizing the excuse of a bomb explosion on the South Manchuria Railway, moved his army from Korea into Manchuria and overran that great Chinese province. The Japanese government, which had not authorized this ' Manchuria Incident,' was forced to acquiesce under threat of assassination, and in 1933 Japan declared Manchuria the independent kingdom of Manchukuo, under a puppet monarch.

All this was, of course, a clear violation of treaties, the Kellogg Pact, and the Covenant of the League of Nations, by all of which

Japan was bound; all but the last of these concerned the United States. Secretary of State Henry L. Stimson tried to meet Japanese aggression with firmness. He proposed to join with Britain and the League in the threat of economic sanctions against Japan. But President Hoover was alarmed equally by the prospect that we might get into war with Japan or that we might get involved in too close an association with the League. When the British minister, Sir John Simon, asked for assurance of American co-operation with League of Nations sanctions, Hoover refused on the ground that such co-operation might ' give the impression of too strong an alliance with the League. . . . The sanctions of the League are those of force, either economic or military, whereas the United States could not and would not enter into force sanctions.' What began therefore as the Stimson doctrine of non-recognition backed by sanctions ended up as the Hoover doctrine of non-recognition without any backing at all, and what began as a joint Anglo-American protest which might have carried some weight ended up as a unilateral expression of disapproval which had no influence, for Japan went right ahead with her aggressions. President Hoover's conduct in this episode is a classic example of the futility of relying on purely moral suasion when dealing with international banditry. Hoover observed, in 1932, that while he ' would fight for Continental United States he would not fight for Asia.' Just twenty years later his party waged a presidential campaign on the issue that the Democrats had failed to ' fight for Asia '; it is not wholly impossible that had Hoover backed up Stimson in 1932 we might not have had to fight in 1941 or 1950.

Without American support, the League of Nations was equally helpless. The League appointed a commission to investigate, and its report (September 1932) condemned the Japanese aggression against China on every count. Japan replied by withdrawing from the League. In the meantime, the militarists consolidated their power by assassinating the Japanese premier and other important ministers of state, and entered on a vigorous program of economic and military preparation for invading China proper.

4. The Metamorphosis of the Monroe Doctrine

Modification of the Monroe Doctrine had been inaugurated, in theory at least, by Wilson's administration. The Mobile address had held out the promise of a new Latin-American policy, and the A.B.C. Conference at Niagara Falls and Colonel House's plan of a Pan-American League of Nations recognized the right of South American states to co-operate in the formulation of policies affecting the Western Hemisphere. Yet Wilson himself, as we have seen, was not constant to his ideal; the occupation of Vera Cruz and intervention in Nicaragua and Hispaniola caused his sincerity to be seriously questioned south of the Rio Grande. To his successors he left a heritage not only of fine principles but of tough problems, such as the protection of oil and mineral investments in Mexico, the Caribbean occupations, and the struggle for markets and raw material in South America. His successors subscribed to his principles but liquidated his problems.

Mexico was the center of trouble for six years. Article 27 of the Constitution of 1917 had vested in the Mexican nation ownership of all mineral and oil resources, and limited future concessions to Mexican nationals. American investments in mining and oil amounted to about $300 million; if Article 27 should be interpreted as retroactive, all that would be confiscated. President Obregon, who succeeded Carranza in 1919, would not at once commit himself in regard to the interpretation of this article. Consequently President Wilson refused to recognize his government, and the Harding administration declined to do so unless Mexico gave formal guarantees that American interests would not suffer. Obregon, resenting this demand as an affront to Mexican sovereignty, refused. There followed a war of hard words for two years, during which American troops were deployed along the Rio Grande, and war seemed imminent. At this juncture a timely decision of the Mexican Supreme Court, holding that Article 27 was not retroactive, averted a crisis, and negotiations in the summer of 1923 resulted in the resumption of friendly relations between the two nations.

The new President, Plutarco Calles, favored nevertheless a retroactive interpretation of the troublesome Article 27, and at the same time promoted agrarian legislation that threatened American land investments and ecclesiastical legislation that affronted Roman Catholics. Secretary Kellogg, who had succeeded Hughes in the State Department, declared:

The government of Mexico is now on trial before the world. . . . We have been patient and realize, of course, that it takes time to bring about a stable government, but we cannot countenance violation of her obligations and failure to protect American citizens.

Despite this threat, the Calles government remained firm. Secretary Kellogg, unable to enlist popular support for an aggressive defense of American oil interests, early in 1927 dragged the red herring of Communism across the controversy and, further to complicate the issue, accused the Mexican government of opposing American policy in Nicaragua. Nevertheless, on 25 January 1927 the Senate voted unanimously to arbitrate the Mexican controversy. Sobered by this rebuke, President Coolidge appointed as ambassador to Mexico his Amherst classmate, Dwight W. Morrow, a member of the House of Morgan who had publicly avowed his opposition to 'dollar diplomacy.' Through a remarkable combination of character, intelligence, shrewdness, and charm, Mr. Morrow succeeded in repairing most of the damage that his predecessors in Mexico City and his superiors in Washington had done. In response to new Supreme Court rulings the Mexican Congress modified some of its oil and mineral legislation in line with American objections, while Morrow obtained an adjustment of land questions, claims, and the Church question. Throughout the decade of the 1930's this new understanding so auspiciously inaugurated by Morrow remained undisturbed, while in the United States a widespread admiration for Mexican culture (especially the paintings of Rivera and Orozco), and a growing appreciation of the social ideals of the Mexican revolution, made a good base for the future. And, in contrast to World War I, when Mexico was a center of German propaganda, the Southern Republic loyally supported the United States in World War II.

Elsewhere in the Caribbean the United States declined to pick up the 'big stick' that Theodore Roosevelt, Taft, and Wilson had successively brandished. Impatience of public opinion with 'dollar diplomacy' was back of it, but the Caribbean countries co-operated by an awakened sense of order, and American investments in them increased to a point where their direct influence on the local governments rendered the old cry 'Send the Marines!' unnecessary. Americans owned about one-third of the wealth of Cuba, while investments in Haiti amounted to $75 million, in the Santo Dominican Republic $90 million, and in Central America almost $300 million. In 1924 the Dominican flag displaced the American in that distracted Republic. In 1925 United States marines were withdrawn from Nicaragua;

they returned again the following year to put down a revolution and supervise elections, but the acrimonious criticism which greeted this brief revival of intervention led to a more circumspect policy and eventually to a final withdrawal in 1933. Haiti was not freed from American military control until 1934, and that same year Franklin D. Roosevelt's ' good neighbor ' policy was dramatized by the abrogation of the Platt Amendment — those clauses in the 1903 treaty with Cuba that gave the United States the right to intervene at its own judgment for the preservation of order.

It was the Republicans, however, who sloughed off the embarrassing Theodore Roosevelt corollary to the Monroe Doctrine. A State Department memorandum of December 1928, prepared by J. Reuben Clark and promulgated by President Hoover in 1930, asserted that

the doctrine states a case of the United States vs. Europe, and not of the United States vs. Latin America. . . . So far as Latin America is concerned, the Doctrine is now, and always has been, not an instrument of violence and oppression, but an unbought, freely bestowed, and wholly effective guaranty of their freedom, independence, and territorial integrity against the imperialistic designs of Europe.

And shortly thereafter the Assistant Secretary of State, William R. Castle, admitted that ' the Monroe Doctrine confers no superior position on the United States.' It was upon this foundation that Franklin Roosevelt built his Good Neighbor Policy.

BIBLIOGRAPHY

1. THE LEAGUE, EUROPE, AND WAR DEBTS. Samuel F. Bemis, *Diplomatic History of the United States;* C. A. Berdahl, *Policy of the United States with Respect to the League of Nations;* Carl Bergmann, *History of Reparations;* Richard Current, *Secretary Stimson;* Charles G. Dawes, *Journal of Reparations;* R. W. Dunn, *American Foreign Investments;* D. F. Fleming, *United States and World Organization 1920–1933;* J. C. Grew, *The Turbulent Era;* Manley O. Hudson, *The World Court;* David Hunter Miller, *The Peace Pact of Paris;* C. C. Morrison, *The Outlawry of War;* H. G. Moulton & Leo Pasvolsky, *World War Debt Settlements;* W. S. Myers, *The Foreign Policies of Herbert Hoover 1929– 1933;* Allan Nevins, *The United States in a Chaotic World;* Dexter Perkins, *America and Two Wars;* James T. Shotwell, *War as an Instrument of Policy;* Frank Simonds, *American Foreign Policy in the Post-War Years* and *How Europe Made Peace without America;* Harold and Margaret Sprout, *Toward a New Order of Sea Power;* Henry L. Stimson, *The Pact of Paris;* Henry L. Stimson & McGeorge Bundy, *On Active Service in Peace and War;* R. W. Van Alstyne,

American Crisis Diplomacy; J. W. Wheeler-Bennett, *The Wreck of Reparations* and *Disarmament and Security;* B. H. Williams, *The United States and Disarmament.*

2. FAR EASTERN AFFAIRS. George H. Blakeslee, *The Pacific Area;* Dorothy Borg, *American Policy and the Chinese Revolution 1925–1928;* Raymond L. Buell, *The Washington Conference;* H. C. Bywater, *Sea Power in the Pacific;* John K. Fairbank, *The United States and China;* A. Whitney Griswold, *The Far Eastern Policy of the United States;* Y. Ichihashi, *The Washington Conference and After;* A. E. Kane, *China and the Washington Conference;* George F. Kennan, *American Diplomacy;* Grayson Kirk, *Philippine Independence;* R. W. Paul, *The Abrogation of the Gentlemen's Agreement;* E. O. Reischauer, *The United States and Japan;* Sara Smith, *The Manchurian Crisis 1931–32.*

3. LATIN AMERICA AND THE MONROE DOCTRINE. Samuel F. Bemis, *The Latin American Policy of the United States;* Raymond L. Buell, *American Occupation of Haiti;* Howard Cline, *The United States and Mexico;* A. H. Feller, *The Mexican Claims Commission 1923–1934;* C. E. Hughes, *Our Relations to the Western Hemisphere;* C. L. Jones, *Mexico and Its Reconstruction;* Edgar McInnis, *The Unguarded Frontier: A History of American-Canadian Relations;* A. C. Millspaugh, *Haiti Under American Control;* Harold Nicholson, *Dwight Morrow;* Dexter Perkins, *The United States and the Caribbean* and *Hands Off! A History of the Monroe Doctrine;* O. E. Smith, *Yankee Diplomacy in Argentina;* Henry L. Stimson, *American Policy in Nicaragua;* Edgar Turlington, *Mexico and Her Foreign Creditors.*

4. THE ECONOMICS OF FOREIGN POLICY. R. W. Dunn, *American Foreign Investments;* Herbert Feis, *Diplomacy of the Dollar 1919–1932;* M. F. Jollife, *United States as a Financial Centre 1919–1933;* M. A. Marsh, *The Bankers in Bolivia;* Hiram Motherwell, *The Imperial Dollar;* J. Fred Rippy, *The Capitalists and Colombia;* B. H. Williams, *Economic Foreign Policies of the United States;* Max Winkler, *Investments of United States Capital in Latin America.*

5. DOCUMENTS. R. J. Bartlett, *Record of American Diplomacy;* H. S. Commager, *Documents,* nos. 447–9, 457, 460, 466, 467, 469; J. W. Gantenbein, *Evolution of Latin-American Policy.*

For further references, *Harvard Guide,* ¶ 250.

'Normalcy' and Reaction

1. Politics and Personalities

THE decade after the First World War, like the decade after the Civil War, was a period of conservatism in politics and in social philosophy. In both eras the Republican party was in almost undisputed control of national affairs. It avowed the philosophy of laissez faire toward business, but in practice made government an instrument of business. Both decades were necessarily taken up with the liquidation of the war: the restoration of industry, transportation, finance and agriculture to a peacetime basis, payment of the public debt, reduction of taxation, and veterans' benefits. Both saw a rapid change in manufacturing and business techniques and a florid but badly distributed industrial prosperity accompanied by agricultural distress and succeeded by acute and prolonged depression. And both were characterized by political and business corruption, a decline in liberalism, apathy toward reform, and an ardent nationalism that took a repressive and intolerant form.

The point of view of the dominant group in the 1920's was best expressed by the titular leaders of the party in power. President Harding called for a ' return to normalcy,' President Coolidge announced that ' the business of the United States is business,' and President Hoover insisted that the ' American system ' was a product of ' rugged individualism.' There was a bold assertion that the nation was in greater danger from ' mistaken government activity ' than from ' lack of legislation,' and an acknowledgment that the government should assist and encourage business — by high tariffs, the search for markets and raw materials, a suspension of embarrassing regulatory legislation, a reduction of taxation, and outright subsidies to merchant marine and aviation.

Yet the philosophy which animated the Harding-Coolidge-Hoover administrations was at no time integrated or consistent, but a curious amalgam of laissez faire and regimentation. During the war the government had organized and integrated industry, transportation, and finance, and placed them at the service of the nation. This wartime control had brought efficiency and had not seriously interfered with profits, as a bumper crop of new millionaires testified. Businessmen now wished a return to private operation of business, but they were disposed to retain the advantages of nation-wide organization and integration, of price-fixing and monopoly. Despite official repudiation of a planned economy, business was willing enough to accept such an economy provided that it could do the planning. It was willing enough to suffer regimentation of the economy, provided it could command the regiments. Actually the regimentation of the American economy, about which so much was to be said during the Franklin D. Roosevelt administration, grew out of the war and postwar years; many of the NRA codes, for example, were mere copies of codes under which trade organizations had been operating for years. So during the era of Republican reaction we have the paradox of the triumph of the philosophy of laissez faire and of the policy of economic control.

The Republicans naturally argued that their philosophy of conservatism had been endorsed by an overwhelming majority of the American people in 1920; clearly it was so endorsed in 1924 and 1928. For while the precise issues of the election of 1920 were obscure, the general issue was clear. Howsoever the electorate might be confused by the equivocal position of the Republican party on foreign affairs, there was no ambiguity about its economic philosophy. James Cox of Ohio, the Democratic standard-bearer, was not himself a man of strong liberal principles, but as a successor for Wilson he represented the remaining liberalism of the Democratic party. Warren G. Harding, nominated after Governor Frank Lowden and General Leonard Wood had exhausted each other, because ' there was nothing against him and the delegates wanted to go home,' was the choice of the Republican Old Guard — Boies Penrose, Reed Smoot, Joseph R. Grundy, and the members of the ' Ohio gang.' A vice-presidential candidate was then offered to the convention by the same crowd, but the delegates gagged at this second course, and with some show of independence nominated Calvin Coolidge. Fame had recently thrust herself upon Governor Coolidge when, in the course of a Boston police strike, he declared that there was ' no right to strike against the public safety by anybody, anywhere, anytime.' This resounding declaration caught the imagination of a public jittery about the ' Red menace.'

During the election campaign the voters knew that Harding represented a return to conservatism, and Cox a continuation of Wilsonian progressivism; they gave Harding 16,152,200 votes and Cox 9,147,-353. Eugene V. Debs, intellectually the most respectable of the three candidates, received a little less than a million votes. Since at that time he was serving a term in the federal penitentiary at Atlanta for sedition, this vote constituted a tribute rather than a reflection upon his character. Although less than half the potential electorate had troubled to go to the polls, the election indicated that the temper of the country was no less reactionary than that of the successful candidate.

Warren Gamaliel Harding of Marion, Ohio, was a small-town politician and newspaper editor whose appearance and career recalled that of his old neighbor William McKinley. Like McKinley, Harding seemed to represent virtues dear to the American heart: simplicity, friendliness, generosity. He was a thoroughly commonplace person, without intellectual or social pretensions, disposed to let well enough alone, and sure that in the United States everything was well enough. Like McKinley, too, he was politically regular, convinced that the Republican party was the only one fit to rule and that the Old Guard had accumulated most of the wisdom of the United States. His political advancement, as McKinley's, had been promoted by local bosses and friends who expected gratitude, and Harding was not inclined to disappoint them. But unlike McKinley, Harding was morally weak, unable to resist the influence of stronger and more unscrupulous wills or to deny the importunities of his friends.

When Harding moved into the White House he took with him his Ohio friends, and for three years the ' Ohio gang' had pretty much their own way in national politics. One of them, Harry Daugherty, was awarded the position of Attorney-General. The other cabinet appointments aroused mixed emotions. The country looked with satisfaction upon the choice of Charles E. Hughes for the State Department and of Herbert C. Hoover for the Commerce Department, and businessmen were gratified to see the aluminum millionaire, Andrew W. Mellon, take over the Treasury. No one objected to the appointment of J. W. Weeks to the War Department and H. C. Wallace to the Agriculture Department, but that of a long-time opponent of conservation, Albert B. Fall, to the Department of the Interior aroused dismay except among his senatorial colleagues and the oil interests.

'There can be not doubt,' wrote William Allen White, 'that oil controlled the Republican convention of 1920.' This is something of an exaggeration; the manufacturing interests, represented by Joseph Grundy of Pennsylvania, were scarcely less influential. But the oil interests made history, and the Harding administration will be longest remembered not for the Fordney-McCumber tariff or even for the Washington Conference, but for the Teapot Dome. It is unnecessary to retrace here the tortuous and sordid details of the oil scandals of the Harding administration, but the evidence of the various civil and criminal prosecutions makes it clear that Secretary Fall, with the connivance of Secretary of the Navy Denby, entered into a corrupt alliance with the Doheny and Sinclair oil interests to give them control of immensely valuable naval oil reserves. The Elk Hill oil reserve in California was leased to Doheny's company; the Teapot Dome oil reserve in Wyoming to Sinclair's. In return the government obtained some oil storage tanks in Pearl Harbor, Hawaii, and Fall got at least $100,000 from Doheny and $300,000 from Sinclair. Investigations conducted by Senator Walsh of Montana forced the resignations of Denby and Fall; civil prosecutions in the federal courts brought the cancellation of the oil leases; criminal prosecutions sent Fall and Sinclair to prison and threw a lurid light upon the activities of other oil men connected with the Sinclair and Doheny interests.

Other scandals, too, besmirched the Harding administration. Colonel Charles R. Forbes, director of the Veterans' Bureau, was charged with the corrupt sale of government property, liquor, and narcotics, and misconduct in office, and sentenced to a term in the federal penitentiary. Colonel Thomas W. Miller, the alien-property custodian, who sold valuable German chemical patents for a song, was dismissed from office and convicted of a criminal conspiracy to defraud the government. Daugherty, who regarded his office as an opportunity to reward his friends and smite the 'Reds,' was dismissed for misconduct involving the illegal sale of liquor permits and pardons; a Senate committee found him guilty of these and other malpractices, but on a criminal trial he escaped conviction.

Harding seems to have been personally innocent of participation in or profit from this orgy of corruption, but he could not have been entirely unaware of it or of the consequences when the inevitable exposures came. Demoralized by these betrayals, his health broke; a trip to Alaska failed to restore him, and on 2 August 1923 he died. Eight years later, at the belated dedication of the Harding Memorial at Marion, Ohio, President Hoover said, ' Warren Harding had a dim realization that he had been betrayed by a few men whom he trusted, by men whom he had believed were his devoted friends. It was later proved in the courts of the land that these men had betrayed not alone the friendship and trust of their staunch and loyal friend, but they had betrayed their country. That was the tragedy of the life of Warren Harding.' Considering the occasion and the fact that Mr. Hoover had served in the Harding cabinet since it was formed, this admission is worth pondering.

Harding was succeeded by Vice-President Coolidge, and Republicans breathed a sigh of relief. For Calvin Coolidge, whatever his limitations, represented probity and economy; if he displayed little zeal in tracking down the malefactors who had wrecked the Harding administration, he did not permit a continuation of their malpractices, and it was possible for the Republican party to go before the electorate in a reformed if not repentant mood. Yet, as the event proved, even reform was probably unnecessary. The efforts of the Democrats to capitalize on the scandals of Harding's administration were completely futile. It was not merely that the country was apathetic and that Coolidge was himself invulnerable; the Democrats themselves were involved in the whole sorry mess. The oil-leasing policy had been inaugurated under a law passed in Wilson's administration; Doheny was a loyal Democrat, and for years he had paid an annual retainer of $50,000 to William McAdoo's law firm. In 1924 the nomination of Coolidge to succeed himself was not seriously contested, nor, for that matter, was the election. After the convention was deadlocked for 103 interminable ballots between Governor ' Al ' Smith of New York and Wilson's son-in-law William McAdoo, the Democrats repeated the mistake of 1904 when they tried to compete with the Republicans by nominating an ultraconservative. John W.

HOME RELIEF STATION *by Louis Ribak*

Davis ' of West Virginia,' the Democratic nominee in 1924, had been Solicitor-General in Wilson's administration and Ambassador to Great Britain; but he was also the head of a highly successful firm of New York lawyers. The choice of Charles W. Bryan, brother to the 'Great Commoner,' as Davis's running-mate did little to remove from the nomination the taint of Wall Street.

Despairing of both major parties, leaders from the ranks of labor and farming joined with the Socialists to organize a third party — the Conference for Progressive Political Action — and called on ' Fighting Bob ' LaFollette to run on his own platform. That platform included public ownership of water power, downward revision of the tariff and railway rates, farm relief, abolition of the injunction in labor disputes, a federal child labor amendment, the election of all federal judges, legislation permitting Congress to override a judicial veto, the abolition of conscription, and a popular referendum on declarations of war. Almost 5 million votes for LaFollette testified to the strong undercurrent of liberal sentiment in the country, but 15,725,000 voters were satisfied with the Coolidge policies and 8,385,600 were content to follow their traditional allegiance to the Democratic party. The electoral college vote was even more lopsided; 382 for Coolidge, 136 for Davis, and only 13 for LaFollette.

Calvin Coolidge was the first President from New England since Franklin Pierce. Like Pierce he came from a small farming community in the hills, worked his way through college, became a small-town lawyer, and made his way cautiously and painfully from the lower to the higher brackets of state politics. It was Coolidge luck that made the vice-presidency, which for most men is the gate to oblivion, a step to the presidency. A person of respectable mediocrity, he had little to his credit in the way of constructive legislation or political ideas, and equally little to his discredit. So completely negative a man never before lived in the White House; it is characteristic that Coolidge is best remembered for his vetoes and his silence. Yet this dour, abstemious, and unimaginative figure became one of the most popular of all American Presidents. For ' Silent Cal ' was the symbol of what Americans wanted to be. His frugality, unpretentiousness, and taciturnity gave vicarious satisfaction to a generation that was extravagant, pretentious, and voluble. To people who had pulled up their roots and were anxiously engaged in ' keeping up with the Joneses,' there was something vaguely comforting about

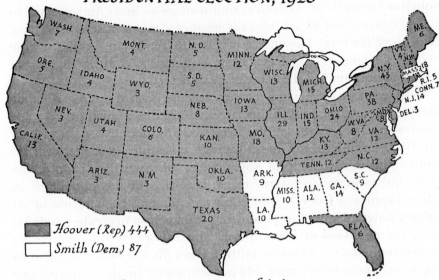

PRESIDENTIAL ELECTION, 1928

WASH. 7
ORE. 5
IDAHO 4
MONT. 4
N.D. 5
MINN. 12
WYO. 3
S.D. 5
WISC. 13
MICH. 15
ME. 6
VT. 4
N.H.
MASS. 18
R.I. 5
CONN. 7
N.Y. 45
NEV. 3
UTAH 4
NEB. 8
IOWA 13
PA. 38
N.J. 14
DEL. 3
MD.
CALIF. 13
COLO. 6
KAN. 10
MO. 18
ILL. 29
IND. 15
OHIO 24
W.VA. 8
VA. 12
KY. 13
ARIZ. 3
N.M. 3
OKLA. 10
ARK. 9
TENN. 12
N.C. 12
S.C. 9
MISS. 10
ALA. 12
GA. 14
TEXAS 20
LA. 10
FLA. 6

Hoover (Rep) 444
Smith (Dem.) 87

Figures indicate number of electors

PRESIDENTIAL ELECTION, 1932

WASH. 8
ORE. 5
IDAHO 4
MONT. 4
N.D. 4
MINN. 11
WYO. 3
S.D. 4
WISC. 12
MICH. 19
ME. 5
VT. 4
N.H. 3
MASS. 17
R.I. 4
CONN. 8
N.Y. 47
NEV. 3
UTAH 4
NEB. 7
IOWA 11
PA. 36
N.J. 16
DEL. 3
MD.
CALIF. 22
COLO. 6
KAN. 9
MO. 15
ILL. 29
IND. 14
OHIO 26
W.VA. 8
VA. 11
KY. 11
ARIZ. 3
N.M. 3
OKLA. 11
ARK. 9
TENN. 11
N.C. 13
S.C. 8
MISS. 9
ALA. 11
GA. 12
TEXAS 23
LA. 10
FLA. 7

Hoover (Rep) 59
Roosevelt (Dem.) 472

624

the fact that Coolidge had been born in a village named Plymouth, that his first name was Calvin, that he had attended an old-fashioned New England college, that he had been content with a modest law practice and half of a two-family house in a small Massachusetts city, and that the oath of office which inducted him into the presidency had been administered in a Vermont farmhouse by his aged father, and by the light of a kerosene lamp. Actually Coolidge was democratic by habit rather than by intellectual conviction; his frugality indicated no distrust of wealth; his taciturnity no philosophic serenity; his simplicity no depth. The Yankee traits left out in Coolidge were idealism, a desire to make the world better, and a fighting devotion to a cause. He believed in the *status quo,* and regarded the entire progressive movement since Theodore Roosevelt's day with cynical distrust. Consequently, although he had a moral integrity wanting in his predecessor, there was no break in administrative continuity between the Harding and the Coolidge administrations; no change in political or economic policy. More fully even than Harding's, the administration of Coolidge represented a return to ' normalcy.' Under his auspices the policies of high tariff, tax reduction, and government support to industry were pushed to extremes, and the high plateau of prosperity was attained. In time, businessmen came to long for a restoration of the good old days of Coolidge as they once had longed for those of McKinley.

Coolidge's success can best be gauged by the election of 1928. He had early announced, with an emphatic old Yankee phrase which the country insisted upon regarding as equivocal, that he did not ' choose to run '; and the Republicans turned perforce to the logical successor, Herbert C. Hoover. By his brilliantly successful administration of relief organizations in Belgium, Russia, and the Mississippi valley, Mr. Hoover had earned the reputation of a great humanitarian; by his active and progressive administration of the Commerce Department he had won the confidence of business and — what was equally to his credit — the distrust of the Old Guard. Innocent of any previous elective office, Hoover seemed to be a new type of political leader, a socially minded efficiency expert, able and ready to chart a new Utopia. The people who had come to regard wealth as the infallible hallmark of success, did not resent the fact that he had become a millionaire; a society which had come to regard the mechanics of life as of primary importance took pride in the fact that he was a world-famous mining engineer. And though Hoover was a man of wealth and of the world, that he had been born on an Iowa farm and had worked his way to success gave him the right to speak of ' rugged individualism ' and satisfied the American demand for democracy.

The Democratic nominee Alfred E. Smith represented a different and less traditional type of democracy. A product of the ' Sidewalks of New York ' and of the Fulton fish market, he was the first lifetime city dweller and the first Catholic ever to receive the presidential nomination of a major party. ' Al ' Smith, rising superior to his Tammany associates, made a brilliant record as governor of New York, and won golden opinions from liberals and social workers, without losing his common touch or his transcendent ability as urban vote-getter. He had acquired a real comprehension of administrative problems and government finance; on questions of power regulation, labor, and social reform he was thoroughly progressive; on the prohibition issue, then agitating American politics, he was an out-and-out ' wet.' Smith had been a leading contender for the Democratic nomination in 1920 and again in 1924; in 1928 he was no longer to be denied. Franklin D. Roosevelt, who had nominated him in 1924, emerged from a long bout with polio to nominate him again, as ' the Happy Warrior,' and he won the nomination on the first ballot.

The campaign of 1928 was more exciting than any in American politics since 1896, but the radio had altered the character of campaigning and there were none of those whirlwind speaking tours with which an earlier generation had been familiar. Governor Smith addressed immense and enthusiastic crowds in the cities of the North and the East, but when he invaded the rural regions of the South and West he met a chill reception. Both parties raised enormous campaign funds, the Republicans over $10 million, the Democrats over $7 million, but it was not money that defeated ' Al ' Smith. He carried all the great urban centers, yet Hoover won by the decisive vote of 21 million to 15 million, and by an electoral college vote of 444 to 87, carrying all the states but eight, and smashing the Solid South. Explanations of this overwhelming defeat are not hard to find. The average businessman was prosperous; and farmers who were not prosperous refused to vote for a Tammany Catholic! As a Catholic, a Tammany brave, a New Yorker, and a wet, Mr. Smith was alien to small-town, middle-class, and rural America. The kind of Protestant who belonged to the Ku Klux Klan feared that if ' Al ' were elected, the Pope would move from Rome to Washington; Southern drys expected him to open a saloon at every crossroads; and there was a general feeling of apprehension that Tammany methods would be introduced into national politics.

2. LIQUIDATING THE WAR

'When the war closed,' said Herbert Hoover, fatuously, 'the most vital of all issues both in our own country and throughout the world was whether governments should continue their wartime ownership and operation of many instrumentalities of production and distribution.' It was in fact a question of little importance but of considerable complexity. The principle involved in the issue was easily settled; the details required careful and prolonged attention. Even Wilson had called for a rapid liquidation of governmental activities, and legislation returning the railroads to private operation and promoting privately owned merchant marine was passed during his administration. The Republicans took an advanced position in favor of private ownership and operation even of such things as airmail and hydroelectric power. 'We want,' said Harding, 'a period in America with less government in business and more business in government,' and the sentiment was echoed, in varying forms, by his successors.

The most immediate problem concerned the railroads which, under the act of 21 March 1918, had been taken over and operated by the Federal Government. That act had been definitely of an emergency character, but it was felt that the roads should not be relinquished to private operation without some positive guarantees that the advantages of unified operation, achieved under government control, should be retained. The Esch-Cummins Transportation Act of 28 February 1920 differed from previous railroad regulation in that it sought to encourage rather than discourage consolidation. Dealing with the railroad system of the nation as a unit, it provided that the Interstate Commerce Commission should evaluate all railroad property and fix a 'fair return' to the stockholders and fair rates on freight and passenger traffic. A so-called recapture clause provided that all net earnings over 6 per cent should be divided equally between the carrier and the government, the latter to use such earnings as a revolving fund for the benefit of weaker roads. The clause proved unworkable and was repealed. Furthermore, the commission was given complete jurisdiction over the financial operations of the railways in order to protect the investing public and its stockholders. A Railway Labor Board was established to mediate all disputes about wages, hours, or working conditions.

This act, together with subsequent Supreme Court decisions, effectually deprived the states of control over a large part of even intrastate commerce, and thus wrote finis to a question which had agitated the courts since the Granger cases. With the railroad system considered as a unit, it became almost impossible to distinguish between interstate and intrastate commerce. ' Commerce is a unit and does not regard state lines,' said Chief Justice Taft in 1922, ' and when the supreme authority of the nation cannot exercise complete effective control over interstate commerce without incidental regulation of intrastate commerce, such incidental regulation is not an invasion of state authority.' [1]

Under plenary government regulation the necessity for artificial competition was ended, and the railways were authorized and encouraged to combine with a view to economical operation. In order to further this end, the Interstate Commerce Commission, under the guidance of Professor W. Z. Ripley, worked out a plan for the consolidation of all railroads into 19 major systems. The revolutionary character of the Esch-Cummins Act is perhaps best indicated by the fact that this Ripley plan called for the consolidation of the Northern Pacific, Great Northern, and Chicago, Burlington and Quincy railroads into one system — which had been prohibited by the Northern Securities decision of 1904 — and for the combination of Central and Southern Pacific railroads — which had been attempted in 1911 but forbidden by the Supreme Court in 1922. Three years later a federal co-ordinator of railroads, Joseph B. Eastman, undertook to work out a scheme for the combination of all the railroads in the country in regional systems. Yet consolidation came slowly, and almost forty years later the major Eastern roads were still finding difficulty in gaining I.C.C. approval for consolidations.

The other features of the Transportation Act did not work well. The Railway Labor Board was unable to prevent the railway shopmen's strike of 1922, and it was replaced, in 1926, by boards of adjustment, mediation, and arbitration with which the Federal Govern-

[1] *Railroad Commission of Wisconsin v. C.B. & Q.R.R. Co.* 257 U.S. 563 (1922).

ment had only the most tenuous connection, and the attempt to fix a 'fair rate' of return ran afoul of the old difficulty of evaluation. The effort of the Interstate Commerce Commission to estimate values upon reproduction costs of 1914 — which was thought to be near 'actual original costs' — encountered bitter opposition from the carriers who much preferred an estimate based upon costs in the 1920's. This difference of opinion — involving billions of dollars — was threshed out in the Supreme Court, and in the O'Fallon decision of 1929 the Court sustained the contention of the roads.[2]

Meantime the whole railroad problem was changing fundamentally. For almost sixty years state and federal governments had fought to regulate railroad rates and curb railroad malpractices, and during most of that time the railroads had fought back. Now the railroads were faced with new and more formidable threats. A network of highways, built at public expense, covered the country; buses and private cars competed for passenger traffic; trucks took away freight; pipelines carried oil. Within a few years airplanes were to make railway travel almost an anachronism.[3] Within a quarter-century the railroads were to throw in the sponge, invite federal intervention and solicit federal aid.

Another step toward the liquidation of the wartime structure was taken with the passage of the Jones Merchant Marine Act of 5 June 1920. Nothing better indicates the effect of the war on nationalism than the fact that this law, embodying eighteenth-century principles of mercantilism, received the signature of a President who had originally confessed free-trade sympathies. The act permitted the Shipping Board to sell the government-owned merchant fleet to private companies, and Albert D. Lasker, the chairman of the Shipping Board who had characterized government ownership as 'poison ivy in the garden of industry,' hastened to dispose of the government ships on liberal terms. Yet the Act of 1920 failed to revive the languishing merchant marine, and in 1928 Congress passed the Jones-White Bill, increasing mail subsidies, appropriating $250 million for construction loans, and authorizing the sale of the remaining government-owned vessels. This act permitted private companies to obtain first-class ships at about one-tenth original cost and underwrote the

[2] *St. Louis and O'Fallon Railway Co. v. United States* 279 U.S. 461 (1929).

[3] In 1930 railways carried 708 million passengers; in 1957, 413 million. In 1934 airplanes carried 475,000 passengers; in 1957, 48 million.

construction of 68 new vessels. The drastic decline of international trade which set in with the depression made it impossible to know whether our merchant marine might have prospered under these liberal arrangements, and the United States was further from having a self-sufficient merchant marine in 1940 than in 1920.

Aviation was deliberately encouraged by a policy of government subsidy to private operation. The first airmail lines had been operated by the government, but from the beginning the ultimate objective of private operation was kept in view; in 1925 Congress authorized contracts for the transfer of airmail to private air lines, and during the following years the shift was effected. Encouraged by airmail subsidies of approximately $8 million annually and by municipal and federal construction of airports for the use of commercial companies, the airplane industry prospered. Charles Lindbergh's solo flight across the Atlantic in the *Spirit of St. Louis,* in May 1927, had caught the public imagination as nothing had since the joining of the Transcontinentals sixty years earlier, and the American public became increasingly air-minded. In 1934 the Black Committee of the Senate revealed that during the Hoover administration the government had co-operated with private companies to discourage competitive bidding, encourage monopoly, and enlarge subsidies, a policy which brought dizzy financial rewards to favored speculators but did little to foster aviation. As a result of these disclosures President Roosevelt, in 1934, canceled all airmail contracts and turned over to the Army Air Corps the task of carrying airmail. A series of disasters, resulting in eleven fatalities, led to the restoration of the airmail to private companies.

A far more vexatious problem created by the war was that of veterans' benefits. The experience of the Civil War demonstrated that the government's account with its soldiers was not closed when they received their discharge. As late as 1932, 23,000 Civil War veterans and 125,000 Civil War widows were receiving nearly $100 million in pensions from the Federal Government. In the years after the First World War, agitation for veterans' benefits took two forms; disability compensation and adjusted compensation for war service. To the first there could be no reasonable objection, and from the beginning the government adopted a liberal policy toward disabled soldiers and their dependents, providing not only outright pensions and hospitalization, but vocational rehabilitation. By 1936 almost 500,000

World War veterans and dependents were receiving aid, and appropriations to the Veterans Administration were over $600 million.

Of a different character was the demand for adjusted compensation, commonly called a bonus. Many soldiers who had served for $30 a month while their civilian friends were earning $10 or $12 a day in industry felt that the government owed them additional compensation. On the conclusion of the war seventeen states provided bonuses ranging from $10 to $30 for each month of service; but the veterans wanted something more liberal than this and looked to the Federal Government for satisfaction. In 1922 representatives of the American Legion pushed through Congress a bill calling for a bonus of $50 for each month of service, but were unable to override the presidential veto. Two years later Congress passed over Coolidge's veto an Adjusted Compensation Act, which gave every World War veteran an endowment and insurance policy computed at the rate of $1.25 for each day of overseas service and $1.00 for each day of home service. Some 3.5 million veterans thus received policies whose average value was about $1000; though the nation was prosperous, no provision was made for carrying this additional burden of $3.5 billion on the public debt.

The depression brought a demand for the immediate payment of the face value of these endowment policies, and in June 1932 a 'bonus army' marched on Washington to present its 'petition on boots.' Camping on the flats within sight of the Capitol building this bonus army seemed to President Hoover an offense against the dignity of the government and with singular ineptitude he called on the National Guard to break up the camp and drive out the bonus marchers. The army performed this task with a thoroughness that shocked public opinion and gained for Hoover the enmity of many who had little sympathy with the bonus army but less with measures that smacked of militarism.

From 1932 to 1936 the bonus question continued to agitate American politics. The Patman Bill providing for the payment of bonus certificates through currency inflation passed Congress in 1935 but was vetoed by President Roosevelt; only its inflationary provision prevented its passage over the presidential veto. In January 1936 a simple bonus act, innocent either of inflationary or taxation features, was passed over Roosevelt's veto, and the Treasury was called upon to find the $1.5 billion immediately necessary to meet this new obligation. The bonus question was thus finally eliminated from American politics; it had the unique distinction of having elicited vetoes from four successive Presidents.

One other inheritance from the war proved equally troublesome until removed from the political arena: prohibition. The roots of prohibition, to be sure, go back deep into the nineteenth century, but it was the war psychology that made it possible to write prohibition into the Constitution. The Eighteenth Amendment, forbidding the 'manufacture, sale or transportation of intoxicating liquors' went into effect in January 1920. The Volstead Act of 28 October 1919 defined intoxicating liquor as any beverage containing over one-half of 1 per cent alcohol and provided stringent regulations for the enforcement of prohibition.

Once national prohibition was a fact the country seemed to regret its gesture of self-denial. The Federal Government made spasmodic efforts to enforce the Volstead Act: in the ten years from 1920 to 1930 prohibition officers made over half a million arrests and the courts secured over 300,000 convictions. Yet drinking continued, and even became fashionable: the corner saloon gave way to the speakeasy and home-brewing became a national pastime. Opposition to prohibition, once strongest among foreign-born workingmen, spread through every class of society, and the thirst for liquor was sublimated into a philosophy of 'personal liberty.' The recalcitrance of the public was not the only cause for the collapse of prohibition. States with large urban populations sabotaged prohibition laws just as Northern states had once nullified the fugitive slave laws. Agents of the Prohibition Bureau entered into corrupt alliance with 'bootlegging' interests, and the Bureau itself became enmeshed in party politics. There was a breakdown not only of law but of respect for the law.

Both parties tried to avoid the troublesome issue, but without success. The Republican party, in office during most of the life of national prohibition, and strongest in the rural communities and among the middle and upper classes of the cities, was inclined to stand behind what Hoover called, 'an experiment noble in motive and far-reaching in purpose.' The Democrats were in a quandary. Their strength was drawn in almost equal proportions from Southern constituencies which were immovably dry and Northern industrial constituencies which were incurably wet. This division almost split the party in 1924 when for 103 ballots the drys supported McAdoo and the wets Smith; the nomination of Davis did nothing to heal the breach. By 1928 the wets had gained the upper hand in the Democratic party; Smith's nomination was not seriously contested and in his campaign he boldly proposed the abandonment of national prohibition enforcement and the return of the problem to the states. His stand on the prohibition question was largely responsible for his spectacular success in the urban centers of the North and his victory in Rhode Island and Massachusetts; it was partly responsible, too, for his loss of traditional Democratic states such as Virginia, North Carolina, Florida, and Texas.

President Hoover made a genuine effort to enforce the prohibition laws, and at the same time appointed a commission to investigate the whole question of law observance and enforcement. This Wickersham Commission submitted, in January 1931, a confused report to the effect that federal prohibition was unenforceable but should be enforced, that it was a failure but should be retained — a conclusion which inspired one columnist to observe that ' the distinguished jurists seem t'feel that if we'd let 'em have it the problem o' keepin' 'em from gettin' it would be greatly simplified.' By 1932 opposition to federal prohibition had gone so far that the Republican party favored a ' revision ' of the Eighteenth Amendment with a view to returning the question to the states, and the Democrats demanded outright repeal. Following Roosevelt's overwhelming victory, Congress passed, in February 1933, the Twenty-first Amendment repealing federal prohibition and within less than a year it was ratified by the requisite number of states. The problem of liquor control was thus back where it had been before the First World War — in the hands of the local authorities.

3. Economic Policies

It was in the realm of economic policy that the conservatism of the Harding, Coolidge, and Hoover administrations was most apparent. The progressive principles of the prewar era were in part discredited, in part outmoded. The new ideal, as elaborated during these twelve years, was to foster economic self-government and economic nationalism. ' The sole function of government,' said President Hoover, ' is to bring about a condition of affairs favorable to the beneficial development of private enterprise.' At the same time the traditional

Republican policies of tax reduction, high tariffs, the promotion of foreign trade, and the encouragement of private ownership of utilities were reasserted and enforced.

The war had left a public debt of $24 billion. The Civil War debt had been liquidated within a generation, and the prosperity of the 'twenties justified the expectation that the World War debt might be paid off with equal rapidity. Secretary Mellon, however, was primarily interested in reducing taxes, and the Congress faithfully reflected his philosophy. A series of revenue acts from 1921 to 1929 wiped out excess profits taxes, drastically reduced surtaxes, granted rebates on ' earned income ' and refunds to corporations of over $3.5 billion. One effect of this policy was to encourage speculation. Another was to transfer the main burden of taxation from the rich to the middle and poorer classes. Thus under Mellon's benign direction taxes on incomes of a million dollars fell from $600,000 to $200,000. Yet notwithstanding these reductions, the national debt was lowered by 1930 to $16 billion. No wonder the business community asserted with one voice that Andrew W. Mellon was ' the greatest Secretary of the Treasury since Hamilton.'

This policy of tax reduction, however, was not maintained with respect to the most pervasive of all taxes — the tariff. The Underwood tariff had never really been tried under normal conditions, for the war itself afforded protection to American manufactures and fostered the establishment of new industries. On the conclusion of the war these new ' infant ' industries — chemicals, dyes, toys, hardware, rayon, and so forth — clamored for protection. In May 1919 President Wilson assured Congress that ' there is, fortunately, no occasion for undertaking in the immediate future any general revision of import duties.' The Republicans, however, thought differently. Fearful that the United States would be inundated with the produce of depressed European labor, a Republican Congress, in March 1921, pushed through an emergency tariff bill which was promptly vetoed by Wilson. ' If there ever was a time when America had anything to fear from foreign competition,' he observed in his veto message, ' that time has passed. If we wish to have Europe settle her debts, governmental or commercial, we must be prepared to buy from her.' But it took fifteen years for this elementary logic to sink in.

Within a month of his accession to the presidency, Harding announced that ' the urgency for an instant tariff cannot be too much emphasized.' Congress responded with the emergency tariff of 27 May 1921, historically important because its prohibitive agricultural schedules, while affording no actual relief to farmers with surplus crops to sell, did commit them to the principle of protection. More important was the Fordney-McCumber tariff of 19 September 1922, which established rates higher than ever before in our history: duties on sugar, textiles, pig iron, rails, and chinaware were restored to the old Payne-Aldrich level, while increases on toys, hardware, chemicals, dyes, and lace ranged from 60 to 400 per cent. In order to provide some degree of elasticity, the law authorized the President, on recommendation of the tariff commission, to raise or lower duties as much as 50 per cent. This provision proved to be of little practical value. Altogether, Presidents Harding and Coolidge used their discretionary authority thirty-seven times. Thirty-two of these changes, including such things as butter, cheese, pig iron, and chemicals were upward; on five articles duties were reduced. These five were mill feed, bob-white quail, paint-brush handles, cresylic acid, and phenol, but there was no Finley Peter Dunne to see the joke.

The economic consequences of the Fordney-McCumber tariff were threefold: it fostered the growth of monopolies in the United States, prevented Europe from paying her obligations to us in the form of goods, and brought reprisals from France and Britain. The ensuing tariff war had important repercussions in American economy. It cut seriously into our foreign trade, persuaded many manufacturers to establish branch plants abroad, and inspired among the large manufacturers and bankers their first serious misgivings as to the wisdom of protection.

Continued prosperity, however, confirmed the Republicans in their devotion to high tariffs and the shift in Democratic strength from the rural South to the industrial North tempered that party's traditional hostility to protection. In the campaign of 1928 the Republicans reaffirmed their faith in the economic blessings of high tariffs and the Democrats hedged shamelessly on the issue. There was no urgent need for further tariff revision, but no sooner was Hoover inaugurated than he summoned Congress in special session to consider farm relief and ' limited changes in the tariff.' The new Hawley-Smoot tariff bill represented increases all along the line, but particularly in minerals, chemicals, dyestuffs, and textiles. Objections from the American Bankers Association and from industries with foreign markets were brushed aside and a vigorous protest from 1028 econo-mists had no effect on President Hoover, who signed the bill on 17 June 1930. The reaction was immediate: within two years twenty-five countries established retaliatory tariffs, and American foreign trade took a further slump.

Yet the Republican administrations could not be impervious to considerations of foreign markets, raw material, and investments. During the First World War the position of the United States had changed from a debtor to a creditor nation. American private invest-ments abroad, estimated at less than $3 billion before the war, in-creased to $14 billion by 1932. These investments were distributed over all parts of the globe and in every variety of business: govern-ment bonds, railroads, utilities, manufactures, mines, oil, fruit, sugar, rubber, and so forth. Part of this investment reflected the determina-tion of American industry to control its own sources of raw material, and in this policy the government co-operated, just as governments had co-operated in the mercantilism of the seventeenth and eight-eenth centuries. It encouraged foreign trade associations, discovered new trade opportunities abroad, and helped American oil interests obtain concessions in Latin America and in the Middle East. Per-haps the most illuminating example of this neo-mercantilism of the 1920's was the struggle for oil.

The United States in the postwar years produced, and consumed, about three-fourths of the world's petroleum, but mounting con-sumption threatened her oil reserves and geologists mistakenly pre-dicted their exhaustion within a generation. Inevitably American producers scrambled to obtain concessions in oil fields abroad. They encountered few difficulties in Mexico or South America, but many in Persia, Mesopotamia, and the Dutch East Indies, where they had to meet the competition of British and Dutch oil interests. An oil war loomed on the international horizon, but when the United States threatened retaliation, the British and Dutch conceded the Standard Oil interests a cut in the gigantic Turkish Petroleum Company, and permitted them to exploit oil reserves in the Dutch East Indies.

The most characteristic example of the new economic philosophy was the official encouragement of large-scale combinations in business. The theory of competition, embodied in the Sherman and Clayton anti-trust laws, had long been discredited by businessmen; it was now scuttled by the government.

Herbert Hoover, as Secretary of Commerce, inaugurated a policy of 'alliance with the great trade associations and the powerful corporations.' His sense of engineering efficiency was outraged at the spectacle of competition with its inevitable waste, and in his first report as Secretary of Commerce he proposed modifications of the Sherman Act to permit business organizations to combine for purposes of information, standardization, arbitration of industrial disputes, elimination of unfair practices, transportation, and research. He placed his department at the disposal of business as a clearing house for exchange of information, and under his auspices, trade associations not only pooled information, advertising, insurance, traffic, and purchases, but drew up codes of fair practice. Over two hundred such codes were in existence at the end of the Hoover administration, and the cotton, woolen, carpet, and sugar codes later accepted by the NRA were copies of those already in use. 'We are passing,' said Hoover perspicaciously, 'from a period of extreme individualistic action into a period of associated activities.'

In part as a result of this official encouragement, the concentration of control in American industry and banking grew apace. The decade from 1919 to 1929 saw 1268 combinations in manufacturing and mining, involving the merging of some 4000 and the disappearance of some 6000 firms. The same process was discernible in the field of utilities, finance, transportation, and trade. In the eight years after the war, for example, 3744 public utility companies disappeared through merger. In 1920 there were 30,139 banks; fifteen years later the number had been reduced by failures and mergers to 16,053. In 1920 the twenty largest banking institutions in the country held about 14 per cent of all loans and investments; ten years later the proportion had increased to 27 per cent. One great corporation came to dominate the telephone, and one the telegraph systems. Even in the realm of retail trade, chain stores ate heavily into the business of the independent shopkeeper. The inevitable result of this process of combination and consolidation was the domination of American industry, transportation, and finance by giant corporations. In 1933, some 594 corporations, each capitalized at $50 million or more, owned 53 per cent of all corporate wealth in the country; the other 387,970 owned the remaining 47 per cent.

The concentration of control extended, inevitably, to the field of natural resources. By the 1920's four companies owned over one-half of the copper resources of the country, the International Nickel Company of Canada owned nine-tenths of the world nickel supply, the Aluminum Company of America held a practical monopoly of bauxite deposits; eight corporations owned three-fourths of the anthracite coal, and five companies produced one-third of the oil.

In few fields had concentration gone further than in the realm of hydroelectric power, which best revealed the economic philosophy of the Republican party. In the years after World War I the electric light and power industry grew with extraordinary rapidity; between 1917 and 1932 production increased more than threefold and capitalization more than fourfold, to over $12 billion. Largely through the holding-company device, control over power production was concentrated in the hands of six giant financial groups — General Electric, Insull, Morgan, Mellon, Doherty, and Byllesby.

Senators Walsh of Montana, LaFollette of Wisconsin, and the indomitable Norris of Nebraska led the most important contest in this sphere, that for government operation of the water-power dams at Muscle Shoals on the Tennessee river. These had been constructed to furnish power for nitrate plants during World War I, at the conclusion of which conservative interests insisted on turning them over to private companies. President Coolidge recommended that the property be sold to the highest bidder and vetoed a bill providing for government operation of the dams. But the high cost of privately produced electricity and the depression kept the power issue alive, and in 1931 the Norris bill calling for the construction of a second dam on the Tennessee river, and for government manufacture and sale of fertilizer and power, once more passed Congress. President Hoover issued a preliminary statement that ' this happens to be an engineering project, and . . . is subject to the cold examination of engineering facts. I am having these facts exhaustively determined by the different departments of the government.' The exhaustive determination took three days; on 3 March 1931 came the anticipated veto, a reiteration of the doctrine of rugged individualism:

I am firmly opposed to the Government entering into any business the major purpose of which is competition with our citizens. . . . This bill raises one of the important issues of Federal Government ownership and operation of power and manufacturing business not as a minor by-product but as a major purpose. . . . I hesitate to contemplate the future of our institutions, of our country, if the preoccupation of its officials is to be no longer the promotion of justice and equal opportunity but is to be devoted to barter in the markets. That is not liberalism, it is degeneration.

Even this *ex cathedra* statement as to the nature and purposes of government, however, did not settle the matter. Two years later, with the creation of the Tennessee Valley Authority the Roosevelt administration entered jauntily upon the course of 'degeneration.'

4. LABOR

The insatiable demands of war, the manpower shortages, and a friendly administration in Washington, made it possible for labor to share some of the prosperity that war had brought to business and farming. By the close of the war, labor unions counted over 5 million members, and could boast distinct advances both in their economic and their legal position. The return of millions of veterans to their jobs, the threat of cheap labor and cheap products from abroad, and the cancellation of wartime contracts with its resulting drastic readjustments in industry, all led to industrial unrest which erupted into over 3000 strikes involving over 4 million workers in 1919, and almost as many the following year. There was a concerted effort by business, and some elements in the government, to establish the 'open shop' and to break the power of the unions, once and for all. During the 'twenties the position of organized labor deteriorated steadily; membership in unions declined from 5.1 million in 1920 to 3.6 million in 1929, and the unions themselves lost more and more of their strikes.

A series of spectacular strikes in steel, coal, railways, and textiles marked the beginning and the end of this decade of 'normalcy.' The most dramatic of the 1919 strikes was in the steel industry. One-third of all steel workers still labored twelve hours a day, seven days a week, and most of the rest worked a ten-hour day. Partly because the workers lived in company towns and were at the mercy of their corporate overlords, partly because they were drawn from such a mixture of nations and races and faiths, Big Steel had so far been able to resist unionization. The giant corporation that dominated the steel industry set itself with adamantine stubbornness against unionization now, and when the steel workers demanded an eight-hour day, Judge Gary of the U.S. Steel Corporation refused even to discuss the matter with them: it was the Pullman-strike situation all over again. An impartial commission of the Federal Council of Churches reported that the grievances of labor were acute: ' the average week of 68.7 hours . . . and the underpayment of unskilled labor, are all inhumane. The " boss system " is bad, the plant organization is military, and the control autocratic.' The strike was attended with the customary violence on both sides, and in Pennsylvania the Constitution was, in effect, suspended. The Steel Corporation managed to persuade public opinion that the strike was the entering wedge of Communism, and it collapsed. Though within a few years U.S. Steel inaugurated an eight-hour day, it successfully resisted unionization of its workers until 1937.

The coal industry had long been sick, in the United States as in England. Coal miners worked without adequate safeguards in dangerous underground pits, and the record of accidents and deaths was appalling; the work was seasonal and many miners could count on only two or three days' work a week; miners who lived in company-owned towns could call neither their homes nor their souls their own. When in 1919 the coal miners of West Virginia went out on strike, President Wilson pronounced the strike a violation of wartime regulations, and the Governor of West Virginia used state militia to smash it. Three years later another and more widespread coal strike exploded in the ' massacre ' of imported strikebreakers at Herrin, Illinois. President Harding set up a commission to study the coal situation; its report sustained most of the complaints of the miners but no one in Congress or in the government paid any attention to it. So shattered was the United Mine Workers by this series of strikes, and by hard times in the mines, that between 1920 and 1932 it declined from half a million to 150,000 members.

The railroads were the third major business affected by the industrial unrest. Railroad workers had won a signal victory in the Adamson Act of 1916, but by 1920 their wages lagged behind those of comparable labor groups, and that year the newly created Railway Labor Board authorized a substantial increase in wages. Two years later, however, a new board appointed by President Harding took a fresh look at the situation, and voted a slash in wages instead. The railway shopmen, 400,000 strong, went out on strike. The President set up a mediation board whose terms were accepted by the shopmen but rejected by the railway operators, or the bankers who controlled them, and the strike continued. At this juncture Attorney-General Daugherty invoked the law, not against the operators but against the strikers; he obtained a sweeping injunction which outlawed any word or gesture that encouraged or aided the strike in any way. The injunction was probably unconstitutional, but the strike was over before this could be determined.

The textile industry, like coal mining, was in chronic difficulties. Originally centered in New England, which had the water power and the skills, it was now shifting to the South where there was no nonsense about limitations on hours of labor or on child labor. Successful strikes in New England and in Paterson, New Jersey, persuaded the United Textile Workers that the time had come to invade the South. They were mistaken, for here they had a hard nut to crack. Southern textile companies owned not only their mills but the mill villages, and usually the local sheriffs and politicians as well. A strike in 1927, in Elizabethton, Tennessee, where girls worked 56 hours a week for 18 cents an hour, was smashed by a combination of local vigilantes, company militia, and state troops. In 1929 the union tried to organize the textile workers of North Carolina and Virginia, but once again the familiar combination of vigilantes and police smashed both strike and strikers.

In all this it was not difficult to discern a distinct pattern of government and business partnership. In almost every instance of industrial conflict the government threw its support to the side of management. It backed boards and commissions; co-operated with business in its evasion of the restrictions of the Sherman Act, but issued injunctions against workers whose right to strike and to picket had presumably been guaranteed by the Clayton Act; and made available federal troops to break strikes. This conduct, says the historian of this era, John D. Hicks, 'was far more scandalous than the merely political depravity for which the Harding regime was noted.'[4]

Even the courts caught the contagion of reaction. The Supreme Court held two child-labor laws unconstitutional, one of them on grounds so untenable that they were wholly repudiated a generation later; it struck down a minimum wage law for women; sustained yellow-dog contracts; voided a Kansas statute authorizing an impartial court to set wages in business affecting the public health and safety; assessed triple damages against an unincorporated union;

[4] John D. Hicks, *Republican Ascendancy*, p. 73.

and threw out an Arizona anti-injunction law. Not until 1932 when the Democrats controlled both houses of Congress did the Norris-LaGuardia law erect effective safeguards against the misuse of the injunction in labor disputes and against the yellow-dog contract.

In only one arena did labor have its way, and that because here labor's goals fitted into the prevailing mood of nationalism, isolationism, and conservatism. Organized labor had long agitated against unlimited immigration, with only moderate success. Now the well-grounded fear of an immense influx of emigrants and refugees from war-stricken Europe brought a variety of pressure-groups to the support of labor's campaign: sociologists who had convinced themselves that the ' new ' immigration was responsible for grave social problems, progressives traditionally sympathetic to labor's demands, and anti-Semitic and anti-Catholic organizations like the Ku Klux Klan. These pressures proved irresistible, and during the 'twenties Congress enacted three sweeping laws which erected quantitative and, it was supposed, qualitative barriers against immigrants. The Act of 1921 limited the total number of aliens who would be admitted from outside the Western Hemisphere to 357,000; the more drastic Act of 1924 set up a quota system that discriminated sharply in favor of the ' old ' and against the ' new ' immigration; the Act of 1929 reduced the total who might come in to 150,000 a year. As a result of this legislation, of Department of Labor rulings excluding any who might become a public charge, and, above all, as a result of the depression, immigration from the Old World fell to about 35,000 during the decade of the 'thirties, while during that decade almost 100,000 more aliens returned to their homes than came to America.

5. AGRICULTURAL DISTRESS

The prosperous condition of American business during the 1920's was not reflected in agriculture. During most of this decade the farmer was in distress, and the end of the period of Republican domination coincided with an agrarian depression deeper and more serious than any since the early 1890's. Between 1920 and 1932 total farm income declined from $15.5 billion to $5.5 billion. Wheat which sold for $1.82 a bushel in 1920 brought 38 cents in 1932; corn fell from 61 cents to 32 cents; cotton from 16 cents a pound to 6 cents a pound.

The size of the cereal and cotton crops of 1920 and 1932 was approximately the same; the 1932 value was slightly over one-third that of 1920.[5]

This collapse of agricultural prosperity is to be accounted for by a number of factors. The values in 1920 were abnormally high, 1932 values abnormally low, not only in agriculture but in business of all kinds, and it is not remarkable that farming should have shared the wartime prosperity and the later depression. Yet the farmers got the short end of prosperity and the long end of depression. Even in 1920 the farmer received only 15 per cent of the national income; in 1933 he received only 7 per cent. High war prices had resulted in expansion, with an increase in borrowings and mortgage indebtedness, but farm prosperity did not last long enough to enable farmers to liquidate their debts. Even more important was the lowering of the world price for cereals and cotton and the collapse of the foreign market. Partly as a result of the impact of the Hawley-Smoot tariff on European purchasing power, farm exports, which had averaged over $2 billion annually from 1917 to 1925, fell to an average of three-quarters of a billion from 1931 to 1935.

The Republican panacea for agricultural depression was the tariff, but since the American farmers raised a large exportable surplus, increases of duties on farm products were futile. The farmers themselves came up with schemes which would enlist government support to agriculture as the tariff enlisted its support to industry. Out of the medley of plans two emerged: the equalization fee and the export debenture. The first, which became the controversial McNary-Haugen bill, created a government corporation which would buy selected farm products at a ' parity ' price, and sell the surpluses at a lower price in the world market; the costs would be paid by an ' equalization fee ' on processing and by the taxpayer. Passed in 1927 this plan was vetoed by President Coolidge. The export debenture plan provided a ' bounty ' on six agricultural commodities, to be paid

[5] *Statistical Abstract of the U.S.*, 1936, pp. 632 ff:

	1920		1932	
	Production	*Value*	*Production*	*Value*
	1000 bu.	*1000 dollars*	*1000 bu.*	*1000 dollars*
Wheat	843,277	1,539,584	756,927	289,096
Corn	3,070,604	1,899,136	2,926,871	934,682
Oats	1,444,291	777,179	1,250,955	195,826
Cotton (bales)	13,429,000	1,069,257	13,003,000	424,013

in ' export debentures ' that could be used for paying tariff duties. Hoover managed to defeat this bill by the threat of a veto.

Hoover's solution for the farm problem was embodied in the Agricultural Marketing Act of 15 June 1929. This act authorized a new Federal Farm Board to extend loans to agricultural co-operatives, create stabilization corporations for the purpose of controlling surpluses, and insure both co-operatives and stabilization corporations against losses. In an effort to peg the price of wheat and cotton these corporations bought altogether over 300 million bushels of wheat and 1.3 million bales of cotton, losing in these operations not less than $184 million, and they lost in addition another $165 million on loans to marketing organizations. Yet farm prices were lower at the end than at the beginning of the experiment.

6. COLLAPSE AND DEPRESSION

President Hoover came to office committed to the ideal of abolishing poverty. ' We in America are nearer to the final triumph over poverty,' he said during the campaign, ' than ever before in the history of any land. . . . We have not reached the goal, but, given a chance to go forward with the policies of the last eight years, we shall soon with the help of God be in sight of the day when poverty will be banished from this nation.' Swept into the presidency by an overwhelming majority, Hoover prepared to go forward with the policies of the previous eight years which he had, in large measure, inspired. His election was the signal for a boom on the Stock Exchange, and most businessmen and investors prepared to reap still higher profits and to enjoy a still higher standard of living.

For a time their confidence seemed justified. The average value of common stocks soared from 117 in December 1928 to 225 the following September, and a few stocks such as U.S. Steel and General Electric rose to dizzy heights. Inspired by these dazzling profits, stockbrokers increased their bank borrowings from $3.5 billion in 1927 to $8.5 billion two years later and bought more extravagantly than ever before. The public appeared willing and able to absorb limitless quantities of stock: in the single month of January 1929 no less than a billion dollars' worth of new securities were floated. Factory employment, freight car loadings, construction contracts, bank loans, almost all the indices of business, showed a marked upward swing.

Even as Hoover announced in his inaugural address that ' in no nation are the fruits of accomplishment more secure,' shrewd investors were cashing in on their paper profits and pulling out of the market, but the Federal Reserve Board, though alarmed at the speculative mania, did little to reverse the policy of easy credit which it had inaugurated in 1927. There were, indeed, many factors to excite concern. The world economic situation was discouraging. War debts were uncollectable, foreign trade had declined precipitously, and the interest on billions of dollars of private investments was in default. Prosperity, even during the height of the boom, was a spotty affair. Agriculture was depressed and the farmers' purchasing power severely reduced. Industries such as the coal and textile had not shared in the general well-being, while technical improvements worked hardships on many older industries and created temporary unemployment. Unemployment was a constant throughout the decade; in 1921 it was estimated at over 4 million, and at no time did it fall below 1.5 million. Much of the new wealth had gone to the privileged few, and 5 per cent of the population enjoyed one-third of the income. But consumer purchasing power had not materially increased; between 1923 and 1928 the index of wages rose from 100 to 112 while the index of speculative profits jumped from 100 to 410! Meantime public and private debts had mounted to staggering sums; by 1930 the total debt burden was estimated at between $100 billion and $150 billion — approximately one-third the national wealth. Above all, debts, installment buying, and speculation had strained credit to the breaking point, and because few understood the dangers involved in the process, credit was gravely abused. Too many Americans were living on the margin of existence, or worse yet, on the future. When confidence in the future disappeared, they discovered their error.

The crash came in October 1929. On the twenty-first of that month the prices of stocks began to sag; on the twenty-fourth over 12 million shares changed hands; on 29 October came a catastrophic crash. In less than a month stocks suffered an average decline of 40 per cent. Sage observers regarded this deflation of values as inevitable, but the collapse caught the country as a whole unprepared, and the first reaction was one of shocked incredulity.

Once under way the spiral of the depression swept out in an everwidening curve. Millions of investors lost their savings; thousands were forced into bankruptcy. Debts mounted, purchases declined, factories cut down production, workers were dismissed, wages and salaries slashed. Farmers, already hard hit, were unable to meet their obligations, and mortgages were foreclosed, often with losses to all concerned. Real estate sagged in value and tax collections dropped alarmingly, forcing governments to cut essential services. Commercial failures increased from 24,000 in 1928 to 32,000 in 1932, and over 5000 banks closed their doors in the first three years of the depression. By 1930 there were slightly over 3 million unemployed; in 1933 the number was variously estimated at from 12 to 15 million. Factory payrolls fell to less than half the level of 1929 and the total wages paid out declined from $55 billion in 1929 to $33 billion in 1931. Construction work, except for government operations, practically ceased. Foreign trade declined in three years from $9 billion to $3 billion. Only taxes and incomes from dividends and interest held up. Government expenditures in 1929 were $13 billion; by 1932 public works and relief had pushed them up to $15 billion. And interest and dividend payments reached in 1931 an all-time high of $8 billion; at no time during the depression did they fall below the 1928 level. Since the whole national income declined from an estimated $85 billion in 1929 to an estimated $37 billion in 1932, it can be seen that the burden of the depression fell upon the less privileged groups.

As the depression wore on, conditions became increasingly desperate; society itself seemed to be on the verge of disintegration. There was open warfare on the labor front, in the steel and automobile industries and in the mines; Iowa farmers staged a revolt that conjured up recollections of Shays's Rebellion of 1787; in drought-stricken Arkansas starving tenant-farmers broke into Red Cross storehouses and stole food; swords in hand, cavalrymen rode down the bonus marchers and their wives and children, burning their hovels on the Anacostia flats and scattering their pitiful possessions; Pennsylvania coal miners froze in the midst of mountains of coal, while their children lived on weeds and dandelions. Two million vagrants took to the roads, riding the rods and living in hobo jungles, a quarter of a million of them boys and girls. Women workers in textile mills in Tennessee got $2.29 a week for a fifty-hour week which was better than the $1.10 a week paid young girls for sweatshop labor in progressive Connecticut. Grown men worked for 5 cents an hour in sawmills, lumbermen in Arkansas got 10 cents. By 1932 the unemployed passed the 10-million mark, and was growing daily. Relief payments were down to $2.40 a week in New York; Toledo, Ohio, paid 2.14 cents per meal, but only one-fourth of the out-of-work were on relief. The week the RFC made $90 million available to Mr. Dawes's Central Republican Bank in Chicago, Washington turned down a request for more relief funds from Chicago's Mayor Cermak. The magisterial historian of these tragic years has described the second winter of the depression:

The cold was bitter in unheated tenements, in the flophouses smelling of sweat and Lysol, in the parks, the empty freight cars, along the windy water-fronts. With no money left for rent, unemployed men and their entire families began to build shacks where they could find unoccupied land. Along the railroad embankment, beside the garbage incinerator, in the city dumps, there appeared towns of tar-paper and tin, old packing-boxes and old car-bodies. . . . Symbols of the New Era, these communities quickly received their sardonic name: they were called Hoovervilles. And, indeed, it was in many cases only the fortunate who could find Hoovervilles. The unfortunate spent their nights huddled together in doorways, in empty packing cases, in box-cars. At the bread lines and soup kitchens, hours of waiting would produce a bowl of mush, often without milk or sugar, and a tin cup of coffee. The vapours from the huge steam cookers mingling with the stench of wet clothes and steaming bodies made the air foul. But waiting in the soup kitchen was better than scavenging in the dump. Citizens of Chicago could be seen digging into heaps of refuse with sticks and hands as soon as the garbage trucks pulled out. On June 30, 1931, the Pennsylvania Department of Labor reported that nearly one-quarter of the labor force of the state was out of work. 'Have you ever heard a hungry child cry?' asked Lillian Wald of Henry Street.[6]

The Hoover administration adopted a policy of discounting the seriousness of the depression. To those who had guided the destinies of the nation throughout the unprecedented prosperity of the 1920's, it seemed inconceivable that the economic structure should collapse. The panic, they were convinced, was a stock-market panic, induced by speculation and precipitated by fear. All that was necessary for a return of prosperity was a restoration of confidence. To this end the administration directed its energies. In conference after conference with the industrial leaders of the country, President Hoover urged the maintenance of employment and wages; in speech after speech

[6] Arthur Schlesinger, Jr., *The Crisis of the Old Order*, p. 177.

he exhorted the nation to keep a stiff upper lip. The President did recommend a modest program of public works, the Federal Farm Board extended aid to depressed farmers, and Congress voted relief to those who had been made destitute by the great drought of 1930. Yet these half-hearted measures were largely nullified by other administrative policies, notably the Hawley-Smoot tariff and feeding relief to banks and railroads rather than directly to the people.

'As a nation,' said President Hoover just a year after the crash, 'we *must* prevent hunger and cold to those of our people who are in honest difficulties.' But the administration was unwilling to grant direct relief; that burden was one for local governments and private charity to shoulder. In vain did Progressives like LaFollette, Costigan, and Cutting plead for large-scale program of public works, financed directly by federal funds. In vain did they present statistics proving the breakdown of private charity and the inability of municipal and state authorities to carry the burden any longer. Every proposal for generous relief was met by the stubborn opposition of Bourbon Democrats and Republican Tories whose devotion to the fictions of states' rights and the shibboleth of a balanced budget blinded them to realities. When the House threatened to pass a bill appropriating some $2 billion for public works, the President himself intervened with the warning that 'This is not unemployment relief. It is the most gigantic pork-barrel ever perpetrated by the American Congress.'

Not until 1932, when the Democrats controlled the House and a coalition of Democrats and Republican progressives ran the Senate, were measures taken to cope with the depression. The most important of these was the Reconstruction Finance Corporation, an enterprise proposed by Eugene Meyer and adopted by the President with utmost reluctance. The Act of January 1932, authorized the RFC to lend money to railroads, banks, agricultural agencies, industry and commerce. By subsequent amendments the RFC was authorized to purchase preferred stock of banks, and extend loans to local government agencies for self-liquidating projects; during the Roosevelt administration it became the banker for many of the new relief and recovery agencies. It inaugurated at once that policy of ' priming the pump ' which should have been adopted two years earlier.

In the course of the next three years the RFC came to the aid of over 7000 banks and trust companies, to the tune of $3.5 billion.

Loans to mortgage-loan companies amounted to some $300 million and to insurance companies another $100 million. Advances of some $700 million to railroads enabled many of them to refinance their outstanding obligations and greatly to improve their facilities. Loans to industry totaled over $100 million, and to agriculture, in one form or another, over $2.5 billion. Altogether authorizations and commitments of the RFC, including advances to other government agencies and disbursements for relief, came to over $11 billion.

This timely assistance to banks, mortgage and insurance companies, railroads and industries, undoubtedly saved many of them from serious losses and to that extent checked the downward spiral of the depression, while assistance to city and state governments enabled many of them to meet their more pressing payroll obligations. At the same time, by setting up certain standards to which borrowers must conform, the RFC was able to introduce minor reforms into banking, transportation, and industry. On the other hand, many of the loans, especially those extended to banks during 1932, merely put off the day of reckoning and involved investors and depositors in losses which might have been avoided by a more circumspect policy. And the RFC gave little effective relief to those who needed it most urgently. For the theory behind it was that of the protective tariff — that prosperity would somehow trickle down from banks and industries to the workingmen at the base of the economic pyramid. Mounting figures of unemployment proved the theory fallacious and indicated the necessity for a more realistic view of the whole economic problem.

One of the casualties of the depression was confidence in business leadership. Possibly nowhere else in the world had the titans of finance and the moguls of industry enjoyed such prestige, or their titles to leadership been so uncritically accepted, as in the United States. But by 1932 business leadership lay in ruins. It was not merely that the great figures of the world of finance and industry confessed themselves as bewildered as simple folk by the catastrophe that had overtaken the country, nor even that their own responsibility for that catastrophe became increasingly clear. It was rather that so many of them revealed themselves derelict in duty and guilty of grave malpractices and even of outright corruption. As late as October 1932 President Hoover had asserted that all Americans could find inspiration in the devotion to duty of ' our great manufactures, our rail-

ways, utilities, business houses and public officials.' But the disclosures of the Pecora Committee which investigated banking and stock
exchange practices in 1933 emphasized that the devotion of the business community had been to its own interests rather than to the national interest. The public learned with astonishment that the dignified House of Morgan kept a ' preferred list ' of influential public
men to whom it sold securities below the market price, and that in
the depression years of 1930 and 1931 not a single partner of that
banking firm had paid any income tax; that Charles E. Mitchell of
the great National City Bank of New York made $2.5 million of
stockholders' money available to bank officers for speculation, without interest or security; that great banking houses palmed off on
gullible investors South American bonds that they knew to be almost
worthless; and that a powerful banker like former Vice-President
Charles E. Dawes used his position and influence to obtain favors for
his bank. Even more damaging was the record of the great utilities
tycoon Samuel E. Insull of Chicago; chairman of 65 companies and
director of 85, he had built up by methods that could not bear the
light of day a utilities empire that controlled one-eighth of the nation's electric power. When it collapsed, taking down with it thousands of little investors, Insull fled to Greece — which had no extra-
dition treaty with the United States — to avoid a jail sentence. No
wonder the millionaire Joseph P. Kennedy could lament that ' the
belief that those in control of the corporate life of America were
motivated by ideals of honorable conduct was completely shattered ';
it was a conclusion that was not wholly lost on his 15-year-old son
John. Not for another quarter of a century did the business community recover something of its former prestige.

The Hoover administration is significant in American history not
so much for the great depression — which would have come no matter who had been President, though not necessarily in such a desperate fashion — but because it represented the last stand of rugged
individualism and the beginnings of the welfare state. It constituted
therefore a watershed between the old and the new, and will doubtless serve to demarcate an historical era. For Hoover was at once a
Manchester liberal who subscribed to laissez faire and an engineer
who had faith in social and economic planning; and he attempted a
synthesis of the two incompatible philosophies. He envisioned a nation where unrestrained individual enterprise was directed solely
toward social good, where a balanced economy was achieved by co-

operative action, and where order and liberty were reconciled; and to this vision he gave the name 'the American system.' The reconciliation of order and liberty is, to be sure, one of the great themes of American history; but Hoover's concept of liberty was narrow and doctrinaire, and the methods by which he sought to implement his philosophy were unrealistic. Equally unrealistic was Hoover's theory that government was a science rather than an art, and that it was a mechanical rather than a political science. He placed his faith not so much in the traditional instrumentalities of democracy as in blueprints, charts, graphs, and commissions — like the notorious Wickersham Commission. Faced with the sharpest economic crisis in the history of the country, Hoover, for all his engineering skill, failed to organize in any comprehensive or effective fashion the resources of the country in the fight against the depression, and left to his successor the tasks he was unable or unwilling to perform.

BIBLIOGRAPHY

1. GENERAL: POLITICS. Fred L. Allen, *Only Yesterday;* Charles A. Beard, *America in Midpassage;* H. U. Faulkner, *From Versailles to New Deal;* Claude Fuess, *Calvin Coolidge;* Oscar Handlin, *Al Smith;* John D. Hicks, *The Republican Ascendancy;* Herbert Hoover, *The New Day, American Individualism,* and *Memoirs,* vol. 2; Kenneth McKay, *The Progressive Movement;* W. S. Myers & W. H. Newton, *The Hoover Administration;* George Norris, *Fighting Liberal;* Fred L. Paxson, *The Post War Years: Normalcy 1918–1923;* Henry Pringle, *Alfred E. Smith: A Critical Study;* Merlo Pusey, *Charles Evans Hughes* (2 vols.) ; M. E. Ravage, *The Story of Teapot Dome;* Karl Schriftgiesser, *This Was Normalcy;* Preston Slosson, *Great Crusade and After;* George Soule, *Prosperity Decade;* Lincoln Steffens, *Autobiography* (2 vols.) ; Morris Werner, *Privileged Characters;* William A. White, *Masks in a Pageant* and *Puritan in Babylon;* R. L. Wilbur & A. M. Hyde, *The Hoover Policies.*

2. SOCIAL DEVELOPMENTS. Roger Burlingame, *Peace Veterans;* Theodore Draper, *The Roots of American Communism;* Marquis James, *History of the American Legion;* Charles Merz, *The Dry Decade;* E. M. Morgan, *The Legacy of Sacco and Vanzetti;* Robert Murray, *Red Scare: A Study in National Hysteria;* Peter Odegard, *Pressure Politics;* W. F. Ogburn (ed.) , *Recent Social Changes in the United States;* David Shannon, *The Socialist Party of America;* Frank Tannenbaum, *Darker Phases of the South;* W. W. Waters, *B. E. F.: The Whole Story of the Bonus Army;* Dixon Wecter, *When Johnny Comes Marching Home.*

3. ECONOMIC POLICIES. A. A. Berle, *Twentieth Century Capitalist Revolution;* A. A. Berle & G. C. Means, *Modern Corporation and Private Property;* A. R. Burns, *The Decline of Competition;* Charles Chapman, *Development of American Business and Banking Thought;* Thomas C. Cochran & William Miller, *The Age of Enterprise;* Merle Fainsod & Lincoln Gordon, *Government and the American Economy;* John K. Galbraith, *American Capitalism;* Louis

Hacker, *Triumph of American Capitalism;* Harry Jerome, *Mechanization in Industry;* D. M. Keezer & Stacy May, *Public Control of Business;* J. C. Kerwin, *Federal Water Power Legislation;* W. I. King, *Wealth and Income of the People of the United States;* Simon Kuznets, *The National Income and Its Composition 1919–1938;* H. W. Laidler, *Concentration of Control in American Industry;* W. W. Leontief, *The Structure of American Economy 1919–1929;* D. B. Locklin, *Railroad Regulation since 1920;* R. MacVeagh, *The Transportation Act of 1920;* Allan Nevins & Frank E. Hill, *Ford: Expansion and Challenge 1915–1933;* G. W. Nutter, *Extent of Enterprise Monopoly 1899–1931;* James W. Prothro, *The Dollar Decade: Business Ideas in the 1920s;* H. S. Rauschenbush, *The Power Fight;* W. Z. Ripley, *Main Street and Wall Street;* E. E. Schattschneider, *Politics, Pressures and the Tariff;* W. M. W. Splawn, *Government Ownership and Operation of Railroads;* The President's Committee, *Recent Economic Changes in the United States* (2 vols.).

4. LABOR AND AGRICULTURE. Harold Barger & Hans Landsberg, *American Agriculture 1899–1939;* J. D. Black, *Agricultural Reform in the United States;* Arthur Capper, *The Agricultural Bloc;* John R. Commons, et al., *History of Labor,* vol. 4; J. D. Durand, *The Labor Force, 1890–1960;* Nathan Fine, *Labor and Farmer Parties in the United States;* Gilbert Fite, *George Peek and the Fight for Farm Parity;* C. O. Gregory, *Labor and the Law;* B. H. Hibbard, *Effects of the Great War upon Agriculture in the United States;* Matthew Josephson, *Sidney Hillman;* Russell Lord, *The Wallaces of Iowa;* K. D. Lumpkin & D. S. Douglas, *Child Workers in America;* Carey McWilliams, *Ill Fares the Land;* Russel Nye, *Midwestern Progressive Politics;* Liston Pope, *Millhands and Preachers: Gastonia;* Theodore Saloutos & John D. Hicks, *Agricultural Discontent in the Middle West;* E. R. A. Seligman, *The Economics of Farm Relief;* Philip Taft, *The A.F. of L. in the Time of Gompers;* A. G. Taylor, *Labor Policies of the N.A.M.;* Mary H. Vorse, *Passaic Textile Strike, 1926–27;* J. A. Wechsler, *Labor Baron: John L. Lewis;* E. E. Witte, *Government in Labor Disputes;* Leo Wolman, *Ebb and Flow in Trade Unionism.*

5. THE DEPRESSION. Irving Bernstein, *The Lean Years: A History of the American Worker 1920–1933;* J. C. Brown, *Public Relief 1929–1939;* C. J. Enzler, *Some Social Aspects of the Depression;* John K. Galbraith, *The Great Crash;* William E. Leuchtenburg, *The Perils of Prosperity;* Arthur Mann, *LaGuardia;* Broadus Mitchell, *Depression Decade;* Ferdinand Pecora, *Wall Street Under Oath;* Lionel Robbins, *The Great Depression;* Arthur M. Schlesinger, Jr., *The Crisis of the Old Order;* David Schneider & Albert Deutsch, *History of Public Welfare in New York State;* J. A. Schumpeter, *Business Cycles;* Gilbert Seldes, *The Years of the Locust* (America, 1929–1932); Rexford Tugwell, *Mr. Hoover's Economic Policies.*

6. DOCUMENTS. H. S. Commager, *Documents,* nos. 424, 430–34, 438–41, 450–56, 458, 459, 461–2, 465, 468, 470–72; David J. and Bertha T. Saposs, *Readings in Trade Unionism;* A. R. Ellingwood and W. Coombs, *The Government and Railroad Transportation;* James M. Landis and Marcus Manoff (eds.), *Cases on Labor Law.*

For further references, *Harvard Guide,* ¶¶ 245–9, 251, 253.

American Society between Wars

1. PROSPERITY AND DISILLUSIONMENT

WORLD War I, like the Civil War, was followed by a decade of materialism, and its manifestations were scarcely less gaudy and even more pervasive. Disillusion and cynicism spread to almost every part of the social body, inducing both irresolution and irrationality. There was widespread distrust of reason, and as men lost faith in reason they almost ceased to use it. They lost faith, too, in many of those values that earlier generations had taken for granted, and lost even the capacity to believe in values. There were few grand ideas, but a sophisticated rejection of ideas; there was little faith, but a superstition masquerading as faith. For all its cascading energy the age was negative rather than affirmative, incontrovertible in repudiation but weak on affirmation. Never before had so many men known so many arguments for rejecting the heritage of the past; seldom has a generation bequeathed so little that was of permanent value and so much that was troublesome to the future.

Weary of reform and of the crusade for democracy, Americans turned with unashamed enthusiasm to the business of getting rich and enjoying themselves. During the piping years of the 'twenties they succeeded in realizing these ends. Population grew by 17 millions in a decade — the largest absolute increase in history until then — and the increase in national wealth was equally spectacular; those who enjoyed this new prosperity congratulated themselves that it was universal and permanent, and that the millennium had arrived.

The wealth of the nation was unevenly distributed: 25 million families — or over 87 per cent of the population — had incomes of less than $2500, while only about a million families — or less than 3 per cent — had incomes of over $5000. Yet if there was still a great deal of real inequality, there was little ostentatious inequality, and if it was true that the rich grew richer, it was equally true that there was little they could do with their money to distinguish them from those who were not rich. Technology provided a standardized product, advertising looked to a mass market, and social habits and philosophy put a premium on formal equality. The gap that separated white from black remained deep, but the lines that distinguished different classes of whites were increasingly blurred.

The war had made this generation conscious of change and impermanence and impatient for the gratification of wants and the indulgence of appetites. Even the President's Committee on Social Trends took note of this ' new attitude towards hardship as a thing to be avoided by living in the here and now, utilizing installment credit, and other devices, to telescope the future into the present.' Business co-operated with these desires by building obsolescence into its products, and providing credit that was easy if not always liberal, and the public responded by buying what it wanted on the installment plan. No longer inclined to regard thrift as a virtue or even a sound economic policy, they speculated avidly on the stock market or in Florida real estate. Mass optimism, or recklessness, was reflected in mounting debts and taxes as Americans cheerfully charged current benefits to future earnings or windfalls, piling up debts that they expected their children to pay. With the depression this extravagance continued, of necessity.

As the depression deepened the birth rate dropped, from 25 per 1000 in 1915 to 16 per 1000 twenty years later — probably the sharpest drop in our history. Marriage came to seem less permanent than had long been supposed; even the remarkable upswing in the Catholic population did not seriously retard the mounting divorce rate. In 1890 out of every one hundred marriages, six ended in divorce; forty years later eighteen of every one hundred marriages were thus terminated, and that year some 200,000 couples were legally separated. In many other respects family life came to seem less stable. Those who continued to live in the town where they were born became objects of curiosity, and for the inhabitants of the large cities, moving came to be an almost annual junket, while the shift from roomy Victorian houses to city flats made it difficult for large families — the grandparents and the maiden aunts — to live together.[1] With the

---

[1] Soon the expatriate poet, Ezra Pound, made a virtue of this:

O, how hideous it is,
To see three generations of one house gathered together!

Oliver Wendell Holmes *by Charles Hopkinson*

passing of the family homestead, many of the old bonds and disciplines that had molded generations of young men and women slipped away, and the cities furnished no immediate substitute. For millions of Americans the depression was to reveal that

> Home is the place where, when you have to go there,
> They have to take you in.[2]

For millions it was that, and nothing more.

Socially perhaps the most notable phenomenon of this period was urbanization. The process of city growth can be read in statistics; for its significance we have to go to sociological studies and to imaginative literature. In 1890 the population was 65 per cent rural; in 1930 it was 56 per cent urban, and if metropolitan areas were included, well over that. Many cities, especially in Florida and California, increased tenfold during these years, while increases in the larger cities of the older parts of the country were spectacular.[3]

The whole nation became urbanized — in its psychology as well as in its economy. Big towns copied the cities, and little towns copied the big towns, while few villages were so small or isolated as to be without moving pictures and supermarkets and parking problems. Nearly half the population of the country lived within easy access of cities of 100,000 inhabitants or more; these cities became the shopping, entertainment, educational, and cultural centers of the country. To this process the automobile especially, as well as the radio, the moving picture, and the newspaper contributed. At the close of World War I there were some 9 million motor cars in use; a decade later the number had soared to 26 million, and, even in the depression decade, the number continued to increase. Originally a luxury, the automobile quickly became a necessity; when hard times hit a family, the car was the last thing to go, and with the return of prosperity it was not a house but a car that the workingman bought.

---

2 Robert Frost, ' Death of the Hired Man.'
3 Thus, in thousands:

	1890	1930		1890	1930
Atlanta, Ga.	65	270	Minneapolis, Minn.	164	464
Detroit, Mich.	205	1568	Pittsburgh, Pa.	238	669
Grand Rapids, Mich.	60	170	Rochester, N.Y.	130	320
Hartford, Conn.	60	150	Syracuse, N.Y.	88	209
Indianapolis, Ind.	105	305	Toledo, O.	81	290
Kansas City, Mo.	130	400	Washington, D.C.	189	487

For many Americans the automobile was a symbol of freedom, a badge of equality, useful for transportation but essential for social intercourse and self-respect.

With the automobile the national characteristics of mobility and restlessness and the mania for speed were given new and easy outlets.[4] The automobile did more than carry restless city-folk out into the country and country-folk to the city in ceaseless and futile interchange; it broke down isolation and provincialism, promoted standardization, accelerated the growth of the city at the expense of the village and then the growth of the suburbs at the expense of the city, trained young Americans to mechanical ingenuity, created a hundred new industries and millions of new jobs, and required the destruction of large parts of the country to make way for roads and by-passes. It precipitated new problems of morals and of crime; and took an annual toll of life and limb as high as that exacted by the First World War. Henry Adams, who had seen in the dynamo the symbol of the twentieth century, was vindicated.

The radio, like the automobile, began as a plaything and became a necessity, and a promoter of social and economic change. The first broadcasting station opened at Pittsburgh in 1920; within a decade there were almost 13 million radios in American homes, and by 1940 there were close to 900 broadcasting stations and 52 million receiving sets. Radio commanded an even wider audience than the newspaper, and radios were in almost continuous use. The statistics of the radio business can be readily computed; it is more difficult to evaluate their significance. Notwithstanding the multiplicity of broadcasting stations, most of the wave-lengths were controlled by a few great networks — the Columbia, the National, and the Mutual leading the field,[5] for here, as elsewhere in American business, concentration of control went on apace.

From the beginning radio was privately owned and controlled, and

---

[4] Thus Santayana wrote:

> No space for noonday rest or midnight watches,
> No purest joy of breathing under heaven!
> Wretched themselves, they heap, to make them happy,
>   Many possessions.

Poems, Chas. Scribner's Sons, p. 73.

[5] Eventually these gave way to the big three: National Broadcasting Company, Columbia Broadcasting System, and American Broadcasting Corporation, which exercised a virtual monopoly in radio and television.

not — as in Britain and on the Continent — in public hands, and the success of municipal stations such as New York's famous WNYC did not convert the average listener to the European policy of government-ownership. Indeed even government regulation was tardy, feeble, and fragmentary. Not until 1927 did Congress establish a Federal Radio Commission to license stations, assign wave-lengths, and supervise policies. In 1934 this commission was abolished and general supervision over radio assigned to the Federal Communications Commission. This body has, in theory, exclusive control over both radio and television broadcasting; though it is prohibited from exercising any form of ' censorship ' over radio or television, it is authorized to require that all radio and television broadcasts conform to the ' public interest, convenience and necessity.' This requirement has always been loosely and amiably interpreted.

Over the air waves went forth the most varied agglomeration of entertainment, news, advertisement, and propaganda that had ever assailed the ears of men. The entertainment, though most prominent, was probably the least important. More significant was the rapid development of news broadcasting and commentary. News commentators were heard daily by millions who never read newspaper editorials, and judicious and conscientious commentators like Raymond Gram Swing and Elmer Davis, as well as demagogues like Father Coughlin and Gerald Smith, came to wield an influence comparable to that exercised by Horace Greeley a century earlier. The radio — soon to be dramatically augmented by television — brought world affairs into the living room, and by making it possible for every American to hear the ' fireside chats ' of Roosevelt, the bitter harangues of Hitler, and the somber eloquence of Churchill, did a great deal to break down provincialism and isolation. Because the radio competed with the newspaper, newspaper owners began to acquire radio, and later television, stations; in many cities a single company came to control all the media of news.

Second only to the radio as entertainment and diversion, but well behind it as education, were the ' movies.' Invented by the resourceful Thomas Edison at the turn of the century, the motion picture grew steadily in popularity. David Griffith's *The Birth of a Nation*, shown to rapt audiences in 1915, revealed unsuspected possibilities of drama and technique in this new art, and introduced the spectacle film which another producer, Cecil B. de Mille, shortly made his peculiar property. Stars of the silent screen supplanted luminaries of the ' legitimate ' stage in the democratic heavens: Mary Pickford, ' America's sweetheart '; Charles Chaplin, greatest of comedians; Douglas Fairbanks, handsome and acrobatic; Bill Hart, always in cowboy costume; Pearl White, whose endless series of escapades left her audience palpitating each week for the next installment; and a host of others now forgotten except by old-timers. Sound, introduced in 1927, greatly expanded film potentialities (as television later did radio), and allied movies to the theater. Many former stars disappeared, and talking cinema increasingly recruited artists and adapted dramas from the more sophisticated boards. Film versions of *David Copperfield, Wuthering Heights, Anna Karenina, Little Women,* and other books introduced millions to classics they would never have read; Greta Garbo, Charles Laughton, W. C. Fields, Katherine Hepburn, gave performances worthy of the best stage tradition. The development of the cartoon movie by Walt Disney, creator of Mickey Mouse and Donald Duck, delighted adults as well as children, and opened up a new dimension of the art. By 1937 the motion-picture industry was fourteenth in volume of business and eleventh in assets among the industries of the nation; some 75 million persons visited the movies every week, and Hollywood competed with New York and Washington for public attention. By then television had already been invented, but though Hollywood moguls — the type was limned by F. Scott Fitzgerald in *The Last Tycoon* — delighted in exploiting the Old Testament on the screen, none of them read the handwriting on the wall.

Inevitably the mores and the vocabulary of the movies were imitated by those to whom they represented the fulfillment of every ambition. They set the popular fashion in dress, home furnishings, play, morals, even in marriage and family life; and increasingly human nature came to conform to commercial art. But circumscribed as they were by the requirements of the box office, directed to vast and uncritical audiences, subjected to a censorship that managed to be both naïve and prurient, the movies hesitated to give a realistic picture of life as it actually was in the United States. Hollywood movies advertised the gaudier aspects of American life to every country of the globe, but their documentary value was a by-product of their function as entertainment.

Every other form of entertainment revealed the same quality of commercialization. Sport became big business. Professional baseball teams played to capacity crowds, and so too did boxers and wrestlers. Intercollegiate football attracted millions of spectators who thus came to appreciate one of the advantages of higher education, and many university presidents could not resist the demand of their communities or alumni for a football team of hired oafs. High-school basketball tournaments became events of state-wide importance, and few Americans saw any connection between the exaltation of competitive sports and the low standards of public education. Daylight-saving time and the five-day week gave a new popularity to tennis and golf, while such old-fashioned games as croquet, which required well-kept lawns and family groups, all but disappeared. Card games, once looked upon as a form of gambling, became fashionable, and adeptness at bridge came to be as important an ingredient in social success as membership in a country club. No previous generation had made such progress in the art of being amused; none had been less capable of amusing itself; to judge by the literature of the day, few had been so bored.

It is as difficult to fix a date for the ' emancipation ' of women, as it is to define that term, but almost everyone agrees that there was such an emancipation, and that it was finally achieved in the years after the First World War. Women had been in process of winning the suffrage ever since Wyoming Territory granted them the vote back in 1869. With the introduction of co-education in Oberlin in the 1830's and the admission of women to the Universities of Iowa, Michigan, and Cornell after the Civil War they had won something like equality in education. They had long enjoyed the privilege of working, side by side with children of both sexes, in textile mills, and the invention of the typewriter and the telephone opened up to them new worlds of office work. Gradually, too, they had made their way into the professions of medicine, law, and the ministry, and had pretty much taken over elementary and high-school teaching. All of these things came to a head in the years of the First World War, when manpower shortages put a premium on woman power. Woman suffrage came on with a rush, and was written into the Constitution in time to help elect Warren G. Harding; millions of women crowded into jobs in factory and office; and increasing numbers of them took part in public life. A generation that observed Jane Addams and Eleanor Roosevelt could not seriously believe women less

competent than men in public affairs. The greatest changes came in
the social and psychological realms. Labor-saving devices emanci-
pated millions of women from the stove and the wash-tub, and
knowledge of birth control from the demands of large families, while
education and prosperity opened up new possibilities in private and
public careers. As women won freedom from the kitchen and the
nursery, and won economic independence as well, they succeeded in
replacing the old double standard of morality with a single standard,
and both sexes agreed in relaxing the standard. Conservatives had
looked upon all this with deepest misgivings, predicting the collapse
of morality and of the family. Morality seemed to survive, and woman's position in the family was strengthened by her new competence;
soon sociologists were muttering darkly about an American matri-
archy, while comic strips, the radio, and James Thurber's cartoons
presented the American male as dithering and childish and the American woman as firmly in command. These stereotypes were probably
as inaccurate as most of the Victorian stereotypes of the sexes; what
is interesting is that they should have been so widely accepted.

2. Intolerance and Civil Liberties

Busily engaged in getting and enjoying wealth, and confident that
they were at last on the road to utopia, Americans of this generation
were peculiarly intolerant of criticism or heterodoxy. The seeds of
intolerance had been planted during the war, and in the postwar
years they sprouted strange and noxious weeds. So admirable did this
business civilization appear to those who enjoyed its benefits that
they found it difficult to understand how honest men could find fault
with it, and fault-finding was ascribed to depravity or disloyalty;
criticism itself was a sign of un-Americanism. Nationalism, glorified
during the war, took on virulent form. It manifested itself in a bewildering variety of ways — the revision of history and history textbooks, the requirement that school teachers subscribe to loyalty oaths,
denial of citizenship to pacifists, deportation of aliens, suppression of
economic unrest through laws against syndicalism and anarchism,
purging of legislatures, harassing of suspect organizations, suspicion
of liberalism in literature and the arts or of modernism in religion —
all made possible by the legislative and judicial emasculation of state
and federal bills of rights.

Religious fundamentalism took on an aggressive form. Colleges and theological seminaries were purged of ' modernists.' Under the leadership of William J. Bryan, now turned crusader for religious orthodoxy, several Southern states enacted laws forbidding the teaching of evolution in state-supported schools. These laws were challenged in the famous Scopes trial, at Dayton, Tennessee, where Clarence Darrow pitted his skill against Bryan himself; but even the notoriety of this trial failed to erase the legislation from the statute books for some years. Censorship and ' Comstockery ' burgeoned under official sanction. A number of states established state boards of censors for moving pictures — enough to control a product dependent upon nation-wide favor — and the Treasury Department and the Post Office connived with self-appointed guardians of the public morals to protect the public from ' immoral ' books and works of art.

The most notorious chapter in the history of intolerance was written by the Ku Klux Klan. This secret society, organized in Atlanta, Georgia, in 1915, had nothing in common with the Klan of Reconstruction days but a name and a purpose to keep the Negro down. It made little progress during the war years, but in the 1920's it flourished like the green bay tree. During these years it dedicated itself to the old Know-Nothing program of nativism and anti-Catholicism and added, for bad measure, anti-Semitism. The Klan's cult of secrecy, elaborate rituals and ceremonials, and gaudy paraphernalia appealed to many who were indifferent to its objectives, and it soon spread from Georgia throughout the South and into the Middle West; even on the rolling hills of Pennsylvania and in eastern Massachusetts fiery crosses blazed against evening skies. At its height the Klan boasted some 6 million members; it went into politics, intimidated candidates for office throughout the South and in Indiana, and elected governors and senators sympathetic to its fears and prejudices. For a decade the Klan went its violent way, and thoughtful men saw in it the potential basis for an American fascist movement. It declined, in the end, from internal rot rather than from external pressure.

The Klan represented a widespread hostility to minority and non-conformist groups. Rarely had that emphasis upon conformity, which Tocqueville had discerned in the 1830's, been so insistent, or the bills of rights proved so impotent as barriers against persecution. The demand for conformity and orthodoxy was proclaimed in a bewildering body of laws, and where the laws were impotent, vigilante groups acted for them. In the South, Negroes were denied rights guaranteed to them by the Fourteenth Amendment. Jim Crow laws, segregation ordinances, denial of equal facilities in education or in public services were all but universal, and archaic legislation from slavery or Reconstruction days were resurrected as a weapon to break Negro labor and tenant-farmer organizations. ' Grandfather ' clauses, party control of primary elections, poll taxes, and sheer intimidation were used to circumvent the Fifteenth Amendment's guarantee of the right to vote.

Startled by the triumph of the Bolsheviks in Russia, alarmed by the threat of the Third International to spread Communism throughout the world, and shocked by the activities of the I.W.W., nation and states joined in a vigorous campaign to wipe out radicalism — which was glibly equated with Communism. Twenty-four states enacted criminal-syndicalism or criminal-anarchy laws directed chiefly at radical labor agitators; and West Virginia safeguarded future generations by making unlawful any teachings of ' ideals hostile to those now or *henceforth* existing under the constitution and laws of this State.' California outlawed any doctrine advocating the use of force to accomplish a change in industrial ownership, and under the esoteric terms of this law over five hundred persons were arrested in a period of five years. One of them, the venerable and distinguished social worker, Anita Whitney, was arrested for the crime of attending a meeting of the Communist Labor Party in order to oppose its program. Miss Whitney's sentence of one to fourteen years in the penitentiary evoked from Justice Brandeis an eloquent protest:

Those who won our independence believed that the final end of the state was to make men free to develop their faculties; and that in its government the deliberative forces should prevail over the arbitrary. They valued liberty both as an end and as a means. They believed liberty to be the secret of happiness, and courage to be the secret of liberty. They believed that freedom to think as you will and to speak as you think are means indispensable to the discovery and spread of political truth; that without free speech and assembly, discussion would be futile; that with them, discussion affords ordinarily adequate protection against the dissemination of noxious doctrine; that the greatest menace to freedom is an inert people; that public discussion is a political duty; and that this should be a fundamental principle of the American government. But they knew that order cannot be secured merely through fear of punishment for its infraction; that it is hazardous to discourage thought, hope, and imagination; that fear breeds repression, that repression breeds hate; that hate menaces stable government; that the path of safety lies in the opportunity to discuss freely supposed grievances and proposed remedies; and that the fitting remedy for evil counsels is good ones. Believing in the power of reason as applied through public discussion, they eschewed silence coerced by law — the argument of force in its worst form. Recognizing the occasional tyrannies of governing majorities, they amended the Constitution so that free speech and assembly should be guaranteed.[6]

The most sensational attack upon persons entertaining radical ideas came with the deportation delirium of 1919–20. President Wilson had predicted, ' once lead this people into war and they'll forget there ever was such a thing as tolerance '; and his Attorney-General, A. Mitchell Palmer, hastened to embrace the opportunity of justifying that prediction. After the war was over, Palmer, whose role in the cabinet had been insignificant but who entertained presidential ambitions, tried to make political hay by persecuting alien radicals. Using private spies and *agents provocateurs,* Palmer conducted a series of lawless raids on private houses and labor headquarters, rounded up several thousand aliens, and subjected them to drumhead trials.

In one city [writes William Leuchtenberg] prisoners were handcuffed, chained together, and marched through the streets. In New England hundreds of people were arrested who had no connection with radicalism of any kind. In Detroit 300 people were arrested on false charges, held for a week in jail, forced to sleep on the bare floor of a vile corridor, and denied food for twenty-four hours, only to be found innocent of any involvement in a revolutionary movement. Not for half a century had there been such a wholesale violation of civil liberties.[7]

In the end only some five hundred aliens were deported — many of them quite illegally; the vast majority of those arrested were found to be harmless.

The courts, too, felt the repercussions of the war and of postwar hysteria, and in two notable cases construed the wartime Espionage and Sedition Acts severely to limit freedom of speech in time of national danger. *Schenck v. United States* [8] involved criticism of conscription; the defendant was found guilty but the decision is mem-

[6] *Whitney v. California* 274 U.S. 357, at 375.
[7] *The Perils of Prosperity,* p. 78.
[8] 249 U.S. 47 (1919).

orable for the establishment of the criterion of ' clear and present danger ' as the only justification for qualifying the constitutional guarantee of freedom of speech. This standard, however, was not adhered to in the more controversial case where a miserable garment-worker, Jacob Abrams, was sentenced to twenty years' imprisonment for distributing a pamphlet calling on the workers of the world to rise against the American military expedition to Siberia — an expedition conceived in folly, conducted in vain, and abandoned in disorder. The opinion of the Court in this case evoked from Justice Holmes the most moving of his many eloquent dissents:

When men have realized that time has upset many fighting faiths, they may come to believe even more than they believe the very foundations of their own conduct that the ultimate good desired is better reached by free trade in ideas — that the best test of truth is the power of the thought to get itself accepted in the competition of the market, and that truth is the only ground upon which their wishes can be safely carried out. That at any rate is the theory of our Constitution. It is an experiment, as all life is an experiment. Every year if not every day we have to wager our salvation upon some prophecy based upon imperfect knowledge. While that experiment is part of our system I think that we should be eternally vigilant against attempts to check the expression of opinions that we loathe and believe to be fraught with death, unless they so imminently threaten immediate interference with the lawful and pressing purposes of the law that an immediate check is required to save the country.[9]

Socialism as well as Communism and pacifism came under the ban, and in 1920 the Empire State distinguished itself by expelling five Socialist members from the state legislature. It was not alleged that the party was an illegal one or that the Socialist members were guilty of any crime, but merely that Socialism was ' absolutely inimical to the best interests of the State of New York and of the United States.' This palpable violation of elementary constitutional rights inspired vigorous protests from liberals and conservatives alike. The distinguished Charles Evans Hughes, later to be elevated to the chief justiceship, hastened to expose the illogic of the Albany legislature, but his call for sanity fell on deaf ears. Even the Supreme Court shortly revealed a spirit scarcely more enlightened than that of legislative bodies. In two notable cases [10] it denied citizenship to a woman and to an elderly professor in a theological school who proclaimed their

[9] *Abrams v. U.S.* 250 U.S. 616 (1919).
[10] *U.S. v. Schwimmer* 279 U.S. 644, and *U.S. v. Macintosh* 283 U.S. 605.

pacifism. ' I would suggest,' wrote Justice Holmes in one of the last of his many dissenting opinions — subsequently accepted by the Court — ' that the Quakers have done their share to make the country what it is, that many citizens agree with the applicant's belief, and that I had not supposed hitherto that we regretted our inability to expel them because they believed more than some of us do in the teachings of the Sermon on the Mount.'

As often before in our history, radical ideas were called ' alien ' and ' aliens ' were associated with radical ideas and were therefore suspect. Legislation in the 'twenties had already cut down drastically on the number of immigrants who could be admitted, and discriminated in favor of the old and against the new immigration, though by no stretch of the imagination could immigration be considered a threat to anything in the 'thirties: the total excess of immigration over emigration in that decade was a paltry 68,000. Yet when tens of thousands of victims of Nazi and Fascist persecution — Jews, Poles, liberals, democrats, and other minority groups — sought asylum in the United States, the American response, except to a small minority of distinguished scientists and artists, was not generous. When President Roosevelt tried to open the gates to these victims of persecution, patriotic societies, veterans' organizations, and organized labor rallied to oppose any relaxation of restrictions, even in the name of humanity. Even the proposal to admit 20,000 children of refugees was defeated by these groups. ' If we are going to keep this country as it is and not lose our liberty,' said one of their spokesmen, ' we have got to keep not only these children out, but the whole damned Europe.' Not until the Truman administration was a more enlightened policy adopted.

Hostility to radicals, antipathy to foreigners, and a jealous protection of the status quo were revealed in the most sensational murder case since that of the Haymarket anarchists — the Sacco-Vanzetti case (1920–27). The principals, again, were foreigners and philosophical anarchists — Nicola Sacco and Bartolomeo Vanzetti — accused of murdering a paymaster at South Braintree, Massachusetts. Although appearances were against them, the evidence against them was slight and their alibis convincing. When they were convicted and sentenced to death there was a widespread belief that the jury had been moved more by their radical views and their evasion of military service than by the evidence. For seven years men and women of all shades of opinion and in almost every country labored to obtain a retrial, and Governor Fuller of Massachusetts so far heeded this opinion as to appoint an investigating committee consisting of the presidents of Harvard and Massachusetts Institute of Technology and a judge of probate. Although this committee found the trial judge guilty of ' grave breach of official decorum,' it reported that justice had been done. When Sacco and Vanzetti were electrocuted on 23 August 1927, a cry of horror at the injustice of it went around the world, and citizens of Massachusetts who loved justice remembered John Adams and the Boston massacre case and Judge Sewall's retraction in the case of the Salem witches, and hung their heads in shame. For such people Edna St. Vincent Millay spoke in her sonnet:

> As men have loved their lovers in times past
> And sung their wit, their virtue and their grace,
> So have we loved sweet Justice to the last,
> That now lies here in an unseemly place.
> The child will quit the cradle and grow wise
> And stare on beauty till his senses drown;
> Yet shall be seen no more by mortal eyes
> Such beauty as here walked and here went down.
> Like birds that hear the winter crying plain
> Her courtiers leave to seek the clement south;
> Many have praised her, we alone remain
> To break a fist against the lying mouth
> Of any man who says this was not so;
> Though she be dead now, as indeed we know.[11]

There was poetic license here; justice was wounded but not dead. For in the main, the record of the Supreme Court during these years gratified those who still cherished the guarantees of the Bill of Rights. Conservative on most economic issues, it was distinctly liberal on questions involving personal liberties. Particularly notable was a series of decisions extending federal protection to the right of minority groups to freedom of speech, freedom of assembly, and a fair trial. Thus in *De Jonge v. Oregon*, the Court voided a criminal-syndicalism law which would have made mere attendance at a Communist meeting a crime. ' The greater the importance of safeguarding the community from incitements to the overthrow of our institutions by force and violence,' said Chief Justice Hughes, ' the more imperative

[11] Edna St. Vincent Millay, *Wine from These Grapes*, p. 43 (Harper & Brothers).

is the need to preserve inviolate the constitutional right of free speech, free press, and free assembly in order to maintain the opportunity for free political discussion, to the end that government may be responsive to the will of the people and that changes, if desired, may be obtained by peaceful means.' Again, in *Herndon v. Lowry,* the Court ruled that the mere possession of Communist literature could not be held to be an ' incitement to riot.' *Thornhill v. Alabama* interpreted picketing as a form of expression and extended to it the constitutional guarantees of free speech and *Hague v. C.I.O.* vindicated the right of liberal groups to hold public meetings in boss Frank Hague's bailiwick, Jersey City. Two notable decisions went far to assure Negroes a fair trial in the South: *Powell v. Alabama* — the notorious Scottsboro case — held that failure to include Negroes on the panel from which jurors were drawn constituted in effect a denial of due process; while in *Chambers v. Florida* a unanimous court, speaking through the new Associate Justice of Alabama, Mr. Hugo Black, reversed the conviction of a Negro obtained through the use of the ' third degree.'

Equally significant was the judicial insistence upon a broad reading of the guarantee of a free press. American devotion to freedom of the press was deep-rooted, and not until the First World War was there any serious challenge to the principle that there should be no previous restraint upon any publication. When, in 1925, Minnesota provided punishment without jury trial for any ' malicious, scandalous and defamatory ' newspaper article, making truth a defense only in *Near v. Minnesota* if the motives were good and the ends justifiable, the Supreme Court voided the law. A more dangerous, because more subtle, attack upon the freedom of the press came when Huey Long's pliant legislature in Louisiana imposed a discriminatory tax upon newspapers with a circulation of over 20,000 — a tax neatly designed to embarrass the few papers still opposed to the Long regime. Refusing to be diverted by the vexatious question of the taxing power of the state, the Court in *Grosjean v. American Press Co.* nullified the act squarely on the ground of its conflict with the guarantees of the First Amendment.

In thus striking down state legislation impairing personal liberties, the Court was aided by a new constitutional weapon which it had only recently forged. That was the doctrine whereby the federal Bill of Rights was interpreted as a limitation upon state as well as upon national action. Ever since *Barron v. Baltimore,* back in 1833, it had been assumed that the Bill of Rights limited only the national Congress, and this position was long unchallenged. Beginning, however, in the 1920's — and definitely with the case of *Gitlow v. New York* in 1925 [12] — the Court intimated that the rights of ' life, liberty and property,' guaranteed against state impairment by the Fourteenth Amendment, might be presumed to embrace those rights set forth in the federal Bill of Rights. This dictum, at first only cautiously advanced, was within a decade completely incorporated into constitutional law. Since, historically, most limitations upon personal liberties had come from the states, this new principle of law gave support to the hope that the Fourteenth Amendment might at last be interpreted to mean what its framers had originally intended.

3. LITERARY INTERPRETATIONS

In the early years of the new century Mark Twain, William Dean Howells, and Henry James were still lords of the ascendant, but new luminaries were coming up over the literary horizon, whose brilliance was soon to fill the heavens.

It was a day when almost everything was ' new '; there was the new poetry, the new criticism, the new art, the ' New Freedom,' the ' New Nationalism,' the new history. A new generation was getting ready to break new paths, launch new ventures, think new thoughts, and discover new worlds. Harriet Monroe founded *Poetry* in Chicago; Herbert Croly established the *New Republic;* and Max Eastman and Art Young started the socialistic *Masses,* and soon the staid *Dial* moved from Chicago to New York and found a new youthfulness. Freud and Jung lectured at Clark University and American literature promptly went Freudian; Walter Lippmann published his *Preface to Politics,* followed with *Drift and Mastery,* and there was a new political philosophy; and Joel Spingarn, who had written the *New Criticism,* organized the NAACP. Alfred Stieglitz opened his New York gallery and displayed new dimensions in photography, and in 1913 the Ar-

---

12 The citations are: *De Jonge v. Oregon* 299 U.S. 353 (1937); *Herndon v. Lowry* 301 U.S. 242 (1937); *Thornhill v. Alabama* 310 U.S. 88 (1940); *Hague v. C.I.O.* 307 U.S. 496 (1939); *Powell v. Alabama* 287 U.S. 45 (1932); *Chambers v. Florida* 309 U.S. 227 (1940); *Near v. Minnesota* 283 U.S. 697 (1931); *Grosjean v. American Press Co.* 297 U.S. 233 (1936); *Gitlow v. N.Y.* 268 U.S. 652 (1925).

mory Show exploded traditional art; the Provincetown Players welcomed young Eugene O'Neill; William C. Handy composed the 'Memphis Blues' and jazz was born, and Serge Diaghileff brought the Russian Ballet to America. It was an American Renaissance and, wrote Ezra Pound from London, 'it would make the Italian Renaissance look like a tempest in a teapot.' Actually it was the American Renaissance that was more like a tempest in a teapot.

'The fiddles are tuning up all over America,' wrote John Butler Yeats. So they were, but it was in Chicago that Harriet Monroe whipped them together into a kind of orchestra. This indomitable woman of fifty decided that poetry had been too long neglected and that it ought to have a subsidy and a magazine, and in 1912 she launched *Poetry: A Magazine of Verse,* and a parlor revolution in poetry was under way. Within six years almost all the poets who were to dominate the literary scene for the next fifty years made their bow, and most of them in the pages of this little magazine: the 'prairie' poets, Carl Sandburg and Vachel Lindsay; the imagists, Amy Lowell and Conrad Aiken; the lyricists, Sara Teasdale and Edna St. Vincent Millay and Elinor Wylie; and Freudians like Edgar Lee Masters; and Robinson Jeffers, who went his own way. And over in England three Americans who were to achieve fame in their lifetime — Ezra Pound and T. S. Eliot and Robert Frost — were publishing their first books. Not since New England's golden day had there been anything like it.

Carl Sandburg was not the most original of the 'prairie' poets, but he had more to say than any of the others, and he had staying power. When he published 'Chicago' in *Poetry:*

> Hog Butcher for the World,
> Tool Maker, Stacker of Wheat,
> Player with Railroads and the Nation's Freight Handler;
> Stormy, husky, brawling,
> City of the Big Shoulders

a jaundiced critic wrote that 'the typographical arrangement for this jargon creates a suspicion that it is intended to be taken as some form of poetry.' So it was. A disciple of Whitman, Sandburg thought nothing too undignified for poetry; in this he was like the members of the 'Ash-Can' school, who thought nothing too undignified to paint. Born of Swedish parents, Sandburg was as authentically American as Lincoln, whose biography he later wrote in six huge volumes; like

Lincoln he was instinctively equalitarian, and his most important collection of poetry is called *The People, Yes.*

Another son of Illinois, Vachel Lindsay, was a mixture of poet and minstrel who wandered from town to town preaching the ' Gospel of Beauty,' and ' trading his rhymes for bread.' In 1913 he brought out a volume called *General Booth Enters Heaven* which contained his moving tribute to Governor Altgeld, the ' Eagle Forgotten,' and thereafter the famous ' Congo ' and ' The Chinese Nightingale.' His poems were mostly folk songs, made to be chanted rather than read, and they had the swing and lilt of true ballads.

Imagism was an altogether more sophisticated affair, intellectually closer to abstract painting and to modern music than to the kind of poetry being written by Vachel Lindsay. It was a revolt against sentiment, tradition, and the superfluous word; it was inspired by Greek, Chinese, and modern French verse; it tried to be concrete and scientific. Its high priest was Ezra Pound; when he wearied of it Amy Lowell — sister to Harvard's President Lowell — assumed and retained leadership of the group. Its philosophy was set forth by the poet-critic Conrad Aiken:

It is a sort of absolute poetry of detached waver and brilliance, a beautiful flowering of language alone, a parthenogenesis, as if language were fertilized by itself rather than by thought or feeling. Remove the magic of phrase and sound, and there is nothing left; no thread of continuity, no relations between one page and the next; no thought, no story, no emotion.

The Idaho-born Ezra Pound and the Missouri-born T. S. Eliot were both in London when Miss Monroe launched *Poetry;* Pound became its London editor, and Eliot contributed to it his first important poem, ' The Love Song of J. Alfred Prufrock.' Impetuous and scholarly, adventurous and reactionary, Pound spent a lifetime trying to work out new techniques of verse, immersing himself in new intellectual interests, and living in new countries. He took command of the imagists — and surrendered it; championed Eliot, Hart Crane, James Joyce, and a score of other writers; edited little magazines; and poured out a steady stream of translations, criticisms, and original verse — notably the endless series of *Cantos* composed with brilliant and calculated obscurity. Where Pound dissipated his talents, Eliot grew in stature and in influence until he became one of the commanding figures of his age. Like Henry James he lived by preference in London, and eventually became a British citizen; like James, too, he became increasingly the champion of traditionalism. Equally distinguished as a poet, a dramatist, and a critic, Eliot did as much to change the nature and character of modern poetry as had Wordsworth and Whitman in earlier generations, and his *The Waste Land* (1922), subtle and profound, became the *vade mecum* of a whole generation.

The American traditionalists looked to James rather than to Eliot for inspiration, notably the three intrepid women who bridged the gap between the realism of Howells and the social protest of a Dos Passos or a Steinbeck: Edith Wharton, Ellen Glasgow, and Willa Cather. Mrs. Wharton wrote of New York in the age of gaslight and horses, and of the Hudson Valley when the dominant architecture was Hudson River bracketed. In a series of novels that began with *The House of Mirth* (1905) and concluded with *Hudson River Bracketed* (1929), she presented complex social problems against a background of fashionable New York where Civil War profiteers and the new rich were crashing the gates of society, shattering old standards of elegance and taste, and calling in question old moralities. She was fascinated by the impact of the clash of cultures, and though she began as a rebel against the traditional social standards, she ended as something of an apologist for them. Even when, as in *Ethan Frome* and *Summer,* she turned from the New York scene to rural New England, it was the moral implications of the violation of custom and code that interested her, and *Ethan Frome* might have been a poem by E. A. Robinson. Like James, too, Mrs. Wharton was a master of the short story and of the ghost story; like him she lived much abroad; like him she was, for all the documentation of her novels, primarily a moralist.

Ellen Glasgow was the literary historian of the South and, until Faulkner, the most comprehensive and penetrating. She began, at the turn of the century, as a simple chronicler of the Old South, describing its lingering pretentions with ironic detachment; she moved on to trace in elaborate detail the rise of the plain people of the New South and the clash of cultures and values that accompanied this rise. By the 'twenties the threat to those values which she herself cherished came not so much from the sentimentality of the Old South, but from the absence of tradition in the New. Beginning with *Barren Ground* (1925), Miss Glasgow expressed a mounting distaste for the emptiness of the new day, and a grudging appreciation of the older virtues; with *The Sheltered Life* (1932) the appreciation was ardent; and with *Vein of Iron* (1935) there was an open appeal for the re-creation of the older values. As Miss Glasgow herself tells us:

Although in the beginning I had intended to deal ironically with both the southern Lady and the Victorian tradition, I discovered as I went on, that my irony grew fainter, while it yielded at last to sympathetic compassion.

As a historian of the South, Miss Glasgow overlaps but never quite connects with William Faulkner, and few things better illustrate the changes in literary methods and philosophy that were going on in these years than a comparison of Miss Glasgow's chronicle of Virginia and Mr. Faulkner's history of Yoknapatawpha County.

Willa Cather, too, recorded and celebrated the virtues of the past — the recent past of Nebraska, the historic past of Spanish New Mexico and of French Quebec; to her, as to Ellen Glasgow, the past was significant for its moral qualities rather than for its romance or antiquity. All her novels and stories — those of the Arcadian Virginia of her childhood, the golden Nebraska of her youth, the shimmering Southwest of Bishop Lamy, the Quebec of the Ursulines — were animated by this single theme: the superiority of the moral values of the past over the material interests of the present. Willa Cather shared with Miss Glasgow a passion for the land — as she said of Alexandra Bergson in *O Pioneers!* ' it fortified her to reflect upon the great operations of nature.' She was fascinated, too, by the great Rock of Acoma — the ' utmost expression of human need,' she called it, ' the highest comparison of loyalty in love and friendship,' and so too by the rocks of Quebec on which the French had built their city. ' When an adventurer carries his gods with him into a remote and savage country,' she wrote, ' the colony he founds will have grace, tradition, riches of the mind and spirit. Its history will shine with bright incidents, slight perhaps, but precious, as in life.' This was what she found in the American West — that West which had been settled

by dreamers, great hearted adventurers who were unpractical to the point of magnificence; a courteous brotherhood strong in attack but weak in defence, who could conquer but could not hold . . .

All this now was gone; industry, business, and speculation had destroyed it: that was the moral of the most nearly perfect of her books, *A Lost Lady,* and of *The Professor's House.*

All three of these writers counted themselves disciples of Henry James. In a sense James, too, belongs to this period, for it was only now that he came into his own. The rediscovery of Henry James was both a sign of growing maturity in American readers — the new generation could take both Ezra Pound and T. S. Eliot in its stride — and, more deeply, a sign of nostalgia for the traditions which James championed, and for the subtlety and depth of his insights into human nature. Equally illuminating was the fame of E. A. Robinson in these years. Robinson had been quietly writing ever since the mid-'nineties without much public acclaim (except, briefly, from President Roosevelt), but now he seemed to speak to and for the new generation. It was in these postwar years that he wrote the great Arthurian trilogy of *Merlin, Lancelot,* and *Tristram.*

The greatest poet of this generation was both classicist and modernist, traditionalist and innovator, and he defies easy classification. Robert Frost made his first appearance just as the fiddles were tuning up, but he belonged to no school, took part in no movements, fits into no pattern. For half a century he went his own way, growing steadily in stature and in fame, developing a philosophy deceptively homespun and a style deceptively simple, the bard, the seer, the critic, the orator, an odd mixture of Homer and Voltaire. After a period of farming and school-teaching Frost had gone to England, where he published his first two volumes of poetry: *A Boy's Will* (1913), and *North of Boston* (1914), with the famous ' Mending Wall,' ' Death of the Hired Man,' ' Home Burial ' — poems not surpassed in our literature for beauty and insight. In 1916 came *Mountain Interval,* with ' The Road Not Taken,' ' Birches,' and others — colloquial, philosophical, lyrical. All through the 'twenties and 'thirties, Frost gathered strength and fame, in book after book: *New Hampshire, West Running Brook, A Further Range,* until by the end of this period he was the grand old man of American letters, and with yet another quarter-century of honors ahead of him. No American poet since Longfellow had been so widely read; no poet except Robinson had had so much to say or had said it so well.

If the second decade of the new century had been one of experimentation and affirmation, the decade of the 'twenties was one of disillusionment and revolt. Reaction against the idealism of the war and the hopefulness of the early years took varied forms: revolt against what H. L. Mencken called the ' booboisie ' — which turned out to be hatred of democracy itself; revolt against the village and the small town; revolt against Puritanism; and protest against the industrial order.

The most vociferous critic of his generation was Henry L. Mencken of Baltimore, who made it his special business to expose bourgeois complacency and whose ' Americana ' column in the *American Mercury* recorded with melancholy faithfulness the fatuousness and vulgarity of contemporary American life. Through the *American Mercury,* and through the well-named *Prejudices,* Mencken imposed his style on smart young writers, and his iconoclastic views on a large part of the nation. Those views were almost all malicious, for Mencken was catholic in his dislikes: he disliked the rich and the poor, the ignorant and the intelligent, the mob and the elite, fundamentalism and advanced thought, devotion to the past and confidence in the future. ' From Boy Scouts, and from home cooking, from Odd Fellows' funerals, from Socialists, and from Christians — Good Lord, deliver us ': it was typical of the prayers he sent up. He was a kind of domestic Ezra Pound who seceded from the United States not by going abroad, but by staying home and finding every one out of step. While his influence was for the most part negative, Mencken made some positive contributions: a magazine that attracted the brightest writers of the day; a free-swinging and irreverent style that went far to liberate writing from pedantic pretentiousness; and three learned volumes on *The American Language.*

There was nothing new about the ' revolt from the village ' when Mencken set out to make the small town ridiculous. Ed Howe had already set the pattern in his mordant *Story of a Country Town* in 1883, and Mark Twain had painted a classic portrait in black in *The Man that Corrupted Hadleyburg.* What was new in the second decade of the century was a livelier awareness of sociology and of sex, and it is a bit difficult to know whether to classify such books as *The Spoon River Anthology* and *Winesburg, Ohio,* as social or psychiatric documents. In *The Spoon River Anthology* (1915) Edgar Lee Masters recorded, in the spirit of the Greek Anthology, the drab existence of some two hundred victims of life in a little Illinois town — a kind of prairie Tilbury Town — where dreamers were always defeated and idealists ended as cynics. It was a theme to which Masters returned again and again; in the well-named *Doomsday Book,* for example, and in a biography which managed to take a dim view of Abraham Lincoln. Sherwood Anderson combined social protest and

Freudianism better perhaps than any of his contemporaries. *Winesburg, Ohio,* which caused something of a sensation when it was published in 1919, was a kind of literary declaration of war against the small town, the factory, industry, the ties of marriage and of family; and almost all other conventions. Anderson played variations on this theme in book after book, notably *Poor White* and *Many Marriages.*

It was Sinclair Lewis, however, whose *Main Street* (1920) and *Babbitt* (1922) made the revolt against the small town and against business something like a popular crusade. Lewis was the Mencken of the American novel; his function to satirize the ideals of the smug middle-class society to which he had been born, and in which he moved so uneasily. His satire was of manner rather than of fundamentals; his revolt was against the dullness and provincialism of Gopher Prairie and Zenith City rather than against the moral anarchy of the industrial order which they represented. It was not hard to discover in him a grudging affection for the characters he ridiculed, and, like Mark Twain, he was very much a part of the world he repudiated. He had an unerring ear for the verbal and psychological idiom of the average American, and the devastating accuracy of his reporting caught the imagination of a generation educated by journalism to prefer photography to art.

Meantime, inspired by Sigmund Freud of Vienna, whose books and teachings were becoming increasingly known at first or second hand, the revolt against Puritanism and rationalism flared all along the literary front. Freudianism took the form of exaggerated respect for the irrational and the unconscious, fascination with the primitive and with violence, obsession with sex, and a search for new forms and a new vocabulary with which to express new ideas and impulses. Its influence can be traced in such varied writers as Sara Teasdale, Edna Millay, Elinor Wylie, and Robinson Jeffers among the poets, Fitzgerald, Hemingway, and Faulkner among the novelists, and Eugene O'Neill among the playwrights.

Not since Emily Dickinson — almost unknown in her lifetime — had America produced any women poets to rank with the three who now appeared on the literary scene. The simultaneous appearance of these distinguished women poets was in part a product of the 'emancipation' of women which loomed so large in these years, and in part a revolt against Puritanism. Sara Teasdale's was the earliest, and the thinnest, talent, but in *Rivers to the Sea* and *Love Songs,* she made permanent contributions to our literature. Edna St. Vincent Millay was, peculiarly, the poetess of her generation — of love and youth and sophistication and, in the end, idealism. She was not only the gay spirit who boasted that she burned her candle at both ends because it gave a lovely light, but the idealist who protested movingly against the injustice to Sacco and Vanzetti and, in a series of late poems — *Conversation at Midnight*, and *Huntsman, What Quarry?* — called on her generation to rediscover its spiritual roots. Elinor Wylie was more purely a lyrical poet, and a kind of American Shelley, the most finished master of the sonnet in the whole of our literature; her ' Angels and Earthly Creatures ' is one of the masterpieces of American poetry. Robinson Jeffers, with Frost and Eliot the most considerable American poet of his time, was clearly a Freudian and a determinist. His poetry expressed, in uncompromising form, that revolt against society and civilization, and that fascination with Nature and violence and death, that we associate with the last years of Mark Twain and with much of Hemingway. Man is born to pain — so says Jeffers in ' The Double-Axe ' — as are all living things, but man alone adds depravity to the pain; man alone is inhuman.

> Lord God, exterminate
> The race of man. For only man in all the world, except a few kinds of
>   insect, is essentially cruel.
> Therefore slay also these if you will . . . the driver ant,
> And the slave-maker ant, and the slick wasp
> That paralyzes living meat for her brood; but first
> The human race.

The most significant and most widely read writers of this generation were those who confessed that theirs was a ' lost generation.' ' Lost, and forever writing the history of their loss, they had become specialists in anguish,' writes Alfred Kazin. They were the victims, in a sense, of a new kind of pathetic fallacy, not the application of human emotions to Nature but the application of Science to human emotions. The writers of the lost generation — Fitzgerald, Hemingway, Dos Passos — had passed beyond rebellion into acquiescence, and beyond that to a kind of nihilism. Theirs was the generation of ' the hollow men, the stuffed men,' and their spiritual home was ' the waste land.' Some, like Robinson Jeffers, rejected all human values and found delight in an amoral universe; others, like Hemingway, took refuge in physical violence — in the bull fight or the prize ring or hunting big game in Africa, or in war. A few cherished, like the Victorians Browning and Arnold, the dignity of fortitude. All of them might have said, with Eugene O'Neill, that ' the writer must dig at the roots of the sickness of today as he feels it — the death of the old God and the failure of science and materialism to give any satisfactory new one for the surviving religious instinct to find a new meaning in life.'

The most gifted writer of his generation was F. Scott Fitzgerald, who became the chronicler of the peculiar disillusionment that afflicted the very rich, idle or otherwise, in the postwar years that he taught us to call the Jazz Age. *This Side of Paradise,* published in 1920, became a kind of Baedeker of the new cynicism, a cynicism that was self-conscious and clever, but aimless. Fitzgerald was the historian of the world of glitter and of wealth, the world of Princeton and the St. Regis roof, the Riviera and the Ritz Bar in Paris, West Egg and Hollywood. He is the historian, too, of manners that are never gentle, of ambition that cannot be gratified, of wealth that in the end makes no difference, of pleasures that bring ennui and passion that cannot achieve lasting love. Almost all of his characters are perpetual adolescents; they indulge eagerly in sin, but sin is cocktail parties and girls, not the nightmare that broods over the novels of a Kafka or a Camus; for all their wealth and sophistication, in the vacuity of their lives and the aimlessness of their loves, they differ little from the denizens of Gopher Prairie or Zenith City. In Fitzgerald's books the beautiful are always damned, the young men are always sad, the night is tender but morning brings disillusionment; and his characters are always doomed to be on this side of paradise. In *The Great Gatsby* (1925) one of the notable novels of the generation, Fitzgerald wrote a melancholy commentary on the Jazz Age that is a curious counterpart of Willa Cather's *A Lost Lady,* and with implications for the whole American scene that are as wide.

The year after the appearance of *The Great Gatsby,* the 28-year-old Ernest Hemingway published his first novel, *The Sun Also Rises;* it carried a quotation from Gertrude Stein on the title page, ' You are all a lost generation.' Hemingway was, like Fitzgerald, the historian of the lost generation, but his characters were more hopelessly and desperately lost than were the playboys and girls who disport themselves across Fitzgerald's tinseled stages. He was the chronicler of all those who wanted to be counted out of this society, of their generation; all of his characters, except possibly the idealist Robert Jordan in *For Whom the Bell Tolls*, were engaged in a massive repudiation of their society. They were all like the dubious hero of ' Soldier's Return ' who ' did not want any consequences. He wanted to live along without consequences,' and all of them might have repeated the prayer of the old waiter in ' A Clean Well-Lighted Place ' — ' Hail nothing full of nothing, nothing is with thee.' All this was more than disenchantment, it was nihilism.

As the life of the mind was meaningless, Hemingway celebrated instead sheer physical activity: fighting in the trenches of Italy and behind the barricades in Madrid, the primitive warfare of the prize ring and the artistic warfare of the bull ring; hunting, fishing, eating, drinking — anything that might serve as a refuge from thought. Like Robinson Jeffers, and Faulkner too, Hemingway was obsessed with violence, pain, and death. These are the themes that run through *The Sun Also Rises*, which shifts frenetically from Paris to the bull rings of Spain; *A Farewell to Arms* which is set against the background of the Italian retreat after Caporetto; *For Whom the Bell Tolls*, which caught something of the passion and despair of the Spanish Civil War; *The Green Hills of Africa;* the last of his books, *The Old Man and the Sea*, which won him the Nobel Prize in literature in 1954; and in collections of short stories like *Men Without Women* and *Winner Take Nothing*.

Hemingway was to become a legend even during his own lifetime. ' For the young men born between 1918 and 1924,' wrote one of them, ' there was a special charm about Hemingway. By the time most of us were old enough to read him, he had become a legendary figure, a kind of twentieth century Lord Byron.' This was in part because he was a picturesque and flamboyant figure, in part because he lived the life which was the stuff of his novels and stories — driving an ambulance in war-torn Italy, fighting in the Spanish Civil War, hunting big game in Africa — and partly because he remained a man apart, independent and uninvolved.

It was not this that gave Hemingway his great influence, however, but his literary style. He had gone to school to Mark Twain, he had practiced journalism, he had come under the influence of Gertrude Stein and Ezra Pound; but his style was his own achievement. ' I was always embarrassed,' says one of his characters, by the words sacred, glorious, and sacrifice, and the expression in vain. . . . There were many words that you could not stand to hear and finally only the names of places had dignity. Certain numbers were the same way and certain dates and these with the names of the places were all you could say and have them mean anything. Abstract words such as glory, honor, courage, or hallow were obscene beside the concrete names of villages . . . the names of rivers, the numbers of regiments and the dates.[13]

He hammered out a style that was direct, pithy, nervous, idiomatic, simple, and honest. Though no others quite mastered it, almost all the writers of his generation imitated it.

The third major literary figure of the 'twenties, Eugene O'Neill, has the distinction of being the first, and perhaps the only, American dramatist to achieve the kind of fame accorded Ibsen and Chekhov and Bernard Shaw. Born of a theatrical family and trained at the famous Harvard Workshop and in the Provincetown Theater, O'Neill combined a high order of technical competence with imagination, passion, and a sense of the theater. Very much a child of his age, he reflected almost all the intellectual currents of the day, responding — as he put it — to the ' discordant, broken, faithless rhythms of our time.' He indulged himself in naturalism in his early plays of the sea and the waterfront — *Annie Christie, The Hairy Ape, The Moon of the Caribbees;* participated in the revolt from the village — particularly the New England village — in *Beyond the Horizon* and *Desire Under the Elms;* took his fling at Babbitry in *Marco's Millions* and *The Great God Brown;* confessed a brief nostalgia for a homespun past which he had never known in the charming *Ah! Wilderness;* took refuge in symbolism in the mystical *Lazarus Laughed;* immersed himself in Freudianism in *Diff'rent* and *Strange Interlude,* and in *Mourning Becomes Electra* where he boldly invited comparison with the Agamemnon trilogy of Aeschylus. When he died he left a searing autobiographical drama, *Long Day's Journey into Night,* which returned to the naturalism of his early plays and confessed once again his deep debt to August Strindberg.

A note of desperation resounds in the best of O'Neill's plays — *Strange Interlude, The Iceman Cometh, Mourning Becomes Electra* — and in the final autobiographical *cri du cœur* there is a sense of

---

13 *A Farewell to Arms,* p. 196 (Scribners).

hopelessness and of doom. In this, in his repudiation of his own society, in the role he assigns to violence, madness, and death, O'Neill is at one with Fitzgerald and Hemingway, and with his other great contemporary, William Faulkner.

The fourth major figure to emerge during these postwar years, Faulkner came in time to share with Hemingway dominion of the American literary scene and, like Hemingway, to win the Nobel Prize in literature. Faulkner was in a sense a regionalist; all of his books are laid in the South, and most of them in that Yoknapatawpha County which he created — the most famous and most misspelled country in literature since Swift's Brobdingnag. It was clearly his own Mississippi — for Faulkner resisted the all but universal tendency of Southern writers to come north — and just as clearly the whole South from Virginia to Texas, from its pre-Civil War origins to the present day. Like Ellen Glasgow, Faulkner is the historian of the transformation of the Old South into the New, of the disintegration of the social and moral values of the Old and the failure of the New to create substitutes for those that were gone, but in their philosophy and their style the two writers are as far apart as Trollope and Virginia Woolf.

For Faulkner is the greatest of American literary experimenters — a writer of dazzling virtuosity who can reproduce the folk speech of the poor white and the rhetoric of the Old Testament, the crude, and often perverse, humor of a Mark Twain and the complex symbolism of a T. S. Eliot. He had learned something from Proust, something from James Joyce, but his use of the stream of consciousness technique, of the flashback, of a jig-saw puzzle technique, of symbolism, is all his own.

Faulkner's technical virtuosity reflects a comparable intellectual and moral intensity. Over the years, beginning with *The Sound and the Fury* (1929), and including such masterpieces as *As I Lay Dying, Light in August,* and *The Hamlet,* he has traced the pathology of the South, Old and New — the collapse of standards, the ineffectiveness of the old families — like his own Falkners — and the irredeemable vulgarity and corruption of the new — like the Snopeses and the Sutpens, the class warfare and the race hatred. What he gives us is a southern Waste Land — a region wracked by a sense of guilt, permeated by an all but universal debasement; and he shares with Hemingway and Robinson Jeffers an obsession with violence, pain, and madness. For thirty years he has attempted, by a kind of literary catharsis, to

> Minister to a mind diseased,
> Pluck from the memory a rooted sorrow,
> Raze out the written trouble of the brain
> Cleanse the stuff'd bosom of that perilous stuff
> That weights upon the heart.

But in vain.

A host of lesser writers, successors to Garland and Norris and Dreiser, addressed themselves to the social and economic crises that bedeviled the postwar years. Four made a powerful impression on their own generation: John Dos Passos, James Farrell, Thomas Wolfe, and John Steinbeck. Dos Passos's great, sprawling *U.S.A.* trilogy is the most extensive commentary on American society and economy of the war and the boom years that has yet been written (except Upton Sinclair's interminable Lanny Budd series), a kind of calendar of sin for American society. It portrays a society that is rootless and disintegrated, hurrying to wealth and pleasure without faith or purpose, and its pages are crowded with as repulsive a group of characters as can be found in the modern novel. James Farrell was perhaps Dreiser's most faithful disciple; his *Studs Lonigan* series — another massive and formless social document — depicts the Chicago of the 'twenties with unrelenting bitterness.

Thomas Wolfe, the promise of whose *Look Homeward, Angel* (1929) was never wholly fulfilled in his later and more popular books, belongs only marginally to this group. Gargantuan, tempestuous, capable of both bathos and beauty inextricably intermixed, Wolfe was something of a genius and something of a charlatan; what he did manage to provide was a sense of the clamorous life of Boston and New York during these exciting years, and through them of the whole of America. Coming up from North Carolina to Harvard and New York City, he experienced at first hand the tragedy of the depression and

The staggering impact of this black picture of man's inhumanity to his fellow men, the unending repercussions of these scenes of suffering, violence, oppression, hunger, cold, and the filth and poverty going on unheeded in a world in which the rich were still rotten with their wealth, left a scar upon my life.

Forever a young man — he died at 38 — Wolfe was a kind of American Rousseau in his volatile passions, his public confessions, his torrential eloquence, and his hatred of injustice.

John Steinbeck's greatest work, too, came out of the depression. In the Frank Norris rather than the Dreiser tradition, his early books — *Tortilla Flat, In Dubious Battle,* and the enchanting *Red Pony* — revealed a high technical skill and a deep understanding of the Mexican Americans and the migratory workers of California. His *Grapes of Wrath* (1939), a moving saga of the trek of the Joad clan from their dust-blown Oklahoma farm to the promised land of California, was the one great story to come out of the depression that caught the tragedy of the Dust Bowl, the gallantry as well as the meanness of the rural proletariat. It was a modern version of *The Octopus,* more penetrating and more panoramic, a tribute to enduring fortitude in time of tribulation.

There had been something artificial about the studied cultivation of despair with which so many of the writers reacted to the materialism of the 'twenties. The long depression of the 'thirties, and the challenge of totalitarianism, tested the American writer and artist as had nothing since the Civil War. In a notable tract, ' The Irresponsibles,' the poet Archibald MacLeish called on men of letters to turn away from themselves and meet the challenge of the day. When, after 1935, the shadows of totalitarianism spread over the skies, and a long night threatened to blot out the values of Western civilization, many of the leading poets and novelists rallied to the defense of the things they had long taken for granted. Thus Sinclair Lewis sounded an alarm bell to a lethargic democracy in *It Can't Happen Here* — which sought to show that it could. Ernest Hemingway turned briefly to celebrate the life and death struggle of the Spanish Loyalists in their fight against Franco; Thomas Wolfe recorded the destruction of the older Germany in *The Web and the Rock;* and Dos Passos, who had long wandered aimlessly about the *U.S.A.* found at last *The Ground We Stand On* — democracy and freedom; and Steinbeck celebrated Norwegian resistance to Nazi tyranny in *The Moon Is Down.* The poets, too, returned to the tradition of Whittier and Lowell and William Vaughn Moody. Carl Sandburg reaffirmed his faith in *The People, Yes.* In a series of eloquent poems — ' Public Speech,' ' The Land of the Free ' — MacLeish called on the people to summon up courage for a fight for survival; Edna Millay, in ' Conversation at

Midnight,' and ' Huntsman, What Quarry? ' sounded a new battle-cry of freedom; and in his solemn ' Nightmare at Noon ' Stephen Vincent Benét reminded his people that

> There are certain words,
> Our own and others', we're used to, words we've used,
> Heard, had to recite, forgotten,
> Rubbed shiny in the pocket, left home for keepsakes,
> Inherited, stuck away in the back-drawer. . . .
> Liberty, equality, fraternity.
> To none will we sell, refuse or deny, right or justice.
> We hold these truths to be self-evident.
>
> I'm merely saying — what if these words pass?
> What if they pass and are gone and are no more.[14]

4. PAINTING AND MUSIC

A new chapter in American art began when the Armory Show opened its doors in February 1913. In the next month or so over a hundred thousand New Yorkers — and others, too, for this was a national event — crowded into the vast hall to gaze with incredulity or indignation at paintings by Impressionists and post-Impressionists, Fauvists and Cubists and Modernists of all kinds. Here for the first time Americans could see the paintings of Cezanne and Matisse, Toulouse-Lautrec and Redon, Van Gogh and Picasso as well as that forever baffling ' Nude Descending the Staircase ' by Marcel Duchamp. The new sculptors were there too — figures by Epstein and Maillol and the baffling Brancusi as well as by the newly Americanized Gaston Lachaise. This new art deeply shocked the conservatives; Royal Cortissoz, dean of art critics, called it ' not a movement, or a principle, but unadulterated cheek,' but the ever-versatile Theodore Roosevelt, emerging as an art critic, welcomed a departure from the conventional. The Armory Show performed a number of services: it introduced America to modern art; it made art a subject of popular interest and discussion; it induced a few far-sighted collectors and museums to nibble timidly at the Modernists; it gave a certain respectability to the heretofore neglected New York realists who now came to seem quite safe and conventional in contrast to the true Modernists.

14 *Selected Works of Stephen Vincent Benét*, Vol. I, p. 466 (Farrar & Rinehart, Inc.) .

For the day of the Modernists was still well ahead. The realists continued to dominate the field — the Ash-Can School of painters, Henri and Bellows and Sloan and Luks, who were now astonished to find themselves Old Masters. Alongside them grew up a new school of regionalists and social critics who formed the artistic equivalent of the Steinbecks, Thomas Wolfes, and Sherwood Andersons.

It was this preoccupation with the social scene that was most pronounced, if not most significant, in American painting of these decades. In 1936 the artist George Biddle, reviewing an exhibition of contemporary American and French painting, found that while among the French pictures there was not one that was concerned with social problems, among the American works ' seventy-four dealt with the American scene or with a social criticism of American life; six with strikes or with strikebreakers; six with dust, sand, erosion, drought, and floods. There were no nudes, no portraits, and two still lifes. Out of the hundred not one could be said to enjoy, reflect, participate in our inherited democratic-capitalist culture.'[15] Certainly in Biddle's own work this preoccupation with the social scene is ever present. So, too, with those abler artists, Charles Burchfield and Edward Hopper. Burchfield spread before us a panorama of ugliness — the ugliness of the small town in Ohio or Indiana, of the factory in that Buffalo where he chose to live, of rain-swept nights on dreary streets. He set himself, writes Sam Hunter, ' the task of exploring in humble visual metaphors the failures behind the American success story, the corruption of the landscape that followed in the wake of industrial progress and which most Americans had managed to ignore.' [16] So too with Edward Hopper, painter of the commonplace life of the great cities, a kind of artistic O. Henry. The same social criticism is to be found in the political cartoons of William Gropper, in Henry Varnum Poor's murals of labor; in Alexandre Hogue's graphic pictures of the Dust Bowl which might have served as illustrations for *Grapes of Wrath;* in Reginald Marsh's gaudy pictures of Coney Island, the Bowery, and other gathering places of those who have nowhere to go; and in Ben Shahn's Daumier-like commentary on the political and economic scene.

The regionalists were closely identified with the social critics, but not always in revolt against what they portrayed. Thomas Hart Ben-

15 *An American Artist's Story*, p. 292.
16 *Modern American Painting and Sculpture*, p. 111.

ton was as authentically American as his ancestor the statesman; like Mark Twain, he transcribed the social history of the Mississippi, of the South and the West. John Steuart Curry chose the plains of Kansas and the cottonfields of Dixie to celebrate; Waldo Peirce was at his best in depicting the coast of Maine; Edward Bruce divided his allegiance between New York and California; Grant Wood bathed the rolling hills and the gimcrack houses of Iowa in rich color and sentiment, though in such paintings as ' American Gothic ' and ' Daughters of the Revolution ' he showed that he too could indulge in social criticism.

Meantime the Modernists were on the way. Mere representational art was already becoming passé: art should not copy Nature but respond to it imaginatively; painting, like music, had its own vocabulary. There was a short transition period, dominated by craftsmen like Jonas Lie and Bernard Karfoil and John Marin — painters who still clung to representational art, but were moving into new experiments in the use of color or — as with Charles Sheeler — in geometric designs. ' To the attentive eye,' Ralph Waldo Emerson had written, ' each moment of the year has its own beauty, and in the same field it beholds, every hour, a picture which was never seen before, and which shall never be seen again.' That was the picture which the Modernists wanted to capture — artists like Max Weber and Marsden Hartley and Charles Demuth and Stuart Davis and the brilliant Georgia O'Keefe. And, after them, the pure abstractionists like Mark Tobey and Jackson Pollock were just around the corner.

By now the emergence from colonialism, inaugurated by Homer and Eakins, was complete, and American art was beginning to be almost as fashionable as French. In 1929 a group of seven collectors opened the Museum of Modern Art which went in heavily for Americans, and the next year Gertrude Vanderbilt Whitney founded the first museum in the country devoted exclusively to native art. On the eve of the war Maxim Karolik presented the first of a series of great collections of folk art, genre painting, silver, and furniture to the Boston Museum of Fine Arts.

It was in the 'thirties, too, that the Federal Arts project employed hundreds of impecunious artists to decorate court houses and post offices, circulate art exhibits, teach art appreciation, and compile a vast and impressive record of American folk art. It proceeded ' on the principle that it is not the solitary genius but a sound general movement which maintains art as a vital, functioning part of any cultural scheme,' and it is significant as the first genuine recognition of the fact that artists could make a contribution to society and that society and government had a responsibility to art.

The Federal Arts project subsidized music as well as painting, and if the results were less impressive, the explanation was to be found in the relative immaturity of American music rather than in any want of zeal or of talent.

For, with the notable exceptions of folk music and Negro spirituals, America had always imported her music and her musicians, and the most determined efforts to cultivate here a ' native ' music had failed. Writing a century ago, the editor of the *Musical Journal* urged that ' no fine art can flourish at second hand. We believe it must be rendered national, and in the case of music, be presented through the language the people understand. . . . We believe further that Europe cannot supply this country habitually with singers. Whatever may be the first and absorbing use to which the opera house may be put, it should be obliged to produce original works.' As far as ' singers ' were concerned, the situation was remedied soon enough: the United States produced its own crop of nightingales. But the demand for original works was fulfilled only quantitatively. Before the First World War ambitious compositions were produced by John Knowles Paine, George Chadwick, Arthur Foote, and Horatio Parker, and Edward MacDowell's sonatas and concertos were applauded on two continents. But most of the music of this generation now seems second-rate and derivative.

More vitality and more native quality appeared in the new generation of composers that came to maturity after World War I — John Powell, Virgil Thomson, John Alden Carpenter, Roy Harris, Aaron Copland, Jerome Kern, and George Gershwin. Powell, Harris, and Gershwin exploited the resources of folk music and Negro spirituals, while Carpenter and Copland, influenced by such modernists as Stravinsky and Schönberg, were interested in exploring the symphonic possibilities of jazz or in translating into music the nervous and explosive character of our mechanical civilization. Many of these experiments were interesting sociologically rather than musically, but Harris's *American Overture,* Schelling's *Victory Ball,* Rodgers and Hammerstein's *Oklahoma,* Kern's *Show Boat,* and Gershwin's *Rhapsody in Blue* and *Porgy and Bess* are nominated for permanence.

The American genius was not best revealed in music in the classical forms — sonata, quartet, symphony, opera. It was rather in folk melodies and their modern equivalents, ragtime, jazz, blues, and swing, that the authentic native note was sounded. The wealth of Negro folk music was first exploited by one of the greatest of American composers, Stephen Foster, and his melodious compositions remain our most widely loved songs. Blues and jazz, too, are heavily indebted to the Negroes, and the Jubilee Singers of Fisk University was the first American choir to be well received in Europe. This was the era when for the first time in America composers and performers became popular heroes. Benny Goodman and Duke Ellington and Louis Armstrong won a loyal following among millions of Americans ranging from ' bobby-soxers ' to musical sophisticates. No less important is the wealth of folk music only now being discovered and exploited. Lumberjacks, miners, cowboys, sailors, Appalachian mountaineers, canal boys, all had their own body of songs, while each of our wars had produced a crop of patriotic songs — none more than the Civil War. As the musician Virgil Thomson said, ' The United States is the one country in the world that produces all kinds of music. Only here do composers write in every possible style.'

What we have lacked in music of our own has been made up for in appreciation of the music of others. The tradition of appreciation was an old one, and throughout the nineteenth century American audiences had given enthusiastic welcome to European artists and had listened appreciatively to classical concerts. Early in the nineteenth century, Lowell Mason introduced singing into the public schools, but it was not until World War I that music became a normal part of the curriculum of every school, and it was in 1911 that the Harvard Glee Club set a new fashion for collegiate singing, choosing the most difficult compositions of Bach and Palestrina rather than the sentimental college songs of earlier generations.

The new generation of boys and girls revealed an affection for and a ready mastery of such instruments as the saxophone, the trombone, and the clarinet, astonishing to those who recalled their own resistance to the violin and the piano. The radio enabled the whole nation to enjoy symphonies and operas, and even chamber music found appreciative audiences. Supplementing the 50 million radios were some 4 million phonographs, and during the 'thirties and 'forties the sales of phonograph records reached almost astronomical heights. Few cities were so benighted as to lack a symphony orchestra — no less than eighty-four new ones were established in the depression decade — and if the nation could support few opera companies, that was rather a comment on the decline of the leisure-class tradition than an indictment of musical taste. Particularly encouraging was the growing support to native talent, while the totalitarian terror recruited to our shores some of the most distinguished of contemporary European composers — Stravinsky, Hindemith, Bartók, Schönberg, to mention only a few. Musical conservatories like the Juilliard, Eastman, and Curtis flourished, and great foundations like the Guggenheim stood ready to give such patronage to budding genius as Mozart and Schubert never knew.

5. Science, Natural and Social

It is possible that American civilization during these years will be judged neither by material achievements nor by arts and letters, but by contributions to science. Certainly these contributions affected larger numbers of the people, and affected them more immediately, than did any in the field of the arts. It is suggestive that while the Nobel Prize in literature went to Americans only three times before 1945 (Sinclair Lewis, Eugene O'Neill, Pearl Buck), eight Americans received the prize in physics, seven in medicine, and three in chemistry.

Tocqueville had observed, back in the 1830's, that ' in America the purely practical part of science is admirably understood, and careful attention is paid to the theoretical portion which is immediately requisite to application . . . but hardly any one in the United States devotes himself to the essentially theoretical and abstract portion of human knowledge.' That was still true, a century later, yet by then not only universities but industry were liberally underwriting research in pure science. What is more, the United States greatly benefited from the migration of European scientists, and other intellectuals, which set in with the advent of Hitler to power in 1932; Einstein was merely the most famous of hundreds of physicists, chemists, and medical men who found in America refuge from oppression and an opportunity to pursue their researches in the most favorable circumstances.

It is difficult — indeed it is almost meaningless — to speak of an

' American ' science, for science and medicine (as Franklin had recognized in setting up the American Philosophical Society) are not
national but universal, and the intellectual interdependence of the
modern world is nowhere more self-evident than in the scientific
realm. As Raymond Fosdick of that Rockefeller Foundation which
operates so magnanimously throughout the globe reminded us:

In peace as in war we are all of us the beneficiaries of contributions to
knowledge made by every nation in the world. Our children are guarded
from diphtheria by what a Japanese and a German did; they are saved
from rabies because of a Frenchman; they are cured of pellagra through
the researches of an Austrian. From birth to death they are surrounded
by an invisible host — the spirits of men who never thought in terms of
flags or boundary lines, and who never served a lesser loyalty than the welfare of mankind.[17]

The most striking advances were in the fields of astronomy and of
physics. Working with the giant telescope of Mt. Wilson Observatory,
which enabled them to plot thousands of new galaxies, astronomers
postulated an expanding universe. Physicists, meantime, invented the
cyclotron to break down the composition of the atom and rearrange
its elements, and held out the hope that we might obtain from some
of these elements — uranium, for example — fabulous new sources of
energy that would end dependence on fuel. Yet, able as they were to
chart a new universe of infinite vastness or to penetrate to the secret
of the atom, the new generation of scientists held out no assurance of
ultimate understanding of the laws that governed the universe or
even that there were any laws. Under the impact of the new science
ancient certainties faded, and with them the illusions that the cosmos
was governed by laws that man could comprehend. According to Professor Percy W. Bridgman:

The physicist finds himself in a world from which the bottom has
dropped clean out; as he penetrates deeper and deeper it eludes him and
fades away by the highly unsportsmanlike device of just becoming meaningless. No refinement of measurement will avail to carry him beyond the
portals of this shadowy domain which he cannot even mention without
logical inconsistency. A bound is thus forever set to the curiosity of the
physicist. What is more, the mere existence of this bound means that he
must give up his most cherished convictions and faith. The world is not
a world of reason, understandable by the intellect of man, but as we
penetrate ever deeper, the very law of cause and effect, which we had

[17] *The Rockefeller Foundation, A Review for 1941*, p. 11.

thought to be a formula to which we could force God Himself to subscribe, ceases to have any meaning. The world is not intrinsically reasonable or understandable; it acquires these properties in ever-increasing
degree as we ascend from the realm of the very little to the realm of everyday things; here we may eventually hope for an understanding sufficiently
good for all practical purposes.[18]

The average man lived ' in the realm of everyday things ' and these
melancholy testaments of science did not seriously disturb him, nor
did they exercise any conspicuous effect in upsetting traditional
faiths, religious or philosophical. To the average man science meant
applied science, and here it continued to substantiate the notion of
progress. It meant a host of inventions and techniques that contributed enormously to his convenience and his physical well-being: electrical refrigeration, air conditioning, fluorescent lighting, television,
frequency modulation, microfilming, the use of glass and of plastics
for a thousand new purposes, the development of synthetic rubber, of
new methods of cracking oil, of soil-less agriculture, the construction
of bigger bombers and of more accurate bomb-sights.

Above all, it meant progress in the realm of medicine and public
health. Throughout this generation doctors and chemists and bacteri-
ologists, working in the laboratories of universities, the Federal Government, or the great foundations, waged war against diseases that
had baffled medical science for centuries. The results were little less
than spectacular. In the first third of the century, infant mortality declined in the United States by two-thirds and life expectancy increased from forty-nine to fifty-nine years. The death rate for tuberculosis dropped from 180 to 49 per 100,000, for typhoid from 36 to 2,
for diphtheria from 43 to 2, for measles from 12 to 1, while pneumonia fatalities decreased from 158 to 50 and were still going down rapidly; sulfa drugs and, later, penicillin almost ended them. Yellow fever and smallpox were practically wiped out, and the war on malaria,
pellagra, hookworm, and similar diseases was brilliantly successful.

A new study of the role of the glandular system led to the discovery of specifics against endocrine disorders. Within a few years in-
sulin had cut the death rate of diabetes from over 700 to 12 per 1000
cases. Pernicious anemia, long regarded as fatal, yielded readily to
the use of liver and liver extracts and, later, to vitamins. Adrenalin
proved helpful in cardiac disorders and gave relief to sufferers from

[18] ' The New Version of Science,' *Harper's Magazine,* March 1929.

asthma. Tannic acid was found to work cures on apparently fatal burns. In the study of anesthesia, too, where Americans had long occupied a distinguished position, the perfection of avertin and cyclopropane made possible new miracles of surgery. Chemistry opened the way to an appreciation of the role of vitamins in maintaining health and building up resistance to diseases; numerous ailments like pellagra and rickets yielded to vitamin treatment, and the discovery led to very general dietary reforms, as well as to considerable proprietary quackery.

Indubitably the most sensational development in the field of medicine was the successful fight against coccus infections. In 1935 the German Dr. Domagk announced that prontosil was effective in arresting streptococcal infection. At the Pasteur Institute in Paris, prontosil was broken down and sulfanilamide isolated as the effective ingredient. English and American doctors promptly experimented with sulfanilamide and its numerous derivatives and found that it could be used with spectacular success against a host of coccal infections — streptococcus, meningitis, gonorrhoea, gangrene, pyelitis, and, above all, pneumonia.

These immense advances in medical science put better health within the reach of all, yet the general health of the American people was not a matter for complacency. Infant mortality was still higher than in such countries as Norway and Sweden, and the draft statistics of the early 'forties revealed that an astonishingly high proportion of American men suffered from poor eyesight, bad teeth, and other ailments caused by poverty or neglect, and that the incidence of venereal disease was shockingly high, especially in the rural counties of the South. Investigation discovered a clear correlation between health and income, and suggested the desirability of government support to a public health program comparable with that given to public education.

Advances in the social sciences did not compare favorably with those in the natural sciences. Perhaps never before had social institutions been so elaborately studied, but rarely had the findings been more diverse or conflicting. Sociologists like A. G. Keller of Yale University published monumental studies of *The Science of Society,* but no one was deceived by the title. The most significant contributions were doubtless case studies like the Lynds's *Middletown* and *Middletown in Transition,* and critical analyses like Lewis Mumford's trenchant studies, *Technics and Civilization* and *The Culture of Cities*. No grand ideas illumined the economic landscape except those emanating from John Maynard Keynes's study in Cambridge. Yet those who persisted in regarding laissez faire as part of the economic cosmic system and those who put their faith in a planned economy were still locked in mortal combat, and while they quarreled the most effective instruction in economics came from politicians in Washington. In law, sociological jurisprudence continued to dominate the thinking of jurisprudents; the contributions of the legal ' realists ' were rather extensions of this gospel than challenges to it.

The most interesting, if not the most important, contributions were in the realm of history. If no one took up Henry Adams's challenge to formulate laws of history in harmony with the laws of the stellar universe, this was perhaps just as well, for Adams's own attempt was not designed to encourage others. Three scholars dominated the historical scene: Frederick Jackson Turner, Charles A. Beard, and Vernon L. Parrington. Though all three came out of the Middle Border, and all were deeply influenced by the Populist revolt and the Progressive movement, they responded with very different formulas. In a series of epoch-making essays Turner argued that what chiefly differentiated America from the Old World was the frontier — the wilderness — which took a European and transformed him into an American. ' American democracy,' he wrote, ' is fundamentally the outcome of the experience of the American people in dealing with the West.' Turner's habit of looking at American history from the vantage point of the West made for emphasis on environment rather than on heredity, and encouraged many of those pressures that put a premium on isolation and the concept of uniqueness.

Beard's emphasis, too, was environmental; in a prodigious flow of books and articles he read an economic interpretation into much of American history from the making of the Federal Constitution to American participation in two world wars. A crusader as much as an historian, Beard was incessantly active in public affairs, and used scholarship as a weapon in the struggle for Progressivism and reform, and eventually for isolationism.

Parrington, too, was a rebel and a reformer who refought all the battles of the past in the light of his Jeffersonian principles. As a man of letters he was in the European tradition — a disciple of Hippolyte Taine and of Georg Brandes, whose great work on European thought provided him with the title for his own three-volume masterpiece: *Main Currents of American Thought*. His contribution to American scholarship — and to the American mind — was twofold: to broaden the concept of literature to embrace all forms of expression — theology, law, politics, economics, criticism, journalism — and to use this vast and amorphous body of literature for purposes of social and historical documentation. Both history and literary criticism were to move rapidly away from Parrington's methods, and from his findings, too, but in his day he explained much that had seemed obscure, and inspired in many younger men a new concept of cultural history.

Meantime two younger scholars emerged on the historical scene: Douglas S. Freeman and Allan Nevins. Freeman, who edited the Richmond *News-Leader* in his spare time, dedicated his life to the study of the Confederacy, and in four volumes on *R. E. Lee* and three on *Lee's Lieutenants* wrote not only the classic account of the war in Virginia and the definitive biography of General Lee, but the greatest biography in American literature. Allan Nevins, too, came out of journalism to sweep the whole field of American history: biographies of Grover Cleveland and Hamilton Fish and John C. Frémont; histories of Rockefeller and his empire and of Ford and his industry; studies of the American States during the Revolution, and of Reconstruction, a multi-volumed history of the Civil War which at once supplanted all its predecessors, and a philosophical study of the nature of history. He was a modern Ranke, a historian who combined massive erudition, an encyclopedic range of interest, intellectual originality, and a felicitous literary style; he was, as an English scholar observed, 'a phenomenon of Nature, like Niagara Falls,' and like Niagara Falls he was equally remarkable for the power he displayed and the power he generated.

BIBLIOGRAPHY

1. PROSPERITY AND DISILLUSIONMENT. Frederick Lewis Allen, *Only Yesterday* and *The Big Change;* H. S. Commager, *The American Mind;* John Gunther, *Inside U.S.A.;* Joseph Wood Krutch, *The Modern Temper;* Max Lerner, *America as a Civilization;* William Leuchtenberg, *The Perils of Prosperity;* Robert and Helen Lynd, *Middletown;* Margaret Mead, *Male and Female;* Broadus Mitchell, *Depression Decade, 1929–1941;* Bernard Rosenberg & David White, *Mass Culture: The Popular Arts in America;* Leo Rosten, *Hollywood;* Gilbert Seldes, *The Seven Lively Arts;* Preston Slosson, *The Great Crusade and*

After, 1914–1928; Harold Stearns (ed.), *Civilization in the United States;* Lionel Trilling, *The Liberal Imagination;* Dixon Wecter, *The Age of the Great Depression, 1929–1941.*

2. INTOLERANCE AND CIVIL LIBERTIES. John W. Caughey, *In Clear and Present Danger;* Zechariah Chafee, *Free Speech in the United States;* H. S. Commager, *Freedom, Loyalty, and Dissent;* Robert Cushman, *Civil Liberties in the United States;* Morris Ernst, *The First Freedom;* Osmond Fraenkel, *Our Civil Liberties* and *The Sacco-Vanzetti Case;* Felix Frankfurter, *The Case of Sacco and Vanzetti;* Walter Gellhorn, *American Rights;* Learned Hand, *The Spirit of Liberty;* Frederick Howe, *Confessions of a Reformer;* Samuel Konefsky, *The Legacy of Holmes and Brandeis, Justice Stone and the Supreme Court,* and *The Constitutional World of Mr. Justice Frankfurter;* Robert MacIver, *Academic Freedom in Our Time;* Alpheus T. Mason, *The Supreme Court from Taft to Warren* and *Harlan Fiske Stone;* Wallace Mendelson, *Justices Black and Frankfurter;* Gunnar Myrdal, *An American Dilemma* (2 vols.) ; Leo Pfeffer, *The Liberties of an American;* John P. Roche, *Courts and Rights: The American Judiciary in Action;* Norman Thomas, *The Test of Freedom.*

3. LITERATURE. Carlos Baker, *Hemingway: The Writer as Artist;* Van Wyck Brooks, *The Confident Years;* H. M. Campbell & R. E. Foster, *William Faulkner: A Critical Appraisal;* Oscar Cargill, *Intellectual America;* Richard Chase, *The American Novel and Its Tradition;* Malcolm Cowley, *After the Genteel Tradition;* Bernard Duffey, *Chicago Renaissance in American Letters: A Critical History;* Leslie Fiedler, *Life and Death in the American Novel;* Maxwell Geismar, *Rebels and Ancestors, The Last of the Provincials,* and *Writers in Crisis;* Rudolf Gilbert, *Shine, Perishing Republic: Robinson Jeffers;* Donald Heiney, *Recent American Literature;* Frederick J. Hoffman, *Freudianism and the Literary Mind* and *The Twenties: American Writing in the Post-war Decade;* Irving Howe, *William Faulkner: A Critical Study;* Randall Jarrell, *Poetry and the Age;* Matthew Josephson, *Portrait of the Artist as an American;* Alfred Kazin, *On Native Grounds;* Amy Lowell, *Tendencies in Modern American Poetry;* William Manchester, *Disturber of the Peace: H. L. Mencken;* E. L. Masters, *Vachel Lindsay;* Henry F. May, *The End of American Innocence;* Arthur Mizener, *The Far Side of Paradise: Biography of F. Scott Fitzgerald;* Harriet Monroe, *A Poet's Life;* Herbert J. Muller, *Thomas Wolfe;* Emery Neff, *Edwin Arlington Robinson;* William V. O'Connor, *The Tangled Fire of William Faulkner;* Albert Parry, *Garrets and Pretenders: A History of Bohemianism in America;* Stow Persons, *American Minds;* Houston Peterson, *The Melody of Chaos;* Lawrence C. Powell, *Robinson Jeffers;* Arthur H. Quinn, *History of the American Drama from the Civil War to the Present;* Mark Schorer, *Sinclair Lewis;* Robert E. Spiller, *et al., Literary History of the United States,* vol. 2; Allen Tate, *Selected Essays, 1928–1955;* Edmund Wilson, *The Shores of Light: A Literary Chronicle of the Twenties and Thirties.*

4. ART, PAINTING, AND MUSIC. John Baur, *Revolution and Tradition in American Art;* Milton Brown, *American Paintings from the Armory Show to the Depression;* Elizabeth Cary, *George Luks;* Martha Cheney, *Modern Art in America;* E. O. Christensen, *Index of American Design;* Aaron Copland, *Our New Music;* Waldo Frank, *et al., America and Alfred Stieglitz;* Ira Glackens, *William*

Glackens and The Ashcan School; Robert Henri, *The Art Spirit;* John R. Howard, *Our Contemporary Composers;* Sam Hunter, *Modern American Painting and Sculpture;* Sidney Janis, *Abstract and Surrealist Art in America;* Samuel Koontz, *Modern American Painters;* Walt Kuhn, *The Story of the Armory Show;* Oliver Larkin, *Art and Life in America;* Grace Overmyer, *Government and the Arts;* Constance Rourke, *Charles Sheeler;* James T. Soby, *Contemporary Painters;* Wilson Whitman, *Bread and Circuses.*

5. SCIENCE AND SOCIAL SCIENCE. L. Barrett, *The Universe and Dr. Einstein;* Helen Clapesattle, *The Doctors Mayo;* Bernard Crick, *The American Science of Politics;* Joseph Dorfman, *The Economic Mind in American Civilization,* vol. 4; S. R. and F. T. Flexner, *William Henry Welch and the Heroic Age of American Medicine;* George Gray, *The Advancing Front of Medicine;* Bernard Jaffe, *Men of Science in America;* Lewis Mumford, *Technics and Civilization;* Howard Odum (ed.), *American Masters of Social Science;* S. R. and L. F. Rosen, *Technology and Society;* Morton White, *Social Thought in America;* Harvey Wish, *The American Historian.*

The New Deal

1. THE ELECTION OF 1932

THE Republican program for liquidating the depression was as too late for political purposes as for economic results; every indication pointed to a Democratic victory in 1932. This prospect dampened Republican zeal; Hoover's renomination was neither contested nor greeted with enthusiasm, and the platform was ambiguous and evasive. A very different situation obtained in the Democratic camp where competition for the nomination was sharp. Alfred E. Smith's large popular vote in the previous election justified him in believing that he might now overcome the handicaps that had then thwarted him, and lead his party to victory. Others regarded the anti-Catholic prejudice as insuperable and called for new leadership. By far the most prominent of the several aspirants was Franklin Delano Roosevelt.

A distant connection of the famous T.R., and married to the former President's niece, Franklin D. Roosevelt had more than the magic of his name to commend him. He was born to wealth and position, educated at Groton School, Harvard University, and the Columbia Law School; his interest in public affairs dictated a political career, and his money enabled him to forego private practice and enter the political arena. Like all the Roosevelts except the Oyster Bay branch, he was born a Democrat. At the age of 29 he was elected state senator from the 'silk-stocking' Dutchess County district where he had inherited a country estate, and promptly distinguished himself by a successful fight against the election of Boss Murphy's candidate to the United States Senate. After supporting Wilson in 1912, he was appointed Assistant Secretary of the Navy. Contact with Wilson served to deepen Roosevelt's liberal convictions, companionship with Bryan and Daniels broadened his democratic sympathies, while acquaintance with party leaders taught him the political ropes. In 1920 he was nominated as Cox's running mate; the following year his promising political career was apparently ended by a severe case of infantile paralysis. During the next seven years, while he stubbornly fought his way back to health, he used his enforced retirement for study, thought, and correspondence; his convictions were deepened and his character strengthened. He returned to politics in 1928 rugged in health, rejuvenated in spirit, better known in the party than before, and one of the best-informed men in the country on a wide range of subjects.

Governor Smith persuaded Roosevelt to re-enter politics. The friendship between the ' happy warrior ' from the sidewalks of New York and the gentleman-democrat of Hyde Park had begun early; Roosevelt had nominated Smith for the presidency twice. New York was a critical state and Smith was convinced that Roosevelt's candidacy for the governorship would materially strengthen the national ticket. It did; in 1928, the voters of New York elected Roosevelt governor when they rejected Smith for President. Two years later Governor Roosevelt was re-elected by a majority of 700,000 and thus became the leading contender for the next presidential nomination. Smith, embittered, broke with his former friend; but the drift toward Roosevelt was irresistible, and when the convention met he was nominated on the fourth ballot.

The Democratic platform promised unemployment relief, labor legislation, and the ' restoration of agriculture '; the conservation and development of power resources in the public interest; federal regulation of holding companies, securities exchanges, and utility rates; reciprocal trade agreements and other efforts to secure world peace; a balanced budget and a sound currency; and a prompt repeal of the Eigheeenth Amendment. The ' continuous responsibility of government for human welfare ' was held up as a guiding principle.

The radio had made possible a new type of campaign, but Roosevelt, partly to prove his physical vigor, partly to capitalize on his personal magnetism, chose to embark upon an old-fashioned stump-speaking tour which took him into almost every state of the Union. In his address to the Commonwealth Club in San Francisco, he set forth a comprehensive scheme of reform and recovery, embracing the repeal of prohibition, unemployment relief, government operation of Muscle Shoals, and legislation to save agriculture, rehabilitate the

Year of Election	SENATE			HOUSE		
1928	39		56	167		267
1930	48		47	220		211
'32	60		35	313		113
'34	69		23	318		104
'36	76		16	330		90
'38	69		23	261		164
1940	66		28	268		162
'42	58		37	218		208
'44	56		38	242		190
'46	51		45	245		188
'48	54		42	263		171
1950	49		47	234		199
'52	47		48	211		221
'54	48		47	232		203
'56	49		47	233		200
'58	64		34	283		153
1960	64		35	262		174

☐ Democratic   ■ Republican

COMPOSITION OF CONGRESS SINCE 1928. Other parties and independents are shown by white at the end of bar.

698

railroads, protect consumers and investors, and slash government expenses. The keynote was a ' new deal ' to the ' forgotten man.'

President Hoover, laboring under the dead-weight of hard times, could only recite his efforts to cope with the depression, prophesy that a Democratic victory would mean that ' the grass will grow in the streets of a hundred cities, a thousand towns,' and reaffirm his faith in rugged individualism and the American system. In his last speech of the campaign he set forth his conception of the choice before the people:

It is a contest between two philosophies of government. . . . Our opponents . . . are proposing changes and so-called new deals which would destroy the very foundations of our American system . . . You cannot extend the mastery of government over the daily life of a people without somewhere making it master of people's souls and thoughts.

Too many voters feared that the foundations of the American system were already being destroyed by attrition to take seriously this impassioned warning. On election day Roosevelt received almost 23 million votes, Hoover a little less than 16 million votes. Roosevelt's victory in the electoral college was even more decisive, for he carried every state but six, four of them in New England. Democratic control of both houses of Congress was complete. No President or party ever came into power with a clearer popular mandate to break with past policies and inaugurate new ones, but just what the new program should be was still to be worked out.

2. The Philosophy of the New Deal

When Roosevelt took the oath of office the depression had reached its lowest level and most dramatic stage. The efforts of the RFC had been insufficient to avert a banking crisis; by March 1933 two-thirds of the banks of the country had been closed by official proclamation, and the shock of this financial disaster was being felt throughout American economy. The new President made no effort to minimize the danger. He said, in his inaugural address:

Values have shrunk to fantastic levels; taxes have risen; our ability to pay has failed; government of all kinds is faced by serious curtailment of income; the means of exchange are frozen in the currents of trade; the withered leaves of industrial enterprise lie on every side; farmers find no markets for their produce; the savings of many years in thousands of families are gone. More important, a host of unemployed citizens face the grim problem of existence and an equally great number toil with little return. Only a foolish optimist can deny the dark realities of the moment.

There followed an excoriation of the 'unscrupulous money changers' who 'stand indicted in the court of public opinion,' and of the 'false leadership' which had attempted to solve problems through exhortation. 'They have no vision,' said Roosevelt, who like Bryan and Woodrow Wilson knew the value of biblical phrases, 'and where there is no vision the people perish.'

Roosevelt had no intention of emulating his predecessor in relying upon exhortation. 'This nation,' he said, 'asks for action, and action now! ' Setting forth a general program which he promised shortly to elaborate in detail, he warned Congress and the country that the emergency called for emergency measures.

It is to be hoped that the normal balance of executive and legislative authority may be wholly adequate to meet the unprecedented task before us. But it may be that an unprecedented demand and need for undelayed action may call for temporary departure from that normal balance of public procedure. I am prepared under my constitutional duty to recommend the measures that a stricken nation in the midst of a stricken world may require.

If Congress failed to support these recommendations,

I shall not evade the clear course of duty that will then confront me. I shall ask the Congress for the one remaining instrument to meet the crisis — broad executive power to wage a war against the emergency as great as the power that would be given me if we were in fact invaded by a foreign foe. . . . The people of the United States have asked for discipline and direction under leadership. They have made me the present instrument of their wishes.

The speech, with its criticism of the old order and its promise of executive leadership toward a new, had a Wilsonian flavor, just as the New Deal recalled the New Freedom. If Franklin D. Roosevelt recalled his cousin Theodore in personality, he was closer to Woodrow Wilson in political philosophy. A liberal rather than a radical, he was a genuine democrat, whose confidence in the common people was as instinctive as Bryan's and as rationalized as Wilson's.

Franklin D. Roosevelt combined qualities that perhaps no President since Jefferson possessed in such happy proportion. He had political acumen, the ability to work through established political machinery and to champion reform without antagonizing party bosses. He had personal charm equally effective in social intercourse, public appearances, or over the radio. A cultivated gentleman, he did not distrust scholarship in politics and was able to command the services of an enthusiastic and loyal group of experts to furnish ideas, formulate legislation, and implement policies. He combined audacity and courage; tenacious of ultimate ends, he was almost recklessly opportunist as to means, but he preferred compromise to strife. He knew how to dramatize himself and his policies and how to create a favorable climate of opinion in which to work, and he inspired loyalty to his ideas as well as to his person.

Those ideas, as they were unfolded to a bewildered nation, were a consummation of campaign promises, popular expectations, and ideas formulated by Roosevelt's embryonic ' Brains Trust.' Conservatives were alarmed, but the mass of common people agreed that the desperate emergency justified radical measures. They felt that the Federal Government had been given back to them. Within a year Congress, under the relentless leadership of the President, had enacted a far-reaching program of social and economic legislation; at the end of four years that program had assumed the outlines of a revolution.

And yet the legislation of the first Roosevelt administration did not constitute a revolution. The popular name, New Deal, is more correct. From the perspective of a generation it is obvious that the Roosevelt philosophy was deeply rooted in the American tradition and the Roosevelt methods modeled on American precedents. The New Deal seemed revolutionary not because it introduced fundamental changes into American politics or economy but because it was carried through with such breathless speed. Speed was imperative because of both the emergency situation and the legislative lag which dated from the period of World War I. The abandonment of laissez faire and the development of social control, which had gone on steadily in both state and national politics from the middle 'eighties to the Wilson administration, had been interrupted by World War I and stalled by the postwar reaction. The twelve years of ' normalcy ' had in fact been years of reaction that rejected government intervention in business, and refrained from tampering with the existing system or even questioning its ultimate validity.

The legislation of the Roosevelt administration, then, was an at-

tempt to catch up the political lag of twenty years and to articulate government to the facts of a depressed economy. Three bodies of
precedents illuminated the course of the New Deal: the federal regulation of business and railroads dating back to the 1880's; the social
legislation of progressive states such as Massachusetts, New York,
Wisconsin, and Oregon; and the experiments in social welfare carried on by some of the more progressive nations of Northern Europe
and the British Commonwealth; while the organization of American
industry and business, which had long accepted such practices as
price-fixing agreements, codes, and cartels, provided antecedents for
some of the economic regulations.

In so far, then, as the New Deal was directed toward an extension
of government control over national economy, it was in the progressive tradition; in so far as it was directed toward improving the welfare of the common man, it was in the democratic tradition. Taken
as a whole, the New Deal legislation contributed greatly to both recovery and reform, improved the status of the farmer and the laborer, prepared the way for a more equitable distribution of wealth,
brought business, banking, securities, utilities, and transportation
under more effective regulation and, most important of all, helped to
salvage the natural resources of the nation. At the same time it interfered with the freedom of business enterprise, inaugurated far-
reaching controls over labor and farming, encouraged the growth of
bureaucracy, stimulated class antagonisms, greatly increased the national debt, and at some points challenged traditional readings of the
Constitution. However the historian may wish to strike the balance
between credits and debits, three things are clear: the New Deal, in
one form or another, was inevitable; it was directed toward preserving capitalistic economy rather than substituting another system;
and the methods employed were in the American tradition. Com-
parisons with European dictatorships are misleading, for American
democracy has always accomplished its purposes through powerful
leaders — Jefferson, Jackson, Lincoln, and the Roosevelts — without
seriously menacing the constitutional system. The logic of the New
Deal, and of Roosevelt's leadership, was suggested over a century
earlier by William Ellery Channing:

There are seasons, in human affairs, of inward and outward revolution,
when new depths seem to be broken up in the soul, when new wants are
unfolded in multitudes, and a new and undefined good is thirsted for.

There are periods when the principles of experience need to be modified, when hope and trust and instinct claim a share with prudence in the guidance of affairs, when, in truth, *to dare* is the highest wisdom.[1]

3. MONEY, BANKING, AND SECURITIES LEGISLATION

Roosevelt's first act upon assuming office was to decree a national bank holiday and place an embargo upon the export of gold and silver. Congress met in special session on 9 March 1933, and there followed a series of banking, financial, and revenue measures that went far to fulfill the presidential promise of ' strict supervision of all banking and credits and investments . . . and an end to speculation with other people's money.' An Emergency Banking Law of 9 March provided for the early termination of the bank holiday, facilitated the reopening of liquid banks under proper regulation, and liberalized the powers of the Federal Reserve Banks with respect to the issue of bank notes. The following day Congress listened to a presidential message proposing drastic economies in administrative expenses and veterans' payments. Too disconcerted to offer serious objections, Congress granted authority to slash department budgets 25 per cent, cut federal salaries up to 15 per cent, and reduce pension and benefit payments. These economies were effected, but within a short time Congress recovered sufficiently from its lapse to restore salary cuts, put practically all veterans back on the pension rolls and, eventually, vote a veterans' bonus; the economy measure, therefore, has a mere antiquarian interest.

It was clear, too, that with Great Britain and many other European nations off the gold standard, the United States could no longer afford to maintain it. On 5 April the President exercised his authority to forbid the hoarding of gold and gold certificates, and two weeks later the nation formally abandoned gold. A Joint Resolution of 5 June, designed to avoid the difficulties which had attended Civil War legal tender, canceled the gold clauses in all government and private obligations and made all debts payable in legal tender. The validity of this repudiation of gold contracts was challenged in the courts. A long series of precedents gave the Court no choice but to sustain congressional power over legal tender, and though it held that the cancellation of the gold clauses in government contracts was

[1] *The Complete Works of William Ellery Channing*, p. 459.

both illegal and immoral it added that the plaintiff had suffered no damages and had no ground for suit.[2] The chief object of New Deal financial legislation, however, was to raise commodity prices, and it was in this direction that the administration now moved. Under the terms of the Farm Relief and Inflation Act of 12 May, the President might, at his discretion, inflate the currency by the addition of $3 billion of new treasury notes, or reduce the gold content of the dollar up to 50 per cent. Before exercising either alternative the President awaited the results of the London Economic Conference. Upon the failure of that conference — a failure due largely to his own refusal to consider international stabilization — he experimented with a ' managed currency.' His object was ' to establish and maintain a dollar which will not change its purchasing and debt-paying power.' This effort to establish a dollar which would have a fixed and constant relation to commodity prices and which would stay put had its champions among contemporary economists; but its real inspiration came from the spirits of James B. Weaver and William Jennings Bryan.

Currency manipulation did not effect any appreciable increase in commodity prices, and in January 1934 the President, ' to make possible the payment of public and private debts at more nearly the price level at which they had been incurred,' obtained authority to devaluate the dollar, impound all gold in the Treasury and the Federal Reserve Banks, and create out of the accruing profit a stabilization fund of $2 billion. He fixed the value of the dollar at 59.06, and the nation returned to this modified gold standard. Friends of the administration credited improvement of commodity prices to this dollar devaluation; critics averred that improvement would have come in any event, and that devaluation worked unwarranted hardship upon security holders. Perhaps the only indisputable effect was to attract much of the world's gold to the United States, where it was buried in the vaults of Fort Knox, in Kentucky. None could deny, however, that the goal of controlled inflation had been carried through with utmost caution or that the dangers of printing-press money had been skillfully avoided.

In line with this inflationary policy was the effort to establish more generous credit facilities. High interest rates and frozen credit had

[2] *Perry v. United States* 294 U.S. 330.

forced an alarming number of foreclosures on both rural and urban properties, involving staggering losses to both owners and investors. In order to reverse this process, the Reconstruction Finance Corporation was allotted additional funds to place at the disposal of business, industry, and agriculture. A new Farm Credit Administration directed by Henry Morgenthau made possible the refunding of farm loans at drastically lower rates of interest, provided more than $100 million for new mortgages in a few months, and set up machinery for equitable adjustment of farm debts. In June 1933 Congress established a Home Owners' Loan Corporation to refinance small mortgages on privately owned homes; within a year this corporation had approved over 300,000 loans amounting to almost a billion dollars. Subsequent legislation to ameliorate municipal and farm bankruptcies was voided by the Supreme Court,[3] but a corporation bankruptcy act stood the test of constitutionality.

Reform rather than recovery was the object of the banking and securities exchange legislation of the Roosevelt administration. The demand for banking reform went back to the decade of the 'twenties, but the congressional investigations of banking and securities practices under the skillful direction of Ferdinand Pecora, which revealed conditions characterized as ' scandalous,' and the banking collapse of 1932–33 dramatized the need and furnished the opportunity for reform. A group of Senators led by LaFollette of Wisconsin and Bronson Cutting of New Mexico tried to persuade the President to seize the opportunity to nationalize the entire banking system of the country, but the proposal was either too radical or too novel to meet presidential approval. Instead he threw his support behind the Glass-Steagall Banking Act of 16 June 1933. This measure, the most important since the Federal Reserve Act of 1913, provided for the separation of commercial and investment banking, severe restrictions on the use of bank credit for speculative purposes, and the expansion of the Federal Reserve System to embrace banks heretofore excluded. To prevent a recurrence of the epidemic of bank failures of the 1920's the act set up a Federal Deposit Insurance Corporation to insure bank deposits up to a fixed sum. The American Bankers Association denounced the proposal as ' unsound, unscientific, unjust and dangerous,' but it turned out to be one of the most constructive devices

[3] *Louisville v. Radford* 295 U.S. 555.

of the whole New Deal era, and bank failures, which had averaged a thousand a year in the previous decade, became almost non-existent.

In accordance with platform and campaign promises the administration undertook a thoroughgoing reform of the whole security and investment business. In his message to Congress, the President called for supervision of the purchase and sale of all property dealt in on exchanges, and legislation to correct unethical and unsafe practices on the part of officers and directors of banks and other corporations. Legislation modeled closely upon the British Companies Act and Directors' Liability Act, which had stood the test of long experience, was formulated by Professor Felix Frankfurter of the Harvard Law School and passed, as the Securities Act, on 27 May 1933. It provided that all new securities offered or advertised for interstate sale should be registered before the Federal Trade Commission — subsequently the Securities and Exchange Commission; that every offering should contain full information to enable the prospective purchaser to judge the value of the issue and the condition of the corporation; and that the directors and officers of the corporation were to be criminally liable for any deliberate omission of significant information or any wilful misstatement of fact.

The following year came legislation to curb malpractices on the stock exchange which the stock exchange itself either could not or would not end. The financial community was outraged at this interference but had nothing to propose in its stead. An act of 6 June 1934 created a Securities and Exchange Commission, licensed stock exchanges and required the registration of all securities in which they dealt, prohibited pools, options, and other devices for manipulating the market, and empowered the Federal Reserve Board to determine the extension of credit for marginal and speculative loans. Joseph P. Kennedy of Boston, financier and speculator, was appointed chairman of the commission because, as Roosevelt said, he knew the tricks of the trade. Subsequent legislation extended and greatly enlarged the authority of the Securities Commission over public utilities companies.

4. FARM RELIEF

The efforts of the Hoover administration to alleviate farm distress had been unsuccessful, and 1932, as we have seen, marked the nadir of the agricultural depression. Prompt and drastic remedial action was necessary if the collapse were not to turn into catastrophe. With the assistance of advisers long familiar with the farm problem — Secretary Wallace, George Peek, and Mordecai Ezekiel — Roosevelt prepared a farm relief plan of unexpected boldness and, urging that ' an unprecedented condition calls for the trial of new means to rescue agriculture,' invited Congress to enter ' a new and untrod path.' Congress responded to the invitation and on 12 May the Agricultural Adjustment Act became law. This act, the first of a series which involved the reconstruction of American economy, was intended to re-establish equality between agriculture and industry by raising the level of agriculture commodity prices and easing the credit and mortgage load. Its most interesting provisions authorized the Secretary of Agriculture to make agreements with farmers whereby, in return for government subsidies, they undertook to reduce production of certain staple commodities. The original act contemplated reduction of cotton, wheat, corn, hogs, rice, tobacco, and milk; subsequent amendments extended the provisions of the act to rice, flax, barley, peanuts, grain sorghums, sugar, and beef cattle. Reductions were to be effected by renting to the government land taken out of cultivation or by benefit payments on restricted allotments grown. The costs of these payments were to be met from taxes on the processing of the products involved.

It was expected that this plan would not only bring cash payments but would raise the entire price level of agricultural commodities, and in this expectation farmers hastened to avail themselves of its benefits. Almost three-fourths of the cotton growers agreed to reduce their acreage by approximately one-third in return for cash payments of from $7 to $20 an acre or an option on the purchase of cotton held by the government up to the extent of their reduction the previous year. Altogether, in 1933, slightly over 10 million acres of land were taken out of production, thus reducing the cotton crop by at least 4 million bales. For this reduction planters received from the government some $200 million in benefit payments. In addition the price of cotton rose from 5.5 to 9.5 cents a pound. The total cash income of the cotton farmers for 1933 was thus more than double the income of the previous year. Subsequent arrangements, in 1934 and 1935, buttressed by the Bankhead Cotton Control Act of April 1934, held the cotton crop down to about 10 million bales, continued generous benefit payments to planters, and maintained the price at 10 cents a pound or better.

The program for the reduction of wheat acreage was equally successful. Contracts with over 550,000 wheat farmers removed some 8 million acres from production, brought the co-operating wheat growers over $100 million in benefit payments, and contributed to an increase in the price of wheat and in the total income of wheat growers of approximately 100 per cent. The drought of 1934 and adverse crop conditions in 1935 necessitated a modification of the crop reduction program, and by the end of this period the government had disposed of surplus stocks held over from the Federal Farm Board operations, and the nation was importing wheat. The effort to reduce corn acreage and remove hogs from the market was attended with even greater success. In 1933 over a million corn and hog producers signed contracts with the AAA to reduce acreage by approximately 25 per cent; at the same time the government purchased and slaughtered for relief or other purposes some 6 million pigs and hogs. The result was the smallest corn crop since 1881, benefit payments totaling over $300 million, and higher prices for corn and pork. The reduction of the tobacco crop was spectacularly successful — from the farmers' point of view. Over 95 per cent of Southern farmers entered into agreements to cut tobacco production by almost one-third. Southern tobacco growers, who had received $56 million for their 1930 and $43 million for their 1933 crop, got $120 million for their 1934 crop. Comparable results were attained in other less important farm commodities. In part because of the AAA program of crop reduction, in part because of drought and government payments, and in part because of the devaluation of the dollar, the national farm income increased from $5,562,000,000 in 1932 to $8,688,000,000 in 1935.

On 6 January 1936 the Supreme Court invalidated the AAA as an improper exercise of the taxing power and an invasion of the reserved rights of states.[4] 'This is coercion by economic pressure,' said Justice Roberts, who conjured up the terrifying consequences

4 *United States v. Butler, et al., Receivers of Hoosac Mills Corp.* 297 U.S. 1.

that would flow from the taxation of one part of the community for the benefit of another.

The expressions of the framers of the Constitution, the decisions of this court interpreting that instrument, and the writings of great commentators will be searched in vain for any suggestion that there exists . . . in the Constitution the authority whereby every provision and every fair implication from that instrument may be subverted, the independence of the individual states obliterated, and the United States converted into a central government exercising uncontrolled police power in every state of the Union, superseding all local control or regulation of the affairs or concerns of the states.

But Justice Stone, in his powerful dissenting opinion, protested that this objection ' hardly rises to the dignity of argument,' pointed out that ' the present levy is held invalid, not for any want of power in Congress to lay such a tax . . . but because the use to which its proceeds are put is disapproved,' warned his colleagues against a ' tortured construction of the Constitution,' and observed, with some asperity, that ' courts are not the only agency of government that must be assumed to have capacity to govern.' Where judges confessed such irreconcilable differences on the meaning of the Constitution, laymen might well be confused.

The philosophy behind the AAA was that of national self-sufficiency. It correctly assumed that the loss of foreign markets was one of the major causes of the agricultural depression, but it entertained little hope that those markets could be permanently recovered. It looked, therefore, rather to the development of a self-sufficient agrarian economy, independent — so far as that was possible — of the vicissitudes of foreign markets. Such a philosophy presupposed a ' planned economy.' It required not only a reduction of farm crops but of the number of farmers; [5] it proposed the removal of millions of acres of ' marginal ' land from cultivation and the resettlement of ' marginal ' farmers on more fertile soil or in small semi-industrial communities; and it demanded that those farmers who were to continue farming be relieved of their burden of mortgage indebtedness and given a new impulse toward independence. Administrative opposition to this philosophy of autarchy and serious doubts as to the expediency of a planned agricultural economy prevented any whole-

[5] Oddly enough, the number of farmers remained constant during the decade of the 'thirties, but declined sharply during and after the war.

hearted effort to carry this scheme into effect, but some parts of it were given a trial. In 1935 the President set up a Resettlement Administration which, under the guidance of Rexford Tugwell, embarked upon a program of rehabilitation. It removed from cultivation some 10 million acres of marginal land; gave financial aid to 635,000 farm families, and adjusted farm mortgages to save debtors over $25 million; built model farmhouses, suburban developments, and camps for migratory workers; and, through the development of health, education, and recreation services, attempted to make rural life more attractive.

An even more ambitious plan to rehabilitate agriculture was embodied in a presidential proposal of 1937 to rid the country of the curse of tenant farming. In the five years between 1930 and 1935 the number of tenant farmers had increased by 200,000; in the latter year two-fifths of the farmers of the country — and in eight Southern states over one-half — were tenants. Efforts to organize the tenant farmers of the South had resulted in disorder and in violent reprisals, but had dramatized to the country a situation which called for prompt remedial measures. Representatives from some Southern states looked askance at federal interference in this new ' peculiar ' institution, but it was everywhere admitted that only the national government could institute the necessary reforms. In July 1937 Congress passed a bill providing that the Federal Government subsidize the purchase of farms for tenants on easy terms. By 1950 only one state — Mississippi — reported more than half of her farms held by tenants; in the nation as a whole the figure had dropped to one-fourth.

Equally important was legislation affording farm mortgage relief. In the five years from 1927 to 1932 not less than 10 per cent of the farm property of the country had been foreclosed at auction; in certain sections of the West these foreclosures had become so numerous that farmers banded together to intimidate prospective purchasers, close courts, and terrorize judges, recalling the scenes of Shays's Rebellion a century and a half earlier. The Federal Farm Loan Act of May 1933 authorized the Federal Land Banks to issue bonds up to $2 billion for the refinancing of farm loans at 4 per cent interest which was guaranteed by the Federal Government; the following year the extension of the government guarantee to both principal and interest permitted a reduction of interest rate to 3 per cent. Meantime the Reconstruction Finance Corporation organized a Commodity Credit Corporation to lend money directly to farmers. The liberal policies pursued by these agencies brought an end to the epidemic of foreclosures and, together with higher commodity prices, enabled hundreds of thousands of farmers to liquidate their debts.

At the same time Secretary of State Cordell Hull, unsympathetic to the philosophy of national autarchy, was exploring the possibilities of the recapture of foreign markets through reciprocity agreements, a solution President McKinley had proposed in 1901. Under the terms of the Trade Agreements Act of June 1934, Secretary Hull negotiated unconditional most-favored-nation reciprocity treaties with Cuba, Canada, France, Russia, and some twenty other countries. The results of this new trade policy were gratifying: within a year trade with Cuba had doubled, and trade with Canada, Sweden, France, and South American and Central American countries had improved materially. It was the hope of Mr. Hull that the new commercial policy would operate not only for economic improvement at home and abroad but that it would break down nationalist barriers and advance international understanding and peace. These hopes were largely realized. Reciprocity became a permanent feature of American economic policy. As long as the Democrats controlled Congress, presidential discretion was not seriously challenged. In the 'fifties, however, Congress wrote some restrictions on presidential power in making reciprocity agreements, and by the Act of 1958 the President was limited to reductions of not more than 20 per cent. By 1960 the reciprocity program embraced some forty countries, while others enjoyed some of the benefits of reciprocity through participation in the General Agreement on Tariffs and Trade of 1948.

5. INDUSTRY UNDER THE NEW DEAL

The most spectacular, though not the most significant, of New Deal experiments was the effort through the NRA to rehabilitate and regiment industry for purposes of recovery and reform. There was nothing essentially new in the regimentation of industry: when he was Secretary of Commerce, Mr. Hoover had given official encouragement to the formation of codes of fair practices and price-fixing agreements. What was new in the Roosevelt program was the attempt to extend this type of organization to all types of industry, small as well as large, to protect labor and the consumer, and to insist upon effective government supervision of the process.

The National Recovery Act of 16 June 1933, like so many of the New Deal measures, had the dual purpose of recovery and reform. It was designed to speed up industrial production, spread employment, reduce hours and raise wages, and provide money for a system of public works and emergency relief. It proposed, at the same time, to eliminate child labor, throw new safeguards about the rights of labor, and reduce the waste of competition without encouraging monopolies.[6] Section 1 of the act, formulated with an eye on the Supreme Court, declared the existence of ' a national emergency productive of widespread unemployment and disorganization of industry,' and announced the policy of Congress

to remove obstructions to the free flow of . . . commerce; to provide for the general welfare by promoting the organization of industry for the purpose of cooperative action among trade groups, to induce and maintain united action of labor and management under adequate governmental sanctions and supervision, to eliminate unfair competitive practices, to promote the fullest possible utilization of the present productive capacity of industries, to avoid undue restriction of production, . . . to increase the consumption of industrial and agricultural products by increasing purchasing power, to reduce and relieve unemployment, to improve standards of labor, and otherwise to rehabilitate industry and to conserve natural resources.

To attain these laudable ends the law provided for the organization of industries through the mechanism of codes drawn up by representatives of the industries concerned in conjunction with government administrators, and subject to approval by the President. Monopolies or monopolistic practices were specifically prohibited, but at the same time the operation of the anti-trust laws was suspended during the duration of the act. Pending the formulation of codes for major industries, the President was authorized to impose upon industry a blanket code. This blanket code, promulgated 27 July, was expected to serve as a model for industrial code-makers; it prohibited child labor, fixed the hours of labor at 36 for industrial and 40 for clerical workers, established a minimum wage of 40 cents an hour, and in-

6 ' It is not stretching the point to state categorically that there was not a major industry in the United States in the spring of 1933 that was not suffering either from over-production, or destructive competition, or unfair practices, or complete lack of planning.' President Roosevelt, in *On Our Way*, p. 85.

cluded the mandatory protection to labor provided for in the famous
Section 7a of the NRA.[7]

In the hot summer months of 1933 thousands of representatives of
American industry descended on Washington to discuss, argue, and
frame codes. The task was a titanic one and exhausted even the cascading energy of the national administrator, General Hugh Johnson. The problems which government authorities faced were bewildering and complex; codes had to be drawn up for hundreds of
industries and businesses, each presenting special technical problems.
The NRA administrators were familiar only with the general principles of the new program, businessmen and their legal advisers were
familiar with all the details; the inevitable result was that business
wrote its own codes of law and that big business imposed its ideas
upon small business. Yet out of the welter of conference and debate
there emerged a pattern of industrial organization that met most of
the requirements laid down by the NRA law and the President's
blanket code. To rally support, Johnson hit on the Blue Eagle as a
symbol of compliance with the wage and hour provisions of the
codes, and for a short time the Blue Eagle was almost as popular as
the flag. Within a year some 500 codes had been adopted and some
200 more were in process of formulation, and it was estimated that
over 23 million workers were under codes, and that over 4 million
unemployed had been reabsorbed in industry.

The ideal of the new program was industrial self-government, with
the NRA as a basic constitution and the codes as laws. It was hoped
that self-interest and public opinion would persuade industry to conform to both constitution and laws; in the event of non-conformity
the codes could be enforced through a complex system of national,
regional, state, and local compliance boards with ultimate recourse
to the federal courts. Three features of the NRA presented peculiar
difficulties: the labor provisions (Section 7a) created confusion and
excited opposition; the suspension of the anti-trust laws strengthened
large business at the expense of small and raised prices; and doubts
as to the constitutionality of the law encouraged non-compliance.
The problem of labor under the NRA requires separate treatment;
the other two may be noted here.

Shortly after the enactment of the NRA, President Roosevelt appealed to business to defer price increases until recovery was under

[7] See below, Section 6.

way. But industry was unwilling to defer profits, and for the most part Roosevelt's appeal was disregarded. Even more ominous was the growth of monopoly and the continuance of unfair practices under the NRA codes, proved conclusively by investigations of Clarence Darrow's Committee, which in July 1934 reported that the codes were controlled by the larger firms and were employed to foster and protect monopoly. Reforms were promptly inaugurated, but were ineffective, and during 1934 and 1935 the NRA was assailed with increasing bitterness from all sides: by large businessmen who resented government control of their labor relations; by small businessmen dismayed at the growth of monopoly; by liberals who lamented the suspension of the anti-trust laws and feared the long-range consequences of a ' planned economy ' regulated by a bureaucracy; by consumers outraged at price increases; by labor disappointed in the practical results of the codes; and by lawyers who insisted that the whole experiment was unconstitutional.

The NRA, then, was breaking down of its own weight when in May 1935 the Supreme Court destroyed it by undermining its legal foundations in the Schechter case.[8] The opinion of the Court was unanimous, and its decision so sweeping that it left no salvage. The NRA, said the Court, involved an illegal delegation of power, for ' Congress cannot delegate legislative power to the President to exercise an unfettered discretion to make whatever laws he thinks may be needed or advisable for the rehabilitation and expansion of trade or industry.' It constituted an improper exercise of the commerce power and an invasion by the Federal Government of the realm reserved to the states, for ' if the commerce clause were construed to reach all enterprises and transactions which could be said to have an indirect effect upon interstate commerce, the federal authority would embrace practically all the activities of the people and the authority of the state over its domestic concerns would exist only by sufferance.' And neither of these palpable violations of the Constitution could be justified on any plea of a ' national emergency,' for the Constitution was designed for emergencies as well as for periods of peace and prosperity.

Thus came to an end a law which President Roosevelt had described with palpable exaggeration as ' the most important and far-reaching ever enacted by the American Congress.' Though many

8 *Schechter Poultry Corp. v. United States* 295 U.S. 495.

liberals felt that the Schechter decision had saved the administration from embarrassment, Roosevelt himself was reluctant to admit defeat or to abandon an experiment so hopefully inaugurated. The reappearance of destructive industrial competition, the hasty abandonment of wage and hour standards, the widespread re-employment of child labor, and the judicial nullification of the Guffey Coal Act [9] and the Railroad Retirement Act,[10] created a demand for the substitution of some new form of industrial regulation for the NRA. Before the end of his first administration Roosevelt was appealing for new wage and hour legislation, and early in his second administration the Black-Connery Act made feeble gestures in this direction.

6. Labor Under the New Deal

Labor had suffered reverses even during the prosperous 'twenties; the depression brought not only unemployment and wage slashes but the extension of the stretch-out system, the sweatshop, and child labor, the widespread flouting of factory laws, and a concerted attack upon labor unions. Roosevelt came to office pledged to the reversal of the illiberal policies of his predecessor, and the appointment of Frances Perkins, distinguished social reformer, to the post of Secretary of Labor augured well for the fulfillment of that pledge. The first and most important effort toward the rehabilitation of labor was the NRA which attempted to spread employment, raise wages, reduce hours, eliminate child and sweatshop labor, and safeguard the right of organization and collective bargaining. This latter policy was embodied in the famous Section 7a of the National Recovery Act which provided that

Employees shall have the right to organize and bargain collectively, through representatives of their own choosing, and shall be free from the interference, restraint, or coercion of employers of labor, or their agents, in the designation of such representatives or in self-organization or in other concerted activities . . . and that no employee and no one seeking employment shall be required as a condition of employment to join any company union or to refrain from joining . . . a labor organization of his own choosing.

To effectuate this policy there was created, in August 1933, a National Labor Board to investigate violations of Section 7a and settle

[9] *Carter v. Carter Coal, et al.* 298 U.S. 238.
[10] *R. R. Retirement Board v. Alton R. R. Co.* 295 U.S. 330.

controversies between employers and workers. In this it was highly successful: in the first year of its existence the NLB entertained 3755 grievances of which 3061 were arbitrated. In June 1934 it was replaced by a National Labor Relations Board which, with its affiliated industrial boards, had jurisdiction over all controversies arising under the NRA and was authorized to determine which of competing unions represented the majority of workers in any industry.

Under the impetus of the NRA, organized labor more than recovered all the losses which it had suffered in the preceding decade, and by 1936 the A.F. of L. boasted a membership of over 4 million. When employers refused to accept the rulings of the NLRB, labor struck, and an epidemic of strikes and lockouts swept the country. Labor, sure that the government stood behind it, presumed upon its new position and antagonized public opinion; industry, determined to recoup depression losses and unintimidated by the New Deal, employed the traditional weapons of the company union, the injunction, and violence. During 1934 the country witnessed a great strike in the automobile industry, a nation-wide textile strike, and a general strike in San Francisco; all three were unsuccessful, and the latter two were smashed by the militia and by self-constituted vigilantes. The government itself suffered a severe setback when the Wierton Steel Company invoked the Norris-LaGuardia Anti-Injunction Act to prevent the NLRB from supervising a vote of employees on union representation. Emboldened by this successful defiance of the government, corporations initiated a massive counteroffensive against labor.

The invalidation of the NRA appeared to justify this counteroffensive, on legal grounds at least, but some of the labor provisions of that law were promptly re-enacted in the Wagner Act of 5 July 1935. This act set up an independent National Labor Relations Board authorized to investigate complaints and issue 'cease and desist' orders against unfair practices in labor relations affecting interstate commerce. These 'unfair practices' included interference with or coercion of employees in collective bargaining, domination of a labor union through financial contributions, discrimination against union members in employment or tenure, and refusal to bargain collectively with employees. Within two years this revamped NLRB handled over 5000 cases involving 'unfair practices.' Yet in many instances business, relying upon the precedent of the Schechter case, refused to comply with the terms of the law. In April 1937, however, the Supreme Court, by a 5–4 decision, sustained the validity of the Wagner Act.[11]

The fact remains [said Chief Justice Hughes] that the stoppage of those operations by industrial strife would have a most serious effect upon interstate commerce. It is idle to say that the effect would be indirect or remote. It is obvious that it would be immediate and might be catastrophic. We are asked to shut our eyes to the plainest facts of our national life and to deal with the question of direct and indirect effects in an intellectual vacuum. . . . When industries organize themselves on a national scale, making relation to interstate commerce the dominant factor in their activities, how can it be maintained that their industrial labor relations constitute a forbidden field into which Congress may not enter when it is necessary to protect interstate commerce from the paralyzing consequences of industrial war?

This opinion was so sweeping that it blurred the line between interstate and intrastate business and constituted a partial modification of the Schechter decision.

The most important development in labor, however, was the emergence in 1935 and 1936 of the Committee (later Congress) of Industrial Organizations. The C.I.O., as it came to be known, was a secession from the A.F. of L. by workers impatient with the cautious policy of that organization; it represented, too, a revival of the philosophy of industrial unionism espoused in the decade of the 1880's by the Knights of Labor. Under the turbulent leadership of John L. Lewis, President of the United Mine Workers, the C.I.O. set out to unionize skilled, unskilled, and white-collar workers in industries that had heretofore successfully resisted unionization, such as the steel, automobile, textile, and public utilities. Its success was, for a time, phenomenal. Union after union seceded from the A.F. of L. to the new organization. By mid-summer 1937 it was estimated that the C.I.O. had a membership of 4 million, and students predicted that it would, in the near future, supplant its older rival as the spokesman for American labor, a prediction that proved entirely erroneous.

Heady with success, Mr. Lewis instituted a series of strikes directed not so much to improvement in hours and wages as to the closed shop and the right of exclusive representation in collective bargaining. Disdaining traditional methods, strikers employed the new technique of the ' sit-down,' seizing possession of the machinery and prop-

[11] *National Labor Relations Board v. Jones & Laughlin Steel Corp.* 301 U.S. 1 (1937).

erty of employers and refusing to yield until their demands had been granted. To this new weapon many employers capitulated at once, and the acquiescence of the U.S. Steel Corporation in the demands of the C.I.O., in March 1937, was of historic significance. Others, notably the General Motors and Republic Steel corporations, challenged the legality of the sit-down, and called upon the courts to rescue their property. The courts responded with injunctions, and when workers resisted the court orders, violence ensued. The intervention of Governor Murphy of Michigan prevented widespread violence in the automobile industries of that state, but in June 1937 the nation was shocked by the outbreak of open warfare at the Republic Steel Company in South Chicago. Though a Senate committee under Robert LaFollette scored the Chicago police for brutality, public opinion turned against the C.I.O. and the sit-down, and by mid-summer 1937 it appeared that the new organization might forfeit many of the gains it had achieved in its first year.

7. CONSERVATION AND THE TVA

No part of the New Deal program was more imaginative or constructive than that which looked to the conservation of natural resources; none, certainly, was closer to the heart of the President. Conservation was, in a sense, a family tradition: if the first Roosevelt had not actually invented it, he had taken it over and attached his name to it historically. Because the intervening administrations, Democratic and Republican, had been on the whole indifferent to the exploitation and the erosion of natural resources, Franklin D. Roosevelt pretty much picked up where T.R. had left off. A country gentleman, he was passionately interested in the preservation of soil, forests, water, and wild life; his ideal for the American people was really a ' balanced civilization ' in which all workers had a stake in the land and all farmers enjoyed the advantages of urban life. The contrast between President Hoover's veto of the Muscle Shoals Bill in 1931 (' it is degeneration ') and Roosevelt's sponsorship of the TVA in 1933 is the measure of the change in political and social philosophy that occurred in two years. The change involved not only a large-scale effort to save and restore the national domain but also a cheerful acceptance of government control of public utilities, and a commitment to a far-reaching experiment in economic planning.

The conservation work of the Roosevelt administration was directed both to emergency relief and to permanent reform, and constituted the most scientific effort yet made to preserve and restore the soil, forest, water power, and wild life of the nation. The initial step in this policy was the creation (31 March 1933) of the Civilian Conservation Corps designed to give emergency work relief to young men from 17 to 25 and to carry through a program of conservation. In the eight years of its existence the CCC enlisted almost 3 million young men, who, under the direction of army officers and foresters, added over 17 million acres of new forest land, checked forest fires, fought plant and animal diseases, stocked hatcheries with over a billion fish, built 6 million check dams to halt soil erosion, and by mosquito control helped stamp out malaria. And — as President Roosevelt said — ' no one will ever be able to estimate in dollars and cents the value to the men themselves and to the nation in morale, in occupational training, in health, and in adaptability to later competitive life.'

The recurrent droughts and floods of the 1930's led to the enactment of an Omnibus Flood Control Bill, the construction of a large number of reservoir and power dams and check dams along smaller streams. The alarming spread of the ' dust bowl ' on the high plains inspired the planting of a 100-mile-wide shelter belt of trees, stretching from Texas to Canada. The program to stop soil erosion enlisted one-fourth the farmers of the country and embraced almost 300 million acres. Other contributions to conservation were the creation of numerous game and bird sanctuaries, the closing of grazing lands to homestead entries, and the addition of 12 million acres to the national forests.

Of all New Deal measures possibly the most important, and certainly the most dramatic, was that establishing the Tennessee Valley Authority and building the TVA. The problem of Muscle Shoals had been inherited from the Hoover administration; the repudiation of Hoover persuaded Senator Norris to bring his project forward once again. Roosevelt not only embraced it, but outlined a project larger and more ambitious than any imagined by the venerable Senator. Not content with government operation of Tennessee river dams for nitrate production, he insisted on expanding the program to a vast experiment in regional reconstruction. The law of 18 May 1933 created the Tennessee Valley Authority, with power to acquire, construct, and operate dams in the Tennessee valley, manufacture nitrate and fertilizer, generate and sell electric power, inaugurate flood control, withdraw marginal lands from cultivation, develop the river for navigation, and in general ' advance the economic and social well-being of the people living in the said river basin.' Never before in our history had the general welfare clause of the Constitution been given such literal application.

The Tennessee valley embraces an area of some 40,000 square miles in seven states; a natural geographical unit, it presented a tempting challenge to long-range economic and social planning. It was a region rich in natural resources which were rapidly being exhausted, and in water power which was going to waste. Once the Promised Land, it had been cruelly exploited and neglected and ravaged; its soil was depleted, its once beautiful forests heedlessly cut or destroyed by fire; its people living in primitive economy, scratching a precarious living from the soil. Could all this be changed? Could the intelligence of science and the resources of government combine to restore the natural richness of the region and to rehabilitate its people? Certainly the experiment of government operation of power plants, regulation of agriculture, preservation of water resources, co-operation with industry, might be expected to throw some light on the problem of a planned economy. Success would point to an extension of the experiment, failure a return to rugged individualism.

To direct the destinies of the new agency the President appointed Arthur Morgan, president of Antioch College and an engineer with a long record of idealism and reform and with a predilection for a planned society. To balance him on the three-man commission were Harcourt Morgan, President of the University of Tennessee and a practical agriculturalist, and the brilliant young David Lilienthal, chairman, at 36, of the Wisconsin Public Service Commission. The directors, interpreting the act as giving them broad authority to provide a new deal for the people of the valley, undertook to make the project a laboratory for social and economic experiment, and for an experiment, too, in the regeneration of local government. They acquired or constructed in the course of time some 25 dams for flood control, nitrate production, and the generation of electric power; to these they eventually added a series of steam generator plants. Altogether the government built some 5000 miles of transmission lines, and sold surplus power to nearby communities at rates low enough to ensure widespread consumption, and a subsidiary of the TVA promoted this scheme by financing rural electrification. In 1932 only two farms out of one hundred in the valley were electrified; five years later the proportion was one out of seven, and by 1960 electrification was well-nigh complete.

As an agency to foster 'an orderly and proper physical, economic, and social development' of the valley, the TVA withdrew marginal lands from cultivation, resettled marginal farmers, promoted public health and recreational facilities, encouraged local industry and in a general way 'used the facilities of the controlled river to release the energies of the people.' All this was done in close co-operation with the people of the valley, for the TVA was from the beginning dedicated to the principle of decentralized administration. The program was successful beyond the expectations of its sponsors. Within a few years millions of abandoned acres were returned to cultivation, forests grew in burnt-over land, industry returned to the valley, vacationers crowded its artificial lakes, and the river, navigable now over its entire length from Knoxville to the Ohio river, became one of the busiest streams in the country. The valley itself became a kind of model which attracted the attention and emulation of the whole world.

The Tennessee Valley Authority was the most notable of several such experiments in the generation of hydroelectric power in regional rehabilitation. Almost as important for the future was the ambitious program for the Columbia river basin. In 1933 the government began construction work on the Grand Coulee Dam, some 90 miles west of Spokane, and in 1937 on the Bonneville Dam on the lower Columbia. These were expected to develop some 2.5 million kilowatts of electric power, and to make possible the irrigation and reclamation of over a million acres of farm land.

Government competition with private power companies and the use of the 'yardstick' to determine fair rates inspired acrimonious criticism and challenge. Wendell Willkie, president of the Commonwealth and Southern, a great holding company, was the most prominent and effective of critics. TVA was attacked on economic grounds as a threat to the $12 billion invested in private utilities; on social grounds as tending to undermine private initiative and enterprise; and on legal grounds as an exercise of unauthorized power. The first two issues were fought out in the arena of public opinion and politics, and in both arenas the government policy was endorsed. The third came before the Supreme Court for adjudication. In a notable decision of 17 February 1936 the Court, with only McReynolds dissenting, sustained the government on every major point.[12]

The TVA presented one form of approach to the utilities problem. A more direct and positive control was provided in the Wheeler-Rayburn Act of 26 August 1935. This law authorized the Federal Water Power Commission to regulate the production, transmission, and sale of electric power in interstate commerce, and the Federal Trade Commission to exercise the same authority over gas. In its original form the act contained a ' death sentence ' provision designed to separate holding companies from their subsidiaries; this provision was defeated by a powerful lobby, but the act as finally passed authorized the commission to dissolve all holding companies contrary to the public interest.

8. RELIEF AND SECURITY

The most urgent problem facing the administration was that of relief for the 12 million to 15 million unemployed victims of the depression. Roosevelt had promised during his campaign that no one should starve, but millions of Americans were perilously near starvation, and the resources of state and local governments and of private charities were well-nigh exhausted. The emergency was clearly one that called for the energetic intervention of the Federal Government. What form that intervention should take was a matter of dispute. Outright relief had the advantages of economy and efficiency; work relief, on the other hand, promised to maintain morale, repair and improve the economic plant, and facilitate the transfer of workers to private industry. Relief, however, no matter how generously contributed or how intelligently directed, offered no solution to the problem of unemployment nor guarantee of security, and from the beginning President Roosevelt took the position that it must be succeeded by a permanent program of security.

In a message to Congress in mid-March he proposed three types of relief: the enrollment of workers by the Federal Government for public employment; grants to the states for relief work; and a broad program of public works. Congress adopted all three. The first step

12 *Ashwander v. Tennessee Valley Authority* 297 U.S. 288.

in emergency relief was the creation of the Civilian Conservation Corps. In May Congress adopted the second proposal by setting up the Federal Emergency Relief Administration to make grants to state and local governments to get public projects under way; where necessary the FERA made direct grants to the needy. To administer the new agency Roosevelt 'borrowed' the experienced social-work administrator, Harry Hopkins, from Governor Lehman of New York. In the two years of its existence the FERA disbursed $4 billion for relief purposes, three-fourths from federal and one-fourth from local funds.

The third major program of relief was provided by two agencies whose functions, like their names, overlapped: the Public Works Administration and the Works Progress Administration. The NRA of June 1933 had authorized a comprehensive system of public works embracing the construction of highways and parks, river and harbor improvement, slum clearance, and similar projects. Under the terms of this act a Public Works Administration was set up to co-ordinate the whole system of relief work. Under the leadership of Secretary Harold Ickes it eventually set some 4 million men to work on a great variety of construction — and some clerical — projects, at wages adjusted to prevailing rates in local communities. The PWA engaged in such diverse enterprises as the construction of schools, flood control, the rebuilding of aircraft carriers and submarines, and the construction of army posts. It gave Kansas City a municipal auditorium, Denver a new water-supply system, and the state of Washington a set of university buildings. In the six years of its existence it helped build two-thirds of all new school buildings in the nation, and one-third of the new hospitals. In addition to this, the government contributed direct relief to victims of drought and floods, and set up a U.S. Employment Service to co-ordinate state employment facilities.

In January 1935 President Roosevelt proposed that a distinction be made between employables and unemployables, that new and more satisfactory provision be made for the former, and that the burden of supporting the latter be transferred to state and local authorities. In accordance with these suggestions, Congress created a Works Progress Administration, and appropriated $4880 million to be expended for relief, loans and grants on non-federal projects, reforestation, flood-control, housing and slum clearance, public health, rural electrification, and education. The purposes of the new program were to stimulate private business by 'pump-priming' and to inaugurate reforms that states were unable to subsidize. The responsibility for carrying through this immense enterprise was assigned to the dynamic Harry Hopkins, whose influence with the President was growing apace. Inevitably it was attended with confusion and waste: administrative costs were high, construction was often shoddy, some of the projects were ridiculous, and politics influenced the hiring of some workers. Yet what is most impressive is the scope and variety of the projects actually carried through. By 1943 when the WPA terminated its activities, it had given work to over 8 million unemployed, and spent $11 billion on a bewildering variety of projects. These included 600,000 miles of highways, 125,000 public buildings, 8000 parks, 850 airport landing fields, and thousands of hospitals, municipal power plants, and school buildings.

Particularly novel were federal arts, writers', and theater programs. Unemployed writers prepared state, regional, and city guides, organized state and local archives, indexed newspaper files, and undertook useful sociological and historical investigations. Artists decorated hundreds of post offices, schools, and other public buildings with mural paintings. Unemployed musicians organized symphony orchestras and community singing, and brought music to communities where it had been known only through the radio, while scores of stock companies toured the country with repertories of old and new plays.

The depression hit the middle class, too, and millions of families who had borrowed money to build or buy houses found themselves unable to keep up mortgage payments or finance necessary repairs. The Home Owners' Loan Corporation which refinanced mortgages at low rates of interest came to the rescue of over a million home owners. A Federal Housing Administration assumed the risk of insuring existing mortgages. By 1940 it had covered over $4 billion in mortgages. And in 1937 Congress created the U.S. Housing Authority to assist local communities in slum clearance and the construction of low-cost housing. This program was fought bitterly by the real estate interests, and by 1941 only 120,000 family dwelling units, designed for the lower-income groups, had been completed. Then war put an end to further construction and the housing shortage remained to plague the next generation.

The chief obstacle to the indefinite continuation of these relief projects was the expense. Altogether in the three fiscal years of 1934, 1935, and 1936 the Federal Government appropriated $8681 million for relief and public works. This sum represented, to be sure, merely one-third the cost of World War I, and Roosevelt had promised, in his inaugural address, to ' treat the task as we would treat the emergency of a war '; yet it was generally supposed that the American people could not afford an indefinite continuation of such expenditures. No popular supposition was more speedily or more conclusively disproved.

As early as 1934 the President had called for a broad program of old-age and unemployment insurance. ' There is no reason,' he said to Secretary Frances Perkins, ' why every child from the day he is born, shouldn't be a member of the social security . . . cradle to grave — they ought to be in a social insurance system.' Investigations conducted by his Committee on Economic Security and hearings before House and Senate committees indicated the urgent nature of the problem. Between 1920 and 1936 population had increased by approximately 20 per cent; in the same period the number of industrial jobs had declined by 25 per cent. At the same time the increase in life expectancy and the decline in the birth rate resulted in a disproportionate rise in the number of persons over 65 years of age. But industry was unwilling to employ men of advanced years; investigations of several hundred industrial establishments revealed that few of them hired workers over 50 years of age, and the situation in professional and white-collar establishments was much the same. The conclusion was inescapable that the aged would, in the future, constitute an ever-growing burden on the community. That burden was, indeed, already a present one. In 1937 the Social Security Board reported that ' one-fifth of the aged in the United States were receiving old-age assistance, emergency relief, institutional care, employment under a works program, or some other form of aid from public or private funds; two-fifths to one-half were dependent on friends and relatives. . . . Approximately three out of four persons 65 or over were probably wholly or partially dependent on others for support.'

Beginning in 1929 a number of states passed old-age pension laws, and by 1934 twenty-eight states provided old-age pensions to some 180,000 beneficiaries over 65. Despite the efforts of Mr. Roosevelt, when Governor of New York, to bring other states into a joint system of unemployment insurance, only Ohio and Wisconsin had such legislation. It was clear that old-age and unemployment insurance placed an unequal burden upon those states which adopted and gave an unfair advantage to those states which rejected such a program. Pressure was also exerted by advocates of the so-called Townsend Plan of old-age pensions and the Lundeen Plan of unemployment compensation. The first, concocted by Dr. Francis Townsend of California, provided for monthly payments of $200 to all persons over 60 years of age, on the sole provision that they retire from work and spend the money; it was championed by Townsend Clubs claiming close to a million members. The second, sponsored by Farmer-Labor Congressman Ernest Lundeen of Minnesota, called for payments at prevailing wages of all unemployed workers; supported chiefly by Communists and radical labor leaders, its distinguishing feature was that under its terms relief would be administered not by the government but by commissions of workers and farmers' organizations. Each would have cost the national treasury not far from $10 billion annually — approximately one-fourth the total national income during the depression years! There was never the remotest chance that either would pass Congress, but pressure for such legislation made moderate social security legislation appear conservative.

The President had first proposed social security legislation to the Congress in June 1934, but so complex were the issues and so heated the debate between those who supported the 'Wisconsin' plan of state administration and those who preferred national coverage and administration, that the final bill did not pass until 14 August 1935. This memorable act was a kind of omnibus bill providing for pensions to needy aged, old-age insurance, unemployment insurance, benefit payments to the blind, dependent mothers and children, and crippled children, and extensive appropriations for public health work. Pensions of not more than $15 a month were to be extended to indigent persons over 65 on the understanding that co-operating states would contribute a like amount. The system of old-age insurance provided benefits to participants in accordance with a complicated system of graduated premiums paid by both employer and employee. The unemployment insurance plan was designed to persuade the states to establish systems of unemployment insurance; to this end it required payments by employers of a percentage of their payroll for insurance purposes, but provided that 90 per cent of the federal levy should be returned to states whose insurance plans conformed to standards approved by a Social Security Board. In addition the act appropriated to the states $25 million for aid to dependent children and called for annual appropriations of $25 million for maternal and child health service, crippled children, the blind, state and local public health service, and vocational rehabilitation.

Few other pieces of New Deal legislation inspired such misgivings among the conservatives. It was, said the otherwise judicious Representative Wadsworth of New York, ' a power so vast, so powerful, as to threaten the integrity of our institutions and to pull the pillars of the temple down upon the heads of our descendants.' A quarter of a century later a Republican President was to boast to those descendants that he had extended social security coverage to 2 million Americans.

In the course of the next two years every state set up old-age pensions and unemployment insurance systems that met the requirements fixed by the Social Security Board. Inevitably the Social Security Act was challenged on constitutional grounds, and conflicting opinions in inferior federal courts created uncertainty as to the effectiveness of the law. In a series of notable decisions handed down on 24 May 1937,[13] the Supreme Court sustained all the crucial provisions of the act, and announced a concept of national welfare so broad that it constituted, in theory if not in effect, a reversal of many of the conservative decisions of the early New Deal period and a return to the Marshall interpretation of the Constitution. Thus Justice Cardozo, sustaining the unemployment insurance provisions of the Security Act, observed of unemployment that,

The states were unable to give the requisite relief. The problem had become national in area and dimensions. There was need of help if the people were not to starve. It is too late today for the argument to be heard with tolerance that in a crisis so extreme the use of the moneys of the nation to relieve the unemployed and their dependents is a use for any purpose narrower than the promotion of the general welfare.

Such an interpretation of the Constitution, had it been adopted earlier, might have sustained the AAA and Railway Pension legislation. Not the least significant aspect of the Social Security legislation was that it discovered a method of implementing nationalism.

For Bibliography for this chapter see the Bibliography at the end of Chapter XXVI, page 750.

---

[13] *Carmichael et al. v. Southern Coal & Coke Co.* 301 U.S. 495; *Charles C. Steward Machine Co. v. Davis* 301 U.S. 548; *Helvering et al. v. Davis* 301 U.S. 619.

Domestic Issues of the Second Administration

1. THE ELECTION OF 1936

THE congressional elections of 1934 strengthened the Democratic control of Congress and dramatized the popularity of the New Deal. Yet as the presidential election approached, signs of discontent multiplied; and as prosperity in some measure returned, business-men became increasingly critical. The charges against President Roosevelt and the New Deal were numerous, varied, and urgent. Conservatives asserted that the President was destroying the ' American system ' of individualism, undermining enterprise, and insinuating socialism, if not communism, into American economy. His policies, it was urged, had discouraged rather than encouraged recovery; there were still millions of unemployed and, despite extravagant government expenditures, the number was not being appreciably reduced. High taxes shackled industry, critics asserted, the Securities Act prevented new stock flotations; the TVA would ruin the private utility business, the Home Owners' Loan Corporation undermine mortgage investments, the Wagner Act foment labor disorders, the monetary policy impede the recovery of foreign trade, and the reciprocity treaties injure the farmer. The President, it was alleged, had ignored the platform and flouted campaign promises. The platform had committed the party to ' sound money ' and the party had promptly taken the nation off the gold standard and repudiated financial obligations; it had promised reduction in government expenses, and expenses had increased with every fiscal year. Money had been thrown away on relief, millions of men had been encouraged in idleness, a monstrous bureaucracy had developed, taxes had mounted, and the national debt had reached the staggering sum of $35 billion. The Constitution, it was said, had been betrayed, and there was the authority of the Supreme Court to prove that much of the new legislation was unconstitutional. The Bill of Rights had been violated, the jurisdiction of the states ruthlessly invaded, and the federal system shattered! The President was reaching toward dictatorship, Congress was a rubber stamp, the independence of the judiciary was threatened, and the tripartite division of the government ignored! The billions poured out for relief purposes constituted a party slush fund, and Postmaster-General Farley had introduced Tammany methods into the national government!

Much of this criticism emanated from members of the Democratic party. The President's former friend Alfred E. Smith led a small but distinguished procession of Democrats including John W. Davis, presidential candidate in 1924, and Bainbridge Colby, Secretary of State under Wilson, in ' taking a walk ' away from the Democratic camp. These men appealed to the party to preserve the traditional faith, and when their appeal was ignored, organized the ' Jeffersonian Democrats.'

Potentially far more serious was thunder on the extreme left which — as it turned out — was almost indistinguishable from the extreme right, just as Communism and Fascism were almost indistinguishable abroad. By 1936 Dr. Townsend broke irretrievably with Roosevelt and, boasting a following of twenty million, threatened to organize his own party. Discredited by a congressional investigation of his organization he struck a strange alliance with the equally discredited Gerald K. Smith, hatemonger extraordinary and putative successor to Huey Long. The third figure in this triumvirate was Father Coughlin, the rabble-rousing radio priest of Detroit who had, or claimed to have, a nation-wide following and who decided, now, to back North Dakota's William Lemke for the presidency on a Union party ticket. Had the effervescent Huey Long lived he might have welded these three dissident groups into the semblance of a party. After all they shared a common hatred of Roosevelt, bankers, and Harvard University, and a common zeal for a more equal distribution of the wealth. But neither Townsend nor Smith nor Father Coughlin could impose any kind of discipline on the inherent anarchy of their followers, and nothing but an uneasy coalition emerged — a coalition without either party or candidates. In the end even the coalition crumbled, and all three of its leaders were discredited.

Throughout 1936 criticism mounted, becoming shriller every day.

The din and clamor pouring from hundreds of radio stations and thousands of platforms seemed impressive, and some Republicans went so far as to prophesy defeat for the New Deal. It was incumbent upon the Republicans to find a candidate satisfactory alike to liberals and conservatives, and in Alfred M. Landon, Governor of Kansas, they thought they had found one. He was in the oil business, yet appeared to understand the farm problem; he had followed Theodore Roosevelt in 1912, but had returned with him to the ' G.O.P. '; he was thrifty, ' folksy '; in a word, a Midwestern ' Cal ' Coolidge. When the Republican convention met, Landon was nominated on the first ballot, and on a platform which asserted that

America is in peril. The welfare of American men and women and the future of our youth are at stake. We dedicate ourselves to the preservation of their political liberty, their individual opportunity and their character as free citizens, which today for the first time are threatened by the government itself.

The platform, however, promised to do all the things the Democrats had done, but in a different spirit and without violation of the Constitution or destruction of the ' American system of free enterprise, private competition, and equality of opportunity.' The party pledged itself to speed up employment, maintain relief, obtain old-age security, foster agriculture, destroy monopolies, regulate business, protect the civil service, and preserve a ' sound currency '; it would at the same time reduce expenditures, balance the budget, and free business from New Deal trammels. It was not to be expected that the platform should be more specific than this, but the nominee, in his speeches, was equally positive about the program and equally vague about the methods by which these apparently contradictory ends were to be achieved.

The Democrats met in a jubilant mood. The convention dispensed with the hundred-year-old two-thirds rule, renominated Franklin D. Roosevelt by acclamation, endorsed the entire New Deal program, and promised its continuation and expansion, through legislative action if possible, through constitutional amendment if necessary. It declared:

The Republican platform proposes to meet many pressing national problems solely by action of the separate States. We know that drought, dust storms, floods, minimum wages, maximum hours, child labor and working conditions in industry, monopolistic and unfair business practices cannot be adequately handled exclusively by forty-eight separate State legislatures, forty-eight separate States administrations and forty-eight separate State courts. Transactions and activities which inevitably overflow State boundaries call for both State and Federal treatment.

Though the campaign was heated, its outcome was a foregone conclusion. Governor Landon showed himself lacking in political finesse and personal magnetism; Roosevelt again revealed consummate skill in his appeal to public opinion. Most newspapers of the country supported Landon, as did a large proportion of professional and academic groups, and almost all businesses. So energetic was the Republican attack upon the New Deal that when 'straw votes' conducted by the *Literary Digest* and the Hearst press predicted Landon's election, many were inclined to doubt the evidence of their senses and accept the prophecy. Mr. Farley, unimpressed by these straw votes, predicted that Roosevelt would carry every state but two. His prediction was fulfilled. In the greatest landslide in American political history, Roosevelt polled a popular majority of ten million votes and carried every state but Maine and Vermont. Democratic victory in state and congressional elections was equally overwhelming.

2. COURT REFORM AND CONSTITUTIONAL REVOLUTION

No more impressive vote of confidence [1] had ever been given a candidate; his mandate to continue policies already inaugurated was unmistakable. In the last speech of the campaign the President declared ' we have just begun to fight,' and when Congress met in January 1937, he presented it with a series of far-reaching proposals designed to complete the structure of the New Deal: bills on farm tenancy, wages and hours of labor, housing, taxation, and hydro-electric development, together with a plan for sweeping administrative reorganization. Weakened but not chastened, the Republican minority was unable to offer effective opposition to these proposals. The elephant then lifted his eyes to the Supreme Court.

For the Republicans had ' retired into the judiciary as a stronghold, and from that battery all the works of republicanism were to be beaten down and erased.' So Jefferson had said of the Federalists over a century earlier, and his successor in the White House had rea-

[1] Harding actually polled a larger percentage of the vote in 1920, but the Harding vote was not a vote of confidence in him, but a vote of no-confidence in the Democrats.

son to echo the bitter charge. Never before had the Supreme Court worked such havoc with a legislative program as it did in 1935 and 1936 with that of the New Deal nor in so short a time invalidated so many acts of Congress. It overthrew the NRA on the novel ground of improper delegation of power. It struck down the AAA through what a dissenting justice called a ' tortured construction of the Constitution,' which created a no-man's land where neither federal nor state power might be applied. It rejected the railroad retirement plan on the curious theory that there was no legitimate connection between interstate commerce and the welfare of those who conducted it, while the Bituminous Coal Act went into the judicial wastebasket because the Court insisted that coal mining was a purely local business. It invalidated congressional legislation to protect farm mortgages on the ground of conflict with the esoteric ' due process ' clause of the Fifth Amendment, and nullified the Municipal Bankruptcy Act on the assumption that such legislation invaded the domain of the states — even though the Act required state consent, which many states had already given. The Federal Government had long been denied the power to enact minimum-wage legislation; now a twilight zone of political impotence was conjured up by denying this power to the states as well. In the realm of administration the Court rejected the clear implications of the Myers decision and denied to the President power to remove a recalcitrant member of the Federal Trade Commission. Even in the two cases where the Court sustained the New Deal — the gold clause and the TVA cases — it did so on narrow grounds and with ill-grace.

Thus the highest court had undermined the legislative structure of the New Deal. And ' what was worse,' as Roosevelt insisted, ' the language and temper of the decisions indicated little hope for the future. Apparently Marshall's conception of our Constitution as a flexible instrument — adequate for all times and therefore able to adjust itself as the new needs of new generations arose — had been repudiated.' So it had and the prospect was a bleak one, for the 1935–36 decisions were so sweeping in character that they appeared to foreclose amendment of the objectionable legislation and to foredoom further legislation along liberal lines. The Court, in fact, had taken upon itself the responsibility of nullifying the electoral verdicts of 1932 and 1934 and of negating in advance any consequences of a comparable verdict in 1936.

What to do? The question was not a new one; it had confronted Jefferson, Jackson, Lincoln, and Theodore Roosevelt, and had commanded the attention of a long line of political thinkers from Taylor of Caroline to Borah of Idaho. Yet the most anxious study of the problem had not yielded a solution. Impeachment had failed, with the acquittal of Justice Chase in 1805; withdrawal of jurisdiction had been tried during Reconstruction and proved dangerous; proposals to require more than a mere majority of votes for the nullification of legislative acts or to permit Congress, by a two-thirds vote, to override such nullifications, were of dubious constitutionality; the process of constitutional amendment was slow and uncertain. In the past the judiciary had been brought to tardy acquiescence in majority will only by the uncertain process of new appointments.

Roosevelt had early announced his determination to find constitutional sanctions for what the nation required, and he had been confirmed in this determination by the spectacle of democracies abroad yielding to dictatorship because ' too weak or too slow to fulfill the wants of their citizens.' Opportunistic in tactics, he confined himself to the immediate issues. ' I know,' he said, ' that the Constitution was not to blame, and that the Supreme Court as an institution was not to blame. The only trouble was with some of the human beings on the Court.' Seven of the nine members of the Court had been appointed by Republican predecessors, and although six of the judges were over seventy years of age Mr. Roosevelt had not yet been able to make a single appointment, and in Justices McReynolds, Van Devanter, Sutherland, and Butler there was a solid nucleus of the Court which appeared to think that the Fifth and Fourteenth Amendments had ' enacted Herbert Spencer's *Social Statics*,' in fact done just what Justice Holmes once denied.[2]

If the trouble was merely in the weakness of the Court, that could be remedied by appointing new members. So at least Roosevelt thought, and this was the crucial part of the proposal for the reform of the federal judiciary which he submitted to a startled Congress on 5 February 1937.

In the proposed bill the ' addition of younger blood ' was to be obtained by the appointment of one new judge, up to a maximum of

---

[2] Dissenting opinion in *Lochner v. New York* 198 U.S. 45: ' The Fourteenth Amendment does not enact Mr. Herbert Spencer's Social Statics.'

six, for every justice of the Supreme Court who, having passed the age of seventy and served for ten years, failed to retire.

The proposal was simplicity itself, and on this score, at least, had much to commend it. It fixed upon seventy as the logical retirement age, and if the examples of Holmes and Brandeis made this age seem premature, the rules in effect in the civil service, the army and navy, universities, hospitals, and similar institutions, suggested that it was not unreasonable. The presidential proposal did not compel retirement at seventy, but merely provided an additional judge for every incumbent over seventy; if the incumbent wished to avoid an enlarged court he had the alternative of resigning, at full pay. The bill raised no constitutional question, for the power of Congress to control membership was clear. Nor was its method without precedent; the number of judges had been changed six times in the past.

Nevertheless, the proposal was greeted with cries of alarm and dismay. It was denounced as a plan to ' pack ' the Supreme Court; as an attack on the independence of the judiciary; as the end of constitutional government in the United States. Conservatives rejoiced that they could now identify opposition to presidential policies with the defense of the Constitution; Southern Bourbons, long restless under the New Deal lash, found here an opportunity for opposition that had a powerful emotional appeal. Liberals like Senators Wheeler, Borah, and Johnson, who had long held something of a monopoly on criticism of the highest court, ranged themselves on the side of judicial supremacy, and it was clear that hostility to the President was making strange bedfellows.

Throughout the spring and summer of 1937 as the debate went on, it became clear that the tide of public opinion was rising against the presidential proposal. Yet in the end it was not logic that brought about the defeat of the bill, but rather the strategic retreat of the Court itself. For even as the bill was under consideration, and before there had been any change in its membership, the Court found ways of making the constitutional sun shine on legislation which had heretofore been under a judicial cloud. Nine months after the Court had struck down the New York minimum-wage law, it sustained a similar act of the state of Washington. On the same day it approved a revised farm-mortgage act and a new Railway Labor Act. A few weeks later came five decisions, all upholding various provisions of the National Labor Relations Act which a committee of sixty distinguished lawyers had advised their clients to disregard as incontestably unconstitutional. A month later, and the controversial Social Security legislation was vouchsafed judicial blessing. In vain did a consistent, if stubborn, minority argue that these decisions were reversals of those recently announced. The new majority, made possible by a timely switch by Justice Roberts, was determined to be liberal!

Convinced, now, that reform had already been achieved and confident that public opinion would not support the presidential plan, the Senate Judiciary Committee voted 10–8 to reject it, and the bill went no further. The President, at the height of his power and his popularity, had suffered a stinging rebuke.

Although Roosevelt lost this battle, he won the campaign. And so too, oddly enough, did the Court. Even while the Court debate was under way, Justice Van Devanter announced his retirement, and his example was shortly followed by Sutherland and Butler as well as the revered Brandeis, intellectual godfather of so much of the New Deal. Within a few years, the Court was entirely remade. To fill vacancies created by retirement and death President Roosevelt appointed Hugo Black of Alabama, distinguished for his fight against the power trust; Stanley Reed of Kentucky, former solicitor-general; Felix Frankfurter of the Harvard Law School, teacher of a generation of social-minded lawyers and jurists; William Douglas of the Yale Law School and the Securities and Exchange Commission; Attorney-General Robert Jackson of New York; and Frank Murphy, former governor of Michigan and Governor-General of the Philippine Islands; while the talents and tolerance of Mr. Justice Stone were recognized by his elevation to the chief justiceship.

This new court hastened to retreat from the untenable constitutional positions seized by its predecessor, back to the tradition of Marshall, Story, Taft, and Holmes. There was a quick return to that broad interpretation of the commerce and the tax clauses which had made possible the adaptation of the Constitution to the varied needs of national growth, and to that judicial continence, best exemplified in Holmes, which preserved the equality and independence of the three departments and the dependence of all three upon the Constitution.

The unrealistic limitation on the commerce power written into the Constitution by *Hammer v. Dagenhart* was repudiated and a series of decisions interpreting the Wagner Labor Act and the Fair

Labor Standards Act finally nullified the curious divorce of commerce from manufacturing affirmed in the Schechter and Guffey coal cases. Another series of decisions, in 1939, swept away any lingering doubts about the power of the Federal Government to regulate agricultural production through marketing agreements. The limitation imposed upon congressional spending power by the Butler decision was withdrawn; uncertainties about federal control over navigable rivers and water power, conjured up in the TVA decision, were abandoned and the right of the Federal Government to regulate even potentially navigable streams and to exercise general jurisdiction over the development of hydroelectric power re-established.

The judicial fiction of ' liberty of contract ' endorsed in the Adkins case went by the board. The judicial amendment of the ' rule of reason ' to the Sherman anti-trust law was, in effect, repealed, and the complicated doctrine of ' fair value ' formulated in *Smythe v. Ames* abandoned as useless or misleading. Limitations on federal regulation of primary elections were dissipated, and congressional authority over the whole process of federal elections was established. In the Phelps-Dodge case the court held that those earlier monuments to judicial conservatism respecting labor legislation, *Adair v. United States* and *Coppage v. Kansas,* were ' completely sapped of their authority,' while the Hutcheson decision announced that the prohibitions on the use of the injunction in labor disputes provided for by the Clayton and the Norris-La Guardia Acts should be interpreted to mean what they said. Congressional authority to enact bankruptcy legislation, presumably fixed by the clear terms of the Constitution but denied in two recent decisions, was restored; congressional jurisdiction over the business of employment agencies, heretofore seriously circumscribed, was enlarged. *Collector v. Day* and its successors, which had long served to create fields of reciprocal tax immunity, gave way to realism in the realm of taxation, and both state and federal governments were permitted to tax each other's employees where such taxation did not impose an improper burden upon any governmental function.

Nor were all the new decisions in the direction of the enlargement of federal powers. The Court took a sympathetic attitude toward the exercise of state police power, while in the complex and controversial domain of taxation, it acquiesced in the search for new sources of revenue through discriminatory taxation of the business of out-of-state corporations. And, finally, *Swift v. Tyson,* which for a century had permitted the federal courts to disregard decisions of the state courts on matters of state law, was formally pronounced mistaken.

Within a few years the Supreme Court had carried through a constitutional revolution, but it was a conservative revolution, inspired by respect not only for the great traditions of constitutional interpretation but for the other two co-equal departments of the government. None who observed the functions of the government and the character of the commonwealth after ridding the Constitution of the judicial gloss of recent years could doubt that democratic government under law had met and surmounted one of its most crucial tests.

3. NEW DEAL FINANCES AND THE RECESSION OF 1937

All through the 'twenties the government had enjoyed a revenue surplus; after 1929 this turned into a deficit, and in 1932 the deficit reached what then seemed the staggering sum of almost $3 billion. Roosevelt came to office committed to a program of government retrenchment and a balanced budget. He tried this, briefly, but the political and economic repercussions were so unfavorable that he gave it up, and thereafter accepted a high level of government spending and an unbalanced budget as an unpleasant necessity. All through the New Deal years expenses exceeded income, and the national debt mounted. By 1936 there was a deficit of $4 billion; the gap closed a bit in 1937 and 1938, then widened once more to $4 billion by 1940. This meant of course a steady augmentation of the national debt which soared from $22 billion when Roosevelt first took office to almost $36 billion at the beginning of his second term, and by 1940 to an unprecedented $42 billion. All this staggered a generation brought up on Micawber's simple prescription for happiness, yet five years later that same generation accepted a debt of $258 billion without visible perturbation.

The crucial problem, as Roosevelt saw it, was low prices and low wages, and the solution consisted simply in raising prices: then farmers and workingmen could start buying again, investors would come back into the market, business would flourish, and money would once more flow into the coffers of the government. As government economies clearly did not achieve these ends, Roosevelt tried three other devices long familiar from the days of the Greenbackers and the Populists: devaluation of the dollar; an increase in the circulating medium; and large-scale government spending. As we have seen Roosevelt cut the gold content of the dollar until it was worth only 59 cents; at the same time government spending policies and more liberal Federal Reserve credit pumped more money into circulation: in 1930 circulation was $37 per capita, by 1940 it was $59.[3] As Roosevelt himself put it:

Following 1933 the fiscal policy of the Government was more realistically adapted to the needs of the people. All about were idle men, idle factories, and idle funds, and yet the people were in desperate need of more goods than they had the purchasing power to acquire. The Government deliberately set itself to correct these conditions by borrowing funds to put idle men and idle factories to work.

These measures, together with heavy spending for public works and relief, seemed to do the job. Farm prices increased, in four years, by 86 per cent; industrial production was up by 77 per cent; and dividends mounted by a comfortable 90 per cent. In 1937 the President was persuaded that he could safely return to more conservative fiscal policies, and he even entertained himself with the mirage of a balanced budget. The Federal Reserve Board contracted credit, and government spending was radically slashed. The reaction of the economy was convulsive. Farm prices dropped, unemployment soared, government revenues took a tailspin, and within months a full-scale recession was under way.

Always quick to learn lessons of political expediency, Roosevelt promptly dropped his brief flirtation with conservative economics, and called a special session of Congress to cope with the problems of the recession. The Federal Reserve Board eased credit, government spending was increased by almost $2 billion, and the administration pushed through a series of measures designed to stimulate the economy — large-scale farm relief, minimum wages and maximum hours legislation, and $3 billion more for a vast public works program. The economy rebounded, and by mid-summer of 1938 recovery was once more in full swing. Thereafter war orders from abroad and at home poured in on American factories, unemployment fell rapidly, and the economy righted itself.

All this was later to be interpreted as a vindication of the teachings

[3] And in 1945 it was $191, with no untoward results.

of the distinguished English economist, John Maynard Keynes, of Cambridge University; and in a sense it was. Keynes argued that in time of depression a government should not economize, but spend, and that a large-scale public works program was the key to recovery: every man employed on government works would provide employment for two men in private industry. Keynes had many friends and disciples in the United States, but there is no evidence that Roosevelt was directly influenced by his teachings, or that he was familiar with the magisterial *General Theory of Employment, Interest and Money* in which the Cambridge economist set forth his economic philosophy. It is far more probable that in his fiscal thinking Roosevelt was influenced by a school of American economists: Irving Fisher of Yale University, who had long championed the ' commodity dollar '; George Warren of Cornell University, whose book *Prices* argued the necessity of devaluing gold; and a group of University of Chicago professors including Paul Douglas — later Senator from Illinois — who in 1933 published an appeal for deficit spending as the cure for the depression.

4. FARM AND LABOR LEGISLATION

The long and acrimonious debate on judicial reform had sidetracked consideration of many of the measures which the President had recommended to Congress at the beginning of his second administration. Of these perhaps the most urgent and certainly the most clamorous was the farm problem. The Agricultural Act of 1933 had been voided by the Court, and the Soil Conservation Act of 1936 was admittedly only a stopgap until farm representatives and congressional leaders could formulate a comprehensive program that would meet judicial approval. The first step in that program was the Bankhead Farm Tenant Act of July 1937. It set up a Farm Security Administration to make loans to tenant farmers and sharecroppers eager to own their own farms; built camps for the migratory farm workers whose unhappy lot was so movingly depicted in *The Grapes of Wrath;* subsidized co-operative homestead communities; and came to the relief of underprivileged farm groups in many other ways. The next year came a more comprehensive measure to replace the judicially slaughtered act of 1933. The Agricultural Adjustment Act of February 1938 had five principal features. It authorized the Secretary

of Agriculture, with the approval of two-thirds of the farmers involved, to fix the acreage to be planted in crops and establish marketing control of surplus crops; set up a system of ' parity payments ' to
producers who agreed to limit their crops; continued conservation
payments to farmers who planted within certain acreage allotments
and practiced soil conservation; made available commodity loans on
surplus crops and set up storage facilities to ensure an ' ever normal
granary ' — a provision that went right back to the Populist platform
of the 1890's; and provided federal insurance on wheat. Although the
result of this ambitious attack upon the problem of farm surpluses
was at first disappointing, the program came to command the approval of the vast majority of the farmers involved, which is not surprising when one views the results. The Secretary of Agriculture reported that between 1932 and 1939 cash income from wheat had
doubled, and income from corn and cotton had increased fourfold.

Meantime the administration moved vigorously to deal with the
recession on the labor front. A new Bituminious Coal Act replaced
the outlawed Guffey Bill, and stood the test of judicial scrutiny. The
Wagner-Steagall Act created a Federal Housing Authority to finance
slum clearance and construct low-cost housing; if the quantitative
results were disappointing — for somehow slums grew faster than
they could be torn down — it was at least important to establish the
principle that the Federal Government has an obligation here as in
other areas of public welfare. These measures were designed to
' prime the pump ' of private business; so, too, to expand the WPA
rolls by $3 million; to increase Reconstruction Finance Corpora-
tion loans to business; and to initiate the ' desterilization ' of more
than $3 billion in gold that the Treasury had ' captured ' when the
dollar was devalued.

The problem of wages and hours remained — a problem affecting
the health of the whole economy. The invalidation of the NRA had
removed all semblance of federal control over hours and wages, and
the recession further threatened the gains which labor had made
since the advent of the New Deal. The year 1937 was one of widespread industrial disorder and of declining wages. The efforts of
the newly organized C.I.O. to organize the heretofore invulnerable
steel, automobile, and textile industries met with bitter opposition.
Industrial unionism — and especially the new weapon of the sit-
down strike — evoked charges of radicalism and Communism from

management. In Pennsylvania and Ohio the militia was employed to break strikes, at the River Rouge plant of the Ford Company near Detroit vigilante organizations beat up labor organizers, and at the Republic Steel works in South Chicago striking steel workers were killed by police in the Memorial Day massacre. Altogether 1937 witnessed a total of almost 5000 strikes, involving some 2 million workers.

In July 1937 the Senate passed a bill drawn by Senator Black of Alabama designed to put 'a ceiling over hours and a floor under wages.' The bitter opposition of Southern Democrats delayed enactment until June 1938. This Fair Labor Standards Act had as its objective the ' elimination of labor conditions detrimental to the maintenance of the minimum standards of living necessary for health, efficiency, and well being of workers.' It provided for an eventual maximum working week of 40 hours and an eventual minimum wage of 40 cents an hour for all employees engaged in or producing goods for interstate commerce. No less important was the prohibition of child labor in all industries engaged in producing goods for interstate commerce and the severe limitation on the labor of boys and girls between 16 and 18 in hazardous occupations.

Inevitably its constitutionality was challenged by those who relied upon the precedent of *Hammer v. Dagenhart,* but in a unanimous opinion the Supreme Court reversed the Dagenhart case and sustained the new law.[4]

Labor, meantime, was winning other victories in the courts scarcely less significant. The authority of the National Labor Relations Board sustained perhaps the most persistent and severe attack that had ever been directed against any of the New Deal agencies. Yet the record of the board was good. In the five years ending January 1941, it handled some 33,000 cases involving over 7 million workers and including some 22,000 charges of unfair labor practices and over 11,000 petitions to determine collective bargaining agencies. More than 10 per cent of all these cases were disposed of amicably, and of the 3166 strikes certified to the board, 2383 were settled peaceably. In the judicial arena, too, the success of the NLRB was little less than spectacular. In case after case its findings were sustained by the Supreme Court; the percentage of reversals was the smallest in the history of any of the independent commissions. Sus-

[4] *U.S. v. Darby Lumber Co.* 312 U.S. 100.

tained by these triumphs in the labor and the judicial arenas, the board successfully beat back all attempts to repeal its authority or curtail its powers and, by the beginning of the third Roosevelt administration, the opposition was silenced if not converted.

5. POLITICAL AND ADMINISTRATIVE REFORM

The history of the NLRB was symbolic of a development long in existence but not yet appreciated by the average citizen: the expansion of governmental functions and the burgeoning of administrative agencies. The number of civil servants in the employ of the Federal Government had increased from some 370,000 before World War I to over half a million during the Hoover administration. Under the New Deal, with the establishment of new boards and bureaus and the enlargement of old ones, the number rose from 583,000 in 1932 to 920,000 in 1939. Both the increase in governmental activity and in the number of civil servants had every appearance of permanence.[5]

This situation was regarded with misgivings by many whose thinking about government had been molded by the laissez faire philosophy. But with most people the older notion that that government was best which governed least had given way to a more realistic appreciation of government as the servant of the people and the instrument of national welfare. The ' necessary evil ' of Thomas Paine had become so necessary that it had ceased to be an evil. More and more Americans came to look to government to perform whatever individuals and groups were powerless to do for the control of national economy and the protection of society. Farmers looked to it to save them from the consequences of the vagaries of the weather or of the world market; the unemployed to provide them with jobs or relief; the old and infirm for security; distressed borrowers to save their homes; the middle class to guarantee bank deposits; investors to safeguard investment; workingmen to protect labor organizations and regulate wages and hours; teachers to keep the schools open; scholars to keep them in school; while the whole people took for granted that government would regulate business and transportation, develop water power, preserve the soil and the forest resources, and generally supervise most aspects of national life.

[5] As indeed it was; by 1940 the total had passed 1 million and by 1950 it passed 2 million.

Yet the government which had thus come to play so crucial a part in the life of the nation had developed in an opportunistic and haphazard fashion. Every student of government knew that the administrative machinery was inefficient and extravagant, while to the layman bureaucracy was synonymous with red tape. Scientific management, which had been applied to the business of large corporations, had never been tried out in this largest and most important of all businesses. Every President since Theodore Roosevelt had been aware of the problem and anxious for reform, but none had been able to achieve more than piecemeal improvement.

By almost any standards Roosevelt was a poor administrator. He did not work through channels, or a chain of command, but through any persons or methods that caught his fancy; his intellectual processes were not orderly but intuitive, and he liked to match his 'hunches' against the logic of his advisers. He allowed a thicket of overlapping and even conflicting bureaus and agencies to grow up almost in the White House grounds; he found it difficult to fire anyone, and those who had outlived their usefulness were often kicked upstairs to make further trouble. He liked to play his assistants off against each other; he had a pawky sense of humor; he was by turns confiding and secretive, generous and vindictive, clear cut and deliberately fuzzy. Yet in a larger sense he was wonderfully effective: he got things done. He made Washington so exciting that first-rate men left good jobs and came to work for him, and he inspired them with such loyalty that they worked far beyond the ordinary call of duty. Superficially less efficient than President Hoover, Roosevelt was in fact far more effective, and his presidency dramatized once again the vital principle that politics is neither a business nor a science, but an art.

Roosevelt was convinced that a thorough overhauling of the executive branch of the government was imperative, and in 1936 he appointed a Committee on Administrative Management to formulate plans for reform. Early the next year he laid their recommendations before Congress: a reorganization of the civil service and an extension of the merit system; the addition of two new departments of cabinet rank; the establishment of budget and efficiency agencies, and of a planning agency through which the President might coordinate executive functions; an increase in the White House staff; and the creation of an independent auditing system for the executive departments. These reforms, the President asserted, would ' increase efficiency, minimize error, duplication and waste, and raise the morale of the public service.'

The proposals were innocuous enough, but Congress, alarmed by the presidential ' attack ' on the Supreme Court, jealous of any enlargement of executive authority, and sensitive to the bogey of dictatorship, rejected them. The President, however, persisted, and in 1939 — after the Supreme Court issue had been settled and the congressional elections were safely out of the way — had the satisfaction of obtaining congressional approval for most of this program.

One important aspect of the problem remained — that concerned with the extension of the merit system and the divorce of administration from politics. Although the total number of federal employees covered by the merit system had increased steadily during the New Deal, the percentage had declined, and it was generally believed that many of the relief agencies had engaged in politics. To prevent any such exploitation of government employees or relief workers, Senator Hatch of New Mexico introduced and Congress passed two bills forbidding federal employees or state employees paid from federal funds to engage in ' pernicious political activities.' More specifically these bills made it unlawful for any officeholder to coerce or intimidate any voter, or ' to use his official authority or influence for the purpose of interfering with an election or affecting the result thereof.' Just what these esoteric words meant was not entirely clear, nor was their meaning clarified in the following decade.

If politics was to be divorced from spoils, it seemed logical that it should then be closely wedded to principles and issues. This, at any rate, was the view which the President announced with reference to the congressional elections of 1938. Exasperated by the persistent hostility of some reactionary Democrats to the New Deal program, and anxious that party labels should have meaning and that the Democratic party should be a liberal one, Roosevelt undertook what he thought was a vindication of political principles and what his critics called a ' purge.' Speaking — so he insisted — as party leader rather than as President, he appealed for the defeat of three conservatives in the Democratic primaries: George of Georgia, Tydings of Maryland, and O'Connor of New York. If parties really represented principles and if the Wilsonian theory of presidential responsibility as party leader was sound, the appeal was both logical and laudable. But

American politics are not governed by considerations of logic or principles of political philosophy, and critics were quick to stigmatize the presidential intervention as dictatorial and to appeal to state pride to defeat it. The appeal was successful, notably in Georgia and Maryland, where the ' purge ' was repudiated and George and Tydings triumphantly returned to the Senate. There was rejoicing among the Republicans, yet with the Democrats holding a majority of 262 to 169 in the House and 69 to 23 in the Senate, even the most credulous could not delude themselves that the President's popularity was seriously impaired.

6. The New Deal: An Evaluation

With the farm and labor legislation of 1938 the domestic reform program of the Roosevelt administration was rounded out. Much, to be sure, remained to be done, but what remained was in the nature of an extension and elaboration of policies already inaugurated rather than of new projects. Certainly by the close of the second Roosevelt administration the philosophical principles of the New Deal had been firmly established, the process of public education carried through, the political and administrative machinery set in effective motion, many essential economic and social reforms achieved, and prosperity largely restored. Much of the crusading fervor was gone, too. Some of the original crusaders, alarmed by the scope and the cost of the New Deal, had gone over to the opposition; some had grown tired, or dropped by the wayside; others were content with their accomplishments and more concerned to institutionalize them and preserve them than to extend them. There were internal fissures and internecine quarrels in the administration. Roosevelt himself had shifted his center of interest to foreign affairs. He was to win a third term in which to consummate his program, but that third term was concerned almost exclusively with war; in 1943 he formally bade goodbye to ' Dr. New Deal ' and embraced ' Dr. Win-the-War.' After all, the reform impulse had lasted six or seven years: longer than it had lasted under either Theodore Roosevelt or Woodrow Wilson! The end of the second administration thus furnishes an appropriate opportunity for an evaluation of the New Deal.

What, then, is the significance of the New Deal in our history, and what are its permanent contributions? First there is the physical rehabilitation of the country. A century from now this may well seem the most important single contribution on the domestic front. For generations Americans had been laying waste their natural resources without restoring them; earlier efforts to halt this process had been unsuccessful. The New Deal attack on this problem was both ambitious and thoroughgoing; it involved a frontal attack on soil erosion, the building of dams and the planting of trees to prevent flood, the reclamation of the grass lands of the Great Plains and of millions of acres of sub-marginal lands, the development of water-power resources, and the inauguration of vast regional reconstruction enterprises like the TVA and the Columbia river projects. All this changed the face of the country and restored to productive use much of the national domain.

Second, accomplishments in human rehabilitation: the establishment of the principle that government has responsibility for the health, welfare, and security, as well as for the protection and education of all its citizens. This principle was implicit in the New Freedom, but only with the New Deal did it receive general application in federal and state governmental activities. These embraced social security, public health, and housing, and entered the domain of agriculture and labor, and of the arts and sciences. Verbal and ceremonial opposition persisted for the next generation, but in fact the new principle was accepted by the Republican as well as the Democratic party after 1940, and it is difficult to imagine any serious challenge to this enlarged concept of general welfare.

Third, three major developments in the realm of politics and government. One of these was the strengthening of the executive branch and the reassertion of presidential leadership characteristic of every period of progressivism in our history: Roosevelt made clear — as had his forceful predecessors from Jackson through Wilson — that the presidential power was pretty much what the President made it. Another was the revitalization of the political party as a vehicle for the popular will and as an instrument for effective action; a vindication of the American party system as the chief agency for harmonizing section and class conflicts, pressures and interests. A third development was the demonstration that Big Government was not incompatible with a flourishing grass-roots democracy. Federal centralization had been under way for a long time, but it was sharply accelerated by the compulsions of the depression, the practices of the

New Deal, and after 1939 by the requirements of national defense. The growth of centralization was apparent in the number of civil servants and in expenditures, as well as in the entry of government into relatively new fields of activity such as public works, health, and the arts. It was ratified judicially by the reapplication of a ' broad construction ' to the Constitution where federal authority was involved. Yet federal centralization and Big Government were attended by a corresponding growth of regional administrative activities — of which the TVA was the most publicized — and the accommodation of administration to geographical and economic realities. State boundary lines lost some of their earlier importance; state powers, while not diminished in their totality or in their reach, were not permitted to interfere with the activities of the Federal Government in matters that ' concerned more states than one.'

One of the most interesting New Deal experiments was in economic and social planning. Most Americans were suspicious of governmental planning, and their distaste for it was accentuated by the reaction against the series of Russian ' five year plans ' which somehow associated the whole thing with Communism. Yet the immense tasks of physical and human rehabilitation, the incoherence and confusion attendant on merely opportunistic reform, and the practical necessities of co-operation between state and federal governments and between different departments brought home to students the necessity of some kind of planning. Tried out locally, as by city planners, or regionally, as in the Great Plains or the Rio Grande valley, planning seemed more reasonable, and came to lose some of its socialistic connotations.

Yet the notion that the New Deal tried to commit the country to a planned economy is erroneous. Some of those who constituted the original ' brains trust ' — men like Moley and Tugwell, Donald Richberg and Hugh Johnson — did try to bring about a centralized control of the national economy, but they never really won Roosevelt's support for this program. The failure of the NRA dramatized the failure of their approach, and after 1935 they rapidly lost influence. What is sometimes called ' the second New Deal ' — a phrase that exaggerates differences — was committed to the principle of government regulation within the competitive system, a principle which differed only in degree from that espoused by Theodore Roosevelt and Wilson. Three social philosophers dominated the formal thinking of the ' second New Deal ': Justice Brandeis, who was a life-long opponent of bigness in any form and whose students and dis-ciples — Felix Frankfurter, Thomas Corcoran, David Lilienthal, to name a few — came to occupy key posts after 1935; Walter Lippmann, whose *Good Society* was the most vigorous and influential assault on the whole concept of a planned economy; and the English economist John Maynard Keynes, who converted some of the New Dealers to the program of regulating the economy through government spend-ing rather than by the police power.

Nevertheless the expansion of governmental regulation and func-tions meant a steady socialization of the economic life of the nation — a socialization going forward under the auspices of private enter-prise as well. The immediate impulse to socialization came from practical considerations of the inability of private enterprise to un-dertake necessary large-scale social and economic programs; its mani-festations were chiefly in the economic realm such as government de-velopment of hydroelectric power, operation of merchant marine, and partnership in banking. Equally significant was the growing gov-ernment participation in business activities that came with the de-pression and the defense program of the late 'thirties. During the early years of the depression the Federal Government had to come to the rescue of banks, railroads, utilities and industries, and inevitably financial aid involved supervision and effective partnership. As the attempt to manage the whole economy was abandoned, regulation of particular departments of the economy became stricter. The Wheeler-Rayburn Public Utilities Act of 1935 gave the government effective control and veto-power over holding companies; and the Eccles Banking Act of the same year transferred to the Federal Re-serve Board substantial control over all market transactions in gov-ernment bonds. War brought a vast expansion of governmental activity — the financing and operation of defense industries, construc-tion of low-cost housing, and so forth. States, too, expanded not only their regulatory activities but their participation in economic life, setting up systems of state insurance and employment agencies, while cities took on such diverse activities as transportation, the sale of gas and electricity, the distribution of milk, and radio broadcasting.

It would be a mistake to suppose that this socialization was devel-oped at the expense of private enterprise. On the contrary, the New Deal did more to strengthen than to weaken the capitalist economy.

That economy had broken down in many countries abroad, and its collapse contributed to the rise of totalitarian governments which completely subordinated business to the state. The system was on the verge of collapse in the United States during the Hoover administration, and the demagoguery of Huey Long, Father Coughlin, Francis Townsend, and Gerald K. Smith suggest that had the collapse been permitted to occur it would have been followed by an economic system fundamentally different from that of the past. Historically, Franklin Roosevelt did for twentieth-century American capitalism what Theodore Roosevelt had done for the traditional nineteenth-century private enterprise: he saved the system by ridding it of its grosser abuses and forcing it to accommodate itself to the public interest and the general welfare. History may eventually record Franklin D. Roosevelt as the greatest American conservative since Hamilton.

Closely associated with these political and economic developments was the expansion and extension of democracy under the New Deal. Except for the Negroes — a very large exception — political democracy had been largely achieved before 1933; it was the function of the New Deal to bring home to the American people the fact that the common man must be assured of security as well as suffrage. In speech after speech Roosevelt pointed what he thought was the moral of recent European history: that given a choice between liberty and bread, men will choose bread, and that it was the responsibility of democracy to provide the bread as well as to secure liberty. In a ' fireside chat ' of 1938 Roosevelt said:

Democracy has disappeared in several other great nations, not because the people of those nations disliked democracy, but because they had grown tired of unemployment and insecurity, of seeing their children hungry while they sat helpless in the face of government confusion and government weakness through lack of leadership in government. Finally, in desperation, they chose to sacrifice liberty in the hope of getting something to eat. We in America know that our democratic government is equal to the task of protecting the security of the people . . . The people of America are in agreement in defending their liberties at any cost, and the first line of that defense lies in the protection of economic security.

To this task of providing economic and psychological security Roosevelt devoted the major energies of his administration.

Even more significant than the extension of democracy in the domestic realm was the maintenance of a democratic system of government and society in a world swept by confused alarms of struggle and flight. ' The only sure bulwark of continuing liberty,' Roosevelt had observed, ' is a government strong enough to protect the interests of the people, and a people strong enough and well enough informed to maintain its sovereign control over its government.' The proof that in the United States it was possible for such a government to exist and such a people to flourish was of fateful significance, and it helped restore the United States to its traditional position as ' the hope of the human race.' For in the 'thirties it became doubtful whether liberty or democracy could survive in the modern world, and at the end of that decade totalitarian states felt strong enough to challenge the democracies in a war for survival. It was of utmost importance to the peoples of the world that the American democracy had withstood the buffetings of depression and the vicissitudes of world affairs and emerged strong and courageous; that the American people were refreshed in their faith in the democratic order, prepared to defend it at home and to fight for it wherever it was threatened.

BIBLIOGRAPHY

1. GENERAL. Charles and Mary Beard, *America in Midpassage;* John M. Blum, *From the Morgenthau Diaries 1928–1938;* Denis Brogan, *The Era of Franklin D. Roosevelt;* James McG. Burns, *Roosevelt: The Lion and the Fox;* James F. Byrnes, *Speaking Frankly;* Mario Einaudi, *The Roosevelt Revolution;* Frank Freidel, *Franklin D. Roosevelt* (3 vols.) ; Daniel R. Fusfeld, *The Economic Thought of Franklin D. Roosevelt and the Origins of the New Deal;* John Gunther, *Roosevelt in Retrospect;* Cordell Hull, *Memoirs* (2 vols.) ; Harold Ickes, *The Autobiography of a Curmudgeon* and *The Secret Diary of Harold Ickes* (3 vols.) ; Broadus Mitchell, *Depression Decade, 1929–1941;* Dexter Perkins, *The New Age of Franklin D. Roosevelt;* Frances Perkins, *The Roosevelt I Knew;* Basil Rauch, *History of the New Deal, 1933–1938* and *Roosevelt from Munich to Pearl Harbor;* Eleanor Roosevelt, *This is My Story* and *This I Remember;* Arthur M. Schlesinger, Jr., *The Age of Roosevelt:* vol. 1, *The Crisis of the Old Order,* vol. 2, *The Coming of the New Deal,* and vol. 3, *The Politics of Upheaval;* Robert Sherwood, *Roosevelt and Hopkins: An Intimate History;* Henry Stimson, *On Active Service in Peace and War;* Rexford Tugwell, *The Democratic Roosevelt.*

2. POLITICS AND ELECTIONS. Joseph Barnes, *Willkie;* John M. Blum, *From the Morgenthau Diaries;* J. F. Dinneen, *Purple Shamrock: Curley of Boston;* James Farley, *Jim Farley's Story* and *Behind the Ballots;* E. J. Flynn, *You're the Boss;* Herbert Hoover, *Addresses on the American Road 1933–1938;* Donald Bruce Johnson, *The Republican Party and Wendell Willkie;* V. O. Key, *Politics,*

Parties and Pressure Groups; Louis W. Koenig, *The Invisible Presidency;* Alfred M. Landon, *America at the Crossroads;* Samuel Lubell, *The Future of American Politics;* Charles Michelsen, *The Ghost Talks;* Louise Overacker, *Presidential Campaign Funds;* Roy V. Peel & T. C. Donnelly, *The 1932 Election;* E. E. Robinson, *They Voted for Roosevelt: The Presidential Vote 1931–1944;* Fred Rodell, *Democracy and the Third Term;* Samuel Rosenman, *Working with Roosevelt;* Charles Stein, *The Third Term Tradition;* R. G. Tugwell, *The Battle for Democracy;* Henry Wallace, *New Frontiers;* George Wolfskill, *The Revolt of the Conservatives: A History of the American* and *Liberty League.*

3. THE RECOVERY PROGRAM: AGRICULTURE. M. R. Benedict, *Farm Policies of the United States;* D. C. Blaisdell, *Government and Agriculture;* Stuart Chase, *Rich Land, Poor Land;* Alvin Hansen, *America's Role in World Economy;* Russell Lord, *The Wallaces of Iowa;* Carey McWilliams, *Factories in the Field* and *Ill Fares the Land;* E. G. Nourse, *Government in Relation to Agriculture;* E. G. Nourse, et al., *Three Years of the AAA;* J. C. Pearson, *Reciprocal Trade Agreements;* A. F. Raper, *Preface to Peasantry;* John Steinbeck, *The Grapes of Wrath;* Rex G. Tugwell, *Stricken Land;* Henry Wallace, *New Frontiers* and *America Must Choose;* Waller Wynne, *Five Years of Rural Relief.*

4. THE RECOVERY PROGRAM: INDUSTRY AND SECURITIES REGULATION. A. A. Berle, et al., *America's Recovery Program;* Wendell Berge, *Cartels;* A. R. Burns, *The Decline of Competition;* A. W. Crawford, *Monetary Management under the New Deal;* W. O. Douglas, *Democracy and Finance;* M. F. Gallagher, *Government Rules Industry;* G. G. Johnson, *The Treasury and Monetary Policy 1933–1938;* Hugh Johnson, *Blue Eagle, from Egg to Earth;* David Lynch, *The Concentration of Economic Power;* L. S. Lyon, et al., *The National Recovery Administration;* Broadus Mitchell, *The Depression Decade;* Arthur Nussbaum, *Money and the Law;* Ferdinand Pecora, *Wall Street Under Oath;* Sidney Ratner, *The Social History of Taxation;* J. R. Reeve, *Monetary Reform Movements;* C. F. Roos, *NRA Economic Planning;* Emmanuel Stein, *Government and the Investor.*

5. THE RECOVERY PROGRAM: SOCIAL SECURITY AND LABOR. Edith Abbott, *Public Assistance;* Grace Adams, *Workers on Relief* and *From Relief to Social Security;* Carol Aronovici, *Housing the Masses;* R. R. Brooks, *Unions of Their Own Choosing;* Josephine C. Brown, *Public Relief;* Evalina M. Burns, *American Social Security;* Horace R. Cayton, *Black Workers and the New Unions;* Milton Derber & Edwin Young (eds.), *Labor and the New Deal;* Carroll Dougherty, *Labor under the NRA;* Paul Douglas, *Social Security in the United States;* Paul Douglas & A. Director, *The Problem of Unemployment;* Abraham Epstein, *Insecurity* and *The Challenge of the Aged;* Walter Galenson, *The C.I.O. Challenge to the A.F. of L.* and *Rival Unionism;* Herbert Harris, *American Labor;* Seymour E. Harris, *The Economics of Social Security;* Donald S. Howard, *The WPA and Federal Relief Policy;* Harold L. Ickes, *Back to Work;* G. R. Leighton, *Five Cities;* Betty and E. K. Lindley, *A New Deal for Youth;* L. L. Lorwin, *Youth Work Programs;* Robert and Helen Lynd, *Middletown in Transition;* Lewis Meriam, *Relief and Social Security;* Grace Overmyer, *Government and the Arts;* Selig Perlman, *Labor in the New Deal Decade;* L. H. Pink, *The New Day in Housing;* Louis Post, *The Challenge of Housing;* Joseph

Rosenfarb, *The National Labor Policy and How It Works;* I. M. Rubinow, *The Quest for Security;* L. G. Silverberg, *The Wagner Act;* Emmanuel Stein, et al., *Labor and the New Deal;* Marietta Stevenson & Ralph Spear, *The Social Security Program;* Nathan Straus, *Four Years of Public Housing;* Philip Taft, *The A.F. of L. from the Death of Gompers;* Mary H. Vorse, *Labor's New Millions;* Willson Whitman, *Bread and Circuses;* J. K. Williams, *Grants in Aid under Public Works Administration.*

6. THE TVA AND CONSERVATION. R. G. Baumhoff, *The Damned Missouri Valley;* H. H. Bennett, *Conservation Farming Practices and Flood Control;* James C. Bonbright, *Public Utilities and the National Power Policies;* Gordon R. Clapp, *The T.V.A., An Approach to the Development of a Region;* C. L. Hodge, *The Tennessee Valley Authority;* William E. Leuchtenburg, *Flood Control Politics;* David E. Lilienthal, *The TVA: Democracy on the March;* Richard L. Neuberger, *Our Promised Land;* R. L. Neuberger & S. B. Kahn, *Integrity: The Life of George W. Norris;* C. H. Pritchett, *The Tennessee Valley Authority: Study in Public Administration;* H. S. Raushenbush, *The Power Fight;* H. S. Raushenbush & H. W. Laidler, *Power Control;* Paul B. Sears, *Deserts on the March;* Philip Selznick, *TVA and the Grass Roots;* Rufus Terral, *The Missouri Valley;* Willson Whitman, *God's Valley* and *David Lilienthal.*

7. THE COURT REFORM PROGRAM. Irving Brant, *Storm over the Constitution;* F. V. Cahill, Jr., *Judicial Legislation;* Robert K. Carr, *The Supreme Court and Judicial Review;* H. S. Commager, *Majority Rule and Minority Rights;* E. S. Corwin, *The Twilight of the Supreme Court, Court Over Constitution, The Supreme Court and the Commerce Power,* and *Constitutional Revolution, Ltd.;* Charles P. Curtis, *Lions under the Throne;* E. McK. Eriksson, *Supreme Court and the New Deal;* J. P. Frank, *Mr. Justice Black;* Eugene C. Gerhart, *America's Advocate Robert H. Jackson;* Samuel Hendel, *Charles Evans Hughes and the Supreme Court;* Robert Jackson, *Struggle for Judicial Supremacy;* Alvin Johnson & Frank Yost, *Separation of Church and State in the United States;* S. J. Konefsky, *Chief Justice Stone and the Supreme Court* and *Constitutional World of Mr. Justice Frankfurter;* Alpheus T. Mason, *Harlan Fiske Stone;* Alpheus T. Mason & William M. Beaney, *The Supreme Court in a Free Society;* C. Herman Pritchett, *The Roosevelt Court;* Milo J. Pusey, *Charles Evans Hughes* (2 vols.) and *The Supreme Court Crisis;* Bernard Schwartz, *The Supreme Court: Constitutional Revolution in Retrospect;* Virginia Wood, *Due Process of Law 1932–1949;* Benjamin Wright, *The Course of American Constitutional Law;* Carl Zollman, *American Church Law.*

8. DOCUMENTS. Joseph Blau (ed.), *Cornerstones of Religious Freedom in America;* H. S. Commager, *Documents,* nos. 475–87, 493–520, 529, 542, 543, 549, 555; *Hearings* of the Senate Judiciary Committee on the Supreme Court Reform Bill, 75th Cong. 1st Sess. (6 vols.); J. M. Landis and Marcus Manoff (eds.), *Cases on Labor Law;* F. D. Roosevelt and Samuel Rosenman (eds.), *The Public Papers and Addresses of Franklin D. Roosevelt* (13 vols.).

For further references *Harvard Guide,* ¶¶ 256–64.

Gathering Storm

1. The Challenge of the Dictators

IF there was one principle upon which the vast majority of the American people agreed in 1937, it was that what was happening in Europe was no concern of theirs; and that if Europe were so wicked or stupid as to get into another war, America would resolutely stay out of it. Even the President reflected this feeling by failing to mention foreign relations in his second inaugural address, which, owing to the ratification of the Twentieth Amendment to the Constitution, was delivered on 20 January 1937 instead of the traditional 4 March. Yet within two years, developments in Europe and Asia made a mockery of this negative attitude.

A system known as collective security was supposed to maintain the territorial and other settlements made after World War I, but to make minor adjustments necessary to serve justice and prevent any new war. It worked well enough until challenged by demagogues and dictators whose main object was unrestrained power. In pursuance of their several ambitions they set up totalitarian regimes in which the rule of law, and traditional liberties such as freedom of speech, assembly, elections, and the press, were suppressed, and the citizen became powerless under a monster state. Russia, Communist since 1918, fitted this category, but Russia in the 1930's did not threaten the peace of the world. Stalin was too deeply concerned with his country's problems to brandish the spear, and in 1934 he had joined the League of Nations and used his influence to check Hitler. Benito Mussolini also had set himself up as *duce* of Italy in 1922, but waited until the rise of Hitler before taking a first step to ' restore the Roman Empire ' by attacking helpless Ethiopia.[1]

[1] The other dictators — Franco in Spain, Salazar in Portugal, Perón in Argentina, Trujillo in the Dominican Republic, Castañeda in Guatemala — were relatively powerless outside their own countries, although the three Latin Americans nourished a ' fifth column ' of Nazis who were potentially dangerous to the New World.

Mussolini would have been powerless to upset the peace of Europe but for the rise of Adolf Hitler. The hold of that uneducated paranoiac over the German people, with their long tradition of culture and decency (to which they have since returned), is a phenomenon which even the Germans themselves have been unable to explain. In part, no doubt, it was due to the poverty and disorganization of Germany after her defeat in World War I; but other nations, notably Austria and Poland, had suffered even more than Germany, and made little trouble. Hitler rose on a tide of resentment over the Treaty of Versailles; but the victor powers had redressed most of the severities imposed by that treaty, and (with the aid of American loans) they had relieved Germany from the burden of war reparations before Hitler reached power. There was much talk of *Lebensraum,* room for expansion; but the Netherlands and Scandinavia suffered similar pressures without trying to wreck the European world. Possibly the conclusion that Franklin D. Roosevelt reached is the right one. Hitler, a frustrated fanatic, based his National Socialist (Nazi) party on the residuary hatred, barbarism, and cruelty inherent in modern society. He hated the Jews, he hated democracy, he hated the Christian religion in which he was reared, he hated all foreigners, and in general anything that was good, true, or beautiful. For brutality, sadistic cruelty, and villainy he may be compared only with Genghis Khan in ancient days, or to Stalin in ours. As Winston Churchill wrote, Hitler ' called from the depths of defeat the dark and savage furies latent in the most numerous, most serviceable, ruthless, contradictory, and ill-starred race in Europe.' [2]

Hitler's objective was to reunite all Germans at home and abroad as a ' master race ' which would rule Europe and dictate to the world. He was willing only to tolerate rulers whose objectives in other areas were similar to his. When Marshal von Hindenberg, President of the German Republic, allowed Hitler to take office as Chancellor on 30 January 1933, it was as if President Roosevelt, seeing his end approaching, had abdicated in favor of Huey Long or Gerald Smith. And when Hindenberg died (2 August 1934) Hitler made himself chief of state, using his party title of *Fuehrer.* He promptly abolished the republican constitution, made Germany a military dictatorship in which he was the source of all authority, and surcharged the German flag with the party swastika.

[2] *The Second World War,* pp. 170–71.

Hitler had a devilish ability to play off rivals against each other and to profit by their weakness and folly. The only nations capable of stopping him in his early aggressions were Great Britain and France; and in both countries, decimated as they had been by the First World War (France lost some million and a half men, and the British Empire a million) sound leadership was wanting; lassitude, timidity, and class hatred were paramount, especially in France. The Western powers acquiesced in one aggression after another, in the vain hope of ' appeasing ' Hitler, until the time came when they had to dig in and fight. Nor can our country escape censure. If American influence had been exerted in time, directly or through the League of Nations, it might have galvanized flabby British politicians like MacDonald, Baldwin, and Chamberlain, timid French politicians like Daladier and Georges Bonnet, into action; and there were still elements in Germany, especially in the army, who wanted only encouragement from abroad to liquidate Hitler.

Never since Jefferson's time had America, and never in recorded history had England, been in so pacifist a mood; and Hitler was canny enough to play upon this. He pronounced President Roosevelt's speech of 16 May 1933, outlining American plans and hopes for peace, disarmament, and the abolition of heavy weapons, a ' ray of comfort.' Two years later, Hitler delivered an oration on peace which was greeted by the London *Times* with almost hysterical joy. Hitler, Stalin, and the war lords of Japan secretly worked for war but publicly advocated ' peace,' and although this fooled the democracies, no hypocrisy was intended. For their concept of peace was as different from ours as Soviet ' democracy ' is from real democracy. For Hitler, peace meant getting all he wanted for Germany; for Japan, it meant a ' feudal peace ' of all Eastern Asia under Japanese hegemony; for Stalin (as now for Khrushchev) , peace meant the peace of death that would follow when the whole world went Communist. The American public never understood this; they supposed that when some foreign ruler talked peace, he meant peace in their sense.

America's pacifist mood received official sanction in 1934 from a Senate investigation into the bankers and munitions makers during World War I. Although the findings of this Nye commission failed to prove anyone's responsibility for the war, they did reveal scandalously high profits, and the public concluded that Wall Street wanted the war for financial reasons. Historians like Charles A. Beard, journalists like Colonel McCormick of the Chicago *Tribune* and William Randolph Hearst, converted a substantial part of public opinion to the naïve view that America had been stampeded into war in order to make money for ' merchants of death,' and that our intervention in any future European war would be a crime.

2. 'For Whom the Bell Tolls'

Here, in briefest outline, are the successive triumphs achieved by Hitler's craft and cunning against his neighbors and the peace of Europe. In 1934 he withdrew Germany from the League of Nations. Next year he denounced the Treaty of Versailles, and defiantly announced that Germany would rearm. This was ignored. That fall Mussolini launched his armies against Ethiopia. The League of Nations imposed half-hearted sanctions, which were ineffective, and the British government, which could have closed the Suez Canal to Italian transports and warships, tamely let them pass. In March 1936 Hitler's army reoccupied the Rhineland, which had been forbidden by the Treaty of Versailles and the subsequent Locarno treaties. France and England, which then could easily have checked him, did nothing. ' After all, they are only going into their own back garden,' commented a British statesman, ignoring the strategic value of the Rhineland. After taking this step, as after every other, Hitler assured the world that he wanted nothing more; in July 1936 he even signed a non-aggression pact with Austria, his next intended victim.

In October and November 1936, Hitler concluded a German-Italian pact creating the ' Berlin-Rome Axis,' and the Anti-Comintern pact, a defensive-offensive alliance between Germany, Italy, and Japan, directed primarily at Russia. Presently the Axis had a new partner — Spain. In 1931 the Spanish Republic had been established, with the support of most of the brave and free spirits in that country, and the good will of the Western world. But no representative government could rule so individualistic a people; Spain broke up into angry factions of anarchists, communists, syndicalists, monarchists, Fascists, and Catalan nationalists. The ' popular front ' government, formed by all leftist factions in 1936, could not keep order or stop violence, such as the burning of churches and massacre of priests and landowners. Thus it lost the support of the middle class, which, as in most countries, prized order above liberty. The army under General

Franco revolted; and civil war began in July. The western European nations and the United States virtuously proclaimed neutrality and prevented the supply of arms and munitions to the republicans; Russia alone helped them, and as Russia always does when ' helping ' a country or a faction, she had her aid distributed by Communists, who thus acquired ascendancy over the republican government. On the other hand, Hitler and Mussolini actively supported the rebels. They won in early 1939; but only after a conflict so vicious that Spain has sullenly endured Franco's Fascist rule for a quarter-century rather than risk another miserable conflict.

This Spanish civil war had the same relation to World War II as ' bleeding Kansas ' had to the American Civil War, or the Balkan wars to World War I. Ernest Hemingway, who had covered the Spanish war for American newspapers, and, along with thousands of young Americans and Englishmen, volunteered to fight for the republican cause, recalled in his novel *For Whom the Bell Tolls* the solemn words of John Donne. The bell in Spain tolled not only for that unhappy country; ' *it tolls for thee.*'

We may now conclude what Churchill calls ' the long, dismal, drawling tides of drift and surrender, of wrong measurements and feeble impulses.' Unknown to anyone but the participants, Hitler at a meeting with his foreign minister and his top generals, had announced his plans for conquest on 5 November 1937. His object, he said, was to obtain *Lebensraum,* new territory for Germans to live on, in Europe's heartland. This could only be done by force. It was the Fuehrer's unalterable resolve to apply force in 1943 if the opportunity did not occur sooner, as he expected it would. The generals and the foreign minister who objected were dismissed, and Hitler decided to step up his program.

The bell tolled for Austria in March 1938, when Hitler invaded that hapless remnant of the Hapsburg empire and annexed it to Germany; nobody stopped him. The next victim was Czechoslovakia. This secession state from the old Austro-Hungarian Empire had prospered since 1920 under the able rule of statesmen such as Masaryk and Beneš. But in its western part, the old kingdom of Bohemia, the so-called Sudeten Germans, once the ruling class under Austrian domination, regarded the Slavic Czechs and Slovaks with hatred and contempt, and hailed Hitler as the German savior who would put them in the saddle again. Czechoslovakia had a strong, well-trained army and valuable munitions works which would have been a danger to Hitler when he attacked France and Russia, as he intended to do. In May 1938 he decided to move on this country and divide or annex it. Neville Chamberlain, the British prime minister, thrice visited Hitler in September 1938, and was completely fooled by the Fuehrer's promise that he wanted only a fringe of the German-speaking part of Czechoslovakia. In the final meeting at Munich on 28–29 September, Chamberlain, Mussolini, and the French premier Daladier, agreed to Hitler's terms; and Chamberlain returned to England, announcing cheerily ' it is peace in our time.'

In the one year 1938 Hitler had annexed and brought under his absolute rule 6.7 million Austrians and 3.5 million Sudeten Germans. And these were not annexations in the traditional sense, giving full rights to the annexed people, and a year's time or more for objectors to sell out and leave. The Czechs or Austrians who did not relish joining the German Reich had to flee, or be liquidated; the Jews were liquidated anyway.

Hitler was not yet appeased. In March 1939, again breaking solemn promises, he moved his army into Prague, made the rest of Czechoslovakia two German satellite states, and cynically announced again that he now had all he wanted. Mussolini followed suit by seizing Albania.

These sorry episodes made Chamberlain and his inevitable umbrella figures of contempt, and ' appeasement ' a pejorative word in the language of politics.

3. Hakko Ichiu

On the other side of the world the Japanese militarists, resurrecting from their dim and distant past the slogan *Hakko ichiu* — ' bringing the eight corners of the world under one roof ' — were riding high. Their movement had many points of resemblance to Hitler's Nazism, in its contempt for democracy, liberty, and most of the peaceful virtues. It entertained the same enticing ambition of wide dominion; in this instance, a Manchu-like empire of East Asia. Dissolving China offered a good start toward eventually bringing all Asiatic colonies or dependencies of Europe and America — India, Burma, Indonesia, Indo-China, the Philippines — under Japanese hegemony. Emperor Hirohito deplored these tendencies, but was helpless before a movement that continually invoked his name and used his moral authority over the Japanese nation.

After inconvenient liberal leaders had been assassinated, a militarist cabinet was set up, and the ' China incident ' of 7 July 1937 was provoked. This led to war between Japan and China; but Japan did not wish to call it a war, since that was contrary to the nine-power treaty for the integrity of China. Prince Konoye, the premier, declared on 27 July, ' Japan never looks upon the Chinese people as an enemy '; her sole object is ' to preserve the peace of East Asia.' Such talk sounded like gross hypocrisy, especially in China, where the Japanese military organized battues of unarmed peasants and conducted themselves with a savagery worthy of Hitler's exterminators. But it made sense to the Japanese. Assuming Japan's divine mission to bring about a *pax Nipponica* of East Asia, Chinese resistance was a sin against the light; and those who failed to co-operate in the beneficent work had to be eliminated.

For two years the American government concentrated on diplomatic efforts to ' bring Japan to her senses,' and restore peace in China. The attempt proved to be as futile as Chamberlain's at Munich; but that is not to say that it was foolish. There was always hope that the increasing difficulty and expense of making war on China would discredit the Japanese army and bring a liberal government back into power. Moreover, President Roosevelt and everyone else in a responsible position knew that the American people would never go to war merely to save China from conquest or partition.

The Japanese militarists, from 1937 on, made a concerted effort to drive American and European missionary, educational, medical, and cultural activities out of China permanently, as the Chinese Communists have since done. American churches, hospitals, schools, and colleges were bombed despite flag markings on their roofs; American missionaries and their families were killed; there were so many ' accidents ' of this sort that cynical Chinese reported the most dangerous spot in an air raid to be an American mission. A small river gunboat of the American navy's Yangtze river patrol, U.S.S. *Panay*, was ' accidentally ' bombed and sunk by Japanese naval planes on 12 December 1937. When the Japanese government apologized and offered to pay indemnity to the victims, a sigh of relief passed over the length and breadth of America. In a Gallup poll conducted during the second week of January 1938, 70 per cent of the American voters who

were interviewed and had an opinion on the subject, favored complete withdrawal from China — Asiatic Fleet, marines, missionaries,
medical missions, and all.

Well, why not? the reader may ask, since that is what Mao Tse-
tung's government has forced us to do in the end. Would not a China
under Japanese rule have been better for the world than a Communist China? Possibly; for the end product of communizing China is
not yet in sight. But no responsible American statesman could contemplate going back on our plighted word to China, and treating her
as the European powers had treated Czechoslovakia. And they knew
from many historical examples, recent and remote, that militarist
cliques are never satisfied, and that nothing short of the hegemony of
all Asia and the Pacific Ocean would satisfy the Japanese. We had to
risk a war in the 1940's rather than take on an infinitely stronger
enemy later.

In 1939 the Japanese captured Shanghai and proceeded to make
life intolerable for Americans and Europeans in the international
settlement there. President Roosevelt now contemplated the imposition of economic sanctions on Japan to make her leaders stop, look,
and listen. His first step, on 26 July 1939, was to denounce the existing treaty of commerce with Japan. This received almost unanimous
approval, even from isolationists.

There matters stood in the Far East when war broke out in Europe. Stalemate in China; Japan and the United States getting ready
for the next move.

4. A Fortress on a Paper Pad

> Longing to wed with Peace, what did we do? —
> Sketched her a fortress on a paper pad;
> Under her casement twanged a love-sick string;
> Left wide the gate that let her foemen through.[3]

The bell also tolled for the United States, but its somber notes fell
dim and muffled on American ears. To threats of the war lords the
average American was indifferent. He thought of Europe as decadent,
given to secret diplomacy, class conflict, and evasion of debts. He was
sorry for ' John Chinaman ' and detested the ' Japs,' but he felt that

[3] Edna St. Vincent Millay, *Make Bright the Arrows*, Harper & Brothers, 1942, copy-
right 1939, 1940 by the author.

if 450 million Chinese could not defend themselves against 73 million Japanese there was nothing he should or could do about it. Isolationism was not so much a reasoned principle as an instinctive belief in our safety behind ocean barriers. The world was indeed out of joint, but what obligation had we to set it right? The argument of self-determination, invoked to justify German annexation of Austria and the seizure of the Sudetenland, seemed plausible; Ethiopians were said to be uncivilized; perhaps it was the mission of Japan to unite distracted China. In many quarters Hitler and Mussolini seemed fresh and hopeful examples of the typical American ' poor boy making good,' rejuvenating decrepit Europe. Never, since ' Young America ' days, had America been so smugly complacent about herself, or so sneeringly indifferent to the rest of the world.

The popular reaction to the events in Europe and Asia that we have described was to create a demand for a thoroughgoing revision of the laws of neutrality. Three neutrality acts, passed in the years 1935–37, were designed to prevent the involvement of the United States in any European or Asiatic war. They prohibited private loans or credits to belligerent nations or parties to a civil war, placed an embargo upon direct or indirect shipments of arms or munitions to belligerents, and required that they ' pay cash and carry ' any other articles. The 1939 act, passed after the war began in Europe, extended the ' cash and carry ' provision to munitions, but forbade American citizens to travel upon belligerents' ships, prohibited the arming of American merchantmen, and forbade them to enter designated ' danger zones.' Law could not have gone further to ' keep us out of war '; and as President Roosevelt, who disapproved the neutrality bills, but not strongly enough to veto them, later observed, ' Our arms embargo played right into the hands of the aggressor nations.' Germany, Japan, and to a lesser degree Italy, were feverishly preparing for land, sea, and air warfare; England, France, and Russia were barely beginning to do so; and American neutrality legislation assured the Axis that when they got ready to strike, their victims would be shut off from obtaining implements of war from America.

The President and Secretary Hull continued to build up hemispheric solidarity. In 1935 they concluded with six Latin American nations a treaty of non-aggression and conciliation which reaffirmed the Kellogg-Briand pact outlawing war, provided machinery for its enforcement, and pledged the signatories not to recognize territorial changes effected by force. Next year President Roosevelt attended the Pan-American conference at Buenos Aires which provided for mutual consultation on all matters affecting the peace of the Americas. Both Italy and Germany were nourishing ' fifth columns ' in Latin America, but this time Uncle Sam won the propaganda battle.

Hemispheric solidarity also developed northward. Roosevelt renewed efforts to strengthen ties between the United States and Canada, and between himself and the perennial premier of Canada, W. L. Mackenzie King, who was wrestling with the same problems of depression and foreign affairs. Reciprocal trade agreements were enacted in 1935 and 1938. At Kingston, Ontario, in August 1938, President Roosevelt promised ' that the people of the United States will not stand idly by if domination of Canadian soil is threatened by any other Empire.'

Roosevelt was watching with growing concern the menaces to peace in Europe and Asia. Speaking at Chicago, the heart of the isolationist camp, shortly after the beginning of the ' China incident ' in 1937, he called for a quarantine against aggressor nations. If lawlessness and violence rage unrestrained, he warned, ' let no one imagine that America will escape, that America may expect mercy, that this Western Hemisphere will not be attacked.' These prophetic words seemed to awaken no popular response, and in many quarters the President was denounced as a ' warmonger.' In January 1938 he proposed to the British government a conference of leading powers in Washington to discuss the underlying causes of turmoil in Europe. Chamberlain brushed him off; he preferred the appeasement approach to Hitler, and was indifferent to Japan's doings in China. After the war Churchill declared that this rebuff to Roosevelt lost ' the last frail chance to save the world from tyranny otherwise than by war.' On 26 September 1938 the President reminded all signatory nations of their ' outlawry of war ' under the Kellogg-Briand pact, and appealed for arbitration of the Sudeten question. On 14 April 1939, he sent a personal message to Hitler and Mussolini asking them to promise not to attack some twenty small countries in Europe during the next ten years. Hitler made an insulting reply, and then bullied some of the countries (which he was about to gobble up) into assuring Roosevelt that they had no cause to fear good neighbor Germany. Mussolini at first refused to read the message, then sneered at it before his underlings as ' a result of infantile paralysis.'

America had tried to maintain peace by isolation, by arms limitation, by neutrality legislation, and now by exhortation. Nothing short of a hard-and-fast military alliance like NATO could have stopped Hitler; nothing short of war could have stopped Japan.

5. 'And the War Came'

Hitler, far from sated with Czechoslovakia, early in 1939 turned his hungry glare on Poland, a state with which he had signed a non-aggression pact. At the end of World War I Poland had been granted a 'corridor' to the Baltic, which separated East Prussia from West Prussia, and a small territory around the old German seaport of Danzig had been set up as a free state under League of Nations protection. Poland allowed German trains and cars free transit across the corridor; but to Hitler this was a degrading situation. In North American terms it was as if the United States felt insulted because trains from Buffalo to Detroit cross the Ontario Peninsula, and demanded that Canada cede that territory up to and including Toronto.

The British and French governments, now cured of their delusions about Hitler by the rape of Czechoslovakia, completely reversed their policy and (31 March) made too late the rash move of guaranteeing against aggression Poland and then Romania, whom they were incapable of helping. The guarantee would have made sense if English and French diplomacy had made a partner of Russia, as eventually they were forced to do; for the one thing Hitler then feared was a war on two fronts. Litvinov, the veteran Soviet foreign minister, who had consistently supported a policy of containing Hitler, offered on 16 April 1939 to sign a pact with Great Britain to protect Poland. Instead of encouraging this offer, Chamberlain's government fiddled around with it, Poland quibbled about details, and in early May Litvinov, having played his last card, was flung out of office by Stalin and replaced by Molotov. That able, cold-blooded Communist, with his cannon-ball head and poker face, had survived all the hazards and ordeals to which the Bolshevik leaders were subjected; even survived the death of Stalin to become one of Khrushchev's right-hand men until he fell out of favor in 1957. Unable to do business with the Western democracies, he promptly began negotiations with Ribbentrop, Hitler's foreign affairs secretary, for a pact at the expense of

Poland. On 24 August 1939, the Western world was stupefied by the news that Stalin and Hitler, who had been violently abusing each other for five years, had shaken hands in a non-aggression pact. The world did not yet know the secret clauses, that they also agreed to partition Poland.

After his usual preparatory propaganda of fake frontier incidents, Hitler launched his attack on Poland on 1 September 1939. Two days later, Great Britain and France declared war on Germany. The British dominions followed suit shortly. World War II was on.

For two dreadful weeks the German mechanized army smashed through Poland in a ' Blitzkrieg ' without parallel in earlier warfare, while bombing planes reduced Polish towns and villages to rubble. The Russians moved in from the east, taking over what they held to be Russian Poland. Attacked from both sides by overwhelming force, with no military aid from anyone, Poland capitulated before the end of September. Germany and Russia divided the country between them. At comparatively slight cost Hitler had acquired 21 million more subjects, together with vast agricultural and industrial resources.

In the west, Germany stood securely behind the newly completed Siegfried line, while Britain and France, the one unable and the other unwilling to take the offensive,[4] relied upon an imperfect blockade to bring her to terms. Hitler refrained from a Western offensive because he hoped to buy peace with the sacrifice of Poland. There ensued a period of inaction which Senator Borah called the ' phony war,' and which Churchill named ' the winter of illusion.' Any illusions about Russia were dispelled when Stalin picked a quarrel with his democratic neighbor Finland, and in March 1940 forced her to yield large slices of territory. Shortly after, Stalin annexed the three other Baltic states (Estonia, Latvia, Lithuania) and recovered Bessarabia and the Bukovina from Romania; thus completing, as he thought, a barrier defense against a possible change of policy by Hitler.

Early in April 1940, the phony war came to a dramatic end. Without warning Germany moved into Denmark, a nation with whom Hitler had just recently concluded a non-aggression pact, and then

---

[4] After the war was over it turned out that the French, with 85 divisions, were opposed by 43 German divisions, of which only 11 were fully trained. It was like the ' all quiet along the Potomac ' period in the American Civil War.

into Norway. This attack was well planned, and the co-operation of the Norse traitor Quisling almost resulted in that government's being taken over. The king escaped to England, and the British tried to help; but their efforts were ' too little and too late '; within less than two months they had been driven out, and Hitler controlled Norway.

One month after the invasion of Scandinavia came the blow in the West. Here the French army, already weakened by Communist and Fascist propaganda, trusted to a series of modern forts, called the Maginot line after its designer. But the Maginot line ended at the frontier of Belgium, whose king was so scrupulously neutral and so eager to keep out of war that he neglected even rudimentary defense. On 10 May the German army invaded his country and neutral Holland, while the *Luftwaffe*, the German air force, rained death on those countries and on northeastern France. In five days the Netherlands was conquered, Rotterdam laid in ruins by a cruel air assault. Three days later Antwerp fell. Already the German Panzer (armored) divisions, slipping around the end of the Maginot line, had crashed through the Ardennes Forest, enveloped a French army, and smashed ahead toward the channel ports. On 21 May — only eleven days after the attack on Holland — the Germans reached the English Channel, cutting off the British expeditionary force which had been rushed to the aid of Belgium and France. A week later Belgium surrendered, and the British were left to their fate. Their evacuation has well been called ' the miracle of Dunkirk.' Every available warship, yacht, power boat, fisherman, barge, and tug, to the number of 848, was pressed into service; and with a suicide division holding the front and the Royal Air Force screening, 338,000 men were transported to England. But they did not bring their weapons, and evacuations do not win wars.

The German army now swung south, and in two weeks cut the French army to pieces. On 10 June 1940 Mussolini, with his jackal instinct to be in at the kill, entered the war. Five days later Paris fell, and Premier Reynaud, in desperation, appealed to Roosevelt for ' clouds of planes.' But Roosevelt could give only sympathy, and a hastily formed French government under the aged Marshal Pétain sued for peace. Hitler exacted a savage price. He occupied half of France, leaving the southern part to be ruled, from Vichy, by Pétain and Laval, who were forced to collaborate with the victors, even to recruit workers for German war industry and to deliver French Jews to torture and death. In one month Hitler's mechanized armies had done what the forces of William II had been unable to accomplish in four years.

Now England stood alone. ' We have just one more battle to win,' said Hitler's propaganda minister Goebbels to cheering thousands; but Hitler, having foolishly counted on England's not fighting, was not prepared with landing craft and equipment to launch a massive amphibious operation. While these instruments were being built and assembled in northern France, Hitler's air force leader Marshal Goering tried to ' soften up ' England by massive bombing attacks. All that summer and fall the German bombs rained on Britain. In September 1940 this air assault rose to a furious crescendo. Cities like London, Coventry, and Birmingham suffered massive destruction; civilian casualties ran into the tens of thousands. England at that juncture was saved by her scientists, such as Watson-Watt and Tizard, who developed radar and persuaded the government to set up a chain of radar warning posts about southern and eastern England; and by the gallantry of her Spitfire and Hurricane fighter pilots, who exacted an insupportable toll of the invaders. By October the German air force had to acknowledge that it had failed.

In this hour of mortal peril England found her soul, under the inspiration of a great leader. The reins of government, on 11 May 1940, had passed from the faltering hands of Chamberlain into the iron grip of Winston Churchill, who announced, when he took office, that he had naught to offer his countrymen but ' blood, sweat, and tears.' Undismayed by disaster, he confronted life with antique courage, and infused that courage into freedom-loving peoples everywhere. At the threat of invasion, he thus hurled defiance at the German legions: ' We shall not flag or fail, we shall go on to the end, we shall fight in France, we shall fight on the seas and oceans . . . we shall fight on the landing grounds, we shall fight in the fields and in the streets, we shall fight in the hills; we shall never surrender. And even if . . . this island . . . were subjugated and starving, then our Empire beyond the seas, armed and guarded by the British Fleet, would carry on the struggle, until, in God's good time, the new world, with all its power and might, steps forth to the rescue and liberation of the old.'

Would America respond? President Roosevelt did so. In a speech to the graduating class of the University of Virginia, on 10 June

1940, he announced, ' We will extend to the opponents of force the material resources of this nation; and, at the same time . . . speed up the use of these resources in order that we . . . in the Americas may have equipment and training equal to the task of any emergency. . . .'

6. AMERICA MOVES TOWARD WAR

Americans were not neutral in thought to this war. An overwhelming majority desired the defeat of Hitler and his satellites, but also wanted to keep out of the war. One concession, however, was wrung from a reluctant Congress — a modification of neutrality legislation which permitted belligerents to obtain war materials from this country on a ' cash and carry ' basis. Britain and France promptly took advantage of the new law by placing large orders with American manufacturers, but it would be months or years before tanks began to roll off assembly lines and planes out of hangars in sufficient quantity to match German production.

During the winter of 1939–40, few Americans worried about that consideration. It was assumed that the French army, supposed to be the world's best, could take care of Hitler with the help of British sea power. But the German conquest of France, the Low Countries, and Scandinavia made the nation shudder. What would happen if the British navy fell into German hands, and the United States was attacked both in the Atlantic and, by Japan, in the Pacific? That gloomy prospect, under the spur of presidential prodding, resulted in Congress's voting immense sums for defense. We began to build a two-ocean navy and thousands of planes, and to raise and equip a great army. Within a year after the invasion of the Low Countries, Congress appropriated $37 billion for rearmament and aid to the Allies — a sum larger than the total cost to the United States of World War I.

This, however, was a long-range program. Not until 1943, it was thought, would planes come out in sufficient numbers to enable the United States to meet attack from any direction, and not until 1945 would the two-ocean navy be in commission. Until then the safety of the United States would depend upon the ability of Britain to hold out, and the ability of American diplomats to appease Japan.

The President was prepared for even bolder steps, and he announced them with the utmost frankness. The myth built up by pacifist historians like Beard to the effect that he made a ' covenant ' with the American people to ' keep them out of war ' has no foundation in fact. His radio ' fireside chat ' of 26 May 1940, his Charlottesville speech of 10 June which we have already quoted, gave fair notice that the administration was no longer neutral; merely nonbelligerent. At the same time (June 1940) he replaced the colorless Secretaries of War and of the Navy in his cabinet with two prominent Republicans — the 72-year-old Henry M. Stimson, who had been Secretary of War under Taft and Secretary of State under Hoover, and Frank Knox, who had been the vice-presidential candidate in 1936. By the end of 1940 there were also new and stronger Democratic faces in the cabinet: Frank Walker replaced Jim Farley as Postmaster General, Robert H. Jackson came in as Attorney-General, Jesse Jones in Commerce.

In pursuance of the new presidential policy came a series of diplomatic, executive, and legislative acts. The Act of Havana of 29 July 1940 extended protection to European colonies in America, giving notice that the transfer of British, French, or Dutch colonies to Nazi overlords would be resisted. In August the United States and Canada set up a joint board to pool their defense facilities. In mid-September Congress passed the first peacetime conscription in our history — the Burke-Wadsworth Bill, providing for the registration of all men between the ages of 21 and 35 and the induction into the armed services of 800,000 draftees. That same month President Roosevelt announced an arrangement whereby the United States transferred to Britain 50 World War I destroyers and received in return 99-year leases on a series of naval and air bases in the British West Indies.[5] It was, said the President, ' an epochal and far-reaching act of preparation for continental defense in the face of grave danger.'

Nor was Anglo-American co-operation a one-way affair. A British scientific mission, headed by Sir Henry Tizard, reached Washington in August 1940, with blueprints of radar and the latest secret weapons (rockets, underwater detectors, etc.) which they were authorized to place at the disposition of our armed forces; and the National Defense Research Committee, organized that summer and including such distinguished scientists as Vannevar Bush and James B. Conant, reciprocated.

[5] The Argentia (Newfoundland) and Bermuda bases were free gifts, and the U.S. Navy also transferred ten Coast Guard cutters to Britain.

It was charged, both in this country and by the Axis powers, that these measures were unneutral, which indeed they were; openly so. The Attorney-General advised the President that Hitler could no longer invoke the protection of international law, after successively violating the neutrality of Denmark, Norway, Belgium, and Holland. But this did not lessen our respect for the neutrality of other nations. Switzerland successfully maintained hers throughout the war, doing business with both sides. Temptation was great, after we entered the war, to recover the British naval bases in the Irish Free State, which Chamberlain had improvidently given up, and to seize a base in the Azores, to help the fight against enemy submarines. But De Valera was allowed defiantly to maintain Irish neutrality, even protesting against American troops' using Northern Ireland, which was outside his jurisdiction; and Dr. Salazar did not relax the neutrality of Portugal until he was fairly certain that the Axis was not going to win.

The destroyer-bases deal met with general approval. But Roosevelt's foreign policy sharply divided American opinion and precipitated one of the greatest debates in American history. Critics charged that it was dragging the United States inexorably into an ' imperialistic ' war with which we had no legitimate concern; supporters insisted that only by helping Britain and France to defeat Hitler could we save democracy from destruction and ourselves from ultimate attack. The issue was fought out in the halls of Congress, in the press, over the radio, on public platforms, and in private houses. Party lines were shattered, labor organizations split, business relations were strained, old friendships broken. William Allen White's Committee to Defend America by Aiding the Allies organized branches in a thousand towns, sent out hundreds of speakers and millions of letters and pamphlets to arouse the nation to its danger. The opposition organization, the America First Committee, top-billing Charles Lindbergh, paraded, picketed, protested, and preached an amalgam of isolationism and pacifism, with overtones of anti-Semitism; and it came out after the war that the ' American Firsters ' accepted financial support from Germany. Newspapers like the New York *Times* and *Herald-Tribune* ranged themselves behind the presidential policy, while the Chicago *Tribune* found itself in a congenial alliance with the Hearst papers ringing the alarm-bell against ' being dragged into war to save England.'

7. The Election of 1940

In the midst of this debate came the presidential election. Back in 1919 the Republican party had espoused isolationism, and ever since had clung to that unheroic position. Political considerations now appeared to dictate consistency in that policy. The three leading contenders for the presidential nomination — Senator Robert Taft of Ohio, Senator Arthur Vandenberg of Michigan, and District Attorney Thomas Dewey of New York — were isolationists in varying degree. But, in the meantime, a group of amateur politicians had been building up a political maverick, Wendell Willkie, a Wall Street lawyer who had never been active in politics. Willkie was a liberal conservative, critical not of the principles animating the New Deal but of its extravagance and inefficiency. He was no isolationist, but a frank proponent of aid to the Allies. His sincerity and personal charm appealed to an electorate wearied with political clap-trap, and inspired a devotion such as no other Republican has enjoyed between ' Teddy ' and ' Ike.' When the Republican convention met at Philadelphia in June, seasoned politicians found that they could not hold the rising tide of Willkie sentiment. On the sixth ballot he was nominated.

The Democrats were in a quandary. The President had never been more popular, or his leadership more essential, than in this crisis. Democratic state conventions called for his renomination. But would he accept the nomination for a third term, and would the American people acquiesce in this challenge to the sacrosanct two-term tradition? Roosevelt himself maintained an inscrutable silence. The Democratic convention, without guidance, renominated him on the first ballot. Roosevelt replied by radio that ' in the face of the danger which confronts our time ' he had no right to refuse; but there is no doubt that F.D.R. loved power and gladly accepted responsibility in the most ticklish situation his country had been in since 1861.

Since Jack Garner had had more than enough of the vice-presidency, Roosevelt's able Secretary of Agriculture, Henry Wallace of Iowa, received second place.

The campaign that followed lacked real issues, since Willkie supported the President's ' short of war ' measures, and most of the New Deal domestic reforms. It was not clear that Willkie could do better what Roosevelt was doing well, and he labored under the handicap of the support of odd-balls, such as followers of the rabble-rousing Gerald Smith, and of Father Coughlin, who accused Roosevelt of Communism. Although many Southern bourbons disliked the New Deal because it was supposed to be doing too much for the Negroes, the South in general, with its gallant traditions, applauded the President's determination to help the Allies; and, ahead of any other part of the country, prepared mentally for the war that the nation had to fight.

In the November election Roosevelt received 449 electoral votes, Willkie only 82. Apart from *semper fideles* Maine and Vermont, the Republicans carried only the isolationist heartland of the Midwest.[6] The third-term tradition had been shattered; it required Amendment XXII to the Constitution, the Republicans' posthumous slap at F.D.R., to put it together again.

8. YEAR OF DECISION

The President naturally interpreted re-election as an endorsement of his foreign as well as his domestic policies. When Congress met early in January 1941 he appealed to it for support of nations who were fighting in defense of what he called the Four Freedoms — freedom of speech, freedom of religion, freedom from want, freedom from fear. Four days later he submitted a program designed to circumvent the limitations of the neutrality legislation and make American war material immediately available to the fighting democracies. This was the Lend-Lease Act, which authorized the President to ' sell, transfer, exchange, lease, lend ' any defense articles ' to the government of any country whose defense the President deems vital to the defense of the United States.' It also made available to such nations the facilities of American shipyards. Although the President argued for his proposal with a simile that reached the popular understanding — ' Suppose my neighbor's house catches fire, and I have a length of garden hose . . .' — it touched off a prolonged and bitter debate which reached its nadir in Senator Burton K. Wheeler's statement that Lend-Lease ' will plow under every fourth American boy.' After the isolationists had had their say, administration supporters passed the bill by substantial majorities and it became law 11 March 1941.

6 The popular vote was Roosevelt, 27,243,466; Willkie, 22,304,755.

Lend-Lease really made the United States the 'arsenal of democracy.' Under its provisions America not only made available to the enemies of the Axis billions of dollars worth of arms, foodstuffs, and services,[7] but geared her own production to war needs and officially abandoned any pretense at neutrality.

Events now moved speedily. A few weeks after the passage of Lend-Lease the United States seized all Axis shipping in American ports. In April 1941 it took Greenland under protection and announced that the navy would patrol the sea lanes in defense zones. In May came the transfer of 50 oil tankers to Britain, and, after the sinking of an American freighter by a U-boat, the proclamation of an 'unlimited national emergency.' In June the United States froze all Axis assets in this country and closed all Axis consulates. And on 24 June the President announced that Lend-Lease would be extended to a new ally — Russia. For on 22 June, Hitler, in one of the astounding about-faces common to dictators, broke his 1939 pact and set out to conquer that vast country. It was one of those colossal mistakes in strategy which undid the earlier mistakes of England and France. Now they had an ally capable of pinning down the bulk of the German army on an Eastern front. And all left-wing elements in America, which had been sneering at the 'imperialist war,' now demanded our participation in a 'crusade.'

The United States moved toward a war basis and complete involvement, despite bitter opposition from isolationists and others. An administration bill to extend conscription for the duration of the emergency, and keep under the colors the national guard regiments then receiving training, passed the House only by a majority of one vote. Many Congressmen who voted to 'send the boys home' were really for having them stay, but feared the wrath of their constituents.[8] A group of leading citizens, including Herbert Hoover and John L. Lewis of the C.I.O., proclaimed that America had no stake in the outcome of this war. But public opinion was hardening. And when, after a battle on 4 September between *U-642* and U.S.S. *Greer,* the President ordered the navy to 'shoot on sight' any German submarine en-

---

[7] The original appropriation was $7 billion; altogether Lend-Lease aid totaled $50,226,845,387.

[8] The Republicans in the House voted 133 to 21 against this selective service bill, 143 to 21 against repeal of the arms embargo, and 135 to 24 against Lend-Lease.

countered, the nation applauded. From that date, the United States was engaged in a *de facto* naval war with Germany.

In the meantime, President Roosevelt, like Wilson a generation earlier, had moved to obtain a statement of war aims from the Allies. On 14 August 1941 he and Winston Churchill met afloat in Argentia Bay, Newfoundland, and there drew up the Atlantic Charter, containing certain 'common principles' on which they based 'their hopes for a better future for the world.' These included the already proclaimed Four Freedoms, a renunciation of territorial aggrandizement, a promise of the restoration of self-government to those deprived of it, and to all equal access to trade and raw materials. This was essentially a restatement of Wilson's principles; and, as the Fourteen Points met death in the hands of their friends, so the Atlantic Charter received only a limited application, since Russia wanted no piece of it, and the Western powers, desperate for her aid in the war, acquiesced in her breaking these principles with respect to Poland and the Baltic republics.

For Bibliography for this Chapter see the General World War II Bibliography at the end of Chapter XXX, page 846.

World War II: The Defensive Phase

1. PEARL HARBOR — 7 DECEMBER 1941

FOR over a year, tension had been mounting in the Far East. The Japanese war lords, meeting unexpected resistance in China, now planned to swing south and gobble up the Philippines, Malaya, and Indonesia. In order to realize this ' Greater East Asia Co-Prosperity Sphere,' as they called it, Japan had to risk fighting Great Britain, France, the Netherlands, and the United States, which controlled the coveted territories. The Japanese government was of two minds about risking open war with the West. It still had considerable respect for the United States Navy. But after the German victories of May–June 1940, it became more difficult for moderate elements in Japan to restrain the militarists. Now that France and Holland were conquered, Indo-China and the Netherlands East Indies were ripe for the picking; Malaya, Burma, and even India looked easy, when and if Hitler invaded Britain. In the summer of 1940 Japan wrested permission to build airfields in Indo-China from the helpless Vichy government of France. The United States struck back with a small loan to China and a partial embargo on exports to Japan. Congress, in the Act to Expedite the Strengthening of the National Defense (July 1940), gave the President power to restrict the export of any war materials required for American defense or to license export to friendly nations. In the same month, Congress passed the Two-Ocean Navy Act. Very cautiously, Roosevelt began imposing embargoes on various strategic materials, including scrap iron; and a Gallup poll indicated 96 per cent popular approval. So things went for almost a year.

In July 1941 events began moving toward a crisis. On the 25th, Japan announced that she had assumed a protectorate of the whole of French Indo-China. Next day, President Roosevelt took three momentous steps. He received the armed forces of the Philippine Commonwealth into the United States Army, appointed General Douglas MacArthur to command all army forces in the Far East, and issued an executive order freezing Japanese financial assets in the United States. Great Britain and the Netherlands followed suit, cutting off Japan's source of credit and imports of rubber, scrap iron, and fuel oil. The Japanese war lords decided to make war on these three countries within three or four months, unless the flow of oil and other strategic supplies was restored. For Japan was 'eating her own tail' in the matter of oil; the armies must have fuel or evacuate the mainland, and the military could not contemplate any such loss of face. It was the embargo on oil and credit that brought Japan to the point of war. After one hundred and thirty years Thomas Jefferson, in a sense, was vindicated, but the end product was a war more terrible than anything he ever imagined.

The final negotiations were a mere sparring for time by two governments that considered war all but inevitable. The Japanese wanted time to organize their military and naval push to the south; the United States wanted time to prepare the defense of the Philippines and strengthen the navy. Through the summer and fall of 1941 Secretary Hull made it clear that Japan could have all the goods and credits she wanted from America, if she would begin a military evacuation of China and Indo-China. Prince Konoye, the Japanese premier, on 14 October asked General Tojo, the war minister, to begin at least a token withdrawal. Tojo refused. He was confident that Japan could beat America, Britain, and any other country that stood in her way; and a few days later Tojo became prime minister. On 20 November he presented Japan's ultimatum. He promised to occupy no more Asiatic territory if the United States would stop reinforcing the Philippines; he would evacuate southern Indo-China only if the United States would cut off aid to Chiang Kai-shek and 'unfreeze' Japanese assets in the United States, leaving Japan free to complete her subjugation of China. Tojo did not expect that the United States would accept such terms, which were suitable only for a defeated nation, and his plans for further aggression were already hardened. On 26 November 1941 the Japanese striking force of six big carriers carrying 423 planes (of which 353 were available for the attack), two battleships, two heavy cruisers, and eleven destroyers sortied from its rendezvous in the Kurile Islands for the fatal destination of Pearl Harbor.

No inkling even of the existence of that force leaked out. A few days earlier, however, Japanese troop-laden transports with escorting warships were reported steaming south off Formosa, and on 27 November Washington sent a 'war warning' message to Pearl Harbor and Manila, indicating an amphibious attack against either the Philippines, Thailand, or the Malay Peninsula, but nobody suspected that Pearl Harbor would be attacked.

Oahu was in a relaxed Sunday morning mood at 7:55 December 7, when the bombs began to drop. Despite the war warning of 27 November, Admiral Kimmel had not interrupted his training schedules or canceled week-end leave and liberty; General Short had his army planes parked wing-to-wing, fearing only danger from sabotage. A midget submarine launched from an advance Japanese force was sighted off Pearl Harbor at 3:42 A.M. 7 December and sunk at 6:45, but the word did not reach naval headquarters for over an hour. An army search radar on northern Oahu picked up scouting planes from the Japanese carriers at 6:45, and the first wave of attack planes at 7:02; but the watch officer laughed off the report. General Marshall and Admiral Stark, in Washington, hearing that the Japanese ambassador was about to present a note breaking off diplomatic relations to Secretary Hull, at an hour corresponding to 7:30 A.M. at Pearl Harbor, sent out an alert to the effect that something, they knew not what, was about to happen; the alert, sent by commercial wire, was delivered after the attack.

At the end of this sad and bloody day, the 'day that shall live in infamy' as President Roosevelt called it, 2403 American sailors, soldiers, marines, and civilians had been killed, and 1178 more wounded; 149 planes had been destroyed on the ground or in the water; battleship *Arizona* was shattered and sunk beyond repair; *Oklahoma* shattered and capsized; *Tennessee, West Virginia,* and *California* were resting on the bottom; *Nevada* run aground to prevent sinking; two naval auxiliaries destroyed; three destroyers and a few other vessels badly damaged. All at a cost of fewer than 30 planes and about the same number of men to the Japanese striking force, which returned undetected to its home waters.

Nor was this all. Although General MacArthur's Far Eastern command was notified of the attack on Pearl Harbor at 3:00 A.M. 8 December (corresponding to 8:00 A.M. 7 December at Oahu), a Japanese bomber attack from Formosa caught the army air force grounded on fields near Manila at noon, and all but wiped it out. At 8:30 A.M. Guam was bombed from nearby Saipan, and before dawn Japanese troops landed on the Malay Peninsula.

To millions of Americans, sitting down to Sunday dinner, or with radios tuned in to some musical program, this news of disaster after disaster came as something fantastic and incredible. As the awful details poured in, hour after hour, incredulity turned to anger and an implacable determination to avenge these ' unprovoked and dastardly ' attacks. Next day Congress declared a state of war with Japan; on 11 December Germany and Italy, faithful to their tripartite pact with Japan, declared war on the United States.

President Roosevelt delivered his war message to the nation on the 9th. Reviewing American efforts for peace and the events that led up to the attack on Pearl Harbor, he reminded the people that this was a war of survival, not only for their nation but for democracy and for spiritual values which Americans had always cherished and defended. It is indeed painful to contemplate what would have happened to the United States if the Axis and Japan had won World War II. Yet, conversely, the victory of the Allies freed their enemies from dictatorships, and gave them a far happier future than they could have enjoyed under regimes of conquest and oppression.

The American people were not content merely to avenge Pearl Harbor; they wished to know why it happened. Investigations followed, culminating in an exhaustive one by Congress after the war was over, with testimony and reports filling forty volumes. In these investigations, and in discussion in Congress and in the press, every effort was made by pacifists and Roosevelt-haters to prove that the administration was responsible; that it withheld vital news of Japanese ship movements from the commanders at Pearl Harbor, either from sheer stupidity or from a vicious design to get the country into full-fledged war, since Hitler seemed determined not to resent our unneutral aid to Great Britain. It may confidently be asserted, after twenty years have elapsed, that no scrap of evidence exists to support this amazing hypothesis.

Naval and army intelligence had broken the Japanese secret code, and were ' reading the mail ' that passed between Tokyo and Japanese representatives abroad; but the Japanese war lords never let their consuls or their ambassadors at Washington in on the secret. The United States government knew that frequent and detailed reports were being sent from the Japanese consulate at Honolulu about American ship movements; but similar reports were being sent by Japanese consuls from every important world port, and nobody noticed that those from Honolulu also gave the exact position of every ship in Pearl Harbor. Washington knew that mighty Japanese forces were moving south — that was the reason for the 27 November war warning to Admiral Kimmel and General Short — but none of the ' top brass ' thought that Japan was capable of launching another attack eastward. Nor, putting themselves in the place of Japan, could they imagine that any nation in its senses would dare bring the United States, angry and united, into war; for the isolationists in Congress would very likely have prevented a declaration of war on Japan had she attacked only British or Dutch possessions. Peacetime relaxation in Hawaii was matched by Sunday somnolence in Washington. General Marshall, chief of the army general staff, did not omit his Sunday morning horseback ride on 7 December, although he had been warned that something was about to break. Two ranking officers of the war plans division of the Navy Department, when they heard the terrible news, decided to go down to the department and get secret war plans out of the safe. They found that the combination had a time-lock which would not be released until Monday morning!

In attacking Pearl Harbor, Japan actually conferred a moral and strategic favor on the nation which was the chief object of her rage and hatred. Senator Arthur Vandenberg of Michigan, who had been one of the leading isolationists before December 1941, remarked five years later that Pearl Harbor ' drove most of us to the irresistible conclusion that world peace is indivisible. We learned that the oceans are no longer moats around our ramparts. We learned that mass destruction is a progressive science which defies both time and space and reduces human flesh and blood to cruel impotence.'

2. How the War Was Directed

Supposing those officers in Washington had been able to read the war plan on Pearl Harbor Sunday, it would have done them no good. This plan called for the Pacific Fleet, on the outbreak of war with Japan, to sail westward, capture selected Japanese bases in the Marshall and Caroline Islands, and then relieve MacArthur's army in the Philippines. This, it was calculated, would take from three to five months. If the battle fleet had not been sunk in shoal water in Pearl Harbor, it would undoubtedly have been sunk in deep water by Japanese bomber planes based on the Marshalls; for on 10 December

1941 the Japanese air force did just that to H.M.S. *Prince of Wales* and *Repulse* off the Malay Peninsula. These disasters proved that capital ships were incapable of defending themselves against bombing aircraft. That was one of the many things that the United States and British navies set out to remedy.

Owing to ample warning of impending hostilities on two oceans, and the administration's foresight, the United States was relatively better prepared for a world-wide war in 1941 than she had been for a limited one in 1917. In that year the United States Navy had entered the war with no plans, and no agreement with associated nations how to operate. But early in 1941, warned by the German blitz on neutral nations of Europe, the United States Joint Chiefs of Staff (as the heads of army, navy, and army air force shortly became) initiated a secret staff conference with their British opposite numbers. The resulting ' ABC-1 ' staff agreement of 27 March 1941 set forth that, if and when America entered the war, her primary military effort would be exerted in the European theater.

This concept of ' Beat the Axis First ' was arrived at, because the Axis, by knocking out France, had control of the entire western coast of Europe, thus threatening with her U-boats sea communication between the Old World and the New; because Germany had a greater war potential than Japan, and it was feared she might uncork some devastating secret weapon if given the time — as indeed she did, but too late to win; and because Japan was fighting only China and there was still hope of keeping her from further aggressions. This decision, which dictated the major strategy of World War II, became the more pressing after Hitler attacked Russia; for if Germany obtained control over Russian manpower and resources, the geopolitical ' heartland ' would be under Hitler's control, from Finisterre to Vladivostok, and from the North Cape to the bulge of Africa.

The informal alliance thus formed continued throughout the war, through the American Joint Chiefs of Staff and the British Chiefs of Staff. Meeting together, these were called the Combined Chiefs of Staff. They, under President Roosevelt and Prime Minister Churchill, initiated strategy, drafted plans, allocated forces, and directed the war. Russia was represented by Marshal Stalin, and China by Chiang Kai-shek, at the Teheran and Cairo C.C.S. conferences, respectively; but each of these two allies fought his own war, not without aid from the others, but with little regard to their wishes or strategy.

America was fortunate in having very able war direction. The vital members of the Joint Chiefs of Staff throughout the war were General H. H. (' Hap ') Arnold, head of the air force, which until after the war was part of the army; the army chief of staff General George C. Marshall, a Virginian who combined in his character the patient wisdom of a Washington with the strategic savvy of a Lee; Admiral Ernest J. King, chief of naval operations and commander in chief of the fleet (Cominch), a hard-bitten, experienced naval officer who took a world-wide view of strategy, and seldom, if ever, made a mistake.[1] These three in concert with President Roosevelt formed a winning team. There had been nothing like that in American history since the Lincoln-Grant-Farragut team of 1864–65.

At the cabinet level, America was equally strong. Cordell Hull of Tennessee, Secretary of State, was becoming rather infirm, but he had an energetic under secretary, Sumner Welles, and several able assistant secretaries, such as Dean Acheson and Adolf Berle, Jr.; Henry M. Stimson, the elderly Secretary of War, was still full of brains and energy, and profited by his cabinet experience under two earlier presidents. Frank Knox, Secretary of the Navy, also had an able under secretary, James Forrestal, who handled all matters of procurement for the navy, as assistant secretary Robert Patterson did for the army. Forrestal succeeded Knox after the latter's death in 1944, and later became the first Secretary of Defense. Over these staffs and heads of departments, and also over innumerable boards and committees which dealt with various phases of the war, were Churchill and Roosevelt. The ' P.M.' was Britain's greatest war leader since the elder Pitt. His energy and pluck saved England in her darkest hour, which he, in his remarkable history of the war, characteristically calls ' Her Finest Hour.' He called leading scientists, in the persons of Sir Henry Tizard and F. A. Lindemann, into consultation at the very top levels of government. He visited every British front to give the soldiers and sailors of King George VI the inspiration of his presence, always smoking a long cigar and making the ' V for Victory ' sign with two upraised fingers.

Roosevelt, too, was a great war President, in a class with Lincoln; and, like Lincoln's, his greatness came from a capacity to lead and

[1] Their British opposite numbers were Field Marshal Sir Alan Brooke, Admiral Sir Dudley Pound (relieved by Admiral Lord Cunningham in 1943), and Air Chief Marshal Sir Charles Portal.

inspire, rather than from skill in administration. He was an opportunist, with a flair for the possible and the attainable, rather than, as
in the case of Wilson, for the ideal; but, no less than Wilson, he
looked ahead to a world of peace and justice. He kept a boyish zest
for life, and his courage and energy triumphed over the crippling disease of his young manhood and enabled him for twelve years to carry
the greatest burden that any modern statesman has been called upon
to bear. His warm understanding of other nations enabled him to
deal successfully with Latin America, neutrals, and representatives of
the overrun democracies; at his death, when victory was in sight, he
was almost universally mourned. He respected his military advisers,
and his considered judgment was almost always sound. He sometimes
worked in devious ways, as through his much detested but amazingly
wise confidential assistant, Harry Hopkins; but the wisdom of the
serpent was necessary to deal with clashing personalities and opposing
interests. It was F.D.R. who glimpsed the dangers of Axis and Japanese militarism before any other American leader, and who, with tact
and patience, persuaded a reluctant Congress and a pacifist-indoc-
trinated people to prepare for war.

3. PROCUREMENT AND PRODUCTION

Although much had been accomplished in military preparedness
when Pearl Harbor broke — far more, relatively, than in 1812, 1846,
or 1917 — yet even more remained to be done. Congress promptly
repealed its prohibition against sending draftees outside the Western
Hemisphere, and extended their period of service to six months after
the war's end — no ' three months men ' in this war. All men between
18 and 45 were made liable to military service. Standards of physical
fitness and intelligence were exacting, and many failed to qualify. Re-
jections ran from less than 25 per cent in Iowa, Kansas, Wyoming,
and Utah, to over 40 per cent in Georgia and the Carolinas. Including
voluntary enlistments, over 15 million people served in the armed
forces during the war; 10 million in the army, 4 million in the navy
and coast guard, 600,000 in the marine corps. About 216,000 women
served as nurses, and in the auxiliary ' Waves ' and ' Wacs,' or as lady
marines.

There was a great deal of discussion about the place of the Negro
in the armed services. Although not confined to labor battalions, as

he largely had been in World War I, he was not completely integrated with the whites, except on bases and in small units and ships. And, for want of education, Negro aviators and officer candidates were few. In two specialized activities Negroes excelled: in naval anti-aircraft fire, and in driving the ' dukws,' the amphibious trucks used in amphibious assaults on the beaches. Facilities on bases were, however, integrated; and, in general, war service gave the Negro race in America a social and economic lift which made the denial of political rights and economic opportunity, still practiced in states of the former Confederacy, very difficult to maintain.

The problem of training was prodigious. The first consideration was morale. This was easier to achieve for the navy and the marine corps, whose recruits were volunteers. It never seemed to occur to them that they could be defeated. But the average ' G.I.' (General Issue), the nickname for infantrymen in this war, was a more or less unwilling draftee, who had been brought up in a pacifist atmosphere. He could be trained *to* fight, but it was well said of General Patton that he alone could make them *want* to fight. And more was required of the G.I. than of the ' doughboy' of World War I, or the ' boys in blue' — or gray — of 1861. In those days all that a man needed to become a soldier was close-order drill and the manual of arms; modern warfare required him to be something of an athlete, a mechanic, and a scientist as well as a fighting man. A sailor had to be taught almost everything except to sail — basic navigation, ship handling, and gunnery; but modern warships are as complicated as the modern industrial state, and new devices like sonar, radar, and loran were constantly being added. There were any number of specialized forces, such as the army rangers for raiding, and the navy's UDT's or ' frogmen,' who swam up to enemy-held beaches, made soundings, and blew obstacles. Air forces had already become highly specialized. There were fighter planes, high-level bombers, torpedo- and dive-bombers, operating both from ships and shore, and several other types, for which pilots and crewmen had to be trained. And since flying was relatively new, we required an enormous amount of research to replace plane types which proved unequal to their tasks, by newer, faster, and bigger ones. To fight a global war it was necessary to build dozens of naval bases and hundreds of airfields all over the world. Specially packaged units called Lions, Cubs, Oaks, and Acorns were organized with men and matériel all ready to rush in and build a base or airfield as soon as a site was secured.

The work of the service forces was no less important. In this war the average soldier required at least double the World War I equipment. An infantry division of 8000 fighting men required 6000 more to keep it fed, supplied, paid, doctored, amused, transported, and its equipment repaired. And by the end of the war, so many heavy artillery and other elements were added that a 'reinforced' infantry division totaled 20,000 or more men. Remarkable progress was made by the medical corps. Infection and disease had always been the bane of armies, and in every American war before 1917 had accounted for many more deaths than did actual battle. Thanks to abundant food, proper clothing, and hospitals competently staffed, the health of the armed forces in World War II compared favorably with that of the civilian population in the same age groups. The development of sulfa drugs and penicillin, given by injections, the use of plasma for transfusions, control of mosquitoes and other insects, new techniques for the treatment of the terrible burns incident to bursting shells and Japanese kamikaze tactics, and prompt evacuation of the wounded, reduced the death rate from wounds to less than half that of World War I, and enabled about two-thirds of all wounded to return to duty. The increasing role of the artillery shell and the bomb in warfare is shown by the fact that, whilst 94 per cent of wounds in the Civil War were caused by rifle bullets, 72 per cent of those in the two world wars and the Korean War were inflicted by shell fragments.

The United States Navy entered the war well prepared except for anti-aircraft and antisubmarine defense, which happened to be among its most pressing needs. Fortunately, in conjunction with the marines, it had undertaken training for amphibious warfare. That ancient branch of conflict had received a black eye in World War I, owing largely to the British failure at the Dardanelles. As early as 1933 the navy realized that in Asia certainly, and Europe probably, delivering troops to a fighting area would be no simple matter of transporting them by sea and landing them on a wharf; men, supplies, and heavy equipment would have to be landed under fire on enemy-held beaches. Consequently the navy began building a new line of vessels specially designed for amphibious warfare: the 460-foot LSD (Landing Ship, Dock), which spawned loaded landing craft from a miniature lake in its bowels; the 330-foot LST (Landing Ship, Tank), a two-decker floating garage, which became the workhorse of the fleet; the 180-foot LCI (Landing Craft, Infantry) for bringing soldiers directly to a beach; and a variety of small landing craft that could be carried on the davits of a big transport. After 1940, with money available for high wages and overtime in the shipyards, it became possible to build a destroyer in five months instead of a year, and a big carrier in 15 months instead of 35.

The Maritime Commission, created by Congress in 1936 and headed by Rear Admiral Emory S. Land, received new powers in July 1941, and drew up blueprints for an emergency freighter that could be built quickly and inexpensively. The first of these Liberty ships — appropriately named *Patrick Henry* — was launched in September, and 139 more came out that year. The bigger and faster Victory ship followed. The United States Merchant Marine Cadet Corps, established in 1938, was expanded to provide officers; the national maritime union, with the slogan ' Keep 'em Sailing,' co-operated in keeping merchant seamen on their jobs despite losses to U-boats. In November 1941, when Congress repealed the Neutrality Act forbidding merchantmen to arm in self-defense, the navy began installing naval guns with bluejacket crews on freighters.

In the realm of production the United States enjoyed advantages over every other country that enabled it to became an ' arsenal of democracy ' while fighting the war. Lend-Lease and the big defense appropriations of 1940–41 had already added 6 million workers to the payrolls, wiping out unemployment. Yet there were ominous lags and shortages. Donald Nelson, the merchandising expert who became director of procurement in 1940 under the Treasury Department — because no other department was equipped to handle it — said ' we almost lost the war before we ever got into it.' Many leading industrialists, distrusting ' that man in the White House,' could not believe that the country would ever go to war, and hung back from incurring the expense of conversion. The War and Navy Departments were sometimes slow to place orders for tanks, planes, and weapons, lest current models become obsolete before they could be used. The steel industry did not expand its capacity quickly enough, and the automobile industry was reluctant to shift from pleasure cars to war vehicles when restored prosperity released a flood of new car orders. Pearl Harbor galvanized American industry into a confusion of high-

PRODUCTION OF SELECTED WAR ITEMS *
1 JULY 1940 – 31 JULY 1945

	1 July 1940 –Dec. 1941	1942	1943	1944	1 Jan.– 31 July 1945	Total
Military airplanes and special purpose aircraft	23,228	47,859	85,930	96,359	43,225	296,601
Naval ships excluding landing craft	1,341	8,039	18,431	29,150	14,099	71,060
Displacement tonnage of above	270,000	846,000	2,569,000	3,224,000	1,341,000	8,250,000
Merchant shipping	136	760	1,949	1,786	794	5,425
Dead-weight tonnage of above	1,551,000	8,090,000	19,296,000	16,447,000	7,855,000	55,239,000
Machine guns	126,113	666,820	830,384	798,782	302,798	2,724,897
Tanks	4,258	23,884	29,497	17,565	11,184	86,388

* From S. I. Rosenman, *Public Papers of F. D. Roosevelt*, the 1942 volume.

speed planning and production, which had to be straightened out by the War Production Board before anything useful could be accomplished. But in 1942 the curve of production rose sharply, as reference to the table preceding this page indicates. American industry produced not only enough matériel and weapons for the United States, but supplied the deficiencies of Allies besides Britain, whose receipts were not few — many thousands of planes, over 100,000 trucks and jeeps, 6 million tons of steel, a billion dollars' worth of ordnance. Stalin, at the Teheran Conference in December 1943, remarked that sixty of his mobile armored divisions, which could be shifted rapidly from place to place on Russia's extended front, constituted his margin of superiority over the Germans; but it is doubtful whether they could have been moved, except in trucks from America.

Adequate stockpiles of bauxite, aluminum, and chrome, which would have to reach America through submarine-infested waters, were lacking in 1941. Japan's quick conquests cut off the Western world's principal sources of rubber, quinine, and manila fiber, and one of the chief sources of oil. As iron and horses had been essential to earlier wars, so steel, oil, and rubber were to this; armies no longer ‘ marched on their stomachs,’ as Napoleon remarked, or wriggled ahead on their bellies, as in World War I, but rolled in motor vehicles on rubber tires; naval vessels were no longer fired by coal, but by black or diesel oil; high-test avgas was required for the ‘ airy navies grappling in the central blue.’ Oil production had to be vastly increased in the United States and in Venezuela. New synthetic rubber plants, reworked tires, and wild caoutchouc imports from the Amazon lifted rubber production to over a million tons in 1944.

Mighty as America's effort was, it did not add up to total war, as the term was understood in the British Commonwealth, Germany, or Japan. There was no firm control over manpower, no conscription of women, little direction of talent to useful activities. A few edibles were rationed, but most Americans ate more heartily than before. Gasoline and tires were rationed, but hundreds of thousands of cars managed to stay on the road for purposes remotely connected with the war. Personal and corporation taxes were increased, but there was no limit on profits, or to what workers could earn, if they chose to work overtime; and as prices of most essentials were kept down, the standard of living rose. The country was never invaded, except by U-boats penetrating the three-mile limit, and a large measure of the

' blood, sweat, and tears ' that Churchill promised his countrymen, were spared to his country's ally.

Congress successfully resisted the President's demand that the war be financed primarily by taxes. Only about 40 per cent of the cost was met by taxation, the rest by borrowing; about $97 billion were subscribed in government bonds. The United States Treasury went into the red by over $40 billion annually, and borrowed freely from banks at 1 to 1.5 per cent interest — rates which would have astounded Salmon P. Chase. The national debt soared to $250 billion. Total cost of the war, exclusive of postwar pensions, interest payments, Marshall plan, etc., came to about $350 billion, tenfold the cost of World War I.

Thanks to Pearl Harbor, and to Hitler's attack on Russia, which put all the ' commies ' and left-wing pacifists on our side, the United States had far less trouble with dissident groups than in World War I. What trouble there was came from ideological rather than racial motives. The three most prominent traitors were the poet Ezra Pound, who broadcasted for Mussolini, a former American newspaper correspondent in Berlin who tried to help Hitler, and an American-born Japanese girl whom our sailors called ' Tokyo Rose.' None appear to have had any results for their efforts; Pound's stuff was so crazy that few could understand it, and Tokyo Rose's daily score of American ships sunk was so fantastic that few cared to miss it. The major exception to a clean record on civil liberties in this war was the wholesale deportation of Japanese-Americans from the west coast to prison camps in the interior. This was reluctantly consented to by the President largely for political reasons, because the West-coast public clamored for it. In Hawaii, where the Japanese-born population was far greater in proportion than on the west coast, not one act of sabotage was performed; and the young Nisei, organized in an infantry battalion, proved to be the toughest of all fighters for America in the Italian campaign.

It is useless to pretend that war is completely horrible, although in the future it may well be that, or worse. World War II had its high, proud moments of *gaudium certaminis* — the joy of battle that in some sense is in every man — shooting down an enemy plane before it can get you; storming ashore on a coral-reefed beach; forcing a company of tough Germans to cry for quarter; blasting a group of die-hard Japs out of a cave. But in many respects it well illustrated

Justice Holmes's dictum, ' War is organized boredom.' Such were guarding a convoy or patrolling an ocean area against U-boats that might never show up; manning one of the many thousand anti-aircraft guns that the War Department uselessly spotted along the coast; practicing jungle warfare or amphibious assaults day after day for months. On the whole it was a grim, austere war for the American fighting forces, compared with World War I. No brass bands or bugles, no ' Over There ' or marching songs, no flaunting colors; not even a ship's bell to mark the watches. It was typical that when the Japanese surrendered on board *Missouri* on 2 September 1945 ' The Star-Spangled Banner ' had to be played from a disk over the intercom system and Admiral Halsey had no better beverage than coffee to offer his guests.

4. At Bay in the Atlantic

Hitler, in one of his more flagrant and (for us) fortunate misjudgments, did not expect to fight England before 1944. He concentrated German naval efforts on building up a high-seas fleet to challenge the ' mistress of the seas ' at that distant date, when he expected to have all Europe in his grasp. In September 1939 he had fewer than fifty U-boats ready to fight, half of them too small for oceanic work. But this submarine fleet, under command of the young and daring Rear Admiral Karl Doenitz, served notice on the first day of the war that no holds would be barred, and no treaties respected. A U-boat torpedoed and sank the unescorted, unarmed, and lighted British passenger ship *Athenia,* with the loss of 112 lives, many of them women and some of them Americans. German propaganda then compounded the felony by claiming that the British sunk her themselves, to get America into the war.

The Royal Navy, though ill-prepared for defense, got on top of the submarine problem very quickly. Merchantmen on the most vital trade routes were organized into convoys, and Canadian corvettes helped to escort them. A separate Coastal Command of the Royal Air Force was specially trained to hunt submarines. Echo-ranging sound gear (' sonar ') was installed on escort vessels, to detect submarines.[2]

---

[2] The 10-mm or microwave radar for submarine-hunting aircraft, which Doenitz declared to be the most important gadget for defeating U-boats, was also a British invention, adopted in early 1943. All these methods and inventions were freely given to the United States.

During the first ten months of the war, the Germans destroyed more British, French, and neutral ships by surface raids, mines, and aircraft than by submarines, and the total loss was staggering — 616 vessels, amounting to 2.2 million tons.

By June 1940 the fall of France enabled the Germans to construct bombproof submarine pens in the harbors of Brest, Lorient, Saint-Nazaire, and La Pallice, which doubled the range of their U-boats. Admiral Doenitz worked out the technique of night attack on convoys by ' wolf-packs ' of eight to twenty U-boats. A pack would dog a convoy for days, submerging in daylight; and its success prompted the first countermeasures taken by the United States — the destroyer-naval bases deal, the occupation of Greenland and Iceland, the intensive training of sailors in antisubmarine warfare, and help in escorting convoys as far as Iceland. These ' short of war ' measures, as we have seen, gradually merged into a shooting war; [3] but the situation was still very ' sticky ' when Hitler declared war on the United States, 11 December 1941. During the first eleven months of 1941 almost a thousand Allied or neutral merchantmen, totaling over 3.6 million tons, had been lost by enemy action, half of it by U-boats, and very few of those noxious craft were being forfeited. The British by this time had chased submarines out of the narrow seas, but the U-boats had moved out to mid-ocean and were actively supporting General Rommel's offensive in North Africa.

Since the basic strategic decision was to beat the Axis first, the Atlantic sea lanes had to be kept open for supplies, and for building up a United States army in England for eventual invasion of the Continent. American destroyers now helped to escort convoys all the way across, and used the excellent training facilities of the British bases in Northern Ireland. Sinkings in the North Atlantic fell off promptly; soon we knew why. Admiral Doenitz was moving wolf-packs over to the American east coast, where he rightly anticipated rich pickings from non-convoyed tankers and merchantmen. The navy, pressed to build more carriers and cruisers, had neglected small vessels suitable for coastal convoying, hoping to improvise them if

[3] The first hostile contact, unknown at the time, was on 20 June 1941, *U-203* attempting to torpedo U.S.S. *Texas*. The *Greer* incident, already mentioned, occurred on 4 September. U.S.S. *Kearny* was torpedoed but not sunk by a U-boat on 17 Oct. On the 31st, U.S.S. *Reuben James* was torpedoed and sunk by *U-562* about 600 miles west of Iceland. Also, seven American merchantmen were sunk by enemy action prior to the declaration of war.

the need arose; but the Germans were not so accommodating as to wait.

The U-boat offensive opened on 12 January 1942 off Cape Cod, and a severe one it was. Most United States destroyers were tied to North Atlantic escort duty; only five subchasers were in commission; there were fewer than a hundred planes to patrol coastal waters between Newfoundland and New Orleans; no merchantmen had yet been armed. Under these conditions, frightful destruction was wrought by the submarines in shipping lanes between the Canadian border and Jacksonville. During January–April 1942, almost 200 ships were sunk in North American, Gulf, and Caribbean waters, or around Bermuda. Doenitz then shifted his wolf-packs to the Straits of Florida, the Gulf of Mexico, and the Caribbean; and in those waters 182 ships totaling over 751,000 tons were sunk in May and June 1942. Vessels were torpedoed 30 miles off New York City, within sight of Virginia Beach, off the Passes to the Mississippi, off the Panama Canal entrance. Since tourist resorts from Atlantic City to Miami Beach were not even required to turn off neon signs and waterfront lights until 18 April 1942, or to black out completely for another month, hapless freighters and tankers passing them were silhouetted for the benefit of the U-boats. Over half the victims in southern waters were tankers, the sinking of which not only roasted the water-borne survivors in burning oil, but threatened the success of military operations in Europe and the Pacific. Puerto Rico suffered from inability to move crops or import necessary food; sugar and coffee had to be rationed in the United States; 'good neighbors' in Latin America began to doubt big neighbor's ability to win. The north-south sea lane, along the east coast through the Caribbean to Rio de Janeiro and the River Plate, had to be maintained equally with the west-east line to Great Britain, and the Pacific sea lanes. But the U-boats were knocking down the ships like tenpins. New construction of merchantmen in Allied and neutral countries amounted to less than 600,000 tons in June 1942 when the total loss almost touched 800,000 tons; and in half a year the British and American navies had sunk less than one month's production of new U-boats. Obviously, if this ratio continued, a 'torpedo curtain' would soon be dropped between the United States and Europe.

Fortunately Admiral Ernest J. King, who as 'Cinclant' had directed the 'short of war' phase, became 'Cominch,' commander in chief of the United States fleet, on 20 December 1941. At once he took energetic measures to combat the submarine menace. The first need was for small escort vessels. The slogan ' sixty vessels in sixty days ' was nailed to the mast in April 1942; and 67 vessels actually came through by 4 May, when a second 60–60 program was already under way. Scientists were mobilized to find more efficient means of tracking and sinking U-boats. Inshore and offshore patrols were organized with converted yachts — the ' Hooligan Navy ' as it was nicknamed. As more escorts became available, an interlocking convoy system was worked out; the trunk line New York to Key West was fed freight by numerous branch lines which extended north to Canada and south to Brazil. In the second half of 1942 coastal convoys lost only 0.5 per cent of their ships; the transatlantic convoys lost only 1.4 per cent in a whole year. By April 1943 there were every day at sea in the American half of the North Atlantic, an average of 31 convoys with 145 escorts and 673 merchant ships, as well as 120 ships traveling alone and unescorted, and the heavily escorted troop convoys. There was nothing like a well-escorted convoy to ' bait ' the U-boats, or a well-equipped destroyer to kill them with depth charges, or the forward-throwing ' hedgehog '; but you had to have enough destroyers so that some of them could peel off and hunt. A big, fast, four-engined plane like the Liberator, equipped with guns, microwave radar, and depth bombs, was an effective instrument to sink a submarine, especially when they could be located by radio transmission.

It took time for these new methods and weapons to be adopted or produced in sufficient quantities to be effective. Throughout 1942 the U-boats enjoyed a succession of field days at our expense. And, in the meantime, this battle had extended into the Arctic Ocean and the South Atlantic. The first, the most dangerous and disagreeable of all convoy routes, had to be used to get Lend-Lease goods to Russia through Murmansk or Archangel. Although the British navy did most of the escorting over this route — losing in that service eleven warships — about half the merchantmen concerned were American, and their losses were severe. Another extension of the Atlantic battle lay southward. Most of the Latin American nations broke relations with or declared war on the Axis and Japan,[4] and Brazil gave

[4] All Central American republics declared war on the Axis and Japan, and Colombia and Venezuela broke diplomatic relations with them, in December 1941. Ecuador and

792 GROWTH OF THE AMERICAN REPUBLIC

the Allies substantial aid. She declared war on the Axis in August 1942, after Doenitz pulled a minor Pearl Harbor on her by sinking five Brazilian ships within sight of shore. In conjunction with the Brazilian navy, with the British naval command in West Africa, and using an airfield built by United States Army engineers on lonely Ascension Island, an effective air-sea patrol of the Atlantic Narrows was then established.

5. RETREAT IN THE PACIFIC

When the results of the Japanese strike on Pearl Harbor were assessed, it was evident that the situation in Hawaii was not so bad as it seemed; but the consequences of other Japanese attacks in the Far East were much worse. The expensive and valuable installations at Pearl Harbor, the oil tanks filled with 2.5 million gallons of temporarily irreplaceable fuel were spared; the three carriers, *Lexington, Enterprise,* and *Saratoga,* were providentially not at Pearl. These and their air groups actually constituted a striking force far more valuable than the lost battleships, all but two of which were salvaged.

In the Far East, on the other hand, the news was calamitous. Thailand surrendered to the Japanese, who promptly landed troops at various points on the Malay Peninsula and began a relentless march on the British base at Singapore. On 10 December the Rising Sun flag was hoisted on Guam, which had been bravely but pitifully defended by a few hundred Americans and Chamorros. Other Japanese task forces occupied the British Gilbert Islands, captured Hong Kong, and jumped the Borneo oilfields. Japanese bombers based on Indo-China eliminated British naval strength in the Pacific. On Wake Island, lonely outpost in the Central Pacific, Commander W. S. Cunningham and a small marine defense force beat off a Japanese attack on 11 December, only to be overwhelmed by another on the 23rd, before the navy managed to come to their rescue. In the Philippines, after the blitz of 8 December, American air forces in Luzon were reduced to about 17 bombers and 40 fighters. Two days later, Japanese bombers destroyed Cavite navy yard. During the seventeen days before Christmas the enemy made nine amphibious landings in the Philip-

Peru broke relations in January 1942, Mexico in May. Chile broke relations in January 1943. Argentina broke relations only a year later. The countries who had not yet done so declared war in 1945 in order to be among the United Nations.

pines, five of them on Luzon. General MacArthur evacuated Manila on 27 December, withdrew his army to the Bataan Peninsula, and set up headquarters on the island fortress of Corregidor.

The defense of Bataan and Corregidor, valiant and inspiring though it was, had no other effect than to deny the use of Manila Bay to the enemy for three months. The campaign was a melancholy confirmation of Mahan's theory of sea power. The Japanese, controlling all sea approaches and the air too, enveloped both peninsula and Rock in a tight blockade, and landed fresh troops behind the American lines almost at will. Over half the fighting men were disabled by wounds or by disease, and all were at the point of starvation by early April. On the 8th the ' battling bastards of Bataan,' about 12,500 Americans and over 60,000 Filipinos, had to surrender unconditionally. Only a couple of thousand escaped to Corregidor before the ranks of the prisoners were thinned by the infamous 65-mile ' death march ' from Bataan to Japanese prison camps. In the hope of restoring confidence to the Australians, who now expected a Japanese invasion themselves, President Roosevelt ordered General MacArthur to leave the Philippines and set up headquarters in the sub-continent. He left by motor torpedo boat on 11 March 1942, promising to return; as he did. On 6 May, after the Japanese had captured the main defenses of Corregidor, General Jonathan M. Wainwright was forced to surrender the Rock together with its 11,000 defenders, and a Philippine army of over 50,000 on the Visayas and Mindanao. There had been no such capitulation in American history since that of Appomattox. Many troops in the southern islands refused to surrender and continued guerilla resistance to the Japanese with supplies sent from Australia by submarine.

In the meantime the Japanese had won all their objectives in Southeast Asia. Rabaul in New Britain fell in January 1942. The Malay barrier (Sumatra, Java, Bali, Timor, and smaller islands), which barred the enemy from the Indian Ocean and Australia, was desperately defended by soldiers, sailors, and aviators of the United States, Great Britain, the Netherlands, and Australia under a combined ' Abda ' command. But this loose-jointed command had a hopeless task. The Japanese would seize a strategic point in Borneo or Celebes, operate or build an airfield there, soften up the next objective by air bombing, and then occupy it with an amphibious force and go on to the next. Admiral Hart's Asiatic Fleet, with British and

Dutch allies, fought a series of valiant engagements in January and February 1943 — Balikpapan, Bali, Badung Strait, Java Sea — always greatly outnumbered, always defeated. The great naval base of Singapore, on which England had lavished millions of pounds, fell on 15 February. On Java and in the surrounding waters the soldiers, sailors, and aviators of the three united nations fought and fought until they could fight no more. On 9 May 1942 Java surrendered. Rangoon, capital and chief seaport of Burma, had been occupied by the Japanese the day before. The Japanese were now the rulers of East Asia, west to British India and south to the waters adjacent to Australia and Fiji. India, as threatened by nationalists within as by enemies without, and Australia were tremblingly aware that their turn might come next.

Never in modern history has there been so quick and valuable a series of conquests; even Hitler's were inferior. The prestige of the white races fell so low that even victory over Japan could not win it back; and the areas that the Japanese conquered, though no longer Japanese, are now also independent of Europe.

For Bibliography for this Chapter see the General World War II Bibliography at the end of Chapter XXX, page 846.

First Offensives, West and East

1. 'VICTORY DISEASE'

ON Christmas Eve 1941 Admiral King warned, 'The way to victory is long; the going will be hard.' And hard it was. Admiral Chester W. Nimitz, who at the same time received the command of the Pacific Fleet, was forced to bide his time until new naval construction and more trained troops gave him adequate reinforcements. Since no British fleet remained in the Pacific, the Combined Chiefs of Staff entrusted the conduct of the Pacific war to the American Joint Chiefs of Staff, and they perforce adopted a strategy of active defense. A glance at the map of the Pacific will show why. Distances were immense, and the only hope of eventually defeating Japan was to hold fast to what we still had, and prepare for future offensives. Islands still in American possession such as the Hawaiian and Samoan groups had to be defended; the sea-air lanes to New Zealand and to Australia had to be protected; and that meant tying up a large part of the fleet to escort transports and supply ships. Nothing much could be done for five months except to make hit-and-run raids with carrier planes. Of these the most spectacular was the air assault on Tokyo 18 April 1942. That was delivered by Colonel James H. Doolittle's B-25's from carrier *Hornet,* a base that President Roosevelt humorously called ' Shangri-La,' after the mystery city in James Hilton's *Lost Horizon.* The planes did little damage, and most of their crews had to bail out over China; but the news that Tokyo had actually been bombed lifted American morale, and encouraged the Japanese high command to retrieve face by an imprudent offensive. America learned more from adversity than Japan did from victory.

Instead of sitting pretty in their new conquests until attacked, and organizing their resources to make their country invincible, the Japanese succumbed to what one of their admirals after the war ruefully called ' victory disease.' They decided to wrest more Pacific territory — Papua, Fijis, New Caledonia, Solomons, western Aleutians, Midway Island — from the Allies and set up an impregnable ' ribbon defense.' These islands, in connection with those that Japan already held, were near enough to one another for patrol planes to protect, and as bases for disrupting the lifeline between the United States and the British antipodes.

Admiral Yamamoto, greatest Japanese sea lord since Togo, wished to provoke a major battle with our Pacific Fleet. A good prophet, he pointed out that the United States Navy must be annihilated, if ever, in 1942, before American productive capacity replaced the Pearl Harbor losses. He expected that after another defeat, the ' soft ' American people would force their government to quit and leave Japan in possession of her most valuable conquests. Then she could proceed at her leisure to conquer the rest of China and so become the most powerful empire in the world, capable of defying even Germany, if Hitler conquered all Europe.

The Japanese navy in 1942 was, by any standards, a great navy. Japan had the two largest and most powerful battleships in the world, displacing 68,000 tons, with 18-inch guns; the American *Iowa* class, none of which were completed before 1943, were of 45,000 tons with 16-inch guns. She had a fleet of fast and powerful 8-inch gunned cruisers built in defiance of former treaty restrictions, comparable to the later American *Baltimore* class. She had the fastest and most modern destroyers, twice as many big carriers as the American navy, and her carrier planes were superior in the fighter and torpedo-bomber types. Japanese torpedoes were faster, more powerful, and more sure-firing than those made in the United States, and employment of them was at once more lavish and more intelligent. Japanese naval gunnery was excellent; Japanese warships were intensely trained for night fighting, as the Americans were not. They lacked only radar, which American ships began to install in 1942. Flushed with triumph after triumph in the Southwest Pacific, the Japanese army and navy were confident of victory.

Why, then, did Japan fail? Because, owing to a combination of stupid strategy on her part and good strategy and good luck on ours, the numerically inferior Pacific Fleet defeated her in the battles of the Coral Sea, Midway, and Guadalcanal. And after 1942 it was too late, as Yamamoto predicted. The United States Navy had learned many salutary lessons, acquired unprecedented strength, and become an irresistible force in the air, on the surface, and under water.

2. BATTLES OF CORAL SEA AND MIDWAY: MAY–JUNE 1942

The Battle of the Coral Sea (7–8 May 1942) frustrated the first forward lunge in the new Japanese offensive, to capture Port Moresby, a strategic base in Papua, New Guinea. This was the first naval battle in which no ship of either side sighted one of the other; the fighting was done by carrier plane against carrier plane, or carrier plane against ship. Admiral Nimitz, commanding the Pacific Fleet, sent carriers *Lexington* and *Yorktown* and a support group of cruisers into the Coral Sea, under the command of Rear Admiral Frank Jack Fletcher. The resulting engagement was almost a comedy of errors. Each side in this new sort of naval warfare made mistakes, but the Japanese made more; and although their losses were inferior to ours, they dared not press on to occupy Port Moresby. For Australia, Coral Sea was the decisive battle, saving her from possible invasion.

In the next and more vital Japanese offensive, Yamamoto went all-out. Personally assuming command, he brought with him almost every capital ship of the Japanese navy except two carriers damaged in the Coral Sea. His first objective was to capture Midway, a tiny atoll at the tip end of the Hawaiian chain, 1134 miles northwest of Pearl Harbor, where the United States had an advanced naval and air base. Yamamoto wanted Midway as a staging point for air raids to render Pearl Harbor untenable by the Pacific Fleet. Minor objectives were Attu and Kiska, two barren islands in the western Aleutians which he wanted as the northern anchor of the new ribbon defense. Yamamoto's dearest object, however, was to force Nimitz to give battle with his numerically inferior Pacific Fleet. He had his wish, but this time the battle did not go to the strong.

Nimitz guessed what Yamamoto was up to, but had only a small fleet to stop him. First, he reinforced Midway with planes to the saturation point. Next, he sent out Rear Admiral Raymond A. Spruance to command carriers *Enterprise* and *Hornet* with their attendant cruisers and destroyers; Rear Admiral Fletcher in carrier *Yorktown* (damaged in the Coral Sea but promptly repaired) hastened to join. On 4 June 1942, the Japanese four-carrier force, advancing undetected under a foul-weather front, was near enough Midway to batter the air base. A brave group of 26 obsolete marine fighter planes, together with anti-aircraft guns on the island, disposed of about one-third of the enemy attackers. The rest bombed Midway severely but not lethally.

Admiral Nagumo, the Japanese carrier-force commander, had a painful surprise on the morning of 4 June, when he learned from a reconnaissance plane that American flattops were approaching. Nagumo then made the fatal decision of the battle. He ordered his reserve attack group, then arming for a second strike on Midway, to be rearmed with the different sort of bombs used against ships, and turned his prows northeastward to close with the American carriers. Spruance and Fletcher already had several flights of torpedo- and dive-bombers flying toward the Japanese; and, owing to Nagumo's mistake, they had the good fortune to catch three of his four carriers in the vulnerable situation of rearming and refueling planes. But the carrier-plane battle opened ill for the Americans. Nagumo's combat air patrol of fast fighter planes shot down 35 of the 41 slow torpedo-bombers that came in first. Minutes later, the American dive-bombers hit three carriers and left them exploding and burning. The fourth Japanese carrier, *Hiryu,* unseen by the American fliers, got off two plane strikes, which found and disabled *Yorktown.* Fletcher's flagship, however, was promptly avenged, for an attack group from her deck and from *Enterprise* jumped *Hiryu* that afternoon and put her down. A lucky shot by a Japanese submarine later sank *Yorktown* as she was under tow.

Yamamoto, having lost his four best carriers, ordered a general retirement of his vast fleet. He had sustained the first defeat to the Japanese navy in modern times. The carriers and their air groups were wiped out, and the Stars and Stripes still flew over Midway; Kiska and Attu — poor consolation prizes — had been taken by a Japanese task group. The ambitious plans for capturing New Caledonia, the Fijis, and Samoa, had to be scrapped; and the Japanese high command was forced into an unaccustomed defensive position.

This glorious Battle of Midway on 4 June 1942, marked a clean-cut ending to the defensive phase in the Pacific war. For two months there was an ominous pause, each contestant licking his wounds. There then broke out a bloody and desperate six months' campaign over two focal points — Buna-Gona in New Guinea, and Guadalcanal.

3. OPERATION 'TORCH' — THE RECONQUEST OF NORTH AFRICA

While Winston Churchill was conferring with President Roosevelt in June 1942, news came of the German capture of Tobruk in North Africa. Publicly, Churchill described the situation as 'a bit disconcerting'; privately, he confessed that he was the most miserable Englishman in America since the surrender of Burgoyne. For the fall of Tobruk opened a German road into Egypt and beyond. If Alexandria and the Suez Canal fell to the Axis, nothing short of a miracle could keep them out of India, on whose eastern frontier the Japanese were already poised.

At their White House meeting neither Roosevelt nor Churchill nor their military advisers could agree on the time or place of the first combined military operation against the Axis. The Americans wanted a cross-channel operation in France to come first; a beachhead to be secured in 1942, and the big invasion in 1943. The British opposed any such attempt before the Allies had overwhelming air and ground forces and plenty of amphibious equipment, lest it be thrown back with heavy loss. Roosevelt, who had received Molotov at the White House just before Churchill arrived, was deeply impressed with the effort being made by Russia and the need for a second front in Europe to prevent Russia's being overrun. Something had to be done in 1942 — Churchill and Roosevelt could not stand the obloquy of fighting another ' phony war.' They decided, overriding most of their military advisers, on an occupation of French North Africa (25 July 1942) — Operation ' Torch.'

Oran and Algiers on the Mediterranean, and Casablanca on the Atlantic coast of Morocco, were selected as the three strategic harbors to be seized by amphibious forces. General Dwight D. Eisenhower was appointed commander in chief, with Admiral Sir Andrew Cunningham as over-all commander of naval forces.

With less than four months in which to plan, equip, and launch this operation, it was very risky. The United States and Great Britain had to train thousands of troops for amphibious warfare, divert hundreds of ships to new duties, and, as General Eisenhower wrote, occupy ' the rim of a continent where no major military campaign had been conducted for centuries.'

On 23 October General Sir Bernard Montgomery launched the second battle of El Alamein against Rommel, and on the same day Rear Admiral H. Kent Hewitt, commanding the Western Naval Task

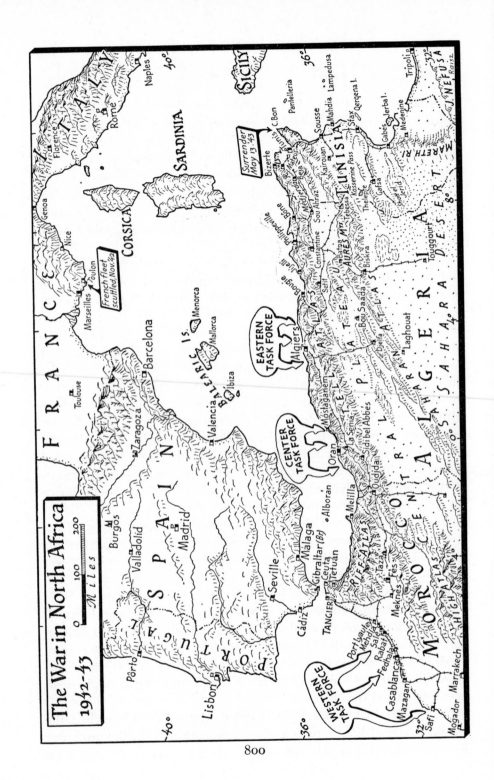

The War in North Africa
1942-43

0   100 200
Miles

FRANCE

Toulouse

Marseilles

Toulon
French fleet
scuttled, Nov.'42

Nice

Genoa

Florence

Rome

ITALY

Naples

SARDINIA

CORSICA

SICILY

Surrender
May 13 '43

C. Bon

Pantelleria

Lampedusa

Bizerte

Tunis

Sousse

Mahdia

Sfax

Qerqena I.

TUNISIA

MARETH RI.

Gabès

Jerba I.

Medenine

Tripoli

J. NEFUSA

Raisz.

PORTUGAL

Porto

Lisbon

Valladolid

Burgos

Madrid

SPAIN

Zaragoza

Barcelona

Valencia

BALEARIC IS.

Menorca

Mallorca

Ibiza

EASTERN TASK FORCE

Algiers

Bougie

Djidjelli

Philippeville

Bône

Médjez-el-Bab

Béja

Constantine

Sétif

Sou Ahras

Tébessa

Kasserine Pass

Thelepte

Gafsa

AURES MT.

Biskra

Bou Saâda

Djelfa

Laghouat

Touggourt

SAHARA DESERT

ALGERIA

CENTER TASK FORCE

Oran

Mostaganem

La Senia

Sidi bel Abbès

Oudjda

Séville

Málaga

Gibraltar (Br)

Ceuta

Tetuán

TANGIER

Cádiz

Tlemcen

Melilla

Alborán

RIF ATLAS

Fès

Meknès

Taza

Marrakech

HIGH ATLAS

WESTERN TASK FORCE

Port Lyautey

Mehdia

Salé

Rabat

Fedhala

Casablanca

Mazagan

Safi

Mogador

MOROCCO

TELL PLATEAU

GREAT ATLAS

800

Force, sailed from Hampton Roads. Back in Jefferson's day America
had invaded Africa, and Africa had come to America, in the persons
of her sable sons and daughters; but never before had an amphibious
operation been projected across an ocean. The complex operation
went like clockwork. By midnight 7–8 November all three task forces
(the two for Oran and Algiers under British command) had reached
their destinations, unscathed and unreported. The French — all except a few patriotic leaders who were in on the secret — the Spaniards, the Germans, and the Italians were caught completely off
guard. Admiral Hewitt had to fight a naval battle with the French
fleet off Casablanca, and sink most of it, in order to get General Patton's troops ashore safely, but there was little resistance from the
French army. By a happy coincidence Admiral Darlan, second to
Marshal Pétain in the Vichy government, happened to be in Algiers.
He was so impressed by the strength of the Anglo-American landings
that Eisenhower was able to persuade him to issue a cease-fire order
to all French forces in North Africa, on 11 November.

This ' Darlan deal,' as it was called, aroused vicious attacks on the
sincerity of Eisenhower, Roosevelt, and Churchill from left-wing elements in America, England, and elsewhere. The leaders were accused of compromise with Fascism, as represented by Darlan and
Pétain. They had yielded to the enemy. Nobody knew until the end
of the war that Marshal Pétain, although forced by German pressure
publicly to denounce the invasion, privately ordered Darlan to co-
operate. By this Darlan deal the United States and Great Britain
saved thousands of their soldiers' lives and gained new bases, the support of the French in North Africa, and eventually a new ally.

Although caught flat-footed by the invasion, the Germans reacted
promptly, flying 20,000 men across the Sicilian straits within a few
days, and establishing fighter and bomber bases on Tunisian airfields.
General Eisenhower moved, too, but the difficulties he faced from
mountain and desert, narrow twisting roads, the rainy season which
grounded his aircraft, and, not least, from half-trained troops, prevented his reaching Bizerte and Tunis in 1942.

Early in January 1943 Roosevelt and Churchill and the Combined
Chiefs of Staff met at Casablanca to plan future operations. For the
first time Allied prospects seemed favorable; this was, as Churchill
said, ' the end of the beginning.' The Russians had turned the tide
at the decisive battle of Stalingrad; Auchinleck and Montgomery had

saved Egypt; air and naval forces were fast being built up in Morocco and Algeria; Mussolini could no longer call the Mediterranean *mare nostrum.*

Allied chiefs at Casablanca gave antisubmarine warfare top priority, decided to invade Sicily as soon as Tunisia was secured, gave America the green light to start Admiral Nimitz and General Mac-Arthur on an offensive against the Japanese, and promised ' to draw as much weight as possible off the Russian armies by engaging the enemy as heavily as possible at the best selected point.' And they made the momentous announcement that the war would end only with ' unconditional surrender' of all enemies, European and Asiatic. That formula, borrowed from General Grant's declaration before Fort Donelson, was the second major strategic decision of the war. Not well thought out as to the consequences, it may have been a mistake. The reasons prompting it were the failure of the armistice of 11 November 1918 to eliminate the German menace, propaganda about the Darlan deal, suggesting that Roosevelt and Churchill were contemplating a similar deal with Mussolini and Hitler, and a desire to reassure Russia that we would not let her down. On Mussolini the formula had no effect, since he was almost ready to quit, but it may have helped Hitler to persuade his people to fight to the bitter end.

While Roosevelt and Churchill were discussing grand strategy, the Germans seized the initiative. Swift counterattacks and the arrival of Rommel's Afrika Korps gave them ground superiority, which Rommel exploited in brilliant fashion. On 14 February 1943 he hurled his armor through the Kasserine Pass, turned northward toward Tebessa, and threatened to cut the Allied armies in two. The untried American forces were badly beaten for a time. But General Patton, the timely arrival of two armored divisions from Oran, the employment of powerful new tanks, and clearing skies that permitted the North African Air Force to deliver punishing blows, turned the tide.

This was Rommel's last offensive. Montgomery had caught up with him, and the two antagonists squared off for a last round. Hammered front and rear, pounded by the most devastating aerial attack of the North African campaign, Rommel acknowledged defeat and retreated northward into Tunisia. The Allied armies, now half a million strong, closed in for the kill. Then, as Montgomery broke the German lines in the south and raced for Tunis, Omar Bradley, commanding II Corps, United States Army, smashed into Bizerte. Each city fell on 7 May 1943. Cornered on Cape Bon, the German army still 275,000 strong, surrendered on 13 May. It was the greatest victory that British and American arms had yet won.

Now that North Africa was cleared of the enemy, the Mediterranean became open to Allied merchant ships throughout its entire length, though still subject to air attack from Italy and southern France, which the Germans occupied as soon as they heard of the Darlan deal. The now spliced lifeline of the British Empire to India through Suez made it possible to reinforce Russia via the Persian Gulf. And the way was open at last for a blow at what Churchill mistakenly called ' the soft underbelly ' of Europe.

4. The Guadalcanal and Papua Campaigns

After the Coral Sea and Midway victories, Allied forces in the Pacific were based mainly at four points. Operating from Dutch Harbor in Alaska, a small force of the United States Navy watched the Japanese in the western Aleutians. At Pearl Harbor the main Pacific Fleet was based, and on Oahu and other Hawaiian islands several army divisions were being trained for jungle warfare. At Nouméa in New Caledonia and at Espiritu Santo, which the Free French had made available, was based the South Pacific force, at first under Admiral Ghormley, later relieved by the dashing leader Admiral Halsey. In Brisbane, Australia, General MacArthur headed the Southwest Pacific command, American, Australian and New Zealand troops, together with a small United States and Australian naval force.

In July 1942 the Japanese still held Tulagi on Florida Island in the Solomons, and Rabaul on New Britain. These were anchors to a formidable barrier — the Bismarck Archipelago barrier — to an Allied advance toward Japan. The islands are so close to one another that the surrounding waters could be controlled by land-based planes. The Joint Chiefs of Staff decided that this barrier must be breached if ever we were to defeat Japan. And the campaign to do this was sparked off by the news that the Japanese had taken Buna and Gona on the north coast of Papua, and were building an airfield on Guadalcanal, whence they would be able to batter our advance base at Espiritu Santo. Since massive naval, ground, and air forces were being assembled for the invasion of North Africa, the South Pacific command got only what was left; the campaign was well nick-

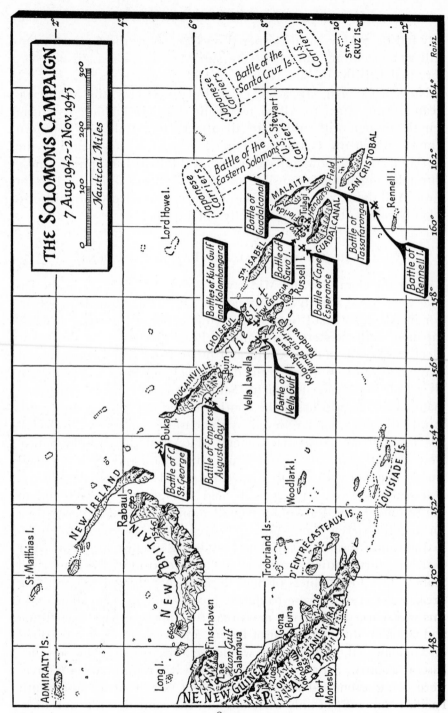

THE SOLOMONS CAMPAIGN
7 Aug. 1942 – 2 Nov. 1943

Nautical Miles

0   100   200   300

Battle of the Santa Cruz Is.

Japanese Carriers

U.S. Carriers

STA. CRUZ IS.

Raisz

Battle of the Eastern Solomons

Japanese Carriers

U.S. Stewart I. Carriers

Lord Howe I.

Battle of Guadalcanal

MALAITA

Henderson Field

SAN CRISTOBAL

Florida I.

Tulagi

Battle of Savo I.

Rennell I.

Battles of Kula Gulf and Kolombangara

STA. ISABEL

Russell I.

GUADALCANAL

Battle of Tassafaronga

Battle of Cape Esperance

Battle of Rennell I.

The Slot

New Georgia

Kolombangara I.

Munda airstrip

Rendova I.

Battle of Vella Gulf

CHOISEUL

Vella Lavella

BOUGAINVILLE

Buin

Battle of Empress Augusta Bay

Buka I.

Battle of C. St. George

Woodlark I.

LOUISIADE IS.

NEW IRELAND

Rabaul

NEW BRITAIN

Trobriand Is.

D'ENTRECASTEAUX IS.

St. Matthias I.

ADMIRALTY IS.

Long I.

Finschaven

Lae

Huon Gulf

Salamaua

6660

Gona

Buna

OWEN STANLEY RANGE

Kokoda

2109

226

PAPUA

Port Moresby

NE. NEW GUINEA

named Operation 'Shoestring.' Presently nineteen transports, escorted by cruisers and destroyers, with an air-support force of three carriers, were converging on the mountainous, jungle-clad Solomon Islands, whose very names were almost unknown in America. On 7 August 1942, the 1st Marine Division under General Alexander A. Vandegrift landed at Tulagi and Guadalcanal, surprised the enemy, and seized the harbor of the one island and the airfield on the other.

There then began the prolonged and bloody struggle for Guadalcanal; an island worthless in itself — like the battlefield of Gettysburg in 1863 — but even more violently contested. The Japanese could not afford to let us establish a base there and we could not afford to let it go. Ships, planes, and troops were committed by both sides. Seven major naval battles were fought,[1] until Iron Bottom Bay, as our sailors named Savo Island Sound, was strewn with the hulls of ships and the bodies of sailors. Every few nights the Japanese ran fast reinforcement echelons, the 'Tokyo Expresses,' down the central channel, the Solomons' 'Slot'; every few days American reinforcements came in, and daily air battles became routine. On shore, the marines, reinforced by army divisions, fought stubbornly and, in the end, successfully. On 9 February 1943, six months after the landings, the Japanese evacuated Guadalcanal.

In this campaign American soldiers took the measure of the supposedly invincible Japanese foot-soldiers, who had overrun half of Eastern Asia, and found that they could be beaten. And the navy learned, the hard way, how to fight night battles and shoot down en-

---

[1] (1) Battle of Savo Island, 7 Aug. 1942, won by Admiral Mikawa against a cruiser force commanded by Rear Adm. Crutchley, R.N., with a loss of three U.S. and one Australian heavy cruisers; (2) Battle of the Eastern Solomons, 24 Aug., in which carriers *Saratoga* and *Enterprise* under Vice Adm. F. J. Fletcher beat off a Japanese carrier force under Vice Adm. Kondo and sank one; (3) Battle of Cape Esperance, 11–12 Oct., in which a cruiser force under Rear Adm. Norman Scott defeated a reinforcement group under Rear Adm. Goto, sinking four destroyers and losing one; (4) Battle of the Santa Cruz Islands, 26–27 Oct., in which a carrier force under Rear Adm. Thomas C. Kinkaid beat off Kondo again, but lost *Hornet*; (5) the two-night naval Battle of Guadalcanal, 12–15 Nov., in which Rear Admirals D. J. Callaghan, Norman Scott, and Willis A. Lee sank two Japanese battleships, a cruiser, two destroyers, and 11 transports, but paid for it with the lives of Callaghan and Scott, two cruisers, and seven destroyers; (6) Battle of Tassafaronga, 30 Nov., in which we lost a cruiser but frustrated an attempt at reinforcement; (7) Battle of Rennell Island, 29–30 Jan. 1943, in which we lost cruiser *Chicago* to air attack. The final score was 24 warships lost to each side. There was almost continuous fighting by ground troops on the island itself, scores of air battles, and frequent night bombardments by Japanese warships.

emy planes. After this deadly island had been secured, the navy won every battle with the Japanese fleet.

In the meantime the western prong of this Japanese offensive had been stopped on the north coast of Papua, New Guinea, in the villages of Buna, Gona, and Sanananda. This was done by General MacArthur's command, executed by American and Australian troops under Generals Eichelberger and Sir Edmund Herring. The fighting, in malaria-infested mangrove swamps against a trapped and never-surrendering enemy, was the most horrible of the entire war. With the aid of air power the combined armies won through, and by the end of January 1943 Papua up to Huon Gulf was in Allied hands. The defensive period in the war with Japan finally came to an end.

5. The Tide Turns Against the U-boat

At the Casablanca conference in January 1943 the Combined Chiefs of Staff gave antisubmarine warfare number one priority. In terms of construction, this meant that American shipyards had to slow up on production of beaching and landing craft for amphibious operations, and concentrate on escort vessels, especially the new DE (destroyer-escort) and the CVE (escort or 'jeep' carrier), which could carry bombing planes into submarine-infested waters.

The crucial period in the Battle of the Atlantic came in the first half of 1943. At the turn of the year Hitler appointed as head of the German navy his submarine expert, Admiral Doenitz, and concentrated on producing more and better U-boats. The number operating in the Atlantic more than doubled, and their effectiveness was increased by sending big supply subs — 'milch cows' — into waters around the neutral Azores, enabling U-boats to replenish without returning to France. But the number of Allied ships and planes capable of dealing with them more than quadrupled. The North African campaign required so many troop and supply convoys to Casablanca and Algiers that the United States Navy took charge of them, while the British and Canadian navies escorted the North Atlantic merchant convoys. A fresh German blitz on this and other routes, in March 1943, accounted for 108 merchant ships aggregating over 625,-000 tons. Echelons of wolf-packs, preceded by U-boats whose sole duty was to shadow convoys, attacked by day as well as night. These sinkings, occurring at the worst season in the North Atlantic when the temperature of the water hovers around 30° F, were accompanied by heavy loss of life. And although the United States Navy, which escorted transatlantic troop transports, lost none of those going to and from Great Britain or the Mediterranean, it lost three army transports en route to Greenland and Iceland; one of these, the *Dorchester,* on 3 February 1943, with heavy loss, including four army chaplains.

The big question in mid-1943 was whether the existing U-boat types could be mastered in time to enable America to get enough men and weapons across and beat Germany to her knees before the new U-boats got into production. It was a race against time. By April 1943 the Allies were definitely ahead. At a conference with Hitler on the 11th, Doenitz admitted the loss of 40 U-boats and 6 Italian submarines since the New Year.

The increased number of convoys and escorts, improved devices and training, and the work of scientists and technicians were getting results. The British put on a great drive in the Bay of Biscay against U-boats that were approaching or departing from their French bases. This, in conjunction with successes elsewhere, brought the total bag up to 41 in May. At the same time the United States began using her new escort carriers in convoys between Norfolk and the Mediterranean. These, screened by the new DE's, went out after every submarine detected within 300 miles of the convoy route and sank a considerable number, even some of the big 'milch cows.' The latter were already driven from their pastures when Portugal permitted the Allies to use air bases in the Azores; that closed the last stretch in the North Atlantic which long-range bomber planes had been unable to reach. And merchant ship new construction was now well ahead of losses.

Germany built 198 U-boats between 1 May 1943 and the end of the year, and lost 186. Transatlantic convoys were now so well defended that tonnage losses during these eight months totaled only 592,000 tons, less than in the single months of June and November 1942. Admiral Doenitz, feeling that he must make a tonnage score, no matter where, now began sending his best long-legged U-boats into the Indian Ocean, where as yet there were no convoys. But he kept enough in home waters, occasionally to send wolf-packs full cry after transatlantic traffic; the Battle of the Atlantic was not over until Germany surrendered.

6. THE INVASION OF SICILY AND ITALY

If the North African campaign could have been concluded early in 1943, it might have been possible to invade the continent of Europe that year; but operation ' Torch ' flickered too long to permit that, and ' Overlord,' the invasion of Normandy, had to be postponed to 1944. ' Something ' had to be done during the rest of 1943, or the people would howl for action, and Russia might quit; and that ' something ' obviously had to start from the newly won Allied base in North Africa.

The plan selected was to overrun Sicily, cross the Strait of Messina to Calabria, and work up the Italian peninsula. This offered the chance of complete control of the Mediterranean, as well as an objective dear to Churchill's heart, knocking Italy out of the war. D-day for the attack on Sicily was set for 10 July, General Eisenhower was designated to run the show; under him Admiral of the Fleet Sir A. B. Cunningham, General Sir Harold Alexander, and Air Chief Marshal Tedder were the top naval, ground-force, and air commanders.

The invasion of Sicily was the biggest amphibious assault of the war, not excepting ' Overlord.' About 250,000 British and American troops landed simultaneously, eight divisions abreast, and in black darkness. The 350,000 Italian and German defenders of Sicily were surprised and thrown off balance. The American Seventh Army (General Patton) was put ashore by the American Eighth Fleet (Admiral Hewitt) on the southwestern shore of Sicily; the British Eighth Army (General Montgomery) , which included a Canadian division, landed on the American right flank and up to a short distance from Syracuse. The new LST and other beaching craft, here employed in large numbers for the first time, assisted in getting troops, tanks, and field artillery ashore so promptly that within a few hours the invaders controlled 150 miles of coastline, and substantial beachheads. The smoothness with which these landings were carried off, the celerity with which enemy opposition was overwhelmed, deeply impressed the German and Italian high commands. The Germans concluded that only a delaying operation was possible; the Italians decided that it was time for them to get out of the war.

After a sharp battle at the Gela beachhead with a German armored division, the Seventh Army swept across Sicily, marching at a rate

INVASION OF ITALY
July 1943 to the end
of the War

0   100
Miles

SWITZERLAND

Brenner Pass AUSTRIA

Turin
Milan
L. Garda
Verona
Venice
Trieste
Rijeka (Fiume)
Po R.
Parma
Genoa
Bologna
GOTHIC LINE
Ravenna
Spezia
Pisa
Florence
Winter Line 1944-45
Leghorn 19 July
12 Aug.
Siena 3 July
Perugia
Ancona 19 July
Elba
Viterbo
Pescara
Winter Line 1943-44
Line of Oct. '43
Rome 5. June
Anzio
Cassino 19. May
Foggia
Bari
Landing Jan. 44
Naval diversion Sep. '43
Volturno R.
Naples 1. Oct.
Salerno
Potenza
Brindisi
Taranto
Main attack 9 Sep. '43
CORSICA Oct. '43
42°
TYRRHENIAN
SARDINIA Sep. '43
SEA
Cosenza
Crotone
Naval diversion Sep. '43
39°
Cagliari
from Oran
22. July Palermo
17. Aug Messina
CALABRIA
Règgio
Bizerte
SICILY
Etna
C. Bon
Seventh Army July '43. ff.
Licata
Catania
Augusta
Syracuse
Tunis
Gela
Pantelleria 11 June '43
C. Passero
From Tripoli
Eighth Army July '43
36°
Sousse
Malta
TUNISIA
12°
Lampedusa
15°
Raisz
18°

APENNINES

ADRIATIC SEA

Sangro R.

YUGOSLAVIA

Sarajevo

Split (Spalato)

Dubrovnik (Ragusa)

42°

36°

809

that matched Stonewall Jackson's 'foot cavalry' in the Civil War. On 22 July General Patton made his triumphal entry into Palermo and set up headquarters in the ancient palace of the Norman kings, whence, much like old Roger II in the twelfth century, he directed the campaign along the north coast of Sicily.

In the meantime Montgomery's Eighth Army had slashed into the ancient city of Syracuse, seized Augusta, but met a sharp check from the Germans on the Catania plain. That gave the enemy a week to take up good defensive positions. But by 17 August the great island was in Allied hands. Unfortunately some 40,000 German troops escaped across the Strait of Messina with most of their weapons and equipment.

Italy, though not mortally wounded, was heartily sick of the war into which Mussolini had forced her. On 25 July, six days after Allied air forces had delivered a 560-plane bombing raid on Rome, King Victor Emmanuel III summoned up enough courage to force Mussolini to resign. Marshal Badoglio, who told the king that the war was *perduto, perdutissimo* (absolutely and completely lost), now headed the government and began to probe for peace with the Allies. Owing to the Italian love of bargaining and the Allies' 'unconditional surrender' slogan, which made bargaining difficult, negotiations dragged along until 3 September. This gave the Germans, who suspected what was cooking, plenty of time to rush reinforcements into Italy and to seize key points such as Genoa, Leghorn, and Rome.

General Eisenhower had already been ordered to plan an invasion of Italy at the earliest possible date. Salerno, south of the Sorrento Peninsula, was chosen for the main landing in Italy, as the point farthest north where Allied fighter planes could protect amphibious forces from German air attack. In early September 1943 the Allied Fifth Army, commanded by General Mark W. Clark, with two British and two American infantry divisions in the assault, took off from a dozen ports between Oran and Alexandria. En route to the objective the familiar voice of General ' Ike ' was heard broadcasting news of the Italian surrender, so all hands expected a walk-over. They had a bitter surprise. Some very tough and unco-operative Germans were at the beachhead, and reinforcements were being rushed in from beyond the mountains. D-day for Salerno, 9 September, was very costly. Beachheads were established with difficulty, and held precariously. The German air force was active and enterprising, and tried a new weapon, the radio-guided bomb, which put several ships out of business. A Panzer division laid on a series of vicious tank attacks designed to divide the American divisions from the British divisions. These were thwarted by the invaders, ably assisted by naval gunfire, and on 16 September the Germans started an orderly retirement northward. Fifth Army on 1 October entered Naples, which the Germans had done their best to destroy. Commodore William A. Sullivan, with a mixed Anglo-American salvage team, did a remarkable job in clearing the bay and the waterfront, so that by the end of the year more tonnage was being discharged in Naples than in time of peace.

Here, at the Volturno line north of Naples, with the great harbor secured, and the Foggia airdrome on the other side of Italy in Allied hands, the Italian campaign should have been halted. But Churchill and Alan Brooke, whose idea it was to fight all the way up the ' boot,' justified continuing on the ground that the battle of Italy pinned down and used up German divisions which might resist the Normandy landing in 1944. Actually the Italian campaign failed to draw German reserves from France, and by June 1944 the Allies were employing in Italy double the number of the Germans in that area. It developed, as General Sir Henry Wilson said, into a ' slow, painful advance through difficult terrain against a determined and resourceful enemy, skilled in the exploitation of natural obstacles by mines and demolition.' Marshal Kesselring, fighting a series of delaying operations along prepared mountain entrenchments, exploited these natural advantages to the full; and none of the Allied generals except Guillaume, who commanded a French army corps, showed much ability to cope with this terrain or with German tactics. From Naples to Rome is but a hundred miles; yet the Allies, with numerical superiority on land and in the air, and with control of adjacent waters, took eight months to cover that ground. Fighting in the Apennines was vividly described by the war correspondent Ernie Pyle, as consisting of ' almost inconceivable misery,' in mud and frost. GIs ' lived like men of prehistoric times, and a club would have become them more than a machine gun.'

Rome was the objective of the winter campaign of 1943–44, but some of the most mountainous terrain in Europe barred the way. Churchill persuaded the C.C.S. to try and break the stalemate by an amphibious landing in the rear of the Germans at Anzio, 37 miles south of Rome. Although the Anzio landing (22 January 1944) by one British division and the United States 3rd Infantry Division was a complete surprise, Marshal Kesselring reacted swiftly; his air force sank a number of British and American transports and warships, and the troops had to dig into an open plain, where they were subjected to constant air and infantry counterattack. Anzio beachhead, which should have been a spearhead, became instead a beleaguered fort.

To the south, the Eighth Army launched a series of savage attacks against the ancient monastery of Monte Cassino, anchor of the German ' Gustav line.' For three months the Allies wore themselves out in futile attempts to take the place by storm. Finally, the Eighth Army, which by this time included American, British, Polish, Indian, and French divisions, enveloped and captured Monte Cassino (19 May); a Canadian force advanced up the Adriatic coast; Mark Clark's Fifth Army burst through the iron ring around Anzio on 25 May, and advanced north against stubborn rear-guard resistance.

By the morning of 4 June 1944, as Kesselring's forces were retiring toward a new defense line, columns of Allied troops were rushing along all roads that led to Rome. By midnight the Fifth Army was there.

For one brief day the liberation of Rome held the attention of the Allied nations. Then, on 6 June, came the news that the Allies had landed on the coast of Normandy.

7. FORWARD IN THE PACIFIC

For five months after Guadalcanal was secured in early February 1943, there was a lull in the Pacific war. The principal reason for this delay, apart from our efforts in Africa and the build-up for invading Italy, was lack of aircraft carriers. By mid-1943, when the new *Essex* class carriers began to join the fleet, it was ready to go.

Japan was the final objective, but before invasion of her tightly defended home islands, positions had to be taken within air-bombing distance. But how to get there? The short northern route, via the Aleutians, was ruled out by bad flying weather.[2] Hundreds of atolls

---

[2] The western Aleutians, however, were first reconquered for their nuisance value. Following the naval victory by Rear Adm. Charles A. McMorris off the Komandorski Islands on 24 March 1943, the 7th Infantry Division was landed on Attu and after a very tough fight cleared out the enemy, which then evacuated Kiska. These Aleutians and Adak were then developed as air bases.

and thousands of islands — the Gilberts, Marshalls, Carolines, Marianas, and Bonins — plastered with airfields and bristling with defenses, sprawled across the ocean like a maze of gigantic spider webs, blocking all Central Pacific routes. South of the equator, Japan held the Bismarck Archipelago, the Solomons north of Guadalcanal, and all New Guinea except its slippery tail. General MacArthur wished to advance by what he called the New Guinea-Mindanao axis; but Rabaul, planted like a baleful spider at the center of a web across that axis, would have to be eliminated first. And as long as Japan held the island complex on MacArthur's north flank, she could throw air and naval forces against his communications at will. So it was decided that Admiral Nimitz must take a broom to the Gilberts, the Marshalls, and the Carolines, while MacArthur and Halsey cleaned out the Bismarcks. All could then join forces for a final push into the Philippines and on to the coast of China.

Accordingly the plans for mid-1943 to mid-1944 began with preliminary operations to sweep up enemy spiders' webs. The central Solomons were the first objective. After three sharp naval actions up the Solomons' Slot in July (battles of Kula Gulf, Kolombangara, and Vella Gulf) and a number of motor torpedo boat actions (in one of which President Kennedy distinguished himself), the United States Navy won control of surrounding waters, and Munda field with adjacent positions was captured by the army after a tough jungle campaign. In New Guinea and on Cape Gloucester, New Britain, a series of shore-to-shore amphibious operations secured the main passage from the Coral Sea through the Bismarcks barrier into the Western Pacific.

Japan could now be approached in a series of bold leaps instead of a multitude of short hops. Independently, General MacArthur and Rear Admiral Theodore S. Wilkinson thought up 'leap-frogging,' or, as Wilkinson called it in baseball phraseology, ' hitting 'em where they ain't.' The essence of this strategy was to by-pass the principal Japanese strongpoints like Truk and Rabaul, sealing them off with sea and air power, leaving their garrisons to ' wither on the vine,' while we constructed a new air and naval base in some less strongly defended spot several hundred miles nearer Japan. After the war was over General Tojo told General MacArthur that leap-frogging, the success of United States submarines against the Japanese merchant marine, and the projection of fire power by aircraft carriers deep

The
JAPANESE WAR
1941 ~ 1945

XII.'41 ——— Japanese control Dec.7,'41
VIII.'42 ——— Aug.7,'42
III.'44 ——— March 1,'44
III.'45 ——— March 1,'45

Jap. controlled land VIII.'42
   "   "   "   III.'45

Sea of Okhotsk

U. S. S. R

Amur

Nikolayevsk
SAKHALIN
Khabarovsk
KARAFUTO
KAMCHATKA
Petropavlovsk

Tsitsihar
MANCHURIA
Harbin

Changchun

INNER MONGOLIA
JEHOL
Wolf
Peiping
Great
Suchow
Lanchow
Tientsin
Dairen
Mukden
Vladivostok

Sea of Japan
Keijo (Seoul)
Pusan
Hiroshima
Tokyo
Kyoto
Osaka
18

TIBET
CHINA
Chengtu
Yangtze R. Gorges
Hankow
Nanking
Shanghai
Chungking
Changsha
Wenchow
Nagasaki
Kyushu

THE HUMP
ASSAM
Ledo
Kweiyang
Kweilin
Kunming
Foochow
RYUKYU
Okinawa
15

BONIN Is.
Iwo Jima
14
Marcus I.

INDIA
Imphal
Lashio
Mandalay
BURMA
ROAD
Canton
Amoy
Hong Kong
TAIWAN
(FORMOSA)

III.'45

Rangoon
SIAM
Hanoi
Hué
FRENCH INDO CHINA
Lingayen
13
LUZON
Manila
2

MARIANA Is.
Saipan
Tinian
Guam
10

Eniwetok

Bangkok
Saigon
SOUTH CHINA SEA
SAMAR
LEYTE
12
Yap I.
Ulithi I.
11
CAROLINE Is.
Ponape
Truk I.

Kota Bharu
MALAYA
Kuala Lumpur
Singapore
BORNEO
SARAWAK
Tarakan
17
MINDANAO
Davao
PALAUS
Peleliu I.
Angaur I.
16

SUMATRA
Palembang
Batavia
JAVA
BALI
BORNEO
Balikpapan
CELEBES
19
Morotai
Halmahera
XII.'41
Biak
9
DUTCH NEW GUINEA
Hollandia
Aitape
NEW IRELAND
Rabaul
Bougainville
5

DUTCH EAST INDIES
Dili
TIMOR
(Port.)
VIII.'42
Torres Str.
NEW GUINEA
NEW BRITAIN
Lae
Buna
Port Moresby
SOLOMONS
3

Christmas I.
Cocos I.
INDIAN OCEAN

Defense HWY
Darwin
AUSTRALIA
CORAL SEA
Townsville
Rockhampton

Pre-war XII.'41 Japanese control

Equator XII.'41

100°   120°   140°   160°

814

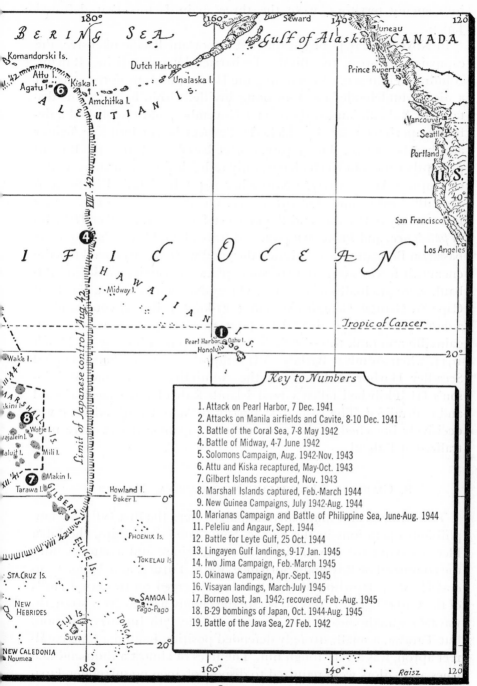

The following labels appear on the map:

BERING SEA

Komandorski Is.
'42 Attu I.
Agatu I. ⑥ Kiska I.
Amchitka I.
ALEUTIAN IS.

Dutch Harbor
Unalaska I.

160° Seward 140° Juneau 120°
Gulf of Alaska CANADA
Prince Rupert

Vancouver
Seattle
Portland
U.S.

San Francisco

PACIFIC OCEAN

Los Angeles

HAWAIIAN IS.
Midway I.

④

Limit of Japanese control Aug. '42

Tropic of Cancer
20°

Pearl Harbor Oahu I.
Honolulu ①

Wake I.

MARSHALL Is.
Bikini I. ⑧
Wotje I.
Kwajalein I.
Jaluit I. Mili I.

Makin I. ⑦
Tarawa I. GILBERT IS.

Howland I.
Baker I.
0°

PHOENIX Is.

ELLICE Is.

TOKELAU Is.

STA. CRUZ Is.

NEW HEBRIDES

FIJI Is.
Suva

TONGA Is.

SAMOA Is.
Pago-Pago

20°

NEW CALEDONIA
Noumea

180° 160° 140° Raisz 120°

Key to Numbers

1. Attack on Pearl Harbor, 7 Dec. 1941
2. Attacks on Manila airfields and Cavite, 8-10 Dec. 1941
3. Battle of the Coral Sea, 7-8 May 1942
4. Battle of Midway, 4-7 June 1942
5. Solomons Campaign, Aug. 1942-Nov. 1943
6. Attu and Kiska recaptured, May-Oct. 1943
7. Gilbert Islands recaptured, Nov. 1943
8. Marshall Islands captured, Feb.-March 1944
9. New Guinea Campaigns, July 1942-Aug. 1944
10. Marianas Campaign and Battle of Philippine Sea, June-Aug. 1944
11. Peleliu and Angaur, Sept. 1944
12. Battle for Leyte Gulf, 25 Oct. 1944
13. Lingayen Gulf landings, 9-17 Jan. 1945
14. Iwo Jima Campaign, Feb.-March 1945
15. Okinawa Campaign, Apr.-Sept. 1945
16. Visayan landings, March-July 1945
17. Borneo lost, Jan. 1942; recovered, Feb.-Aug. 1945
18. B-29 bombings of Japan, Oct. 1944-Aug. 1945
19. Battle of the Java Sea, 27 Feb. 1942

into enemy territory, were the three main factors that defeated Japan.

In November 1943 began the first important Pacific offensive, the campaign to break the Bismarcks barrier by neutralizing Rabaul. Admiral Wilkinson, commanding the III Amphibious Force, selected a slice of undefended coast on Bougainville, within fighter-plane distance of Rabaul, landed there on 1 November, and established a defensive perimeter inside which the Seabees began building fighter and bomber strips. The Japanese fleet based on Truk and Rabaul promptly came out to challenge, only to be decisively beaten (Battle of Empress Augusta Bay, 2 November 1943) by Admiral A. Stanton Merrill's cruiser and destroyer force. On the 5th and 11th, planes from stately old ' Sara ' and the new carriers *Essex, Bunker Hill, Independence,* and *Princeton* pounded Rabaul, and ' Airsols ' bombers based on Bougainville continued the good work day by day. Thus the enemy air forces, even after stripping planes off carriers to defend Rabaul, were gradually worn away. On 25 November in the Battle of Cape St. George, Captain Arleigh (' 31-knot ') Burke, commanding a destroyer squadron, defeated a Japanese attempt to reinforce Bougainville and sank three of their five destroyers. Thus, by 25 March 1944, when Admiral Barbey's VII Amphibious Force had occupied Seeadler Harbor at Manus in the Admiralty group, and Wilkinson's III 'Phib had taken Green Island, Rabaul was ringed around and neutralized. The Bismarcks barrier to MacArthur's advance was decisively breached, and almost 100,000 Japanese troops were neutralized at Rabaul.

8. GILBERTS, MARSHALLS, NEW GUINEA, MARIANAS

The Gilberts and Marshalls campaigns were the first full-scale amphibious operations in the Pacific. Some 200 sail of ships, the Fifth Fleet carrying 108,000 soldiers, sailors, marines, and aviators under the command of Raymond Spruance, Kelly Turner, and Major General H. M. (' Howling Mad ') Smith, converged on two coral atolls of the Gilbert group. Makin, where the enemy had no great strength, was taken methodically by a regiment of the 27th Infantry Division, but Tarawa, a small, strongly defended position behind a long coral-reef apron, was a very tough nut. The lives of almost a thousand marines and sailors were required to dispose of 4000 no-surrender Japanese on an islet not three miles long. But Tarawa taught invaluable lessons for future landings, and provided another airfield. The Gilberts became bases from which aircraft helped to neutralize the seven Japanese air bases in the Marshalls. These islands were sealed off by the fast carrier forces under Rear Admiral Marc Mitscher, which roved about the group, ships pounding and aircraft bombing. Consequently, not one Japanese plane was available in the Marshalls on D-day, 31 January 1944. Massive amphibious forces under Admirals Harry Hill and Turner, with close air and gunfire support, covered landings at both ends of the great atoll of Kwajalein. On 17 February 1944 another force moved into Eniwetok, westernmost of the Marshalls. The Japanese troops, as usual, resisted to the last man; but the Marshalls not only cost many fewer casualties than tiny Tarawa, but were conquered without the loss of a single United States ship. The Japanese navy dared not challenge because its air arm had been sliced off to defend Rabaul; and on 20 February 1944 its capital ships and aircraft were chased out of the important naval base of Truk, with heavy loss, by a round-the-clock carrier raid.

Mobile surface forces and mobile naval air power needed mobile logistics, and got them. Outstanding in the pattern for Pacific victory was the mobile supply base — Service Squadron 10, a logistic counterpart to the fast carrier forces. While the flattops carried the naval air arm to within striking distance of the enemy, ' Servron 10,' composed of tankers, ammunition ships, refrigerator ships, repair ships, fleet tugs, escort carriers with replacement planes, and several other types of auxiliaries, acted as a traveling annex to Pearl Harbor in order to provide the fleet with food, fuel, bullets, spare parts, and spare planes. Thus, the United States Pacific Fleet recovered that independence of land bases which had been lost when sail gave way to steam.

While Spruance and Turner were crashing through the Gilberts and Marshalls, ' MacArthur's navy,' the Seventh Fleet under Admirals Kinkaid and Dan Barbey, were leap-frogging along the New Guinea coast. Hollandia and Aitape airfields were secured by the end of April. Biak Island, posed like a fly over the neck of the New Guinea bird, fell on 17 May 1944. Admiral Toyoda, commander in chief of the Japanese fleet (Yamamoto having been shot down over Bougainville), planned to stop the Americans right there with his two super-battleships; but before he got around to it, a more dangerous American movement engaged his attention, and VII 'Phib was able to take Noemfoor, Cape Sansapor, and Morotai, by 15 September. MacArthur's air forces were now within bombing distance of the Philippines.

The new offensive that engaged Toyoda's attention was directed against the Marianas, of which the principal islands were Saipan and Tinian, which Japan had acquired in World War I, and Guam, which she had wrested from the weak American garrison in December 1941. This group, with the Bonins, and the Philippines, was part of Japan's inner line of defense. Saipan was within flying distance of southern Japan by the new B-29 bombers. So, when the victorious team of Spruance, Turner, Mitscher, and H. M. Smith moved into Saipan on 15 June, Japan had to do something better than the last-ditch local resistance she had offered in the Marshalls. And her fleet by now had trained new air groups.

Deploying into the Philippine Sea, Vice Admiral Ozawa commanded nine carriers, with five battleships and seven heavy cruisers. The Spruance-Mitscher fleet (seven *Essex*-class and eight light carriers, seven battleships, three heavy and six light cruisers) moved out to meet him, preceded by a screen of submarines. Spruance played his usual cool game, taking risks boldly when they seemed commensurate with the damage he might inflict, yet never forgetting that his main duty was to protect the amphibious forces at Saipan. The Battle of the Philippine Sea broke at 10 A.M., 19 June 1944, when hundreds of Japanese planes were detected flying toward the American carriers, then about 100 miles northwest of Guam. The resulting clash proved that American carrier planes and pilots were now vastly superior to the enemy's, both in tactics and in performance. Sixty miles out, Hellcat fighters intercepted Japanese planes, only 40 of which broke through; and the anti-aircraft fire of Spruance's ships was so accurate and deadly that these scored only two hits, on tough battleships that suffered little damage. As a result of this day's fighting, the Japanese lost over 345 planes at the cost of only 17 American aircraft. Our sailors called this ' the great turkey shoot.' The enemy lost three carriers, two of them to United States submarines; Ozawa's air groups were wiped out, and he had no time to train new ones before the next great battle, in October.

Now the conquest of the Marianas could proceed without outside interference. On 6 July, the Japanese general and his staff committed suicide, and the rest of his army jumped off cliffs or holed up in caves. Turner's amphibious forces then proceeded to assault and capture Tinian and Guam, which were much less strongly held than Saipan. By 1 August 1944 these three big islands of the Marianas were in American possession. Airfield and harbor development went on briskly, Admiral Nimitz moved his headquarters to the hills above Agaña, and by fall, Marianas-based B-29's were bombing southern Japan.

The more sagacious Japanese now knew they were beaten; but they dared not admit it, and nerved their people to another year of bitter resistance in the vain hope that America might tire of the war when victory was within her grasp.

For Bibliography for this Chapter see the General World War II Bibliography at the end of Chapter XXX, page 846.

Victory in Europe and in the Pacific

1. THE AIR ASSAULT ON GERMANY

WHILE waiting for an appropriate moment to launch the cross-channel invasion of Hitler's 'Fortress Europe,' the R.A.F., in conjunction with the United States Army Air Force, was doing its best to render invasion unnecessary by bombing Germany into submission. On 30 May 1942 came the first 1000-bomber raid against Cologne. In 1943 the Americans began taking an increasing share. Largely British, but assisted by B-17's of the VIII Air Force, was the most destructive air bombing of the European war — the series of attacks on Hamburg in July–August 1943, which, by using incendiary bombs, wiped out over half the city, killed 42,600, and injured 37,000 people. 'Those who sowed the wind are reaping the whirlwind,' said Winston Churchill.

They certainly were, and worse was to come; but this strategic air offensive never succeeded as an alternative to land invasion. The bombing of German cities, almost nightly by the R.A.F. and every clear day by the A.A.F., did not seriously diminish Germany's well-dispersed war production, and conspicuously failed to break civilian morale. It was also frightfully expensive. In six days of October 1943, culminating in a raid on the ball-bearing plants at Schweinfurt, deep in the heart of Germany, the VIII Air Force lost 148 bombers and their crews, mostly as a result of battles in the air.

During 1944 the strategic bombing effort was far better directed. On New Year's day America's most famous aviator, General Carl Spaatz, was appointed commander of the United States Strategic Air Force in Europe. Air power, besides obstructing the movement of German armies, was now applied with increasing precision and violence to the key centers of German war production. One reason for the heavy casualties of October 1943 was the lack of fighter planes long-legged enough to escort the bombers; by the spring of 1944 we had the P-38 Lightning, P-47 Thunderbolt, and P-51 Mustang, which could fly to Berlin and back, fighting a good part of the way. In the ' Big Week ' of 19–25 February 1944, 3300 heavy bombers of the England-based VIII, and over 500 of the Italy-based XV Air Force, escorted by about the same number of fighter planes, attacked twelve targets important for the German aircraft industry, as far south as Ratisbon and Augsburg. Our losses were 226 bombers, 28 fighters, and about 2600 men; but some 600 German planes were shot down in the air. German aircraft production recuperated to be sure; but these February bombing missions did deny many hundreds of aircraft to the enemy when he needed them most; and the names of Major Generals Frederick A. Anderson and William Kepner USA, who organized them, should be gratefully remembered. By 14 April, when the almost two-year-old Combined Bomber Offensive ended, and control of the U.S. Strategic Air Forces in Europe passed to General Eisenhower, the Allied air forces had established a thirty-to-one superiority over the German air force, and during the next seven weeks, before the Normandy invasion, they co-operated to make that operation a success. On D-day, ' Ike ' told his troops, ' If you see fighting aircraft over you, they will be ours,' and they were.

The air war in Europe was very expensive, costing the lives of some 158,000 British, Canadian, and American aviators. Many mistakes were made; but the Germans made even more. It must be remembered that this was a new dimension in warfare, and that without victory in the air there could have been no victory anywhere.

2. Operation ' Overlord,' June–July 1944

Planning for the continental invasion began at London early in 1943, by an Anglo-American staff under the direction of General Sir Frederick Morgan. In May the Combined Chiefs of Staffs set the date a year ahead. Roosevelt and Churchill decided to appoint General Eisenhower, who in the conduct of North African and Mediterranean operations had revealed military and diplomatic talents of a high order, to command all invasion forces of both nations. In January 1944 ' Ike ' flew to London where he received his directive from the Combined Chiefs of Staff: ' You will enter the continent of Europe and, in conjunction with the other United Nations, undertake operations aimed at the heart of Germany and the destruction of her armed forces.'

Never before in modern times had an invading army crossed the English Channel against opposition, and Hitler's coastal defenses were formidable: underwater obstacles and mines, artillery emplacements, pill boxes, wire entanglements, tank traps, land mines, and other hazards designed to stop the invaders on the beaches. Behind these defenses were stationed 58 divisions, 17 of them in the Pas de Calais, 14 in Normandy and Brittany. Yet the Allies had reason for confidence. They could select their point of attack. For six weeks Allied air forces had been smashing roads and bridges in northern France, reducing the transportation system to chaos. The Allied force of soldiers, sailors, aviators, and service amounted to 2.8 million men, all based in England; that little country almost sagged under a stockpile of 2.5 million tons of supplies. Thirty-nine divisions and 11,000 planes were available for the initial landings, and the Allied supporting fleet was overwhelmingly superior to anything the Germans could deploy; the U-boats had been so neutralized by the Allied navies that not one got in a lick at the thousands of vessels engaged in the invasion. The German army, fighting on three fronts, lacked strategic reserves, and the German high command was riddled with dissension. Hitler's army commanders, fooled by an elaborate deception devised by the British, to the effect that a major army group under General Patton, in southeast England, was about to cross the bottleneck to the Pas de Calais, concentrated their strongest forces on the wrong stretch of coast.

The Allied command selected as target a 40-mile strip of beach along the Normandy coast between the Orne river and the Cotentin peninsula. The eastern sector was assigned to the British, the western to the Americans. By the end of May southern England was one vast military camp, crowded with soldiers awaiting the final word to go, and piled high with supplies and equipment awaiting transport to the far shore of the Channel. This ' mighty host,' wrote Eisenhower, ' was as tense as a . . . great human spring, coiled for the moment when its energy should be released.' Shortly after midnight 5 June three paratroop divisions were flown across the Channel to drop behind the beaches. During the night the invasion fleet of 600 warships and 4000 supporting craft, freighted with 176,000 men from a dozen different ports, the British commanded by Admiral Sir Philip Vian and General Sir Miles Dempsey, the Americans by Admiral Alan Kirk and General Omar Bradley, moved over to the Norman coast. The transports and large landing craft anchored off the invasion beaches at 3:00 A.M.; battleships, cruisers, and destroyers closed the beaches and began hurling shells ashore at 5:30. Before naval bombardment ended, landing craft, lowered from transports over ten miles from shore, began their approach. It was D-day, 6 June.

The first assault troops, who touched down at 6:30, achieved tactical surprise. On the American right — designated Utah Beach — VII Corps (including Brigadier General Theodore Roosevelt, Jr.) got ashore against light opposition, surmounted barriers of marsh and swamp, and linked up with elements of the 82nd Airborne Division. But V Corps, assigned a four-mile strip designated Omaha Beach, found the going tough. Heavy overcast had prevented the air force from bombing that beach; naval bombardment had not destroyed German artillery emplacements; underwater obstacles were numerous and formidable. For a time the issue was in doubt. Soldiers were wounded in a maze of mined underwater obstacles, and drowned by the rising tide; those who got through had to cross a 50-yard-wide beach, exposed to cunningly contrived cross-fire from concrete pill boxes that supporting naval gunfire could not initially reach; men huddled for protection under a low sea wall until company officers rallied them to root the defenders out of their prepared positions. Plain guts and training saved the day at Omaha, not forgetting the naval gunfire support that rained shells on the Germans as soon as the shore fire control parties were able to indicate targets.

The numerically superior British assault force under General Dempsey had a somewhat less difficult landing on beaches Gold, Juno, and Sword, but it bore the brunt of the next week's fighting. Caen was the hinge of the Allied beachhead, and the Germans counterattacked strongly at that point. In both sectors paratroops played an essential part, by confusing the Germans and harassing their communications. All in all, the D-day assault on that ever memorable 6th of June was a brilliant if costly success.

Once the initial landings had been effected, the Allies rushed over men, armor, and supplies to build up the invading army faster than the Germans could reinforce theirs. By 12 June the Allies controlled a continuous beachhead some 70 miles in length and from five to fifteen miles in depth. On the left the British were battling for Caen;

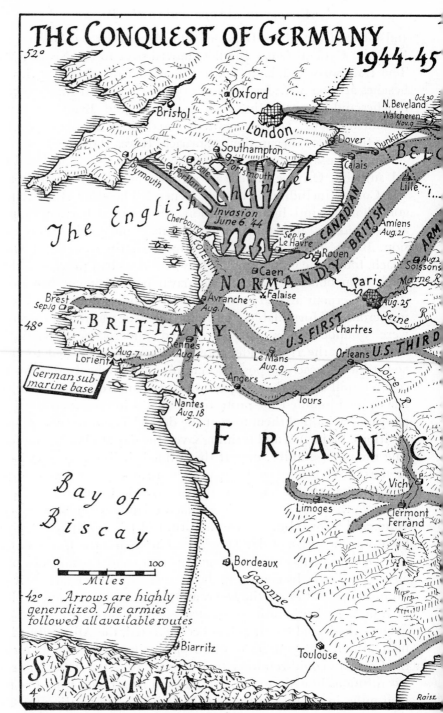

THE CONQUEST OF GERMANY
1944-45

52°

Oxford

Bristol

London

N. Beveland *Oct. 30*
Walcheren *Nov. 9*

Dover
Dunkirk

Southampton

Portland
Portsmouth
Poole

Calais

BEL

Plymouth

The English Channel

Lille

Cherbourg

Invasion
June 6 '44

Sep. 13
Le Havre

Amiens
Aug. 21

ARM

COTENTIN

Caen

Rouen

Aug. 2
Soissons

NORMANDY

Paris

Marne R.

Brest
Sep. 19

48°

BRITTANY

Avranches
Aug. 1

×Falaise

Aug. 25

Seine R.

Chartres

U.S. FIRST

Lorient

Rennes
Aug. 4

Aug. 7

Le Mans
Aug. 9

Orleans

U.S. THIRD

*German sub-
marine base*

Angers

Tours

Loire R.

Nantes
Aug. 18

F R A N C

Vichy

*Bay of
Biscay*

Limoges

Clermont
Ferrand

0   100
Miles

42° – Arrows are highly
generalized. The armies
followed all available routes

Bordeaux

Garonne

Biarritz

Toulouse

S P A I N

4°

Raisz

824

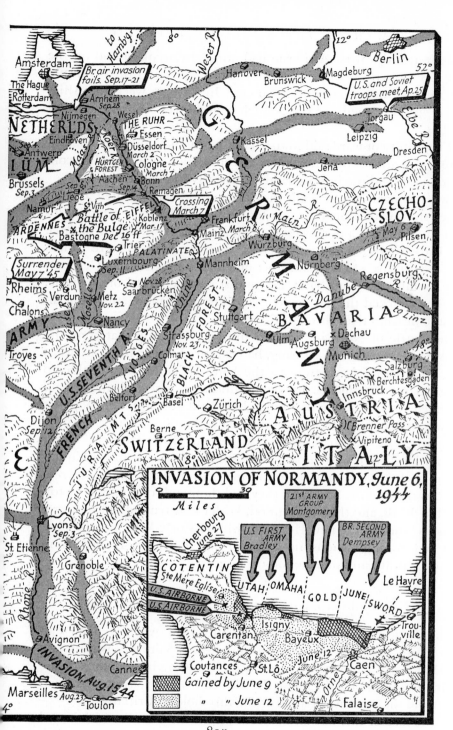

Amsterdam
The Hague
Rotterdam
Br. air invasion fails. Sep.17-21
Arnhem Sep.28
NETHERLDS.
Nijmegen
Wesel
THE RUHR
Essen
Düsseldorf March 2
Cologne March 7
HÜRTGEN FOREST
Aachen Sep.8
Bonn Sep.14
Remagen
Crossing March 7
Eindhoven
Antwern Sept.
Brussels Sep.3
Namur
Liège
St.Vith
Battle of EIFFEL the Bulge
Bastogne Dec.16 ff
Koblenz Mar.17
Trier
PALATINATE
Luxembourg Sep.11
Frankfurt
Mainz March 8
Wurzburg
Mannheim
Nürnberg
ARDENNES
Surrender May'45
Rheims
Verdun
Chalons
Metz Nov.22
Nov.28
Saarbrücken
Nancy
Strassburg Nov.23
Colmar
Stuttgart
Ulm Augsburg
Dachau
Munich
BAVARIA
Regensburg
Danube to Linz
Salzburg
Berchtesgaden
Innsbruck
AUSTRIA
Brenner Pass
Vipiteno L.
ITALY

to Hamburg
Weser R.
Hanover
Brunswick
Magdeburg
Berlin
U.S. and Soviet troops meet.Ap.25
Torgau
Leipzig
Dresden
Kassel
Jena
GERMANY
R. Main
May 6
Pilsen
CZECHO-SLOV.

Troyes
ARMY
Dijon Sep.12
St. Etienne
Grenoble
Lyons Sep.3
Avignon
Cannes
INVASION. Aug.15.'44
Marseilles Aug.23
Toulon
FRENCH
VOSGES MTS.
U.S.SEVENTH A.
Belfort
Basel
Zürich
Berne
SWITZERLAND
JURA MTS.
BLACK FOREST
Rhine
Moselle R.
Meuse R.
Rhone

825

INVASION OF NORMANDY, June 6, 1944

Miles 30

21ST ARMY GROUP Montgomery
U.S. FIRST ARMY Bradley
BR. SECOND ARMY Dempsey

Cherbourg June 27
COTENTIN
Ste Mère Eglise
U.S. AIRBORNE
U.S. AIRBORNE
UTAH OMAHA
GOLD
JUNE
SWORD
Le Havre
Trouville
Carentan
Isigny
Bayeux
June 12
Caen
Coutances
St.Lô
Falaise
Orne

Gained by June 9
" " June 12

in the center the 101st Airborne had entered Carentan; and on the right VII Corps was pushing swiftly across the Cotentin peninsula and sweeping north toward Cherbourg. In a single week the Allies landed 326,000 men, 50,000 vehicles, and over 100,000 tons of supplies.

' The history of war,' said Marshal Stalin, in one of his rare compliments to his allies, ' does not know any undertaking so broad in conception, so grandiose in scale, and so masterly in execution.'

Two artificial harbors off the landing beaches created out of sunken ships with connecting pontoon units, facilitated a rapid build-up of supplies; but a northwest gale blew up on 19 June and in three days badly damaged the ' mulberrys,' as these harbors were called. Now the capture of Cherbourg became highly urgent. The Germans there, bombarded from land, air, and sea, surrendered on 26 June. But they wrecked the harbor first, and for weeks more stuff came in over the beaches than through Cherbourg.

The Battle of Normandy lasted until 24 July. By that time the British, after very tough fighting, had captured Caen; the Americans had taken Saint-Lô, gateway to the South. The enemy, unable to bring up reinforcements, his communications wrecked and planes grounded, was bewildered. Rommel thought the situation hopeless and was preparing to try to negotiate with Eisenhower for a separate peace when he was arrested and killed, on Hitler's orders. Other high-ranking officers attempted to assassinate Hitler at his headquarters on 20 July, to take over the German government, and to surrender; but the Fuehrer survived, they and thousands of others were tortured to death, and the war went on. Hitler now trusted to his ' secret weapons ' such as the new U-boat to win. His new V-1 ' buzz bombs,' launched from positions in Belgium and northern France, were spreading death and destruction on London.

3. NORMANDY TO THE RHINE, JULY–SEPTEMBER 1944

The battle for France began on 25 July 1944, when General Patton's Third Army hit the German lines west of Saint-Lô. Within two days VII Corps had reached Coutances, hemming in remnants of the German army along the coast. By the end of July, Avranches had fallen and the Americans stood at the threshold of Brittany.

In the face of this fast and furious attack the German withdrawal turned into something like a rout. And after the breakthrough came the breakout. One wing of Patton's army turned west and within a week overran Brittany, stopping only at Brest, Lorient, and Saint-Nazaire, which were left for leisurely reduction. Another wing turned east, and within two weeks reached the Loire and Le Mans. In a desperate gamble Hitler ordered the German Seventh Army to break through the funnel of the American army at Avranches. Most of it was destroyed in the ensuing Battle of the Falaise gap; only remnants of armor fought their way through and sped east to prepare for the defense of Germany.

On 15 August, as the Germans were being ground to bits in the Falaise gap, the Allies launched their long-awaited invasion of southern France. General Eisenhower insisted on this Operation ' Dragoon ' for two reasons: to deploy General Patch's American Seventh Army and General de Lattre de Tassigny's First French Army on his southern flank for the final invasion of Germany; and to capture the major port of Marseilles for logistic supply. The French Riviera coastline was lightly defended, and Operation ' Dragoon,' commanded by Admiral Hewitt, was a push-over. Toulon and Marseilles were soon taken by the French, while the Seventh Army rolled up the Rhône valley, captured Lyon and raced to close the German escape corridor at the Belfort gap. By mid-September Patch had linked up with Patton.

' Liberate Paris by Christmas and none of us can ask for more,' said Churchill to Eisenhower. General Hodges's First Army raced for the Seine; Patton's Third boiled out onto the open country north of the Loire, and swept eastward through Orléans to Troyes. Paris rose against her hated masters, and with the aid of General Leclerc's 2nd Armored Division, was liberated on 25 August, four months ahead of Churchill's request. General Charles de Gaulle entered the city in triumph and assumed the presidency of a French provisional government.

Only lack of gasoline could stop Patton. His spearheads reached the Marne on 28 August, pushed through Château-Thierry (where an American army had fought in 1918), overran Rheims and Verdun. To the north, Montgomery's British and Canadians pushed along the coast into Belgium, by-passing Calais and Dunkirk. They captured Brussels and entered Antwerp 4 September; but that great port was no use while the Germans blocked the lower Scheldt. By

11 September the American First Army had liberated Luxembourg and near Aachen crossed the border into Germany. Within six weeks all France had been cleared of the enemy, and from there to Switzerland Allied armies stood poised for the advance into Germany. The Germans had lost almost half a million men; but Hitler's amazing hold over them had not relaxed, and they were ready for a last counterblow that cost the Allies dear.

On other fronts, the German position was becoming equally bad. The Russian offensive that began in July 1943 had recovered most of the invaded territory, and in the spring of 1944 the Red armies reached the Dnieper river in the north and the Carpathians in the south. Stalin had promised to launch a new offensive when the Allies entered Normandy, and on 23 June he began it, along an 800-mile front from Leningrad to the Carpathians. In the space of five weeks the Russians swept across the Ukraine and Poland and up to the gates of Warsaw, where, despicably, they paused instead of helping Polish patriots to liberate their capital, hoping to reduce Poland to a satellite state; as they did. Rumania threw in the sponge when another Red army crossed her borders, and so deprived the Germans of their last source of crude oil. By October the Russians had linked up with partisan forces in Yugoslavia. With most of the Balkans overrun, the road to Austria and Czechoslovakia was open. In Italy, too, the Germans were being driven back on their last line of defense, the Gothic line guarding the Po valley — a formidable barrier, which held up further advance in 1944.

Although the Allies still held the initiative in France, they were unable to exploit it. They had run into a serious problem of logistics; the speed of their advance had outrun supply, and a stubborn defense still denied them the water approach to Antwerp.

This situation presented Eisenhower with one of his most difficult strategic decisions. Montgomery wanted to push ahead through Holland into the heart of Germany; he was confident that with proper support he could plunge through to Berlin. Patton was no less confident of his ability to smash into Germany from the south. Logistics permitted a modest advance on a broad front, or a deep stab on a single front, but not both. Because Eisenhower deemed it essential to clear the way to Antwerp, capture Calais and Dunkirk, and overrun the V-1 and V-2 bomb emplacements, which were raining guided missiles on London, priority in the scarce gasoline supply was given to Montgomery, who wasted it. But the root of Allied trouble at this moment of supreme opportunity was lack of foresight. The top planners, not having anticipated the collapse of German resistance in France in August, had made no preparation for exploiting it instantly. Thus, by mid-September, when airborne forces dropped on Arnhem were definitely defeated, and the ground offensive stopped in its tracks, the sad prospect of another winter's campaign in Europe loomed ahead.

4. LEYTE, OCTOBER 1944

By 1 August 1944, when the three largest Marianas and the entire northern coast of New Guinea were in American hands, the question of the next move became acute. All previous plans for victory had counted on establishing an Allied base somewhere on the coast of China as a springboard for invading Japan, as Great Britain had been a springboard for invading Germany. But the Japanese army, in a fresh offensive starting in April 1944, captured most of the airdromes from which General Chennault's XIV Army Air Force had been operating, and sealed off the China coast.

How then could the Allies get at Japan? The question was virtually decided in July 1944, in a conference at Honolulu, between General MacArthur, Admiral Nimitz, and President Roosevelt. The President, pointing to Saipan on the map, said, ' Douglas, where do we go from here? ' — ' Leyte, Mr. President; and then Luzon! ' And that is how it was done.

The Joint Chiefs of Staff first set the date for the invasion of Leyte as 20 December 1944. At the suggestion of the aggressive Admiral Halsey, and with General MacArthur's glad approval, the timetable was stepped up two months. While amphibious forces were marshaling at the Admiralties and Hollandia, and slowly approaching their target, the fast carrier forces — four groups under Mitscher comprising nine fleet and eight light carriers, with their attendant battleships, cruisers, and destroyers — rendezvoused in the Philippine Sea on 7 October, and embarked on a three-day ' knock-down, drag-out fight,' as Halsey described it, over the Ryukyus and Formosa. They destroyed over 500 planes at the cost of 89 aircraft and 64 aviators lost, and two cruisers damaged. None of the supposedly vulnerable carriers was touched, although the Japanese claimed over the radio to have sunk them all — to which Halsey retorted in a dispatch to

Nimitz, ' Ships reported sunk by Tokyo have been salvaged and are now retiring toward the enemy.'

Now the Central Pacific forces under Admirals Nimitz and Halsey, and the Southwest Pacific forces under General MacArthur and Admiral Kinkaid, were combined in one massive thrust into Leyte. Early in the morning of 20 October 1944, 73 transports and 50 LST's, covered by a dozen battleships and cruisers and a flock of escort carriers, destroyers, and small craft, entered Leyte Gulf — where Magellan, 423 years before, had discovered the Philippines. The landings on Leyte were handsomely conducted by Admirals Barbey and Wilkinson, and Sixth Army, commanded by Lieutenant General Walter Krueger, promptly secured a 20-mile beachhead. That afternoon General MacArthur and President Osmeña of the Philippines splashed ashore from a landing craft. Before a microphone, MacArthur delivered an impressive liberation speech beginning, ' People of the Philippines, I have returned.'

He certainly had; but how long could he stay? The Japanese were not taking this lying down. At Tokyo the war lords decided that now was the time to commit the entire Japanese fleet, defeat American forces afloat, and isolate MacArthur, so that he would be virtually back at Bataan. From that decision there resulted, on 25 October, the battle for Leyte Gulf, greatest sea fight of this or of any other war.

Admiral Toyoda put in execution a plan based on ruse and surprise, factors dear to Japanese strategists; but his plan required a division of the Japanese fleet into three forces, which proved to be fatal. Admiral Nishimura's Southern Force of battleships and cruisers was to come through Surigao Strait, break into Leyte Gulf at daybreak 25 October, and there rendezvous with Kurita's more powerful Center Force, which was to thread San Bernardino Strait and come around Samar from the north. Either separately was strong enough to make mincemeat of Admiral Kinkaid's amphibious forces in Leyte Gulf and cut off General Krueger's troops from their seaborne lifeline. Way was to be cleared for Kurita by Admiral Ozawa's Northern Force built around four carriers, whose mission was to entice Halsey's Task Force 38, the American carrier force, up north.

That part of the plan worked only too well, but the rest of it worked not at all. Admiral Kinkaid deployed almost every battleship, cruiser, and destroyer that had supported the Leyte landings, and placed them under the command of Rear Admiral Jesse Oldendorf, to catch Nishimura as he came through Surigao Strait in the early hours of 25 October. First a flock of motor torpedo boats fired their ' fish,' missed, but sent word ahead. Then, two destroyer torpedo attacks nicked Nishimura of one battleship and three destroyers. What was left of his ' T ' was crossed by Oldendorf's battleships and cruisers. Their high-calibre fire sank the other enemy battleship and killed Admiral Nishimura; and what was left of the Southern Force fled, most of it to be harried and sunk after dawn by carrier planes. This superb night victory was the battlewagons' revenge for Pearl Harbor — five of the six there engaged had been sunk or grounded on 7 December 1941.

Scarcely was the Surigao Strait battle won when the most critical of the three actions began. Kurita's massive Center Force, built around his biggest battleships and heavy cruisers, had been damaged and delayed en route, first by two American submarines in Palawan Passage, then by carrier planes in the Sibuyan Sea, on 24 October. Halsey overestimated the damage that his bombers had done; and, after his search planes had found Admiral Ozawa's Northern Force of carriers coming down from Japan (with the express mission of luring him north), Halsey could think of just one thing — to sink those carriers. So, without leaving even a destroyer to watch San Bernardino Strait, Halsey tore up north to dispose of the enemy flattops.

Thus, Kurita, to his great astonishment, was able to thread the strait unopposed, and approach the northern entrance to Leyte Gulf undetected. At one of the critical moments of the war, off the island of Samar, at 6:45 A.M., 25 October, Kurita ran smack into a force of six escort carriers under Rear Admiral Clifton Sprague. One of three groups of ' baby flattops ' that were providing air cover for the amphibious forces in Leyte Gulf, they had no idea or intimation that they would have to fight a force of battleships, heavy cruisers, and destroyers. The ensuing battle off Samar was the most gallant naval action in our history, and the most bloody — 1130 killed, 913 wounded. Kurita, who still had the 18-inch-gunned *Yamato* and three more battleships, eight cruisers, and ten destroyers, should have been able to destroy Sprague's feebly armed escort carriers; but as soon as the Japanese big guns opened at a range of 14 miles, Sprague turned into the wind to launch planes, called for help from two other escort carrier groups, and sent his destroyers and DE's to make desperate gunfire and torpedo attacks. After a running fight of an hour and a half, two American destroyers and a DE were sunk; but the American bombs and torpedoes had sunk three Japanese heavy cruisers and, by repeated air attacks relentlessly pressed home, so badly mauled and scattered the other enemy ships that Admiral Kurita broke off action and retired. Thus, because the enemy commander lacked gumption, and Sprague had plenty; and, still more, because the Japanese had no air support, a fleet more than ten times as powerful as the Americans in gunfire power was defeated.

Up north, Admiral Mark Mitscher's carriers were slicing off bombers and fighter planes against Ozawa's carriers which had decoyed him and Halsey up north. In this battle off Cape Engaño, all four Japanese carriers (including the last survivor of those which had struck Pearl Harbor) were sunk, with a trifling loss of planes and pilots on our side.

This three-part battle for Leyte Gulf on 25 October 1944 left the United States Navy in complete command of Philippine waters; never again could the Japanese navy offer a real threat. But two months' fighting ashore were required against the hard-fighting, no-surrender Japanese infantry, before Leyte and Samar were in Mac-Arthur's hands.

5. POLITICAL INTERLUDE

As the Allied armed forces fought ahead, another presidential election came up — the first in wartime since 1864. Eighty years earlier the Democratic party had nominated a disgruntled general, attacked the conduct of the war, and called for a compromise peace; in 1944 a hard core of isolationists, supported by the Chicago *Tribune* and the Hearst press, attacked the basic strategic decision of beating the Axis first, and tried to promote General MacArthur, as a supposed ' martyr ' to Roosevelt's ' jealousy,' for the Republican presidential nomination. This was a sequel to repeated efforts by Senator A. B. (' Happy ') Chandler of Kentucky, Senator Arthur Capper of Kansas, and others, to have Admiral Nimitz's Pacific command placed under MacArthur. But the General, though he felt that the Southwest Pacific had been slighted, was now on the eve of fulfilling his promise to return to the Philippines, and gave his political admirers no encouragement.[1] Apart from this small though influential group, the

---

[1] One of the inexplicable facets of the isolationist mind was a desire to drop the war in Europe but go ' all out ' in the Pacific; their island had only one coast! Frazier

Republicans supported the war and endorsed a postwar international organization, without being reconciled to the New Deal. In the 1942 congressional elections they increased their strength in the House 30 per cent, which gave them high hopes of winning the presidency in 1944.

Wendell Willkie by now was a world figure, owing to his many visits to Allied countries, and his inspiring speeches in support of the Allied cause. But he made the tactical error of entering the presidential primary in Wisconsin, where the voters wanted no advocate of ' One World,' but an isolationist who would promise to ' bring the boys home ' from Europe. There he met a stunning defeat, and withdrew from the race. Governor Thomas E. Dewey of New York, who had proved himself a competent administrator, was nominated by the Republican convention on the first ballot. The Republican platform criticized the technique rather than the substance of the New Deal, promised to take the government out of business and to ' re-establish liberty ' at home, but pledged the party to support a postwar international organization. Their political strategy was to concentrate on the argument that no party could safely be entrusted with office for more than twelve years without getting hardening of the political arteries, and that the country needed younger men for the tasks of peace and reconstruction. Respecting the President's health the charge was only too true; but his physicians reported him still to be fit as a fiddle; and the hardening of the physical arteries from which he was really suffering had so unpredictable a prognosis and duration that the doctors expected him to survive a fourth term. The Democratic party convention renominated him on the first ballot. There was a battle over the second place on the ticket. Senator Harry Truman of Missouri, politically the most acceptable of the applicants, got the nod from President Roosevelt and was nominated on the second ballot.

Dewey, wanting the personal charm that made Willkie and F.D.R. so formidable, was a poor campaigner, and the 'issue was never in doubt. Roosevelt carried 36 states with 432 electoral votes; Dewey, 12 states with 99 electoral votes; Roosevelt's popular plurality was about 3.5 million; the Democrats won 242 seats in the House, as

---

Hunt's *MacArthur*, p. 312, states that in Sept. 1943 a Gallup poll in the farm areas, especially the Middle West, gave MacArthur a 12 per cent preference over F.D.R. as the next President.

against 190 Republicans. That marked the end of isolationism as a potent political factor. But, in a sense, it 'went underground,' to emerge nastily as McCarthyism.

6. VICTORY IN EUROPE, SEPTEMBER 1944–MAY 1945

After the failure of the Arnhem air drop, the war temporarily lost its momentum and settled down to what General Eisenhower called 'the dirtiest kind of infantry slugging.' The Germans now held their strongest defensive positions since the beginning of the invasion. Rundstedt and Kesselring, ablest of their generals, were now commanders in the West and in Italy. And the winter of 1944–45 was one of the worst in memory: floods, cold, and snow combined to help the defense.

In the confused fighting that stretched from October to mid-December 1944 we can distinguish a series of battles, each as bitter as any of those that had been fought since Tunisia, and as costly. The first, taking them in geographical order, was the battle for the Scheldt estuary. The task of clearing the enemy out of the islands, whose possession by the Germans prevented Allied use of Antwerp, was assigned to the Canadian First Army. South Beveland was overrun by 30 October. Walcheren was a tougher nut to crack, and its reduction cost the Allies more casualties than the conquest of Sicily. Minesweeping and harbor clearance took so long that not until the end of November could Allied ships unload at Antwerp, and so shorten the logistics line.

The second major battle was for Aachen, near the junction of Belgium, Holland, and Germany. General Courtney H. Hodges's American First Army launched the attack on 2 October, fighting through five miles of Siegfried line fortifications. By the middle of the month the city was surrounded; then came a week of street fighting before the ancient capital of Charlemagne capitulated. It was the first German city to fall to the Allies.

General Omar Bradley now brought the Ninth Army north to cooperate with the First in a campaign to capture the Roer river dams — third of the major battles. An assault by seventeen divisions through the Hürtgen Forest toward Düren failed to do it. The country was not unlike that Wilderness in which Grant and Lee had tangled eighty years earlier. Three divisions alone, the 4th, 9th and

28th, suffered almost 13,000 casualties. The Americans reached the Roer river on 3 December, and there they were stalled until early February.

To the south, General Patton's Third Army jumped off early in November to capture Metz, northern Lorraine, and the industrial Saar basin. Only once before in modern times — in 1871 — had the fortress city of Metz fallen to an invader. Patton proved that if need be, he could be methodical, instead of dashing. First he enveloped Metz, reducing one by one the forts that encircled it. Then came a week of street fighting. The city fell on 22 November and the Third Army, fighting its way through the heaviest fortifications of the Siegfried line, plunged into the Saar. This campaign cost the Americans 29,000 battle casualties, but netted them 37,000 prisoners.

In conjunction with Patton's advance, General Devers's Sixth Army Group launched an attack into Alsace; Strasbourg fell on 23 November. The French then turned north along the Rhine, the Americans south. These operations, obscured by the more dramatic fighting to the north, cost the Allies 33,000 more casualties.

By mid-December the Allied armies were poised all along the border from Holland to Switzerland, ready to plunge into Germany. Then came a dramatic change of fortune: a German counteroffensive. Rundstedt's name was given to this desperate thrust through the Ardennes Forest, but the idea was Hitler's. His objective was to split the Allied army groups, drive through to the coast, and recapture Antwerp. Eisenhower had taken the calculated risk of spreading thin his forces in the rugged Ardennes, through which Rundstedt had crashed with his main force in May 1940. Now the Germans prepared to repeat that successful campaign. Because the bad weather prevented Allied air reconnaissance, they achieved surprise and initial success along a 50-mile front, on 16 December. After the first shock, Allied resistance stiffened. The Germans concentrated on the center of the Allied line. Here they achieved their most spectacular success, thrusting toward the Meuse, which they almost reached on 26 December. But they were checked at Bastogne, a name long to be remembered. This little Belgian town, headquarters of General Troy Middleton's VIII Corps, was a focal point of a network of roads essential to the Germans. Middleton decided to hold it at all costs, without adequate forces. Late in the night of 17 December the 101st Airborne Division, then in a rest center 100 miles behind the lines, was ordered to Bastogne; the men piled into trucks and jeeps and pulled into Bastogne on the 18th, just before the German tide flooded around the town. This reinforcement beefed up the strength of the defenders to some 18,000 men.

There followed one of the fiercest land battles of the war. The Americans seized outlying villages, and set up a perimeter defense. For six days the enemy hurled armor and planes at them, persistently probing for a weak spot, and found not one. Foul weather prevented aerial reinforcement of the defenders. On 22 December the American situation appeared hopeless and the Germans presented a formal demand for surrender, to which General ' Tony ' McAuliffe of the 101st Airborne gave the simple answer ' Nuts! ' Next day the weather cleared, and planes began dropping supplies; by Christmas Eve, with bomber and fighter support, the situation looked more hopeful. In the meantime, Patton's Third Army had made a great left wheel and started pell-mell north to the rescue of the besieged garrison. On 26 December his 4th Armored Division broke through the German encirclement and Bastogne was saved. The Battle of the Bulge, as we named it, was not over, but by 15 January 1945 the original lines of mid-December had been restored. Rundstedt had held up the Allied advance by a full month, but at a cost of 120,000 men, 1600 planes, and a good part of his armor. Never thereafter were the Germans able to put up an effective defense.

At the end of January, Eisenhower regrouped his armies and resumed advance toward the Rhine. In the meantime the Russians had sprung their winter offensive, which surpassed the campaign in the West in numbers involved and territory recaptured. The Russian army jumped off on a thousand-mile front early in January, crossed the Vistula, and swept toward Germany. While one group of armies in the center took Warsaw and raced across Poland to the Oder river, others stabbed into Germany from the north and south, moved into Hungary and Czechoslovakia and threatened Vienna. This gigantic pincer movement inflicted over a million German casualties.

In the final Allied campaign in the West we can distinguish three stages: the advance to the Rhine, from late January to 21 March; the crossing of the Rhine and the Battle of the Ruhr, 21 March to 14 April; and the annihilation of all enemy opposition, 14 April to the surrender on 7 May.

First came a series of systematic mopping-up operations designed to clear the Germans out of all territory west of the Rhine. The Canadian First Army launched an attack in the north and reached the Rhine at Kleve. The American First and the Ninth fought through the Hürtgen Forest, crossed the Roer river, and plunged on toward Cologne. Patton's Third Army, wheeling to the right again after the Ardennes battle, fought its way through the Siegfried line into Trier, and further south the French First Army cleared out the Colmar pocket. By the first week of March the Allied armies occupied the left bank of the Rhine from Holland to Switzerland, except in the triangle formed by the Eifel and the Palatinate.

That triangle did not remain long in German hands. Early in March Patton broke loose again and drove forward in a great sweeping advance. Within five days he reached the Rhine, then wheeled south and raced through the Palatinate, mopping up over 60,000 prisoners at a cost of less than 800 men killed. ' No defeat suffered in the war, except possibly Tunisia,' wrote Eisenhower, ' was more devastating in the completeness of the destruction inflicted ' on enemy forces. The 7th of March 1945 was one of the dramatic days of the war. On that day a detachment of the 9th Armored Division of the First Army captured the bridge over the Rhine at Remagen, just as the Germans were about to blow it. A fleet of navy landing craft were brought up in trucks to help the First Army cross, and once across the Rhine it fanned out, securing the highway running south to Munich. And on 22 March Patton began crossing the Rhine at Oppenheim, beating ' Monty ' to the historic river, as he had hoped.

The next move after vaulting the Rhine barrier was to encircle the Ruhr. Moving at breakneck speed — the 3rd Armored Division covered 90 miles in a single day — Hodges's First Army swung north, Simpson's Ninth turned south, and a giant pincer closed on the Ruhr, trapping some 400,000 Germans. Encircled, pounded on all sides, hammered day and night by swarms of bombers, the German armies caught in the pocket disintegrated. By 18 April the bag of prisoners reached a total of 325,000, and organized resistance ceased in the Ruhr. It was, said General Marshall, the largest envelopment operation in the history of American warfare; and it should be noted that this was Marshall's idea, violently opposed by Alan Brooke and ' Monty,' who wanted all Allied ground forces to be concentrated in one knifelike thrust across northern Europe; a concept which would have caused an impossible congestion and left the Ruhr in enemy hands.

Now Montgomery drove toward Bremen and Hamburg, Patton raced for Kassel, and Patch sped through Bavaria toward Czechoslovakia.

As the Allied armies drove deep into Germany, Austria, and Poland, they came upon one torture camp after another — Buchenwald, Dachau, Belsen, Auschwitz, Linz, Lublin — and what they reported sickened the whole Western World. These atrocity camps had been established in 1937 for Jews, gypsies, and anti-Nazi Germans and Austrians; with the coming of the war the Nazis used them for prisoners of all nationalities, civilians and soldiers, men, women, and children, and for Jews rounded up in Italy, France, Holland, and Hungary. All were killed in the hope of exterminating the entire race. In these camps, hordes of prisoners had been scientifically murdered; other multitudes had died of disease, starvation, and maltreatment. Much of this wholesale murder was done in the name of ' science,' and with the criminal collusion of German physicians, who appear to have absorbed the Nazi contempt for humanity. Nothing in their experience had prepared Americans for these revelations of human depravity; many are still incredulous. But the evidence is conclusive that the total number of civilians done to death by Hitler's orders exceeded 6 million. And the pathetic story of one of the least of these, the diary of the little German girl Anna Frank, has probably done more to convince the world of the hatred inherent in the Nazi doctrine than the solemn postwar trials.

As German resistance crumbled and victory appeared certain, the Western World was plunged into mourning by the news that a great leader had died. President Roosevelt, returning from the Yalta conference of the Combined Chiefs of Staff in February a sick man, went to his winter home in Warm Springs, Georgia, to prepare for the inauguration of the United Nations at San Francisco, which he hoped would usher in a new era of peace and justice. On 12 April, as he was drafting a Jefferson Day address, he suffered a cerebral hemorrhage which brought instant death. The last words he wrote were an epitome of his career: ' The only limit to our realization of tomorrow will be our doubts of today. Let us move forward with strong and active faith.'

The end was now in sight for Hitler's Germany. The Western Allies were rolling unopposed to the Elbe; the Russians were thrusting at Berlin. Advance detachments of the two armies met at Torgau on 25 April, severing Germany. On the last day of April, Hitler died a coward's death, killing first his mistress and then himself in a bomb-proof bunker under Berlin. German resistance was also collapsing in northern Italy. On 4 May General Mark Clark's Fifth Army, which had fought all the way up the boot of Italy, met, at the Brenner Pass, General Patch's Seventh, coming down through Austria, and next day German resistance in Italy ceased. Italian partisans had already captured Mussolini, complete with mistress, and killed them, on 28 April. Thus ended, in ruin, horror, and despair the Axis that pretended to rule the world, and the Reich which Hitler had boasted would last a thousand years.

Admiral Doenitz, Hitler's designated heir and second Fuehrer, tried desperately to arrange a surrender to the Western Allies, instead of Russia. Loyalty to our Eastern ally — a loyalty not reciprocated — caused General Eisenhower sternly to decline these advances. And on 7 May General Jodl signed an unconditional surrender at Allied headquarters in Rheims, and the war came to an end in the West.[2]

7. Victory over Japan, 1945

Well before the landings at Leyte on 20 October 1944, the Joint Chiefs of Staff decided that as soon as the Third Fleet, with its carriers, could be relieved from supporting MacArthur in the Philippines, it should be used to secure island bases for a final assault on Japan. Tokyo, Saipan, and Formosa make an isosceles triangle with legs 1500 miles long. The eastern leg, Saipan-Tokyo, was already being used by the B-29 Superforts to bomb the Japanese homeland, but a halfway house was wanted through which fighter support could stage, or where these Superforts could call if damaged. Iwo Jima fitted the bill. After a two weeks' preliminary bombardment, a three-day intensive naval and carrier-plane bombardment drove the Japanese from the landing beaches, and Kelly Turner's seasoned Fifth Fleet team, with Major General Harry Schmidt commanding the marines, went in on 19 February 1945. Mount Surabachi, scene of the famous flag-raising, was captured on 23 February; after that it was a

---

[2] V–E Day is celebrated on 8 May because the surrender became effective at 2301 that day, Central European time.

steady, bloody advance of the marines against the holed-up enemy, with constant naval fire support. Even before organized resistance ceased on 14 March, the B-29's began using the Iwo airfields; and it is estimated that by this means thousands of American lives were saved. But Iwo Jima cost the navy and marine corps 6855 deaths and 21,000 other casualties.

In the meantime another angle of the triangle, whose apex was Tokyo, had been shifted to Okinawa in the Ryukyus, several hundred miles nearer Japan than is Formosa, and less stoutly defended. Sixty-mile long Okinawa, where Commodore Perry had called in 1853, was an integral part of Japan. It was expected that when we attacked the Japanese would 'throw the book at us,' and they did. They had few warships left and American command of the sea prevented reinforcement of the island garrison; but they had plenty of planes and self-sacrificing pilots to employ the deadly kamikaze tactics. The Kamikaze ('Divine Wind') Corps was organized as a desperate expedient after the use of proximity-fuzed anti-aircraft shells by the United States Navy had made it almost impossible for a conventional bomber to hit a ship. The kamikaze pilots were trained to crash a ship, which meant certain death for a large part of its crew, and probable loss of the vessel. These tactics had already been tried in the Philippines campaign, with devastating success, and no defense against them had yet been found, except to station radar picket destroyers around the fleet, to take the rap and pass the word.

The Spruance-Turner team was in charge of the amphibious assault on Okinawa, with General Simon B. Buckner (who lost his life there), commanding Tenth Army. And, as the war in Europe was drawing to a close, the British contributed a task force built around four carriers with steel decks — useful insurance against kamikaze-kindled fires — which neutralized the Japanese airfields between Okinawa and Formosa.

American amphibious technique was now so perfected that when the four divisions went ashore on Okinawa on Easter Sunday, 1 April, the Japanese abandoned beaches and airfields and retired to prepared positions on the southern end of the island. Here they put up a desperate resistance, exacting a heavy toll of American lives, before the island was finally conquered late in June. In the meantime the navy, which had to cover the operation and furnish fire support, took a terrible beating from the kamikaze planes. Twenty-seven ships, fifteen of them destroyer types, were sunk, and sixty-one others were so badly damaged as to be out of the war; casualties were heavy even on the ships that survived. The fleet-carrier Task Force 58, besides supporting this operation, made carrier-plane raids on Tokyo and on Japanese airfields, and when the super-battleship *Yamato* sortied in early April, she was promptly sunk by air attack. Seven carriers were badly damaged by kamikazes — *Franklin, Wasp,* and *Bunker Hill* between them lost 2211 men killed and 798 wounded — but not one was sunk. The total cost to us of the invasion of Okinawa was over 12,500 killed and over 62,500 wounded; but the island as a base was indispensable not only in the closing weeks of World War II but in the cold war that followed.

Germany was now defeated and the Allies could give their undivided attention to knocking out Japan. A new British offensive, by land and sea, captured Mandalay and Rangoon in the spring of 1945 and soon pushed the Japanese out of Burma. While in great secrecy scientists were preparing the atomic bombs at Los Alamos, the navy and the army air force redoubled the fury of their attacks on the Japanese home islands. There were bombings by carrier planes, naval bombardments, and B-29 bombing raids. Large parts of Tokyo and other industrial cities were destroyed by incendiary bombs.

During the bloody assaults on the outlying Japanese islands, General Eichelberger's Eighth Army and Admiral Kinkaid's Seventh Fleet — both under General MacArthur — were completing the liberation of the Philippines. They captured the ruins of Manila, where the Japanese made a house-to-house defense, on 4 March 1945. There the Philippine Commonwealth, soon to become the Philippine Republic, was promptly re-established. But MacArthur did not feel that he had redeemed his promise until the rest of the archipelago was liberated; and before Japan surrendered, Palawan, Panay, Negros, Cebu, Bohol, Mindanao, and Sulu had been taken by a series of assaults spearheaded by Admiral Dan Barbey's VII 'Phib.

Nor must one forget a tribute to the submarines of the Pacific Fleet, whose destruction of merchant shipping was one of the three main factors that brought victory over Japan. The 50 American submarines (at a maximum) operating daily in the Pacific, in 1944, were almost twice as effective as over 100 German U-boats operating daily in the Atlantic in 1942–43. Japan had 6 million tons of merchant shipping at the start of the war and added another 4 million tons by conquest and new construction; but at the end she had left only 1.8 million tons, mostly small wooden vessels in the Inland Sea, and was completely cut off from her early conquests. United States forces alone sank 2117 Japanese merchant vessels of almost 8 million tons during the war, and 60 per cent of this was done by submarines, of which 50 were lost in action. The Japanese I-boats and RO-boats picked off a few valuable warships (e.g. *Yorktown, Wasp, Indianapolis*), but inflicted slight damage on the American merchant marine; and the Japanese lost 128 submarines, U.S.S. *England* sinking six in thirteen days of May 1944. Admiral Charles A. Lockwood, commanding all submarines of the United States Pacific Fleet, was one of our outstanding naval leaders in the war.

The Combined Chiefs of Staff, meeting at Quebec in September 1944, figured that it would take eighteen months after the surrender of Germany to defeat Japan. Actually, the war in the Pacific ended with a terrific bang only three months after V-E Day. President Truman and Winston Churchill, meeting with the C.C.S. at Potsdam, presented Japan with an ultimatum on 26 July 1945. The surrender must be complete, and must include an Allied occupation of Japan, and the return of all Japanese conquests since 1895 to their former owners. But the Japanese people were assured that the occupation would end as soon as ' a peacefully inclined and responsible government ' was established, and that they would neither ' be enslaved as a race or destroyed as a nation.' The alternative was ' prompt and utter destruction.' If the government of Suzuki, the Japanese premier, had made up its mind promptly to accept the Potsdam declaration as a basis for peace, there would have been no atomic bomb explosion over Japan. But Suzuki was more afraid of the Japanese militarists than he was of American power.

The fearful consequences were the end product of long experiment and development in atomic fission. In 1939 Albert Einstein, Enrico Fermi, Leo Szilard, and other physicists who had sought refuge in the United States from tyranny in their native countries, warned President Roosevelt of the danger of Germany's obtaining a lead in uranium fission. The President entrusted a project of that nature to the Office of Scientific Research and Development, set up in May 1941 under the direction of Vannevar Bush and James B.

Conant.[3] By December, Fermi and others, working at the University of Chicago, achieved the first self-sustaining nuclear chain reaction, halfway mark to the atomic bomb. Army engineers under General Graves then took over, under the code name 'Manhattan District,' and built a small city at Oak Ridge, Tenn., for producing the atomic bomb. By 1944 research had so progressed that a special physics laboratory was erected at Los Alamos, N. M., for which J. R. Oppenheimer was responsible; and on 16 July 1945 the first atomic bomb was exploded there. President Truman conveyed the news at Potsdam to Winston Churchill, who remarked ' This is the Second Coming, in wrath.'

That, indeed, it was for Japan; eventually, perhaps, for the entire world.

We had it, but whether or not to use it was another question. President Truman's committee of high officials and top atomic scientists recommended that atomic bombs be exploded over Japan at once, and without warning. On 24 July the President issued the necessary order to the XX Army Air Force at Saipan, whither the first two bombs had been sent, to prepare to drop them at the first favorable moment after 3 August, if Japan had not accepted surrender. He and Secretary Byrnes hoped that the enemy would reconsider his scornful answer to the Potsdam declaration; but, as he did not, Truman issued the fateful order ' Execute! ' on 2 August.

' Enola Gay,' as the chosen B-29 was called, was commanded by Colonel Paul W. Tibbets; Captain William S. Parsons, a naval ordnance expert, went along to make the final adjustments to the bomb. At 9:15 A.M., 6 August, it was toggled out at an altitude of 31,600 feet, at a speed of 328 m.p.h., over Hiroshima. This city had been given the tragic target assignment as the second most important military center in Japan. The bomb wiped out the Second Japanese Army to a man, razed four square miles of the city, and killed 60,175 people, including the soldiers. And around noon 9 August, a few hours after Russia had declared war on Japan, the second atomic bomb was exploded over Nagasaki, killing 36,000 more.[4]

Although many Americans have expressed contrition over explod-

---

[3] See J. P. Baxter, *Scientists Against Time,* for relation between this and the earlier National Defense Research Committee.

[4] Official Japanese statement of 31 July 1959 for Hiroshima. Samuel Glasstone, *Effects of Nuclear Weapons* (Atomic Energy Commission), June 1957, p. 455, for Nagasaki.

ing the first atomic bombs, it is difficult to see how the war with Japan could otherwise have been concluded promptly, or what difference it would have made after the war if the secret had temporarily been withheld. The explosion over Hiroshima caused fewer civilian casualties than the repeated B-29 bombings of Tokyo, and those big bombers would have had to wipe out one city after another if the war had not ended in August. Japan had enough military capability — more than 5000 planes with kamikaze-trained pilots and at least 2 million ground troops — to have made our planned invasion of the Japanese home islands in the fall of 1945 an exceedingly bloody affair for both sides. And that would have been followed by a series of bitterly protracted battles on Japanese soil, the effects of which even time could hardly have healed. Moreover, as Russia would have been a full partner in these campaigns, the end result would have been division of Japan with the Communists, as happened in Germany.

Even after the two atomic bombs had been dropped, and the Potsdam declaration had been clarified to assure the Japanese that they could keep their emperor, the surrender was a very near thing. Hirohito had to override his two chief military advisers, Admiral Toyoda and General Umezu, and take the responsibility of accepting the Potsdam terms. That he did at 10:50 P.M., 14 August. Even thereafter, a military coup d'état to sequester the emperor, kill his cabinet, and continue the war, was narrowly averted. Hirohito showed great moral courage; and the promise to retain him in power despite the wishes of Russia (which wanted the war prolonged and Japan given over to anarchy), was perhaps the wisest high-level decision of the war.

After preliminary arrangements had been made at Manila with General MacArthur's and Admiral Nimitz's staffs, an advance party was flown into Atangi airfield near Tokyo on 28 August. Scores of ships of the United States Pacific Fleet, and of the British Far Eastern Fleet, then entered Tokyo Bay. On 2 September 1945 General MacArthur, General Umezu, the Japanese foreign minister, and representatives of Great Britain, China, Russia, Australia, Canada, New Zealand, the Netherlands, and France, signed the surrender documents on the deck of battleship *Missouri,* a few miles from the spot where Commodore Perry's treaty had been signed 82 years before.

At 9:25 A.M., as the formalities closed, a flight of hundreds of air-

craft swept over *Missouri* and her sister ships. General MacArthur
then addressed a broadcast to the people of the United States. ' A
great tragedy has ended. A great victory has been won. . . . A new era
is upon us. . . . Men since the beginning of time have sought
peace . . . military alliances, balances of power, leagues of nations,
all in turn failed, leaving the only path to be by the way of the crucible of war. . . . The utter destructiveness of war now blots out
this alternative. We have had our last chance. If we do not devise
some greater and more equitable system, Armageddon will be at
our door. . . .'

In this stern and solemn setting, Japan acknowledged her total defeat in a war forced upon her by a clique of ambitious and reckless
militarists.

BIBLIOGRAPHY

1. THE WAR'S APPROACH, DIPLOMACY, INTERNATIONAL RELA-
TIONS. Winston S. Churchill, *The Gathering Storm* and *Their Finest Hour*
(The Second World War, vols. 1, 2) ; John R. Deane, *The Strange Alliance . . .
Wartime Co-operation with Russia;* John K. Fairbank, *The United States and
China* (2nd ed.) ; Herbert Feis, *The Road to Pearl Harbor, The China Tangle,
Churchill-Roosevelt-Stalin, The Potsdam Conference,* and *Japan Subdued;* Jo-
seph C. Grew, *Ten Years in Japan;* Toshikazu Kase, *Journey to the Missouri;*
George F. Kennan, *Russia and the West under Lenin and Stalin;* William L.
Langer & S. Everett Gleason, *The Challenge to Isolation 1937–1940* and *The
Undeclared War 1940–1941;* Fleet Admiral William D. Leahy, *I Was There;*
Basil Rauch, *Roosevelt from Munich to Pearl Harbor;* E. O. Reischauer, *The
United States and Japan;* Gaetano Salvemini, *Prelude to World War II;* Paul W.
Schroeder, *The Axis Alliance and Japanese-American Relations;* William L.
Shirer, *The Rise and Fall of the Third Reich.*

2. SHORT HISTORIES OF THE ENTIRE WAR. Maj. Gen. J. F. C. Fuller,
The Second World War, 1939–45. A Strategic and Tactical History; Capt. B. H.
Liddell Hart (in preparation) , *A History of the Second World War;* Hans-Adolf
Jacobsen, Jürgen Rohwer, *et al., Entscheidungsschlachten des zweiten Welt-
krieges;* Walter Millis (ed.) , *The War Reports of General George C. Marshall,
General H. H. Arnold, and Admiral E. J. King.*

3. SHORT NAVAL HISTORIES. Rear Adm. Paul Auphan & Jacques Mordal,
The French Navy in World War II (in preparation) ; Cdr. M. A. Bragadin, *The
Italian Navy in World War II;* Lt. Cdr. P. K. Kemp, RN, *Key to Victory: The
Triumph of British Sea Power in World War II;* S. E. Morison, *Anchors Aweigh*
(in preparation) ; Cdr. E. B. Potter & Fleet Admiral Chester W. Nimitz, *The
Great Sea War;* Capt. S. W. Roskill, RN, *White Ensign: The British Navy at
War;* Friedrich Ruge, *Der Seekrieg: The German Navy's Story, 1939–45;* U.S.
Strategic Bombing Survey, Naval Analysis Div., *The Campaigns of the Pacific
War* (ed. by Rear Adm. R. M. Ofstie) .

4. SHORT HISTORIES OF OTHER ARMS AND ASPECTS. J. Phinney Baxter 3rd, *Scientists Against Time;* Bureau of the Budget, *The U.S. at War: Development and Administration of the War Program; Building the Navy's Bases in World War II* (History of the Bureau of Yards & Docks, vol. I) ; Edwin S. Corwin, *Total War and the Constitution;* Rear Adm. Henry E. Eccles, *Logistics in the National Defense;* Walter D. Edmonds, *They Fought with What They Had* (Air Force in Southwest Pacific) ; Kent R. Greenfield (ed.) , *Command Decisions,* a series of essays; F. H. Hinsley, *Hitler's Strategy;* Jeter A. Isely & Philip A. Crowl, *The U.S. Marines and Amphibious War;* George H. Johnston, *The Toughest Fighting in the World* (New Guinea) ; Frederic C. Lane, *Ships for Victory;* Anthony Martienssen, *Hitler and his Admirals;* S. E. Morison, *Strategy and Compromise;* Donald M. Nelson, *Arsenal of Democracy;* Theodore Roscoe, *U.S. Submarine Operations, World War II;* Robert Sherrod, *History of Marine Corps Aviation, World War II;* Jacobus ten Broek, *et al., Salvage: Japanese American Evacuation and Resettlement;* War Production Board, *Industrial Mobilization for War,* vol. 1.

5. PERSONAL ACCOUNTS. General H. H. Arnold, *Global Mission;* General Omar Bradley, *A Soldier's Story;* Lewis H. Brereton, *The Brereton Diaries: The War in the Air, in the Pacific, Middle East and Europe, 1941–1945;* James F. Byrnes, *Speaking Frankly;* Winston S. Churchill, *The Grand Alliance, The Hinge of Fate, Closing the Ring,* and *Triumph and Tragedy* (The Second World War, vols. 3-6) ; Charles R. Codman, *Drive* (with Patton) ; Admiral of the Fleet Viscount Cunningham of Hyndhope, *A Sailor's Odyssey;* Grand Admiral Doenitz, *Memoirs: Ten Years and Twenty Days;* Anthony Eden, *Full Circle;* General Robert L. Eichelberger, *Our Jungle Road to Tokyo;* General of the Army Dwight D. Eisenhower, *Crusade in Europe;* Desmond Flower & James Reeves (eds.) , *The Taste of Courage, The War, 1939–45* (anthology of participants' accounts) ; Walter Millis (ed.) , *The Forrestal Diaries;* Sir Francis de Guingand, *Operation Victory;* Fleet Admiral William F. Halsey & Lt. Cdr. J. Bryan 3rd, *Admiral Halsey's Story;* Captain B. H. Liddell Hart, *The Other Side of the Hill: The German Generals Talk* and (ed.) , *The Rommel Papers;* S. L. A. Marshall, *Blitzkrieg, Bastogne, Island Victory,* and *Night Drop* (Normandy) ; Viscount Montgomery of Alamein, *The Memoirs;* Lt. Gen. Sir Frederick Morgan, *Overture to Overlord;* Ernie Pyle, *Brave Men;* Grand Admiral Erich Raeder, *My Life;* Marshal of the R. A. F. Sir John Slessor, *The Central Blue;* Theodore White (ed.) , *The Stilwell Papers;* Henry L. Stimson & McGeorge Bundy, *On Active Service* (2 vols.) ; General Albert C. Wedemeyer, *Wedemeyer Reports.*

6. BIOGRAPHIES OF LEADING PARTICIPANTS. Arthur Bryant, *The Turn of the Tide* and *Triumph in the West* (2 vols.) , based on diaries of Field Marshal Viscount Alanbrooke; E. J. King & Walter Whitehill, *Fleet Admiral King: A Naval Record;* Elting E. Morison, *Turmoil and Tradition: The Life and Times of Henry L. Stimson;* Robert Payne, *The Marshall Story;* Robert E. Sherwood, *Roosevelt and Hopkins: An Intimate History;* H. R. Trevor-Roper, *The Last Days of Hitler.*

7. COMPREHENSIVE OFFICIAL AND SEMI–OFFICIAL HISTORIES.
AUSTRALIA. *Australia in the War of 1939–1945.* Series 1 (Army) , 7 vols.; Series 2 (Navy) , 2 vols.; Series 3 (Air) , 4 vols.; Series 4 (Civil) , 5 vols.; Series 5 (Medical) , 4 vols.

CANADA. Col. C. P. Stacey, *The Canadian Army 1939–1945, An Official Historical Summary,* and *History of the Canadian Army* (3 vols.) ; Gilbert N. Tucker, *The Naval Service of Canada* (2 vols.) .

GREAT BRITAIN. J. R. M. Butler (ed.) , *History of the Second World War, U.K. Military Series,* includes 6 vols. on *Grand Strategy* by Butler & John Ehrman, 4 vols. on *The War at Sea* by S. W. Roskill, and the sensational *Strategic Air Offensive against Germany* (4 vols.) by Sir Charles Webster & Noble Frankland.

JAPAN. Col. Takushiro Hattori, *Dai Toa Sanso Zenshi* (Complete History of the Greater East Asia War, 8 vols.) , Tokyo.

U.S. ARMY. Kent R. Greenfield, *et al.* (eds.) , *The U.S. Army in World War II,* 35 vols. published or in preparation on individual campaigns, and vols. on Military Administration, Engineers and other Corps, the Supreme Command, etc. (*Master Index, Reader's Guide II,* published in 1960, gives an analysis of each vol.) ; *The American Forces in Action* (14 paper-bound vols.) ; Wesley F. Craven & J. L. Cate (eds.) , *The Army Air Forces in World War II* (7 vols.) .

U.S. MARINE CORPS. *History of U.S. Marine Corps Operations in World War II,* 5 vols. published or in preparation; *Marine Corps Monographs,* 14 vols. on campaigns in the Pacific.

U.S. NAVY AND COAST GUARD. Rear Adm. Julius A. Furer, *Administration of the Navy Dept. in World War II;* S. E. Morison, *History of United States Naval Operations in World War II* (15 vols.) ; M. F. Willoughby, *The United States Coast Guard in World War II.*

For further references, *Harvard Guide,* ¶¶ 265–71.

Domestic Issues
of the Truman Administration

1. Reconversion

WHEN, on 12 April 1945, Franklin D. Roosevelt died and the Vice-President took the oath of office as President, there were some who affected to ask, ' Who is Harry S. Truman? ' just as a century earlier some had asked, ' Who is James K. Polk? ' At both times the questions were rhetorical. Harry S. Truman came to the presidency with longer experience in politics than Theodore Roosevelt, Woodrow Wilson, or Herbert Hoover. Twelve years in Missouri state politics had trained him to appreciate the realities of party organization and patronage, and two terms in the United States Senate had quickened his mind and enlarged his views, and transformed him into a national statesman. He seemed — as he looked — the very epitome of the average small-town American: pithy and idiomatic in speech, easy-going, friendly, and self-confident, hating all pretense and injustice. Like Lincoln and Wilson, once in office he revealed an astonishing capacity for growth. In matters of domestic politics and personalities he often spoke, and acted, impulsively; intensely loyal to his friends he was inclined to overlook even their more flagrant shortcomings; passionately devoted to his party he was disposed, like Bryan, to ' reward faithful Democrats.' But these failings seemed venial when contrasted with his virtues: staunchness, boldness, decisiveness, and courage. Truman's domestic record, which seemed modest by comparison with that of his predecessor, came to seem more respectable when compared with that of his successor, and no other President in our history — not even Roosevelt himself — did so much to give shape to our foreign policy, or to set the stage on which the drama of world politics was to be played out as did this unassuming man from Missouri who had come so unexpectedly to the pinnacle of power.

The first and most urgent task on the domestic front was reconversion from war to peace. This reconversion presented fewer and less onerous problems than had been anticipated. Twelve million service men and women were absorbed into civilian life with no greater difficulty than half that number in 1919, and though the war had, inevitably, vastly enhanced the role and the power of the military, it did not leave a heritage of militarism, nor did the American character appear to be affected very deeply by the military experience. Industry changed over easily enough from a war to a peace basis. Neither a depression nor a runaway inflation materialized. There was no political reaction comparable to that which had been dramatized by the change from Lincoln to Grant, and from Wilson to Harding, no social upheaval, no jazz age; but there was something even more unpleasant: the cold war and the security hysteria.

The most impressive fact about the domestic scene was the continuation and expansion of wartime prosperity. Those who remembered the sharp recession of 1921 and the agricultural malaise that persisted throughout the decade of the 'twenties had feared a repetition of this economic crisis. This fear was not justified. Veterans had little difficulty finding work, and unemployment remained low; reconversion to civilian economy was swift; the dammed-up demand for consumer goods seemed insatiable. In the five years after the war national production increased from $213 billion to $284 billion, national income from $181 billion to $241 billion, and consumer income from $151 billion to $208 billion. More important than these general indications of continued prosperity were the maintenance of full employment, high wages, and high farm prices. What this meant was an acceleration of the redistribution of national income that was under way with the war itself. In 1935 over one-half the workers of the country earned less than $1000; by 1950 only one-tenth of the workers were in this unhappy category. In 1935 only one out of six American families enjoyed an income of over $2000 a year, and only 6 per cent over $3000; by 1950 three-fourths of all families earned over $2000, and half over $3000, a year. A sharp increase in the cost of living, to be sure, qualified these statistics, but even so it was clear that the war and postwar prosperity, together with new tax policies, had achieved a greater approach to economic equality than Americans had known since the Civil War.

Even the farmers, the group most sensitive to the economic cycle, continued to enjoy unprecedented prosperity. Sustained by an insatiable demand for foodstuffs abroad, by higher standards of living at home, and by government subsidies, farm income actually increased by $5 billion between 1945 and 1948: total farm income in 1948

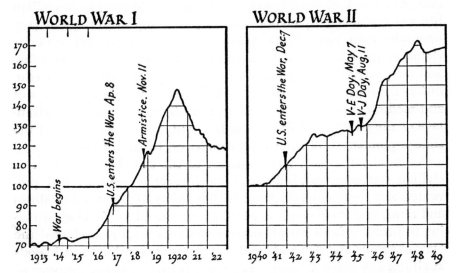

CONSUMERS' PRICE INDEX in two World Wars for moderate-income families in large cities, 1935–39 = 100. From *U.S. Bureau of Labor Statistics*

was over $30 billion as compared with $11 billion in 1941 and $5.5 billion in 1933. This meant a decline both in tenancy and in farm mortgages. Total farm mortgages fell by $2 billion between 1940 and 1950, and farm tenancy to the lowest point in the twentieth century.

What was the explanation of this phenomenon, which appeared to justify the claims of private enterprise and to confound the Communists, who had confidently expected an economic collapse in the United States? It was, in part, that five years of war had created a vast demand for consumer and durable goods; in part, the market for American surpluses assured by the program of relief and reconstruction abroad; in part, the continuation of heavy government spending after the war. At the depth of the depression the Federal Government had spent about $9 billion; five years after the war the federal budget was over $40 billion, and most of this was pumped into the domestic economy.

Neither demobilization nor reconversion created the problems that had been expected. Demobilization got under way with the surrender of Germany and proceeded swiftly — perhaps too swiftly — after victory in the Pacific. Within a year the armed services had been reduced from 12 million to 3 million, and by 1950 to well below 1 million. The shock of the transition from the armed services to civilian life was cushioned by elaborate laws providing mustering-out pay, unemployment pay for one year, job reinstatement and seniority rights, civil-service preferment, insurance, loans for home building and the purchase of farms or businesses, generous subsidies for education or apprentice training, and elaborate provision for health and medical care. Eventually some 12 million veterans took advantage of the education subsidies of the ' G.I. Bill of Rights,' and the college population of the country increased by over a million.

Potentially the most serious threat to the orderly resumption of civilian economy was inflation. Wartime price controls had prevented any spectacular increase in the prices of basic commodities and rents, and these controls were retained until 1946. Then, yielding to pressure from manufacturers and farmers who preferred the ' law of supply and demand,' and from consumers who wanted goods at almost any price, Congress enacted a price-regulation measure so feeble that President Truman vetoed it. In three weeks prices increased more than in the previous three years. A stop-gap law, which Truman reluctantly signed, was ineffective, except for rents, which increased from an index of 108 in 1945 to 117 in 1948, while the food index soared from 139 to 210 in this period. By 1949, however, production had caught up with demand in most fields, and, even with higher wages and corporation profits, prices were stabilized.

Closely related to the problem of inflation was that of the national debt and of tax policy. Under the impact of war the federal debt had soared to the astronomical figure of $269 billion; the carrying charges on this debt alone came to over $5 billion. After World War I government expenditures had declined from $18 billion to $6 billion, permitting a reduction in both debt and taxes. Congress hastily cut taxes by about $6 billion, but government expenditures dropped to about $34 billion in 1948, when there was a surplus of $8 billion. The next year expenses rose to $40 billion. Without either additional taxes or a sharp increase in taxable income, this spelled a deficit, and neither measure was forthcoming. On the contrary, political pressure led to slight reductions in income and excise taxes, and as the demands for national defense and international reconstruction remained high, the richest nation on earth resorted once again to deficit financing. With the Korean War, the cold war, and mounting costs of nuclear weapons, the budget doubled in the 'fifties, and by the end of the decade Americans had resigned themselves to a budget of over $80 billion.

2. The Fair Deal

Franklin D. Roosevelt had picked Truman as his potential successor because he was confident that Truman shared both his domestic and his foreign policy principles; that confidence was not misplaced. Because in his early days Truman had been associated with Tom Pendergast's unsavory political machine out in Missouri, there were some who thought that he would be less interested in policies and principles than in politics and patronage and who doubted the sincerity of his commitment to reform. In his address to Congress of 6 September 1945 Truman hastened to clarify his position, outlining a twenty-one point program of far-reaching reforms. ' Every segment of our population, and every individual,' he said, ' has a right to expect from his government a fair deal,' and that was the term he hopefully adopted as a substitute for Roosevelt's New Deal.

In part because his own position was weak, in part because the temper of the country was increasingly conservative, and in part because the cold war and the Korean War diverted attention to great issues of foreign policy, Truman was not able to make much progress with his Fair Deal program. Nor did he receive very effective aid from his own party. Alarmed by the President's advocacy of an effective civil rights bill, the Southern Bourbons struck an alliance with Republican conservatives to frustrate the Truman program. During the next six years this conservative alliance managed to chalk up a good many impressive victories: among them the Taft-Hartley Labor Act, the McCarran Internal Security bill, the McCarran-Walters Immigration bill, and the end of price controls.

Yet Truman and his followers did manage to write a respectable body of progressive legislation onto the statute books. It will be sufficient to note some of these achievements in four areas: labor, natural resources, administration, and civil rights.

Both the Civil War and the First World War had been followed by depressions from which labor suffered acutely. The depression of the early 1870's had broken the National Labor Union and retarded the growth of the Knights of Labor, reduced wages, and spread unemployment. The 1920's had seen a steady decline in the membership

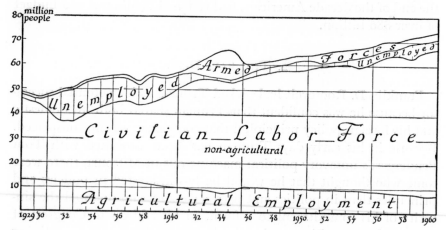

EMPLOYMENT IN THE UNITED STATES 1929–60. Seasonal fluctuations are disregarded (from *Economic Report of the President 1961*).

of the A.F. of L. and other labor unions, and a marked weakening of labor's bargaining power. The two powerful labor organizations — A.F. of L. and C.I.O. — were determined to avoid a repetition of this history after World War II. Fear of rising costs of living, the prospect of a return to the 40-hour week with consequent loss of overtime pay, and the belief that labor had not shared as fully in the general prosperity as had capital, brought a demand for substantial wage increases. Clearly, too, this was the ideal time to strike: business was eager to get back to normal production, and ready enough to pass higher costs on to the consumer; the public was eager to buy at almost any price.

During the war the unions had faithfully observed the no-strike pledge; with the end of the war the lid was off, and within a month after victory over Japan half a million workers were out on strike, while the year 1946 saw 4.6 million workers on strike, with a loss of 116 million man-days of work. Almost every major industry was affected, but the most serious strikes were in coal, automobile, steel, and electrical industries and on the railroads. The strike of bituminous coal miners, threatening not only American industry but European recovery, caused such grave concern that the government took over the mines. When the union leader John L. Lewis refused to order his men back to work, a federal court slapped a fine of $3.5 million on the union — a fine later reduced to $700,000. Yet eventually Lewis won almost all of his demands.

The stoppages in the coal industry with their repercussions on industry generally, and a strike by the Railway Brotherhoods which threatened a nation-wide tie-up of transportation, together with a widespread feeling that labor was irresponsible, that it indulged in wasteful practices like featherbedding, that it was tainted with corruption and permeated with Communism, all combined to produce a sharp anti-labor reaction in public opinion and in the Congress. This reaction found expression first in President Truman's threat to use the army to run the railroads, and next in the Case bill of May 1946, which required a 60-day cooling-off period in labor disputes and compulsory bargaining by the unions. Truman, who had himself cooled off a bit after his denunciation of the railroad unions, vetoed this bill. The Republican Eightieth Congress of 1947, however, enacted the controversial Taft-Hartley Act. This elaborate act outlawed the closed shop and the secondary boycott; made unions liable for breach of contract or damages resulting from jurisdictional disputes; required a 60-day cooling-off period for strikes; authorized an 80-day injunction against strikes that might affect national health or safety; forbade political contributions from unions, featherbedding, and excessive dues; required union leaders to take a non-Communist oath; and set up a conciliation service outside the Labor Department, which was suspected of being too friendly to labor. Truman vetoed this bill on the ground that it would

reverse the basic direction of our national labor policy, inject the government into private economic affairs on an unprecedented scale, and conflict with important principles of our democratic society. Its provisions would cause more strikes, not fewer. It would contribute neither to industrial peace nor to economic stability and progress. . . . It contains seeds of discord which would plague this nation for years to come.

Congress, however, re-enacted the bill by thumping majorities. Whether the Taft-Hartley bill 'plagued the nation' or not, it certainly plagued the parties: in the election of 1948 organized labor returned many Republican supporters of the act to private life. Yet the most energetic efforts to repeal it proved unavailing, and it lingered on as an issue for future elections.

The most serious labor crisis of the Truman years came when steel workers gave notice of an intention to strike in December 1951, in the midst of the Korean War. The Wage Stabilization Board recommended an increase of 18 cents an hour without corresponding increases in steel prices. When the operators refused this solution and labor called a strike, President Truman stepped in and took over the mills under what he assumed to be wartime authority. One of the mills — Youngstown Sheet and Tube Company — challenged the constitutionality of this act and asked for an injunction against it; a district court granted the injunction and the case came on appeal to the Supreme Court.[1] The Court struck down the presidential order on the ground that it constituted executive lawmaking; Chief Justice Vinson filed a powerful dissent which won support from many eminent legal scholars.

One interesting feature of the postwar labor scene was the growing demand for those welfare payments and fringe benefits long common in business and the professions, the military and the civil service. The pattern, originally set by the social security program, was taken over by John L. Lewis who in 1946 persuaded the coal industry to set aside a ' royalty ' of 20 cents on every ton of coal, to be used for health and welfare and pensions of $100 a month. This demand was quickly taken up by workers in the steel, automobile, and other industries. As only those who had been with their companies for long periods would be eligible for these benefits, the pension system put a premium on stability in labor, and indicated that the day of the casual laborer was a thing of the past.

The unrest of the 'forties should not obscure the advances that labor made in that decade. By mid-century the A.F. of L. numbered well over 7 million members, the C.I.O. over 6 million, and another 2.5 million belonged to the independent unions. Total union membership had almost doubled since 1940. Organized labor generally had secured the 40-hour week, vacations with pay, welfare benefits, and in some major industries old-age pensions as well. A federal act of October 1949 raising minimum wages to 75 cents an hour gave

[1] *Youngstown Sheet & Tube Co. v. Sawyer* 343 U.S. 579 (1952) .

added protection to the mass of unorganized labor, and new social security legislation embraced another 10 million workers in the social security system. And although Congress persisted in its refusal to enact a permanent Fair Employment Practices Act, at least ten states passed laws forbidding discrimination in employment because of race, color, creed, or national origins.

Truman's contributions to the conservation of natural resources were largely in vain. He supported the expansion of the TVA, and recommended comparable hydroelectric projects for the Columbia and the Missouri river valleys. He gave such support as he could to federal rather than private construction and operation of the Hell's Canyon dam on the Snake river. More important — though in the end futile — was his effort to preserve for the United States the immensely valuable oil and natural gas under the tidelands. The Geological Survey had estimated the oil reserves in these areas at 15 billion barrels: who held title to them, and who should develop and exploit them? As early as the 'thirties Texas and Louisiana began to deed these lands to private companies. That sleepless watchdog of the national interests, Secretary Ickes, brought suit to establish federal rights to these tidelands mineral deposits, and in two decisions the Supreme Court sustained the paramount interest and right of the Federal Government and struck down the claims of the states.[2] In 1946 and again in 1952 Congress passed bills giving rights to oil and natural gas within their ' historic ' limits to the states, but Truman vetoed both bills. In the campaign of 1952 Eisenhower came out in favor of state title to the submerged oil lands, and early in 1953 Congress for the third time passed an act which assigned federal rights to the states: Texas, Louisiana, Florida, and California were the chief beneficiaries.

Few administrations made more important contributions to governmental efficiency than the Truman administration. In order to make sure that whoever succeeded a Vice-President in the presidential chair represented a popular rather than a personal choice, a Presidential Succession Act of 1947 provided that the Speaker of the House and the President of the Senate should be next in line of presidential succession after the Vice-President. That same year Congress voted to establish a committee to study the whole problem of governmental administration; Truman appointed Herbert Hoover chair-

[2] *United States v. California* 332 U.S. 19; and *United States v. Louisiana* 339 U.S. 699.

man of the committee, and the Hoover Committee made a series of reports recommending the reduction of federal departments and agencies from 65 to 23 and the creation of a Department of Health and Welfare. Congress authorized the President to submit plans for reorganization which would go into effect unless it disapproved — an interesting and unusual formula — and under this arrangement Truman submitted no less than 36 reorganization plans, all of which went through except the one calling for the Department of Health and Welfare: that was blocked temporarily by Southern votes.

More difficult was the effort to put an end to the bickering, jealousy, and competition between the army, navy, and air force. An act of 1947 created a single National Defense Establishment under a Secretary of Defense; two years later this was reorganized as the Department of Defense. The appointment of the distinguished George Marshall to the post of Secretary of Defense in 1950 gave it prestige, but even Marshall's immense dignity and authority could not unify the three rival departments. Another new governmental agency as influential as the Department of Defense was the Atomic Energy Commission, created by act of 15 November 1946. Less important, as it proved, was the establishment of a Council of Economic Advisers to co-operate with the President and the Congress in maintaining full employment.

It would be a mistake to suppose that these measures ' streamlined ' the government or brought it to a new peak of efficiency. Government continued to grow faster than the capacity of Congress or the President to control it; as with Alice and the Red Queen, Congress would have to run twice as fast if it expected to get anywhere.

That was true of civil rights as well. In 1946 Truman appointed a Civil Rights Commission which issued a notable report, *To Secure These Rights,* and recommended far-reaching congressional and executive action on behalf of civil and political rights of minorities, particularly Negroes. In 1948 the President presented a ten-point program of civil rights which embraced a permanent Civil Rights Commission, a federal Fair Employment Practices Act, and legislation to protect the right to vote, do away with poll taxes, and prevent lynching. These recommendations, plus Truman's firm stand for a civil-rights plank in the 1948 Democratic platform, were chiefly responsible for the bolt by Southern delegates and the organization of the Dixiecrat party. If Congress was unprepared to support the Truman program, Truman himself was quite prepared to push ahead without congressional approval. By ending discrimination in the armed services, discouraging it in government employment, and directing that no defense contracts should go to any firm that discriminated against Negroes, the President in effect wrote a kind of informal federal employment practices act.

The Truman administration made two other contributions to civil liberties of a less direct character. One was new immigration legislation which liberalized the terms for the admission of Displaced Persons from Europe and did away with the specific prohibition against the admission of Asiatics. The other was the ratification of the Universal Declaration of Human Rights.

3. POLITICS AND THE ELECTION OF 1948

Every past war had been followed by political reaction, and most observers assumed that history would now repeat itself. And, after all, the Democrats had controlled the presidency for 16 years and the Congress for 14 years, and that was as long a tenure as any party had enjoyed since Reconstruction. Expectation of change was strengthened by the consideration that the country had weathered both depression and war and was now entering a new era, that the New Deal program had been largely achieved, and that the great leader who had so long proved politically irresistible was gone.

When the magnetic Roosevelt was replaced by the prosaic Truman, Republican hopes mounted. Truman's position, weak when he assumed office, appeared to grow progressively weaker. A loyal Democrat, there was as yet no convincing evidence that he was a loyal New Dealer, and the speed with which he replaced Roosevelt's cabinet with one of his own choosing and his appointment of conservatives to key positions in the administration [3] and in the judiciary suggested that he would find his natural allies in the more conservative wing of the Democratic party and thus forfeit much of the labor, liberal, and Negro vote that had contributed so generously to Roosevelt's successive victories. His Fair Deal speech of September 1945 outraged conservatives who had hoped for an end to reform, while

[3] When Truman appointed the oil magnate Ed Pauley to be Under Secretary of the Navy, Harold Ickes resigned in disgust.

his dismissal of Henry Wallace shocked many liberals unaware of the extent to which the Secretary had lost touch with reality.

The congressional election of 1946 appeared to confirm the expectation that the Democrats were on the way out. Exasperated by the slowness of demobilization, high prices, high taxes, inexplicable shortages,[4] and political incompetence, and doubtless wearied by long Democratic tenure, the voters turned to the Republican party for the first time since 1930. The Eightieth Congress numbered 51 Republicans and 45 Democrats in the Senate, 246 Republicans and 188 Democrats in the House.

The Republicans, however, misread the moral of this election. Having campaigned with the query ' Had enough? ' they not unnaturally interpreted their victory as a hearty ' yes.' Actually the election was an expression of impatience with the paucity of Truman's achievements rather than a demand for a return to normalcy. The temper of the country remained fundamentally liberal.

Yet so sure were the Republicans of capturing the presidency in 1948 that, for the first time in their history, they renominated a defeated candidate, Thomas E. Dewey. They had offered the nomination to Eisenhower, to be sure, but he thrust the crown from him with the observation that ' the necessary and wise subordination of the military to civil power will be best sustained when life-long professional soldiers abstain from seeking high office.' And so confident was Dewey of victory that in his campaign he deliberately avoided any discussion of issues that might commit him to a particular policy or obligate him to particular groups, and treated Truman with patronizing pity. Despairing of success, the Democratic Convention met in an atmosphere of gloom. A revolt led by James Roosevelt of California fizzled out; a last minute attempt to persuade General Eisenhower to take the nomination failed; and Truman was renominated by default. When Justice William O. Douglas refused to be a candidate for the vice-presidency, the nomination went to 70-year-old Senator Alben Barkley of Kentucky who was thought to be acceptable to the Southern wing of the party.

Democratic prospects were further dimmed by a revolt both of the right and of the left, which threatened to disintegrate the party. Henry Wallace, last remaining member of the original Roosevelt

---

[4] Wrote the commentator David Cohn, ' A housewife who cannot get hamburger is more dangerous than Medea wronged.'

cabinet, broke with Truman in the fall of 1946 over the administration's Russian policy, organized a Progressive party, and ran for the presidency. While there was little likelihood that his candidacy would develop any substantial strength throughout the country, it seemed probable that his aggressive championship of the interests of labor and of the Negro might wean enough votes from the Democratic ticket to swing such states as New York, Michigan, Illinois, and California into the Republican column. The revolt from the right was of longer standing. Woodrow Wilson had had trouble with the Bourbon Democracy of the South, and Franklin Roosevelt had been able to hold it in line only by his proved capacity to win elections. Truman inherited Bourbon enmity to Roosevelt, but not the ability to silence or to surmount it. When — for valid political as well as moral reasons — he took over Roosevelt's advocacy of a civil-rights program, forcing a strong civil-rights plank into the party platform, many Southern Democrats revolted. Convinced that Truman was doomed to defeat in any event, and waving Confederate flags, they left the party and organized at Montgomery, Alabama, a state-rights or Dixiecrat party. Their candidate was Strom Thurmond of South Carolina, their platform state rights, and their method to exclude the regular Democrats from the ticket wherever possible.

Threatened thus from both right and left, Truman's chances of re-election seemed negligible. Largely abandoned by his own party, with inadequate campaign funds, and in the face of general apathy, Truman waged an aggressive campaign. He attacked relentlessly the record of the Republican party as revealed in the Eightieth Congress and reaffirmed the principles of the New Deal — now named the Fair Deal. He defied the Dixiecrats and so held the Negro vote of Northern cities. He countered the Wallace attack with an aggressive defense of his foreign policy and a strong intimation of a determination to seek military alliances with the nations of western Europe.

To the astonishment of almost every prognosticator, Truman won a resounding popular and electoral-college victory.[5] The Dixiecrats — though they garnered 39 electoral votes — proved less for-

[5] The vote was:	Popular	Electoral College
Truman	24,045,052	304
Dewey	21,896,927	189
Thurmond	1,168,687	38
Wallace	1,137,957	0

midable than had been anticipated; Mr. Wallace was less popular with labor and the Negroes than had been supposed. Dewey's popular vote fell below that of 1944, and though he carried such powerful states as New York and Pennsylvania, he lost Ohio, Iowa, and Wisconsin, which he had carried four years earlier.

The Democrats, too, recaptured control of both houses of Congress, winning a majority of 12 in the upper chamber and of 93 in the House. Particularly interesting was the victory of such liberals as Kefauver of Tennessee, Humphrey of Minnesota, Douglas of Illinois, and Murray of Montana. The gubernatorial contests followed the national trend: the Democrats won 21 out of 33 contests, and among the Democratic victors were prominent liberals like Chester Bowles in Connecticut and Adlai Stevenson in Illinois.

The 1948 elections confirmed what had long been taken for granted under Roosevelt; that Americans do not take kindly to splinter parties; that labor, and the Negro, were still loyal to the Democratic party; that the Midwestern farm vote was by no means irretrievably committed to the Republican party; that the political temper of the country was still liberal; and that loyalty to Franklin Roosevelt was a factor to be reckoned with in the future.

4. CIVIL RIGHTS, LOYALTY, AND SECURITY

In his famous Peoria speech Abraham Lincoln had charged that slavery

deprives our republican example of its just influence in the world; enables the enemies of free institutions with plausibility to taunt us as hypocrites; causes the real friends of freedom to doubt our sincerity; and forces so many good men among ourselves into an open war with the very fundamental principles of civil liberty.

The denial of civil and political rights to Negroes and other minority groups during World War II and after had much the same effect. As Dean Acheson observed:

The existence of discrimination against minority groups in this country has an adverse effect upon our relations with other countries. . . . Frequently we find it next to impossible to formulate a satisfactory answer to our critics in other countries; the gap between the things we stand for in principle and the facts of a particular situation may be too wide to be bridged.

The war at once exacerbated race relations and advanced racial equality. Its total effect was to bring the whole issue of minority rights out into the open, expose the gap between the pretense of equality and the reality of inequality, and force the government to take action toward bridging that gap.

Notwithstanding official disapproval, segregation and discrimination persisted in the armed forces. Not until July 1948 did President Truman direct the armed forces to end segregation and inequality of opportunity for appointment and promotion. More serious was discrimination in employment, exercised by both management and labor. Even before Pearl Harbor President Roosevelt had required that all defense contracts include a non-discrimination clause, and set up a Fair Employment Practices Committee to enforce the order. In response to this policy Negro employment in war industries increased from 3 per cent to 8 per cent of the whole, while employment in the Federal Government jumped from 40,000 to over 300,000. Labor proved, in fact, more recalcitrant on this issue than management, and it required court action to force the Railroad Brotherhoods to abandon their practice of writing racial discrimination into their contracts. Although the establishment of a permanent Fair Employment Practices Committee was endorsed by both parties and supported, at all times, by a majority in both houses of Congress, every attempt to pass an FEPC law was frustrated by filibusters from Southern Democrats.

Politically, too, the Negro made moderate advances during the war and postwar years. Southern states had long circumvented the Fifteenth Amendment and, except in some of the larger urban centers and in the border states, few Negroes voted. Eight Southern states limited voting in Democratic primaries to white men; eleven required the payment of poll taxes — in some instances cumulative; others excluded Negroes from the polls by discriminatory application of literacy tests, requiring them to explain things in the Constitution that not even the Supreme Court has been able to explain. These laws and practices kept not only Negroes but whites from voting: thus in 1944 the population of the state of Washington was slightly under that of South Carolina, but 856,328 voted in Washington and 103,375 in South Carolina. This discrepancy between poll-tax and non-poll-tax states was general: 18 per cent of those entitled to vote in poll-tax states actually voted, but 69 per cent in the non-poll-tax states.

A series of Supreme Court decisions — notably *Nixon v. Herndon* [6] and *Smith v. Allwright* [7] — nullified white primary laws, and when South Carolina attempted to evade these decisions by repealing all primary laws and maintaining the Democratic party as a purely private organization, the District Court rejected the subterfuge. ' Racial distinctions,' the court said,

cannot exist in the machinery that selects the officers and lawmakers of the United States; and all citizens of this State and Country are entitled to cast a free and untrammeled ballot in our elections, and if the only material and realistic elections are clothed with the name ' primary ' they are equally entitled to vote there.[8]

Poll taxes, however, resisted both political and constitutional attack, though between 1921 and 1948 four Southern states — North Carolina, Louisiana, Florida, and Georgia — abandoned them. There are no adequate statistics of Negro voting, but it seems clear that more Southern Negroes voted in the election of 1948 than in any up to that time since Reconstruction.

It was perhaps inevitable that the war with the Axis powers and then the cold war with Russia should inspire fear of subversive activities in the United States. The totalitarian nations, Fascist and Communist alike, had perfected the technique of the ' fifth column,' and Communism, at least, inspired in some of its inherents a fanatical loyalty that superseded national allegiance. There was a widespread suspicion that Communists had infiltrated into government service, labor unions, and schools, and that they were hiding behind the guarantees of the Bill of Rights to destroy freedom.

Even before the outbreak of the fighting war, Congress took two steps to frustrate disloyal or subversive activities in the United States. As early as 1938 the House established a committee on un-American activities. This committee, which at no point in its long and shabby career defined the term ' un-American,' embarked upon a relentless search for subversive activities — chiefly communistic and radical. Although it distracted congressional attention from more important matters, spent millions of dollars, produced voluminous reports, and made the headlines of newspapers with great regularity, it found

[6] 273 U.S. 536 (1927).   [8] *Rice v. Elmore* 165 Fed. 2nd, 387 (1947).
[7] 321 U.S. 649 (1944).

nothing that was not already known to the Department of Justice. The second measure was the enactment, in 1940, of the Smith Registration Act, which was, in reality, a sedition act. While the purpose of the act was to prohibit the advocacy of revolution by violence, the act itself departed from Anglo-American traditions by embracing the doctrines of guilt by intent and guilt by association.

In part to counteract the excessive zeal and loose standards of the Un-American Activities Committee, President Truman in 1947 provided for an orderly investigation of the loyalty of civil servants in the executive department of the government. While this order set up intelligent standards and procedural safeguards and provided for non-judicial review, it, too, embraced the doctrines of guilt by intention and by association. Under its terms activities that might be evidence of disloyalty included ' membership in, affiliation with, or sympathetic association with . . . any organization, movement, group or combination of persons, designated by the Attorney General as having adopted a policy of approving the commission of acts of force or violence to deny other persons their rights under the Constitution.' On the whole the enforcement of the order was characterized by moderation. Of the 3 million persons passed on, only a few thousand were actually investigated. Of these, 212 were dismissed, but none, apparently, had committed offenses serious enough to warrant prosecution. Potentially the most ominous feature of the executive order was the one authorizing the Attorney-General to prepare lists of subversive organizations and giving these lists a quasi-legal character. ' If there is any fixed star in our constitutional constellation,' Justice Jackson had said in the second flag-salute case, ' it is that no official, high or petty, can prescribe what shall be orthodox in politics, nationalism, religion or other matters of opinion, or force citizens to confess by word or act their faith therein.' [9] The most serious practical consequence of the executive order was to discourage independence, originality, and criticism in government employees, put a premium on conformity, and dissuade many valuable citizens from entering government service.

In 1948 the security issue got out of hand, and the whole of Truman's second term was plagued by the tensions, anxieties, and neuroses we have come to call McCarthyism.

The election of 1948 left the Republicans feeling embittered: to

[9] *West Virginia Board of Education v. Barnette* 319 U.S. 624 (1943).

be beaten by Roosevelt was disappointing but familiar; to be rejected in favor of Truman seemed intolerable. And then two prodigious events upset the global balance of power shortly after the election: the final defeat and retreat of Chiang Kai-shek, and the Soviet detonation of the atomic bomb. On top of this came the Korean War. How did it happen? How did we 'lose' China, and the atomic monopoly all at once, and then come close to losing the Korean War as well? To the average American it was unthinkable that Communism could win on its own, and incredible that Soviet scientists were as clever as American or British. The answer must lie elsewhere. It must lie in subversion and treachery.

A handful of extremists had alleged that it was President Roosevelt himself who had somehow 'sold out' to the Communists at Yalta, but only men bereft of their senses took any stock in this notion. But might it not be some of his, or Truman's, appointees — intellectuals and 'one-worlders' in the State Department who were secret sympathizers with Russia, or atomic scientists who had sold themselves to the Communists or been seduced by them into treason? Was it not all part of a monstrous conspiracy — a conspiracy, said Senator McCarthy, 'so immense, an infamy so black, as to dwarf any previous such venture in the history of man'?

To support this fantastic interpretation of history came first the Hiss case and then the treason of Klaus Fuchs. In August 1948 Whittaker Chambers, onetime editor of *Time* magazine, accused Alger Hiss of being a Communist spy and of passing secret government documents to the Russians. Hiss, a graduate of the Harvard Law School, had been a State Department official, and had been with Roosevelt at Yalta, before becoming President of the Carnegie Endowment for International Peace. He denied all of Chambers's charges; a New York grand jury indicted him for perjury; Chambers produced some of the stolen documents — out of a pumpkin! — and after two trials Hiss was found guilty and sentenced to five years in jail.

Hiss had been a minor official in the State Department and it was highly improbable that he had ever influenced policy in any way. But he was tailor-made for the role of a villain: a Harvard 'egghead,' a New Dealer, a friend of Secretary Acheson, an international 'do-gooder'; even his name suggested perfidy! Clearly he was 'fit for treasons, stratagems, and spoils.' And if Hiss, why not scores of others?

Then two weeks after Hiss's conviction came news from England that Klaus Fuchs, an atomic physicist who had worked at the Los Alamos laboratory, had been found guilty of systematically feeding atomic information to the Russians. Here was the explanation of Russian success with the atomic bomb!

At almost the same time eleven top Communists — the 'Politburo' of the American party — were brought to trial on the charge of violating the Smith Act of 1940, which made it a crime to conspire to 'advocate and teach' the violent overthrow of government. The defendants challenged the constitutionality of the act itself, but the Supreme Court accepted Judge Learned Hand's modification of the 'clear and present danger' test: 'in each case courts must ask whether the gravity of the evil, discounted by its improbability, justifies such invasion of free speech as is necessary to avoid the danger,' — and concluded that the Smith Act was constitutional and that the Communists were in fact guilty of conspiracy to advocate the overthrow of government.[10]

This was the background of that phenomenon known as McCarthyism: the 'loss' of China, the Russian possession of the bomb, the Hiss affair, the treason of Klaus Fuchs, the Communist trials, and the Korean War. Senator McCarthy himself was a finished demagogue of a type more familiar to Europe than to America: brutal, unscrupulous, cunning, and adroit, he hoped to achieve power by exploiting the Communist issue; his methods were wild charges, fake evidence, innuendoes and lies, appeals to ignorance, prejudice, hatred, and fear. On 9 February 1950 he alleged that he had the names of 205 — or was it 57? — 'card-carrying Communists' in the State Department. He never actually produced any of these names, but he did charge that Professor Owen Lattimore of the Johns Hopkins University, one of the leading experts on Far Eastern affairs, was 'Russia's top espionage agent' in the United States. Lattimore denied under oath that he was a Communist, or a 'follower of the communist line'; when some years later Attorney-General Herbert Brownell, who was still playing McCarthy's game, indicted Lattimore for perjury, the case was contemptuously thrown out of court.

In July 1950 a Senate committee under Senator Tydings of Maryland, investigating the McCarthy charges, reported that they were 'a fraud and a hoax perpetrated on the Senate of the United States

[10] *Dennis v. United States* 341 U.S. 494 (1951).

and on the American people. They represent perhaps the most nefarious campaign of half-truth and untruth in the history of the Republic.' McCarthy's reply was to charge the Tydings Committee itself with being ' soft ' on Communism! Then, nothing daunted, he moved on to larger game. ' It was Moscow,' he cried, ' which decreed that the United States should execute its loyal friend, the Republic of China. The executioners were that well-defined group headed by Acheson and George Marshall.'

Out of the sense of panic aroused by McCarthy, and by the course of events, came the McCarran-Nixon Internal Security bill of 1950. This act required all Communist-front organizations to register with the Attorney-General, excluded Communists from employment in defense plants, made it illegal to *conspire* to perform any act that would ' substantially contribute ' to the establishment of a dictatorship in the United States, debarred from the United States any one ever affiliated with a totalitarian organization, or with organizations looking to the revolutionary overthrow of government, and authorized deportation for aliens involved in suspect organizations. Truman vetoed the bill, alleging that it was ' worse than the Sedition Acts of 1798,' but Congress passed it over his veto by acclamation.

Loyalty investigations and purges, and the requirement of loyalty oaths, were extended into many other fields, notably those of labor and education. The Taft-Hartley Act required union officials to take a non-Communist oath and inspired a wholesome housecleaning in some unions. A number of states and cities, convinced that the schools were rife with Communism, required loyalty oaths of teachers and of university professors, and two states made the flag salute compulsory for school children, until the Supreme Court struck down the regulation.[11] State legislatures set up committees to parallel the work of the House Un-American Activities Committee; the Tenney Committee in California and the Broyles Committee in Illinois convulsed their states with wild charges of Communism in the schools and the churches. Scholars and artists, pacifists and Quakers and Unitarians, reformers and internationalists, non-conformists of every stripe, were suspect. Organizations like the American Legion and the Minute Women joined in the crusade to destroy all those who did not come up to their standards of loyalty and Americanism.

11 The Gobitis case, 310 U.S. 586; and *West Virginia v. Barnette* 319 U.S. 624.

5. THE ELECTION OF 1952

By the spring of 1952 Americans were ready to listen to the Republican's contention that it was ' time for a change ' from twenty years of Democratic administration. Disillusionment, anxiety, and frustration gripped the American people, even in the midst of prosperity. Prices were too high; there was a ' mess in Washington '; the Russians had the atom bomb; the State Department had ' lost ' China; the war in Korea was at a stalemate, and nothing in their experience had prepared Americans for a war which they could not hope to ' win.' It was not surprising that many people came to believe that they were the victims not of circumstances, or even of Communist aggression, but of subversion and incompetence in high places.

The restless mood of the country was evident to the most casual of observers. What was not clear was how deep the dissatisfaction went, and how wide it spread. The right wing of the Republican party, rallying behind Senator Robert Taft of Ohio, contended that the Republicans had failed to capture the presidency in the three previous elections because they had offered no real alternative to the Roosevelt-Truman policies, and they called now for a complete repudiation of those policies and a return to the ' rugged individualism ' associated with President Hoover. Liberal Republicans were convinced that the nomination of a member of the Old Guard would be disastrous, and that what was needed was the kind of progressive conservatism associated with Theodore Roosevelt. They looked to General Eisenhower to provide this kind of leadership.

Both parties had made overtures to Eisenhower in 1948, but without success. When, in 1951, Governor Dewey of New York and Governor Sherman Adams of New Hampshire approached him once again, the General declared that his duties as commander in chief of NATO prevented him from undertaking a campaign for the nomination, but did nothing to discourage his supporters. They promptly entered him in the New Hampshire primary election, which he won handily. When Taft carried the primaries in Wisconsin, Ohio, and West Virginia, Eisenhower abandoned his pose of aloofness and came home to take an active part in the campaign.

At the Republican Convention which met in Chicago the Taft forces gave the impression that they were acting like the Taft forces back in 1912: deals, intrigues, steam-rollers, and smoke-filled rooms!

Eisenhower, by contrast, was remote and aloof, above partisanship and above the battle. Governor Dewey marshaled the Eisenhower cohorts, wavering delegates fell in line under a conviction that only ' Ike ' could win; and the General was uproariously named on the first ballot. Senator Richard Nixon of California, who had distinguished himself by his zeal in exploiting the issue of ' subversion,' was nominated for Vice-President.

The Democrats, who followed the Republicans to Chicago, were faced with the necessity of choosing a candidate acceptable to the dissident groups in the party and yet not too closely identified with the Truman administration. From a field which included Senator Kefauver of Tennessee, Governor Harriman of New York, and Vice-President Barkley, Adlai Stevenson of Illinois emerged as the only one who appealed to all shades of opinion and who seemed able to command a national following. He was, moreover — as his welcoming address to the convention revealed — a man of wit, charm, intelligence, and eloquence. The fact that he was not a candidate only enhanced his appeal since it meant that he would be free of commitments to the outgoing administration. And no candidate had wider or more varied experience. He was born to Democratic politics — his grandfather had been Vice-President in Cleveland's second term; he had served in the Navy Department, in the State Department, as delegate to the United Nations, and as reform governor of Illinois. He could count on the support of President Truman, of organized labor, and of the intellectuals who wanted another Roosevelt in the White House.

Stevenson was nominated on the third ballot, with John Sparkman of Alabama as his running-mate. In his acceptance speech the nominee promised to tell the American people that —

sacrifice, patience, understanding and implacable purpose may be our lot for years to come. Let's tell the American people that there are no gains without pains, that we are now on the eve of great decisions, not easy decisions, like resistance when you're attacked, but a long, patient, costly struggle which alone can assure triumph over the great enemies of man — war, poverty and tyranny — and the assaults upon human dignity which are the most grievous consequences of each.

The Republican platform, reflecting the views of Senator Taft, denounced the Truman administration for failing to maintain Chiang Kai-shek, inviting aggression in Korea, and pursuing the 'negative' policy of containment, but Eisenhower at first showed himself unwilling to repudiate policies which he had helped to shape. After a momentous meeting with Senator Taft, however, Eisenhower began to give aid and comfort to the more extreme right wing of his party. He accepted the support of demagogues like McCarthy and Senator Jenner of Indiana, denounced the Truman administration for harboring subversives, charged Acheson with responsibility for the Communist attack on Korea, and poured scorn on the 'eggheads' who had rallied to the support of Stevenson. It was to no avail that Stevenson reminded the country that 'Korea, corruption, and communists in government are really not controversial issues between the two candidates at all. No one is running on a pro-corruption ticket or in favor of treachery.'

Once again, as so often in the past, the Republicans enjoyed the support of three-fourths or more of the nation's newspapers. With ample funds at their command they exploited to the full the possibilities of television which, for the first time, played an important part in a presidential campaign. Thus when Nixon was accused of having solicited a campaign fund from wealthy Californians who might expect to benefit from his election to the vice-presidency, he converted the liability into an asset by a dramatic television appearance giving a full account of his financial situation, and of his private as well as his public life. But the greatest advantage the Republicans enjoyed was neither control of the mass media, the smoke screen of 'subversion,' or even Korea, but simply Eisenhower himself. 'The crowd is with him,' wrote one correspondent. 'Idolatry shows in their solemn, upturned faces.'

So great was the General's popularity that much of the traditional Democratic support went to him: labor, for example, and the big-city vote. Most of those whom Eisenhower called 'eggheads' rallied to the Democratic candidate, but even here the division was by no means clear; some far-sighted students of American politics accepted Walter Lippmann's argument that the Republicans should be returned to power in order to restore to them, or impose upon them by stern necessity, a sense of order and responsibility, and that Eisenhower alone could rescue the party from reactionaries like Senators Taft and Knowland and demagogues like Senators Jenner and McCarthy.

The election returns provided an accurate index of the General's popularity. Eisenhower won with 33,824,352 votes to Stevenson's 27,314,987, and carried 39 states with 442 electoral votes, while Stevenson carried only 9 states with 89 votes. Most interesting was Eisenhower's success in winning four states of the not so solid South: Virginia, Tennessee, Texas, and Florida. The personal nature of Eisenhower's triumph was apparent when contrasted to the congressional vote. In spite of all the advantages they enjoyed, the Republican party barely carried the House by a majority of 8, and managed no better than a tie in the Senate. Clearly the election was less a verdict on the Democrats than a vote of confidence in Eisenhower himself, and if the support of the people is the secret of presidential power the new President should have been one of the strongest of American executives.

BIBLIOGRAPHY

1. PRESIDENT TRUMAN. Jonathan Daniels, *The Man of Independence;* C. A. M. Ewing, *Presidential Elections from Lincoln to F.D.R.;* Eric Goldman, *The Crucial Decade;* John Gunther, *Inside the U.S.A.;* William B. Hesseltine, *The Rise and Fall of Third Parties;* M. B. Schnapper (ed.), *The Truman Program;* Harry S. Truman, *Memoirs* (2 vols.).

2. POLITICS. James M. Burns, *Congress on Trial;* N. F. Busch, *Adlai E. Stevenson;* Arthur H. Compton, *The Atomic Quest;* R. A. Dahl & R. S. Brown, *The Domestic Control of Atomic Energy;* A. A. Ekirch, *The Citizen and the Military;* Frank Gervasi, *Big Government: The Hoover Commission Report;* Samuel P. Huntington, *The Soldier and the State;* V. O. Key, *Southern Politics in State and Nation;* Walter Millis, *Arms and Men;* J. R. Newman & B. S. Miller, *Control of Atomic Energy;* Lindsay Rogers, *The Pollsters;* Clinton Rossiter, *The Supreme Court and the Commander-in-Chief;* Richard Rovere & A. M. Schlesinger, *The General and the President;* Arthur M. Schlesinger, Jr., *The Vital Center;* Adlai E. Stevenson, *Major Campaign Speeches.*

3. THE FAIR DEAL. D. I. Ash & George Rifkin, *The Taft-Hartley Law;* Stephen K. Bailey, *Congress Makes a Law;* E. R. Bartley, *The Tidelands Oil Controversy;* J. M. Clark, *The Demobilization of Wartime Economic Controls;* Paul H. Douglas, *Economy in the National Government;* Peter F. Drucker, *The Concept of the Corporation;* John K. Galbraith, *American Capitalism* and *The Affluent Society;* Seymour E. Harris, *National Health Insurance;* David E. Lilienthal, *Big Business;* Harold Metz, *The Labor Policy of the Federal Government;* H. A. Millis & E. C. Brown, *From the Wagner Act to Taft-Hartley;* Joel Seidman, *American Labor from Defense to Reconversion;* G. W. Stocking & M. W. Watkins, *Monopoly and Free Enterprise;* Philip Taft, *The A.F. of L. from the Death of Gompers;* C. E. Warne & K. W. Lumpkin, *et al.,* *Labor in Post War America;* A. Widick, *The U.A.W. and Walter Reuther.*

4. CIVIL LIBERTIES. Alan Barth, *The Loyalty of Free Men;* Eleanor Bontecou, *The Federal Loyalty-Security Program;* Richard K. Carr, *Federal Protection of Civil Rights, The House Committee on Un-American Activities,* and *To Secure These Rights;* Henry S. Commager, *Freedom, Loyalty, Dissent;* Alastair Cooke, *A Generation on Trial;* M. R. Davie, *Refugees in America;* Theodore Draper, *The Roots of American Communism;* Osmond D. Fraenkel, *Supreme Court and Civil Liberties;* Walter Gellhorn, *Security, Loyalty, and Science, The States and Subversion,* and *American Rights;* Learned Hand, *The Spirit of Liberty;* Milton Konvitz, *The Constitution and Civil Rights;* Owen Lattimore, *Ordeal by Slander;* C. H. Moehlman, *The Wall of Separation;* J. M. O'Neill, *Catholicism and American Freedom;* C. H. Pritchett, *Civil Liberties and the Vinson Court;* Frank Reel, *The Case of General Yamashita;* Lillian Smith, *Killers of the Dream;* S. A. Stouffer, *Communism, Conformity and Civil Liberties.*

5. DOCUMENTS. H. S. Commager, *Documents,* nos. 567–73, 576, 578–85, 588, 592, 594–5, 597–605.

For further references, *Harvard Guide,* ¶¶ 274–6.

The Responsibilities of World Power

1. THE NEW WORLD

THE problems of the postwar years were so many and so complex that neither the American people nor their government seemed able to understand or to master them: witness, for example, the turns and twists of American policy toward Palestine, Spain, Yugoslavia, and the Argentine in the five years after the close of the war. It was not merely that large areas of the globe had been laid waste and were ravaged by famine, disease, and anarchy, though this in itself placed a heavy responsibility upon the United States. Nor was it merely that Russia and the Western powers seemed unable to agree upon the solution of any of the important problems created by the war and by victory, though this disagreement threatened to prolong world unrest indefinitely. It was rather that profound and revolutionary changes were under way throughout the globe. Russia, like the United States, emerged from the war as a world power, and Communism as a world force. The British Empire was losing power, and Britain could no longer play her historic role or exercise her traditional influence in politics and economy. The so-called backward peoples of Asia and Africa were bursting out of the inferior position to which they had so long been condemned, and claiming the right to govern themselves and to have a voice in world affairs. Science and technology were binding nations ever closer together in time and space, making them at once more interdependent and more vulnerable than ever before.

Yet amid the vast confusion that obtained, the swift changes of light and shadow, it was possible to perceive a pattern that was almost elementary. In a century and a half — a short time in history — the United States had vaulted from insignificance to dominance, and from isolation to leadership. Not ambitious for power, America had achieved power. Rejecting responsibility, she had been unable to escape it. Inclined to parochialism, she had been thrust into the center of internationalism. Fundamentally peaceable, she had been led by circumstances to become the arsenal of the Western world. The only great nation to emerge from the war materially unscathed, she elected to assume responsibility for relief and reconstruction, and to put her technological skills and wealth at the disposal of less fortunate peoples. The only democratic power able to resist the advance of Communism, she was required to commit herself to that perilous task throughout the world.

As the global map underwent kaleidoscopic changes, the familiar features of global politics seemed to dissolve. National gave way to ideological antipathies, and the conflict was no longer between nations but between systems and philosophies. World War II, with its terrible destruction of the material, political, and spiritual resources of mankind, created immense vacuums into which American and Russian power poured almost as if in response to natural forces. The titanic conflict between Russian and American systems which Henry Adams had foreseen materialized. That Atlantic Community familiar to the Founding Fathers was re-created. A shift in the center of gravity from the Atlantic to the Pacific which Homer Lea had prophesied came to pass.

Because America felt compelled to feed, clothe, and sustain the peoples of the Old World, to occupy parts of Germany, Austria, and Korea, defend Greece, rearm Turkey, sustain Bolivia and Brazil, establish air and naval bases across the world, become an Atlantic power, a Pacific power, and a Hemispheric power all at once, she stretched not only her physical but her intellectual resources thin. Because American wealth was essential to recovery almost everywhere, many Americans assumed that all that was needed for recovery was American wealth. Because so many ancient nations appeared unable to exist without American support, Americans were tempted to forget the force of tradition and history and assume that they could rearrange European politics as simply as they rearranged their own. Because American military might was the most formidable the world had ever seen, many Americans thought that it was absolute, and argued the necessity of using it wherever democracy or liberty was challenged by hostile forces.

But as the United States advanced in strength, so too did Russia. As the United States poured financial aid into western Europe, Russia revolutionized the economies of eastern Europe and of China through the application of Communism. As the United States built up a system of alliances, Russia gained allies through military or ideological conquest. And as the United States made atom bombs, so too did the Russians. With the emergence of the atom and the hydrogen bombs as absolute weapons, it became clear that notwithstanding her might, the United States was as vulnerable as any of her rivals. At the moment in history when Americans attained their greatest power, they were confronted with implacable limits on power.

Thus Americans were called on to make multiple adjustment. They had to adjust themselves first to the notion and the practice of world responsibility, and then to a host of particular problems connected with the exercise of that responsibility. This required a swift education in global affairs, and that education was inevitably superficial and confused. Americans who had barely acquainted themselves with the geography of their own country had to learn overnight about Burma and Indo-China, Pakistan and India, Eritrea and Ethiopia, Iran and Iraq, Palestine and Transjordan, Manchuria and Korea, as well as about the geopolitics of a new Europe. They had to learn about foreign trade and currency controls, the intricacies of British, French, and Italian politics, the economy of a divided Germany, the strategic importance of the Scandinavian states, of Greece, Palestine, North Africa, Korea, and Formosa. They had to learn to work with new international organizations and administrations, and to acquire a new vocabulary and grammar of international politics. World responsibility meant, too, a new political orientation at home: a bipartisan foreign policy, a vastly enlarged State Department, a closer correlation between foreign and domestic policy and between civilian and military economy than ever before, the elaboration of far-reaching security controls, and the creation of an alert, intelligent, and prudent public opinion. The cost of national defense and the financing of relief, reconstruction, and defense abroad meant a terrific tax burden. Americans were called upon to display a degree of political maturity such as they had displayed only once before — in the Revolutionary generation, 1765–1800.

It was asking a good deal to expect Americans to learn all this at once. If the student were to judge by what appeared in the press or by what was said in Congress or in political campaigns, he might well conclude that it was asking too much. If he judged, however, by what was actually accomplished in the years after the war, he would necessarily reach a more favorable conclusion. For, to an impressive degree, the American nation did fulfill the obligations that had been thrust upon it, and did seek, with patience and good will, the road to peace.

We are sometimes so impressed by the problems war creates that we forget those it solves. Just as World War I was followed by an era of disenchantment in which Americans argued that their participation had been a mistake, so within a few years of victory over Germany and Japan there were some who asserted that American participation in World War II had been an avoidable mistake. In some quarters it was thought clever to say that the United States had won the war but had lost the peace. For the most part this attitude was inspired by the exigencies of partisan politics, but some of it was inspired by a deep disillusionment with the postwar world, and by the fear that Communist Russia and China posed as great a threat to world peace as had Nazi Germany and militarist Japan. It is perhaps sufficient answer to these assertions to suggest the consequences to America had Germany and Japan been victorious, as they would inevitably have been had the United States stood aloof from the war. Shortly after Pearl Harbor President Roosevelt, asked to give a name to the conflict, suggested ' The War for Survival.' It was a good name, and however vexatious the problems of the postwar years, it is well to keep in mind that the United States and Britain survived, and with them a chance for democracy and freedom and for civilization itself in the modern world.

2. LIQUIDATING THE WAR

It was the irrepressible Winston Churchill who said, ' We shall not make the same mistakes after this war that we made after the last; we shall make a lot of new ones.' As it turned out, we made plenty of them and many of the old ones as well. The peacemaking of 1919, long the object of criticism and contempt, came to seem almost statesmanlike by comparison with the lack of it after 1945. The leaders of the Western democracies, Roosevelt and Churchill, had given — as we now know — immense thought and effort to laying the foundations for peace and an international organization, and a whole series of conferences — Quebec, Moscow, Teheran, Cairo, Crimea — had presumably prepared the way for the creation of a secure future. Yet fifteen years after victory no permanent settlements had been achieved for Germany. Disagreements among the victors, restrained during the war itself, broke out virulently after the war, and grew increasingly acrimonious with the passing years.

The unconditional surrender formula, announced at Casablanca and reiterated at Moscow and Yalta, and imposed on the Germans and the Japanese, was no more than just that — a formula for surrender. Certainly it was not a formula for peace. Even as a formula for surrender it required very considerable elaboration, for the surrender of an army and a navy, and the dissolution of a government, is a complex and delicate process. And clearly the victors had to go on from there. They had to provide the mechanism for demobilization, dispose of the millions of prisoners of war, set up military government during the interregnum between surrender and peace, and get temporary civil government under way. They had to start the economy functioning once more, supply food and clothing, heat and shelter, medicine and protection for the defeated populations, and re-create such social institutions as church, schools, and the press.

What was to be the Allied policy toward Germany? World War I afforded no precedent; when Germany quit, in November 1918, a German government was functioning and German economy was intact. Italy furnished no satisfactory precedent; her territory had not been devastated nor her economy shattered as had the German, and she had achieved the status of co-belligerent. The Allies — already by mid-1945 as much rivals as allies — had to tailor their policies to fit new and unpredictable circumstances. Unconditional surrender was not a conclusion but merely a point of departure. Two plans were discussed in the United States: the Welles plan of breaking Germany up into a group of small states, and the Morgenthau plan of reducing her to a pastoral economy. The first was never seriously considered; the second was tentatively endorsed at the Quebec Conference — over the protest of the British — and was then abandoned.

Some sort of plan was, however, essential. The Moscow Conference of 1943 set up a European Advisory Commission, which worked out the basic principles for the treatment of Germany after the war: the destruction of German militarism and military potential; the dissolution of the Nazi party and the punishment of war criminals;

creation of zones of control; and the payment of reparations ' to the greatest extent possible.' The Yalta Conference reaffirmed these principles, added the provision that France might share in the occupation, named, as a basis for discussion only, the sum of $20 billion for reparations, and tentatively conceded the territory east of the Curzon line to Russia and the right of Poland to compensation from German territory. At the Potsdam Conference, held in July 1945, Truman, Stalin, and Clement Attlee — who had replaced Churchill as spokesman for the British government — spelled out the details of these agreements and added certain others. That conference created a Council of Foreign Ministers, which was to draw up peace treaties with Italy and the Axis satellites; regularized an Allied Control Council for the military administration of Germany; gave Poland administrative control over all German territory east of the Oder and Neisse rivers; decided that notwithstanding the division into occupation zones Germany should be treated as an economic unit; and provided that each occupying power should take reparations from its own zone but that, in addition, the U.S.S.R. might receive reparations in the form of industrial equipment from the West in exchange for food and other products from the East. The Soviets demanded recognition of the Communist governments of Hungary, Rumania, and Bulgaria; when Truman called for free elections in these satellites, Stalin replied that ' any free elected government would be anti-Soviet and that we cannot permit.'

Joint occupation was already under way, and was already revealing its inadequacies, yet it is difficult to know what alternative there was. Eastern Germany, including Brandenburg, Mecklenburg, Saxony, and Thuringia, was assigned to Russia; northwestern Germany, including Westphalia, Hanover, and Holstein, to Britain; southwestern Germany, including Bavaria, Württemberg, and Hesse, to the United States; while France received two smaller areas — Baden and the Saar. Austria, too, was carved up into four occupation zones, while both Berlin and Vienna were parceled out to the victors. None of these zones was self-sufficient economically, and the principle of treating Germany as an economic unit broke down almost immediately. The Russians stripped their zone of whatever they thought they were entitled to, and made heavy demands for factories, power plants, rolling stock, and tools on the British and American zones. But the Potsdam declaration had included a precautionary clause to the effect

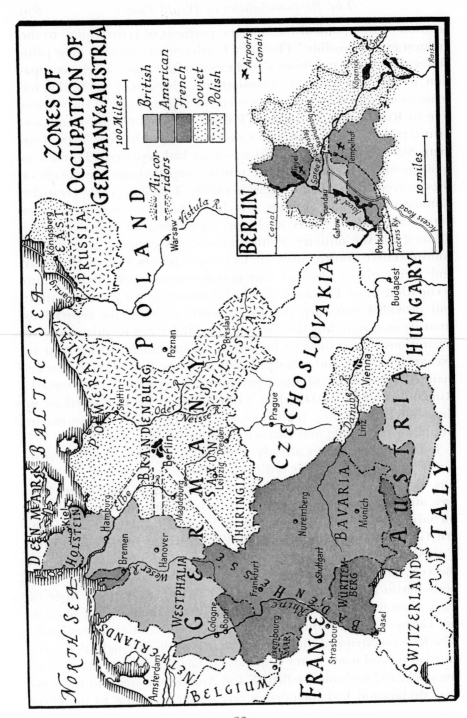

ZONES OF OCCUPATION OF GERMANY & AUSTRIA

British
American
French
Soviet
Polish

100 Miles

Air corridors

BERLIN

Airports
Canals

10 miles

Havel
Spree R.
Reichstag
Brandenburg Gate
Köpenick
Raisz
Tempelhof
Spandau
Havel R.
Gatow
Potsdam
Access Ry.
Access Road
Canal

BALTIC SEA
NORTH SEA
DENMARK
Königsberg
EAST PRUSSIA
Danzig
POLAND
Warsaw
Vistula R.
Poznan
Breslau
SILESIA
Stettin
POMERANIA
Odet
Neisse R.
BRANDENBURG
Berlin
SAXONY
Dresden
Leipzig
Magdeburg
Elbe
THURINGA
Prague
CZECHOSLOVAKIA
Budapest
HUNGARY
Vienna
Linz
Danube R.
AUSTRIA
ITALY
Munich
BAVARIA
Nuremberg
Stuttgart
WÜRTEM-BERG
BADEN
Basel
SWITZERLAND
Strasbourg
Rhine R.
Frankfurt
HESSEN
Luxembourg (SAAR)
Bonn
Cologne
WESTPHALIA
GERMANY
Hanover
Bremen
Weser R.
Hamburg
HOLSTEIN
Kiel
NETHERLANDS
Amsterdam
BELGIUM
FRANCE

880

that the conquerors ' should leave enough resources to enable the German people to subsist without external assistance.' If Britain and the United States permitted their zones to be gutted, German economy would collapse and Germany would become a permanent burden on their taxpayers. Furthermore, if the industrial potential of the Ruhr and the Saar were destroyed, the consequences for European recovery generally would be disastrous. As a result of these considerations, and of growing antagonism between Russia and the Western Allies, reparations slowed down, and then stopped altogether in 1947.

Behind these sharp differences of opinion on reparations lay even sharper differences of general policy. The Russians made clear from the first that they aimed at nothing less than the Communization of the whole of Central Europe — Germany and Austria included. They proceeded as if the purely provisional agreements at Yalta and Potsdam were permanent. Thus Russia took over not only the Baltic states seized during the war — Estonia, Latvia, and Lithuania — but part of East Prussia as well and the whole of Poland east of the Curzon line, and undertook a vigorous campaign to win eastern Germany for Communism. Poland regarded her occupation of Germany west of the Oder-Neisse line as equally permanent, and proceeded to oust some 10 million Germans living in that rich area. This mass expulsion worked grave hardship on its victims, but in the long run it was highly beneficial to them and to the West; it permitted millions of Germans to live under freedom rather than under Communist dictatorship and it greatly strengthened the West German economy. In the circumstances, genuine co-operation between the East and the West appeared impossible. So within two years of the defeat of Hitler's Reich, Russia and the Western Allies were bidding against each other for control of the German people.

American policy, at first confused, was somewhat clarified by Secretary of State Byrnes in a speech at Stuttgart in September 1946. ' The American government,' he said, ' is unwilling to accept responsibility for the needless aggravation of economic distress that is caused by the failure of the Allied Control Council to agree to give the German people a chance to solve some of their most urgent economic problems.' The United States was unwilling to turn Germany into a poorhouse, and if Russia would not observe the terms of the Potsdam agreement, the whole reparations program would

have to be revised. As a further gesture, Byrnes added that the
United States would support revision of the eastern frontier, and regarded the Ruhr and the Rhineland as irretrievably German. ' It
is not in the interest of the German people,' he asserted, ' that Germany should become a pawn or a partner in a military struggle for
power between the East and the West.' Yet that is precisely what
Germany had become!

Meantime every effort to write peace treaties for Germany and
Austria failed, but some progress was made on the lesser treaties. It
would be tedious to follow these in detail. In accordance with instructions from the Potsdam Conference, the Council of Foreign
Ministers — representatives of the Big Three with occasional spokesmen from France and China — met at London, Moscow, and Paris
to air their differences and dramatize their disagreement. Pressure
from other members of the United Nations, however, finally forced
action, and in the closing weeks of 1946 the council hammered out
treaties with Italy, Finland, Hungary, Rumania, and Bulgaria. Russia acquired the Karelian Isthmus and part of Petsamo from Finland,
and Bessarabia from Rumania, and the Dodecanese Islands were
ceded to Greece. The settlement of Trieste and its hinterland — a
question that had plagued the Peace Conference of 1919 — was the
knottiest problem the council faced; it was finally decided to make
Trieste a free port under international control and cede the hinterland to Yugoslavia, but within a year this decision was revised, and
Italy was encouraged by the Western powers to win back Trieste.

Meantime the Big Three went ahead with the trial of major war
criminals, and the Western powers with their denazification program and with the re-establishment of a German government. From
the beginning of the war Churchill and Roosevelt had made clear
their determination to bring Nazi war criminals to trial. That Associate Justice Robert Jackson was appointed to represent the United
States in establishing an International Military Tribunal and to
serve as chief counsel for the prosecution was an indication of the
importance that Roosevelt and Truman attached to these trials. Jackson's report designated three major types of crime: violations of international law, crimes against humanity and against established
criminal law, and aggressive warfare in violation of the Kellogg Pact
and other international commitments. Jackson proposed the trial not
only of major war criminals, but of criminal organizations such as

the Gestapo, the SS, and the Nazi party as well, but left to military tribunals and to the German courts the punishment of lesser criminals.

The London Agreement of August 1945 accepted these proposals and established an international judicial tribunal with representatives from the four occupying powers. The International Military Tribunal then presented indictments against 24 major criminals and six criminal organizations. The trials, lasting ten months, published the whole ghastly record of Nazi aggression, atrocities, mass murders, looting, and destruction. Nineteen war criminals were found guilty, and twelve, including such notorious figures from the Nazi high command as Goering, Keitel, Jodl, Ribbentrop, and Seyss-Inquart, sentenced to death. In addition there were numerous trials of lesser war criminals by the military authorities and by denazified German courts. The Americans conducted a series of 12 trials, each centered on an occupational group — doctors and lawyers, military leaders, SS and police, industrialists, and government ministers. All the members of these groups were tried individually for specific crimes: 35 were acquitted, 24 given death sentences, and 128 condemned to varying terms of imprisonment.

The war trials came in for heavy criticism in Britain and the United States. It was alleged that by making aggressive warfare a crime the tribunal was guilty of *ex post facto* legislation, that trials by judges from the victor nations did not deserve the term ' judicial,' and that trials by military tribunals were equally flawed with impropriety. To this it was replied that the legal justification for the trials lay in the Kellogg-Briand Pact which had outlawed war, and the trials therefore were not *ex post facto;* and that the tribunals which tried the accused observed the highest standards of due process. Whatever the validity of these charges and justifications, much was to be said for the attempt to make aggressive warfare a crime; and by adopting the Universal Declaration of Human Rights, the United Nations in effect endorsed the principles and the findings of the Nuremberg tribunals.

While these trials were proceeding to their somber conclusion, the work of sterilizing German society of its Nazi infection went ahead. The Potsdam declaration had looked not only to the outlawing of the Nazi party and all of its affiliates, but to the elimination of Nazis from the civil service, schools, industries, and all important private organizations, and their replacement by persons capable of developing genuine democratic institutions in Germany. This was easier said than done. The Nazi regime had so extended itself into every field of social and economic activity that almost the only Germans free of Nazi taint were those in exile, concentration camps, or cemeteries. Confronted with this situation, the military administration was forced to compromise, and the denazification that had begun with a bang petered out with a whimper. Notorious Nazis were ousted from places of authority and, in some instances, punished, but most of the small fry went free or were subjected to mild penalties. Under the Germans, denazification became something of a joke. Thus of the 836,000 Nazis tried, less than 0.1 per cent were classified as major offenders, and as of May 1948 only 1677 were serving jail sentences.[1]

Notwithstanding the difficulties of denazification, the military government made substantial progress in the restoration of German economy and government in the years after the war. The task was one for which Americans were almost wholly without experience, and the wonder is not that so much was done badly, but that so much was done well. Even in the most favorable circumstances it would have been difficult to restore Germany economy; with the amputation of the agricultural east and Silesia by the Russians and of the Saar by the French, the influx of 12 million German refugees from the Russian and Polish areas and from East Germany, the division of the west into three administrative zones, the reduction of German industry to the 1932 level, and the drain of reparations, complete restoration seemed impossible. After 1946 some of these obstacles to recovery were removed. The level of industrial production was raised; Britain and America combined their zones into an

---

[1] The figures may be of interest: in the American Zone

    12,753,000 registered
     3,209,000 were processed
     2,373,000 received amnesty without trial
       836,000 were tried
       503,360 were convicted
       430,890 were fined less than 1000 RM
        27,413 were sentenced to perform some community work
         7,768 were given short sentences in labor camps
        18,503 were pronounced ineligible to hold office
        20,865 suffered partial property confiscation

See J. H. Herz, *Political Science Quarterly*, December 1948.

economic 'bizonia'; the United States poured half a billion dollars annually into western Germany and, in 1948, made it eligible for Marshall Plan aid. With spectacular speed economic life revived and western Germany moved toward a self-supporting economy and then to such prosperity as no other European power enjoyed.

The establishment of German governments proved at first difficult. The collapse of the Nazi regime had left a complete political vacuum in Germany, and for the time being the military had to improvise administration as best it could, a task aggravated by the absence of any over-all policy and of clear-cut directives, and by the fact that the occupation zones cut athwart traditional state boundaries. The creation of a government for the whole of western Germany took three years. A Parliamentary Council of elected delegates met at the university city of Bonn in September 1948 to draft a Basic Law; after six months of debate and negotiation a constitution creating a democratic federal state was finally hammered out, accepted by the occupation authorities, and adopted in May 1949.

The occupation of Japan was simple compared with that of Germany. The Imperial government was still functioning, the Japanese people were subservient and co-operative; their economy had not been destroyed as had the German; and there was no problem of divided authority: General MacArthur handled the whole thing himself.[2] Japan, too, had surrendered unconditionally; the Potsdam Conference made clear that this did not involve the destruction of the Japanese nation, and subsequently it was decided that it did not involve the deposition of the Emperor. Within a few months after the surrender, General MacArthur in co-operation with liberal elements in Japan revolutionized Japanese society and government. He demobilized 4 million Japanese soldiers, destroyed Japanese military potential, purged the civil service, abolished the secret police and 'patriotic' societies, broke up cartels and the family trusts, democratized the landowning system, ended press censorship, prohibited racial and religious discrimination, abolished Shintoism as a state religion, and required the Emperor to repudiate his own divinity. Meantime an International Tribunal tried the leading war criminals, and sen-

[2] There were, however, two advisory bodies: a Far Eastern Commission in Washington and an Interallied Council for Japan in Tokyo. Each of the four major powers in the Far Eastern Commission had a veto, and if the commission failed to agree, the American military administration could act unilaterally, as it almost always did; the Allied Council was limited to making recommendations.

tenced Prime Minister Tojo and a dozen of the leading generals to death for their part in war crimes and atrocities. High ranking officers of the army and navy were tried by local tribunals for offenses against the laws of war; 4200 of them were convicted and no less that 720 of them were executed.

At the same time MacArthur inaugurated far-reaching reforms. A new Diet, elected under a law permitting woman suffrage, drafted a democratic constitution that provided for popular sovereignty and parliamentary government, reduced the Emperor to a figurehead, and included a bill of rights and a permanent renunciation of war — which was shortly modified by the Americans themselves. Efforts to write a peace treaty were long frustrated by Russia, but in 1951, after the outbreak of the Korean War, John Foster Dulles drafted a treaty which put a formal end to the war and the occupation. Another treaty of the same day permitted the United States to maintain troops and air bases on the Japanese islands.

Military occupation was as unsuccessful in Korea as it was successful in Japan. Long part of China, then briefly independent, the ' Hermit Kingdom ' had been annexed to Japan in 1910; the Cairo Conference had promised Koreans freedom ' in due course.' Russia's last-minute declaration of war against Japan enabled her to move troops into the Korean peninsula, and Korea, like Germany, was divided into zones of occupation: the United States in the more populous south, and Russia in the north. All efforts to unify either administration or economy proved vain; as the Russians proceeded to communize their area, the American authorities threw their support to the conservative elements of South Korea, represented by the aged and stubborn Syngman Rhee, a kind of Korean Chiang Kaishek. Late in 1946 the administration was turned over to the Koreans, and in 1948 a popular election adopted a Republican constitution. Syngman Rhee was elected President for what proved to be a 12-year term, and the American military occupation came to an end. The triumph of the Communists in the north and in China, however, made Korea's strategic position highly vulnerable, while economically the nation continued to be a heavy drain on the American taxpayer. The stage was set for trouble, yet when it came it took Americans by surprise.[3]

[3] For the Korean War see section 7 below.

3. ORGANIZATION FOR PEACE

We seek peace — enduring peace. More than an end to war, we want an end to the beginnings of all wars— yes, an end to this brutal, inhuman and thoroughly impractical method of settling the differences between governments. . . . We are faced with the pre-eminent fact that, if civilization is to survive, we must cultivate the science of human relationships — the ability of all peoples, of all kinds, to live together and work together in the same world, at peace. . . . Today, as we move against the terrible scourge of war — as we go forward toward the greatest contribution that any generation of human beings can make in this world, — the contribution of lasting peace — I ask you to keep up your faith.

These were the last words that Franklin Roosevelt wrote, and they were eloquent of that profound concern for peace, and for the creation of machinery to keep it, that possessed him throughout the war years. Roosevelt's interest in peace went back to his service in the Wilson administration during World War I and to his candidacy, on a League of Nations platform, in 1920. That he had been deeply impressed by Wilson's idealism is clear; that he was determined not to repeat Wilson's mistakes is equally clear; ' the tragedy of Wilson,' wrote Robert Sherwood, ' was always somewhere within the rim of his consciousness.'

The Atlantic Charter had called for ' the establishment of a wider and permanent system of general security,' and thereafter, it is no exaggeration to say, the construction of a peaceful postwar order was second in Roosevelt's thoughts only to the war, and never wholly separated from it. The great coalition that was to guarantee peace took embryonic form in the wartime United Nations of 1 January 1942, and thereafter every major conference of the Allied leaders gave increasing attention to this problem, and to its solution. All through 1944 the United States State Department and foreign-office officials of the major Allied powers were busily engaged in drafting proposals for a postwar international organization, and in August of that year their representatives met at Dumbarton Oaks, in Washington, and drew up the blueprint which was adopted, with some changes and additions, as the Charter of the United Nations.

The discussions at Yalta — the last and most important of the Roosevelt-Churchill-Stalin conferences — had addressed themselves to three major topics: the final defeat of the Axis powers, the problems of occupation (including what should be occupied and who

should do the occupying), and the creation of an international organization. It was the last which Roosevelt emphasized in his report
to Congress, and in the light of the subsequent breakdown of world
peace, that report takes on an almost tragic character. ' I come from
the Crimea Conference,' he said,

with a firm belief that we have made a good start on the road to a world
of peace. . . . This time we are not making the mistake of waiting until
the end of the war to set up the machinery of peace. . . . The Conference
in the Crimea was a turning point — I hope in our history and therefore
in the history of the world. There will soon be presented to the Senate
of the United States and to the American people a great decision that
will determine the fate of the United States — and of the world — for
generations to come. There can be no middle ground here. We shall have
to take the responsibility for world collaboration, or we shall have to
bear the responsibility for another world conflict.

Roosevelt died on 12 April, but invitations had already gone out
for a United Nations Conference to meet at San Francisco to draft a
charter for the new international organization, and late in that
month delegates from 50 nations gathered at that city whose very
choice suggested the new importance of the Pacific area. Secretary of
State Stettinius headed the American delegation, Anthony Eden the
British, and — in the end — Molotov the Russian. Determined not
to make the mistake Wilson had made in ignoring both the Republicans and the Congress, Roosevelt had appointed two Republicans —
Senator Vandenberg and Representative Eaton — and two Democrats — Senator Connally and Representative Bloom — to fill out
the American delegation.

The conference lasted for two months, and was marked by many
sharp disagreements over such matters as the Polish delegation, the
admission of Argentina, separate votes for the Ukraine and White
Russia, and the veto power; it ended on a note of surface harmony
with all 50 nations signing the Charter, whose preamble announced
the purpose of the organization:

To save succeeding generations from the scourge of war . . . and to reaffirm faith in fundamental human rights, in the dignity and worth of
the human person, in the equal rights of men and women and of Nations
large and small, and to establish conditions under which justice and
respect for the obligations arising from treaties and other sources of international law can be maintained, and to promote social progress and
better standards of life in larger freedom, and . . . to ensure, by the

acceptance of principles and the institution of methods, that armed force shall not be used, save in the common interest, and to employ international machinery for the promotion of the economic and social advancement of all peoples.

The United States was already committed to the Charter in principle by the Fulbright-Connally Resolutions of 1943, and the Senate ratified the document on 28 July 1945 with only two votes in opposition. By October, 29 nations had ratified and the Charter went into effect.

The United Nations Charter was, in many respects, like the Covenant of the League of Nations. Like the League, it created an Assembly, whose functions were largely deliberative, and a Council whose functions were executive; like the League, it provided for a system of mandates, an International Court of Justice, a Secretariat, and other affiliated organizations; and like the League, too, it recognized the validity of regional agreements. It was unlike the League, however, in several important respects. It was not tied to the peace treaties, but existed independently of any that might be made; it permitted any one of the five great powers (the United States, Britain, Russia, France, and China) to exercise a veto on any but procedural questions — a power which Soviet Russia grossly abused; and it authorized the use of force against aggressor nations.

Specifically the Charter provided for a General Assembly in which each nation had one vote, and whose functions were limited almost entirely to discussion, investigation, and advice, and a Security Council to consist of five permanent [4] and six elected members, which alone had power to act in international disputes. The Assembly could call to the attention of the Council any situation likely to endanger peace, recommend measures for the settlement of disputes, and promote international co-operation in economic, social, and cultural fields. The Council, to which was assigned ' primary responsibility for the maintenance of peace and security,' was authorized to hear complaints from member nations, investigate disputes that might lead to war, and take such measures ' by air, sea or land forces ' as might be necessary to preserve peace. All members agreed to make available to the Council such armed forces and facilities as

[4] Great Britain, France, Russia, the United States, and China. The kind of problem presented, after 1950, by the existence of Nationalist and Communist governments each claiming to represent China was neither anticipated nor provided for in the Charter.

were agreed on and called for. Article 52 of the Charter permitted the creation of regional agreements and agencies, and it was in accordance with this permissive article that the Rio de Janeiro and the North Atlantic treaties were subsequently negotiated.

The Charter created a number of agencies designed to ease international tensions and promote co-operation of a constructive nature. There was to be an International Court of Justice with powers comparable to those formerly exercised by the World Court; an Economic and Social Council to promote social and cultural welfare and human rights; a trusteeship system to replace the unsatisfactory mandate system of the old League; a permanent Secretariat; a Military Staff Committee composed of the chiefs of staffs of the great powers and with authority over such military contingents as might be placed under it; and later an Atomic Energy Commission. Under the Economic and Social Council there was a proliferation of special agencies — UNESCO, a Food and Agricultural Organization, an International Labor Organization, a World Health Organization, and eventually many others of a technical character. The revolution in American opinion which had come in a scant quarter-century could be gauged by the keen competition among American cities to be headquarters for the United Nations. In the end the strategic value of locating the organization in the largest American city and the timely gift of millions of dollars for land and buildings by John D. Rockefeller were decisive in bringing it to New York City.

Launched with high hopes, the United Nations soon ran into the dangerous waters of the East-West conflict. Yet in the first few years of its existence it had some substantial accomplishments to its credit. It succeeded in settling — after a fashion — three major disputes: that between Russia and Iran, the series of problems connected with the emergence of Israel as a nation, and the complex and inflammable Indonesia issue. In addition, it took cognizance of the problem of Communist-inspired guerrilla warfare in Greece, the presence of British and French troops in Syria and Lebanon, and a claim of Britain against Albania. Its principal achievements were not, however, in the settlement of explosive disputes, but in serving — in Senator Vandenberg's phrase — as a ' town meeting of the world,' and as a vehicle for important social and economic reforms. In a quiet way such agencies as the International Health and the International Labor Organizations performed important services for the whole world.

Yet it could not be denied that the United Nations disappointed those who had hoped that it would succeed where the League had failed. The ostensible difficulty was the veto; designed for use only in emergencies, and then to avoid a rupture between the great powers, it was invoked by Russia some 50 times in the first four years, often for purposes that were trivial. The real difficulty of the United Nations was, of course, not mechanical but substantial: the division of the world into hostile camps led by the United States and the Soviet Union. This division was dramatized by the Russian boycott of the Trusteeship Council, and her veto on applications for membership from Ireland, Portugal, and Finland; the failure to bring important disputes before the International Court of Justice; and — most ominously — the failure of the Security Council to agree on the momentous question of the control of atomic energy.

4. THE CONTROL OF ATOMIC ENERGY

The atom bomb, so soon to be detonated at Los Alamos, was the subject of Secretary Stimson's last talk with President Roosevelt. ' I went over with him,' Stimson records,

the two schools of thought that exist in respect to the future control after the war of this project . . . one of them being the secret close-in attempted control of the project by those who control it now, and the other being the international control based upon freedom both of science and of access. I told him that those things must be settled before the first projectile was used. . . . He agreed to that.[5]

This basic question of control was not, however, settled; that failure remained to plague the world and perhaps to condemn it to destruction.

On the day the United Nations Conference convened at San Francisco, Stimson presented to President Truman a memorandum on the bomb, which pointed out that

The world, in its present state of moral advancement, compared with its technical development, would be eventually at the mercy of such a weapon. . . . Modern civilization might be completely destroyed. To approach any world peace organization of any pattern now likely to be considered without an appreciation by the leaders of our country of the power of this new weapon would seem to be unrealistic. No system

[5] Henry Stimson, *On Active Service*, p. 616.

of control heretofore considered would be adequate to control this menace. . . . Our leadership in the war and in the development of this weapon has placed a certain moral responsibility upon us which we cannot shirk without very serious responsibility for any disaster to civilization which it would further.[6]

The explosions at Hiroshima and Nagasaki and the 1946 experiments in the Bikini Lagoon [7] justified the truth of this prophecy and the validity of this warning. Thoughtful men everywhere in the world realized that atomic energy might be the Frankenstein monster that would destroy mankind. At the same time it was clear that, properly safeguarded and used for beneficent ends, atomic energy might usher in a new era of prosperity and well-being for the peoples of the earth. How to prevent the use of atomic energy for destructive purposes and encourage its use for constructive purposes was the most urgent problem that confronted the statesmen of the world at mid-twentieth century.

It was a problem of peculiar difficulty as well as of peculiar urgency. In the first place, there were no 'secrets' about the atom bomb; physicists everywhere in the world knew how to make the bomb, and it was certain that within a few years any country that cared to spend the money and effort could have bigger and more devastating bombs than those that had already been exploded. Within a few years Russia, Britain, and France all had 'the bomb.' In the second place, given existing international machinery, there was no effective means of controlling either the manufacture of atom bombs or nuclear experiments; any method that would be effective required some surrender of national sovereignty. In the third place, there was no defense against an atomic attack except the desperate defense of counterattack.

American policy on atomic energy, first outlined by Secretary Stimson, was clearly formulated by two committees headed by Dean Acheson and David Lilienthal. This Acheson-Lilienthal Plan, published in March 1946, called for the creation of an International Atomic Development Authority, which should have exclusive control over such raw materials as uranium and thorium and over every

---

[6] Ibid. p. 638.

[7] There were two tests. One bomb, dropped from the air, sank five ships and heavily damaged the superstructure of many more. The second, exploded under water, sank two battleships and an aircraft carrier and did major damage to many other vessels; it also created radioactivity in the water that lasted for several months.

stage of the production of atomic energy throughout the world, and should act as custodian of atomic weapons and stockpiles of fissionable materials.

Meantime, at its first session the General Assembly of the United Nations created an Atomic Energy Commission to consist of representatives of all eleven of the members of the Security Council plus Canada. President Truman appointed the sage Bernard Baruch as American representative on this commission, and in a notable address in June 1946 Baruch presented a proposal that incorporated the main features of the Acheson-Lilienthal Plan plus provision for rigid international inspection and for the elimination of the veto in cases involving illegal manufacture of atomic bombs. Under the Baruch Plan, the proposed International Atomic Authority would control the whole field of atomic energy through ownership, licenses, operation, inspection, research, and management, and concern itself not only with the prevention of the manufacture of atomic weapons but with the production of atomic energy for peaceful benefits. If this program were adopted, the United States stood ready to destroy its stock of atom bombs, stop further manufacture of bombs, and share its scientific knowledge with the rest of the world. When it is remembered that at this time the United States had a monopoly on the atomic bomb, it will be conceded that this proposal was not only enlightened but magnanimous.

The United Nations Atomic Energy Commission endorsed the American plan by a vote of 10–0; Russia and Poland abstained from voting. Russia rejected it for two reasons: inspection would be an intolerable invasion of national sovereignty, and the suspension of the veto would destroy the unanimity principle that was the very basis of the Security Council. Gromyko proposed an alternative plan: the immediate destruction of all atom bombs and the prohibition of the manufacture of atomic weapons. Obviously such a plan was unacceptable to the United States or to her Western associates. It required the surrender of almost the only effective weapon the West had to restrain Russian aggression and, in the absence of inspection, gave no corresponding assurance that Russia would not proceed with the manufacture of atomic weapons behind her Iron Curtain.

Russian intransigence on the veto and on inspection condemned the work of the United Nations Atomic Energy Commission to futility, and in July 1949 the commission suspended its deliberations.

Meantime the United States pushed steadily ahead with her own atomic program. The atom bomb had originally been made by civilian scientists, but under the jurisdiction of the military. With the end of the war there was strong pressure for civilian control of the whole field of atomic energy. The plan worked out by Congress, after lengthy debate, placed the atomic-energy program under the jurisdiction of a five-man civilian Atomic Energy Commission but provided for close military liaison and elaborate security measures; the AEC was to have a monopoly on all fissionable materials, processes, facilities, patents, and technical information. Lilienthal, whose administrative abilities had been tested by his work as head of the TVA, was appointed first chairman of the new commission.

The whole atomic situation was changed radically by the announcement, in September 1949, that the Russians had detonated an atomic bomb. Clearly the Baruch Plan was outmoded, and some new plan, which recognized Russia's altered position, was called for. The necessity of reopening the whole question of international control was dramatized by the announcement, a few months later, that the atom bomb would eventually be supplanted by the hydrogen bomb, a thousandfold as powerful. With the hydrogen bomb the annihilation of the human race became a grim possibility. Speaking with deep solemnity, the venerable philosopher-scientist Albert Einstein, who had originally called President Roosevelt's attention to the potentialities of nuclear fission, warned the world,

The armament race between the U.S.A. and the U.S.S.R., originally supposed to be a preventive measure, assumes hysterical character. On both sides, the means to mass destruction are perfected with feverish haste, behind respective walls of secrecy. The H-bomb appears on the public horizon as a probably attainable goal. . . . If successful, radio-active poisoning of the atmosphere and hence annihilation of any life on earth has been brought within the range of technical possibilities. The ghost-like character of this development lies in its apparently compulsory trend. Every step appears as the unavoidable consequence of the preceding one. In the end, there beckons more and more clearly general annihilation.

5. RELIEF AND RECONSTRUCTION

The most pressing problem at the close of the war was to bring relief to the stricken millions of the Old World. For five years the Nazis and the Communists had systematically looted and destroyed wherever they went. Tens of millions of workers had been drawn into non-productive war industries; perhaps 20 million men and women had been killed in battle, or in the rubble of cities, or in concentration camps. Food production had fallen to half the prewar level. Towns and cities were destroyed, factories smashed up, power plants wrecked, mines flooded, ports clogged, shipping sunk, railroads torn up, and rolling stock in ruins; money was almost worthless. Ten to twelve million bewildered refugees wandered aimlessly on the roads, or clung to the camps that had been hastily established for them. Herbert Hoover, sent abroad to survey the food situation, reported that ' It is now 11:59 o'clock on the clock of starvation.' Most continental Europeans were living on less than 1500 calories a day: the American average was 3500. Starvation, disease, and anarchy threatened to take more lives and to leave worse scars than war itself. Over large parts of Asia, too, the situation was desperate, and with crop failures in 1946, it grew worse: it was estimated that almost 400 million people of Asia were close to starvation.

The burden of relief fell most heavily upon the United States, which alone of major nations had a transportation system and shipping intact, and surplus food. As early as June 1943 the United States proposed to her Allies the creation of an international relief organization, and out of this proposal came the United Nations Relief and Rehabilitation Administration (UNRRA), of November 1943, to which 48 nations eventually adhered. Under the vigorous leadership first of ex-Governor Herbert Lehman of New York and then of Fiorello LaGuardia, UNRRA distributed not only food and clothing, but seed, fertilizer, livestock, machinery, and medicine. Altogether, in four years of troubled existence, UNRRA spent some $4 billion for relief purposes; of this sum the United States gave $2.75 billion. In addition the U.S. Army fed large areas of occupied Europe, Lend-Lease continued to pour foodstuffs and other supplies into Allied countries, and private gifts and CARE supplemented governmental contributions on a generous scale. Yet if the United States did much for relief, she did less than her resources permitted; there was no postwar rationing, cereals continued to be fed to livestock rather than exported direct to the starving abroad, and Lend-Lease was abruptly terminated in August 1945, one week after the capitulation of Japan.

A major part of UNRRA's task was responsibility for the millions of refugees who came to be known as Displaced Persons. At the close of the war there were perhaps ten million of these hapless victims of modern war; many of them had been pressed into Nazi military service and were mingled with other prisoners of war; others were labor slaves, or inmates of prison camps. By the end of 1946 the military had repatriated most of these refugees, but there remained a hard core of perhaps a million non-repatriables: Jews who wanted to go to Palestine, or Balts, Poles, Yugoslavs, and Russians who had fought Communism and were unable or unwilling to return to their own countries. Many of these were eventually resettled in Palestine, New Zealand, Brazil, Colombia, Australia, and other countries who were ready to welcome the labor and skills that they possessed. The United States lagged badly behind in this program of resettlement of Displaced Persons, admitting only some 6000 by the end of 1947. In 1948 Congress passed legislation to admit an additional 200,000, on terms far from generous; in 1950 this legislation was liberalized and another 200,000 refugees admitted.

The reconstruction of the war-shattered economy of western Europe called for boldness, imagination, and intelligence. Yet complex as was the problem of economic reconstruction, its broad outlines were essentially simple. Europe needed everything but was able to buy nothing; the United States had — or was capable of producing — almost everything, but could sell nothing to a bankrupt Europe. If the European economy collapsed, the American economy would take a tailspin. Some method must be found, therefore, not only of getting the European economy functioning on an emergency basis, but of putting it on a permanently self-supporting basis, so that European countries could resume their traditional role in international trade. Clearly, too, more was involved than economic prosperity. If the United States stood idly by while western Europe plunged into economic chaos, she would be faced, within a few years, with a Soviet-dominated Continent.

Tinkering with tariffs, credits, and investment policies could ameliorate the immediate effects of the economic malaise, but could not cure it. The United States moved on many fronts to ease restrictions on trade, stabilize currencies, and encourage investments. The Reciprocal Trade Agreements, inaugurated in 1934, had been renewed in 1945, and in 1947 some 40 nations, meeting at Geneva, agreed on sweeping reductions in tariffs. Under the terms of this agreement the United States cut duties on thousands of items; the general effect was to reduce duties to the 1913 level. At the same time the United States took the lead in establishing an International Trade Organization to promote the expansion of world trade. In response to these moves American imports increased from a prewar average of less than $3 billion to a total of over $7 billion in 1948. Yet this still left a gap of almost $8 billion between what the rest of the world bought and what it sold to the United States: if trade were to continue, this gap would have to be closed.

Closely connected with the problem of trade was that of credit and currency. As early as 1943 the Treasury Department began laying plans for stabilizing national currencies and making available credit for international trade and investment, and in the summer of 1944 a United Nations Monetary and Financial Conference met at Bretton Woods, New Hampshire, to crystallize these plans. This conference set up and Congress ratified two new agencies: an International Monetary Fund and an International Bank for Reconstruction. The first, designed to maintain stable exchange rates and discourage restrictions on the transfer of funds from nation to nation, was provided with a capital of $8.8 billion, to which the United States contributed one-fourth. The World Bank, as it came to be called, was authorized to borrow and lend money and to underwrite private loans for production purposes. Its achievements were, up to 1950, disappointing: by that time the bank had made loans of only $700 million and had been unable to attract private capital to any large-scale investment in European recovery.

One step that contributed to orderly economic reconstruction was the prompt settlement of Lend-Lease accounts. Lend-Lease had been terminated, with what Europeans thought unnecessary abruptness, in August 1945, but existing obligations called for the delivery of some 2 billion dollars' worth of material and services during the following year. The final reckoning showed total Lend-Lease grants of some $50 billion, and reverse Lend-Lease to the value of a little less than $8 billion.[8] Roosevelt and Truman were both determined to avoid the war-debt business that had plagued America's relations with her Allies after World War I, so Lend-Lease was settled on the simple principle of wiping all wartime debts and credits off the books, and requiring repayment only of postwar grants, and that on

[8] See Table in Appendix.

easy terms. Settlements were speedily concluded with Britain, France, China, and other wartime associates; for a long time Russia refused to discuss the matter.

The end of Lend-Lease precipitated a serious economic crisis in Britain. The British had not only lost most of their foreign investments, but incurred heavy debts abroad; they had lost one-third of their shipping as well as a substantial part of their foreign markets; and their industry was partially destroyed and almost wholly run down. They could neither recapture their export market nor pay for imports with accumulated capital. At the same time they were unable to escape heavy external financial commitments: occupation costs in Germany and Austria, military expenses in Palestine, Greece, and the Far East, assistance to their colonies, contributions to the World Bank, and so forth. To ward off a catastrophe the British asked for a loan of $5 billion from the United States. After protracted negotiations a sum of $3.75 billion was agreed upon, plus an additional credit for the $650 million outstanding on Lend-Lease; the loan was to run for 50 years and carry interest at 2 per cent. It had been hoped that the loan would carry Britain through the next five years but, notwithstanding the maintenance of wartime austerity and heroic efforts to regain foreign markets, the money ran out in two years, and by 1947 Britain was again faced with economic disaster.

The British crisis, together with the persistence of economic conditions that encouraged Communism in Italy and France, finally led to the formulation of a really adequate program of American aid: the Marshall Plan. This famous plan did not spring full-blown from the brain of Secretary Marshall. Many minds went into its making. Perhaps George Kennan — who during these years contributed as much as any American outside the White House to the formulation of foreign policy — was chiefly responsible. As early as 1946 he had admonished our government to

put forward for other nations a more positive and constructive picture of the sort of world we would like to see. . . . It is not enough to urge people to develop political processes similar to our own. Many foreign peoples are tired and frightened by experiences of the past and are less interested in abstract freedom than in security. They are seeking guidance rather than responsibilities. We should be better able to give them this. And unless we do the Russians certainly will.[9]

[9] Quoted in W. C. Mallalieu, ' Origin of the Marshall Plan,' 73 *Pol. Sci. Qt.* 481.

The next year Secretary Marshall set up a policy-planning staff headed by Kennan; this staff recommended short-term aid to stop further deterioration of the European economy, and a long-range program looking to European economic integration. Early in May 1947 Dean Acheson announced that national self-interest required that western European nations become self-supporting, and that to this end the United States must be prepared to contribute. Speaking at a Harvard Commencement in June Secretary Marshall summed up all of these recommendations by advising Europe to work out a joint plan for reconstruction. ' Our policy,' he said, ' is directed against hunger, poverty, desperation and chaos. Its purpose should be the revival of a working economy in the world so as to permit the emergence of political and social conditions in which free institutions can exist.' Any government willing to assist in the task of recovery, he added, would find full co-operation on the part of the United States.

This was what Europe had been waiting for. The Prime Ministers of Britain and France promptly issued an invitation to 22 nations, including Russia, to meet at Paris the following month to draw a blueprint for European recovery. Though Molotov came to Paris with a staff of 89 economic experts to discuss preliminaries, it quickly appeared that while he was willing to accept American aid on a gigantic scale as nothing less than Europe's due, he thought America's role should be strictly limited to paying the bill. When it became clear that this delusion was shared by neither Britain nor France — to say nothing of the United States — Molotov withdrew, and all the Soviet satellites followed; poor Czechoslovakia, which had already accepted an invitation to the Paris conference, sent regrets.

In the end representatives of 16 nations met at Paris and, under the leadership of the Oxford philosopher Sir Oliver Franks, drafted an elaborate plan for European recovery. This plan fixed new production targets, promised financial and monetary stability, advised the abandonment of trade barriers, called for the restoration of the industrial economy of western Germany, and fixed the bill at approximately $22 billion over a period of four years; it was assumed that most of this would come from the United States.

In December 1947 President Truman submitted this plan to Congress together with his own recommendations for an appropriation of $17 billion over a four-year period. The debate, in and out of Congress, was comparable to that over the not dissimilar Lend-Lease bill of 1941. The opposition came chiefly from those who felt that the American economy could not stand so heavy a burden and those who regarded any further aid to the Old World as ' Operation Rathole.' It was led by Senator Taft, who was rapidly reverting to his prewar isolationism and who had his eye on the Republican nomination that summer. Liberals of both parties as well as powerful business, farm, and labor organizations rallied to the bill, whose leading senatorial champion was Senator Vandenberg, architect of the bipartisan foreign policy and most internationally minded of Republican leaders since Willkie. What finally turned the tide was not so much economic arguments as the Communist coup in Czechoslovakia in March 1948, together with new Russian demands on Finland. A program to halt the advance of Communism appealed to many who were immune to an appeal on mere economic or humanitarian grounds, and the Foreign Assistance Act — providing an immediate grant of $5.3 billion for European recovery plus $463 million for China and $275 million for Greece and Turkey — passed both houses of Congress by thumping majorities and became law on 3 April 1949. Thus once more, in the great words of Churchill, ' the new world with all its power and might, stepped forth to the rescue and liberation of the old.'

Thus was inaugurated the most effective counterattack on poverty, despair, and disintegration in modern history. Altogether Congress voted some $12 billion to carry out the Marshall Plan; what is more, the Marshall Plan became a pattern for Truman's Point Four program, and for much of the foreign aid of the 'fifties. When the Economic Cooperation Administration — set up to administer Marshall aid money — reported in 1951 it could point to an over-all increase in production in Marshall-aid countries of 37 per cent, an increase in agricultural production of 25 per cent, ' steel production nearly doubled in less than four years; coal production 17 per cent higher than in 1947, aluminum, copper, and cement production up 69, 31, and 90 per cent from 1947; electrical production up from 13 to 20 million kilowatt hours per month,' and so forth. All of this was important. More important was the dramatic change in morale. As the economy rebounded, so did the spirits and the confidence of the peoples of western Europe, confidence not only in their ability to fend for themselves, but in their democratic institutions.

6. The Cold War

The wartime alliance between Russia and the Western powers was clearly a marriage of convenience, not of love. Yet it was no less effective for that. When Hitler invaded Russia, Churchill at once announced that ' any man or state who fights against Nazidom will have our aid,' and in this view Roosevelt concurred. The Western powers promised aid and fulfilled their promises: witness the $11 billion of Lend-Lease that went to Russia, most of it freighted by British and American ships through the perilous North Atlantic and Arctic seas or on the long voyage around Africa and to the Persian Gulf. During the whole of the wartime alliance the leaders of the West hoped that after the war Russia, freed from the fear of Germany and Japan, protected by friendly border states, and strengthened by American help, might abandon her policy of isolation and hostility and associate herself with the work of creating a new international order. These expectations, it must be admitted, animated Roosevelt rather than Churchill, who was more cynical, or more realistic. Roosevelt saw clearly the importance of Russian co-operation to assure peace after the defeat of the Axis; he did not see so clearly the forces in Russia and in Communism militating against such co-operation. In short, he consulted his hopes rather than his fears; being Roosevelt, he could not have done otherwise.

Relations between Russia and the West were strained even during the war. Sharp differences over such matters as the sharing of military secrets, co-operation in the air war, the policy toward the Polish Army in Exile and the Polish underground and toward the contending forces in Yugoslavia, the timing of the second front, the treatment of Italy, and many other matters all foreshadowed the even deeper divisions that emerged after the war. Roosevelt hoped that these frictions would yield to the emollient of wartime comradeship, and that particular misunderstandings could be cleared up by personal consultations, and to this end he went to Teheran and to the Crimea.

The Yalta Conference of February 1945 in the Crimea appeared to have achieved the end to which Roosevelt so ardently looked. Later Yalta came to be regarded as a defeat for the West, but it was not so regarded at the time, nor is there any convincing evidence that it was so in fact. The Yalta agreements involved mutual concessions from Russia and the Western powers; on paper the concessions from the West seemed more far-reaching than those from Russia, but in reality the West conceded nothing substantial that Russia could not have taken anyway, while Russia yielded on important points to the Western point of view. Of primary importance was Russia's agreement to enter the war against Japan ' within two or three months ' of the defeat of Germany. In return she was promised the Kurile Islands, the southern half of Sakhalin, and privileges in Manchuria and at Port Arthur and Dairen: in all probability she could have taken all these as easily without as with Anglo-American permission. Nor should it be forgotten that when this agreement was made, the Allied armies had not yet crossed the Rhine, nor had the atom bomb been exploded at Los Alamos, and Roosevelt's military advisers anticipated that the war with Japan would go on for at least another year. As for the other postwar arrangements, Stalin acquiesced in the American formula for the admission of Latin American states to the United Nations and for their voting in the Security Council, withdrew his preposterous demand for 16 votes in the General Assembly, agreed to permit France a zone of occupation in Germany, accepted the reparation figure as tentative only, and — presumably — left open to further negotiation the reorganization of the Polish government. Roosevelt and Churchill conceded the Curzon line as Russia's western boundary, accepted a tentative reparations figure far beyond what they thought proper, promised Russia three votes in the General Assembly, and left open for future negotiation such thorny questions as Russian rights in the Dardanelles and in Iran, the future of the Baltic countries, and the disposition of Italian colonies.

Roosevelt, and his adviser Harry Hopkins, thought that the Yalta agreements ushered in a new era of peace and hope. ' We really believed in our hearts,' said Hopkins,

that this was the dawn of the new day we had all been praying for and talking about for so many years. We were absolutely certain that we had won the first great victory for peace — and by we I mean *all* of us, the whole civilized human race. The Russians had proved that they could be reasonable and farseeing and there wasn't any doubt in the minds of the President or any of us that we could live with them peacefully for as far into the future as any of us could imagine.[10]

Actually the conference was neither a victory nor a defeat for peace. Its principal achievements were in committing Russia to enter the

[10] Sherwood, *Roosevelt and Hopkins*, p. 870.

war against Japan and to support the United Nations. As it turned out, the atom bomb made Russian entry an embarrassment rather than a help, and Russian membership proved an obstacle to the United Nations. It is doubtful whether the course of history was changed in any important particulars by the Yalta Conference.

The breakdown in East-West relations came after Yalta, and for reasons not clear except on the assumption that Communism was implacably hostile to the West, and that nothing could heal the antagonism. Wartime co-operation, never wholly effective, came to an end with the defeat of Germany. Thereafter — even in the war on Japan — Russia and the West were rivals, not partners. As Winston Churchill said in a notable speech at Fulton, Missouri, on 5 March 1946, ' From Stettin in the Baltic to Trieste in the Adriatic an iron curtain has descended across the continent.' Then, whether impelled by a sense of power, or by fear, or by the iron logic of Communism, Russia embarked upon a policy of defiance and aggression. She engineered Communist revolutions in Hungary, Bulgaria, and Rumania, and finally Czechoslovakia, reducing those countries to the position of satellites; Finland resisted, and kept her independence in domestic but not in foreign affairs — witness her inability to join in the Marshall Plan. In the Far East, too, Russia's policy was one of unblushing aggression. She engineered a Communist revolution in northern Korea, stripped Manchuria of her industrial wealth, brought Outer Mongolia into her orbit, supported the Chinese Communists in their successful war against Chiang Kai-shek, inspired revolutionary movements in Indo-China, Malaysia, Burma, and Indonesia, and threatened Iran and even India.

It was in Asia that Communism scored its most spectacular success. The Chiang Kai-shek regime, torn by dissension, corroded by corruption, and without strong popular support, proved wholly unable to stem the tide of Chinese Communism. Even during the war the Chinese had been as zealous to fight among themselves as to fight the Japanese; after the war, as the Japanese moved out, Russian and Chinese Communist armies moved in. Resolute efforts by the United States to reform and strengthen the Nationalist regime and to force some settlement of the Chinese civil war proved abortive. Early in 1946 General Marshall arranged a truce between the Nationalists and the Communists, but it was speedily violated by both and, pronouncing a plague on both houses, Marshall withdrew American troops from China and washed his hands of the whole muddle. Yet notwithstanding this official shift in policy, the United States continued to pour military and financial aid into Nationalist China as long as there was any of it left, and thereafter into Formosa. Altogether this aid came to some $2 billion by 1950; its effect was to excite Nationalist hopes for further assistance, and to embitter the Communists. When, in 1949, the Communists swept the whole of the mainland and Chiang Kai-shek took refuge on the island of Formosa, the problem of Chinese membership in the United Nations and representation on the Security Council served further to embitter Soviet-American relations.

The deterioration of Russian relations with the Western powers, and especially with the United States, need not be traced in detail. From the Russian point of view American military might, air and naval bases in far-flung quarters of the globe, and control of the atomic weapon, as well as American support to capitalism and socialism abroad, all constituted a threat to Communism; for Stalin clearly accepted Lenin's dictum that ' the existence of the Soviet Republic side by side with the imperialistic states for a long time is unthinkable. In the end either one or the other will conquer.' Soviet conduct, in any event, revealed a settled purpose to create a *cordon sanitaire* around Russia and aggrandize her territorial holdings, and to subvert democratic governments and extend Communism throughout the globe. Particular manifestations of Soviet policy fitted this pattern: Communist-inspired attacks on Greece, pressure on Turkey, invasion of Iran, demand for Italian colonies, revolution in Czechoslovakia, intransigence on the Polish boundary and the Polish-government issues, refusal to make peace with Austria, breakdown of four-power control in Germany, blockade of Berlin, the creation of the Cominform in 1947, boycotting of many agencies of the United Nations and of the Marshall Plan, frequent resort to the veto in the UN, scuttling of the Atomic Energy Commission, and Communist infiltration into western European states, Latin America, and even the United States.

It was in the Mediterranean and Near East that the first showdown came. The importance of the Mediterranean lifeline had been proved by the war, and the prospect of Russian dominance in this area raised questions of basic political and military strategy. If Russia could take over Iran with its rich oil resources, bring Turkey and

Greece into her orbit, retain her strong ties with Yugoslavia, and get a foothold in North Africa, she would turn the flank of the West. Italy would be unable to resist Communism; the Near and Middle East would fall to Russia; the whole Moslem world would be threatened; and India would be open to attack from north, east, and west.

The British, who kept a tenuous foothold in Greece and Palestine, announced early in 1947 that they could no longer carry this burden, and proposed to pull out. In desperation Greece and Turkey turned to the United States for financial and military assistance. On 12 March, President Truman sent a message to Congress embodying not only a request for appropriations for Greece and Turkey, but what came to be known as the Truman Doctrine. ' One of the primary objectives of the foreign policy of the United States,' he said,

is the creation of conditions in which we and other nations will be able to work out a way of life free from coercion. We shall not realize our objectives unless we are willing to help free peoples to maintain their free institutions, and their national integrity against aggressive movements that seek to impose on them totalitarian regimes. . . . I believe that it must be the policy of the United States to support free peoples who are resisting attempted subjugation by armed minorities or by outside pressures.

It was to be noted — and Russia did note — that while this doctrine affected immediately only Greece and Turkey, it was potentially world-wide in its application.

Congress voted the money — eventually close to $700 million — and American power moved into the vacuum created by Britain in the Near East. After prolonged fighting the Greek guerrillas were beaten, Greek government and economy were reformed, Turkish defenses were strengthened, and Russia withdrew from Iran. Palestine achieved her independence, and Truman hastened to extend recognition to the new state of Israel. Italy swung to the moderate de Gasperi government, and the situation in the Mediterranean was stabilized.

With the Truman Doctrine and Marshall aid the United States took the offensive. What came to be regarded as official American policy was shortly stated by George Kennan of the State Department in an ' inspired ' article in *Foreign Affairs,* which announced that

the main element of any United States policy toward the Soviet Union must be that of a long-term patient but firm and vigilant containment of Russian expansive tendencies. . . . The United States has it in its power to increase enormously the strains under which the Soviet policy must operate, to force upon the Kremlin a far greater degree of moderation and circumspection than it has had to observe in recent years, and in this way to promote tendencies which must eventually find their outlet in either the breakup or the gradual mellowing of Soviet policy.[11]

The next few years were to reveal that this represented, to some extent, wishful thinking: there was no ' mellowing ' of Soviet policy. All through 1947 relations between the East and the West became increasingly exacerbated. Early in 1948 a complete deadlock developed; when the Western powers decided to go ahead and establish a West German government, the Soviet representative on the Control Council charged that the four-power machinery had broken down and that the council no longer existed. A crisis came in the summer of 1948 when Russia countered Western plans for the rehabilitation of western Germany with a blockade of Berlin. Through some inexplicable oversight the Allied Control Council had not guaranteed the Western Allies access to their zones of Berlin, and as a result the Russians were able to cut all land communication by the simple device of erecting road blocks and stopping railroad trains. Confronted with the alternatives of mass starvation for the 2 million Germans of the western zones of Berlin or an ignominious evacuation of that city, the American Commander, General Lucius Clay, rejected both. ' We have lost Czechoslovakia,' he said,

Norway is threatened. We retreat from Berlin. When Berlin falls, western Germany will be next. If we mean to hold Europe against Communism we must not budge. . . . If we withdraw, our position in Europe is threatened. If America does not understand this now . . . then it never will, and communism will run rampant. I believe the future of democracy requires us to stay.

The American and British governments accepted this advice, and embarked upon an ' airlift ' operation to supply the beleaguered capital not only with food but with coal and other necessities. To the consternation of the Russians the airlift was a spectacular success: by the spring of 1949 American and British planes were flying in up to 10,000 tons of supplies daily; altogether the British and Americans flew 2.5 million tons of supplies into the beleaguered city. Confronted by the implacable determination of the West to supply Berlin indefinitely by this method — a method that incidentally provided ad-

11 *Foreign Affairs*, July 1947.

mirable training for pilots and a dramatic display of power for continental Europe — Russia ended the blockade and negotiated the minor differences that had inspired it. It was a moral victory for the West, but there was no assurance that Russia might not reimpose the blockade at any time.

It was against this background of crisis and conflict that the Truman administration embarked upon ambitious plans for the economic and military rehabilitation of Europe and, eventually, of free nations throughout the globe. The Marshall Plan was the first step. No sooner was it launched than Truman began negotiations for a military alliance that would weld western Europe into unified force. The Brussels Pact of 1948, joining Britain, France, Belgium, and the Netherlands in a defensive alliance provided the springboard. That June the Senate adopted Arthur Vandenberg's resolution pledging American support to collective security arrangements between the free nations of the West, and President Truman promptly opened negotiations to implement this resolution. The result was the North Atlantic Treaty of 4 April 1949 which brought together the United States and Canada and ten nations of western Europe in an alliance against aggression; eventually it embraced several Mediterranean nations as well. The treaty pledged that an armed attack against any one member would be considered an attack upon them all.

The North Atlantic Treaty Organization (NATO) brought together about 350 million people, occupying the most highly industrialized areas of Europe and North America and possessing the most advanced technological and scientific skills, in an alliance to protect the West against Communist aggression. Never before had the United States gone so far in a practical surrender of part of its sovereign power, or so clearly recognized that its frontier henceforth lay overseas along the lines that divided free nations from the Soviet Union. The overwhelming public support for the pact was measured by the alacrity with which the Senate ratified it, by a vote of 82 to 13. The administration then proposed a military assistance program, giving NATO authority to spend over a billion dollars on arms and other military needs, and giving further aid to Greece and Turkey — soon to join the organization — and Iran, still threatened by Russian encroachment.

The next year saw NATO make a real beginning in armed power. The first American shipments of arms reached Europe in April;

Great Britain and France both undertook to rearm; and General Eisenhower was persuaded to resign the presidency of Columbia University and become Supreme Commander of NATO forces. Within a few years Germany, now on her own, was admitted to NATO and her armed forces integrated into the NATO army. Not surprisingly, Russia looked upon the creation of NATO as an open declaration of hostility, and upon the rearming of Germany and her admission to the new international organization as an act of defiance.

7. THE KOREAN WAR

While Americans were preoccupied with the problems of European recovery, the control of the atomic bomb, and the organization of NATO, the Far East burst into flames.

The fate of Korea had not been settled at the close of the war, and the division of the country into Communist North and non-Communist (it would be an exaggeration to say democratic) South along the illogical 38th parallel persisted. The Communists regarded South Korea as a threat and an affront — just as the Russian Communists regarded Czechoslovakia as a threat — and when they failed to destroy it by subversion, they resorted to force. On 25 June 1950 North Korean troops launched a full-scale attack upon the South, and within three days they had captured the capital at Seoul, and threatened to overrun the entire country. It was a challenge as critical as that of the Berlin blockade, for had it succeeded it would have marked the beginning of a campaign to conquer or subvert the whole of eastern Asia, and possibly the Philippines and Japan as well.

Stalin and the Chinese leader Mao Tse-tung probably believed that the United States would not and that the United Nations could not intervene. The United States was, after all, 7000 miles distant; her nearest troops were in Japan; and a war in Asia would seriously weaken her just at a time when she was trying to build up her strength in Europe. What is more, Secretary Acheson had omitted South Korea from his ' defense perimeter ' in the Pacific,[12] and Gen-

[12] Outlining the 'defense perimeter,' Acheson added that 'so far as the military security of other areas in the Pacific is concerned, it must be clear that no person can guarantee these areas against military attack.' But two months later he seriously modified this statement: ' The Chinese people should understand that . . . they can only bring grave trouble on themselves and their friends, if they are led by their new rulers into aggressive or subversive adventures beyond their borders. . . . I say this so that

eral MacArthur had said that 'anyone who commits the American army on the mainland of Asia ought to have his head examined.'

Once again, as at the time of the threat to Berlin, President Truman reacted decisively. On 27 June he announced that he was sending American air and naval forces to the aid of the South Koreans. That same day the United Nations Security Council — with Russia momentarily absent on a boycott — called on member nations to repel aggression in Korea. Truman ordered American troops to the battlefront, and within a few days a dozen other members of the United Nations responded to the appeal and in time sent contingents to the front. When the Security Council asked Truman to create a unified command, he appointed General MacArthur commander in chief of the United Nations forces, and before long the UN banner waved over a motley world army — the first of its kind in history.

For nearly six weeks North Korean armies advanced down the peninsula driving the smaller South Korean and American forces before them. Fighting desperately, the outnumbered defenders retreated over jagged mountains, across tangled ravines, and through malodorous rice paddies to the southernmost tip of Korea. There they held firm while re-enforcements poured into the port of Pusan from Japan and the United States, and MacArthur built up naval and air support to a counteroffensive. Then, in mid-September, while American and British fliers destroyed supply depots behind the enemy lines and warships poured shells into coastal areas, the United Nations armies came out of their defenses and moved forward on Seoul. Blasted from all sides the North Korean lines collapsed and the stricken armies retreated to the north. On 26 September Seoul was once more in South Korean hands, and the United Nations armies were pounding on the North Korean border.

The United States had gone to war when North Koreans crossed the 38th parallel; would China go to war when South Koreans — and Americans — crossed it going the other direction? Washington hesitated, and so, too, did the United Nations, but not MacArthur. Convinced that the only way to end the war was to conquer North Korea, he drove ahead and on 20 October captured the North Korean capital

---

there may be no mistake about the attitude of the United States, no opportunity to distort or twist it, and so that all in China may know who would be responsible for all that such adventures might bring to pass.' McG. Bundy, ed., *The Pattern of Responsibility*, pp. 189, 200.

of Pyongyang. By the end of the month he was approaching the Manchurian border, while the battleship *Missouri* bombarded Chongjin, only 50 miles from Siberia. Belatedly both the United Nations and the State Department agreed on the invasion, but tried to limit it to a kind of defensive-offensive so that the Chinese would not be tempted to enter the conflict. So concerned was President Truman with the threat of Chinese intervention that in mid-October he flew to Wake Island for a conference with the victorious MacArthur. The General assured him that the war was already won; that the Chinese would not attack; and that if they did they would meet defeat. He was wrong on all three counts.

Even as the President and the General conferred, the Chinese were getting ready to intervene, and within a week of MacArthur's return a vast Chinese army of three-quarters of a million was massing for an attack. MacArthur wanted to seize the initiative by destroying bridges across the Yalu river which was the boundary between China and North Korea, and by bombing Chinese supply depots behind the lines, but neither the President nor the Chiefs of Staff were prepared to risk broadening a local war into a world war in this fashion, and his proposals were rejected.

Notwithstanding evidence of the massive Chinese build-up, MacArthur confidently launched a new offensive at the end of November, boasting that it would all be over by Christmas. Within a few days, however, the attackers were being attacked — and engulfed. An army of almost a quarter-million Chinese, provided with the best arms and equipment and supported by ample air power, poured across the Yalu river, smashed the United Nations lines, and sent MacArthur's armies reeling back across the 38th parallel in what threatened to turn into a disaster.

It did not. The new United Nations commander, General Matthew B. Ridgway fell back slowly to below Seoul, exacting a terrible price for every yard; then he halted, regrouped his lines, and waited for air support. That winter of 1951 saw some of the cruelest warfare in American history. The fierce cold and blinding storms, the rugged terrain of jagged mountains, treacherous swamps and unbridged streams, the ferocity of the enemy giving no quarter, the power of Russian tanks and planes, the desperate nature of many of the battles, the inhuman treatment of prisoners — all this added a new dimension to terror.

THE KOREAN WAR, 1950-53

MANCHURIA

U.S.S.R.

Changpai Shan 9003   Musan   Najin

Mukden   ✗ Fushun   Tunghua   Linchiang   Chongjin

Penki   Manpo   Hyesan

Liaoyang   Anshan   Kanggye   Farthest U.N. advance, Nov.'50

Chinhsien   Yinkow   Reservoir   Songjin

LIAOTUNG   Chinese con centration Nov.'50   Changjin   Battle of the Reservoir, Nov-Dec.'30

Antung   Sinui   Hamhun

Hungnam   Evacuation Dec.'30

Anju

Nov.'50   Wonsan   U.N. landing Oct. 26 '30

Dairen   Russian-Chinese Naval Area   Pyongyang

Port Arthur   Sariwon   The Iron Triangle   Kosong

YELLOW   Kumhwa   Truce line June '31

SEA   Chorwon

Ongjin   Panmunjom   Chunchon   Chinese advance Jan.'51

Chefoo   Samchok

SHANTUNG (Japan)   Inchon   Seoul   Wonju

Armistice July 27.'53

Landing July 5,'30
Lost June 28'50
Regained Sep.29'50
Lost Jan.4 '51
Regained March 14'51

Perimeter Sep.15,'30

EAST   Taejon   Andong

Kunsan   Taegu

CHINA   Main U.N. Base

Mokpo   Kwangju   Pusan

Yosu

SEA   Tsushima (Japan)

CHEJU   JAPAN

U.N. Base

126° (Quelpart)   Sasebo

0   100
Miles

122°   124°   128°   Raisz   130°

Next spring Ridgway was ready to launch a counterattack, which carried him back into Seoul, and by mid-April he was once more across the 38th parallel. For two months the fighting seesawed desperately back and forth, then dragged to a halt. On 25 June 1951, the first anniversary of the war, the Communists held 2100 fewer square miles than when they began their attack.

When the Chinese threw their fresh divisions into the war, General MacArthur wanted to counter by launching full-scale operations against them. He proposed not only bombing supply depots and lines of communication in Manchuria, but a blockade of the Chinese coast, air attacks on the densely populated industrial cities of the Chinese mainland, and an invasion of China by the well-trained but untested armies of Chiang Kai-shek. Clearly all this spelled not only a major war with China but — as Russia was bound to China by the closest of ties — the beginning of World War III. There is no substitute for victory, said MacArthur, but General Omar Bradley, the Chief of Staff, replied that this would be the wrong war, at the wrong time, in the wrong place, with the wrong enemy. President Truman firmly rejected MacArthur's policy of extending the war and announced that ' our goal is not war but peace.'

Unhappily MacArthur was unwilling to accept the policy laid down by the President and the Chiefs of Staff. When March 1951 brought a turn in the tide of war Truman prepared a statement that with South Korea again cleared of the enemy, the time had come to make peace. Before he released this statement General MacArthur issued a declaration that Red China had been defeated, and that the time had come to deliver a knock-out blow against her. Shocked by this attempt to usurp civilian power of negotiation and diplomacy, Truman ordered MacArthur to refrain from further public statements; MacArthur countered with a letter to Republican minority leader Joseph Martin criticizing the presidential policy and reiterating his conviction that ' there is no substitute for victory.' It was the boldest challenge to civilian authority since McClellan had tried to take direction of the war out of Lincoln's hands; and it was equally intolerable, and even more dangerous, for what was at stake this time was not merely American peace but world peace. After consulting with Secretary Marshall and General Bradley, Truman dramatically dismissed General MacArthur from command.

The General came home to receive tumultuous ovations, address both houses of Congress, and defend his position in elaborate hearings conducted by the Congress and in speeches throughout the country. In all of these he made clear that he was indifferent to the fate of Europe, thought the United States could get along without European allies, and felt that the future destiny of America lay in the Pacific and Asiatic theaters.

Nor did MacArthur speak for himself alone. As Walt Rostow says:

Beyond the recently remembered clashes of policy and personality, MacArthur symbolized that part of American history which, since the early days of the China trade, had looked out over the Pacific to Asia as a region where the American nation could express its enterprise — missionary, commercial, and military — relatively untrammeled with ties to old Europe.[13]

Ever since Seward's 'large' policy in the Pacific and McKinley's 'open door' policy in China, the Republican party had been deeply committed to intervention in Pacific affairs; the isolationism upon which it embarked in 1919 did not embrace Asia, and indeed the very consciousness of isolationism toward Europe tended to exaggerate the vigor of interventionism in the Far East. MacArthur's position was endorsed by the two most powerful figures in the Republican party: Herbert Hoover and Robert A. Taft. Even as the General was trying to impose his program upon the President, Hoover urged that the United States withdraw its forces from Europe, and become a 'Western Hemisphere Gibraltar,' and Taft supported Senator McCarthy's wild attacks upon Secretary Acheson and the State Department for 'losing' China. The presidential election was just a year away: would the Hoover-Taft wing dominate the Republican convention, name the candidate — perhaps MacArthur himself? — and capture the government?

The Korean conflict was deadlocked, and when in June 1951 the Soviet delegate to the United Nations suggested that it was time for an armistice with mutual withdrawal behind the 38th parallel, Washington welcomed the proposal. Early the next month the leaders of the opposing forces began discussions looking to an armistice; these dragged on interminably over two issues: the exact boundary line between North and South, and the fate of prisoners. The first was settled by accepting the current status quo, which meant the United Nations forces would be a bit north of the famous parallel; the sec-

[13] *The United States in the World Arena*, p. 240.

ond proved more vexatious. The United Nations held some 132,000 prisoners; the Chinese admitted to only 11,502, of which 3198 were Americans; either the Chinese lists were incomplete, or they had killed most of their prisoners. Now the Communists insisted on mutual repatriation of all prisoners. But most of the North Koreans and Chinese did not want to be repatriated. The armistice negotiators were at an impasse when the timely 'escape' of some 20,000 North Koreans from their prisons, the election of Eisenhower to the presidency, and the death of Stalin, brought about a change of atmosphere. In a more conciliatory mood the Communists accepted a plan of voluntary repatriation, and on 27 June 1953 a truce put an end to the three-year war.

The war had cost the United States some 54,000 dead, over 100,000 wounded, and over 10,000 missing. South Korean casualties were well over a million, and North Korean and Chinese were estimated at a million and a half. Thus this wanton and futile war had cost 3 million casualties. Korea itself lay in ruins, North and South alike; it was to be another decade before South Korea would achieve some kind of recovery, and a stable government, while the chains that bound North Korea to China were tightened. In return for all this South Korea was saved from Communism; the Communist timetable was deranged; and the prestige of the United Nations was enhanced.

BIBLIOGRAPHY

1. GENERAL. Raymond Aron, *The Century of Total War;* Raymond Danson, *The Decision To Help Russia;* Jules Davids, *America and the World in Our Time;* W. Phillips Davison, *The Berlin Blockade;* Donald M. Dozer, *Are We Good Neighbors?;* Herbert Feis, *The China Tangle from Pearl Harbor to the Marshall Mission;* Henry Kissinger, *Nuclear Weapons and Foreign Policy;* Gunther Moltmann, *Amerikas Deutschland Politik im Zweiten Weltkrieg;* Jeannette Muther, *A History of the United Nations Charter: The Role of the U.S.;* Walt W. Rostow, *The United States in the World Arena;* Richard P. Stebbins, *The United States in World Affairs* (annual volumes) ; Harry S. Truman, *Memoirs,* vol. 2; Allen S. Whiting, *China Crosses the Yalu.*

2. LIQUIDATING THE WAR. Ruth Benedict, *The Chrysanthemum and the Sword;* V. H. Bernstein, *Final Judgment: The Story of Nuremberg;* Robert Butow, *Japan's Decision To Surrender;* James F. Byrnes, *Speaking Frankly;* Lucius Clay, *Decision in Germany;* W. Phillips Davison, *The Berlin Blockade;* W. Friedman, *Allied Military Government of Germany;* Sheldon Glueck, *The Nuremberg Trials and Aggressive War;* Robert Jackson, *The Case Against the Nazi War Criminals;* William L. Neumann, *Making the Peace, 1941–1945;* Saul K. Padover,

Experiment in Germany; A. Frank Reel, *The Case of General Yamashita;* Theodore White, *Fire in the Ashes;* Robert Woetzel, *Nuremberg Trials in International Law;* Harold Zink, *American Military Government in Germany.*

3. ORGANIZATION FOR PEACE AND THE CONTROL OF ATOMIC WEAPONS. Percy Bidwell, *The United States and the United Nations;* P. M. Blackett, *Fear, War and the Bomb;* David Bradley, *No Place to Hide;* Bernard Brodie, *The Absolute Weapon;* Floyd A. Cave, *et al., Origins and Consequences of World War II;* E. S. Corwin, *The Constitution and World Organization;* Norman Cousins, *Modern Man Is Obsolete;* Vera M. Dean, *The Four Cornerstones of Peace;* Herman Finer, *The U.N. Social and Economic Council;* Herman Kahn, *On Thermonuclear War;* Henry Kissinger, *Nuclear War and Foreign Policy;* P. McGuire, *Experiment in World Order;* Jeannette Muther, *History of the United Nations Charter.*

4. RELIEF AND RECOVERY. T. Besterman, *UNESCO;* Blair Bolles, *Big Change in Europe;* W. A. Brown, *American Foreign Assistance;* Merle Curti & Kendall Birr, *Prelude to Point Four: American Missions Overseas;* Seymour Harris, *European Recovery Program* and *Foreign Economic Policy for the United States;* Eugene Kulischer, *Europe on the Move;* George Woodbridge (ed.), *UNRRA* (2 vols.).

5. THE COLD WAR. E. H. Carr, *Soviet Impact on the Western World;* W. Phillips Davison, *The Berlin Blockade;* J. R. Deane, *The Strange Alliance;* Herbert Feis, *Potsdam;* D. L. Fleming, *The Cold War* (2 vols.); Norman Graebner, *The New Isolationism;* B. H. Ivanyi & A. Bell, *The Road to Potsdam;* Ernest Lefever, *Ethics and United States Foreign Policy;* Walter Lippmann, *The Cold War;* John Lukacs, *A History of the Cold War;* Drew Middleton, *The Defense of Western Europe;* Henry L. Roberts, *Russia and America;* Robert Sherwood, *Roosevelt and Hopkins;* Walter B. Smith, *My Three Years in Moscow;* John L. Snell (ed.), *The Meaning of Yalta;* Edward Stettinius, *Roosevelt and the Russians.*

6. THE KOREAN WAR. Mark Clark, *From the Danube to the Yalu;* Herbert Feis, *The China Tangle;* Leland M. Goodrich, *Korea: A Study in U.S. Policy;* R. T. Oliver, *Why War Came to Korea;* Richard Rovere & A. M. Schlesinger, Jr., *The General and the President;* John Spanier, *The Truman-MacArthur Controversy;* Harry Truman, *Memoirs,* vol. 2; Allen Whiting, *China Crosses the Yalu;* Courtney Whitney, *MacArthur;* C. A. Willoughby & J. Chamberlain, *MacArthur, 1944–1951.*

7. DOCUMENTS. Ruhl Bartlett (ed.), *Record of American Diplomacy,* 1954; Z. Chafee (ed.), *Documents on Fundamental Human Rights;* H. S. Commager, *Documents,* nos. 557–58, 562–66, 571–75, 577, 583, 586–93, 596, 599–602.

For further references, *Harvard Guide,* ¶¶ 272–73.

Society and Culture in the Postwar Years

1. GROWTH

'THE time will come,' wrote Tocqueville in 1835, ' when 130 millions of men will be living in North America, equal in condition, the progeny of one race, owing their origin to the same cause, and preserving the same civilization, the same language, the same religion, the same habits, the same manners, imbued with the same opinions propagated under the same forms. The rest is uncertain, but this is certain.' A century after Tocqueville, demographers anxiously scanning the birth rate predicted that the population of the United States might reach 150 millon by the 1960's, and thereafter barely hold its own. For reasons not wholly clear, but connected with the war and the vast upswing of prosperity, the total population reached 150 million by 1950, and then jumped to 180 million ten years later. This astonishing increase resulted largely from higher birth and lower death rates. The birth rate which had been only 16 per thousand in 1935 reached 25 per thousand twenty years later, and held fairly steady; at the same time the death rate fell from 12 to 9 per thousand. Even during the war early marriages and larger families began to make up for the sharp falling off of immigration; and the boom in babies showed no sign of slowing up after the war. It had taken 250 years for the population of the United States to reach 29 million; the single decade of the 'fifties added about that number. Gratification over the disclosures of the census of 1960 was tempered by the prospect of a population of 300 million by the year A.D. 2000. All this was part of a world-wide ' population explosion,' but no European country, except possibly Portugal, increased as did the United States.

With this growth in population came a shift in racial and national composition that approached Tocqueville's prediction of 'one race . . . the same language.' Europe generally failed to fill the immigration quotas set by earlier restrictive legislation. More than three million immigrants were admitted to the United States in the fifteen years after the end of the war, about half of them from the countries of the Western Hemisphere. By 1960, 95 per cent of the American population was native-born, and the overwhelming majority of Americans belonged to families who had lived in this country at least two generations. There was a sharp increase in the numbers coming from Puerto Rico — which was part of the United States — and from Mexico. There were now more Puerto Ricans in New York City than in San Juan and more Mexicans in Los Angeles than in any Mexican city except the capital. As most of these newcomers were poor, and many uneducated and unaccustomed to the ways of urban life, their presence gave grave concern to those who were faced with the responsibility of city government and of education; but objective opinion held that these newcomers did not differ in quality from the poor European immigrants who had earlier sought homes in America. The increase in the Negro population kept pace with the white, but the 19 million Negroes of 1960 were no longer concentrated in the South; New York boasted the largest Negro population of any state in the Union, and sufficient numbers of Negroes had moved to Philadelphia, Detroit, Chicago, and other large cities of the North to hold the balance of power in presidential elections.[1]

The most marked shifts in the population were from the Northeast to the South and West, and from country and small town to city. During the 'fifties the population of New England increased only 12 per cent, and that of the South Central states only 5 per cent, while some of the plains states barely held their own; but the population of California increased 50 per cent, and Florida, which in 1920 had not one million inhabitants, passed the five million mark and became one of the ten largest states of the Union. By 1960 the statistical center of population had moved to the edge of the Mississippi river, and it was clear that in another decade California would pass New York and become the first state in the Union.

Even more spectacular was the flight from farm and village to the cities and their burgeoning suburbs. By 1960 some 70 per cent of

[1] The largest Negro cities in the country in 1960 were: New York City, 1,087,931; Chicago, 812,637; Philadelphia, 529,240; Detroit, 482,223; Washington, 411,737.

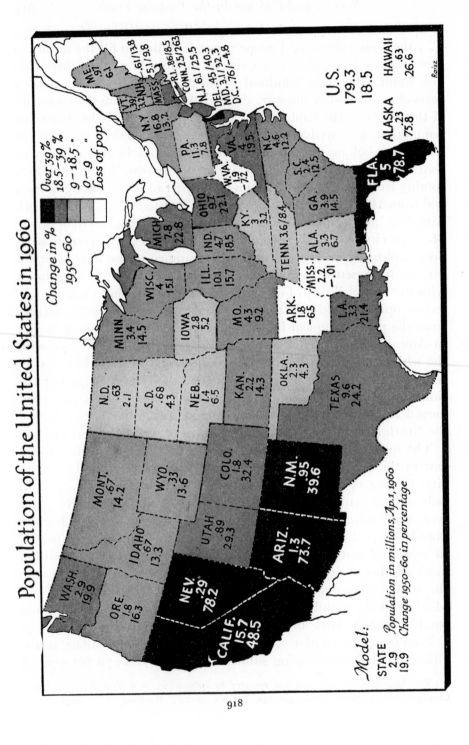

Population of the United States in 1960

Change in %
1950-60

Over 39 %
18.5-39 %
9 - 18.5 "
0 - 9 "
Loss of pop.

U.S.
179.3
18.5

HAWAII
.63
26.6

ALASKA
.23
75.8

FLA.
5
78.7

N.J. 6.1/25.5
DEL. 45/40.3
MD. 3.1/32.3
D.C. .76/-4.8

CONN. 2.5/26.3
R.I. .86/8.5
MASS. 5.1/9.8
N.H. .61/13.8
VT. .39/3.2
ME. .97 6.1

N.Y.
16.8
13.2

PA.
11.3
7.8

W.VA.
1.9
-7.2

VA.
4
19.5

N.C.
4.6
12.2

S.C.
2.4
12.5

GA.
3.9
14.5

ALA.
3.3
6.7

MISS.
2.2
-.01

TENN. 3.6/8.4

KY.
3
3.2

OHIO
9.7
22.1

IND.
4.7
18.5

ILL.
10.1
15.7

MICH.
7.8
22.8

WIS.
4
15.1

MINN.
3.4
14.5

IOWA
2.8
5.2

MO.
4.3
9.2

ARK.
1.8
-6.5

LA.
3.3
21.4

N.D.
.63
2.1

S.D.
.68
4.3

NEB.
1.4
6.5

KAN.
2.2
14.3

OKLA.
2.3
4.3

TEXAS
9.6
24.2

MONT.
.67
14.2

WYO.
.33
13.6

COLO.
1.8
32.4

N.M.
.95
39.6

IDAHO
.67
13.3

UTAH
.89
29.3

ARIZ.
1.3
73.7

WASH.
2.9
19.9

ORE.
1.8
16.3

NEV.
.29
78.2

CALIF.
15.7
48.5

Model:

STATE
2.9   Population in millions, Ap.1, 1960
19.9   Change 1950-60 in percentage

Rásiz

the population lived in metropolitan areas, and the United States was as unmistakably urban as Britain or Germany. While some of the major cities actually declined in population, their ragged metropolitan areas spread and grew uncontrollably. The New York metropolitan area, which sprawled across three states, passed the 14 million mark; Los Angeles reached almost 7 million; Chicago over 6 million, and Philadelphia 4. By 1960 the ten largest metropolitan areas — if we include the Washington-Baltimore complex among them — embraced 50 million people.

There was also political growth. After the admission of New Mexico and Arizona to statehood in 1912, it was assumed that the Union had crystalized permanently into forty-eight States. World War II and the Cold War proved the strategic and economic importance of Hawaii and Alaska. Both territories had long agitated for statehood. Alaska, with almost 600,000 square miles but only 225,000 people had the size; Hawaii with over 600,000 inhabitants but only 6400 square miles, the population. Because neither of them was contiguous with the American mainland, and both vindicated their claims by appeal to strategic considerations, their applications were coupled; both were admitted in 1959.[2] Unless Puerto Rico evolves from its preferred commonwealth status and demands statehood, and unless (as is extremely unlikely) other Caribbean islands demand annexation, it would seem that the United States has reached its maximum territorial limits.

2. THE DECLINE OF THE CITY

The census of 1960 revealed what had long been foreseen — the erosion of the great cities: eight of the ten largest cities actually declined in population between 1950 and 1960. As population fled to the suburbs, newcomers from the cotton fields of Mississippi, the mountains of West Virginia, and the teeming villages of Puerto Rico poured in to fill the void partially. Business and industry followed population to outlying areas, thus depriving the central cities of essential services and financial support; residential districts declined

[2] Neither the political fears of those who had opposed nor the hopes of those who had favored their admission were fulfilled. The two new states proved their normalcy by dividing precisely down the middle in the election of 1960. Alaska went Republican by 1200 votes, Hawaii went Democratic by 115 votes!

into slums, thus cutting off tax support. Yet city demands for schools, law enforcement, roads, sanitation, and welfare services loomed much larger than in the prewar years. Thus a vicious circle was set up where declining revenues led to poorer schools and lax law enforcement and these, by driving business and the middle classes to the suburbs, brought a still further decline in revenues.

The basic reason for the blight that descended on American cities in these postwar years was the absence of an urban tradition and the want of a patriciate, or burgher, class such as had flourished in the Old World and for centuries had preserved the beauty and civic vigor of Florence, Frankfurt, Bordeaux, Bruges. There had been something similar in colonial and federal Charleston, Philadelphia, Boston, and Salem, but descendants of the old city patricians had given up the struggle and moved out to suburbs, and there were few left who cared to devote themselves to the almost hopeless struggle to preserve the beauties and amenities of the old cities and resist the ravages of industrialism, and of the automobile. The automobile not only made it possible to live in the suburbs, or far out in the country, and do business in the city, but also, by creating insoluble traffic problems, ruining public transportation, making insatiable demands for space for highways and parking lots (two-thirds of central Los Angeles has been given over to streets, freeways, parking lots, and garages) and filling the air with noxious fumes, made it disagreeable to live in the central city. As prosperous families moved to the suburbs, middle-class residential areas declined into slums, with concomitants of crime and juvenile delinquency. Unregulated building of skyscrapers — laissez faire carried to the verge of anarchy — aggravated already desperate problems of transportation and housing. Antiquated government, such as the palpable paradox of dividing the administration of metropolitan areas among a score or a hundred independent jurisdictions, made it all but impossible to solve the most elementary problems of politics and administration. Appeals for help to state legislatures, most of which are dominated by representatives from rural areas, for the most part have been in vain.

A few cities, such as Boston, St. Louis, Rochester, Pittsburgh, have been partially successful in arresting the erosion that was eating them away, but for the most part the efforts of cities to stop decay were like those of Alice in her race with the Red Queen: they found that they had to run twice as fast if they expected to get anywhere. The chief difficulty was financial. Increasingly the cities turned to the Federal Government for financial assistance in slum clearance, new housing, and urban renewal, but the sums forthcoming were insufficient. A recognition of the desperate nature of the urban crisis persuaded President Kennedy, early in 1962, to recommend the creation of a new Department of Urban Affairs.

The movement to the suburbs began well before the war, but after 1945 it became something like a mass migration. Driven by the urge for space and privacy, better schools and recreation facilities, and by the desire for status as well, by 1960 some 40 or 50 million Americans had found refuge in suburbia or, as the fringes came to be called, ' exurbia.' Uniformity characterized the suburbs from Portland, Maine, to Portland, Oregon. They displayed the same ' ranch houses ' on single or split levels, with picture windows, television antennae, and a two-car garage; the same well-manicured back gardens with little swimming pools; the same country clubs and shopping centers and supermarkets, all built to a pattern. Almost all the men commuted to nearby cities, society was matriarchal, and the well-protected young gravitated from the local high or country-day school to the state university or the Ivy League college of the East. For many Americans suburbia represented a new way of life — one that contrasted sharply with the older habits of the countryside or the city. As Max Lerner observed:

The suburbanites found new roots for their lives in a new sense of neighborhood which was closer than anything in previous American experience except college dormitories or fraternities or the communal settlements of the early nineteenth century. . . . Not only did the doors within houses tend to disappear, but the outside doors ceased to have much function. . . . Newcomers were expected to be ' outgoing ' and to ' join the gang '; introversion was frowned upon, and the society of ex-introverts was like the society of ex-sinners. There was intensive ' joining ' in club work and community participation, including greatly increased church membership. . . . Instead of ' conspicuous consumption ' the rule became ' inconspicuous consumption ' so that no one would embarrass anyone else. There were car pools for shuttling children to school and back; there was an almost communal use of bicycles, books, and baby toys; there was an enforced intimacy so that everyone's life was known to everyone, and no one had to face his problems alone.[3]

[3] Max Lerner, *America as a Civilization,* p. 178.

Suburbia even developed a literature. Novelists like John Marquand and Sloan Wilson and poets like Phyllis McGinley described suburban life as a Dreiser or a Sandburg had described the city, a Sinclair Lewis or an Edgar Lee Masters the village, a generation earlier, but more sympathetically; and a new school of sociologists — William Whyte and Vance Packard and others — found in the suburbs the materials for drawing a portrait of the 'organization man' and the Status Seekers of the new day.

But, as the city itself declined, the country became citified, and the old rural patterns and stereotypes, which had loomed so large in American economy, politics, and literature, almost disappeared. No parts of the country were so remote as to be denied the advantages of good roads and electricity; if they were, they became abandoned by their impatient inhabitants. Electricity brought efficiency, convenience, leisure, and recreation into every farmhouse, while the automobile and paved roads ended isolation. For generations farmers had clamored for the establishment of agricultural colleges and taken pride in sending their children to these institutions; now these schools dropped the word 'agricultural' from their names, and the students turned to everything except tilling the soil. The romantic or sentimental images drawn from Whittier's poems, Currier and Ives prints, and a century of political oratory faded out, as did the counter-images of the city slicker and Wall Street.

3. THE ECONOMY

The economy, too, was growing and expanding. From 1945 to 1960 the gross national product increased from $213 billion to $500 billion — a figure which has to be qualified by an inflation of at least 25 per cent. Other economic statistics were almost equally impressive: an upsurge in electrical energy in the twenty years after 1940 from 150 to 800 trillion kilowatt hours, and a 100 per cent increase in the production of natural gas and petroleum, and an increase in the labor force to 70 million. More than twice as many automobiles and trucks crowded the roads in 1960 as in 1940, and 180 million Americans owned no fewer than 200 million radio and television sets, more than all the rest of the world combined.

To business, at least, these statistics were gratifying, but not surprising; after all the American economy had been growing for a long time. If growth continued, so did concentration. Big business grew steadily bigger, the giant corporation came to be more and more gigantic, and notwithstanding the most zealous efforts of the anti-trust division of the Department of Justice, mergers and combinations spread into almost every field of the economy. The ten years after 1948 saw no fewer than 2191 mergers and combinations of corporations worth over $10 million. Between 1940 and 1960 bank deposits increased fourfold, but the number of banks declined by over one thousand and branch banking came to be almost as common in the United States as in Great Britain. Three great corporations — General Motors, Ford, and Chrysler — dominated the automobile industry, though in the 'fifties a fourth, American Motors, entered the competition. Three networks all but monopolized the air; six tobacco companies fed the insatiable appetite of Americans for cigarettes; ailing railroads — even giants like the Pennsylvania and the New York Central — tried to avoid bankruptcy by mergers; half a dozen giant grocery chains all but put the independent grocer and butcher out of business. Even in the realm of news the process seemed inexorable. In 1910 almost 700 cities and towns in the United States had competing daily newspapers; by 1954 the number had fallen to 87, and 18 states were without any locally competing newspapers. In many cities the same individual or company owned not only the newspaper but the radio and television station as well, thus monopolizing local and state news. Americans still yearned for the day of small business, and both major parties made dramatic gestures toward aiding the independent businessman, such as the Fair Trade laws in 45 states and the McGuire Act of 1952, but these gestures have proved to be almost entirely futile.

Along with concentration went major shifts in economic activities. As fewer and fewer farmers and workers produced the food and goods that were needed by an affluent society, the service industries swiftly became central to the economy. The census of 1960 revealed some 35 million workers in service, sales, professional, and managerial jobs — what had once been called ' white collar ' — and fewer than 32 million working on the farms or in factories, shops, and mines. There were far-reaching changes in the older industries, too. As the automobile, the bus, the truck, and the airplane took over much of the passenger and freight service, railroads, which had long dominated the economy of the nation, fell into desperate straits. Between 1940 and 1960 total railroad mileage actually declined by 17,000, and many parts of the nation which had been well served by railroads in 1890 found themselves isolated in 1960. The railroad companies, which had once fought federal intervention, now appealed, almost desperately, for federal aid; the Federal Government, which had once fought combinations as ' conspiracies in restraint of trade,' now encouraged mergers. In the meantime, partly in response to military usefulness, air service expanded rapidly; every city had an airport and some needed two or three to handle the traffic that filled the skies. Transatlantic air freight even threatened transatlantic shipping, and great monarchs of the sea that had excited the imaginations of an earlier generation, like the *Queen Mary* or the *Ile de France,* were destined to be scrapped for anonymous jet planes.

Automation increased apace and brought more problems than it solved. This was not just a continuation of that speeding-up process introduced by the industrial revolution, but something new, for it tended to supplant not only the operative but the boss as well — to provide thinking and judgment as well as labor. Walter Reuther has described its workings in one of the Ford plants:

I went to work in the automotive industry back in 1927. At that time, it took us about twenty-four hours to take a rough engine block, as it was cast in the foundry, and to machine that block, ready for assembly. . . . We kept making progress. We cut it down to 18 hours, and then 14 hours, then 12, then 9 hours. If you'll go through the Cleveland Ford engine plant, which is fully automated, you will see a Ford V-engine, 8 cylinders — a very complicated piece of mechanism — in which the rough castings are automatically fed into this automated line, and in fourteen and six-tenths minutes later, it is fully machined, without a human hand touching it. . . . There are acres and acres of machines, and here and there you will find a worker standing at a master switchboard, just watching green and yellow lights blinking off and on, which tell the worker what is happening in the machine.[4]

Automation presented labor with the prospect of falling employment — and industry with the prospect of declining purchasing power among workers; it made inevitable the shorter working day, week, and year; it gave rise to an urgent demand for the annual wage; it created a massive problem of leisure. Oddly enough, though

4 Walter P. Reuther, *Selected Papers,* Henry M. Christman (ed.), pp. 178, 180.

it cut down drastically on labor costs, it did not seem to produce cheaper products, and industries which relied heavily on automation led the way to higher rather than lower prices. At a time when the numbers of young and old were growing at the expense of the numbers in between, it denied employment to the young and retired the old, thus putting on the 20- to 55-year-olds an ever increasing burden of support for the rest of the community.[5]

Automation in industry, mechanization on the farm, and labor-saving devices in the home combined to make leisure not so much a reward as a major problem. For thousands of years most men and women, and many children too, had worked from sun-up to sundown; now, abruptly, the work day was cut to six or seven hours, and the work week to five days or even less. Industries catering to leisure flourished: radio and television, golf, skiing, camping, touring, and swimming pools. Travel became a national habit, and the winter vacation almost as normal as the summer, as Americans indulged their mania for relaxation. Because calculated relaxation was more tiring than hard work, 30 million Americans turned hopefully to adult — now renamed ' continuing ' — education, immersing themselves in the study of the Hundred Great Books, or indulging in amateur music, painting, and ceramics, or working toward that college degree which was almost as essential to social respectability as a marriage license.

America had never known an economy of scarcity in the Old World sense of the term, but in the past it had always been able to dispose of its abundance by a steady increase in the standards of living, and by exports. Now the capacity of farm and factory to produce far more than could normally be consumed created a new series of problems. Four solutions, or techniques, suggested themselves, and were adopted in whole or in part. One was to build obsolescence into the product itself, thus making reasonably sure that there would be a continuous demand for new models. A second was to create new consumer wants: this task was the special responsibility of the advertisers, who rose to so prominent a position in American life that the term ' Madison Avenue ' came to take on some of the connotations that ' Wall Street ' had held a generation earlier. A third solution was

---

[5] Between 1950 and 1960 the number of persons under 18 increased by 37 per cent and the number over 65 increased by 35 per cent, while the number between the ages 19 to 64 increased by only 7 per cent.

to ship vast quantities of surplus goods abroad — to give wheat or airplanes, dynamos or books, to ' needy ' nations. These were the more conventional solutions. The fourth, ardently advocated by the economist-diplomat John Galbraith in his widely read *The Affluent Society,* was to place less emphasis on the private and more on the public economy: to divert an ever larger part of the economy to the providing of schools, hospitals, museums, playgrounds, public housing, and the like. Because this smacked of the welfare state, business did not approve it. Yet it was government expenditures in the public area — highways, airports, the military, the exploration of outer space, foreign aid — which helped keep the economy going.

The new economy of the second half of the century was not only vaster, but far more complex than the old. It was not only national but international; increasingly American corporations bought control of great automobile, drug, or electrical companies overseas. It devoted an ever larger part of its energies to ' services ' rather than to production, and required a growing army of technicians and experts. It created a new type of employee — the ' organization man ' whose talents were primarily adaptability and team work rather than independence and ingenuity; and it discouraged dominant personalities, even at the top. Just as the academic system no longer produced strong presidents like Charles W. Eliot, Nicholas Murray Butler, and William R. Harper, and the military no longer produced great generals like Grant, Sherman, and Lee, so the new economy did not seem to bring to the fore any new Rockefellers, Carnegies, McCormicks, and Morgans.

Even in organized labor, where the tradition of personal leadership was strong, warriors like Samuel Gompers and John L. Lewis and idealists like Terence Powderly and Eugene Debs gave way to bureaucrats who ran large and flourishing organizations from comfortable well-staffed offices. Of all labor leaders of this generation only Walter Reuther of the United Automobile Workers emerged as a statesman. In the postwar years organized labor achieved both prosperity and stability. In 1955 when the A.F. of L. and the C.I.O. merged, they boasted a joint membership of 17 million; if that was still only one-fourth of the entire labor force, it was well over one-half of the so-called ' blue collar ' workers, who had always been the core of labor strength. Not only was labor increasingly prosperous but, as it abandoned much of its former militancy, it became increasingly conservative. By mid-century all but the most intransigent were willing to concede that labor shared with business, finance, and government the responsibility for maintaining the economy on an even keel.

One reason that the old militancy had gone was that there was less and less to fight about. Automation, to be sure, glared over every horizon, but it glared with equal intensity at business.[6] Almost every traditional goal of labor had been won, either by collective bargaining or by law; just as the welfare state pulled the rug out from under the old political machines, so it usurped the role of the old labor leader and changed the character and the goals of organized labor. Beginning with the New Deal, and continuing without a serious setback, government had written most of labor's goals into law: the right to organize and to bargain collectively, workmen's compensation, minimum wages, old age pensions, unemployment insurance, limitations on hours, the prohibition of the injunction, and so forth. Along with this came increasing government intervention in union affairs, first in the Taft-Hartley Act and then in the Labor Act of 1959, which set up codes of ethical practices for labor and provided federal supervision of many of the internal affairs of the union.[7]

Changes in the character of organized labor came so fast that neither labor nor capital took in what was happening. By 1961 two major developments were under way. First, as government took over responsibility for broad areas of social welfare and the protection of the rights of workers, labor turned to new objectives that involved it deeply in the whole national economy. The more important were the guaranteed annual wage, a redistribution of work

[6] Mr. Reuther tells us that one of the management who conducted him through the new fully automated Cleveland plant, ' with a slightly gleeful tone in his voice said to me, " How are you going to collect union dues from all these machines? " And I replied, " You know, that is not what's bothering me. I'm troubled by the problem of how to sell automobiles to all these machines." ' *Selected Papers*, p. 180.

[7] ' For about a decade beginning in the mid-1930's the unions had enjoyed the best of both possible legal worlds. On the one hand they were permitted to negotiate for closed shops by statutory authority . . . on the other, they continued to enjoy the status of voluntary, nonprofit associations. . . . Then, in 1947, Congress opened the shops to a very considerable degree, thereby obliging the unions better to qualify . . . as voluntary organizations. But in 1959 the community decided that the internal affairs of unions, even in open shops, could not be closed to regulation and supervision. As Gompers had predicted in the last century, the price of governmental protection was governmental control.' Lloyd Ulman, ' Unionism and Collective Bargaining,' in Seymour Harris (ed.) , *American Economic History*, p. 471.

time to fit the new pattern of automation, profit sharing and management sharing, co-operation with business to preserve vested interests in particular areas, and a livelier concern with global economy and international economic policies. It was safe to predict that within the foreseeable future organized labor would come to be one of the great conservative forces in American economy and politics.

4. SOCIETY AND THE CLASS STRUCTURE

Tocqueville had predicted that American society would become ' equal not only in condition, but preserving the same civilization, habits and manners.' But in the 1940's and 1950's a new school of sociologists was impressed with the inequalities of American society, and distinguished no less than nine categories, or classes, ranging from lower-lower and middle-lower to middle-upper and upper-upper. They discovered indices of class in such common denominators as family background, education, residence, work, profession, church and club affiliations, and similar stigmata. Other sociologists were impressed with the frenetic quest for status which, so they thought, pervaded the whole of American society, but particularly suburbia. Still others discovered the emergence of a new power elite, made up of closely interrelated leaders in politics, finance, industry, communications, and the military: it was this small and tightly knit group, they asserted, which exercised effective power and made crucially important decisions.

Yet the most impressive social development from the mid-nineteenth to the mid-twentieth century was the growth, rather than the decline, of equalitarianism. Nineteenth-century American society, equalitarian by Old World standards, contained certain class distinctions, and the gap between rich, white, native-born Protestants and poor immigrants and Negroes was wide and deep. That gap persisted after emancipation, and even widened, through immigration from southern and eastern Europe and the burgeoning of urban slums to which so many of the newcomers gravitated. The America described as late as 1900 by an Upton Sinclair or an Edith Wharton, a Theodore Dreiser or a Henry James, was in many respects a stratified and class-conscious society.

In the course of the twentieth century the gap between rich and poor, native and foreign-born, Protestant, Catholic, and Jew, gradually narrowed, and after World War II the progress toward equalitarianism was spectacular. The general leveling of standards of living, the increase in real wages, the cessation of large-scale immigration, the advent of all but universal high school education and the enormous increase in college and university enrollments, the standardization of consumer products — all of these developments tended to make American society at mid-twentieth century more equalitarian than at any time since the Revolution.

Old families and first families alike disappeared, as representatives of newer stocks like Felix Frankfurter and Mayor Wagner, Senator DiSalle and Governor Rosellini, Secretary Ribicoff and Secretary Goldberg, moved into the seats of power. 'The other side of the track' became a figure of speech, as one-class housing developments sprawled around every city, and even the tracks themselves disappeared. With 95 per cent of the population native-born, only Puerto Ricans and Mexicans remained in any substantial numbers to remind Americans of their earlier habits of associating class with place of birth. And as Negroes achieved an ever larger measure of economic, political, and educational equality, it became increasingly difficult to deny them social equality. Technology, mass production, and advertising brought a leveling up and standardization of almost all products, from automobiles to nylon stockings and from canned foods to reproductions of the Old Masters. Where, in England, a Morris and a Rolls-Royce clearly proclaimed their class affiliations, in the United States Fords and Cadillacs came to look more and more alike. Almost every one went to the same schools, dressed in the same ready-made clothes, shopped in the same supermarkets, ate the same packaged foods, drank the same beverages, listened to the same radio and television programs, read the same mass-produced magazines, drove the same cars, vacationed on the same beaches (only some were 'exclusive'). Differences in wealth remained very great, but differences in what money would buy were negligible.

Aside from overt differences between white and colored, old stock and new stock, of occupation and speech, it became increasingly difficult to find classes in the historic sense of the term. Fluidity and mobility were most characteristic of the American social scene. That the so-called power elite drew heavily on those who had inherited money and had graduated from Ivy League colleges was demonstrated; but it was still easy to make money, and access to Ivy League colleges was open to all who had the necessary intellectual qualifications, and there was no conclusive evidence that the 'power elite' was in fact an elite or in fact exercised power. And where class distinctions persisted, even in a democratic society like that of the English, in such things as church and chapel, Oxbridge and Redbrick, barrister and solicitor, 'U' and 'non-U,' American society acknowledged no decisive class distinctions other than those fixed by color.

It is no wonder that this society was preoccupied with status, because no one therein was condemned to a fixed position, and status was determined by native ability — or by luck. The fact that the search for status was so widespread implied, too, that almost everyone could not only seek but find it. It could be achieved in a hundred ways that were open to all. It could be achieved — so many Americans believed — by gestures such as living in the right neighborhood, or joining the right club, or even reading the right books and listening to the right music. As these gestures were all easy and simple, almost anyone could hope to win some kind of status.

5. The Search for Security

The Cold War persisted, and the frustrations that it entailed. Every year the United States was called on to do more and more, and in the most remote parts of the globe; every year Russian power grew, and that of Communist China, and as Communist power spread, the 'uncommitted' nations became ever more reluctant to take sides. Because the issues that divided the two giant contenders for power were so fundamental, the familiar instruments on which nations had heretofore relied — negotiation and diplomacy — became ineffective. At the same time the hydrogen bomb meant that the traditional alternative of war could no longer be relied on to accomplish anything but the annihilation of mankind. No wonder all of those tensions and anxieties that had afflicted parts of American society ever since the breakdown of the Yalta agreements persisted and fermented.

Senator McCarthy had died in 1957, discredited and almost forgotten, but McCarthyism remained. One heritage of McCarthyism was a large body of laws and administrative practices, based on the notion that there were litmus tests for such things as loyalty, security, and Americanism, and that it was the business of governments, at all levels, to apply these tests to all those who served in any public capacity. ' Un-American activities ' committees functioned without ever defining either ' American ' or ' Un-American '; there were ' loyalty ' tests and oaths without any clear notion of what loyalty meant; elaborate ' security ' screenings which sought to assure security by aimless inquiries into the private activities, beliefs, and intellectual interests of civil servants. A person's conduct, which since the Middle Ages had been considered the only proper test of loyalty or security, was now discarded in favor of inquests into a person's intentions, ideas, associations, and other tests so vague as to guarantee confusion and error.

What was new in the 'fifties was not American impatience with nonconformity — Tocqueville had noted that as far back as the 1830's — but the notion that it was the government's business to set up standards of conformity and force citizens to live up to them.[8] The elaborate apparatus improvised in the 'forties now hardened as a permanent engine of the American security system. To the Smith Act of 1940 and the Internal Security Act of 1950 was added the Communist Control Act of 1954 outlawing the Communist party. President Eisenhower enlarged the Truman security program by extending it to all government agencies, and added a new criterion of ' security risk ' to the earlier one of ' disloyalty ' as a basis for dismissal.

Much of the crusade for loyalty and security was unofficial rather than official. Self-appointed guardians of ' true ' Americanism — patriotic, filiopietistic, and ultra-conservative organizations of all stripes — joined to preserve the true marrow of Americanism. They attempted to censor books and magazines, films, radio, and television in order to protect the public from ' subversive ' ideas; ransacked libraries to remove ' subversive ' books; and were so successful in censoring textbooks in the social sciences and in requiring them to present orthodox versions of history, politics

[8] Thus Senator McCarthy charged the distinguished lawyer and judge, Dorothy Kenyon, with being ' affiliated with ' 28 Communist-front organizations. A congressional committee exonerated her from this charge, but nevertheless undertook to criticize her for being ' less than judicious ' in her choice of associates and organizations. The notion that a congressional committee may supersede individual judgment in the choice of friends, clubs, churches, or organizations is certainly an innovation not only in constitutional law but in American history.

and economics that they managed to make American history the dullest subject in the curriculum.

Just as in pre-Civil War days Southern hostility to abolition gradually became hostility to all liberal nineteenth-century ideas, such as free public schools and woman suffrage, so now hostility to ' subversion ' became also a bitter opposition to the United Nations and UNESCO, to those who championed the rights of Negroes, favored recognition of Communist China, supported federal aid to schools and medical care for the aged, or even — as Arthur Schlesinger said — those who believed in the income tax, the fluoridation of water, and the twentieth century.

Many aspects of these security programs raised important constitutional questions, and increasingly in the 'fifties the federal courts found themselves preoccupied with civil liberties cases. The Supreme Court tended to divide sharply in interpreting such cases, with Justice Frankfurter speaking for one group — usually the majority — and Justice Black or Chief Justice Warren for the other. The philosophical difference between the two groups was subtle but important.[9] The Frankfurter group tended to support the right of the legislature to qualify or suspend some of the guarantees of the First Amendment where it felt that the security of the commonwealth was at stake. The Black group felt that because security was ultimately best served by the exercise of freedom, legislatures should not be permitted to plead the necessity of security as a justification for overriding what formerly were considered firm constitutional guarantees. This was part of the never-ending attempt to balance freedom and liberty against authority and security; a contest which, as we have seen, began in America in colonial days.

In the Dennis case of 1951 the Court had found the balance of interest to be on the side of security — as interpreted by the Congress — rather than of freedom. After 1954 there was a shift toward a more restrictive view of governmental power and a stronger empha-

9 It would be naïve to characterize these two groups as ' liberal ' and ' conservative.' No judges were in favor of license or (the Birch Society to the contrary) were dupes of Communism; no judges were against the guarantees of the Bill of Rights. The real issue, as men like Frankfurter and Douglas saw it, was whether the Court or the legislature should determine, in the last analysis, whether the balance of interest was to be found in the preservation of particular freedoms or in the supposed security of society. This particular issue may have been factitious, but not the issue whether it should be decided by the legislatures or by the courts!

sis on the guarantees of the First Amendment. The next four or five years saw a series of decisions that substantially enlarged the area of freedom. In 1955 the federal courts rejected — and rebuked — the blundering attempt of Attorney-General Brownell to indict the scholar Owen Lattimore for perjury because he had denied Communist affiliations. The next year, in *Cole v. Young* the Court drastically curtailed the scope of the executive security program by restricting it to 'sensitive' positions only, and also in 1956, in *Pennsylvania v. Nelson,* it invalidated a state security program on the ground that the Federal Government had already pre-empted the field. *Yates v. United States* (1957) curtailed the scope of the Dennis opinion by holding that even advocacy of forcible overthrow of government was not illegal if it confined itself to mere advocacy and made no effort to inspire action. The same year *Watkins v. United States* curbed the authority of the Un-American Activities Committee to punish unco-operative witnesses at will, and in two notable cases — *Kent v. Dulles* and *Dayton v. Dulles* — the Court denied the State Department the right to deny passports on arbitrary grounds. In *Sweezy v. New Hampshire* the Court rejected the claims of a state attorney-general that he had a right to spy on state university professors in quest of subversive doctrines; in *NAACP v. Alabama* (1958) the Court nullified an Alabama ordinance requiring full disclosure of membership and activities of that organization, as an unconstitutional interference with freedom of association. That same year, too, the courts invalidated a California law requiring clergymen to take loyalty oaths as the price of tax exemption for their churches.[10]

With the sharpening of the Cold War after 1958 there was a perceptible shift to the side of security. Thus in the Barenblatt, the Uphaus, and the Wilkinson cases the Court sustained the activities of legislative investigating committees even when these were palpably bent on exposure rather than on acquiring information, or when the relevance of the information they accumulated was negligible. It upheld the constitutionality of a requirement that subversive organizations register with the Department of Justice (*Communist Party v. Subversive Activities Board*) and applied the penal provisions of the membership clause in that act, thus all but

[10] Almost all of these cases can be found in H. S. Commager (ed.), *Documents,* 7th ed., 1962.

officially endorsing the doctrine of guilt by association (*Scales v. United States*). In two decisions (*Konigsberg v. State Bar of California* and *In re Anastaplo*) it sustained the right of a state to exclude from the bar candidates otherwise qualified if they refused to answer questions about their associations and affiliations. Perhaps the most far-reaching — and potentially the most dangerous — decision was one that attracted very little attention: *Perez v. Brownell*.[11] This decision sustained an Act of Congress depriving a native-born American of citizenship because he voted in an election of a foreign country. As Congress has control of foreign affairs, said Mr. Justice Frankfurter, it may punish actions which embarrass the conduct of foreign affairs.

The most violent expression of intolerance, as the nation moved into the 'sixties, came from the extreme right — a term loosely applied to the various groups of political reactionaries, ideological states'-righters, white racists, anti-semites, Ku-Kluxers, religious fanatics, even an American Nazi group boldly displaying the swastika — who were united by common hatreds, suspicions, and confusions rather than by a common program. As President Kennedy said,

They look suspiciously at their neighbors and their leaders. They call for a ' man on horseback ' because they do not trust the people. They find treason in our finest churches, in our highest court, and even in the treatment of our water. They equate the Democratic party with the welfare state, the welfare state with socialism, and socialism with communism.

The absence of any positive program, the appeal to scattered groups of malcontents, and a leadership that was not above contempt, condemned these ' right ' groups to ultimate futility, but they were well financed and clamorous, and their capacity to make trouble almost limitless.

Despite Frederick Jackson Turner's theory of the West being the liberal, forward-looking section of America, these groups were strongest in Southern California, Arizona, and Texas; and contrary to earlier prophecies that the ' submerged tenth ' would rise up against the American system, these same groups were almost entirely composed of the well-to-do and the wealthy, and those

[11] Citations for these cases: *Perez v. Brownell* 356 U.S. 44, *Uphaus v. Wyman* 360 U.S. 72, *Barenblatt v. U.S.* 360 U.S. 109, *Wilkinson v. U.S.* 365 U.S. 399, *Konigsberg v. California* 81 S. Ct. 997, *In re Anastaplo* 81 S. Ct. 978, *Scales v. U.S.* 81 S. Ct. 1496, *Communist Party v. Subversive Activities Board* 81 S. Ct. 1537.

whose education was insufficient to discount the alarmist propaganda issued by these self-styled and largely anonymous saviors of society.

6. EDUCATION

America was the first country in modern history where each generation was better educated than its forebears — an elementary consideration which goes far to explain that child-centered society which puzzled foreign observers. The familiar process of enlarging both the base and the height of the educational pyramid was greatly accelerated in the years after the Second World War. Prosperity, the G.I. Bill of Rights — which sent over ten million veterans to school — leisure, the achievement of equality for women and the beginnings of equality for Negroes, the urgent demands for expertise and professional skills — all of these combined to give a powerful impetus to education, particularly at the secondary and higher levels. In the twenty years after 1940 the educational level of the country as a whole rose by two or three years. By 1960 the college occupied about the same position in the educational enterprise as the high school in 1920 and the junior college in 1940. Between 1920, and 1960, when the population increased by about 75 per cent, the high school population increased by 500 per cent. Figures for college and university population pointed the same lesson. The total number of students at institutions of higher education in 1920 was less than 600,000, and that year universities granted some 53,000 degrees. By 1960 the university population was 3.6 million, and of these, 479,000 earned degrees — a sixfold increase in enrollment, and a ninefold increase in earned degrees. Nor did the general raising of the levels of education stop here. Substantial numbers of college graduates — in some colleges as high as 85 or 90 per cent of graduates — moved on to graduate professional schools, and thus spent six to eight years beyond high school in completing their academic education.

The new demands on schools and universities raised many perplexing problems, of which the most urgent was money. How were the American people to finance twice as much education for twice the number of students as they had for an earlier generation? Total public school expenditures in 1950 were around $6 billion — not an impressive sum when compared with the $7 billion spent for liquor, to be sure, but heavy enough to cause widespread complaint. Yet by 1960 public school expenditures had increased to over $15 billion. The average varied greatly from state to state. In 1958 New York spent over $500 per pupil, Oregon and Delaware over $400, but Mississippi, South Carolina, and Arkansas less than $200; nevertheless Southern states were actually spending a larger proportion of their tax income on schools than were their rich Northern and Western neighbors.

Inability, assumed or real, of the poorer states to support public schools adequately led to a widespread demand for federal aid to education. This demand was based on the argument that the whole nation had a stake in the training and intelligence of all young people — an argument proved by the experience of World War II, when states with a high illiteracy rate contributed less than their share to the armed services. In the late 'forties Senator Taft of Ohio, otherwise deeply suspicious of federal centralization, introduced a bill appropriating up to $250 million a year to aid public schools in the poorer states and guaranteeing appropriations for $40 a year for every school child in the country. But this and similar proposals from Presidents Eisenhower and Kennedy encountered intractable opposition. States'-righters argued that federal aid would lead inevitably to federal control; Southerners feared that it might be an instrument for forcing integration on their schools; Catholics refused to go along unless their parochial schools, which provided education to almost five million children, obtained a share of the federal bounty; while those who supported the ' wall of separation ' between church and state warned that federal aid to parochial schools would fatally breach that wall. The Kennedy administration came to office committed to an ambitious program of aid to public education at all levels — school construction, teachers' salaries, scholarships, but ran into stormy weather when the Catholic hierarchy blasted its proposals as inequitable.

These material problems of education reflected deeper and more important intellectual ones. Education had been controversial ever since Plato's day, and it was not to be expected that society would cease to debate its character, content, or purposes when it became ' universal.' What troubled many Americans at mid-century was that somehow education had failed to educate: that a generation of which almost everyone went to high school and unprecedented numbers to the university, was still content with largely pictorial journalism, television programs fit for imbeciles, politics conducted with the technique of the circus, and race relations that reflected the tribal enmities of primitive peoples. If it was not quite true that ' Johnny couldn't read,' it was true that he preferred TV to books, and ' comics ' to real books. But then so did his parents.

Disillusion was sharpened by anxiety when, in 1957, the Soviets launched their first Sputnik and, in 1961, succeeded in orbiting a man about the earth, dramatizing the superiority of their engineers. Russia was spending a larger proportion of her income on education than was the United States, and Russian and Western European students who left school at eighteen were better educated than the average American of college age and experience. The inadequacies of American schools were charged, somewhat wildly, to ' progressive ' education, and a few critics went so far as to blame it all on John Dewey. Some of the criticism was inspired by the conviction that progressive educators had neglected old-fashioned disciplines like spelling and arithmetic; some by a belief that progressive education inspired in the young a critical attitude toward authority and the status quo; some by the simple desire to recapture not only the pastoral pleasures of the ' little red schoolhouse ' with its McGuffey Readers and Blue-backed Spellers, but its modest budgets as well.

Dissatisfaction centered on the high school. It was charged that it taught badly in four years what should be learned well in two or three; that it failed to provide a sound knowledge of mathematics, English grammar, or a foreign language; that it encouraged social and athletic activities at the expense of intellectual; that it favored mediocrity at the expense of excellence and laid waste the talents of its brighter students. The most judicious critic of the high schools, James B. Conant — formerly president of Harvard University — in his *The Child, the Parent, and the State* (1959) supported some of these charges, recommended increased emphasis on mathematics and foreign languages and endorsed the comprehensive high school. In his *Slums and Suburbs* (1961) he warned against the development of two school systems in America, one for the poor children of the slums and the other for the privileged children of the suburbs — a division which would dangerously exacerbate social divisions in American life.

Higher education was in a much sounder condition. Our thousand or more colleges and universities presented a fantastically varied pattern, from vocational institutions which were inferior to a good high school academy, to some of the best universities in the world. Whilst in the nineteenth century Americans eager for post-graduate instruction had to go to German or French universities, and in the twentieth many continued to do so, there was now a reverse movement — thousands of graduates of the universities of Latin America and the Old World flocked to the universities and technological institutes of the United States and Canada.

Colleges and universities were confronted by as great a pressure of students as the high schools — the three million or so of 1960 promised to grow to five million by 1970, beyond which few cared to peer. It was not too difficult to cope with the physical problem, and as armies of students invaded the great state universities, dormitories and student unions, field houses and university airports mushroomed over the landscape. Private philanthropy and public generosity, together with increased tuition charges, helped meet the mounting costs. Older universities like Harvard and Yale, newer institutions like Chicago and Stanford, counted their endowments by the hundred million, while many state universities, not to be outdone, rejoiced in annual appropriations of $50 or $60 million. During the war the Federal Government began to farm out research to the universities — Manhattan Project which produced the atomic bomb was carried through at Stagg Field at the University of Chicago — and the universities in turn found this a convenient way to pay for scientific research. By 1960 the Federal Government was financing most of the basic research going on in the universities with contributions that had passed the billion dollar mark. California Tech and Michigan received almost half their income from this source; and, with federal funds, a single institution like M.I.T. was enabled to spend more money on scientific research than all the universities of the British Isles combined. This development caused grave misgivings. Could the universities remain independent, faithful to their responsibility for the arts and the humanities as well as science, devoted to that ' pure ' research which, in the past, had produced the most important scientific findings; or would they gradually become adjuncts of the Federal Government, depending on its largess for their existence, and taking orders from bureaucrats? Fortunately a century-long experience with government financing of research in agriculture, public health, and other subjects had created a pattern of freedom which could be, and so far has been, followed rather than the individual-crushing German or Russian patterns.

Great foundations like the Ford, the Rockefeller, and the Guggenheim added to this stream of Americans studying overseas, and within a few years the American student was as familiar a sight on the Boul' Mich' of Paris, or Rome's Via Veneto, as the American scholar in the archives of Vienna or the museums of Florence. Another interesting postwar development has been the creation of American university centers abroad — the Salzburg center of American studies in Austria, a branch of the Johns Hopkins in Bologna, outposts of Stanford and Syracuse universities in Florence, Frankfurt, and Japan. All of these activities — the interchange of students and scholars, the transplanting of educational facilities, the beneficent work of the foundations, the activities of UNESCO — went far to re-create that community of Western learning which had flourished from the Middle Ages to the rise of modern nationalism; and in all this the United States played a generous and enlightened role.

More serious than the fiscal or even the political problems of education was the intellectual. American graduate schools had not turned out enough first-rate scholars to take care of the two million or so students of the 1940's; by the 'sixties the shortage of talent was alarming, and it promised to become desperate. Two developments exacerbated this shortage of talent: the growing complexity of science and the rapid enlargement of the areas of knowledge. The facts of biology, physics, chemistry, and other sciences were increasing faster than men's ability to absorb them; the areas and disciplines which Americans were expected to master — the Near East, the Far East, Indonesia, the African languages and Indian languages, Japanese culture, the economics of the Common Market — all of these clamored for attention. At the same time foundations, business, and government all competed with universities for such talent as was available. Scholars could take some satisfaction in the reflection that ' egg-head ' was no longer a term of opprobrium, and that professors now jostled doctors and lawyers in the prestige ratings that the sociologists solemnly compiled.

Not the least interesting development in this realm was the response of education to the world responsibilities of the United States. Originally universities had been cosmopolitan in character, and some European universities, like Paris, Göttingen, and Edinburgh, had continued this tradition of cosmopolitanism throughout their history; but not until after the Second World War did American universities begin to attract large numbers of students from abroad or to take on formal responsibility for training foreign students. Provisions of the Smith-Mundt and other congressional acts brought tens of thousands of students, chiefly from Germany, to American campuses, and by 1960 there were well over 50,000 foreign students enrolled in American universities — most of them in graduate and professional schools. Individual institutions like Columbia, Michigan, and California numbered their foreign students by the thousand. At the same time the Fulbright Act of 1946, revised and enlarged in 1961, enabled thousands of American students and scholars to study and teach in universities throughout the world.

7. Literature and the Arts

The most conspicuous feature of the cultural landscape in the postwar years was its barrenness. The new generation was still living on the capital accumulated by the old, or busy dissipating it. No new novelists emerged to replace Hemingway or to supplant Faulkner; no major poet took up the torch which had been held aloft for so long by Robert Frost, Archibald MacLeish, and Robinson Jeffers; neither Eugene O'Neill nor Thornton Wilder had any worthy successor in the theater, although Tennessee Williams rang the changes on the familiar theme of frustration, decay, and violence in the South. Most of the major critics were hold-overs from an earlier generation: the cosmopolitan Edmund Wilson, gathering strength with the years, Lionel Trilling, a kind of American Georg Brandes, the learned Richard Blackmur, and the iconoclastic Yvor Winters. In music and architecture the auspices were more hopeful. Architects, after a long period of enthrallment with Frank Lloyd Wright, began to emancipate themselves from the functional and return to the imaginative, while the musical renaissance launched in the 'thirties flourished and gathered strength.

It is difficult to believe that the decline of creative talent in these years was wholly fortuitous. The explanation was in part materialism and affluence, yet the Victorian age had been materialistic and affluent but still intellectually vigorous. It was in part disillusion with the war and frustration by the postwar world; but the European countries that had suffered most from the war were enjoying the liveliest intellectual life. It was in part that first-rate talents were being attracted increasingly into science and public affairs, but this, too, was a general, not a purely American, phenomenon. It was in part the pressure to conform that afflicted American society during the McCarthy era. It was doubtless, too, a reflection of the growing depersonalization of life that accompanied automation, outer space, atomic wars, and mass destruction: it is difficult to celebrate life when the public mind is obsessed with death. Novelists, when not preoccupied with sex, were fascinated by futility and death and, as they became increasingly analytical, ceased to present heroes and heroines and all but ceased to have plots. Much of what they wrote appeared to be

> shape without form, shade without colour,
> paralyzed force, gesture without motion.

Poets, painters, and musicians, too, rebelled against the narrative, the dramatic, and the representational — from the sonnet to the images that words conjured up, or to symbolism; from the musical form to the instrument and the sound; from the picture to the paint. Films took refuge in 'spectaculars' or surrendered wholly to the supposed claims of television, while television ceased to present real people, and displayed instead cardboard characters contrived by advertisers who themselves had ceased to be real.

Americans congratulated themselves that their literature had vitality, and even English critics, deprecating their own preoccupation with form and style, accepted this estimate, but most of the postwar novels had little to recommend them except vitality. There was power and vigor in such writers as Saul Bellow, Irwin Shaw, John O'Hara, but their novels were documentary, in the Dreiser or the Steinbeck tradition, rather than imaginative. As Mr. Bellow himself wrote, 'The American desire for the real has created a journalistic sort of novel which has a *thing* excitement, a glamor of *process;* it specializes in information, satisfies the readers' demand for knowledge. It seldom has much independent human content and it is more akin to popularized science or history than to the fiction of Balzac or Chekhov.' [12] The Second World War, as clearly as the Civil War, involved moral issues, but these somehow failed to command interest or allegiance, and the war itself evoked only a meager and ineffectual literary response. The novels of World War II were longer and stronger than those of World War I, but there was no *Sun Also Rises,* no *Soldiers' Pay,* no *Enormous Room,* and very little war poetry that caught the imagination; while the only war song that any one could remember was ' Lili Marlene,' taken from the Germans. The voluminous and highly personal writing about the war reflected mostly resentment of the military or disillusionment with the war itself; it was not so much a resentment of war as of the officers who happened to be running the war, and not a philosophical but a highly personal disillusionment. Representative war novels such as John Burns's *The Gallery* or Norman Mailer's *The Naked and the Dead* observed with monotonous reiteration that war was hell, but it was hard to escape the impression that the worst thing about the war was what it did to the authors. Almost alone of the war novelists, John Hersey caught something of its tragic heroism: *The Wall,* the story of the ill-fated uprising of the Warsaw Jews and their destruction by the Germans, had qualities of dignity and compassion worthy of the subject.

Perhaps the most interesting literature of these postwar years was a product of Southern self-consciousness. William Faulkner continued to dominate the literary scene: *Intruder in the Dust, Requiem for a Nun, The Town,* and *The Mansion* continued that study of the pathology of the South which Faulkner had inaugurated in the early 'thirties, and which now became the most elaborate literary analysis of one segment of American society since Henry James. Faulkner's influence was pervasive, but he had few disciples; most of the new Southern writers traced their lineage to Ellen Glasgow or Willa Cather or even to Stark Young rather than to him. Certainly Anne Goodwin Winslow (*A Quiet Neighborhood, The Springs, A Winter in Geneva*) belonged to the Willa Cather tradition, and had something of Miss Cather's sensitiveness to atmosphere, her stylistic elegance, and her moral seriousness. In *Delta Wedding, The Ponder Heart,* and a large number of short stories, Eudora Welty showed herself one of the most faithful interpreters of the present-day South;

[12] New York *Times Book Review,* 18 Feb. 1962.

her mastery of the idiom and her feeling for the life of the affections connected her with the Stark Young of *So Red the Rose* and *River House*. Carson McCullers (*Reflections in a Golden Eye, The Heart Is a Lonely Hunter, The Member of the Wedding*), perhaps the most brilliant of the younger generation of writers, combined psychological insight with an impressive technical competence. The most substantial of the Southern writers was doubtless Robert Penn Warren, a Kentuckian and a member of the remarkable Vanderbilt University group (which included the poet John Crowe Ransom and the critic Allen Tate). In a series of novels outwardly historical but fundamentally philosophical, Warren examined critical episodes of history that dramatized Southern traits of character. *Night Riders* re-created the war between the tobacco farmers and the companies in the early years of the century; *World Enough and Time* explored the passions involved in a famous Kentucky murder case more than a century earlier; *All the King's Men* was a fictional tour de force about the career of Huey Long.

Warren was one of the most skillful practitioners of the new historical genre. For as the sociological novel declined in interest the historical novel took on a new maturity. Novelists like Conrad Richter and Esther Forbes abandoned the costume pieces which had delighted readers of an earlier generation and penetrated as deeply into the life of the past as had Stendhal or Tolstoy. Miss Forbes's *The Running of the Tide* — a story of Salem in the opening years of the nineteenth century — A. B. Guthrie's *The Way West,* Conrad Richter's *The Trees, The Fields,* and *The Town,* McKinlay Kantor's *Andersonville,* combined a firm grasp on history with philosophical maturity new in the American historical novel.

A group of younger writers whose talents were dazzling but thin emerged in the 'fifties. What distinguished them from the older novelists was an interest in eccentricity and in the more exotic manifestations of sex, cosmopolitanism, and humor. The most popular of them was probably J. D. Salinger, whose *Catcher in the Rye* and *Franny and Zooey* were the preferred reading of the sophisticated adolescent. No less talented were Bernard Malamud, whose *The Assistant* caught unfamiliar aspects of the Jewish character; Vladimir Nabokov, whose *Lolita* was an international scandal; Paul Bowles, who turned from a distinguished career in music to the portrayal of Fitzgerald-like characters disporting themselves under African skies; and Truman Capote, whose *Other Voices, Other Rooms* conjured up a faintly perverse world of fantasy not unlike that created in Alain Fournier's classic *The Wanderer*. Most of these writers belonged to what might be called the *New Yorker* school of fiction; their stories — like most of the writing in that magazine — were characterized by a sophisticated wit, a sharp intelligence, and inability to take the institutions or practices of American society very seriously. What they lacked was solidity, direction, and significance. These limitations do not apply to the most distinguished *New Yorker* writer, James Thurber, whose gifted pen ushered in a new era in American humor.

Many of the older poets — Robert Frost, Carl Sandburg, Conrad Aiken, John Crowe Ransom, Marianne Moore (all born before 1890) — lingered on into the 'sixties with no apparent diminution of powers, providing examples of orthodoxy and tradition that inevitably challenged the younger poets. Rarely had poetry had so many practitioners; never had they demanded so much of their readers. Younger poets like Robert Lowell and Theodore Roethke, Richard Eberhart and Richard Wilbur, W. H. Auden and Karl Shapiro combined an astonishing technical competence, an intricate and allusive style, and philosophical maturity. Like so many of the painters and sculptors of the day they were non-representational, divorced themselves and their art from common experience, and so had to be content with a critical rather than a popular success.

With the passing of Frank Lloyd Wright a new group of architects, some trained in Europe but transplanted to America, came to the fore: Eero Saarinen, Mies van der Rohe, Walter Gropius, George Binshaft, and Walter Harrison. The postwar years saw a reaction against both the functionalism of Wright and the mechanical impersonality of the all-glass skyscrapers that turned out to be so tiresome, and back to some of Louis Sullivan's ideas of decoration. This can be seen in the American Embassy at New Delhi erected by Harrison and Abramowitz, Saarinen's American Embassy building in London, George Binshaft's Lever building and Mies van der Rohe's Seagram building in New York's midtown area, and Walter Harrison's United Nations Secretariat building alongside the East river in New York. No less original was the new airport architecture — which could be seen at its best in St. Louis, Minneapolis, and at Idlewild in New York — and the combination of functional interiors, decorative exteriors, and landscaping in the complex of the Connecticut General Life Insurance buildings outside Hartford planned by Skidmore, Owings and Merrill and landscaped by the gifted Isamu Noguchi.

The musical renaissance which had set in after the First World War, with the coming of distinguished European refugees like Paul Hindemith, Arnold Schoenberg, Igor Stravinsky, Bela Bartók, and Darius Milhaud, flourished and gathered strength. One of the most interesting developments here was the assumption of responsibility for creative music by colleges and universities. Nothing dramatized this more strikingly than the appointment of so many distinguished composers to university faculties: Randall Thompson and Walter Piston at Harvard, Roger Sessions at Princeton, Douglas Moore at Columbia, Lukas Foss at California, Darius Milhaud at Mills College in California, and Leonard Bernstein at Brandeis University. Although America still could not boast an opera company as good as Vienna or the Scala in Milan, the number of small, local opera companies and small-town symphony orchestras increased tremendously.

From Haydn and Mozart to Dvořak and Brahms, musicians had drawn on folk music for their compositions; now this same process was under way in the United States. George Gershwin based *Porgy and Bess* largely on Negro songs of the sea islands; Aaron Copland wrote ' native ' music for Steinbeck's *Red Pony* and for Emily Dickinson's poems, and drew on folk music for his own ballets. Leonard Bernstein, gifted conductor of the New York Philharmonic, composed the music for *On the Town* and *West Side Story* out of familiar materials. Douglas Moore, who provided probably the largest operatic repertory of anyone of his generation, composed in authentic American style *The Ballad of Baby Doe, The Devil and Daniel Webster, Giants in the Earth,* and *The Wings of the Dove,* based on Henry James's novel. The Italian-born Gian-Carlo Menotti wrote, for the American stage, *Amahl and the Night Visitors, The Medium,* and *The Saint of Bleecker Street.* Meantime Lerner and Loewe's *My Fair Lady* not only promised to be a permanent fixture on Broadway — and in every other major city of the country — but conquered the world.

8. The Challenge of Science

In a lecture on ' The Two Cultures,' in 1959, the British novelist C. P. Snow admonished his contemporaries not to think of ' culture ' exclusively in traditional terms of art, music, and letters, but to remember that science, too, is a culture, with its own traditions, laws, and empire. There is no doubt that America has made significant contributions to this scientific culture, increasingly so to theory and principle rather than to those ' purely practical arts ' toward which Tocqueville thought that the American genius would be exclusively directed. ' Today, in almost all fields of natural science,' wrote Robert Oppenheimer, ' our country is pre-eminent in theory as it is in experiment, invention, and practice. . . . Today the young man wishing the best training in theoretical physics, or mathematics, theoretical chemistry or biology, will be likely to come to this country, as three decades ago he would have gone to the schools of Europe.' Science, to be sure, is universal, and scientific findings are the product of co-operative action spread over many countries and long periods of time. Yet no period of American history has seen more far-reaching advances in science than the two decades after the outbreak of World War II. Americans made notable contributions in atomic physics, the exploration of outer space and of the seas, calculating machines, medicine and public health. It is suggestive that during the years from 1945 to 1961 only two Americans (Faulkner and Hemingway) won the international Nobel prize in literature, while ten won it in chemistry and twelve in physics.

Doubtless the most spectacular development was in the realm of atomic physics. The preliminary work had been done long before the war by Rutherford of Cambridge, Niels Bohr of Copenhagen, Otto Hahn of Göttingen, Enrico Fermi of Rome, and Lise Meitner of Berlin, and by Americans like Ernest Lawrence, Robert Oppenheimer, Harold Urey, and Isidor Rabi. It was the co-operation of American and European scientists that made possible Manhattan Project, and the first nuclear explosions. The association of atomic fission with military purposes was strengthened when American physicists perfected the incomparably powerful hydrogen bomb, which had its first full-scale test on the Pacific island of Eniwetok in November 1952. The wartime use of the atomic bomb to destroy Hiroshima and Nagasaki had induced a sense of guilt in many Americans; the perfection of the hydrogen bomb added an awesome sense of responsibility, for it placed a weapon of infinite power in the hands of finite men. Fear was added to guilt and responsibility when, in mid-summer 1953, the Russians too exploded a hydrogen bomb. By 1960 not only these two great powers but Britain and France — and possibly China — were in a position to ' destroy the great globe itself ' and ' leave not a rack behind.'

In the meantime it became clear that the peaceful uses of atomic energy either through fission (the atomic bomb) or fusion (the hydrogen bomb) held out the most dazzling prospects to mankind. One pound of uranium could provide the power of 1300 tons of coal, and five pounds of hydrogen could create enough energy to meet all the power requirements of New York City for twenty-four hours. Uranium was in short supply, but the supply of hydrogen, processed from water, was limitless. Once fully harnessed, nuclear fusion could take care of the power needs of the entire world for all time.

This was the theme of the ' Atoms for Peace ' speech which President Eisenhower made to the United Nations in December 1953, in an effort to ward off what he feared would become a fatal atomic race between the United States and Russia. In this address the President proposed that the major scientific nations of the world jointly contribute to a United Nations pool of atomic power to be used exclusively for peaceful purposes. ' Experts would be mobilized,' he said, ' to apply atomic energy to the needs of agriculture, medicine, and abundant electrical energy in the power-starved areas of the world.' The proposal, accompanied by a suggestion for disarmament and international controls, fell afoul of Soviet distrust and suspicion. Yet all through the 'fifties there was progress in the application of atomic power to peaceful uses. By the end of the decade there were atomic power reactors in the United States, Britain, France, and Russia, and atomic energy was being used to speed up the desalination of ocean water, for logging oil wells and detecting gas-bearing and oil-bearing geological strata, for combating agricultural pests and diseases, in many fields of medicine, and in electronics and engineering.

For thousands of years mankind had lived in an economy of scarcity, and even optimistic Americans, with a continent at their disposal, were haunted by the specter of the exhaustion of natural resources. Now science was able to dissipate most of these fears. Vast deposits of oil were discovered in the off-shore and tidal lands of the

Gulf States and California, and by the 1960's this oil was being pumped out. Science has also found the way to extract oil from the inexhaustible slate mountains of Colorado, although as yet the cost of such an operation is prohibitively high. Reforestation and check dams slowed up soil erosion; chemical fertilizers restored the fertility of worn-out land; and new sources of food such as the ocean gave some reassurance that the world-wide ' population explosion ' would not mean starvation for mankind.

Science is on the verge, too, of solving the most ancient problem in the history of man's struggle to master his environment: that of water. Two developments account for an almost universal water shortage. Reckless deforestation and other abuse of the land for centuries have turned once rich and fertile regions, like North Africa, into semi-deserts, and the concentration of population in great cities, as well as the demands of industry, have been taxing the water resources even of well-watered nations like the United States. Surveying this problem at mid-century, Professor Walter Webb [13] concluded that before long Americans might have to give up farming in much of the plains area, and that even cities like Los Angeles would eventually be defeated by lack of water. But even as Webb wrote, programs of desalination of sea water through vapor compression, solar distillation, or more complex processes run by atomic power, were holding out the bright promise of enough water to make ancient deserts once again blossom as gardens, and to meet the needs of cities and industry. Israel is about to win back the Negev desert, and desalination plants in Texas and California are providing millions of gallons of water daily for irrigation and industry.

As spectacular as the development of atomic energy, and even more exciting to the imagination, was the exploration of outer space, which got under way in the 'fifties. What the discovery of America had been to the imagination of the sixteenth century, the exploration of space promised to be to the twentieth and the twenty-first. It was the realization of the dream of Icarus, which had bemused generations of astronomers, physicists, and philosophers, and the result of the most elaborate, and hard-headed scientific and engineering planning. In 1957 the Russians launched a satellite into outer space, and soon both Russian and American satellites were photographing the moon, and relaying messages from space. In 1961 the Russians

[13] Author of the classic study of *The Great Plains*.

put a man in orbit about the globe; in February 1962, Colonel John Glenn USMC circled the earth three times in less than five hours. The significance of this penetration of outer space is not merely practical activities such as satellite communication, long-range weather prediction, or launching sites for lethal weapons; but that for the first time it enables man to penetrate the mysteries of the stellar universe and holds out hope that man may in time establish contact with other planets. Thus, at the very moment in history when man peered into the abyss of total self-destruction through atomic weapons, there was opened to his eyes a glimpse of the farthest reaches of the universe, and to his ears the music of the spheres mingled with the clang from beyond phenomena.

Less spectacular, but more immediately practical, were the voyages of two nuclear-powered United States submarines. *Nautilus* (Commander William R. Anderson) submerged 1 August 1958 north of Alaska, steamed for 1800 miles under the polar ice cap, and emerged on the 5th on the European side of the pole. *Triton* (Captain Edward L. Beach) circumnavigated the globe under water between 16 February and 10 May 1960, breaching only twice in the 84 days — once to land a sick seaman at Montevideo, and once at Cadiz to honor the memory of Magellan, whose course she had followed.

There were far-reaching developments in the science of electronics. Computers capable of combining thousands of separate items in a single formula, of solving almost instantly mathematical questions beyond the control or even the grasp of the human mind, and of directing the most delicate machines in the most complicated processes — all these promised to extend the mental powers of man as steam and electricity had extended his physical powers in the nineteenth century. Already on the horizon were computing machines that would not only work on material fed into them, but would 'think' for themselves on subjects formulated for them. Inevitably these and similar technological inventions conjured up a world in which the machine itself would take over direction of some of the most meaningful activities of life — the kind of world imagined by George Orwell in *1984* or by Huxley in his *Brave New World*.

Of many scientific discoveries and advances during these years it may be said that their malevolent qualities are more apparent than their benevolent — that having proved their capacity to destroy life they yet have to prove their capacity to enrich it. The decades in which war, implemented by science and technology, destroyed many million lives, also saw advances in medicine that wiped out long-familiar diseases, reduced infant mortality, extended the life span, and made those added years more useful and comfortable than old age had ever been.

In 1920, 82 out of every 1000 white babies and 131 out of every 1000 Negro babies born in the United States died at birth or in their first year. By 1959 infant mortality had been reduced to 23 out of 1000 white babies and 44 out of 1000 colored. Thus a 1960 baby had about four times the chance of survival of a 1920 baby. Figures for life expectancy were almost equally dramatic. The average child born in 1850 could expect to live only to the age of 40; the child born in 1900 might live to be 47; but the child born in 1960 should — if atomic war can be avoided — live out the Biblical three score and ten.

Medicine is the least national of scientific activities, yet it is eloquent testimony to medical research in the United States that since 1945 the Nobel prize in medicine has gone to fourteen Americans — four of them European-born. Dr. Herman Muller's discovery of DDT made possible a world-wide attack on malaria; the Russian-born Dr. Selman Waksman discovered streptomycin; Doctors Jonas Salk and Albert Sabin developed vaccines that promised to wipe out poliomyelitis; Dr. Max Theiler found a vaccine against the ancient scourge of yellow fever. New techniques of anesthetics and new surgical refinements made possible open-heart surgery, the grafting of arteries and veins, massive blood transfusions, and the transplanting of eye corneas and of other vital organs. Vitamin research went back to the early years of the century, as did the discovery that diseases like pellagra were caused by vitamin deficiencies; the postwar years saw steady advances in vitamin research and discovery, the development of cortisone for treating arthritis, and of orinase for diabetes. The Atomic Energy Commission sponsored research into the effect of radiation on cancer, and for its diagnosis and treatment made available radio-isotopes.

Much of this research was made possible by lavish appropriations from the Federal Government. That government had long interested itself in some fields of science — geology, oceanography, paleontology, and botany, for example — but during the war and the postwar years it entered boldly into almost every area of scientific activity.

This new alliance of government and science was dictated in the first instance by the exigencies of national defense; as it became clear that no aspect of science from cancer research to the exploration of outer space was unrelated to national security, government came to be the chief support to research of all kinds. By 1960 the Federal Government was subsidizing research in universities to the tune of over a billion dollars a year; the cost of atomic research and the probing of outer space was of course far larger. There were two serious dangers here: that government subsidies might deflect research into those areas that seemed most important to government officials rather than encourage it in those areas that appealed to the scientists themselves, and that the governmental insistence on supervision, regulation, and security would endanger scientific and academic independence. In the years immediately after the war these dangers were very real, and persuaded many universities and scientists to refuse government contracts on the terms which then obtained. Within a decade government officials learned that if they expected to get results they must respect academic freedom and the independence of scientists, and by the 1960's government support to science was not only generous but enlightened.

BIBLIOGRAPHY

1. GROWTH AND THE ECONOMY. A. A. Berle, *The Twentieth Century Revolution;* Roger Burlingame, *Backgrounds of Power: The Story of Mass Production;* Peter Drucker, *America's Next Twenty Years* and *The New Society;* James K. Finch, *Engineering and Western Civilization;* Kenneth Galbraith, *The Affluent Society* and *American Capitalism: The Countervailing Power;* Horace Gray, *Monopoly in America: The Government as Promoter;* Walton Hamilton, *Politics and Industry;* Robert Jungk, *Tomorrow Is Already Here;* Max Lerner, *America as a Civilization;* Walter P. Reuther, *Selected Papers;* Philip Taft, *Structure and Government of Labor Unions.*

2. THE CITY. Luther Gulick, *The Metropolitan Problem;* Jane Jacobs, *The Death and Life of Great American Cities;* Lewis Mumford, *The City in History* and *The Culture of Cities;* A. C. Spectorsky, *The Exurbanites;* Christopher Tunnard & Henry H. Reed, *American Skyline.*

3. SOCIETY AND THE CLASS STRUCTURE. Frederick L. Allen, *The Big Change;* Bernard Barber, *Social Stratification;* Reinhard Bendix & Seymour Lipset, *Class, Status and Power;* August Hollingshead, *Elmtown's Youth;* Howard Mumford Jones, *The Pursuit of Happiness;* Alfred C. Kinsey, et al., *Sexual Behavior in the Human Male;* Russell Lynes, *A Surfeit of Honey;* Kurt Mayer, *Class and Society;* C. Wright Mills, *The Power Elite* and *White Collar;* Vance

Packard, *The Status Seekers;* David Riesman, *et al., The Lonely Crowd;* W. Lloyd Warner, *American Life: Dream and Reality* and *Social Class in America;* William H. Whyte, *The Organization Man.*

4. THE SEARCH FOR SECURITY. Alan Barth, *Government by Investigation;* Daniel Bell (ed.), *The New American Right;* John W. Caughey, *In Clear and Present Danger;* H. S. Commager, *Freedom, Loyalty, Dissent;* Frank J. Donner, *The Un-Americans;* Erwin Griswold, *The Fifth Amendment Today;* Morton Grodzins, *The Loyal and the Disloyal;* Robert MacIver, *Academic Freedom in Our Time;* Edward A. Shils, *The Torment of Secrecy;* Telford Taylor, *Grand Inquest.*

5. EDUCATION. Jacques Barzun, *The House of Intellect* and *Teacher in America;* James Conant, *The American High School Today* and *Slums and Suburbs;* Scott Fletcher (ed.), *Education for Public Responsibility;* Robert Hutchins, *Conflict of Education in a Democratic Society;* David Riesman, *Constraint and Variety in American Education;* Mark Van Doren, *Liberal Education.*

6. ARTS AND LETTERS. John Aldridge, *After the Lost Generation;* I. H. Baur, *Revolution and Tradition in Modern American Art;* Leo Gurko, *Heroes, Highbrows and the Popular Mind;* Talbot Hamlin, *Forms and Functions of Twentieth Century Architecture;* Randall Jarrell, *Poetry and the Age;* Archibald MacLeish, *Poetry and Experience;* Andrew C. Ritchie, *Abstract Painting and Sculpture in America;* Bernard Rosenberg & David M. White (eds.), *Mass Culture: Popular Arts in America;* Gilbert Seldes, *The Public Arts;* Lionel Trilling, *The Liberal Imagination.*

7. SCIENCE. Charles Curtis, *The Oppenheimer Case;* Walter Gellhorn, *Security, Loyalty, and Science;* Siegfried Giedion, *Mechanization Takes Command;* Bernard Jaffe, *Men of Science in America* and *The New World of Chemistry;* Robert Millikan, *Autobiography;* Ruth Ellen Moore, *The Coil of Life: Great Discoveries in the Life Sciences; Scientific American Reader:* see, too, files of *The Scientific American,* especially September 1950; Mitchell Wilson, *American Science and Invention.*

Politics and Policies of the Eisenhower Administration

1. President Eisenhower

PRESIDENT Eisenhower, who was 62 years old when he took office, personified the American success story. Born in Denison, Texas, in 1890, into a humble family of Pennsylvania-Dutch descent, Dwight Eisenhower grew up in Abilene, Kansas, long one of the famous 'cow-towns' of the West, still very much part of the frontier. Appointed to West Point at the age of 21, Eisenhower spent the whole of his adult life in government service. From 1915 to 1941 he rose methodically through the grade of the army, serving for four years on General MacArthur's staff in the Philippines, and in Washington. The outbreak of World War II found him Chief of the War Plans Division of the General Staff; his work there brought him to the attention of General Marshall who recommended him to the President for the command of the Allied forces invading North Africa. Eisenhower's success in this enterprise led to his appointment as Supreme Commander of the Allied Forces in Europe, a post which he filled with distinction. After the war General Eisenhower remained Chief of Staff until 1948, when he became, briefly, president of Columbia University and, from 1950 to June 1952, Supreme Commander of NATO. In all of these posts he displayed a transparent honesty, integrity, prudence, good judgment, a talent for mediating among men of diverse views and inspiring loyalty among subordinates and confidence among associates.

Eisenhower belonged to what might be called the McKinley-Taft rather than the Roosevelt-Wilson tradition of the presidency. He thought of the President as neither a party nor a popular leader, but as a combination chief of staff, mediator, and symbol. Unlike his Democratic predecessors and successor in the White House he disliked politics and politicians, and tried to keep aloof from the contest for power and patronage, the Billingsgate of campaigns, and the sharp clash of personal and political opinions. He was, in short, unsuited for the exacting and importunate role of President in time of crisis. Thoroughly American as 'Ike' was, he nevertheless conceived his role to be somewhat like that of a constitutional monarch: he was to be an image and a symbol above the battle. It was his hope to smooth over party differences, to offend nobody in Congress, to preside over a scene of harmony and peace, to use his immense popularity, like President Monroe, to bring about a new 'Era of Good Feelings.'

Eisenhower's long military experience predisposed him toward a 'staff' system, which he had used so successfully in Europe. He preferred to work through subordinates whose business it was to shelter him from demands on his time and thought, and to protect him from personal involvement in the hurly-burly of politics. This was the function of his assistant Sherman Adams, who became a kind of unofficial alter-ego of the President himself. Members of his cabinet like Secretaries Dulles and Humphrey who enjoyed his confidence exercised more power than had been customary in the history of the American presidency. Impatient of detail and of administrative routine, Eisenhower was not disposed to probe deeply into any subject; and he liked to have every problem, even the most complex, summarized for him on a single sheet of paper. Because he so successfully insulated himself from public affairs, he was often taken by surprise on learning things that almost everyone knew — book burning by the Department of State underlings in American overseas libraries, for example, or sit-down strikes by colored students in the South, or the issues involved in the Dixon-Yates power contract.

Conservative by instinct and by training, Eisenhower (like General Grant) admired men of business, and preferred them for his political and private associates. Six members of his first cabinet were prominent businessmen, and several were multimillionaires. Secretary of Defense Charles E. Wilson, who had been head of the General Motors Corporation, achieved a kind of immortality by his public statement that 'what's good for our country is good for General Motors, and vice versa.' Arthur Summerfield, also of General Motors, distinguished himself as Postmaster-General by trying to put the department on a 'businesslike footing' regardless of the impact on postal service, and by his crusades against books that he considered too 'obscene' for the mails. The new Secretary of the Interior, Douglas MacKay of Oregon, was an automobile salesman with a long record of hostility to conservation and public power. Secretary of Commerce Sinclair Weeks of Massachusetts began his administration by firing the head of the Bureau of Standards, Dr. Allen Astin, because he was oblivious to 'the business point of view'; but in the face of nation-wide protests Secretary Weeks reversed himself and restored Dr. Astin to his job. Secretary of the Treasury George Humphrey, president of a large iron and steel company, was committed to a balanced budget as the supreme test of economic statesmanship. The new Secretary of Agriculture, Ezra Taft Benson, a devout elder of the Mormon Church, had strong convictions about the dangers of federal centralization and the welfare state. Attorney-General Herbert Brownell, a prominent New York lawyer, enforced the federal security program in a confused and spotty manner, and was ready to put his office in the service of partisan politics. In this atmosphere it is little wonder that the Secretary of Labor Martin Durkin, a Stevenson Democrat and union official, felt thoroughly out of place, and resigned within a few months; his post was filled by James P. Mitchell of New Jersey, a former personnel manager.

The leader of the cabinet, and the man in whom Eisenhower reposed limitless confidence, was John Foster Dulles of New York. Grandson of the Secretary of State under President Harrison, Dulles was born and bred to the foreign service. He had helped draft the 'war-guilt' clause of the Treaty of Versailles, placing the entire blame for World War I on Germany. Dulles later came to doubt the wisdom of American participation in that, or any European war, and not until after the attack on Pearl Harbor was he converted to intervention and internationalism. One of the architects of the United Nations, and of the peace treaty with Japan, Dulles had a vital stake in the foreign policies of the outgoing administration which made it probable that there would be substantial continuity in the conduct of foreign relations.

As his special assistant Eisenhower chose one of his original backers, Governor Sherman Adams of New Hampshire. This dour Yankee wielded a power all out of proportion to his official position, for under the Eisenhower staff system he controlled access to the President: 'The Governor' decided who could see the President, and selected letters and papers to be submitted to his consideration. He was to Eisenhower what Colonel House had been to Wilson and Harry Hopkins to Roosevelt, and had far more power than either, owing to Eisenhower's declining physical vigor and lack of positive policy. 'I need him,' Eisenhower said when Adams's position was threatened through his indiscretions. Increasingly, as the President took refuge on his Gettysburg farm from routine work and social demands, the burden of running the presidential office fell on the hardworking Adams. On the whole he performed his thankless task well.

After Dulles, Humphrey, and Adams, the most powerful figure in the new administration was doubtless Senator Taft. Son of an ' Old Guard' President, and himself perennial favorite of the Old Guard for the presidency, Robert Taft was known affectionately as 'Mr. Republican.' No other Senator enjoyed such respect among his colleagues as this shrewd, homespun, clever, and industrious Ohioan: defeated for the nomination in 1952, he remained powerful enough to impose on General Eisenhower agreement with his own program, and now he proposed to see that the President lived up to his agreement. Not illiberal in domestic policies — he supported federal aid to housing and to education — in foreign policy Taft was the leader and spokesman for that large and powerful element who were opposed to further entanglements in the affairs of the Old World, but determined on American involvement in the affairs of Asia. For a short time Taft threatened to be to Eisenhower what Stephen A. Douglas had been to Buchanan; his death, in July 1953, removed not only a dangerous rival but almost the one man on whom the President could rely to mediate between the different wings of the Republican party.

2. Old-Fashioned Conservatism

Eisenhower's election marked the return of the Republican party to power after twenty years; many Republicans who remembered an era when it was normal for Republicans to rule the nation regarded this long exclusion as contrary to the laws of nature. They persuaded themselves that it was due, not to any fault of the G.O.P., but to the beguiling charm of F.D.R., to a wholesale ' bribery ' of the electorate by ' welfare ' measures, to the improper activity of organized labor in politics, and to corruption. There was also a very widespread belief, fanned by Senator McCarthy, that the Democratic administrations, extensively infiltrated by Communists, had ' betrayed ' the American people by helping Russia win a dominating position in Europe, ' handing over ' China to the Reds, and recalling General MacArthur just as he was about to win the Korean War. President Eisenhower did not share these delusions, but many of his associates high in party councils did. Now they determined to expose the alleged misdeeds of men who had so long excluded them from the seats of power, to hold them up to public scorn, and reverse their policies — all in the name of ' Americanism,' although this attempt to smear the defeated party and take revenge for its success had no more savory precedent than Reconstruction. It was in deep contrast to Jefferson's magnanimous attitude in 1801, or Lincoln's in 1861.

Thus, there were senseless attacks on Secretary Acheson and other high officials who supported his views and on George Kennan, who was probably the American who knew Russia best. Other veterans of the Foreign Service were forced out of it because they had given unpalatable advice, which later developments proved to be sound. A vague feeling of ' betrayal ' inspired the attack on Robert Oppenheimer, the distinguished atomic physicist who had directed the laboratories at Los Alamos and was now excluded from further participation in the atomic program because of his onetime Communist associations and his misgivings about the hydrogen bomb. Revenge inspired the persecution of the Far Eastern expert, Owen Lattimore, of the Johns Hopkins University, because his views on China ran counter to those of the Republican right. Many respectable Republicans such as Senator Taft, who ordinarily would not have associated with a demagogue like Senator McCarthy, supported him because he seemed to be convincing the public that the years of Democratic rule were ' twenty years of treason.' These and similar gestures, worked grave injury to innocent men, lowered the standards of public service by discouraging officials from presenting honest views, and distracted statesmen from serious issues that clamored for attention. They accomplished nothing positive, they uncovered no traitors or subversives, and even brought little satisfaction to those who instigated these ' witch hunts.' The Republican platform of 1952 charged that the Democratic party had ' by a long succession of vicious acts, so undermined the foundations of our Republic as to threaten its existence,' but investigations which covered the whole field of Democratic administrations failed to find anything remotely justifying this hyperbole.

The politics of revenge took formal guise in two amendments to the Constitution, one enacted and the other defeated. The first was the Twenty-second Amendment, passed and ratified after little public discussion, which limited future Presidents to two terms of office; a piece of retroactive vindictiveness against F.D.R., as President Eisenhower himself said. The so-called Bricker Amendment, sponsored by Senator John Bricker of Ohio, provided that 'a treaty or other international agreement shall become effective as internal law in the United States only through legislation by the Congress,' unless the Senate specifically waived the two-thirds rule. This was supported by isolationist elements in both parties, and by Southerners who conjured up fears that their domestic institutions might somehow be subject to international agreements like the Declaration of Human Rights. Had this been incorporated in the Constitution it would have hampered the conduct of foreign relations, as under the Articles of Confederation; President Eisenhower observed that it would make it difficult for the United States to negotiate agreements with other nations for our mutual defense and common interests. The amendment was defeated, but by the narrowest of margins; in the crucial vote no fewer than sixty Senators, from both parties, voted to write this anachronism into the Constitution.

Many Republicans looked forward to a complete reversal of Democratic policies which (their platform asserted) led toward socialism and the wrecking of the free enterprise system. Both New Deal and Fair Deal to be discredited and scrapped; no more welfare-state ' creeping socialism '; an end to unbalanced budgets and sky-rocketing debt; a reversal to centralization and the invasion of states' rights; and, in foreign policy, no more ' giveaways '; a tough line with the Reds and the ' unleashing ' of Chiang to overthrow Mao. Yet, once in power, the Republicans found they could do no more than modify principles, policies, and practices which had been woven into the fabric of American life, through the inescapable needs of the age. For better or worse, both government and people were irretrievably committed to many elements of the welfare state, such as federal responsibility for full employment, social security, economic health, control of natural resources, supervision of banking and finance. There could be no major reversal. So, too, the United States was now a world power, inextricably involved in the affairs of every quarter of the globe. Moderate Republicans like Eisenhower, Nixon, and Dulles knew that it was no more possible to scrap the welfare state or return to isolation than to reverse the twentieth century.

Eisenhower himself said that in domestic areas the true role of government was ' to stabilize the economy and encourage the free play of our people's genius for individual initiative.' His two favorite phrases were ' middle of the road ' and ' dynamic conservatism.' He meant that while he would not try to reverse the achievements of the past twenty years, neither would he carry them forward; while he would not try to dismantle the welfare state, neither would he enlarge it; while he would not actively discourage public enterprise, he would encourage private enterprise. It was not to be expected that the Republican party would deny itself all fruits of victory; but it is surprising how few it harvested. The new conservatism can best be traced in appointments, cabinet posts, and ambassadorships, and in such subjects as taxation, finance, natural resources, water power, atomic energy, and in the administration's attitude toward the regulatory commissions.

These regulatory commissions — the Interstate Commerce Commission, the Federal Power Commission, the Federal Communications Commission, the Atomic Energy Commission — had long been considered independent and non-partisan. Under Eisenhower they lost in both respects. After James Landis had surveyed them, in 1960, he concluded that ' careful scrutiny of agency members from the standpoint of their qualifications was too often replaced by a consideration of what political obligations could be repaid through appointments,' and that ' top administrative positions appear to have been sought as stepping stones to further political preference or to positions of importance within the industries subject to regulation.' President Eisenhower not only evaded the legal requirements of bipartisan appointments by appointing ' Eisenhower Democrats ' to fill the posts normally reserved for Democrats, but appointed members who did not believe in government regulation at all. Thus John C. Doerfer, new chairman of the Federal Communications Commission, was opposed to regulation of radio or television by the government. ' A strong suspicion exists,' wrote Mr. Landis, ' that far too great an influence is exercised over the Commission by the networks,' and in the end Mr. Doerfer had to be dropped because of his intimacy with network officials. The Federal Power Commission was stacked with opponents of public power, and William B. Conole, who had fought against increases in the price of natural gas, and whose dissenting opinions in cases before the Federal Power Commission had been sustained by the Supreme Court, was dismissed because the President thought him too deeply committed ' to the consumer point of view.' The policies of the Civil Aeronautics Board, favoring the major airlines at the expense of the smaller ones, practically put the ' nonscheduled ' independent airlines out of business. Indeed so readily did these commissions yield to political or business pressures and depart from their original quasi-judicial character, that many economists believed that they had outlived their usefulness.

Nowhere did the new conservatism express itself more emphatically than in the attitude toward natural resources. The disposition of off-shore oil was a case in point. President Truman had twice vetoed bills giving control to the states over the underseas oil deposits lying off their shores. In 1947 and 1950 the Supreme Court, while recognizing the special claims of Texas, held that these oil resources belonged to the entire nation.[1] In 1952 Truman assigned underseas oil to the navy as a reserve for use in time of war. The Republican platform of 1952 called for ' *restoration* to the States of their rights to all lands and resources beneath navigable inland and offshore waters '; and Eisenhower was committed to the same principle. Within a few months of his accession he had the satisfaction of signing a Submerged Lands Act which nullified all earlier arrangements and assigned federal rights to the off-shore oil to the seaboard states — three miles in the Atlantic and Pacific Oceans and ten and one-half miles in the Gulf of Mexico.

In the realm of atomic energy also, private interests gained. The Atomic Energy Act of 1954 provided for government financing of atomic research, but farmed out the operation of the new atomic energy plants to private corporations: General Electric at Hanford (Washington), Union Carbide at Oak Ridge (Tennessee). ' In turning a twelve billion dollar investment over to private industry,' wrote Walter Adams and Horace Gray, ' the statute was a milestone in government abdication from the public domain.' [2]

---

[1] *U.S. v. California* 332 U.S. 19; *U.S. v. Louisiana* 339 U.S. 699; *U.S. v. Texas* 339 U.S. 707.

[2] *Monopoly in America: The Government as Promoter.*

If there was one thing that almost all Republicans agreed upon it was the paramount importance of private enterprise in the production of hydroelectric power. President Hoover characterized the proposed TVA as ' the negation of the ideals upon which our civilization has been based '; President Eisenhower declared that the question of power was not primarily an economic but a moral issue. Not only would federal control of hydroelectric power paralyze local enterprise, it would ' pose a threat deadly to our liberties.' And the President, promoting the issue to a celestial plane, added, ' there are spiritual as well as physical values to protect.' The Eisenhower administration cut the budget of the various federal power administrations, abandoned projects already approved by Congress, and jettisoned a Democratic plan for a federally built and controlled dam at Hell's Canyon on the Snake river in Idaho in favor of a series of small dams to be built and operated by the Idaho Power Company.

When, early in his administration, Eisenhower was asked for an example of that ' creeping socialism ' against which he so insistently warned his countrymen, he cited the TVA, and Clarence Manion, whom he had appointed chairman of the Commission on Inter-governmental Relations, went so far as to advocate the sale of it to private industry. That was going too far even for the President, but his attitude was reflected in two illuminating statistics. Between 1952 and 1960 appropriations for the TVA fell from $185 million to $12 million, and the number of employees from 21,300 to 15,000. It was the administration's reluctance to expand this great enterprise that led in 1954–55 to the Dixon-Yates imbroglio. When Congress denied the TVA money to build a new generating plant to serve the needs of Memphis and its vicinity, the Atomic Energy Commission signed a contract for the generating plant with two private utilities, represented by Edgar Dixon and Eugene Yates. The terms of the contract were more than generous. Dixon and Yates were required to contribute only $5.5 million of a total investment of $107 million; the AEC guaranteed a 9 per cent return and exempted them from all taxes. When a congressional investigation revealed that the contract had been written by a consultant to the Bureau of the Budget who, by an odd coincidence, was also vice-president of the corporation which would finance the operation, the Atomic Energy Commission voided the contract and President Eisenhower cancelled it.

Devotion to private enterprise, and suspicion of public, persisted throughout the Eisenhower administration. Shortly after assuming office the President ended all price and rent controls, and did away with the Reconstruction Finance Corporation. He vetoed a school construction bill which he thought interfered unduly with local autonomy, acquiesced in a sharp reduction in federal aid to public housing, and opposed medical insurance amendments to social security bills. It was not that ' Ike ' disliked all ' welfare ' legislation — as his extension of social security proved — but that he wanted the states, not the nation, to assume major responsibility for it, as they had always done under Republican regimes. This came out clearly in his veto of a bill to check the pollution of rivers by sewage and industrial wastes:

Because water pollution is a uniquely local blight, primary responsibility for solving the problem lies not with the Federal Government but rather must be assumed and exercised . . . by State and local governments. . . . Polluted water is a threat to the health and well being of all our citizens. Yet, pollution and its correction are so closely involved with local industrial processes and with public water supply and sewage treatment that the problem can be successfully met only if State and local governments and industry assume the major responsibility for cleaning up the nation's rivers and streams.[3]

3. Dynamic Conservatism

Almost all Republicans agreed that their predecessors had carried centralization to dangerous extremes, and — in the words of the platform — ' turned loose upon the country a swarm of arrogant bureaucrats.' So it is not surprising that few new domestic programs are associated with the Eisenhower administration. Indeed, the average adult American who lived through these eight years would have some difficulty in recalling a single important piece of legislation sponsored by the administration. However, Eisenhower's State of the Union message of 2 February 1953 did outline a somewhat vague domestic program. The true role of government, he said, was to stabilize the economy and encourage the free play of the people's genius for individual initiative. A reduction in taxes was desirable but debt reduction was more important; inflation should be met by limitations on credit, not by wage or price ceilings; government should stay out of the rooms where unions and management were bargaining unless there

[3] Veto of 23 February 1960.

was a threat to the national welfare; flexible price controls were preferred to rigid ones for the farmer. He advocated an extension of social security, amendment of the McCarran Immigration Act, and the development of natural resources through a happy partnership of public and private enterprise.

This was no clarion call to a new freedom, deal, or frontier, but a cautious recommendation of the minimum that a ' welfare '-spoiled public might accept. And the administration's record was not wholly negative. Under Eisenhower's prodding — at times merely with his tacit approval — Congress extended reciprocal trade agreements; enlarged social security to embrace some ten million additional persons in agriculture, government employment, and domestic work; raised the minimum wage to a dollar an hour; enacted drastic legislation to end corruption and racketeering in labor unions and to assure a greater degree of freedom of choice for workers; pushed through two civil-rights bills designed to extend federal guarantees of the political rights of Negroes; established a new Department of Health, Education and Welfare; created an Air Force Academy; authorized a far-reaching reorganization of the Department of Defense; substituted for the Reconstruction Finance Corporation a Small Business Administration; carried through some modest tax reductions; provided for the admission of an additional 214,000 refugees outside the normal immigration quotas; and authorized the construction of a St. Lawrence river seaway which was actually completed by the United States and Canada within the decade.

At his first press conference Eisenhower discussed the perennial farm problem. Production was going up but prices were going down, and the farmers — who mostly agreed with Eisenhower on the danger of bureaucratic controls — were clamoring for relief. The President recommended and Congress reluctantly adopted flexible instead of rigid price supports for leading agricultural commodities, and a program which enabled the government to dispose of mounting surpluses to needy foreign countries. These measures alleviated, but did not solve, the farm problem. In 1954 Minnesota's Senator Humphrey revived Henry Wallace's idea of paying farmers to take their land out of production. This ' soil bank ' idea was at first rejected by Eisenhower, but in 1956 he came around to it, and even persuaded Congress to adopt it. There were two parts to the new program. Under the short-term Acreage Reserve Plan farmers agreed to take farm land out of production in return for certificates to be redeemed either in cash or in produce. Under the long-range Conservation Reserve Plan the government agreed to pay a large part of the cost of taking land out of agricultural production and reserving it for forest, forage, or water storage.

Although the Republican platform of 1952 had charged the Democrats with using ' tax money to make farmers dependent upon goverment,' federal expenditures for agriculture increased during Eisenhower's two terms from 20 to 30 per cent of all expenditures for civil benefits, and by 1959 the government was paying approximately $5 billion for farm supports of one kind or another.

The rising cost of farm subsidies was typical of the kind of problem that bedeviled the Eisenhower administration for eight years. It was an axiom of Republican orthodoxy that an unbalanced budget was the road to ruin, and to this Eisenhower himself subscribed with almost religious fervor. Nothing in Eisenhower's message of February 1953 excited more approval among his followers than his plea for a balanced budget, but he soon discovered that it was one thing to preach the virtues of economy and another to practice them. It proved to be impossible to carry out the campaign promise of a 10 per cent reduction in government employees; there was a minor reduction of less than 100,000 people, but rising costs canceled out the hoped-for-savings. Inasmuch as almost two-thirds of federal expenditures went into defense, the budget could be pruned only at the risk of jeopardizing national security. As a result of expanding military costs, economic recession, and the consequent reduction of tax revenue, the administration achieved a balanced budget in only three of its eight years. In 1959 the deficit reached a peacetime record of $12.9 billion, and in the eight years of the Eisenhower administration the total of deficit over surplus came to some $20 billion.

The Republicans had promised not only to balance the budget, but to reduce taxes as well; they speedily discovered that the two policies were incompatible. Yet in 1954 by eliminating excess-profits taxes, lowering taxes on incomes from dividends, and increasing deductions in the lower income brackets, the Treasury managed to cut taxes a bit. It gave some relief to hard-pressed industrialists by liberal depreciation ' write-offs,' and by depletion allowances for oil companies. Thus in 1953, thirty-five oil companies, with a revenue of some $20 billion, were able to charge off to depletion and other expenses some $17 billion; on the remaining $3 billion they paid $981 million in taxes — 30 per cent of net income compared to the 52 per cent required of corporations generally. Equally helpful to business was an accelerated amortization policy which enabled corporations to write off the total cost of privately built facilities 'necessary to the national defense'; in five years the Treasury permitted industry to 'write off' some $30 billion of such facilities, a saving to the owners — according to Secretary Humphrey — of some $880 million a year.

For one of the long-needed accomplishments of the administration, the Senate rather than the President was responsible. That was the liquidation of Senator McCarthy as an effective force — though not, as yet, the liquidation of McCarthyism. The Republican victory of 1952 owed not a little to the guerrilla warfare tactics of the junior Senator from Wisconsin, and if Eisenhower did not endorse them, neither did he repudiate them. ' By the Administration's appeasement of Communism at home and abroad,' said the Republican platform, ' it has permitted Communists and their fellow travelers to serve in many key agencies and to infiltrate our American life.' Shortly after taking office Eisenhower undertook to substantiate this charge by extending the security system to all agencies of the government,[4] by replacing the earlier criterion of ' loyalty ' with a broader and vaguer criterion of ' security risk,' and by authorizing the discharge of any person whose employment was not ' clearly consistent with the interests of national security.' Between May 1953 and October 1954 no fewer than 6926 ' security risks ' were ' separated ' from their government jobs. Very few of these were even charged with subversion, and not one had committed any crime or breach of duty for which he was brought to trial in a court of law.

All this display of zeal, however, failed to assuage McCarthy, who, not impressed with the administration's house-cleaning, now trained his guns on the administration itself. McCarthy was both impartial and indiscriminate in his attacks: he objected to Eisenhower's new Ambassador to Russia, Charles Bohlen, because he had been at Yalta; he charged that the Army Signal Corps at Fort Monmouth was riddled with subversion; he sent to Europe two semi-illiterate assistants to track down and destroy ' subversive ' literature (such as the works of Emerson and Thoreau) in libraries of the American In-

---

[4] In 1956 the Supreme Court held that this order applied only to workers in ' sensitive ' positions. *Cole v. Young* 351 U.S. 536.

formation Service — a usurpation of State Department authority in which Secretary Dulles readily acquiesced in the hope of appeasing McCarthy. Early in 1954, McCarthy seized on the case of an obscure army dentist, a major who had been given an honorable discharge from the Army notwithstanding a suspicion of Communist sympathies. In the course of an investigation of this trivial episode McCarthy browbeat the major's superior, General Zwicker, and then turned on Robert Stevens, Secretary of the Army, who allowed himself to be bullied into signing a ' memorandum of agreement ' with the Senator. No wonder Adlai Stevenson called the Republican party ' half McCarthy, half Eisenhower.' But by this time the Senator had gone too far for the moderates in his own party. In March the army struck back with the charge that McCarthy had demanded preferential treatment in the army for one of his book-burning aides who had been drafted. The Senator counterattacked with forty-six charges against the army, and the war was on. The month-long hearings to determine the facts were televised on national networks, and the whole country watched with a kind of horrified fascination the spectacle of McCarthy bullying witnesses, even high officials and army officers. When it became clear that public opinion was turning against McCarthy, the administration's backbone stiffened, and when the Senator arrogantly asserted that government employees were ' duty bound ' to give him ' information even though some bureaucrat may have stamped it secret,' Eisenhower was moved to denounce usurpation by an individual who undertook ' to set himself above the laws of our land or to override orders of the President of the United States.' No sooner was the investigation concluded than Republican Senator Flanders of Vermont moved that the Senate formally censure McCarthy for improper conduct. A Senate committee headed by Watkins of Utah, another Republican, recommended censure, and on 2 December 1954 the Senate formally ' condemned ' McCarthy by a vote of 67 to 22. That ended McCarthy's power, and he died three years later.

4. Desegregation and Civil Rights

Notwithstanding the solemn guarantees of the Fourteenth and Fifteenth Amendments, and the supposed safeguards of the Civil Rights bills, Negroes, as the centenary of the Civil War approached, were still second-class citizens throughout the South and in parts of the North too. Negro children were fobbed off with schools that were not only segregated but physically and academically inferior, and Negro youths were denied entrance to the state universities they helped to support by taxation. When Negroes traveled they were forced to use segregated waiting rooms and sections of buses and denied access to Pullman cars. They were not permitted to sit with white people in theaters, movies, restaurants, or at lunch counters; even in many churches. Half a century after Booker T. Washington's famous Atlanta speech calling for economic and industrial partnership between white and black, Negroes were mostly tenant farmers or unskilled laborers, excluded from the skilled jobs by the labor unions, North and South alike. Urban Negroes lived in slums that would have been called ghettos had they been in Warsaw or Prague. Their right to vote was flouted by various devices, and without fellow Negroes on juries it was impossible for many to obtain a fair trial.

The New Deal made the first substantial dent in this façade of white exclusiveness, and World War II broke down segregation in the armed forces. To prevent a return of discrimination after the war, President Truman proclaimed, by executive order, ' equality of treatment and opportunity for all persons in the armed services without regard to race, color, religion or national origins.' During the war many Negroes had enjoyed being treated as equals in countries of the Old World, so it is not surprising that when peace came they were reluctant to go back to the old position of enforced inferiority. Moreover, peace brought an end to the heavy concentration of color in the South. Between 1940 and 1960 Negroes in the North increased from 2.8 to 7.2 million, while in the South they barely held their own. New York now had more Negroes than any other state, and among the cities with the largest Negro population were New York, Philadelphia, Chicago, Washington, and Detroit. This meant that economically and politically the Negroes were a power to be reckoned with, for it was not practical to deny social rights to those who had achieved economic independence, or political rights to those who might hold the balance of power. What is more, the great increase in the number of Negro intellectuals and college graduates provided a new Negro leadership, which no longer looked to Booker T. Washington for inspiration.

In the meantime the conscience of the American people had been deeply disturbed by what the great Swedish sociologist, Gunnar Myrdal, called the American Dilemma — the dilemma of commitment to both equality and to white superiority — and by the spectacle of the ravages of racism in Nazi Germany. Nor was the problem wholly moral. At a time when the colonial peoples of Africa and Asia were bursting their bonds and emerging into the sunshine of liberty, and when the United States was trying to win them to the side of the democracies, it was embarrassing, and even stultifying, to maintain at home a policy that made a dark skin a badge of inferiority.

The new attitude toward the Negro was foreshadowed by a series of state and federal laws and executive orders forbidding racial discrimination in employment, both in civil service and in industry, and by Supreme Court decisions chipping away at the stone wall of separation and prejudice erected by the states of the South. One series of Court decisions looked to the practical implementation of due process and fair trial by requiring Negro representation on juries; another required political parties to act as public, not private bodies; a third announced the beginning of the end of discrimination in public facilities such as housing and interstate transportation.

The climax of the judicial assault on white supremacy, and one of the historic decisions of the Supreme Court, was the decision in the school segregation case, *Brown v. Board of Education of Topeka,* of 1954.[5] Back in 1896 the Supreme Court had held — over the protest of Justice Harlan — that the Fourteenth Amendment did not require that Negroes and whites share all public facilities, and that it was not illegal for such facilities to be ' separate ' as long as they were ' equal.' The principle of this ruling, though subject to serious qualification, had survived. In the Brown case a unanimous Court, speaking through Chief Justice Warren, reversed this decision and held that ' separate educational facilities are inherently unequal.' It followed this ruling with another in May 1955 which required that Southern states proceed with desegregation ' with all deliberate speed,' and assigned to the lower courts responsibility for applying this principle in the school districts of the South.[6]

In the event, the deliberateness became more apparent than the speed. In the border states — except Virginia — desegregation encountered only sporadic resistance. In the Deep South, however, the

[5] *Brown v. Board of Education of Topeka* 347 U.S. 483.   [6] 349 U.S. 294.

segregationists stood firm, hoping that district judges would find some legal means to frustrate the Supreme Court decision, or to delay its implementation. When, in decision after decision, the courts ordered school boards to proceed with integration, the beleaguered defenders of segregation resorted to less formal and more drastic measures. Organizing themselves into White Citizens' Councils, they whipped up the already sensitive public opinion to fever pitch, brought pressure on state officials and on congressmen, and, in the words of Senator Byrd of Virginia, confronted the federal authorities — and the Negroes — with ' massive resistance.' In March 1956 one hundred Southern congressmen sought to throw a mantle of legality over these acts of defiance by a ' Declaration ' of constitutional principles. ' We commend the motives of those states,' it said, ' which have declared the intention to resist forced integration by any lawful means. . . .' Southern legislatures hastily threw up a barricade of legislation and regulation designed to impede integration: within a few months five Southern states adopted forty-two segregation measures. Georgia made it a felony for any school official to spend tax money for public schools in which the races were mixed; Mississippi made it a crime for any organization to institute desegregation proceedings in the state courts; North Carolina withheld school funds from any school district which integrated its public schools. Some states sanctioned segregation on the ground not of ' race ' but of ' public health, morals, and good order '; some segregated pupils according to ' scholastic ability '; some put the burden of initiating action for desegregation on the individuals in each school district, thus assuring endless litigation; some made a gesture of purely token integration. Virginia went to the extreme of closing public schools altogether and enrolling white children in segregated ' private ' schools. Where these methods failed, or where Negroes attempted to nullify them, there was resort to force. In 1953 a mob at the University of Alabama had forced the expulsion of a Negro girl; in September 1956 a mob attempting to prevent twelve Negro students from attending classes at the high school in Clinton, Tennessee, had to be restrained by the National Guard.

The issue came to a head in Little Rock, Arkansas, where, in 1957, Governor Orval Faubus called out the state National Guard, not to protect the Negro children in their right to attend the public schools but to prevent them from exercising that right. When these troops were withdrawn on order of the federal district judge, a mob prevented Negro students from entering that local high school, thus neatly vindicating the Governor's contention that the troops had been necessary to preserve order. On 24 September President Eisenhower dispatched federal troops to Little Rock to preserve order and protect Negro children. ' Mob rule,' he said, ' can not be allowed to override the decisions of our courts.' [7] The people of Arkansas, however, rallied to this new nullification by re-electing Faubus to the governorship, and he continued his tactics of obstruction. In June 1958 the Little Rock school board obtained from a federal district judge a delay of two and one-half years for integration. When the Circuit Court of Appeals overturned this decision, the school board appealed to the Supreme Court. On 12 September the Court unanimously refused to permit further delay. ' The constitutional rights [of the children] are not to be sacrificed or yielded to the violence and disorder which have followed the actions of the Governor and Legislature. . . . Law and order are not to be preserved by depriving the Negro children of their constitutional rights.' [8]

This decision seemed to represent the limits of the Court's power to enforce its segregation order. The rest would have to come from the executive branch, and from the people themselves, in their local communities. The executive branch did not know what to do; the white people of the Deep South, contemplating with satisfaction the success of their ' massive resistance,' and closing their eyes to the price they paid for that success, hardened their hearts against compromise or concession. Six years after the Court had called for de-

[7] When Senator Russell of Georgia compared Eisenhower's action with Hitler's use of storm troops, the President replied, ' When a state, by seeking to frustrate the orders of a Federal Court, encourages mobs of extremists to flout the orders of a Federal Court, and when a State refuses to utilize its police powers to protect against mobs persons who are peaceably exercising their right under the Constitution as defined in such Court orders, the oath of office of the President requires that he take action to give that protection. Failure to act in such a case would be tantamount to acquiescence in anarchy and the dissolution of the union.'

[8] *Cooper v. Aaron* 358 U.S. 1. In his concurring opinion Justice Frankfurter was even more vigorous: ' No explanation that may be offered in support of [this] request can obscure the inescapable meaning that the law should bow to force. To yield to such a claim would be to enthrone official lawlessness, and lawlessness if not checked is the precursor of anarchy. . . . Violent resistance to law can not be made a legal reason for its suspension without loosening the fabric of our society. For those in authority thus to defy the law of the land is profoundly subversive not only of our constitutional system but of the presuppositions of a democratic society.'

segregation with ' all deliberate speed,' schools were integrated in the District of Columbia and the border states, and in parts of Oklahoma and Texas; there was token integration in Virginia, Tennessee, North Carolina, and Florida; but there was not a single integrated school in South Carolina, Georgia, Alabama, Mississippi, or Louisiana.

Against the probability that desegregation would prove unenforceable in the Deep South had to be set the growing determination of the Negroes themselves to insist on their moral and constitutional rights. In previous stages of the controversy over civil rights, the Negroes had played a passive rather than an active role. In the decade of the 'fifties Southern Negroes for the first time began to take matters into their own hands. In a number of cities they staged successful demonstrations against segregation in streetcars and buses. Then, in the spring of 1960, Negro students, inspired by the example of Gandhi's passive resistance movement, began to ' sit in ' at lunch counters in drug stores and at shopping centers. Within a few weeks the sit-in movement had swept the South and inspired widespread demonstrations of sympathy in the North among both whites and Negroes. Southern authorities responded with wholesale arrests, but in *Garner v. Louisiana* the Supreme Court voided these arrests on the narrow ground that sit-ins did not constitute a breach of the peace; the larger constitutional question of the obligation of any business engaged in public service to give that service without discrimination was put off for later adjudication. It was largely the pressure of economic boycott by Negroes, particularly on nation-wide business organizations, that put an end to segregation in stores and lunch counters, and in 1961 a more vigorous enforcement policy inaugurated by the new Attorney-General Robert Kennedy outlawed discrimination in interstate travel. The sit-in movement served notice on the South that Negroes intended to claim their legal rights, and that they were prepared to use economic and political as well as legal weapons in that struggle.

5. POLITICS AND THE ELECTION OF 1960

Political analysts like Samuel Lubbell, surveying the political scene in the early 'fifties, and peering into the future, concluded that the outlook for the Democratic party was bleak. The strength of the Democracy, as they saw it, lay in four groups united in uneasy alliance: Southerners still clinging stubbornly to the tradition of a one-party South; Negroes bemused by what Franklin Roosevelt and Harry Truman had done for them; organized labor which had gained much from Democratic administrations and was confident that it would get more; and city voters who, like white Southerners, were creatures of habit and tradition. But, said the analysts, all this was changing. The South was becoming industrialized, and could no longer be counted on to follow tradition; Negroes, outraged by Southern (and therefore Democratic) recalcitrance on racial issues, would swing back to their old Republican allegiance; labor, as it became more prosperous, would move over to the party of business and of prosperity; and as workers moved out of the central cities and into the suburbs, they would quietly shift their allegiance to the Republican party, membership in which gave status.

None of these predictions came true. The Republican party did grow in the South, but not fast enough to shift the balance of power. Negroes remained faithful to the memory of Franklin and Eleanor Roosevelt; organized labor had a lively expectation of favors yet to come from the Democrats; and instead of the suburbs turning newcomers into ' respectable ' Republicans, the newcomers swung many suburbs into the Democratic column.

What is more, the Democratic party discovered a new group of leaders who seemed to have a more realistic sense of the direction of domestic and world affairs than did their political opponents, and more popular appeal as well: elder statesmen like Adlai Stevenson, Chester Bowles, William Fulbright, and Paul Douglas, and younger statesmen like Hubert Humphrey and Eugene McCarthy of Minnesota, Henry Jackson of Washington, William Proxmire of Wisconsin, Richard Neuberger of Oregon, and John F. Kennedy of Massachusetts. No one of these commanded the affection and devotion that Eisenhower aroused, but precisely because Eisenhower chose to be a national and not a party leader, he was unable to transfer his prestige to anyone, even the Vice-President. Republican strength began to decline shortly after Eisenhower's inauguration. The Republicans lost several gubernatorial contests in 1953, and in the congressional elections of 1954 the Democrats obtained control of both houses of Congress. It was, to be sure, only a technical control, because a coalition of Republicans and Southern Bourbons rendered the Democratic party largely impotent through most of the Eisenhower administration.

According to public opinion polls no President — not even F.D.R. — had been more generally liked than ' Ike,' and it was taken for granted that he would win a second term. In the latter part of 1955 he made a remarkable recovery from a heart attack (thanks largely to his physician, Dr. Paul Dudley White), and by January 1956 was back at his desk in the White House. Next month he set speculation at rest by announcing that he would stand for re-election that fall.

The Republican convention, meeting in San Francisco in August of 1956, renominated President Eisenhower by acclamation and, after only token opposition, named Nixon as his running mate; the platform rang the familiar changes on the themes of paternalism, the welfare state, and federal centralization. But if the outcome of the Republican convention was a foregone conclusion, not so the Democratic. In 1952 Governor Stevenson had been ' drafted,' but in 1956 he was obliged to make a fight for it against Senator Kefauver, a Southern liberal whose pose of homespun simplicity masked sharp intelligence and bold independence. He withdrew from the race after Stevenson captured the California primary by almost half a million votes. Notwithstanding a last-minute effort by President Truman to whip up support for Governor Harriman of New York, Stevenson won the nomination on the first ballot.

Both candidates were familiar, as were the issues that they discussed and the issues that they avoided. Only toward the end of the campaign did Governor Stevenson inject some interest into it, with two controversial proposals: that the selective service system be discontinued and the army rely henceforth on a small corps of highly trained professionals; and that the United States suspend hydrogen bomb tests as a practical step toward disarmament and as a moral gesture. Both proposals were sensible enough, and Eisenhower — who dismissed the hydrogen bomb proposal as ' a theatrical gesture ' — actually adopted it within two years but neither was designed to win a serious hearing during the hurly-burly of a presidential campaign.

Stevenson campaigned vigorously, and once again inspired almost fanatical devotion in his followers, but actually he never had a chance. It was not merely that the Republicans had plenty of money, and could count on the support of some 80 per cent of the press; that familiar situation had not prevented Roosevelt and Truman from winning elections. It was rather that Eisenhower had come to seem the very symbol of courage, honesty, fairness, and unity — those virtues which appealed most strongly to the plain people of the country. He had ended the war in Korea; avoided war over Vietnam; ridden out the threat of war with China; he had even silenced McCarthy. Fate herself was on his side. The very week of the election the long-festering Suez crisis came to a head when Israel, France, and Britain sent armed forces against Nasser's Egypt; the United Nations condemned this as aggression. Eisenhower took to the air to recall the West to its moral principles and could claim that he had won a cease-fire agreement — though the Soviets had something to do with it too. That same week the Hungarians revolted against their Communist overlords and Russian tanks poured into the hapless country to suppress the revolt. Clearly this was no time to ' change horses.'

The election was a triumph for Eisenhower — but not for his party. The President polled 35,590,000 votes and swept 41 states with a total electoral vote of 457; Stevenson polled 26,022,000 votes, winning 7 states with 73 electoral votes. It was the most one-sided victory since Roosevelt had defeated Landon in 1936. The President broke into the once-solid South, winning not only Florida, Virginia, and Tennessee, but also Texas, Oklahoma, and Louisiana. He carried most of the large cities of the North — traditionally the strongholds of the Democracy — and made heavy inroads on both the labor and the Negro vote. Yet the Democrats again won the congressional elections, holding their narrow majority of two in the Senate, and increasing their House majority to thirty-three.

So Eisenhower remained in the White House, sustained by an almost unprecedented vote of confidence. By asserting himself he could have carried through almost any reasonable program. Unfortunately he had no program, except the familiar one of peace and prosperity, and with the passing of time it became increasingly difficult for him to maintain either. The new administration was plagued by a severe economic recession in 1957, by a budget that grew ever more unbalanced, by agricultural discontent, a stormy controversy over civil rights, and new and vehement attacks on the Supreme Court.

As a result of these circumstances, his second administration was not so effective as it might have been. Yet its achievements were not inconsiderable: (1) another extension of the Reciprocal Trade Act;

(2) an amendment to the Atomic Energy Act of 1954, permitting more effective co-operation in atomic research and the exchange of scientific information with allied nations; (3) the creation of a National Aeronautics and Space Administration to direct space research; (4) the admission of Hawaii and Alaska to statehood; (5) the enactment of a National Defense Education Act which provided some $887 million for student loans and the support of language and science teaching; (6) the creation of a Civil Rights Commission to investigate deprivations of civil and political rights by reason of race and color; (7) legislation to wipe out corruption in labor unions and protect union members in the right to vote in union elections.

During the last session of Congress in his administration President Eisenhower exercised a more vigorous leadership than he had in the previous six years. This was largely the result of losing his two most trusted lieutenants. In September 1958 Sherman Adams had to resign as confidential assistant to the President after a congressional committee had exposed his indiscreet relations with a shady industrial promotor. And in May 1959 death claimed the Secretary of State John Foster Dulles. Bereft of the two men on whom he had most heavily leaned, Eisenhower discovered in himself an unexpected political resourcefulness. He spoke more freely and more confidently in press conferences, took an active interest in the bills considered by the Congress, acted as his own Secretary of State, and made a foreign tour as far afield as India. Although his popularity remained as high as ever, the country was increasingly restive, and in 1958 the Republicans suffered their third consecutive congressional defeat — an event unprecedented in the history of a party that currently controlled the executive branch. The Democrats increased their congressional majority in the House from 233 to 283 — and in the Senate their numbers rose from 49 to 64. They unseated Republican governors in key states like Maryland, Ohio, Wisconsin, and California, giving them control of thirty-three states. It was the right wing of the party that suffered most. Reactionary Senators like Bricker of Ohio, Payne of Maine, and Revercomb of West Virginia went down to defeat while others like Jenner of Indiana and Malone of Nevada withdrew voluntarily to private life. Only in New York were the Republicans able to breast this current of discontent: there the liberal and internationalist Nelson Rockefeller won an impressive victory over his Democratic opponent. In the words of Walter

Lippmann the election meant that the people ' wanted their government to come alive and to be alert and to show vigor, and not to keep
mouthing the same old slogans and not to dawdle along in the same
old ruts.'

The Twenty-second Amendment now made it impossible for President Eisenhower to succeed himself; whether the President would
have accepted a third nomination is doubtful, but he would doubtless have been re-elected if he had been able to accept it. Republicans
did not have to look far for a candidate. Back in 1952 Eisenhower
had said of Richard Nixon, ' he's my boy,' and the passing years had
not blunted the President's confidence in the Vice-President. As the
Republican convention approached, it became clear that this vigorous
and ambitious young man would have little competition for the nomination. Nelson Rockefeller briefly threatened a contest, but was
easily dissuaded, and at the Chicago convention Mr. Nixon was
named on the first ballot. To balance the ticket with an Easterner
and an internationalist, the convention chose as his running mate
Henry Cabot Lodge of Massachusetts, member of a distinguished
political family and, since his defeat by John F. Kennedy for re-
election to the Senate, the chief United States representative at the
United Nations.

A succession of congressional victories, and a growing discontent
with what seemed to be a policy of drift, had inspired the Democracy
with a vision of victory in 1960. Competition for the presidential
nomination was therefore lively. Adlai Stevenson was still not only
the titular but the moral leader of his party, but he was handicapped
by the burden of two defeats — something no previous candidate had
ever overcome — by the refusal of organized labor and the big city
bosses to support him with any enthusiasm, and by his own procrastination. The early contenders were Senator Lyndon Johnson of Texas,
who represented the more moderate Southern wing of his party;
Senator Hubert Humphrey of Minnesota, who spoke for the uncompromising liberals; and Senator John F. Kennedy of Massachusetts,
who was looked upon as a middle-of-the-roader, but who in fact was
as liberal on both domestic and international issues as Humphrey
himself.

In the beginning almost everything seemed to be against Kennedy.
He was a Roman Catholic and Al Smith's defeat was well remembered; he was only 43 years old, and if elected would be the youngest

man ever to be chosen for the presidency; he came from a state which had not provided a candidate since John Quincy Adams, except for the accidental one of Calvin Coolidge; he was rich and had gone to Choate School and to Harvard College, had written two books, and so was obviously both an aristocrat and an intellectual. These apparent drawbacks were counter-balanced by advantages. Born to politics — his maternal grandfather was Mayor John F. Fitzgerald (' Honey Fitz ') of Boston, his multimillionaire father had been ambassador to Britain — he was young and personable and had a beautiful wife; his war record was dramatic and heroic; he had a talent for organization. The Kennedys — for the entire clan turned out to work for ' Jack ' — caught the popular imagination and inspired confidence; he seemed to old-timers like a new Teddy Roosevelt.

Challenging the older politicians of his own party, Kennedy entered the primaries in seven widely separated states, and won them all. Campaigning indefatigably, with a powerful organization and ample funds, he entered the Democratic convention in Los Angeles as a heavy favorite. Although Stevenson inspired the most fervid acclamation from the galleries, Kennedy had the convention well in hand even before it opened, and managed to win on the first ballot. With characteristic boldness he promptly took command, and persuaded the convention to name Lyndon Johnson, his most formidable rival, to the second place on the ticket, and Johnson to accept — a sagacious move that united the party.

This was the first presidential pair born in the twentieth century. The issues were significant and the differences between the parties not insignificant; yet the campaign itself was dull. The only thing that relieved the general apathy was a television ' debate ' between the two candidates, which showed Kennedy not to be the inexperienced young man that the Republicans had described, but witty, alert, and intelligent, always in command of himself and of the situation.

The election itself was the closest since that of 1916. Early reports showed Kennedy well ahead, but gradually his lead was cut to almost the vanishing point, and not for two or three days was it certain that he had won. His popular majority was only 118,000 out of a total of some 68 million votes, but he rolled up a comfortable majority of 303 to 219 in the electoral college.[9] The narrowness of the victory should

[9] Fifteen votes went to Senator Byrd of Virginia.

PRESIDENTIAL ELECTION 1960.

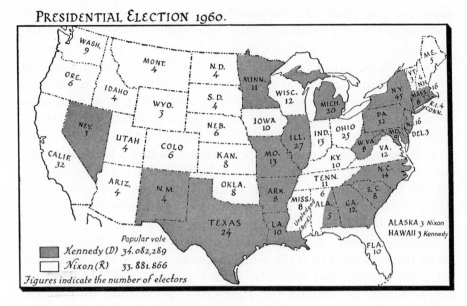

Popular vote
Kennedy (D) 34,082,289
Nixon (R) 33,881,866
Figures indicate the number of electors

not blind us to its astonishing character. Kennedy and Johnson ended eight years of Republican rule at a time when the nation was enjoying both peace and prosperity; they overcame the immense popularity of Eisenhower and the experience of Nixon; they increased the Democratic electoral vote by 230 and the popular vote by over eight million over 1956 — and all this with a handicap of youth, Catholicism, geography, and a discontented South!

Ten weeks later as blustery winds and snow flurries swept across Washington, one hundred million Americans watched the inauguration ceremonies on television, and heard the new President reaffirm their revolutionary inheritance:

Let the word go forth from this time and place, to friend and foe alike, that the torch has been passed to a new generation of Americans — born in this century, tempered by war, disciplined by a hard and bitter peace, proud of our ancient heritage, and unwilling to witness or permit the slow undoing of those human rights to which this Nation has always been committed.

He called for an end to the Cold War, an end to the futile and wasteful competition in arms, and proposed instead co-operation among the great powers:

Let both sides seek to invoke the wonders of science instead of its terrors. Together let us explore the stars, conquer the deserts, eradicate disease, tap the ocean depths and encourage the arts and commerce. Let both sides join in [creating] a new world of law, where the strong are just and the weak secure and the peace preserved.

He called upon his generation

to bear the burden of a long twilight struggle, year in and year out, ' rejoicing in hope, patient in tribulation ' — a struggle against the common enemies of man: tyranny, poverty, disease and war itself.

And he concluded with a characteristic affirmation of confidence and of faith:

I do not believe that any of us would exchange places with any other people or any other generation. The energy, the faith, the devotion which we bring to this endeavor will light our country and all who serve it — and the glow from that fire can truly light the world.

BIBLIOGRAPHY

1. GENERAL. Sherman Adams, *First-Hand Report: Story of the Eisenhower Administration;* J. R. Beal, *John Foster Dulles;* Harry Butcher, *My Three Years with Eisenhower;* Marquis Childs, *Eisenhower: Captive Hero;* Robert J. Donovan, *Eisenhower: The Inside Story;* Eric Goldman, *The Crucial Decade 1945– 1955;* Walter Johnson, *1600 Pennsylvania Avenue;* William R. Kintner, *et al., Forging a New Sword: A Study of the Department of Defense;* Louis Koenig, *The Invisible Presidency;* Martin Merson, *The Private Diary of a Public Servant;* Merlo J. Pusey, *Eisenhower the President;* Richard Rovere, *The Eisenhower Years: Affairs of State.*

2. CONSERVATISM, MODERATE AND DYNAMIC. William Anderson, *The Nation and the States;* E. R. Bartley, *The Tidelands Oil Controversy;* Daniel Bell (ed.) , *The New American Right;* Richard Fenno, *The President's Cabinet;* A. E. Holmans, *United States Fiscal Policy, 1945–1959;* Philip Jessup, *The Law of Territorial Waters;* Richard Rovere, *Senator Joe McCarthy;* J. E. Russell (ed), *National Policies for Education, Health and Social Service;* Michael Straight, *Trial by Television;* Telford Taylor, *Grand Inquest;* Aaron Wildavsky, *Dixon-Yates: A Study in Power Politics;* William R. Willoughby, *The St. Lawrence Waterway;* A. Yarmolinsky, *Case Studies in Personal Security.*

3. DESEGREGATION AND CIVIL RIGHTS. Harry Ashmore, *The Negro and the Schools;* Monroe Berger, *Equality by Statute: Legal Controls over Discrimination;* Walter Gellhorn, *American Rights;* Robert Harris, *The Quest for Equality;* David Loth & Harold Fleming, *Integration North and South;* Walter F. Murphy, *Congress and the Court;* B. A. Nelson, *The Fourteenth Amendment and the Negro since 1920;* William Peters, *The Southern Temper;* Don Shoemaker (ed.) , *With All Deliberate Speed: Segregation — Desegregation.*

4. POLITICS AND THE ELECTION OF 1960. Dean Acheson, *A Democrat Looks at His Party;* Nathan Blumberg, *One Party Press: Press Coverage of the 1952 Campaign;* Stuart G. Brown, *Conscience in Politics: Adlai Stevenson;* James McG. Burns, *John F. Kennedy;* L. Harris, *Is There a Republican Majority?;* Walter Johnson, *How We Drafted Adlai Stevenson;* John F. Kennedy, *Let Us Begin* and *The Strategy of Peace,* ed. by Allan Nevins; Arthur Larson, *A Republican Looks at His Party;* Samuel Lubbell, *The Future of American Politics* and *The Revolt of the Moderates;* Richard M. Nixon, *Six Crises;* Arthur E. Rowse, *Slanted News;* Adlai Stevenson, *The New America;* Theodore White, *The Making of the President, 1960.*

5. DOCUMENTS. H. S. Commager, *Documents,* nos. 606–33; *The Public Papers of Dwight D. Eisenhower* (8 vols.) ; Kirk Porter & Donald B. Johnson, *National Party Platforms 1840–1960.*

World Power in the Nuclear Age

1. THE NEW LOOK AND THE OLD VIEW

THE administrations of Roosevelt and Truman had been the most troubled in American history since Lincoln's, and the election of Eisenhower, if not a mandate for ' normalcy ' such as that of Harding in 1920, was clearly a vote for peace and security. The campaign attempted to fasten responsibility for the war, subversion, the advance of Communism, and the ' loss ' of China on the Democrats; and there was a lively expectation that with the return of the Republicans history would reverse itself. This was explicit in the Republican platform and implicit in President Eisenhower's observation in his State of the Union message that ' our country has come through a painful period of trial and disillusionment since the victory of 1945. We anticipated a world of peace and co-operation. . . . calculated pressures have forced us, instead, to live in a world of turmoil.'

But alas for expectations, nothing was changed by the election and Americans continued to live in a world of turmoil. It is no wonder that the 'fifties was a decade of mounting tensions. It was ushered in by a kind of stalemate in Korea. Even in 1815 Americans had persuaded themselves that they had won the late war; now for the first time in their history they had to be content with something less than victory. That was prophetic of much to come. The eight years of the Eisenhower administration, in foreign affairs, were to be filled with danger and strife, compromise and concession, disappointment and frustration. Yet if there was no dramatic reversal of the lava flow of history, there was, at least, a kind of peace. In the circumstances that was almost a triumph.

All around the globe there was crisis: crisis in Vietnam, in the Straits of Formosa, in Jordan and Saudi Arabia, in Hungary, in the Middle East and Suez, in Berlin, in Kashmir, in the Argentine, in Guatemala, in the Congo, in Cuba — turn where you would, there

was crisis. Inevitably the United States was involved in every one —
such was the price of power. And all the time, filling the horizon and
darkening the skies, was the never-ending crisis presented by the implacable growth of Soviet and Chinese power, and the relentless threat
of atomic annihilation. A people who for generations had come to
expect peace and security and who, in every major struggle, had imposed their will on the seeming chaos of history, now had to learn to
live with fear and insecurity. No wonder that there was a mounting
sense of exasperation and of impatience. After trying for a decade to
build a peaceful world, after convulsive efforts to strengthen military
defenses, after subsidies to our allies and associates of over $50 billion
— after all this we still found ourselves embattled and beleaguered.
With the best of intentions the new administration of 1953 was able
to provide neither certitude nor peace nor help for pain — and the
same could be said of the new administration of 1961!

In a sense the Republicans were the prisoners of their campaign
propaganda. They were pledged to the dogma of ' betrayal ' at Yalta
and in China, and as a result were committed to the support of
Chiang Kai-shek. Because the doctrine of ' containment ' was associated with the Truman administration, they felt it incumbent on them
to replace it by the principle of ' liberation ' — which they were
unable to implement. Because they had persuaded themselves that
Russian advances in atomic science were the product not of Russian scientific skill but of the betrayal of atomic secrets by American
Communists, they were unprepared for the Russian invention of the
hydrogen bomb and for Russian leadership in satellites and missiles.
Because they had told themselves that the State Department was riddled with subversives, they played into the hands of extremists like
Senator McCarthy, who demoralized the Department and the Foreign
Service, and deprived themselves of experienced diplomats and experts just when most needed. And because they were pledged to economy, they attempted to buy security by concentrating on atomic
weapons at the expense of conventional arms.

But the new administration speedily discovered that there was far
less room for maneuver in the conduct of foreign affairs than they
had imagined. The great forces that surrounded and glared upon
them were not to be outwitted by shifts in pace, or evaded by subterfuge, or exorcised by pious words. There was a ' New Look,' to be
sure, but the view remained dismally the same. There it was, spread

before them: the might of Russia, the immensity of China, the ambitions of France, the intransigence of Germany, the nationalist revolts of the non-European peoples against imperialism and colonialism, the hostility of the Arabs to Israel, of Pakistan to India, the pull of neutralism, the population explosion, the technological revolution, the threat of atomic fission. These were the stubborn facts and forces that fixed the latitude and the longitude of foreign policy.

Nor was the conduct of foreign policy by the new administration circumscribed by these external factors alone. It wanted clear military supremacy — but a balanced budget. It needed the best scientific and political talents in the country, but followed policies of harassment and persecution which made it increasingly difficult to attract such talents to government service. It hoped to ' liberate ' oppressed peoples, but was unable to do so without the danger of war, and this conflict between hope and realism gave an impression of insincerity. It desired closer ties with our European associates, and with the uncommitted countries, but by identifying the American version of private enterprise with freedom, it antagonized important elements in those countries. It recognized that the real struggle was for the minds of men, but put emphasis — and money — on the military rather than on economic or cultural programs. It looked for long-range solutions, but was impatient for quick returns. It championed the United Nations, but worked through regional or bilateral agreements which tended to weaken that organization. It encouraged change and progress, but yearned for stability; encouraged revolution, but expected that revolution to be respectable, and in fact misjudged such revolutions as occurred, notably in Cuba. It supported such friends as Chiang Kai-shek, Syngman Rhee, Batista, and Trujillo, even though such support forfeited the confidence of liberal elements elsewhere on the globe and challenged the sincerity of our own commitment to reform.

The foreign aid and containment policies of the Truman administration had succeeded in their primary objective of strengthening the non-Communist countries and preventing further extension of Communism by force. In Iran, Turkey, Greece, Berlin, and Korea, the Reds had discovered that no such easy victories lay open to them as had been achieved by Hitler as a result of Western apathy. But Communism was both more flexible and more ingenious than Nazism. Balked in attempts at military expansion, the Communists turned

WORLD ALIGNMENT 1962. All nations, except Germany, China, Korea, Vietnam, Switzerland, and some small countries, are members of the United Nations. All American countries, except Canada are members of the Rio Pact of 1947. All

Communist nations, except Yugoslavia, are members of the Warsaw Pact of 1955. The division of Germany, Korea, Laos, and Vietnam and the seizure of Estonia, Latvia, Lithuania, and Tibet are not recognized by the West.

instead to exploiting the grievances of Asian and African people emerging from the long night of colonialism into the uncertain day of national independence. In the struggle for the support of these peoples, the Communists played upon the hostility of ex-colonials toward the West and the resentment of colored peoples against the whites; and upon the fact that the Reds were newcomers on the international scene.

Would Western policy prove sufficiently resourceful to meet these challenges? The logical response was that of the Marshall Plan and the Point Four program — to support the economies of new nations so that they would themselves be strong enough to defeat aggression and stamp out subversion. This called for a heavy concentration on economic aid, for a strong information program which would make clear the different methods and objectives of the free and the Communist worlds, and above all for patience and understanding. But to the new administration, this seemed negative and sterile. Some of their spokesmen yielded, naturally enough, to the temptation to substitute words for deeds and promises for policies. During the presidential campaign Dulles had spoken of ‘liberating’ the captive peoples; and later, as Secretary of State, he fell back on phrases like ‘massive retaliation,’ or ‘unleashing’ Chiang Kai-shek, or a ‘dynamic’ foreign policy. All this gave the appearance of action without actually committing the country to action.

In the end the Eisenhower foreign policies differed little from those of Truman. But the spirit — and the method — was very different. The President shared Dulles's faith in ‘personal’ diplomacy; not only was everything to be talked out in front of microphones and television lights, but the participants should be principals, not subordinates. Eisenhower inaugurated this ‘new’ diplomacy successfully by flying to Korea to arrange an armistice, and thereafter he preferred, when possible, to negotiate ‘at the summit’; while Dulles, flitting from continent to continent, turned out to be the most traveled Secretary of State in American history.[1]

2. The Far East and the Summit Conference

The Korean truce did not really settle anything — except a cease-fire, which after all was something. That stricken country, divided

---

[1] During the seven years of his secretaryship he flew 480,000 miles outside the bounds of the United States.

absurdly at the waist, faced an uncertain and gloomy future. It was threatened hourly by the ' People's Republic ' on its northern boundary, and by Communist China and Russia on its flanks; it lacked a sound economic basis and was sustained only by the vast sums — some $4.5 billion altogether — which the United States poured into it as economic and military aid. It was governed by the patriot leader Syngman Rhee, who grew more and more dictatorial with the passing years and was eventually ousted by a popular rebellion. But the United States was committed to support this unhappy Republic by a mutual defense treaty, by far-reaching political and military considerations, and by deep moral obligations.

A comparable situation confronted the United States in Formosa, whither Chiang Kai-shek and the Chinese Nationalists had betaken themselves when driven by the Reds from the mainland in 1949. Whereas Dr. Rhee had at least the formal credentials of a popular election, Chiang ruled as if by divine right. The United States, already bound to him by a wartime alliance, by compelling considerations of a common front against Chinese Communism, and now by the exigencies of American politics, found itself committed to the theory that Chiang, representing the true and rightful government of all China, would eventually recross the Formosa Strait and reconquer the mainland. With the passing of years, this became an increasingly unrealistic policy, but the Eisenhower administration — and its successor, to date — refused to recognize the existence of Red China and opposed her admission to the United Nations. Even had President Eisenhower wished to modify these policies he could not have done so, for a powerful element in his own party, led by the chairman of the Foreign Affairs Committee, Senator Knowland, was unalterably devoted to the support of the Nationalist cause. Support of Chiang, both military and economic, involving the use of the Seventh Fleet, between 1949 and 1961 cost the American taxpayer some $5 billion.

The problem of Taiwan (the Chinese name for Formosa) was complicated by the fact that Chiang occupied not only the nearby Pescadores Islands but a group of smaller islands — Quemoy, Matsu, and Tachen — close in to the Chinese mainland. Chiang took the position that these islands were essential to the defense system of Taiwan, as they commanded one of the few places on the China coast where the Reds could mount an amphibious operation. On his accession to the presidency, Eisenhower announced that he was lifting the ' blockade ' of Taiwan by the U.S. Seventh Fleet, thus ' un-leashing ' Chiang Kai-shek for an attack upon the mainland. The Chinese premier, Chou En-lai, responded with a declaration that Taiwan was part of China proper, and that the Nationalist regime there must be liquidated. When, in the summer of 1954, the Communists began a heavy bombardment of the off-shore islands, the United States negotiated a ' mutual defense ' treaty with Chiang, and the President told the Congress that ' in the interest of peace the United States must remove any doubt regarding our readiness to fight.' Congress responded with a somewhat ambiguous resolution declaring that ' an attack against territories . . . in the region of Formosa and the Pescadores, would be dangerous to the peace and safety ' of the United States, and authorizing the President to use the armed force of the nation ' as he deems necessary ' for the defense of this region. This was one of the few times in history that Congress formally gave the Executive power to involve the nation in war at his discretion.

The danger passed, but the problem remained. Were the off-shore islands of Quemoy and Matsu part of those ' territories ' to whose defense the United States now stood committed? When, in August 1958, the Communists opened another and heavier bombardment on the islands, Secretary Dulles promptly declared that an attack on them would be a prelude to an attack on Formosa, and that the United States stood ready to repel it, and the Seventh Fleet was assigned as naval escort to troops which Chiang rushed to garrison the beleaguered islands. Public opinion at home and abroad reacted sharply to the threat of war over these islands, which were almost as close to the Chinese mainland as Staten Island is to New York; were they really worth an atomic war — or even a ' conventional ' war? The Eisenhower administration, however, stood firm; the Chinese Communists tapered off their bombardment; and the skies cleared. But the basic problem remained, and loomed up, ever more formidable, on the international horizon: the problem of the non-recognition of Communist China and her exclusion from the United Nations.

In 1954 the revolution against colonialism which was sweeping Asia and Africa presented the West with another crisis. For almost seven years Communist guerrillas known as the Viet-Minh had been waging war against the French in the jungles of Indo-China. By the summer of 1953 they had overrun much of the northern half of

Vietnam, largest of the three states comprising French Indo-China, and threatened the neighboring state of Laos. Fearful that the Communist wave might engulf the whole of southeastern Asia, and eager to take the pressure off the French in order to enable them to fulfill their obligations toward the European Defense Community, the United States greatly increased its financial aid to the French in Vietnam and stepped up its indirect military aid. With the continued success of the Viet-Minh, Dulles seriously considered the use of American ground troops. As he subsequently explained

You have to take chances for peace, just as you must take chances in war. Some say that we were brought to the verge of war. Of course we were brought to the verge of war. The ability to get to the verge of war without getting into the war is the necessary art. If you cannot master it, you inevitably get into wars. If you try to run away from it, if you are scared to go to the brink, you are lost. We've had to look it square in the face — on the question of enlarging the Korean War, on the question of getting into the Indo-China war, on the question of Formosa. We walked to the brink and we looked it in the face.

In this particular instance events moved too swiftly for international action. On 7 May the fortress of Dienbienphu fell, and the French decided to give up the unequal struggle and settle for a compromise line, as the United States had done in Korea. That summer a conference of the great powers — which for the first time included Red China — drew up an Indo-Chinese settlement which provided for the independence of Cambodia, temporarily relieved the pressure on Laos, and divided Vietnam in two along the 17th parallel.

Secretary Dulles met this crisis by the creation of an Asiatic defense community to parallel NATO. In November 1954, Pakistan, Thailand, and the Philippines joined with the United States, Britain, France, Australia, and New Zealand to set up a Southeast Asia Treaty Organization (SEATO). The treaty provides that in the event of a threat of armed aggression the members would ' meet in order to agree on the measures which should be taken for common defense.' SEATO maintains a secretariat and a planning group at Bangkok and a permanent consultation group consisting of the ambassadors of the signatory powers to Thailand. It is a live organization, but differs from NATO in two important respects. Neither we nor any of our allies in the Southeast Asia organization have significant armed forces for waging a general war in the treaty area, and there is no

permanent command structure and no standing military organization, such as NATO maintains in Paris.

By 1955 a series of events combined to bring about a mild thaw in
the Cold War: truce in Korea; a cease-fire in the Formosa Strait; a
compromise peace in Vietnam. Eisenhower himself became a symbol
of peace. In a dramatic gesture before the United Nations Assembly
he proposed that atomic power be dedicated to peace not war, and
on four crucial occasions — Korea, Taiwan, Indo-China, and in negotiations with China over prisoners [2] — he had thrown the weight
of his influence to the side of peace. The European defense community was now a reality. A wave of prosperity surged through Western Europe, giving West Germany, France, and Italy self-confidence
and greatly diminishing fear of Communist subversion or aggression.
Russia, having detonated a hydrogen bomb, showed signs of a more
reasonable relationship with the West. Stalin had died, and while the
official repudiation of him awaited the advent to power of the bold
Nikita Khrushchev, the new government was already proving itself
less intransigent. Meantime Russia badly needed a period of internal
calm in which to settle the question of succession, and a period of
peace in which to reconsider relations with China — a junior partner
now threatening to take over the firm. As if to dramatize the new
spirit, the Soviet Union in May 1955, ended its long and harsh
occupation of Austria and gave that little nation its freedom. Thus
the stage was set for the 'summit' conference at Geneva in mid-
summer 1955.

As early as May 1953 Winston Churchill had proposed a conference of the heads of major states, but neither Russia nor the United
States was then ready for it. The British Foreign Minister, Harold
Macmillan, reopened the issue in a more favorable climate of opinion; and President Eisenhower, Sir Anthony Eden, Bulganin, and

[2] Discussing the Chinese detention of thirteen American fliers, on 2 December 1954,
the President said: 'In many ways the easy course for a President . . . is to adopt a
truculent, publicly bold, almost insulting attitude. A President experiences exactly the
same resentments, the same anger, the same kind of sense of frustration . . . when
things like this occur to other Americans, and his impulse is to lash out. [But] when
one accepts the responsibilities of public office, he can no longer give expression freely
to such things; he has got to think of results. That would be the easy way. . . .
The hard way is to have the courage to be patient, tirelessly to seek out every single
avenue open to us in the hope of finally leading the other side to a little better understanding of the honesty of our intentions.' *Public Papers of President Eisenhower*, 1955,
pp. 1075–6.

Edgar Faure agreed to represent their respective countries. On 18 July, Eisenhower opened the conference on a note of hope and of good will:

The American people want to be friends with the Soviet peoples. There are no natural differences between our peoples or our nations. There are no territorial or commercial rivalries. Historically our two countries have always been at peace. . . . It is time that all curtains whether of guns or laws or regulations should begin to come down.

Specifically, Eisenhower proposed a new approach to the problem of German unification, free communication between the East and the West, the peaceful use of atomic power, with some practical contributions to disarmament. It was the disarmament plan that caught the popular imagination, for it called upon Russia and the United States to:

give each other a complete blueprint of our military establishments, from beginning to end, from one end of our countries to the other; lay out the establishments and provide the blueprints to each other. Next to provide within our countries facilities for aerial photography to the other country, ample facilities for aerial reconnaissance where you can make all the pictures you choose and take them to your own country to study, you to provide exactly the same facilities for us, and we to make these examinations, and by this step to convince the world that we are providing as between ourselves against the possibility of great surprise attack, thus lessening danger and relaxing tension.

' What I propose,' he added, ' would be but a beginning.'

Bulganin, in turn, proposed a prohibition of the manufacture of atomic weapons, and a limitation of the armies of the United States and the U.S.S.R. to 1.5 million men. But Russia would not even hear of Eisenhower's generous proposal. The Russian proposal of prohibiting atomic weapons meant nothing once they would not admit inspection, and in modern conditions of warfare a limitation of the size of the ground force was completely anachronistic. So nothing came of the Geneva conference.

3. CRISIS IN THE MIDDLE EAST

The ' spirit of Geneva ' which had inspired such high hopes in the West — and possibly even in the East — quickly evaporated under the hot sun of power politics. Within a few months events in Central

Europe and in the Middle East again strained East-West relationships to the breaking point.

At the celebration of the Twentieth Communist Party Congress, in February 1956, Nikita Khrushchev, the new leader of the U.S.S.R., startled the world by a savage attack on his predecessor, Stalin. Josef Stalin, he asserted, had been a tyrant and a monster, brutal, savage, and cruel. That kind of leadership, Khrushchev implied, was a thing of the past. Seven months later the festering discontent of the Poles broke out into the open, and under the leadership of Wladyslaw Gomulka, the Poles demanded freedom from Soviet bayonets and autonomy within the Communist system. When Khrushchev accepted these demands for a new kind of partnership it looked like the dawn of a new and better day.

But alas for all such hopes. When that same autumn, the long-suffering Hungarians revolted against Communist misrule, Khrushchev showed no inclination to acquiesce in a new order. Khrushchev's response to the Hungarian challenge would have done credit to Stalin whom he had just denounced. Two hundred thousand soldiers and thousands of tanks poured into the hapless country, and while the United Nations passed frantic resolutions of protest, and the West looked on in despair, this heroic revolt of the Hungarians was ruthlessly stamped out. Tens of thousands of Hungarian patriots were killed, and almost 200,000 fled across the border into Austria, eventually into other Western countries.

A minor casualty of the Hungarian revolt was the ' spirit of Geneva.'

The crisis in the Middle East had been long in the making. That vast area, stretching from the Mediterranean to the Caspian Sea, and from the Hellespont to the Gulf of Oman, and embracing some twelve countries,[3] was seething with unrest. Long the pawn of European politics, its peoples governed by distant rulers, and its rich oil resources exploited for the benefit of distant economies, it was now quickened into new life — and revolt — by the currents of anti-colonialism, nationalism, and religion that were roaring through the whole non-European world. World War II accelerated these pressures. In Iran, Dr. Mossadegh nationalized oil; and although he was later ousted (with the help of the West) the oil remained national-

---

[3] Turkey, Lebanon, Syria, Iraq, Iran, Jordan, Israel, Egypt, and Saudi Arabia; also Kuwait, Yemen, and the Sudan.

ized. Syria and Lebanon asserted their independence, and in 1946 the last French troops left these two Arab nations. In 1948 the British gave up their mandate in Palestine; the Israelis struck for freedom and, when invaded by the combined forces of Egypt, Lebanon, Jordan, and Syria, broke the invaders and emerged victorious into independence. Egypt was then swept by revolt; in 1952 the fat King Farouk was driven into exile, and two years later Colonel Gamal Abdel Nasser took over the government.

All this marked an upsurge of Arab nationalism which rapidly became a religious crusade supported by the whole Moslem world, from Morocco halfway across the globe to Pakistan and Indonesia. Both the Soviet Union and the West watched these developments with the liveliest interest.

The crisis was precipitated in 1953–54 by the attempt of Secretary Dulles to create a regional defense against Soviet penetration into the Middle East which would parallel NATO in the Atlantic and SEATO in the Pacific areas. The result was the Baghdad Pact of 1954 to which Turkey, Iraq, Iran, and Pakistan adhered, but not the United States! The Pact did not in fact intimidate the Soviets; it did, however, antagonize Nasser, who saw it as a deliberate attempt to undermine his own leadership and to split the Arab, or at least the Moslem, world in two.

Under pressure to vindicate his newly won position, Nasser was now following the well-worn precedent of distracting his people from their difficulties at home by creating crises abroad. His first step was to negotiate with Britain for the withdrawal of all British troops from the Suez Canal zone, a withdrawal to be completed by 1956. Second came the formation of a close military alliance with Syria, Jordan, and Saudi Arabia. Third was a deal with Czechoslovakia for arms — presumably to use against the Israelis; and fourth a war of nerves — and of attrition — against Israel by denying Israeli ships passage through the Suez Canal, by subversion, and by ceaseless threats of destruction. Finally came a constructive gesture — a project for a vast dam and irrigation system at Aswan on the upper Nile; it was to be the largest dam in the world. As Egypt was quite unprepared to finance this herself, Nasser entered on the dangerous game of inviting the United States and the U.S.S.R. to bid against each other for the privilege of financing the enterprise.

As it turned out, neither great power wanted that privilege — or was prepared to pay the price for it. Nasser then precipitated a major world crisis in 1956 by seizing the Suez Canal in clear violation of treaty agreements. Faced with the prospect of being cut off from essential Middle East oil supplies, the British and French determined to use force to recover control of the Canal. This provided Israel with an opportunity to launch her own offensive against Egypt; Nasser having denied Israel access to the Canal on the grounds that the two countries were at war, the Israeli legal and moral position seemed strong. On 29 October, as Russian tanks were rumbling into the streets of Budapest, Israeli troops invaded the Sinai peninsula, scattered a much larger Egyptian army, and within a few days were across the peninsula and on the banks of the Canal. Britain and France joined hastily in the war with aerial attacks on the Egyptian air force; Nasser responded by sinking enough ships in the Canal to close it to traffic for an indefinite time.

Here were the makings of another major war. The whole Arab world was aroused; India and the Soviet bloc denounced the war as ' imperialist aggression,' and threatened to pile in unless there was an immediate cease-fire. A possibly fatal rift between East and West was avoided when the United Nations, too, denounced the war as aggression and the United States supported the U.N. position. ' We believe these actions [of Britain and France] to have been taken in error,' said Eisenhower. ' We do not accept the use of force as a proper instrument for the settlement of international disputes.' Confronted by the prospect of a long and wearing war in Egypt, by the threat of retaliation from Russia, by disapproval from the United States and India, and by condemnation by the United Nations, England and France bowed to the inevitable and brought their hostilities to a close.

Israel, however, was reluctant to withdraw her troops from their advanced positions until she had obtained assurances of equitable treatment. Eisenhower assured the Israelis that if they withdrew their troops, the United States would support their efforts to end Egyptian hostility and the exclusion of Israeli ships from the Canal. This commitment became binding when Israel complied with the President's request; but, nothing was done. The Suez crisis drove a wedge between the United States and her allies, dramatized the growing power of the Soviet Union, enhanced the prestige — but not the strength — of Israel, and played into the hands of Nasser, whose propaganda machine made the whole thing look like a military as well as a moral victory, and who now presented himself as the very symbol of Arab nationalism in its struggle against Western imperialism. The peaceful settlement was a victory for Eisenhower; but a few more victories of that kind, and the Western alliance would be in ruins.

The Suez crisis had created a situation favorable to the extension of Communist influence throughout the Middle East. Eisenhower now turned his attention to that threat and, in a message of 5 January 1957, warned that if the nations of the Middle East should

lose their independence, if they were dominated by alien forces hostile to freedom, that would be both a tragedy for the area and for many other free nations whose economic life would be subject to near strangulation. Western Europe would be endangered just as though there had been no Marshall Plan, no NATO. The free nations of Asia and Africa, too, would be placed in serious jeopardy. . . . All this would have the most adverse, if not disastrous, effect upon our own nation's economic life and political prospects.

To avoid such a catastrophe, the President asked for authority to extend economic and financial assistance to any Middle Eastern nation needing and asking for such help, and to use the armed forces of the nation to protect the integrity and independence of any nation ' threatened by aggression from any country controlled by international communism.' This was the so-called Eisenhower Doctrine. On 9 March Congress made it official, and authorized some $200 million for economic and military aid. The response from the West generally was enthusiastic, but not so from the rest of the world. Prime Minister Nehru said that ' if there is a power vacuum in West Asia (the Middle East), it is to be filled by the countries in that region through their internal strength and unity,' and the leaders of four Middle Eastern countries, meeting in Cairo, resolved ' never to allow their countries to become a sphere of influence for any foreign power.' The Russians countered with a doctrine of their own: the liquidation of all foreign bases and the withdrawal of all foreign troops from the Middle East, and a refusal to supply arms to any Middle East country. Nasser's and Soviet influence grew all through that stormy region. The Eisenhower Doctrine could not prevent the capture of the government of Syria by a clique favorable to Nasser, the forced retirement of the pro-Western king of Saudi-Arabia, or the assassination of King Faisal of Iraq and the establishment there of a pro-

Nasser government. It was this revolt in Iraq that once again brought the simmering Mid-Eastern pot to a boil.

When in the spring of 1958 Syria and Egypt undertook to subvert the pro-Western government of Lebanon, President Chamoun appealed to the United Nations for help. As usual the United Nations machinery worked slowly. The revolt in Iraq gave a new urgency to the crisis, and Chamoun turned to the United States for help. There was some doubt about the applicability of the Eisenhower Doctrine, but Eisenhower responded immediately by ordering the Sixth Fleet to steam into the eastern Mediterranean and by dispatching 9000 — eventually 14,000 — marines to Lebanon. An American proposal to turn the whole problem over to the United Nations was vetoed by the Soviets. When the nearby Arab states agreed to refrain from armed intervention in Lebanon, and Chamoun consented to retire, peace returned to the beleaguered country, and in October Eisenhower withdrew the marines. Eisenhower's decisiveness had brought an American victory in the Middle East. Russia hurriedly countered by announcing that she would help finance Egypt's Aswan dam.

4. The Good Neighbor Policy Tested and Reconstructed

Eisenhower and Dulles speedily discovered what Truman and Acheson had already known, that the penalty of wealth and power was responsibility and trouble. The United States was expected to provide leadership, but not to exercise authority; to protect free peoples everywhere, but not to be militaristic; to provide limitless sums of money, but not to exact an accounting. It was impossible to satisfy all demands or meet all objections. If we financed the rebuilding of Taiwan or Vietnam, we were accused of backing the wrong governments. If we built airfields in Spain, we favored Fascism; if we helped Yugoslavia we were contributing to Communism. If we subsidized Pakistan we were hostile to India, and if we responded to the needs of Israel we were anti-Arab. When we poured billions into France, we subsidized a colonial power, but when we sided with Angola against Portugal we were fomenting revolution in a friendly state. When we spent money in Italy we were accused of buying elections; when we spent money in neutralist countries we were pouring money down the drain. If we stayed on good terms with a Trujillo or a Batista we were supporting dictatorships, but if we countenanced revolution — as in Guatemala — we were violating the principle of non-intervention. When we opposed the use of force in the Suez we betrayed our friends; when we ourselves used force in Lebanon we were imperialists.

No aspect of the conduct of foreign policy aroused more misgivings or inspired more resentment than foreign aid. Large-scale military and economic aid had long been one of the major instruments of American foreign policy. There were antecedents in Lend-Lease, in UNRRA, and in other emergency relief programs, but the real beginnings came with the Marshall Plan, the success of which commended it as a model for the future. Over the years the foreign aid program was enlarged and expanded by one device or another until it came in time to be the most familiar and the most effective of all instruments of foreign policy. Yet it never had smooth going, at home or abroad. There was unremitting criticism at home, and every proposal to renew the program had to run the gauntlet of congressional critics bent on beating it down. Even those who approved it in principle rarely agreed on the form it took or on its administration. Some preferred military aid to economic, others thought military aid rather a waste; some took for granted that we would attach strings to our aid, others felt that any attempt to buy support was doomed to boomerang. Nor were the recipients always happy. Many felt that they did not receive their proper share of largesse; others resented whatever restrictions were attached to the expenditure of the grants; almost all assumed that there were hidden motives — imperialistic of course — behind the grants of aid. In a very short time President Eisenhower learned that the way of the benefactor is hard.

Nowhere was discontent with American policy livelier than in the states of Latin America. During the Roosevelt administration — the era of the Good Neighbor policy — there had been a honeymoon in Hemispheric affairs. The Monroe Doctrine had been transformed into a Hemispheric doctrine, and a long series of conferences and Declarations had almost wholly dispelled much traditional suspicion of Yankee imperialism. But the end of the war put a heavy strain on the Good Neighbor policy. All through the 'fifties Latin America, outside Mexico, was in the throes of a major crisis. The abrupt cessation of wartime purchases dealt a heavy blow to Latin American economies; the population explosion was pressing implacably on existing resources; the gap between rich and poor was growing wider;

and forces of nationalism and of revolutionary equalitarianism were sweeping across the continent as peoples long suffering under poverty and misgovernment sought to improve their lot.

Preoccupied with world affairs, the United States government failed to take note of what was happening at her very doorstep — in the Caribbean, and in Central and South America. There was no hostility to our South American neighbors — merely indifference and a feeling that, since they had not been ravaged in World War II or even deeply involved in it, they should be able to handle their problems without outside aid. After all, Canada, which had suffered more from the war than ourselves, did not demand foreign aid. And because of the non-intervention doctrine to which we had been faithful since World War I, we acquiesced in military dictatorships which we liked no more than the people concerned did, and so got in bad with the liberals. We took Latin American friendship for granted. Down to 1951 all the Latin American republics together had received about the same amount of foreign aid as Greece; and in the next ten years Latin America received only $3.4 billion out of a total of some $80 billion in aid: that was less than Japan, Taiwan, or Korea got.

Events in Guatemala shocked the United States out of its complacency. For years that little Central American state had groaned under the dictatorship of General Jorge Castañeda; in 1944 he was overthrown and after a period of confusion the government came under the control of Jacobo Arbenz, who was sympathetic to Communism and used to its methods. He and his followers carried through a wholesale confiscation of land, dominated the labor unions, ran the government-owned newspapers, and — when threatened by revolutionary discontent — appealed to Poland for arms, and got them. Alive to the proximity of Guatemala to the Panama Canal, Dulles moved to check Communist infiltration; mindful of the prohibition against intervention in the internal affairs of any American state, he worked through the existing machinery of the Organization of American States. The tenth Inter-American Conference condemned ' any dominion or control of the political institutions of any American state by the international Communist movement.' On the basis of this resolution — and of the Monroe Doctrine — Dulles then shipped arms in to the Guatemalan rebels gathering along the Honduras border, and on 18 June 1954 these forces invaded Guatemala, overthrew the Arbenz government, and set up a government under a liberal constitution, but led by an ultra-conservative group. What looked to Secretary Dulles like a triumph for constitutionalism, and for Hemispheric solidarity, looked to most Latin Americans like old-fashioned intervention, and the reaction was generally critical.

South America was making progress toward freedom. In the Bogotá Charter of the Organization of American States, all the Latin American republics pledged themselves to the principle of representative democracy. There was something of a social revolution in Bolivia in 1952; in 1955 Argentina ousted the dictator Peron and elected the moderate President Frondizi (who, in turn, was swept aside in 1962). Peru, Colombia, and Venezuela got rid of dictators, and replaced them with liberal constitutional Presidents.

' I suppose we devote as much time and thought to the problems of the Americas as we do to the problems of any other region in the world,' said Secretary Dulles. Perhaps it was not thought that the Latin Americans wanted, however, but action.[4] When in 1958 Vice-President Nixon visited South America on a good will tour he met, instead, manifestations of ill will. ' The fiercely hostile demonstrations that greeted Nixon,' wrote Richard Stebbins, ' were only the most acute symptom of what appeared to be a deep-seated and general discontent with United States policy in both economic and political matters.' They were, even more, a symptom of Communism in student bodies.

Now, with becoming magnanimity and exemplary dispatch, the United States applied itself to mending its Latin American fences. It stepped up foreign aid; helped set up an Inter-American Development Bank with a capital of one billion dollars; encouraged the creation of a free-trade area in the major Latin American states; and at the Bogotá conference authorized a grant of $500 million to advance social and economic welfare throughout Latin America. To dramatize this aid, President Eisenhower himself made a visit to South America in 1960. ' We are not saints,' he said at Santiago. ' We know we make mistakes, but our heart is in the right place.'

Cuba provided a hard test. That long-suffering island had been ruled for years by a ruthless military dictator, Fulgencio Batista. Although evidence of his cruelty was overwhelming, the United States

[4] ' A kiss on the wrist is all very well, but a diamond bracelet lasts forever,' said the heroine of Anita Loos's *Gentlemen Prefer Blondes*.

continued to recognize him as the legitimate governor until 1958. Two years earlier a student leader, Fidel Castro, had launched an invasion from Mexico; taking refuge in the remote mountains of the Sierra Maestra, he gathered support from long-oppressed peasants and the middle classes. Within a year he succeeded in ousting Batista. A ' fellow traveler' from the first, and influenced by his Argentine Communist economic adviser, ' Che' Guevara, Castro apparently planned to turn the ' Pearl of the Antilles' into the first Communist country in the New World. This was not evident for some time. Castro, who had been hailed as a hero and liberator by the American press, made a triumphant tour of the eastern states in 1959, and in Washington was promised foreign aid by Secretary Herter for rebuilding Cuban schools and social services, and helping the economy. But Castro had other views. He held no elections, threw thousands of Cubans who opposed his ruthlessness into jail, and expropriated sugar plantations, major industries, utilities, and banks, with scarcely a pretense at compensation. When the United States protested Castro adopted a policy of overt hostility to the northern neighbor which had given his country her independence, and moved ever closer to Khrushchev, who was only too delighted to establish a Communist beachhead only a few hours steaming from the United States. The Russian Deputy Premier Mikoyan visited Cuba in 1960, extended a credit of $100 million, arranged to buy five million tons of Cuban sugar over a five-year period, and provided technical — and eventually military — assistance. Goaded by these acts of hostility, the United States broke off relations with the dictator and tried to rally the Organization of American States for counter-measures against him. In the meantime tens of thousands of exiles had fled a dictatorship as harsh and bloody as that of Batista, and taken refuge in the United States and several Caribbean countries. Early in 1961 several thousand refugees — who had trained with the connivance of American authorities — launched an invasion of Cuba which Castro not only repulsed but annihilated. This ill-fated episode drove Castro even further into the embraces of the Communists and raised suspicions throughout Latin America about our readiness to abide by the non-intervention provisions of the OAS charter.

A reconsideration of Latin American policy was in order. President Kennedy, hoping to recover the ground lost in the previous decade and in the Cuban debacle, proposed the creation of an Alliance for Progress, a great co-operative effort for the economic and social rehabilitation of the southern continent. The new program, to which the United States pledged an initial billion dollars, was not unlike the Marshall Plan. It was designed to stimulate economic recovery in the Latin American countries, to make them strong enough to resist Communism themselves, and to encourage them to carry through long-needed reforms. As Kennedy said, in a review of the program in March 1962:

For too long my country, the wealthiest nation on a poor continent, failed to carry out its full responsibilities to its sister republics. We have now accepted that responsibility. In the same way those who possess wealth and power in poor nations must accept their own responsibilities. They must lead the fight for those basic reforms which alone can preserve the fabric of their own societies. Those who make peaceful revolution impossible will make violent revolution inevitable.

5. THE THREAT OF NUCLEAR WARFARE

Throughout all the vicissitudes of the 'fifties one overwhelming menace loomed over mankind; the danger that the two great powers, the United States and the U.S.S.R., would plunge the world into nuclear war and shatter the great globe itself. Driven by mutual fears and animosities, these two powers piled up the most formidable armories in the history of mankind, and, like figures of classical Greek tragedy, called on the innermost secrets of nature, long imprisoned in stone and water, to serve them for purposes of mutual destruction. How to avoid war, and the use of nuclear weapons in the event there was a war — that was the question that haunted the minds of statesmen and dictators throughout these years. It was to no avail that they won a cease-fire in Korea, patched up an evanescent settlement in Vietnam, laid waste Hungary, or barricaded Berlin while this great question awaited an answer.

The central problem of the 'fifties, and the one that most persistently threatened to burst into war, was that of Germany. The Potsdam Conference of leading Allies, in July 1945, divided defeated Germany down the middle, and the division was given an insane kind of reflection, as in those distorting mirrors at popular beach resorts, by the parallel division of the city of Berlin. The separation into East and West Germany was originally designed to last only during the Allied occupation, but like other temporary arrangements it gradually took on permanence. That it did so was the product of the failure to write a formal peace treaty; of the fear of a resurgent Germany that was deeply ingrained in the peoples of Central and Eastern Europe she had victimized in the past; of Russian insistence on a thick padding of satellite states along her western border; and of the Communists' belief that they could extend their system by this kind of political osmosis. Under the auspices of Russia the Communists took over East Germany — as they had taken over Poland and Czechoslovakia. They hoped to make it not only a willing satrapy in the Communist empire but a kind of show-place of Communism which would win over the hesitant neighbors in the West. To their intense mortification this plan did not work out. East German economy never recovered; few East Germans were converted to Communism, and every week thousands of them escaped into West Germany, while few West Germans went east. West Germany prospered beyond any other European state, and it was West Berlin, a glittering jewel in the drab fabric of East Germany, that was the showpiece.

The situation was explosive. Communism by its very nature was aggressive and expansive, and looked westward; West Germany had never acquiesced in the division and refused to recognize an East German government. At the same time a rearmed West Germany, its NATO forces possibly equipped by the United States with nuclear weapons, was a threat which the Communist bloc regarded with grave misgivings.

In 1958 Khrushchev denounced ' the continuation of the old, unrealistic policy which contradicts common sense,' and delivered an ultimatum to Berlin and the Germanies: either negotiate a settlement within six months, recognizing the permanent partition of Germany, or Russia would make a separate treaty with East Germany, giving her control of East Berlin and the air lanes into West Berlin. Committed to the defense of West Germany, and of Berlin as an outpost of freedom, and dependent on West Germany's contribution to the European defense system, the United States refused to back down. No way out of this impasse has yet (1962) been found.

Asia, too, presented a new menace with every passing year. Nothing had really been settled by the stalemate in Vietnam, Korea, and the Formosa Strait. Every year Red China grew bigger and more dangerous: her population reached 700 millions, her industry was rapidly modernized, her power to make trouble for her neighbors was practically unlimited, and there was good reason to expect that she would have nuclear weapons within a few years. And meantime she was threatening in all directions — pressing southward into Vietnam and Laos, westward on the borders of India, and even northward along the Siberian frontier. The United States continued to pour hundreds of millions of dollars in military supplies and economic aid into the beleaguered countries of the Far East, but the situation there showed little improvement, and as the curtain lifted on the 'sixties American entanglement in Vietnam and Laos was deeper than it had been at any previous time.

Now Africa, too, burst into flame. The currents of anti-colonialism, anti-imperialism, and nationalism flowed swiftly through the continent, and after centuries of subjugation and exploitation the Africans were ready to throw off their bonds. The situation was desperately complicated in the far north and the far south, where substantial numbers of Europeans had established themselves for a long period of time and were unwilling either to leave their ancestral homes or to admit the native peoples — the Arabs in the north and the Negroes in the south — to the government or to society. In between, in the vast area of tropical Africa, one former colony after another won its independence: Nigeria, Ghana, the Ivory Coast, Cameroun, Mali, Sudan, and others. In some states the transfer of authority from European to native governments was carried through with a minimum of unpleasantness and a maximum of co-operation — notably in some of the former French and British colonies. In two places, however, the transfer of power was attended with prolonged violence: Algeria and the Congo. In Algeria, where almost two million Europeans had established themselves, the Arabs waged a deadly guerrilla warfare on the French which took a toll of some hundreds of thousands of Arab and French-Algerian lives; by the time de Gaulle had negotiated a cease-fire in 1962, the right-wing Algerian French had organized a secret revolutionary army (the O.A.S.) which waged its own private war against both the Arabs and the de Gaulle government. When, in response to urgent demands for independence, the Belgians pulled abruptly out of the Congo, that vast nation — or congeries of tribes — fragmented three ways, and burst into civil war. Confronted by the twin dangers that the war might spread

through tropical Africa and be metamorphosed into a race war, and
that the Congolese might be used as pawns in a game of power politics played by Russia and the West, the United Nations stepped in.
Under the leadership of the far-sighted and intrepid Dag Hammarskjöld the U.N. raised an international military force to maintain the
peace. In the process of negotiating a settlement, Hammarskjöld
himself lost his life. His sacrifice was not in vain: foreign interests
that had bedeviled the internal politics of the Congo were persuaded
to withdraw, the war was brought under control, and the Congo set
on the road to nationhood. The Congo crisis dramatized the necessity
of preparation for independence and provided a frightening example
of what might happen if East and West permitted themselves to exploit native discontents for their own advantage. And it provided the
United Nations, for the first time, with a really effective military
force of its own — possibly the precursor for an international or
United Nations army.

What chance was there for effective disarmament — or even for
the control of arms — in such a world? Almost every one agreed on
the imperative necessity of controlling the arms race, but when it
came to ways and means ' their weak noddles,' as Benjamin Franklin
had said almost two centuries earlier, ' are perfectly distracted.'

As early as 1953 Russia had detonated a hydrogen bomb, and
pulled abreast of the United States in the arms race. Thereafter she
never fell behind. Every year the two great powers devoted more and
more of their resources to building nuclear weapons — and defenses
against nuclear weapons. The 'fifties saw the development not only
of bigger and more devastating hydrogen bombs, but of Polaris-
equipped nuclear submarines, rockets, guided missiles, and anti-
missile missiles, and a revelation of the staggering potentialities of
outer space for military purposes. In this contest the Russians, who
were able to concentrate their scientific talents more exclusively on
weapons, made more rapid progress than the United States. In 1957
they announced that they had put their first satellite — Sputnik I — in
orbit around the globe; in 1959 they fired a rocket past the moon and
in orbit about the sun; and in the spring of 1961 they launched two
astronauts into outer space, one of whom circled the globe seventeen
times in twenty-five hours and returned safely to Russia. Within a
few months of Sputnik the United States, too, had launched a whole
series of rockets; in December 1958 we sent a monkey into outer

space and brought him safely home; and in the spring of 1962, amidst nation-wide rejoicings, Colonel John Glenn orbited the earth thrice in a space capsule. It became clear that neither major power could hope to win a resounding lead over the other, and that if they were not to exhaust and bankrupt themselves, they would do well to consider co-operation instead of competition.

The danger that confronted the world was twofold: nuclear war and radioactive fall-out. ' Today,' said President Kennedy in a speech to the United Nations in September 1961, ' every inhabitant of this planet must contemplate the day when this planet may no longer be habitable. Every man, woman and child lives under a nuclear sword of Damocles, hanging by the slenderest of threads, capable of being cut at any moment by accident or miscalculation or madness.' Everyone agreed that no head of state would deliberately launch a nuclear war, but madness or miscalculation might bring it on. A generation that had known a Hitler and a Stalin could not wholly discount madness in a dictator; and Walter Lippmann warned that collective madness might even infect an otherwise sensible people. ' Though nuclear war would be lunacy,' he said,

it is an ever-present possibility. Why? Because however irrational it may be to commit suicide, a nation can be provoked and exasperated to a point where its nervous system cannot endure inaction, where only violence can relieve its feelings. . . . There is a line of intolerable provocation beyond which the reactions are uncontrollable. Here lies the greatest danger of miscalculation, and therefore of war.

Nuclear weapons — unlike all earlier weapons — were dangerous in peace as in war. To ' keep up' in the nuclear race required continuous experiments in underground and atmospheric tests, and these tests threatened to spread radioactive materials through the atmosphere, which might do incalculable damage not only to this but to future generations. This was demonstrated in 1954 when the United States exploded a 20-megaton hydrogen bomb in the Bikini atoll in the Pacific, spreading a lethal amount of radioactive material over an area of 7000 square miles. Another seven years and the Russians would be exploding 50-megaton bombs — and boasting bombs of 100 megatons, powerful enough to destroy the largest metropolitan areas in the world. While members of the Atomic Energy Commission talked about ' tolerable' levels of radioactivity, geneticists made clear that all radioactivity was harmful, and that the damage from it was cumulative. The problem, critical for the peoples of the United States and Russia, took on a special urgency from the elementary fact that it was impossible to confine the damage from radioactive fall-out to particular countries; like the rain, it falls alike upon the just and the unjust.

After the death of Secretary Dulles, President Eisenhower embarked upon a more conciliatory policy, in Europe as in Latin America and the Far East. Khrushchev, too, seemed more conciliatory. Confident that person-to-person talks would solve problems that defied conventional diplomacy, Eisenhower invited Khrushchev to the United States to see for himself how well-intentioned the American people really were, and to discuss with him the most urgent problems of world politics. In the fall of 1959 the Russian dictator made his first visit to the United States; he toured the country, talked with workingmen, farmers, shopkeepers, and housewives, and wound up his trip with a visit at President Eisenhower's rural retreat, Camp David. The two leaders appeared to get along famously, and the ' spirit of Camp David ' supplanted the defunct ' spirit of Geneva,' as the Western world prepared for yet another summit meeting to lay the foundations for a permanent settlement of the problems of Berlin, nuclear weapons, and disarmament.

Once again everything went wrong. On 5 May 1960, just two weeks before the summit conference was to have convened in Paris, Khrushchev announced that the Russians had brought down an American U-2 reconnaissance plane in the heart of Russia. And they had captured the pilot, Francis Powers, who admitted that he was employed by the U.S. Central Intelligence Agency and engaged in aerial photographic espionage, as the Secretary of State eventually confirmed. This was clearly a violation of international law, and so, too, the use of neutral territory — Turkey and Norway — for take-off and landing. Khrushchev, although he had indicated at Camp David that he knew about these flights, chose to use this incident as an excuse to wreck the summit conference before it ever got under way. And a month later, the Russians broke up the ten-nation disarmament conference in Geneva. In the meantime the trial of Francis Powers for espionage was exploited to make out a case against the United States as a militaristic and lawless nation, hell-bent for war. But if Russia had consented, as the United States had been proposing since 1946 and is still proposing, to allow neutral inspections of nuclear plants, these attempts to find out through aerial photography what she was doing would have been unnecessary.

Everywhere clouds drew over the international skies. Chinese Reds infiltrated Laos and set up a rival Communist government there. The civil war in Vietnam continued. A revolution in South Korea overthrew Syngman Rhee, but did not lead to civil war. The Congo was embroiled in civil war; Castro and the United States came to a parting of ways. As President Eisenhower prepared to lay down his office, the international scene was one of confusion and disarray. Progress toward freedom and peace, he said in his farewell address, ' is persistently threatened by the conflict now engulfing the world. It commands our whole attention, absorbs our very beings. We face a hostile ideology — global in scope, atheistic in character, ruthless in purpose, and insidious in method. The danger it poses promises to be of indefinite duration.'

Certainly the danger continued into the next administration. The crisis in Berlin flared up once again, and in aggravated form as a great concrete wall knifed its way through the heart of the stricken city. The war in Laos and Vietnam spread and became more demanding. Castro openly avowed his adherence to Communism, and the new administration was no more able to solve the Cuban problem than the old. There was trouble in Brazil, the Argentine, Chile, Bolivia, Panama, and Guatemala. The threat of nuclear destruction continued to hang over mankind. Khrushchev did his best to paralyze the United Nations since he could not control it. And on 18 September 1961 Dag Hammarskjöld met his death in the jungles of the Congo.

President Kennedy seized that occasion to make an impassioned plea for disarmament. His plan embraced: (1) a ban on atmospheric testing, even without inspection, in order to save the human race from radioactive fall-out; (2) an end to the production of all fissionable materials for use in weapons; (3) a prohibition of the transfer of nuclear weapons or materials to states that do not now have them; (4) the destruction of existing stocks of nuclear weapons; (5) the creation of special ' peace-keeping ' units in all national armies, to be made available to the United Nations; (6) the establishment of a new International Disarmament Organization to supervise disarmament ' until it has abolished all armies and all weapons except those needed for internal order and a new United Nations Peace Force.'

Even as the President made this hopeful gesture, the Soviets broke a two-year truce in nuclear testing by conducting a series of atmospheric tests, detonating altogether some thirty bombs, one of 25 and one of 50 megatons. Public opinion in the United States and throughout the world was aghast at this reckless assault on the health and the peace of mankind. Yet so deep was the fear that Russian experiments might have given her a decisive lead in the nuclear race, that President Kennedy felt compelled to order the renewal of atmospheric tests by the United States. Thus the prospects of a nuclear holocaust continued to glare upon mankind.

It was a sobering prospect that Americans looked out upon as they moved into the final third of that century which might prove to be their last — sobering but by no means desperate. For as Americans looked back over the long road that they had traveled since the bombs ceased to rain down over Berlin and Tokyo, they might be forgiven a sense of pride, and indulged in a sense of hope. They had survived. They had avoided a major and fatal war. They had helped to create and sustain a great world organization for peace. They had played a not ignoble part in lifting the standards of living for the poor and oppressed throughout the globe, giving of their wealth with unprecedented generosity. Nor had they confined their gifts to material goods alone: in a hundred ways — through the United Nations, through Point Four, through the Peace Corps, through beneficent work of the great Foundations, the Universities, the churches — they were trying to obey the command of Isaiah to undo the heavy burdens and let the oppressed go free. They had pledged themselves to prospering freedom — freedom from ignorance, from disease, from hunger, from tyranny. They were wholeheartedly committed to one of the most exhilarating enterprises in the history of mankind — to help the neglected and the backward peoples of three-quarters of the globe close, in a single generation, the gap of centuries that separated them from the more fortunate peoples of the European world. Conscious of their own failures in generations past, they were wiping out the last vestiges of slavery and discrimination against their own minority groups. Out of their affluence they were building school systems designed to give education to all who could profit from it. They were trying to salvage their countryside and to rebuild their cities. They had penetrated more deeply into the mysteries of the universe than any previous generation in history. Perhaps the forces that they had unleashed would destroy them, and the civilization which had been built up through the ages, and which they had inherited, would dissolve and leave not a rack behind. But perhaps, too, they would be able to control those dread forces, and putting behind them the animosities and parochialisms of the past, join with their fellow men throughout the globe in common enterprises of benevolence and magnanimity. Then, what Oliver Wendell Holmes so finely said of the Civil War generation, could be said of this a century later, that

Through our great good fortune, in our youth our hearts were touched with fire. It was given to us to learn at the outset that life is a profound and passionate thing. . . . We have seen with our own eyes, beyond and above the gold fields, the snowy heights of honor.

BIBLIOGRAPHY

1. GENERAL. Dean Acheson, *Power and Diplomacy;* Percy Bidwell, *The United States and the United Nations;* Blair Bolles, *Big Change in Europe;* Chester Bowles, *Ideas, People and Peace;* W. A. Brown, *American Foreign Assistance;* James McG. Burns, *Kennedy;* William G. Carleton, *Revolution in American Policy;* Jules Davids, *America and the World of Our Time: U.S. Diplomacy in the 20th Century;* Vera M. Dean, *Builders of Emerging Nations* and *The Four Cornerstones of Peace;* Lionel Gelber, *America in Britain's Place;* Norman Graebner, *The New Isolationism;* Grove Haines (ed.), *European Integration;* George F. Kennan, *The Realities of American Foreign Policy;* J. M. Lasky (ed.), *The Hungarian Revolution;* Charles B. Marshall, *The Limits of Foreign Policy;* Drew Middleton, *The Defense of Western Europe;* Hans Morgenthau, *Dilemmas of Politics* and *Politics Among the Nations;* Robert Osgood, *Limited War: The Challenge to American Strategy;* Walter W. Rostow, *The United States in the World Arena;* Richard Stebbins, *The United States in World Affairs* (annual volumes) ; Harry S. Truman, *Mr. Citizen* and *Truman Speaks;* Barbara Ward, *The Rich Nations and the Poor Nations;* Theodore White, *Fire in the Ashes;* Arnold J. Zurcher, *The Struggle To Unite Europe, 1940–1958.*

2. FAR EAST AND SUMMIT CONFERENCE. Carl Berger, *The Korea Knot: Military-Political History;* John K. Fairbanks, *The United States and China;* Herbert Feis, *The China Tangle;* E. J. Hammer, *The Struggle for Indo-China;* Charles T. Joy, *How Communists Negotiate;* R. C. North, *Moscow and the Chinese Communists;* Edwin Reischauer, *The United States and Japan;* Willard Thorpe (ed.), *The United States and the Far East;* Donald Zagoria, *The Sino-Soviet Conflict.*

3. MIDDLE EAST. Hanson Baldwin, *The Middle East in Turmoil;* John Campbell, *Defense of the Middle East;* Jacob Hurewitz, *Diplomacy in the Near and Middle East* (2 vols.) ; Walter Laqueur, *Communism and Nationalism in the Middle East;* Emil Lengyel, *Egypt's Role in World Affairs;* Richard Stebbins, *The United States in World Affairs, 1956.*

4. LATIN AMERICA. Robert Alexander, *Communism in Latin America;* George Blanksten, *Péron's Argentine;* Donald M. Dozer, *Are We Good Neighbors? 1930–1960;* Karl Meyer & Tad Szulc, *The Cuban Invasion;* C. Wright Mills, *Listen, Yankee: The Revolution in Cuba;* Harold Osborne, *Bolivia: A Land Divided;* J. Fred Rippy, *Globe and Hemisphere: Latin America's Place in the Foreign Relations of the United States;* Morris H. Rubin, ' Latin America: Dynamite on Our Doorstep,' *Progressive* (June 1961) ; Ronald Schneider, *Communism in Guatemala;* Arthur P. Whitaker, *Argentine Upheaval* and *The United States and Latin America: The Northern Republics.*

5. THREAT OF NUCLEAR WARFARE. Robert Batchelder, *The Irreversible Decision 1939–1950;* P. M. Blackett, *Fear, War, and the Bomb;* Bernard Brodie, *The Absolute Weapon;* Harrison Brown, *The Challenge of Man's Future;* Pierre Gallois, *The Balance of Terror;* George Gamow, *Atomic Energy in Cosmic and Human Life;* James M. Gavin, *War and Peace in the Space Age;* Herman Kahn, *On Thermonuclear War;* George Kennan, *Russia, the Atom and the West;* Henry Kissinger, *Nuclear Weapons and Foreign Policy;* Ralph Lapp, *Atoms and Peace;* Joseph Lash, *Dag Hammarskjöld;* Pieter Lessing, *African Kaleidoscope;* Willy Ley, *Rockets, Missiles, and Space Travel;* Herbert Spiro, *Politics in Africa;* Charles Thayer, *The Unquiet Germans;* Henry Wallich, *Mainsprings of the German Revival;* James Warburg, *Disarmament: The Challenge of the 1960's;* Arthur Waskow, *The Limits of Defense;* Richard Witkin (ed.) , *The Challenge of the Sputniks;* Harold Zink, *The United States in Germany, 1944–1955.*

6. DOCUMENTS. Council on Foreign Relations, *Documents on American Foreign Relations* (annual vols.) ; Dwight D. Eisenhower, *Public Papers* (8 vols.) .

For recent foreign relations, files of *Foreign Relations; Current History; The Reporter Magazine; The Progressive; The New Republic;* and the ' Headline Series ' of the Foreign Policy Association are indispensable.

GENERAL BIBLIOGRAPHY

1. GENERAL REFERENCE WORKS

The American Historical Association's *Guide to Historical Literature,* judicious but skimpy on American materials.

Roy Basler, *et al., A Guide to the Study of the United States of America: Representative Books . . . ,* covers a broad range of literature, but is somewhat arbitrary in judgment and selection and neglects older works.

H. P. Beers (ed.), *Bibliographies in American History,* the standard work though by now somewhat out of date.

Henry S. Commager (ed.), *Documents of American History* (7th ed.) provides bibliographical annotations with each document.

Marion Dargan, *Guide to American Biography* (2 vols.).

Philip M. Hamer (ed.), *A Guide to the Archives and Manuscripts in the United States.*

Oscar Handlin, *et al., Harvard Guide to American History,* the most satisfactory single bibliographical guide.

U.S. Bureau of the Census, *Historical Statistics of the United States, Colonial Times to 1957* and *Statistical Abstract of the United States* (82 vols., through 1961).

ENCYCLOPEDIAS AND REFERENCE WORKS

J. T. Adams & R. V. Coleman, *Dictionary of American History* (6 vols.).

John R. Commons (ed.), *Documentary History of American Industrial Society* (10 vols.).

A. B. Hart & A. C. McLaughlin, *Cyclopedia of American Government* (3 vols.).

Allen Johnson & Dumas Malone (eds.), *The Dictionary of American Biography* (20 vols. and two supplements).

Paul Monroe (ed.), *A Cyclopedia of Education* (5 vols.).

Richard B. Morris (ed.), *Encyclopedia of American History* (rev. ed.).

E. A. R. Seligman & Alvin Johnson (eds.), *Encyclopaedia of the Social Sciences* (8 vols.).

HISTORICAL JOURNALS

The American Historical Review (1895 –) reviews all new historical literature.

American Heritage (1954) is less scholarly and more popular, but handsomely illustrated.

The American Political Science Review (1906 —).
Journal of Economic History (1941 —).
Journal of the History of Ideas (1940 —).
Journal of Southern History (1935 —).
Mississippi Valley Historical Review (1914 —).
New England Quarterly (1928 —).

2. HISTORIES OF THE UNITED STATES

Charles A. and Mary Beard, *The Rise of American Civilization* (4 vols.).

Daniel J. Boorstin (ed.), *The Chicago History of Civilization* (in process).

H. S. Commager & R. B. Morris (eds.), *The New American Nation Series* (the latest co-operative history of the United States will cover the period to 1960 in some fifty volumes).

E. M. Coulter & Wendell Stephenson (eds.), *A History of the South* (10 vols.).

Henry David, *et al.* (eds.), *Economic History of the United States* (9 vols.).

Arthur M. Schlesinger & Dixon R. Fox (eds.), *History of American Life* (13 vols.).

3. ECONOMIC AND SOCIAL HISTORY

GENERAL. Joseph Dorfman, *Economic Mind in American Civilization* (5 vols.); Harold U. Faulkner, *American Economic History;* Edward C. Kirkland, *A History of American Economic Life;* Max Lerner, *America as a Civilization;* Fred A. Shannon, *America's Economic Growth;* Frederick J. Turner, *The Frontier in American History;* Chester W. Wright, *Economic History of the United States.*

LABOR. John R. Commons, *et al., History of Labour in the United States* (4 vols.); H. Harris, *American Labor;* Selig Perlman, *A History of Trade Unionism in the United States.*

IMMIGRATION. Louis Adamic (ed.), *The Peoples of America* (9 vols.); Maurice Davie, *World Immigration;* Oscar Handlin, *The Uprooted;* Marcus L. Hansen, *The Immigrant in American History;* Carl Wittke, *We Who Built America: The Saga of the Immigrant.*

TRAVEL. H. S. Commager (ed.), *America in Perspective;* Oscar Handlin (ed.), *This Was America;* Allan Nevins (ed.), *America Through British Eyes.*

4. FOREIGN RELATIONS

Ruhl J. Bartlett (ed.), *The Record of American Diplomacy,* a documentary collection.

Samuel F. Bemis, *A Diplomatic History of the United States.*

Samuel F. Bemis (ed.), *American Secretaries of State and Their Diplomacy* (10 vols.).

Samuel F. Bemis & G. G. Griffin (eds.), *Guide to the Diplomatic History of the United States, 1775–1921.*

Council on Foreign Relations, *Documents on American Foreign Relations* (since 1952) and *The United States in World Affairs* (since 1931).

Department of State, *Papers Relating to the Foreign Relations of the United States,* one or more annual volumes since 1870.

Donald C. McKay (ed.), *The American Foreign Policy Library* (15 vols.), a series of more popular monographs by specialists.

James T. Shotwell (ed.), *The Relations of Canada with the United States* (14 vols.).

Foreign Affairs (1922–) is indispensable.

5. SCIENCE AND INVENTION

Bernard Jaffe, *Men of Science in America;* Waldemar Kaempffert, *Popular History of American Inventions* (2 vols.); F. R. Packard, *A History of Medicine in the United States* (2 vols.); Charles Singer, *et al., A History of Technology,* vols. 4 and 5.

6. GOVERNMENT AND CONSTITUTIONAL HISTORY

Source Material. U.S. Supreme Court, *Reports* (some 370 volumes published); E. S. Corwin (ed.), *The Constitution of the United States* (annotated); Thomas Emerson & David Haber, *Political and Civil Rights in the United States: A Case-Book;* John B. Moore (ed.), *History and Digest of International Arbitration* (6 vols.); James M. Smith & Paul Murphy (eds.), *Liberty and Justice.*

General. W. P. Binkley, *American Political Parties;* Louis Boudin, *Government by Judiciary* (2 vols.); James Bryce, *The American Commonwealth* (2 vols.); A. H. Kelly & W. A. Harbison, *The American Constitution, Origins and Development;* Andrew C. McLaughlin, *Constitutional History of the United States; Selected Essays on Constitutional Law* (4 vols.); Carl B. Swisher, *American Constitutional Development;* Alexis de Tocqueville, *Democracy in America* (2 vols.); Charles Warren, *The Supreme Court in United States History.*

7. DOCUMENTS AND SOURCES

Ruhl J. Bartlett (ed.), *The Record of American Diplomacy;* H. S. Commager (ed.), *Documents of American History,* 7th ed. (parallels this work) and *Living Ideas in America;* Merle Curti, *et al.* (eds.), *American Issues* (2 vols.); Louis Hacker (ed.), *The Shaping of the American Tradition;* Marvin Meyers, *et al., Sources of the American Republic* (2 vols.); David Miller (ed.), *Treaties and Other International Acts of the United States; Public Papers of the Presidents* (a new series now under way, one volume for each year of the Truman and Eisenhower administrations).

8. GEOGRAPHY AND ATLASES

J. T. Adams, *Atlas of American History;* Ralph H. Brown, *Historical Geography of the United States;* V. J. Esposito, *West Point Atlas of American Wars; Harper's Atlas of American History;* A. B. Hulbert (ed.), *Historic Highways of America* (16 vols.); C. E. Lord & E. H. Lord, *Historical Atlas of the United States;* Howard Odum, *Southern Regions of the United States;* C. O. Paullin, *Atlas of the Historical Geography of the United States;* C. L. Skinner & Carl Carmer (eds.), *The Rivers of America* (c. 40 vols.); J. R. Smith, *North America.*

9. LITERATURE, PHILOSOPHY, AND RELIGION

LITERATURE. W. R. Benét & N. H. Pearson, *Oxford Anthology of American Literature;* Van Wyck Brooks, *Makers and Finders: A History of the Writer in America* (5 vols.); Harry H. Clark (ed.), *The American Writers Series* (*c.* 30 vols.); James D. Hart (ed.), *Oxford Companion to American Literature;* Jay Hubbell, *The South in Literature, 1607–1900;* Frank Luther Mott, *History of American Magazines* (4 vols.); F. O. Matthiessen, *American Renaissance;* V. L. Parrington, *Main Currents of American Thought* (3 vols.); Henry Pochmann, *German Culture in America;* R. E. Spiller, *et al.* (eds.), *Literary History of the United States* (3 vols.); W. P. Trend (ed.), *Cambridge History of American Literature* (4 vols.); Stanley Williams, *The Spanish Background of American Literature.*

PHILOSOPHY. Joseph Blau (ed.), *American Philosophical Addresses* and *Men and Movements in American Philosophy;* Merle Curti, *Growth of American Thought;* Herbert Schneider, *History of American Philosophy;* Stow Persons, *American Minds.*

RELIGION. Nelson Burr, *Critical Bibliography of Religion in America* (2 vols.); James W. Smith, *et al.* (eds.), *Religion in American Life* (3 vols.); Anson P. Stokes, *Church and State in the United States* (3 vols.).

10. THE FINE ARTS

Wayne Andrews, *Architecture in America;* John Burchard & Albert Bush Brown, *The Architecture of America;* L. C. Elson, *The History of American Music;* J. T. Howard, *Our American Music;* John Kouwenhoven, *Made in America;* Oliver Larkin, *Art and Life in America;* Russell Lynes, *The Tastemakers;* Lewis Mumford, *The Culture of the Cities, The City in History, Sticks and Stones,* and *Technics and Civilization;* E. P. Richardson, *Painting in America;* Lorado Taft, *History of American Sculpture.*

11. THE HISTORY OF HISTORY

Herman Ausubel, *Historians and Their Craft;* H. Hale Bellot, *American History and Historians;* William T. Hutchinson (ed.), *The Marcus Jernegan Essays in American Historiography;* Michael Kraus, *A History of American History;* Allan Nevins, *The Gateway to History;* David Van Tassel, *Recording America's Past;* Harvey Wish, *The American Historian.*

STATISTICAL TABLES

ADMISSION OF STATES TO THE UNION

State	Ent'd Union	State	Ent'd Union
Alabama	1819	Montana	1889
Alaska	1958	Nebraska	1867
Arizona	1912	Nevada	1864
Arkansas	1836	New Hampshire	1788
California	1850	New Jersey	1787
Colorado	1876	New Mexico	1912
Connecticut	1788	New York	1788
Delaware	1787	North Carolina	1789
Florida	1845	North Dakota	1889
Georgia	1788	Ohio	1803
Hawaii	1959	Oklahoma	1907
Idaho	1890	Oregon	1859
Illinois	1818	Pennsylvania	1787
Indiana	1816	Rhode Island	1790
Iowa	1846	South Carolina	1788
Kansas	1861	South Dakota	1889
Kentucky	1792	Tennessee	1796
Louisiana	1812	Texas	1845
Maine	1820	Utah	1896
Maryland	1788	Vermont	1791
Massachusetts	1788	Virginia	1788
Michigan	1837	Washington	1889
Minnesota	1858	West Virginia	1863
Mississippi	1817	Wisconsin	1848
Missouri	1821	Wyoming	1890

URBAN AND RURAL POPULATION, 1870–1960

Census Year	Urban Number (In Thousands)	Urban Per Cent of Total	Rural Number (In Thousands)	Rural Per Cent of Total
1870	9,902	25.7	28,656	74.3
1880	14,129	28.2	36,026	71.8
1890	22,106	35.1	40,841	64.9
1900	30,159	39.7	45,834	60.3
1910	41,998	45.7	49,973	54.3
1920	54,157	51.2	51,552	48.8
1930	68,954	56.2	53,820	43.8
1940	74,423	56.5	57,245	43.5
1950	96,467	59.0	54,229	41.0
1960	125,268	69.9 *	54,054	30.1 *

* New definition of urban; including urban-fringe areas and unincorporated places of 2,500 or more population.
Source: *Statistical Abstract of the United States, 1961.* p. 26, No. 15.

FOREIGN–BORN POPULATION BY COUNTRY OF BIRTH

COUNTRY OF BIRTH	FOREIGN-BORN WHITE				
	1950	1940	1930	1920	1910
ALL COUNTRIES	10,158,854	11,419,138	13,983,405	13,712,754	13,345,545
NORTHWESTERN EUROPE.........	2,226,887	2,825,671	3,726,844	3,828,876	4,237,373
England......................	554,625	621,975	808,684	812,828	876,455
Scotland.....................	244,200	279,321	354,323	254,567	261,034
Wales........................	30,060	35,360	60,205	67,066	82,479
Northern Ireland..............	15,398	106,416	178,882	} 1,087,238	1,352,155
Ireland (Eire).................	504,961	572,031	744,810		
Norway......................	202,294	262,088	347,852	363,862	403,858
Sweden......................	324,944	445,070	595,250	625,580	665,183
Denmark.....................	107,897	138,175	179,474	} 189,154	181,621
Iceland......................	2,455	2,104	2,764		
Netherlands..................	102,133	111,064	133,133	131,766	120,053
Belgium.....................	52,891	53,958	64,194	62,686	49,397
Luxembourg..................	5,590	6,886	9,048	12,585	3,068
Switzerland..................	71,515	88,293	113,010	118,659	124,834
France......................	107,924	102,930	135,265	152,890	117,286
CENTRAL AND EASTERN EUROPE...	4,218,903	4,958,368	5,897,795	6,134,825	6,013,720
Germany.....................	984,331	1,237,772	1,608,814	1,686,102	2,811,085
Poland......................	861,184	993,479	1,268,583	1,139,978	937,884
Czechoslovakia...............	278,268	319,971	491,638	362,436	....
Austria......................	408,785	479,906	370,914	575,625	845,506
Hungary.....................	268,022	290,228	274,450	397,282	495,600
Yugoslavia...................	143,956	161,093	211,416	169,437	....
U. S. S. R...................	894,844	1,040,884	1,153,624	)	
Latvia.......................	31,590	18,636	20,673	} 1,400,489	}
Estonia......................	10,085	4,178	8,550		} 1,184,382
Lithuania....................	147,765	165,771	198,606	135,068	)
Finland.....................	95,506	117,210	142,478	149,824	129,669
Rumania....................	84,952	115,940	146,393	102,823	65,920
Bulgaria....................	9,615	8,888	9,399	10,477	11,453
Turkey in Europe.............	....	4,412	2,257	5,284	32,221
SOUTHERN EUROPE.............	1,706,640	1,896,886	2,093,976	1,902,781	1,528,934
Greece......................	169,083	163,252	174,526	175,972	101,264
Albania.....................	10,510	....	....	....	....
Italy........................	1,427,145	1,623,580	1,790,424	1,610,109	1,343,070
Spain.......................	45,565	47,707	59,033	49,247	21,977
Portugal....................	54,337	62,347	69,993	67,453	57,623
OTHER EUROPE................	15,670	19,819	25,065	11,509	12,851
Danzig......................	....	....	....	....	....
Europe, not specified..........	....	....	....	....	....
ASIA........................	179,900	149,909	157,580	110,450	64,314
Armenia.....................	....	....	....	....	}
Palestine....................	540	7,047	6,135	3,202	
Syria.......................	35,325	50,859	57,227	51,900	} 59,702
Turkey in Asia................	71,730	52,479	46,651	11,014	
China......................	11,985	....	....	....	) ....
Japan.......................	4,650	....	....	....	....
India.......................	5,370	....	....	....	....
Other Asia...................	50,300	39,524	47,567	44,334	4,612
AMERICA.....................	1,564,139	1,509,855	2,011,224	1,656,801	1,453,186
Canada-French...............	238,409	273,366	370,852	307,786	385,083
Canada-Other................	756,153	770,753	907,660	810,092	810,987
Newfoundland................	....	21,361	23,071	13,242	5,076
Cuba.......................	29,295	15,277	16,089	12,848	12,869
Other West Indies.............	22,735	15,257	15,511	13,526	10,300
Mexico.....................	450,562	377,433	639,017	478,383	219,802
Central America..............	28,375	7,638	7,791	4,074	1,507
South America................	43,510	28,770	30,333	16,855	7,562
All other.......................	146,715	58,630	70,921	67,512	40,167

POPULATION OF THE UNITED STATES, 1870–1960

Estimates taken from the

STATE	1870	1880	1890	1900	1910
NEW ENGLAND					
Maine..........	626,915	648,936	661,086	694,466	742,371
New Hampshire..	318,300	346,991	376,530	411,588	430,572
Vermont........	330,551	332,286	332,422	343,641	355,956
Massachusetts...	1,457,351	1,783,085	2,238,947	2,805,346	3,336,416
Rhode Island....	217,353	276,531	345,506	428,556	542,610
Connecticut.....	537,454	622,700	746,258	908,420	1,114,756
MIDDLE ATLANTIC					
New York.......	4,382,759	5,082,871	6,003,174	7,268,894	9,113,614
New Jersey......	906,096	1,131,116	1,444,933	1,883,669	2,537,167
Pennsylvania....	3,521,951	4,282,891	5,258,113	6,302,115	7,665,111
SOUTH ATLANTIC					
Delaware.......	125,015	146,608	168,493	184,735	202,322
Maryland.......	780,894	934,943	1,042,390	1,188,044	1,295,346
Dist. of Columbia	131,700	177,624	230,392	278,718	331,069
Virginia.........	1,225,163	1,512,565	1,655,980	1,854,184	2,061,612
West Virginia....	442,014	618,457	762,794	958,800	1,221,119
North Carolina...	1,071,361	1,399,750	1,617,949	1,893,810	2,206,287
South Carolina...	705,606	995,577	1,151,149	1,340,316	1,515,400
Georgia.........	1,184,109	1,542,180	1,837,353	2,216,331	2,609,121
Florida..........	187,748	269,493	391,422	528,542	752,619
SOUTH CENTRAL					
Kentucky.......	1,321,011	1,648,690	1,858,635	2,147,174	2,289,905
Tennessee.......	1,258,520	1,542,359	1,767,518	2,020,616	2,184,789
Alabama........	996,992	1,262,505	1,513,401	1,828,697	2,138,093
Mississippi......	827,922	1,131,597	1,289,600	1,551,270	1,797,114
Arkansas........	484,471	802,525	1,128,211	1,311,564	1,574,449
Louisiana.......	726,915	939,946	1,118,588	1,381,625	1,656,388
Oklahoma.......	....	....	258,657	790,391	1,657,155
Texas..........	818,579	1,591,749	2,235,527	3,048,710	3,896,542
NORTH CENTRAL					
Ohio...........	2,665,260	3,198,062	3,672,329	4,157,545	4,767,121
Indiana.........	1,680,637	1,978,301	2,192,404	2,516,462	2,700,876
Illinois.........	2,539,891	3,077,871	3,826,352	4,821,550	5,638,591
Michigan........	1,184,059	1,636,937	2,093,890	2,420,982	2,810,173
Wisconsin.......	1,054,670	1,315,497	1,693,330	2,069,042	2,333,860
Minnesota.......	439,706	780,773	1,310,283	1,751,394	2,075,708
Iowa...........	1,194,020	1,624,615	1,912,297	2,231,853	2,224,771
Missouri.......	1,721,295	2,168,380	2,679,185	3,106,665	3,293,335
North Dakota...	\} 14,181	135,177	\} 190,983	319,146	577,056
South Dakota....			\} 348,600	401,570	583,888
Nebraska.......	122,993	452,402	1,062,656	1,066,300	1,192,214
Kansas.........	364,399	996,096	1,428,108	1,470,495	1,690,949
MOUNTAIN					
Montana........	20,595	39,159	142,924	243,329	376,053
Idaho..........	14,999	32,610	88,548	161,772	325,594
Wyoming.......	9,118	20,789	62,555	92,531	145,965
Colorado........	39,864	194,327	413,249	539,700	799,024
New Mexico.....	91,874	119,565	160,282	195,310	327,301
Arizona.........	9,658	40,440	88,243	122,931	204,354
Utah..........	86,786	143,963	210,779	276,749	373,351
Nevada.........	42,491	62,266	47,355	42,335	81,875
PACIFIC					
Washington.....	23,955	75,116	357,232	518,103	1,141,990
Oregon..........	90,923	174,768	317,704	413,536	672,765
California.......	560,247	864,694	1,213,398	1,485,053	2,377,549
Alaska..........	....	....	....	....	63,592
Hawaii..........	....	....	....	....	154,001
Total.........	38,558,371	50,155,783	62,947,714	75,994,575	92,228,496

POPULATION OF THE UNITED STATES, 1870–1960 — *Continued*

United States censuses

STATE	1920	1930	1940	1950	1960
NEW ENGLAND					
Maine.........	768,014	797,423	847,226	913,774	969,265
New Hampshire..	443,083	465,293	491,524	533,242	606,921
Vermont........	352,428	359,611	359,231	377,747	389,881
Massachusetts...	3,852,356	4,249,614	4,316,721	4,690,514	5,148,578
Rhode Island....	604,397	687,497	713,346	791,896	859,488
Connecticut.....	1,380,631	1,606,903	1,709,242	2,007,280	2,535,234
MIDDLE ATLANTIC					
New York.......	10,385,227	12,588,066	13,479,142	14,830,192	16,782,304
New Jersey......	3,155,900	4,041,334	4,160,165	4,835,329	6,066,782
Pennsylvania....	8,720,017	9,631,350	9,900,180	10,498,012	11,319,366
SOUTH ATLANTIC					
Delaware.......	223,003	238,380	266,505	318,085	446,292
Maryland.......	1,449,661	1,631,526	1,821,244	2,343,001	3,100,689
Dist. of Columbia	437,571	486,869	663,091	802,178	763,956
Virginia.........	2,309,187	2,421,851	2,677,773	3,318,680	3,966,949
West Virginia....	1,463,701	1,729,205	1,901,974	2,005,552	1,860,421
North Carolina...	2,559,123	3,170,276	3,571,623	4,061,929	4,556,155
South Carolina...	1,683,724	1,738,765	1,899,804	2,117,027	2,382,594
Georgia.........	2,895,832	2,908,506	3,123,723	3,444,578	3,943,116
Florida.........	968,470	1,468,211	1,897,414	2,771,305	4,951,560
SOUTH CENTRAL					
Kentucky.......	2,416,630	2,614,589	2,845,627	2,944,806	3,038,156
Tennessee.......	2,337,885	2,616,556	2,915,841	3,291,718	3,567,089
Alabama........	2,348,174	2,646,248	2,832,961	3,061,743	3,266,740
Mississippi.....	1,790,618	2,009,821	2,183,796	2,178,914	2,178,121
Arkansas........	1,752,204	1,854,482	1,949,387	1,909,511	1,786,272
Louisiana.......	1,798,509	2,101,593	2,363,880	2,683,516	3,257,022
Oklahoma.......	2,028,283	2,396,040	2,226,434	2,233,351	2,328,284
Texas..........	4,663,228	5,824,715	6,414,824	7,711,194	9,579,677
NORTH CENTRAL					
Ohio...........	5,759,394	6,646,697	6,907,612	7,946,627	9,706,397
Indiana........	2,930,390	3,238,503	3,427,796	3,934,224	4,662,498
Illinois..........	6,485,280	7,630,654	7,897,241	8,712,176	10,081,158
Michigan........	3,668,412	4,842,325	5,256,106	6,371,766	7,823,194
Wisconsin.......	2,632,067	2,939,006	3,137,587	3,434,575	3,951,777
Minnesota.......	2,387,125	2,563,953	2,792,300	2,982,483	3,413,864
Iowa...........	2,404,021	2,470,939	2,538,268	2,621,073	2,757,537
Missouri........	3,404,055	3,629,367	3,784,664	3,954,653	4,319,813
North Dakota...	646,872	680,845	641,935	619,636	632,446
South Dakota....	636,547	692,849	642,961	652,740	680,514
Nebraska.......	1,296,372	1,377,963	1,315,834	1,325,510	1,411,330
Kansas.........	1,769,257	1,880,999	1,801,028	1,905,299	2,178,611
MOUNTAIN					
Montana........	548,889	537,606	559,456	591,024	674,767
Idaho..........	431,866	445,032	524,873	588,637	667,191
Wyoming........	194,402	225,565	250,742	290,529	330,066
Colorado........	939,629	1,035,791	1,123,296	1,325,089	1,753,947
New Mexico.....	360,350	423,317	531,818	681,187	951,023
Arizona.........	334,162	435,573	499,261	749,587	1,302,161
Utah..........	449,396	507,847	550,310	688,862	890,627
Nevada.........	77,407	91,058	110,247	160,083	285,278
PACIFIC					
Washington.....	1,356,621	1,563,396	1,901,874	2,378,963	2,853,214
Oregon..........	783,389	953,786	1,089,604	1,521,341	1,768,687
California......	3,426,861	5,677,251	6,907,387	10,586,223	15,717,204
Alaska..........	64,356	55,036	59,278	72,524	226,167
Hawaii..........	191,874	255,881	368,300	422,770	632,772
Total.........	106,021,537	123,202,624	132,164,569	151,325,798	179,323,175

IMMIGRATION BY COUNTRY OF ORIGIN, 1820–1960

Source: Immigration and Naturalization Service.

(Figures are totals, not annual averages, and were tabulated as follows: 1820–67, alien passengers arrived; 1868–91 and 1895–97, immigrant aliens arrived; 1892–94 and 1898 to present, immigrant aliens admitted. Data before 1906 relate to country whence alien came; since 1906, to country of last permanent residence.)

COUNTRIES	1820–1910	1911–1920	1921–1930	1931–1940	1941–1950	1951–1960	1820–1960
Europe: Albania [1]	....	....	1,663	2,040	85	59	3,847
Austria [2]	3,172,461	453,649	32,868	3,563	24,860	67,106	3,754,507
Belgium	103,796	33,746	15,846	4,817	12,189	18,575	188,969
Bulgaria [3]	39,440	22,533	2,945	938	375	104	66,335
Czechoslovakia [1]	....	3,426	102,194	14,393	8,347	918	129,278
Denmark	258,053	41,983	32,430	2,559	5,393	10,984	351,402
Estonia [1]	....	....	1,576	506	212	185	2,479
Finland [1]	....	756	16,691	2,146	2,503	4,925	27,021
France	470,868	61,897	49,610	12,623	38,809	51,121	684,028
Germany [2]	5,351,746	143,945	412,202	114,058	226,578	477,765	6,726,294
Great Britain: England	2,212,071	249,944	157,420	21,756	112,252	156,171	2,909,614
Scotland	488,749	78,357	159,781	6,887	16,131	32,854	782,759
Wales	59,540	13,107	13,012	735	3,209	2,589	92,192
Not specified [4]	793,741	....	....	....	....	3,884	797,625
Greece	186,204	184,201	51,084	9,119	8,973	47,608	487,189
Hungary [2]	....	442,693	30,680	7,861	3,469	36,637	521,340
Ireland	4,212,169	146,181	220,591	13,167	26,967	57,332	4,676,407
Italy	3,086,356	1,109,524	455,315	68,028	57,661	185,491	4,962,375
Latvia [1]	....	....	3,399	1,192	361	352	5,304
Lithuania [1]	....	....	6,015	2,201	683	242	9,141
Luxemburg [1]	....	....	727	565	820	684	2,796
Netherlands	175,943	43,718	26,948	7,150	14,860	52,277	320,896
Norway [5]	665,189	66,395	68,531	4,740	10,100	22,935	837,890
Poland [6]	165,182	4,813	227,734	17,026	7,571	9,985	432,311
Portugal	132,089	89,732	29,994	3,329	7,423	19,588	283,055
Rumania [7]	72,117	13,311	67,646	3,871	1,076	1,039	159,060
Spain	69,296	68,611	28,958	3,258	2,898	7,894	180,915
Sweden [5]	1,021,165	95,074	97,249	3,960	10,665	21,697	1,249,810
Switzerland	237,401	23,091	29,676	5,512	10,547	17,675	323,902
Turkey in Europe	85,800	54,677	14,659	737	580	2,653	159,106
U.S.S.R. [8]	2,359,048	921,201	61,742	1,356	548	584	3,344,479
Yugoslavia [3]	....	1,888	49,064	5,835	1,576	8,225	66,588
Other Europe	2,605	8,111	9,603	2,361	3,983	8,155	34,818
Total Europe	25,421,929	4,376,564	2,477,853	348,289	621,704	1,328,293	34,574,632
Asia: China	326,060	21,278	29,907	4,928	16,709	9,657	408,539
India	5,409	2,082	1,886	496	1,761	1,973	13,607
Japan [9]	158,344	83,837	33,462	1,948	1,555	46,250	325,396
Turkey in Asia [10]	106,481	79,389	19,165	328	218	866	206,447
Other Asia	16,942	5,973	12,980	7,644	11,537	88,707	143,783
Total Asia [15]	613,236	192,559	97,400	15,344	31,780	147,453	1,097,772
America: Canada & New-foundland [11]	1,230,501	742,185	924,515	108,527	171,718	377,952	3,555,398
Central America	10,365	17,159	15,769	5,861	21,665	44,751	115,570
Mexico [12]	77,645	219,004	459,287	22,319	60,589	299,811	1,138,655
South America	29,385	41,899	42,215	7,803	21,831	91,628	234,761
West Indies	233,146	123,424	74,899	15,502	49,725	123,091	619,787
Other America [13]	....	....	31	25	29,276	59,711	89,043
Total America	1,581,042	1,143,671	1,516,716	160,037	354,804	996,944	5,753,214
Africa	9,581	8,443	6,286	1,750	7,367	14,092	47,519
Australia & New Zealand	31,654	12,348	8,299	2,231	13,805	11,506	79,843
Pacific Islands [15]	8,859	1,079	427	780	5,437	4,698	21,280
Countries not specified	252,691[14]	1,147	228	....	142	12,493	266,701
Total all countries	27,918,992	5,735,811	4,107,209	528,431	1,035,039	2,515,479	41,840,961

[1] Countries established since beginning of World War I are theretofore included with countries to which they belonged. [2] Data for Austria-Hungary not reported until 1861. Austria and Hungary recorded separately after 1905. Austria included with Germany 1938–45. [3] Bulgaria, Serbia, Montenegro first reported in 1899. Bulgaria reported separately since 1920. In 1920, separate enumeration for Kingdom of Serbs, Croats, Slovenes; since 1922, recorded as

PUBLIC ELEMENTARY AND SECONDARY SCHOOL STATISTICS, 1870–1958

	1870	1880	1890	1900	1910	1920
Total population............	38,558,371	50,155,783	62,622,250	75,602,515	91,972,266	105,710,620
Population 5–17 years, inclusive	12,055,443	15,065,767	18,543,201	21,404,322	24,239,948	27,728,788
Pupils enrolled in public schools	6,871,522	9,867,505	12,722,581	15,503,110	17,813,852	21,578,316
Per cent of population 5–17, inclusive..................	57.00	65.50	68.61	72.43	73.49	77.8
Number of teachers..........	200,515	286,593	363,922	423,062	523,210	679,533
Total expenditure for education (thousands of dollars).......	63,397	78,095	140,507	214,965	426,250	1,036,151
Per capita of total population..	$1.64	$1.56	$2.24	$2.84	$4.64	$9.80
Per capita of enrollment.......	$9.23	$7.91	$11.04	$13.87	$23.93	$48.02

	1930	1936	1940	1950	1958	
Total population............	122,775,046	128,429,000	131,669,275	148,665	170,295	
Population 5–17 years, inclusive	31,571,322	31,547,000	29,745,246	30,168	40,164	
Pupils enrolled in public schools	25,678,015	26,367,098	25,433,542	25,111	33,529	
Per cent of population 5–17, inclusive..................	81.3	83.6	85.5	82.3	83.5	
Number of teachers..........	854,263	870,963	875,477	962	1,333	
Total expenditure for education (thousands of dollars).......	2,316,790	1,968,898	2,344,049	5,858	13,569	
Per capita of total population..	$18.87	$15.33	$17.77	$39.27	$79.68	
Per capita of enrollment.......	$90.22	$74.38	$91.64	$208.83	$341.14	

Source: U.S. Office of Education

AREAS OF PERFECTED HOMESTEAD ENTRIES,

Years ending JUNE 30

	ACRES		ACRES		ACRES		ACRES		ACRES
1868	355,086	1885	3,032,679	1902	4,342,748	1919	6,524,760	1936	1,764,958
1869	504,302	1886	2,663,532	1903	3,576,964	1920	8,372,696	1937	1,914,806
1870	519,728	1887	2,749,037	1904	3,232,717	1921	7,726,740	1938	1,361,943
1871	629,162	1888	3,175,401	1905	3,419,387	1922	7,307,034	1939	1,088,938
1872	707,410	1889	3,681,709	1906	3,526,749	1923	5,594,259	1940	652,484
1873	1,224,891	1890	4,060,593	1907	3,740,568	1924	4,791,436	1941	389,970
1874	1,585,782	1891	3,954,588	1908	4,242,711	1925	4,048,910	1942	187,507
1875	2,068,538	1892	3,259,897	1909	3,699,467	1926	3,451,105	1943	101,529
1876	2,590,553	1893	3,447,232	1910	3,795,863	1927	2,583,627	1944	50,506
1877	2,407,828	1894	2,929,947	1911	4,620,197	1928	1,815,549	1945	34,692
1878	2,662,081	1895	2,980,809	1912	4,306,068	1929	1,700,950	1946	29,368
1879	2,070,842	1896	2,790,242	1913	10,009,285	1930	1,371,073	1947	25,987
1880	1,938,235	1897	2,778,404	1914	9,291,121	1931	1,352,861	Total	247,466,340
1881	1,928,205	1898	3,095,018	1915	7,180,982	1932	1,209,894		
1882	2,219,454	1899	3,134,140	1916	7,278,281	1933	906,578		
1883	2,504,414	1900	3,477,843	1917	8,497,390	1934	1,123,673		
1884	2,945,575	1901	5,241,121	1918	8,236,438	1935	1,640,393		

Source: Commissioner of the General Land Office

Yugoslavia. [4] United Kingdom not specified; for 1901–51, included in "Other Europe." [5] Norway included with Sweden 1820–68. [6] Included with Austria-Hungary, Germany and Russia 1899–1919. [7] No record of immigration until 1880. [8] Since 1931, U.S.S.R. has been broken down into European Russia and Siberia or Asiatic Russia. [9] No record of immigration until 1861. [10] No record of immigration until 1869. [11] Includes all British North American possessions 1820–98. [12] No record of immigration 1886–93. [13] Included with "Countries not specified" prior to 1925. [14] Includes 32,807 persons returning in 1906 to their homes in U.S. [15] From 1952, Asia included Philippines. From 1934–51, Philippines included in Pacific Islands; before 1934, recorded in separate tables as insular travel.

PRESIDENTIAL VOTE, 1860–1960

Year	Candidate	Party	Popular Vote	Per Cent	Electoral Vote
1860	**Lincoln**	**Republican**	1,866,352	39.91	180
	Douglas..................	Democratic............	1,375,157	29.40	12
	Breckinridge.............	Democratic............	845,763	18.08	72
	Bell......................	Union.................	589,581	12.61	39
1864	**Lincoln**	**Republican**............	2,216,067	55.06	216
	McClellan................	Democratic............	1,808,725	44.94	21
1868	**Grant**....................	**Republican**............	3,015,071	52.67	214
	Seymour.................	Democratic............	2,709,613	47.23	80
1872	**Grant**....................	**Republican**............	3,597,070	55.63	292
	Greeley..................	Democratic............	2,834,079	43.83	66
	O'Conor.................	Ind. Democratic.......	29,408	.45	...
	Black....................	Temperance............	5,608	.09	...
1876	Tilden...................	Democratic............	4,284,885	50.94	184
	Hayes...................	**Republican**............	4,033,950	47.95	185
	Cooper..................	Greenback.............	81,740	.97	...
	Smith....................	Prohibition............	9,522	.11	...
	Walker..................	American..............	2,636	.03	...
1880	**Garfield**.................	**Republican**............	4,449,053	48.31	214
	Hancock.................	Democratic............	4,442,035	48.23	155
	Weaver..................	Greenback.............	307,306	3.34	...
	Dow.....................	Prohibition............	10,487	.11	...
	Phelps...................	American..............	707	.01	...
1884	**Cleveland**...............	**Democratic**............	4,911,017	48.89	219
	Blaine...................	Republican............	4,848,334	48.27	182
	St. John.................	Prohibition............	151,809	1.51	...
	Butler...................	Greenback.............	133,825	1.33	...
1888	Cleveland...............	Democratic............	5,540,050	48.66	168
	Harrison................	**Republican**............	5,444,337	47.82	233
	Fisk.....................	Prohibition............	250,125	2.20	...
	Streeter.................	Union Labor...........	146,897	1.29	...
	Cowdrey.................	United Labor..........	2,808	.03	...
1892	**Cleveland**...............	**Democratic**............	5,554,414	46.04	277
	Harrison.................	Republican............	5,190,802	43.02	145
	Weaver..................	People's..............	1,027,329	8.51	22
	Bidwell..................	Prohibition............	271,058	2.24	...
	Wing....................	Socialist..............	21,164	.19	...
1896	**McKinley**................	**Republican**............	7,035,638	50.88	271
	Bryan....................	Democratic............	6,467,946	46.77	176
	Levering.................	Prohibition............	141,676	1.03	...
	Palmer...................	Nat. Democratic.......	131,529	.95	...
	Matchett.................	Socialist Labor.........	36,454	.27	...
	Bentley..................	National..............	13,969	.10	...
1900	**McKinley**................	**Republican**............	7,219,530	51.69	292
	Bryan....................	Democratic............	6,358,071	45.51	155
	Woolley..................	Prohibition............	209,166	1.49	...
	Debs.....................	Socialist Democrat......	94,768	.67	...
	Barker...................	People's..............	50,232	.37	...
	Malloney.................	Socialist Labor..........	32,751	.23	...
	Ellis.....................	Union Reform..........	5,098	.04	...
	Leonard.................	United Christian........	518	.00	...
1904	**Roosevelt**...............	**Republican**............	7,628,834	56.41	336

PRESIDENTIAL VOTE, 1860–1960—*Continued*

YEAR	CANDIDATE	PARTY	POPULAR VOTE	PER CENT	ELECTORAL VOTE
	Parker....................	Democratic............	5,084,401	37.60	140
	Debs.....................	Socialist..............	402,460	2.98	...
	Swallow..................	Prohibition............	259,257	1.91	...
	Watson...................	People's...............	114,753	.85	...
	Corregan.................	Socialist Labor........	33,724	.25	...
	Holcomb..................	Continental............	830	.00	...
1908	**Taft**.....................	**Republican............**	7,679,006	51.58	321
	Bryan....................	Democratic............	6,409,106	43.05	162
	Debs.....................	Socialist..............	420,820	2.83	...
	Chafin...................	Prohibition............	252,683	1.69	...
	Hisgen...................	Independence..........	83,562	.56	...
	Watson...................	People's...............	28,131	.19	...
	Gillhaus.................	Socialist Labor........	13,825	.10	...
	Turney...................	United Christian.......	461	.00	...
1912	**Wilson**...................	**Democratic............**	6,286,214	41.82	435
	Roosevelt................	Progressive............	4,126,020	27.45	88
	Taft.....................	Republican............	3,483,922	23.17	8
	Debs.....................	Socialist..............	897,011	5.97	...
	Chafin...................	Prohibition............	208,923	1.39	...
	Reimer...................	Socialist Labor.........	29,079	.20	...
1916	**Wilson**...................	**Democratic............**	9,129,606	49.28	277
	Hughes...................	Republican............	8,538,221	46.07	254
	Benson...................	Socialist..............	585,113	3.16	...
	Hanly....................	Prohibition............	220,506	1.19	...
	Reimer...................	Socialist Labor.........	13,403	.07	...
	Misc.....................	....	41,894	.23	...
1920	**Harding**..................	**Republican............**	16,152,200	61.02	404
	Cox......................	Democratic............	9,147,353	34.55	127
	Debs.....................	Socialist..............	919,799	3.47	...
	Watkins..................	Prohibition............	189,408	.72	...
	Cox......................	Socialist Labor........	31,175	.12	...
	Christensen..............	Farmer Labor..........	26,541	.10	...
	Macauley.................	Single Tax............	5,837	.02	...
1924	**Coolidge**.................	**Republican............**	15,725,016	54.1	382
	Davis....................	Democratic............	8,385,586	28.8	136
	LaFollette	Independent, Progressive, and Socialist	4,822,856	16.6	13
	Faris....................	Prohibition............	57,551		...
	Johns	Socialist Labor........	38,958		...
	Foster...................	Workers'..............	33,361	.5	...
	Nations..................	American..............	23,867		...
	Wallace..................	Com. Land............	2,778		...
1928	**Hoover**...................	**Republican............**	21,392,190	58.2	444
	Smith....................	Democratic............	15,016,443	40.8	87
	Thomas..................	Socialist..............	267,420		...
	Foster...................	Workers'..............	48,770		...
	Reynolds.................	Socialist Labor........	21,603	1.0	...
	Varney...................	Prohibition............	20,106		...
	Webb....................	Farm-Labor............	6,390		...
1932	**Roosevelt**................	**Democratic............**	22,821,857	57.3	472
	Hoover...................	Republican............	15,761,841	39.6	59

PRESIDENTIAL VOTE, 1860–1960—*Continued*

Year	Candidate	Party	Popular Vote	Per Cent	Electoral Vote
	Thomas..................	Socialist...............	884,781	⎫	...
	Foster....................	Communist.............	102,991	⎪	...
	Upshaw.................	Prohibition............	81,869	⎬ 3.1	...
	Harvey..................	Liberty................	53,425	⎪	...
	Reynolds................	Socialist Labor........	33,276	⎪	...
	Coxey..................	Farm-Labor............	7,309	⎭	...
1936	**Roosevelt**................	**Democratic**...........	27,751,612	60.7	523
	Landon.................	Republican............	16,681,913	36.4	8
	Lemke..................	Union.................	891,858		...
	Thomas.................	Socialist..............	187,342	⎫	...
	Browder................	Communist............	80,181	⎬ 2.9	...
	Colvin..................	Prohibition...........	37,609	⎪	...
	Aiken..................	Socialist Labor........	12,729	⎭	...
1940	**Roosevelt**................	**Democratic**...........	27,243,466	54.7	449
	Willkie..................	Republican............	22,304,755	44.8	82
	Thomas.................	Socialist..............	99,557	⎫	...
	Babson.................	Prohibition...........	57,812	⎬ .5	...
	Browder................	Communist............	46,251	⎪	...
	Aiken..................	Socialist Labor........	14,861	⎭	...
1944	**Roosevelt**................	**Democratic**...........	25,602,505	52.8	432
	Dewey..................	Republican............	22,006,278	44.5	99
	Thomas.................	Socialist..............	80,518	⎫	...
	Watson.................	Prohibition...........	74,758	⎬ 2.7	...
	Teichert................	Socialist Labor........	45,336	⎪	...
	Misc. Independent........	....	216,289	⎭	...
1948	**Truman**.................	**Democratic**...........	24,045,052	50.5	304
	Dewey..................	Republican............	21,896,927	43.75	189
	Thurmond...............	States Rights..........	1,168,687	⎫	38
	Wallace.................	Progressive............	1,137,957	⎪	...
	Thomas.................	Socialist..............	95,908	⎬ 5.75	...
	Watson.................	Prohibition...........	95,075	⎪	...
	Misc. Independent........	....	49,611	⎭	...
1952	**Dwight D. Eisenhower**.....	**Republican**............	33,936,234	55.2	442
	Adlai E. Stevenson.......	Democratic............	27,314,992	44.5	89
	Vincent Hallinan.........	Progressive............	140,023	⎫	...
	Stuart Hamblen..........	Prohibition...........	72,949	⎪	...
	Eric Haas...............	Socialist Labor.........	30,267	⎪	...
	Darlington Hoopes.......	Socialist..............	20,203	⎬ .3	...
	Douglas A. MacArthur.....	Constitution..........	17,205	⎪	...
	Farrell Dobbs.............	Socialist Workers.......	10,312	⎭	...
1956	**Dwight D. Eisenhower**.....	**Republican**............	35,590,472	57.4	457
	Adlai E. Stevenson.......	Democratic............	26,022,752	42.0	73*
	T. Coleman Andrews.......	States Rights..........	107,929	⎫	...
	Eric Haas...............	Socialist Labor........	44,300	⎬ .6	...
	Enoch A. Holtwick.......	Prohibition...........	41,937	⎭	...
1960	**John F. Kennedy**..........	**Democratic**...........	34,221,463	49.7	303
	Richard M. Nixon........	Republican............	34,108,582	49.5	219
	Orval Faubus.............	National States Rights...	227,881	⎫	...
	Eric Haas................	Socialist Labor........	48,031	⎪	...
	Rutherford B. Decker......	Prohibition...........	46,197	⎬ .8	...
	Farrell Dobbs.............	Socialist Workers........	39,692	⎭	...
	Harry F. Byrd.............	....	....	.....	15†

* In 1956 in Alabama one Democratic elector refused to vote for Stevenson and cast his ballot for Walter B. Jones.
† Six unpledged electors from Alabama, eight from Mississippi and one Oklahoma Republican who refused to vote for Nixon.

POLITICAL CONTROL IN THE PRESIDENCY AND IN CONGRESS, 1865–1961

Congress	Year	President	Senate	House
39	1865–1867	Johnson R	R	R
40	1867–1869		R	R
41	1869–1871	Grant R	R	R
42	1871–1873		R	R
43	1873–1875		R	R
44	1875–1877		R	D
45	1877–1879	Hayes R	R	D
46	1879–1881		D	D
47	1881–1883	Garfield R	37D–37R 1 Independent	R
48	1883–1885	Arthur	R 1 Readjuster	D
49	1885–1887	Cleveland D	R	D
50	1887–1889		R	D
51	1889–1891	Harrison R	R	R
52	1891–1893		R	D
53	1893–1895	Cleveland D	D	D
54	1895–1897		R	R
55	1897–1899	McKinley R	R	R
56	1899–1901		R	R
57	1901–1903	McKinley R	R	R
58	1903–1905	Roosevelt	R	R
59	1905–1907	Roosevelt R	R	R
60	1907–1909		R	R
61	1909–1911	Taft R	R	R
62	1911–1913		R	D
63	1913–1915	Wilson D	D	D
64	1915–1917		D	D
65	1917–1919		D	D
66	1919–1921		R	R
67	1921–1923	Harding R	R	R
68	1923–1925	Coolidge	R	R
69	1925–1927	Coolidge R	R 48R 1 In. 47D	R
70	1927–1929			R
71	1929–1931	Hoover R	R 48R 1 In. 47D	R
72	1931–1933			D
73	1933–1935	Roosevelt D	D	D
74	1935–1937		D	D
75	1937–1939		D	D
76	1939–1941		D	D
77	1941–1943		D	D
78	1943–1945	Roosevelt D	D	D
79	1945–1947	Truman	D	D
80	1947–1949	Truman D	R	R
81	1949–1951		D	D
82	1951–1953		D	D
83	1953–1955	Eisenhower R	R	R
84	1955–1957		D	D
85	1957–1959		D	D
86	1959–1961		D	D
87	1961–1963	Kennedy D	D	D

Source: *Statistical Abstract of the United States*

SPEAKERS OF THE HOUSE OF REPRESENTATIVES, 1860–1961

Name	Party, State	Tenure
William Pennington	R, N.J.	1860–1861
Galusha A. Grow	R, Pa.	1861–1863
Schuyler Colfax	R, Ind.	1863–1869
James G. Blaine	R, Me.	1869–1875
Michael C. Kerr	D, Ind.	1875–1876
Samuel J. Randall	D, Pa.	1876–1881
Joseph W. Keifer	R, Ohio	1881–1883
John G. Carlisle	D, Ky.	1883–1889
Thomas B. Reed	R, Me.	1889–1891
Charles F. Crisp	D, Ga.	1891–1895
Thomas B. Reed	R, Me.	1895–1899
David B. Henderson	R, Iowa	1899–1903
Joseph G. Cannon	R, Ill.	1903–1911
Champ Clark	D, Mo.	1911–1919
Frederick H. Gillett	R, Mass.	1919–1925
Nicholas Longworth	R, Ohio	1925–1931
John N. Garner	D, Tex.	1931–1933
Henry T. Rainey	D, Ill.	1933–1935
Joseph W. Byrns	D, Tenn.	1935–1936
William B. Bankhead	D, Ala.	1936–1940
Sam Rayburn	D, Tex.	1940–1947
Joseph W. Martin, Jr.	R, Mass.	1947–1949
Sam Rayburn	D, Tex.	1949–1953
Joseph W. Martin, Jr.	R, Mass.	1953–1955
Sam Rayburn	D, Tex.	1955–1961
John C. McCormack	D, Mass.	1961–

RAILROAD MILEAGE

(By decade, 1830–1960)

1830	23	1900	193,346
1840	2,818	1910	240,293
1850	9,021	1920	252,845
1860	30,626	1930	249,052
1870	52,922	1940	233,670
1880	93,262	1950	223,779
1890	163,597	1959	217,565

JUSTICES OF THE UNITED STATES SUPREME COURT

NAME *Chief Justices in Italics*	SERVICE		NAME *Chief Justices in Italics*	SERVICE	
	Term	Yrs.		Term	Yrs.
John Jay, N.Y.............	1789–1795	6	Samuel Blatchford, N.Y....	1882–1893	11
John Rutledge, S.C.	1789–1791	2	Lucius Q. C. Lamar, Miss...	1888–1893	5
William Cushing, Mass.....	1789–1810	21	*Melville W. Fuller*, Ill......	1888–1910	22
James Wilson, Pa...........	1789–1798	9	David J. Brewer, Kan.....	1889–1910	21
John Blair, Va.	1789–1796	7	Henry B. Brown, Mich....	1890–1906	16
Robert H. Harrison, Md....	1789–1790	1	George Shiras, Jr., Pa......	1892–1903	11
James Iredell, N.C.........	1790–1799	9	Howell E. Jackson, Tenn. ..	1893–1895	2
Thomas Johnson, Md.......	1791–1793	2	Edward D. White, La.....	1894–1910	16
William Paterson, N.J......	1793–1806	13	Rufus W. Peckham, N.Y...	1895–1910	14
John Rutledge, S.C.	1795–1795	..	Joseph McKenna, Cal.	1898–1925	27
Samuel Chase, Md.........	1796–1811	15	Oliver W. Holmes, Mass...	1902–1932	29
Oliver Ellsworth, Conn.	1796–1799	4	William R. Day, Ohio.....	1903–1922	19
Bushrod Washington, Va....	1798–1829	31	William H. Moody, Mass..	1906–1910	4
Alfred Moore, N.C.	1799–1804	5	Horace H. Lurton, Tenn. ..	1910–1914	5
John Marshall, Va..........	1801–1835	34	Charles E. Hughes, N.Y....	1910–1916	6
William Johnson, S.C.......	1804–1834	30	Willis Van Devanter, Wyo..	1910–1937	27
Brock. Livingston, N.Y.....	1806–1823	17	Joseph R. Lamar, Ga......	1911–1916	6
Thomas Todd, Ky.........	1807–1826	19	*Edward D. White*, La......	1910–1921	11
Joseph Story, Mass.........	1811–1845	34	Mahlon Pitney, N.J.	1912–1922	10
Gabriel Duval, Md.........	1811–1836	25	Jas. C. McReynolds, Tenn..	1914–1941	27
Smith Thompson, N.Y......	1823–1843	20	Louis D. Brandeis, Mass. ..	1916–1939	23
Robert Trimble, Ky........	1826–1828	2	John H. Clark, Ohio	1916–1922	6
John McLean, Ohio........	1829–1861	32	*William H. Taft*, Conn. ...	1921–1930	9
Henry Baldwin, Pa........	1830–1844	14	George Sutherland, Utah ..	1922–1938	16
James M. Wayne, Ga.......	1835–1867	32	Pierce Butler, Minn.......	1922–1939	17
Roger B. Taney, Md........	1836–1864	28	Edward T. Sanford, Tenn..	1923–1930	7
Philip P. Barbour, Va.	1836–1841	5	Harlan F. Stone, N.Y......	1925–1941	16
John Catron, Tenn.	1837–1865	28	*Charles E. Hughes*, N.Y....	1930–1941	11
John McKinley, Ala.	1837–1852	15	Owen J. Roberts, Pa.......	1930–1945	15
Peter V. Daniel, Va........	1841–1860	19	Benjamin N. Cardozo, N.Y.	1932–1938	6
Samuel Nelson, N.Y.......	1845–1872	27	Hugo L. Black, Ala........	1937–....	..
Levi Woodbury, N.H.......	1845–1851	6	Stanley F. Reed, Ky.......	1938–1957	19
Robert C. Grier, Pa........	1846–1870	24	Felix Frankfurter, Mass....	1939–....	..
Benj. R. Curtis, Mass......	1851–1857	6	William O. Douglas, Conn..	1939–....	..
John A. Campbell, Ala......	1853–1861	8	Frank Murphy, Mich......	1940–1949	9
Nathan Clifford, Me.......	1858–1881	23	*Harlan F. Stone*, N.Y......	1941–1946	5
Noah H. Swayne, Ohio	1862–1881	20	James F. Byrnes, S.C......	1941–1942	1
Samuel F. Miller, Iowa.....	1862–1890	28	Robert H. Jackson, N.Y...	1941–1954	13
David Davis, Ill............	1862–1877	15	Wiley B. Rutledge, Iowa ..	1943–1949	6
Stephen J. Field, Cal.......	1863–1897	34	Harold H. Burton, Ohio...	1945–1958	13
Salmon P. Chase, Ohio	1864–1873	9	*Fred M. Vinson*, Ky.......	1946–1953	7
William Strong, Pa.........	1870–1880	10	Tom C. Clark, Tex........	1949–....	..
Joseph P. Bradley, N.J.	1870–1892	22	Sherman Minton, Ind......	1949–1956	7
Ward Hunt, N.Y...........	1872–1882	10	*Earl Warren*, Calif.........	1953–....	..
Morrison R. Waite, Ohio	1874–1888	14	John M. Harlan, N.Y.	1955–....	..
John M. Harlan, Ky........	1877–1911	34	William J. Brennan, Jr., N.J.	1956–....	..
William B. Woods, Ga......	1880–1887	7	Charles E. Whittaker, Mo..	1957–1962	5
Stanley Matthews, Ohio	1881–1889	8	Potter Stewart, Ohio	1959–....	..
Horace Gray, Mass.........	1881–1902	21	Byron R. White, Colo.....	1962–....	..

LABOR UNION MEMBERSHIP, 1897–1958

YEAR	ALL UNIONS, TOTAL MEMBERSHIP	AMERICAN FEDERATION OF LABOR		CONGRESS OF INDUSTRIAL ORGANIZATION		INDEPENDENT OR UNAFFILIATED UNIONS, TOTAL MEMBERSHIP
		Number of affiliated unions	Total membership	Number of affiliated unions	Total membership	
	1,000 members	Number	*1,000 members*	Number	*1,000 members*	*1,000 members*
1897	440	58	265			175
1900	791	82	548			243
1910	2,116	120	1,562			554
1919	4,046	111	3,260			786
1920	5,034	110	4,079			955
1921	4,722	110	3,907			815
1922	3,950	112	3,196			754
1923	3,629	108	2,926			703
1924	3,549	107	2,866			683
1925	3,566	107	2,877			689
1926	3,592	107	2,804			788
1927	3,600	106	2,813			787
1928	3,567	107	2,896			671
1929	3,625	105	2,934			671
1930	3,632	104	2,961			671
1931	3,526	105	2,890			636
1932	3,226	106	2,532			694
1933	2,857	108	2,127			730
1934	3,249	109	2,608			641
1935	3,728	109	3,045			683
1936	4,164	111	3,422			742
1937	7,218	100	2,861	32	3,718	639
1938	8,265	102	3,623	42	4,038	604
1939	8,980	104	4,006	45	4,000	974
1940	8,944	105	4,247	42	3,625	1,072
1941	10,489	106	4,569	41	5,000	920
1942	10,762	102	5,483	39	4,195	1,084
1943	13,642	99	6,564	40	5,285	1,793
1944	14,621	100	6,807	41	5,935	1,879
1945	14,796	102	6,931	40	6,000	1,865
1950	15,000	107	7,143	30	5,000	2,600
1955	17,749	139		16,062		1,688
1956	18,477	137		16,904		1,573
1957	18,431	184		18,954		1,476
1958	18,081	186		14,993		3,088

UNITED STATES PARTICIPATION IN WORLD WAR I

Total armed forces, including Army, Navy, Marine Corps, etc.	4,800,000
Total men in the Army	4,000,000
Men who went overseas	2,086,000
Men who fought in France	1,390,000
Greatest number sent in one month	306,000
Greatest number returning in one month	333,000
Tons of supplies shipped from America to France	7,500,000
Total registered in draft	24,234,021
Total draft inductions	2,810,296
Greatest number inducted in one month	400,000
Graduates of Line Officers' Training Schools	80,568
Cost of war to April 30, 1919	$21,850,000,000
Cost of Army to April 30, 1919	$13,930,000,000
Battles fought by American troops	13
Months of American participation in the war	19
Days of battle	200
Days of duration of Meuse-Argonne battle	47
Americans in Meuse-Argonne battle	1,200,000
American casualties in Meuse-Argonne battle	120,000
American battle deaths in war	50,000
American wounded in war	206,000
American deaths from disease	57,500
Total deaths in the Army	115,000

From Leonard P. Ayres, *The War with Germany. A Statistical Summary*, p. 11. Washington. Government Printing Office, 1919.

UNITED STATES PARTICIPATION IN WORLD WAR II

(All data are as of 31 August 1945)

ITEM	TOTAL	ARMY (Inc. AAF)	NAVY	MARINE CORPS	COAST GUARD
Registered in Draft [a]	50,680,137	....	....	....	....
Draft Inductions, Total [b]	10,189,773	8,397,356	1,549,285	227,001	16,131
1 Nov. '40 to 31 Aug. '45 only	9,867,707	8,096,248	1,534,241	221,087	16,131
Number Who Served, Total	15,145,115	10,420,000	3,883,520	599,963	241,902
Overseas only [c]	11,411,581	7,300,000	3,378,662	512,788	220,131
Battle Casualties, Total [d]	1,122,879	948,574	83,550	89,194	1,561
Battle Deaths, Total	304,014	237,049	46,469	19,910	586
Killed in Action	} 267,899	{ 175,407	36,488	} 19,641	{ 572
Died of Wounds		26,706	9,072		13
Died while Prisoner or Missing	36,115	34,936	909	269	1
Wounded in Action	673,665	571,822	33,726	67,142	975
Captured or Missing	145,200	139,703	3,355	2,142	....
Died of Disease	21,856	[e] 14,730	[e] 5,862	900	364
Prisoners Captured, Total	3,710,000				
German	3,500,000				
Italian	175,000				
Japanese	35,000				
Enemy Submarines Destroyed, Total	[f] 290	....	....	....	3
German	174	....	....	....	3
Italian	5	....	....	....	0
Japanese	111	....	....	....	0

[a] Represents total registrations of age groups 18–64 years during the period October 1940 through March 1947.
[b] Total figures are for the entire draft period, 1 November 1940–30 November 1946.
[c] Estimated.
[d] Tentative.
[e] Tentative.
[f] Does not include number sunk by mines. A total of 906 enemy submarines were sunk by the Allies during the years 1939–45, of which 893 were sunk by known causes.
Source: U.S. Army Historical Branch.

LEND–LEASE AID, BY COUNTRY, 1941–1945

(In thousands of dollars)

Country	Mar. 11, 1941, to V–J Day (Sept. 2, 1945)	Country	Mar. 11, 1941, to V–J Day (Sept. 2, 1945)
British Empire.............	$30,949,870	American Republics:	
U.S.S.R.....................	11,058,833	Argentina................	o
France and Possessions.......	2,842,082	Bolivia	5,155
China....................	870,435	Brazil...................	326,913
Netherlands and Possessions..	182,000	Chile....................	21,499
Belgium..................	90,278	Colombia................	8,120
Greece...................	71,697	Costa Rica	155
Norway	45,820	Cuba....................	6,083
Yugoslavia	32,000	Dominican Republic	1,594
Turkey....................	27,397	Ecuador	6,979
Saudi Arabia..............	14,988	Guatemala...............	1,779
Poland	16,874	Haiti....................	1,437
Liberia...................	7,237	Honduras	374
Ethiopia	5,152	Mexico..................	38,468
Iran......................	4,798	Nicaragua...............	902
Iceland...................	4,797	Panama..................	84
Egypt.....................	1,016	Paraguay................	1,963
Czechoslovakia.............	349	Peru....................	18,553
Iraq......................	4	Salvador	894
		Uruguay................	7,132
		Venezuela...............	4,407
		Not charged by country......	1,900,805
		Total Lend-Lease aid....	$48,578,923

MAJOR U.S. GOVERNMENT FOREIGN ASSISTANCE

Postwar Period, 1 July 1945 through 30 June 1961

AREAS AND COUNTRIES	NET TOTAL (In millions of dollars)
TOTAL	$84,710
Investment in international financial institutions	4,949
THROUGH ASSISTANCE PROGRAMS	79,761
Western Europe	39,475
France...........................	9,659
Germany..........................	4,023
Italy............................	5,134
United Kingdom	7,739
Yugoslavia	2,106
Eastern Europe	1,492
Near East	12,641
Greece...........................	2,950
India............................	2,001
Iran.............................	1,068
Israel...........................	646
Pakistan.........................	1,054
Turkey...........................	3,028
Africa	771
Far East and Pacific	20,036
China-Taiwan.....................	4,910
Japan............................	4,044
Korea	4,556
Philippines......................	1,380
Thailand.........................	570
Vietnam..........................	1,910
American Republics	3,430

INDEX

THE CONSTITUTION
OF
THE UNITED STATES OF AMERICA

We the People of the *United States,*
in order to form a more perfect union, establish
Justice, insure domestic tranquility, provide for
the common defence, promote the general Welfare,
and secure the Blessings of Liberty to ourselves
and our Posterity, do ordain and establish this
Constitution for the United States of America.

ARTICLE I

SECTION 1. All legislative Powers herein granted shall be vested in a Congress of the United States, which shall consist of a Senate and a House of Representatives.

SECTION 2. The House of Representatives shall be composed of Members chosen every second Year by the People of the several States, and the Electors in each State shall have the Qualifications requisite for Electors of the most numerous Branch of the State Legislature.

No Person shall be a Representative who shall not have attained to the Age of twenty-five Years, and been seven Years a Citizen of the

United States, and who shall not, when elected, be an Inhabitant of that State in which he shall be chosen.

Representatives and direct Taxes shall be apportioned among the several States which may be included within this Union, according to their respective Numbers, which shall be determined by adding to the whole Number of free Persons, including those bound to Service for a Term of Years, and excluding Indians not taxed, three fifths of all other Persons. The actual Enumeration shall be made within three Years after the first Meeting of the Congress of the United States, and within every subsequent Term of ten Years, in such Manner as they shall by Law direct. The Number of Representatives shall not exceed one for every thirty Thousand, but each State shall have at Least one Representative; and until such enumeration shall be made, the State of New Hampshire shall be entitled to chuse three, Massachusetts eight, Rhode-Island and Providence Plantations one, Connecticut five, New-York six, New Jersey four, Pennsylvania eight, Delaware one, Maryland six, Virginia ten, North Carolina five, South Carolina five, and Georgia three.

When vacancies happen in the Representation from any State, the Executive Authority thereof shall issue Writs of Election to fill such Vacancies.

The House of Representatives shall chuse their Speaker and other Officers; and shall have the sole Power of Impeachment.

SECTION 3. The Senate of the United States shall be composed of two Senators from each State, chosen by the Legislature thereof, for six Years; and each Senator shall have one Vote.

Immediately after they shall be assembled in Consequence of the first Election, they shall be divided as equally as may be into three Classes. The Seats of the Senators of the first Class shall be vacated at the Expiration of the second Year, of the second Class at the Expiration of the fourth Year, and of the third Class at the Expiration of the sixth Year, so that one-third may be chosen every second Year; and if Vacancies happen by Resignation, or otherwise, during the Recess of the Legislature of any State, the Executive thereof may make temporary Appointments until the next Meeting of the Legislature, which shall then fill such Vacancies.

No Person shall be a Senator who shall not have attained to the Age of thirty Years, and been nine Years a Citizen of the United States, and who shall not, when elected, be an Inhabitant of that State for which he shall be chosen.

The Vice President of the United States shall be President of the Senate, but shall have no Vote, unless they be equally divided.

The Senate shall chuse their other Officers, and also a President pro tempore, in the Absence of the Vice President, or when he shall exercise the Office of President of the United States.

The Senate shall have the sole Power to try all Impeachments. When sitting for that Purpose, they shall be on Oath or Affirmation. When the President of the United States is tried, the Chief Justice shall preside: And no Person shall be convicted without the Concurrence of two thirds of the Members present.

Judgment in Cases of Impeachment shall not extend further than to removal from Office, and disqualification to hold and enjoy any Office of honor, Trust or Profit under the United States: but the Party convicted shall nevertheless be liable and subject to Indictment, Trial, Judgment and Punishment, according to Law.

SECTION 4. The Times, Places and Manner of holding Elections for Senators and Representatives, shall be prescribed in each State by the Legislature thereof; but the Congress may at any time by Law make or alter such Regulations, except as to the Places of chusing Senators.

The Congress shall assemble at least once in every Year, and such Meeting shall be on the first Monday in December, unless they shall by Law appoint a different Day.

SECTION 5. Each House shall be the Judge of the Elections, Returns and Qualifications of its own Members, and a Majority of each shall constitute a Quorum to do Business; but a smaller Number may adjourn from day to day, and may be authorized to compel the Attendance of absent Members, in such Manner, and under such Penalties as each House may provide.

Each House may determine the Rules of its Proceedings, punish its Members for disorderly Behavior, and, with the Concurrence of two thirds, expel a Member.

Each House shall keep a Journal of its Proceedings, and from time to time publish the same, excepting such Parts as may in their Judgment require Secrecy; and the Yeas and Nays of the Members of either House on any question shall, at the Desire of one fifth of those present, be entered on the Journal.

Neither House, during the Session of Congress, shall, without the Consent of the other, adjourn for more than three days, nor to any other Place than that in which the two Houses shall be sitting.

SECTION 6. The Senators and Representatives shall receive a Compensation for their Services, to be ascertained by Law, and paid out of the Treasury of the United States. They shall in all Cases, except Treason, Felony and Breach of the Peace, be privileged from Arrest during their Attendance at the Session of their respective Houses, and in going to and returning from the same; and for any Speech or Debate in either House, they shall not be questioned in any other Place.

No Senator or Representative shall, during the Time for which he was elected, be appointed to any civil Office under the Authority of the United States, which shall have been created, or the Emoluments whereof shall have been encreased during such time; and no Person holding any Office under the United States, shall be a Member of either House during his Continuance in Office.

SECTION 7. All Bills for raising Revenue shall originate in the House of Representatives; but the Senate may propose or concur with Amendments as on other Bills.

Every Bill which shall have passed the House of Representatives and the Senate, shall, before it become a Law, be presented to the President of the United States; If he approves he shall sign it, but if not he shall return it, with his Objections to that House in which it shall have originated, who shall enter the Objections at large on their Journal, and proceed to reconsider it. If after such Reconsideration two thirds of that House shall agree to pass the Bill, it shall be sent, together with the Objections, to the other House, by which it shall likewise be reconsidered, and if approved by two thirds of that House, it shall become a Law. But in all such Cases the Votes of both Houses shall be determined by Yeas and Nays, and the Names of the Persons voting for and against the Bill shall be entered on the Journal of each House respectively. If any Bill shall not be returned by the President within ten Days (Sundays excepted) after it shall have been presented to him, the Same shall be a Law, in like Manner as if he had signed it, unless the Congress by their Adjournment prevent its Return, in which Case it shall not be a Law.

Every Order, Resolution, or Vote to which the Concurrence of the Senate and House of Representatives may be necessary (except on a question of Adjournment) shall be presented to the President of the United States; and before the Same shall take Effect, shall be approved by him, or being disapproved by him, shall be repassed by two thirds of the Senate and House of Representatives, according to the Rules and Limitations prescribed in the Case of a Bill.

SECTION 8. The Congress shall have Power To lay and collect Taxes, Duties, Imposts and Excises, to pay the Debts and provide for the common Defence and general Welfare of the United States; but all Duties, Imposts and Excises shall be uniform throughout the United States;

To borrow Money on the credit of the United States:

To regulate Commerce with foreign Nations, and among the several States, and with the Indian Tribes;

To establish an uniform Rule of Naturalization, and uniform Laws on the subject of Bankruptcies throughout the United States;

To coin Money, regulate the Value thereof, and of foreign Coin, and fix the Standard of Weights and Measures;

To provide for the Punishment of counterfeiting the Securities and current Coin of the United States;

To establish Post Offices and post Roads;

To promote the Progress of Science and useful Arts, by securing for limited Times to Authors and Inventors the exclusive Right to their respective Writings and Discoveries;

To constitute Tribunals inferior to the supreme Court;

To define and punish Piracies and Felonies committed on the high Seas, and Offences against the Law of Nations;

To declare War, grant Letters of Marque and Reprisal, and make Rules concerning Captures on Land and Water;

To raise and support Armies, but no Appropriation of Money to that Use shall be for a longer Term than two Years;

To provide and maintain a Navy;

To make Rules for the Government and Regulation of the land and naval Forces;

To provide for calling forth the Militia to execute the Laws of the Union, suppress Insurrections and repel Invasions;

To provide for organizing, arming, and disciplining the Militia, and for governing such Part of them as may be employed in the Service of the United States, reserving to the States respectively, the Appointment of the Officers, and the Authority of training the Militia according to the discipline prescribed by Congress;

To exercise exclusive Legislation in all Cases whatsoever, over such District (not exceeding ten Miles square) as may, by Cession of particular States, and the Acceptance of Congress, become the Seat of the Government of the United States, and to exercise like

Authority over all Places purchased by the Consent of the Legislature of the State in which the Same shall be, for the Erection of Forts, Magazines, Arsenals, dock-Yards, and other needful Buildings; — And

To make all Laws which shall be necessary and proper for carrying into Execution the foregoing Powers, and all other Powers vested by this Constitution in the Government of the United States, or in any Department or Officer thereof.

SECTION 9. The Migration or Importation of such Persons as any of the States now existing shall think proper to admit, shall not be prohibited by the Congress prior to the Year one thousand eight hundred and eight, but a Tax or duty may be imposed on such Importation, not exceeding ten dollars for each Person.

The Privilege of the Writ of Habeas Corpus shall not be suspended, unless when in Cases of Rebellion or Invasion the public Safety may require it.

No Bill of Attainder or ex post facto Law shall be passed.

No Capitation, or other direct, tax shall be laid, unless in Proportion to the Census or Enumeration herein before directed to be taken.

No Tax or Duty shall be laid on Articles exported from any State.

No Preference shall be given by any Regulation of Commerce or Revenue to the Ports of one State over those of another: nor shall Vessels bound to, or from, one State, be obliged to enter, clear, or pay Duties in another.

No Money shall be drawn from the Treasury, but in Consequence of Appropriations made by Law; and a regular Statement and Account of the Receipts and Expenditures of all public Money shall be published from time to time.

No Title of Nobility shall be granted by the United States: And no Person holding any Office of Profit or Trust under them, shall, without the Consent of the Congress, accept of any present, Emolument, Office, or Title, of any kind whatever, from any King, Prince, or foreign State.

SECTION 10. No State shall enter into any Treaty, Alliance, or Confederation; grant Letters of Marque and Reprisal; coin Money; emit Bills of Credit; make any Thing but gold and silver Coin a Tender in Payment of Debts; pass any Bill of Attainder, ex post facto Law, or Law impairing the Obligation of Contracts, or grant any Title of Nobility.

No State shall, without the Consent of the Congress, lay any Im-

posts or Duties on Imports or Exports, except what may be absolutely necessary for executing its inspection Laws: and the net
Produce of all Duties and Imposts, laid by any State on Imports or
Exports, shall be for the Use of the Treasury of the United States;
and all such Laws shall be subject to the Revision and Controul of
the Congress.

No State shall, without the Consent of Congress, lay any Duty of
Tonnage, keep Troops, or Ships of War in time of Peace, enter
into any Agreement or Compact with another State, or with a foreign Power, or engage in War, unless actually invaded, or in such
imminent Danger as will not admit of delay.

ARTICLE II

SECTION 1. The Executive Power shall be vested in a President of the
United States of America. He shall hold his Office during the
Term of four Years, and, together with the Vice President, chosen
for the same Term, be elected, as follows

Each State shall appoint, in such Manner as the Legislature thereof
may direct, a Number of Electors, equal to the whole Number
of Senators and Representatives to which the State may be entitled
in the Congress: but no Senator or Representative, or Person holding an Office of Trust or Profit under the United States, shall be
appointed an Elector.

The electors shall meet in their respective States, and vote by ballot
for two Persons, of whom one at least shall not be an Inhabitant of
the same State with themselves. And they shall make a List of all
the Persons voted for, and of the Number of Votes for each; which
List they shall sign and certify, and transmit sealed to the Seat of
the Government of the United States, directed to the President of
the Senate. The President of the Senate shall, in the Presence of the
Senate and House of Representatives, open all the Certificates, and
the Votes shall then be counted. The Person having the greatest
Number of Votes shall be the President, if such Number be a
Majority of the whole Number of Electors appointed; and if there
be more than one who have such Majority, and have an equal
Number of Votes, then the House of Representatives shall immediately chuse by Ballot one of them for President; and if no Person
have a Majority, then from the five highest on the List the said
House shall in like Manner chuse the President. But in chusing
the President, the Votes shall be taken by States, the Representation from each State having one Vote; A quorum for this Purpose
shall consist of a Member or Members from two thirds of the

States, and a Majority of all the States shall be necessary to a Choice. In every Case, after the Choice of the President, the Person having the greatest Number of Votes of the Electors shall be the Vice President. But if there should remain two or more who have equal Votes, the Senate shall chuse from them by Ballot the Vice President.

The Congress may determine the Time of chusing the Electors, and the Day on which they shall give their Votes; which Day shall be the same throughout the United States.

No Person except a natural born Citizen, or a Citizen of the United States, at the time of the Adoption of this Constitution, shall be eligible to the Office of President; neither shall any Person be eligible to that Office who shall not have attained to the Age of thirty five Years, and been fourteen Years a Resident within the United States.

In Case of the Removal of the President from Office, or of his Death, Resignation or Inability to discharge the Powers and Duties of the said Office, the same shall devolve on the Vice President, and the Congress may by Law provide for the Case of Removal, Death, Resignation or Inability, both of the President and Vice President, declaring what Officer shall then act as President, and such Officer shall act accordingly, until the Disability be removed, or a President shall be elected.

The President shall, at stated Times, receive for his Services, a Compensation, which shall neither be encreased nor diminished during the Period for which he shall have been elected, and he shall not receive within that Period any other Emolument from the United States, or any of them.

Before he enter on the Execution of his Office, he shall take the following Oath or Affirmation: — " I do solemnly swear (or affirm) that I will faithfully execute the Office of President of the United States, and will to the best of my Ability, preserve, protect and defend the Constitution of the United States."

SECTION 2. The President shall be Commander in Chief of the Army and Navy of the United States, and of the Militia of the several States, when called into the actual Service of the United States; he may require the Opinion, in writing, of the principal Officer in each of the executive Departments, upon any Subject relating to the Duties of their respective Offices, and he shall have Power to grant Reprieves and Pardons for Offences against the United States, except in Cases of Impeachment.

He shall have Power, by and with the Advice and Consent of the

Senate, to make Treaties, provided two thirds of the Senators present concur and he shall nominate, and by and with the Advice and Consent of the Senate, shall appoint Ambassadors, other public Ministers and Consuls, Judges of the supreme Court, and all other Officers of the United States, whose Appointments are not herein otherwise provided for, and which shall be established by Law: but the Congress may by Law vest the Appointment of such inferior Officers, as they think proper, in the President alone, in the Courts of Law, or in the Heads of Departments.

The President shall have Power to fill up all Vacancies that may happen during the Recess of the Senate, by granting Commissions which shall expire at the End of their next Session.

SECTION 3. He shall from time to time give to the Congress Information of the State of the Union, and recommend to their Consideration such Measures as he shall judge necessary and expedient; he may, on extraordinary Occasions, convene both Houses, or either of them, and, in Case of Disagreement between them, with Respect to the Time of Adjournment, he may adjourn them to such Time as he shall think proper; he shall receive Ambassadors and other public Ministers; he shall take Care that the Laws be faithfully executed, and shall Commission all the Officers of the United States.

SECTION 4. The President, Vice President and all civil Officers of the United States, shall be removed from Office on Impeachment for, and Conviction of, Treason, Bribery, or other high Crimes and Misdemeanors.

ARTICLE III

SECTION 1. The judicial Power of the United States, shall be vested in one supreme Court, and in such inferior Courts as the Congress may from time to time ordain and establish. The Judges, both of the supreme and inferior Courts, shall hold their Offices during good Behaviour, and shall, at stated Times, receive for their Services, a Compensation, which shall not be diminished during their Continuance in Office.

SECTION 2. The judicial Power shall extend to all Cases, in Law and Equity, arising under this Constitution, the Laws of the United States, and Treaties made, or which shall be made, under their Authority; — to all Cases affecting Ambassadors, other public Ministers and Consuls; — to all Cases of admiralty and maritime

Jurisdiction; — to Controversies to which the United States shall be a Party; — to Controversies between two or more States; — between a State and Citizens of another State; — between Citizens of different States, — between Citizens of the same State claiming Lands under Grants of different States, and between a State, or the Citizens thereof, and foreign States, Citizens or Subjects.

In all Cases affecting Ambassadors, other public Ministers and Consuls, and those in which a State shall be Party, the supreme Court shall have original Jurisdiction. In all other Cases before mentioned, the supreme Court shall have appellate Jurisdiction, both as to Law and Fact, with such Exceptions, and under such Regulations as the Congress shall make.

The Trial of all Crimes, except in Cases of Impeachment, shall be by Jury; and such Trial shall be held in the State where the said Crimes shall have been committed; but when not committed within any State, the Trial shall be at such Place or Places as the Congress may by Law have directed.

SECTION 3. Treason against the United States, shall consist only in levying War against them, or in adhering to their Enemies, giving them Aid and Comfort. No Person shall be convicted of Treason unless on the Testimony of two Witnesses to the same overt Act, or on Confession in open Court.

The Congress shall have Power to declare the Punishment of Treason, but no Attainder of Treason shall work Corruption of Blood, or Forfeiture except during the Life of the Person attainted.

ARTICLE IV

SECTION 1. Full Faith and Credit shall be given in each State to the public Acts, Records, and judicial Proceedings of every other State. And the Congress may by general Laws prescribe the Manner in which such Acts, Records and Proceedings shall be proved, and the Effect thereof.

SECTION 2. The Citizens of each State shall be entitled to all Privileges and Immunities of Citizens in the several States.

A person charged in any State with Treason, Felony, or other Crime, who shall flee from Justice, and be found in another State, shall on Demand of the executive Authority of the State from which he fled, be delivered up, to be removed to the State having Jurisdiction of the Crime.

No Person held to Service or Labour in one State, under the Laws thereof, escaping into another, shall, in Consequence of any Law or Regulation therein, be discharged from such Service or Labour, but shall be delivered up on Claim of the Party to whom such Service or Labour may be due.

SECTION 3. New States may be admitted by the Congress into this Union; but no new State shall be formed or erected within the Jurisdiction of any other State; nor any State be formed by the Junction of two or more States, or Parts of States, without the Consent of the Legislatures of the States concerned as well as of the Congress.

The Congress shall have Power to dispose of and make all needful Rules and Regulations respecting the Territory or other Property belonging to the United States; and nothing in this Constitution shall be so construed as to Prejudice any Claims of the United States, or of any particular State.

SECTION 4. The United States shall guarantee to every State in this Union a Republican Form of Government, and shall protect each of them against Invasion; and on Application of the Legislature, or of the Executive (when the Legislature cannot be convened) against domestic Violence.

ARTICLE V

The Congress, whenever two thirds of both houses shall deem it necessary, shall propose Amendments to this Constitution, or, on the Application of the Legislatures of two thirds of the several States, shall call a Convention for proposing Amendments, which, in either Case, shall be valid to all Intents and Purposes, as Part of this Constitution, when ratified by the Legislatures of three fourths of the several States, or by Conventions in three fourths thereof, as the one or the other Mode of Ratification may be proposed by the Congress; Provided that no Amendment which may be made prior to the Year One thousand eight hundred and eight shall in any Manner affect the first and fourth Clauses in the Ninth Section of the first Article; and that no State, without its Consent, shall be deprived of its equal Suffrage in the Senate.

ARTICLE VI

All Debts contracted and Engagements entered into, before the Adoption of this Constitution, shall be as valid against the United

States under this Constitution, as under the Confederation.

This Constitution, and the Laws of the United States which shall be made in Pursuance thereof; and all Treaties made, or which shall be made, under the Authority of the United States, shall be the supreme Law of the Land; and the Judges in every State shall be bound thereby, any Thing in the Constitution or Laws of any State to the Contrary notwithstanding.

The Senators and Representatives before mentioned, and the Members of the several State Legislatures, and all executive and judicial Officers, both of the United States and of the several States, shall be bound by Oath or Affirmation, to support this Constitution; but no religious Test shall ever be required as a Qualification to any Office or public Trust under the United States.

ARTICLE VII

The Ratification of the Conventions of nine States, shall be sufficient for the Establishment of this Constitution between the States so ratifying the Same.

DONE in Convention by the Unanimous Consent of the States present the Seventeenth Day of September in the Year of our Lord one thousand seven hundred and Eighty seven and of the Independence of the United States of America the Twelfth. IN WITNESS whereof We have hereunto subscribed our Names.

G° WASHINGTON
Presid^t and deputy from Virginia

AMENDMENTS
ARTICLE I

[THE FIRST TEN ARTICLES PROPOSED 25 SEPTEMBER 1789; DECLARED IN FORCE 15 DECEMBER 1791]

Congress shall make no law respecting an establishment of religion, or prohibiting the free exercise thereof; or abridging the freedom of speech, or of the press; or the right of the people peaceably to assemble, and to petition the Government for a redress of grievances.

ARTICLE II

A well regulated Militia, being necessary to the security of a free State, the right of the people to keep and bear Arms, shall not be infringed.

ARTICLE III

No Soldier shall, in time of peace, be quartered in any house, without the consent of the Owner, nor in time of war, but in a manner to be prescribed by law.

ARTICLE IV

The right of the people to be secure in their persons, houses, papers, and effects, against unreasonable searches and seizures, shall not be violated, and no Warrants shall issue, but upon probable cause, supported by Oath or affirmation, and particularly describing the place to be searched, and the persons or things to be seized.

ARTICLE V

No person shall be held to answer for a capital, or otherwise infamous crime, unless on a presentment or indictment of a Grand Jury, except in cases arising in the land or naval forces, or in the Militia, when in actual service in time of War or public danger; nor shall any person be subject for the same offence to be twice put in jeopardy of life or limb; nor shall be compelled in any Criminal Case to be a witness against himself, nor be deprived of life, liberty, or property, without due process of law; nor shall private property be taken for public use, without just compensation.

ARTICLE VI

In all criminal prosecutions, the accused shall enjoy the right to a speedy and public trial, by an impartial jury of the State and district wherein the crime shall have been committed, which district shall have been previously ascertained by law, and to be informed of the nature and cause of the accusation; to be confronted with the witnesses against him; to have compulsory process for obtaining Witnesses in his favor, and to have the Assistance of Counsel for his defence.

ARTICLE VII

In suits at common law, where the value in controversy shall exceed twenty dollars, the right of trial by jury shall be preserved, and no fact tried by a jury shall be otherwise re-examined in any Court of the United States, than according to the rules of the common law.

ARTICLE VIII

Excessive bail shall not be required, nor excessive fines imposed, nor cruel and unusual punishments inflicted.

ARTICLE IX

The enumeration in the Constitution, of certain rights, shall not be construed to deny or disparage others retained by the people.

ARTICLE X

The powers not delegated to the United States by the Constitution, nor prohibited by it to the States, are reserved to the States respectively, or to the people.

ARTICLE XI

[PROPOSED 5 MARCH 1794; DECLARED RATIFIED 8 JANUARY 1798]

The Judicial power of the United States shall not be construed to extend to any suit in law or equity, commenced or prosecuted against one of the United States by Citizens of another State, or by Citizens or Subjects of any Foreign State.

ARTICLE XII

[PROPOSED 12 DECEMBER 1803; DECLARED RATIFIED 25 SEPTEMBER 1804]

The Electors shall meet in their respective states, and vote by ballot for President and Vice-President, one of whom, at least, shall not be an inhabitant of the same state with themselves; they shall name in their ballots the person voted for as President, and in distinct ballots the person voted for as Vice-President, and they shall make distinct lists of all persons voted for as President, and of all persons voted for as Vice-President, and of the number of votes for each, which lists they shall sign and certify, and transmit sealed to the seat of the Government of the United States, directed to the President of the Senate; — The President of the Senate shall, in the presence of the Senate and House of Representatives, open all the certificates and the votes shall then be counted; — The person having the greatest number of votes for President, shall be the President, if such number be a majority of the whole number of Electors appointed; and if no person have such majority, then from the persons having the highest numbers not exceeding three on the list of those voted for as President, the House of Representatives shall choose immediately, by ballot, the President. But in choosing the President, the votes shall be taken by states, the representation from each state having one vote; a quorum for this purpose shall consist of a member or members from two-thirds of the states, and a majority of all the states shall be necessary to a choice. And if the House of Representatives shall not choose a President whenever the right of choice shall devolve upon them, before the fourth day of March next following, then the Vice-President shall act as President, as in the case of the death or other constitutional disability of the President. The person having the greatest number of votes as Vice-President, shall be the Vice-President, if such number be a majority of the whole number of Electors appointed, and if no person have a majority, then from the two highest numbers on the list, the Senate shall choose the Vice-President; a quorum for the purpose shall consist of two-thirds of the whole number of Senators, and a majority of the whole number shall be necessary to a choice. But no person constitutionally ineligible to the office of President shall be eligible to that of Vice-President of the United States.

ARTICLE XIII

[PROPOSED 1 FEBRUARY 1865; DECLARED RATIFIED 18 DECEMBER 1866]

SECTION 1. Neither slavery nor involuntary servitude, except as a punishment for crime whereof the party shall have been duly convicted, shall exist within the United States, or any place subject to their jurisdiction.

SECTION 2. Congress shall have power to enforce this article by appropriate legislation.

ARTICLE XIV

[PROPOSED 16 JUNE 1866; DECLARED RATIFIED 28 JULY 1868]

SECTION 1. All persons born or naturalized in the United States, and subject to the jurisdiction thereof, are citizens of the United States and of the State wherein they reside. No State shall make or enforce any law which shall abridge the privileges or immunities of citizens of the United States; nor shall any State deprive any person of life, liberty, or property, without due process of law; nor deny to any person within its jurisdiction the equal protection of the laws.

SECTION 2. Representatives shall be apportioned among the several States according to their respective numbers, counting the whole number of persons in each State, excluding Indians not taxed. But when the right to vote at any election for the choice of electors for President and Vice President of the United States, Representatives in Congress, the Executive and Judicial officers of a State, or the members of the Legislature thereof, is denied to any of the male inhabitants of such State, being twenty-one years of age, and citizens of the United States, or in any way abridged, except for participation in rebellion, or other crime, the basis of representation therein shall be reduced in the proportion which the number of such male citizens shall bear to the whole number of male citizens twenty-one years of age in such State.

SECTION 3. No person shall be a Senator or Representative in Congress, or elector of President and Vice President, or hold any office, civil, or military, under the United States, or under any State, who, having previously taken an oath, as a member of Congress, or as an officer of the United States, or as a member of any State legislature, or as an executive or judicial officer of any State, to support the Constitution of the United States, shall have engaged in insurrection or rebellion against the same, or given aid or comfort to the enemies thereof. But Congress may by a vote of two-thirds of each House, remove such disability.

SECTION 4. The validity of the public debt of the United States, authorized by law, including debts incurred for payment of pensions and bounties for services in suppressing insurrection or rebellion, shall not be questioned. But neither the United States nor any State shall assume or pay any debt or obligation incurred in aid of insurrection or rebellion against the United States, or any claim for the loss or emancipation of any slave; but all such debts, obligations and claims shall be held illegal and void.

SECTION 5. The Congress shall have power to enforce, by appropriate legislation, the provisions of this article.

ARTICLE XV

[PROPOSED 27 FEBRUARY 1869; DECLARED RATIFIED 30 MARCH 1870]

SECTION 1. The right of citizens of the United States to vote shall not be denied or abridged by the United States or by any State on account of race, color, or previous condition of servitude.

SECTION 2. The Congress shall have power to enforce this article by appropriate legislation.

ARTICLE XVI

[PROPOSED 12 JULY 1909; DECLARED RATIFIED 25 FEBRUARY 1913]

The Congress shall have power to lay and collect taxes on incomes, from whatever source derived, without apportionment among the several States, and without regard to any census or enumeration.

ARTICLE XVII

[PROPOSED 16 MAY 1912; DECLARED RATIFIED 31 MAY 1913]

The Senate of the United States shall be composed of two senators from each State, elected by the people thereof, for six years; and each Senator shall have one vote. The electors in each State shall have the qualifications requisite for electors of the most numerous branch of the State legislature.

When vacancies happen in the representation of any State in the Senate, the executive authority of such State shall issue writs of election to fill such vacancies: PROVIDED, That the legislature of any State may empower the executive thereof to make temporary appointments until the people fill the vacancies by election as the legislature may direct.

This amendment shall not be so construed as to affect the election or term of any senator chosen before it becomes valid as part of the Constitution.

ARTICLE XVIII

[PROPOSED 18 DECEMBER 1917; DECLARED RATIFIED 29 JANUARY 1919]

After one year from the ratification of this article, the manufacture, sale, or transportation of intoxicating liquors within, the importation thereof into, or the exportation thereof from the United

States and all territory subject to the jurisdiction thereof for beverage purposes is hereby prohibited.

The Congress and the several States shall have concurrent power to enforce this article by appropriate legislation.

This article shall be inoperative unless it shall have been ratified as an amendment to the Constitution by the legislatures of the several States, as provided in the Constitution, within seven years from the date of the submission hereof to the States by the Congress.

ARTICLE XIX

[PROPOSED 4 JUNE 1919; DECLARED RATIFIED 26 AUGUST 1920]

The right of citizens of the United States to vote shall not be denied or abridged by the United States or by any States on account of sex.

The Congress shall have power, by appropriate legislation, to enforce the provisions of this article.

ARTICLE XX

[PROPOSED 2 MARCH 1932; DECLARED RATIFIED 6 FEBRUARY 1933]

SECTION 1. The terms of the President and Vice-President shall end at noon on the twentieth day of January, and the terms of Senators and Representatives at noon on the third day of January, of the years in which such terms would have ended if this article had not been ratified; and the terms of their successors shall then begin.

SECTION 2. The Congress shall assemble at least once in every year, and such meeting shall begin at noon on the third day of January, unless they shall by law appoint a different day.

SECTION 3. If, at the time fixed for the beginning of the term of the President, the President-elect shall have died, the Vice-President-elect shall become President. If a President shall not have been chosen before the time fixed for the beginning of his term, or if the President-elect shall have failed to qualify, then the Vice-President-elect shall act as President until a President shall have qualified; and the Congress may by law provide for the case wherein neither a President-elect nor a Vice-President-elect shall have qualified, declaring who shall then act as President, or the manner in which one who is to act shall be selected, and such person shall act accordingly until a President or Vice-President shall have qualified.